The Baseball Bibliography
Second edition

The Baseball Bibliography

Second Edition

MYRON J. SMITH, JR.

Foreword by JOHN KUENSTER

Volume 4

G. Individual Biography, Oyley–Zwissig
Journals, Periodicals and Magazines Examined
Index of Names and Subjects

McFarland & Company, Inc., Publishers
Jefferson, North Carolina, and London

4

LIBRARY OF CONGRESS CATALOGUING-IN-PUBLICATION DATA

Smith, Myron J.
The baseball bibliography / Myron J. Smith, Jr. ; foreword by John Kuenster. — 2nd ed.
p.   cm.
Previous ed. published as: Baseball : a comprehensive bibliography.
Jefferson, N.C. : McFarland, 1986 [and two supplements, 1993 and 1998].
Includes bibliographical references and index.

ISBN 0-7864-1531-2 (4 volume set : softcover : 50# alkaline paper)

ISBN 0-7864-2408-7 (v. 1 : library binding : 50# alkaline paper)
ISBN 0-7864-2409-5 (v. 2 : library binding : 50# alkaline paper)
ISBN 0-7864-2636-5 (v. 3 : library binding : 50# alkaline paper)
ISBN 0-7864-2637-5 (v. 4 : library binding : 50# alkaline paper)

1. Baseball — United States — Bibliography.
2. Baseball — Canada — Bibliography.
I. Smith, Myron J. Baseball.   II. Title.
Z7514.B3S64   2006   [GV863.A1]   016.796357 — dc22   2005016989

British Library cataloguing data are available

Cover image ©2005 Photospin.com

Manufactured in the United States of America

McFarland & Company, Inc., Publishers
Box 611, Jefferson, North Carolina 28640
www.mcfarlandpub.com

VOLUME 4 : 0-7864-2637-5
FOUR VOLUME SET : 0-7864-1531-2

SUMMARY TABLE OF CONTENTS

CONTENTS

Raymond Francis ("Ray") Oyler

SS. (B: Aug. 4, 1938, Indianapolis, IN–D: Jan. 26, 1981). Detroit (AL), 1965–1968; Seattle (AL), 1969; California (AL), 1970. Remarks: Obtained 221 hits (15 homers) and two stolen bases in 542 games in six years; in 1968, established MLB record for lowest season batting average by a starting SS (.135), 1968; had homer to win first Seattle (AL) home game; coach, Salt Lake City (PCL), 1971–1972, Hawaii (PCL), 1973; retired to run a Bellevue, WA-area bowling alley and died of a heart attack.

46995. "Rodriguez's Forefather: Seattle's First Shortstop Sensation." *Sports Illustrated,* LXXXV (September 30, 1996), 14, 16.

46996. Rubin, Bob. "A Ray of Hope." *Sport,* XLIX (January 1970), 8–9.

Daniel Leonard ("Danny" or "Ike") Ozark

MGR. (B: Nov. 26, 1923, Buffalo, NY). Remarks. Minor league player and manager, 1946–1964; coach, Los Angeles (NL), 1965–1972, 1980–1982, and San Francisco (NL), 1983; manager, Philadelphia (NL), 1973–1979 and San Francisco (NL), 1984, winning 618 games and losing 542 (.533); also coach, Los Angeles (NL), 1980–1982 and San Francisco (NL), 1983–1984.

46997. Jordan, Pat. "The Game is Meant to Be Fun: Danny Ozark, Manager of the Philadelphia Phillies." *Sport,* LXVII (August 1978), 37–40+.

46998. Rossi, John P. "Daniel Leonard 'Danny' Ozark." In: Vol. G-P of David L. Porter, ed. *Biographical Dictionary of American Sports: Baseball.* Rev. and enlarged ed. Westport, CT: Greenwood Press, 2000. Pp. 1158–1159.

John Lewis Pacella

P. (B: Sept. 15, 1956, Brooklyn, NY). New York (NL), 1977, 1979–1980; New York (AL) and Minnesota (AL), 1982; Baltimore (AL), 1984; Detroit (AL), 1986. Remarks: Had four victories and 10 defeats, with three "saves," in six big league season; also, hurled no-hitter, Jackson (TL), April 1977.

46999. Shannon, Mike. "John Pacella." In: his *Tales from the Ballpark: More of the Greatest True Baseball Stories Ever Told.* Lincolnwood, IL: Contemporary Books, 1999. Pp. 152–160.

Thomas Marian ("Tom") Paciorek

OF-1B. (B: Nov. 2, 1946, Detroit, MI). Los Angeles (NL), 1970–1975; Atlanta (NL), 1976–1978; Seattle (AL), 1978–1981; Chicago (AL), 1982–1985; New York (NL), 1985; Texas (AL), 1986–1987. Remarks: Obtained 1,162 hits (86 homers) and 55 stolen bases in 1,392 big league games in 18 years; also played for Albuquerque (PCL), where he was Minor League Player of the Year, 1971.

47000. Paciorek, Tom, as told to George Vass. "The Game I'll Never Forget." *Baseball Digest,* XLIV (November 1985), 56–58.

Andrew ("Andy or "Pruschka" or "Handy Andy") Pafko

OF-SCOUT. (B: Feb. 26, 1921, Boyceville, WI). Chicago (NL), 1943–1951; Brooklyn (NL), 1951–1952; Milwaukee (NL), 1953–1959. Remarks: Obtained 1,796 hits (213 homers) and 38 stolen bases in 1,832 games in 17 years; had five RBIs in one game, July 2, 1950; coach and scout, Milwaukee (NL), 1960–1963; minor league manager, 1964–1968; scout, Montreal (NL), 1969–1970; was PCL MVP in 1943 with Los Angeles.

47001. "Andy Pafko." In: Carrie Muskat, ed. *Banks to Sandberg to Grace: Five Decades of Love and Frustration with the Chicago Cubs.* Chicago, IL: Contemporary Books, 2001. Pp. 11–14.

47002. Chapman, Lou. "Andy Pafko Still Remembers

Shot Heard 'Round the World." *Baseball Digest,* LI (November 1992), 68–74.

47003. DeLillo, Don. "Pafko at the Wall." In: George Plimpton, ed. *Home Run.* San Diego, CA: Harcourt, 2001. Chapter 11.

47004. Green, Paul M. "Andy Pafko." In: his *Forgotten Fields.* Waupaca, WI: Parker Publications, 1984. Pp. 190–200.

47005. Gross, Milton. "Pafko Pays Off." *Sport,* XIII (September 1952), 26–27+.

47006. Hoffman, John C. *Andy Pafko, the Solid Man.* New York: A.S. Barnes, 1951. 25p.

47007. _____. "We Want Pafko." *Baseball Digest,* X (June 1951), 5–9.

47008. Kahn, Roger. "The Sandwich Man." In: his *The Boys of Summer.* New York: Harper & Row, 1972. Pp. 262–270.

47009. Kelley, Brent P. "Andy Pafko: Handy Andy." In: his *The Early All-Stars: Conversations with Standout Baseball Players of the 1930s and 1940s.* Jefferson, NC: McFarland & Co., Inc., 1997. Pp. 103–113.

47010. Kessler, Gene. "Andy, the Handiest Cub." *Baseball Digest,* IV (October 1945), 5–7.

47011. Meany, Thomas. "Andy Patko, Milwaukee's Bouncing 'Check." *Baseball Digest,* XIII (September 1954), 36–41.

47012. _____. "Local Boy Makes Hits (Andy Pafko). In: his *Milwaukee's Miracle Braves.* New York: A.S. Barnes, 1954. Pp. 130–142.

47013. Miller, Hub. "Center Fielder Deluxe." *Baseball Magazine,* LXXXVI (February 1951), 315–317.

47014. Pafko, Andrew. "I'm Lucky to Be a Brave." *Sport,* XVI (June 1954), 26–27+.

47015. Phalen, Rick. "Andy Pafko." In: his *Our Chicago Cubs.* South Bend, IN: Diamond Communications, 1992. Pp. 19–25.

47016. Richelson, Bob. "Handy and Y of the Cubs." *Sport,* VIII (April 1950), 42–43+.

47017. Sargent, Jim. "Andy Pafko." *Oldtyme Baseball News,* VII, no. 4 (1995), 6–7.

47018. Smith, Duane A. "Andrew 'Pruschka,' 'Handy Andy' Pafko." In: Vol. G-P of David L. Porter, ed. *Biographical Dictionary of American Sports: Baseball.* Rev. and enlarged ed. Westport, CT: Greenwood Press, 2000. Pp. 1161–1162.

47019. Spalding, John E. "Andy Pafko." In: his *Pacific Coast League Stars, Vol. II: Ninety Who Made It to the Majors, 1905–1957.* San Jose, CA: John E. Spalding, 1997. Pp. 132–133.

47020. Westcott, Rich. "Andy Pafko — Solid as a Rock." In: his *Diamond Greats.* Westport, CT: Meckler Books, 1988. Pp. 371–375.

47021. Wilbert, Warren and William Hageman. "Andrew Pafko —1948." In: their *Chicago Cubs: Seasons at the Summit, the 50 Greatest Individual Seasons.* Champaign, IL: Sagamore Publishing, 1997. Pp. 161–164.

47022. Wolf, Bob. "A Diving Catch Was Andy Pafko's Trademark." *Baseball Digest,* XXXIX (February 1980), 80–86.

David Percy ("Dave") Pagen

P. (B: Sept. 15, 1949, Nipawen, Canada). New York (AL), 1973–1976; Baltimore (AL), 1976; Seattle (AL) and Pittsburgh (NL), 1977. Remarks: in five big league seasons, had four victories, nine defeats, and four "saves."

47023. Gallagher, Danny. "1987 Inductees to Saskatchewan Baseball Hall of Fame: Dave Pagan of Nipawin — Player." In: *Saskatchewan Historical Baseball Re-*

view 1987. Battleford, SK: Saskatchewan Baseball Hall of Fame and Museum Association, 1987. Pp. 86–87.

Joseph Francis ("Joe" or "Fireman" or "The Gay Reliever") Page

P. (B: Oct. 28, 1917, Cherry Valley, PA–D: April 21, 1980). New York (AL), 1944–1950; Pittsburgh (NL), 1954. Remarks: Won 57 games and lost 49, with 76 "saves," in eight years; hero for Yankees in 1947, 1948, and 1949 World Series; *Sport Magazine* "Athlete of the Year," 1947; also hurled for Kansas City (AA), San Francisco (PCL), and Syracuse (IL), 1951–1953.

47024. Akin, William E. "Joseph Francis 'Joe,' 'Fireman' Page." In: Vol. G-P of David L. Porter, ed. *Biographical Dictionary of American Sports: Baseball.* Rev. and enlarged ed. Westport, CT: Greenwood Press, 2000. Pp. 1162–1163.

47025. Daniel, Daniel M. "Joe Page, Perhaps the Greatest Southpaw Relief Specialist the Game Has Seen." *Baseball Magazine,* LXXXIII (November 1943), 403–405.

47026. Epstein, Ben. "Joe Page." In: his *My Greatest Baseball Game.* New York: A.S. Barnes, 1950. Pp. 114–119.

47027. _____. "Page Just Wasn't 'Hip' This Year." *Baseball Digest,* IX (November 1950), 31–34.

47028. Gallagher, Mark. "Joe Page." In: his *50 Years of Yankee All-Stars.* New York: Leisure Press, 1984. Pp. 145–147.

47029. Goldman, Steve. "A Blip on the Radar Screen." *Yankees Magazine,* XX (May 1999), 114–123.

47030. Graham, Frank. "Brightest Page in the Book." *Baseball Digest,* VII (January 1948), 12–15.

47031. Heinz, W.C. "The Fireman." In: his *Once They Heard the Cheers.* Garden City, NY: Doubleday, 1979. Pp. 225–241.

47032. Jacobs, Bruce. "Answer to Casey's Prayers." In: Bruce Jacobs, ed. *Baseball Stars of 1950.* New York: Lion Books, 1950. Pp. 134–142.

47033. "Joe Page." In: *Current Biography, 1950.* New York: H.W. Wilson Co., 1950. Pp. 437–439.

47034. Page, Joseph F. "I Was Baseball's Bad Boy." *Saturday Evening Post,* CCXX (May 22, 1948), 28+.

47035. Parker, Dan. "My Friend Joe Page." *Sport,* VIII (March 1950), 16–17+.

47036. Shapiro, Milton J. "Hugh Casey-Joe Page." In: his *Heroes of the Bullpen: Baseball's Greatest Relief Pitchers.* New York: Julian Messner, 1967. Pp. 40–46.

47037. Trachtenberg, Leo. "When Joe Page Came Striding In." *Yankee Magazine,* XLVII (February 1983), 20+.

Theodore Roosevelt ("Ted") Page

OF-1B. (B: April 22, 1903, Glasgow, KY–D: Dec. 1, 1984). Toledo Tigers, 1923; Buffalo Giants, 1924–1925; Newark Stars, 1926; Chappie Johnson's Stars, 1927–1928; Mohawk Giants, 1928; Brooklyn Royal Giants, 1929–1930; Baltimore Black Sox, 1929–1930; Homestead Grays, 1930–1931; New York Black Yankees, 1932; Pittsburgh Crawfords, 1932–1934; Newark Eagles, 1935; Philadelphia Stars, 1935–1937. Remarks: Career .335 hitter and speedy baserunner; post-baseball, bowling alley owner and columnist on the subject for the Pittsburgh *Courier;* murdered during a burglary attempt.

47038. Bernstein, David. "Theodore Roosevelt 'Ted' Page." In: Vol. G-P of David L. Porter, ed. *Biographical Dictionary of American Sports: Baseball.* Rev. and enlarged ed. Westport, CT: Greenwood Press, 2000. Pp. 1163–1165.

47039. Holway, John. "Ted Page." In: his *Voices from the Great Black Baseball Leagues.* Rev. ed. New York: Da Capo Press, 1992. Pp. 140–168.

James Vincent ("Jim" or "Pug") Pagliaroni

C-BROADCASTER. (B: Dec. 11, 1937, Dearborn, MI). Boston (AL), 1960–1962; Pittsburgh (NL), 1963–1967; Oakland (AL), 1968–1969; Seattle (AL), 1969. Remarks: Had 622 hits (90 homers) and four stolen bases in 949 games in 11 campaigns; had three homers in two days, including a grand slam, June 17–18, 1961; later Red Sox broadcaster.

47040. Abrams, Al. "Jim Pagliaroni: 'Pug' Catches on to [Manny] Mota and the Bucs." *Baseball Digest,* XXII (June 1963), 57–69.

47041. McHugh, Roy. "The Semi-Continental Pirate." *Sport,* XLII (August 1966), 54–57.

Michael Timothy ("Mike" or "Pags") Pagliarulo

3B. (B: March 15, 1960, Medford, MA). New York (AL), 1984–1989; San Diego (NL), 1989–1990; Minnesota (AL), 1991–1993; Baltimore (AL), 1993; Seibu Lions (Japan League), 1994; Texas (AL), 1995. Remarks: Obtained 942 hits (134 homers) and 18 stolen bases in 1,246 U.S. big league games over 11 years; had game winning homer in Game Three of 1991 ALCS; later a Massachusetts high school coach who, with Willie Fraser, formed IScouts, Inc., a technology-enabled scouting service that delivers custom professional scouting information and video to baseball organizations around the world, in 2002.

47042. Berney, Louis. "Mike Pagliarulo Hopes to Restore the Power in His Bat." *Orioles Gazette,* III (August 27, 1993), 14–15.

47043. Klein, Moss. "Mike Pagliarulo Hits the Comeback Trail." *Baseball Digest,* XLVIII (June 1989), 59–61.

47044. Lauber, Scott. "Home from the Hot Corner." *Yankees Magazine,* XX (September 1999), 102–107.

47045. Nash, Bruce and Allan Zullo. "Mike Pagliarulo." In: their *Little Big Leaguers: Amazing Boyhood Stories of Today's Baseball Stars.* New York: Little Simon, 1990. Pp. 88–89.

47046. Wendel, Tim. "In a Pinch, Twins' Pagliarulo Delivers." *USA Today Baseball Weekly,* I October 18, 1991), 22–23.

47047. Wilder, Steve. "Yankees' Mike Pagliarulo: He Strives for Perfection." *Baseball Digest,* XLV (November 1986), 78–79.

Leroy Robert ("Satchel") Paige★

P. (B: July 7, 1906, Mobile, AL–D: June 5, 1982). Chattanooga Black Lookouts, 1926–1927; Birmingham Black Barons, 1927–1930; Baltimore Black Sox, 1930; Cleveland Cubs, 1931; Pittsburgh Crawfords, 1931–1934; Kansas City Monarchs, 1935–1937; Pittsburgh Crawfords and Ciudad Trujillo Santo Domingo team, 1937; Newark Eagles, 1938; Satchel Paige's All-Stars, 1939; Kansas City Monarchs, 1939–1942; New York Black Yankees and Memphis Red Sox, 1943; Kansas City Monarch, 1944–1945; Philadelphia Stars, 1947; Kansas City Monarchs, 1948; Cleveland (AL), 1948–1949; Kansas City Monarchs and Philadelphia Stars, 1950; Chicago American Giants, 1951; St. Louis (AL), 1951–1953; Kansas City Monarchs, 1955; Miami (IL), 1956–1958; Portland (PCL), 1961; Kansas City (AL), 1965; Peninsula (Carolina League), 1966; Indianapolis Clowns, 1967; coach, Atlanta (NL), 1968. Remarks: One of the most colorful and wealthy players of the Negro Leagues, Paige, who earned his nickname at age 7 carrying suitcases from the Mobile train station, did not pitch in the white majors until age 42, thus becoming MLB's oldest rookie when he simultaneously became the first African American pitcher in an AL game, Aug. 13, 1948; first African American hurler to appear in a World Series contest, pitching 2/3 inning of relief, Oct. 10, 1948; won one game and lost three with Kansas City in 1965 at age

59 , earning honors as the oldest man to pitch a big league game; major league career total of 29 wins and 31 losses deceiving, as Paige himself estimated that he had also appeared in some 2,600 Negro League contests (winning 2,000) and hurled perhaps 300 shutouts, including 55 no-hitters; named to Missouri Sports Hall of Fame, 1979; elected to National Baseball Hall of Fame in 1971 (the first former Negro League player inducted), where his plaque reads: "Paige was one of the greatest stars to play in the Negro baseball Leagues. Thrilled millions of people and won hundreds of games. Struck out 21 major leaguers in an exhibition game. Helped pitch Cleveland Indians to the 1948 pennant in his first big league year at age 42. His pitching was a legend among major league hitters."

47048. Bankes, James. "Master Satch." In: his *The Pittsburgh Crawfords*. Dubuque, IA: Wm. C. Brown Publishers, 1991. Pp. 31–43.

47049. Blackburn, Paul. "A Long Range Interview with Satchel Paige, the Man of Age." In: *Io: The Baseball Issue*. Cape Elizabeth, ME: Io Publications, 1971. Pp. 144–146.

47050. Bontemps, Arna. "Leroy (Satchel) Paige." In: his *Famous Negro Athletes*. New York: Dodd, Mead, 1964. Pp. 71–80.

47051. "Brainiest Man in Baseball: Leroy 'Satchel' Paige is One of the National Game's Sharpest Players Both on and off the Field." *Ebony*, VII (August 1952), 26–28.

47053. Broeg, Bob. "Satch." In: his *My Baseball Scrapbook*. St. Louis, MO: River City Publishers, 1983. Pp. 48–50.

47054. Brosnan, Jim "A Good Pitch is Better Than a Wild Swing." *National Review,* XII (June 1962), 446–448.

47055. _____. "Satchel Paige." In: his *Great Baseball Pitchers*. New York: Random House, 1965. Pp. 63–73.

47056. Bryson, Bill. "The Clubhouse Was Satchel's Bullpen." *Baseball Digest*, XX (July 1961), 91–92.

47057. Burchard, S.H. "Satchel Paige." In: his *Book of Baseball Greats*. New York: Harcourt, Brace, Jovanovich, 1983. Pp. 60–63.

47058. Cline-Ransome, Lesa. *Satchel Paige*. New York: Simon and Schuster, 2000. 32p.

47059. Cobbledick, Gordon. "Old Satch: He's Really-Got It." *Sport*, V (December 1948), 32–35+.

47060. _____. "Satch a Natch for the Hall of Fame." *Baseball Digest*, XI (October 1952), 31–33.

47061. Cohane, Tim. "Ancient Satchel" *Look*, XVII (April 7, 1953), 65–66.

47062. Creamer, Robert W. "Fine Paige Out of History." *Sports Illustrated*, LIV (June 1, 1981), 55+.

47063. Daley, Arthur. "Forever is a Long Time." In: his *Sports of The Times: The Arthur Daley Years*. New York: Quadrangle/The New York Times Book Co., 1975. Pp. 274–276.

47064. _____. "Satch Proved Self in Brief Role." *Baseball Digest*, IX (May 1950), 55–57.

47065. Davis, Mac. "Satchel Paige: The Ageless Wonder." In: his *Pacemakers in Baseball*. Cleveland, OH: World Publishing Company, 1968. Pp. 30–33.

47066. De Bourbon, Caucus & Mitzi Herrera. *Satchel Paige*. San Diego, CA: Revolutionary Comics, 1993. 30p.

47067. Donovan, Richard E. "The Fabulous Satchel Paige." *Collier's*, CXXXI (May 30–June 13, 1941), 62+, 20–24, 54–59. Reprinted in Charles Einstein, ed., *The Fireside Book of Baseball* (New York. Simon and Schuster, 1956), pp. 75–95.

47068. Fitzgerald, Ed. "Let's Get Old Satch into the Hall of Fame." *Sport*, XIII (November 1952), 16–19.

47069. Fox, W.P. "A Conversation with Satchel Paige." *Holiday*, XXXVIII (August 1965) 18+.

47070. Grady, Sandy. "The Return of Satchel Paige." *Baseball Digest,* XXVII (October 1969), 32–30.

47071. Grayson, Harry. "Leroy (Satchel) Paige." In: *They Played The Game*. New York: A.S. Barnes, 1944. Pp. 132–133.

47072. Gretschier, Steven P. "The Short, Sweet Indian Summer of Satchel Paige." *Timeline,* Vi (April-May 1989), 44–56.

47073. Gustkey, Earl. "Satchel Paige Breaks His Own Rule and Looks Back." *Baseball Digest*, XXXIX (March 1980), 78–97.

47074. Hart, Stan. "Satchel Paige." In: *Scouting Reports: The Original Reviews of Baseball's Greatest Stars*. New York: Macmillan, 1995. Pp. 99–109.

47075. Herskowitz, Mickey. "Paige Near the End of the Book." *Baseball Digest*, XXIII (April 1964), 46–49.

47076. Holway, John B. *Josh and Satch: The Life and Times of Josh Gibson and Satchel Paige*. Baseball and American Society, no. 6. Westport, CT: Meckler, 1991. 238p.

47077. _____. "Satchel Paige." *TV Guide*, XXIX (May 30, 1981), 30–32.

47078. Humphrey, Kathryn Long. *Satchel Paige*. New York: Watts, 1988. 110p.

47079. Klima, John. "Shutout the Whispers: Bill Wright vs. Satchel Paige (August 20, 1948)." In: his *Pitched Battle: 35 of Baseball's Greatest Duels from the Mound*. Jefferson, NC: McFarland & Co., Inc., 2002. Pp. 77–81.

47080. Lardner, Rex. "*Sport's* Hall of Fame: The Ageless Satchel Paige." *Sport*, XLVII (January 1969), 44–47.

47081. "The Law Tells Satch: 'Win or Jail.'" *Ebony*, XIII (September 1958), 77–82.

47082. Lebovitz, Hal. "The Day Old Satch Made the Majors." *Sport*, XXIV (September 1957), 70–74.

47083. Leiker, Ken. "26–1971: Satchel Paige Becomes the First Player Inducted Into the Hall of Fame for His Negro League Accomplishments." In: his *Major League Baseball Memorable Moments: The Most Memorable Moments in Major League Baseball History*. New York: Ballantine Books, 2002. Pp. 130–135.

47084. "Leroy (Robert) Paige." In: *Current Biography Yearbook, 1952*. New York: H.W. Wilson Co., 1952. Pp. 458–460.

47085. Lester, Larry, with John "Buck" O'Neil. "Satch Vs. Josh [Gibson]." *The National Pastime*, XIII (1993), 30–33.

47086. Lewis, Allen. "For Satchel, It Was Always 'in the Bag.'" *Baseball Digest*, XIX (August 1960), 10–11.

47087. Lewis, Franklin. "Past or No, It's Still Satchmo." *Baseball Digest*, X (October 1951), 35–37.

47088. Lewis, Lloyd. "Satchel Paige." In: his *It Takes All Kinds*. New York: Harcourt, 1947. Pp. 177–184.

47089. Lowitt, Bruce. "Satchel Paige–If Only He'd Been White." In: Associated Press. *Sports Immortals*. Englewood Cliffs, NJ: Prentice-Hall, 1974. Pp. 146–151.

47090. Macht, Norman L. *Baseball Legends: Satchel Paige*. New York: Chelsea House, 1991. 64p.

47091. Manning, Max. "Satchel Paige." In: Danny Peary, ed. *Cult Baseball Players*. New York: Simon and Schuster, 1990. Pp. 301–307.

47092. _____. "Satchel Paige." In: Danny Peary, ed. *Baseball's Finest: The Greats, the Flakes, the Weird and the Wonderful*. North Dighton, MA: The JG Press, 1990. Pp. 301–307. Both Peary books are identical.

47093. Marasco, David. "Apocrypha in Pittsburgh." *The National Pastime*, XVII (1997), 134–137.

47094. McKissack, Patricia and Frederick. *Satchel Paige: The Best Arm in Baseball*. Hillside, NJ: Enslow, 1992. 32p.

47095. Moffi, Larry and Jonathan Kronstadt. "Leroy Robert 'Satchel' Paige." In: their *Crossing the Line: Black Major Leaguers, 1947–1959*. Jefferson, NC: McFarland & Co., Inc., 1994. Pp. 32–35.

47096. Molter, Harry. "Leroy (Satchel) Paige: Baseball's Living Legend." In: his *Famous American Athletes of Today*. 13th Series. New York: Page, 1953. Pp. 205–222.

47097. O'Neil, John ("Buck"). "Unforgettable Satchel Paige." *Reader's Digest,* CXXIV (April 1984), 89–93.

47098. Paige, Leroy ("Satchel"), as told to David Lipman. *Maybe I'll Pitch Forever: A Great Baseball Player Tells the Hilarious Story Behind the Legend*. Garden City, NY: Doubleday, 1962. 285p. Excerpted in *Saturday Evening Post*, CCXXXIV (March 11, 1961), 39–39+ and reprinted by the University of Nebraska Press at Lincoln in a 295-page 1993 edition, which contains a foreword by John B. Holway.

47099. _____., as told to Hal Lebovitz. *Pitchin' Man*. New York: H.P. Lebovitz, 1948. 96p.

47100. _____. *Pitchin' Man: Satchel Paige's Own Story*. Westport, CT: Meckler Publishing, 1992. 121p.

47101. _____. "My Greatest Day in Baseball." *National Baseball Hall of Fame and Museum Newsletter*, IV (July 1982), 4+.

47102. _____. "Rules for Staying Young." In: Nicholas Dawidoff, ed. *Baseball: A Literary Anthology*. New York: The Library of America, 2002. Pp. 318–319.

47103. _____. *Satchel Sez: The Wit, Wisdom and World of Leroy "Satchel" Paige*. Edited by David Sterry and Arielle Eckstut. New York: Crown, 2001. 112p.

47104. _____, as told to Ernest Mehl. "My Greatest Day in Baseball." In: John P. Carmichael, ed. *My Greatest Day in Baseball*. New York: A.S. Barnes, 1945. Pp. 148–152. First published In the *Chicago Daily News*.

47105. "A Philosopher's Consolation." *Sports Illustrated*, XX (January 27, 1964), 17.

47106. Powers, Jimmy. "Satchel Paige." In: his *Baseball Personalities*. Chicago, IL: Field, 1949. Pp. 283–288.

47107. Ransome, Lesa-Cline. *Satchel Paige*. New York: Simon & Schuster Books for Young Readers, 2000. Unpaged.

47108. Reidenbaugh, Lowell. "Satchel Paige." In: his *Cooperstown: Where Legends Live Forever*. St. Louis, MO: The Sporting News, 1983. Pp. 206–207.

47109. Ribowsky, Marty. *Don't Look Back: Satchel Paige in the Shadows of Baseball*. New York: Simon and Schuster, 1994. 351p. Reprinted by the Cambridge, MA, firm of De Capo Press in 2000.

47110. Richman, Milton. "Ironman Extraordinary." In: Bruce Jacobs, ed. *Baseball Stars of 1953*. New York: Lion Books, 1953. Pp. 91–97.

47111. Roper, Scott. "Uncovering Satchel Paige's 1935 Season." *The Baseball Research Journal*, XXIII (1994), 51–54.

47112. Rubin, Bob. *Satchel Paige: All-Time Baseball Great*. New York: G.P. Putnam, 1974. 157p.

47113. Ruck, Robert L. "Leroy Robert 'Satchel' Paige." In: Vol. G-P of David L. Porter, ed. *Biographical Dictionary of American Sports: Baseball*. Rev. and enlarged ed. Westport, CT: Greenwood Press, 2000. Pp. 1165–1167.

47114. _____. "Satchel Paige." In: John A. Garrity and Marsh C. Carries, eds. *American National Biography*. 24 vols. New York: Oxford University Press, 1999. XVI, 914–916.

47115. Rust, Art, Jr. "Satchel Paige." In: his *Get That Nigger Off the Field*. New York: Delacorte, 1976. Pp. 106–119.

47116. "Satch Makes the Big Leagues." *Life*, XXV (July 26, 1949), 49–50+.

47117. "Satchel Paige." In: Joseph J. Vecchione, ed. *The New York Times Book of Sports Legends*. New York: Times Books, 1991. Pp. 239–244.

47118. "Satchel Paige Pitches Bismarck to Semipro Title." In: Dean A. Sullivan, ed. *Middle Innings: A Documentary History of Baseball, 1900–1948*. Lincoln, NE: University of Nebraska Press, 1998. Pp. 157–159. Reprinted from the *Wichita Eagle*, Aug. 28, 1935.

47119. "Satchel the Great." *Time*, LII (July 19, 1948), 56+.

47120. Schmidt, Julie. *Satchel Paige*. Baseball Hall of Famers of the Negro League. New York: Rosen Publishing Group, 2002. 112p.

47121. Shane, Ted. "Old Satchel Man." In: Al Silverman, ed. *True's 1953 Baseball Yearbook*. Greenwich, CT: Fawcett Publications, 1953. Pp. 66–61.

47122. _____. "Satchel Man." *Reader's Digest*, LIV (June 1949), 39–42.

47123. Shapiro, Milton J. "General." In: his *Heroes of the Bullpen: Baseball's Greatest Relief Pitchers*. New York: Julian Messner, 1967. Pp. 15–29.

47124. Shirley, David. *Satchel Paige*. New York: Chelsea House Publishers, 1993. 102p.

47125. Shury, Dave. "The Last Barnstormer: An All-Time Great Appears in North Battleford." In: William Humber and John St. James, eds. *All I Thought About was Baseball: Writings on a Canadian Pastime*. Toronto and Buffalo, NY: University of Toronto Press, 1996. Pp. 273–274.

47126. _____. *Satch in Saskatchewan*. Battleford, SK: Saskatchewan Baseball Hall of Fame, 1996. 38p.

47127. Silverman, Al. "Satchel Paige Sounds Off." *Sport*, LIII (January 1972), 44–46.

47128. Sinclair, Ed. "Satchel Paige MVP in Last East-West Negro All-Star Game." In: Dean A. Sullivan, ed. *Late Innings: A Documentary History of Baseball, 1945–1972*. Lincoln, NE: University of Nebraska Press, 2002. Pp. 164–166. Reprinted from the *New York Herald-Tribune*, Aug. 21, 1961.

47129. Skipper, John C. "Epilogue: A Special Tribute to Satchel Paige." In: his *Inside Pitch: A Closer Look at Classic Baseball Moments*. Jefferson, NC: McFarland & Co., Inc., 1996. Pp. 179–182.

47130. Sloate, Susan. "Satchel Paige: From Rocks to Records." In: her *Hotshots: Baseball Greats of the Game When They Were Kids*. Boston, MA: Little, Brown, 1991. Pp. 48–53.

47131. "Slow: Satchel Paige." *The New Yorker*, XXVIII (September 1, 1952), 32–33.

47132. Smith, Ira L. "Leroy (Satchel) Paige." In: his *Baseball's Famous Pitchers*. New York: A.S. Barnes, 1954. Pp. 298–302.

47133. Smith, Robert. "Leroy (Satchel) Paige." In: his *Pioneers of Baseball*. Boston, MA: Little, Brown, 1978. Pp. 135–149.

47134. Smith, Ron. "Satchel Paige 19." In: his *The Sporting News Selects Baseball's 100 Greatest Players*. St. Louis, MO: The Sporting News, 1998. Pp. 46–47.

47135. Stainback, Berry. "Dang, Nobody Liked Hitting His 'Ole Trouble Ball." *Panorama*, I (September 1980), 82–85.

47136. Stann, Francis. "Satchel Paige: Hall of Famer." *Baseball Digest*, XXXI (January 1972), 78–81.

47137. Turner, Glennette T. "Satchel Paige." In: her *Take a Walk in Their Shoes*. New York: Cobblehill Books, 1989. Pp. 149–160.

47138. Van Blair, Rick. "Was Satchel Paige as Great as They Said He Was?" *Baseball Digest,* LV (June 1996), 68–71.

47139. Veeck, William Jr., as told to George Vass. "The Game I'll Never Forget." *Baseball Digest,* XXXI (March 1972), 41–44. This account of the August 13, 1949 major league debut of Satchel Paige was reprinted in John Kuenster, ed., *From Cobb to Catfish* (Chicago: Rand McNally, 1975), pp. 174–175.

47140. Walbum, Lee. "Satchel Might Be Gaining on Us." *Atlanta,* XX (August 1980), 79+.

47141. Ward, Geoffrey C. and Ken Burns. "Satchel Paige." *U.S. News & World Report,* CXVII (August 29, 1994), 84–85.

47142. Washington, Chester L. "Satchel's Back in Town." In: David K. Wiggins and Patrick B. Miller, eds. *The Unlevel Playing Field: A Documentary History of the African American Experience in Sport.* Champaign, IL: University of Illinois Press, 2003. Pp. 93–98.

47143. Wheatley, Tom. "Who Was Satchel Paige?" *Beckett Baseball Card Monthly,* VI (September 1989), 75–77.

47144. "When Batters Wobble." *Newsweek,* LII (July 14, 1958), 57–58.

47145. Whittaker, Andrea N. and James A. Riley. "Paige Out of History." *Sports Illustrated for Kids,* XIV (July 2002), 58–61.

47146. Wolf, Al. "A Bookful in a Paige." *Baseball Digest,* XIII (April 1954), 65–67.

47147. Young, Andrew S. N. "A Black Athlete in the Golden Age of Sports." *Ebony,* XXIV (March 1969), 122–124+.

47148. _____. "Satchel Paige." In: his *Great Negro Baseball Stars and How They Made the Major Leagues.* New York: A.S. Barnes, 1953. Pp. 73–91.

47149. _____. "Satchel Paige." In: his *Negro Firsts in Baseball.* New York: Johnson Publishing Co., 1963. p. 214.

Stephen Michael ("Steve" or "Stevie") Palermo
UMP-BROADCASTER. (B: Oct. 9, 1949, Worcester, MA). Remarks: A. L. arbiter, 1977–1991; Elected to Texas Baseball Hall of Fame, 1992; broadcaster, Seattle (AL), 1992–1994; broadcaster/analyst, MSG Network, 1994–; special asst., Major League Baseball Executive Council, 1994–1999; Umpire Supervisor, Major League Baseball, 2000–; recipient of various awards for heroism in wake of injuries received on July 7, 1991 while attempting to aid mugging victims in a Dallas parking lot.

47150. Demaret, Kent. "The Umpire Won't Call Himself Out: Steve Palermo Paralyzed While Attempting to Stop a Mugging." *People Weekly,* XXXVII (April 27, 1992), 105–108.

47151. Gerlach, Larry R. "Stephen Michael 'Steve,' 'Stevie' Palermo." In: Vol. G-P of David L. Porter, ed. *Biographical Dictionary of American Sports: Baseball.* Rev. and enlarged ed. Westport, CT: Greenwood Press, 2000. Pp. 1167–1168.

47152. Knopf, David. "Inch by Inch: Three-and-a-Half Years After Being Partially Paralyzed by a Mugger's Bullet, Steve Palermo Still Fights for What He Hopes Will Be a Full Recovery." *Referee,* XX (February 1995), 28–35.

47153. Marazzi, Rich. "The Heroic Story of Disabled AL Umpire Steve Palermo." *Sport Collector's Digest,* XXIII (October 11, 1996), 90–91.

47154. _____. "Steve Palermo's Incredible Comeback from Tragedies." *Sport Collector's Digest,* XXIII (October 18, 1996), 80–81.

47155. Newman, Bruce. "Pain and Progress." *Sports Illustrated,* LXXVII (July 6, 1992), 28–33.

47156. Palermo, Steve. "Interview." *Referee,* XIV (October 1989), 20–23.

47157. "Umpire Steve Palermo Was Left Paralyzed When He Was Shot During a Robbery Attempt." *Sports Illustrated for Kids,* V (April 1993), 24–25.

47158. Will, George F. "Steve Palermo's Game of Inches." In: his *Bunts: Curt Flood, Camden Yards, Pete Rose and Other Reflections on Baseball.* New York: Touchstone Books, 1998. Pp. 218–220.

David Michael ("Dave") Pallone
UMP. (B: Oct. 5, 1951, Waltham, MA). Remarks: NL arbiter, 1979–1988.

47159. Eberly, Tim. "Whatever Happened to Dave Pallone?" *Referee,* XXV (July 2000), 40+.

47160. Isherwood, Christopher. "Strike, He's Out! Former Umpire Dave Pallone Talks About Gay Life in the Big Leagues." *Advocate: The National Gay & Lesbian Newsmagazine,* no. 555 (July 17, 1990), 50–53.

47161. Pallone, David M. "Interview." *Referee,* V (May 1981), 11–17, 55.

47162. _____., with Alan Steinberg. *Behind the Mask: My Double Life in Baseball.* New York: Viking Press, 1990. 331p.

47163. Wulf, Steve. "30 Days." *Sports Illustrated,* LXVIII (May 9, 1988), 22–25. Pallone and Pete Rose.

Rafael Palmeiro
OF-1B. (B: Rafael Palmeiro Corrales, Sept. 24, 1964, Havana, Cuba). Chicago (NL), 1986–1988; Texas (AL), 1989–1993; Baltimore (AL), 1994–1998; Texas (AL), 1999–2003; Baltimore (AL), 2004–. Remarks: Through 2004, has had 2,922 hits (572 homers) and 95 stolen bases in 2,721 games; had grand slam homer, July 27, 1996; AL doubles leader, 1991; became spokesman for Viagra, 2002.

47164. Agliardo, Peter. "The Sweet Swing of Success." *LifeDrive,* (Winter 2002), 30–33.

47165. Brandt, Ed. *Rafael Palmeiro: At Home with the Baltimore Orioles.* Childs, MD: Mitchell Lane Publishers, 1998. 128p.

47166. Eisenberg, John. "Rafael Palmeiro Wants to Do More to Spark Orioles." *Baseball Digest,* LVI (July 1997), 60–61.

47167. Elliott, Josh. "Raffy Joins the Club: The Rangers' Rafael Palmeiro Celebrated His 500th Home Run and Accepted Long Overdue Recognition in Typically Understated Fashion." *Sports Illustrated,* XCVIII (May 19, 2003), 52–57.

47168. Fraley, Gerry. "Palmeiro Needs Armed Posse of Rangers for Shoot-Out In West." In: George Leonard, ed. *Athlon's Baseball '91.* Nashville, TN: Athlon Sports Communications, 1991. Pp. 162–165.

47169. Howard, Johnette. "A Star in the Shadows." *Sports Illustrated,* LXXXVII (September 8, 1997), 42–47.

47170. Koenig, Bill. "Pillar of Strength: Orioles Slugger Rafael Palmeiro Isn't Dwelling on His Lack of Notoriety." *USA Today Baseball Weekly,* VI (January 15, 1997), 20–23.

47171. Kurkjian, Tim. "The Third Man." *Sports Illustrated,* LXXIX (August 16, 1993), 46–47.

47172. Marvis, Barbara. *Rafael Palmeiro.* Childs, MD: Mitchell Lane Publishers, 1998. 32p.

47173. McMurray, John. "Rafael Palmeiro — Quietly Swinging into the Record Books." *Baseball Digest,* LXIII (September 2004), 52–55.

47174. Newton, Brad. "Superstar Gallery: Rafael Palmeiro." *Beckett Baseball Card Monthly,* VIII (November 1991), 11–13.

47175. Palmeiro, Rafael. "When I was a Kid." *Junior League Baseball,* no. 58 (July-August 2004), 20+.

47176. Pearlman, Jeff. "A Nifty Pickup: the Rangers Unwittingly Made the Play of the Off-season By Signing Free-agent Rafael Palmeiro." *Sports Illustrated*, XCI (July 19, 1999), 46–47.

47177. Reichman, Victor. "A Second Look: Rafael Palmeiro." *Beckett Baseball Card Monthly*, IX (April 1992), 101–102.

47178. Rogers, Phil "The Hidden Profit Behind a Deal: The Cubs' Trade of Rafael Palmeiro to Texas in 1988 Remains Unpopular with Chicago Fans, but It Led to the Acquiring of Sammy Sosa." *Baseball Digest*, LXI (September 2002), 60–63.

47179. _____. "Interview: Rafael Palmeiro." *Inside Sports*, XVI (May 1994), 24–31.

47180. Smith, Duane A. "Rafael Palmeiro." In: Vol. G-P of David L. Porter, ed. *Biographical Dictionary of American Sports: Baseball.* Rev. and enlarged ed. Westport, CT: Greenwood Press, 2000. Pp. 1168–1169.

47181. Sorci, Rick. "Baseball Profile: First Baseman Rafael Palmeiro." *Baseball Digest*, LIV (December 1995), 47–48.

47182. Weinberg, Rick. "Texas Terror." *Sport*, LXXXIII (May 1992), 38–40.

47183. Williams, Mark D. "Majors' Overlooked Star." *Baseball Digest*, LIX (May 2000), 52–55.

Dean William Palmer
3B. (B: Dec. 27, 1968, Tallahassee, FL). Texas (AL), 1989, 1991–1997; Kansas City (AL), 1997–1998; Detroit (AL), 1999–2002. Remarks: Had 1,217 hits (275 homers) and 48 stolen bases in 1,331 games in 13 years; had grand slam homer, April 21, 1996.

47184. Iverson, Kurt. "Fire Tested." *Beckett Focus on Future Stars*, II (April 1992), 6–9.

James Alvin ("Jim") Palmer★
P-BROADCASTER. (B: Oct. 15, 1945, New York City). Baltimore (AL), 1965–1967, 1969–1984. Remarks: Won 268 games and lost 152, with four "saves," in 19 seasons; AL Cy Young Award, 1973, 1975–1976; hurled no-hitter, Aug. 13, 1969; ABC baseball broadcaster, 1984 and his television commercials for Jockey Underwear are still remembered; elected to National Baseball Hall of Fame in 1990, where his plaque reads: "High-kicking, smooth-throwing symbol of Baltimore's six championship teams of 1960's, 70's, and 80's. Impressive numbers include 268 wins with .638 pct., eight 20-win seasons, 2.86 ERA and no grand slams allowed over entire 19 year career. Intensity was trademark of 3-time Cy Young winner, who combined strength, intelligence, competitiveness and consistency to become Orioles' all-time winningest hurler."

47185. Allen, Maury. "Jim Palmer (1965–Present)." In: his *Baseball's 100.* New York: Galahad Books, 1981. Pp. 149–151.

47186. Boswell, Thomas. "Palmer vs. Palmer." In: *his Why Time Begins on Opening Day.* Garden City, NY: Doubleday, 1984. Pp. 223–238.

47187. Broeg, Bob. "Pin Up Pitcher." In: his *My Baseball Scrapbook.* St. Louis, MO: River City Publishers, 1983. Pp. 178–180.

47188. Butler, Hal. "Jim Palmer." In: his *Baseball's Champion Pitchers.* New York: Julian Kessner, 1974. Pp. 65–77.

47189. Cohen, Joel H. *Jim Palmer, Great Comeback Competitor.* New York: G.P. Putnam, 1978. 192p.

47190. Cohen, Scott. "Jim Palmer." In: his *Jocks.* New York: Fireside Books, 1983. Pp. 84–87.

47171. Condon, David. "The Orioles' Jim Palmer: Baseball's Greatest Pitcher." *Baseball Digest*, XXXVIII (July 1979), 70–73.

47172. Deford, Frank. "In a Strike Zone of His Own." *Sports Illustrated*, XLV (July 26, 1976), 28–34.

47173. Durslag, Melvin. "Jim Palmer Views the Pinch Hitter Rule." *Baseball Digest*, XXXII (May 1973), 42–44.

47174. Elderkin, Phil "How Jim Palmer Sizes Up His Pitching." *Baseball Digest*, XXXVI June 1977), 30–31.

47175. Fimrite, Ron. "Kings of the Hill Again: Tom Seaver and Jim Palmer." *Sports Illustrated*, XLIII (July 21, 1975), 14–17.

47176. Frommer, Harvey and Frederick J. "Jim Palmer." In: their *Growing Up Baseball: An Oral History.* Dallas, TX: Taylor Publishing Co., 2001. Pp. 176–178.

47177. Gerlach, Larry R. "James Alvin 'Jim' Palmer." In: Vol. G-P of David L. Porter, ed. *Biographical Dictionary of American Sports: Baseball.* Rev. and enlarged ed. Westport, CT: Greenwood Press, 2000. Pp. 1169–1170.

47178. Goldman, Mike. "A Final Look: Jim Palmer." *Beckett Baseball Card Monthly*, VII (April 1990), 94–95.

47179. Henneman, Jim. "Jim Palmer Recalls the Lean Days." *Baseball Digest*, XXXIII (January 1974), 45–47.

47180. Herman, Jack. "Who's Better?: Seaver or Palmer?" *Baseball Digest*, XXXVI (July 1977), 28–31.

47181. Hoffer, Richard. "Hope Flings Eternal." *Sports Illustrated*, LXXIV (March 11, 1991), 24–27.

47182. Honig, Donald. "Jim Palmer." In: his *The Greatest Pitchers of All Time.* New York: Crown Publishers, Inc., 1988. Pp. 134–139.

47183. Jablow, Paul. "Jim Palmer: All-Around Oriole." In: Ray Robinson, ed. *Baseball Stars of 1974.* New York: Pyramid Books, 1974. Pp. 78–83.

47184. "Jim Palmer." In: *Current Biography Yearbook, 1980.* New York: H. W. Wilson Co., 1980. Pp. 301–303.

47185. Lapin, Jackie. "Jim Palmer of the Orioles." *Sport*, LX (March 1975), 66, 71–77.

47186. Marx, Larry. "Audubon Never Saw One Like Him: Jim Palmer Is the Oriole with the Colorful Underwear." *People Weekly*, XVIII (October 4, 1982), 110–112.

47187. McKay, Joe. "Jim Palmer: From Oblivion to Greatness." In: his *The Great Shutout Pitchers: 20 Profiles of a Vanishing Breed.* Jefferson, NC: McFarland & Co., Inc., 2004. Pp. 170–176.

47188. Paceli, Lee C. "Jim Palmer: Fit and 'Famed' at 45." *Physician and Sportsmedicine*, XVIII (March 1990), 135–136.

47189. Palmer, Jim. "The Inside Pitch." *Inside Sports*, XVI (May 1994), 48–51.

47190. _____. *Pitching.* Edited by Joel H. Cohen. New York: Atheneum, 1975. 211p.

47191. _____, as told to George Vass. "The Game I'll Never Forget." *Baseball Digest*, XXXV (March 1976), 81–83.

47192. _____, with Jack T. Clary. *Jim Palmer's Way to Fitness.* New York: Harper and Row, 1985. 169p.

47193. _____, with Jim Dale. *Together We Were Eleven Foot Nine: The Twenty Year Friendship of Hall of Fame Pitcher Jim Palmer and Orioles Manager Earl Weaver.* Kansas City, MO: Andrews and McMeel, 1996. 169p.

47194. _____, with Mark Ribowsky. "Interview." *Sport;* LXVIII ((May 1979), 72+; LXXIV (April 1983), 21+.

47195. _____, with Tracy Ringolsby. "Making the Final Stride." *Inside Sports*, XVI (April 1994), 28+.

47196. Plummer, William and Don Sider. "Refusing to Go Gentle Into Life's Dugout, Jim Palmer Plots a Comeback." *People Weekly*, XXXV (February 25, 1991), 53–54.

47197. Reed, Susan K. "How Do You Sell Unmentionables?" *Savvy*, IV (July 1983), 34–39.

47198. Ribowsky, Mark. "Jim Palmer." *Sport*, LXVIII (May 1979), 69–75.

47199. Ritter, Lawrence and Donald Honig. "Jim Palmer." In: their *The 100 Greatest Baseball Players of All Time.* New York: Crown Publishers, 1981. Pp. 14–15.

47200. Rubin, Bob. "Jim Palmer: Not Just Another Pretty Face in the Booth." *Inside Sports,* VIII (July 1986), 15–17.

47201. Smith, Ron. "Jim Palmer 64." In: his *The Sporting News Selects Baseball's 100 Greatest Players.* St. Louis, MO: *The Sporting News,* 1998. Pp. 140–141.

47202. Steadman, John F. "Jim Palmer's Career Almost Ended Before It Started." *Baseball Digest,* XLIX (May 1990), 47–51.

47203. _____. "Jim Palmer: The Orioles' Pitching Symphony." *Baseball Digest,* XXXVI (January 1977) 79–81.

47204. Urban, Darren. "Jim Palmer: The Pride of Scottsdale." In: Mike Holden, ed. *Mining Towns to Major Leagues: A History of Arizona Baseball.* Cleveland, OH: The Society for American Baseball Research, 1999. Pp. 30–31.

47205. Ward, Robert. "Jim Palmer." *Sport,* LXXIV (April 1983), 21–26.

47206. Wulf, Steve. "Biggest Bird in the Bushes." *Sports Illustrated,* LIX (August 15, 1983), 44–45.

47207. Young, Ken. "Jim Palmer: Consistency and Grace." In: his *Cy Young Award Winners.* New York: Walker and Co., 1994. Pp. 76–89.

47208. Zanger, Jack "The Arm That Came Back." *Sport,* XLVIII (August 1969), 44–47.

Joseph ("Joe") Paparella
UMP. Remarks: AL arbiter, 1946–1965.

47209. Gerlach, Larry R. "Joe Paparella." In: his *The Men in Blue: Conversations with Umpires.* New York: Viking Press, 1980. Pp. 129–150. Reprinted by the University of Nebraska Press in 1994.

Milton Steven ("Milt" or "Gimpy") Pappas
P. (B: May 11, 1939, Detroit, MI). Baltimore (AL), 1957–1965; Cincinnati (NL), 1966–1968; Atlanta (NL), 1968–1970; Chicago (NL), 1970–1973. Remarks: Won 209 games and lost 164, with four "saves," in 17 years; pitched no-hitter (Sept. 2, 1972), which would have been a perfect game if 9th inning walk not issued; had 20 career homers, including two in one game, Aug. 27, 1961.

47210. Condon, David. "Milt Pappas Next to Join the Elite?" *Baseball Digest,* XXXII (June 1973), 29–32.

47211. Fehler, Gene. "Milt Pappas." In: his *Tales from Baseball's Golden Age.* Champaign, IL: Sports Publishing Co., 2000. Chapter 39.

47212. Isaacs, Stan. "Milt Pappas, Pitching Prodigy." *Sport,* XXXIV (June 1962), 44–45+.

47213. Martin, Douglas D. "Milton Stephen 'Milt,' 'Gimpy' Pappas." In: Vol. G-P of David L. Porter, ed. *Biographical Dictionary of American Sports: Baseball.* Rev. and enlarged ed. Westport, CT: Greenwood Press, 2000. Pp. 1170–1172.

47214. Pappas, Milton S. "The Game I'll Never Forget." *Baseball Digest,* XXXVI (February 1977), 62–65.

47215. _____., with Larry Names. *Out at Home: Triumph and Tragedy in the Life of a Major Leaguer.* Oshkosh, WI: LKP Group, 2000. 350p.

47215. Rogin, Gilbert. "'I'm the Worst That's Ever Been'-Baltimore's Milt Pappas." *Sports Illustrated,* XX (April 27,1964), 54–56+.

47216. Steadman, John F. "His Head Has Caught Up with His Arm: Milt Pappas, 16-Win Oriole, Has Outgrown His Brash Kid Days." *Baseball Digest,* XXIV (May 1965), 47–49.

47217. Tanton, Bill. "Nineteen, Cocky—and Good." *Baseball Digest,* XVII (October 1958), 16–21.

47218. Westcott, Rich. "Milt Pappas—A Winner in Two Leagues." In: his *Diamond Greats.* Westport, CT: Meckler Books, 1988. Pp. 300–304.

Craig Harold Paquette
3B-OF-SS. (B: March 28, 1969, Long Beach, CA). Oakland (AL), 1993–1995; Kansas City (AL), 1996–1997; New York (NL), 1998; St. Louis (NL), 1999–2001; Detroit (AL), 2002–. Remarks: Through 2003, had 620 hits (99 homers) and 27 stolen bases in 814 games; had five RBI's in one game, June 27, 1997.

47219. Doyle, Al. "Super Sub: Cardinals' Craig Paquette—a Utilityman with Power." *Baseball Digest,* LX (November 2001), 75–77.

Chan Ho Park
P. (B: June 30, 1973, Kongiu, South Korea). Los Angeles (NL), 1994–2001; Texas (AL), 2002–. Remarks: Through 2004, has won 94 games and lost 72; first South Korean player to appear in a MLB game, as well as the first Korean pitcher to win a big league contest; first 20th century hurler (and only 2nd all time) to surrender two grand slam homers in same inning, April 23, 1999; surrendered the season's 71st homer by Barry Bonds (q.v.), Oct. 5, 2001.

47220. Enrico, Dottie. "Living Well on Park Place: Korean Pitcher Comes into His Own in L.A." *USA Today Baseball Weekly,* VIII (July 29, 1998), 28–30.

47221. Johnston, Jeff. "Deeper Look: Chan Ho Park." *Beckett Baseball Card Monthly,* XI, no. 112 (July 1994), 20–21.

47222. Weinstock, Jeff. "Chan Ho Park." *Sport,* LXXXIX (August 1998), 76–79.

Ace Parker *see* **Clarence McKay ("Ace") Parker**
Clarence McKay ("Ace") Parker
SS-2B. (B: May 17, 1912, Portsmouth, VA). Philadelphia (AL), 1937–1938. Remarks: Had 37 hits (two homers) and one stolen base in 94 games in two years; pinch hit homer in first regular season big league AB, April 30, 1937; gave up pro baseball for pro football, playing for Brooklyn (N.F.L.), 1937–1941 and Boston (N.F.L.), 1945; New York (AAF.C.), 1945; N.F.L. MVP Award, 1940; elected to Pro Football Hall of Fame, 1972.

47223. Meany, Thomas. "'Baseball Is My Game,' says Ace Parker." *Sport,* I (December 1946), 50–52+.

Daniel Francis ("Dan") Parker
WRITER. (B: July 1, 1893, Waterbury, CT-D: May 20, 1967). Remarks: Reporter, *Waterbury Republican,* 1912–1913 and *Waterbury American,* 1913–1920; reporter, later sports editor and columnist, *New York Daily Mirror,* 1920–1963; columnist, *New York Journal,* 1963–1967; strong opponent of baseball's color line, elected to National Association of Sportswriters and Sportscasters Hall of Fame, 1975.

47224. Harper, James W. "Daniel Francis 'Dan' Parker." David L. Porter, ed. *Biographical Dictionary of American Sports: 1992–1995 Supplement for Baseball, Football, Basketball and Other Sports.* Westport, CT: Greenwood Press, 1995. Pp. 351–353.

David Gene ("Dave" or "The Cobra") Parker
OF. (B: June 9, 1951, Jackson, MS). Pittsburgh (NL), 1973–1983; Cincinnati (NL), 1984–1987; Oakland (AL), 1988–1989; Milwaukee (AL), 1990; California (AL) and Toronto (AL), 1991. Remarks: Had 2,712 hits (339 homers) and 154 stolen bases in 2,466 games in 19 years; led NL in doubles, 1977 and 1985; NL MVP Award, 1978; NL batting champion, 1977–1978; All-Star Game MPV award, 1979; NL RBI champion, 1985; coach, St. Louis (NL), 1998.

47225. Allen, Maury. "Dave Parker (1973–Present)." In: his *Baseball's 100*. New York: Galahad Books, 1981. Pp. 232–233.

47226. Bennett, Gaymon L. "David Gene 'Dave,' 'The Cobra' Parker." In: Vol. G-P of David L. Porter, ed. *Biographical Dictionary of American Sports: Baseball*. Rev. and enlarged ed. Westport, CT: Greenwood Press, 2000. Pp. 1172–1173.

47227. Brosnan, Jim. "Dave Parker: Peerless Pirate: 'Whatever He's Done, He Thinks He Can Do Better.'" *Boy's Life,* LXX (October 1980), 32–35.

47228. Buck, Ray. *Dave Parker: The Cobra's Swirl.* Chicago, IL: Children's Press, 1981. 42p.

47229. Clark, Tom. "Dave Parker." *Baseball.* Berkeley, CA: Figures, 1976. Pp. 54–55.

47230. Collier, Ken. "Dave Parker." In: Ken Collier, ed. *The Baseball Book, 1986*. Scottsdale, AZ: Jalart House, 1986. Pp. 11–13.

47231. Dalton, Joe. "For Sale: Dave Parker." *Sport,* LXXIV (October 1983), 41–48.

47232. Downey, Mike. "Dave Parker Left His Anger, Not His Talent, in Pittsburgh." *Baseball Digest,* XLIV (November 1985), 30–34.

47233. Elderkin, Phil "Dave Parker: Baseball's Next Great Hitter?" *Baseball Digest,* XXXV (August 1976), 30–33.

47234. Granger, Dave. "The Anatomy of an At-Bat." *Sport,* LXXVIII (July 1987), 26–29. Parker vs. Mike Scott.

47235. Gutman, Bill. "Dave Parker." In: his *Baseball's Belters: Jackson, Schmidt, Parker, Brett*. New York: Grosset and Dunlap, 1981. Pp. 118–158.

47236. _____ "Dave Parker." In: his *Pro Sports Champions*. New York: Julian Messner, 1981. Pp. 36–60.

47237. Haudricourt, Tom. "Brewers' Steep Falloff Will Stop if They Rally Around Parker." In: George Leonard, ed. *Athlon's Baseball '91*. Nashville, TN: Athlon Sports Communications, 1991. Pp. 120–123.

47238. Honig, Donald. "1978: Dave Parker." In: his *National League MVP's*. New York: Bantam Books, 1989. Pp. 99–100.

47239. Kuenster, John. "Dave Parker of the Pirates: Best of the Big Hitters of the Majors." *Baseball Digest,* XXXVI (July 1977), 16–19.

47240. Lawson, Earl. "Coming Home." In: Jim Ferguson, and Jon Braude, eds. *Cincinnati Reds 1984 Yearbook Magazine*. Cincinnati, OH: Public Relations Department, Cincinnati Reds, 1984. Pp. 112–13. Parker and Tony Perez.

47241. Leo, Joseph. "Dave Parker Checklist." *Baseball Cards,* IX (February 1989), 70–77.

47242. Masterson, Dave and Timm Boyle. "1978." In: their *Baseball's Best: The MVPs*. Chicago, IL: Contemporary Books, 1985. Pp. 292–297.

47243. McDonnell, Joe. "The World's Greatest Baseball Player: National League General Managers Vote Dave Parker Best in the Game." *Sepia,* XXVII (November 1978), 73–77.

47244. Mendelson, Abby. "Can Dave Parker Find Happiness in Pittsburgh Earning Only $200,000 a Year?" *Baseball Quarterly,* II (Spring 1978),14–13.

47245. Musick, Phil "I'm Pursuing the Ultimate'— Dave Parker." *Sport,* LXVIII (June 1979), 12–13+.

47246. Newhouse, Dave. "For Dave Parker, '89 was a Redeeming Year." *Baseball Digest,* XLIX (January 1990), 43–45.

47247. O'Brien, Jim. "'I'm the Best Player in Baseball'— Dave Parker." *Sport,* LXXII (June 1981), 13–18.

47248. Parker, David G. ("Dave"). "Interview." *Baseball Magazine,* New Series V (May 1981), 18–21.

47249. _____. as told to George Vass. "The Game I'll Never Forget." *Baseball Digest,* XLIV (April 1985), 79–82.

47250. Perotto, John. "Final Look: Dave Parker." *Beckett Baseball Card Monthly,* X, no. 99 (June 1993), 130–131.

47251. "Plutocrat from Pittsburgh." *Time,* CXII (April 16, 1979), 88+.

47252. Resciniti, Angelo G. "Dave Parker." In: his *Stars of the Diamond*. Mississauga, Ontario: School Book Fairs, 1981. Pp. 90–99.

47253. Reveron, Derek A. "Dave Parker: Big Man, Big Bat, and Baseball's Biggest Salary." *Ebony,* XXXIV (October 1979), 84–92.

47254. Ribowsky, Mark. "Dave Parker is the Closest Thing to Perfection." *Black Sports,* VII (May 1978), 44–47.

47255. Ritter, Lawrence and Donald Honig. "Dave Parker." In: their *The 100 Greatest Baseball Players of All Time*. New York: Crown Publishers, 1981. Pp. 158–161.

47256. Rushin, Steve. "Big Brew Ha-Ha: Old Hands Don Baylor and Dave Parker are Showing the Brewers How to Stay Loose and Win." *Sports Illustrated,* LXXII (June 11, 1990), 24–26, 31.

47257. Sahadi, Lou. "Dave Parker: Interview." *Penthouse,* XX (September 1988), 89+.

47258. Shapiro, Barry. "Dave Parker." *Sport,* LXXVII (June 1986), 15–18.

47259. Vecsey, George. "The Taming of 'Crazy Horse.'" *Sport,* LXXI (July 1980), 44–45+.

47260. Wheeler, Lonnie. "Dave Parker: His Image is Hitting .300 Again." *Inside Sports,* VIII (January 1986), 20–24.

47261. Weinberg, Robert. "One-on-One: Dave Parker." *Sport,* LXXXII (August 1991), 27–28.

Doc Parker *see* **Harley Park Parker ("Doc") Parker**

Harley Park Parker ("Doc") Parker

P. (B: June 14, 1872, Theresa, NY-D: March 3, 1941). Chicago (NL), 1893, 1895–1898; Cincinnati (NL), 1901. Remarks: Had five victories, nine defeats, and one "save" in six seasons; surrendered a NL record 21 runs on 26 hits in one game, June 21, 1901; brother of Jay Parker (below).

47262. Cardello, Joseph. "The Parker Brothers and Other Cincinnati Oddities." *The Baseball Research Journal,* XXIV (1995), 21–24.

Jay Parker

P. (B: July 8, 1874, Theresa, NY-D: June 8, 1935). Pittsburgh (NL), 1899. Remarks: Played in only one game; brother of Harley Park Parker ("Doc") Parker (above).

47263. Cardello, Joseph. "The Parker Brothers and Other Cincinnati Oddities." *The Baseball Research Journal,* XXIV (1995), 21–24.

Maurice Wesley ("Wes" or "Tiger") Parker

OF-BROADCASTER. (B: Nov. 13, 1939, Evanston, IL). Los Angeles (NL), 1964–1972. Remarks: Obtained 1,110 hits (64 homers) and 40 stolen bases In 1,288 games in eight years; noted fielder who voluntarily retired with .996 fielding average; first-and last to date — L.A. Dodger to hit for cycle, May 7, 1970; radio broadcaster, Cincinnati (NL), 1970; minor league instructor for Los Angeles (NL), 1973; also played for Nankai (Japan League), 1974 and became television actor, with substantial role in 1977 series *All That Glitters* and in 1986 made-for-TV movie *Cry from the Mountain*.

47264. Goren, Charles. "Good Play by a First Baseman." *Sports Illustrated,* XXIV (April 18, 1966), 110–111.

47265. "Letterman Talks with Wes Parker." *Letterman,* II (October 1971), 12–13.

47266. Libby, Bill. "Wes Parker: A 'Tiger' in Disguise." *Sport,* LI (January 1971), 20–29+.

47267. Newhan, Ross. "Wes Parker-Suddenly a Complete Player." *Baseball Digest,* XXX (May 1971), 42–46.

47268. Weiskopf, Donald C. "First Base and Wes Parker: An Interview." *Athletic Journal,* LI (January 1971), 42–46+.

Wes Parker *see* **Maurice Wesley ("Wes" or "Tiger") Parker**

Leroy Earl ("Roy" or "Bud" or "Tarzan") Parmelee
P. (B: April, 25, 1901, Lamberville, MI-D: Aug. 29, 1981). New York (NL), 1929–1935; St. Louis (NL), 1936; Chicago (NL), 1937; Philadelphia (AL), 1939. Remarks: Won 59 games and lost 55, with three "saves," in a decade; had grand slam homer to win a game, July 17, 1934.

47269. Murdock, Eugene C. "Some Called Him Tarzan." *The Baseball Research Journal,* X (1981), 106–111.

Melvin Lloyd ("Mel" or "Dusty") Parnell
P-COACH-BROADCASTER. (B: June 13, 1922, Now Orleans, LA). Boston (AL), 1947–1956. Remarks: Won 123 games (including 25 in 1949 and 21 in 1953) and lost 75, with 10 "saves," in a decade; pitched one no-hitter, July 14, 1956; Tulane University baseball coach, 1958; manager, New Orleans (SA), 1959; scout, Boston (AL), 1960; manager, Alpine (Sophomore League), 1961, York (EL), 1962, and Seattle (PCL), 1963; broadcaster, Boston (AL), 1965–1968 and Chicago (AL), 1969; elected to Louisiana Sports Hall of Fame, 1963; named to Boston Red Sox Hall of Fame, Sept. 1997.

47270. Bloodgood, Clifford. "Parnell Now Pitching for the Red Sox." *Baseball Magazine,* LXXXI (September 1948), 339–341.

47271. Fay, Bernard. "Fabulous Mel, Pitcher with a Bat." *Collier's,* CXXIV (July 30, 1949), 42+.

47272. Frommer, Harvey and Frederic J. "Mel Parnell." In: their *Growing Up Baseball: An Oral History.* Dallas, TX: Taylor Publishing Company, 2001. Pp. 179–183.

47273. Heiman, Lee, Dave Weiner and Bill Gutman. "Mel Parnell." In: their *When the Cheering Stops.* New York: Macmillan, 1990. Pp. 36–39.

47274. Hirshberg, Al. "Pitching for Boston: Mel Parnell." *Sport,* VII (September 1949), 50–53+.

47275. _____. "Yankee-Tamer Parnell." *Sport,* XVI (May 1954), 26–27+.

47276. Holbrook, Bob. "Double Trouble in the Hub." In: Bruce Jacobs, ed. *Baseball Stars of 1950.* New York: Lion Books, 1950. Pp. 143–151.

47277. _____. "Red Sox Meal Ticket." *Complete Baseball,* IV (July 1952), 10–17+.

47278. Hurwitz, Hy. "He'll Jack Up Red Sox Hurling." *Baseball Digest,* VII (May 1948), 83–65.

47279. Kelley, Brent P. "Mel Parnell: The Fenway Southpaw." In: his *The Early All-Stars: Conversations with Standout Baseball Players of the 1930s and 1940s.* Jefferson, NC: McFarland & Co., Inc., 1997. Pp. 115–128.

47280. Macht, Norman L. "How Red Sox Lefty Mel Parnell Mastered the 'Green Monster.'" *Baseball Digest,* LII (August 1993), 64–69.

47281. McClelland, Marshall K. "Mel Parnell Tells — 'How to Blank the Yanks.'" *Baseball Digest,* XIII (May 1954), 44–49.

47282. Moffi, Larry. "Mel Parnell: 'Get That Little Skinny Kid Back on the Mound." In: his *This Side of Cooperstown: An Oral History of Major League Baseball in the 1950s.* Iowa City, IA: University of Iowa Press, 1996. Pp. 129–146.

47283. Mule, Marty. "Mel Parnell: They Called Him the 'Yankee Killer.'" *Baseball Digest,* XL (January 1981), 90+.

47284. Newville, Todd. "Mel Parnell Wasn't Awed by Fenway's 'Green Monster.'" *Baseball Digest,* LVI (March 1997), 77–79.

47285. Spoehr, Luther W. "Melvin Lloyd 'Mel,' 'Dusty' Parnell." In: Vol. G-P of David L. Porter, ed. *Biographical Dictionary of American Sports: Baseball.* Rev. and enlarged ed. Westport, CT: Greenwood Press, 2000. Pp. 1175–1176.

47286. Westcott, Rich. "Mel Parnell — The Epitome of the Stylish Lefthander." In: his *Diamond Greats.* Westport, CT: Meckler Books, 1988. Pp. 305–311.

47287. Wilber, Cynthia J. "Mel Parnell." In: her *For the Love of the Game: Baseball Memories from the Men Who Were There.* New York: William Morrow, 1992. Pp. 248–257.

James Arthur ("Rube") Parnham
P. (B: Feb. 1, 1894, Heidelberg, PA-D: Nov. 25, 1963). Philadelphia (AL), 1916–1917. Remarks: In two big league seasons, won two games and lost two; career minor leaguer, who, while hurling for Baltimore (IL) in 1923, won 33 games and lost only seven.

47288. Ross, M. "Rube Parnham: He May Have Been the Game's Best Pitcher in 1923." *The Baseball Research Journal,* XXIV (1995), 92–93.

Lance Michael Parrish
C-BROADCASTER. (B: June 16, 1956, McKeesport, PA). Detroit (AL), 1977–1986; Philadelphia (NL), 1987–1988; California (AL), 1989–1992; Seattle (AL), 1992; Cleveland (AL), 1993; Pittsburgh (NL), 1994; Toronto (AL), 1995. Remarks: Had 1,782 hits (324 homers) in 1,988 games in 19 seasons; had grand slam homer, Aug. 21, 1984; served for a period as bodyguard to singer Tina Turner; coach, Detroit (AL), 1999–2001, 2003–; color analyst, UPN-50 for Detroit (AL), 2002.

47289. Appleton, Sheldon L. "Lance Michael Parrish." In: Vol. G-P of David L. Porter, ed. *Biographical Dictionary of American Sports: Baseball.* Rev. and enlarged ed. Westport, CT: Greenwood Press, 2000. Pp. 1174–1175.

47290. Cohen, Irwin. "Talkin' Baseball — Lance Parrish and George Kell." *Baseball Cards,* III (Fall 1983), 62–64.

47291. Gage, Tom. "Lance Parrish, Baseball's Most Dominant Catcher." *Baseball Digest,* XLIII (June 1984), 19–22.

47292. Hochberg, Wally. "Now Lance Parrish Has It All." *Sports World,* XXIII (August 1984), 18–19.

47293. Kionke, Bob. "Lance Parrish: Baseball's Beat Catcher Leads by Example." In: Gerald Kavanagh, ed. *Street and Smith's Official 1984 Baseball Yearbook.* New York: Conde Nast Publications, 1964. Pp. 44–47.

47294. Lidz, Franz. "Finally Earning His Stripes." *Sports Illustrated,* LVII (August 30, 1982), 46+.

Larry Alton ("Gov") Parrish
3B-OF-MGR. (B: Nov. 10, 1953, Winter Haven, FL). Montreal (NL), 1974–1981; Texas (AL), 1982–1988; Boston (AL), 1988. Remarks: Had 1,789 hits (256 homers) in 1,891 games in 15 years; hit three grand slam homers in a week, July 4–10, 1985; Yakult Swallows (Japan League), 1989; Hanshin Tigers (Japan League), 1990); manager, Niagara Falls (New York-Pennsylvania League), 1992–1993; manager, Toledo (IL), 1994–1995; manager, Jacksonville (SL), 1996; coach, Detroit (AL), 1996–1998; manager, Detroit (AL), 1998–1999, winning 82 games and losing 104 (.441); scout, Detroit (AL), 1999–2002; manager, Toledo (IL), 2003–.

47295. Gordon, Daniel. "Larry Parrish." In: Tommy Kay, ed. *Tommy Kay's 1980 Baseball Factbook.* Scottsdale, AZ: Jalart House, 1980. Pp. 64–77.

47296. O'Reilly, P. "Back to the Bushes." *Dugout,* I (October 1993), 5–7.

47297. Rasmussen, Larry F. "Larry Parrish Joined Select Home Run Club in '87." *Baseball Digest,* XLVII (January 1988), 38–39.

47298. Rosenberg, Victor. "Larry Alton 'Gov' Parrish." In: Vol. G-P of David L. Porter, ed. *Biographical Dictionary of American Sports: Baseball.* Rev. and enlarged ed. Westport, CT: Greenwood Press, 2000. Pp. 1175–1176.

47299. Whicker, Mark. "How Expos' Larry Parrish Silenced His Critics." *Baseball Digest,* XXXIX (February 1980), 70–73.

Harold Francis Parrott
WRITER-EXEC. (B: 1909–D: 1987) Remarks: Baseball writer, *Brooklyn Eagle,* 1929–1943; traveling secretary, Brooklyn (NL), 1944–1950; ticket sales director and publicist, Brooklyn/Los Angeles (NL), 1951–1960; exec., Seattle (AL), San Diego (NL) and California (AL), 1962–1970s; remembered as friend of and ghost writer for Jackie Robinson (q.v.).

47300. Holtzman, Jerome. "Harold Parrott." In: his *No Cheering in the Press Box.* New York: Holt, Rinehart And Winston, 1974. Pp. 230–242.

47301. Parrott, Harold. *The Lords of Baseball: A Wry Look at a Side of the Game the Fan Seldom Sees — the Front Office.* New York: Praeger Publishers, 1976. 265p. Reissued by the Atlanta, GA, firm of Longstreet Press in a 256-page 2002 edition.

47302. Scott, GIL "Rap with Harold Parrott." *Black Sports,* VI (July 1976), 34–37.

Roy Robert Partee
C. (B: Sept. 17, 1917, Los Angeles, CA-D: Dec. 26, 2000). Boston (AL), 1943–1944, 1946–1947; St. Louis (AL), 1948. Remarks: In five seasons, obtained 273 hits (two homers) and two stolen bases in 367 games; Enos Slaughter (q.v.), in his famous "Mad Dash," slid by him to score a winning run in 1946 World Series.

47303. Kelley, Brent P. "Roy Partee: If Only the Throw Had Been Good (1943–1948)." In: his *The Pastime in Turbulence: Interviews with Baseball Players of the 1940s.* Jefferson, NC: McFarland & Co., Inc., 2002. Pp. 145–162.

Camilo Alberto Y Lus ("Little Potato") Pascual
P. (B: Jan. 20, 1934, Havana, Cuba), Washington (AL) and Minnesota (AL), 1954–1966; Washington (A.L), 1967–1969; Cincinnati (NL), 1969; Los Angeles (NL), 1970; Cleveland (AL), 1971. Remarks: Won 174 games and lost 170, with 10 "saves," in 18 campaigns, coach, Minnesota (AL), 1978–1980, Latin American scout, Los Angeles (NL), 1980s and 1990s; remembered for his curveball; elected to Cuban Baseball Hall of Fame, 1993.

47304. Addie, Bob. "Pascual May Be the Best." *Sport,* XXX (August 1960), 24–25+.

47305. Furlong, William B. "A Cure for Camilo Pascual." *Sport,* XXXIV (December 1962), 42–45.

47306. Gordon, Dick. "Pascual Finds It Doesn't Pay to Advertise." *Baseball Digest,* XXI (March 1962), 17–21.

47307. Pascual, Camilo. "How to Throw Curveballs." *Sport,* XL (August 1965), 104–105.

47308. Rubin, Bob. "Camilo Pascual: He was a Master of the Curveball." *Baseball Digest,* LII (July 1993), 44–47.

47309. Stann, Francis. "Camilo Pascual: Much Stuff, Little Success." *Baseball Digest,* XVIII (June 1959), 23–27.

47310. Welch, James E. "Camilo Alberto y Lus 'Little Potato' Pascual." In: Vol. G-P of David L. Porter, ed. *Biographical Dictionary of American Sports: Baseball.* Rev. and enlarged ed. Westport, CT: Greenwood Press, 2000. Pp. 1176–1177.

47311. Westcott, Rich. "Camilo Pascual — Master Curveballer." In: his *Diamond Greats.* Westport, CT: Meckler Books, 1988. Pp. 312–316.

Larry John Pashnick
P. (B: April 25, 1956, Lincoln Park, MI). Detroit (AL), 1982–1983; Minnesota (AL), 1984. Remarks. Won seven games and lost eight in three seasons.

47312. "Larry Pashnick is Every One of US." *Inside Sports,* VI (June 1984), 12+.

47313. "The Struggles of Pashnick (Continued)." *Inside Sports,* VII (February 1985), 16+.

George Henry ("Dode" or "Honey Boy") Paskert
OF. (B: Aug. 28, 1881, Cleveland, OH-D: Feb. 12, 1959). Cincinnati (NL), 1907–1910; Philadelphia (NL), 1911–1917; Chicago (NL), 1918–1920; Cincinnati (NL), 1921. Remarks: Obtained 1,613 hits (40 homers) and 293 stolen bases in 1,715 games in 15 seasons; stole home plate, May 23, 1910; went 4-for-4 in one game, July 5, 1911; noted fielder; minor league player, 1922–1924; rescued 15 children from burning Cleveland building In 1920, suffering injuries.

47314. Kofoed, J.C. "A Fly Ball Expert." *Baseball Magazine,* XVI (February 1916), 45–47.

47315. Phelps, Frank V. "George Henry 'Dode' Paskert." In: Vol. G-P of David L. Porter, ed. *Biographical Dictionary of American Sports: Baseball.* Rev. and enlarged ed. Westport, CT: Greenwood Press, 2000. Pp. 1177–1178.

Daniel Anthony ("Dan") Pasqua
OF. (B: Oct. 17, 1961, Yonkers, NY). New York (AL), 1985–1987; Chicago (AL), 1988–1994. Remarks: Obtained 638 hits (117 homers) and seven stolen bases in 905 big league games in a decade; IL MVP Award, 1985.

47316. Cohen, Irwin. "Baseball Beat: Dan Pasqua." *Baseball Cards,* VIII (September 1988), 86+.

Claude William Passeau
P. (B: April 9, 1909, Waynesboro, MS-D: August 30, 2003). Pittsburgh (NL), 1936; Philadelphia (NL), 1936–1939; Chicago (NL), 1939–1947. Remarks: Won 162 games and lost 150, with 21 "saves," in a 13-year pro career; defied superstition by wearing uniform no. 13; had 15 career homers; surrendered game winning homer by Ted Williams (q.v.) in 1941 All Star Game; played entire 1945 season with bone chip in elbow, but still had eight-game winning streak (July) and threw one-hitter in Game Three of World Series; holds all-time pitchers' fielding record of 273 consecutive errorless chances, Sept. 21, 1941–May 20, 1946; manager, Centralia (Midwest League), 1948; elected to Mississippi Sports Hall of Fame.

47317. "Claude Passeau." In: Carrie Muskat, ed. *Banks to Sandberg to Grace: Five Decades of Love and Frustration with the Chicago Cubs.* Chicago, IL: Contemporary Books, 2001. Pp. 17–22.

47318. Fagen, Herb. "Claude Passeau: He Usually Finished What He Started." *Baseball Digest,* LIV (December 1995), 84–90.

47319. Hines, Rick. "Claude Passeau: Ex-cub Ace Recalls ML Career." *Sports Collector's Digest,* XVIII (March 8, 1991), 200–201.

47320. Macht, Norman L. "Claude Passeau: He Pitched a World Series One-Hitter." *Baseball Digest,* LII (November 1993), 75–85. 1945.

47321. Passeau, Claude, as told to George Vass. "The Game I'll Never Forget." *Baseball Digest,* XXXVIII (August 1979), 87–89. Reprinted in George Vass, ed. *The Game I'll Never Forget* (Chicago, IL: Bonus Books, 1999), pp. 181–185.

47322. Phalen, Rick. "Claude Passeau." In: his *Our Chicago Cubs*. South Bend, IN: Diamond Communications, 1992. Pp. 8–12.

47323. Smith, Duane A. "Claude William Passeau." In: Vol. G-P of David L. Porter, ed. *Biographical Dictionary of American Sports: Baseball*. Rev. and enlarged ed. Westport, CT: Greenwood Press, 2000. Pp. 1178–1179.

47324. Wilbert, Warren and William Hageman. "Claude Passeau —1940." In: their *Chicago Cubs: Seasons at the Summit, the 50 Greatest Individual Seasons*. Champaign, IL: Sagamore Publishing, 1997. Pp. 81–84.

David Pasti

AGENT. (B: 1952, Derwood, MD). Rockwood, MD, attorney turned minor league talent agent.

47325. Naughton, Jim. "The Long Shot: If Anything Tests Your Faith More Than Being a Minor Minor Leaguer, It's Being His Agent." *The Washington Post Magazine*, (May 26, 2002), 10–15, 23–27.

Frank Enrico Pastore

P. (B: Aug. 21, 1957, Alhambra, CA). Cincinnati (NL), 1979–1985; Minnesota (AL), 1986. Remarks: Had 48 victories and 58 defeats, with six "saves," in eight years; hurled winning game allowing Reds to capture 1979 NL West title.

47326. Elderkin, Phil "Frank Pastore: The Reds Groom Another Young Star." *Baseball Digest*, XXXIX (September 1980), 62–65.

47327. Hill, Terry. "Frank Pastore: 'Johnny Bench Ran Out, And I Jumped into His Arms.'" In: his *Batting a Thousand*. New York: T. Nelson, 1987. Pp. 90–95.

Frederick Joseph ("Freddie" or "The Flea" or "Moochie") Patek

SS. (B: Oct. 9, 1944, Oklahoma City, OK). Pittsburgh (NL), 1968–1970; Kansas City (AL), 1971–1979; California (AL), 1980–1981. Remarks: Obtained 1,340 hits (41 homers) and 385 stolen bases in 1,650 games in 14 campaigns; hit for cycle, July 9, 1971; AL stolen base champion, 1977; had three homers in one game, June 20, 1980; at one point, the smallest player in the majors; elected to Missouri Sports Hall of Fame, 1999.

47328. Allen, Maury. "Smallest Big Leaguer: Fred Patek." *Baseball Digest*, XXVIII (September 1969), 62–65.

47329. Ballew, Bill. "Fred Patek." In: his *The Pastime in the Seventies: Oral Histories of 16 Major Leaguers*. Jefferson, NC: McFarland & Co., Inc., 2002. Pp. 164–176.

47330. Brosnan, Jim. "Fast Freddie from Kansas City." *Boy's Life*, LXIX (April 1979), 14+.

47331. Christine, Bill. "How to Be 5-Foot-4 and a Big Leaguer." In: Zander Hollander, ed. *Popular Sports Grand Slam, 1973*. New York: Popular Library, 1973. Pp. 36–39.

47332. Debs, Victor, Jr. "Fred Patek." In: his *"That Was Part of Baseball Then": Interviews with 24 Former Major League Baseball Players, Coaches, and Managers*. Jefferson, NC: McFarland & Co., Inc., 2002. Pp. 151–155.

47333. Elderkin, Phil "Fred Patek. Mighty Mite on the Diamond." *Baseball. Digest*, XXXVII (October 1978), 64–68.

47334. Garrity, John. "Gutsiest Player in Baseball." *Sport*, LXVI (May 1978), 23+.

47335. McGuff, Joe. "Fred Patek: Mighty Mite of the Royals." *Baseball Digest*, XXXV (September 1976), 58–61.

47336. Murray, Jim. "Freddie Patek: Kansas City's Mighty Mite." *Baseball. Digest*, XXXI (February 1972), 33–30.

Max ("The Clown Prince of Baseball") Patkin

COACH-ENTERTAINER (B: Jan. 10, 1920, Philadelphia, PA-D: Oct. 30, 1999). Remarks: Former minor league pitcher in White Sox farm system, 1941–1942 and for Wilkes-Barre (EL), 1945; discovered by Bill Veeck (q.v.) and asked to coach as well as entertain Cleveland (AL) crowds, beginning a pantomime career (primarily before minor league crowds) lasting until August 1993; assumed title of "Clown Prince of Baseball" in 1982 and appeared in 1988 motion picture *Bull Durham*; an off-field dance exhibitionist, he taught jitter-bug to the film's lead actress, Susan Sarandon; elected to Philadelphia Jewish Sports Hall of Fame, 1998.

47337. Cunneff, Tom and David Hutchings. "Max Patkin, the Goofball Laureate of Baseball, Scores in *Bull Durham* and — Holy Cow — It's a Grand Slam." *People Weekly*, XXX (June 11, 1988), 61–62.

47338. Jaffe, Michael. "Honored." *Sports Illustrated*, LXXIV (April 29, 1991), 85+.

47339. Lieb, Frederick G. "Max Patkin: Physical Makeup Great Asset." In: his *Comedians and Pranksters of Baseball*. St. Louis, MO: *The Sporting News*, 1958. Pp. 36–38.

47340. Patkin, Max, with Stan Hochman. *The Clown Prince of Baseball*. Waco, TX: WRS Publications, 1994. 167p.

47341. Schacht, John. "Jokers Wild." *Oakland Athletics Magazine*, VIII, no. 2 (1988), 105–113. Patkin and the author's father, Al Schacht.

47342. Wilson, John R. M. "Max Patkin." In: Paul Betz and Mark C. Carnes, eds. *American National Biography: Supplement I*. New York: Oxford University Press, 2002. Pp. 472–473.

47343. Wulf, Steve. "Max: After More Than 40 Years, the 'Clown Prince of Baseball,' Max Patkin, Still Leaves 'Em Laughing." *Sports Illustrated*, LXIX (June 6, 1988), 98–107.

Gilbert Patten

WRITER. (B: Oct. 25, 1866, Corinna, Maine-D: Jan 16, 1945). Remarks: Dime-novelist and creator of the Frank Merriwell youth baseball novel series; had 15 pseudonyms, wrote 1,500 works, with a total of 40 million words! Among his boys' novels are the 16 volumes of the Big League Series, written for the Stratemeyer Syndicate between 1914 and 1928.

47344. Cox, J. Randolph. "Bibliographical Notes: The Merriwells After *Tip Top Weekly*." *Dime Novel Roundup: A Magazine Devoted to the Collecting, Preservation and Study of Old-Time Dime and Nickel Novels, Popular Story Papers, Series Books, and Pulp Magazines*, LXX (June 2001), 97–101.

47345. Cox, J. Randolph. "Bibliographical Notes: Play Ball!: The Story of Frank Merriwell's Double Shoot." *Dime Novel Roundup: A Magazine Devoted to the Collecting, Preservation and Study of Old-Time Dime and Nickel Novels, Popular Story Papers, Series Books, and Pulp Magazines*, LXI (June 2002), 30+.

47346. Cutler, John Levi. *Gilbert Patten and His Frank Merriwell Saga: A Study in Sub-Literary Fiction, 1896–1913*. University of Maine Studies, Second series, no. 31. Orono, ME: Printed at the University Press, 1934. 123p. Includes a partial Merriwell bibliography, pp. 111–117.

47347. Gowen, William R. "Gilbert Patten: A Look Beyond the Merriwells." *Newsboy*, XXXII (September-October 1994), 11–19.

47348. Kolb, Harold H., Jr. "Gilbert Patten." In: Supplement III of Edward T. James, ed. *Dictionary of American Biography*. New York: Charles Scribner's Sons, 1973. Pp. 585–587.

47349. Moses, Sid. "The Merriwell Miracle Man." *Dime*

Novel Roundup: A Magazine Devoted to the Collecting, Preservation and Study of Old-Time Dime and Nickel Novels, Popular Story Papers, Series Books, and Pulp Magazines, LX (June 1991), 20+.

47350. Patten, Gilbert. *Frank Merriwell's "Father": An Autobiography by Gilbert Patten ("Burt L. Standish").* Edited by Harriet Hinsdale. Norman, OK. University of Oklahoma Press,1964. 331p. Published posthumously.

47351. Praeger, Arthur. *Rascals at Large; or, The Clue in the Old Nostalgia.* Garden City, NY: Doubleday, 1971. A look at the series books of the Golden Age of children's literature including Frank Merriwell.

47352. "Roaring Mike," pseud. "A Merriwell Genealogy; or, 'You Can't Tell the Players Without a Scorecard.'" *Dime Novel Roundup: A Magazine Devoted to the Collecting, Preservation and Study of Old-Time Dime and Nickel Novels, Popular Story Papers, Series Books, and Pulp Magazines,* LIX (August 1990), 10+.

47353. Scharnhorst, Gary. "Gilbert Patten." In: Vol. XVII of John A. Garrity and Mark C. Carnes, eds. *American National Biography.* New York: Oxford University Press, 199. Pp. 126–128.

Andrew Lawrence ("Pat") Patterson
SS-2B-3B-OF. (B: Dec. 19, 1911, Chicago, IL-D: May 1984). Pennsylvania Red Caps, Cleveland Red Caps, and Homestead Grays, 1934; Pittsburgh Crawfords, 1935; Kansas City Monarchs, 1936; Pittsburgh Crawfords, 1937; Philadelphia Stars, 1938–1939; Mexico City (Mexican League), 1940; Kansas City Monarchs, 1941; Newark Eagles, 1946–1947; Houston Eagles, 1949. Remarks: Highly-regarded third sacker and four time Negro League All-Star; later high school coach and educator and Houston school system superintendent, becoming the first Black coach selected to Texas Coaches Hall of Fame.

47354. Heaphy, Leslie. "Andrew Lawrence 'Pat' Patterson." In: Vol. G-P of David L. Porter, ed. *Biographical Dictionary of American Sports: Baseball.* Rev. and enlarged ed. Westport, CT: Greenwood Press, 2000. Pp. 1179–1180.

Corey Patterson
C. (B: August 13, 1979, Atlanta, GA). Chicago (NL), 2000–. Remarks: Through 2004, has obtained 452 hits (57 homers) and 71 stolen bases in 463 games; had four hits in one game, Oct. 3, 2001.

47355. Thompson, Jim. "Everybody Loves Corey." *Beckett Baseball Card Monthly,* XVII (June 2000), 116–119.

Pat Patterson *see* **Andrew Lawrence ("Pat") Patterson**
Gabriel Howard ("Gabe") Paul, Sr.
EXEC. (B: Jan. 4, 1910, Rochester, NY-D: April 26, 1998). Remarks: Publicity director, Rochester (IL), 1928–1933; road secretary, Rochester (IL), 1934–1936; publicity director, then traveling secretary, Cincinnati (NL), 1937–1948; pres. assistant, then vp, Cincinnati (NL), 1948–1949; president, Cincinnati (NL), 1950–1960; GM, then president, Cleveland (AL), 1961–1972; president, New York (AL), 1973–1977 and Cleveland (AL), 1978–1984; executed over 500 trades during his long career.

47356. Martin, Douglas D. "Gabriel Howard 'Gabe' Paul, Sr." In: Vol. G-P of David L. Porter, ed. *Biographical Dictionary of American Sports: Baseball.* Rev. and enlarged ed. Westport, CT: Greenwood Press, 2000. Pp. 1180–1182.

47357. McMillan, Ken. "Gabe Paul." In: his *Tales from the Yankee Dugout: A Collection of the Greatest Yankee Stories Ever Told.* Champaign, IL: Sports Publishing, Inc., 2001. Pp. 128–129.

47358. Werber, Bill. "Shirley Povich and Gabe Paul:

Legends Off the Field." In: his *Memories of a Ballplayer: Bill Werber and Baseball in the 1930s.* Cleveland, OH: The Society for American Baseball Research, 2001. Pp. 203–210.

Carl Pavano
P. (B: Jan. 8, 1976, New Britain, CT). Montreal (NL), 1998–2002; Florida (NL), 2002. Remarks: In five major league seasons, won 27 games and lost 37; surrendered the season's 70th homer to Mark McGwire (q.v.), Sept. 27, 1998.

47359. O'Rourke, Larry. "Pavano Takes It Easy: Thunder Ace Draws Raves During 11-Game Summer Stretch." *Boston Baseball,* VII (September 1996), 38–39.

Joan Whitney Payson
EXEC. (B: Feb. 5, 1903, New York City-D: Oct. 4, 1975). Remarks. Philanthropist and principal owner, New York (NL), 1962–1975.

47360. Amory, Cleveland. "Mrs. Payson's Ball Park." *Vogue,* CXLIV (September 15, 1964), 144+.

47361. Dempsey, D. "Says Mrs. Payson of the Mets: 'You Can't Lose Them All.'" *The New York Times Magazine* (June 23, 1968), 20–31+. Abridged *in Reader's Digest,* XCIV (June 1969), 201–202 as "Mrs. Payson and Her Lovable Mets."

Dickey Pearce *see* **Richard J. ("Dickey") Pearce**
Richard J. ("Dickey") Pearce
SS-MGR. (B: Feb. 29, 1836, Brooklyn, NY-D: Oct. 12, 1908). New York (N.A.), 1871–1872; Brooklyn (N.A.), 1873–1874; St. Louis (N.A.), 1875; St. Louis (NL), 1876–1877. Remarks: Regarded as first great shortstop; obtained 334 hits (two homers) and 12 stolen bases in 291 games in seven seasons; player-manager, New York (N.A.), 1872 and St. Louis (N.A.), 1875, winning 73 games and losing 49 (.598); NL umpire, 1878–1882.

47362. Smith, Duane A. "Dickey Pearce: Baseball's First Great Shortstop." *The National Pastime,* IX (1990), 38–42.

47363. _____. "Richard J. 'Dickey' Pearce." In: Vol. G-P of David L. Porter, ed. *Biographical Dictionary of American Sports: Baseball.* Rev. and enlarged ed. Westport, CT: Greenwood Press, 2000. Pp. 1182–1183.

47364. Smith, Robert. "Dickey Pearce: Fair is Foul and Foul is Fair." In: his *Heroes of Baseball.* Cleveland, OH: The World Publishing Co., 1952. Pp. 17–23.

Albert Gregory ("Albie") Pearson
OF. (B: Sept. 12, 1934, Alhambra, CA). Washington (AL), 1958–1959; Baltimore (AL), 1959–1960; Los Angeles (AL) and California (AL), 1961–1966. Remarks: Had 831 hits (28 homers) and 77 stolen bases in 988 games in nine seasons; AL Rookie of the Year Award, 1958; had one grand slam homer, April 23, 1960; first player to go hitless in 11 ABs in a doubleheader (both 9-inning games), July 1, 1962; also played for San Francisco (PCL), 1957; later became golf pro, disc jockey, and radio evangelist.

47365. Addie, Bob. "Fadeout for Little Albie Pearson." *Baseball Digest,* XIX (August 1960), 79–81.

47366. Brosnan, Jim. "Albie Pearson: Rookie of the Year—1958—American League." In: his *Great Rookies of the Major Leagues.* New York: Random House, 1966. Pp. 95–108.

47367. Cohn, Howard. "Pearson and [Roy] Sievers." In: Ray Robinson, ed. *Baseball Stars of 1959.* New York: Pyramid Books, 1959. Pp. 125–130.

47368. Fox, Larry. "Albie Pearson: 'What Have They Sent Me?'" In: his *Little Men in Sports.* New York: W. W. Norton, 1968. Pp. 214–223.

47369. Hano, Arnold. "...And the Angel Swings." *Sport,* XXXIII (February 1962), 42–47.

47370. Hefley, James C. "Albie Pearson." In: his *Sports Alive.* Grand Rapids, MI: Zondervan, 1986. Pp. 57–63.

47371. Herskowitz, Mickey. "Albie Pearson. He Starts in Short Grass." *Baseball Digest,* XXII (June 1963), 61–63.

47372. Honig, Donald. "1958: Albie Pearson." In: his *American League Rookies of the Year.* New York: Bantam Books, 1989. Pp. 25–26.

47373. Pearson, Albert G. ("Albie"). "Midget in the Majors." *Baseball Digest,* XVII (October 1958), 11–13.

47374. Povich, Shirley. "The Littlest Big Leaguer." *Saturday Evening Post,* CCXXXI (May 16, 1959), 34+.

47375. Rogin, Gilbert. "Albie Pearson, the Littlest Angel." *Sports Illustrated,* XVIII (May 27, 1963), 62–64.

47376. Spalding, John E. "Albie Pearson." In: his *Pacific Coast League Stars, Vol. II: Ninety Who Made It to the Majors, 1905–1957.* San Jose, CA: John E. Spalding, 1997. Pp. 145–147.

47377. Stann, Francis. "Pearson Shows 'Em a Little Man Can Make It Big." *Baseball Digest,* XXIII (March 1964), 25–27.

47378. Stern, Chris. "Albie Pearson." In: his *Where Have They Gone?* New York: Tempo Books, 1979. Pp. 9–13.

47379. Stevens, Bob. "The Night Little Albie Pearson Became a Man." *Baseball Digest,* XVIII (April 1959), 37–41.

47380. Stump, Al. "Albie Pearson: The Angels' Tiny Terror." *True: The Men's Magazine,* XLIV (June 1963), 54–55+.

47381. Vecsey, George. "Albie Pearson: Half Pint." In: Ray Robinson, ed. *Baseball Stars of 1964.* New York: Pyramid Books, 1964. Pp. 85–90.

Monte Pearson *see* **Montgomery Marcellus ("Monte") Pearson**

Montgomery Marcellus ("Monte") Pearson

P. (B: Sept. 2, 1909, Oakland, CA–D: Jan. 27, 1978). Cleveland (AL), 1932–1935; New York (AL), 1936–1940; Cincinnati (NL), 1941. Remarks: Obtained 100 victories, 42 defeats, and four "saves" in a decade; won four World Series games, 1936–1939; had one no-hitter, Aug. 27, 1938; also played for Oakland (PCL), 1930–1931.

47382. Gallagher, Mark. "Monte Pearson." In: his *50 Years of Yankee All-Stars.* New York: Leisure Press, 1984. Pp. 148–149.

47383. Giglio, James N. "Montgomery Marcellus 'Monte' Pearson." In: Vol. G–P of David L. Porter, ed. *Biographical Dictionary of American Sports: Baseball.* Rev. and enlarged ed. Westport, CT: Greenwood Press, 2000. Pp. 1183–1184.

47384. Ison, Jim. "Monte Pearson." In: his *Mormons in the Major Leagues.* Cincinnati, OH: Action Sports, 1991. Pp. 152–157.

47385. Pearson, Monte. "Secrets of a Champion Pitcher." *Popular Mechanics,* LXXI (May 1939), 674–679.

47386. Spalding, John E. "Monte Pearson." In: his *Pacific Coast League Stars, Vol. II: Ninety Who Made It to the Majors, 1905–1957.* San Jose, CA: John E. Spalding, 1997. Pp. 114–115.

Roger Thorpe Peckinpaugh

SS–MGR–EXEC. (B: Feb. 5, 1891, Wooster, OH–D: Nov. 17, 1977). Cleveland (AL), 1910–1913; New York (AL), 1913–1921; Washington (AL), 1922–1926; Chicago (AL), 1927. Remarks: Obtained 1,876 hits (48 homers) and 207 stolen bases in 2,012 games in a 17-year playing career; hit winning double, Game Two, 1924 World Series; AL MVP award, 1925; made eight errors during 1925 World Series; manager, New York (A.L.), 1914 (at age 23, the all-time youngest in big leagues) and Cleveland (AL),

1928–1933 and 1941, winning 500 games and losing 491 (.505); also played for Portland (PCL), 1910; minor league manager, 1934; AL promotion bureau, 1935–1938 and 1940; minor league club official, 1940; vice president–GM, Cleveland (AL), 1942–1946; GM, Rochester (IL), 1947.

47387. Drebinger, John. "More Pressure for Peck." *Baseball Magazine,* LXVI (January1941), 339–341.

47388. Fullerton, Hugh S. "Peckinpaugh's Greatest Thrill: A Baseball Classic of 1921." *Liberty,* VI (May 4, 1929), 67–68.

47389. Givens, Horace R. "Roger Thorpe Peckinpaugh." In: Vol. G–P of David L. Porter, ed. *Biographical Dictionary of American Sports: Baseball.* Rev. and enlarged ed. Westport, CT: Greenwood Press, 2000. Pp. 1184–1185.

47390. Honig, Donald. "Roger Peckinpaugh." in: his *The Man in the Dugout: Fifteen Big League Managers Speak Their Minds.* Chicago, IL: Follett Publishing Co., 1977. Pp. 213–229.

47391. Lane, Ferdinand C. "Roger Peckinpaugh: The Plodder Who Became a Star." *Baseball Magazine,* XXIV (February 1920), 533–535.

47392. Langford, Walter. "Errors That Lost the Series." *Sports Heritage,* I (November 1987), 24–26. Peckinpaugh and Johnny Pesky.

47393. Murdock, Eugene C. "Roger Peckinpaugh: He Was the Youngest 'Boy Manager.'" *Baseball Digest,* XLI (March 1982), 59–64.

47394. _____. "Roger Peckinpaugh: The Youngest Boy Manager." In: his *Baseball Between the Wars: Memories Of The Game by The Men Who Played It.* Westport, CT: Meckler Publishing, 1992. Pp. 1–22.

47395. _____. "The Youngest Boy Manager." *The Baseball Research Journal,* IV (1975), 29–33.

47396. Peckinpaugh, Roger. "The Decisive Importance of the Double-Play." *Baseball Magazine,* XXXV (November 1925), 543–545.

47397. _____. "The Manager's Dream—a Well-Balanced Ball Club." *Baseball Magazine,* XLV (July 1930), 351–352.

47398. _____. "Try to Outguess the Batter." In: *Secrets of Baseball Told by Big League Players.* New York: D. Appleton and Co., 1927. Pp. 102–110.

47399. Santa Maria, Michael and James Costello. "Behind the Eight Balls." In: their *In the Shadows of the Diamond.* Dubuque, IA: The Elysian Fields Press, 1992. Pp. 29–34.

47400. Spalding, John E. "Roger Peckinpaugh." In: his *Pacific Coast League Stars, Vol. II: Ninety Who Made It to the Majors, 1905–1957.* San Jose, CA: John E. Spalding, 1997. Pp. 31–32.

47401. Turner, Ken C. "Roger Peckinpaugh: Fate and Ol' Peck." *Vintage & Classic Baseball Collector,* no. 5 (January 1996), 30–32.

47402. Weiss, Peter. "Roger Peckinpaugh." In: his *Baseball's All-Time Goats: As Chosen by America's Top Sportswriters.* Holbrook, MA: Bob Adams, Inc, 1992. Pp. 132–135.

Francis Westbrook Pegler

WRITER. (B: August 2, 1894, Minneapolis, MN–D: June 24, 1969). Remarks: sports writer, United Press, 1920–1925; sports writer/editor, *Chicago Tribune/New York Daily News,* 1925–1933 and occasional ghostwriter for Babe Ruth (q.v.); political columnist, New York *World Telegram* and Sun, 1933–1944; syndicated columnist, King Features Syndicate, 1944–1962; freelance writer and journalist, 1962–1969; won Pulitzer Prize, 1941; lost libel case against fellow journalist Quentin Reynolds, 1951.

47403. Brown, Warren. "Good Morning, Judge." In: his *Win, Lose, or Draw: Thirty Years Behind the Sports Scene.* New York: G.P. Putnam's Sons, 1947. Pp. 157–164.

47404. Farr, Finis. *Fair Enough: The Life of Westbrook Pegler.* New Rochelle, NY: Arlington House, 1975.

47405. Orodenker, Richard. "Westbrook Pegler." In: Richard Orodenker, ed. *Dictionary of Literary Biography, Volume 171: Twentieth-Century American Sportswriters.* A Bruccoli Clark Layman Book. Detroit, MI: The Gale Group, 1996. Pp. 264–274.

47406. Pegler, Westbrook. "From the Woman's Angle." In: Charles Einstein, ed. *The Fireside Book of Baseball.* New York: Simon & Schuster, 1956. Pp. 263–264.

47407. Pilat, Oliver. *Pegler: Angry Man of the Press.* Boston, MA: Beacon Press, 1963.

47408. Smith, Walter ("Red"). "Pegler Scoffed at 1926 Yanks!: 'No Players, No Manager.'" *Baseball Digest,* XIII (March 1954), 81–82.

Westbrook Pegler see **Francis Westbrook Pegler**

Edward Charles ("Eddie") Pellagrini
SS-2B-3B. (B: March 13, 1918, Boston, MA). Boston (AL), 1946–1947; St. Louis (AL), 1948–1949; Philadelphia (NL), 1951; Cincinnati (NL), 1952; Pittsburgh (NL), 1953–1954. Remarks: Obtained 321 hits (20 homers) and 13 stolen bases in 563 games in eight years; hit homer in first big league AB, April 22, 1946.

47409. Hernon, Jack. "It's a Life of 13's for Pellagrini." *Baseball Digest,* XII (August 1953), 92–93.

47410. Lautier, Jack. "Eddie Pellagrini." In: his *Fenway Voices.* Camden, ME: Yankee Books, 1990. Pp. 39–44.

47411. Swank, Bill. "Eddie Pellagrini." In: his *Echoes from Lane Field: A History of the San Diego Padres 1936–1957.* Paducah, KY: Turner Publishing Company, 1997. Pp. 45–46.

Antonio Francesco Padilla ("Tony") Pena
C. (B: June 4, 1957, Monte Cristi, Dominican Republic). Pittsburgh (NL), 1980–1986; St. Louis (NL), 1987–1989; Boston (AL), 190–1993; Cleveland (AL), 1994–1997; Houston (NL), 1997. Remarks: Had 1,687 hits (107 homers) in 1,988 games in 17 campaigns; remembered for trademark one-leg-out crouch; player-manager, Cibao (Dominican League), 1997; manager, New Orleans (PCL), 1999–2002; manager, Kansas City (AL), 2003–, through 2004, has won 190 games and lost 260 (.422).

47412. Andre, Lee. "Love is What Makes Tony Pena Tick." *Sports World,* XXIII (August 1984), 16–17.

47413. Elderkin, Phil "Tony Pena-a Good Catch for the Pirates." *Baseball Digest,* XLI (December 1982), 46–47+.

47414. McCallum, John. "Pittsburgh's Prize Catch." *Sports Illustrated,* LVI (May 3, 1982), 51–52.

47415. Olmsted, Frank J. "Antonio Francisco Padilla 'Tony' Pena." In: Vol. G-P of David L. Porter, ed. *Biographical Dictionary of American Sports: Baseball.* Rev. and enlarged ed. Westport, CT: Greenwood Press, 2000. Pp. 1185–1186.

47416. Ruck, Rob. "Tony Pena: In the Game to Win." *Pittsburgh,* (April 1986), 65–72.

47417. "Tony Pena, Buc Belter." In: Tommy Kay, ed. *Tommy Kay's Big Book of Baseball.* Scottsdale, AZ: Jalart House, 1985. Pp. 118–119.

47418. Wendel, Tim. "Staying in Tuna, Pena Helps Deliver Perfect Pitch." *USA Today Baseball Weekly,* I (November 15, 1991), 24–25.

Orlando Gregory Pena
P. (B: Nov. 17, 1933, Victoria de las Tunas, Cuba). Cincinnati (NL), 1958–1960; Kansas City (AL), 1962–1965; Detroit (AL), 1965–1966; Cleveland (AL), 1967;

Pittsburgh (NL), 1970; Baltimore (AL), 1970–1971, 1973; St. Louis (N.L), 1973–1974; California (AL), 1974–1975. Remarks. Won 56 games and lost 77, with 40 "saves," in a 14-year major league career; as a minor leaguer, won 146 games and lost 85; elected to Cuban Baseball Hall of Fame, 1996.

47419. Hochman, Stan. "Pena's Secret: Bam, Bam." *Baseball Digest,* XXVII (October 1968), 45–47.

47420. Moffi, Larry and Jonathan Kronstadt. "Orlando Gregory Pena." In: their *Crossing the Line: Black Major Leaguers, 1947–1959.* Jefferson, NC: McFarland & Co., Inc., 1994. Pp. 189–190.

Tony Pena see **Antonio Francesco Padilla ("Tony") Pena**

James Edward ("Jim") Pendleton
OF. (B: Jan. 7, 1924, St. Charles, MO-D: March 20, 1996). Chicago American Giants, 1948; St. Paul (AA), 1949–1951; Montreal (IL), 1952; Milwaukee (NL), 1953–1956; Pittsburgh (NL), 1957–1958; Cincinnati (NL), 1959; Houston (NL), 1962. Remarks: In all or parts of eight big league seasons, obtained 240 hits (19 homers) and 11 stolen bases in 444 games; had three homers in a game, Aug. 30, 1953; first African American player with Houston (NL), April 13, 1962.

47421. Appel, Marty. "Jim Pendleton." In: his *Yesterday's Heroes: Revisiting the Old-Time Baseball Stars.* New York: William Morrow, 1988. Pp. 166–169.

Terry Lee Pendleton
2B. (B: July 16, 1960, Los Angeles, CA). St. Louis (NL), 1984–1990; Atlanta (NL), 1991–1994; Florida (NL), 1995–1996; Atlanta (NL), 1996; Cincinnati (NL), 1997; Kansas City (AL), 1998. Remarks: Had 1,897 hits (140 homers) and 127 stolen bases in 1,893 games in 15 summer campaigns; NL MVP Award, 1991; had homer in Game Two of 1993 NLCS; had five hits in one game, May 29, 1995; had grand slam homer, May 13, 1996; coach, Atlanta (NL), 2000–.

47422. Pendleton, Terry. "Pendleton's Season: Agony and Ecstasy." *USA Today Baseball Weekly,* I (January 3, 1992), 5–6.

47423. "The Real Thing." In: Joe Hoppel, ed. *The Sporting News 1993 Baseball Yearbook.* St. Louis, MO: The Sporting News, 1993. Pp. 46–48.

47424. Rosenberg, I. J. "A Second Look: Terry Pendleton." *Beckett Baseball Card Monthly,* IX, no. 93 (December 1992), 105–107.

47425. Schlossberg, Dan. "From Bum to Hero." *Topps Magazine,* (Fall 1992), 22–27.

47426. Sonderegger, John. "Cardinals' Terry Pendleton Comes of Age as a Hitter." *Baseball Digest,* XLVI (October 1987), 42–47.

47427. Strauss, Joe. "Terry Pendleton: The Braves' Indispensable Man." In: George Leonard, ed. *Athlon's 1992 Pro Baseball.* Nashville, TN: Athlon's, 1992. Pp. 146–148.

Arthur David ("Art" or "Superman") Pennington
1B-OF. (B: May 18, 1923, Memphis, TN). Chicago (Negro American League), 1940–1946, 1949–1951; also played for Portland (PCL), 1949, St. Petersburg (Florida State League), 1958; and Modesto (California League), 1959. Remarks: Incomplete records show that, in 1,074 games, had 1,243 hits (92 homers) and 140 stolen bases.

47428. Salin, Tony. "Superman: Art Pennington." In: his *Baseball's Forgotten Heroes: One Fan's Search for the Games Most Interesting Overlooked Players.* Lincolnwood, IL: Masters Press, 1999. Pp. 169–178.

Brad Lee Pennington
P. (B: April 14, 1969, Salem, IN). Baltimore (AL),

1993–1995; Cincinnati (NL), 1995; Boston (AL), California (AL), and Tampa Bay (AL), 1996. Remarks: Won three games, lost six, and had four "saves" in four years.

47429. Krapf, Christine. "Relieving Could Be Brad Pennington's Ticket to Stardom." *Orioles Gazette,* II (July 23, 1992), 24–25.

Herbert Jefferis ("Herb" or "The Knight of Kennett Square") Pennock★
P-EXEC. (B: Feb. 10, 1894, Kennett Square, PA-D: Jan. 30, 1948). Philadelphia (A.L), 1912–1915; Boston (AL), 1915–1922; New York (AL), 1923–1933; Boston (AL), 1934. Remarks: Won 241 games and lost 162, with 32 "saves," in 22 seasons; surrendered the first Yankee homer of George Herman ("Babe") Ruth (q.v.), May 1, 1920; won five World Series games and lost none; coach, Boston (AL), 1936–1940 and supervisor of the Red Sox farm system, 1941–1943, GM, Philadelphia (NL), 1944-death; elected to National Baseball Hall of Fame in 1948, where his plaque reads: "Outstanding left handed pitcher in the AL and executive of Philadelphia NL club. Among rare few who made jump from prep school to majors. Saw 22 years service with Philadelphia, Boston and New York teams in AL Recorded 240 victories, 161 4efeats. Never lost a World Series game, winning five. In 1927, pitched 7 1/3 innings without allowing hit in third game of Series."

47430. Allen, Lee, and Thomas Meany. "Herb Pennock." In: their *Kings of the Diamond.* New York: G.P. Putnam, 1965. Pp. 65–67. Frank Vaccaro's profile is a number in the online SABR Biography Project http://bioproj.sabr.org/bioproj.cfm?a=v&v=l&bid=450&pid=11053.

47431. Barton, Jerry. "Herbert Jeffries Pennock." In: his *A Treasure Chest of the Hall of Fame.* Boston, MA: The Wilson-Hill Co., 1952. Pp. 102–103.

47432. Bloodffood, Clifford. "The Yankees' Number Two Southpaw." *Baseball Magazine,* LII (May 1934), 557–559. Written before his trade to Boston.

47433. Briley, Ron. "Herb Pennock." In: John A. Garrity and Marsh C. Carries, eds. *American National Biography.* 24 vols. New York: Oxford University Press, 1999. XVII, 303–304.

47434. Broeg, Bob. "Herb Pennock." In: his *Super Stars of Baseball.* St. Louis, MO : The Sporting News, 1971. Pp. 195–200.

47435. Graham, Frank. "Herb Pennock." *Baseball Digest,* VII (April 1948), 28–48.

47436. _____. "Herb Pennock." In: his *Baseball's Greatest Pitchers.* New York: A.S. Barnes, 1951. Pp. 205–214.

47437. _____. "When Pennock Got the Bees-Ness." *Baseball Digest,* VI (July 1947), 41–42.

47438. Hickey, David and Kerry Keene. "Herb Pennock." In: their *The Proudest Yankees of All: From the Bronx to Cooperstown.* Lanham, MD: Taylor Trade Pub., dist. by National Book Network, 2003. Chapter 34.

47439. Lindthurst, B. Randolph. "Herbert Jeffries 'Herb,' 'The Knight of Kennett Square' Pennock." In: Vol. G-P of David L. Porter, ed. *Biographical Dictionary of American Sports: Baseball.* Rev. and enlarged ed. Westport, CT: Greenwood Press, 2000. Pp. 1188–1189.

47440. Meany, Thomas. "The Country Gentleman." In: his *Baseball's Greatest Pitchers.* New York: A.S. Barnes, 1951. Pp. 205–216.

47441. Pennock, Esther F. "If You Marry a Big-League Pitcher, You'll Be Both Wife and Widow." *Good Housekeeping,* XCVII (August 1933), 32–35.

47442. Pennock, Herb. "Herb Pennock's Theories of Successful Pitching." *Baseball Magazine,* XVIII (December 1926), 293–294. Comments from a Hall of Famer.

47443. _____. "How to Pitch." Edited by Sol Metzger. *Youth's Companion,* CIII (April 1929), 204–206.

47444. _____. "How to Pitch." Edited by Sol Metzger. *Youth's Companion,* CIII (April 1929), 204–206.

47445. Ritter, Lawrence and Donald Honig. "Herb Pennock." In: their *The 100 Greatest Baseball Players of All Time.* New York: Crown Publishers, 1981. Pp. 256–257.

47446. Robinson, Ray. "Herb Pennock: The Stylist." In: his *Greatest Yankees of Them All.* New York: G.P. Putnam's Sons, 1969. Pp. 97–108.

47447. Smith, Ira. "Herbert Jefferies Pennock." In: his *Baseball's Famous Pitchers.* New York: A.S. Barnes, 1954. Pp. 145–150.

47448. Ward, John J. "Herb Pennock: The Man Who Twice Dashed the Giants' Hopes." *Baseball Magazine,* XXXII (December 1923), 299–301.

Joseph Anthony ("Joe" or "Pepi") Pepitone
1B-OF. (B: Oct. 9, 1940, Brooklyn, NY). New York (AL), 1962–1969; Houston (N.L), 1970; Chicago (NL), 1910–1973; Atlanta (NL) and Yakult Atoms (Japan League), 1973. Remarks: Had 1,315 hits (219 homers) and 41 stolen bases in 1,397 games in a dozen years; established several records — but caused club officials concern by periodically "quitting" the game, 1969 and 1972; had three homers in one game, including a grand slam, Aug. 29, 1964; had grand slam homer in Game Four of 1964 World Series; coach, New York (AL), 1982.

47449. Axthelm, Pete. "When the Boys of Summer Go Sour." *Newsweek,* CV (April 1, 1985), 70–71.

47450. Feeney, Charlie. "No Pressure on Joe Pepitone." *Baseball Digest,* XXIX (August 1970), 48–51.

47451. Furillo, Bud. "Pepitone Remembered Tommy Davis." *Baseball Digest,* XXII (September 1963), 69–71.

47452. Gallagher, Mark. "Joe Pepitone." In: his *50 Years of Yankee All-Stars.* New York: Leisure Press, 1984. Pp. 150–151.

47453. Gross, Milton. "Joe Pepitone-Pep Tune from Him Now?" *Baseball Digest,* XV (May 1966), 85–89.

47454. "Joe Pepitone." In: *Current Biography Yearbook 1973.* New York. H.W. Wilson Co., 1973. Pp. 330–333.

47455. McMillan, Ken. "Joe Pepitone." In: his *Tales from the Yankee Dugout: A Collection of the Greatest Yankee Stories Ever Told.* Champaign, IL: Sports Publishing, Inc., 2001. Pp. 130–133.

47456. Obojski, Robert. "Pepitone, [Ed] Kranepool Had the Big Apple in Their Eye." *Sport Collector's Digest,* XXV (October 16, 1998), 130–131.

47457. O'Connor, Dick. "Man Behind the Beard and the New League." *Sport,* XIX (September 1970), 70+.

47458. Pepe, Phil "Joe Pepitone: Next Yankee Superstar?" In: Zander Hollander, ed. *Baseball Yearbook, 1964.* New York: Popular Library, 1964. Pp. 33–36.

47459. Pepitone, Joseph A., with Berry Stainback. *Joe, You Coulda Made Us Proud.* Chicago, IL: Playboy Press, 1975. 246p.

47460. _____., with Tom Capezzuto. "It Was Fun While It Lasted." *Baseball Digest,* L (February 1991), 61–64.

47461. Robinson, Murray. "Yankee Question, Who's on First?" *Baseball Digest,* XXII (February 1963), 15–17.

47462. Schneider, Armand. "Joe Pepitone: The Cubs' New Matinee Idol." *Baseball Digest,* XXX (September 1971), 16–19.

47463. Shecter, Leonard. "Joe Pepitone, a Four-Sewer Yankee." *Baseball Digest,* XXI (August 1962), 71–73.

47464. Sleget, Morris. "Pepitone Eager for Recognition." *Baseball Digest,* XVIII (June 1968), 41–43.

47465. Smith, Leverett T., Jr. "Joseph Anthony 'Joe,' 'Pepi' Pepitone." In: Vol. G–P of David L. Porter, ed. *Biographical Dictionary of American Sports: Baseball.* Rev. and enlarged ed. Westport, CT: Greenwood Press, 2000. Pp. 1189–1191.

47466. Stainback, Berry. "The Freshest Rookie I Ever Saw." *Sport,* XXXVI (December 1963), 40–42.

47467. Vecsey, George. "Peace, Joe Pepitone." *Sport,* XLIX (April 1970), 42–46.

June Peppas

P-OF-2B-1B. (B: June 16, 1929, Kansas City, MO). Fort Wayne and Racine (All-American Girls Professional Baseball League), 1949; Racine (AAGPBL), 1950; Battle Creek and Kalamazoo (AAGPBL), 1951; Kalamazoo (AAGPBL), 1952–1954. Remarks: In six playing years, won 18 games and lost 31; as a fielder, obtained 572 hits, 21 homers, and 70 stolen bases in 581 games.

47468. Sargent, Jim. "June Peppas and the All-American League." *The National Pastime,* XXII (2002), 9–13.

Troy Eugene Percival

P. (B: Aug. 9, 1969, Fontana, CA). California (AL), 1995–1996; Anaheim (AL), 1997–2004; Detroit (AL), 2005–. Remarks: Through 2004, has won 29 games and lost 38, with 316 "saves."

47469. Johnson, Paul M. "Heavenly Heat." *Sport,* LXXXVII (May 1996), 92+.

47470. McDevitt, Scott. "How Dominant Was Percival?" In: STATS, Inc. *STATS 1996 Baseball Scoreboard.* Skokie, IL: STATS Publishing, 1996. Pp. 160–162.

Atanasio Rigal ("Tony" or "Mr. Clutch") Perez★

1B-3B. (B: May 14, 1942, Camaguey, Cuba). Cincinnati (NL), 1964–1976; Montreal (NL), 1977–1979; Boston (AL), 1980–1982; Philadelphia (NL), 1983; Cincinnati (NL), 1984–1986. Remarks: Had 2,732 hits (379 homers) and 49 stolen bases in 2,777 games in 23 seasons; All-Star Game MVP award, 1967; became U.S. citizen in 1971; belted three home runs in 1975 World Series, including key shot in Game Seven; coach, Cincinnati (NL), 1987–1992; manager, Cincinnati (NL) 1993 and Florida, 2001, winning 74 games and losing 84 (.468); director of international relations, Florida (NL), 1994–1997; special assistant to president, Florida (NL), 1998–; enshrined in Cuban Baseball Hall of Fame, 1997; father of Educardo Perez (below); elected to the National Baseball Hall of Fame in 2000, where his plaque reads: "A clutch performer throughout an illustrious 23-year career, he tormented the opposition with his ability to consistently drive in runs. His composure under pressure led to 379 home runs, 505 doubles and 1,652 RBI, including seven 100-RBI seasons and 954 RBI in the 1970s. A catalyst of Cincinnati's talented Big Red Machine teams during the 1970s. His subtle leadership and timely hitting helped pace those clubs to five division titles, four pennants and two World Series championships."

47471. Banks, Lacy J. "Vet-Rookie Duo Sparks Cincinnati Machine: Perez, [Wayne] Simpson Energize Reds' Pennant Drive." *Ebony,* XXV (September 1970), 70–73.

47472. Berke, Art. "Tony Perez." In: his *Unsung Heroes of the Major Leagues.* New York: Random House, 1976. Pp. 134–147.

47473. Dowling, Tom. "Tony Perez, Silent Cog in the 'Big Red Machine.'" *Sport,* L (October 1970), 70–99.

47474. Herzel, Bob. "Tony Perez, the Biggest Bargain of Them All." *Baseball Digest,* XXXIV (December 1975), 44–47.

47475. _____. "Why the Reds Call Tony Perez 'The Big Dog.'" *Baseball Digest,* XXXII (August 1973), 42–45.

47476. Hochman, Stan. "Game No. 5: Tony Perez Finally Had His Moment of Glory." *Baseball Digest,* XXXV (January 1976), 28–29.

47477. Lawson, Earl. "Coming Home." In: Jim Ferguson and Jon Braude, eds. *Cincinnati Reds 1984 Yearbook Magazine.* Cincinnati, OH: Public Relations Department, Cincinnati Reds, 1984. Pp. 12–14. Perez and Dave Parker.

47478. Libby, Bill. "Tony Perez." In: his *Heroes of the Hot Corner.* New York: Franklin Watts, 1972. Pp. 36–44.

47479. McHugh, Roy. "Is Perez Burning." *Sport,* XLIV (October 1967), 54–55+.

47480. Padwe, Sandy. "Tony Perez: Baseball's Little-Known Superstar." *Baseball Digest,* XXIX (September 1970), 42–47.

47481. Perez, Anansio R. ("Tony"). "A Conversation with Tony Perez: 'It's Just Like You Have a New Toy and You Want to Try It.'" *Reds Report,* VI (March 1993), 14–15.

47482. _____, with George Vass. "The Game I'll Never Forget." *Baseball Digest,* XXXIII (August 1974), 58–61. Reprinted in George Vass, ed., The Game I'll Never Forget (Chicago, IL: Bonus Books, 1999), pp. 187–191.

47483. Rathgeber, Bob. "Man's Best Friend: Tony Perez." In: his *Cincinnati Reds Scrapbook.* Virginia Beach, VA: J.C.P. Corp. of Virginia, 1982. Pp. 132–133.

47484. Reed, William F. "Seeing Red in Cincinnati." *Sports Illustrated,* LXXVIII (June 7, 1993), 28–30.

47485. Regalado, Samuel O. "Atanasio Rigal 'Tony,' 'Mr. Clutch' Perez." In: Vol. G–P of David L. Porter, ed. *Biographical Dictionary of American Sports: Baseball.* Rev. and enlarged ed. Westport, CT: Greenwood Press, 2000. Pp. 1191–1192.

47486. Richman, Milton. "Tony Perez: He's Still a Baseball Favorite." *Baseball Digest,* XXXVIII (July 1979), 48–51.

47487. Rogers, Phil "Call to the Hall: Carlton Fisk and Tony Perez to Be Honored in Cooperstown." *Baseball Digest,* LIX (April 2000), 64–75.

47488. Sala, K. J. "Every Dog Has His Day." In: Richard Levin, ed. *2000 World Series Program.* New York: Major League Baseball Promotion Corp., 2000. Pp. 156–159.

47489. Sorci, Rick. "Baseball Profile: Coach Tony Perez of the Reds." *Baseball Digest,* LI (December 1992), 57–59.

47490. Van Hyning, Thomas. "Number 24 Was a Puerto Rico Winter League Hall of Famer: Remembering 'Tany' (Tony) Perez's Puerto Rico Winter League Career." In: *From McGillicuddy to McGwire: Baseball in Florida and the Caribbean.* Cleveland, OH: Society for American Baseball Research, 2000. Pp. 32–34.

47491. Verschoth, A. "Tony Perez." *Sports Illustrated,* LXIV (June 30, 1986), 62–63.

Carlos Perez

P. (B: April 14, 1971, Nigua, Dominican Republic). Montreal (NL), 1995–1997; Los Angeles (NL), 1998–2001. Remarks: Although out with injuries in 1996 and 2001, won 40 games in his big league career, while losing 53; pitched three shutouts in four starts, May-June 1997; brother of Milido Perez and Pascual Perez (below).

47492. Epstein, Eddie. "Carlos Perez." In: STATS, Inc. *The STATS 1995 Minor League Scouting Notebook.* Skokie, IL: STATS Publishing, 1995. Pp. 129–130.

47493. Winston, Lisa. "Expos' Newest Perez Has Same Dance and the Same Trigger." *USA Today Baseball Weekly,* IV (October 26, 1994), 17–18.

Eduardo Atanasio Perez

3B-OF. (B: Sept. 11, 1969, Cincinnati, OH). California (AL), 1993–1995; Cincinnati (NL), 1996–1998; St. Louis

(NL), 1999–2003; Tampa Bay (AL), 2004–. Remarks: Through 2004, has obtained 357 hits (50 homers) and 19 stolen bases in 597 games; Achilles' tendon operation ended his season, May 2004; son of Atanasio ("Tony") Perez (above).

47494. Nightengale, Bob. "Prime Time Talent." *Beckett Focus on Future Stars,* IV, no. 38 (June 1994), 18–19.

Melido Perez

P. (B: Feb. 15, 1966, San Cristobal, Dominican Republic). Kansas City (AL), 1987; Chicago (AL), 1988–1991; New York (AL), 1992–1996. Remarks: Obtained 78 victories and 85 defeats, with one "save," in a decade; had six-inning, rain-shorted no hitter, later removed from record books, May 12, 1990; brother of Carlos Perez (above) and Pascual Perez (below).

47495. Dewan, John and Don Zminda. "Who Pitched Better in 1992?—Tom Glavine or Melido Perez." In: STATS, Inc. *STATS 1993 Baseball Scoreboard.* New York: Harper Perennial, 1993. Pp. 178–180.

Pascual ("Pete") Perez

P. (B: May 17, 1957, San Cristobal, Dominican Republic). Pittsburgh (NL), 1980–1981; Atlanta (NL), 1982–1985; Montreal (NL), 1987–1989; New York (AL), 1990–1991; San Diego (NL), 1992–1993. Remarks: Won 67 games and lost 68 in 14 seasons; had rain-shortened five-inning no hitter, later removed from record books, Sept. 24, 1988; remembered for antics on and off the field; brother of Carlos Perez and Milido Perez (above).

47496. Garrity, John. "He Has Found the Way to Go." *Sports Illustrated,* LVIII (May 23, 1983), 72+.

47497. Langston, Steve. "Pascual Perez: Headed in the Right Direction." *Braves Banner,* II (June 1983), 11+.

47498. Winston, Lisa. "Expos' Newest Perez Has Same Dance and the Same Trigger." *USA Today Baseball Weekly,* IV (October 26, 1994), 17–18.

Pete Perez *see* **Pascual ("Pete") Perez**

Robert Perez

OF. (B: Robert Alexander Perez Jimenez, June 4, 1969, Bolivar, Venezuela). Toronto (AL), 1994–1997; Seattle (AL) and Montreal (NL), 1998; New York (AL) and Milwaukee (NL), 2001. Remarks: In six big league seasons, obtained 126 hits (eight homers) and three stolen bases in 221 games.

47499. Kirst, Sean Peter. "Mother's Voice Guides Player." In: his *The Ashes of Lou Gehrig and Other Baseball Essays.* Jefferson, NC: McFarland & Co., Inc., 2003. Pp. 196–197.

Tony Perez *see* **Atanasio Rigal ("Tony" or "Mr. Clutch") Perez**

Louis Robert ("Lou") Perini

EXEC. (B: Nov. 29, 1903, Ashland, MA-D: April 16, 1972). Remarks: President of Boston (NL) and Milwaukee (NL) clubs, 1945–1957.

47500. Kaese, Harold. "They're Digging a Pennant in Boston." *Saturday Evening Post,* CCXIX (June 28, 1947), 26–28.

47501. Stainback, Barry, and Fred Katz. "Lou Perini: Absentee Owner." *Sport,* XXXIII (May 1962), 47–48.

Matthew Alan Perisho

P. (B: June 6, 1975, Burlington, IA). Anaheim (AL), 1997; Texas (AL), 1998–2000; Detroit (AL), 2001–2002; Florida (NL), 2004–. Remarks: Through 2004, won nine games and lost 17.

47502. Perisho, Matt. "Perisho Gets Fresh Start with Rangers: Lefty Pitcher is Waiting for His First ML Victory." *Sports Collector's Digest,* XXVII (May 10, 2000), 72–73.

Broderick Phillip ("Outfield Patrol") Perkins

1B-OF. (B: Nov. 23, 1964, Pittsburg, CA). San Diego (NL), 1978–1982; Cleveland (AL), 1983–1984. Remarks: Had 340 hits (eight homers) and nine stolen bases in 516 games over seven seasons.

47503. Newman, Bruce. "Fairest of Them All?" *Sports Illustrated,* LIV (June 1, 1981), 56+.

Harry Walter Perkowski

P. (B: Sept. 6, 1922, Dante, VA). Cincinnati (NL), 1947, 1949–1954; Chicago (NL), 1955. Remarks: Won 33 games, including 12 straight, in 1952–1953, while losing 40 and saving five.

47504. Cole, Robert. "I Remember Harry." *The National Pastime,* II (1983), 86–88. Reprinted in John Thorn, ed. *The National Pastime* (New York: Bell Publishing Co., 1987), pp. 265–271.

Ronald Peter ("Ron") Perranoski

P. (B: Ronald Peter Perzanowski, April 1, 1936, Paterson, NJ). Los Angeles (NL), 1961–1967; Minnesota (AL), 1988–1971; Detroit (AL), 1971–1972; Los Angeles (NL), 1972; California (AL), 1973. Remarks: Won 79 games and lost 74, with 179 "saves," in a 13–year big league career; never pitched a complete game as employed exclusively in relief; minor league instructor, 1973–1980; pitching coach, Los Angeles (NL), 1981–1994; pitching coach, San Francisco (NL), 1997–2002.

47505. Bennett, Gaymon L. "Ronald Peter 'Ron' Perranoski." In: Vol. G-P of David L. Porter, ed. *Biographical Dictionary of American Sports: Baseball.* Rev. and enlarged ed. Westport, CT: Greenwood Press, 2000. Pp. 1192–1193.

47506. Cairns, Bob. "Ron Perranoski." In: his *Pen Men: Baseball's Greatest Bullpen Stories told by the Men who Brought the Game Relief.* New York: St. Martin's Press, 1992. Pp. 218–227.

47507. Donnelly, Joe, "Ron Perranoski: A Study in Confidence." *Sport,* XXXVI (April 1963), 30–32.

47508. Hochman, Stan. "Perranoski at Best When Arm is Tired." *Baseball Digest,* XXII (March 1964), 33–35.

47509. Park, Charlie. "Ron Perranoski: Dodgers' Grenadier." *Baseball Digest,* XXII (November 1961), 27–30.

47510. Peables, Dick. "Big Deal at Mesa." *Baseball Digest,* XXIII (May 1964), 61–63.

47511. Perranoski, Ronald P, as told to George Vass. "The Game I'll Never Forget." *Baseball Digest,* XLI (December 1982), 78–81.

47512. Peters, Nick. "No Dodger Blues for Perranoski." *Official San Francisco Giants Magazine,* X, no. 1 (1985), 66–68.

47513. Laughlin, Bob, with Budd Theobald. *Ron Perranoski: Southpaw Rookie Makes Good.* New 1961 Dodger Family series. Los Angeles, CA: Union Oil Company of California, 1961. 14p.

47514. Shapiro, Milton J. "Ron Perranoski." In: his *Heroes of the Bullpen: Baseball's Greatest Relief Pitchers.* New York. Julian Messner, 1967. Pp. 159–172.

47515. Thorn, John. "The Ten Best: Perranoski." In: his *The Relief Pitcher.* New York: E.P. Dutton, 1979. Pp. 126–133.

47516. Vecsey, George. "Ron Perranoski: Bullpen King." In: Ray Robinson, ed. *Baseball Stars of 1964.* New York: Pyramid Books, 1964. Pp. 42–47.

William Dayton ("Pol") Perritt

P. (B: Aug. 310, 1892, Arcadia, LA-D: Oct. 15, 1947). St. Louis (NL), 1912–1914; New York (NL), 1915–1921; Detroit (A.L.), 1921. Remarks: Had 91 victories and 78 defeats, with eight "saves," in a decade; won a shut-out game while giving up 12 hits, Sept. 14, 1917.

47517. Lane, Ferdinand C. "Pol Perritt, Pitcher." *Baseball Magazine*, XV (June 1910), 29–32.

Gaylord Jackson Perry★

P-COACH. (B Sept- 15, 1938, Williamston, NC). San Francisco (N-L), 1962–1971; Cleveland (A.L), 1972–1975; Texas,(AL), 1975–1977; San Diego (NL), 1978–1979; Texas (AL) and New York (AL), 1980; Atlanta (NL), 1981; Seattle, (AL), 1982–1984 Kansas City (AL), 1983. Remarks: Won 314 games and lost 265 in 22 seasons; A.L Cy Young Award, 1972; NL Cy Young Award, 1978; pitched no-hitter, Sept. 17, 1968; also played for St. Cloud (Northern League), 1958, Corpus Christi (TL), 1959, Harlingen (TL), 1960, Tacoma (PCL), 1961–1963; coach, Limestone College (SC), 1987–1990; brother of Jim Perry (below); named to Missouri Sports Hall of Fame, 2000; elected to the National Baseball Hall of Fame in 1991, where his plaque reads: "Achieved pitchers' magic numbers with 314 wins and 3,534 strikeouts. Playing mind games with hitters through array of rituals on mound was part of his arsenal. 20-game winner 5 times with lifetime ERA of 3.10. No-hit Cards for Giants 9/18/68. Outstanding competitor. Only Cy Young winner in both leagues."

47518. Allen, Maury. "Gaylord Perry (1962–Present)." In: his *Baseball's 100*. New York: Galahad Books, 1981. Pp. 119–121. Mark Armour's profile is a number in the online SABR Biography Project http://bioproj.sabr.org/bioproj.cfm?a=v&v=l&bid=448&pid=11112.

47519. Ames, Steve. "When the Perry Brothers Made History." *Baseball Digest*, XXXIII (June 1974), 66–69.

47520. Axthelm, Pete. "Conquering Con Man." *Newsweek*, XCIX (May 17, 1982), 89–90.

47521. Bloom, Bob. "King of Grease." *Sport*, LXXIII (August 1982), 55–59+.

47522. Blount, Roy, Jr. "Return of the Natives: The Perry Boys of Williamston, NC" *Sports Illustrated*, XXXIV (March 20, 1971), 56–60+.

47523. Butler, Hal. "Gaylord Perry." In: his *Baseball's Champion Pitchers*. New York: Julian Messner, 1974. Pp. 39–51.

47524. Chesson, Parker. "A Gaylord Perry Story." In: Chris Holaday, ed. *Baseball in the Carolinas: 25 Essays in the States' Hardball Heritage*. Jefferson, NC: McFarland & Co., Inc., 2002. Pp. 33–36.

47525. Collier, Phil "Gaylord Perry: Still Wet Behind the Ears." In: Gerald Kavanagh, ed. *Street and Smith's Official 1983 Baseball Yearbook*. Now York: Conde Nast Publications, 1983. Pp. 14–21.

47526. Dolgan, Bob. "Gaylord Perry: Portrait of a Winner." *Baseball Digest*, XXXI (September 1972), 22–27.

47527. Elderkin, Phil "Gaylord Perry Still One of the Best at Ago 40." *Baseball Digest*, XXXVIII (January 1979), 70–73.

47528. Fimrite, Ron. "Bound for Glory." *Sports Illustrated*, LV (August 24, 1981), 92–96+.

47529. "Gaylord Perry." In: *Current Biography Yearbook, 1982.*New York: H.W. Wilson Co., 1982. Pp. 315–319.

47530. Green, Paul M. "Baseball and Gaylord Perry." *Sports Collector's Digest*, XI (January 6, 1984), 72+.

47531. Hickey, David and Kerry Keene. "Gaylord Perry." In: their *The Proudest Yankees of All: From the Bronx to Cooperstown*. Lanham, MD: Taylor Trade Pub., dist. by National Book Network, 2003. Chapter 8.

47532. Jordan, Pat. "Forkballers of the Year." *Sports Illustrated*, . XL (June 17, 1984), 39+.

47533. Kuenster, John. "Gaylord Perry — Next, 300 Game Winner in the Majors?" *Baseball Digest*, XXXIX (May 1980), 19–21.

47534. Lawson, Earl. "Gaylord Perry Next in Line to Win 300 Games." *Baseball Digest*, XL (August 1981), 40–43.

47535. Matos, Fred. "Gaylord Perry — 1972." In: his *Baseball's Top 100: The Best Individual Seasons of All Time*. Wilton, CT: Diamond Library, 1996. Pp. 221–225.

47536. McCallum, John. "Prime of the Ancient Mariner." *Sports Illustrated*, ILVI.(May 17, 1982), 26–29.

47537. McKay, Joe. "Gaylord Perry: The Master of Deception." In: his *The Great Shutout Pitchers: 20 Profiles of a Vanishing Breed*. Jefferson, NC: McFarland & Co., Inc., 2004. Pp. 177–186.

47538. McMillan, Ken. "Gaylord Perry." In: his *Tales from the Yankee Dugout: A Collection of the Greatest Yankee Stories Ever Told*. Champaign, IL: Sports Publishing, Inc., 2001. Pp. 134–135.

47539. Pepe, Phil "How Gaylord Learned to Pitch." *Sport*, XLII (November 1966), 62–63+.

47540. Perry, Gaylord J., with Bob Sudyk. *Me and the Spitter: An Autobiographical Confession*. New York: Saturday Review Press, 1974. 222p. Excerpted In *Baseball Digest*, XXXIII (August 1974), 30–35, and *Sport*, LVI (September 1973), 40–53; LVII (April and June 1974), 97–108, 81–89.

47541. Pickard, Chuck. "Perrys First Brothers to Win 20 Games." *Baseball Digest*, XXX (April 1971), 74–81. Both Gaylord and Jim won 20+ in 1970.

47542. Post, Paul. "Hall of Fame, But No World Series." *Sports Collector's Digest*, XXIV (March 7, 1997), 184–185.

47543. Pratt, John L. "Gaylord Perry." In: his *Baseball All-Stars*. Garden City, NY: Doubleday, 1967. Pp. 103–104.

47544. Robinson, Ray. "Gaylord Perry: Gone is the Greaseball!" In: Ray Robinson, ed. *Baseball Stars of 1975*. New York: Pyramid Books, 1975. Pp. 93–98.

47545. Schlossberg, Dan. "Gaylord." *Baseball Cards*, XI (July 1991), 126–131.

47546. Smith, Leverett T., Jr. "James Evans 'Jim' Perry [and] Gaylord Jackson Perry." In: Vol. G-P of David L. Porter, ed. *Biographical Dictionary of American Sports: Baseball*. Rev. and enlarged ed. Westport, CT: Greenwood Press, 2000. Pp. 1193–1195.

47547. Smith, Ron. "Gaylord Perry 97." In: his *The Sporting News Selects Baseball's 100 Greatest Players*. St. Louis, MO: *The Sporting News*, 1998. Pp. 208–209.

47548. Sudyk, Bob. "The Perrys Greatest Brother Pitching Combo." *Baseball Digest*, XXXIV (April 1975), 62–64.

47549. Taylor, Keith R. "A Final Look: Gaylord Perry." *Beckett Baseball Card Monthly*, VII (May 1990), 94–95.

47550. _____. "Gaylord Perry Recalls His Career as a 300-Game Winner." *Baseball Digest*, XLIX (May 1990), 73–75.

47551. Valerie, Joseph. "End of the Line for Gaylord Ferry?" *Baseball Digest*, XXXV (December 1976), 54–56.

47552. Westcott, Rich. "Gaylord Perry — Few Pitchers Were More Durable." In: his *Diamond Greats*. Westport, CT: Meckler Books, 1988. Pp. 317–321.

47553. _____. "Gaylord Perry: Master of Mind Games." In: his *Winningest Pitchers: Baseball's 300-Game Winners*. Philadelphia, PA: Temple University Press, 2002. Pp. 127–136.

James Evan ("Jim") Perry

P. (B: Oct. 3, 1936, Williamston, NC). Cleveland (AL), 1959–1963; Minnesota (AL), 1963–1972; Detroit (AL), 1973; Cleveland (AL), 1974–1976; Oakland (AL), 1975. Remarks: Had 215 victories and 174 defeats, with 10 "saves," in 17 seasons; AL Cy Young Award, 1970; brother of Gaylord Perry (above).

47554. Ames, Steve. "When the Perry Brothers Made History." *Baseball Digest,* XXXIII (June 1974), 66–69.

47555. Blount, Roy, Jr. "Return of the Natives: The Perry Boys of Williamston, NC" *Sports Illustrated,* XXXIV (March 20, 1971), 56–60+.

47556. Gibbons, Frank. "Jim Perry: Pugger from the Peanut Patches." *Baseball Digest,* XIX (April 1960), 37–39.

47557. Jordan, Pat. "Forkballers of the Year." *Sports Illustrated,* . XL (June 17, 1984), 39+.

47558. Lebovitz, Hal. "Jim Perry Lives Up to His Promises." *Baseball Digest,* XXIX (December 1970), 20–22.

47559. McAuley, Ed. "Jim Perry: The Character Who Isn't One." *Baseball Digest,* XIX (September 1960), 27–31.

47560. Mann, Jack. "Jim Perry's Will to Win." *Sport,* XXXII (July 1961), 22–24+.

47561. Perry, Jim. "It's a Long Road to 20 Wins." In: Vito Stellino, ed. *Sports All-Stars 1971 Baseball.* New York: Maco Publishing Co., 1971. Pp. 64–68.

47562. Pickard, Chuck. "Perrys First Brothers to Win 20 Games." *Baseball Digest,* XXX (April 1971), 74–81.

47563. Smith, Leverett T., Jr. "James Evans 'Jim' Perry [and] Gaylord Jackson Perry." In: Vol. G-P of David L. Porter, ed. *Biographical Dictionary of American Sports: Baseball.* Rev. and enlarged ed. Westport, CT: Greenwood Press, 2000. Pp. 1193–1195.

47564. Sudyk, Bob. "The Perrys Greatest Brother Pitching Combo." *Baseball Digest,* XXXIV (April 1975), 62–54.

Robert Alan Person

P. (B: Jan. 8, 1969, Lowell, MA). New York (NL), 1995–1996; Toronto (AL), 1997–1999; Philadelphia (NL), 1999–2002; Boston (AL), 2003; Chicago (AL), 2004–. Remarks: Through 2003, had won 51 games and lost 42, with eight "saves"; hit two homers in one game, June 2, 2002; Achilles tendon rupture forced him to miss 2003 season.

47565. Epstein, Eddie. "Robert Person." In: STATS, Inc. The STATS 1995 Minor League Scouting Notebook. Skokie, IL: STATS Publishing, 1995. Pp. 130–131.

John Michael ("Johnny") Pesky

SS-3B-2B-MGR-BROADCASTER. (B: John Michael Paveskovich, Sept. 27, 1919, Portland, OR). Boston (AL), 1942, 1946–1952; Detroit (AL), 1952–1954; Washington (AL), 1954. Remarks: Had 1,455 hits (17 homers) and 53 stolen bases in a decade of play; AL Rookie of the Year award, 1942; established or tied several AL records, including that of becoming the first to score six runs in one game, May 8, 1946; is also remembered for late throw in Game Seven of 1946 World Series; struck out only 218 times in entire career; also played for Rocky Mount (Piedmont League), 1940 and Louisville (AA), 1941; player-coach, Denver (AA), 1955; manager, Durham (Carolina League), Birmingham (SA), Lancaster (EL), Knoxville (South Atlantic League), Victoria (TL), and Seattle (PCL), 1956–1962; manager, Boston (AL), 1963–1964 and Boston (AL), 1980, winning 147 games and losing 178 (.452); coach, Pittsburgh (NL), 1965–1967 and Boston (AL), 1975–1984; manager, Columbus (IL), 1968; broadcaster, Boston (AL), 1969–1974; named to Oregon Sports Hall of Fame, 1980; special assistant to GM, Boston (A.L), 1988–1992; named to Boston Red Sox Hall of Fame, Nov. 1995; special assistant for player development, Boston (AL), 1993–1999.

47566. Allen, Ethan. "Signing Off." *Scholastic Coach,* XVI (February 1947), 7–8. Signs as demonstrated by Pesky.

47567. Berry, Henry. "Players: Johnny Pesky." In: his *Baseball's Great Teams: Boston Red Sox.* New York: Collier Books, 1975. Pp. 151–158.

47568. Debs, Victor, Jr. "Johnny Pesky." In: his *"That Was Part of Baseball Then": Interviews with 24 Former Major League Baseball Players, Coaches, and Managers.* Jefferson, NC: McFarland & Co., Inc., 2002. Pp. 20–27.

47569. DiMeglio, John E. "John Michael 'Johnny' Pesky." In: Vol. G-P of David L. Porter, ed. *Biographical Dictionary of American Sports: Baseball.* Rev. and enlarged ed. Westport, CT: Greenwood Press, 2000. Pp. 1195–1196.

47570. Drohan, John. "That Pesky Kid." *Baseball Magazine,* LIX (October 1942), 495–497.

47571. Eichmann, J. K. "Johnny Pesky: A Forgotten Star." *Sports Scoup,* II (September 1974), 10+.

47572. Frommer, Harvey and Frederick J. "Johnny Pesky." In: their *Growing Up Baseball: An Oral History.* Dallas, TX: Taylor Publishing Co., 2001. Pp. 184–188.

47573. Hirshberg, Al. "The Popular Pesky." *Sport,* XII (June 1952), 26–27.

47574. Holway, John B. "The Myth of Pesky's [1946 World Series] Throw." In: his *The Ol' Ball Game.* Harrisburg, PA: Stackpole Books, 1990. Pp. 118–125.

47575. Kaese, Harold. "He's Pesky All Right." *Baseball Digest,* V (July 1946), 37–41.

47576. Langford, Walter. "Errors That Lost the Series." *Sports Heritage,* I (November 1987), 24–26. Pesky and Roger Peckinpaugh.

47577. Lautier, Jack. "Johnny Pesky." In: his *Fenway Voices.* Camden, ME: Yankee Books, 1990. Pp. 33–38.

47578. Miller, Hub. "Pesky Has Always Set a Fast Pace." *Baseball Magazine,* LXXVII (July 1944), 257–259.

47579. Nowlin, Bill and Jim Prime. *Mr. Red Sox: The Johnny Pesky Story.* Boston, MA: Rounder Books, 2004. 388p. Nowlin's profile is a number in the online SABR Biography Project http://bioproj.sabr.org/bioproj.cfm?a=v&v=l&bid=456&pid=11123.

47580. Santa Maria, Michael and James Costello. "He Who Hesitates." In: their *In the Shadows of the Diamond.* Dubuque, IA: The Elysian Fields Press, 1992. Pp. 57–63.

47581. Stump, Al. "Johnny Pesky: Peskiest Little Guy." In: his *Champions Against Odds.* New York: MacRae Smith, 1952. Pp. 57–66.

47582. _____. "Pesky—the 'Peoples' Pet." *Sport,* II (May 1947), 46–50.

47583. Van Blair, Rick. "Johnny Pesky." In: his *Dugout to Foxhole: Interviews with Baseball Players Whose Careers Were Affected By World War II.* Jefferson, NC: McFarland & Co., Inc., 1994. Pp. 160–170.

47584. Weiss, Peter. "Johnny Pesky." In: his *Baseball's All-Time Goats: As Chosen by America's Top Sportswriters.* Holbrook, MA: Bob Adams, Inc, 1992. Pp. 136–139.

47585. Wilber, Cynthia J. "Johnny Pesky." In: her *For the Love of the Game: Baseball Memories from the Men Who Were There.* New York: William Morrow, 1992. Pp. 210–218.

Gary Charles Peters

P. (B: April 21, 1937, Grove City, PA). Chicago (A.L), 1959–1969; Boston (AL), 1970–1972. Remarks: Won 124 games and lost 105 in 14 seasons; AL Rookie of the Year award, 1963; good hitting pitcher who had 289 hits and eight homers in 1,222 at bats, including three homers in one game, Sept. 27, 1970.

47586. Appel, Marty. "Gary Peters." In: his *Yesterday's Heroes: Revisiting the Old-Time Baseball Stars.* New York: William Morrow, 1988. Pp. 170–173.

47587. Falls, Joe. "Gary Peters: Boomerangs and Baseballs." *Sport,* XXXVII (January 1964), 40–42.

47588. Furlong, William B ("Bill"). "Gary Peters & Juan Pizarro: Southpaw Sorcery." In: Ray Robinson, ed. *Baseball Stars of 1965.* New York: Pyramid Books, 1965. Pp. 125–133.

47589. _____. "Gary Peters-Pete Ward: White Sox Wonder Boys." In: Ray Robinson, ed. *Baseball Stars of 1964.* New York: Pyramid Books, 1964. Pp. 138–144.

47590. Graybar, Lloyd J. "Gary Charles Peters." In: Vol. G-P of David L. Porter, ed. *Biographical Dictionary of American Sports: Baseball.* Rev. and enlarged ed. Westport, CT: Greenwood Press, 2000. Pp. 1197–1198.

47591. Heiman, Lee, Dave Weiner and Bill Gutman. "Gary Peters." In: their *When the Cheering Stops.* New York: Macmillan, 1990. Pp. 283–293.

47592. Holtzman, Jerome. "Gary Peters, Seven Years on the Way." *Baseball Digest,* XXII (December 1963), 67–71.

47593. Honig, Donald. "1963: Gary Peters." In: his *American League Rookies of the Year.* New York: Bantam Books, 1989. Pp. 35–36.

47594. Kaese, Harold. "Why Red Sox Wanted to Get Gary Peters." *Baseball Digest,* XXIX (April 1970), 95–98.

47595. Vanderberg, Bob. "Gary Peters: The Joker Went Wild." In: his *Sox—From Lane and Fain to Zisk and Fisk.* Chicago, IL: Chicago Review Press, 1982. Pp. 297–102.

47596. Wolf, Bob. "If Peters Loses Pitching Touch, He Can Hit." *Baseball Digest,* XXVII (June 1968), 77–79.

Henry J. ("Hank") Peters
EXEC. (B: Sept. 16, 1924, St. Louis, MO). Remarks: Asst. dir., farm system, St. Louis (AL), 1946–1953; GM, Burlington (Three-I League), 1954; farm director, Kansas City (AL), 1955–1960 and Cincinnati (NL), 1961; asst. GM, Kansas City (AL), 1962–1964; GM, Kansas City (AL), 1965; VP/Player personnel, Cleveland (AL), 1966–1971; president, National Association of Professional Baseball Leagues, 1972–1975; exec VP/GM, Baltimore (AL), 1976–1987; president, Cleveland (AL), 1987–1991.

47597. Glassman, Brian. "Life in Tower A." *Minneapolis Review of Baseball,* VIII (Fall 1989), 17–19.

Russell Dixon ("Rusty") Peters
2B-SS-3B-OF. (B: Dec. 14, 1914, Roanoke, VA-D: February 21, 2003). Philadelphia (AL), 1936–1938; Cleveland (AL), 1940–1946; St. Louis (AL), 1947. Remarks: Obtained 289 hits (eight homers) and nine stolen bases in 471 games in 10 big league seasons; went 4-for-5 in one game, Aug. 14, 1937, also played for Albany (IL), 1935, Columbus (AA), 1936, Atlanta (SA), 1938–1939, Toledo (AA), 1948, Indianapolis (AA), 1948–1951; worked for U.S. Post Office, 1952–1975 .

47598. Sargent, Jim. "Russ 'Rusty' Peters: From Roanoke to the Big Leagues." *Oldtyme Baseball News,* VIII, no. 2 (1996), 14–15. Sargent's profile is a number in the online SABR Biography Project http://bioproj.sabr.org/bioproj.cfm?a=v&v=l&bid=696&pid=11134.

Rusty Peters *see* **Russell Dixon ("Rusty") Peters**
Fred Ingels ("Fritz") Peterson
P. (B; Feb. 8, 1942, Chicago, IL). New York (AL), 1966–1974; Cleveland (AL), 1974–1976; Texas (AL), 1976. Remarks: Had 133 victories, 131 defeats, and one "save" in an 11-year big league career; remembered for wife-trading episode of 1973 with fellow Yankee pitcher Mike Kekich (q.v.).

47599. Condon, David. "How Extra Pitch Helped Fritz Peterson." *Baseball Digest,* XXX (June 1971), 28–31.

47600. Fitzgerald, Ray. "The Night Fritz Peterson Won His 20th Game." *Baseball Digest,* XXX (January 1971), 33–36.

47601. Gallagher, Mark. "Fritz Peterson." In: his *50 Years of Yankee All-Stars.* New York: Leisure Press, 1984. Pp. 152–153.

47602. McMillan, Ken. "Fritz Peterson." In: his *Tales from the Yankee Dugout: A Collection of the Greatest Yankee Stories Ever Told.* Champaign, IL: Sports Publishing, Inc., 2001. Pp. 136–137.

47603. Meyer, Thomas L. and David L. Mason. "The Pick-Off." *Athletic Journal,* XLIX (February 1969), 33–36. As demonstrated by Peterson.

47604. Rubin, Bob. "You Tell Me Your Dream." *Sport,* XLVI (December 1968), 4–5.

47605. Smith, C. S. "Yankee-Panky." *New York,* XXIV (January 14, 1991), 24–25.

Fritz Peterson *see* **Fred Ingels ("Fritz") Peterson**
Rick Peterson
COACH (B: 1955, Pittsburgh, PA). Remarks: Minor league pitching coach in Pittsburgh (NL), Cleveland (AL), and Chicago (AL) systems, 1980–1995; coach, Chicago (AL), 1994–1995, Toronto (AL), 1996–1997; Oakland (AL), 1998–2003; New York (NL), 2004–.

47606. Macht, Norman L. "A's Coach Rick Peterson: Using a Philosophical Approach to Teaching." *Baseball Digest,* XLII (January 2003), 38–43.

John Petrakis
EXEC. Owner, Dubuque Packers (Midwest League), 1954–1976; John Petrakis Field at Dubuque named in his honor in 1967.

47607. Slocum, Bill. "Baseball's Unlikely Magnate." *Saturday Evening Post,* XXXVIII (May 5, 1956), 38–41.

Americo Peter ("Rico") Petrocelli
SS-38-BROADCASTER. (B: June 27, 1943, Brooklyn, NY). Boston (AL), 1963–1976. Remarks. Obtained 1,352 hits (210 homers) and 10 stolen bases in 13 seasons; catch clinched "Impossible Dream" Red Sox pennant, Oct. 1, 1967; had two homers in Game Six, 1967 World Series; with 40 homers in 1969, set AL record for most homers in a season by a shortstop, while simultaneously tying a then-standing record for fewest errors by a shortstop (14); had grand slam homer, June 21, 1972; broadcaster, Boston (AL), 1979–1985; manager, Appleton (Midwest League) 1986; manager, Birmingham (SL), 1987–1988; manager/instructor, Pawtucket (IL), 1992–1994; broadcaster, NESN, 1996–; named to Boston Red Sox Hall of Fame, Sept. 8, 1997.

47608. Abrams, Al. "A Look at Rico Petrocelli." *Baseball Digest,* XXVII (August 1968), 57–58.

47609. Crehan, Herbert F. and James W. Ryan. "Rico Petrocelli." In: their *Lightning in a Bottle: The Sox of '67.* Boston, MA: Branden Publishing Co., 1992. Pp. 155–170.

47610. Devaney, John. "Rico Petrocelli: A Small Change in the Iron Butterfly." *Sport,* XLIX (June 1970), 62–73.

47611. Elderkin, Phil "Red Sox Balance Wheel." *Baseball Digest,* XXVI (August 1967), 55–57.

47612. _____. "Rico Petrocelli, Newest Minibrute in the Majors." *Baseball Digest,* XXVIII (September 1969), 68–70.

47613. Fitzgerald, Joe. "Ricky: The Brooding but Brilliant Red Sox." *Baseball Quarterly,* II (Fall 1978), 12–15.

47614. Hirshberg, Al. "How Rico Put 'Pop' in His Game." *Sport,* XLIV (September 1967), 26–27+. Coach Edward Popowski.

47615. Libby, Bill. "Rico Petrocelli." In: his *Heroes of the Hot Corner.* New York: Watts, 1972. Pp. 117–123.

47616. Marshall, Ron. "Rico's Record." *Boston Baseball,* VII (September 1996), 54–55.

47617. McDermott, Joe. "Petrocelli Pulls Up His Sox." *Sports Illustrated,* XXXVI (April 3, 1972), 67, 70.

47618. Porter, David L. "Americo Peter 'Rico' Petrocelli." In: Vol. G-P of David L. Porter, ed. *Biographical Dictionary of American Sports: Baseball*. Rev. and enlarged ed. Westport, CT: Greenwood Press, 2000. Pp. 1198–1199.

Rico Petrocelli *see* **Americo Peter ("Rico") Petrocelli**

Daniel Joseph ("Dan" or "Peaches") Petry

P. (B: Nov. 13, 1958, Palo Alto, CA). Detroit (AL), 1979–1987; California (AL), 1988–1989; Detroit (AL), 1990–1991; Atlanta (NL) and Boston (AL), 1992. Remarks: Had 125 victories, 104 defeats, and one "save" in 14 years; lost Game Two of 1984 World Series.

47619. English, John T. "Daniel Joseph 'Dan,' 'Peaches' Petry." In: Vol. G-P of David L. Porter, ed. *Biographical Dictionary of American Sports: Baseball*. Rev. and enlarged ed. Westport, CT: Greenwood Press, 2000. P. 1199.

Gary George Pettis

OF. (B: April 3, 1958, Oakland, CA). California (AL), 1982–1987; Detroit (AL), 1988–1989; Texas (AL), 1990–1991; San Diego (NL) and Detroit (AL), 1992. Remarks: Obtained 855 hits (21 homers) and 354 stolen bases in 1,183 games in 11 seasons; had nine hits in 1986 ALCS; coach, Chicago (AL), 2001–2002; coach, New York (NL), 2003; coach, Nashville (AA), 2004–.

47620. Anderson, Bruce. "An Angel in the Outfield." *Sports Illustrated*, LXIII (July 8, 1985), 48–49.

47621. Thornton, K. D. "Gary Pettis." In: Ken Collier, ed. *The Baseball Book, 1986*. Scottsdale, AZ: Jalart House, 1986. Pp. 126–127.

George William Paul ("Lefty") Pettit

P. (B: Nov. 29, 1931, Los Angeles, CA). Pittsburgh (NL), 1951 and 1953. Remarks: Highly touted major league "phenom" who won one game and lost two of the dozen involved in.

47622. Bisher, Furman, "Dixie's Wild About Pettit." *Sport*, XIV (March 1953), 44–45+.

47623. "California Gold Rush." *Newsweek*, XXXV (February 13, 1950), 76.

47624. Chapin, Dwight. "Paul Pettit Survives Fall from Glory." *Baseball Digest*, XXX (December 1971), 60–63.

47625. Hernon, Jack. "The End Nears for $100,000." *Baseball Digest*, XIII (April 1954), 43–45.

47626. Johnson, Vance. "Will Bucs' Lefty Jinx' Haunt Pettit?" *Baseball Digest*, IX (May 1950), 59–61.

47627. Lardner, John. "Art, Bloodhounds, and Pirate Gold." *Newsweek*, XXXV (March 27, 1960), 81+.

47628. "Ten Years to Nowhere." *Sport*, XXIX (January 1960), 48–50.

47629. Wolf, Al. "Pettit, 100-G Arm Flop, Tries with Bat." *Baseball Digest*, XIV (April 1955), 38–41.

Andrew Eugene ("Andy") Pettitte

P. (B: June 15, 1972, Baton Rouge, LA). New York (AL), 1995–2003; Houston (NL), 2004–. Remarks: Through 2004, has won 155 games and lost 82; won Game Five of 1996 ALCS; won Game Six of 1996 World Series; lost Game Three of 1998 ALCS; won Game Four of 1998 World Series; won Game Three of 1999 ALCS; won Game Three of 2000 ALCS; Won Games One and Five, 2001 ALCS; ALCS MVP Award, 2001; lost Games Two and Six of 2001 World Series; won Game Two of 2003 ALCS; won Game Two and lost Game Six of 2003 World Series.

47630. Capezzuto, Tom. "Yankee's Andy Pettitte Learns the Fine Art of Pitching." *Baseball Digest*, LV (November 1996), 34–37.

47631. Curry, Jack. "Andy Pettitte Joins Yankee Lefty Legends." In: Zander Hollander, ed. *The Complete Baseball Handbook, 1997*. New York: Signet Books, 1997. Pp. 16–23.

47632. Glickson, Grant. "By Any Means Necessary." In: Tony Gervino, ed. *Hardball*. New York: Harris Pub. Co., 1997. Pp. 28–33.

47633. Klapisch, Bob. "Ace in the Hole." *Yankees Magazine*, XX (May 1999), 28–37.

47634. _____. "Pumped Up." *Yankees Magazine*, XXII (July 2001), 20–31.

47635. Klima, John. "The Country Boy: Andy Pettitte vs. John Smoltz (October 24, 1996)." In: his *Pitched Battle: 35 of Baseball's Greatest Duels from the Mound*. Jefferson, NC: McFarland & Co., Inc., 2002. Pp. 175–179.

47636. Koenig, Bill. "Three of a Kind: Yanks' Modest Young Stars [Jeter, Bernie Williams, and Pettitte] Have Plenty of Incentive to Pursue Second World Title." *USA Today Baseball Weekly*, VII (March 26, 1997), 8–10.

47637. Pettitte, Andy. "When I was a Kid: Interview." *Junior League Baseball*, no. 12 (November-December 1997), 10+.

47638. Sorci, Rick. "Baseball Profile: Yankee Pitcher Andy Pettitte." *Baseball Digest*, LVI (August 1997), 64–65.

Timothy ("Tim") Pettorini

COACH. (B: 1951, Columbus, OH). Remarks: Head baseball coach, The College of Wooster, 1981–; through 2004, has had a record of 720–283-6 (.717); coached 1,000th game, April 24, 2004; NCAC Coach of the Year, 1987–1988, 1990, 1995, 2002, 2004.

47639. Finn, John. "Pushing to the Top." *Wooster Magazine*, (Spring 2001), 32–34.

Jesse Lee ("The Silver Fox") Petty

P. (B: Nov. 23, 1894, Orr, OK-D: Oct. 23, 1971). Cleveland (AL), 1921; Brooklyn (NL), 1925–1928; Pittsburgh (NL), 1929–1930; Chicago (NL), 1930. Remarks: Had 67 victories and 78 defeats, with four "saves," in seven seasons; in 1926, won 17 games — and lost 17 games.

47640. Ward, John J. "Jesse Petty and His Southpaw Speedball." *Baseball Magazine*, XXXVIII (February 1927), 409–410.

47641. _____. "Petty, the Unlucky." *Baseball Magazine*, XLIII (August 1929), 390–391.

Edward Joseph ("Jeff" or "Hassen") Pfeffer

P-UMP. (B: March 4, 1888, Seymour, IL-D: Aug. 15, 1972). St. Louis (AL), 1911; Brooklyn (NL), 1913–1921; St. Louis (NL), 1921–1924; Pittsburgh (NL), 1924. Remarks: Obtained 158 victories, 112 defeats, and 10 "saves" in 11 big league seasons; also hurled for Grand Rapids (Central League), 1912–1913, San Francisco (PCL), 1925, and Toledo (AA), 1926–1927; AA umpire, 1928–1930.

47642. Matz, David S. "Edward Joseph 'Jeff,' 'Hassen' Pfeffer." In: Vol. G-P of David L. Porter, ed. *Biographical Dictionary of American Sports: Baseball*. Rev. and enlarged ed. Westport, CT: Greenwood Press, 2000. Pp. 1200–1201. John Bennet's profile is a number in the online SABR Biography Project http://bioproj.sabr.org/bioproj.cfm?a=v&v=l&bid=932&pid=11171.

Fred Pfeffer *see* **Nathaniel Frederick ("Fred" or "Dandelion") Pfeffer**

Jeff Pfeffer *see* **Edward Joseph ("Jeff" or "Hassen") Pfeffer**

Nathaniel Frederick ("Fred" or "Dandelion") Pfeffer

2B-SS-MGR. (B: March 17, 1860, Louisville, KY-D: April 10, 1932). Troy (NL), 1882; Chicago (NL), 1883–1889; Chicago (P), 1890; Chicago (NL), 1891; Louisville (NL), 1892–1895; New York (NL), 1896; Chicago (N.L), 1896–1897. Remarks: Obtained 1,671 hits (95 homers) and 362 stolen bases in 1,670 games in 16 seasons; had three hits in one inning, Sept. 6, 1883; NL home run champion, 1884; first infielder to cut off a catcher's throw to second base on a double-steal attempt and throw out the runner at the plate; manager, Louisville (NL), 1892, winning 42 games and losing 56 (.429); manager, Decatur (3I League), 1902; author early baseball instructional, *Scientific Ball,* 1889; Chicago saloon keeper, 1898–1920.

47643. Ahrens, Arthur R. "Fred Pfeffer, Stonewall Second Baseman" *The Baseball Research Journal,* VIII (1979), 46–51.

47644. Pfeffer, N. Frederick. "Reminiscences of an Old-Timer." *Baseball Magazine,* XXI (August 1918), 358–359+.

47645. _____. *Scientific Ball.* Chicago, 1889. 83p. Thoughts and advice.

47646. Ray, DeWitt. "Biography of the Author." In: N. Frederick Pfeffer. *Scientific Ball.* Chicago, 1889. Chapter 1. Profile of Pfeffer, who was one of the first baseball book authors.

47647. Smith, Leverett T., Jr. "Nathaniel Frederick Pfeffer." In: Vol. G-P of David L. Porter, ed. *Biographical Dictionary of American Sports: Baseball.* Rev. and enlarged ed. Westport, CT: Greenwood Press, 2000. Pp. 1201–1202.

John Albert ("Jack" or "Jack the Giant Killer") Pfiester
P. (B: John Albert Hagenbush, May 24, 1878, Cincinnati, OH–D: Sept. 3, 1953). Pittsburgh (NL), 1903–1904; Chicago (NL), 1906–1911. Remarks: In eight big league seasons, won 72 games and lost 44; struck out 17 batters in a 15-inning game, May 30, 1906; lost Games Three and Five of 1906 World Series; won Game Two of 1907 World Series; won Game Three of 1908 World Series; also played for Spokane (Pacific Northwest League), 1902, San Francisco (PCL), 1903, Omaha (WL), 1904–1905, Sioux City (WL), 1916.

47648. Smith, Duane A. "John Albert 'Jack' Pfiester." In: Vol. G-P of David L. Porter, ed. *Biographical Dictionary of American Sports: Baseball.* Rev. and enlarged ed. Westport, CT: Greenwood Press, 2000. Pp. 1202–1203. Stuart Schimler's profile is a number in the online SABR Biography Project http://bioproj.sabr.org/bioproj.cfm?a=v&v=l&bid=915&pid=11173.

William A. Phelon
WRITER. (B: 1871–D: 1925). Remarks: Baseball writer, *Chicago Tribune* and *New York Morning Telegraph,* 1889–1909; baseball writer, Cincinnati *Times-Star,* and *Baseball Magazine,* 1910–1925; founding member, Baseball Writers Association of America.

47649. Phelon, William A. "The Trials of a Baseball Prophet: The Sad Lot of the Scribe Who Picks the Losing Team." *Baseball Magazine,* VIII (January 1912), 3–6.

Ernest Gordon ("Babe" or "Blimp") Phelps
C-1B. (B: April 19, 1908, Odenton, MD–D: Dec. 10, 1992). Washington (AL), 1931; Chicago (NL), 1933–1934; Brooklyn (NL), 1935–1941; Pittsburgh (NL), 1942. Remarks: In 11 big league seasons, had 657 hits (54 homers) and nine stolen bases in 726 games; went 5-for-6 in one game, May 31, 1937; refused to fly to away games.

47650. Phelps, Frank V. "Ernest Gordon 'Babe,' 'Blimp' Phelps." In: Vol. G-P of David L. Porter, ed. *Biographical Dictionary of American Sports: Baseball.* Rev. and enlarged ed. Westport, CT: Greenwood Press, 2000. Pp. 1203–1204. Cort Vitty's profile is a number in the online SABR Biography Project http://bioproj.sabr.org/bioproj.cfm?a=v&v=l&bid=718&pid=11183.

David Earl ("Dave") Philley
OF-1B. (B: May 16, 1920, Paris, TX). Chicago (A.L), 1941, 1946–1951; Philadelphia, (AL), 1951–1953; Cleveland (AL), 1954–1955; Baltimore (AL), 1955–1956; Chicago (AL), 1956–1957; Detroit (AL), 1957; Philadel-

phia (NL), 1958–1960; San Francisco (NL), 1960; Baltimore (AL), 1960–1961; Boston (AL), 1962. Remarks: In an 18-year career with-nine big league teams, had 1,700 hits (84 homers) and 102 stolen bases in 1,904 games; remembered as pinch hitter who had nine consecutive pinch hits end of 1958 season-beginning of 1959.

47651. Grosshandler, Stanley. "Dave Philley: He was a Versatile Fielder and Hitter." *Baseball Digest,* LI (March 1992), 46–48.

47652. Hillman, John. "David Earl 'Dave' Philley." In: Vol. G-P of David L. Porter, ed. *Biographical Dictionary of American Sports: Baseball.* Rev. and enlarged ed. Westport, CT: Greenwood Press, 2000. Pp. 1204–1205.

47653. Moffi, Larry. "Dave Philley: 'They Called Me Grumpy.'" In: his *This Side of Cooperstown: An Oral History of Major League Baseball in the1950s.* Iowa City, IA: University of Iowa Press, 1996. Pp. 76–93.

47654. Pickard, Chuck. "Dave Philley: In His Day, a Premier Pinch-Hitter." *Baseball Digest,* XXXIV (May 1975), 68–44.

Charles Louis ("Deacon") Phillippe
P-MGR. (B: May 23, 1872, Rural Retreat, VA-D: March 30, 1952). Louisville (NL), 1899; Pittsburgh (NL), 1900–1911. Remarks: Won 189 games and lost 109, with 12 saves," in 13 seasons; had one no-hitter, May 25, 1899; pitched five 1903 World Series contests, winning Games One, Three, and Four; manager, Pittsburgh Filipinos (United States League), 1912, winning 16 games and losing eight; manager, Pittsburgh (F), 1913.

47655. Katz, Lawrence S. "Pittsburgh's Pitching Twins." *The Baseball Research Journal,* XXVI (1997), 133–135. Phillippe and Sam Leever. Mark Armour's profile is a number in the online SABR Biography Project .

47656. Pisano, Carmen. "Baseball's First World Series Hero." *Oldtyme Baseball News,* II, no. 5 (1990), 12–13.

47657. Smith, Duane A. "Charles Louis 'Deacon' Phillippe." In: Vol. G-P of David L. Porter, ed. *Biographical Dictionary of American Sports: Baseball.* Rev. and enlarged ed. Westport, CT: Greenwood Press, 2000. Pp. 1205–1206.

Adolfo Emilio Phillips
OF. (B: Dec. 16, 1941, Bethania, Panama). Philadelphia (NL), 1964–1966; Chicago (N.L.), 1966–1969; Montreal (NL), 1969–1970; Cleveland (AL), 1972. Remarks: Had 463 hits (59 homers) and 92 stolen bases in 649 games in eight-years; had four consecutive homers in a doubleheader (three in one game), June 11, 1967.

47658. McKean, William J. "Bravo Adolpho, Bravo." *Look,* XXXII (June 25, 1968), M10–M13.

47659. Vecsey, George. "Waiting for Adolfo." *Sport,* XLV (May 1968), 48–51.

Bill Phillips *see* **William ("Bill") Phillips**
Damon Roswell ("Dee") Phillips
SS-3B. (B: June 8, 1919, Corsicana, TX). Cincinnati (NL), 1942; Boston (NL), 1944, 1946. Remarks: In three big league seasons, obtained 144 hits (one homer) and one stolen base in 112 games.

47660. Kelley, Brent P. "Damon 'Dee' Phillips: Double or Nothing (1942–1946)." In: his *The Pastime in Turbulence: Interviews with Baseball Players of the 1940s.* Jefferson, NC: McFarland & Co., Inc., 2002. Pp. 108–123.

David Robert ("Dave") Phillips
UMP. (B: Oct. 8, 1943, St. Louis, MO). Remarks: AL arbiter, 1971–2003; supervisor of Metro Conference basketball officials during off-season.

47661. "A Big Tail Wind." *Sports Illustrated,* LXVII (October 26, 1987), 2–3.

47662. "Dave Phillips, American League Umpire Who is Also Supervisor of Basketball Officials for the Metro Conference." *Referee,* VIII (May 1983), 8–11.

47663. "Dave Phillips Retires." *Referee,* XXVIII (May 2003), 10, 13.

47664. Mueller, Tom. "Dave Phillips, You are There: July 12, 1979, Disco Demolition Night." *Referee,* XXI (August 1996), 38+.

47665. Phillips, Dave, with Rob Rains. *Center Field on Fire: An Umpire's Life with Pine Tar Bats, Spitballs, and Corked Personalities.* Chicago, IL: Triumph Books, 2004. 244p.

Dee Phillips *see* **Damon Roswell ("Dee") Phillips**

E. Lawrence Phillips
ANNOUNCER. Remarks: Griffith Stadium announcer, ca. 1910–1920s.

47666. Hardy, Robert. "The Megaphone Man; Washington's E. Lawrence Phillips." *The National Pastime,* XVII (1997), 131–133.

Harold Ross ("Lefty") Phillips
MGR. (B: May 16, 1919, Los Angeles, CA–D: June 10, 1972). Remarks: Scout, Cincinnati (NL), 1949–1960, Brooklyn (NL) and Los Angeles (NL), 1952–1964; coach, Los Angeles (NL), 1964–1969; manager, California (AL), 1969–1971, winning 222 games and losing 225 in three piloting years.

47667. Blount, Roy, Jr. "Lefty Makes the Angels Sing." *Sports Illustrated,* XXXII (June 8, 1970), 28–29.

47668. Libby, Bill. "Lefty Phillips." In: his *The Coaches.* Chicago:. Regnery, 1972. Pp. 99–106.

Keith Anthony ("Tony") Phillips
OF. (B: April 25, 1959, Atlanta, GA). Oakland (AL), 1982–1989; Detroit (AL), 1990–1994; California (AL), 1995, Chicago (AL), 1996–1997; Toronto (AL) and New York (NL), 1998; Oakland (AL), 1999. Remarks: In 18 seasons, had 2,023 hits (160 homers) and 177 stolen bases in 2,161 games; first Oakland (AL) player to hit for cycle, May 16, 1986; on July 6, 1986, tied nine-inning game MLB with 12 assists at 2B; had five hits in one game, June 14, 1995; in 1999, had game-winning homer on his birthday.

47669. Guss, Greg. "All the Rage." *Sport,* LXXXVII (October 1996), 71–73.

47670. Hecht, A. "The A's Get a Tony Award." *Sports Illustrated,* LXIV (June 2, 1986), 78+.

47671. Howard, Johnette. "Dynamite." *Sports Illustrated,* LXXXVI (June 30, 1997), 64–66, 71.

47672. Kurkjian, Tim. "A Short Fuse." *Sports Illustrated,* LXXXIV (June 10, 1996), 86, 88.

47673. Pearlman, Jeff and Stephen Cannella. "An Ageless A." *Sports Illustrated,* XC (May 24, 1999), 79–80.

47674. Ryan, Bob. "Tony Phillips Masters the Art of Gaining a Winning Edge." *Baseball Digest,* LIV (December 1995), 70–73.

47675. Stier, Kit. "[Alfredo] Griffin [to] Phillips." *Oakland Athletics Magazine,* V, no. 4 (1985), 100–102.

Lefty Phillips *see* **Harold Ross ("Lefty") Phillips**

Richie Phillips
EXEC. (B: 1946). General Counsel/CEO, Major League Baseball Umpires Association, 1979–2000. Remarks: Led disastrous mass arbiter resignation strategy of 1999 and removed from office when his followers formed a new union.

47676. Huber, R. "A Really Bad Call." *Referee,* XXVII (August 2002), 24–31.

47677. Phillips, Richie. "Interview." *Referee,* XIV (June 1989), 20–23.

47678. "Richie Phillips: General Counsel to the Major

League Baseball Umpire's Association." *Referee,* XXI (October 1996), 56+.

47679. Will, George F. "Them are the Bases." In: his *Bunts: Curt Flood, Camden Yards, Pete Rose and Other Reflections on Baseball.* New York: Touchstone Books, 1998. Pp. 292–293.

Taylor Phillips *see* **William Taylor ("T-Bone") Phillips**

Tony Phillips *see* **Keith Anthony ("Tony") Phillips**

Walter ("Flops") Phillips
SEMI-PRO PLAYER.

47680. Clifton, Merritt F. "Baseball in the Berkshires: The 'Flops' Phillips Story." *Baseball History,* II (Spring 1987), 14–27.

William ("Bill" or "Whoa Bill" or "Silver Bill") Phillips
P. (B: 1857 in St. John, NB, Canada–D: Oct. 7, 1900). Cleveland (NL), 1879–1884; Brooklyn (AA), 1885–1887; Kansas City (AA), 1888. Remarks: Obtained 1,130 hits (17 homers) and 39 stolen bases in 1,038 games in a decade; first Canadian-born player in U.S. big leagues, May 1, 1879; also played for Hamilton (IL), 1889; well-regarded fielder who died of syphilis; elected to Canadian Baseball Hall of Fame, 1988.

47681. Shearon, Jim. "Bill Phillips of Saint John, New Brunswick, First Canadian in the Big Leagues." In: his *Canada's Baseball Legends: True Stories, Records and Photos of Canadian-born Players in Baseball's Major Leagues.* Kanata, Ontario: Malin Head Press, 1994. Pp. 3–6. Readers should also consult William E. Akin's "William B. Phillips (Silver Bill)," in Frederick Ivor-Campbell, Robert Tieman, Mark Rucker, eds., *Baseball's First Stars* (Cleveland, OH: SABR, 1996), p. 127 which also appears as a number in the SABR Biography Project online at < http://bioproj.sabr.org/bioproj.cfm?a=v&v=l&bid=461&p id=11193>.

William Taylor ("T-Bone") Phillips
P. (B: June 18, 1933, Atlanta, GA). Milwaukee (NL), 1956–1957; Chicago (NL), 1958–1959; Philadelphia (NL), 1959–1960; Chicago (AL), 1963. Remarks: In all or parts of six big league seasons, won 16 games and lost 22, with six "saves"; also hurled for Atlanta (SA), 1965; later sold insurance.

47682. Bisher, Furman. "The Pitcher from Otwell Insurance." In: Furman Bisher, ed. *The Burman Bisher Collection.* Dallas, TX: Taylor Publishing Co., 1989. Pp. 14–16. Reprinted from the April 25, 1965 issue of the Atlanta *Journal-Constitution.*

Thomas Harold ("Tom") Phoebus
P. (B: April 7, 1942, Baltimore, MD). Baltimore (AL), 1968–1970; San Diego (NL), 1971–1972; Chicago (N.L), 1972. Remarks: Won 56 games and lost 52, with six "saves," in seven years; had one no-hitter, April 27, 1968.

47683. Poiley, Joel. "Whatever Happened To...Tom Phoebus?" *Orioles Gazette,* IV (February 1994), 14–15.

47684. Schultz, Randy. "Where Are They Now?: Tom Phoebus." *Baseball Digest,* XLV (March 1986), 67–68.

47685. Sheldon, Harold. "The New 'O' Man of the O's." *Baseball Digest,* XXVI September 1967), 77–78.

Michael Joseph ("Mike") Piazza
C. (B: Sept. 4, 1968, Norristown, PA). Los Angeles (NL), 1992–1998; Florida (NL), 1998; New York (NL), 1998–. Remarks: Through 2004, has had 1,829 hits (378 homers) and 17 stolen bases in 1,590 games; A. L. Rookie of the Year Award, 1993; had six RBIs in a game thrice, June 29, 1996, Aug. 27, 1997 and April 30, 2002; All-Star Game MVP Award, 1996; first big league catcher to obtain 201

hits in a season, 1997; had grand slam homers in consecutive games, April 9–10, 1998; had 24-game hitting streak, 1998; first major leaguer to earn $13 million per year, 1998; had 15-game hitting streak, 2000; had homer in Game Four of 2000 NLCS; had two homers in 2000 World Series; hit 350th homer, April 22, 2003; has had 14 career grand slam homers.

47686. Bannon, Joseph J. Jr., ed. *Piazza*. Champaign, IL.: Sports Publishing, 2000. 128p.

47687. *Beckett Tribute: Mike Piazza.* Dallas, TX: Beckett Publications, 1997. 64p.

47688. Berlind, William. "The Season That Wasn't: Mike Piazza." *The New York Times Magazine,* (August 11, 2002), 42–45.

47689. Broder, John. "Metal Mike." *ESPN: The Magazine,* V (July 8, 2002), 70–71.

47690. Brown, Robert J. "Michael Joseph 'Mike' Piazza." In: Vol. G-P of David L. Porter, ed. *Biographical Dictionary of American Sports: Baseball.* Rev. and enlarged ed. Westport, CT: Greenwood Press, 2000. Pp. 1206–1208.

47691. Chen, Albert. "First Move." *Sports Illustrated,* XCIX (August 25, 2003), 80–81.

47692. Cunningham, Bob. "Deeper Look: Mike Piazza." *Beckett Baseball Card Monthly,* XI, no. 110 (May 1994), 120–121.

47693. _____. "Ready for Class to Begin: The Dodgers' Mike Piazza Wants to Disprove the Sophomore Jinx Theory." *Fantasy Baseball,* V (May 1994), 106–107.

47694. "Fox's First Order of Business is to Sign Piazza to Contract." *Dodgers Dugout,* XIII (March 1998), 1–2.

47695. Francis, C. Phillip. "Tale of Two Dodgers." In: Joseph M. Wayman, ed. *Grandstand Baseball Annual, 1996.* Downey, CA: Joseph M. Wayman, 1996. Pp. 197–198. Piazza and Roy Campanella (q.v.).

47696. Fry, George B., 3rd. "Catching the Beat." *Sports Illustrated for Kids,* VII (June 1995), 32–38.

47697. Gould, Mark T. "Fantasy Revisited: Baseball's Antitrust Exemption Gets Hit by a Pitch." *Entertainment and Sports Lawyer,* XI (Fall 1993), 11–14. Piazza v. Major League Baseball.

47698. Hoffer, Richard. "Catch a Rising Star." *Sports Illustrated,* LXXXIV (May 13, 1996), 74–77.

47699. Holtzman, Jerome. "Dodger Trade of Mike Piazza Over-Rated as a 'Blockbuster.'" *Baseball Digest,* LVII (September 1998), 72–75.

47700. James, Brent. *Mike Piazza.* Philadelphia, PA: Chelsea House, 1997. 63p.

47701. Keown, Tim. "MVPiazza." *ESPN: The Magazine,* III (September 4, 2000), 48–51.

47702. Langill, Mark. "No Backing Off." *Beckett Focus on Future Stars,* III, no. 21 (January 1993), 6–9.

47703. _____. "Rookie Report: Mike Piazza." *Beckett Baseball Card Monthly,* X, no. 97 (April 1993), 20–21.

47704. Manoloff, Dennis. "Mike Piazza: Best Hitting Catcher in the Majors." *Baseball Digest,* LVII (April 1998), 22–25.

47705. Marini, Victoria J., ed. *Piazza / Daily News.* Champaign, IL: Sports Publishing, 2000. 127p. Reprinted articles and photos from the *New York Daily News.*

47706. McCarver, Tim, with Danny Peary. "Mike Piazza." In: his *The Perfect Season: Why 1998 Was Baseball's Greatest Year.* New York: Villard Books, 1999. Pp. 44–51.

47707. "Mike Piazza." In: *Current Biography Yearbook, 1999.* New York: H. W. Wilson, 1999. Pp. 442–445.

47708. Morrissey, Michael. "Mike Piazza: Mets' Catcher Comes Up Big." *Baseball Digest,* LIX (December 2000), 48–51.

47709. Nightengale, Bob. "Work Ethic Thrusts Dodgers' Mike Piazza Among Elite Catchers." *Baseball Digest,* LV (July 1997), 32–35.

47710. Noble, Marty. *Mike Piazza: Mike and the Mets.* Champaign, IL: Sports Publishing, 1999. 86p.

47711. Olney, Buster. "Dodgers' Mike Piazza Ignores Rookie of Year Hype." *Baseball Digest,* LII (October 1993), 33–36.

47712. Owens, Thomas S. *Mike Piazza: Phenomenal Catcher.* Sports Greats Series. New York: Rosen Pub. Group's PowerKid's Press, 1997. 24p.

47713. Patrick, Dan. "Mike Piazza." In: his *Outtakes.* Edited by John Hassan. New York: ESPN Books/Hyperion, 2000. Chapter 3.

47713a. Pellowski, Michael. *Mike Piazza.* Super Sports Star Series. Hillside, NJ: Enslow Publishers, 2004. 48p.

47714. Piazza, Mike, with Jeff Bradley. "I'm Not Moving." *ESPN: The Magazine,* V (April 15, 2002), 52–55.

47715. Pierce, Charles P. "Hardball." *GQ-Gentlemen's Quarterly,* LXIV (May 1994), 67–72.

47716. Romano, John. "Dodger Catcher Mike Piazza Hits at a High Level." *Baseball Digest,* LV (January 1996), 40–43.

47717. Rosenthal, Ken. "Mike Piazza." In: his *Best of the Best, Baseball: 35 Major League Superstars.* Indianapolis, IN: Masters Press, 1998. Pp. 118–121.

47718. Rubalcava, Tomas. "Mike Piazza: Best-Hitting Catcher Ever?" *The Baseball Research Journal,* XXV (1996), 100–102.

47719. Sandground, Grant. "Player's Choice: Mike Piazza." *Beckett Baseball Card Monthly,* XVI (September 1999), 92–93.

47720. Savage, Jeff. *Mike Piazza: Hard-Hitting Catcher.* Minneapolis, MN: Lerner Publications, 1997. 64p.

47721. Schwarz, Alan. "Closer Look: Mike Piazza." *Beckett Baseball Card Monthly,* X, no. 105 (December 1993), 8–16.

47722. _____. "Interview: Mike Piazza." *Inside Sports,* XIX (May 1997), 22–27.

47723. Singer, Tom. "One-on-One [with] Mike Piazza." *Sport,* LXXXV (May 1994), 26+.

47724. Smith, L. "Piazza with Crust." *GQ-Gentlemen's Quarterly,* LXIX (April 1999), 184–189.

47725. Spander, Deborah L. "The Impact of Piazza on the Baseball Antiturst Exemption." *UCLA Entertainment Law Review,* II (Winter 1995), 113+.

47726. "Take Control. Dig Deeper." *Boys' Life,* LXXXIV (May 1994), 16–17.

47727. Taragano, Martin. "Piazza — More Than Talent." *Listen Magazine,* (June 1996), 8+.

47728. Verducci, Tom. "Catch This!: Mike Piazza Isn't Just the Best-Hitting Backstop of All Time, He's Also the Leading Man on Baseball's Hottest Team." *Sports Illustrated,* XCIII (August 21, 2000), 38–43.

47729. Whiteside, Kelly. "A Piazza with Everything." *Sports Illustrated,* LXXIX (July 5, 1993), 12–17.

Billy Pierce *see* **Walter William ("Billy") Pierce**

Jack Pierce *see* **Lavem Jack Pierce**

Lavem Jack Pierce

1B. (B: June 2, 1949, Laurel, MS). Atlanta (NL), 1973–1974; Detroit (AL), 1975. Remarks: Obtained 42 hits (eight homers) in 45 big league games in three years.

47730. Cartwright, Gary. "Chasing the Red Eagle." *Texas Monthly,* XXI (August 1993), 92–97.

Sean Pierce

OF. (B: Nov. 26, 1978, Covina, CA). Great Falls (Pioneer League) and Wilmington (Carolina League), 2001;

South Georgia Waves (South Atlantic League), 2002; South Georgia Waves (South Atlantic League) and Vero Beach Dodgers (Florida State League), 2003; Vero Beach Dodgers (Florida State League), 2004. Remarks: Minor leaguer drafted by Los Angeles (NL) in 2001.

47731. Bradley, J. E. "Uncertain Prospects." *Sports Illustrated,* XCV (September 17, 2001), 98–110.

Walter William ("Billy") Pierce

P. (B: April 2, 1927, Detroit, MI). Detroit (A.L.), 1945, 1948; Chicago (AL), 1949–1961; San Francisco (NL), 1962–1964. Remarks: In an 18-year big league career, had 211 victories, 169 defeats, and 32 "saves"; won 12-straight games in Candlestick Park, 1962; worked for Continental Envelope Company, 1974–1997; uniform no. (19) retired by White Sox in 1987; has also served as a scout and member of Chicago (AL) community relations department speakers' bureau.

47732. Berke, Art. "Hall of Fame Billy?" In: Paul Jensen, ed. *Chicago White Sox 1987 Yearbook.* Chicago, IL: Public Relations Department, Chicago White Sox, 1987. Pp. 29–31.

47733. Cohane, Tim. "Billy Pierce: Chicago's South Side Southpaw." *Look,* XXII (May 27, 1958), 102–104.

47734. Condon, David. "Chicago's Good Little Lefty." *Sport,* XV (October 1953), 32–33+.

47735. Devine, Tommy. "Billy Pierce — Snubbed to Stardom." *Baseball Digest,* XIII (April 1954), 23–28.

47736. Enright, Jim. "Billy the Kid's a Man Now." *Baseball Magazine,* LXXXIX (November 1952), 12–14.

47737. Fagen, Herb. "Walter William Pierce: They Called Him Billy." *Oldtyme Baseball News,* VIII, no. 4 (1997), 26–29.

47738. Furlong, William B. ("Bill"). "Billy Pierce." In: Bruce Jacobs, ed. *Baseball Stars of 1958.* New York: Lion Books, 1958. Pp. 89–95. Reprinted Charles Einstein, ed., *The Second Fireside Book of Baseball.* (New York: Simon and Schuster, 1958), pp. 149–152.

47739. Hilton, George W. "Walter William 'Billy' Pierce." In: Vol. G-P of David L. Porter, ed. *Biographical Dictionary of American Sports: Baseball.* Rev. and enlarged ed. Westport, CT: Greenwood Press, 2000. Pp. 1208–1209.

47740. Hoffman. John C. "Billy Pierce, Doctor on the Mound." *Baseball Digest,* XV (September 1968), 53–57.

47741. Jacobs, Bruce. "Low Road for a Lefty: Billy Pierce." In: Bruce Jacobs, ed. *Baseball Stars of 1957.* New York: Lion Books, 1957. Pp. 139–144.

47742. Kinlaw, Francis. "No Place Like Home: Billy Pierce's 1962 Season." In: *Northern California Baseball History.* Cleveland, OH: Society for American Baseball Research, 1998. Pp. 35–37.

47743. Mandel, Mike. "Billy Pierce." In: his *The San Francisco Giants: An Oral History.* Santa Cruz, CA: Mike Mandel, 1979. Pp. 108–112.

47744. Munzel, Edgar. "Billy Pierce's Pitching Tips." *Baseball Digest,* XIX (April 1960), 22–25.

47745. _____. "Pitching's 10 Commandments Spelled Out by Billy Pierce." *Scholastic Coach,* XXIX (February 1960), 28–29.

47746. Pierce, Walter W. ("Billy"). "Billy Pierce's Story." *Baseball Digest,* XI (March 1950), 21–25.

47747. _____. "I Love Baseball, But — Bowling Is More Fun!" *National Bowlers' Journal and Billiard Review,* XLIII (November 1956), 14–15+.

47748. _____, as told to George Vass. "The Game I'll Never Forget." *Baseball Digest,* XXXVIII (February 1979), 80–85.

47749. Povich, Shirley. "If Pierce Were Only Pierce." *Baseball Digest,* XV (May 1956), 18–21.

47750. Ralph, John. "Where are They Now?: Former Pitcher Billy Pierce Ranked Among the Best of His Era." *Baseball Digest,* LXI (June 2002), 62–65.

47751. Schaap, Dick. "What Makes a Bonus Kid Worth $110,000?" *Sport,* XXVI (July 1958), 26–27+.

47752. Vanderberg, Bob. "Billy Pierce: Fastballs, Sliders and Ed Fitzgerald." In: his *Sox — From Lane and Fain to Zisk and Fisk.* Chicago, IL: Chicago Review Press, 1982. Pp. 137–145.

47753. Zanger, Jack. "Billy Pierce." In: John Devaney, ed. *Official Baseball Annual, 1963.* Greenwich, CT: Fawcett Publications, 1963. Pp. 38–41.

Tony Michael Pierce

P. (B: Jan. 29, 1946, Brunswick, GA). Kansas City (AL), 1967; Oakland (AL), 1968. Remarks: Won three games and lost four, with seven "saves," in two big league seasons.

47754. Pierce, Tony. "Hot Dog Diary: Our Candlestick Correspondent Takes Us Out to the Ballpark." *Bay Sports Review,* VII (July 1997), 10–11.

Marion Paul ("Chick") Pieretti

P. (B: Sept. 23, 1920, Lucca, Italy-D: Jan. 30, 1981). Washington (A.L.), 1945–1946; Chicago (AL), 1948–1949; Cleveland (AL), 1950. Remarks: Won 30 games and lost 38, with eight "saves," in half a dozen seasons; worked off-seasons killing cattle in a slaughterhouse; also played for Sacramento (PCL) in the early 1950s.

47755. Flaherty, Vincent X. "Slaughter on the Mound." *Baseball Digest,* IV (September 1945), 29–31.

47756. Spalding, John E. "Marino Pieretti." In: his *Pacific Coast League Stars: One Hundred of the Best, 1903–1957.* San Jose, CA: John E. Spalding, 1994. Pp. 117–118.

A. J. Pierzynski

C. (B: Dec. 30, 1976, Bridgehampton, NY). Minnesota (AL), 1998–2003; San Francisco (NL), 2004; Chicago (AL), 2005–. Remarks: Through 2004, has had 558 hits (37 homers) and six stolen bases in 561 games; led NL in grounding into double plays (27), 2004.

47757. Souhan, Jim. "Catcher A. J. Pierzynski Puts Spark in Twins' Game." *Baseball Digest,* LXII (March 2003), 62–63.

Juan Pierre

OF. (B: August 14, 1977, Mobile, AL). Colorado (NL), 2000–2002; Florida (NL), 2003–. Remarks: Through 2004, has had 859 hits (seven homers) and 210 stolen bases in 683 games; had five hits in one game twice, Sept. 4, 2000 and Sept. 21, 2002; NL stolen base champion, 2001, 2003; led NL in triples, 2004.

47758. Doyle, Al. "Speed, the Name of the Game for Florida's Juan Pierre." *Baseball Digest,* LXIII (June 2004), 62–65.

47759. Olney, Buster. "Stealing Home." *ESPN: The Magazine,* VI (December 8, 2003), 84–88.

James Anthony ("Jimmy") Piersall

OF-BROADCASTER. (B: Nov. 14, 1929, Waterbury, CT). Boston (A.L.), 1950–1958; Cleveland (A.L.), 1959–1961; Washington (AL), 1962–1963; New York (N.L), 1963; Los Angeles (AL) and California (AL), 1963–1967. Remarks: Had 1,604 hits (104 homers) and 115 stolen bases in 1,734 games in 17 years; went 6-for-6 in one game, June 10, 1953; suffered well-chronicled mental breakdown in 1952; recovered and remembered, thereafter, for zaniness; went six-for-six in one game, June 10, 1953; GM, Roanoke (Atlantic Coast Football League),

1968–1969; public relations official for California (AL) and Oakland (AL), 1970–1972; manager, Orangeburg (West Carolinas League), 1973; broadcaster, Chicago (AL), 1977–1983; minor league instructor, Chicago (NL), 1995–1999.

47760. "Baseball's Greatest Outfielder." *Look,* XVIII (May 19, 1964), 53–55.

47761. Bingham, Walter. "A Here of Many Moods." *Sports Illustrated,* XII (June 20, 1960), 28–35.

47762. Birtwell, Roger. "Teammates Key to Piersall's Fate." *Baseball Digest,* XII (March 1953), 17–19.

47763. Borst, William A. ("Bill"). "James Anthony 'Jimmy' Piersall." In: Vol. G-P of David L. Porter, ed. *Biographical Dictionary of American Sports: Baseball.* Rev. and enlarged ed. Westport, CT: Greenwood Press, 2000. Pp. 1209–1210.

47764. "Breakdown in Ball Park: Piersall's Comeback to Sanity is Told in Heartwarming Film." *Life,* XLII (April 1, 1957), 56–59.

47765. Carmichael, John P. "Peerless Piersall." *Baseball Digest,* XV (January 1950), 27–29.

47766. Cohane, Tim. "Jimmy Piersall: Baseball's Greatest Outfielder." *Look,* XVIII (May 18, 1954), 53–55.

47767. Connolly, Ed. "Jimmy Piersall Speaks Out on Outfield Defense." *Baseball Digest,* XLVIII (June 1989), 28–32.

47768. Dolgan, Bob. "One of a Kind." *Baseball Digest,* LX (December 2001), 68–71.

47769. Goddard, Joe. "The World of Baseball According to Jimmy Piersall." *Baseball Digest,* L (June 1991), 26–29.

47770. Green, Paul M. "Jimmy Piersall: Interview." *Baseball Cards,* VII (October 1987), 79+.

47771. Hirshberg, AL. "Boston's Boy Bandit." *Sport,* XVI (March 1954), 26–31.

47772. _____. "Jimmy Piersall Answers His Critics." *Sport,* XXXIII (March 1962), 18–21.

47773. _____. "Jimmy Piersall's Greatest Day." In: Charles Einstein, ed. *The Second Fireside Book of Baseball.* New York: Simon and Schuster, 1959. Pp. 199–201.

47774. _____. "The Strange Case of Jimmy Piersall." *Sport,* XIV (May 1953), 60–51+.

47775. Horgan, Tim. "Jimmy Piersall." In: Danny Peary, ed. *Cult Baseball Players.* New York: Simon and Schuster, 1990. Pp. 276–283.

47776. _____. "Jimmy Piersall." In: Danny Peary, ed. *Baseball's Finest: The Greats, the Flakes, the Weird and the Wonderful.* North Dighton, MA: The JG Press, 1990. Pp. 276–283. Both Peary books are identical.

47777. "Jimmy Piersall." In: Carrie Muskat, ed. *Banks to Sandberg to Grace: Five Decades of Love and Frustration with the Chicago Cubs.* Chicago, IL: Contemporary Books, 2001. Pp. 154–160.

47778. Lebovitz, Hal. "Piersall is Still Battling." *Sport,* XXVIII (July 1959), 23–25.

47779. Lewis, Whitey. "Piersall Plays 'Em Close." *Baseball Digest,* XIII (March 1964), 5–7.

47780. Linn, Ed. "Jimmy Piersall's Second Fight with Fear." *Sport,* XXXI (March 1961), 12–13+.

47781. Meany, Thomas. "Specialist in Armed Robbery: Jimmy Piersall, the Red Sox's Star Outfielder." *Collier's,* CXXXIII (February 5,1954), 26–31. Reprinted in his *Mostly Baseball* (New York: A.S. Barnes, 1968), pp. 327–338.

47782. Newcombe, Jack. "Jimmy Piersall: Tormented Tribesman." In: Ray Robinson, ed. *Baseball Stars of 1961.* New York: Pyramid Books, 1961. Pp. 66–72.

47783. Orr, Jack. "Jimmy Piersall: Capital Gains." In: Ray Robinson, ed. *Baseball Stars of 1962.* New York: Pyramid Books, 1962. Pp. 63–68.

47784. Piersall, Jim. "Interview." Edited by John Schulian. *Sport,* LXIX (August 1979), 53+.

47785. _____., as told to Al Hirshberg. "Sure, I'm a Pest, but...." *Sport,* XXXV (February 1963), 38–41.

47786. _____., as told to George Vass. "The Game I'll Never Forget." *Baseball Digest,* XXXVI (March 1977), 81–84.

47787. _____., with Al Hirshberg. *Fear Strikes Out: The Jim Piersall Story.* Boston, MA: Little, Brown, 1955. 217p. Reprinted by the University of Nebraska Press in 1999 in a 224-page edition, with a new afterword by Piersall. Also made into a 1957 motion picture starring Anthony Perkins and abridged in *Saturday Evening Post,* CCXXVII (January 29–February 1, 1955), 17–19+, 27+, as "They Called Me Crazy—and I Was!" and excerpted in John L. Pratt, ed. *Sport, Sport, Sport* (New York: Franklin Watts, 1960), pp. 125–155.

47788. _____. "From *Fear Strikes Out.*"In: Charles Einstein, ed. *The New Baseball Reader: An All-Star Lineup from The Fireside Book of Baseball.* New York: Penguin Books, 1992. Pp. 296–301.

47789. _____. "How the Home Team Cheats." *Baseball Monthly,* I (April 1962), 21–27.

47790. _____., with Dick Whittingham. *The Truth Hurts.* Chicago, IL: Contemporary Books, 1985. 183p. The story of his struggle with bipolar disorder.

47791. Piersall, Mary. "Why Do They Call My Husband Crazy?" Edited by Al Hirshberg. *Saturday Evening Post,* CCXXXV (March 31, 1962), 52–53+.

47792. Richman, Milton. "He Robs 'Em in the Outfield." In: Bruce Jacobs, ed. *Baseball Stars of 1954.* New York: Lion Books, 1954. Pp. 92–98.

47793. Sheldon, Harold. "Piersall—Model Rookie of 1952." *Baseball Digest,* XI (July 1952), 43–47.

47794. Vass, George. "Jimmy Piersall." In: *his Champions of Sports: Adventures in Courage.* Chicago: Reilly and Lee, 1970. Pp. 50–61.

47795. Westcott, Rich. "Jimmy Piersall: Versatile, Volatile Outfielder." In: *his Splendor on the Diamond: Interviews with 35 Stars of Baseball's Past.* Gainesville, FL: The University Press of Florida, 2000. Pp. 283–290.

47796. Whitmarsh, F. E. "Jim Piersall: Jumping Jim." In: *Famous American Athletes of Today.* 14th Series. Boston, MA: L.C. Page, 1956. Pp. 181–194.

Anthony Francis ("Tony") Piet

2B-3B. (B: Anthony Francis Pietruszka, Dec. 7, 1906, Barwick, PA-D: Dec. 1, 1981). Pittsburgh (NL), 1931–1933; Cincinnati (NL), 1934–1935; Chicago (AL), 1935–1937; Detroit (AL), 1938. Remarks: Had 717 hits (23 homers) and 80 stolen bases in 744 games in an eight-year major league career.

47797. Bloodgood, Clifford. "The Leading Basestealer of the Pirates." *Baseball Magazine,* L (February 1932), 404–405.

47798. Murdock, Eugene. "He Posed with Paderewski: Tony Piet." In: *his Baseball Players and Their Times: Oral Histories of the Game, 1920–1940.* Westport, CT: Meckler Publishing, 1991. Pp. 264–288

Emil Pietrangeli

UMP. All-American Girls Professional Baseball League

47799. "When Ballplayers Wore Skirts." *Referee,* XVIII (April 1993), 36+.

Lipman ("Lip" or "The Iron Batter") Pike

OF-MGR. (B: May 25, 1845, New York City-D: Oct.

10, 1893). Troy (N.A.), 1871; Baltimore (N.A.), 1872–1873; Hartford (N.A.), 1874; St. Louis (N.A.), 1875; St. Louis (NL), 1876; Cincinnati (NL), 1877–1878; Providence (NL), 1878; Worcester (NL), 1881; New York (AA), 1887. Remarks: Obtained 637 hits (20 homers) and 47 stolen bases in 425 games in 10 playing seasons; first paid ballplayer (considered first professional baseball player); also a famous runner, becoming Maryland State 100-yard champion, 1872; manager, Troy (N.A.), 1871; Hartford (N.A.), 1874, and Cincinnati (NL), 1877, winning 20 games and losing 51 (.282).

47800. Brody, Seymour. "Lip Pike." In: his *Jewish Heroes in America.* New York: Shapolsky, 1991. Pp. 65–66.

47801. Geduld, Herb. "Lipman at the Bat." *Jewish World Review,* (Oct. 22, 1998), 10+.

Duane Pillette

P. (B: July 24, 1922, Detroit, MI). New York (AL), 1949–1950; St. Louis (AL), 1950–1953; Baltimore (AL), 1954–1955; Philadelphia (NL), 1956. Remarks: Won 38 games and lost 66, with two "saves" in eight years.

47802. Kelley, Brent P. "Duane Pillette." In: his *They Too Wore Pinstripes: Interviews with 20 Glory-Days New York Yankees.* Jefferson, NC: McFarland & Co., Inc., 1998. Pp. 147–163.

Herman Polycarp ("Old Folks") Pillette

P. (B: Dec. 26, 1895, St. Paul, OR-D: April 30, 1960). Cincinnati (NL), 1917; Detroit (AL), 1922–1924. Remarks: Had 34 victories, 32 defeats, and three "saves" in four big league seasons; won a game before the smallest crowd (68) in Fenway Park history, July 13, 1922.

47803. Swank, Bill. "Herman Pillette." In: his *Echoes from Lane Field: A History of the San Diego Padres 1936–1957.* Paducah, KY: Turner Publishing Company, 1997. Pp. 17–18.

Babe Pinelli *see* **Ralph Arthur ("Babe" or "The Soft Thumb") Pinelli**

Ralph Arthur ("Babe" or "The Soft Thumb") Pinelli

3B-UMP. (B: Oct. 18, 1895, San Francisco, CA-D: Oct. 22, 1984). Chicago (AL), 1918; Detroit (AL), 1920; Cincinnati (NL), 1922–1927. Remarks: In an eight-year playing career, obtained 723 hits (five homers) and 71 stolen bases in 744 games; became PCL umpire, 1933–1934, and NL arbiter, 1935–1956; plate umpire who called Don Larsen's perfect game in 1956 World Series.

47804. Connolly, Will. "Small Strike Zone Makes Game Drag'—['Babe'] Pinelli." *Baseball Digest,* XVI (August 1957), 79–81.

47805. Gerlach, Larry R. "Babe Pinelli: Mr. Ump." In: *Northern California Baseball History.* Cleveland, OH: Society for American Baseball Research, 1998. Pp. 43–45.

47806. _____. "Ralph Arthur 'Babe', 'The Soft Thumb' Pinelli." In: Vol. G-P of David L. Porter, ed. *Biographical Dictionary of American Sports: Baseball.* Rev. and enlarged ed. Westport, CT: Greenwood Press, 2000. Pp. 1210–1211.

47807. Graham, Frank. "Hidden-Ball King: Pinelli." *Baseball Digest,* VII (November 1948), 53–55.

47808. Molen, Sam. "Pinelli was a Bloomer Girl." *Baseball Digest,* VIII (February 1949), 77–79.

47809. Pinelli, John J. "From San Francisco Sandlots to the Big Leagues: Babe Pinelli." In: Robert Elias, ed. *Baseball and the American Dream: Race, Class, Gender and the National Pastime.* New York: M. E. Sharpe, 2001. Pp. 135–140.

47810. Pinelli, Ralph A. ("Babe"). "Philosophy of Babe Pinelli." *Sports Illustrated,* X (February 16, 1959), 21–22.

47811. _____. "The Toughest Game I Ever Umpired." *Sport,* XVIII (April 1956), 76–79.

47812. _____., as told to Al Stump. "Babe Pinelli Blasts Crybaby Ballplayers." *True,* XL (August 1959), 64–70.

47813. _____. "Kill the Umpire—Don't Make Me Laugh." In: Charles Einstein, ed. *The Second Fireside Book of Baseball.* New York: Simon and Schuster, 1958. Pp. 278–283.

47814. _____, as told to Joe King. *Mr. Ump.* New York: Westminster Press, 1953.184p.

47815. Rathgeber, Bob. "Quick Hands and Temper at Third: Babe Pinelli." In: his *Cincinnati Reds Scrapbook.* Virginia Beach, VA: J.C.P. Corp. of Virginia, 1982. Pp. 58–59.

47816. Simons, Herbert. "The Babe in Blue." *Baseball Magazine,* LXVIII (February 1942), 401–402.

47817. Spalding, John E. "Babe Pinelli." In: his *Pacific Coast League Stars, Vol. II: Ninety Who Made It to the Majors, 1905–1957.* San Jose, CA: John E. Spalding, 1997. Pp. 68–70.

Louis Victor ("Sweet Lou" or "Lou") Piniella

OF-MGR-EXEC. (B: Aug. 28, 1943, Tampa, FL). Baltimore (AL), 1964; Cleveland (AL), 1968; Kansas City (AL), 1969–1973; New York (AL), 1974–1984. Remarks: Had 1,705 hits (102 homers) and 32 stolen bases in 1,747 games in 17 playing seasons; AL Rookie of the Year Award, 1969; had double, triple, and homer in one game, Sept. 8, 1978; coach, New York (AL), 1981–1985; manager, New York (AL), 1986–1988; GM and special assistant, New York (AL), 1988–1989; manager, Cincinnati, 1990–1992; Seattle (AL), 1993–2002, Tampa Bay (AL), 2003–; through 2004, has won 1,452 games and lost 1,325 (.523); made good on standing challenge to have his salt-and-pepper locks dyed with blond highlights when the Rays put together their first three- game winning streak, July 6, 2004.

47818. Bamberger, Michael. "Safe at Home: Why Would Lou Piniella Leave a Winner in Seattle to Manage the Tampa Bay Devil Rays, the Worst Team in Baseball?—to be with His Family." *Sports Illustrated,* XCVIII (March 3, 2003), 56+.

47819. Buckley, Steve. "One on One [with] Lou Piniella: Interview." *Sport,* LXXXIV (June 1993), 20–21.

47820. Chass, Maury. "Case of the Pinstriped Volcano." *Sport,* LXX (May 1980), 34–39.

47821. DeFord, Frank. "Sweet & Lou: Age, Success and a Good Woman Have Mellowed Mariners Mangers Lou Piniella." *Sports Illustrated,* XCIV (March 1, 2001), 88–90, 92, 96, 98, 101–102.

47822. Gullo, Jim. "Getting to Know Him." *Seattle,* X (July-August 2001), 38+.

47823. Honig, Donald. "1969: Lou Piniella." In: his *American League Rookies of the Year.* New York: Bantam Books, 1989. Pp. 50–53.

47824. Jordan, Pat. "Winning Used to Be Everything." *The New York Times Magazine,* (July 20, 2003), 24–27.

47825. Jozwik, Thomas D. "Louis Victor 'Lou', 'Sweet Lou' Piniella." In: Vol. G-P of David L. Porter, ed. *Biographical Dictionary of American Sports: Baseball.* Rev. and enlarged ed. Westport, CT: Greenwood Press, 2000. Pp. 1211–1213.

47826. Klein, Jim. "Sweet Lou." *New York,* XIX (March 24, 1986), 38–45.

47827. Lidz, Franz. "Mirror, Mirror on the Wall." *Sports Illustrated,* LVII (September 20, 1982), 56+.

47828. McMillan, Ken. "Lou Piniella." In: his *Tales from the Yankee Dugout: A Collection of the Greatest Yankee Stories Ever Told.* Champaign, IL: Sports Publishing, Inc., 2001. Pp. 137–143.

47829. Montville, Leigh. "The Edge of Rage." *Sports Illustrated*, LXXIII (October 1, 1990), 34–37.

47830. Nauen, Elinor. "Lou Piniella." In: Danny Peary, ed. *Cult Baseball Players*. New York: Simon and Schuster, 1990. Pp. 290–293.

47831. _____. "Lou Piniella." In: Danny Peary, ed. *Baseball's Finest: The Greats, the Flakes, the Weird and the Wonderful*. North Dighton, MA: The JG Press, 1990. Pp. 290–293. Both Peary books are identical.

47832. Piniella, Lou. "The Mechanics of a Home Run." *Popular Mechanics,* CLXVIII (April 1991), 40–43.

47833. _____. and Maury Allen. *Sweet Lou*. New York: G. P. Putnam, 1986. 300p.

47834. _____.,as told to George Vass. "The Game I'll Never Forget." *Baseball Digest*, XLI (November 1982), 70–73. Reprinted in George Vass, ed. *The Game I'll Never Forget* (Chicago, IL: Bonus Books, 1999), pp. 193–198.

47835. Whittlesey, Merrell. "The Breaks Begin to Even Up for Lou Piniella." *Baseball Digest*, XXIX (August 1970), 74–76.

47836. Wilner, Barry. "Sweet Lou Piniella Proves His Point." In: *Major League Baseball Yearbook*. New York: Reliance Publications, 1991. Pp. 22–24.

Vada Edward Pinson, Jr.
OF (B: Aug. 8, 1939, Memphis, TN). Cincinnati (NL), 1958–1968; St Louis (NL), 1969; Cleveland (AL), 1970–1971; California (AL), 1972–1973; Kansas City (AL), 1974–1975. Remarks: In 18 seasons, Pinson had 2,757 hits (166 homers) and 305 stolen bases in 2,469 games; led NL in doubles, 1959–1960; had two triples in one game, May 27, 1960; led NL in triples, 1963; had 27-game hitting streak, 1967; had five hits in one game, Aug. 4, 1972; had eight career grand slam homers; retired with most hits of any player not in the Baseball Hall of Fame; also played for Wausau (Northern League), 1956, Visalia (California League), 1957, Seattle (PCL), 1958; coach and minor league batting instructor, Seattle (AL), 1977–1980, Chicago (AL), 1981; Seattle (AL), 1982–1984, Detroit (A.L), 1985–1991, and Florida (NL), 1993–1994; elected to Bay Area Sports Hall of Fame, 1996.

47837. Allen, Maury. "Vada Pinson." In: his *Baseball: The Lives Behind the Scenes*. New York: Macmillan, 1990. Pp. 65–79.

47838. Bisher, Furman. "Is He the Nearest-Perfect Player?" *Saturday Evening Post*, CCXXXIII (July 16, 1960), 72–78.

47839. Burick, Si. "Vada Pinson Bats .300 for Job Corps." *Baseball Digest*, XXVII (May 1968), 84–87.

47840. "Cincinnati's Vada Pinson." *Look,* XXV (August 29,1961), 37–42.

47841. Cohane, Tim. "Cincinnati's Vada Pinson: the Red Go Sign." *Look,* XXV (August 29, 1961), 84–86.

47842. Collett, Ritter. "Vada Pinson: Faster Than a TV Headache Cure." *Baseball Digest,* XVIII (July 1959), 31–33.

47843. Elderkin, Phil "Veda Pinson, Baseball's Scientific Hitter." *Baseball Digest*, XXXII (September 1973), 40–42.

47844. Gann, Cory. "Vada Pinson." In: Danny Peary, ed. *Cult Baseball Players*. New York: Simon and Schuster, 1990. Pp. 120–126.

47845. _____. "Vada Pinson." In: Danny Peary, ed. *Baseball's Finest: The Greats, the Flakes, the Weird and the Wonderful*. North Dighton, MA: The JG Press, 1990. Pp. 120–126. The entries in both Peary books are identical.

47846. Herman, Jack. "Pinson Adds Grace to Cards' Outfield." *Baseball Digest,* XXVII (May 1969), 24–26.

47847. Izenberg, Jerry. "Vada Pinson and the Man Who Never Was." *Sport,* XL (October 1965), 68–76.

47848. Libby, Bill. "A Fresh Start in Another Town." *Sport*, XLVIII (November, 1969), 54–57.

47848a. Moses, Ralph C. "Vada Pinson." *The Baseball Research Journal*, XXV (1996), 88–89. Moses' profile appears as a number in the online SABR Biography Project.

47849. Orr, Jack. "Pinson Made It in a Hurry." *Sport*, XXX (July 1960), 48–49+.

47850. Pinson, Veda, as told to George Vass. "The Game I'll Never Forget." *Baseball Digest*, XXVIII (January 1979), 74–81.

47851. Robinson, Ray. "Veda Pinson: Soph Sensation." In: Ray Robinson, ed. *Baseball Stars of 1960*. New York: Pyramid Books, 1960. Pp. 48–53.

47852. _____. "Veda Pinson: The Unexpected Goat." In: Ray Robinson, ed. *Baseball Stars of 1962*. New York: Pyramid Books, 1962. Pp. 89–94.

47853. "Rookie with a Whallop." *Newsweek,* LIII (April 27, 1959), 100+.

47854. Schaap, Dick. "Norm Cash and Veda Pinson: On the Spot in '62." *Sport*, XXXIII (April 1962), 20–23.

47855. Skipper, James K., Jr. "Vada Edward Pinson, Jr." In: Vol. G-P of David L. Porter, ed. *Biographical Dictionary of American Sports: Baseball*. Rev. and enlarged ed. Westport, CT: Greenwood Press, 2000. Pp. 1213–1214.

47856. Stump, Al. "Veda Pinson: Problems of a Ballplayer." *Sport*, XXXVII (May 1964), 32–39+.

47857. Terrell, Roy. "Baseball Is a Breeze for Vada Pinson." *Sports Illustrated,* XI (August 31, 1959), 45–46.

47858. "Vada Pinson: Missile-Fast Youngster Races Toward Stardom." *Ebony,* XV (September 1960), 84–87.

47859. "Vada Pinson of the Cincinnati Reds." *Ebony,* XV (September 1960), 86–87.

47860. Vecsey, George. "Vada Pinson: Punch Hitter." In: Ray Robinson, ed. *Baseball Stars of 1964*. New York: Pyramid Books, 1964. Pp. 151–155.

47861. "Viva Vada." *Sports Illustrated,* XV (September 11, 1961), 7–8.

George William Pipgras
P-UMP. (B: Dec. 20, 1899, Ida Grove, IA-D: Oct. 19, 1986). New York (AL), 1923–1933; Boston (AL), 1933–1935. Remarks: Had 102 victories, 73 defeats, and 12 "saves" in 11 years; had homer in a game, June 12, 1927; undefeated in World Series play in 1927–1928 and 1932; AL umpire, 1938–1945; later named to Iowa Sports Hall of Fame.

47862. Gerlach, Larry R. "George Pipgras." In: his *The Men in Blue: Conversations with Umpires*. New York: Viking Press, 1980. Pp. 75–92. Reprinted by the University of Nebraska Press in 1994.

47863. Givens, Horace R. "George Pipgras: He Pitched for the Greatest [Yankee] Team of All." *Baseball Digest,* XLI (December 1942), 85–89.

47864. Honig, David. "George Pipgras." In: his *Baseball. When the Grass was Real*. New York: Coward, McCann, Geoghegan, 1975. Pp. 126–133.

47865. Trachtenberg, Leo. "The Hard-Throwing Viking." *Yankees Magazine,* XXII (August 2001), 70–89.

47866. Ward, John J. "Pipgras the Persistent." *Baseball Magazine,* XLIV (May 1930), 547–548+.

Walter Clement ("Wally") Pipp
1B. (B: Feb. 17, 1893, Chicago, IL-D: Jan. 11, 1985). Detroit (AL), 1913; New York (AL), 1915–1925; Cincinnati (NL), 1926–1928; Newark (IL), 1929–1931. Remarks: Had 1,941 hits (90 homers) and 125 stolen bases in 1,872 big league games in 15 years; AL home run champion, 1916–1917; had one grand slam homer, May 14, 1923, first by a Yankee; took day off on June 1, 1925 and the man sent

in to substitute took his Yankee position permanently—Lou Gehrig (q.v.); also played for Providence (IL) and Scranton (New York State League), 1913 and Rochester (IL), 1914.

47867. Anderson, Bruce. "Just a Pipp of a Legend." *Sports Illustrated,* LXVI (June 29, 1987), 78–82.

47868. Balter, Sam. "Gehrig-and Pipp's Strange Return." *Baseball Digest,* VII (August 1958), 45–47.

47869. Borst, William A. ("Bill"). "Walter Clement 'Wally' Pipp." In: Vol. G-P of David L. Porter, ed. *Biographical Dictionary of American Sports: Baseball.* Rev. and enlarged ed. Westport, CT: Greenwood Press, 2000. Pp. 1214–1215.

47870. Pipp, Walter C. "First-Hand Impressions of a Star First Baseman." *Baseball Magazine,* XXXII (April 1924), 488–489.

47871. Robinson, Murray. "Wally Pipp: The Guy Before Gehrig." *Baseball Digest,* XXIV (March 1965), 25–27.

47872. Santa Maria, Michael and James Costello. "In the Shadow of Giants." In: their *In the Shadows of the Diamond.* Dubuque, IA: The Elysian Fields Press, 1992. Pp. 35–38.

47873. Smith, Ira L. "Walter Clement Pipp." In: his *Famous First Basemen.* New York: A.S. Barnes, 1956. Pp. 123–130.

47874. Ward, John J. "The Yankees' Chief Slugger." *Baseball Magazine,* XVIII (January 1917), 37–40.

Juan Roman (Cordova) Pizarro

P. (B: Feb. 7, 1938, Santuree, Puerto Rico). Milwaukee (NL), 1957–1960; Chicago (AL), 1961–1966; Pittsburgh (NL), 1967–1968; Boston (AL), 1968–1969; Cleveland (AL), 1969; Oakland (AL), 1969; Chicago (NL), 1970–1973; Houston (NL), 1973, Pittsburgh (NL), 1974. Remarks: Pitched for eight different teams in 18 years, winning 131 games and losing 105, with 28 "saves"; one of only two pitchers to hurl one-hitters for both the Cubs and the White Sox.

47875. Furlong, William B. ("Bill"). "Gary Peters & Juan Pizarro: Southpaw Sorcery." In: Ray Robinson, ed. *Baseball Stars of 1965.* New York: Pyramid Books, 1965. Pp. 125–133.

47876. Hirshberg, Al. "The Rough Rise of Juan Pizarro." *Sport,* XXXVII (December 1964), 62–65.

47877. Kiersh, Edward. "Juan Pizarro: Here Comes the Coconut Cowboy." In: his *Where Have You Gone, Vince DiMaggio?* New York: Bantam Books, 1983. Pp. 130–137.

47878. McGuff, Joe. "Pizarro Fans His Critics." *Baseball Digest,* XXII (October/November 1963), 33–35.

47879. Walfoort, Cleon. "The Mystery of Juan Pizarro." *Baseball Digest,* XVIII (May 1959), 5–10.

47880. Wright, Jerry J. "Juan Roman 'Cordova' Pizarro." In: Vol. G-P of David L. Porter, ed. *Biographical Dictionary of American Sports: Baseball.* Rev. and enlarged ed. Westport, CT: Greenwood Press, 2000. Pp. 1215–1216.

Edward Stewart ("Eddie" or "Gettysburg Eddie") Plank ★

P. (B: Aug. 31, 1875, Gettysburg, PA-D: Feb. 24, 1926). Philadelphia (A.L.), 1901–1914; St. Louis (F.L.), 1915; St. Louis (AL), 1916–1917. Remarks: Won 327 games and lost 192, with 25 "saves," in 17 major league seasons; traded to New York (AL), 1919, but did not report; in off-seasons, Gettysburg farmer and battlefield guide; later operated automobile dealership; his brother, Ira D., served as head baseball coach at Gettysburg College from 1912–1947; elected to National Baseball Hall of Fame in 1946, where his plaque reads. "One of greatest lefthanded pitchers of

major leagues. Never pitched for a minor league team, going from Gettysburg College to the Philadelphia team with which he served from 1901 through 1914. Member of St. Louis F.L. in 1915 and St. Louis AL in 1916–17. One of few pitchers to win more than 300 games in big leagues. In eight of 17 seasons, won 20 or more games."

47881. Allen, Lee, and Thomas Meany. "Eddie Plank." In: their *Kings of the Diamond.* New York: G.P. Putnam, 1965. Pp. 48–50.

47882. Barton, Jerry. "Edward Stewart Plank." In: his *A Treasure Chest of the Hall of Fame.* Boston, MA: The Wilson-Hill Co., 1952. Pp. 86–87.

47883. Dexter, Charles. "Knuckler Won Him 26 in 1912." *Baseball Digest,* VIII (October 1959), 61–66.

47884. Grayson, Harry. "Edward S. (Eddie) Plank." In: his *They Played The Game.* New York: A.S. Barnes, 1944. Pp. 39–41.

47885. _____. "Plank Greatest,' Says (Eddie] Collins." *Baseball Digest,* II (July 1943), 41–43.

47886. Honig, Donald. "Eddie Plank." In: his *The Greatest Pitchers of All Time.* New York: Crown Publishers, 1988. Pp. 20–25.

47887. Klima, John. "Man at Work: Joe McGinnity vs. Eddie Plank (October 13, 1905)." In: his *Pitched Battle: 35 of Baseball's Greatest Duels from the Mound.* Jefferson, NC: McFarland & Co., Inc., 2002. Pp. 8–12.

47888. Kofoed, J.C. "The Crossfire King." *Baseball Magazine,* XIV (November 1914), 33–36.

47889. Lane, Ferdinand C. "The Passing of a Master Pitcher." *Baseball Magazine,* XXVI (May 1926), 553–554.

47890. Lawler, Joseph. "Eddie Plank." In: John A. Garrity and Marsh C. Carries, eds. *American National Biography.* 24 vols. New York: Oxford University Press, 1999. XVII, 578–579.

47891. _____. "Edward Stewart 'Eddie,' 'Gettysburg Eddie' Plank." In: Vol. G-P of David L. Porter, ed. *Biographical Dictionary of American Sports: Baseball.* Rev. and enlarged ed. Westport, CT: Greenwood Press, 2000. Pp. 1216–1218.

47892. Lieb, Frederick G. "Edward S. Plank." *Baseball Magazine,* VII (May 1911), 16–20.

47893. Mason, Ward. "Plank the Perpetual." *Baseball Magazine,* XVIII (February 1917), 22–24.

47894. McKay, Joe. "Eddie Plank: The First Great Left-Hander." In: his *The Great Shutout Pitchers: 20 Profiles of a Vanishing Breed.* Jefferson, NC: McFarland & Co., Inc., 2004. Pp. 51–61.

47895. Meany, Thomas. "The Fidgety One." In: his *Baseball's Greatest Pitchers.* New York: A.S. Barnes, 1951. Pp. 217–224.

47896. _____. "King of Fidgets." *Baseball Digest,* XI (May 1952), 25–31.

47897. Murphy, Jim. "Pitcher: Eddie Plank." In: his *Baseball's All-Time All-Stars.* New York: Clarion Books, 1984. Pp. 95–97.

47898. Pickard, Chuck. "The Hall of Fame Pitcher Who Fooled His College Coach." *Baseball Digest,* XXXIV (December 1975), 54–57.

47899. Ritter, Lawrence and Donald Honig. "Eddie Plank." In: their *The 100 Greatest Baseball Players of All Time.* New York: Crown Publishers, 1981. Pp. 258–259.

47900. Roy, Paul. "A Useful Monument to the Memory of Eddie Plank." *Baseball Magazine,* XXXVII (September 1928), 463–465.

47901. Salant, Nathan. "Eddie Plank." In: his *Superstars, Stars, and Just Plain Heroes.* New York: Stein and Day, 1982. Pp. 161–165.

47902. Smith, Ira L. "Edward Stewart Plank." In: his *Baseball's Famous Pitchers.* New York: A.S. Barnes, 1954. Pp. 81–86.

47903. Smith, Ron. "Eddie Plank 68." In: his *The Sporting News Selects Baseball's 100 Greatest Players.* St. Louis, MO: *The Sporting News,* 1998. Pp. 148–149.

47904. Westcott, Rich. "Eddie Plank: A Hitter's Nightmare." In: his *Winningest Pitchers: Baseball's 300-Game Winners.* Philadelphia, PA: Temple University Press, 2002. Pp. 69–76.

Phillip Alan ("Phil") Plantier

OF. (B: Jan. 27, 1969, Manchester, NH). Boston (AL), 1990–1992; San Diego (NL), 1993–1994; Houston (NL) and San Diego (NL), 1995; Oakland (AL), 1996; San Diego (NL) and St. Louis (NL), 1997. Remarks: Had 457 hits (91 homers) and 13 stolen bases in 610 big league games in eight years; also played for Pawtucket (IL), 1991; Las Vegas (PCL), 1997.

47905. Shalin, Mike. "A Closer Look: Phil Plantier." *Beckett Baseball Card Monthly,* IX (March 1992), 6–7.

47906. Williams, Pete. "Right at Home: San Diego's Son, Phil Plantier, Takes the Long Way Around to Find His Roots." *USA Today Baseball Weekly,* III (March 9, 1994), 4–5.

Daniel Thomas ("Dan" or "Sac-Man") Plesac

P. (B: Feb. 4, 1962, Gary, IN). Milwaukee (AL), 1988–1992; Chicago (NL), 1993–1994; Pittsburgh (NL), 1995–1996; Toronto (AL), 1997–1999; Arlington (AL), 1999–2000; Toronto (AL), 2001; Toronto (AL) and Philadelphia (NL), 2002–2003. Remarks: In 18 seasons, won 65 games and lost 71, with 158 "saves"; appeared in 1,064 games (4th on all time list) and was last Phillies pitcher to record an out at Veterans Stadium.

47907. Cairns, Bob. "Dan Plesac." In: his *Pen Men: Baseball's Greatest Bullpen Stories told by the Men who Brought the Game Relief.* New York: St. Martin's Press, 1992. Pp. 373–379.

47908. Madden, Dan. "Brewers' Dan Plesac Aims to Be Best of AL Relievers." *Baseball Digest,* XLVI (October 1987), 68–74.

Rance Pless

1B-3B. (B: Dec. 6, 1925, Greeneville, TN). Kansas City (AL), 1956. Remarks: In a single big league season, had 23 hits in 48 games; the year previous, he had won the AA batting championship (.337) while also hitting 26 homers for the Minneapolis Millers (AA); while playing for the Denver Bears (AA) in 1957, hit four grand slam homers in a 33-day period.

47909. White, G. H. "Rance Pless Gets Tough: 'High-Class Gent' Started 'Basebrawl for the Ages." *The National Pastime,* XI (2001), 14–16.

Herbert Eugene ("Herb") Plews

2B-SS-3B. (B: June 14, 1928, Helena, MT). Washington (AL), 1956–1959; Boston (AL), 1959. Remarks: Had 266 hits (four homers) in 346 games in four major league years; also played for Toronto (IL), 1960.

47910. Fehler, Gene. "Herb Plews." In: his *Tales from Baseball's Golden Age.* Champaign, IL: Sports Publishing Co., 2000. Chapter 40.

George Ames Plimpton

WRITER. (B: March 18, 1927, New York City-D: Sept 25, 2003). Remarks: Sports writer, literary editor, essayist, humorist, novelist, commentator, and free lance writer, particularly for *Sports Illustrated;* greatest exponent of the "I Feel" school of involved sports writing initially founded by Paul Gallico (q.v.).

47911. Fitzgerald, Mark. "An April Fool's Day Hoax."

Editor & Publisher, (April 20, 1985), 7–8. Plimpton's biography of the fictional pitcher Sidd Finch (q.v.)

47912. "Focus on George Plimpton." *Harper's Bazaar,* (November 1973), 103, 134–135, 142.

47913. Nadel, Alan. "'My Mind Is Weak but My Body is Strong': George Plimpton and the Boswellian Tradition." *Midwest Quarterly,* XXX (Spring 1989), 372–386.

47914. Orodenker, Richard. "George Plimpton." In: Richard Orodenker, ed. *Dictionary of Literary Biography, Volume 241: American Sportswriters and Writers on Sport.* A Bruccoli Clark Layman Book. Detroit, MI: The Gale Group, 2001. Pp. 205–216.

47915. Plimpton, George. "Dreams of Glory on the Mound." *Sports Illustrated,* XIV (10 April 1961), 112–114, 116, 118, 120, 122, 125–126, 128, 131–132, 134.

47916. _____. "From *Out of My League.*" In: Charles Einstein, ed. *The New Baseball Reader: An All-Star Lineup from The Fireside Book of Baseball.* New York: Penguin Books, 1992. Pp. 301–305.

47917. _____. "A Love of Fungo." In: Ron Fimrite, ed. *Birth of a Fan.* New York: Macmillan, 1993. Pp. 160–165.

47918. _____. *Out of My League.* New York: Harper & Row, 1961. 150p. An amateur author, to get the feel of pitching in the big leagues, is allowed to hurl to two all-star lineups, one captained by Mickey Mantle and one by Willie Mays; excerpted in *Sports Illustrated,* XIV (April 10, 1961) under the title, above, "Dreams of Glory on the Mound."

47919. Riley, Sam G. "George Plimpton." In: Arthur J. Kaul, ed. *Dictionary of Literary Biography, Volume 185: American Literary Journalists, 1945–1995.* First Series. A Bruccoli Clark Layman Book. Detroit, MI: The Gale Group, 1997. Pp. 217–232.

47920. Whelton, Clark. "Paper Plimpton." *Esquire,* LXXXV (January 1976), 115–117, 142, 144, 146.

Bill Plummer *see* **William Francis ("Bill") Plummer**

William Francis ("Bill") Plummer

C-MGR. (B: March 21, 1947, Anderson, CA). Chicago (NL), 1968; Cincinnati (NL), 1970–1977; Seattle (AL), 1978. Remarks: Had 168 hits (14 homers) and four stolen bases in 367 games in a decade; spent his Cincinnati playing years as backup to Johnny Bench (q.v.); had seven RBIs in one game, June 6, 1976; manager, Wausau (Midwest League), 1981; coach, Seattle (AL), 1982–1983; manager, Calgary (PCL), 1986–1987; coach, Seattle (AL), 1988–1992; manager, Seattle (AL), 1992, winning 64 games and losing 98 (.395); coach, Colorado (NL), 1993–1994 and Jacksonville (South Atlantic League), 1995–1996; manager, Chico (WL), 1997–1999 and Yuma (WL), 2000–2002; manager, Lancaster (California League), 2002; manager, Yakima (Northwest League), 2003–2004; manager, Lancaster (California League), 2005–.

47921. McDermott, Joe. "Few Things Come to Him Who Waits." *Sports Illustrated,* XLVII (July 18, 1977), 54–55.

Terry Pluto

WRITER. (B: 1958, Cleveland, OH). Remarks: Reporter/columnist, *Akron Beacon Journal,* 1985–.

47922. Pluto, Terry. *Our Tribe: A Baseball Memoir.* New York: Simon & Schuster, 1999. 288p. Postwar history of the Cleveland Indians in an examination of his relationship with his father.

John Joseph ("Johnny") Podres

P. (B: Sept. 30, 1932, Witherbee, NY). Brooklyn , (NL) and Los Angeles (NL, 1953–1955, 1957–1966; Detroit (AL), 1966–1967; San Diego (NL), 1969. Remarks: In a 15-year big league career, had 148 victories, 116 defeats, and

11 "saves"; won Games Three and Seven of 1955 World Series; World Series MVP award, 1955; pitching coach, San Diego (NL), 1970–1974; pitching instructor, farm system, Boston (AL), 1975–1979; pitching coach, Boston (AL), 1980 and Minnesota (AL), 1981–1985; pitching instructor, farm system, Los Angeles (NL), 1986–1989; pitching coach, Philadelphia (NL), 1992–1996.

47923. Barra, Allen. "Arms and the Man — Pitching Coach Johnny Podres Has Worked Wonders with Retreads Such as Terry Mulholland as the Phillies Battle Their Bleak History." *Inside Sports,* XV (October 1993), 72–75.

47924. Carman, Jimmy. "The Hot Hand." In: Charles Einstein, ed. *The Fireside Book of Baseball.* New York: Simon and Schuster, 1956. Pp. 43–44.

47925. Creamer, Robert W. "Sportsman of the Year: Johnny Podres." *Sports Illustrated,* IV (January 2, 1956), 18–22.

47926. Dexter, Charles. "Southpaw Johnny Podres: Moundman from Mineville." *Baseball Digest,* XIII (June 1954), 25–29.

47927. Henneman, Jim. "Johnny Podres: The Pitcher Who Revived the Changeup." *Baseball Digest,* XL (September 1981), 71–79.

47928. "Hero." *Sports Illustrated,* III (October 17, 1955), 11–12.

47929. Honig, Donald. "Johnny Podres." In: his *The October Heroes.* New York: Simon and Schuster, 1979. Pp. 203–215.

47930. Hye, Allen E. "John Joseph 'Johnny' Podres." In: Vol. G-P of David L. Porter, ed. *Biographical Dictionary of American Sports: Baseball.* Rev. and enlarged ed. Westport, CT: Greenwood Press, 2000. Pp. 1218–1219.

47931. Jacobs, Bruce. "Johnny-on-the-Spot: Johnny Podres." In: Bruce Jacobs, ed. *Baseball Stars of 1956.* New York: Lion Books, 1956. Pp. 7–14.

47932. Klima, John. "Keys to the Cathedral: Johnny Podres vs. Tommy Byrne (October 4, 1955)." In: his *Pitched Battle: 35 of Baseball's Greatest Duels from the Mound.* Jefferson, NC: McFarland & Co., Inc., 2002. Pp. 87–91.

47933. Kurkjian, Tim. "Johnny Podres." *Sports Illustrated,* LXXIX (October 25, 1993), 26–27. As pitching coach.

47934. Laughlin, Bob, with Budd Theobald. *Johnny Podres: He Pitches the Big One.* Meet the Dodger Family series. Los Angeles, CA: Union Oil Company of California, 1960. 13p.

47935. Libby, Bill. "The Ten Years of Johnny Podres." *Sport,* XXXVI (August 1963), 38–39+.

47936. Lucas, Edward. "Johnny Podres' High Mark: World Series Win in '55." *Baseball Digest,* LI (August 1992), 68–71.

47937. Meany, Thomas. "The Big Win." In: his *The Artful Dodgers.* New York: Grosset & Dunlap, 1958. Pp. 122–129. 1955 World Series.

47938. Murray, Jim. "Proud Podres Never Won 20." *Baseball Digest,* XXVIII (July 1969), 80–83.

47939. Podres, Johnny. "I Pitched and I Prayed." Edited by Frank Eck. *Saturday Evening Post,* CCXXVIII (January 21, 1956), 28–29+.

47940. ____., as told to George Vass. "The Game I'll Never Forget." *Baseball Digest,* XXXII (October 1973), 62–64. 1955 World Series.

47941. Rosenthal, Harold. "The Dodgers' Unbinding Lefty." *Sport,* XX (November 1955), 24–25+.

47942. "The Ten Years of Johnny Podres." *Sport,* XXXVI (August 1963), 39–41. Pictorial.

47943. Westcott, Rich. "Johnny Podres: Hurled Dodgers to First World Championship." In: his *Splendor on the Diamond: Interviews with 35 Stars of Baseball's Past.* Gainesville, FL: The University Press of Florida, 2000. Pp. 155–163.

47944. Whitmarsh, F. E. "Johnny Podres: Hard-Luck Hero." In: *Famous American Athletes of Today.* 14th Series. Boston, MA: L.C. Page, 1956. Pp. 195–207.

47945. Young, Dick. "Podres Popped into Majors." *Baseball Digest,* XII (October 1953), 19–21.

Scott Podsednik
OF (B: March 18, 1976, West, TX). Seattle (AL), 2001–2002; Milwaukee (NL), 2003–2004; Chicago (AL), 2005–. Remarks: Through 2004, has had 336 hits (22 homers) and 113 stolen bases in 327 games; with 70, led NL in stolen bases, 2004.

47946. Cline, Steve. "Scott Podsednik: Milwaukee's Aggressive Lead-Off Man." *Baseball Digest,* LXIII (October 2004), 46–49.

Boots Poffenberger *see* **Cletus Elwood ("Boots" or "The Baron") Poffenberger**
Cletus Elwood ("Boots" or "The Baron") Poffenberger
P. (B: July 1, 1915, Williamsport, MD-D: Sept. 1, 1999). Detroit (AL), 1937–1938; Brooklyn (NL), 1939. Remarks: Won 16 games and lost 12, with four "saves," in three big league years; an unmanageable eccentric.

47947. Crichton, Kyle S. "Poffenberger Pitching." *Collier's,* CII (August 6, 1938), 20–22.

47948. Steadman, John. "Boots' Poffenberger: Last of Great Baseball Characters." *Baseball Digest,* LI (December 1992), 89–95.

Carl R. Pohlad
EXEC. (B: 1916). Remarks: President, Marquette Bancshares and owner, Minnesota (AL), 1985–.

47949. Houston, Patrick. "The Twins Have Clinched Stardom for Carl Pohlad." *Business Week,* (October 26, 1987), 79–80.

Spottswood ("Spot") Poles
OF. (B: Nov. 7, 1889, Winchester, VA-D: Sept. 12, 1962). Harrisburg Colored Giants, 1906–1908; Philadelphia Giants, 1909–1910; New York Lincoln Giants, 1911–1914; New York Lincoln Stars, 1914–1916; New York Lincoln Giants and Hilldale Daisies, 1917 and 1920; New York Lincoln Giants and New York Bacharach Giants, 1919; New York Lincoln Giants, 1920–1923; Richmond Giants, 1923. Remarks: Called the "Black Ty Cobb," with speed compared to that of Cool Papa Bell (q.v.), retired with a lifetime batting average of approximately .400 against all competitors; post-baseball, owned Harrisburg taxi company and coached semipro Harrisburg Giants.

47950. Holway, John B. "Spottswood Poles." *The Baseball Research Journal,* IV (1975), 66–68.

47951. ____. "Spottswood Poles." In: John A. Garrity and Marsh C. Carries, eds. *American National Biography.* 24 vols. New York: Oxford University Press, 1999. XVII, 619–620.

47952. Riley, James A. "Spottswood 'Spot' Poles." In: Vol. G-P of David L. Porter, ed. *Biographical Dictionary of American Sports: Baseball.* Rev. and enlarged ed. Westport, CT: Greenwood Press, 2000. Pp. 1219–1220.

Howard Joseph ("Howie") Pollet
P. (B. June 26, 1921, New Orleans, LA-D: Aug. 8, 1974). St. Louis (NL), 1941–1943, 1946–1961; Pittsburgh (NL), 1951–1953; Chicago (NL), 1953–1955; Chicago (AL) and Pittsburgh (NL), 1966. Remarks: Had 131 victories, 116 defeats, and 20 "saves" in 14 seasons; winning pitcher in first-ever NL playoff game, Oct. 1, 1946; coach, St. Louis

(NL), 1959–1964 and Houston (NL), 1965; elected to Louisiana Sports Hall of Fame, 1981.

47953. Dress, Donald H. "Pollet-Pitcher of Polish." *Baseball Digest,* V (October 1946), 7–12.

47954. Lieb, Frederick G. "Pollet Pitching." *Sport,* II (March 1947), 18+.

47955. Olmsted, Frank J. "Howard Joseph 'Howie' Pollet." In: Vol. G-P of David L. Porter, ed. *Biographical Dictionary of American Sports: Baseball.* Rev. and enlarged ed. Westport, CT: Greenwood Press, 2000. Pp. 1220–1221.

47956. Smith, Walter ("Red"). "Pollet is Granting Good Again." *Baseball Digest,* VII (May 1948), 13–15.

Crip Polli *see* **Louis Americo ("Crip") Polli**

Louis Americo ("Crip") Polli

P. (B: July 9, 1901, Baveno, Italy-D: Dec. 19, 2000). St. Louis (NL), 1932; New York (NL), 1944. Remarks: In two big league seasons, the Barre, VT resident appeared in 24 games and lost two; also played for Barre-Montpelier (Green Mountain League), 1923–1924, later managed a semi-pro team in Halifax, NS, worked in the granite quarries near and served as constable, tax collector and town agent for his home town of Barre.

47957. Simon, Tom. "Crip Polli." In: Tom Simon, ed. *Green Mountain Boys of Summer: Vermonters in the Major Leagues, 1882–1993.* Shelburne, VT: The New England Press, 2000. Pp. 128–132.

Alice ("Al") Pollitt

3B. (B: July 19, 1929, Lansing, MI). Rockford Peaches (All American Girls Professional Baseball League), 1947–1953. Remarks: In seven seasons, obtained 555 hits (eight homers) and 181 stolen bases in 606 games.

47958. Johnson, Susan E. ("Susie"). "Alice 'Al' Pollitt." In: her *When Women Played Hardball: Professional Lives and Personal Stories from the All-American Girls Professional Baseball League, 1943–1954.* Seattle, WA: Seal Press, 1994. Pp. 85–123.

Luis Andrew Polonia

3B. (B: Dec. 10, 1964, Santiago, Dominican Republic). Oakland (AL), 1987–1988; New York (AL), 1989–1990; California (AL), 1990–1993; New York (AL), 1994–1995; Atlanta (NL), 1995; Baltimore (AL) and Atlanta (NL), 1996; Detroit (AL), 1999–2000; New York (AL), 2000. Remarks: Obtained 1,417 hits (36 homers) and 321 stolen bases in 1,379 games in 12 years; had inside-the-park grand slam homer, Aug. 14, 1995; tied AL record when thrown out three times on attempted steals in one game, May 24, 1993; had five hits in one game, May 27, 1999.

47959. Kurkjian, Tim. "Fallen Angel." *Sports Illustrated,* LXXIV (June 3, 1991), 71+.

Arlie Pond *see* **Erasmus Arlington ("Arlie") Pond**

Erasmus Arlington ("Arlie") Pond

P. (B: Jan. 19, 1872, Rutland, VT-D: Sept. 19, 1930). Baltimore (NL), 1895–1898. Remarks: With the old Orioles, won 35 games, lost 19, and "saved" two; died from complications of a failed appendectomy.

47960. Simon, Tom. "Arlington Pond." In: Tom Simon, ed. *Green Mountain Boys of Summer: Vermonters in the Major Leagues, 1882–1993.* Shelburne, VT: The New England Press, 2000. Pp. 28–33.

Sidney Ponson

P. (B: Nov. 2, 1976, Noord, Aruba). Baltimore (AL), 1998–2003; San Francisco (NL), 2003; Baltimore (AL), 2004–. Remarks: Through 2004, has won 69 games and lost 80, with one "save"; led big leagues in complete games (five), shutouts (two), hits allowed (265), and earned runs allowed (127), 2004.

47961. Habib, Daniel G. "Deadline Dealin." *Sports Illustrated,* XCIX (August 11, 2003), 52–55.

James Richard ("Jim") Poole

P. (B: April 28, 1966, Rochester, NY). Los Angeles (NL), 1990; Texas (AL) and Baltimore (AL), 1991; Baltimore (AL), 1992–1994; Cleveland (AL), 1995–1996; San Francisco (NL), 1996–1998; Cleveland (AL), 1998–1999; Philadelphia (NL), 1999; Detroit (AL) and Montreal (NL), 2000. Remarks: Won 22 games and lost 12, with four "saves," in 11 years; won Game One of 1995 ALCS; lost Game Two of 1997 World Series; lost Game Four of 1998 ALCS.

47962. Heller, Mick. "His Comic Book Collection is No Longer Jim Poole's Ace in the Hole." *Orioles Gazette,* III (August 13, 1993), 13–14.

David ("Dave") Pope

OF. (B: June 17, 1921, Talladega, AL-D: Aug. 28, 1999). Homestead Grays, 1946; Farnham (Provincial League), 1948–1949; Wilkes Barre (AA), 1950–1951; Indianapolis (AA) and Cleveland (AL), 1952; Indianapolis (AA), 1953; Cleveland (AL), 1954–1955; Baltimore (AL), 1955–1956; Cleveland (AL) and Indianapolis (AA), 1956; San Diego (PCL), 1957–1958. Remarks: Obtained 146 hits (12 homers) and seven stolen bases in 230 games in all or parts of four major league years; elected to Ohio Baseball Hall of Fame, 1994.

47963. Moffi, Larry and Jonathan Kronstadt. "David 'Dave' Pope." In: their *Crossing the Line: Black Major Leaguers, 1947–1959.* Jefferson, NC: McFarland & Co., Inc., 1994. Pp. 78–79.

Edwin Pope

WRITER. (B: April 11, 1928, Athens, GA). Remarks: Sports publicity director, University of Georgia, 1944–1946; sports editor, *Athens Banner-Herald,* 1944–1948; southern sports editor, United Press, 1949–1950; sports writer, *Atlanta Constitution,* 1950–1953; executive sports editor, *Atlanta Journal,* 1954–1955; sports editor, *Miami Herald,* 1955–; recipient, Red" Smith Memorial Award for Lifetime Achievement, 1989.

47964. Pope, Edwin. *The Edwin Pope Collection.* Dallas, TX: Taylor Publishing Co., 1988. 288p.

Thomas Arthur ("Tom") Poquette

OF. (B: Oct. 30, 1951, Eau Claire, WI). Kansas City (AL), 1973, 1976–1979; Boston (AL), 1979 and 1981; Texas (AL), 1981. Remarks: Had 320 hits (10 homers) and 12 stolen bases in 428 games in six big league years; had five hits and scored five runs in one game, June 15, 1976; manager, Eugene (Northwest League), 1991, Appleton (Midwest League), 1992, Memphis (AA), 1993, Charleston (South Atlantic League), 1999, Spokane (Northwest League), 2000–2002; coach, Kansas City (AL), 1997–1998.

47965. Vogelaer, Dean. "Tom Poquatte, He Won the Hearts of KC Fans." *Baseball Digest,* XXXVI (February 1977), 84–87.

Darrell Ray ("Dee") Porter

C. (B: Jan. 17, 1952, Joplin, MO-D: Aug. 5, 2002). Milwaukee (A.L), 1971–1976; Kansas City (A-.L), 1977–1980; St. Louis (NL), 1981–1985; Texas (AL), 1986–1987. Remarks: Had 1,369 hits (188 homers) and 39 stolen bases in 1,782 games in 17 seasons; had grand slam homer, June 17, 1973; second catcher (after Mickey Cochrane) to obtain 100+ runs, RBI, and walks in a season, 1979; NLCS MVP award, 1982; World Series MVP award, 1982; elected to Missouri Sports Hall of Fame, 2000; battled drug addiction and was found dead in a KC parking lot from a condition known as excited delirium, which causes the body to overheat and heart to stop.

47966. Bove, Vincent. "Darrell Porter." In: his *Playing His Game.* South Plainfield, NJ: Bridge Publishing, 1984. Pp. 195–197.

47967. Garrity, John. "Out from Behind the Mask." *Baseball Magazine,* New Series IV (October 1980), 19–23.

47968. Hummel, Rick. "Darrell Porter's Greatest Victory." In: Zander Hollander, ed. *1983 Season: The Complete Handbook of Baseball.* New York: New American Library, 1983. Pp. 24–30.

47969. Irish, Arnold. "Darrall Porter: He Has a Talent for Guiding Pitchers." *Baseball Digest,* XLII (August 1981), 80–85.

47970. Lewis, Gregory. "Darrell Porter." In: Ken Collier, ed. *The Baseball Book, 1983.* Scottsdale, AZ: Jalart House, 1983. Pp. 119–121.

47971. Olmsted, Frank J. "Darrell Ray Porter." In: Vol. G-P of David L. Porter, ed. *Biographical Dictionary of American Sports: Baseball.* Rev. and enlarged ed. Westport, CT: Greenwood Press, 2000. Pp. 1222–1223.

47972. Porter, Darrell R., with William Deerfield. *Snap Me Perfect: The Darrell Porter Story.* Nashville, TN: Thomas Nelson Publishers, 1984. 224p.

47973. Rasmussen, Larry P. "Darrell Porter Joins a Select Group of Catchers.*" Baseball Digest,* XXXIX (January 1980), 60–63.

Henry Porter
P. (B: June 1858, Vergennes, VT-D: Dec. 30, 1906). Milwaukee (U), 1884; Brooklyn (AA), 1885–1887; Kansas City (AA), 1888–1889. Remarks: Won 96 games and lost 107 in six AA seasons; with 18, established MLB record for most strikeouts in a nine-inning game by a losing pitcher which stood until 1969, Oct. 3, 1884.

47974. Nelson, Walt. "Henry Porter." In: Tom Simon, ed. *Green Mountain Boys of Summer: Vermonters in the Major Leagues, 1882–1993.* Shelburne, VT: The New England Press, 2000. Pp. 13–14.

J.W. ("Jay") Porter
C-OF-1B. (B: Jan 17, 1933, Shawnee, OK). St. Louis (AL), 1952; Detroit (AL), 1955–1957; Cleveland (AL), 1958; Washington (AL) and St. Louis (NL), 1959. Remarks: Had 124 hits (eight homers) and four stolen bases in 229 games in six seasons; J. W. in his name have no meaning.

47975. Fehler, Gene. "J. W. Porter." In: his *Tales from Baseball's Golden Age.* Champaign, IL: Sports Publishing Co., 2000. Chapter 41.

47976. Heiman, Lee, Dave Weiner and Bill Gutman. "J.W. Porter." In: their *When the Cheering Stops.* New York: Macmillan, 1990. Pp. 273–282.

Bob Porterfield *see* **Erwin Collidge ("Bob" or "Blue Ridge Bob") Porterfield**
Erwin Collidge ("Bob" or "Blue Ridge Bob") Porterfield
P. (B: Aug. 10, 1923, Newport, VA-D: April 28, 1980). New York (AL), 1948–1951; Washington (AL), 1951–1955; Boston (A.L), 1956–1957; Pittsburgh (NL), 1958–1959; Chicago (NL), 1959. Remarks: Won 87 games and lost 97, with eight "saves," in 12 years; had three homers in 1953 (half of career total), including his first, a May 5 grand slam; led AL in complete games, 1953–1954.

47977. Furlong, William B, "The Senators' Prize Castoff." *Saturday Evening Post,* CCXXVII (August 14, 1954), 30+.

47978. Hann, Ralph. "The Making of 'Blue Ridge Bob.'" *Sport,* XVI (February 1954), 32–33+.

47979. Maxwell, Jocko. "Rookie of '49 — Porterfield." *Baseball Digest,* VII (August 1949), 57–59.

47980. Meany, Thomas. "Luck — All Kinds (Bob Porterfield)." In: his *The Boston Red Sox.* New York: A.S. Barnes, 1956. Pp. 133–144.

47981. Nason, Jerry. "The Snakebite Kid." *Baseball Digest,* XI (September 1952), 55–57.

47982. Povich, Shirley. "Hard-Luck Hurler." In: Bruce Jacobs, ed. *Baseball Stars of 1953.* New York: Lion Books, 1953. Pp. 24–26.

47983. _____. "Hard Luck to Happy Days." In: Bruce Jacobs, ed. *Baseball Stars of 1954.* New York: Lion Books, 1954. Pp. 98–101.

47984. _____. "Porterfield's Due." *Complete Baseball,* IV (July 1952), 20–21.

47985. _____."Porterfield's Out to Rescue His Rescuer." *Baseball Digest,* XIII (August 1954), 69–71.

47986. Sheldon, Harold. "Bob Porterfield: Senator from Virginia." *Baseball Digest,* XI (April 1952), 83–87.

47987. White; Russ. "Farewell to a Boyhood Hero: Bob Porterfield." *Baseball Digest,* XXXIX (August 1960), 40–43.

Mark ("Porch") Portugal
P. (B: Oct. 30, 1962, Los Angeles, CA). Minnesota (AL), 1985–1988; Houston (NL), 1989–1993; San Francisco (NL), 1994–1995; Cincinnati (NL), 1995–1996; Philadelphia (NL), 1997–1998; Boston (AL), 1999. Remarks: Had 109 victories, 95 defeats, and five "saves," in 15 years.

47988. Barnes, Taylor. "Player Profile: Mark Portugal." *Houston Astros Magazine,* IV, no. 6 (1991), 30–35.

Jorge Posada
C. (B: Jorge Rafael Posada Villeta, August 17, 1971, Santurce, P.R.). New York (AL), 1995–. Remarks: Through 2004, has obtained 910 hits (156 homers) and 10 stolen bases in 1,003 games; had homer in Game One of 1998 ALCS; had homer in Game Two of 1998 World Series; homered in Game Seven of 1999 ALCS; had homer in Game Two of 2000 ALCS; had grand slam homer, April 8, 2001; had homer in Game Three of 2001 World Series; led AL in grounding into double plays, 2002, 2004; had seven hits in 2004 ALCS.

47989. Davidoff, Ken. "Yankees' Jorge Posada: At Home Behind the Plate." *Baseball Digest,* LXIII (June 2004), 48–49.

47990. Girardi, Joe, as told to Pat McEvoy." What Ceiling?" *Yankees Magazine,* XIX (October 1998), 70–77.

47991. Klapish. Bob. "No Place Like Home." *Yankees Magazine,* XXIV (December 2003), 20–29.

47992. Mandrake, Mark. "Mr. Everything." *Yankees Magazine,* XXII (June 2001), 14–23.

Bob Poser *see* **John Falk ("Bob") Poser**
John Falk ("Bob") Poser
P. (B: March 16, 1910, Columbus, WI-D: May 21, 2002). Chicago (AL), 1932; St. Louis (AL), 1935. Remarks: In parts of two big league seasons, won one game and lost one; later became medical doctor.

47993. Wilson, Nick. "Bob Poser." In: his *Voices from the Pastime: Oral Histories of Surviving Major Leaguers, Negro Leaguers, Cuban Leaguers, and Writers, 1920–1934.* Jefferson, NC: McFarland & Co., Inc., 2000. Pp. 104–108.

Cumberland Willis ("Cum") Posey, Jr.
OF-MGR-EXEC. (B: June 20, 1890, Homestead, PA-D: March 28, 1946). Homestead Grays, 1910–1946. Remarks: Player to 1916 and manager/owner thereafter; also well known as a basketball player and promoter.

47994. Baxter, Terry A. "Cumberland Willis 'Cum' Posey, Jr." In: Vol. G-P of David L. Porter, ed. *Biographical Dictionary of American Sports: Baseball.* Rev. and enlarged ed. Westport, CT: Greenwood Press, 2000. Pp. 1223–1225.

47995. Holway, John B. "Cum Posey and Gus Greenlee: The Long Gray Line." In: his *Blackball Stars.* Westport, CT: Meckler Corp., 1988. Pp. 299–328.

47996. Ruck, Rob. "Cum Posey." In: John A. Garrity and Marsh C. Carries, eds. *American National Biography.* 24 vols. New York: Oxford University Press, 1999. XVII, 721–723.

Walter Charles ("Wally") Post
OF. (B: July 9, 1929, St. Wendelin, OH–D: Jan. 6, 1982). Cincinnati (NL), 1949–1957; Philadelphia (NL), 1958–1960; Cincinnati (NL), 1960–1963; Minnesota (AL), 1963; Cleveland (AL), 1964. Remarks: Obtained 1,064 hits (210 homers) and 19 stolen bases in 1,204 games in 15 seasons; had four homers in a doubleheader, April 28, 1956; had homer in Game Five of 1961 World Series; only player to twice throw out two runners from the OF in one inning, June 28, 1959; hit first homer in Dodger Stadium, April 10, 1962; began as a 17–7 hurler with Muncie (Ohio State League) in 1946; died of cancer.

47997. Miller, Richard D. "Walter Charles 'Wally' Post." In: Vol. G-P of David L. Porter, ed. *Biographical Dictionary of American Sports: Baseball.* Rev. and enlarged ed. Westport, CT: Greenwood Press, 2000. Pp. 1225–1226.

47998. Paxton, Henry T. "The Redlegs' Hardest Hitter." *Saturday Evening Post,* CCXXVIII (June 19, 1956), 31–32+.

47999. Silverman, Al. "Everyone Wants Wally Post." *Sport,* XXIII (April 1956), 40–41, 80–83.

48000. Stern, Chris. "Wally Post." In: his *Where Have They Gone?* New York: Tempo Books, 1979. Pp. 107–108.

Pamela ("Pam") Postema
UMP. (B: 1954, Willard, OH). Remarks: Arbiter, Gulf Coast League, Florida State League and Texas League, 1977–1983; umpire, Pacific Coast League, 1983–1989; arbiter in Baseball Hall of Fame Game, 1988; amidst much controversy, released from her contract by Triple-A Alliance, 1989; became FedEx truck driver in California and welder for Mansfield, Ohio-based Newman Technology after filing against the A.L and NL a Federal discrimination case, *Postema v. National League of Professional Baseball Clubs,* 799 F. Supp 1475 (1992), which was settled in 1997 for an undisclosed sum.

48001. Berlage, Gai I. "Women Umpires as Mirrors of Gender Roles." *The National Pastime,* XIV (1994), 34–38.

48002. Boga, Steve. "Against All Odds." *Referee,* XI (August 1986), 28–32.

48003. Brown, Rusty. "Call to Glory." *Ms,* XVII (April 1989), 34+.

48004. Comte, Liz. "She Calls It as She Sees It." *Inside Sports,* XV (April 1993), 18–19.

48005. Garrity, John. "Waiting For the Call." *Sports Illustrated,* LXVIII (March 14, 1988), 26–28.

48006. Joosse, Wayne. "One for the Knepper." *Reformed Journal,* XXXVIII (April 1988), 7–8.

48007. Keenan, Sandy. "The Umpress Strikes Back." *Sports Illustrated,* LXI (July 30, 1984), 44–45. Profile.

48008. McEvoy, Sharlene A. "When the Umpire Strikes Out: Gender Discrimination in Professional Baseball." *Women Lawyer's Journal,* LXXIX (September 1993), 17+.

48009. McGuire, Mark and Michael Sean Gormley. "Pam Postema." In: their *Moments in the Sun: Baseball's Briefly Famous.* Jefferson, NC: McFarland & Co., Inc., 2001. Pp. 137–143.

48010. Neff, Craig. "Goodbye to a Pioneer." *Sports Illustrated,* LXXI (December 25, 1989), 24+.

48011. Obojski, Robert. "Is Big League Baseball Ready for Lady Umpires?" In: his *Baseball's Strangest Moments.* New York: Sterling Publishing Co., 1988. Pp. 26–28. Postema

48012. Postema, Pam and Gene Wojciechowski. *"You Got to Have Balls to Make It in This League": My Life as an Umpire.* New York: Simon and Schuster, 1992. 256p. Reprinted by Lincoln, NE-based Bison Books in 2003.

48013. Reed, Susan and Lyndon Stambler. "The Umpire Strikes Back." *People Weekly,* XXXVII (May 25, 1992), 87–88.

Shirley Lewis Povich
WRITER. (B: July 15, 1905, Bar Harbor, ME–D: June 8, 1998). Remarks: Sports editor, 1924–1933 then columnist, 1933–1974, *Washington Post;* member, Baseball Writers Association of America (president, 1956); J. G. Taylor Spink Award, 1976.

48014. Beard, Gordon. "Shirley Povich Has Been Fighting Deadlines for 70 Years." *Orioles Gazette,* III (August 13, 1993), 11–12. Ralph Berger's profile appears as a number in the online SABR Biography Project < http://bioproj.sabr.org/bioproj.cfm?a=v&v=l&bid=870&pid=1693.

48015. Harper, James W. "Shirley Lewis Povich." In: David L. Porter, ed. *Biographical Dictionary of American Sports: 1992–1995 Supplement for Baseball, Football, Basketball and Other Sports.* Westport, CT: Greenwood Press, 1995. Pp. 353–354.

48016. Holtzman, Jerome. "Shirley Povich." In: his *No Cheering in the Press Box.* New York: Holt, Rinehart And Winston, 1974. Pp. 114–128.

48017. Kaufman, James C. "Shirley Povich." In: Richard Orodenker, ed. *Dictionary of Literary Biography, Volume 171: Twentieth-Century American Sportswriters.* A Bruccoli Clark Layman Book. Detroit, MI: The Gale Group, 1996. Pp. 275–281.

48018. Lach, Edward L., Jr. "Shirley Povich." In: Paul Betz and Mark C. Carnes, eds. *American National Biography: Supplement I.* New York: Oxford University Press, 2002. Pp. 488–489.

48019. Povich, Shirley. *All These Mornings: The Famed Columnist for the Washington Post Recalls 40 Lively Years on the National Sports Scene.* Englewood Cliffs, NJ: Prentice-Hall, 1969. 240p.

48020. Werber, Bill. "Shirley Povich and Gabe Paul: Legends Off the Field." In: his *Memories of a Ballplayer: Bill Werber and Baseball in the 1930s.* Cleveland, OH: The Society for American Baseball Research, 2001. Pp. 203–210.

Abner Powell *see* **Charles Abner Powell**
Alvin Jacob ("Jake") Powell
OF. (B: July 15, 1908, Silver Spring, MD–D: Nov. 4, 1948). Washington (AL), 1930, 1934–1936; New York (AL), 1936–1940; Washington (AL), 1943–1945; Philadelphia (NL), 1945. Remarks: Obtained 689 hits (22 homers) and 65 stolen bases in 888 games in 11 years; policeman during off season; made national headlines with and suspended for 10 days for anti-Black slurs during postgame radio interview, July 29, 1938; while being questioned in a D.C. police station for passing bad checks, drew a revolver and killed himself.

48021. Crepeau, Richard. "The Jake Powell Incident and the Press: A Study in Black and White." *Baseball History,* I (Summer 1986), 32–46.

48022. Goldman, Steve. "A Troubled Man." *Yankees Magazine,* XIX (March 1999), 60–71.

48023. Hylton, J. G. "Jake Powell Incident a Shaky Precedent." *For the Record,* XI (February-March 2000), 1–5, 8.

48024. Lamb, Chris. "L'Affaire Jake Powell: The Minority Press Goes to Bat Against Segregated Baseball." *Journalism & Mass Communication Quarterly,* LXXVI (Spring 1999), 21+.

Boog Powell *see* **John Wesley ("Boog") Powell**
Charles Abner Powell
P-EXEC. (B: Dec. 15, 1860, Shenandoah, PA-D: Aug. 7, 1953). Washington (Union), 1884; Baltimore (AA) and Cincinnati (AA), 1886. Remarks: In two seasons, won eight games and lost 18; later, owner, New Orleans Pelicans.

48025. Hoag, Edwin. "Baseball's Great Innovator." *Sports Illustrated,* XXXVIII (March 19, 1973), M6–M8.

Ernest ("Willie") Powell
P. (B; Oct. 30, 1903, Eutaw, AL-D: May 16, 1987). Chicago American Giants, 1925–1929; Detroit Wolves, 1930–1931; Chicago American Giants, 1932; Indianapolis ABCs, 1933; Cleveland Red Sox, 1934. Remarks: In Negro League play, won 49 games and lost 42.

48026. Clark, Dick and John B. Holway. "Willie Powell: An American Giant." In: his *The National Pastime,* IV (Winter 1985), 28–34.

48027. Holway, John B. "An American Giant: Ernest "Willie" Powell." In: his *Black Diamonds: Life in the Negro Leagues From the Men Who Lived It.* Baseball and American Society, no. 4. Westport, CT: Meckler, 1989. Pp. 39–54.

Grover David Powell
P. (B: Oct. 10, 1940, Sayre, PA-D: May 21, 1985). New York (NL), 1963. Remarks: Was one and one in one big league season.

48028. Schwarz, Alan. "Wuz You Born in Poland?: The Grover Powell Story." *The Baseball Research Journal,* XIX (1990), 15–17.

Jack Powell *see* **John Joseph ("Jack") Powell**
Jake Powell *see* **Alvin Jacob ("Jake") Powell**
John Joseph ("Jack") Powell
P. (B: July 9, 1874, Bloomington, IL-D: Oct. 17, 1944). Cleveland (NL), 1897–1898; St. Louis (NL), 1899–1901; St. Louis (AL), 1902–1903; New York (AL), 1904–1905; St. Louis (AL), 1906–1912, 1918. Remarks: Had 245 victories (including 23 in 1898) and 254 losses in 16 big league seasons; also hurled for Louisville (AA), 1913 and Venice (PCL), 1914; top Browns record-holder in several statistical categories.

48029. Evers, John L. "John Joseph 'Jack' Powell." In: Vol. G-P of David L. Porter, ed. *Biographical Dictionary of American Sports: Baseball.* Rev. and enlarged ed. Westport, CT: Greenwood Press, 2000. Pp. 1226–1227.

John Wesley ("Boog") Powell
1B-OF. (B: Aug. 17, 1941, Lakeland, FL). Baltimore (AL), 1961–1974; Cleveland (AL), 1975–1976; Los Angeles (NL), 1977. Remarks: Had 1,776 hits (330 homers) and 20 stolen bases in 2,042 games in 17 big league seasons; AL MVP award, 1970; thrice hit three homers in one game; had a record 11 RBIs in a doubleheader, July 6, 1966); though 6' 4," 250-pound, had inside-the-park homer, Aug. 16, 1969; homered in Games One and Two of 1970 World Series; had two homers in Game Two of 1971 ALCS; post-baseball, entered the food industry, operating a food concession at Oriole Park at Camden Yards; years earlier as a pitcher, in 1954, surrendered 16 runs in title game of Little League World Series.

48030. Bilovsky, Frank. "Boog is Back Where He Belongs." *Orioles Gazette,* II (May 1, 1992), 21–22. Postwar career in food industry.

48031. Bobrow, Norm. "Boog Powell: Nice Guy Boog."

In: Ray Robinson, ed. *Baseball Stars of 1970.* New York: Pyramid Books, 1970. pp. 87–92.

48032. Devaney, John. "A Bit of a Boy, Isn't He?" *Sport,* LI (June 1971), 58–60+.

48033. _____. "Boog Powell." In: his *Where Are They Today?: Great Sports Stars of Yesteryear.* New York: Crown Publishers, 1985. Pp. 163–166.

48034. Epstein, Eddie. "Boog—One of Baltimore's Best." *Orioles Gazette,* II (August 18, 1992), 15–16.

48035. Forman, Ross. "Boog Powell: From Baseball Star to TV Celebrity." *Sports Collector's Digest,* XVIII (August 2, 1991), 54–55.

48036. Furillo, Bud. "22 Out of 24 Scouts Nixed Boog Powell." *Baseball Digest,* XXI (August 1962), 89–90.

48037. Goldman, Alan. "Boog Powell: One-Man Wrecking Crew." In: Alan Goldfarb, ed. *Baseball Illustrated, 1971.* New York: Complete Sports, 1971. Pp. 21–30.

48038. Hanners, John. "John Wesley 'Boog' Powell." In: Vol. G-P of David L. Porter, ed. *Biographical Dictionary of American Sports: Baseball.* Rev. and enlarged ed. Westport, CT: Greenwood Press, 2000. Pp. 1227–1228.

48039. Honig, Donald. "1970: Boog Powell." In: his *American League MVP's.* New York: Bantam Books, 1989. Pp. 84–85.

48040. Isenberg, Jerry. "The Burden of Boog Powell." *Sport,* XXXVI (August 1963), 30–31+.

48041. Kiersh, Edward. "Boog Powell: Barracudas, Whales and Sassafras." In: his *Where Have You Gone, Vince DiMaggio?* New York: Bantam Books, 1983. Pp. 328–332.

48042. Klein, Dave. "Boog Powell and Willie McCovey." In: his *Great Infielders of the Major Leagues.* New York: Random House, 1972. Pp. 21–39.

48043. Masterson, Dave and Timm Boyle. "1970." In: their *Baseball's Best: The MVPs.* Chicago, IL: Contemporary Books, 1985. Pp. 244–249.

48044. O'Leary, Ted. "Getting a Belt Out of Boog." *Sports Illustrated,* XLIII (September 1, 1974), 43–44.

48045. Ottum, Bob. "Boog! the Big Baseball Musical." *Sports Illustrated,* XXXV (July 19, 1971), 50–60.

48046. Powell, John W. ("Boog"). "Power Makes a Champion." In: Vito Stellino, ed. *1971 Baseball Guidebook.* New York: Maco Publishing Co., 1971. Pp. 18–24.

48047. _____. "Boog Powell: Baseball's Tom Sawyer." *Baseball Digest,* XXVIII (September 1969), 16–19.

48048. _____. "Boog Powell: The Orioles' Meal Ticket." *Baseball Magazine,* XCIV (November 1964), 26–31.

48049. _____. *Mesquite Cookery.* New York: McGraw-Hill Book Co., 1986. Spiral bound.

48050. _____., as told to George Vass. "The Game I'll Never Forget." *Baseball Digest,* XLVI (February 1987), 86–89.

48051. Reed, J. D. "Always Ready to Chew the Fat." *Sports Illustrated,* XXXIX (July 16, 1973), 65–72, 74.

48052. Stainback, Berry. "Something About a Phenom." *Sport,* XXXIV (July 1962), 11–13.

48053. Steadman, John F. "John Powell: Picture-Swing with Power." *Baseball Digest,* XXIII (September 1964), 24–29.

48054. Vecsey, George. "Behind the Boog Powell Boom." *Sport,* XLII (November 1966), 30–33.

48055. Zanger, Jack. "Killebrew and Powell: Why There's Still a Place for the Old-Fashioned Slugger." *Sport,* XLVIII (November 1969), 30–33+.

Ted Henry Power
P. (B: Jan. 31, 1955, Guthrie, OK). Los Angeles (NL), 1981–1982; Cincinnati (NL), 1983–1987; Kansas City (AL)

and Detroit (AL), 1988; St. Louis (NL), 1989; Pittsburgh (NL), 1990; Cincinnati (NL), 1991; Cleveland (AL), 1992–1993; Seattle (AL), 1993–1994. Remarks: Won 68 games and lost 69, with 70 "saves," in 14 big league seasons, the last of which was spent injured.

48056. Nash, Bruce and Allan Zullo. "Ted Power." In: their *More Little Big Leaguers: Amazing Boyhood Stories of Today's Baseball Stars.* New York: Little Simon, 1991. Pp. 76–77.

48057. Shannon, Mike. "Ted Power." In: his *Tales from the Ballpark: More of the Greatest True Baseball Stories Ever Told.* Lincolnwood, IL: Contemporary Books, 1999. Pp. 160–166.

Victor Pellot ("Vic") Power
1B-2B-OF-3B. (B: Victor Felipe Pellot Pove, Nov. 1, 1931, Arecibo, Puerto Rico). Philadelphia (AL),1954; Kansas City (AL), 1955–1958; Cleveland (AL), 1958–1961; Minnesota (AL), 1962–1964; Los Angeles (AL) and Philadelphia (NL), 1964; California (AL), 1965. Remarks: Had 1,716 hits (126 homers) and 45 stolen bases in 1,627 games in a dozen campaigns; stole home twice in one game, Aug. 14, 1958; suspended and fine for spitting on umpire Jim Honochick, July 11, 1964; minor league manager in Mexican League during late 1960's and early 1970's; scout, California (AL), 1979–1982; also played for Kansas City Blues (AA), 1952–1953, winning that league's batting title the latter year.

48058. Bjarkman, Peter C. "Vic Power: The First Flashy Latin Big League Hero." *Oldtyme Baseball News,* VIII, no. 4 (1997), 18–20.

48059. Figone, Albert J. "Victor Pellot 'Vic' Power." In: Vol. G-P of David L. Porter, ed. *Biographical Dictionary of American Sports: Baseball.* Rev. and enlarged ed. Westport, CT: Greenwood Press, 2000. Pp. 1228–1229.

48060. Graham, Frank, Jr. "Power Proves His Case." *Sport,* XXII (August 1956), 44–47.

48061. Haag, Ken. "The Wrightfield Line." *Sports Collector's Digest,* XVIII (March 29, 1991), 180–181. Time with St. Paul Saints in 1945.

48062. Hall, John. "Vic Power Seeks to Change 'Ee-Mage.'" *Baseball Digest,* XXIV (May 1965), 83–85.

48063. Jacobs, Bruce. "Everything's Up to Date in Kansas City: Vic Power." In: Bruce Jacobs, ed. *Baseball Stars of 1956.* New York: Lion Books, 1956. Pp. 156–159.

48064. Kiersh, Edward. "Vic Power: Bill Cosby Teams Up with Martin Luther King." In: his *Where Have You Gone, Vince DiMaggio?* New York: Bantam Books, 1983. Pp. 173–179.

48065. Lebovitz, Hal. "The True Story of Vic Power." *Sport,* XXVIII (August 1959), 32–34+.

48066. Linn, Ed. "Vic Power, Master at First." *Saturday Evening Post,* CCXXIV (July 29, 1961), 30–31+.

48067. Marazzi, Rich. "The Yankees Passed on Slick-Fielding Vic Power." *Sports Collector's Digest,* XXVI (January 15, 1999), 76–77.

48068. Moffi, Larry. "Vic Power: 'I Don't Want to Eat Negros, I Just Want Rice and Beans.'" In: his *This Side of Cooperstown: An Oral History of Major League Baseball in the 1950s.* Iowa City, IA: University of Iowa Press, 1996. Pp. 93–110.

48069. _____., and Jonathan Kronstadt. "Vic Pellot Power." In: their *Crossing the Line: Black Major Leaguers, 1947–1959.* Jefferson, NC: McFarland & Co., Inc., 1994. Pp. 117–119.

48070. Orr, Jack. "Were the Yankees Wrong on Vic Power?" *Sport,* XVII (September 1954), 21+.

48071. Peary, Danny. "Vic Power." In: his *Cult Baseball Players.* New York: Simon and Schuster, 1990. Pp. 344–350.

48072. _____. "Vic Power." In: his *Baseball's Finest: The Greats, the Flakes, the Weird and the Wonderful.* North Dighton, MA: The JG Press, 1990. Pp. 344–350. Both Peary books are identical.

48073. Power, Vic. "Interview." In: Danny Peary. *Cult Baseball Players.* New York: Simon and Schuster, 1990. Pp. 352–370.

48074. Robinson, Jackie. "Vic Power." In: his *Baseball Has Done It.* Philadelphia: Lippincott, 1964. Pp. 164–172.

48075. Shecter, Leonard. "Vic Power's New, Wonderful World." *Sport,* XXXV (May 1963), 64–65+.

48076. Stainback, Berry. "The 'Clubhouse Lawyer' as a Key Man." *Sport,* XXXIV (November 1962), 7–8.

Albert ("Al" or "Uncle Al") Pratt
P-OF-MGR-UMP. (B: Nov. 19, 1847, Pittsburgh, PA-D: Nov. 21, 1937). Cleveland Forest Cities (N.A.), 1871–1872. Remarks: Won 13 games and lost 27 in 41 games as a hurler; also played the outfielder four times and had a career total of 51 hits; arbiter, NL, 1879 and AA, 1880–1881; manager, Pittsburgh (AA), 1882–1883 and Pittsburgh (NL), 1890.

48077. Pietrusza, David. "Al Pratt: Present at the Creations." *Elysian Fields Quarterly,* XIV (Spring 1995), 43–47.

Derrill Burnham ("Del") Pratt
2B. (B: Jan. 10, 1888, Walhalla, SC-D: Sept. 30, 1977). St. Louis (AL), 1912–1917; New York (AL), 1918–1920; Boston (AL), 1921–1922; Detroit (AL), 1923–1924. Remarks: In a 13-year pro career, had 1,996 hits (43 homers) and 247 stolen bases in 1,835 games; led AL in games played, 1913–1916 and 1920; AL RBI champion, 1916; also played for Montgomery (SA), 1910–1912; player-manager, Waco (TL), 1925–1930; manager, Galveston (TL), 1931–1932 and Fort Worth (TL), 1933–1934; named to Alabama Sports Hall of Fame, 1972.

48078. Borst, William A. ("Bill"). "Derrill Burnham 'Del' Pratt." In: Vol. G-P of David L. Porter, ed. *Biographical Dictionary of American Sports: Baseball.* Rev. and enlarged ed. Westport, CT: Greenwood Press, 2000. Pp. 1229–1230. Steve Steinberg's profile appears as a number in the online SABR Biography Project < http://bioproj.sabr.org/bioproj.cfm?a=v&v=l&bid=1124&pid=11446>.

48079. Kofoed, J. C. "The Star of the Browns' Infield." *Baseball Magazine,* XV (May 1915), 49–52.

Todd Alan Pratt
C. (B: Feb. 9, 1967, Bellevue, NE). Philadelphia (NL), 1992–1994; Chicago (NL), 1995); New York (NL), 1996–2001; Philadelphia (NL), 2001–. Remarks: Through 2004, has had 332 hits (38 homers) and five stolen bases in 540 games; hit into triple play, Aug. 19, 2004.

48080. Frommer, Harvey and Frederick J. "Todd Pratt." In: their *Growing Up Baseball: An Oral History.* Dallas, TX: Taylor Publishing Co., 2001. Pp. 189–192.

John Arthur Pregenzer
P. (B: Aug. 2, 1935, Burlington, VT). San Francisco (NL), 1963–1964. Remarks: In two big league seasons, won two games without a defeat and "saved" another.

48081. Laiolo, Tony. "A Great Cup of Coffee: The John Pregenzer Story." *Elysian Fields Quarterly,* XIII (Winter 1994), 38–50.

Eugene Miles Prentice, 3rd
EXEC. (B: August 27, 1942, Glen Ridge, NJ). Remarks: Owner, Kansas City (AL), 1998–.

48082. Roth, Stephen. "Prentice Seeks Recognition as a Local Owner of Royals." *The Kansas City Business Journal,* XVI (August 21, 1998), 1–2.

48083. _____. "Prentice Wins with Spunk, Brains." *The Kansas City Business Journal,* XVII (November 27, 1998), 1–2.

Joseph Edward ("Joe" or "Little Joe") Presko
P. (B: Oct. 7, 1928, Kansas City, MO). St. Louis (NL), 1951–1954; Detroit (AL), 1957–1958. Remarks: Won 23 games and lost 37, with five "saves," in six years.
48084. Burnes, Robert L. "Presko's Two Big Innings." *Baseball Digest,* XV (January-February 1956), 19–21.
48085. Veech, Ellis J. "Baby Joe of the Gashouse Gang." *Baseball Magazine,* LXXXVIII (September.1951), 15–17.

Forest Charles ("Tot") Pressnell
P. (B: Aug. 8, 1908, Findlay, OH-D: Jan. 6, 2001). Brooklyn (NL), 1938–1940; Chicago (NL), 1941–1942. Remarks: In five big league years, obtained 32 victories, 30 defeats, and 12 "saves"; first game a shutout victory, April 21, 1938.
48086. Kelley, Brent P. "Tot Pressnell: Milwaukee Mainstay." In: his *In the Shadow of the Babe: Baseball Players Who Played with or Against Babe Ruth.* Jefferson, NC: McFarland & Co., Inc., 1995. Pp. 185–192.
Tot Pressnell *see* **Forest Charles ("Tot") Pressnell**
Jackie Price *see* **John Thomas Reid ("Johnny" or "Jackie") Price**

John Thomas Reid ("Johnny" or "Jackie") Price
SS. (B: Nov. 13, 1912, Winborn, MS-D: Oct. 2, 1967). Cleveland (AL), 1946. Remarks: Had three hits in seven big league games; remembered for losing two 5' snakes on a train carrying his team in a prank which cost him his career, March 1947.
48087. Lieb, Frederick. "Jackie Price: Used Snakes in His Act." In: his *Comedians and Pranksters of Baseball.* St. Louis, MO: The Sporting News, 1958. Pp. 32–36.

Gerald Edward ("Jerry") Priddy
SS-2B. (B: Nov. 9, 1919, Los Angeles, CA-D: March 3, 1980). New York (AL), 1941–1942; Washington (AL), 1943, 1946–1947; St. Louis (AL), 1948–1949; Detroit (AL), 1950–1952. Remarks: In 11 seasons, had 1,252 hits (61 homers) and 44 stolen bases in 1,296 games; started record five double plays in first five innings of a game, May 20, 1950.
48088. Graybar, Lloyd J. "Gerald Edward 'Jerry' Priddy." In: Vol. G-P of David L. Porter, ed. *Biographical Dictionary of American Sports: Baseball.* Rev. and enlarged ed. Westport, CT: Greenwood Press, 2000. Pp. 1230–1231.
Jerry Priddy *see* **Gerald Edward ("Jerry") Priddy**
Curtis John Pride
OF. (B: Dec. 17, 1968, Washington, DC). Montreal (NL), 1993, 1995; Detroit (AL), 1996–1997; Boston (AL), 1997; Atlanta (NL), 1998; Salt Lake City (PCL), 1999; Boston (AL), 2000; Montreal (NL), 2001; Nashville (AA), 2002; Nashua (Atlantic League), Columbus (AA), New York (AL), 2003; Anaheim (AL), 2004. Remarks: In all or parts of nine big league seasons, had 192 hits (19 homers) and 29 stolen bases in 388 games; first deaf player at major league level in nearly half a century and only the fifth ever.
48089. Bowker, Michael. "The Loudest Cheer." *Reader's Digest,* CXLIV (May 1994), 79–83. Pride's success despite his deafness.
48090. Giuliotti, Ed. "Pride of the Expos." *Beckett Focus on Future Stars,* IV, no. 35 (March 1994), 14–16.
48091. Jordan, Pat. "Pride of the Expos." *Men's Journal,* III (April 1994), 64+.
48092. Marston, C. "The Pride of Curtis." *Dugout,* II (June 1994), 31–32.

48093. Whiteside, Kelly. "Curtis Pride." *Sports Illustrated,* LXXIX (July 12, 1993), 57+.
Raymond Lee ("Ray" or "Pop") Prim
P. (B: Dec. 30, 1906, Salitpa, AL-D: April 29, 1995). Washington (AL), 1933–1934; Philadelphia (NL), 1935; Chicago (NL), 1943, 1945–1946. Remarks: Won 22 games and lost 21, with four "saves," in six big league years; lost Game Two of 1945 World Series; also played for Los Angeles (PCL), 1936–1942.
48094. Spalding, John e. "Ray Prim." In: his *Pacific Coast League Stars: One Hundred of the Best, 1903-1957.* San Jose, CA: John E. Spalding, 1994. Pp. 82–83.
Robert ("Bob" or "Gunner") Prince
BROADCASTER. (B: July 1, 1916, New York City-D: June 10, 1985). Remarks: radio broadcaster for Pittsburgh (NL), 1948–1975, 1985 and Houston (NL) 1976 and ABC-TV, 1977–1982, and Home Sports Entertainment, 1983–1985; Ford C. Frick Award, 1986.
48095. Cope, Myron. "The Prince of Pittsburgh." *Sports Illustrated,* XXIII (September 13, 1965), 84–87. James Forr's profile is a number in the online SABR Biography Project http://bioproj.sabr.org/bioproj.cfm?a=v&v=l&bid=794&pid=16922.
48096. Meyers, Robert. "Bob Prince, Eccentric Sportscaster." *TV Guide,* XXI (August 4, 1973), 33–34.
48097. O'Brien, Jim. *We Had 'Em All the Way: Bob Prince and His Pittsburgh Pirates.* Pittsburgh, PA: James P. O'Brien Publishing, 1998. 432p.
48098. Spoehr, Luther W. "Robert Ferris 'Bob,' 'The Gunner' Prince." In: David L. Porter, ed. *Biographical Dictionary of American Sports: 1989–1992 Supplement for Baseball, Football, Basketball and Other Sports.* Westport, CT: Greenwood Press, 1992. Pp. 357–358.
Mark William Prior
P. (B: Sept. 7, 1980, San Diego, CA). Chicago (NL), 2002–. Remarks: Through 2004, has won 30 games and lost 16; lost Game Two of 2003 NLCS.
48099. Cannella, Stephen. "A Matter of Time." *Sports Illustrated,* XCVI (April 1, 2002), 72–73.
48100. Couch, Greg. "Cubs' Mark Prior Has All the Ingredients to Be a Winner." *Baseball Digest,* LXI (December 2002), 54–57.
48101. Latack, Andy. "Poison Ivy." *ESPN: The Magazine,* V (July 22, 2002), 52–55.
Luke Prokopec
P. (B: Feb. 23, 1978, Blackwood, Australia). Los Angeles (NL), 2000–2001; Toronto (AL), 2002. Remarks: Won 11 games and lost 17 in three big league seasons; also played for Great Falls Dodgers (Pioneer League), 1995; Savannah Sandgnats (South Atlantic League),1996; San Bernardino Stampede (California League), 1997–1998.
48102. Weber, R. "Cool Hand Luke: There's a Very Short List of Aussies Who've Pitched in the US Major Leagues — Add One Intense 23-year-old South Australian, Luke Prokopec, a Dodgers Rookie who Could Surpass all Their Efforts in the Run Up to This year's World Series Play-Offs." *Inside Sport* (Sydney), no. 117 (October 2001), 114–115, 118–121.
Hubert Shelby ("Hub" or "Shucks") Pruett
P. (B: Sept. 1, 1900, Malden, MO-D: Jan. 28, 1982). St. Louis (AL), 1922–1924; Philadelphia (NL), 1927–1928; New York (NL), 1930; Boston (NL), 1932. Remarks: Won 29 games and lost 48, with 13 "saves," in all or parts of seven major league seasons; struck out George Herman ("Babe") Ruth (q.v.) in 10 of first 13 match-ups (nine of first 10 before surrendering a homer); medical student in

off-season who left the game after graduation to establish his practice.

48103. Holway, John B. "Hub Pruett: The Pitcher Who Baffled Babe Ruth." *Baseball Digest,* XLVI (September 1987), 86–89.

48104. Stewart, Wayne. "The Man Who 'Owned' the Babe and Other Tales of Success Against the Babe." In: Peter Levine, ed. *Baseball History 2.* Westport, CT: Meckler, 1989. Pp. 78–85.

Kirby ("Stub") Puckett★

OF. (B. March 14, 1961, Chicago, IL). Minnesota (AL), 1994–1997. Remarks: Had 2,304 hits (207 homers) and 217 stolen bases in 1,783 games; had four hits in first big league game, May 8, 1984; hit for the cycle, Aug. 1, 1986; had six hits in one game, Aug. 30, 1987; led AL in hits, 1987–1989, 1992; had six doubles in two games, May 13–14, 1989; first $3 million player, Nov. 22, 1989; AL batting champion, 1989; homered in Games Three and Four of 1991 ALCS; had three hits and three RBIs in Game Six, 1991 World Series; had seven RBIs in one game twice in one season, May 24 and Aug. 10, 1994; AL RBI champion, 1994; received Branch Rickey Award, 1993; on Sept. 28, 1995, hit in the face by a pitched ball; diagnosed with glaucoma on March 28, 1996 and placed on injured reserve, prior to retiring on July 12; had more hits in his first 10 years than any 20th century player; ALCS MVP award, 1991; World Series MVP award, 1991; exec. VP, Minnesota (AL), 1997–. Elected to National Baseball Hall of Fame in 2001, where his plaque reads: "A proven team leader with an ever-present smile and infectious exuberance who led the Twins to World Series titles in 1987 and 1991. Over 12 seasons hit for power and average batting .318 with 414 doubles and 207 home runs. Also a prolific run producer, scored 1,071 runs and drove in 1,085 in 1,783 games. A six-time Gold Glove winner who patrolled center field with elegance and style, routinely scaling outfield walls to take away home runs. The 10-time All-Star's career ended abruptly due to irreversible retinal damage in his right eye."

48105. Aaseng, Nathan. *Sports Great Kirby Puckett.* Hillside, NJ: Enslow, 1993. 64p.

48106. Aschburner, Steve. "For Kirby Puckett, Success a Product of Hard Work." *Baseball Digest,* LI (October 1992), 20–23.

48107. _____. "Kirby Puckett of the Twins Fools the Skeptics Again." *Baseball Digest,* XLVII (October 1988), 72–73.

48108. Bauleke, Ann. *Kirby Puckett: Fan Favorite.* Minneapolis, MN: Lerner Publications, 1993. 64p.

48109. Blount, Roy, Jr. "Standing Tall." *Sports Illustrated,* LXXVI (April 6, 1992), 110–124.

48110. Brown, Doug. "An $93 Taxi Fare for Twins' Kirby Puckett Was Well Spent." *Baseball Digest,* XLIII (November 1984), 48–50.

48111. Caple, Jim. "Deeper Look: Kirby Puckett." *Beckett Baseball Card Monthly,* X, no. 97 (April 1993), 112–113.

48112. Carlson, Chuck. *Puck! Kirby Puckett: Baseball's Last Warrior.* Lenexa, KS: Addax Publishing Group, 1998. 195p.

48113. Carpenter, Jerry and Steve DiMeglio. *Kirby Puckett.* Bloomington, MN: Abdo & Daughters, 1988. 32p.

48114. Cohen, Irwin. "Kirby Puckett: Interview." *Baseball Cards,* VII (December 1987), 62–65.

48115. Coplon, J. "The Secret of My New Success." *Sport,* LXXVIII (November 1987), 50–51+.

48116. Crasnick, Jerry. "Farewell to Kirby Puckett, One of the Game's Class Acts." *Baseball Digest,* LV (November 1996), 62–65.

48117. Deford, Frank. "The Rise and Fall of Kirby Puckett." *Sports Illustrated,* XCVIII (March 17, 2003), 58–62, 64, 67–69.

48118. DeLand, Dave. "A Closer Look: Kirby Puckett." *Beckett Baseball Card Monthly,* VI (May 1989), 6–7.

48119. _____. "Deeper Look: Kirby Puckett." *Beckett Baseball Card Monthly,* XI, no. 114 (September 1994), 22–24.

48120. Dewan, John and Don Zminda. "Minnesota Twins: Will Kirby Reach 3000?" In: STATS, Inc. *STATS Baseball Scoreboard 1994.* New York: HarperPerennial, 1994. Pp. 24–25.

48121. Dooher, Doug. "Opponent Feature: Minnesota's Kirby Puckett: 'I Came to Play....'" *Texas Rangers 1996 Souvenir Program,* XXV, no. 25 (1996), pp. 57–60.

48122. _____. "Puckett by the Numbers." *Twins Magazine,* IX (September 1996), 18–27.

48123. _____. "Tell Dr. Kirby Where It Hurts, Man." *Minneapolis/St. Paul Magazine,* XXV (September 1997), 19–20.

48124. Enders, Eric. "Night and Day: 2001 Hall of Fame Inductees Kirby Puckett and Dave Winfield Had Little in Common—Until Now." In: Michael J. McCormick, ed. *2001 League Championship Series Official Program.* New York: Major League Baseball Promotion Corp., 2001. Pp. 32–43.

48125. Gutman, Bill. "Kirby Puckett." In: his *Baseball's Hot New Stars.* New York: Pocket Books, 1988. pp. 36–54.

48126. Henderson, John. "Where are They Now?: Former Twins Star Kirby Puckett." *Baseball Digest,* LIX (November 2000), 56–61.

48127. Heyman, Jon. "Kirby Puckett: A Star Who Doesn't Act Like One." *Baseball Digest,* LI (February 1992), 24–25.

48128. Hood, Robert E. "Baseball's Mighty Puck." *Boys' Life,* LXXXIII (April 1993), 8–9.

48129. Italia, Bob. *Kirby Puckett, MVP.* Edina, MN: Abdo & Daughters, 1993. 32p.

48130. Kaplan, Jim "Cal (Griffith) Can Bring 'Em up Right." *Sports Illustrated,* LXI (July 23, 1984), 56–57.

48131. Kennedy, K. "Baseball's Loss." *Sports Illustrated,* LXXXIV (June 3, 1996), 13–14.

48132. Leavy, Walter. "Puckett: On a New Mission." *Ebony,* LII (October 1997), 174+.

48133. Lenihan, Jef. "A Closer Look: Kirby Puckett." *Beckett Baseball Card Monthly,* IX (June 1992), 6–7.

48134. Linkugel, Wil A. and Edward J. Pappas. "Blurred Vision: Kirby Puckett." In: their *They Tasted Glory: Among the Missing at the Baseball Hall of Fame.* Jefferson, NC: McFarland & Co., Inc., 1998. Pp. 61–71.

48135. Lupica, Mike. "The Short, Happy Life of Kirby Puckett." *Esquire,* CXVII (April 1992), 61–62.

48136. Murphy, Brian. "Hall of Fame Election: Twin's 'Overachiever' Kirby Puckett Gets Call to Glory." *Baseball Digest,* LX (April 2001), 72–73.

48137. Nash, Bruce and Allan Zullo. "Kirby Puckett." In: their *More Little Big Leaguers: Amazing Boyhood Stories of Today's Baseball Stars.* New York: Little Simon, 1991. Pp. 16–17.

48138. Newhan, Ross. "Kirby Puckett: AL's Best All-Around Player." *Baseball Digest,* XLVIII (July 1989), 34–39.

48139. Puckett, Kirby. *I Love the Game: My Life and Baseball.* New York: HarperCollins, 1993. 238p.

48140. _____. "Kirby Talks Baseball." *Minnesota Monthly,* XXVII (March 1993), 46–47+.

48141. _____. "My Greatest Day in Baseball." In: Eliot Cohen, ed. *My Greatest Day in Baseball.* New York: Little Simon, 1991. pp. 84–86.

48142. _____. "When I was Your Age." *KidSports,* IV, no. 4 (1992), 28–29.

48143. _____. and Andrew Gutelle. *Kirby Puckett's Baseball Games.* New York: Workman Publishers, 1996. 100p. Instructional and biographical.

48144. _____., as told to George Vass. "The Game I'll Never Forget." *Baseball Digest,* LII (November 1993), 37–39.

48145. _____., as told to Greg Brown. *Be the Best You Can Be.* Minneapolis, MN: Waldman House Press, 1993. 38p.

48146. Rambeck, Richard. *Kirby Puckett.* Mankato, MN: Child's World, 1993. 31p.

48147. Reusse, Patrick. "The Puck." In: Tom Barnidge, ed. *The Sporting News 1987 Baseball Yearbook.* St. Louis, MO: The Sporting News, 1987. Pp. 28–32.

48148. Robson, Britt. "Watch Him While You Can." *Minneapolis,* XXI (June 1993), 49+.

48149. Rushin, Steve. "A Bright Outlook." *Sports Illustrated,* LXXXVI (May 19, 1997), 74–76, 79–80.

48150. _____. "Does the Puck Stop Here?" *Sports Illustrated,* LXXVI (June 22, 1992), 22–24, 29–30.

48151. Sinker, Howard. "Kirby Puckett of the Twins: The Best is Yet to Come." *Baseball Digest,* XLVI (July 1987), 43–46.

48152. Smith, Ron. "Kirby Puckett 86." In: his *The Sporting News Selects Baseball's 100 Greatest Players.* St. Louis, MO: The Sporting News, 1998. Pp 186–187.

48153. Steinberg, Alan. "Interview: Kirby Puckett." *Sport,* XI (April 1989), 22–29.

48154. Sullivan, George. "Kirby Puckett." In: his *Glovemen: Twenty-Seven of Baseball's Greatest.* New York: Atheneum, 1996. Pp. 8–9.

48155. Telander, Rick. "Minny's Mighty Mite." *Sports Illustrated,* LXVI (June 15, 1987), 46–49.

48156. Thornton, K. D. "Kirby Puckett." In: Ken Collier, ed. *The Baseball Book, 1987.* Scottsdale, AZ: Jalart House, 1987. Pp. 92–93.

48157. Wee, David L. "The English Professor Goes to the 1987 World Series: A Medley — the Glove Song of Our Kirby Puckett." *Minneapolis Review of Baseball,* VIII (January 1988), 48–49. Poem.

48158. Welch, James E. "Kirby Puckett." In: Vol. G-P of David L. Porter, ed. *Biographical Dictionary of American Sports: Baseball.* Rev. and enlarged ed. Westport, CT: Greenwood Press, 2000. Pp. 1231–1232.

48159. Wendel, Tim. "Curtain Falls on Kirby Era: Puck was the Pastime's Best Ambassador." *USA Today Baseball Weekly,* VI (July 17, 1996), 3–4.

48160. _____. "Puckett's Heroics End Tense Struggle: Fans' Favorite Comes Through in Clutch." *USA Today Baseball Weekly,* I (November 1, 1991), 9–10.

48161. "Winfield, Puckett Head Baseball's Class of 2001 Hall of Fame Inductees." *Jet,* C (August 20, 2001), 52–53.

48162. Young, A. D. "Doc." "Coping." *People Weekly,* XLVII (March 3, 1997), 67+. Glaucoma drives Puckett from the game.

Timothy Dean ("Tim") Pugh

P. (B: Jan. 26, 1967, Lake Tahoe, CA). Cincinnati (NL), 1992–1996; Kansas City (AL), 1996; Detroit (AL), 1997. Remarks: Won 25 games and lost 28 in six years.

48163. Pugh, Tim. "Tim Pugh's Spring Training Dairy." *Reds Report,* VI (April-May 1993), 16–17, 16–17.

Terry Stephen ("T. P.") Puhl

OF. (B: July 8, 1956, Melville, Canada). Houston (NL), 1977–1990; Kansas City (AL), 1991. Remarks. Obtained 1,361 hits (62 homers) and 217 stolen bases in 1,531 games in 15 years; had record .526 batting average in 1980 NLCS; had .993 career fielding average, making only 18 errors; through date of retirement, played in more MLB games than any other Canadian-born player; became financial broker upon retirement; elected to Canadian Baseball Hall of Fame, 1995.

48164. Joyce, G. "Lone Star Canadian." *MVP Magazine,* II (September-October 1986), 40–45.

48165. Keller, Garnet. "1993 Inductees into the Saskatchewan Baseball Hall of Fame: Terry Puhl." In: *Saskatchewan Historical Baseball Review 1993.* Battleford, SK: Saskatchewan Baseball Hall of Fame And Museum Association, 1993. Pp. 48–50.

48166. Kendall, Brian. "October 12, 1980: Terry Puhl Bats a Playoff Record .526." In: his *Great Moments in Canadian Baseball.* Toronto, Ont.: Lester Publishing, 1995. Chapter 16.

48167. Nash, Bruce and Allan Zullo. "Terry Puhl." In: their *More Little Big Leaguers: Amazing Boyhood Stories of Today's Baseball Stars.* New York: Little Simon, 1991. Pp. 86–87.

48168. Puhl, Terry, as told to George Vass. "The Game I'll Never Forget." *Baseball Digest,* XLVIII (August 1989), 50–55. 1980 NLCS.

48169. Robertson, John. "Terry Stephen Puhl." In: Vol. G-P of David L. Porter, ed. *Biographical Dictionary of American Sports: Baseball.* Rev. and enlarged ed. Westport, CT: Greenwood Press, 2000. P. 1233.

48170. Shearon, Jim. "Terry Puhl of Melville, Pride Of Saskatchewan." In: his *Canada's Baseball Legends.* Kanata, Ontario: Malin Head Press, 1994. Pp. 198–202.

48171. Turner, Dan. "Terry Puhl." In: his *Heroes, Bums and Ordinary Men.* Toronto: Doubleday Canada Ltd., 1988. Pp. 183–192.

Albert ("Prince Albert" or "Phat Albert") Pujols

OF-1B-3B. (B: Jan. 16, 1980, Santo Domingo, Dominican Republic). St. Louis (NL), 2001–date. Remarks: Through 2004, has had 787 hits (160 homers) and 13 stolen bases in 629 games; NL Rookie of the Year Award, 2001; achieved 30-game hitting streak, 2002; had two homers in 2002 NLCS; NL batting champion, 2003, while simultaneously leading his league in extra-base hits and doubles; had two doubles and four homers in 2004 NLCS; NLCS MVP Award, 2004; first player in history with 30 or more homers in each of his first four seasons, and the third player with 500 RBIs in his first four years.

48172. Etkin, Jack. "National League 2003 Batting Champion: Albert Pujols." *Baseball Digest,* LXIII (February 2004), 38–45.

48173. Fialkov, Harvey. "Cardinals' Albert Pujols Shows No Complacency in His Play." *Baseball Digest,* LXI (November 2002), 48–51.

48174. Habib, Daniel G. "Albert the Great." *Sports Illustrated,* XCVIII (June 30, 2003), 32–34, 36. Pujols.

48175. Hummell, Rick. "Phat Albert." *Sports Illustrated for Kids,* XV (June 2003), 36–37.

48176. Le Batard, Dan. "God Only Knows: How Good is Albert Pujols?" *ESPN: The Magazine,* VI (July 21, 2003), 44–48, 50, 52.

48177. McHale, Mutt. "Albert Pujols." *Baseball Digest,* LXII (October 2003), 22–25.

48178. Muskat, Carrie. "No Ordinary Rookie." *Baseball Digest,* LX (December 2001), 46–49.

48179. Verducci, Tom. "Card Trick: No Mac? No Sweat, as Rookie Albert Pujols Led Reshuffled St. Louis to a Sweep of Arizona." *Sports Illustrated,* XCIV (April 16, 2001), 48–49.

Harry Clay Pulliam

EXEC. (B: Feb. 8, 1869, Scottsville, KY–D: July 29, 1909). Remarks: Club secretary, Louisville (NL), 1899 and Pittsburgh (NL), 1900–1902; NL president, 1902 until his death by suicide.

48180. Akin, William E. "Harry Clay Pulliam." In: Vol. G-P of David L. Porter, ed. *Biographical Dictionary of American Sports: Baseball.* Rev. and enlarged ed. Westport, CT: Greenwood Press, 2000. Pp. 1233–1234.

48181. Richter, Francis C. "The Passing of Pulliam." *Sporting Life,* (August 7, 1909), 10+.

Bill Pulsipher *see* **William Thomas ("Bill") Pulsipher**

William Thomas ("Bill") Pulsipher

P. (B: Oct. 9, 1973, Clifton, VA). New York (NL), 1995, 1998; Milwaukee (NL), 1998–1999; New York (NL), 2000; Boston (AL) and Chicago (AL), 2001. Remarks: Had 13 victories and 19 defeats in five years; injured in 1996–1997.

48182. Lingo, Will. "Hard Nut to Crack." *Beckett Focus on Future Stars,* V, no. 47 (March 1995), 74–75.

48183. Schwartz, Alan. "Rookie Report: Bill Pulsipher." *Beckett Baseball Card Monthly,* XII, no. 124 (July 1995), 126–127.

John Nolan Purdin

P. (B: July 16, 1942, Lynx, OH). Los Angeles (NL), 1964–1965, 1968–1969. Remarks: In four big league years, had six victories, four defeats, and two "saves."

48184. Lawson, Earl. "Dodgers Can Thank College Prof for 'Second Erskine': Scouted Purdin, Rookie Star in Germany." *Baseball Digest,* XXIV (April 1965), 59–60.

Robert Thomas ("Bob") Purkey

P. (B: July 14, 1929, Pittsburgh, PA).Pittsburgh (NL), 1954–1957; Cincinnati (NL), 1958–1964; St. Louis (NL), 1965; Pittsburgh (NL), 1966. Remarks: Obtained 129 victories, 115 defeats, and nine "saves" in 13 years; knuckleball artist; had grand slam homer, Aug. 1, 1959; gave up 11 hits and still won a game, Aug. 15, 1961; lost Game Four of 1961 World Series.

48185. Appel, Marty. "Bob Purkey." In: his *Yesterday's Heroes: Revisiting the Old-Time Baseball Stars.* New York: William Morrow, 1988. Pp. 174–177.

48186. Kamm, Herb. "Bob Purkey." In: Jack Orr, ed. *Baseball's Greatest Players Today.* New York: Watts, 1963. Pp. 50–57.

48187. Kaplan, Dave. "Bob Purkey." In: Ray Robinson, ed. *Baseball Stars of 1959.* New York: Pyramid Books, 1959. Pp. 109–112.

48188. Perkins, Steve. "Cincinnati's Pitching Con Man — Some Pitchers Make the Batters Fear Them; Bob Purkey Doesn't. He Seems to be Grooving the Ball, Which Is Part of the Success Secret." *Sport,* XXXIV (October 1962), 30–31.

48189. Pille, Bob. "Bob Purkey — a Right-Purkey Hurler." *Baseball Digest,* XVII (June 1958), 69–72.

48190. Rathgeber, Bob. "The Era of the Dancing Knuckler: Bob Purkey." In: his *Cincinnati Reds Scrapbook.* Virginia Beach, VA: J.C.P. Corp. of Virginia, 1982. Pp. 126–127.

48191. Thackeray, Frank W. "Robert Thomas 'Bob' Purkey." In: Vol. G-P of David L. Porter, ed. *Biographical Dictionary of American Sports: Baseball.* Rev. and enlarged ed. Westport, CT: Greenwood Press, 2000. Pp. 1234–1235.

Craig Pursley

ARTIST. (B: 1954). Remarks: Staff artist, *Orange County Register,* 1983–; baseball card artist.

48192. Stein, M. L. "Sports Illustrator's Reputation Grows: *Orange County Register* Craig Pursley Has Drawn a Second Career for Himself by Painting Player Pictures for Topps Cards." *Editor & Publisher,* CXXIV (May 4, 1991), 16–17.

Patrick Edward ("Pat") Putnam

1B. (B: Dec. 3, 1953, Bethel, VT). Texas (AL), 1977–1982; Seattle (AL), 1983–1984; Minnesota (AL), 1984. Remarks: In eight big league years, obtained 508 hits (63 homers) and 10 stolen bases in 577 games.

48193. Purtell, Jeff. "Pat Putnam." In: Tom Simon, ed. *Green Mountain Boys of Summer: Vermonters in the Major Leagues, 1882–1993.* Shelburne, VT: The New England Press, 2000. Pp. 165–167.

Frank Ralph ("Guido") Quilici

2B-3B-MGR. (B: May 11, 1939, Chicago, IL). Minnesota (AL), 1965, 1967–1970. Remarks: In five big league seasons, had 146 hits (five homers) and three stolen bases in 405 games; manager, Minnesota (AL), 1972–1975, winning 280 games and losing 287 (.494).

48194. Hutton, Shirley. "This Month: Frank Quilici." *Minnesota Sports Fan,* I (December 1972), 20–21.

48195. Quilici, Frank. "Quilici Plays Q. and A.— After 40 Games at the Helm: Interview." *Minnesota Sports Fan,* I (September 1972), 10–12.

Jack Quinn *see* **John Picus ("Jack") Quinn**

John Picus ("Jack") Quinn

P. (B: John Quinn Picus July 5, 1884, Jeanesville, PA-D: April 17, 1946). New York (AL), 1909–1912; Boston (NL), 1913; Baltimore (F.L.), 1914–1915; Chicago (AL), 1918; New York (AL), 1919–1921; Boston (AL), 1922–1925; Philadelphia (AL), 1925–1930; Brooklyn (NL), 1931–1932; Cincinnati (NL), 1933; Hollywood (PCL), 1934. Remarks: Hurling for eight different big league teams in 23 seasons, Quinn won 241 games, lost 216 and had 59 "saves"; manager, Johnstown (Middle Atlantic League), 1935; oldest regular-roster player in MLB history, who won final game at age 48.

48196. Davids, L. Robert. "John Pincus 'Jack' Quinn." In: Vol. Q-Z of David L. Porter, ed. *Biographical Dictionary of American Sports: Baseball.* Rev. and enlarged ed. Westport, CT: Greenwood Press, 2000. Pp. 1237–1238.

48197. Ford, William R. Sr. "Remembering Mr. Quinn." *Oldtyme Baseball News,* IV, no. 6 (1994), 2–3.

48198. Lane, Ferdinand C. "The Dean of Major League Pitchers." *Baseball Magazine,* XXVIII (March 1927), 453–455.

48199. Lewis, Allen. "John Quinn Recalls His Biggest Disappointment" *Baseball Digest,* XXXI (October 1972), 65–69.

Luis Raul Quinones

3B-2B-SS. (B: April 28, 1962, Ponce, PR). Oakland (AL), 1983; San Francisco (NL), 1986; Chicago (NL), 1987; Cincinnati (NL), 1988–1991; Minnesota (AL), 1992. Remarks: Obtained 227 hits (19 homers) and nine stolen bases in 442 games in a decade; had one hit in 1990 NLCS.

48200. Quinones, Luis, as told to George Vass. "The Game I'll Never Forget." *Baseball Digest,* LI (July 1992), 63–64. 1990 NLCS.

Arthur Lincoln ("Art") Quirk

P. (B: April 11, 1938, Providence, R.I.). Baltimore (AL), 1962; Washington (AL), 1963. Remarks: Won three games and lost two in two seasons.

48201. Horn, Huston. "Springtime Trials of a Rookie." *Sports Illustrated,* XVI (April 16, 1962), 40–45.

James Patrick ("Jamie") Quirk

C. (B: October 22, 1954, Whittier, CA). Kansas City

(AL), 1975–1976; Milwaukee (AL), 1977; Kansas City (AL), 1978–1982; St. Louis (NL), 1983; Chicago (AL) and Cleveland (AL), 1984; Kansas City (AL), 1985–1988; New York (AL), Oakland (AL) and Baltimore (AL), 1989; Oakland (AL), 1990–1991. Remarks: In 18 seasons, obtained 544 hits (43 homers) and five stolen bases in 984 games; coach, St. Louis (NL), 1984; had one hit each in 1976 and 1990 ALCS.

48202. Will, George F. "A Professional Catcher." In: his *Bunts: Curt Flood, Camden Yards, Pete Rose and Other Reflections on Baseball.* New York: Touchstone Books, 1998. Pp.126–128.

Daniel Raymond ("Dan" or "Quiz") Quisenberry
P. (B: Feb. 7, 1963, Santa Monica, CA–D: Sept. 30, 1998). Kansas City (AL), 1979–1988; St. Louis (NL), 1988–1989; San Francisco (NL), 1990. Remarks: Submarine pitcher; won 56 games and lost 46, with 244 "saves," in 12 seasons; established short-lived major league record for most "saves" in a season (45 in 1983); elected to NAIA Hall of Fame in 1984; elected to Missouri Sports Hall of Fame, 1997; published poet and a victim of brain cancer.

48203. Angell, Roger. "Profiles: Dan Quisenberry." *The New Yorker,* LXI (September 30, 1985), 41–42+.

48204. Coffey, Wayne. "Interview: Dan Quisenberry." *Sport,* LXXV (May 1984), 21–27.

48205. Collier, Ken. "Dan Quisenberry." In: Ken Collier, ed. *The Baseball Book, 1984.* Scottsdale, AZ: Jalart House, 1984. Pp. 65–67.

48206. Friedman, Jack. "Here's an Underhanded Quiz." *People Weekly,* XXV (April 7, 1986), 49–50+.

48207. Gammons, Peter. "Royals' Reliever Gives His Foes That Sinking Feeling." *Baseball Digest,* XLIII (December 1984), 43–47.

48209. Hye, Allen E. "Daniel Raymond 'Dan' Quisenberry." In: Vol. Q–Z of David L. Porter, ed. *Biographical Dictionary of American Sports: Baseball.* Rev. and enlarged ed. Westport, CT: Greenwood Press, 2000. Pp. 1238–1239.

48210. Jordan, Pat. "Oh, What a Relief He Is." *Sport,* LXXI (November 1980), 68–71.

48211. Kurkjian, Tim. "Dan Quisenberry: A Royal Submarine Commander." *Baseball Digest,* XLI (September 1982), 71–74.

48212. McCarver, Tim, with Danny Peary. "Dan Quisenberry." In: his *The Perfect Season: Why 1998 Was Baseball's Greatest Year.* New York: Villard Books, 1999. Pp. 59–61.

48213. McGuff, Joe. "Dan Quisenberry: He Does It with Aplomb." *Baseball Digest,* XLII (October 1983), 84–87.

48214. McKenzie, Mike. "'Quiz Show' Is a Box Office Smash in K.C." In: Dick Kaegel, ed. *The Sporting News 1984 Baseball Yearbook.* St. Louis: *The* Sporting News, 1984. Pp. 88–92.

48215. Quisenberry, Dan. "The Land of Stupid Dances: An Intimate Guide to Life and Lunacy in Big League Bullpens, from a Pitcher Who Has Seen Them All." *Sports Illustrated,* LXXII (April 15, 1990), 56–60.

48216. _____. *On a Day Like This: Poems.* Kansas City, MO: Helicon Nine Editions, 1998. 90p.

48217. _____,as told to George Vass. "The Game I'll Never Forget." *Baseball Digest,* XLVIII (September 1989), 71–73. Reprinted in George Vass, ed. *The Game I'll Never Forget* (Chicago, IL: Bonus Books, 1999), pp. 199–202. 1989 ALCS.

48218. Schlossberg, Dan. "The Ultimate Relievers: Bruce Sutter and Dan Quisenberry." *Baseball Digest,* XLIV (July 1985), 49–58.

48219. Wulf, Steve. "Special Delivery from Down Under." *Sports Illustrated,* LIX (July 11, 1983), 74–78+.

Richard Raymond ("Dick" or "The Monster") Radatz
P. (B: April 2, 1937, Detroit, MI–D: March 16, 2005). Boston (AL), 1962–1966; Cleveland (AL), 1966–1967; Chicago (NL), 1967; Detroit (AL) and Montreal (NL), 1960. Remarks: Obtained 52 victories, 43 defeats, and 122 "saves" in seven years; appeared in 381 big league games, but never made a "start"; led AL in "saves" his rookie year; in two innings pitched in 1963 All-Star Game, struck out Willie Mays (q.v.), Dick Groat (q.v.), Duke Snider (q.v.), Willie McCovey (q.v.), and Julian Javier (q.v.); losing pitcher in 1964 All-Star Game; named to Boston Red Sox Hall of Fame, Sept. 1997.

48220. Cairns, Bob. "Dick Radatz." In: his *Pen Men: Baseball's Greatest Bullpen Stories told by the Men who Brought the Game Relief.* New York: St. Martin's Press, 1992. Pp. 246–255.

48221. Gentile, Richard H. "Richard Raymond 'Dick,' 'The Monster' Radatz." In: Vol. Q–Z of David L. Porter, ed. *Biographical Dictionary of American Sports: Baseball.* Rev. and enlarged ed. Westport, CT: Greenwood Press, 2000. Pp. 1241–1242.

48222. Greene, Lee. "Dick Radatz: Send for the Monster." In: Ray Robinson, ed. *Baseball Stars of 1964.* New York: Pyramid Books, 1964. Pp. 73–79.

48223. Hirshberg, Al. "Dick Radatz: Monster at Work." In: Ray Robinson, ed. *Baseball Stars of 1965.* New York: Pyramid Books, 1965. Pp. 134–139.

48224. _____. "'The Monster' of the Red Sox." *Sport,* XXXVI (October 1963), 34–37.

48225. Jares, Joe. "Look, It's 'The Monster.'" *Sports Illustrated,* XXII (April 9, 1960), 101–105.

48226. Kiersh, Edward. "Dick Radatz: Frankenstein Revisited." In: his *Where Have You Gone, Vince DiMaggio?* New York: Bantam Books, 1983. Pp. 221–225.

48227. Lautier, Jack. "Dick Radatz." In: his *Fenway Voices.* Camden, ME: Yankee Books, 1990. Pp. 93–96.

48228. Rumill, Ed. "Big Radatz Proves Massive Shoulders Hold Smart Head." *Baseball Digest,* XXIII (March 1964), 75–77.

48229. _____. "Radatz. Man-Mountain Reliever." *Baseball Digest,* XXII (May 1963), 73–76.

48230. Shapiro, Milton J. "Dick Radatz." In: his *Heroes of the Bullpen: Baseball's Greatest Relief Pitchers.* New York: Julian Messner, 1967. Pp. 143–158.

48231. Sparks, Barry. "Dick Radatz Still Stands Tall Among Relievers." *Baseball Digest,* XLIII (September 1984), 82–84.

48232. Stump, Al. "Dick Radatz: He's in Charge." *Sport,* XXXIX (June 1965), 64–69.

48233. Westcott, Rich. "Dick Radatz: 'The Monster'— a Nickname That Fit." In: his *Splendor on the Diamond: Interviews with 35 Stars of Baseball's Past.* Gainesville, FL: The University Press of Florida, 2000. Pp. 239–245.

Charles Gardner ("Charlie" or "Old Hoss") Radbourn ★
P. (B: Dec. 11, 1854, Rochester, NY–D: Feb. 5, 1897). Providence (NL), 1881–1885; Boston (NL), 1886–889, Boston (P.), 1890; Cincinnati (N.L), 1891. Remarks: Won 308 games and lost 191 in 11 seasons; his victories included 49 in 1883 and an incredible 60 in 1884, including two in one day, May 31, 1884; pitched no hitter, July 25, 1883; began by playing the outfield and second base for Buffalo (NL), 1880; as a batter, had 585 hits (nine homers) and 21 stolen bases in 653 games; lost an eye in an 1894 hunting accident and died of paresis; elected to National Base-

ball Hall of Fame in 1939, where his plaque reads: "Providence, Boston, and Cincinnati national league 1881–1891. Greatest of all 19th Century pitchers. Winning 1884 pennant for Providence, Radbourn pitched last 27 games of season, won 26. Won three straight in World Series."

48234. Allen, Lee, and Thomas Meany. "'Old Hoss' Radbourn." In: their *Kings of the Diamond.* New York: G.P. Putnam, 1965. Pp. 26–28.

48235. Bancroft, Frank G. "'Old Hoss' Radbourn." *Baseball Magazine,* I (July 1908), 12–15.

48237. Harshman, Jack E. "The Radbourne and Sweeney Saga." *The Baseball Research Journal,* XIX (1990), 7–9.

48238. Ivor-Campbell, Frederick. "Charles Gardner 'Charley,' 'Old Hoss' Radbourn." In: Vol. Q-Z of David L. Porter, ed. *Biographical Dictionary of American Sports: Baseball.* Rev. and enlarged ed. Westport, CT: Greenwood Press, 2000. Pp. 1242–1244.

48239. _____. "Charlie Radbourn." In: Frederick Ivor-Campbell, ed. *Baseball's First Stars.* Cleveland, OH: The Society for American Baseball Research, 1996. Pp. 131–132.

48240. _____. "1884: Old Hoss Radbourn and the Providence Grays." *The National Pastime,* IV (Spring 1985), 33–38. Reprinted in John Thorn, ed. *The National Pastime* (New York: Bell Publishing Co., 1987), pp. 156–169.

48241. Joyce, WL. "Never a Wild Pitch." *Yankee,* XXXVII (October 1973), 222–224.

48242. Kull, A. "Baseball's Greatest Pitcher." *American Heritage,* XXXVI (April-May 1985), 102–106+.

48243. Pierson, E. E. "'Old Hoss' Radbourn." *Baseball Magazine,* XIX (August 1917), 423–425.

48244. Radbourn, Charles ("Old Hoss"). "The Greatest Pitcher of the 19th Century." *Illinois Historical Journal,* LXXXI (Winter 1988), 255–268.

48245. Smith, Ira L. "Charles G. 'Old Hoss' Radbourn." In: his *Baseball's Famous Pitchers.* New York: A.S. Barnes, 1954. Pp. 3–8.

48246. Smith, Robert M. "'Old Hoss' Radbourn." In: his *Heroes of Baseball.* Cleveland: World Publishing Co., 1952. Pp. 136–141.

48247. Smith, Ron. "Hoss Radbourn." In: his *Heroes of the Hall: Baseball's Greatest Players.* New York: Contemporary Books, 2002. Pp. 374–375.

48248. Westcott, Rich. "Old Hoss Radbourn: Never Too Tired to Pitch." In: his *Winningest Pitchers: Baseball's 300-Game Winners.* Philadelphia, PA: Temple University Press, 2002. Pp. 25–32.

Raymond Allen ("Rip") Radcliff
OF. (B: Jan. 19, 1906, Kiowa, OK-D: May 23, 1962). Chicago (AL), 1934–1939; St. Louis (AL), 1940–1941; Detroit (AL), 1941–1943. Remarks: Obtained 1,267 hits (42 homers) and 40 stolen bases in 1,081 games in a decade; went 6-for-7 in one game, July 18, 1936; also played for Paris (Lone Star League), 1928; Muskogee (W.A.), 1929; Selma (Southeastern League), 1930; Shreveport (TL), 1931; St. Paul (AA), 1933 Chattanooga (SA, 1946; player- manager, Greensboro (Carolina League), 1948; became machinery salesman; died of heart attack.

48249. Spatz, Lyle. "Raymond Allen 'Rip' Radcliff." In: Vol. Q-Z of David L. Porter, ed. *Biographical Dictionary of American Sports: Baseball.* Rev. and enlarged ed. Westport, CT: Greenwood Press, 2000. Pp. 1244–1245. Mr. Spatz has also prepared a Radcliff profile as part of the SABR Biography Project; it appears online at < http://bioproj.sabr.org/bioproj.cfm?a=v&v=l&bid=711&pid=11581>.

48250. Ward, John J. "The Restless, Hustling Rookie:

Radcliff." *Baseball Magazine,* LVI (February 1936), 395–396.

Alexander ("Alec") Radcliffe
3B-SS. (B: July 26, 1905, Mobile, AL-D: July 18, 1983). Chicago Giants, 1927; Cole's American Giants, 1932–1935; New York Cubans, 1936; Chicago American Giants, 1936–1939; Palmer House All-Stars, 1940; Chicago American Giants, 1941–1944; Indianapolis Clowns, 1944–1945; Memphis Red Sox, 1946; Detroit Senators, 1947. Remarks: One of the Negro Leagues' top third sackers and Negro American League home run champion, 1944–1945; brother of Ted Radcliffe (below).

48251. Lester, Larry. "Alexander 'Alec' Radcliffe." In: Vol. Q-Z of David L. Porter, ed. *Biographical Dictionary of American Sports: Baseball.* Rev. and enlarged ed. Westport, CT: Greenwood Press, 2000. Pp. 1245–1246.

Ted Radcliffe see **Theodore Roosevelt ("Ted" or "Double Duty") Radcliffe**

Theodore Roosevelt ("Ted" or "Double Duty") Radcliffe
P-C-MGR. (B: July 7, 1902, Mobile, AL–D: August 11, 2005). Detroit Stars, 1928–1929, 1931; St. Louis Stars, 1930; Pittsburgh Homestead Grays, 1931, 1933, 1936, 1946; Pittsburgh Crawfords, 1932; Columbus Blue Birds, Cleveland Giants, and New York Black Yankees, 1933; Bismarck, 1934–1935; Chicago American Giants, 1934, 1941–1943, 1949–1950; Brooklyn Eagles, 1935; Cincinnati Tigers, 1936–1937; Memphis Red Sox, 1938–1939, 1941; Birmingham Black Barons, 1942–1946; Kansas City Monarchs, 1945; Harlem Globetrotters, 1947; Louisville Buckeyes, 1949. Remarks: Won 53 games and lost 33, having a lifetime .282 batting average; brother of Alec Radcliffe (above).

48252. Bamberger, Michael. "Where are They Now: Man of a Century, Double Duty Radcliffe." *Sports Illustrated,* XCII (July 15, 2002), 128–129, 131–132.

48253. Holway, John. "Ted 'Double Duty' Radcliffe." In: his *Voices from the Great Black Baseball Leagues.* New York: Da Capo Press, 1992. Pp. 168–186.

48254. Lester, Larry. "Theodore Roosevelt 'Ted,' 'Double Duty' Radcliffe." In: Vol. Q-Z of David L. Porter, ed. *Biographical Dictionary of American Sports: Baseball.* Rev. and enlarged ed. Westport, CT: Greenwood Press, 2000. Pp. 1246–1247.

48255. McNary, Kyle P. *Ted "Double Duty" Radcliffe: 36 Years of Pitching & Catching in Baseball's Negro Leagues.* Minneapolis, MN: McNary Pub., 1994. 277p.

48256. Wilson, Nick. "Ted Radcliffe." In: his *Voices from the Pastime: Oral Histories of Surviving Major Leaguers, Negro Leaguers, Cuban Leaguers, and Writers, 1920–1934.* Jefferson, NC: McFarland & Co., Inc., 2000. Pp. 116–124, 151.

Douglas Lee ("Doug" or "Rojo" or The Red Rooster) Rader
3B-1B-MGR. (B: July 30, 1944, Chicago, IL). Houston (NL), 1967–1975; San Diego (NL), 1976–1977; Toronto (AL), 1977. Remarks: Had 1,302 hits (155 homers) in 1,465 games in an 11-year playing career; had one grand-slam homer, May 17, 1971; coach, San Diego (NL), 1979; manager, Hawaii (PCL), 1980–1982; manager, Texas (AL), 1983–1984; Chicago (AL), 1986; California (AL), 1989–1991, winning 388 games and losing 417 (.482); also coach, Chicago (AL), 1986–1987, 1997, Oakland (AL), 1992, and Florida (NL), 1993–1994; scout, California (AL), 1989–1991.

48257. Berke, Art. "Doug Rader." In: his *Unsung Heroes of the Major Leagues.* New York: Random House, 1976. Pp. 24–37.

48258. Burns, Bob. "Doug Rader, Comic with a Golden Glove." *Life,* XXVII (June 16, 1972), 81–83.

48259. Fimrite, Ron. "He's Not Just a Wild and Crazy Guy." *Sports Illustrated,* LIX (August 8, 1983), 38–41+.

48260. Freeman, Don. "San Diego is Crowing About the Red Rooster." *Sport,* LXIII (September 1976), 57–58+.

48261. Gammons, Peter. "He's an Angel Now." *Sports Illustrated,* LXXI (August 7, 1989), 34–39.

48262. Kiersh, Edward. "Doug Rader: Going Bananas with the Grape Bubble Gum Kid." In: his *Where Have You Gone, Vince DiMaggio?* New York: Bantam Books, 1983. Pp. 47–53.

48263. Libby, Bill. "Doug Rader." In: his *Heroes of the Hot Corner.* New York: Watts, 1972. Pp. 95–96.

48264. Martin, Buddy. "Alias Lou D'Bardini, Alias Dominic Bulganzio, Alias the Red Rooster: Real Name Doug Rader, Occupation: Third Base, Avocation: Flake." *Sport,* LIV (September 1972), 76–77+.

48265. Pate, Steve. "A Good Old Boy Rides the Ranger." *Sport,* LXXIV (April 1983), 47+.

48266. _____. "He's Stranger Than His Rangers." *Sport,* LXXIV (September 1983), 73–74+.

48267. Peebles, Dick. "Doug Rader: A Throwback to the Old Days." *Baseball Digest,* XXVIII (June 1969), 82–85.

48268. Rosenberg, Victor. "Douglas Lee 'Doug,' 'The Red Rooster,' 'Rojo' Rader." In: Vol. Q-Z of David L. Porter, ed. *Biographical Dictionary of American Sports: Baseball.* Rev. and enlarged ed. Westport, CT: Greenwood Press, 2000. Pp. 1247–1248.

Brad William Radke

P. (B: Oct. 27, 1972, Eau Claire, WI). Minnesota (AL), 1995–. Remarks: Through 2004, has won 127 games and lost 118; had 12-game winning streak, May-August 1997; lost one game in 2002 ALCS.

48269. Eisenbath, Mike. "Why Twins' Brad Radke Blossomed into a No. 1 Starter." *Baseball Digest,* LVI (November 1997), 60–61.

Kenneth David ("Ken") Raffensberger

P. (B: August 8, 1917, York, PA-D: Nov. 9, 2002). St. Louis (NL), 1939; Chicago (NL), 1940–1941; Philadelphia (NL), 1943–1947; Cincinnati (NL), 1947–1954. Remarks: In 15 years, won 119 games and lost 154, with 16 "saves"; winning pitcher, 1944 All-Star Game; led NL in shutouts (six), 1949; also played for Cambridge (Eastern Shore League), 1937; Rochester (IL), 1938; Los Angeles (PCL), 1941–1943; and York (Piedmont League), 1954; manager, Lafayette (Evangeline League), 1956; manager, Burlington (3-I League), 1957.

48270. Spalding, John E. "Ken Raffensberger." In: his *Pacific Coast League Stars, Vol. II: Ninety Who Made It to the Majors, 1905–1957.* San Jose, CA: John E. Spalding, 1997. Pp. 133–135. A profile of Raffensberger has also been prepared by Warren Corbett as part of the SABR Biography Project; it can be found online at < http://bioproj. sabr.org/bioproj.cfm?a=v&v=l&bid=1082&pid=11594>.

48271. Sparks, Barry. "Ken Raffensberger: The Pitcher Who Baffled Stan Musial." *Baseball Digest,* LIV (May 1995), 59–60.

48272. Westcott, Rich. "Ken Raffensberger — Crafty Control Artist." In: his *Diamond Greats.* Westport, CT: Meckler Books, 1988. Pp. 322–327.

Timothy ("Tim" or "Rock") Raines

OF-2B. (B: Sept. 14, 1959, Sanford, FL). Montreal (NL), 1979–1990; Chicago (AL), 1991–1995; New York (AL), 1996–1998; Oakland (AL), 1999. Remarks: Had 2,561 hits (168 homers) and 808 stolen bases In 2,353 games in 21 seasons; NL stolen base champion, 1981–1984; NL batting champion, 1986; had grand slam homer, May 2, 1987; All-Star Game MPV award, 1987; hit for the cycle, Aug. 16, 1987; established modern major league record for most stolen bases in rookie season (71) in 1981 and holds record for highest stolen base percentage (84.7%); ranks fifth in MLB history with a career total of 808 stolen bases; minor league instructor, Florida (NL), 2002–2003; manager, Brevard County (Florida State League), 2004; coach, Chicago (AL), 2005–.

48273/48274. Bjarkman, Peter C. "Timothy 'Tim,' 'Rock' Raines." In: Vol. Q-Z of David L. Porter, ed. *Biographical Dictionary of American Sports: Baseball.* Rev. and enlarged ed. Westport, CT: Greenwood Press, 2000. Pp. 1248–1249.

48275. "Dawson and Raines: The Id and the Ego." In: Tom Barnidge, ed. *The Sporting News 1988 Baseball Yearbook.* St. Louis, MO: *The Sporting News,* 1988. Pp. 60–65.

48276. Fimrite, Ron. "Don't Knock the Rock!" *Sports Illustrated,* LX (June 25,1984), 44–56.

48277. Gammons, Peter. "Light Years Ahead of the Field." *Sports Illustrated,* LXV (July 28, 1986), 34–36.

48278. _____. "Who's the Fastest Man in Baseball?" *Sport,* LXXIII (May 1982), 44–45+.

48279. Hill, Bob. "Tim Raines: The Baserunner Who Rattles Enemy Defenses." *Baseball Digest,* XLV (July 1986), 48–49.

48280. Jasner, Phil "Tim Raines: The Majors' New Base-Stealing Sensation." *Baseball Digest,* XL (August 1981), 20–22.

48281. Kaplan, Jim. "Raines Really Pours it On." *Sports Illustrated,* LIV (May 11, 1981), 49–51.

48282. Kuenster, John. "Tim Raines Positioned to Produce Big Runs for White Sox." *Baseball Digest,* L (June 1991), 17–19.

48283. Ladewski, Paul. "Tim Raines: Interview." *Inside Sports,* IX (January 1987), 72+.

48284. Lane, Jon. "Just Happy to Be Here." *Yankees Magazine,* XIX (August 1998), 22–29.

48285. Leerhsen, L. "The Thief of Montreal." *Newsweek,* XCVIII (September 21, 1981), 77+.

48286. McRae, Ed. "Thief: Tim Raines of the Expos Steals Bases More Brilliantly Than Anyone Else in Baseball." *Today Magazine,* (August 14, 1982), 10–12.

48287. Nash, Bruce and Allan Zullo. "Tim Raines." In: their *Little Big Leaguers: Amazing Boyhood Stories of Today's Baseball Stars.* New York: Little Simon, 1990. Pp. 54–55.

48288. Quinn, Hal. "Like a Thief in the Night." *Macleans,* XCIV (June 9, 1981), 38+.

48289. Raines, Tim, as told to George Vass. "The Game I'll Never Forget." *Baseball Digest,* XLIX (November 1990), 37–38.

48290. Whitford, David. "The Last Laugh." *Sport,* LXXVIII (December 1987), 16–18+.

Manuel ("Manny") Ramirez

OF. (B: Manuel Aristides Ramirez Onelcida, May 30, 1972 in Santo Domingo, D.R.). Cleveland (AL), 1993–2000; Boston (AL), 2001–. Remarks: Though 2004, has had 1,760 hits (390 homers) and 33 stolen bases in 1,535 games; had two homers in 1995 ALCS and one homer in 1995 World Series; had grand-slam homers in games on May 17 and Aug. 20, 1996 and June 21, 1997; had one homer in 1997 ALCS and two homers in 1997 World Series; had four consecutive homers in four straight ABs, Sept. 16–17, 1998; had two homers in 1998 ALCS; AL RBI champion, 1999; first $20 million per year player, Dec. 11, 2000; AL batting champion, 2002; had two homers in

2003 ALCS; AL home run champion, 2004; had one homer in 2004 World Series; World Series MVP Award, 2004; also played for Burlington (Appalachian League), Kinston (Carolina League), Akron-Canton (E.L), and Charlotte (IL).

48291. Bechtel, Michael. "Manny of the Year." *Sports Illustrated,* LXXXIX (September 28, 1999), 100–101.

48292. Callahan, Gerry. "Son of Sammy." *Sports Illustrated,* XC (April 5, 1999), 62–66.

48293. Gleisser, Benjamin. "Rookie Report: Manny Ramirez." *Beckett Baseball Card Monthly,* XI, no. 107 (February 1994), 126–127.

48294. Greenberg, Keith Elliot. "Indians' Ramirez Comes Home to Roots." *USA Today Baseball Weekly,* V (August 30, 1995), 8–9.

48295. Hoynes, Paul. "Manny Ramirez: Maturing of a Big League Star." *Baseball Digest,* LVIII (April 1999), 58–63.

48296. Ingraham, Jim. "Manny Who?" *Crain's Cleveland Business,* XXII (March 19, 2001), 110–111.

48297. Le Batard, Dan. "Real Simple." *ESPN: The Magazine,* IV (March 5, 2001), 64–69.

48298. McCarver, Tim, with Danny Peary. "Manny Ramirez." In: his *The Perfect Season: Why 1998 Was Baseball's Greatest Year.* New York: Villard Books, 1999. Pp. 138–141.

48299. Nightengale, Bob. "Ramirez: Quiet, Quirky, Talented." *USA Today Baseball Weekly,* IX (May 12, 1999), 6–7.

48300. Ocker, Sheldon. "Manny Happy Returns." *Beckett Focus on Future Stars,* III, no. 25 (May 1993), 16–17.

48301. Pierce, Charles P. "A Cut Above." *Sports Illustrated,* CI (July 5, 2004), 56–60, 63–65.

48302. Schwarz, Alan. "RBI Machine." *Sports Illustrated for Kids,* XI (September 1999), 66–67.

48303. Scott, David. "Silent but Deadly: Manny Ramirez." *Sport,* XCI (August 2000, 40–43.

48304. Stern, Kate. "Manny Ramiriz." *Current Biography,* LXIII (June 2002), 72–76. Reprinted in *Current Biography Yearbook, 2002.* New York: H. W. Wilson, 2002. Pp. 478–480.

48305. Suttell, Scott. "Manny's Many Virtues." *Crain's Cleveland Business,* XX (March 29, 1999), T3–T4.

48306. Vascellaro, Charlie. *Manny Ramirez.* Latinos in Baseball Series. Childs, MD: Mitchell Lane Publishers, 2000. 64p.

48307. Verducci, Tom. "He's the Manny: In the Battle for the Last Playoff Spot, the Indians Rely on Manny Ramirez, Who Talks Softly but Carries a Big Bat." *Sports Illustrated,* XCIII (October 2, 2000), 112–114, 116.

48308. Ziants, Steve. "Speaking in Volumes: Indians' Manny Ramirez Lets Bat Do His Talking." *Baseball Digest,* LVIII (October 1999), 42–45.

Rafael Emilio Ramirez
SS. (B: Feb. 18, 1959, San 'Pedro de Macoris, Dominican Republic). Atlanta (NL), 1980–1987; Houston (NL), 1988–1992. Remarks: Had 1,432 hits (53 homers) and 112 stolen bases in 1,539 games in 13 years; sixth MLB player to have 30 homers and 30 stolen bases in same year, 1983; had seven RBIs in one game, Aug. 29, 1989; scout, Houston (NL), 1993–.

48309. Korch, Bob. "Move Over Davey [Lopes]." In: Wayne Minshew, ed. *Braves Illustrated '84.* Atlanta, GA: Public Relations Department, Atlanta Braves, 1984. Pp. 14–16.

Pedro Guerra ("Pete") Ramos
P. (B: April 29,1935, Pinar del Rio, Cuba). Washington

(A.L) and Minnesota (A.I.), 1955–1961; Cleveland (AL), 1962–1994; New York (AL), 1964–1966; Philadelphia (NL), 1967; Pittsburgh (NL) and Cincinnati (NL), 1969; Washington (AL), 1970. Remarks: Hurled 117 victories, 160 defeats, and 55 "saves" in 15 years; had a career total of 15 homers, including one grand-slam, (May 30, 1962) and two others in one game (July 31, 1963); named to Cuban Baseball Hall of Fame, 1981.

48310. Addie, Bob. "Everybody Wants Ramos." *Sport,* XXVIII (September 1969), 42–43+.

48311. _____. "Pete Ramos, the Senators' Pistol Pedro." *Baseball Digest,* XIX (March 1960), 65+.

48312. Forker, Dom. "Pedro Ramos." In: his *Sweet Seasons: Recollections of the 55–64 New York Yankees.* Dallas, TX: Taylor Publishing Co., 1989. Pp. 130–133.

48313. Jacobson, Steve. "The Man Who Won the Pennant for the Yankees." *Sport,* XXXIX (January 1965), 42–45.

48314. Kiersh, Edward. "Pedro Ramos: Behind Bars with the Cocaine Cowboy." In: his *Where Have You Gone, Vince DiMaggio?* New York: Bantam Books, 1983. Pp. 212–220.

48315. Shannon, Mike. "Pedro Ramos." In: his *Tales from the Ballpark: More of the Greatest True Baseball Stories Ever Told.* Lincolnwood, IL: Contemporary Books, 1999. Pp. 167–168.

Thomas A. ("Toad" or "Tode") Ramsey
P. (B: Aug. 8, 1864, Indianapolis, IN-D: March 27, 1906). Louisville (AA), 1895–1889; St. Louis (AA), 1889–1890. Remarks: The game's first knuckleballer unfortunately drank himself out of the major leagues after winning 114 games and losing 124 in six seasons; struck out 499 batters in 1886, second highest MLB total ever; became minor league umpire and then bricklayer before dying of pneumonia.

48316. Cava, Peter J. "Thomas A. 'Toad,' 'Tode' Ramsey." In: Vol. Q-Z of David L. Porter, ed. *Biographical Dictionary of American Sports: Baseball.* Rev. and enlarged ed. Westport, CT: Greenwood Press, 2000. Pp. 1249–1250.

48317. Smith, Robert M. "'Toad' Ramsey." In: his *Heroes of Baseball.* Cleveland, OH: World Publishing Co., 1952. Pp. 146–151.

Joseph Gregory ("Joe" or "Joe the Joker") Randa
3B. (B: Dec. 18, 1969, Milwaukee, WI). Kansas City (AL), 1995–1996; Pittsburgh (NL), 1997; Detroit (AL), 1998; Kansas City (AL), 1998–. Remarks: Through 2004, has had 1,335 hits (102 homers) and 42 stolen bases in 1,283 games; had five hits in a game thrice, June 9 and July 9, 1999 and May 12, 2001.

48318. Hunt, John. "Wake Up To Those Sleeper Possibilities: Where to Find Those Hidden Randas." *USA Today Baseball Weekly,* VII (March 18, 1998), 24–25.

Maxine Kline Randall
P. (B: Sept. 16, 1929, North Adams, MI). Fort Wayne Daisies (All American Girls Professional Baseball League), 1948–1954. Remarks: Won 116 games and lost 65; had two no-hitters, June 12, 1949 and June 20, 1954; also played for Bill Allington's All-Americans, 1955–1958.

48319. Clark, Dennis S. "Maxine Kline Randall." In: Vol. Q-Z of David L. Porter, ed. *Biographical Dictionary of American Sports: Baseball.* Rev. and enlarged ed. Westport, CT: Greenwood Press, 2000. Pp. 1250–1251.

Leonard Shenoff ("Lenny") Randle
3B-2B. (B: Feb. 12, 1949, Long Beach, CA). Washington (AL) and Texas (AL), 1971–1976; New York (NL), 1977–1978; New York (AL), 1979; Chicago (NL), 1980;

Seattle (AL), 1981. Remarks Obtained 1,008 hits (27 homers) and 154 stolen bases in 1,108 games in an 11-year big league career; remembered for attacking, in a fit of pique, and hospitalizing his manager, Frank Lucchesi, on March 28, 1977.

48320. Blount, Roy, Jr. "Fighting Side of Baseball." *Esquire,* LXXXVIII (July 1977), 30+.

48321. Hannon, Kent. "One Mindless Moment." *Sports Illustrated,* XLVI (June 6, 1977), 44+.

William Larry ("Willie") Randolph, Jr.
2B-MGR. (B: July 6, 1954, Holly Hill, SC). Pittsburgh (NL), 1974; New York (AL), 1976–1988; Los Angeles (NL), 1989–1990; Oakland (AL), 1990; Milwaukee (AL), 1991); New York (NL), 1992. Remarks: Had 2,210 hits (54 homers) and 271 stolen bases in 2,202 games in 19 years; scored winning run in 1977 World Series; led AL in walks, 1980; asst. GM, New York (AL), 1993; coach, New York (AL), 1994–2004; manager, New York (NL), 2005–.

48322. Brown, Robert J. "William Larry 'Willie' Randolph, Jr." In: Vol. Q–Z of David L. Porter, ed. *Biographical Dictionary of American Sports: Baseball.* Rev. and enlarged ed. Westport, CT: Greenwood Press, 2000. Pp. 1251–1252.

48323. Gallagher, Mark. "Willie Randolph." In: his *50 Years of Yankee All-Stars.* New York: Leisure Press, 1984. Pp. 154–156.

48324. McMillan, Ken. "Willie Randolph." In: his *Tales from the Yankee Dugout: A Collection of the Greatest Yankee Stories Ever Told.* Champaign, IL: Sports Publishing, Inc., 2001. Pp. 144–145.

48325. Randolph, Willie, as told to George Vass. "The Game I'll Never Forget." *Baseball Digest,* XLVIII (October 1989), 43–45.

48326. Thorn, John. "Willie Randolph: 'The Kid from Brooklyn.'" In: his *Baseball's Dream Team.* New York: Ace Tempo Books, 1982. Pp. 28–39.

48327. "Willie Randolph: A True Professional." *Yankees Magazine,* IV (April 12, 1984), 8–12.

Willie Randolph *see* **William Larry ("Willie") Randolph, Jr.**

Goldie Rapp *see* **Joseph Aloysius ("Goldie") Rapp**

Joseph Aloysius ("Goldie") Rapp
3B. (B: Feb. 6, 1892, Cincinnati, OH-D: July 1, 1966). New York (NL), 1921, Philadelphia (NL), 1921–1923. Remarks: In three seasons, had 269 hits (two homers) and 16 stolen bases in 276 games.

48328. Selko, Jamie. "The Strange Case of Rapp's Missing Raps: Something was Not Right About Goldie Rapp's Rookie Hitting Streaks." *The Baseball Research Journal,* XXIV (1995), 134–136.

Victor John Angelo ("Vic" or "The Springfield Rifle") Raschi
P-COACH. (B: March 28, 1919, West Springfield, MA-D: Oct. 14, 1988). New York (AL), 1946–1953, St. Louis (NL), 1954–1955; Kansas City (AL), 1955. Remarks: Hurled 132 victories (including 21 in 1950–51–52) and had 66 defeats in a decade; had seven RBI's in one game, (Aug. 4, 1953), a record for pitchers which lasted until broken by Tony Cloninger (q.v.) in 1966; surrendered the first big league homer hit by Henry ("Hank") Aaron (q.v.), April 23, 1954; baseball coach and high school teacher, Genesco, New York, 1960's.

48329. Bloodgood, Clifford. "Victor — a Good Name for Raschi." *Baseball Magazine,* LXXXIII (June 1949), 235–237.

48330. Broeg, Bob. "Raschi is Right for the Cards." *Sport,* XVII (August 1954), 42–43.

48331. Daley, Arthur. "The Strange Vic Raschi Deal." *Baseball Digest,* XIII (May 1954), 88–92.

48332. Epstein, Ben. "Right and Wrong on Raschi." *Baseball Digest,* VII (August 1948), 75–79.

48333. Forker, Dom. "Vic Raschi." In: his *The Men of Autumn.* Dallas, TX: Taylor Publishing Co., 1989. Pp. 12–22.

48334. Gallagher, Mark. "Vic Raschi." In: his *50 Years of Yankee All-Stars.* New York: Leisure Press, 1984. Pp. 157–159.

48335. Gittleman, Sol. "A Study in Synergy." *The Baseball Research Journal,* XXII (1993), 78–79.

48336. Gross, Milton. "Winning Pitcher Vic Raschi." *Look,* XIII (August 30, 1949), 68–69.

48337. Honig, Donald. "Vic Raschi." In: his *Baseball Between the Lines: Baseball in the Forties and Fifties as Told by the Men Who Played It.* Lincoln, NE: University of Nebraska Press, 1976. Pp. 171–180.

48338. McClure, Arthur F. "Victor John Angelo 'Vic,' 'The Springfield Rifle' Raschi." In: Vol. Q–Z of David L. Porter, ed. *Biographical Dictionary of American Sports: Baseball.* Rev. and enlarged ed. Westport, CT: Greenwood Press, 2000. Pp. 1252–1254.

48339. Meany, Thomas. "Raschi: The Springfield Rifle." *Baseball Digest,* XI (June 1952), 82–86.

48340. _____. "Vic Raschi: The Springfield Rifle." In: his *Baseball's Greatest Pitchers.* New York: A.S. Barnes, 1951. Pp. 227–232.

48341. _____. "Vic Raschi: The Springfield Rifle." In: his *The Magnificent Yankees.* New York: A. S. Barnes, 1952. Pp. 66–74.

48342. Newcombe, Jack. "The Yankees' Dependable Raschi." *Sport,* XI (October 1951), 24–29.

48343. Povich, Shirley. "How's Raschi Doing?" *Baseball Digest,* XI (August 1952), 11–13.

48344. Raschi, Victor J.A. "Pitching Is a Lonesome Business." *Sport,* XXIV (July 1957), 26–27+.

48345. Schultz, Randy. "Vic Raschi: He Was a 'Clutch Pitcher' for the Yankees." *Baseball Digest,* XL (July 1981), 46–49.

48346. Stern, Chris. "Vic Raschi." In: his *Where Have They Gone?* New York: Tempo Books, 1979. Pp. 62–63.

Dennis Lee Rasmussen
P. (B: April 18, 1959, Los Angeles, CA). San Diego (NL), 1983; New York (A.L), 1984–1987; Cincinnati (NL), 1987–1988; San Diego (NL), 1988–1991; Chicago (NL), 1992; Kansas City (AL), 1992–1995. Remarks: In 12 years, won 99 games and lost 77; at 6'7", one of MLB's tallest pitchers.

48347. Nash, Bruce and Allan Zullo. "Dennis Rasmussen." In: their *Little Big Leaguers: Amazing Boyhood Stories of Today's Baseball Stars.* New York: Little Simon, 1990. Pp. 68–69.

Maurice Charles ("Morrie") Rath
2B. (B: Dec. 25, 1887, Mobeetie, TX-D: Nov. 18, 1945). Philadelphia (AL), 1909–1910; Cleveland (AL), 1910; Chicago (AL), 1912–1913; Cincinnati (NL), 1919–1920. Remarks: Had 521 hits (four homers) and 82 stolen bases in 563 games in six big league years; set modern NL record with 13 assists in a 15-inning game, Aug. 26, 1919; hit while leading off in 1919 World Series, a signal from the Black Sox to the gamblers that the fix was on, but scored five runs in that dark classic.

48348. Lane, Ferdinand C. "How Rath the Discard Equaled [Eddie] Collins the Star." *Baseball Magazine,* XXIV (December 1919), 461–463.

Morrie Rath *see* **Maurice Charles ("Morrie") Rath**

Jimmy Rattlesnake
P. (B: 1909, Hobbema Reserve, Alberta, Canada–D: 1972). Well-known amateur baseball player after whom a trophy was named that is now presented annually to Team Canada's senior baseball team.
48349. Zeman, Brenda. "The Smilin' Rattler." In: William Humber and John St. James, eds. *All I Thought About was Baseball: Writings on a Canadian Pastime.* Toronto and Buffalo, NY: University of Toronto Press, 1996. Pp. 327–331.
James France ("Jim" or "String") Ray
P. (B: Dec. 1, 1944, Rock Hill, SC). Houston (NL), 1965–1973; Detroit (AL), 1974. Remarks: Won 43 games and lost 30, with 25 "saves," in nine big league years; won four consecutive games, April–May, 1972.
48350. Heiling, Joe. "Jim Ray: Best Relief Pitcher in the Majors?" *Baseball Digest,* XXXI (August 1972), 41–44.
John Cornelius ("Johnny") Ray
2B-OF. (B: March 1, 1957 in Chouteau, OK). Pittsburgh (NL), 1981–1987; California (AL), 1987–1990; Jakult Swallows (Japan League), 1991–1992. Remarks: In a decade, obtained 1,502 hits (53 homers) and 80 stolen bases in 1,353 U.S. big league games; drove in five runs in one inning, May 15, 1982; NL Rookie of the Year Award, 1982 (first Pirate so honored); led NL in doubles, 1982–1983.
48351. Hertzel, Bob. "When It Comes to Contact Hitters, Look to Johnny Ray." *Baseball Digest,* XLV (June 1986), 23–24.
48352. Porter, David L. "John Cornelius 'Johnny' Ray." In: Vol. Q–Z of David L. Porter, ed. *Biographical Dictionary of American Sports: Baseball.* Rev. and enlarged ed. Westport, CT: Greenwood Press, 2000. P. 1254.
Arthur Lawrence ("Bugs") Raymond
P. (B: Feb. 24, 1882, Chicago, IL–D: Sept. 7, 1912.). Detroit (AL), 1904; St. Louis (NL), 1907–1908; New York (NL), 1909–1911. Remarks: Won 44 games and lost 54 in a six-year MLB career; struggled with alcohol throughout his career; hurling for Charleston (South Atlantic League), pitched no-hitters in morning and afternoon of same day, July 4, 1905; hard drinker, found dead of a brain hemorrhage at Chicago's Hotel Valley two days after suffering a skull fracture in a barroom fight.
48353. Boddington, Clem. "Bugs: The Legendary Mr. Raymond." In: Charles Einstein, ed. *The Second Fireside Book of Baseball.* New York: Simon and Schuster, 1958. Pp. 32–35.
48354. Kavanagh, Jack. "Bugs Raymond." *The Baseball Research Journal,* XXVI (1997), 125–127.
48355. Lesemann, Charles. "The Heroics of 'Bugs' Raymond." *Sport,* XXIV (July 1957), 72–81.
48356. Salsinger, H. G. "'Bugs' Raymond and the Banana Ball." *Baseball Digest,* XIV (October 1955), 11–13.
48357. Watts, A. E. and H. J. Casey. "Arthur L. (Bugs) Raymond." *Baseball Magazine,* IV (March 1910), 67–70.
Bugs Raymond *see* **Arthur Lawrence ("Bugs") Raymond**
Claude Raymond *see* **Joseph Claude Marc ("Frenchy") Raymond**
David Raymond
MASCOT. (B: 1957). Remarks: Phillie Phanatic, 1978–1994; later, Founder & Director of Fun and Games, Acme Mascots.
48358. McCarthy, Gayle. "Former Phanatic Sports New Image." *Delaware Messenger,* III (Spring 1994), 17–18.
48359. Robinson, M. "David Raymond." *Sport Marketing Quarterly,* XII (June 2003), 69–71.

Frenchy Raymond *see* **Jean Claude Marc ("Frenchy") Raymond**
Jean Claude Marc ("Frenchy") Raymond
P-BROADCASTER. (B: May 7, 1937, St. Jean, Canada). Chicago (AL), 1959; Milwaukee (NL), 1961–1963; Houston (NL), 1964–1967; Atlanta (NL), 1967–1969; Montreal (NL), 1969–1971. Remarks: French-speaking relief specialist who had 46 wins, 53 defeats, and 83 "saves" in a dozen summer campaigns; first Canadian-born player to play for a Canadian major league team; broadcaster, Montreal (NL), 1973–1990; coach, Montreal (NL), 2002–2004; elected to Canadian Baseball Hall of Fame, 1984.
48360. Herskowitz, Mickey. "Claude Raymond: Relief with a French Accent." *Baseball Digest,* XXIII (August 1964), 21–24.
48361. Kendall, Brian. "August 19, 1969: Claude Raymond—Return of the Prodigal Son." In: his *Great Moments in Canadian Baseball.* Toronto, Ont.: Lester Publishing, 1995. Chapter 11.
48362. Shearon, Jim. "Claude Raymond, The Best From Quebec." In: his *Canada's Baseball Legends.* Kanata, Ontario: Malin Head Press, 1994. Pp. 169–172.
48363. Turner, Dan. "Claude Raymond." In: his *Heroes, Bums and Ordinary Men: Profiles In Canadian Baseball.* Toronto: Doubleday Canada Ltd., 1988. Pp. 247–256.
Alfred James ("Al") Reach
2B-OF-MGR-EXEC. (B: May 25, 1840, London, England–D: Jan. 14, 1928). Brooklyn Eckfords, 1855–1864; Philadelphia Athletics, 1865–1870; Philadelphia (N.A.), 1871–1875. Remarks: Had 97 hits in 80 N.A. games; manager, Philadelphia (N.A.), 1874–1875, winning 83 games and losing 42; investor, Philadelphia (NL), 1876–1903; interim manager, Philadelphia (NL), 1890, winning four games, but losing seven; founded A. J. Reach & Company cigar, later sporting goods company, in 1880, publishing Reach's Official Base Ball Guide after 1883; concern taken over by Spalding Bros. in 1889, with Reach selling his interest in 1892; member of 1907–1908 National Commission which determined baseball started by Abner Doubleday (q.v.).
48364. Casway, Jerrold. "Alfred James Reach." In: John A. Garrity and Marsh C. Carries, eds. *American National Biography.* 24 vols. New York: Oxford University Press, 1999. XVIII, 225–226.
48365. Middleton, Charles R. "Alfred James 'Al' Reach." In: Vol. Q–Z of David L. Porter, ed. *Biographical Dictionary of American Sports: Baseball.* Rev. and enlarged ed. Westport, CT: Greenwood Press, 2000. Pp. 1254–1256.
Randy Max Ready
3B-OF. (B: Jan. 8, 1960, Fremont, CA). Milwaukee (AL), 1983–1986; San Diego (NL), 1986–1989; Philadelphia (NL), 1989–1991; Oakland (AL), 1992; Montreal (NL), 1993; Philadelphia (NL), 1994–1995; Chiba Lotte Marines (Japan League), 1996 Remarks: In 13 seasons, had 547 hits (40 homers) and 27 stolen bases in 777 games; also played for Vancouver (PCL), 1983–1986; manager, Oneonta (New York-Penn League), 2002–2003; manager, Fort Wayne (Midwest League), 2004–.
48366. Plaschke, Bill. "Ready Now Family's Rock." In: Tom Barnidge, ed. *Best Sports Stories of 1989.* St. Louis, MO: *The Sporting News,* 1989. Pp. 71–77.
Ronald Wilson ("Dutch") Reagan
BROADCASTER-ACTOR-POLITICIAN-PRESIDENT. (B: Feb. 6, 1911, Tampico, IL). Remarks: Iowa radio sports broadcaster, 1932–1937 (broadcast Cubs games, 1933–1936); actor, 1937–1964; governor of Cali-

fornia, 1967–1974; radio commentator/newspaper columnist, 1975–1980; president of the United States, 1981–1989.

48367. Morris, Edmund. *Dutch: A Memoir of Ronald Reagan.* New York: Random House, 1999. 874p.

48368. Reagan, Ronald W. *An American Life.* New York: Simon & Schuster, 1990. 748p.

48369. Roberts, James C. "'Dutch' and the Game: Ronald Reagan Described It, Told Stories About It, and Revered It." *The National Pastime,* XX (2000), 77–81.

48370. Sloane, Irving J. *Ronald W. Reagan, 1911–: Chronology, Documents, Bibliographical Aids.* Presidential Chronology Series, v. 40. Dobbs Ferry, NY: Oceana Publications, 1990. 282p.

48371. Verdi, Bob. "Reagan a Cubs Fan." In: Bob Verdi. *The Bob Verdi Collection.* Dallas, TX: Taylor Publishing Co., 1988. Pp. 239–241.

48372. Will, George F. "The Answer Is: Ronald Reagan — The Question Is: Who is the Only Person to Have Held America's Two Most Difficult Jobs?." In: his *Bunts: Curt Flood, Camden Yards, Pete Rose and Other Reflections on Baseball.* New York: Touchstone Books, 1998. Pp. 43–45.

Beans Reardon *see* **John E. ("Beans") Reardon**

Jeffrey James ("Jeff" or "The Terminator") Reardon
P. (B: Oct. 1, 1955, Pittsfield, MA). New York (NL), 1979–1981; Montreal (NL), 1981–1986; Minnesota (AL), 1987–1989; Boston (AL), 1990–1992; Atlanta (NL), 1992; Cincinnati (NL), 1993; New York (AL), 1994. Remarks: Hurled 73 victories and 77 defeats, with 367 "saves," in 15 years; won one game and lost one in 1987 ALCS; won one game of 1992 NLCS, but lost one game of 1992 World Series; first reliever to record 350 "saves" and first pitcher ever to save 40 games in a season in both big leagues.

48373. Holtzman, Jerome. "Twins' Jeff Reardon Makes His Mark as Top Receiver." *Baseball Digest,* XLVI (September 1987), 70–72.

48374. Kapan, Jim. "Saving Face in Montreal." *Sports Illustrated,* LXII (June 24, 1985), 58–60.

48375. "Knuckling Down." *Reds Report,* VI (May 1993), 7–8.

48376. Newman, Howie. "Jeff Reardon: Montreal's Budding Bullpen Star." *Baseball Digest,* XLI (February 1982), 52–55.

48377. Reardon, Jeff, as told to George Vass. "The Game I'll Never Forget." *Baseball Digest,* LIII (October 1994), 69–73.

48378. Rushin, Steve. "The Pen Ultimate." *Sports Illustrated,* LXXVI (June 8, 1992), 54–57.

48379. Wendel, Tim. "Fingers-Snapping: Reardon on Verge of Save Record." *USA Today Baseball Weekly,* II (May 27, 1992), 4–5.

John Edward ("Jack" or "Beans") Reardon
UMP. (B: Nov. 23, 1897, Taunton, MD-D: July 11, 1984). Remarks: NL arbiter, 1926–1949; colorful umpire, who was behind the plate for Babe Ruth's 714th homer and also appeared in many of the motion pictures of his friend, the actress Mae West.

48380. "Beans." *Referee,* VII (November 1982), 56–57.

48381. Gerlach, Larry R. "Beans Reardon." In: his *The Men in Blue: Conversations with Umpires.* New York: Viking Press, 1980. Pp. 3–26. Reprinted by the University of Nebraska Press in 1994.

48382. _____. "John Edward 'Jack,' 'Beans' Reardon." In: Vol. Q-Z of David L. Porter, ed. *Biographical Dictionary of American Sports: Baseball.* Rev. and enlarged ed. Westport, CT: Greenwood Press, 2000. Pp. 1257–1258.

48383. Gould, James M. "A Man in a Blue Suit." *Baseball Magazine,* XXXVII (July 1941), 347–348, 382.

Dick ("Cannonball") Redding *see* **Richard ("Dick" or "Cannonball Dick") Redding**

Richard ("Dick" or "Cannonball Dick") Redding
P-MGR. (B: 1891, Atlanta, GA-D: 1948). Philadelphia Giants, 1911, New York Lincoln Giants, 1911–1916; Brooklyn Royal Giants, 1916, 1918, 1923–1932, 1938); Chicago American Giants, 1917–1918; Atlantic City Bacharachs, 1919–1921; New York Bacharachs, 1922. Remarks: Won at least 71 games, while losing about 22; credited with 30 no-hitters and development of the no-windup delivery; manager New York Bacharachs, 1921 and Brooklyn Royal Giants, 1927–1932.

48384. Evers, John L. "Richard 'Dick,' 'Cannonball Dick' Redding." In: Vol. Q-Z of David L. Porter, ed. *Biographical Dictionary of American Sports: Baseball.* Rev. and enlarged ed. Westport, CT: Greenwood Press, 2000. Pp. 1258–1259.

48385. Holway, John B. "Dick Redding." In: John A. Garrity and Marsh C. Carries, eds. *American National Biography.* 24 vols. New York: Oxford University Press, 1999. XVIII, 245–246.

48386. _____. *Smokey Joe [Wood] and the Cannonball.* Washington, DC: Capital Press, 1983. 38p.

48387. _____. "The Cannonball." *The Baseball Research Journal,* IX (1980), 99–103.

Jeffrey Scott ("Jeff") Reed
C. (B: Nov. 12, 1962, Joliet, IL). Minnesota (AL), 1984–1986; Montreal (NL), 1987–1988; Cincinnati (NL), 1988–1992; San Francisco (NL), 1993–1995; Colorado (NL), 1996–1999; Chicago (NL), 1999–2000. Remarks: In 17 seasons, had 774 hits (61 homers) and seven stolen bases in 1,234 games; left-handed backstop remembered for three errors made in one inning of Game Five of 1987 NLCS.

48388. Frommer, Harvey and Frederick J. "Jeff Reed." In: their *Growing Up Baseball: An Oral History.* Dallas, TX: Taylor Publishing Co., 2001. Pp. 192–193.

Ronald Lee ("Ron") Reed
P. (B. Nov. 2, 1942, La Porte, IN). Atlanta (NL), 1966–1975; St. Louis (NL), 1975; Philadelphia (NL), 1976–1983; Chicago (AL), 1984. Remarks: Won 146 games and last 140, with 103 "saves," in 19 seasons; had played pro basketball with the Detroit Pistons, 1965 and 1967; won game in which Hank Aaron (q.v.) hit his record 715th homer, April 8, 1984; lost Game Two of 1980 NLCS but saved Game Two of 1980 World Series; named to Indiana Baseball Hall of Fame, 1990.

48389. Ballew, Bill. "Ron Reed: Former Two-Star Athlete Had Two Baseball Careers." *Sports Collector's Digest,* XXI (May 13, 1994), 148–149.

48390. Gagnon, Richard ("Cappy"). "Ronald Lee 'Ron' Lee." In: Vol. Q-Z of David L. Porter, ed. *Biographical Dictionary of American Sports: Baseball.* Rev. and enlarged ed. Westport, CT: Greenwood Press, 2000. Pp. 1259–1260.

48391. Prato, Lou. "Ron Reed: He'll Fight You Any Way He Can." *Sport,* XLVI (September 1968), 36–39.

48392. Reed, Ron, as told to George Vass. "The Game I'll Never Forget." *Baseball Digest,* XLII (November 1983), 73–76.

48393. Rumill, Ed. "Reed Sends His Stock Uphill by Pitching Downhill." *Baseball Digest,* XXVII (August 1968), 47–50.

Calvin ("Pokey") Reese, Jr.
2B-SS. (B: June 10, 1973, Columbia, SC). Cincinnati (NL), 1997–2001; Pittsburgh (NL), 2002–2003; Boston (AL), 2004; Seattle (AL), 2005–. Remarks: Through

2004, has had 704 hits (44 homers) and 144 stolen bases in 856 games; went 5-for-6 in one game, June 22, 1999; had five hits in one game, April 20,2000; had two homers in one game, May 8, 2004.

48394. Bamberger, Michael. "Fast and Loose: Even with Ken Griffey, Jr. as the Potential Prize, the Reds Wouldn't Part with Pokey Reese, Who's Loaded with Talented and Burdened by a Long History of Family Dysfunction." *Sports Illustrated,* XCII (June 12, 2000), 88–92, 94, 96, 99, 102, 104.

48395. Shannon, Mike. "Pokey Reese." In: his *Tales from the Ballpark: More of the Greatest True Baseball Stories Ever Told.* Lincolnwood, IL: Contemporary Books, 1999. Pp. 169–170.

Harold Henry ("Pee Wee" or "The Little Colonel") Reese★

SS-BROADCASTER (B: July 23, 1919, Ekron, KY-D: Aug. 14, 1999). Louisville (AA), 1937–1939; Brooklyn (NL), 1940–1942, 1946–1957; Los Angeles (NL), 1958. Remarks: Nickname came from a common type of marble called a "pee-wee"; obtained 2,170 hits (126 homers) and 232 stolen bases In 2,146 games in 16 big league seasons; had 19-game hitting streak, 1951; NL stolen base champion, 1952; recorded last out of 1955 World Series; coach, Los Angeles (NL), 1959; radio broadcaster, Cincinnati (NL), 1970; died of lung cancer; elected to National Baseball Hall of Fame in 1984, where his plaque reads: "Shortstop and captain of great Dodger teams of 1940's and 50's. Intangible qualities of subtle leadership on and off field, competitive fire and professional pride complemented dependable glove, reliable baserunning and clutch-hitting as significant factors in Dodger pennants. Instrumental in easing acceptance of Jackie Robinson, as baseball's first Black performer."

48396. Allen, Ethan. "General Infield Defense." *Scholastic Coach,* XXII (March 1953), 12–115. Examples illustrated by Reese.

48397. Allen, Maury. "Pee Wee Reese (1940–1958)." In: his *Baseball's 100.* New York: Galahad Books, 1981. Pp. 241–243.

48398. _____. "Pee Wee Stands Tall in the Hall of Fame." *Baseball Digest,* XLIV (January 1985), 91–94.

48399. Bonner, Mary G. "Pee Wee Reese." In: her *Baseball Rookies Who Made Good.* New York. Alfred A. Knopf, 1954. Pp. 93–95.

48400. Borst, William A. ("Bill"). "Baseball's Man for All Seasons." *The Baseball Research Journal,* IV (1975), 39–42.

48401. Creamer, Robert W. "How to Do It Again!" *Sports Illustrated,* IV (March 19, 1956), 22–25.

48402. Daniel, Daniel M. "Reese Named Rookie of the Year." *Baseball Magazine,* LXVI (January 1941), 353–355.

48403. Dexter, Charles. "Reese: Dean of the Dodgers." *Baseball Digest,* XI (June 1952), 35–40.

48404. Eldridge, Larry. "Why Isn't Pee Wee Reese in the Hall of Fame?" *Baseball Digest,* XXXVII (July 1978), 80–85.

48405. Gabriel, Ronald L. "Harold Henry 'Pee Wee,' 'The Little Colonel' Reese." In: Vol. Q–Z of David L. Porter, ed. *Biographical Dictionary of American Sports: Baseball.* Rev. and enlarged ed. Westport, CT: Greenwood Press, 2000. Pp. 1260–1261.

48406. Gershman, Michael. "A Final Look: Pee Wee Reese." *Beckett Baseball Card Monthly,* IX, no. 90 (September 1992), 126–127.

48407. Golenbock, Peter. *Teammates.* San Diego, CA: Gulliver Books, 1990. 30p. Reese and Jackie Robinson.

48408. Goren, Herb. "Next Manager of the Dodgers?" *Baseball Digest,* IX (February 1950), 3–8.

48409. Graham, Frank. "'The Little Colonel' Is a Born Leader." *Sport,* XX (July 1955), 42–45.

48410. Green, Paul M. "The Captain: Pee Wee Reese." *Baseball Cards,* IV (April 1984), 24–29.

48411. Gross, Milton. "Pee Wee Reese Grows Up." *Sport,* X (June 1951), 24–29.

48412. "Harold (Henry) Reese." In: *Current Biography Yearbook, 1950.* New York: H.W. Wilson Co., 1950. Pp. 482–484.

48413. Hirshberg, Al, and Joe McKefiney. "Pee Wee Reese." In: their *Famous American Athletes of Today.* 10th Series, New York: Page, 1947. Pp. 269–282.

48414. Holmes, Tommy. "It's the Same Boyish Reese." *Baseball Digest,* X (October 1950), 84–86.

48415. Honig, Donald. "Pee Wee Reese." In: his *The Greatest Shortstops of All Time.* Dubuque, IA: Wm. C. Brown Publishers, 1992. Pp. 54–60.

48416. Jacobs, Bruce. "Dodger Dynamo: Pee Wee Reese." In: Bruce Jacobs, ed. *Baseball Stars of 1956.* New York: Lion Books, 1956. Pp. 121–128.

48417. _____. "The Old Pro of Flatbush. In: Bruce Jacobs, ed. *Baseball Stars of 1950.* New York: Lion Books, 1950. Pp. 152–160.

48418. Kahn, Roger. "Pee Wee and the Fountain of Youth." *Sport,* XXIII (June 1957), 52–61.

48419. Kaplan, Jim and Dick Perez. "Pee Wee Reese." In: their *The 2nd Official Baseball Hall of Fame Book of Superstars.* New York: Little Simon, 1990. Pp. 37–38.

48420. Klein, Dave. "Pee Wee Reese and Phil Rizzuto." In: his *Great Infielders of the Major Leagues.* New York: Random House, 1972. Pp. 72–89.

48421. Lardner, John. "Reese and [Jackie] Robinson: Team Within a Team." *The New York Times Magazine,* (September 18, 1949), 17+.

48422. Meany, Thomas. "The Little Colonel." In: his *The Artful Dodgers.* New York: A. S. Barnes, 1953. Pp. 111–121.

48423. _____. "[Pete] Reiser and Reese: The Gold-Dust Twins." *Sport,* II (May 1947), 18–19+.

48424. Menke, Frank G. "Good Enough for Brooklyn." In: his *Sports Tales and Anecdotes.* New York: A.S. Barnes, 1953. Pp. 82–83.

48425. Reese, Dorothy Walton (Mrs. Harold). "My Husband Is a Bum!" *American Magazine,* CLIII (February 1952), 37+.

48426. Reese, Harold H. ("Pee Wee"). "Baseball Is a Different Game Now: Furthermore, Says Brooklyn's Star Shortstop, It's a Better Game Than When He Broke in 15 Years Ago — No Matter What the Old-Timers May Say." Edited by Thomas Meany. *Collier's,* CXXXVI (August 19, 1955), 38–39+.

48427. _____. "Exclusive: Pee Wee Reese Writes." *Baseball Magazine,* LXXX (Spring 1953), 6–8+.

48428. _____. "How I Play Shortstop." In: Harold Parrott, ed. *Dodgers 1951 Yearbook.* New York: W&H Baseball Publishing Co., 1951. Pp. 46–47. Reprinted in *Scholastic Coach,* XXIII (April 1954), 9–11.

48429. _____. "Key Plays at Short." *Sport,* XVI (February 1954), 66–71.

48430. _____. "Pee Wee Reese's Own Story: 14 Years a Bum!" *Baseball Digest,* XIII (May 1954), 32–41. First published in *Look,* XVIII (March 9, 1954), 59–61+.

48431. _____, as told to George Vass. "The Game I'll Never Forget." *Baseball Digest,* XXX (February 1971), 35–39. Reprinted in George Vass, ed. *The Game I'll Never Forget (*Chicago, IL: Bonus Books, 1999), pp. 203–207.

48432. Robinson, Rachel. "Rachel Robinson Recalls How the Late Pee Wee Reese Helped Jackie Robinson Integrate Baseball." *Jet,* XCVI (September 13, 1999), 49–50.

48433. Rosenthal, Harold. "Storybook Stars in Brooklyn." In: Bruce Jacobs, ed. *Baseball Stars of 1953.* New York: Lion Books, 1953. Pp. 134–138. Reese and Jackie Robinson.

48434. "The Sacrifice Bunt." *Sports Illustrated,* V (July 2, 1956), 12–13. Illustrated by Reese.

48435. Schoor, Gene. *Pee Wee Reese Story.* New York: Julian Messner, 1956. 190p.

48436. Sher, Jack. "Reese Without [Pete] Reiser." *Sport,* VI (May 1949), 28–31.

48437. Smith, Ron. "Pee Wee Reese." In: his *Heroes of the Hall: Baseball's Greatest Players.* New York: Contemporary Books, 2002. Pp. 375–376.

48438. Sukeforth, Clyde, as told to Donald Honig. "Oh, They Were a Pair." In: Jackie Robinson and Jules Tygiel. *The Jackie Robinson Reader: Perspectives on an American Hero.* New York: E. P. Dutton, 1997. Chapter 5. Reese and Robinson.

48439. Thorn, Hal. "Payroll Combo." In: Bruce Jacobs, ed. *Baseball Stars of 1955.* New York: Lion Books, 1955. Pp. 91–95. Reese and Jackie Robinson.

48440. Westcott, Rich. "Pee Wee Reese: Captain and Sparkplug of the Dodgers." In: his *Splendor on the Diamond: Interviews with 35 Stars of Baseball's Past.* Gainesville, FL: The University Press of Florida, 2000. Pp. 78–86.

48441. Wilson, John R. M. "Pee Wee Reese." In: Paul Betz and Mark C. Carnes, eds. *American National Biography: Supplement I.* New York: Oxford University Press, 2002. Pp. 508–519.

48442. Wind, Herbert W. "Pee Wee Reese: The Heart of the Dodgers." In: his *Gilded Age of Sport.* New York: Simon and Schuster, 1961. Pp. 197–215. Reprinted from *True Magazine.*

James Herman Solomon ("Jimmie") Reese

2B: (B: Oct. 1, 1901, New York City-D: July 13, 1994). New York (AL), 1930–1931; St. Louis (NL), 1932. Remarks: In three big league seasons, had 209 hits (eight homers) and seven stolen bases in 232 games; had a 70-year baseball career, beginning as a batboy for Los Angles (PCL) and closing as a coach for California, 1972–1994; also played for the PCL teams at Los Angeles, Oakland, and San Diego, 1920, 1924–1929, 1933–1938, and 1940; threw out the ceremonial first pitch for the 60th All-Star Game, 1989; at Anaheim Stadium; honorary captain, AL All-Stars, 1992; uniform retired by California (AL), 1995; elected to PCL Hall of Fame, 2003.

48443. Reese, Jimmy and Bob Gibson. *How to Play Baseball the Professional Way.* New York: New York Yankees, 1939–1940. Tips in booklets by Yankee scouts.

48444. Smith, James D., 3rd. "Jimmie Reese." In: *Echoes from Lane Field: A History of the San Diego Padres 1936–1957.* Paducah, KY: Turner Publishing Company, 1997. Pp. 28–30.

48445. _____. "Jimmie Reese: In His Own Words." *The Baseball Research Journal,* XXIV (1995), 89–91.

48446. Spalding, John E. "Jimmie Reese." In: his *Pacific Coast League Stars: One Hundred of the Best, 1903–1957.* San Jose, CA: John E. Spalding, 1994. Pp. 50–51.

48447. Stump, Al. "From Babe Ruth to Nolan Ryan— Jimmy's Still Swinging." *Sport,* LXXXII (January 1991), 14+.

48448. Willman, Tom. "The Baseball Journey of Jimmie Reese." In: *Northern California Baseball History.*

Cleveland, OH: Society for American Baseball Research, 1998. Pp. 57–58.

Jimmie Reese *see* **James Herman Solomon ("Jimmie") Reese**

John D. ("Bonesetter") Reese

TRAINER (B: May 6, 1855, Rhymney, Wales-D: 1931). Remarks: Muscle and ligament manipulation pioneer who treated upwards of 54 pro baseball players, including 28 in the Hall of Fame.

48449. Anderson, David W. "Bonesetter Reese: Youngstown's 'Baseball Doctor.'" *The Baseball Research Journal,* XXX (2000), 18–19.

48450. Strickler, David L. *Child of Moriah: A Biography of John D. "Bonesetter" Reese, 1855–1931.* Albion, MI: Four Corners Press, 1984. 368p. David Anderson's profile is a number in the online SABR Biography Project < http://bioproj.sabr.org/bioproj.cfm?a=v&v=l&bid=869&pid=16948>.

Pee Wee Reese *see* **Harold Henry ("Pee Wee" or "The Little Colonel") Reese**

Pokey Reese *see* **Calvin ("Pokey") Reese, Jr.**

Richard Benjamin ("Rich") Reese

1B. (B: Sept. 29, 1941, Leipsic, OH). Minnesota (AL), 1964–1973; Detroit (AL), 1973. Remarks: Had 512 hits (52 homers) in 866 games in a decade; holds (tie) NL record for most career pinch grand slam homers (three).

48451. Rumill, Ed. "How Quicker Stroke Helped Rich Reese." *Baseball Digest,* XXVIII (December 1969), 36–39.

Philip Raymond ("Phil" or "The Vulture") Regan

P-SCOUT-MGR. (B: April 6, 1937, Otsego, MI). Detroit (AL), 1960–1965; Los Angeles (NL), 1966–1968; Chicago (NL), 1968–1972; Chicago (AL), 1972. Remarks: Won 96 games and lost 41, with 92 "saves," in a 13-year pro career; pitching in relief, gained victories in both ends of a doubleheader, July 7, 1968; coach, Seattle (AL), 1984–1986; advance scout, Los Angeles (NL), 1987–1993; coach, Cleveland (AL), 1994; manager, Baltimore (AL), 1995, winning 71 games and losing 73 (.493); manager, Albuquerque (PCL), 1996; coach, Chicago (NL), 1997–1998; coach, Cleveland (AL), 1999; coach, U.S. Olympic Team, 2000; manager, West Michigan (Midwest League), 2002–.

48452. Cope, Myron. "The Call Him the Vulture." *Sport,* XLIII (January 1967), 34–35+.

48453. "Phil Regan." In: Carrie Muskat, ed. *Banks to Sandberg to Grace: Five Decades of Love and Frustration with the Chicago Cubs.* Chicago, IL: Contemporary Books, 2001. Pp. 122–124.

48454. Regan, Philip R., with James Hefley. *Phil Regan.* Grand Rapids, MI: Zondervan Publishing Co., 1968. 191p.

Frederic Carl ("Rick") Reichardt

OF. (B; March 16, 1943, Madison, WI). Los Angeles (AL) and California (AL), 1964–1970; Washington (A.L.), 1970; Chicago (AL), 1971–1973; Kansas City (AL), 1973–1974. Remarks: Had 864 hits (116 homers) and 42 stolen bases in 997 games in 11 summer campaigns; $200,000 signing made him history's richest "bonus baby"; hit first homer in Anaheim Stadium, April 19, 1966; lost a kidney to illness, August 1966.

48455. Appel, Marty. "Rick Reichardt." In: his *Yesterday's Heroes: Revisiting the Old-Time Baseball Stars.* New York: William Morrow, 1988. Pp. 178–181.

48456. Astor, Gerald. "Rick ('The Ripper') Reichardt, California's Super Angel." *Look,* XXXI (July 25, 1967), 65+.

48457. Bortstein, Larry. "Inside Rick Reichardt's Pressure-Cooker World." *All-Star Sports* II (June 1969), 18–21.

48458. Cope, Myron. "Baseball's Richest Rookie." *Saturday Evening Post,* CCXXXVII (September 19, 1964), 68–69.

48459. ____. "Rick Reichardt. He's Got a Great Baseball Face, Don't He." *Sport,* XLII (September 1966), 70–71+.

48460. Durslag, Melvin. "Rick Reichardt: The Unusual Bonus Infant." *Baseball Digest,* XXV (July 1966), 45–47.

48461. Maher, Charles. "Rick Reichardt: Too Much Too Soon?" *Baseball Digest,* XXVII (September 1968), 39–41.

48462. Rumill, Ed. "The Angels' Real Cool Rick." *Baseball Digest,* XXVII (August 1968), 53–55.

48463. Shrake, E. "Richest Bonus Baby Ever." *Sports Illustrated,* XX (July 6, 1964), 16–21.

Rick Reichardt *see* **Frederic Carl ("Rick") Reichardt**

Joseph Lawrence Reichler
WRITER. (B: Jan. 1, 1915, New York City–D: Dec. 12, 1988). Remarks: Sportswriter, Associated Press (AP), 1942–1965; director of public relations and special assistant to commissioner, Office of the Commissioner of Baseball, 1965–1988; J. G. Taylor Spink Award, 1975; prolific writer and editor of baseball's bible, *The Baseball Encyclopedia* (no. 508).

48464. Reichler, Joseph L., ed. *The Baseball Encyclopedia.* 10th ed., rev. and updated. New York: Macmillan, 1996. 3,026p. Begun in 1969 as the first modern baseball encyclopedia, but now ceased.

John Good ("Long John") Reilly
1B. (B: Oct. 5, 1858, Cincinnati, OH–D: May 31, 1937). Cincinnati Stars (semipro), 1879–1881; New York Metropolitans, 1882; Cincinnati (AA), 1883–1889; Cincinnati (NL), 1890–1891. Remarks: In nine big league seasons, obtained 1,352 hits in 1,142 games; AA home run champion, 1884 (11), 1888 (13); hit for the cycle, Aug. 6, 1890; worked as commercial artist, Strobridge Lithographic Company, 1892–1932

48465. Ivor-Campbell, Frederick. "John Good 'Long John' Reilly." In: Vol. Q–Z of David L. Porter, ed. *Biographical Dictionary of American Sports: Baseball.* Rev. and enlarged ed. Westport, CT: Greenwood Press, 2000. Pp. 1261–1262. David Ball's profile is a number in the online SABR Biography Project < http://bioproj.sabr.org/bioproj.cfm?a=v&v=l&bid=10&pid=11771>.

Kevin Michael Reimer
OF. (B: June 28, 1964, Macon, GA). Texas (AL), 1988–1992; Milwaukee (AL), 1993; Fukuoka Daiei Hawks (Japan League), 1995 Remarks: Grew up Canadian; obtained 387 hits (52 homers) and four stolen bases in 488 U.S. big league games; went 6-for-6 in one game, Aug. 24, 1993.

48466. Shearon, Jim. "Slugging Kevin Reimer: A Canadian Goes to Japan." In: his *Canada's Baseball Legends.* Kanata, Ontario: Malin Head Press, 1994. Pp. 215–217.

Jerry M. Reinsdorf
EXEC. (B: Feb. 25, 1936, Brooklyn, NY). Remarks: Balcor Corporation chairman and principal owner and chairman, Chicago (AL), 1981–.

48467. Aversano, Vince. "Jerry Reinsdorf: Just a Regular Guy — the Owner of the Bulls and the White Sox Says He's Nothing Special, but the Movers and the Shakers in Sports Don't Agree." *Inside Sports,* XV (November 1993), 22–27.

48468. Greising, David. "The Toughest #&?!% in Sports: In Just Over a Decade, Jerry Reinsdorf Has Become a Major Power in Two Major Leagues." *Business Week,* (June 15, 1992), 100–101, 104.

48469. Hill, S. "Playing in the Major Leagues." *Institutional Investor,* XX (June 1986), 23–24.

48470. "Jerry Reinsdorf Pulls a Double Play in Chicago." *Business Week* (October 10, 1983), 53+.

48471. Nightengale, Bob. "His Magical Season: White Sox Chairman Jerry Reinsdorf Talks About His Greatest Passion — Baseball." In: Michael J. McCormick, ed. *2003 All-Star Game Official Program.* New York: Major League Baseball Promotion Corp., 2003. Pp. 126–129.

48472. Vanderberg, Bob. "Jerry Reinsdorf: Looking Ahead — New Uniforms and Superstars to Wear Them." In: his *Sox — From Lane and Fain to Zisk and Fisk.* Chicago, IL: Chicago Review Press, 1982. Pp. 370–376.

Harold Patrick ("Pete" or "Pistol Pete") Reiser
OF. (B: March 17, 1919, St. Louis, MO–D: Oct. 25, 1981). Brooklyn (NL), 1940–1942, 1946–1948; Boston (NL), 1949–1950; Pittsburgh (NL), 1951); Cleveland (AL), 1952. Remarks: Obtained 786 hits (58 homers) and 87 stolen bases in 861 games in a decade; had one grand slam homer, May 25, 1941; led NL in doubles and in triples, 1941; NL batting champion, 1941 (youngest); had homer in 1941 World Series; NL stolen base champion, 1942, 1946; often injured while fielding; manager, Thomasville (Georgia-Florida League); Kokomo (Midwest League); Green Bay (Three-I League); Spokane (PCL), and Dallas-Fort Worth (TL), 1955–1959, 1965–1966; coach, Los Angeles (NL), 1960–1964; Chicago (NL), 1966–1969; California (AL), 1970–1971; Chicago (NL), 1972–1974.

48473. Bisher, Furman. "Pete Reiser, Manager." *Sport,* XX (October 1955), 30–31+.

48474. Burr, Harold C. "Reiser Needs a 'Secretary.'" *Baseball Digest,* V (September 1946), 15–17.

48475. Carmichael, John P. "Mr. Reiser was a Cardinal Fan." *Baseball Digest,* I (October 1942), 6–8.

48476. Daley, Arthur. "Reiser Lacked One Thing — Luck." *Baseball Digest,* IX (May 1950), 47–48.

48477. ____. "Which Reiser Did the Braves Get?" *Baseball Digest,* VIII (April 1949), 65–69.

48478. Green, Gerald. "Pete Reiser." In: Danny Peary, ed. *Cult Baseball Players.* New York: Simon and Schuster, 1990. Pp. 218–221.

48479. ____. "Pete Reiser." In: Danny Peary, ed. *Baseball's Finest: The Greats, the Flakes, the Weird and the Wonderful.* North Dighton, MA: The JG Press, 1990. Pp. 218–221. Both Peary books are identical.

48480. Heinz, W. C. "The Man They Padded the Walls For." In: his *Once They Heard the Cheers.* Garden City, NY: Doubleday, 1979. Pp. 392–415.

48481. ____. "The Rocky Road of 'Pistol Pete.'" In: Charles Einstein, ed. *The Second Fireside Book of Baseball.* New York: Simon and Schuster, 1958. Pp. 190–198. Reprinted in Editors of *True, True, Anthology of True* (New York: Nelson, 1962), pp. 225–235 and in Nicholas Dawidoff, ed., *Baseball: A Literary Anthology* (New York: The Library of America, 2002), pp.275–293. Originally published as a 1958 article in *True: The Men's Magazine.*

48482. Holmes, Tot. *Brooklyn's Best.* Gothenburg, NE: Holmes Publishing, 1988. 104p. Reiser and Jackie Robinson.

48483. Honig, Donald. "Pete Reiser, 1940–1952." In: his *Baseball When the Grass Was Real.* New York: Coward, McCarm, Geoghegan, 1975. Pp. 292–316.

48484. Jacobson, Sidney. *Pete Reiser: The Rough-and-Tumble Career of the Perfect Ballplayer.* Jefferson, NC: McFarland & Co., Inc., 2004. 224p.

48485. Koster, Rich. "Pete Reiser: He Was an Original 'Mr. Hustle.'" *Baseball Digest,* XLI (April 1992), 53–56.

48486. Linkugel, Will A. and Edward J. Pappas. "Hitting the Wall: Pistol Pete Reiser." In: their *They Tasted Glory: Among the Missing at the Baseball Hall of Fame.* Jefferson, NC: McFarland & Co., Inc., 1998. Pp. 24–40.

48487. McGowen, Roscoe. "Powerhouse Pete." In: Charles Dester, ed. *Dodgers' Victory Book, 1942.* New York: W&H. Baseball Publishing Co., 1942. Pp. 42–43.

48488. Meany, Thomas. "Pistol Pete-National Leaguer No. 1." *Saturday Evening Post,* CCXV (September 26, 1942), 19–20+.

48489. _____. "Reiser and [Pee Wee] Reese: The Gold-Dust Twins." *Sport,* II (May 1947), 18–19+.

48490. Moss, Robert A. "Hit It to Me!": Pete Reiser and *The Natural.*" *Elysian Fields Quarterly,* XII (Fall 1993), 92–98.

48491. Olmstead, Frank J. "Harold Patrick 'Pete,' 'Pistol Pete' Reiser." In: Vol. Q–Z of David L. Porter, ed. *Biographical Dictionary of American Sports: Baseball.* Rev. and enlarged ed. Westport, CT: Greenwood Press, 2000. Pp. 1262–1264.

48492. Reiser, Pete. "Hit the Dirt!" In: *Boy's Life,* Editors of. *Baseball as We Played It.* New York: G.P. Putnam, 1969. Pp. 144–151.

48493. Ritter, Lawrence and Donald Honig. "Pete Reiser." In: their *The 100 Greatest Baseball Players of All Time.* New York: Crown Publishers, 1981. Pp. 152–155.

48494. Robinson, Ray. "Pete Reiser: Dodger Who Owned Home Plate." In: his *Speed Kings at the Base Paths.* New York: G.P. Putnam, 1964. Pp. 71–93.

48495. Rogers, C. Paul, 3rd. "Of Outfield Walls and Concussions: The Pete Reiser Story." *Elysian Fields Quarterly,* XIX (Summer 2002), 24–37.

48496. Santa Maria, Michael and James Costello. "Headbanger's Ball." In: their *In the Shadows of the Diamond.* Dubuque, IA: The Elysian Fields Press, 1992. Pp. 175–180.

48497. Stier, Jack. "Reese Without Reiser." *Sport,* VI (May 1949), 28–31.

48498. Simons, Herbert. "Would You Have Walked Reiser?" *Baseball Digest,* VII (January 1948), 29–33.

48499. Tietjen, W. Verrnon. "It May Be Southpaw Reiser!" *Baseball Digest,* V (February 1946), 9–11.

Kenneth John ("Ken" or "The Zamboni Machine") Reitz
3B. (B: June 24, 1951, San Francisco, CA). St. Louis (NL), 1972–1975; San Francisco (NL), 1976; St. Louis (NL), 1977–1980; Chicago (NL), 1981. Remarks: Had 1,243 hits (68 homers) and 10 stolen bases in 1,337 games in a decade; had one grand slam homer, June 28, 1977; highly-regarded fielder who committed only eight errors in 1980.

48500. Borst, William A. ("Bill"). "Kert Reitz: 'The Zamboni Machine.'" *Baseball Digest,* XXXIII (August 1974), 66–71.

48501. Kaplan, Jim. "His Bat Blossoms in the Spring." *Sports Illustrated,* LII May 26, 1980), 69–70.

48502. Reitz, Kenneth J., as told to George Vass. "The Game I'll Never Forget." *Baseball Digest,* XL (August 1981), 67–70.

Joe Louis Reliford
BATBOY. (B: 1939). Remarks: Batboy for Fitzgerald Pioneers (Georgia-Florida League), who, when he pinch hit for the team in 1952 at age 12, became the youngest player ever to appear in a professional baseball game; later an 18-year deputy sheriff for Douglas, GA.

48503. "The Heart and Soul of Georgia." *Reflections: Georgia African-American Historic Preservation Network,* II (June 2002), 6–7.

48504. Reynolds, James E. "The Batboy Who Swung for Equality: The Color Barrier in Georgia Baseball was Dented When a 12-Year Old Stepped Up to Hit." *Sports Illustrated,* LXXIII (July 2, 1990), 74+.

Gerald Peter ("Jerry") Remy
2B-BROADCASTER. (B: Nov. 8, 1952, Fall River, MA). California (AL), 1975–1977; Boston (AL), 1978–1984. Remarks: Obtained 1,226 hits (seven homers) and 208 stolen bases in 1,154 games; went 5-for-5 in one game, May 12, 1979; New England Sports Network Boston (AL) announcer, 1988–.

48505. Lautier, Jack. "Jerry Remy." In: his *Fenway Voices.* Camden, ME: Yankee Books, 1990. Pp. 171–176.

48506. Remy, Jerry. *Watching Baseball : Discovering the Game within the Game.* Boston, MA: Globe Pequot Press, 2004. 384p.

Jerry Remy *see* **Gerald Peter ("Jerry") Remy**
Othello Nelson ("Chico") Renfroe
SS. (B: March 1, 1923, Newark, NJ-D: Sept. 3, 1991). Kansas City Monarchs, 1945–1947; Cleveland Buckeyes, 1948–1949; Indianapolis Clowns, 1949–1950; Mexican League, 1950–1952; Kansas City Monarchs, 1953. Remarks: Monarchs shortstop who succeeded Jackie Robinson in 1946; later, first official scorer for Atlanta (NL).

48507. Holway, John B. "Othello Renfroe." In: his Voices from the Great Black Baseball Leagues. New York: Da Capo Press, 1992. Pp. 339–351.

Big Bill Renna *see* **William Beneditto ("Bill" or "Big Bill") Renna**
William Beneditto ("Bill" or "Big Bill") Renna
OF. (B: Oct. 14, 1924, Hanford, CA). New York (AL), 1953; Philadelphia (AL), 1954; Kansas City (AL), 1955–1956; Boston (AL), 1958–1959. Remarks: Had 219 hits (28 homers) and two stolen bases in 370 big league games.

48508. Fehler, Gene. "Bill Renna." In: his *Tales from Baseball's Golden Age.* Champaign, IL: Sports Publishing Co., 2000. Chapter 42.

48509. Kelley, Brent P. "Bill Renna: Baseball Over Football." In: his *They Too Wore Pinstripes: Interviews with 20 Glory-Days New York Yankees.* Jefferson, NC: McFarland & Co., Inc., 1998. Pp. 163–170.

Laurence Henry ("Dutch") Rennert, Jr.
UMP. (B: June 12, 1934, Oshkosh, WI). Remarks: NL arbiter, 1973–1993, remembered for colorful gestures.

48510. Gerlach, Larry R. "Laurence Henry 'Dutch' Rennert, Jr." In: Vol. Q–Z of David L. Porter, ed. *Biographical Dictionary of American Sports: Baseball.* Rev. and enlarged ed. Westport, CT: Greenwood Press, 2000. Pp. 1264–1265.

48511. Rennert, Laurence ("Dutch"). "Interview." *Referee,* XV (April 1990), 20–23.

48512. Skipper, John C. "Laurence 'Dutch' Rennert." In: his *Umpires: Classic Baseball Stories from the Men who Made the Calls.* Jefferson, NC: McFarland & Co., Inc., 1997. Pp. 31–37.

48513. Watt, R. L. "Memories: An Interview." *Sport,* LXXXIV (July 1993), 70–71.

Edgar Enrique Renteria
SS. (B: August 7, 1975, Barranquilla, Colombia). Florida (NL), 1996–1998; St. Louis (NL), 1999–2004; Boston (AL), 2005–. Through 2004, has obtained 1,423 hits (83 homers) and 237 stolen bases in 1,296 games; 4000th batter struck out by Roger Clemens (q.v.), June 13, 2003; had three doubles in 2004 World Series.

48512. O'Neill, Dan. "Cardinals Look to Edgar Renteria for Leadership." *Baseball Digest,* LXII (July 2003), 56–59.

Mervin Weldon ("Merv") Rettenmund
OF. (B: June 6, 1943, Flint, MI). Baltimore (AL), 1968–1973; Cincinnati (NL), 1974–1975; San Diego (NL), 1976–1977; California (AL), 1978–1980. Remarks: In a 13-year big league career, had 693 hits (66 homers) and 68 stolen bases in 1,023 games; drafted by Dallas Cowboys in 1964 to play N.F.L. pro football; homered in Game Four of 1970 World Series; had home run in Game One of 1971 World Series; had one career grand slam homer, April 12, 1974; minor league instructor, California (AL), 1981–1982; coach, Texas (AL), 1983 and Oakland (AL), 1989–1990, San Diego (NL), 1991–1999; Atlanta (NL), 2000–2001, Detroit (AL), 2002.

48513. Fimrite, Ron. "Well, He's That Kind of Guy." *Sports Illustrated,* XXXV (October 4, 1971), 28–30+.

48514. Freeman, S. "Hit Man." *Atlanta,* XLI (July 2001), 24–26.

48515. Jordan, Pat. "An Oriole-in-Waiting." *Sport,* LI (February 1971), 60–65.

48516. Rettenmund, Merv. "Running and Base Stealing." *Coaching Clinic,* XVIII (January 1980), 2–4.

Adolph John ("Otto") Rettig
P. (B: Jan. 29, 1894, New York City-D: June 16, 1977). Philadelphia (AL), 1922. Remarks: Won one game and lost two of the four big league games he hurled.

48516. Goldberg, Hy. "Rettig's Lone Win Lives On." *Baseball Digest,* IV (February 1945), 65–61.

Edward Marvin ("Ed" or "Big Ed") Reulbach
P. (B: Dec. 1, 1882, Detroit, MI-D: July 17, 1981). Chicago (NL), 1906–1913; Brooklyn (NL), 1913–1914; Newark (F.L.), 1915; Boston (NL), 1916–1917. Remarks: Had 185 victories, 104 defeats, and 11 "saves" in 13 seasons; won 14 consecutive games In 1909 and before that was 60–15 in 1906–1908, including two shutout victories in one day, Sept. 26,1908; his winning percentage for those years remains the NL record; won a game in both the 1906 and 1907 World Series; had 14-game winning streak in 1910.

48517. Dittmar, Joe. "Double Shutout for Reulbach: September 26, 1908." In: his *Box Scores.* Fairview Village, PA: Joseph J. Dittmar, 1988. Pp. 10–11.

48518. Fullerton, Hugh S. "Psychology in Baseball." *Baseball Magazine,* IV (January 1910), 1–5.

48519. Gagnon, Richard ("Cappy"). "Ed Reulbach Remembered." *The Baseball Research Journal,* XI (1982), 77–79.

48520. Karnes, Thomas L "Edward Marvin Reulbach." In: John A. Garrity and Marsh C. Carries, eds. *American National Biography.* 24 vols. New York: Oxford University Press, 1999. XVIII, 357–358.

48521. Kronstadt, Normm "The Day Ed Reulbach Pitched Two Shutouts." *Sport,* XX (July 1965), 68–71.

48522. Lane, Ferdinand C. "Reulbach: The Man Who Ran Out of Baseball." *Baseball Magazine,* XV (May 1915), 63–74.

48523. Reulbach, Edward M. "Making 'Em Bite." *Baseball Magazine,* XIX (June 1917), 303–305.

48524. _____. "Reminiscences of a World Series Pitcher." *Baseball Magazine,* X (November 1912), 27–29.

48525. Rothe, Emil H. "The Day Ed Reulbach Pitched Two Shutouts." *Baseball Digest,* XXXII (January 1973), 70–75.

48526. Slater, Robert. "Edward Reulbach: The Only Man to Ever Pitch Two Shutouts in a Doubleheader." In: his *Great Jews in Sports.* Middle Village, NY: Jonathan David Publishers, 1983. Pp. 171–172.

48527. Smith, Ira L. "Edward Marvin (Ed) Reulbach." In: his *Baseball's Famous Pitchers.* New York: A.S. Barnes, 1954. Pp. 106–111.

48528. Stann, Francis. "When Reulbach Beat Up His Manager." *Baseball Digest,* XX (October 1961), 65–67.

48529. Suehsdorf, Adie D. "Edward Marvin 'Ed,' 'Big Ed' Reulbach." In: Vol. Q-Z of David L. Porter, ed. *Biographical Dictionary of American Sports: Baseball.* Rev. and enlarged ed. Westport, CT: Greenwood Press, 2000. Pp. 1265–1266.

48530. Ward, John J. "The Shutout King." *Baseball Magazine,* IX (October 1912), 45–54.

48531. Wilbert, Warren and William Hageman. "Edward Marvin Reulbach —1905." In: their *Chicago Cubs: Seasons at the Summit, the 50 Greatest Individual Seasons.* Champaign, IL: Sagamore Publishing, 1997. Pp. 123–126.

Rickey Eugene ("Rick" or "Big Daddy") Reuschel
P. (B: May 16, 1949, Quincy, IL). Chicago (NL), 1972–1981; New York (AL), 1981; Chicago (NL), 1983– 1984; Pittsburgh (NL), 1985–1987; San Francisco (NL), 1987–1991. Remarks: In 19 seasons, obtained 214 victories and 191 defeats, with five "saves"; third pitcher to record three put-outs in one inning, 1975; retired 17 consecutive batters, June 16, 1977; pitched two shut-outs in a row, July 22 & 27, 1977; lost one game in 1987 NLCS; won one game and lost one in 1989 NLCS and lost one game of 1989 World Series.

48532. Doyle, Al. "How Perseverance Paid Off for Rick Reuschel." *Baseball Digest,* XLV (May 1986), 34–36.

48534. Findling, John E. "Ricky Eugene 'Rick,' 'Big Daddy' Reuschel." In: Vol. Q-Z of David L. Porter, ed. *Biographical Dictionary of American Sports: Baseball.* Rev. and enlarged ed. Westport, CT: Greenwood Press, 2000. Pp. 1266–1267.

48535. Greenwood, Chuck. "Reuschel Resurrected Career Twice in Minors." *Sports Collector's Digest,* XXV (August 21, 1998), 70–71.

48536. Kravitz, Bob. "Pittsburgh's Golden Oldie." *Sports Illustrated,* LXIII (July 15, 1985), 62, 64.

48537. Taylor, Phil "A Pitcher's Most Desired Requisite: 'Good Stuff.'" *Baseball Digest,* XLVIII (November 1989), 44–47.

48538. Tefertiller, Casey. "Rick Reuschel: He Lets the Batter Get Himself Out." *Baseball Digest,* XLVII (December 1988), 77–79.

48539. Vass, George. "Rick Reusche." In: his *The Game I'll Never Forget.* Chicago, IL: Bonus Books, 1999. Pp. 209–213.

48540. Wilbert, Warren and William Hageman. "Rick Reuschel —1977." In: their *Chicago Cubs: Seasons at the Summit, the 50 Greatest Individual Seasons.* Champaign, IL: Sagamore Publishing, 1997. Pp. 57–60.

Jerry ("Rolls") Reuss
P-BROADCASTER. (B: June 19, 1949, St. Louis, MO). St. Louis (NL), 1969–1971; Houston (NL), 1971–1973; Pittsburgh (NL), 1974–1978; Los Angeles (NL), 1979–1987; Cincinnati (NL) and California (AL), 1987; Chicago (AL), 1988–1989; Milwaukee (AL), 1989; Pittsburgh (NL), 1990. Remarks: Won 220 games and lost 191 in 16 years; pitched no-hitter, June 27, 1980; broadcaster, ESPN, 1991–1993, Las Vegas (PCL), 1994–1995, Anaheim (AL), 1996–1998; coach, Harrisburg (EL), 2000; Iowa (PCL), 2001–2003; Binghampton (EL), 2004-.

48541. Cavender, S. "Crazy with a K." *Inside Sports,* IX (October 1985), 60–70.

48542. Chortkoff, Mitch. "Jerry Reuss: Maturity is Evident." In: Bill Shumard, ed. *1981 Los Angeles Dodgers Yearbook.* Anaheim, CA: Rotary Off-Set Printers, 1981. Pp. 46–47.

48543. Cohen, Irwin. "Baseball Beat: Jerry Reuss." *Baseball Cards,* IX (January 1989), 90–93.

48544. Fimrite, Ron. "Meet the Rolls Reuss of Pitchers." *Sports Illustrated,* LV (August 25, 1980), 44+.

48545. Hartsock, John. "Where are They Now?: Former Pitcher Jerry Reuss." *Baseball Digest,* LIX (September 2000), 74–76.

48546. Herron, Gary. "Jerry Reuss: From Pitcher's Mound to Television Booth." *Sports Collector's Digest,* XVIII (May 10, 1991), 90–91.

48547. Marazzi, Rich. "Jerry Reuss." *Sports Collector's Digest,* XXIV (January 17–24, 1997), 68–69, 70–71.

48548. Olmsted, Frank J. "Jerry Reuss." In: Vol. Q-Z of David L. Porter, ed. *Biographical Dictionary of American Sports: Baseball.* Rev. and enlarged ed. Westport, CT: Greenwood Press, 2000. Pp. 1267–1269.

48549. Reuss, Jerry, as told to George Vass. "The Game I'll Never Forget." *Baseball Digest,* XLVII (September 1988), 69–71. Reprinted in George Vass, ed. *The Game I'll Never Forget* (Chicago, IL: Bonus Books, 1999), pp. 215–219. 1980 no-hitter.

Al Reyes *see* **Rafael Alberto ("Al") Reyes**

Jose Bernabe Reyes
SS. (B: June 11, 1983, Villa Gonzalez, D.R.). New York (NL), 2003–. Remarks: Through 2004, has obtained 140 hits (seven homers) and 32 stolen bases in 122 games; injured much of 2004.

48550. Beaton, Rod. "The Next Great Glove." In: Scott Smith, ed. *Street and Smith's 2004 Baseball Annual.* Charlotte, NC: Street & Smith Group, 2004. Pp. 14–24.

48551. Habib, Daniel G. "José Reyes." *Sports Illustrated,* XCVIII (March 3, 2003), 44–45.

Rafael Alberto ("Al") Reyes
P. (B: April 10, 1971, San Cristobal, D.R.). Milwaukee (AL/NL), 1995–1999; Baltimore (AL), 1999–2000; Los Angeles (NL), 2000–2001; Pittsburgh (NL), 2002; Columbus (AA) and New York (AL), 2003; St. Louis (NL), 2004–. Remarks: Through 2004, has had 15 big league wins, eight losses, and three saves.

48552. Epstein, Eddie. "Alberto Reyes." In: STATS, Inc. *The STATS 1995 Minor League Scouting Notebook.* Skokie, IL: STATS Publishing, 1995. Pp. 138–139.

Allie Pierce ("Superchief") Reynolds
P-EXEC. (B: Feb. 10, 1915, Bethany, OK-D: Dec. 26, 1994). Cleveland (AL), 1942–1946; New York (AL), 1947–1954. Remarks. In a 13-year big league career, this quarter-Creek Indian had 182 victories, 107 defeats, and 49 "saves"; won Game Two of 1947 World Series; won Game One of 1949 World Series; first to pitch two no-hitters in one season (July 12 and September 28, 1951); won Game Four of 1952 World Series; won Game Six of 1953 World Series; established or tied several records, president, American Association, 1969–1971; elected to Oklahoma Sports Hall of Fame, 1986; Allie Reynolds Award, given annually in Oklahoma, established in 1998.

48553. "Allie Reynolds." In: *Current Biography Yearbook, 1952.* New York: H. W. Wilson Co., 1952. Pp. 494–496.

48554. "Allie Reynolds: Yankees' 'Superchief.'" *Yankees Magazine,* V (June 7,1984), 24–27.

48555. Bealmear, Austin. "Lo, the Rich Indian." *Baseball Magazine,* LXXX (June-July 1953), 18–19+.

48556. Bower, Mary G. "Allie Reynolds." In: her *Baseball Rookies Who Made Good.* New York: Alfred A. Knopf, 1964. pp. 95–99.

48557. Coyle, Dale D. "Reynolds, Maglie, Newcombe Toughest to Hit." *Baseball Digest,* XI (March 1952), 26–30.

48558. Dexter, Charles. "Allie Reynolds: The Yankees' 'Mr. Chips.'" *Baseball Digest,* XI (April 1952), 27–31.

48559. Epstein, Ben. "Reynolds Is Tough." *Complete Baseball,* IV (November 1952), 18–27.

48560. Fitzgerald, Ed. "The Pitcher They Called a Quitter." *Sport,* XIII (August 1952), 28–33.

48561. Forker, Dom. "Allie Reynolds." In: his *The Men of Autumn.* Dallas, TX: Taylor Publishing Co., 1989. Pp. 1–11.

48562. Frey, Leonard H. "Allie Pierce 'Superchief' Reynolds." In: Vol. Q-Z of David L. Porter, ed. *Biographical Dictionary of American Sports: Baseball.* Rev. and enlarged ed. Westport, CT: Greenwood Press, 2000. Pp. 1269–1270.

48563. Gallagher, Mark. "Allie Reynolds." In: his *50 Years of Yankee All-Stars.* New York: Leisure Press, 1984. Pp. 160–162.

48564. Green, Paul M. "Baseball and Allie Reynolds." *Sports Collector's Digest,* XI (March 30, 1984), 14+.

48565. Gross, Milton. "Allie Reynolds: The Vanishing American." *Sport,* IX (September 1950), 42–43+.

48566. _____. "Heap Big Chief (Allie Reynolds)." In: his *The Magnificent Yankees.* New York: A.S. Barnes, 1952. Pp. 75–89.

48567. Klima, John. "Number Five is the Hardest: Allie Reynolds vs. Robin Roberts (October 5, 1950)." In: his *Pitched Battle: 35 of Baseball's Greatest Duels from the Mound.* Jefferson, NC: McFarland & Co., Inc., 2002. Pp. 82–86.

48568. Lewis, Franklin. "So Allie was Timid, Eh?" *Baseball Digest,* VIII (November 1949), 15–17.

48569. Martin, Whitney. "A Moment That's Reynolds' Monument." *Baseball Digest,* XIV (April 1955), 13–16.

48570. McMillan, Ken. "Allie Reynolds." In: his *Tales from the Yankee Dugout: A Collection of the Greatest Yankee Stories Ever Told.* Champaign, IL: Sports Publishing, Inc., 2001. Pp. 145–146.

48571. Molter, Harry. "Allie Reynolds." In: his *Famous American Athletes of Today.* 13th Series. New York: Page, 1953. Pp. 225–242.

48572. Nichols, Max J. "Allie Pierce Reynolds." *Chronicles of Oklahoma,* LXXIII (Spring 1995), 4+.

48573. Parr, Royse and Bob Burke. *Allie Reynolds: Super Chief.* Oklahoma City, OK: Oklahoma Heritage Association, 2002. 280p.

48574. Post, Paul. "Allie Reynolds was at His Best When Going Got Tough." *Baseball Digest,* LVIII (May 1999), 68–73.

48575. Robinson, Ray. "Allie Reynolds: Superchief." In: his *Greatest Yankees of Them All.* New York: G.P. Putnam's Sons, 1969. Pp. 84–96.

48576. Stern, Chris. "Allie Reynolds." In: his *Where Have They Gone?* New York: Tempo Books, 1979. Pp. 143–148.

48577. Taylor, Keith R. "Allie Reynolds: He Helped Keep the Yankee Mystique Alive." *Baseball Digest,* L (May 1991), 24–29.

48578. Trimble, Joe. "Reynolds' Secret a 'Half-Baked' Curve." *Baseball Digest,* VII (August 1948), 55–57. The slow pitch of the Yankees' Reynolds.

48579. Westcott, Rich. "Allie Reynolds — Ace of the Yanks' Big Three." In: his *Diamond Greats.* Westport, CT: Meckler Books, 1988. Pp. 328–333.

48580. Wilson, John. "Allie Reynolds Talks About Pitching." *Baseball Digest,* XXX (November 1971), 69–71. Reprinted in John Kuenster, ed., *From Cobb to Catfish* (Chicago: Rand McNally, 1975), pp. 179–180.

Carl Nettles Reynolds
OF. (B: Feb. 1, 1903, LaRue, TX-D: Dec. 29, 1974). Chicago (AL), 1927–1931; Washington (AL), 1932; St. Louis (AL), 1933; Boston (AL), 1934–1936; Washington (AL), 1936; Chicago (NL), 1937–1939. Remarks: Obtained 1,367 hits (80 homers) and 112 stolen bases In 1,222 games in 13 years; had three consecutive homers in one game, including two inside-the-park, July 2, 1930; also played for Los Angeles (PCL), 1940; named to Texas Sports Hall of Fame, 1971.

48581. Bloodgood, Clifford. "Carl Reynolds of Rattlesnake Ranch and Chicago." *Baseball Magazine,* XLVI (March 1931), 449–450.

48582. Hillman, John. "Carl Nettles Reynolds." In: Vol. Q-Z of David L. Porter, ed. *Biographical Dictionary of American Sports: Baseball.* Rev. and enlarged ed. Westport, CT: Greenwood Press, 2000. Pp. 1270–1271.

Craig Reynolds *see* **Gordon Craig Reynolds**
Gordon Craig Reynolds
SS. (B. Dec. 27, 1952, Houston, TX.). Pittsburgh (NL), 1975–1976; Seattle (AL), 1977–1978; Houston (NL), 1979–1989. Remarks: Had 1,142 hits (42 homers) and 58 stolen bases in 1,491 games in 15 years; walked three times in 1980 NLCS; had a record three triples in one game, May 16, 1981.

48583. Hill, Terry. "Craig Reynolds." In: his *Batting a Thousand.* Nashville, TN: Thomas Nelson, 1987. Pp. 78–82.

48584. Newman, Bruce. "Seattle Has a Secret Weapon." *Sports Illustrated,* XLIX (July 10, 1978), 32+.

Harold Craig Reynolds
2B-BROADCASTER. (B: Nov. 26, 1960, Eugene, OR). Seattle (AL), 1983–1992; Baltimore (AL), 1993; California (AL), 1994. Remarks: Obtained 1,233 hits (21 homers) and 250 stolen bases in 1,374 games in 12 years; A. L. stolen base champion, 1987; baseball analyst, ESPN, 1995–; named to Oregon Sports Hall of Fame, 1998.

48585. Alexson, Bill. "Harold Reynolds, Seattle Mariners." In: his *Batting a Thousand, Book 2.* Nashville, TN: Thomas Nelson Publishers, 1990. Pp 76–79.

48586. Berney, Louis. "Harold Reynolds: A True Blue Oriole Already." *Orioles Gazette,* III (January 22, 1993), 16–17.

48587. Nash, Bruce and Allan Zullo. "Harold Reynolds." In: their *Little Big Leaguers: Amazing Boyhood Stories of Today's Baseball Stars.* New York: Little Simon, 1990. Pp. 66–67.

48588. Shalin, Mike. "A Deeper Look: Harold Reynolds." *Beckett Baseball Card Monthly,* VIII (October 1991), 98–99.

48589. Tuthill, Bill. "Harold Reynolds of the Mariners: Good and Getting Better." *Baseball Digest,* XLVII (December 1988), 66–71.

Richard Shane Reynolds
P. (B: March 26, 1968, Bastrop, LA). Houston (NL), 1992–2002; Atlanta (NL), 2003; Arizona (NL), 2004–. Remarks: Through 2004, has won 114 games and lost 96; led NL in games started, 1998–1999.

48590. Klima, John. "Then It Happened: Kerry Wood vs. Shane Reynolds (May 6, 1998)." In: his *Pitched Battle: 35 of Baseball's Greatest Duels from the Mound.* Jefferson, NC: McFarland & Co., Inc., 2002. Pp.180–184.

Shane Reynolds *see* **Richard Shane Reynolds**
Charles Flint ("Shad") Rhem
P. (B: Jan. 24, 1901, Rhem, SC-D: July 30, 1960).St. Louis (NL), 1924–1928, 1930–1932; Philadelphia (NL), 1932–1933; St. Louis (NL), 1934; Boston- (NL),

1934–1936;. St. Louis (N.L), 1936. Remarks: Had 106 victories, 97 defeats, and 10 "saves" In a decade; remembered for improbable 1930 report that that he had gone missing because he was kidnapped by gamblers and forced to drink bootleg whiskey.

48591. Broeg, Bob. "Flint Rhem's 'Thing' was a Sip and a Good Story." *Baseball Digest,* XXVIII (November 1969), 71–73.

48592. Thom, John. "The Kidnapping of Flint Rhem." *The National Pastime,* VI (1990), 79–82. Reprinted in: Mark Alvarez, ed. *The Perfect Game* (New York: Barnes & Noble Books, 1995), pp. 197–203.

Billy Rhines *see* **William Pearl ("Billy") Rhines**
William Pearl ("Billy") Rhines
P. (B: March 14, 1869, Ridgeway, PA-D: Jan. 30, 1922). Cincinnati (NL), 1890–1892; Louisville (NL), 1893; Cincinnati (NL), 1895–1897; Pittsburgh (NL), 1898–1899. Remarks: Submarine hurler who won 113 games and lost 103; also pitched for Grand Rapids (WL), 1894.

48593. McMahon, William F. "William Pearl 'Billy' Rhines." In: Vol. Q-Z of David L. Porter, ed. *Biographical Dictionary of American Sports: Baseball.* Rev. and enlarged ed. Westport, CT: Greenwood Press, 2000. Pp. 1271–1272.

Richard Alan ("Rick") Rhoden
P. (B: May 16, 1953, Boynton Beach, FL). Los Angeles (NL), 1974–1979; Pittsburgh (NL), 1979–1986; New York (AL), 1987–1988; Houston (NL), 1989. Remarks: In 16 years, won 151 games and lost 125 with one "save"; also had nine homers; lost one game of 1977 World Series.

48594. Thackeray, Frank W. "Richard Alan 'Rick' Rhoden." In: Vol. Q-Z of David L. Porter, ed. *Biographical Dictionary of American Sports: Baseball.* Rev. and enlarged ed. Westport, CT: Greenwood Press, 2000. Pp. 1272–1273.

Rick Rhoden *see* **Richard Alan ("Rick") Rhoden**
Arthur Lee Rhodes, Jr.
P. (B: Oct. 24, 1969, Waco, TX). Baltimore (AL), 1991–1999; Seattle (AL), 2000–2003; Oakland (AL), 2004; Cleveland (AL), 2005–. Remarks: Through 2004, has won 72 games and lost 54, with 26 "saves"; lost one game of 2000 ALCS; traded to Pittsburgh (NL) and then to Cleveland (AL), Dec. 2004.

48595. Berney, Louis. "Maturity is Key to Arthur Rhodes' Progress." *Orioles Gazette,* III (May 7,1993), 16–17.

Dusty Rhodes *see* **James Lamar ("Dusty") Rhodes**
Gregory ("Greg") Rhodes
WRITER. (B: Aug. 17, 1946, Richmond, IN). Remarks: High school history teacher in Indiana, Kentucky, and Hawaii; moved to Cincinnati in 1988 to accept position with Cincinnati Historical Society, where he became the "unofficial historian of the Cincinnati Reds."

48596. Shannon, Mike. "Greg Rhodes." In: his *Baseball: The Writer's Game.* 2nd ed. Dulles, VA: Brassy's, Inc., 2002. Pp. 187–210.

James Lamar ("Dusty") Rhodes
OF. (B: May 13, 1927, Mathews, AL-D: June 9, 1984). New York (NL) and San Francisco (NL), 1952–1957, 1959. Remarks: Obtained 206 hits (54 homers) in 576 games in seven seasons; had three consecutive homers in games in a year, Aug. 26, 1953 and July 28, 1954; had two doubles, two homers, and two triples in one game, Aug. 29, 1954; remembered for his four hits (three pinch-hit) in Games One, Two, and Three of the 1954 World Series, particularly the homer in Game One.

48597. Bisher, Furman, "The Dizzy Dean of the Pinch-Hitters." *Sport,* XVIII (April 1955), 8–13.

48598. Drees, Jack and James C. Mullen. "Dusty Rhodes: Four Games in 1954." *Where Is He Now?* Middle Village, NY: Jonathan David Publishers, 1973. Pp. 148–152.

48599. Gergen, Joe. "Lemke to Larsen to Rhodes: From Unsung to World Series Heroes." In: Zander Hollander, ed. *1984: The Complete Handbook of Baseball.* New York: Signet, 1984. Pp. 21–41.

48600. Gould, Stephen Jay. "Dusty Rhodes." In: Danny Peary, ed. *Cult Baseball Players.* New York: Simon and Schuster, 1990. Pp. 222–225.

48601. _____. "Dusty Rhodes." In: Danny Peary, ed. *Baseball's Finest: The Greats, the Flakes, the Weird and the Wonderful.* North Dighton, MA: The JG Press, 1990. Pp. 222–225. Both Peary books are identical.

48602. Hano, Arnold. "The Four Days of Dusty Rhodes." *Sport,* XXVIII (October 1959), 34–38.

48603. Kiersh, Edward. "Dusty Rhodes: All Roads Lead to New York Harbor." In: his *Where Have You Gone, Vince DiMaggio?* New York: Bantam Books, 1983. Pp. 138–147.

48604. Linn, Ed. "Dusty Rhodes Ten Years Later." *Sport,* XXXVIII (November 1964), 40–43.

48605. Miller, Brett C. "Dusty Rhodes." In: Peter Levine, ed. *Baseball History.* Westport, CT: Meckler, 1989. Pp. 13–18.

48606. Rosenthal, Harold. "Punch in the Pinch." In: Bruce Jacobs, ed. *Baseball Stars of 1955.* New York: Lion Books, 1955. Pp. 95–100.

48607. Salant, Nathan. "Dusty Rhodes." In: his *Superstars, Stars, and Just Plain Heroes.* New York: Stein And Day, 1982. Pp. 259–263.

48608. Silverman, Al. "The Fable of Dusty Rhodes." In: his *Heroes of the World Series.* New York: G.P. Putnam's Sons, 1964. Pp. 185–198.

48609. Stern, Chris. "Dusty Rhodes." In: his *Where Have They Gone?* New York: Tempo Books , 1979. Pp. 5–12.

48610. Valenti, Dan. "Dusty Rhodes." In: his *Clout.* New York: Stephen Greene Press, 1989. Pp. 108–116.

Kevin Jay Rhomberg
OF-2B. (B: Nov. 22, 1955, Dubuque, IA). Cleveland (AL), 1982–1984. Remarks: Had 18 hits (one homer) in 41 games in three seasons; had an extraordinary superstition about being touched.

48611. Hannon, Kent. "Chattanooga Choochoo." *Sports Illustrated,* LIII (December 8, 1980), 65–66. Title taken from Rhomberg's time with Chattanooga minor league club.

Delbert W. ("Del") Rice
C-MGR. (B: Oct. 27, 1922, Portsmouth, OH-D: Jan. 26, 1983). St. Louis (NL), 1945–1955; Milwaukee (NL), 1955–1959; Chicago (NL), St. Louis (NL), and Baltimore (AL), 1960, Los Angeles (AL), 1961. Remarks: In a 17-year playing career, had 998 hits (79 homers) in 1,309 games; coach, Los Angeles (AL) and California (AL), 1962–1966; Cleveland (AL), 1967; minor league manager, 1968–1971; manager, California (AL), 1972, winning 75 games and losing 80 (.484).

48612. Broeg, Bob. "Catcher for the Cardinals." *Complete Baseball,* V (September 1953), 44–45+.

48613. Hoffman, Jeane. "Del Rice ChaCha's Way Back to Majors." *Baseball Digest,* XX (July 1961), 49–51.

48614. Veech, Ellis J. "Del Rice — Cards' Daily Dish." *Baseball Digest,* XI (August 1952), 45–50.

Edgar Charles ("Sam") Rice ★
OF. (B: Feb. 20, 1890, Morocco, Ind.-D: Oct., 13, 1974). Washington (AL), 1915–1933; Cleveland (AL), 1934. Re-

marks: Obtained 2,404 hits (34 homers) and 351 stolen bases in 2,404 games in two decades; AL stolen base champion, 1920; began as pitcher winning one game and losing one in 1915–1916; had 31-game hitting streak, 1924; named to Indiana Baseball Hall of Fame, 1979; elected to National Baseball Hall of Fame in 1963, where his plaque reads "At bat 600 or more times eight different seasons. Had 200 or more hits in each of six seasons. Batted .322 for 20-year career and had 2987 hits. Set AL record with 182 singles in 1925. Led AL in number of hits 216 in 1924 and 1926. Led AL in putouts for outfielders with 454 in 1920 and 395 in 1922."

48615. Addie, Bob. "Sam Rice Says: 'I Wouldn't Vote for Myself for Hall [of Fame].'" *Baseball Digest,* XIX (June 1960), 76–77.

48616. Allen, Lee and Tom Meany. "Sam Rice." In: their *Kings of the Diamond.* New York: G.P. Putnam's Sons, 1965. Pp. 210–212.

48617. Daniel, Daniel M. "Sam Rice." *Baseball Magazine,* XCI (May 1955), 25–26.

48618. Kermisch, Al. "Sam Rice's Batting Record Purified." *The Baseball Research Journal,* IX (1981), 70–71.

48619. Lane, Ferdinand C. "That Hardy Perennial — Sam Rice." *Baseball Magazine,* XLVII (July 1931), 347–349.

48620. LeCompte, Mary Lou. "Edgar Charles 'Sam' Rice." In: Vol. Q-Z of David L. Porter, ed. *Biographical Dictionary of American Sports: Baseball.* Rev. and enlarged ed. Westport, CT: Greenwood Press, 2000. Pp. 1273–1274.

48621. _____. "Sam Rice." In: John A. Garrity and Marsh C. Carries, eds. *American National Biography.* 24 vols. New York: Oxford University Press, 1999. XVIII, 423–424.

48622. Peterson, Richard F. "Fair or Foul: The Claims of Oral History on the 1925 World Series." *Nine: A Journal of Baseball History and Social Policy Perspectives,* VII (Fall 1998), 75–83.

48623. Rice, Edgar C. ("Sam"). "Baseball Reflections of an Old-Timer." *Baseball Magazine,* XLIV (February 1930), 393–395.

48624. _____. "How the U.S. Navy Made Me a Professional Ball Player." *Baseball Magazine,* XXV (August 1920), 429–431.

48625. Smith, Ron. "Sam Rice." In: his *Heroes of the Hall: Baseball's Greatest Players.* New York: Contemporary Books, 2002. Pp. 377–378.

48626. Stann, Francis. "Sam Rice: He Was a Picture-Book Player." *Baseball Digest,* XXII (July 1963), 19–21.

48627. Ward, John J. "How Sam Rice Broke the Outfield Record." *Baseball Magazine,* XXVII (June 1921), 295–297.

48628. _____. "The Man Who Gave Washington Their Punch." *Baseball Magazine,* XXXIV (December 1924), 298–299.

48629. Wulf, Steve. "The Secrets of Sam." *Sports Illustrated,* LXXIX (July 19, 1993), 58–64.

Grantland Rice *see* **Henry Grantland Rice**
Harry Francis Rice
OF-3B. (B: Nov. 22, 1901, Ware Station, IL.-D: Jan. 1, 1971). St. Louis (AL), 1923–1927; Detroit (AL), 1928–1930; New York (AL), 1930; Washington (AL), 1931; Cincinnati (NL), 1933. Remarks: Had 1,118 hits (48 homers) and 60 stolen bases in 1,023 games in a decade; noted fielder who also played for Minneapolis (AA), Toronto (IL), Nashville (SA), San Francisco (PCL), Seattle (PCL), and Portland (PCL), 1933–1939.

48630. Akin, William E. "Harry Francis Rice." In: Vol. Q-Z of David L. Porter, ed. *Biographical Dictionary of American Sports: Baseball.* Rev. and enlarged ed. Westport, CT: Greenwood Press, 2000. Pp. 1274–1275.

48631. Lane, Ferdinand C. "Harry Rice: The Versatile Star of the St. Louis Browns." *Baseball Magazine,* XXXVI (March 1926), 451–452.

Henry Grantland ("Grant" or "Granny") Rice
WRITER-BROADCASTER. (B: Nov. 1, 1880, Murfreesboro, TN–D: July 13, 1954). Remarks: editor, *Nashville News,* 1901; reporter, *Forester* magazine and *Atlanta Journal,* 1902–1905; reporter, *Cleveland News,* 1905–1907; reporter, Nashville *Tennessean,* 1907–1910; reporter/columnist, *New York Evening Mail,* 1910–1912; reporter/columnist, *New York Tribune/New York Herald Tribune,* 1913–1930; provided play-by-play for first live World Series game radio broadcast, 1922; column, "The Sportlight," syndicated, 1930–1954; J. G. Taylor Spink Award, 1966.

48632. Brathain, Michelle. "Grantland Rice." In: John A. Garrity and Marsh C. Carries, eds. *American National Biography.* 24 vols. New York: Oxford University Press, 1999. XVIII, 412–413.

48633. Cohane, Tim. "See You at the Chatham, Granny." In: his *Bypaths of Glory.* New York: Harper & Row, 1963. Pp. 130–146.

48634. "The Dean, 1880–1954." *Newsweek,* XLIV (July 29, 1954), 50–51.

48635. "An Evangelist of Fun." *Time,* LXIV (July 26, 1954), 38–39.

48636. Everett, George. "Grantland Rice." In: Perry J. Ashley, ed. *Dictionary of Literary Biography, Volume 29: American Newspaper Journalists, 1926–1950.* A Bruccoli Clark Layman Book. Detroit, MI: The Gale Group, 1984. Pp. 304–309.

48637. Fountain, Charles. *Sportswriter: The Life and Times of Grantland Rice.* New York: Oxford University Press, 1993. 327p.

48638. Harper, William. *How You Played the Game: The Life of Grantland Rice.* Colombia, Mo: University of Missouri Press, 1999. 640p.

48639. Inabinett, Mark. *Grantland Rice and His Heroes: The Sportswriter as Mythmaker in the 1920s.* Knoxville, TN: University of Tennessee Press, 1994. 130p.

48640. Lardner, Ring W. "The Keeper of the Bees; Or, Grant on Diamond and Gridiron." *Collier's,* LXXXIII (May 11, 1929), 28–29.

48641. "One of Baseball's Foremost Scribes." *Baseball Magazine,* IX (July 1912), 55–56.

48642. Rice, Grantland. *Base-Ball Ballads.* Nashville, TN: Nashville Tennessean, 1910. 128p. Poems.

48643. _____. "Casey's Revenge." In: Jeff Silverman, ed. *Classic Baseball Stories.* Guilford, CT: Lyons Press, 2003. Chapter 4.

48644. _____. "The Slide of Paul Revere." In: Jeff Silverman, ed. *Classic Baseball Stories.* Guilford, CT: Lyons Press, 2003. Chapter 22.

48645. _____. *The Tumult and the Shouting: My Life in Sport.* New York: A. S. Barnes, 1954.

48646. Winchell, Mark Royden. "Grantland Rice." In: Richard Orodenker, ed. *Dictionary of Literary Biography, Volume 171: Twentieth-Century American Sportswriters.* A Bruccoli Clark Layman Book. Detroit, MI: The Gale Group, 1996. Pp. 282–292.

James Edward ("Jim") Rice
OF. (B: March 8, 1953, Anderson, SC). Boston (AL), 1974–1989. Remarks. Had 2,452 hits (382 homers) and 58 stolen bases in 2,089 games in 16 seasons; AL MVP award, 1978; AL home run champion, 1977–1978, 1983; AL RBI champion, 1978 and 1983 (tie); only player in MLB history with three consecutive 35 HR-200 hit seasons, 1977–1979; had grand slam homer, July 4, 1984; homered Game Seven of 1986 ALCS; scored six runs in 1986 World Series; also played for Pawtucket, where he won the IL Triple Crown, 1974; coach, Boston (AL), 1994–2000; named to Boston Red Sox Hall of Fame, Nov. 1995; inducted into Ted Williams' Hitters Hall of Fame, February 2001.

48647. Alfano, Pete. "Jim Rice, Boston's Other Rookie." *Baseball Digest,* XXXIV (December 1975), 67–71.

48648. Allen, Maury. *Jim Rice, Power Hitter.* New York: Harvey House, 1980. 71p.

48649. _____. "Jim Rice (1974–Present)." In: his *Baseball's 100.* New York: Galahad Books, 1981. Pp. 302–304.

48650. Benson, John. "Jim Rice —1978." In: his *Baseball's Top 100: The Best Individual Seasons of All Time.* Wilton, CT: Diamond Library, 1996. Pp. 239–240.

48651. Brosnan, Jim. "Jim Rice: Baseball's Hercules." *Boy's Life,* LXX (March 1980), 26–29.

48652. Deane, Bill. "Jim Rice Ready to Join Exclusive Batting Club in '84." *Baseball Digest,* XLIII (April, 1984), 62–65.

48653. Durso, Joseph. "Jim Rice: He's Alone in the Fenway Spotlight." *Baseball Digest,* XLIII (July 1984), 36–41.

48654. Fimrite, Ron. "An Ultrastrong Silent Type." *Sports Illustrated,* L (April 9, 1979), 53–61.

48655. Fitzgerald, Joe. "Jim Rice: A Man for All Seasons." *Baseball Quarterly,* II (Spring 1970), 60+.

48656. Gammons, Peter. "Is It Twilight Time?" *Sports Illustrated,* LXVIII (March 14, 1988), 30–32.

48657. Gutman, Bill. "Jim Rice." In: his *Pro Sports Champions.* New York: Julian Messner, 1981. Pp. 6–35.

48658. Honig, Donald. "1978: Jim Rice." In: his *American League MVP's.* New York: Bantam Books, 1989. Pp. 100–101.

48659. "Jim Rice." In: *Current Biography Yearbook, 1979.* New York: H.W. Wilson, 1979. Pp. 307–309.

48660. Liston, Bill. "Why Pitchers Hate to Face Jim Rice." *Baseball Digest,* XXXVII (August 1978), 24–27.

48661. Masterson, Dave and Timm Boyle. "1978." In: their *Baseball's Best: The MVPs.* Chicago, IL: Contemporary Books, 1985. Pp. 292–297.

48662. Nardinelli, Clark. "James Edward 'Jim,' 'Ed' Rice." In: Vol. Q-Z of David L. Porter, ed. *Biographical Dictionary of American Sports: Baseball.* Rev. and enlarged ed. Westport, CT: Greenwood Press, 2000. Pp. 1275–1276.

48663. O'Donnell, Bob. "Jim Rice: He Prefers to Avoid the Spotlight." *Baseball Digest,* XLVI (September 1987), 73–76.

48664. Rasmussen, Larry F. "These Teammates Finished 1–2 In Home Run Derby." *Baseball Digest,* XLIII (January 1984), 30–32. Rice and Tony Armas.

48665. Resciniti, Angelo G. "Jim Rice." In: his *Stars of the Diamond.* Mississauga, Ontario: School Book Fairs, 1981. Pp. 39–48.

48666. Ribowsky, Mark. "It's Like He's Got 1,000 Votes in That Bat." *Sport,* LXVII (July 1978), 14–15+.

48667. Ritter, Lawrence and Donald Honig. "Jim Rice." In: their *The 100 Greatest Baseball Players of All Time.* New York: Crown Publishers, 1981. Pp. 200–201.

48668. Ryan, Morey. "The Hidden Side of Jim Rice." *Sports World,* XXIII (August 1984), 31–32.

48669. Wezsteon, R. "What's Eating Jim Rice?" *Sport,* LXXVIII (June 1987), 40–41.

48670. Whiteside, Larry. "Jim Rice: The Quiet Superstar." In: Dick Kaegel, ed. *The Sporting News 1984 Baseball Yearbook.* St. Louis: *The Sporting News*, 1984. Pp. 4–11.
48671. Wulf, Steve. "Up Against the Wall" *Sports Illustrated,* LXI (August 6,1984), 62–68.

John Rice
UMP. (B: 1920). AL arbiter, 1955–1973; umpired in first World Series night game and always carried a tape measure while working home plate.
48672. Skipper, John C. "John Rice." In: his *Umpires: Classic Baseball Stories from the Men Who Made the Calls.* Jefferson, NC: McFarland & Co., Inc., 1997. Pp. 24–30.

Sam Rice *see* **Edgar Charles ("Sam") Rice**
Robert E. ("Bob") Rich, Jr.
EXEC. (B: 1941, Buffalo, NY). Remarks: President, Rich Products, Inc., owner/CEO, Buffalo (EL), 1983–.
48673. Fink, James. "After 28 Years, Bisons Still a Hit for Bob Rich, Jr." *Business First of Buffalo,* (March 31, 2003), 1+.

James Rodney ("J.R." or "Jim") Richard
P. (B: March 27, 1950, Vienna, LA). Houston (NL), 1971–1981. Remarks: 6'8" hurler won 107 games and lost 71 in a decade; first NL pitcher to strike out 300 batters in a season, 1978; played for Tucson (PCL), 1982–1983, following stroke in June 1980; elected to Louisiana Sports Hall of Fame, 1988.
48674. Bjarkman, Peter C. "James Rodney 'J.R.' Richard." In: Vol. Q-Z of David L. Porter, ed. *Biographical Dictionary of American Sports: Baseball.* Rev. and enlarged ed. Westport, CT: Greenwood Press, 2000. Pp. 1276–1278.
48675. Collier, Ken. "J. R. Richard." In: Tommy Kay, ed. *Tommy Kay's 1980 Baseball Factbook.* Scottsdale, AZ: Jalart House, 1980. Pp. 96–100.
48676. Didinger, Ray. "J.R. Richard of the Astros: He Specializes In 'Smoke.'" *Baseball Digest,* XXXVII (December 1978), 42–45.
48677. "Former Houston Star Says Bad Investments Left Him Homeless." *Jet,* LXXXVII (February 13, 1995), 47–48.
48678. Francis, C. Philip. "J.R. Richard — From Top to Bottom." In: Joseph M. Wayman, ed. *Grandstand Baseball Annual, 1998.* Downey, CA: Joseph M. Wayman, 1998. Pp. 204–205.
48679. Gilbert, Bill. "J. R. Richard's Aborted Career." *The National Pastime,* XVI (1996), 29–31.
48680. Keith, Larry. "Whiff of Spring in Houston." *Sports Illustrated,* LII (April 21, 1980), 34–36+.
48681. Klawans, Harold L. "The Men with the Not So-So-Golden Arms: J. R. Richard and Whitey Ford." In: his *Why Michael Couldn't Hit and Other Tales of the Neurology of Sports.* New York: W.H. Freeman, 1996. Chapter 9.
48682. Kuenster, John. "J.R. Richard Long Overdue for National Recognition." *Baseball Digest,* XXXIX (June 1980), 17–20.
48683. Lautenslager, George. "Another Inning for J.R. Richard." *Nautilus Magazine,* V (April-May 1983), 70–73.
48684. Linkugel, Will A. and Edward J. Pappas. "A Stroke of Misfortune: J.R. Richard." In: their *They Tasted Glory: Among the Missing at the Baseball Hall of Fame.* Jefferson, NC: McFarland & Co., Inc., 1998. Pp. 144–155.
48685. Nock, William. "J.R.'s Pledge: 'I'm Going to Return.'" *Sports Illustrated,* LIV (March 2, 1981), 26–21+.
48686. _____. "Now Everybody Believes Him." *Sports Illustrated,* LIV (April 18,1981), 12–17.
48687. Prisco, Pete. "J.R. Richard at Peace with His New Lifestyle." *Baseball Digest,* XLIII (December 1984), 77–81.

48688. Reid, Ron. "Sweet Whiff of Success." *Sports Illustrated,* XLIX (September 4, 1978), 66+.
48689. Ribowsky, Mark. "This Pitcher Makes Hitters Tremble." *Sport,* LXIX (July 1979), 8–9+.
48690. Santa Maria, Michael and James Costello. "Is Something Wrong Here?" In: their *In the Shadows of the Diamond.* Dubuque, IA: The Elysian Fields Press, 1992. Pp. 249–255.
48691. Twersky, Marty. "J. R. Richard: So Who's That?" *Black Sports Magazine,* VII (September 1977), 48–51

Ruth ("Richy") Richard
C. (B: Sept. 20, 1928, Argus, PA). Grand Rapids Chicks (All American Girls Professional Baseball League), 1947; Rockford Peaches (AAGPBL), 1948–1954. Remarks: In eight seasons, obtained 608 hits (15 homers) in 725 games.
48692. Clark, Dennis S. "Ruth 'Richy' Richard." In: Vol. Q-Z of David L. Porter, ed. *Biographical Dictionary of American Sports: Baseball.* Rev. and enlarged ed. Westport, CT: Greenwood Press, 2000. P. 1278.

Paul Rapier Richards
C-MGR-EXEC. (B: Nov. 21, 1908, Waxahachie, TX-D: May 4, 1986). Brooklyn (NL), 1932; New York (NL), 1933–1935; Philadelphia (AL), 1935; Detroit (AL), 1943–1946. Remarks: In eight big league playing years obtained 321 hits (15 homers) in 523 games; manager, Buffalo (IL), 1947; Seattle (PCL), 1950–1951; manager, Chicago (AL), 1951–1954, Baltimore (AL), 1955–1961, and Chicago (AL), 1976, winning 923 games and losing 901 (.506); named to Texas Sports Hall of Fame, 1959; GM, Houston (NL), 1962–1965; vice president, Atlanta (NL), 1966–1972; consultant, Texas (AL), 1984–1985.
48693. Bisher, Furman. "The Paul Richards System." *Baseball Digest,* XXV (December 1966), 87–89. Managing.
48694. Carmichael, John P. "Richards-One Year Later." *Baseball Digest,* XV (January-February 1956), 71–73.
48695. _____. "Richards' Two-Point Creed." *Baseball Digest,* XIII (March 1950), 93–95.
48696. Crusinberry, James. "Paul Richards: A Forceful Leader." *Baseball Magazine,* LXXXVI (February 1951), 301–303.
48697. Furlong, William B. "He Put the White Sox Back in the League." *Saturday Evening Post,* CCXXIV (July 21, 1951), 25+.
48698. Hatter, Lou. "Thoughts of Paul Richards." *Baseball Digest,* XIX (December 1960), 40–43.
48699. Hilton, George R. "Paul Rapier Richards." In: Vol. Q-Z of David L. Porter, ed. *Biographical Dictionary of American Sports: Baseball.* Rev. and enlarged ed. Westport, CT: Greenwood Press, 2000. Pp. 1278–1280.
48700. Hoffman, John C. "They Won't Love Richards." *Baseball Digest,* X (January 1951), 20–27.
48701. Honig, Donald. "Paul Richards." In: his *The Man in the Dugout.* Chicago, Il: Follett, 1977. Pp. 118–144.
48702. Linn, Ed. "The Double Life of Paul Richards." *Sport,* XX (August 1955), 48–60.
48703. Maisel, Bob. "A Tribute to Paul Richards." *Orioles Gazette,* II (August 3, 1992), 12–13.
48704. MacDonald, Leo. "That Texas Titer, Paul Richards." *Baseball Magazine,* LXXIII (November 1944), 407–409.
48705. Mulvoy, Mark. "Things Are Different in Atlanta. Paul Richards in Charge of the Braves." *Sports Illustrated,* XXVI (March 27, 1967), 53–54.
48706. Overfield, Joseph M. "The [Paul] Richards-[Sam] Jethroe Caper: Fact or Fiction?" *The Baseball Research Journal,* XVI (1987), 33–35.

48707. Pope, Edwin. "Paul Rapier Richards." In his *Baseball's Greatest Managers.* Garden City, NY- Doubleday, 1960. Pp. 204–218.

48708. Povich, Shirley. "Paul Richards, Translated." *Baseball Digest,* XX (April 1961), 27–29.

48709. _____. "Richards Gets a 'Blank Check.'" *Baseball Digest,* IV (November 1945), 45–51.

48710. Richards, Paul R. "Baserunning Strategy." *Sports Illustrated,* II (June 27, 1955), 47; III (July 18, 1955), 40–41.

48711. _____. "The Bunt and Squeeze." *Sports Illustrated,* II (May 23, 1955), 51–52.

48712. _____. "The Hit-and-Run." *Sports Illustrated,* II (May 30, 1955), 37–38.

48713. _____. "The Intentional Pass." *Sports Illustrated,* III (July 25, 1955), 47+.

48714. _____. *Modern Baseball Strategy.* Englewood Cliffs, NJ: Prentice-Hall, 1955. 214p. The then-new manager of the Baltimore Orioles offers anecdotal advice based on his own experiences.

48715. _____. "On the Use of Pinch Hitters." *Sports Illustrated,* II (June 6, 1955), 45+.

48716. _____. "Secrets of a Baseball Manager." *Collier's,* CXXXV (February 18, 1955), 40–44.

48717. _____. "Smart Baseball." In: *Boy's Life,* Editors of. *Baseball as We Played It.* New York: G.P. Putnam, 1969. Pp. 166–176.

48718. _____. "A Wheeler-Dealer's Trading Secrets." Edited by Furman Bisher. *Sport,* XLV (June 1968), 34–37.

48719. Rosenthal, Harold. "Paul Richards." In: his *Baseball's Best Managers.* New York: Nelson, 1961. Pp. 119–138.

48720. Terrell, Roy. "Hawkeye and His Boy Scouts." *Sports Illustrated,* XIV (April 17, 1961), 68–72+.

48721. "Unorthodox Manager." *Time,* LVII (June 4, 1951), 79–80.

48722. Vanderberg, Bob. "Paul Richards: The Wizard of Waxahachie." In: his *Sox — From Lane and Fain to Zisk and Fisk.* Chicago, IL: Chicago Review Press, 1982. Pp. 59–69.

Abram Harding ("Hardy" or "Old True Blue") Richardson

3B-OF-2B. (B: April 21, 1855, Clarksboro, NJ-D: Jan. 14, 1931). Buffalo (NL), 1879–1885; Detroit (NL), 1886–1888; Boston (NL), 1889; Boston (P.), 1890; Boston (AA), 1891; Washington (NL) and New York (NL), 1892. Remarks: In 14 seasons, obtained 1,688 hits (73 homers) and 163 stolen bases in 1,331 games; NL home run champion (11), 1886; NL RBI champion, 1890.

48723. Akin, William E. "Abram Harding 'Hardy,' 'Old True Blue' Richardson." In: Vol. Q-Z of David L. Porter, ed. *Biographical Dictionary of American Sports: Baseball.* Rev. and enlarged ed. Westport, CT: Greenwood Press, 2000. Pp. 1280–1281.

Bobby Richardson *see* **Robert Clinton ("Bobby") Richardson**

Dorothy Gay ("Dot") Richardson

SS-2B-PHYSICIAN. (B: Sept. 22, 1961, Orlando, FL). Player, Orlando Rebels (ASA League), 1976, and USA Softball Association, 1979–1996; University of Louisville M.D.1995; captain, U.S. Olympic Women's Softball Team, 1996; completed residency, University of Southern California, 1999; elected to Florida Sports Hall of Fame, 1999; member, U.S. Olympic Women's Softball Team, 2000; private practice, 2000–2001; Executive Director / Medical Director, USAT National Training Center, 2002–.

48724. "Dot Richardson: Gold Medal, Softball." *People Weekly,* XLVI (August 19, 1996), 47–48.

48725. King, Kelley. "Playing Hardball: A New Format for the Women's Softball League Shuts Out Some Old Friends." *Sports Illustrated for Women,* III (May 1, 2001), 98+.

48726. Marvel, Mark. "They Throw Like Girls." *Esquire,* CXXVI (July 1996), 26–27.

48727. Murphy, Austin. "Dot Richardson." *Sports Illustrated,* LXXXI (July 18, 1994), 54–55.

48728. Richardson, Dot, with Dianne Hales. "Learning to Win: Before the Olympics, I Had My Share of Failures — Then I Taught Myself to Go for the Gold." *Ladies Home Journal,* CXIV (October 1997), 28–30.

48729. _____., with Don Yaeger. *Living the Dream.* New York: Kensington Books, 1997. 180p.

48730. Roberts, Carolanne Griffith. "The Road to Atlanta. *Southern Living,* XXXI (February 1996), 24–26.

Hardy Richardson *see* **Abram Harding ("Hardy") Richardson**

Robert Clinton ("Bobby") Richardson

2B-COACH-POLITICIAN (B: Aug. 19, 1935, Sumter, SC). New York (AL), 1955–1966. Remarks: Had 1,432 hits (34 homers) and 73 stolen bases in 1,412 games in a dozen seasons; had a grand slam homer and six RBIs in Game Three of 1960 World Series; had two triples in Game Six of 1960 World Series, bringing his number of hits in the series to 11 and his RBI count for this classic to a record 12; World Series MVP award, 1960; had nine hits in 1961 World Series; had record 11 ABs in a 22 inning game, June 24, 1962; gloved last out in Game Seven of 1962 World Series; noted fielder; baseball coach at University of South Carolina, 1970–1977; Coastal Carolina C.C. and Liberty University, 1978–1990; active in Republican Party politics and defeated in a bid for U.S. House of Representatives; elected to South Carolina Hall of Fame, 1996.

48731. Appel, Marty. "Bobby Richardson." In: his *Yesterday's Heroes: Revisiting the Old-Time Baseball Stars.* New York: William Morrow, 1988. Pp. 182–186.

48732. August, Bob. "['64] Series Film Takes One Error Away from Richardson: Bounder That Won Fifth Game Took a Bad Hop." *Baseball Digest,* XXIV (March 1965), 71–72.

48733. Bisher, Furman. "Bobby Richardson: A David Among Goliaths." *Baseball Digest,* XXXI (November 1972), 77–81.

48734. "Bobby Richardson." In: *Current Biography Yearbook, 1966.* New York: H. W. Wilson Co., 1966. Pp. 330–332.

48735. Bryson, Bill. "Bobby Richardson: Runs Driven In — by the Truck." *Baseball Digest,* XX (March 1961), 43–45.

48736. Cohen, Haskell. "Bobby Richardson, Unsung Hero." *Baseball Monthly,* II (April 1960, 24–29.

48737. Deindorter, Bob. "Bobby Richardson: One Man in Off-Year." In: Ray Robinson, ed. *Baseball Stars of 1960.* New York. Pyramid Books, 1960. Pp. 143–147.

48738. Ferdensi, TIL "Yankee Gentleman: Bobby Richardson is a Ballplayer People Respect — Not Only Because of His Skills." *Sport,* XXXIV (September 1962), 48–49+.

48739. Forker, Dom. "Bobby Richardson." In: his *Sweet Seasons: Recollections of the 55–64 New York Yankees.* Dallas, TX: Taylor Publishing Co., 1989. Pp. 1–11.

48740. Gallagher, Mark. "Bobby Richardson." In: his *50 Years of Yankee All-Stars.* New York: Leisure Press, 1984. Pp. 163–165.

48741. Graybar, Lloyd J. "Robert Clinton 'Bobby' Richardson, Jr." In: Vol. Q-Z of David L. Porter, ed. *Biographical Dictionary of American Sports: Baseball*. Rev. and enlarged ed. Westport, CT: Greenwood Press, 2000. Pp. 1281–1282.

48742. Hefley, James C. "Bobby Richardson: The Yankee Glue-man Who Sticks to His Beliefs." In: his *Play Ball*. Grand Rapids, MI: Zondervan Publishing House, 1964. Pp. 20–25.

48743. Iooss, Walter, Jr. "The Double Play." *Sport,* XXXVIII (September 1964), 52–56.

48744. Kaplan, Dick. "Bobby Richardson: Valuable Little Guy." In: Ray Robinson, ed. *Baseball Stars of 1963*. New York: Pyramid Books, 1963. Pp. 54–58.

48745. Keith, Larry. "Nothin' Could Be Finah." *Sports Illustrated,* XLII (June 2, 1975), 55–56.

48746. McCormick, Robert. "Bobby Richardson and Tom Tresh." In: Jack Orr, ed. *Baseball's Greatest Players Today*. New York: Watts, 1963. Pp. 75–81.

48747. McVay, I.R. "Yankee Blockade: Hands Across the Infield." *Look,* XXVII (July 16, 1963), 79–81.

48748. Olson, Stan. "Bobby Richardson Looks Back on the Yankee Dynasty Years." *Baseball Digest,* LIV (September 1995), 64–67.

48749. Post, Paul. "After 30 Years, He's Still a Hit with Fans." *Sports Collector's Digest,* XXIV (April 11, 1997), 160–161.

48750. Richardson, Bobby. *Bobby Richardson Story*. New York: Revell, 1965. 159p.

48751. _____. "How to Play Second Base." *Sport,* XL (October 1965), 114–115.

48752. _____. and Johnny Hunton. *Grand Slam: Principles of Baseball and the Christian Life*. Atlanta, GA: Cross Roads Publications, 1978. 256p.

48753. Rizzuto, Philip F. ("Phil"). "Bobby Richardson: Number One at Second Base." In: Editors of *Boy's Life. Baseball as We Played It*. New York: G.P. Putnam, 1969. Pp. 133–143.

48754. Robinson, Ray. "Bobby Richardson." In: Ray Robinson, ed. *Baseball Stars of 1961*. New York: Pyramid Books, 1961. Pp. 152–153.

48755. Shecter, Leonard. "Bobby Richardson's Drive for Respect." *Sport,* XXXVIII (October 1964), 72–80.

Lance Clayton Richbourg
OF-2B-MGR. (B: Dec. 18, 1897, DeFuniak Springs, FL-D: Sept. 10, 1975). Philadelphia (NL), 1921; Washington (AL), 1924; Boston (NL), 1927–1931; Chicago (NL), 1932. Remarks: In eight big league seasons, obtained 806 hits (13 homers) and 65 stolen bases in 698 games; set NL mark of playing 18 innings in right field without a fielding chance, May 14, 1927; also played for Nashville (SL), 1923; Milwaukee (AA), 1924–1926; player, Nashville (SL), 1933–1935; player-manager, Nashville (SL), 1935–1937.

48756. Richbourg, Lance, Jr. "My Father, Lance Richbourg." *The National Pastime,* XXII (2002) 3–8.

Peter Gerard ("Pete") Richert
P. (B: Oct. 29, 1939, Floral Park, NY). Los Angeles (NL), 1962–1964; Washington (AL), 1965–1967; Baltimore (AL), 1967–1971; Los Angeles (N.L), 1972–1973; St. Louis (NL) and Philadelphia (NL), 1974. Remarks: Won 80 games and lost 73, with 51 "saves," in 13 campaigns; struck out seven-in-a row in one game, April 24, 1966.

48757. Rumill, Ed. "Richert Can Best Anybody." *Baseball Digest,* XXVI (February 1967), 63–65.

Arthur Richman
WRITER-EXEC. (B: 1926, New York City). Remarks: Sportswriter, *New York Daily Mirror*, 1942–1963; PR director/special assistant to GM, New York (NL), 1964–1988; senior VP and media advisor, New York (AL), 1989–; credited with idea to hire mgr. Joe Torre (q.v.).

48758. Lucas, Ed and Paul Post. "Yankees Executive Arthur Richman Recalls His 60 Years in the Game." *Baseball Digest,* LX (July 2001), 76–81.

J. Lee Richmond
P. (B: May 5, 1857, Sheffield, OH-D: Oct. 1, 1929). Boston (NL), 1879; Worcester (NL), 1880–1882; Providence (NL), 1883; Cincinnati (AA), 1886. Remarks: In six years, won 75 games and lost 100, with three "saves"; hurled for both Brown University and Worcester simultaneously; had first perfect game in MLB history, June 12, 1880; also in 1880, pitched 74 of Worcester's 83 games, winning 32 and losing 32; retired from baseball to become medical doctor, subsequently becoming a teacher in the public schools of Toledo, Ohio and, at age 65, Dean of Men at the University of Toledo.

48758a. Brownlee, Kimberly. "The Most Wonderful Game: J. Lee Richmond's Perfect Game." *Timeline,* XXI (May-June 2004), 28–33.

48759. Buckley, James, Jr. "J. Lee Richmond." In: his *Perfect!: The Inside Story of Baseball's Sixteen Perfect Games*. New York: Triumph Books, 2002. Pp. 1–17.

48760. Husman, John R. "The First Perfect Game." *Ohio,* XV (May 1992), 39+. In 1879.

48761. _____. "J. Lee Richmond." In: Vol. Q-Z of David L. Porter, ed. *Biographical Dictionary of American Sports: Baseball*. Rev. and enlarged ed. Westport, CT: Greenwood Press, 2000. Pp. 1282–1283.

48762. _____. "J. Lee Richmond's Remarkable 1879 Season." *The National Pastime,* IV (1985), 65–71.

48763. Lawler, Joseph. "Perfection in June." *Yankee,* L (June 1986) 154–155.

48764. _____. "Pre-Phillies Pitcher Posted Majors' First Perfect Game." *Phillies Report,* IV (April 24, 1986), 21–22.

48765. Mayer, Ronald A. "J. Lee Richmond." In: his *Perfect: Biographies and Lifetime Statistics of 14 Pitchers of "Perfect" Baseball Games, with Summaries and Boxscores*. Jefferson, NC: McFarland & Co., Inc., 1991. Pp. 8–22.

48766. Smith, Ronald A. "J. Lee Richmond, Brown University, and the Amateur-Professional Controversy in College Baseball." *The New England Quarterly,* LXIV (March 1991), 82–99.

Wesley Branch ("The Mahatma") Rickey★
C-OF-MGR-EXEC. (B: Dec. 20, 1881, Stockdale, OH-D: Dec. 9, 1965). St. Louis (AL), 1905–1906; New York (AL), 1907; St. Louis (AL), 1914. Remarks: In four playing years, had 82 hits (three homers) and nine stolen bases in 119 games; manager, St. Louis (A.L), 1913–1915 and St. Louis (NL), 1920–1926, winning 597 games and losing 664 (.473); vice president, St. Louis (AL), 1916; St Louis (NL), 1917–1920 and 1925–1942 (while with Cardinals created the modern minor league farm system), and Brooklyn (NL), 1942–1950 (while the Dodgers broke baseball color line by bringing Jackie Robinson to majors in 1947); GM, Pittsburgh (NL), 1961–1955 and board chairman, Pittsburgh (NL), 1956–1959; organizer and president of the ill-fated Continental League, 1960–1962, which set off era of major league expansion in 1960s-1970s; advisor to president, St. Louis INL), 1963–1965; deeply religious and never played or managed on Sunday; elected to National Baseball Hall of Fame in 1947, where his plaque reads simply: "Founder of farm system which he developed for St. Louis Cardinals and Brooklyn Dodgers. Copied by all other major league teams. Served as executive for Browns, Cardinals, Dodgers and Pirates, Brought Jackie Robinson to Brooklyn in 1947."

48767. Abrams, Al. "Rickey's Flopping: He's Lost His Touch." *Baseball Digest,* XII (May 1960), 5–10.

48768. Abrams, Roger I. "The Owners and the Commissioner: Branch Rickey and Charles O. Finley." In: his *Legal Bases: Baseball and the Law.* Philadelphia, PA: Temple University Press, 1998. Pp. 91–114.

48769. Andersen, Donald Ray. "Branch Rickey and the St. Louis Cardinal Farm System: The Growth of an Idea." Unpublished PhD. Dissertation, University of Wisconsin at Madison, 1975. 291p.

48770. Austin, John R. "A Method for Facilitating Controversial Social Change in Organizations: Branch Rickey and the Brooklyn Dodgers." *The Journal of Applied Behavioral Science,* XXXIII (March 1997), 101–118.

48771. Behn, Robert D. "Branch Rickey as a Public Manager: Fulfilling the Eight Responsibilities of Public Management." *Journal of Public Administration Research and Theory,* VII (January 1997), 1–33.

48772. Bell, Floyd L. "Branch Rickey: The Major League Manager Who Is Different." *Baseball Magazine,* XXIV (April 1920), 646–648.

48773. "Branch Rickey." In: Joseph J. Vecchione, ed. *The New York Times Book of Sports Legends.* New York: Times Books, 1991. Pp. 245–251.

48774. "Branch (Wesley) Rickey." In: *Current Biography Yearbook, 1945.* New York: H.W. Wilson Co., 1945. Pp. 497–500.

48775. Burr, Harold C. "Fly-by-Night Rickey." *Baseball Digest,* VIII (September 1940), 43–45.

48776. Chalberg, John C. *Rickey & Robinson: The Preacher, the Player and America's Game.* Wheeling, IL: Harlan Davidson, 2000. 270p.

48777. Chamberlain, John. "Brains, Baseball, and Branch Rickey." *Harpers,* CXCVI (April 1948), 346–355. Abridged in *Reader's Digest,* LIII (July 1948), 101–105.

48778. Daley, Arthur. "The Mahatma Bows Out." *Baseball Digest,* XIV (November-December 1955), 93–97.

48779. Dexter, Charles. "Branch Rickey: 'Can I Do It Again [at Pittsburgh]?'" *Sport,* X (February 1961), 64+.

48780. _____. "Brooklyn's Sturdy Branch." *Collier's,* CXVI (September 15, 1946), 17+.

48781. _____. "'The Mahatma' and 'The Lip': The Story of Rickey and Durocher." *Baseball Digest,* VII (February 1948), 3–6.

48782. Drebinger, John. "The Rise of Rickey." *Baseball Magazine,* LXX (January 1943), 341–343.

48783. Fitzgerald, Ed. "Branch Rickey, Dodger Deacon." *Sport,* III (November 1947), 58–68.

48784. _____. "*Sport's* Hall of Fame: Branch Rickey." *Sport,* XXXIII. (May 1962), 62–63+.

48785. Fox, Stephen. "The Education of Branch Rickey." *Civilization,* (September-October 1995), 52–57.

48786. "From Rags to Riches: The Success Story of Branch Rickey." *Saturday Evening Post,* CCVI (June 9, 1934 18–17+.

48787. Frommer, Harvey. *Rickey and Robinson: The Men Who Broke Baseball's Color Line.* New York: Macmillan, 1982. 240p. Reprinted in a 256-page edition by the Dallas, TX, firm of Taylor Publishing in 2003.

48788. Gardner, Paul. "'The Mahatma' and the Pirates." In: Ken W. Purdy, ed. *True's 1951 Baseball Annual.* Greenwich, CT: Fawcett Publications, 1951. Pp. 32–33+.

48789. Gietschier, Steven P. "Branch Rickey." In: John A. Garrity and Marsh C. Carries, eds. *American National Biography.* 24 vols. New York: Oxford University Press, 1999. XVIII, 480–481.

48790. Glennon, Fred. "Baseball's Surprising Moral Ex-

ample: Branch Rickey, Jackie Robinson, and the Racial Integration of America." In: his *The Faith of Fifty Million.* Philadelphia, PA: Westminster Press, 2002. Pp. 145–166.

48791. Graham, Frank. "Branch Rickey Rides Again: The Return of 'The Mahatma.'" *Saturday Evening Post,* CCXXXVI (March 0, 1963), 66–68.

48792. Green, Howard. "Branch Rickey." *The National Pastime,* XVI (1996), 104–106.

48793. Greene, Doc. "Rickey: A Study in Humanity." *Baseball Digest,* XX (Auguat.1961), 85–87.

48794. Holland, Gerald. "Mr. Rickey and the Game." *Sports Illustrated,* II (March 7, 1956), 38–41. Reprinted in Herbert W. Wind, ed., *The Realm of Sport* (New York: Simon and Schuster, 1966), pp. 56–62 and in David Halberstam, ed. *The Best American Sports Writing of the Century* (Boston, MA: Houghton, Mifflin, 1999), pp. 219–235.

48795. Holmes, Tommy. "Who Gave Bums Bush to Whom?" *Baseball Digest,* X (February 1951), 29–31.

48796. Honig, Donald. "Branch Rickey." In: his *Baseball America: the Heroes of the Game and the Times of Their Glory.* New York: Macmillan, 1985. Pp. 252–255.

48797. Kamisar, Yale. "The A Student Who Gave Up the Law for Baseball." *Law Quadrangle Notes,* XL (Summer 1997), 48–50.

48798. Lipman, David. *Mr. Baseball: The Story of Branch Rickey.* New York: G.P. Putnam, 1966. 191p.

48799. Mann, Arthur. *Baseball Confidential: Secret History of the War Among Chandler, Durocher, MacPhail, and Rickey.* New York: David McKay, 1951.184p.

48800. _____. *Branch Rickey, American in Action.* Boston: Houghton, Mifflin, 1957. 312p. Abridged in *Look,* XXI (August 20–September 17, 1957), 71–72+, 74–76+, 111+.

48801. _____. "Has Rickey Failed at Pittsburgh?" *Sport,* XVI (June 1954), 16–23.

48802. Meany, Thomas. "The Dodgers Ain't No Accident." *Collier's,* CXXV (June 24, 1950), 23+.

48803. Miller, Hub. "'The Mahatma's' Magic." *Baseball Magazine,* LXXVI (February 1946), 299–301+.

48804. Nason, Jerry. "A Tip of His Own Helmet to Rickey." *Baseball Digest,* XXV (September 1968), 49–51.

48805. O'Toole, Andrew. *Branch Rickey in Pittsburgh: Baseball's Trailblazing General Manager for the Pirates, 1950–1955.* Jefferson, NC: McFarland & Co., Inc., 2000. 213p.

48806. Parrott, Harold. "Meet Mr. Rickey." *Baseball Digest,* II (February 1943), 43–53.

48807. Polner, Murray. *Branch Rickey: A Biography.* New York! Atheneum, 1982. 307p.

48808. Pratkanis, Anthony R. and Marlene E. Turner. "Nine Principles of Successful Affirmative Action: Branch Rickey, Jackie Robinson, and the Integration of Baseball." In: Peter M. Rutkoff, ed. *The Cooperstown Symposium on Baseball and American Culture, 1997 (Jackie Robinson).* Jefferson, NC: McFarland & Co., Inc., 2000. Pp. 151–176.

48809. Puerzer, Richard J. "Engineering Baseball: Branch Rickey's Innovative Approach to Baseball Management." In: William M. Simons, ed. *The Cooperstown Symposium on Baseball and American Culture 2002.* Jefferson, NC: McFarland & Co., Inc., 2003. Pp. 81–94.

48810. Rickey, Branch. *Branch Rickey's Little Blue Book: Wit and Strategy from Baseball's Last Wise Man.* Ed by John J. Monteleone. New York: Macmillan, 1995. 142p. Reprinted by the Kingston, NY, firm of Total Sports Publishing in a 160-page 2004 edition.

48811. _____. "Three Points to Stardom." *Baseball Di-*

gest, XIII (August 1954), 15–19. Thoughts by one of the game's most noted managers/executives.

48812. Riger, Robert. "Branch Rickey." In: his *Athlete.* New York: Simon and Schuster, 1980. Pp. 30–43.

48813. Robinson, Jecide. "Branch Rickey." In: his *Baseball Has Done It.* Philadelphia: Lippincott, 1964. Pp. 40–50.

48814. _____. "The Most Unforgettable Character I've Met." *Reader's Digest*, LXXIX (October 1961), 97–102.

48815. Robinson, Murray. "Branch Rickey's Three Gifts." *Baseball Digest*, XXV (February 1960), 13–15.

48816. Russo, Neal. "The Trouble with Rickey." *Baseball Digest*, XXIII (December 1964), 77–80.

48817. Shannon, Mike. "Branch Rickey." In: his *Tales from the Dugout: The Greatest True Baseball Stories Ever Told.* Lincolnwood, IL: NTC/Contemporary Books, 1997. Pp. 155–157.

48818. Sheed, Wilfrid. "Branch Rickey." *Sport,* LXXVII (December 1986), 29+.

48819. Smith, Ron. "Branch Rickey." In: his *Heroes of the Hall: Baseball's Greatest Players.* New York: Contemporary Books, 2002. Pp. 378–379.

48820. Smith, Walter ("Red"). "The Bending Branch." *Sports Illustrated*, I (August 23, 1954), 68–69.

48821. Stevens, John D. "As the Branch is Bent: Rickey as College Coach at the University of Michigan." *Nine: A Journal of Baseball History and Social Policy Perspective,* II (Spring 1994), 277–286.

48822. Stockton, J. Roy. "The Brain Comes to Brooklyn." *Saturday Evening Post*, CCXV (February 11, 1941), 24–25+.

48823. Thorn, John and Jules Tygiel. "Signing Jackie Robinson." *The National Pastime*, X (1990), 7–12.

48824. Tygiel, Jules. "The Great Experiment Fifty Years Later." In: Peter M. Rutkoff, ed. *The Cooperstown Symposium on Baseball and American Culture, 1997 (Jackie Robinson).* Jefferson, NC: McFarland & Co., Inc., 2000. Pp. 257–270.

48825. Voigt, David Quentin. "Wesley Branch 'The Mahatma' Rickey." In: Vol. Q–Z of David L. Porter, ed. *Biographical Dictionary of American Sports: Baseball.* Rev. and enlarged ed. Westport, CT: Greenwood Press, 2000. Pp. 1283–1285.

48826. Wolf, Al. "Hollywood Goes Rickey." *Baseball Digest*, VIII (August 1949), 65–67.

48827. Woodward, Stan. "In the Rickey Manner." *Baseball Digest*, IX (July 1950), 19–24.

48828. Young, Dick. "Rickey's Tea Party." *Baseball Digest*, VII (June 1948), 9–11.

Greg Riddoch

MGR. (B: July 17, 1945). San Diego (NL), 1990–1992. Remarks: won 200 games and lost 194 (.508); earlier, had served as manager for Seattle (Northwest League), 1974, Eugene (Northwest League), 1975–1976, 1978–1981; asst. then dir. of player development, Cincinnati (NL), 1983–1985; assoc. dir. of player development, San Diego (NL), 1986; coach, San Diego (NL), 1987–1990; established Greg Riddoch Major League Baseball & Softball Academy, 1993–1997; coach, Tampa Bay (AL), 1998–1999; dir. of player development, Milwaukee (NL), 2000–2002; instructor, Higher Ground Softball Camps, Tipton, GA. and defensive coordinator, Clinton (Midwest League), 2003–2004; manager, Spokane (Northwest League), 2005–

48829. Owens, Bill. "New Man in Town." *San Diego Magazine*, XLII (October 1990), 116+.

Steven George ("Steve") Ridzik

P. (B: April 29, 1929, Yonkers, NY). Philadelphia (NL),

1950–1955; Cincinnati (NL), 1955; New York (NL), 1956–1957; Cleveland (AL), 1958; Washington (AL), 1963–1965; Philadelphia (NL), 1966. Remarks: Won 39 games and lost 38, with 11 "saves," in a dozen summer big league campaigns, broken at one point by four years in the minors.

48830. Libby, Bill. "Travails of a Non-Star." *Baseball Digest*, XXIV (February 1965), 55–62.

Steven Allan Riess

WRITER. (B: August 26, 1947, New York City). Remarks: Assistant professor of history, State University of New York College at Brockport, 1974–1975; lecturer in social sciences, University of Michigan — Dearborn, 1975–1976; assistant professor, associate professor, and professor of history, 1976–.

48831. Riess, Steven A. "I Am Not a Baseball Historian." *Rethinking History,* V (March 2001), 27–41.

David Allan ("Dave" or "Rags" or "Snake") Righetti

P. (B: Nov. 28, 1966, San Jose, CA) New York (AL), 1979, 1981–1990; San Francisco (NL), 1991–1993; Oakland (AL) and Toronto (AL), 1994; Chicago (AL), 1995. Remarks: Won 82 games and lost 79, with 252 "saves," in 16 seasons; won one game of 1981 ALCS; threw a no-hitter, July 4, 1981; had MLB-record 46 "saves" in 1986; coach, San Francisco (NL), 2000–date; son of Leo Righetti (below).

48832. Ballen, Kate, et al. "News/Trends: The Righetti Factor." *Fortune*, CXVII (January 18, 1988), 12–14.

48833. Cairns, Bob. "Dave Righetti." In: his *Pen Men: Baseball's Greatest Bullpen Stories Told by the Men who Brought the Game Relief.* New York: St. Martin's Press, 1992. Pp. 355–364.

48834. Cohen, Irwin. "On the Baseball Beat: Dave Righetti." *Baseball Cards,* IV (October 1984), 36–41.

48835. "Dave Righetti: What a Relief." *Yankees Magazine,* V (September 20, 1984), 9–14.

48836. Donnelly, Joe. "Persistence Paid Off for Yankees' Dave Righetti." *Baseball Digest*, XLI (January 1982), 31–35.

48837. Geosits, Stephanie J. "The Riches of Rags." *Yankees Magazine,* XX (January 2000), 34–45.

48838. Honig, Donald. "1981: Dave Righetti." In: his *American League Rookies of the Year.* New York: Bantam Books, 1989. Pp. 86–88.

48839. James, Robert. "Dave Righetti." In: Ken Collier, ed. *The Baseball Book, 1987.* Scottsdale, AZ: Jalart House, 1987. pp. 63–65.

48840. Kaplan, Jim. "He Went from 'Rags' to Riches." *Sports Illustrated*, LIX (July 25, 1983), 46–47.

48841. Lieber, Jill. "The Relief is Not So Sweet." *Sports Illustrated*, LXXII (April 16, 1990), 70–73.

48842. Noble, Marty. "Sacrifice by Dave Righetti a Welcome Relief for Yankees." *Baseball Digest*, XLIV (April 1985), 75–78.

48843. "A Quirk of Fate Brought Dave Righetti to the Yankees." *Yankees Magazine,* IV (September 1, 1983), 14–17.

48844. Ribowsky, Marty. "Stranger Than Paradise." *Inside Sport,* VIII (October 1986), 78–87.

48845. Righetti, Dave, as told to George Vass. "The Game I'll Never Forget." *Baseball Digest,* LII (June 1993), 49–51. 1981 ALCS.

48846. Rubin, Bob. "Dave Righetti: Ready to Put It All Together." *Baseball Digest,* XLII (June 1983), 39–43.

48847. Springsteen, Art. "The Righetti Decision — a Historical Perspective." *Baseball Analyst,* I (August 1984), 10–16.

48848. Weir, Robert E. "David Allan 'Rags,' 'Snake'

Righetti." In: Vol. Q-Z of David L. Porter, ed. *Biographical Dictionary of American Sports: Baseball*. Rev. and enlarged ed. Westport, CT: Greenwood Press, 2000. Pp. 1285–1286.

Leo Righetti
SS. (B: March 3, 1927, San Francisco, CA-D: Feb. 19, 1998). Newark (IL) and Binghampton (EL), 1944; Binghampton (EL), 1946; Victoria (W.I.), 1947; Binghampton (EL) and Augusta (SA), 1948; Augusta (SA), 1948–1949; Sacramento (PCL), 1951; Toledo (AA), 1952; San Francisco (PCL), 1953–1955; Seattle (PCL), 1955–1957. Remarks: In 12 minor league campaigns, obtained 1,201 hits and 42 homers in 1,445 games; father of David Righetti (above).

48849. Kelley, Brent P. "Leo Righetti." In: his *The San Francisco Seals, 1946–1957: Interviews with 25 Former Baseballers*. Jefferson, NC: McFarland & Co., Inc., 2002. Pp. 187–194.

Charles ("Cy" or "Charley") Rigler
UMP. (B: May 16, 1882, Massillon, OH-D: Dec. 21, 1936). Remarks: A star on the original semipro Massillon Tigers football team of 1903, who became a NL arbiter in 1906 and served through 1935, becoming NL umpire supervisor in 1936, just prior to his death; credited with introducing the custom of indicating balls with fingers of left hand and strikes with those on right.

48850. Gerlach, Larry R. "Charles 'Cy,' 'Charley' Rigler." In: Vol. Q-Z of David L. Porter, ed. *Biographical Dictionary of American Sports: Baseball*. Rev. and enlarged ed. Westport, CT: Greenwood Press, 2000. Pp. 1286–1287.

48851. Krueckeberg, Dan. "Take Charge Cy." *The National Pastime*, IV (1985), 7–11.

Cy Rigler *see* **Charles ("Cy" or "Charley") Rigler**
Bill Rigney *see* **William Joseph ("Bill" or "Billy" or "Specs" or "The Cricket") Rigney**
William Joseph ("Bill" or "Billy" or "Specs" or "The Cricket") Rigney
2B-1B-MGR-BROADCASTER. (B: Jan. 29, 1919, Alameda, CA-D: Feb. 2, 2001). New York (NL), 1946–1953. Remarks: Obtained 510 hits (41 homers) and 26 stolen bases in 664 games in eight playing years; led off three innings of a game with hits, May 29, 1948; manager, Minneapolis (AA), 1954–1956; manager, New York (NL) and San Francisco (NL), 1956–1960, 1976; Los Angeles (AL) and California(AL), 1961–1969, Minnesota (AL), 1970–1972, winning 1,239 games and losing 1,321 (.484); broadcaster, Oakland (AL), 1973; scout, San Diego (NL), 1974–1975 and California (AL), 1978–1982; coach, San Diego (NL), 1975; broadcaster and assistant to president, Oakland (AL), 1983–1990; elected to Bay Area Sports Hall of Fame, 1996.

48852. Allen, Maury. "Bill Rigney." In: his *Baseball: The Lives Behind the Seams*. New York: Macmillan, 1990. Pp. 3–16.

48853. Bitker, Steve. "Bill Rigney." In: his *The Original San Francisco Giants: The Giants of '58*. Champaign, IL: Sports Publishing, 1998. Pp. 47–62.

48854. _____. "Local Sage Bill Rigney Reminisces About the Game." *Bay Sports Review*, V (August 1995), 16–20.

48855. Daley, Arthur. "Bill Rigney: Part Ottie [Mel Ott], Part 'Lip' [Leo Durocher]." *Baseball Digest*, XIV (November-December 1955), 77–81.

48856. Freed, Frederick. "Life of a Giant." *Baseball Digest*, VI (October 1947), 47–50.

48857. _____. "Rigney at Second for the Giants." *New Republic*, CXVII (August 11, 1947), 20–24.

48858. Kelley, Brent P. "Bill Rigney: Full Circle." In: his *The Early All-Stars: Conversations with Standout Baseball Players of the 1930s and 1940s*. Jefferson, NC: McFarland & Co., Inc., 1997. Pp. 129–143.

48859. Libby, Bill. "Bill Rigney : The Art of Living Under the Axe." *Los Angeles*, X (August 1965), 51–54.

48860. Linn, Ed. "Year of Decision for Bill Rigney." *Saturday Evening Post*, CCXXXII (June 25, 1980), 25, 103–104.

48861. Lowenfish, Lee. "World Series 2000 A.D.: 50 Years Ago, Branch Rickey Wrote a Magazine Article About the Future of Baseball." In: Richard Levin, ed. *2000 World Series Program*. New York: Major League Baseball Promotion Corp., 2000. Pp. 106–109.

48862. Mandel, Mike. "Bill Rigney." In: his *The San Francisco Giants: An Oral History*. Santa Cruz, CA: Mike Mandel, 1979. Pp. 12–17.

48863. Noble, John Wesley. "Bill Rigney and His Giants." *Sport*, XXVIII (August 1959), 56–57+.

48864. Porter, David L. "William Joseph 'Bill,' 'Specs' Rigney." In: Vol. Q-Z of David L. Porter, ed. *Biographical Dictionary of American Sports: Baseball*. Rev. and enlarged ed. Westport, CT: Greenwood Press, 2000. Pp. 1287–1289.

48865. Rigney, Bill. *Fine Points of Baseball Strategy*. Los Angeles, CA: Union Oil Company of California, 1958. 11p. Booklet of tips.

48866. _____., as told to George Vass. "The Game I'll Never Forget." *Baseball Digest*, XXXIV (October 1975), 75–77.

48867. Swift, E. M. "Up Against the Wall." *Sports Illustrated*, LXXIII (October 29, 1990), 82–84.

48868. Waldmeir, Pete. "'The Manager Belongs in the Dugout'—[Bill] Rigney." *Baseball Digest*, XXVI (July 1967), 21–23.

48869. Will, George F. "Bill Rigney: Baseball's Favorite Uncle." In: his *Bunts: Curt Flood, Camden Yards, Pete Rose and Other Reflections on Baseball*. New York: Touchstone Books, 1998. Pp. 235–239.

48870. Wilson, John R. M. "Bill Rigney." In: Paul Betz and Mark C. Carnes, eds. *American National Biography: Supplement I*. New York: Oxford University Press, 2002. Pp. 514–515.

48871. Wulf, Steve. "Good Man, Sometimes." *Sports Illustrated*, LXXIII (December 31, 1990), 69–70.

Jose Rijo
P. (B: Jose Antonio Rijo Abreu, May 13, 1965, San Cristobal, D.R.). New York (AL), 1984; Oakland (AL), 1985–1987; Cincinnati (NL), 1988–2002. Remarks: Through 2002, had 116 victories, 91 defeats, and three "saves"; Florida State League MVP Award, 1983; struck out 16 batters in one game, April 16, 1986; won one game of 1990 NLCS and two of 1990 World Series; World Series MVP Award, 1990; went seven years between victories, 1995–2002; retired due to elbow injuries.

48872. Crasnick, Jerry. "Jose Rijo: 'The Divorce, the World Series, My Contract — That's All Over Now, I Have to Go Out There and Fight." *Sport*, LXXXII (July 1991), 21–22.

48873. Fitzsimmons, David. "Jose Antonio Rijo." In: Vol. Q-Z of David L. Porter, ed. *Biographical Dictionary of American Sports: Baseball*. Rev. and enlarged ed. Westport, CT: Greenwood Press, 2000. P. 1289.

48874. "Jose, Bip Reds' Best." *Reds Report*, VI (February 1993), 3–4.

48875. McCoy, Hal. "Jose Rijo and the Nasty Boys." In: Zander Hollander, ed. *1991: The Complete Handbook of Baseball*. New York: Signet Books, 1991. Pp. 16–25.

48876. Rijo, Jose, as told to George Vass. "The Game I'll Never Forget." *Baseball Digest*, LIII (August 1994), 53–55.

48877. Shannon, Mike. "Jose Rijo." In: his *Tales from the Dugout: The Greatest True Baseball Stories Ever Told*. Lincolnwood, IL: NTC/Contemporary Books, 1997. Pp. 158–159.

James Joseph ("Jimmy") Ring

P. (B: Feb. 15, 1895, Brooklyn, NY-D: July 6, 1965). Cincinnati (NL), 1917–1920; Philadelphia (NL), 1921–1924; New York (NL), 1925; St. Louis (NL), 1926; Philadelphia (NL), 1927. Remarks: In 12 big league seasons, won 118 games and lost 149, with 11 "saves"; won one game and lost one in 1919 "Black Sox" series.

48878. Ward, John J. "The Man Who Threw the White Sox for a Loss." *Baseball Magazine*, XXIV (May 1920), 674–675.

Billy Ripkin *see* **William Oliver ("Billy") Ripken**

Calvin Edwin ("Cal") Ripken, Sr.

C-OF-MGR. (B: Dec. 17, 1935, Aberdeen, MD-D: March 25, 1999). Remarks: Manager, Fox Cities (Three I League, 1957–1964) and manager, Baltimore (AL) farm system, 1961–1974, winning 904 games; coach, Baltimore (AL), 1976–1984, 1986, 1989–1992; manager, Baltimore (AL), 1985, 1987–1988, winning 68 games and losing 101 (.402); father of Cal Ripken, Jr. and William ("Billy") Ripken (below) and first to simultaneously manage two sons in MLB.

48879. Albin, Larry. "The Baltimore Ripkens: A Big Hit." *50 Plus*, XXIV (June 1984), 26–28+.

48880. Boswell, Thomas. "The Ripken Team, Kith and Kinship." In: Edward Ehre, ed. *The Best Sports Stories of 1984*. St. Louis, MO: *The Sporting News*, 1984. Pp. 14–23. Also published in the author's *Why Time Begins on Opening Day* (Garden City, NY: Doubleday, 1984), pp. 263–274.

48881. Cowherd, Kevin. "Cal Ripken Learns That Father Does Know Best." *Baseball Digest*, XLI (November 1982), 29–42.

48882. Henneman, Jim. "The Ripkens Cal Are the Orioles' First Family." In: Dick Kaegel, ed. *The Sporting News 1984 Baseball Yearbook*. St. Louis: *The Sporting News*, 1984. Pp. 58–62.

48883. Hersch, Hank. "One Big Rip-Roaring Family Affair." *Sports Illustrated*, LXVI (March 9, 1987), 26–28.

48884. Hildreth, Jim. "When a Dad's Dream Finally Comes True." *U.S. News and World Report*, XCIV (June 20,1983), 35–36.

48885. Ripken, Cal, Sr., with Larry Burke. *The Ripken Way: A Manual for Baseball and Life*. New York: Pocket Books, 1999. 224p.

48886. Wulf, Steve. "Let's Play Ball, Dad." *Sports Illustrated*, LVI (March 22, 1982), 30–32+.

Calvin Edwin ("Cal") Ripken, Jr.

SS-3B (B: Aug. 24, 1960, Havre de Grace, MD). Baltimore (AL), 1981–2001. Remarks: Had 3,184 hits (431 homers) and 36 stolen bases in 3,001 games in 21 seasons; AL Rookie of the Year award, 1982; led AL in doubles, 1983; recorded final putout of 1983 World Series; AL MVP award, 1983, 1991; hit for cycle, May 6, 1984; had 95 consecutive errorless games, April 14–July 27, 1990; All-Star Game MVP Award, 1991, 2001; had eight RBIs in one game, May 28, 1996; had two grand slam homers in 1997; had homer in 1997 ALCS; had six hits in one game, June 13, 1999; MLB career-leader in grounding into double plays (324); holds SS records in numerous categories, including total number of homers, extra-base hits, and total bases; played in record 2,632 consecutive games ("The Streak," concluded on Sept. 20, 1998), exceeding previous record held by "Iron Man" Lou Gehrig (q.v.); uniform no. 8 retired by Baltimore (AL), Oct. 6, 2001; owner, Aberdeen Ironbirds (New York-Pennsylvania League), 2002–date; son of Cal Ripken, Sr. (above) and brother of William ('Billy") Ripken (above).

48887. Albin, Larry. "The Baltimore Ripkens: A Big Hit." *50 Plus*, XXIV (June 1984), 26–28+.

48888. Anderson, Dave. "Baseball's Iron Men: Lou Gehrig and Cal Ripken." In: George Leonard, ed. *Athlon Baseball 1995*. Nashville, TN: Athlon, 1995. Pp. 27–34.

48889. *Baltimore Sun*, Editors of and *The Sporting News*, Editors of. *Cal—Celebrating the Career of a Baseball Legend*. St. Louis, MO: *The Sporting News*, 2001. 176p.

48890. Bamberger, Michael. "The Kids are All Right." *Sports Illustrated*, XCVII (September 2 2002), 48–50, 53–4. Ripken's challenge to Little League.

48891. *Beckett Tribute: Cal Ripken, Jr.* Dallas, TX: Beckett Publishers, 1995. 80p.

48892. Bloom, Barry M. "Paradise Lost." *Sport*, LXXXIX (June 1997), 68–72.

48893. _____. "Pride of the Orioles." *Sport*, LXXXVI (September 1995), 84+.

48894. Boswell, Thomas. "Baseball's Best: Cal Ripken at Mid-Career." *Washington Post Magazine*, (March 22, 1992), 14–20.

48895. _____. "Cal Ripken, Jr.: Cracking the Show." In: Dick Wimmer, ed. *The Home Run Game*. Short Hills, NJ: Burford Books, 1999. Chapter 15.

48896. _____. "For Timeless Player, It was Time." In: Richard Ford, ed. *The Best American Sports Writing, 1999*. Boston, MA: Houghton, Mifflin, 1999. Pp. 69–72. Reprinted in Richard Ford, ed., *The Best American Sports Writing, 1999* (Boston, MA: Houghton, Mifflin, 1999), pp. 69–72.

48897. _____. "The Ripken Team, Kith and Kinship." In: Edward Ehre, ed. *The Best Sports Stories of 1984*. St. Louis, MO: *The Sporting News*, 1984. Pp. 14–23. Also published in the author's *Why Time Begins on Opening Day* (Garden City, NY: Doubleday, 1984), pp. 263–274.

48898. Brett, Michael. "Cal Ripken Reveals His Special Delight." *Sports World*, XXIII (August 1984), 29–30.

48899. Broome, Tol. "Jock Talk: Cal Ripken, Jr." *Beckett Baseball Card Monthly*, VII, no. 149 (August 1997), 10+.

48900. Buck, Roy. *Cal Ripken, Jr.: All-Star Shortstop*. Chicago, IL: Children's Press, 1985. 41p.

48901. "Cal Ripken, Jr." In: *Good Sports : Athletes Your Kids Can Look Up To*. Dallas, TX: Beckett Publications, 1999. Chapter 23.

48902. "Cal Ripken, Jr." In: Laurie L. Harris, ed. *Biography Today, 1996: Profiles of People of Interest to Young Readers*. Detroit, MI: Omnigraphics, 1996. pp. 126–137.

48903. "Cal Ripken, Jr. Joins the True Value [Advertising] Team." *Do-It-Yourself Retailing*, CLXX (May 1996), 25–26.

48904. Campbell, Jim. *Today's Stars: Cal Ripken, Jr.* Philadelphia, PA: Chelsea House, 1997. 64p.

48905. Chass, Murray. "Ripken, the Iron Man, to Retire at Season's End." *The New York Times Biographical Service*, (June 2001), 950–952.

48906. Chen, Theo. "A Second Look: Cal Ripken, Jr." *Beckett Baseball Card Monthly*, VI (May 1989), 73–74.

48907. Clary, Jack. "Trammel, Ripken, Blount: How They're Turning Back the Clock." *Sports World*, XXIII (October 1984), 29–31.

48908. Coffey, Wayne. "Baseball's Baby Boom." *Sport,* LXXIII (September 1982), 56–58.

48909. Cowherd, Kevin. "Cal Ripken Learns That Father Does Know Best." *Baseball Digest,* XLI (November 1982), 39–42.

48910. _____. "Should the Orioles Play Cal Ripken, Jr., at Third Base in '86?" *Baseball Digest,* XLV (March 1986), 63–70.

48911. Cramer, Richard Ben. "Cal: End of the Iron Age." *USA Weekend,* (March 2, 2001), 6–9.

48912. _____. "A Native Son's Thoughts." *Sports Illustrated,* LXXXIII (September 11, 1995), 56–64, 66, 68. Reprinted in John Feinstein, ed., *The Best American Sports Writing, 1996* (Boston, MA: Houghton, Mifflin, 1996), pp. 331–344.

48913. Crothers, Tim. "Is It Time to Sit Down?" *Sports Illustrated,* LXXXVII (August 4, 1997), 83–84.

48914. Dodd, Mike. "One-on-One with Baseball 'Ironman' Cal Ripken." *Baseball Digest,* LIV (December 1995), 45–46.

48915. Edelson, Mat. "Cal on the Verge." In: John Feinstein, ed. *The Best American Sports Writing, 1996.* Boston, MA: Houghton, Mifflin, 1996. Pp.314–330.

48916. "Pride of the Orioles." *Washingtonian,* XXX (September 1995), 64–67+.

48917. Eisenberg, John. "Dossier: Cal Ripken, Jr." *Details,* XIX (April 2001), 49+.

48918. Ey, Craig S. "Cal-ebration: Everyone's Cashing in on the Streak." *Baltimore Business Journal,* XIII (August 11, 1995), 1–2.

48919. Felchner, William. "Cal Ripken, Jr., Checklist." *Baseball Cards,* VIII (January 1988), 65–69.

48920. Fimrite, Rm. "He's Done His Daddy Proud." *Sports Illustrated,* LX (April 2, 1984), 34–36.

48921. Gleisser, Benjamin. "A Closer Look: Cal Ripken, Jr." *Beckett Baseball Card Monthly,* VIII (May 1991), 6–7.

48922. Gottlieb, Nat. "How Cal Ripken Proved His Critics Wrong." *Baseball Digest,* LI (July 1992), 51–53.

48923. Gutman, Bill. *Cal Ripken, Jr.: Baseball's Iron Man.* New York: Millbrook Press, 1998. 48p.

48924. Harrison, Don and Carolyn. *Cal Ripken, Jr. Checklist Book, 1980-1995.* Hampton, VA: The 10th Inning, 1995. 175p.

48925. "He Keeps Going and Going." *Sports Illustrated for Kids,* VII (August 1995), 32–42.

48926. Henneman, Jim. "One More Prize for Cal Ripken, Jr.: Major League Player of the Year." In: Bob Sparks, ed. *Baseball '84.* St. Petersburg, FL: National Association of Professional Baseball Leagues, 1984. Pp. 6–8.

48927. _____. "The Ripkens Cal are the Orioles' First Family." In: Dick Kaegel, ed. *The Sporting News 1984 Baseball Yearbook.* St. Louis, MO: *The Sporting News,* 1984. Pp. 58–62.

48928. Herman, Gail "Count on Cal." *Men's Health,* VII (June 1994), 54–57.

48929. _____., et al. *Cal Ripken, Jr.: Play Ball!.* New York: Dial Books. for Young Readers, 1999. 48p.

48930. Hersch, Hank. "One Big Rip-Roaring Family Affair." *Sports Illustrated,* LXVI (March 9, 1987), 26–28.

48931. Hertzel, Bob. "Cal Ripken Redefines the Art of the Classic Shortstop." *Baseball Digest,* XLII (December 1983), 45–49.

48932. Hildreth, Jim. "When a Dad's Dream Finally Comes True." *U.S. News and World Report,* XCIV (June 20, 1983), 35–36.

48933. Hoffer, Richard. "Old Glories: Retirement of Orioles' Cal Ripken, Jr. and Padres Tony Gwynn." *Sports Illustrated,* XCV (October 15, 2001), 50–52.

48934. _____. "Sportsman of the Year." *Sports Illustrated,* LXXXIII (December 18, 1995), 70–76, 78, 83–84, 86–88, 90.

48935. Hood, Robert E. "Cal Ripken: The Perfect Shortstop." *Boy's Life,* LXXXII (August 1992), 22–24.

48936. Joseph, Paul. *Cal Ripken, Jr.* Edina, MN: Abdo and Daughters, 1997. 32p.

48937. Kiersh, Edward. "Interview: Cal Ripken." *Inside Sports,* XIV (June 1992), 22–28.

48938. Kirkpatrick, Curry. "Cal Ripken, Jr." *TV Guide,* XLIII (July 8, 1995), 10–14.

48939. _____. "The Pride of the Orioles." *Newsweek,* CCVI (September 11, 1995), 79+.

48940. Koenig, Bill. "Holy Cal: Ripken Nears the 3,000-hit and 400-home Run Milestones, Culminating His Battle Back from a Tumultuous Spring." *USA Today Baseball Weekly,* IX (August 4, 1999). 8–9.

48941. Ksicinski, Jim. "Silent Cal and Fun-Loving George [Brett]." In: Jim Ksicinski and Tom Flaherty. *Jocks and Socks: Inside Stories from a Major League Locker Room.* Chicago, IL: Contemporary Books, 2001. Pp. 139–148.

48942. Kuenster, John. "Cal Ripken, Jr., an Early Choice as 1991 Player of the Year." *Baseball Digest,* LI (January 1992), 17–21.

48943. Kurkjian, Tim. "Man of Iron." *Sports Illustrated,* LXXXIII (August 7, 1995), 22–32, 34, 37.

48944. _____. "One of a Kind." *ESPN: The Magazine,* IV (October 1, 2001), 52–57.

48945. _____. "Rip on a Tear." *Sports Illustrated,* LXXV (July 29, 1991), 24–26.

48946. _____. "Shortchanging Cal: Why Moving Ripken to Third Would be an Error by the Orioles." *Sports Illustrated,* LXXXIV (June 3, 1996), 74, 76.

48947. Lane-O'Neill, A. "King Cal." *Kid City,* no. 77 (April 1996), 8–9.

48948. Leahy, Michael. "Swing Shift: Cal Ripken, Jr." *The Washington Post Magazine,* (April 2, 2000), 6–11. Reprinted in Bud Collins, ed., *The Best American Sports Writing, 2001* (Boston, MA: Houghton, Mifflin, 2001), pp. 92–114.

48949. Leiker, Ken. "1–1995: Ken Ripken, Jr. Breaks Lou Gehrig's Record for Consecutive Games Played." In: his *Major League Baseball Memorable Moments: The Most Memorable Moments in Major League Baseball History.* New York: Ballantine Books, 2002. Pp. 12–15.

48950. Lord, L. J. "For the Fans, Day In and Day Out." *U.S. News & World Report,* CXIX (September 18, 1995), 16–17.

48951. Lucas, Ed and Paul Post. "Farewell to Greatness: Teammates and Foes Pay Tribute to Cal Ripken's Career." *Baseball Digest,* LX (November 2001), 50–55.

48952. Lupica, Mike. "The Cherry O's." *Esquire,* CXXV (May 1996), 48–49.

48953. _____. "Let's Play 2000." *Esquire,* CXXIII (April 1995), 48+.

48954. Macnow, Glen. *Sports Great Cal Ripken, Jr.* Hillside, NJ: Enslow, 1993. 64p.

48955. Mansfield, Stephanie. "My Husband the Hero." *Ladies Home Journal,* CXIII (August 1996), 98+. Views of Kelly Ripken.

48956. Marx. Jeffrey. "Cal Makes It Real for Dreamers: Ripken's Hands-on Tutorial of Wanna-be Players Spells Fantastic Adventures Under Arizona Sun." *USA Today Baseball Weekly,* VIII (February 10, 1999), 18–19.

48957. McMane, Fred. "Cal Ripken, Jr." In: his *The*

3,000 Hit Club. Champaign, IL: Sports Publishing, 2000. Pp. 167–174.

48958. Montville, Leigh. "The Long Haul: Cal Ripken Reaches the 3,000 Hit Mark." *Sports Illustrated,* XCII (April 24 2000), 52–57. Reaching 3,000 hits.

48959. Nathan, Daniel A. and Mary G. McDonald. "Yearning for Yesteryear: Cal Ripken, Jr., the Streak, and the Politics of Nostalgia." *American Studies,* XLII (Spring 2001), 99–123.

48960. "The New Ripken." *ESPN: The Magazine,* VII (April 26, 2004), 30+.

48961. Nicholson, Lois. *Cal Ripken, Jr.: Quiet Hero.* 2nd ed. Centreville, MD: Tidewater Publishers, 1995. 116p. A 100-page first edition was published in 1993.

48962. Olney, Buster. "2,130 & 2,131: A Scrapbook of Memories from 'The Streak.'" In: George Leonard, ed. *Athlon Baseball 1996.* Nashville, TN: Athlon, 1996. Pp. 136–138.

48963. Palmer, Sally. "People's Choice." *Beckett Future Stars & Sports Collectibles,* VII, no. 75 (July 1997), 10+.

48964. Pavitt, Charles. "Does Cal Ripken Tire?: Another Way to Find Out." *By the Numbers,* VI (March 1994), 9–10.

48965. Pierman, C. J. "Cal Ripken and the Condition of Freedom: Theme and Variation on the American Work Ethic." *Nine: A Journal of Baseball History and Social Policy Perspectives,* VII (Fall 1998), 59–74.

48966. Plummer, William. "Man at Work: Cal Ripken Breaks Consecutive Game Record." *People Weekly,* XLIV (September 18, 1995), 68–70.

48967. Pope, Edwin. "How Reggie Jackson's Advice Helped Cal Ripken." *Baseball Digest,* XLII (June 1983), 18–20.

48968. Porter, David L. "Calvin Edwin 'Cal' Ripken, Jr." In: Vol. Q-Z of David L. Porter, ed. *Biographical Dictionary of American Sports: Baseball.* Rev. and enlarged ed. Westport, CT: Greenwood Press, 2000. Pp. 1290–1292.

48969. Rainie, H. "Chasing Lou Gehrig." *U.S. News & World Report,* CXVII (December 26, 1994), 87–88.

48970. Rambeck, Richard. *Cal Ripken, Jr.* Mankato, MN: Child's World, 1993. 31p.

48971. Ribowsky, Mark, "Cal is in Wonderland." *Inside Sports,* VI (April 1984), 38–45.

48972. Richmond, Paul. "Local Hero." *GQ—Gentlemen's Quarterly,* LXIII (May 1993), 166–171+.

48973. Ripken, Cal, Jr., with Dan Gutman and Mike Bryan. *Cal Ripken, Jr.: My Story.* New York: Dial Books. for Young Readers, 1999. 113 p.

48974. _____. "Learn to Play Cal's Way." *Sports Illustrated for Kids,* IV (June 1992), 28–33.

48975. _____. "My Greatest Day in Baseball." In: Eliot Cohen, ed. *My Greatest Day in Baseball.* New York: Little Simon, 1991. Pp. 87–89.

48976. _____. "Position Perfect." *KidSports,* III, no. 2 (1991), 22–25.

48977. _____. *Ripken: Cal on Cal.* Edited by Mark Vincent. Arlington, TX: Summit Publishing Group, 1995. 112p. Largely pictorial.

48978. _____. "Standing Tall at Short Stop." *KidSports,* III, no. 1 (1991), 14–21.

48979. _____. "When I was a Kid: Interview." *Junior League Baseball,* no. 14 (March-April 1998), 10+.

48980. _____., as told to George Vass. "The Game I'll Never Forget." *Baseball Digest,* LII (January 1993), 69–72.

48981. _____., with Mike Bryan. *The Only Way I Know.* New York: Viking Press, 1997. 326p.

48982. Roberts, S. V. "Remember, Baseball is a Great Game." *U.S. News & World Report,* CXIX (August 14, 1995), 6–7.

48983. Rogers, Phil "Cal Ripken: More Than Baseball's Iron Man." *Baseball Digest,* LIX (September 2000), 54–59.

48984. Rosenfeld, Harvey. *Iron Man: The Cal Ripken, Jr. Story.* New York: St. Martin's Press, 1995. 276p.

48985. Rosenthal, Ken. "The Man Behind the Iron Mask." *Beckett Baseball Card Monthly,* XV (May 1998), 20–23.

48986. Sandground, Grant. "Player's Choice: Cal Ripken, Jr." *Beckett Baseball Card Monthly,* XVII (May 2000), 18–19.

48987. Savage, Jeff. *Cal Ripken, Jr.: Star Shortstop.* Hillside, NJ: Enslow, 1994. 64p.

48988. Schmuck, Peter. "Cal Ripken, Jr.: On Course to Make Baseball History." *Baseball Digest,* LIII (February 1994), 34–37.

48989. _____. "A Matter of Record." *Sport,* LXXXIII (May 1992), 22–27.

48990. _____. "Shortstop of Steel." In: Gary Levy, ed. *The Sporting News 1992 Baseball Yearbook.* St. Louis, MO: The Sporting News, 1992. Pp. 12–14.

48991. _____. "Still Going." In: George Leonard, ed. *Athlon's 1992 Pro Baseball.* Nashville, TN: Athlon's 1992. Pp. 60–75.

48992. Smith, Ron. "Cal Ripken, Jr.-78." In: his *The Sporting News Selects Baseball's 100 Greatest Players.* St. Louis, MO: *The Sporting News,* 1998. Pp. 170–171.

48993. Snyder, Deron. "'The Streak' Clings Like a Second Shadow." *USA Today Baseball Weekly,* III (July 21, 1993), 4–5.

48994. Stadnicki, Michael. "Ripken Museum a Dream Destination for Fans, Collectors." *Sports Collector's Digest,* XXV (December 25, 1998), 74–75.

48995. Stallard, Tracy. "Cal Ripken, Jr., Interview." *Baseball Cards,* VIII (January 1988), 28–35.

48996. Steadman, John F. "Cal Ripken, Jr.: Pride of the Orioles." *Baseball Digest,* L (October 1991), 28–34.

48997. Strauss, Joe. "The Streak is Over, but Cal Ripken's Record Will Endure." *Baseball Digest,* LVIII (January 1999), 44–46.

48998. Strazzabosco, Jeanne. *Learning About the Work Ethic from the Life of Cal Ripken, Jr.* New York: Rosen Pub. Group's PowerKids Press, 1996. 24p.

48999. Summerall, Pat and Jim Moskovitz, with Craig Kubey. "Cal Ripken, Jr." In: their *Pat Summerall's Sports in America: 32 Celebrated Sports Personalities Talk About Their Most Memorable Moments In and Out of the Sports Arena.* New York: HarperCollins, 1996. Pp. 223–236.

49000. Thornton, K. D. "Cal Ripken, Jr." In: Ken Collier, ed. *The Baseball Book, 1984.* Scottsdale, AZ: Jalart House, 1984. Pp. 5–6.

49001. "A True Baseball Hero: Why Cal Ripken, Jr., Stands by His Union." *American Teacher,* LXXIX (April 1995), 3+.

49002. "2131: A Baseball Odyssey." In: Joe Hoppel, ed. *The Sporting News 1995 Baseball Yearbook.* St. Louis, MO: The Sporting News, 1995. Pp. 14–21.

49003. Van Dyck, Dave. "Cal Ripken Puts His Record Streak Behind Him." *Baseball Digest,* LVIII (June 1999), 70–73.

49004. Verducci, Tom. "The Pleasures of His Company: The Worst Thing Anyone Ever Said About Cal Ripken Is That He Never Misses a Game." *Sports Illustrated,* LXXXIII (September 18, 1995), 98+.

49005. _____. "The Solitary Man." *Sports Illustrated,* LXXVIII (June 28, 1993), 40–42.

49006. Weaver, Earl, *et al. Nine Innings with Cal Ripken, Jr.: By the People Who Know Him Best.* Dallas, TX: Beckett Publications, 1998. 179p.

49007. Wiley, Ralph. "A Monumental Streak." *Sports Illustrated,* LXXII (June 18, 1990), 70–74.

49008. Will, George F. "The Defense: Cal Ripken's Information." In: his *Men at Work: The Craft of Baseball.* New York: HarperPerennial, 1991. Pp. 231–292.

49009. ____. "Skill and Mere Will." In: his *Bunts: Curt Flood, Camden Yards, Pete Rose and Other Reflections on Baseball.* New York: Touchstone Books, 1998. Pp. 97–99.

49010. Wulf, Steve. "Iron Bird." *Time,* CXLVI (September 11, 1995), 68–73.

49011. ____. "Let's Play Ball, Dad." *Sports Illustrated,* LVI (March 22, 1982), 30–32+.

49012. ____. "Two for the Show." In: Richard Levin, ed. *2001 World Series Official Program.* New York: Major League Baseball Promotion Corp., 2001. Pp. 72–79. Ripken and Tony Gwynn.

William Oliver ("Billy") Ripken
2B. (B: Dec. 16, 1964, Havre De Grace, MD). Baltimore (AL), 1987–1992; Texas (AL), 1993–1994; Cleveland (AL), 1995; Baltimore (AL), 1996; Texas (AL), 1997; Detroit (AL), 1998. Remarks: In 12 years, had 674 hits (20 homers) and 25 stolen bases in 912 games; brother of Cal Ripkin, Jr., (above), and son of Cal Ripkin, Sr. (above).

49013. Albin, Larry. "The Baltimore Ripkens: A Big Hit." *50 Plus,* XXIV (June 1984), 26–28+.

49014. Hersch, Hank. "One Rip-Roaring Family Affair." *Sports Illustrated,* LXVI (March 9, 1987), 26–28+.

49015. Gammons, Peter. "Billy the Kid Rides Again." *Sports Illustrated,* LXVII (August 3, 1987), 18–19.

49016. Green, Paul M. "Billy Ripken: Interview." *Baseball Cards,* IX (May 1989), 42–49.

49017. Henneman, Jim. "Billy Ripken of the Orioles: Finally His Own Man." *Baseball Digest,* L (July 1991), 47–49.

Charles August ("Swede") Risberg
SS. (B: Oct. 13, 1894, San Francisco, CA-D: Oct. 13, 1975).Chicago (AL), 1917–1920. Remarks: Obtained 394 hits (six homers) and 52 stolen bases in 476 games in four years; also played for Vernon (PCL), 1915–1916; Chick Gandil (q.v.)'s deputy in and last survivor of those involved in the 1919 Black Sox World Series scandal.

49018. Algren, Nelson. "The Swede was a Hard Guy." *Southern Review,* VII (Spring 1942), 873–879.

49019. Spalding, John E. "Swede Risberg." In: his *Pacific Coast League Stars, Vol. II: Ninety Who Made It to the Majors, 1905–1957.* San Jose, CA: John E. Spalding, 1997. Pp. 32–33.

Swede Risberg *see* **Charles August ("Swede") Risberg**
Claude Cassium ("Little All Right") Ritchey
SS-2B-3B. (B: Oct. 5, 1873, Emlenton, PA-D: Nov. 8, 1951). Cincinnati (NL), 1897; Louisville (NL), 1898–1899; Pittsburgh (NL), 1900–1906; Boston (NL), 1907–1909. Remarks: Obtained 1,636 hits (18 homers) and 149 stolen bases in 1,671 games in 13 seasons; had a double, four walks, and two RBIs in the 1903 World Series; also played for Louisville (AA), 1910.

49020. Braun, Jack C. "Claude Cassium 'Little All Right' Ritchey." In: Vol. Q–Z of David L. Porter, ed. *Biographical Dictionary of American Sports: Baseball.* Rev. and enlarged ed. Westport, CT: Greenwood Press, 2000. Pp. 1292–1293.

Todd Everett Ritchie
P. (B: November 7, 1971, Portsmouth, VA). Minnesota (AL), 1997–1998; Pittsburgh (NL), 1999–2001; Chicago (AL), 2002; Milwaukee (NL), 2003; Tampa Bay (AL), 2004–. Remarks: Through 2004, has won 43 games and lost 54; signed minor league contract with Pittsburgh (NL), January 2005.

49021. Paine, Sylvia. "Look Out for Number 1." *Twins Magazine,* IV (June 1991), 45–46.

Wallace Reid ("Wally") Ritchie
P. (B: July 12, 1965, Glendale, CA). Philadelphia (NL), 1987–1992. Remarks: Had six victories, five defeats, and four "saves" in four years.

49022. Ison, Jim. "Wally Ritchie." In: his *Mormons in the Major Leagues.* Cincinnati, OH: Action Sports, 1991. Pp. 162–165.

Wally Ritchie *see* **Wallace Reid ("Wally") Ritchie**
Lawrence Stanley Ritter
WRITER. (B: May 23, 1922, New York City-D: Feb. 15, 2004). Remarks: Instructor/assistant professor of economics, Michigan State University, 1949–1955; economist, Federal Reserve Bank of New York, 1955–1960; professor of finance, New York University, Graduate School of Business Administration, 1960–; in addition to baseball works, has written several texts on money and economics.

49023. Shannon, Mike. "Lawrence S. Ritter." In: his *Baseball: The Writer's Game.* 2nd ed. Dulles, VA: Brassy's, Inc., 2002. Pp. 211–224.

Jim Rivera *see* **Manuel Joseph ("Jim" or "Jungle Jim") Rivera**
Manuel Joseph ("Jim" or "Jungle Jim") Rivera
OF. (B: July 22, 1922, New York City). St. Louis (AL), 1952; Chicago (AL), 1952–1961; Kansas City (AL), 1961. Remarks: Obtained 911hits (83 homers) and 160 stolen bases in 1,171 games in a decade; A. L. stolen base champion, 1955; had two inside-the-park homers in one year, 1958; made famous catch in Game Five of 1959 World Series.

49024. Bamberger, Michael. "Strikeouts by the Boatload." *Sports Illustrated,* LXXXVI (March 24, 1997), 50–53.

49025. Brown, Warren. "Jim Rivera Talking." *Sport,* XX (October I 955), 20–21+.

49026. Grow, Milton. "The Case for Jim Rivera." *Baseball Digest,* XI (April 1952), 91–93.

49027. ____. "The Jim Rivera Story." *Sport,* XII (June 1952), 18–17+.

49028. ____. "Jim Rivera: The Player Who Lives with a Scandal." In: Ralph Daigh, ed. *True's 1956 Baseball Yearbook.* Greenwich, CT: Fawcett Publications, 1956. Pp. 19–19+.

49029. Kiersh, Edward. "Jim Rivera: But Where's Ingrid Bergman?" In: his *Where Have You Gone, Vince DiMaggio?* New York: Bantam Books, 1983. Pp. 165–167.

49030. Richman, Milton. "He Calls It Hustle." In: Bruce Jacobs, ed. *Baseball Stars of 1955.* New York: Lion Books, 1955. Pp. 100–106.

49031. Vanderberg, Bob. "Jim Rivera: Out of the Jungle." In: his *Sox—From Lane and Fain to Zisk and Fisk.* Chicago, IL: Chicago Review Press, 1982. Pp. 154–162.

Mariano Rivera
P. (B: Nov. 29, 1969, Panama City, Panama). New York (AL), 1995–. Remarks: Through 2004, has won 47 games and lost 31, with 336 "saves"; World Series MVP Award, 1999; ALCS MVP Award, 2003; with 53, led AL in "saves," 2004.

49032. Bamberger, Michael. "Strikeouts by the Boatload: Coolheaded Mariano Rivera is Ready to Bring the Heat as the New Closer for the Yankees." *Sports Illustrated,* LXXXVI (March 24, 1997), 50–53.

49033. Bradley, Jeff. "Starring Mo: Rivera Has Secured His Place as Baseball's All-Time Greatest Big-Game Closer." *ESPN: The Magazine,* IV (November 12, 2001), 52–53.

49034. Giannone, John. "Mariano Rivera Faces New Challenges as Yankee Closer." *Baseball Digest,* LVI (June 1997), 70–71.

49035. Klapish, Bob. "Just the Outs, MO" *Yankees Magazine,* XX (July 1999), 58–67.

49036. Kuenster, Bob. "The Terminator." *Baseball Digest,* LIX (February 2000), 22–25.

49037. Pierce, C. P. "The Hammer of God." *Esquire,* CXXXV (June 2001), 62–68.

49038. Sorci, Rick. "Baseball Profile: Yankees' Closer Mariano Rivera." *Baseball Digest,* LX (January 2001), 38–39.

Ruben Rivera
OF. (B: Ruben Rivera Moreno, Nov. 14, 1973, Chorrera, Panama). New York (AL), 1995–1996; San Diego (NL), 1997–2000; Cincinnati (NL), 2001; Texas (AL), 2002. Remarks: Had 334 hits (62 homers) and 49 stolen bases in 631 games in eight years; originally traded to New York (AL) for 2002 season, but released for alleged stealing of items belonging to teammates.

49039. Schwarz, Alan. "Rookie Report: Ruben Rivera." *Beckett Baseball Card Monthly,* XII, no. 122 (May 1995), 126–127.

John Milton ("Mickey" or "Gozzlehead" or "Mick the Quick") Rivers
OF. (B: Oct. 31, 1948, Miami, FL). California (AL), 1970–1975; New York (AL), 1976–1979; Texas (AL), 1979–1984. Remarks. Had 1,660 hits (61 homers) and 267 stolen bases in 1,468 games in 15 seasons; led AL in triples, 1974–1975; A. L. Stolen Base champion, 1975; had two doubles in Game Three of 1977 World Series.

49040. Bechtel, Mark. "Yankee Doodle Dandy." *Sports Illustrated,* XCVIII (June 30, 2003), 64–65.

49041. Calabria, Pat. "Mickey Rivers Keeps the Yankees on the Move." *Baseball Digest,* XXXV (October 1976), 29–32.

49042. Eiderldn, Phil "Mickey Rivers: Fastest Legs in the West." *Baseball Digest,* XXXIV (September 1975), 43–46.

49043. Gallagher, Mark. "Mickey Rivers." In: his *50 Years of Yankee All-Stars.* New York: Leisure Press, 1984. Pp. 166–167.

49044. Hecht, Henry. "Life with the Gozzlehead." *Sports Illustrated,* LIII (October 6, 1980), 94+.

49045. James, Robert. "Mickey Rivers." In: Tommy Kay, ed. *Tommy Kay's 1981 Baseball Factbook.* Scottsdale, AZ: Jalartt House, 1981. Pp. 103–106.

49046. Kowet, Don. "Run, Rivers, Run." *Sport,* LXI (September 1975), 40–43.

49047. Lidz, Franz. "Ol' Man Rivers." *Sports Illustrated,* LXXII (January 29, 1990), 36–38.

49048. McKenzie, Mike. "Mickey Rivers' View of Life Often 'Out of Left Field.'" *Baseball Digest,* XLIII (February 1984), 37–40.

49049. McMillan, Ken. "Mickey Rivers." In: his *Tales from the Yankee Dugout: A Collection of the Greatest Yankee Stories Ever Told.* Champaign, IL: Sports Publishing, Inc., 2001. Pp. 147–149.

49050. Ribowsky, Mark. "'Take the Extra Base' Baseball's Too Slow? Sprinters Like Mickey Rivers, Darting Merrily Around Basepaths, Are Adding Spice to the Grand Old Game." *Black Sports,* V (June 1976), 10–15.

49051. Rivers, Mickey and Michael DeMarco. *Ain't No Sense Worryin': The Wit and Wisdom of "Mick the Quick" Rivers.* Chicago, IL: Sports Publishing, 2003. 200p.

49052. Shannon, Mike. "Mickey Rivers." In: his *Tales from the Dugout: The Greatest True Baseball Stories Ever Told.* Lincolnwood, IL: NTC/Contemporary Books, 1997. Pp. 160–161.

49053. Weir, Robert E. "John Milton 'Mickey,' 'Mick the Quick' Rivers." In: Vol. Q-Z of David L. Porter, ed. *Biographical Dictionary of American Sports: Baseball.* Rev. and enlarged ed. Westport, CT: Greenwood Press, 2000. Pp. 1293–1294.

Mickey Rivers *see* **John Milton ("Mickey") Rivers**

Eppa ("Eppa Jephtha") Rixey, Jr. ★
P. (B. May 3, 1891, Culpeper, VA-D: Feb. 28, 1963). Philadelphia (NL), 19121920; Cincinnati (NL), 1921–1933. Remarks: In a 21-year career, had 266 victories, 261 defeats and 14 "saves"; moved directly from college (University of Virginia) to the majors; served with A.E.F. in France in 1918; win total remained N.L mark until 1959; lost total remains the record for big league lefties; fans voted him all-time left-handed pitcher in Cincinnati history in 1969; elected to National Baseball Hall of Fame in 1963, where his plaque reads: "Won 266-lost 251-pct. 515-ERA 3.15. Set record for most victories by left-handed pitcher. Led league in victories with 25 in 1933. Gave only 182 base on balls in 4494 innings."

49054. Allen, Lee, and Thomas Meany. "Eppa Rixey." In: their *Kings of the Diamond.* New York: G.P. Putnam, 1965. Pp. 63–65. A profile by Jan Finkel appears as a number in the SABR Biography Project and is reproduced online at

49055. Driver, David. "Eppa Rixey: A Son of the Old Dominion." *The National Pastime,* XV (1995), 85–87.

49056. Farmer, Ted. "Eppa Rixey, Virginia Squire." In: Joseph M. Wayman, ed. *Grandstand Baseball Annual, 1996.* Downey, CA: Joseph M. Wayman, 1996. Pp. 57–60.

49057. Fleitz, David L. "Eppa Rixey." In: his *Ghosts in the Gallery at Cooperstown: Sixteen Little-Known Members of the Hall of Fame.* Jefferson, NC: McFarland & Co., Inc., 2004. Pp. 137–150.

49058. Goldblatt, Abe and Robert W. Wentz. "Eppa Rixey: A Virginia Gentleman." In: their *The Great and the Near Great: A Century of Sports in Virginia.* Norfolk, VA: Donning Company, 1976. Pp. 18–19.

49059. Lane, Ferdinand C. "Eppa, Not Jeptha, Rixey." *Baseball Magazine,* XLIV (February 1930), 397–399+.

49060. _____. "Where Height is a Telling Factor." *Baseball Magazine,* XXXV (July 1925), 345–347.

49061. Lawler, Joseph. "Eppa Rixey: One of Phils' Greatest Lefthanders." *Phillies Report,* VII (April 20, 1989), 26–27.

49062. Rathgeber, Bob. "The Pitching Virginia Gentleman: Eppa Rixey." In: *Cincinnati Reds Scrapbook.* Virginia Beach, VA: J.C.P. Corp. of Virginia, 1982. Pp. 52–53.

49063. Smith, Ira L. "Eppa (Jeptha) Rixey." In: his *Baseball's Famous Pitchers.* New York: A.S. Barnes, 1954. Pp. 140–144.

49064. Smith, Ron. "Eppa Rixey." In: his *Heroes of the Hall: Baseball's Greatest Players.* New York: Contemporary Books, 2002. Pp. 380–381.

49065. Weaver, Robert G. "Eppa 'Eppa Jephtha' Rixey, Jr." In: Vol. Q-Z of David L. Porter, ed. *Biographical Dictionary of American Sports: Baseball.* Rev. and enlarged ed. Westport, CT: Greenwood Press, 2000. Pp. 1294–1295.

Philip Francis ("Phil" or "Scooter") Rizzuto★
SS-BROADCASTER. (B: Sept. 25, 1918, New York

City). New York (AL), 1941–1942, 1946–1956. Remarks: Obtained 1,588 hits (38 homers) and 149 stolen bases in 1,661 games in 13 seasons; homered in 1942 and 1951 World Series; led AL in sacrifice hits, 1949–1952; AL MVP award, 1950; established various records; first mystery guest on TV show "What's My Line," Feb. 2, 1950; radio broadcaster, New York (AL), 1957–1996; named to the Sports Hall of Fame of New Jersey, 1993; elected to National Baseball Hall of Fame in 1994, where his plaque reads: "Overcame diminutive size (5'6," 150 lbs.) to anchor superb Yankee teams which won 10 pennants and 8 World Series during his 13 major league seasons. Outstanding shortstop on five consecutive world championship clubs. Skilled bunter and enthusiastic baserunner with sold .273 lifetime batting average. All-Star five times and AL MVP in 1950 when he peaked at .324 with 200 hits and a .439 slugging pct."

49066. Allen, Maury. "Phil Rizzuto (1941–1956)." In: his *Baseball's 100*. New York: Galahad Books, 1981. Pp. 235–237.

49067. Baldassaro, Larry. "Schmoozing with the Scooter: A Conversation with Phil Rizzuto." *Elysian Fields Quarterly*, XIII (Fall 1994), 70–81.

49068. Berkow, Ira. "Too Small to Play, Right Size for Hall." *The New York Times Biographical Service*, XXV (July 1994), 1143–1145.

49069. Bonner, Mary G. "Phil Rizzuto." In: her *Baseball Rookies Who Made Good*. New York: Alfred A. Knopf, 1954. Pp. 18–26.

49070. Borst, William A. ("Bill"). "Philip Francis 'Phil,' 'Scooter' Rizzuto." In: Vol. Q-Z of David L. Porter, ed. *Biographical Dictionary of American Sports: Baseball*. Rev. and enlarged ed. Westport, CT: Greenwood Press, 2000. Pp. 1295–1296.

49071. Cohane, Tim. "Rizzuto: The Yankee Nipper." *Baseball Digest*, IX (July 1950), 5–9.

49072. _____. "Scooter is Still Scooting." *Look*, XXII (August 5, 1958), 31–32.

49073. Corliss, Rich. "Willie, Mickey...and Scooter?" *Time*, CXLIV (August 1, 1994), 56–57.

49074. Davis, Mac. "Sixty-Six Inches of Ballplayer." In: his *The Lore and Legends of Baseball*. New York: Lantern Press, 1953. Pp. 23–24.

49075. Dexter, Charles. "Baseball Has Been Good to the 'Scooter.'" *Sport*, VII (December 1954), 12–15.

49076. _____. *Phil Rizzuto, Baseball Hero*. Greenwich, CT: Fawcett Publications, 1951. 35p.

49077. "Does Phil Rizzuto's Career Measure Up?" *Yankees Magazine*, IV (February 23, 1984), 14–19.

49078. Drebinger, John. "The MVP Winner for 1950." *Baseball Magazine*, LXXXVI (January 1951), 265–237.

49079. _____. "What Makes Rizzuto Great?" *Baseball Magazine*, LXXXIX (June 1952), 14–16.

49080. Forker, Dom. "Phil Rizzuto." In: his *The Men of Autumn*. Dallas, TX: Taylor Publishing Co., 1989. Pp. 43–52.

49081. Fox, Larry. "Phil Rizzuto: 'Get a Shoeshine Box, Kid.'" In: his *Little Men in Sports*. New York: W. W. Norton Co., 1968. Pp. 98–109.

49082. Gallagher, Mark. "Phil Rizzuto." In: his *50 Years of Yankee All-Stars*. New York: Leisure Press, 1984. Pp. 168–171.

49083. Geosits, Stephanie J. "Rizzuto Reflects and Projects." *Yankees Magazine*, XIX (February 1999), 47–49.

49084. Graham, Frank. "The Plays' Coleman, Rizzuto Make." *Baseball Digest*, XV (May 1956), 43–45.

49085. Gross, Milton. "Phil Rizzuto." In. his *Yankee Doodles*. New York, House of Kent, 1948. Pp. 77–87.

49086. Hickey, David and Kerry Keene. "Phil Rizzuto." In: their *The Proudest Yankees of All: From the Bronx to Cooperstown*. Lanham, MD: Taylor Trade Pub., dist. by National Book Network, 2003. Chapter 5.

49087. Hirshberg, Dan. *Phil Rizzuto: A Yankee Tradition*. Champagne, IL: Sagamore Publishing, 1993. 197p.

49088. Honig, Donald. "1950: Phil Rizzuto." In: his *American League MVP's*. New York: Bantam Books, 1989. Pp. 43–44.

49089. James, Bill. "The Scooter." In: his *The Politics of Glory: How Baseball's Hall of Fame Really Works*. New York: Macmillan, 1994. Pp. 425–434.

49090. "Justice is Served: Phil Rizzuto Enters The Hall." In: Gregg Mazzola, ed. *Yankees 1994 Yearbook*. New York: Yankees Magazine, 1994. Pp. 80–84.

49091. Kirst, Sean Peter. "Scooter's Memories on Display at the Met." In: his *The Ashes of Lou Gehrig and Other Baseball Essays*. Jefferson, NC: McFarland & Co., Inc., 2003. Pp. 108–109.

49092. Klein, Dave. "Pee Wee Reese and Phil Rizzuto." In: his *Great Infielders of the Major Leagues*. New York: Random House, 1972. Pp. 72–89.

49093. Lader, Larry. "Professor Rizzuto's Baseball Academy." *Recreation*, XLVI (March, 1953), 581–593. Abridged in *Reader's Digest*, LXII . (March 1953), 26–28.

49094. Martalan, Douglas. "Phil Rizzuto Recalls His Early Years with the Yankees." *Baseball Digest*, XLII (June 1983), 63–64.

49095. McMillan, Ken. "Phil Rizzuto." In: his *Tales from the Yankee Dugout: A Collection of the Greatest Yankee Stories Ever Told*. Champaign, IL: Sports Publishing, Inc., 2001. Pp. 150–154.

49096. Olch, Dan. "Rizzuto Almost Through in Class D." *Baseball Digest*, XI (February 1952), 61–63.

49097. "Phil Rizzuto: The Singular Scooter." *Yankees Magazine*, IV (February 23, 1984), 11–13.

49098. "Phil(ip Francis) Rizzuto." In: *Current Biography Yearbook, 1950*. New York: H. W. Wilson Co., 1950. Pp. 494–496.

49099. Richman, Milton. "Bunting Champ?: Rizzuto." *Baseball Digest*, VIII (September 1949), 69–76.

49100. Rizzuto, Philip F. ("Phil"). "Big League Sliding." *Scholastic Coach*, XXII (March 1953), 26+.

49101. _____. "Don't Tell Me I'm Washed Up." *Sport*, XV (November 1953), 10–11+.

49102. _____. "The Game I'll Never Forget." *Baseball Digest*, XXXIX (February 1980), 39–41.

49103. _____. "Get a Shoeshine Box, Kid." In: Larry Fox, ed. *Lucky Men in Sports*. New York: W.W. Norton, 1968. Pp. 99–110.

49104. _____. "How I Lay Down a Bunt." *Sport*, XII (March 1952), 63–65.

49105. _____. *O Holy Cow!: The Selected Verse of Phil Rizzuto*. Edited by Tom Peyer and Hart Seely. Hopewell, NJ: Ecco Press, 1993. 107p.

49106. _____. "They Made Me a Big Leaguer." Edited by Milton Gross. *Saturday Evening Post*, CCXIV (April 11, 1942), 11+. Reprinted in *Baseball Digest*, V (May 1946), 3–6.

49107. _____. "What Seven World Series Taught Me." Edited by Henry T. Paxton. *Saturday Evening Post*, CCXXVI (October 3, 1953), 27+.

49108. Robinson, Ray. "Phil Rizzuto: Shortstop Supreme." In: his *Greatest Yankees of Them All*. New York: G.P. Putnam's Sons, 1969. Pp. 109–121.

49109. Rosenthal, Harold. "Lucky He's Still a Yankee." In: Bruce Jacobs, ed. *Baseball Stars of 1953*. New York: Lion Books, 1953. Pp. 55–58.

49110. Rubin, Bob. "'Huckleberry' Rizzuto is a Hit in the Bronx." *Inside Sports,* X (July 1986), 12–15.

49111. Sahadi, Lou. "Baseball's Shame." *Penthouse,* XXIV (May 1993), 84–85. On the delay in his Hall of Fame election.

49112. Schulman, Bill. "Phil Rizzuto: 50 Years as a Yankee." In: Gregg Mazzola, ed. *Yankees 1990 Yearbook.* New York: R. R. Donnelley & Sons, 1990. Pp. 62–65.

49113. Seeley, Hart. and Tom Peyer. "The Bard of Baseball." *Harper's Magazine,* CCLXXXIII (October 1991), 30+.

49114. Schoor, Gone. *The Scooter: The Phil Rizzuto Story.* New York: Scribner's, 1982.196p.

49115. "The 'Scooter' Is Still Scooting." *Look,* XXII (August 5, 1958), 31–32+.

49116. Shannon, Mike. "Phil Rizzuto." In: his *Tales from the Dugout: The Greatest True Baseball Stories Ever Told.* Lincolnwood, IL: NTC/Contemporary Books, 1997. Pp. 162–163.

49117. Shapiro, Milton J. *Phil Rizzuto Story.* New York: Julian Messner, 1959. 192p.

49118. Smith, Ron. "Phil Rizzuto." In: his *Heroes of the Hall: Baseball's Greatest Players.* New York: Contemporary Books, 2002. Pp. 382–383.

49119. Smith, Walter ("Red"). "A Man You Can Listen To." In: Verna Reamer, ed. *Best of Red Smith.* New York: Watts, 1963. Pp. 79–82.

49120. Stephens, J.B. "Phil Rizzuto: A Sport Forever Spikemarked." *Baseball Digest,* XVI (June 1957), 81–89.

49121. Trimble, Joe. *Phil Rizzuto: A Biography of the Scooter.* New York: A.S. Barnes, 1951. 184p.

49122. _____. "The Scooter (Phil Rizzuto)." In: his *The Magnificent Yankees.* New York: A.S. Barnes,1952. Pp. 114–133.

49123. Waldman, Frank. "Phil Rizzuto." In: his *Famous American Athletes of Today.* 12th Series. New York: Page, 1951. Pp. 297–316.

49124. Ziegel, Vic. "Little Phil" *New York,* XXIII (December 24, 1990), 91+.

49125. _____. The 'Scooter's' Life and Times." New York, XIV (April 20,1981), 75–76.

Michael Thomas ("Mike") Roarke
C. (B: Nov. 8, 1930, West Warwick, RI). Detroit (AL), 1961–1964. Remarks: Had 113 hits (six homers) In 194 games in four years; coach, Detroit (AL),1965–1967, California (AL). 1968–1970, Chicago (NL), 1978–1980, St. Louis (NL), 1984–1986; San Diego (NL), 1987–1991.

49126. Newman, Charles. "The Arm, the Tutor, and Bruce Sutter." *Sport,* LXXV (June 1984), 85–91.

Douglas W. ("Scotty") Robb
UMP. (B: 1908, Maryland-D: April 10, l969). Remarks. NL arbiter, 1941–1962; involved in shoving incident with Eddie Stanky (q.v.) in 1962, discipline for which brought his resignation; served as AL umpire, 1952–1953.

49127. Durant, John. "Who Wants to Be an Ump?" *Nations Business,* XXXVIII (August 1950), 49–50+.

Bip Roberts *see* **Leon Joseph ("Bip") Roberts**
Curtis Benjamin ("Curt") Roberts
2B. (B: Aug. 16, 1929, Pineland, TX-D: Nov. 14, 1969). Pittsburgh (NL), 1954–1956. In three big league years, obtained 128 hits (one homer) and seven stolen bases in 171 games; first African American player for Pittsburgh (NL), April 13, 1954.

49128. O'Toole, A. "The Forgotten Pirate Pioneer." *Pittsburgh History,* LXXX (Summer 1997), 77–81.

David ("Dave") Roberts
OF. (B: May 31, 1972, Okinawa, Japan). Cleveland (AL),

1999–2001; Los Angeles (NL), 2002–2004; Boston (AL), 2004; San Diego (NL), 2005–. Remarks: Through 2004, has had 335 hits (11 homers) and 135 stolen bases in 422 games; played injured in much of 2003–2004; scored winning run in Game Four of 2004 ALCS.

49129. Cannella, Stephen. "Super Savers: Dave Roberts." *Sports Illustrated,* XCVII (August 5, 2002), 70–71.

David Leonard ("Dave") Roberts
1B-OF (B: June 30, 1933, Panama City, Panama). Houston (NL), 1962, 1964; Pittsburgh (NL), 1966. Remarks: In three big league seasons, obtained 38 hits (two homers) in 91 games; also played for Porterville (Southwest International League), 1952; Grand Forks (Northern League), 1953; Aberdeen (Northern League), 1954; San Antonio (TL), 1955–1956; Vancouver (PCL), Knoxville (South Atlantic League), and San Antonio/Austin (TL), 1957; Austin (TL), 1958; Louisville (AA), 1959; Sacramento (PCL), Austin (TL), 1960, and Dallas/Fort Worth (AA), 1960; Jacksonville (South Atlantic League) and Houston (AA), 1961; Oklahoma City (AA), 1962–1965; Columbus (IL), 1966; Sankei Atoms (Japan League), 1967–1969; Yakult Atoms (Japan League), 1970–1973; Kintetsu Buffaloes (Japan League), 1973 (while playing in Japan, had 764 hits and 183 homers).

49130. Roberts, Dave, as told to Tony Salin. *A Baseball Odyssey: From Panama to Japan.* San Francisco, CA: Embarcadero Press, 2000. 201p.

49131. Salin, Tony. "A Player for the World: Dave Roberts." In: his *Baseball's Forgotten Heroes: One Fan's Search for the Game's Most Interesting Overlooked Players.* Chicago, IL: Masters Press, 1999. Pp. 41–52.

Leon Joseph ("Bip") Roberts, III
2B-BROADCASTER. (B: October 27, 1963, Berkeley, CA). San Diego (NL), 1986–1991; Cincinnati (NL), 1992–1993; San Diego (NL), 1994–1995; Kansas City (AL), 1996–1997; Cleveland (AL), 1997; Detroit (AL) and Oakland (AL). 1998. Remarks: In 12 years, had 1,220 hits (30 homers) and 264 stolen bases in 1,202 games; had 10 consecutive hits, September 1992; doubled in 1997 ALCS; broadcaster, Fox Sports and San Francisco (NL), 2000–.

49132. Banks, Don. "'Mr. Utilityman' Bip Roberts Settles in at Second Base." *Baseball Digest,* LII (July 1993), 36–37.

49133. Crasnick, Jerry. "One-on-One [with] Bip Roberts: Interview." *Sport,* LXXXIV (July 1993), 20–21.

49134. Dewan, John and Don Zminda. "Wasn't Bip a Pip in September?" In: STATS, Inc. *STATS 1993 Baseball Scoreboard.* New York: Harper Perennial, 1993. Pp. 96–99.

Robin Evan Roberts★
P-COACH. (B: Sept. 30, 1936, Springfield, IL). Philadelphia (NL), 1948–1961; Baltimore (A.L), 1962–1965; Houston (NL), 1965–1966; Chicago (NL), 1966–1967. Remarks: Had 286 victories, 245 defeats, and 25 "saves" in a 20-year big league career; lost Game Two of 1950 World Series; noted for pinpoint control; hurled 20 consecutive complete games, 1953; also played for Wilmington (Inter-State League, 1948 and Reading (EL), 1967. head baseball coach, University of South Florida, 1968–1985; coordinator of minor league instruction, Philadelphia (NL), 1985–; elected to National Baseball Hall of Fame in 1976, where his plaque reads. "Won 286 games though usually pitching for second division teams. Gained 20 or more victories six years in a row, 1950–1955, and topped league or tied for lead in victories four successive seasons. Led NL five consecutive years in innings pitched, 1951–1955, and complete games, 1962–1966. Led In shutouts and strikeouts twice each."

49135. Allen, Maury. "Robin Roberts (1949–1966)." In: his *Baseball's 100.* New York: Galahad Books, 1981. Pp. 213–214.

49136. Brown, Hugh. "Did They Overwork Roberts?" *Sport,* XVI (February 1954), 18–19+.

49137. _____. "Mr. Roberts: The Story of a Winner." *Sport,* XXII (August 1956), 52–63.

49138. _____. "Roberts Pitches to Win." In: Al Silverman, ed. *True's 1953 Baseball Yearbook.* Greenwich, CT: Fawcett Publications, 1953. Pp. 6–7+.

49139. "Can Roberts Win 30 in '53." *Baseball Digest,* XII (January 1953), 17–19.

49140. Cartwright, Al. "Robin Roberts, (Blue) Rock of Ages: A Few Weeks in the Minors." *The National Pastime,* XIX (1999), 28–30.

49141. Cohane, Tim. "The Life and Hard Times of Robin Roberts." *Look,* XXV (August 15, 1961), 82–84.

49142. Grady, Sandy. "Roberts' Outside Pitch." *Baseball Digest,* XXVII (May 1968), 55–57.

49143. _____. "Split with [Gene] Mauch Hastened Roberts' Exit from Phils." *Baseball Digest,* XXI (February 1962), 27–29.

49144. Gunther, Curt. "How Roberts Does It." *Sport,* XV (September 1953), 14–21.

49145. Harrow, Richard J. "The Ace." In: Bruce Jacobs, ed. *Baseball Stars of 1955.* New York: Lion Books, 1955. Pp. 107–113.

49146. Heiling, Joe. "Robin Roberts: Leader of the Golden Agers." *Baseball Digest,* XXV (June 1966), 73–75.

49147. Hochman, Stan. "Robin Roberts Remembers the Whiz Kids." *Baseball Digest,* XXXI (July 1972), 35–38.

49148. Honig, Donald. "Robin Roberts." In: his *Baseball Between the Lines: Baseball in the Forties and Fifties as Told By the Men Who Played It.* Lincoln, NE: University of Nebraska Press, 1976. Pp. 230–246.

49149. _____. "Robin Roberts." In: his *The Greatest Pitchers of All Time.* New York: Crown Publishers, 1988. Pp. 102–107.

49150. Huard, Kevin. "Robin Roberts: Representing the Whiz Kids in the Hall of Fame." *Sports Collector's Digest,* XVIII (May 3, 1991), 70–72.

49151. Jacobs, Bruce. "Quaker Kingpin: Robin Roberts." In: Bruce Jacobs, ed. *Baseball Stars of 1956.* New York: Lion Books, 1956. Pp. 68–74.

49152. Kelly, Wilbur. "The Robin Roberts You Didn't Know." *Baseball Magazine,* LXXX (Spring 1953), 14–15+.

49153. Klima, John. "Number Five is the Hardest: Allie Reynolds vs. Robin Roberts (October 5, 1950)." In: his *Pitched Battle: 35 of Baseball's Greatest Duels from the Mound.* Jefferson, NC: McFarland & Co., Inc., 2002. Pp. 82–86.

49154. Lewis, Franklin. "Refreshing Robin Roberts, Model Workman." *Baseball Digest,* XV (June 1956). 25–27.

49155. Lieb, Frederick G. "Best Since Matty: Robin Roberts." *Baseball Magazine,* LXXX (September 1953), 16–17+.

49156. Merchant, Larry. "Pitcher Who Lives in the Past." *Sport,* XXXIII (May 1962), 60–64.

49157. Molter, Harry. "Robin Roberts." In: *Famous American Athletes of Today.* 13th Series. New York: Page, 1953. Pp. 245–260.

49158. Munro, Neil "Great Pitching Seasons — Robin Roberts, 1952." In: Joseph M. Wayman, ed. *Grandstand Baseball Annual, 1998.* Downey, CA: Joseph M. Wayman, 1998. Pp. 82–90.

49158. Newcombe, Jack. "Roberts is the Phillies' Stopper." *Sport,* XII (June 1953), 32–39.

49159. Paxton, Henry T. "Baseball's Biggest Winner." *Saturday Evening Post,* CCXXV (January 10, 1953), 25+.

49160. "The Phillies' Pitching Pals." *Sport,* XV (October 1953), 22–23+. Roberts and Curt Simmons.

49161. Reichler, Joseph L. "The Price of Stubbornness for Robin Roberts." *Sport,* XXV (February 1958), 20–23.

49162. Reidenbaugh, Lowell. "Robin Roberts." In: his *Cooperstown: Where Legends Live Forever.* St. Louis, MO: The Sporting News, 1983. Pp. 215–216.

49163. Richman, Milton. "Best Since [Walter] Johnson." In: Bruce Jacobs, ed. *Baseball Stars of 1954.* New York: Lion Books, 1954. Pp. 101–109.

49164. Ritter, Lawrence and Donald Honig. "Robin Roberts." In: his *The 100 Greatest Baseball Players of All Time.* New York: Crown Publishers, 1981. Pp. 248–249.

49165. Roberts, Robin. "I'll Never Win 30 Games." *Baseball Magazine,* XLVIII (August 1956), 16–17+.

49166. _____., as told to George Vass. "The Game I'll Never Forget." *Baseball Digest,* XXXV (February 1976), 57–63.

49167. _____., with C. Paul Rogers. *My Life in Baseball.* New York: Triumph Books, 2003. 224p.

49168. "Robin (Evan) Roberts." In: *Current Biography Yearbook, 1953.* New York: H. W. Wilson, 1953. Pp. 531–533.

49169. Robinson, Murray. "The Sudden Change-Up." *Baseball Digest,* XXII (July 1963), 45–47.

49170. Seamon, Dick. "The Whole Story of Pitching." In: Charles Einstein, ed. *The Second Fireside Book of Baseball.* New York: Simon and Schuster, 1958. Pp. 319–323. Reprinted from the May 28, 1956 issue of *The New York Times Magazine.*

49171. Shoemaker, Robert H. "Joy in Philly: Robin Roberts." In: his *Best in Baseball.* New York: Crowell, 1959. Pp. 59–76.

49172. Smith, Mayo. "Roberts is the MVP — or There Ain't No Justice!" *Sport,* XX (December 1955), 12–13+.

49173. Smith, Ron. "Robin Roberts." In: his *Heroes of the Hall: Baseball's Greatest Players.* New York: Contemporary Books, 2002. Pp. 384–385.

49174. _____. "Robin Roberts 74." In: his *The Sporting News Selects Baseball's 100 Greatest Players.* St. Louis: The Sporting News, 1998. Pp. 160–161.

49175. Stern, Chris. "Robin Roberts." In: his *Where Have They Gone?* New York: Tempo Books, 1979. Pp. 64–67.

49176. Stewart, Bob. "Comebacks — Robin Roberts and Stan Musial." In: Jack Orr, ed. *Baseball's Greatest Players Today.* New York: Watts, 1963. Pp. 144–150.

49177. Watts, Lew. "Pitching Polish." *Scholastic Coach,* XXV (April 1956), 12–16. As demonstrated by Roberts.

49178. Weaver, Robert G. "Robin Evan Roberts." In: Vol. Q–Z of David L. Porter, ed. *Biographical Dictionary of American Sports: Baseball.* Rev. and enlarged ed. Westport, CT: Greenwood Press, 2000. Pp. 1296–1298.

49179. Wilber, Cynthia J. "Robin Roberts." In: her *For The Love of The Game : Baseball Memories from the Men Who Were There.* New York: William Morrow & Co., 1992. Pp. 303–309.

49180. Williams, Edgar. "The First Robin of Fling." *Baseball Digest,* XII (January 1953), 11–17.

49181. _____. "Has Roberts Lost His Fastball?" *Baseball Digest,* XVI (January-February 1957), 5–10.

49182. _____. "His Control's Built-In." *Baseball Digest,* XII (August 1953), 51–55.

49183. _____. "How Robin Roberts Wrestled Way to Comeback." *Baseball Digest,* XVII (December 1958), 35–41.

49184. _____. "Philadelphia's Mr. Baseball." *Coronet,* XL (June 1956), 41–45.

49185. Yeutter, Frank. "Bonus Baby Pays Off." In: Bruce Jacobs, ed. *Baseball Stars of 1953.* New York: Lion Books, 1953. Pp. 139–142.

49186. _____. "The First Robin of Spring." *Baseball Digest,* VIII (June 1949), 3–7.

Andre Levett Robertson

SS. (B: Oct. 2, 1957, Orange, TX). New York (AL), 1981–1985. Remarks: Had 182 hits (five homers) In 254 games in four seasons; career effectively ended by 1983 automobile accident.

49187. "Andre Robertson is Catching On." *Yankees Magazine,* IV (September 1, 1983), 6–10.

Bob Robertson *see* **Robert Eugene Robertson**

Charles Culbertson ("Charlie") Robertson

P. (B. Jan. 31, 1897, Sherman, TX-D: Aug. 13, 1984). Chicago (AL), 1919, 1922–1925; St. Louis (AL), 1926; Boston (NL), 1927–1928. Remarks: Won 49 games and lost 80 in eight years; pitched baseball's fifth perfect game, April 30, 1922; later served as a college baseball coach.

49188. Buckley, James, Jr. "Charlie Robertson." In: his *Perfect!: The Inside Story of Baseball's Sixteen Perfect Games.* New York: Triumph Books, 2002. Pp. 56–65.

49189. Mayer, Ronald A. "Charlie Robertson." In: his *Perfect! Biographies and Lifetime Statistics of 14 Pitchers of Perfect Games.* Jefferson, NC: McFarland & Co., Inc., 1991. Pp. 80–89.

49190. "The Perfect Game That Rookie Robertson Pitched." *Literary Digest,* LXXIII (May 1922), 54–57.

49191. Salsinger, H.G. "The Recruit Who Pitched a Perfect Game." *Baseball Magazine,* XXIX (July 1922), 351–353.

Dave Robertson *see* **Davis Aydelotte ("Dave") Robertson**

Davis Aydelotte ("Dave") Robertson

OF. (B: Sept. 25, 1889, Portsmouth, VA-D: Nov. 5, 1970). New York (NL), 1912, 1914–1919; Chicago (NL), 1919–1921; Pittsburgh (NL), 1921; New York, (NL), 1922. Remarks: Had 112 hits (47 homers) and 94 stolen bases in 801 games in nine seasons; tied for NL home run championship, 1916–1917; had 11 hits in 22 ABs in 1917 World Series; his .500 batting average in 1917 World Series remained the record until 1953!; hit for the cycle, Aug. 30, 1921.

49192. Lane, Ferdinand C. "How a Brilliant Baseball Career Was Spoiled." *Baseball Magazine,* XXIV (May 1920), 677–680. By trade from Giants to Cubs.

49193. _____. "Ty Cobb's National League Rival." *Baseball Magazine,* XVIII (January 1916), 33–36.

Robert Eugene ("Bob") Robertson

1B-BROADCASTER. (B: Oct. 2, 1946, Frostburg, MD). Pittsburgh (NL), 1967–1976; Seattle (AL), 1978; Toronto (AL), 1979. Remarks: In 11 seasons, had 578 hits (115 homers) and seven stolen bases in 829 games; had five hits in one game, Aug. 1, 1970; had record eight assists in one game, June 21, 1971; obtained a record (tied) four homers in Games Two and Three of the 1971 NLCS, later broadcaster for Tacoma (PCL) and Spokane (Northwest League).

49194. Appel, Marty. "Bob Robertson." In: his *Yesterday's Heroes: Revisiting the Old-Time Baseball Stars.* New York: William Morrow, 1988. Pp. 188–192.

49195. Cosgrove, GIL "Some Baseball from Around Climax." In: *Saskatchewan Historical Baseball Review 1985.* Battleford, SK: Saskatchewan Baseball Hall of Fame and Museum Association, 1985. Pp. 19–22.

49196. Nufer, Doug. "Present at the Re-creation: Bob Robertson Broadcasts Baseball Games the Old-Fashioned Way — Making It Up as He Goes Along." *Sports Illustrated,* LXXV (August 26, 1991), 121–122.

Sherrard Alexander ("Sherry") Robertson

OF-2B-3B-EXEC. (B: Jan. 1, 1919, Montreal, Canada-D: Oct. 23, 1970). Washington (AL), 1940–1943, 1946–1952; Philadelphia (AL), 1952. Remarks: Obtained 346 hits (26 homers) in 597 games in a decade; front office official, Washington (AL), 1953–1957; farm system director, Washington/Minnesota (AL), 1958–1970; killed in automobile accident in South Dakota.

49197. Addie, Bob. "The Strange Case of Sherry." *Baseball Digest,* XI (August 1962), 30–33.

49198. "No Reliefer." *Sports Illustrated,* XXXII (June 8, 1970), 16–17.

49199. Shearon, Jim. "Sherry Robertson, Unlikely Home Run Hero." In: his *Canada's Baseball Legends.* Kanata, Ontario: Malin Head Press, 1994. Pp 91–93.

Aaron Andrew Robinson

C. (B: June 23, 1915, Lancaster, SC-D: March 9, 1966). New York (AL), 1943, 1945–1947; Chicago (AL), 1948; Detroit (AL), 1949–1951; Boston (AL), 1951. Remarks: In eight seasons, had 478 hits (61 homers) in 610 games; lost his Yankees job to Yogi Berra (q.v.).

49200. Bolin, Carl E. "Primer for Catchers." *Scholastic Coach,* XX (March 1951), 12–16. As demonstrated by Robinson.

49201. Gallagher, Mark. "Aaron Robinson." In: his *50 Years of Yankee All-Stars.* New York: Leisure Press, 1984. Pp. 172–173.

49202. Lebovitz, Hal. "Robinson's Rock." In: Irving T. Marsh and Edward Ehre, eds. *Best Sports Stories of 1950.* New York: E. P. Dutton, 1951. Pp. 99–101. Reprinted from an article in the *Cleveland News,* November 25, 1950.

Bill Robinson *see* **William Henry ("Bill") Robinson, Jr.**

Brooks Calbert Robinson, Jr. ★

3B-BROADCASTER. (B: May 18, 1937, Little Rock, AK). Baltimore (AL), 1955–1977. Remarks: Had 2,848 hits (268 homers) and 28 stolen bases in 2,896 games in 25 seasons; hit for the cycle, July 5, 1960; had grand slam homers in consecutive games, May 6 and May 8, 1962; also had a grand slam in 1970; had streak of 463 games played at 3B, 1961–1963; AL RBI champion, 1964; AL MVP award, 1964; All-Star Game MVP award, 1966; established or tied many 3B records, including most games (2,870), best fielding percentage (.971), most putouts (2,697), most assists (6,205), most chances (9,165), and most double plays (618) — and also hit into four triple plays; homered in Games One and Four of 1970 World Series; World Series MVP award, 1970; tied a record by reaching base five consecutive times, Game Two, 1971 World Series; named Baltimore's Man of the Decade in 1972; coach, Baltimore (AL), 1977; uniform no. 5 retired, 1977; color analyst for Oriole games; elected to National Baseball Hall of Fame in 1983 (became board member), where his plaque reads: "Established modern standard of excellence for third basemen, setting major league records at his position for seasons (23), fielding pct. (.971), games, (2,870), putouts (2,697), assists (6,206), and double plays (618). Hit 268 career home runs. Named to 18 consecutive All-Star teams. MVP of 1970 World Series. American League MVP in 1964."

49203. Allen, Maury. "Brooks Robinson (1955–1977)." In: his *Baseball's 100.* New York: Galahad Books, 1981. Pp. 155–157.

49204. Baltimore Orioles, Public Relations Department. *"Thanks Brooks" Day, September 18, 1977, Official Program.* Baltimore, MD, 1977. 8p.

49205. Bodayla, Stephen D. "Brooks Calbert Robinson, Jr." In: Vol. Q-Z of David L. Porter, ed. *Biographical Dictionary of American Sports: Baseball.* Rev. and enlarged ed. Westport, CT: Greenwood Press, 2000. Pp. 1298–1299.

49206. Boswell, Thomas. "Brooks Robinson: A Man of Class Bows Out." *Baseball Digest,* XXXVI (December 1977), 36–39.

49207. _____. "Thomas Boswell on Brooks Robinson." In: *The Baseball Hall of Fame 50th Anniversary Book.* New York: Prentice-Hall, 1988. Pp. 320–328.

49208. Braucher, Bill. "Brooks Robinson Still the Vacuum Cleaner." *Baseball Digest,* XXXIII (July 1974), 54–61. Reprinted in John Kuenster, ed., *From Cobb to Catfish* (Chicago; Rand McNally, 1975), pp. 80–82.

49209. "Brooks Robinson." In: *Current Biography Yearbook, 1973.* New York: H. W. Wilson Co., 1973. Pp. 361–363.

49210. Brown, Dave. "Brooks Robinson's Quiet Success." In: John L. Pratt, ed. *Baseball's All-Stars.* Garden City, NY: Doubleday, 1967. Pp. 49–56.

49211. Bryan, Mike. "Baseball Lives: Orioles Fan Stephanie Vardavas Borrows Brooks Robinson' Uniform For a Halloween Costume." *Sports Illustrated,* LXX (April 24, 1989), 78+.

49212. Burchard, Marshall, and Sue. *Sports Hero: Brooks Robinson.* New York: G.P. Putnam, 1972. 77p.

49213. Cannon, Jimmy. "Too Early to Say Farewell to Brooks Robinson." *Baseball Digest,* IX (July 1970), 18–21.

49214. Cerrone, Rick. "A Conversation with Brooks Robinson." *Baseball Quarterly,* II (Summer 1978), 16–17+.

49215. Cole, Diane. "Brooks Robinson." In: Danny Peary, ed. *Cult Baseball Players.* New York: Simon and Schuster, 1990. Pp. 203–207.

49216. _____. "Brooks Robinson." In: Danny Peary, ed. *Baseball's Finest: The Greats, the Flakes, the Weird and the Wonderful.* North Dighton, MA: The JG Press, 1990. Pp. 203–207. Both Peary books are identical.

49217. Condon, David. "The Incomparable Brooks Robinson." *Baseball Digest,* XXX (January 1971), 22–26.

49218. Craft, David. "Brooks Robinson: Interview." *Baseball Cards,* VIII (October 1988), 74–77.

49219. Dexter, Charles. "Brooks Robinson, Wing Man of the Orioles." *Baseball Digest,* XIX (November-December 1960), 67–72.

49220. Dickmeyer, Lowell A. and Camiel Kannard. *Baseball is for Me.* Minneapolis, MN: Lerner Publications Co., 1978. 47p. A young boy relates his experiences as a first year Little League player and how he comes to meet Brooks Robinson.

49221. Eisenberg, John. "Baseball's Best: Brooks Robinson-The Best at Third Base." *Baseball Digest,* LXIII (September 2004), 60–65.

49222. Green, Paul M. "Baseball and Brooks Robinson." *Sport Collector's Digest,* X (January 21, 1983), 30+.

49223. Hengden, Bill. "Opponents Find No Flaws in Brooks Robinson." *Baseball Digest,* XXVIII (August 1969), 54–56.

49224. Henneman, Jim. "His Niche in Baseball is Framed in Gold." In: Dick Kaegel, ed. *The Sporting News 1983 Baseball Yearbook.* St. Louis: The Sporting News, 1983. Pp. 106–109.

49225. Hirshberg, Al. "Brooks Robinson." In: his *Greatest American Leaguers.* New York: G.P. Putnam, 1970. Pp. 209–218.

49226. Honig, Donald. "1964: Brooks Robinson." In: his *American League MVP's.* New York: Bantam Books, 1989. Pp. 72–73.

49227. Jablow, Paul. "Frank and Brooks Robinson: End of a Partnership." In: Ray Robinson, ed. *Baseball Stars of 1972.* New York: Pyramid Books, 1972. Pp. 86–93.

49228. Kaplan, Dick. "Brooks Robinson." In: Ray Robinson, ed. *Baseball Stars of 1961.* New York: Pyramid Books, 1961. Pp. 92–97.

49229. _____. "Brooks Robinson: Yankee-Baiter." In: Ray Robinson, ed. *Baseball Stars of 1963.* New York:: Pyramid Books, 1963. Pp. 98–102.

49230. Kaplan, Jim and Dick Perez. "Brooks Robinson." In: their *The 2nd Official Baseball Hall of Fame Book of Superstars.* New York: Little Simon, 1990. Pp. 24–25.

49231. Klaff, Harry. "Portrait of World Series Hero Brooks Robinson." *Countrywide Sports,* I (April 1971), 5–11.

49232. Klein, Dave. "Brooks Robinson." In: his *Great Infielders of the Major Leagues.* New York: Random House, 1972. Pp. 120–134.

49233. Kram, Mark. "Discord Defied and Deified: Robinson, Frank and Brooks, of the Baltimore Orioles." *Sports Illustrated,* XXXIII (October 5, 1970), 26–28+.

49234. Kucner, Richard. "Brooks Goes to Cooperstown." In; Rich Kucner, ed. *Orioles Official 1983 Yearbook.* Baltimore, MD: F.A.T.A., Inc., 1983. Pp. 33–39.

49235. Kuenster, Bob. "Baseball Profile: Hall of Famer Brooks Robinson." *Baseball Digest,* XLIX (October 1990), 33–34.

49236. Leggett, William. "Smash New Act of the Season." *Sports Illustrated,* XXIV (May 30, 1966), 28–29.

49237. Leifer, Neil "The Grace of Brooks Robinson." *Sport,* XXXVIII (December 1964), 26–29.

49238. Libby, Bill. "Brooks Robinson." In: his *Heroes of the Hot Corner.* New York: Watts, 1972. Pp. 3–14.

49239. Lichtenauer, Larry. "Brooks to the Rescue." *Sports History,* II (July 1988), 18–27. In the 1970 World Series.

49240. Linn, Ed. "Why Everyone Loves Brooks Robinson." *Sport,* LIII (June 1972), 76–119.

49241. Maisel, Bob. "Brooks Robinson: Most Valuable Oriole." *Baseball Magazine,* XCIV (December 1964), 44–49.

49242. Masterson, Dave and Timm Boyle. "1964." In: their *Baseball's Best: The MVPs.* Chicago, IL: Contemporary Books, 1985. Pp. 208–213.

49243. Murphy, Jim. "Third Base: Brooks Robinson." In: his *Baseball's All-Time All-Stars.* New York: Clarion Books, 1984. Pp. 72–75.

49244. Newsom, Mary. "What Brooks Robinson Believes: An Interview." *Parent's Magazine,* L (May 1975), 36–37+.

49245. O'Shei, Tim. "Tips on Third Base Defense Shared by Brooks Robinson." *Baseball Digest,* LIV (June 1995), 54–57.

49246. Peters, Alexander. "Brooks Robinson." In: his *Heroes of the Major Leagues.* New York: Random House, 1967. Pp. 162–179.

49247. Reidenbaugh, Lowell. "Brooks Robinson." In: his *Cooperstown: Where Legends Live Forever.* St. Louis, MO: The Sporting News, 1983. Pp. 217–218.

49248. Ritter, Lawrence and Donald Honig. "Brooks Robinson." In: their *The 100 Greatest Baseball Players of All Time.* New York: Crown Publishers, 1981. Pp. 196–199.

49249. Robinson, Brooks. "The Hot Corner." In: Sam Andre, ed. *Street and Smith's Official 1968 Baseball Year-*

book. New York: Conde Nast Publications, 1968. Pp. 12–17.

49250. _____. "How to Play Third Base." *Sport*, XXXIX (March 1965), 114–115.

49251. _____. "My Greatest Day in Baseball." In: Eliot Cohen, ed. *My Greatest Day in Baseball*. New York: Little, Simon, 1991. Pp. 90–94.

49252. _____., as told to George Vass. "The Game I'll Never Forget." *Baseball Digest*, XXXI (October 1972), 70–73. Reprinted in George Vass, ed. *The Game I'll Never Forget* (Chicago, IL: Bonus Books, 1999), pp. 221–224. Big league debut.

49253. _____., as told to Jack Mann. "How I Play Third Base." *Boys' Life*, LXI (September 1971), 8–11.

49254. _____., as told to Jack Tobin. *Third Base Is My Home*. Waco, TX: Word Books, 1974. 202p.

49255. _____., with Fred Bauer. *Putting It All Together*. New York: Hawthorn Books, 1971. 207p. Autobiographical recollections of the Orioles' 1971 season.

49256. _____., with Jon Scher. "World Series [1970]: The Human Vacuum Cleaner." *Sports Illustrated*, LXXXIII (October 23, 1995), 51–52, 55–56, 58, 62, 64–66, 69.

49257. _____., and Frank Robinson. "Brooks and Frank Robinson Talk About Each Other." *Sport*, XLII (October 1966), 28–31.

49258. Robinson, Ray. "Brooks Robinson: Fastest Glove in Town." In: Ray Robinson, ed. *Baseball Stars of 1966*. New York: Pyramid Books, 1966. Pp. 115–119.

49259. _____. "Brooks Robinson: Mister Impossible." In: Ray Robinson, ed. *Baseball Stars of 1971*. New York: Pyramid Books, 1971. Pp. 88–93.

49260. _____. "Brooks Robinson: The Other Robby." In: Ray Robinson, ed. *Baseball Stars of 1967*. New York: Pyramid Books, 1967. Pp. 41–46.

49261. _____. "Brooks Robinson: The 'Untouchable.'" In: Ray Robinson, ed. *Baseball Stars of 1965*. New York: Pyramid Books, 1965. Pp. 140–144.

49262. Roush, Chris. "A Final Look: Brooks Robinson." *Beckett Baseball Card Monthly*, VIII (July 1991), 110–111.

49263. "Salute to Brooks Robinson." In: *Baseball '77*. St. Petersburg, FL: National Association of Professional Baseball Leagues, 1977. Pp. 58–59.

49264. Shannon, Mike. "Brooks Robinson." In: his *Tales from the Dugout: The Greatest True Baseball Stories Ever Told*. Lincolnwood, IL: NTC/Contemporary Books, 1997. Pp. 164–165.

49265. Smith, Ron. "Brooks Robinson." In: his *Heroes of the Hall: Baseball's Greatest Players*. New York: Contemporary Books, 2002. Pp. 386–387.

49266. _____. "Brooks Robinson-80." In: his *The Sporting News Selects Baseball's 100 Greatest Players*. St. Louis, MO: The Sporting News, 1998. Pp. 174–175.

49267. Steadman, John F. "Brooks Robinson: Always a Hit with the Fans." *Baseball Digest*, XLII (September 1983), 48–51.

49268. _____. "How the Orioles Signed Brooks Robinson." *Baseball Digest*, XXX (February 1971), 68–75.

49269. Stump, Al. "Brooks Robinson: Untroubled Oriole." *Sport*, XXXVI (October 1963), 56–63.

49270. Sullivan, George. "Brooks Robinson." In: his *Glovemen: Twenty-Seven of Baseball's Greatest*. New York: Atheneum, 1996. Pp. 28–31.

49271. Tanton, Bill. "Brooks Robinson: Future All-Star at Third." *Baseball Digest*, XVII (September 1958), 47–51.

49272. Weiskopf, Donald C. "Third Base and Brooks Robinson." *Athletic Journal*, LII (January 1972), 8–11+.

49273. Westcott, Rich. "Brooks Robinson — The Game's Best Gloveman at Third." In: his *Diamond Greats*. Westport, Ct: Meckler Books, 1988. Pp. 48–52.

49274. Williams, Larry. "Brooks Takes Charge in Baltimore." *Sport*, XXXI (March 1961), 50–51+.

49275. Wolff, Rick. *Baseball Legends: Brooks Robinson*. New York: Chelsea House, 1991. 64p.

49276. Zanger, Jack. *The Brooks Robinson Story*. New York: Julian Messner, 1967. 192p.

Cornelius Randall ("Neil" or "Shadow") Robinson
OF-SS-3B. (B: July 7, 1908, Grand Rapids, MI). Homestead Grays, 1934; Cincinnati Tigers, 1936–1937; Memphis Red Sox, 1938–1952. Remarks: Long-time Memphis fixture who batted in the high .200s.

49277. Riley, James A. "Cornelius Randall 'Neil,' 'Shadow' Robinson." In: Vol. Q-Z of David L. Porter, ed. *Biographical Dictionary of American Sports: Baseball*. Rev. and enlarged ed. Westport, CT: Greenwood Press, 2000. Pp. 1299–1300.

Craig George Robinson
SS-2B. (B: Aug. 21, 1948, Abington, PA). Philadelphia (NL), 1972–1973; Atlanta (NL), 1974–1975; San Francisco (NL), 1975–1976; Atlanta (NL), 1976–1977. Remarks: Obtained 157 hits and 12 stolen bases in 292 games in six years; reserve infielder.

49278. Mednick, Barry L. "He Could Run But Couldn't Walk." *The Baseball Research Journal*, XV(1986), 9–10.

Earl John Robinson
OF-3B. (B: Nov. 3, 1936, New Orleans, LA). Los Angeles (NL), 1958; Baltimore (AL), 1961–1962 and 1964. Remarks: Had 113 hits (12 homers) in 170 games in four big league seasons.

49279. Steadman, John F. "Earl Robinson Didn't Quit." *Baseball Digest*, XXI (March 1962), 55–57.

Eddie Robinson *see* **William Edward ("Eddie") Robinson**

Floyd Andrew Robinson
OF. (B: May 9, 1936, Prescott, AK). Chicago (AL), 1960–1966; Cincinnati (NL), 1967; Oakland (AL) and Boston (AL), 1968. Remarks: In a nine-year pro career, obtained 929 hits (67 homers) and 42 stolen bases in 1,012 games; had grand slam homer, Sept 22, 1961; went six-for-six in one game, July 22, 1962; led AL in doubles, 1962.

49280. Furlong, William B. "Floyd Robinson: Chisox Cleanupper." In: Ray Robinson, ed. *Baseball Stars of 1963*. New York: Pyramid Books, 1963. Pp. 122–127.

49281. Kuenster, John. "Floyd Robinson's Rise: Though He Batted .311 as a Rookie and Appears Headed for One of Baseball's Brightest Careers, the White Sox Outfielder Is Seldom Satisfied with His Play — Says He: 'Sometimes I Think Maybe I Overhustle.'" *Sport*, XXXIV (September 1962), 34–37.

49282. Swank, Bill. "Floyd Robinson." In: his *Echoes from Lane Field: A History of the San Diego Padres 1936–1957*. Paducah, KY: Turner Publishing Company, 1997. Pp. 149–150.

Frank Robinson ★
OF-1B-MGR. (B: Aug. 31, 1935, Beaumont, TX). Cincinnati (NL), 1956–1965; Baltimore (AL), 1966–1971; Los Angeles (NL), 1972; California (A.L), 1973–1974; Cleveland (AL), 1974–1976. Remarks: Had 2,943 hits (586 homers, fourth behind Aaron, Ruth, and Mays on the all-time list) and 204 stolen bases in 2,808 games in 21 playing years; NL Rookie of the Year award, 1956; hit for the cycle, May 2, 1959; homered in second 1959 All-Star Game; NL MVP award, 1961 and AL MVP award,1966 (only player ever to win MVP honors in both leagues); had

grand slam homer, Aug. 28, 1962; AL Triple Crown winner, 1966; AL batting champion, 1961; AL home run champion, 1966;: AL RBI champion, 1966; established major league record for most homers in most major league parks (32 different fields), 1966–1973; World Series MVP award, 1966; had eight RBIs in one game, April 27, 1969; hit two consecutive grand slam homers in one game, June 26, 1970; All-Star Game MPV award, 1971; coach, California (AL), 1977; manager, Rochester (IL), 1978; coach, Baltimore (AL), 1979–1980; manager, Cleveland (AL), 1975–1976 (first African American manager in the big leagues), manager San Francisco (NL), 1981–1984, Baltimore (AL), 1988–1991, Montreal (NL), 2002–2004, and Washington (NL), 2005–, having through 2004 won 913 games and lost 1,004 (.476); named to Bay Area Sports Hall of Fame, 1983; coach, Milwaukee (AL), 1984 and Baltimore (AL), 1985–1987; special assistant to GM, Baltimore (AL), 1992–1995; AL vp of on-field operations, 2000–2001; elected to National Baseball Hall of Fame in 1982, where his plaque reads: "First to be chosen Most Valuable Player in both leagues-NL in 1961 and AL in 1966. Set records by hitting homers in 32 different parks and with pair of grand-slammers in successive innings in 1970. Fourth in homers (586), fifth in extra bases on long hits (2,430), sixth in total bases (5,373), on retiring. Led NL in slugging pct. in 1960–61–62 and AL in batting, homers, runs batted in, total bases, and slugging pct. in 1966."

49283. Adelman, Ken. "When to Cheer." *Washingtonian*, XXIV (August 1989), 65–69.

49284. Allen, Bob, with Bill Gilbert. "Frank Robinson: Underrated?" In: his *The 500 Home Run Club: Baseball's 15 Greatest Home Run Hitters from Aaron to Williams*. Champaign, IL: Sports Publishing, 1999. Pp. 193–213.

49285. Allen, Maury. "Frank Robinson (1956–1976)." In: his *Baseball's 100*. New York: Galahad Books, 1981. Pp. 195–197.

49286. _____. "Frank Robinson — an End to the Mantle Era." In: Lou Sahadi, ed. *Baseball Illustrated, 1967*. New York: Complete Sports, 1967. Pp. 18–19.

49287. Batson, Larry. *Frank Robinson*. Mankato, MN: Amecus Street, 1974. 31p.

49288. Broeg, Bob. "Two-League Terror." In: his *My Baseball Scrapbook*. St. Louis, MO: River City Publishers, 1983. Pp. 157–160.

49289. Brosnan, Jim. "Frank Robinson: Rookie of the Year, 1956, National League." In: his *Great Rookies of the Major Leagues*. New York: Random House, 1966. Pp. 81–93.

49290. "Brothers Three of Baseball: Frank Robinson and His Brothers." *Ebony*, XX (September 1965), 73–74.

49291. Cannella, Stephen. "Mr. Robinson's Neighborhood: Lord of Discipline." *Sports Illustrated*, XCII (May 15, 2000), 99–100.

49292. Cope, Myron. "Frank Robinson: The Facts Behind His Discontent." *Sport*, XXXV (June 1963), 56–73.

49293. Daley, Arthur. "King Frank: Frank Robinson." In: his *All the Home Run Kings*. New York: G.P. Putnam, 1972. Pp. 175–183.

49294. Denlinger, Ken. "Here Comes the Judge: Frank Robinson." *Baseball Digest*, XXVIII (November 1969), 85–87.

49295. Ditky, Julian May. *Frank Robinson: Slugging Toward Glory*. By Julian May, pseud. Mankato, MN: Crestwood House, 1975. 47p.

49296. Donnelly, Joe. "Frank Robinson's New Challenge." In: Zander Hollander, ed. *Baseball Yearbook, 1967*. New York: Popular Library, 1967. Pp. 4–7.

49297. _____, "Frank Robinson's Crusade." *Sport*, XLII (August 1966), 19–23.

49298. Drury, Bob. "Interview: Frank Robinson." *Sport*, LXXVI (June 1985), 29–32+.

49299. Ellison, Nick. "Frank Robinson: Leader of the Birds." In: Ray Robinson, ed. *Baseball Stars of 1970*. New York: Pyramid Books, 1970. Pp. 111–115.

49300. _____. "Frank Robinson: The Pro." In: Ray Robinson, ed. *Baseball Stars of 1971*. New York: Pyramid Books, 1971. Pp. 94–98.

49301. Enders, Eric. "Baseball Legend." In: Michael J. McCormick, ed. *2002 All Star Game Official Program*. New York: Major League Baseball Promotion Corp., 2002. Pp. 32–36.

49302. Enright, Jim. "Why Reds Traded Robinson." *Baseball Digest*, XXV (February 1966), 19–21.

49303. Eskridge, Neal. "When Frank Robinson Led the Orioles to Their First Flag." *Baseball Digest*, XXXVI (February 1977), 77–43.

49304. Evers, John L. "Frank Robinson." In: Vol. Q–Z of David L. Porter, ed. *Biographical Dictionary of American Sports: Baseball*. Rev. and enlarged ed. Westport, CT: Greenwood Press, 2000. Pp. 1300–1302.

49305. Fimrite, Ron. "Jaunty Stride into History." *Sports Illustrated*, XLII (March 4, 1975), 18–19.

49306. "Frank Robinson." In: *Current Biography Yearbook, 1971*. New York: H.W. Wilson Co., 1971. Pp. 350–353.

49307. "Frank Robinson: Baseball's Dean of Discipline." *Ebony*, LV (August 2000) p. 48–50.

49308. "Frank Robinson: Hawk Among the Orioles." *Ebony*, XXI (September 1960), 88–90+.

49309. "Frank Robinson Hiring Draws Queries." *Jet*, LXXIV (May 2, 1988), 46–48.

49310. Gilbert, Bill. "Frank Robinson — 1966." In: his *Baseball's Top 100: The Best Individual Seasons of All Time*. Wilton, CT: Diamond Library, 1996. Pp. 186–188.

49311. Gilligan, Vic. "Frank Robinson: An Interview." *Sport*, LXX (March 1980), 13–14+.

49312. Gleason, Benjamin. "A Final Look: Frank Robinson." *Beckett Baseball Card Monthly*, VII (November 1990), 94–95.

49313. Goldstein, Alan. "Frank Robinson's Dream." *All-Star Sports*, III (April 1969), 28–31.

49314. Graham, Frank, Jr. "Cincinnati's Million-Dollar Baby." *Sport*, XXIV (October 1957), 22+.

49315. Hirshberg, Al. *Frank Robinson, Born Leader*. New York: G.P. Putnam, 1973. 191p.

49316. Honig, Donald. "Frank Robinson." In: his *Baseball America: The Heroes of the Game and the Times of Their Glory*. New York: Macmillan, 1985. Pp. 287–290.

49317. _____."Frank Robinson." In: his *The Power Hitters*. St. Louis, MO: *The Sporting News*, 1989. Pp. 182–193.

49318. _____. "1956: Frank Robinson." In: his *National League Rookies of the Year*. New York: Bantam Books, 1989. Pp. 23–24.

49319. _____. "1961 [and] 1966: Frank Robinson." In: his *National League MVP's*. New York: Bantam Books, 1989. Pp. 65–66, 76–77.

49320. Izenberg, Jerry. "Frank Robinson: Pressures on the Triple-Crown Winner." *Sport*, XLIV (August 1967), 64–71.

49321. Jablow, Paul. "Frank and Brooks Robinson: End of a Partnership." In: Ray Robinson, ed. *Baseball Stars of 1972*. New York: Pyramid Books, 1972. Pp. 86–93.

49322. Jackman, Phil "Frank Robinson Left a Legacy as a Player." *Baseball Digest*, XLI (November 1982), 45–49.

49323. Jacobs, Bruce. "Top Rookie: National League, Frank Robinson. In: Bruce Jacobs, ed. *Baseball Stars of 1957.* New York: Lion Books, 1957. Pp. 38–46.

49324. Jares, Joe. "Indian Tomahawked: The Firing of Manager Frank Robinson." *Sports Illustrated,* XLVH (July 4, 1977), 40+.

49325. Keith, Larry. "Umps Have Given Him the Grumps: Views of Frank Robinson." *Sports Illustrated,* XLV (July 5, 1976), 42+.

49326. Kermisch, Al. "Frank Robinson's Instant Grand Slams for Orioles." *The Baseball Research Journal,* X (1981), 68–69.

49327. Klein, Larry. "Frank Robinson: Target Guy." In: Ray Robinson, ed. *Baseball Stars of 1961.* New York: Pyramid Books, 1961. Pp. 114–121.

49328. Kram, Mark. "Discord Defied and Deified: Robinsons, Frank and Brooks, of the Baltimore Orioles." *Sports Illustrated,* XXXIII (October 5,1970), 26–28+.

49329. Lawson, Earl. "Frank Robinson Comes of Age." *Saturday Evening Post,* CCXXXV (August 26, 1962), 77–79.

49330. Leggett, William. "High Flight for an Oriole: Frank Robinson May Become the Majors' First Negro Pilot." *Sports Illustrated,* XXX (February 3, 1969), 38–39.

49331. Libby, Bill. "Frank Robinson: Enigma in Cincy." In: Ray Robinson, ed. *Baseball Stars of 1965.* New York: Pyramid Books, 1965. Pp. 145–154.

49332. Lindeman, Bard. "Good Leader Strides Hard and Carries a Big Stick." *Saturday Evening Post,* CCXXXIX (August 27, 1966), 74–76. Reprinted In Tom Seaver, ed., *How I Would Pitch to Babe Ruth* (Chicago: Playboy Press, 1974), pp. 199–213.

49333. Liss, Howard. "Frank Robinson." In: his *Triple Crown Winners.* New York: Julian Messner, 1969. Pp. 64–73.

49334. Macht, Norman L. *Baseball Legends: Frank Robinson.* New York: Chelsea House, 1991. 64p.

49335. Masterson, Dave and Timm Boyle. "1961 [and] 1966." In: their *Baseball's Best: The MVPs.* Chicago, IL: Contemporary Books, 1985. Pp. 190–195, 220–225.

49336. Mazur, Roslyn A. "Frank Robinson Inspires Oriole Magic." *The National Pastime,* XI (1992), 77–79.

49337. Moffi, Larry and Jonathan Kronstadt. "Frank Robinson." In: their *Crossing the Line: Black Major Leaguers, 1947–1959.* Jefferson, NC: McFarland & Co., Inc., 1994. Pp. 156–157.

49338. Parr, Jeanne. "The Merry Widow." In: her *The Superwives: Life with the Giant Jocks.* New York: Coward, McCann & Geoghegan, Inc., 1976. Pp. 128–136. Barbara Ann Cole.

49339. Peters, Alexander. "Frank Robinson." In: his *Heroes of the Major Leagues.* New York: Random House, 1967. Pp. 18–19.

49340. Peters, Nick. "Frank. Robinson: A True Blue-Collar Superstar." In: Dick Kaegel, ed. *The Sporting News 1982 Baseball Yearbook.* St. Louis, MO: The Sporting News, 1982. Pp. 98–100.

49341. _____. "The Manager." In: Laurence J. Hyman, ed. *1984 Official San Francisco Giants Yearbook.* San Francisco, CA: Woodford Associates, 1984. Pp. 61–68.

49342. Pille, Bob. "Cincy's Robinson Is Just Starting." *Baseball Digest,* V (September 1956), 31–37.

49343. Post, Paul. "Frank Robinson Revives Some Choice Baseball Memories." *Baseball Digest,* LV (May 1996), 44–47.

49344. Pratt, John L. "Frank Robinson." In: John L. Pratt, ed. *Baseball's All-Stars.* Garden City, NY: Doubleday, 1967. Pp. 127–129.

49345. Pye, Brad. "Frank Robinson: Suitcase Superstar." *Black Sport Magazine,* II (July-August 1972), 14–21.

49346. Rathgeber, Bob. "A Swing Hitched to Stardom: Frank Robinson." In: his *Cincinnati Reds Scrapbook.* Virginia Beach, VA: J.C.P. Corp. of Virginia, 1982. Pp. 120–121.

49347. Reidenbaugh, Lowell. "Frank Robinson." In: his *Cooperstown: Where Legends Live Forever.* St. Louis, MO: The Sporting News,1983. Pp. 219–220.

49348. Ringolsby, Tracy. "Interview: Frank Robinson." *Inside Sports,* XII (April 1990), 22–29.

49349. Ritter, Lawrence and Donald Honig. "Frank Robinson." In: their *The 100 Greatest Baseball Players of All Time.* New York: Crown Publishers, 1981. Pp. 206–207.

49350. Robinson, Frank. "The Day I Settled with Don Drysdale." *Baseball Digest,* XXXIV (October 1975), 33–30.

49351. _____. "How I Won My Biggest Battle." *Sport,* XXXII (December 1961), 20–23.

49352. _____. "I Will Always Be Outspoken." Edited by Roy Blount, Jr. *Sports Illustrated,* XLI (October 21, 1974), 30–32+.

49353. _____. "'In America's National Pastime,' Says Frank Robinson, 'White Is the Color of the Game Off the Field': Interview." *People Weekly,* XXVII (April 27 1987) 46, 51. Reprinted in David K. Wiggins and Patrick B. Miller, eds., *The Unlevel Playing Field: A Documentary History of the African American Experience in Sport.* (Champaign, IL: University of Illinois Press, 2003), pp. 339–341.

49354. _____, and Brooks Robinson. "Brooks and Frank Robinson Talk About Each Other." *Sport,* XLII (October 1966), 28–31.

49355. _____, as told to George Vass. "The Game I'll Never Forget." *Baseball Digest,* XXXII (September 1973), 47–62. Reprinted in John Kuenster, ed., *From Cobb to Catfish* (Chicago, IL: Rand McNally, 1975), pp. 34–35. The May 1966 game in which he hit the first homer ever sent completely out of Baltimore's Memorial Stadium.

49356. _____., with Al Silverman. *My Life in Baseball.* Garden City, NY: Doubleday, 1968. 225p.

49357. _____., with Dave Anderson. *Frank: The First Year.* New York: Holt, Rinehart and Winston, 1976. 270p. Diary account of the Cleveland manager's first year as a pilot.

49358. _____., with Berry Stainback. *Extra Innings.* New York: McGraw-Hill, 1988. 270p.

49359. _____. "Fighting the Baseball Blackout." *Sport,* LXXIX (July 1988), 66–67.

49360. Robinson, Jackie, "Frank Robinson." In: his *Baseball Has Done It.* Philadelphia, PA: Lippincott, 1964. Pp. 152–159.

49361. Robinson, Lawrence. "Frank Robinson Makes Baseball History." *Ebony,* XXX (May 1975), 103–1059+. As first African-American big league pilot.

49362. Robinson, Ray. "Frank Robinson: Indispensable Man." In: Ray Robinson, ed. *Baseball Stars of 1963.* New York: Pyramid Books, 1963. Pp. 71–76.

49363. _____. "Frank Robinson: Year of Decision." In: Ray Robinson, ed. *Baseball Stars of 1962.* New York: Pyramid Books, 1962. Pp. 15–21.

49364. _____. "Frank Robinson: Year of Revenge." In: Ray Robinson, ed. *Baseball Stars of 1963.* New York: Pyramid Books, 1963. Pp. 71–76.

49365. Ross, John M. "They Gave Him a Bat." In: Charles Einstein, ed. *The Second Fireside Book of Baseball.* New York: Simon and Schuster, 1968. Pp. 305–306.

49366. Rust, Art, Jr. "Frank Robinson." In: his *Get That*

Nigger Off the Field. New York: Delacorte, 1976. Pp. 184–189.

49367. Schneider, Russell J. *Frank Robinson: The Making of a Manager.* New York: Coward, McCann, Geoghegan, 1976. 235p.

49368. Shanik, M. "Moody Tiger of the Reds." *Sports Illustrated,* XVIII (June 17, 1963), 33–34.

49369. Shecter, Leonard. "Frank Robinson's Cool Assault on the Black Manager Barrier." *Look,* XXXIV (May 6, 1970), 83–84+.

49370. _____. "Frank Robinson on the Spot." *Sport,* XXXI (June 1961), 20–22+.

49371. Silverman, Al. "Frank Robinson: The Grim Season." In: Ray Robinson, ed. *Baseball Stars of 1968.* New York: Pyramid Books, 1968. Pp. 107–113.

49372. Smith, Ron. "Frank Robinson." In: his *Heroes of the Hall: Baseball's Greatest Players.* New York: Contemporary Books, 2002. Pp. 388–389.

49373. _____. "Frank Robinson 22." In: his *The Sporting News Selects Baseball's 100 Greatest Players.* St. Louis, MO: *The Sporting News,* 1998. Pp. 52–53.

49374. "Sports: Frank Robinson: Baseball's Dean Of Discipline — Now in the Front-Office, Hall of Famer is Making a Point That He Means Business." *Ebony,* LV (October 2000), 48–51.

49375. Stann, Francis. "Cincy's Sore-Armed Kid." *Baseball Digest,* XV (May 1966), 89–91.

49376. Steadman, John F. "Frank Robinson Makes the Difference in the Orioles." *Baseball Digest,* XXX (October 1971), 36–39.

49377. _____. "Frank Robinson Meant the Difference." *Baseball Digest,* XXXI (March 1972), 16–19.

49378. _____. "Frank Robinson: The Magnificent Hitting Machine." *Baseball Digest,* XXVIII (July 1969), 14–17.

49379. Stewart, Bob. "Frank Robinson." In: Jack Orr, ed. *Baseball's Greatest Players Today.* New York: Watts, 1963. Pp. 99–104.

49380. Taylor, Phil "The Heat is On." *Sports Illustrated,* XCVII (July 29, 2002) p. 48–50.

49381. Vecsey, George. "Frank Robinson, the Manager." *Sport,* XLVII (March 1969), 48–51.

49382. Ward, Robert. "Robbie Returns." *Sport,* LXXII (August 1981), 57–59.

49383. Wilber, Cynthia J. "Frank Robinson." In: her *For the Love of the Game: Baseball Memories from the Men Who Were There.* New York: William Morrow, 1992. Pp. 279–286.

49384. Williams, Edgar. "When Reds' Robinson Became All-Year Great." *Baseball Digest,* XX (October 1961), 21–24.

49385. Young, Bernice L *The Picture Story of Frank Robinson.* New York: Julian Messner, 1975. 60p.

Frazier ("Slow") Robinson *see* **Henry Frazier ("Slow") Robinson**

Henry Frazier ("Slow") Robinson

C. (B: May 30, 1916, Birmingham, AL). Satchel Paige's All Stars, 1939; Baltimore Grays, 1942; Kansas City Monarchs, 1942–1943; New York Black Yankees, 1943; Baltimore Elite Giants, 1943, 1946–1950. Remarks: Had .222 batting average in final season.

49386. Robinson, Frazier ("Slow"), and Paul Bauer. *Catching Dreams: My Life in the Negro Baseball Leagues.* Syracuse, NY: Syracuse University Press, 1999. 256p.

Jack Roosevelt ("Jackie") Robinson★

2B-3B-1B-OF-BROADCASTER. (B: Jan. 31, 1919, Cairo, GA-D: Oct. 24, 1972). Kansas City Monarchs, 1945; Montreal (IL), 1946; Brooklyn (NL), 1947–1956.

Remarks: Had 1,518 hits (137 homers) and 197 stolen bases in 1,382 games in a major league decade; first African American player to sign a formal MLB contract, Oct. 23, 1945; first African American minor-player in a game, April 18, 1946; IL batting champion, 1946; first African American player to appear in a modern MLB game, April 15, 1947; first African American to play for the Dodgers; first African American player to get a hit in a modern MLB game, April 16, 1947; first African American player to steal home plate, June 24, 1947; had 14- and 21-game hitting streaks, 1947; NL stolen base champion, 1947 and 1949; NL Rookie of the Year Award, 1947; first African American player to appear in a World Series game, Sept. 30, 1947; hit for the cycle, Aug. 29, 1948; one of first three African American All-Star Game players, July 12, 1949; NL MVP award, 1949 (first won by an African American player); NL batting champion, 1949 (first won by an African American player); had two grand slam homers, June 24 and Aug. 1, 1950; swiped home plate in Game One of 1955 World Series; stole home plate 19 times during career; after playing career, became businessman and active in anti-drug programs; also first African American network (ABC) broadcaster, March 17, 1965; elected to Canadian Baseball Hall of Fame in 1991; second baseball player honored with a U.S. postage stamp, Feb. 18, 1999; elected to the National Baseball Hall of Fame in 1962 (the first African American player so honored), where his plaque reads: "Leading NL batter in 1949. Holds fielding mark for second basemen playing in 150 or more games with .992. Led NL in stolen bases in 1947 and 1949. Most Valuable Player in 1949. Lifetime batting average .311. Joint record holder for most double plays by second baseman, 137 in 1951. Led second basemen in double plays 1949–50–51–52."

49387. Aaron, Henry. "Jackie Robinson." *Time,* CLIII (June 14 1999), 104–107. In the magazine's "Heroes & Icons" special section.

49388. Abraham, Philip. *Jackie Robinson.* New York: Children's Press, 2002. 24p.

49389. Adler, David A. *Jackie Robinson: He was the First.* New York: Holiday House, 1989. 48p.

49390. Adler, Gary A. *A Picture Book of Jackie Robinson.* New York: Holiday House, 1994. 29p.

49391. Allen, Harold C. "Jackie Robinson." In: his *Great Black Americans.* West Haven, CT: Pendulum Press, 1971. Pp. 97–126.

49392. Allen, Lee and Thomas Meany. "Jackie Robinson." In: their *Kings of the Diamond.* New York: G. P. Putnam, 1965. Pp. 130–133.

49393. Allen, Maury. *Jackie Robinson: A Life Remembered.* New York: Watts, 1987. 260p.

49394. _____. "Pepper Street, Pasadena." In: Jackie Robinson and Jules Tygiel. *The Jackie Robinson Reader: Perspectives on an American Hero.* New York: E. P. Dutton, 1997. Chapter 1. An excerpt from the preceding entry.

49395. Alvarez, Mark. *The Official Baseball Hall of Fame Story of Jackie Robinson.* New York: Little, Simon 1990. 96p.

49396. Anderson, B. "Celebrating Jackie Robinson?: Major League Baseball Sees the Limitations of Promotions." *Journal of Promotion Management,* VII (January-February 2001), 215–224.

49397. Angell, Roger. "Box Score: Has Baseball Fulfilled Jackie Robinson's Promise?" *The New Yorker,* LXXIII (April 14, 1997), 5–6.

49398. _____. "The Designated Hero." *The New Yorker,* LXXIII (September 15, 1997), 82–88.

49399. Ardolino, Frank. "Breaking the Color Line: Five Film Representations of Jackie Robinson, 1950–1992." *Aethlon: The Journal of Sport Literature,* XIII (Spring 1996), 49–60.

49400. _____. "Jackie Robinson and the 1941 Honolulu Bears." *The National Pastime,* XV (1995), 68–70.

49401. "Are They Ganging Up on Jackie?" *Our World,* IX (August 1954), 42–46.

49402. Baldwin, Louis. "Jackie Robinson." In: his *Turning Points: Pivotal Moments in the Careers of 83 Famous Figures.* Jefferson, NC: McFarland & Co., Inc., 1999. Pp. 179–180.

49403. Barber, Walter ("Red"). "Lead-off Man." *New Republic,* CLXXXIX (July 4, 1983), 28–31.

49404. _____., with Robert W. Creamer. "He Did Far More for Me." In: Jackie Robinson and Jules Tygiel. *The Jackie Robinson Reader: Perspectives on an American Hero.* New York: E. P. Dutton, 1997. Chapter 4.

49404a. "Baseball Great Jackie Robinson Honored with Congressional Gold Medal." *Jet,* CVII (March 21, 2005), 46–48.

49405. "Baseball Honors Legacy of Jackie Robinson with Special Day." *Jet,* CV (May 3, 2004), 18–21.

49406. "Baseball Remembers Jackie Robinson." In: Richard Levin, ed. *Major League Baseball 1987 All-Star Game Program.* New York: R. R. Donneley & Sons, 1987. Pp. 4–7.

49407. Battema, Doug. "Jackie Robinson as Media's Mythological Black Hero." In: Peter M. Rutkoff, ed. *The Cooperstown Symposium on Baseball and American Culture, 1997 (Jackie Robinson).* Jefferson, NC: McFarland & Co., Inc., 2000. Pp. 199–214.

49408. _____. "Playing Inside the Lines: The Jackie Robinson Mythology as a Discourse of Cultural Power." Unpublished M.A. thesis, The Annenberg School of Communications, University of Pennsylvania, 1995.

49409. Benjamin, Peter. "Then and Now." *The New York Times Magazine,* (April 15, 1962), 84+.

49410. Bergman, Irwin B. *Baseball Legends: Jackie Robinson.* New York: Chelsea House, 1994. 79p.

49411. Bims, H.J. "Black America Says Goodbye, Jackie." *Ebony,* XXVIII (December 1972), 173–174+.

49412. Birmingham, Nan. "Lady, That's Jackie Robinson!" In: Jackie Robinson and Jules Tygiel. *The Jackie Robinson Reader: Perspectives on an American Hero.* New York: E. P. Dutton, 1997. Chapter 22.

49413. Bonner, Mary G. "Jackie Robinson." In: her *Baseball Rookies Who Made Good.* New York: Alfred A. Knopf, 1964. Pp. 131–139.

49414. Bontemps, Arna. "Jackie Robinson." In: his *Famous Negro Athletes.* New York: Dodd, Mead, 1964. Pp. 57–70.

49415. Boston, Talmage. "Jackie Robinson and the Papini Doctrine." *Elysian Fields Quarterly,* XI (Spring 1992), 41–44, 58.

49416. Bowen, C. D. "A Quarter Century: Its Human Triumphs." *Look,* XXV (December 5, 1961), 97–98.

49417. "Branch Breaks the Ice: Brooklyn Signed Jack Roosevelt Robinson, Negro Shortstop." *Time,* XLVI (November 5, 1945), 77+.

49418. Brandt, Keith. *Jackie Robinson: A Life of Courage.* Mahwah, NJ: Troll Associates, 1992. 48p.

49419. Briley, Ronald F. "10 Years After: The Baseball Establishment, Race, and Jackie Robinson." In: Peter M. Rutkoff, ed. *The Cooperstown Symposium on Baseball and American Culture, 1997 (Jackie Robinson).* Jefferson, NC: McFarland & Co., Inc., 2000. Pp. 137–150. Reprinted in

his *Class at Bat, Gender on Deck and Race in the Hole: A Lineup of Essays on 20th Century Culture and America's Game* (Jefferson, NC: McFarland & Co., Inc., 2003), pp. 93–106.

49420. Broeg, Bob. "Jackie Robinson." In: his. *Super Stars of Baseball.* St. Louis, MO: *The Sporting News,* 1971. Pp. 201–208.

49421. "Brooklyn Dodgers Sign First Negro to Play for Organized Baseball." *Life,* XIX (November 26, 1945), 133–134.

49422. Broom, Larry. "The Jackie Robinson Case." In: J.T. Talamini and C. H. Pap, eds. *Sport and Society: An Anthology.* Boston, MA: Little, Brown, 1973. Pp. 234–240.

49423. Brosnan, Jim. "Jackie Robinson." In: his *Great Rookies of the Major Leagues.* New York: Random House, 1966. Pp. 9–25.

49424. Browne, Ray B. "Jackie Robinson." In: Ray B. Browne, ed. *Contemporary Heroes and Heroines.* Detroit, MI: Gale Research, 1990. Pp. 331–336.

49425. Burchard, S.H. "Jackie Robinson." In: his *Book of Baseball Greats.* New York: Harcourt, Brace, Jovanovich, 1983. Pp. 36–39.

49426. Burr, Harold C. "Jackie Robinson Signs with Dodgers." In: Dean A. Sullivan, ed. *Middle Innings: A Documentary History of Baseball, 1900–1948.* Lincoln, NE: University of Nebraska Press, 1998. Pp. 199–201. Reprinted from the *Brooklyn Eagle,* Oct. 24, 1945.

49427. _____. "Jackie Robinson's Major League Debut." In: Dean A. Sullivan, ed. *Middle Innings: A Documentary History of Baseball, 1900–1948.* Lincoln, NE: University of Nebraska Press, 1998. Pp. 215–217. Reprinted from the *Brooklyn Eagle,* April 16, 1947.

49428. Butler, Hal. "Jackie Robinson." In: his *Sports Heroes Who Wouldn't Quit.* New York: Julian Messner, 1978. Pp. 43–53.

49429. "Can Jackie Make the Hall of Fame?" *Negro History Bulletin,* XVII (October 1953), 6+.

49430. Canale, Larry. "The Trailblazer: Jackie Robinson." *Footsteps,* II (March/April 2000), 20–23.

49432. Cannon, Adrienne and Helen Dalrymple. "Values for Living and Records of Life; Family Donates Jackie Robinson Papers." *Library of Congress Information Bulletin,* LX (November 2001), 250–251.

49433. Carpozi, George, Jr. *Jackie Robinson, a Tribute.* New York: Princeton Pub. Co., 1997. 66p. Magazine format.

49434. Chace, S. "The True Color of Heroism." *Good Housekeeping,* CCXXIII (October 1996), 18–19.

49435. Cohen, Barbara and Richard Cuffari. *Thank You, Jackie Robinson.* New York: Lothrop, Lee & Shepard, 1974. 125p. Fiction reprinted in 1988.

49436. "Conference Celebrates Legacy of Jackie Robinson." *Jet,* XCI (April 21, 1997), 51–52. "Jackie Robinson: Race, Sports, and the American Dream" held at Long Island University.

49437. Coombs, Karen M. *Jackie Robinson: Baseball's Civil Rights Legend.* Hillside, NJ: Enslow Publications, 1997. 128p.

49438. Cope, Myron. "Jackie Robinson" In: Zander Hollander, ed. *Great American Athletes of the 20th Century.* New York: Random House, 1966. Pp. 124–127.

49439. Cosell, Howard. "Great Moments in *Sport:* Jackie Breaks the Barrier." *Sport,* XXXI (June 1961), 78–91.

49440. _____, with Mickey Herskowitz. "Jackie Taught Us All." In: his *Cosell.* Chicago, IL: Playboy Press, 1973. Pp. 93–96.

49441. Creamer, Robert W. "Perspective." *Sports Illustrated,* LVII (November 1, 1982), 99–100.

49442. Curvin, Robert. "Remembering Jackie Robinson." *The New York Times Magazine,* (April 4, 1982), 46+.

49443. Daley, Arthur. "Between Two Putouts." *Baseball Digest,* XVI (March 1957), 72–75.

49444. _____. "Jackie Robinson." In: his *Sports of The Times.* New York: E.P. Dutton, 1959. Pp. 113–115.

49445. Davidson, Margaret. *The Story of Jackie Robinson: Bravest Man in Baseball.* New York: Dell, 1988. 92p.

49446. Davis, Hal. "The Court Martial of Jackie Robinson: 50 Years Later, a Defense Lawyer Remembers His Client, the Future Baseball Legend." *National Law Journal,* XVII (September 19, 1994), A12+.

49447. Dawidoff, Nicholas. "Recalling Jackie Robinson: Carl Erskine Visits an Exhibition Celebrating His Teammate." *Sports Illustrated,* LXV (September 28, 1987), 70+.

49448. D'Angelis, Gina. *Overcoming Adversity: Jackie Robinson.* Philadelphia, PA: Chelsea House Publishing, 2001. 112p.

49449. Deford, Frank. "Crossing the [Color] Bar." *Newsweek,* CXXIX (April 14, 1997), 52–55.

49450. DeMarco, Tony. *Jackie Robinson.* New York: Child's World, 2002. 40p.

49451. Denenberg, Barry. *Stealing Home: The Story of Jackie Robinson.* New York: Scholastic Books, 1990. 117p.

49452. Diamond, Arthur. *Jackie Robinson.* San Diego, CA: Lucent Books, 1992. 112p.

49453. Dingle, Derek T. *First in the Field: Baseball Hero Jackie Robinson.* New York: Hyperion, 1998. 48p.

49454. DiTrani, Vinny. "When Jackie Robinson Broke Down the Barriers." *Baseball Digest,* XLVI (August 1987), 64–69.

49455. Dorinson, Joseph and Joram Warmund. *Jackie Robinson: Race, Sports and the American Dream.* Armonk, NY: M. E. Sharpe, 1999. 296p.

49456. Dougherty, Bill. "The Jackie Robinson of Today." *Baseball Digest,* X (July 1951), 25–28.

49457. Douglas, Davison M. "Jackie Robinson." In: John A. Garrity and Marsh C. Carries, eds. *American National Biography.* 24 vols. New York: Oxford University Press, 1999. XVIII, 656–658.

49458. Dowling, Tom. "Jackie Robinson 25 Years Later." *Baseball Digest,* XXXI (March 1972), 72–75.

49459. Doyel, Gregg. "The Five Athletes Who Changed America: No. 4, Jackie Robinson." *Sport,* XC (December 1999), 48–49.

49460. Drier, Peter. "Jackie Robinson's Legacy: Baseball, Race, and Politics" In: Robert Elias, ed. *Baseball and the American Dream: Race, Class, Gender and the National Pastime.* New York: M. E. Sharpe, 2001. Pp. 43–63.

49461. _____. "Remembering Jackie Robinson." *Tikkun,* XII (March-April 1997), 32, 76.

49462. Dunn, Herb, Merly Henderson, and Dan Gutman. *Jackie Robinson: Young Sports Trailblazer.* Childhood of Famous Americans Series. New York: Aladdin Library, 1999. 192p.

49463. Durslag, Melvin. "Leo Durocher and Jackie Robinson." *TV Guide,* XII (July 24, 1966), 12–13.

49464. Early, Gerald. "American Integration, Black Heroism, and the Meaning of Jackie Robinson." *The Chronicle of Higher Education,* XLIII (May 23, 1997), B4–B5. Reprinted in David K. Wiggins and Patrick B. Miller, eds., *The Unlevel Playing Field: A Documentary History of the African American Experience in Sport.* (Champaign, IL: University of Illinois Press, 2003), pp. 215–221.

49465. Ecenbarger, William. "Year of Fire, Year of Grace." *Reader's Digest,* CXLVII (August 1995), 61–65. Rookie season.

49466. Eddings, Jerelyn. "A Grandfather's Greatest Gift: Jackie Robinson Fought to Play, His Grandson [Jesse Simms] Doesn't Have To." *U.S. News & World Report,* CXXII (March 24, 1997), 52–55.

49467. Epstein, Samuel and Sue. *Jackie Robinson: Baseball's Gallant Fighter.* Champaign, IL: Garrard, 1974. 96p.

49468. Falkner, David. *Great Time Coming: The Life of Jackie Robinson, from Baseball to Birmingham.* New York: Simon & Schuster, 1995. 382p.

49469. Findlay, David W. and Clifford E. Reid. "Jackie Robinson and the National Baseball Hall of Fame." In: Peter M. Rutkoff, ed. *The Cooperstown Symposium on Baseball and American Culture, 1997 (Jackie Robinson).* Jefferson, NC: McFarland & Co., Inc., 2000. Pp. 227–256.

49470. Flynn, James J. "Jackie Robinson." In: his *Negroes of Achievement in Modern America.* New York: Dodd, Mead, 1970. Pp. 121–137.

49471. "From First to Fame: Jackie Robinson." *Ebony,* XVII (October 1962), 85–86.

49472. Frommer, Harvey. *Jackie Robinson.* New York: Watts, 1984. 117p.

49473. _____. "Jackie Robinson as a Montreal Royal." In: School of Physical and Health Education, University of Toronto, comp. *Proceedings of the 5th Canadian Symposium on the History of Sport and Physical Education.* Toronto:. University of Toronto, 1982. pp. 122–128. Robinson's tenure in the International League in 1946.

49474. _____. *Rickey and Robinson: The Men Who Broke Baseball's Color Line.* New York: Macmillan, 1982. 240p. Reprinted in a 256-page edition by the Dallas, TX, firm of Taylor Publishing in 2003.

49475. Frost, Helen. *Let's Meet Jackie Robinson.* Philadelphia, PA: Chelsea House Publishers, 2004. 32p. Juvenile.

49476. Fuse, Montye and Keith Miller. "Jazzing the Basepaths: Jackie Robinson and African-American Aesthetics." In: John Bloom and Michael Williard, eds. *Sports Matters: Race, Recreation, and Culture.* New York: New York University Press, 2002. Pp. 119–140.

49477. Gaven, Michael. "Jackie Robinson's Sore Arm." *Baseball Digest,* VII (January 1949), 37–39.

49478. Glasser, Ira. "Baseball and Civil Rights: Branch Rickey and Jackie Robinson." *Current,* no. 454 (July-August 2003), 25–31.

49479. Glasser, R. "Inspiration: Remembering Robinson." *Sports Illustrated,* LXXVI (April 7, 1997), 15–16.

49480. Glennon, Fred. "Baseball's Surprising Moral Example: Branch Rickey, Jackie Robinson, and the Racial Integration of America." In: his *The Faith of Fifty Million.* Philadelphia, PA: Westminster Press, 2002. Pp. 145–166.

49481. Golenbock, Peter. *Teammates.* San Diego, CA: Gulliver Books, 1990. 30p. Robinson and Pee Wee Reese.

49482. Gomez, Rebecca. *Jackie Robinson.* Edina, MN: Abdo Pub., 2003. 32p.

49483. Goren, Herb. "Are They Giving Jackie Robinson the Works?" *Baseball Digest,* XIV (September 1965), 77–82.

49484. _____. "Do the Dodgers Miss Jackie-Robinson?" *Baseball Digest,* XVI (August 1957), 51–55.

49485. _____. "Jackie Robinson Himself Now." *Baseball Digest,* VII (October 1948), 65–69.

49486. Grabowski, Jack F. *Baseball Legends: Jackie Robinson.* New York: Chelsea House, 1991. 64p.

49487. Greene, Carol. *Jackie Robinson: Baseball's First Black Major Leaguer.* Chicago, IL: Children's Press, 1990. 47p.

49488. Griffin, Richard. "Jackie Robinson's 'Real' Anniversary." *World Press Review,* XLVIII (August 1996), 38–39. Breaking color barrier in 1946 while playing for Montreal Royals.

49489. Gross, Milton. "September 30, 1951." In: Jackie Robinson and Jules Tygiel. *The Jackie Robinson Reader: Perspectives on an American Hero.* New York: E. P. Dutton, 1997. Chapter 15.

49490. _____. "Why They Boo Jackie Robinson." *Sport,* XIV (February 1953), 10–13.

49491. Gutman, Bill. "Jackie Robinson." In: his *Famous Baseball Stars.* New York: Dodd, Mead, 1973. Pp. 124–137.

49492. Halberstam, David. "Jackie Robinson." *Sport,* LXXVII (December 1986), 10–14.

49493. Hardy, Stephen. "Where Did You Go Jackie Robinson?; or, The End of History and the Age of Sport Infrastructure." *Sporting Traditions: The Journal of the Australian Society for Sports History,* XVI (November 1999), 85–100.

49494. Harris, Mark. "Jackie Robinson: Major League Baseball's First Black." *TV Guide,* XXV (August 6, 1977), 10–14.

49495. _____. "Where've You Gone, Jackie Robinson?" *The Nation,* CCLX (May 15, 1995), 674–676.

49496. Hayes, Henry L. *Hey Jackie, We Love You.* Nashville, TN: Winston-Drek Pub. Co., 1997.

49497. Head, John. "Great Granddaddy vs. Jackie Robinson." *Southern Exposure,* VII (Fall 1979), 15–18.

49498. Hedin, Mark. "Una Dura Leccion: Despuis de 50 Anes, el Besbel Recuerda Los Remienzos du ru Integracien." *El Mensajero,* XI (22 de Junio 1997), 20–21. How the San Francisco Giants honored Jackie Robinson.

49499. Henry, Patrick. "Jackie Robinson: Athlete and American *Par Excellence." The Virginia Quarterly Review,* LXXIII (Spring 1997), 189–203.

49500. Herzog, Brad. "A Home Run for the Ages." *Sports Illustrated,* LXXXIV (April 1, 1996), 1+.

49501. _____. "Jackie Robinson." In: his *The 20 Greatest Athletes of the 20th Century.* New York: Rosen Pub. Group, 2003. Chapter 16.

49502. Hoffman, Frank W. and William G. Bailey. "Jackie Robinson and Baseball's Color Line." In: their *Sports and Recreation Fads.* Binghampton, NY: Haworth, 1991. Pp. 307–309.

49503. Holmes, Tot. *Brooklyn's Best.* Gothenburg, NE: Holmes Publishing, 1988. 104p. Jackie Robinson and Pete Reiser.

49504. _____. *Jackie 1947.* Gothenburg, NE: Holmes Publishing, 1997. 125p.

49505. Honig, Donald. "Jackie Robinson." In: his *Baseball America: The Heroes of the Game and the Times of Their Glory.* New York: Macmillan, 1985. Pp. 25–267.

49506. _____. "When Baseball Grew Up." In: Jack Canfield and Mark Victor Hansen, eds. *Chicken Soup for the Sports Fan's Soul: 101 Stories of Insight, Inspiration, and Laughter from the World of Sports.* Deerfield Beach, FL: Health Communications, Inc., 2000. Pp. 73–79. When Clyde Sukeforth scouted Robinson for Branch Rickey.

49507. Howerton, Darryl. "Spike [Lee] on Sports: America's Most Famous Fan Talks Reggie Miller, Scottie Pippen, Charles Barkley, Patrick Ewing, and Jackie Robinson." *Sport,* LXXXVI (February 1995), 76+.

49508. Hughes, Langston. "Jackie Robinson." In: his *Famous American Negroes.* New York- Dodd, Mead, 1954. Pp. 139–144.

49509. "Hurray for Jackie Robinson." *Negro History Bulletin,* XVIII (January 1955), 93+.

49510. Hylton, J. Gordon. "American Civil Rights Laws and the Legacy of Jackie Robinson." *Marquette Sports Law Journal,* VIII (Spring 1998), 387–399.

49511. Hyman, Stanley Edgar. "The Other Jackie Robinson." *The New Leader,* LXXX (April 21, 1997), 8–16. First penned in 1960.

49512. "Jack Roosevelt Robinson." In: *Current Biography Yearbook, 1947.* New York: H.W. Wilson Co., 1947. Pp. 544–547.

49513. "Jackie Robinson." In: Arthur Gelb, ed. *The New York Times Great Lives of the 20th Century.* New York: Times Books, 1988. Pp. 529–538.

49514. "Jackie Robinson." In: Joseph J. Vecchione, ed. *The New York Times Book of Sports Legends.* New York: Times Books, 1991. Pp. 252–263.

49515. "Jackie Robinson Congressional Gold Medal Legislation Signed By President Bush." *Jet,* CIV (November 17, 2003), 48–49.

49516. "Jackie Robinson, President Eisenhower, and the Little Rock Crisis." *Social Education,* LXI (April 1997), 218+.

49517. "Jackie Robinson Tribute: Breaking Barriers — Remembering April 15, 1947." In: John J. Ralph, ed. *The National Baseball Hall of Fame and Museum 1997 Yearbook.* Pittsburgh, PA: Geyer Printing Co., 1997. Pp. 2–9.

49518. "Jackie Robinson's Double Play." *Life,* XXVIII (May 8,1950),129–132.

49519. "Jackie Robinson's Grandson Carries on His Sports Legacy." *Jet,* XCI (December 23, 1996), 53–54.

49520. Jerome, Richard. "Man on Fire." *People Weekly,* XLVII (April 28, 1997), 71–74.

49521. Johnson, Spencer. *Value of Courage: The Story of Jackie Robinson.* San Diego, CA: ValueTale, 1977. 64p.

49522. Kahn, Roger. "Jackie Robinson." *Sport,* LXXI (December 1971), 64–87.

49523. _____. "Jackie Robinson." In: Ed Fitzgerald, ed. *Heroes of Sport.* New York: Bartholomew House, 1960. Pp. 137–154.

49524. _____. "The Jackie Robinson I Remember." *Journal of Blacks in Higher Education,* no. 14 (Winter 1999), 88–93.

49525. _____. "The Lion at Dusk." In: Jackie Robinson and Jules Tygiel. *The Jackie Robinson Reader: Perspectives on an American Hero.* New York: E. P. Dutton, 1997. Chapter 23.

49526. _____. "Roger Kahn on Jackie Robinson." In: *The Baseball Hall of Fame 50th Anniversary Book.* New York: Prentice-Hall, 1988. Pp. 214–227.

49527. _____. "The Ten Years of Jackie Robinson." *Sport,* XX (October 1955), 12–13+. Reprinted in Al Silverman, ed., *The Best of Sport, 1946–1971* (New York: Viking Press, 1971), pp. 114–130, in Editors of Sport. *World of Sport* (New York: Holt, Rinehart and Winston, 1962), pp. 43–60, and in Al Silverman and Brian Silverman, eds., *The Twentieth Century Treasury of Sports* (New York: Viking Press, 1992), pp. 334–351.

49528. Kaplan, Dave. "Remembering Jackie Robinson." In: Joe Hoppel, ed. *The Sporting News 1998 Baseball Yearbook.* St. Louis, MO: The Sporting News, 1998. Pp. 10–12.

49529. Kashatus, B. "Baseball's Noble Experiment." *American History,* XXXII (March-April 1997), 32–37+.

49530. Kelley, William G. "Jackie Robinson and the Press." *Journalism Quarterly,* LIII (Spring 1976), 137–139.

49531. Kendall, Brian. "October 4, 1946: Jackie Robinson Finds a Northern Home." In: his *Great Moments in Canadian Baseball.* Toronto, Ont.: Lester Publishing, 1995. Chapter 7.

49532. Kindred, Dave. "Remembering Jackie Robinson." In: Joe Hoppel, ed. *The Sporting News 1997 Baseball Yearbook.* St. Louis, MO: *The Sporting News,* 1997. Pp. 10–11.

49533. Kirst, Sean Peter. "The Worst of Being First' [and] 'Syracuse Faces an Ugly Legacy from the Robinson Era." In: his *The Ashes of Lou Gehrig and Other Baseball Essays.* Jefferson, NC: McFarland & Co., Inc., 2003. Pp. 66–72.

49534. Klingel, Cynthia Fitterer and Robert B. Noyed. *Jackie Robinson.* New York: Child's World, 2002. 24p.

49535. Kuenster, John. "Jackie Robinson: His National Impact Was Greater Than Ruth's." *Baseball Digest,* XXXV (July 1976), 15–20.

49536. _____. "Jackie Robinson Left an Enduring Legacy as a Courageous Pioneer." *Baseball Digest,* LVI (March 1997), 17–19.

49537. Lacy, Sam. "Campy, Jackie as Dodgers." In: David K. Wiggins and Patrick B. Miller, eds. *The Unlevel Playing Field: A Documentary History of the African American Experience in Sport.* Champaign, IL: University of Illinois Press, 2003. Pp. 210–212.

49538. _____. "Hall of Famer Still on Cloud 9." In: Jackie Robinson and Jules Tygiel. *The Jackie Robinson Reader: Perspectives on an American Hero.* New York: E. P. Dutton, 1997. Chapter 19.

49539. Lamb, Charles. "I Never Want to Take Another Trip Like This One': Jackie Robinson's Journey to Integrate Baseball." *Journal of Sport History,* XXIV (Summer 1997), 177–191.

49540. _____. "March 17, 1946: Jackie Robinson Plays His First Game for the Montreal Royals." *The National Pastime,* XIX (1999), 20–23.

49541. Lamb, Chris. *Blackout: The Untold Story of Jackie Robinson's First Spring Training.* Lincoln, NE: University of Nebraska Press, 2004. 176p. In Florida.

49542. Laney, Al. "Regardless of Race, Color or -." In: Irving T. Marsh, ed. *Best Sports Stories of 1945.* New York: E. P. Dutton, 1946. Pp. 270–276. Reprinted from an article in the October 26, 1945 issue of the *New York Herald-Tribune.*

49543. Lardner, John. "[Pee Wee] Reese and Robinson: Team Within a Team." *The New York Times Magazine,* (September 18, 1949), 17+.

49544. Lawson, Barbara Spilman. *Jackie Robinson.* Great American Citizens. Waynesboro, VA : Fun Stuff Publications, 2001. 11p.

49545. Leavy, Walter. "Baseball's Biggest Superstars Salute a 'Legend.'" *Ebony,* LII (July 1997), 52–55.

49546. _____. "The 50th Anniversary of the Jackie Robinson Revolution." *Ebony,* LII (April 1997), 87–90.

49547. Leiker, Ken. "3–1947: Jackie Robinson Breaks the Color Barrier." In: his *Major League Baseball Memorable Moments: The Most Memorable Moments in Major League Baseball History.* New York: Ballantine Books, 2002. Pp. 22–26.

49548. Libby, Bill. "Jackie Robinson." in: his *Heroes of the Hot Corner.* New York: Watts, 1972. Pp. 83–85.

49549. "A Life of Dedication: The Family of Baseball Great Jackie Robinson has Donated His Papers to the Library." *Library of Congress Information Bulletin,* LX (November 2001), 250–251.

49550. Limonchik, Abe, ed. *Jackie Robinson—a Part of Montreal's History: Proceedings of the Symposium on the Removal of Racial Barriers in Professional Baseball.* Montreal, Canada: Organising Committee of the 50th Anniversary Celebration of Jackie Robinson's Presence in Montreal, 2000. 61p.

49551. Lipset, Lew. "Collecting Jackie Robinson." *Baseball Cards,* IV (June 1984), 24–29+.

49552. Lowenfish, Lee E. "Sport, Race and the Baseball Business: The Jackie Robinson Story Revisited." *Arena Review,* II (Spring 1978), 2–16.

49553. Lundquist, Carl. "Drama in Philadelphia: The Catch, the Homer...Jackie Robinson's Forgotten Great Day." *The Baseball Research Journal,* XXVI (1997), 3–4.

49554. Lupica, Mike. "Now Batting for Brooklyn...." *Esquire,* CXXVII (April 1997), 94–98.

49555. Macht, Norman. "Final Look: Jackie Robinson." *Beckett Baseball Card Monthly,* X, no. 100 (July 1993), 126–127.

49556. Major, Gerri. "The Woman Behind Jackie Robinson." *Tan,* VII (June 1957), 34–38. Rachel.

49557. "Major League Baseball Dedicates Season to 50th Anniversary of Jackie Robinson's Breaking Color Barrier." *Jet,* XCI (March 17, 1997), 48–49.

49558. Malec, Michael and Hillary Beckles. "Baseball, Cricket, and Social Change: Jackie Robinson and Frank Worrell." In: Peter M. Rutkoff, ed. *The Cooperstown Symposium on Baseball and American Culture, 1997 (Jackie Robinson).* Jefferson, NC: McFarland & Co., Inc., 2000. Pp. 177–188.

49559. "The Man Who Changed America." *Sports Illustrated for Kids,* IX (February 1997), 24–35.

49560. Mann, Arthur. *Jackie Robinson Story.* New York. Low, 1950. 120p. Excerpted in *Saturday Evening Post,* CCXXII (May 12–20, 1950), 19–21+, 36+, and reprinted by the New York firm of Grosset and Dunlap in an expanded 252-page edition in 1956.

49561. _____. "Say Jack Robinson: Meet the Dodgers' Newest Recruit." *Collier's,* CXVII (March 2, 1946), 67–68. Reprinted in Editors of *Collier's, Greatest Sport Stories.* New York: A.S. Barnes, 1956. pp. 199–204.

49562. _____. "The Truth About the Jackie Robinson Case." In: Editors of *Saturday Evening Post. Sport U.SA* New York: Nelson, 1961. Pp. 381–391.

49563. Mara, Will. *Jackie Robinson.* New York: Children's Press, 2002. 31p.

49564. Massaquoi, Hans. "The Breakthrough Stars." *Ebony,* XLVII (August 1992), 44+.

49565. Mathewson, Alfred Dennis. "Grooming Crossovers." *Journal of Gender, Race and Justice,* IV (Spring 2001), 225–281. Racial athletic role models, especially Robinson.

49566. Mathisen, Chris. "Jackie Robinson vs. Paul Robeson." In: Dean A. Sullivan, ed. *Late Innings: A Documentary History of Baseball, 1945–1972.* Lincoln, NE: University of Nebraska Press, 2002. Pp. 33–36. Reprinted from the *Washington Evening Star,* July 18, 1949.

49567. Maxwell, Jocko. "Robinson's the Name for '47." *Baseball Digest,* V (October 1946), 57–59.

49568. McCollum, S. "Jackie Robinson: Leading the Way." *Scholastic Update,* CXXIX (April 11, 1997), 18–19.

49569. McLeese, Don. *Jackie Robinson.* Vero Beach, FL : Rourke Pub., 2003. 24p.

49570. Meany, Thomas. "Does Jackie Robinson Belong in the Hall of Fame?" *Sport,* XXIV (November 1957), 24–25+.

49571. _____. "Jackie Robinson." In: his *Baseball's Greatest Players.* New York: Grosset and Dunlap, 1953. Pp. 194–204.

49572. _____. "Jackie's One of the Gang." *Sport,* VII (August 1949), 24–27. Reprinted in John L. Pratt, ed., *Sport, Sport, Sport* (New York: Watts, 1960), pp. 19–27.

49573. _____. "What Chance Has Jackie Robinson?" *Sport,* II (January 1947), 12–14+.

49574. _____. and Tommy Holmes. "Jackie Robinson." In: their *Baseball's Best*. New York, Watts, 1964. Pp, 160–168.

49575. Metcalf, George R. "Jackie Robinson." In: his *Black Profiles*. New York: McGraw-Hill, 1968. Pp. 143–147.

49576. Morales, Leslie Anderson. "Jack Roosevelt Robinson: Baseball's First Black Superstar." *AppleSeeds*, II (February 2000), 3–7.

49577. _____. "Young Jackie Robinson." *AppleSeeds*, II (February 2000), 21–23.

49578. Nack, William. "The Breakthrough." *Sports Illustrated*, LXXXVI (May 5, 1997), 56–62, 65–67.

49579. "Nation Celebrates Anniversary of Jackie Robinson's Breaking the Color Barrier." *Jet*, XCI (May 5, 1997), 46–48.

49580. National Baseball Hall of Fame and Museum Library, Staff of. *Jackie Robinson: A Selective Bibliography*. Cooperstown, NY: National Baseball Hall of Fame Library, 1997. 11p. Based on the Robinson sections in the 1985 original edition and 1992 supplement of *Baseball: A Comprehensive Bibliography*.

49581. *New York Amsterdam News*, Editors of. "Thousands Mourn Jackie Robinson (November 4, 1972)." In: Jackie Robinson and Jules Tygiel. *The Jackie Robinson Reader: Perspectives on an American Hero*. New York: E. P. Dutton, 1997. Chapter 24.

49582. O'Connor, Jim. *Jackie Robinson and the Story of All-Black Baseball*. New York: Random House, 1948. 48p. Reprinted by Random House Children's Books in 2003.

49583. Olsen, James T. *Jackie Robinson: Pro Ball's First Black Star*. Mankato, MN: Creative Education, 1974. 29p.

49583. Orr, Jack. "Jackie Robinson: Symbol of the Revolution." *Sport*, XXIX (February 1960), 52–69.

49584. Ostler, Scott. "A Day of Little Challenges." In: Tom Barnidge, ed. *Best Sports Stories of 1988*. St. Louis, MO: *The Sporting News*, 1988. Pp. 87–93.

49585. Ousler, Fulton. "Jackie Robinson." In: his *Why I Know There is a God*. Garden City, NY. Doubleday, 1960. Pp. 67–84.

49586. _____. "Rookie of the Year." *Reader's Digest*, LII (February 1948), 34–38.

49587. Pappas, Doug. "Jackie Robinson and the Red Sox." *Boston Baseball*, VIII (April 1997), 30+.

49588. "Player of the Half Century." *Sport*, LXXXVII (September 1996), 18+.

49589. Parrott, Harold. "The Betrayal of Jackie Robinson." In: Jackie Robinson and Jules Tygiel. *The Jackie Robinson Reader: Perspectives on an American Hero*. New York: E. P. Dutton, 1997. Chapter 11.

49590. Peterson, Richard F. "The Influence of Jackie Robinson on the Serious Baseball Novel." In: Peter M. Rutkoff, ed. *The Cooperstown Symposium on Baseball and American Culture, 1997 (Jackie Robinson)*. Jefferson, NC: McFarland & Co., Inc., 2000. Pp. 215–226.

49591. _____ and Eliot Asinof. "Jackie Robinson and the Serious Baseball Novel." In: their *Extra Innings: Writing on Baseball*. Sport and Society Series. Urbana, IL: University of Illinois Press, 2001. Pp. 112–124.

49592. Pollack, J.K. "Meet a Family Named Robinson." *Parent's Magazine*, XXX (October 1955), 46–47+. Reprinted in Jackie Robinson and Jules Tygiel. *The Jackie Robinson Reader: Perspectives on an American Hero* (New York: E. P. Dutton, 1997), Chapter 17.

49593. Powell, Larry. "Jackie Robinson and Dixie Walker: Myths of the Southern Baseball Player." *Southern Cultures*, VIII (Summer 2002), 56–71.

49594. Pratkanis, Anthony R. and Marlene E. Turner. "Nine Principles of Successful Affirmative Action: Branch Rickey, Jackie Robinson, and the Integration of Baseball." In: Peter M. Rutkoff, ed. *The Cooperstown Symposium on Baseball and American Culture, 1997 (Jackie Robinson)*. Jefferson, NC: McFarland & Co., Inc., 2000. Pp. 151–176.

49594. _____. "The Year Cool Papa Bell Lost the Batting Title: Mr. Branch Rickey, Mr. Jackie Robinson, and the Integration of Baseball." *Nine: A Journal of Baseball History and Social Policy Perspective*, II (Winter 1994), 260–276.

49595. Raatma, Lucia. *Jackie Robinson*. Milwaukee, WI: World Almanac Library, 2002. 48p.

49596. Ralph, John J. "Breaking Barriers: Remembering April 15, 1947." In: Kansas City Royals. *The Kansas City Royals 1997 Yearbook*. Kansas City, M), 1997. Pp. 56–57.

49597. Rampersad, Arnold and Jackie. *Jackie Robinson: A Biography*. New York: Alfred A. Knopf, 1997. 448p.

49598. Rediger, Pat. "Jackie Robinson." In: his *Great African Americans in Sports*. New York: Crabtree Publishing, 1996. Pp. 58–60.

49599. Reese, Harold ("Pee Wee"). "Baseball is a Different Game Now." Edited by Thomas Meany. *Collier's*, CXXXVI (August 19, 1955), 38+.

49600. Reiser, Howard. *Jackie Robinson: Baseball Pioneer*. New York: Franklin Watts, 1992. 64p.

49601. Resnick, Joe. "Jackie Robinson: He Paved the Way for Some of Baseball's Greatest." *Dodgers Scoreboard Magazine*, (May 1987), 12–13.

49602. Rice, Grantland. "The Emancipation of Jackie Robinson." *Sport*, XI (October 1951), 12–15.

49603. Robinson, Jack R. ("Jackie"). "The Best Advice I Ever Had." *Reader's Digest*, LXXII (May 1958), 214–216. From Branch Rickey.

49604. _____. *Breakthrough to the Big Leagues: The Story of Jackie Robinson*. New York: Harper & Row, 1965. 178p.

49605. _____. "The Guts Not to Fight Back." In: Laurence T. Lorimer, ed. *Breaking In*. New York: Random House, 1974. Pp. 173–198.

49606. _____. *I Never Had It Made*. New York: G. P. Putnam, 1972. 287p. Excerpted in Will Balliett and Tom Dyja, eds., *The Hard Way: Writing by the Rebels Who Changed Sports* (New York: Thunder's Mouth Press, 1999), pp. 5–22.

49607. _____. "A Kentucky Colonel [Pee-Wee Reese] Kept Me in Baseball." *Look*, XIX (February 8, 1955), 82–84+.

49608. _____. "My Feud with Leo [Durocher]." *Our Sports*, I (June 1953), 12–13.

49609. _____. *My Own Story*. Edited by Wendell Smith. New York: Greenberg, 1948. 172p.

49610. _____. "Now I Know Why They Boo Me." *Look*, XIX (January 25–February 22,1955); 23–28. Reprinted in Jackie Robinson and Jules Tygiel, *The Jackie Robinson Reader: Perspectives on an American Hero* (New York: E. P. Dutton, 1997), Chapter 16.

49611. _____. "There He Goes." In: *Boy's Life*, Editors of. *Baseball as We Played It*. New York: G.P. Putnam, 1969. Pp. 35–46. Basestealing technique. Reprinted in Editors of *Boy's Life, Baseball as We Played It* (New York: G. P. Putnam, 1969), pp. 36–46.

49612. _____. "Trouble Ahead Needn't Bother You." In: Norman V. Peale, ed. *Faith Made Them Champions*. Englewood Cliffs, NJ: Prentice-Hall, 1955. Pp. 238–241.

49613. _____. "Why I'm Quitting Baseball." *Look*, XXI (January 22, 1957), 91–92. Reprinted in Jackie Robinson and Jules Tygiel, *The Jackie Robinson Reader: Perspectives on an American Hero* (New York: E. P. Dutton, 1997), Chapter 18.

49614. _____ and Malcolm X. "An Exchange of Letters." In: Jackie Robinson and Jules Tygiel. *The Jackie Robinson Reader: Perspectives on an American Hero.* New York: E. P. Dutton, 1997. Chapter 21.

49615. _____. and Wendell Smith. "Jackie Robinson's First Spring Training." in: Stephen A. Reiss, ed. *The American Sporting Experience: An Historical Anthology.* New York: Leisure Press, 1984. Pp. 365–370.

49616. _____., as told to Alfred Duckett. "On Being Black Among the Republicans." In: Jackie Robinson and Jules Tygiel. *The Jackie Robinson Reader: Perspectives on an American Hero.* New York: E. P. Dutton, 1997. Chapter 20.

49617. _____, as told to Fred Down. "20 Years Later." In: Fred Down, ed. *Sports All-Stars 1967 Baseball.* New York: Maco Publishing Co., 1967. Pp. 42–49.

49618. Robinson, Mack. "My Brother Jackie." *Ebony,* XII (July 1957), 75–82.

49619. Robinson, Rachel, and Lee Daniels. *Jackie Robinson: An Intimate Portrait.* New York: Harry N. Abrams, 1996. 240p. Excerpted in *Essence,* XXVII (November 1996), 52+.

49620. Robinson, Ray. "Jackie Robinson." In: his *Speed Kings of the Base Paths.* New York: G.P. Putnam, 1964. Pp. 33–49.

49621. Robinson, Sharon. *Jackie's Nine: Jackie Robinson's Values to Live By — Courage, Determination, Teamwork, Persistence, Integrity, Commitment, Excellence.* New York: Scholastic, 2001. 181p.

49622. _____. *Promises to Keep: How Jackie Robinson Changed America.* New York: Scholastic Books, 2004. 64p.

49623. _____. *Stealing Home: An Intimate Family Portrait by the Daughter of Jackie Robinson.* New York: HarperCollins, 1996. 213p.

49624. "Robinson's Interracial Barnstorming Team Banned by 'Bull' Connor." In: Dean A. Sullivan, ed. *Late Innings: A Documentary History of Baseball, 1945–1972.* Lincoln, NE: University of Nebraska Press, 2002. Pp. 72–73. Reprinted from the *Chicago Defender,* Oct. 17, 1953.

49625. Roeder, Bill. *Jackie Robinson.* New York: A. S. Barnes, 1950. 183p.

49626. "Rookie of the Year." *Time,* L (September 22,1947), 70–76.

49627. Rosenthal, Harold. "Storybook Stars in Brooklyn." In: Bruce Jacobs, ed. *Baseball Stars of 1953.* New York: Lion Books, 1953. Pp. 134–138. Robinson and Pee Wee Reese.

49628. Rossi, John. "Jackie Robinson in the City of Brotherly Love." *Elysian Fields Quarterly,* XV (Spring 1998), 25–31.

49629. Rothe, Emil H. "Jackie Robinson's Major League Debut." *Baseball Digest,* XXXI (December 1972), 82–88.

49630. Rowan, Carl T., with Jackie Robinson. *Wait 'Till Next Year: The Life Story of Jackie Robinson.* New York: Random Home, 1960. 339p.

49631. Rubinstein, William D. "Jackie Robinson and the Integration of Major League Baseball." *History Today,* LIII (September 2003), 20–25.

49632. Rudeen, Kenneth. *Jackie Robinson.* New York: Crowell, 1971. 40p.

49633. _____. *Jackie Robinson.* New York: Harper Trophy, 1996. 53p.

49634. Ruscoe, Michael. "In Jackie's Footsteps: Helping Kids and Honoring a Baseball Hero." *Know Your World Extra,* XXXV (April 26, 2002), 4–6.

49635. Russo, Neat. "Robinson Discovered at 14." *Baseball Digest,* XVIII (October 1959), 52–65.

49636. Rust, Art, Jr. "Jackie Robinson." In: his *Get That Nigger Off the Field.* New York. Delacorte, 1976. Pp. 63–81.

49637. Rutkoff, Peter M. "Jackie Robinson: Baseball, Brooklyn, and Beyond." In: Peter M. Rutkoff, ed. *The Cooperstown Symposium on Baseball and American Culture, 1997 (Jackie Robinson).* Jefferson, NC: McFarland & Co., Inc., 2000. Pp. 3–24.

49638. Rutz, Jonathan Edward. "Fields of Gray: an Examination of Jackie Robinson's First Season in Major League Baseball." Unpublished BA thesis, James Madison University, 1998. 103p.

49639. Sabin, Francene. *Jackie Robinson.* Mahwah, NJ: Troll Associates, 1985. 187p.

49640. Sailer, Steve. "How Jackie Robinson Desegregated America." *National Review,* XLVIII (April 8, 1996), 38+.

49641. Sanford, William R. and Carl R. Green. *Jackie Robinson.* New York: Crestwood House, 1993. 48p.

49642. Santella, Andrew. *Jackie Robinson Breaks the Color Line.* New York: Children's Press, 1996. 32p.

49643. Savage, Jeff. "Jackie Robinson." In: his *Top 10 African-American Men's Athletes.* Berkeley Heights, NJ: Enslow Publishers, 2001. Pp. 34–37.

49644. Schaefer, Lola M. *Jackie Robinson.* Mankato, MN: Pebble Books, 2003. 24p.

49645. Schoor, Gene. "He Broke the Line: Jackie Robinson." In: *his Courage Makes the Champion.* Princeton, NJ: Van Nostrand, 1947. Pp. 49–59.

49646. _____. *Jackie Robinson, Baseball Hero.* New York: G.P. Putnam, 1958. 187p.

49647. Schreiber, Le Anne. "Saviors: Babe Ruth, Jackie Robinson, Larry Bird, Magic Johnson, Pete Rozelle, Tiger Woods." In: Jay Lovinger, ed. *The Gospel According to ESPN: Saints, Saviors & Sinners.* New York: Hyperion, 2002. Chapter 3.

49648. Scott, Richard. *Jackie Robinson.* Black Americans of Achievement Series. Philadelphia, PA: Chelsea House, 1987. 110p.

49649. _____. *Jackie Robinson: First Black in Professional Baseball.* Los Angeles, CA: Melrose Square Publishing Co., 1991. 169p.

49650. Seaver, Tom, with Marty Appel. "The Coming of Jackie Robinson." In: his *Great Moments in Baseball: From the World Series of 1903 to the Modern Records of Nolan Ryan.* New York: Carol Communications, 1992. Pp. 151–156.

49651. Shapiro, Milton J. "Jackie Robinson." In: his *The Year They Won the MVP Award.* New York: Julian Messner, 1966. Pp. 106–125.

49652. _____. *Jackie Robinson of the Brooklyn Dodgers.* New York: Julian Messner, 1973. 192p.

49653. Sheed, Wilfrid. "And Playing Second Base for Brooklyn-Jackie Robinson." *Esquire,* C (December 1983), 91–94+.

49654. Sher, Jack. "Jackie Robinson: The Great Experiment." *Sport,* V (October 1948), 30–31+.

49655. Shorto, Russell. *Jackie Robinson and the Breaking of the Color Barrier.* Brookfield, CT: Millbrook Press, 1991. 28p.

49656. Shumard, Bill. "In Memoriam to Jackie Robinson." In: Bill Shumard, ed. *Los Angeles Dodgers 1987 Yearbook.* Los Angeles, CA: George Rice & Sons, 1987. Pp. 17–19.

49657. Simon, Scott. *Jackie Robinson and the Integration of Baseball.* New York: John Wiley, 2002. 168p.

49658. Simons, William. "Jackie Robinson and the American Mind: Journalistic Impressions of the Reintegration of Baseball." *Journal of Sport History,* XII (Spring 1985), 39–64.

49659. _____. "Jackie Robinson and the American Zeitgeist." In: Peter M. Rutkoff, ed. *The Cooperstown Symposium on Baseball and American Culture, 1997 (Jackie Robinson).* Jefferson, NC: McFarland & Co., Inc., 2000. Pp. 77–108.

49660. Sloate, Susan. "Jackie Robinson." In: her *Hotshots: Baseball Greats of the Game When They Were Kids.* Boston, MA: Little, Brown, 1991. Pp. 42–47.

49661. Slocum, Rob. "My Brush with History: Up Strolls Jackie." *American Heritage,* LII (July-August 2001), 76–78. Receipt of an autographed baseball by author as a seven-year-old youngster.

49662. Smith, Jeffrey A. "Jackie Robinson in Sportsman's Park." *Gateway Heritage,* XVII (Spring 1997), 50–53.

49663. Smith, Robert M. "Jackie Robinson." In: his *Heroes of Baseball.* Cleveland, OH: World Publishing Co., 1952. Pp. 213–224.

49664. _____. "Paul Robeson-Jackie Robinson and a Political Collision." *Journal of Sport History,* VI (Summer 1979), 5–27.

49665. Smith, Ronald A. "Jackie Robinson." In: his *Heroes of the Hall: Baseball's Greatest Players.* New York: Contemporary Books, 2002. Pp. 390–393.

49666. _____. "Jackie Robinson-44." In: his *The Sporting News Selects Baseball's 100 Greatest Players.* St. Louis, MO: *The Sporting News,* 1998. Pp. 98–99.

49667. _____. "The Paul Robeson-Jackie Robinson Saga and a Political Collision." *Journal of Sport History,* VI (Summer 1979), 5–27. Reprinted in Jackie Robinson and Jules Tygiel, *The Jackie Robinson Reader: Perspectives on an American Hero* (New York: E. P. Dutton, 1997), Chapter 14.

49668. Smith, Walter ("Red") . "Jackie Robinson." In: Verna Reamer, ed. *The Best of Red Smith.* New York: Watts, 1963. Pp. 65–69.

49669. Smith, Wendell. "It was a Great Day in Jersey." In: Jackie Robinson and Jules Tygiel. *The Jackie Robinson Reader: Perspectives on an American Hero.* New York: E. P. Dutton, 1997. Chapter 8. Reprinted in Nicholas Dawidoff, ed., *Baseball: A Literary Anthology* (New York: The Library of America, 2002), pp. 195–199. Playing with Montreal in 1946.

49670. _____. "The Jackie, Robinson I Knew." *Baseball Digest,* XXXII (January 1973), 27–30. Reprinted in John Kuenster, ed., *From Cobb to Catfish* (Chicago: Rand McNally, 1975), pp. 144–145.

49671. Stone, Bob. "Jackie Robinson, Pathfinder." *Baseball Digest,* V (February 1946), 19–21.

49672. Stratton, Madeline R. "Jackie Robinson." In: her *Negroes Who Helped Build America.* New York and Chicago: Ginn, 1966. Pp. 144–154.

49673. Strode, Woody and Sam Young. "The Goal Dust Gang." In: Jackie Robinson and Jules Tygiel. *The Jackie Robinson Reader: Perspectives on an American Hero.* New York: E. P. Dutton, 1997. Chapter 2.

49674. Sugar, Bert Randolph. "Jackie Robinson's First Game: Brooklyn Dodgers vs. Boston Braves, April 15, 1947." In: his *Baseball's 50 Greatest Games.* Rev. ed. North Dighton, MA: The JG Press, 1994. Pp. 131–134.

49675. Sukeforth, Clyde, as told to Donald Honig. "Oh, They Were a Pair." In: Jackie Robinson and Jules Tygiel. *The Jackie Robinson Reader: Perspectives on an American Hero.* New York: E. P. Dutton, 1997. Chapter 5. Robinson and Pee Wee Reese.

49676. Sullivan, George. "Jackie Robinson." In his: *Great Lives: Sports.* New York: Scribner's, 1988. Pp. 209–217.

49677. Thorn, Hal. "Payroll Combo." In: Bruce Jacobs, ed. *Baseball Stars of 1955.* New York: Lion Books, 1955. Pp. 91–95. Jackie Robinson and Pee Wee Reese.

49678. Thorn, John. and Jules Tygiel. "Signing Jackie Robinson." *The National Pastime,* IX (1990), 7–12.

49679. _____. "Jackie Robinson's Signing: The Real Untold Story." In: John Thorn and Peter Palmer, eds. *Total Baseball: The Ultimate Encyclopedia of Baseball.* 3rd ed. New York: Harper Perenial, 1993. Pp. 148–153.

49680. _____. "Jackie Robinson's Signing: The Untold Story." In: Mark Alvarez, ed. *The Perfect Game.* New York: Barnes & Noble Books, 1995. Pp. 204–214.

49681. _____. "The Signing of Jackie Robinson: The Untold Story." *Sport,* LXXIX (June 1988), 65–66+. Reprinted in Jackie Robinson and Jules Tygiel, *The Jackie Robinson Reader: Perspectives on an American Hero* (New York: E. P. Dutton, 1997), Chapter 7.

49682. *Time,* Editors of. "Rookie of the Year (September 22, 1947)." In: Jackie Robinson and Jules Tygiel. *The Jackie Robinson Reader: Perspectives on an American Hero.* New York: E. P. Dutton, 1997. Chapter 12.

49683. Torres, John Albert. "Jackie Robinson." In: his *Top 10 Baseball Legends.* Berkeley Heights, NJ: Enslow Publishers, 2001. Pp. 30–33.

49684. Tunney, Jim. "A Classy Guy." In: Jack Canfield and Mark Victor Hansen, eds. *Chicken Soup for the Sports Fan's Soul: 101 Stories of Insight, Inspiration, and Laughter from the World of Sports.* Deerfield Beach, FL: Health Communications, Inc., 2000. Pp. 169–170.

49685. Tygiel, Jules. *Baseball's Great Experiment: Jackie Robinson and His Legacy.* New York: Oxford University Press, 1983. 392p. Reprinted in 1997.

49686. _____. "Beyond the Point [Color Line] of No Return." *Sports Illustrated,* LVIII (June 20–27, 1983), 62–66+, 40–42+.

49687. _____. "The Court-Martial of Jackie Robinson." *American Heritage,* XXXV (September-October 1984), 34–39. Reprinted in Jackie Robinson and Jules Tygiel, *The Jackie Robinson Reader: Perspectives on an American Hero* (New York: E. P. Dutton, 1997), Chapter 3.

49688. _____. "Il a Gagne Ses Epaulets." In: Jackie Robinson and Jules Tygiel. *The Jackie Robinson Reader: Perspectives on an American Hero.* New York: E. P. Dutton, 1997. Chapter 9. Robinson with the Montreal Royals.

49689. _____. "The Great Experiment Fifty Years Later." In: Peter M. Rutkoff, ed. *The Cooperstown Symposium on Baseball and American Culture, 1997 (Jackie Robinson).* Jefferson, NC: McFarland & Co., Inc., 2000. Pp. 257–270.

49690. _____. "Jackie Robinson: 'A Lone Negro' in Major League Baseball." In: Patrick B. Miller and David Kenneth Wiggins, eds. *Sport and the Color Line: Black Athletes and Race Relations in 29th Century America.* New York and London: Routledge, 2004. Pp. 167–190.

49691. _____. "A Spectacular Season: Jackie Robinson Breaks Through." In: *Baseball History from Outside the Lines.* Lincoln, NE: University of Nebraska Press, 2001. Pp. 183–194. Reprinted in John E. Dreifort, ed., *Baseball History from Outside the Lines: a Reader* (Lincoln, NE: University of Nebraska Press, 2001), Chapter 11.

49692. Vass, George. "Jackie Robinson." In. his *Champions of Sports: Adventures in Courage.* Chicago, IL: Reilly and Lee, 1970. Chapter 2.

49693. Voigt, David Quentin. "Jack Roosevelt 'Jackie' Robinson." In: Vol. Q-Z of David L. Porter, ed. *Biographical Dictionary of American Sports: Baseball.* Rev. and enlarged ed. Westport, CT: Greenwood Press, 2000. Pp. 1302–1304.

49694. _____. "They Shaped the Game: Jackie Robinson." *Baseball History,* I (Spring 1986), 5–22.

49695. Waldman, Frank. "Jackie Robinson." In: his *Famous American Athletes of Today.* 11th Series. New York: Page, 1949. Pp. 237–267.

49696. Walker, Sally M. and Rodney Pate. *Jackie Robinson.* On My Own Biographies. Minneapolis, MN: Lerner, 2002. 48p.

49697. Ward, Geoffrey C. and Ken Burns. "Jackie! Jackie! Jackie!" *U.S. News & World Report,* CXVII (April 29, 1994), 85–86+.

49698. Washburn, Pat. "New York Newspaper Coverage of Jackie Robinson in His First Major League Season." Unpublished paper, 63rd Annual Meeting of the Association for Education In Journalism, 1980. This 28-page document is available as ERIC document ED-199617; also revised and published in *Journalism Quarterly,* LVIII (Winter 1981), 640–644.

49699. Weidhorn, Manfred. *Jackie Robinson.* New York: Atheneum, 1993. 207p.

49700. Wheeler, Jill C. *Jackie Robinson.* Edina, MN: ABDO Pub., 2003. 64p.

49701. "When I was a Kid: Jackie Robinson." *National Geographic World,* no. 286 (June 1999), 28–29. Not autobiographical.

49702. White, Walter. "Jackie Robinson on Trial." In: David K. Wiggins and Patrick B. Miller, eds. *The Unlevel Playing Field: A Documentary History of the African American Experience in Sport.* Champaign, IL: University of Illinois Press, 2003. Pp. 207–209. Reprinted from *Chicago Defender,* April 26, 1947.

49703. Wilkins, Roy W. "Jack & Rachel Robinson." *The Nation,* CCLXIV (April 21, 1997), 4–5.

49704. Will, George F. "The Force That Lit the Fire." *Newsweek,* CIX (April 13, 1987), 88+. Reprinted in his *Bunts: Curt Flood, Camden Yards, Pete Rose and Other Reflections on Baseball* (New York: Touchstone Books, 1998), pp. 87–90.

49705. Williams, Alex. "Jackie Under Her Skin: 50 Years After Jackie Robinson Broke Baseball's Color Line, His Widow, Rachel Robinson, Revisits the Man Behind the Legend." *New York,* XXIX (September 23, 1996), 46–47.

49706. Wisendale, Steven. K. "The Black Knight: A Political Portrait of Jackie Robinson." In: Peter M. Rutkoff, ed. *The Cooperstown Symposium on Baseball and American Culture, 1997 (Jackie Robinson).* Jefferson, NC: McFarland & Co., Inc., 2000. Pp. 189–198.

49707. _____. "The Political Wars of Jackie Robinson." *Nine: A Journal of Baseball History and Social Policy Perspectives,* II (Fall 1993), 18–28.

49708. Wolitzer, Hilma. "Jackie Robinson." In: Danny Peary, ed. *Cult Baseball Players.* New York: Simon and Schuster, 1990. Pp. 208–212.

49709. _____. "Jackie Robinson." In: Danny Peary, ed. *Baseball's Finest: The Greats, the Flakes, the Weird and the Wonderful.* North Dighton, MA: The JG Press, 1990. Pp. 208–212. Both Peary books are identical.

49710. Wollenberg, Skip. "Jackie Robinson a Celebrity Endorser Again." *Marketing News,* XXXI (April 28, 1997), 1–2.

49711. Woodward, Stanley W. "One Strike is Out." In:

David Halberstam, ed. *The Best American Sports Writing of the Century.* Boston, MA: Houghton, Mifflin, 1999. Pp. 165–169.

49712. _____. "Reporter Alleges Strike Threat Against Jackie Robinson." In: Dean A. Sullivan, ed. *Late Innings: A Documentary History of Baseball, 1945–1972.* Lincoln, NE: University of Nebraska Press, 2002. Pp. 25–27. Reprinted from the *New York Herald-Tribune,* May 9, 1947.

49713. Young, Andrew S. N. "Black Athlete in the Gold Age of Sports." *Ebony,* XXIV (November-December 1968), 152–154+, 126–128+.

49714. _____. "40th Anniversary: Biggest Breakthrough in Sports." *Ebony,* XLII (May 1987), 66–68+.

49715. _____. "Jackie Robinson." In: his *Great Negro Baseball Stars and How They Made the Major Leagues.* New York: A. S. Barnes, 1953. Pp. 3–49, 105–120.

49716. _____. "Jackie Robinson." In: his *Negro Firsts in Sports.* New York: Johnson Publishing Co., 1963. Pp. 115–161.

49717. _____. "The Jackie Robinson Era." *Ebony,* XI (November 1955), 152–156.

49718. _____. "Jackie Robinson Remembered." *Ebony,* XLII (August 1992), 36–42; LII (February 1997), 103+.

Wilbert ("Uncle Robbie") Robinson★
C-MGR-EXEC. (B: June 2, 1863, Bolton, MA-D: Aug. S, 1934). Philadelphia (AA), 1886–1890; Baltimore (AA), 1890–1891; Baltimore (NL), 1892–1899; St. Louis (NL), 1900; Baltimore (AL), 1901–1902. Remarks: Had 1,398 hits (18 homers) and 163 stolen bases in 1,371 games in 17 playing seasons; had seven hits in one game, June 10, 1892; manager, Baltimore (AL), 1902 and same team as a minor league club in 1903–1904; coach, New York (NL), 1911–1913; manager, Brooklyn (NL), 1914–1931, winning 1,399 games overall and losing 1,398 (.500); president, Brooklyn (NL), 1926–1929; president-manager of Atlanta (Southern Association) 1933 and of Southern Association, 1934; once caught a grapefruit (which splattered upon impact) dropped 400 feet from an airplane carrying the celebrated aviatrix Ruth Law; elected to National Baseball Hall of Fame in 1945, where his plaque reads: "Star catcher for the famous Baltimore Orioles on pennant clubs of 1894, '95 and '96, he later won fame as manager of the Brooklyn Dodgers from 1914 through 1931. Set a record of 7 hits In 7 times at bat in single game."

49719. Allen, Lee, and Thomas Meany. "Wilbert Robinson." In: their *Kings of the Diamond.* New York. G.P. Putnam, 1965. Pp. 223–224.

49720. Barton, Jerry. "Wilbert Robinson." In: his *A Treasure Chest of the Hall of Fame.* Boston, MA: The Wilson-Hill Co., 1952. Pp. 64–65.

49721. Borst, William A. ("Bill"). "Wilbert 'Uncle Robbie' Robinson." In: Vol. Q-Z of David L. Porter, ed. *Biographical Dictionary of American Sports: Baseball.* Rev. and enlarged ed. Westport, CT: Greenwood Press, 2000. Pp. 1304–1305.

49722. Burr, Herold C. "Wilbert Robinson: Uncle? Cousin?" In: Harold Parrott, ed. *Dodgers 1951 Yearbook.* New York: W and H. Baseball Publishing Co., 1951. Pp. 6–7.

49723. Frommer, Harvey. "Wilbert Robinson." In: his *Baseball's Greatest Managers.* New York: Watts, 1985. Pp. 207–215.

49724. Graham, Frank. "John McGraw and Wilbert Robinson." In: his *Baseball Extra.* New York: A.S. Barnes, 1954. Pp. 193–197.

49725. Hoard, Clinton H. "Everybody's Uncle." In:

Clinton H. Hoard and Charles Dexter, eds. *The Dodgers 1941: Yesterday and Today in Brooklyn Baseball.* New York: W. and H. Baseball Publishing Co., 1941. Pp. 42–43, 60.

49726. Kavanagh, Jack. "An Appreciation of Uncle Robbie." *The National Pastime,* XII (1997), 88–90.

49727. ___. "Wilbert Robinson." In: Frederick Ivor-Campbell, ed. SABR. *Baseball's First Stars.* Cleveland, OH: Society for American Baseball Research, 1996. Pp. 140–141.

49728. ___. and Normal L. Macht. *Uncle Robbie.* Cleveland, OH: Society for American Baseball Research, 1999. 200p.

49729. Knight, Tom. "Uncle Robbie and Hugh Casey." *The Baseball Research Journal,* XXII (1993), 105–106.

49730. Lane, Ferdinand C. "Is Wilbert Robinson a Good Manager?" *Baseball Magazine,* XLV (September 1930), 439–441.

49731. ___. "Razzing Uncle Robbie." *Baseball Magazine,* XLVII (September 1931), 437–438.

49732. Meany, Thomas. "Science and Uncle Robbie." *Baseball Digest,* III (May 1944), 42–47.

49733. Pope, Edwin. "Wilbert Robinson." In: his *Baseball's Greatest Managers.* Garden City, NY: Doubleday, 1960. Pp. 210–233.

49734. Robinson, Ray. "Wilbert Robinson." In: his *Baseball's Most Colorful Managers.* New York: G.P. Putnam, 1970. Pp. 130–168.

49735. Robinson, Wilbert. "How Robbie Makes Cast-Off Pitchers Win." *Baseball Magazine,* XXXVI (January 1926), 355–357.

49736. Smith, Ron. "Wilbert Robinson." In: his *Heroes of the Hall: Baseball's Greatest Players.* New York: Contemporary Books, 2002. Pp. 394–395.

49737. "When 'Robbie' Caught for Both Sides." *Literary Digest,* LXXXIX (May 15, 1926), 72–74. Early amateur game.

William Edward ("Eddie") Robinson

1B-EXEC. (B: Dec. 15, 1920, Paris, TX). Cleveland (AL), 1942, 1946–1948; Washington (AL), 1949–1950; Chicago (AL), 1950–1962; Philadelphia (AL), 1953; New York (AL), 1954–1956; Kansas City (AL) and Baltimore (AL), 1956; Detroit (AL), Cleveland (AL) and Baltimore (AL), 1957. Remarks: Obtained 1,145 hits (172 homers) in 1,314 games for seven different teams in a 13-year big league career; had six hits in 1948 World Series; 29 White Sox homers in 1951 remained team record until September 1970; later became "front office" man for Baltimore (AL), Houston (NL), Kansas City (AL), and Atlanta (NL) and director of player personnel for Texas (AL).

49738. Forker, Dom. "Eddie Robinson." In: his *Sweet Seasons: Recollections of the 55–64 New York Yankees.* Dallas, TX: Taylor Publishing Co., 1989. Pp. 149–153.

49739. Graybar, Lloyd J. "William Edward 'Eddie' Robinson." In: Vol. Q-Z of David L. Porter, ed. *Biographical Dictionary of American Sports: Baseball.* Rev. and enlarged ed. Westport, CT: Greenwood Press, 2000. Pp. 1305–1306.

49740. Hines, Rick. "Eddie Robinson: He's Seen Baseball from Every Angle." *Sports Collector's Digest,* XVIII (March 1, 1991), 206–208.

49741. Hoffman, John C. "Has Ed Robinson Convinced 'Em?" *Baseball Digest,* XI (September 1952), 51–54.

49742. ___. "White Sox Slugger." *Sport,* XI (September 1951), 30–35.

49743/49744. McAuley, Ed. "How Jockeys Will Ride Ed Robinson: He Provides Reins Himself." *Baseball Digest,* XIII (March 1954), 63–64.

49745. Povich, Shirley. "Yanks' Trade Has 'Deep'

Meaning: [Harry] Byrd, Robinson Strengthen Mound, Bench." *Baseball Digest,* XIII (March 1954), 11–13.

49746. Rumill, Ed. "Cleveland's 'Robbie' Masters Tough Breaks." *Baseball Magazine,* LXXXI (August 1948), 293–295.

49747. ___. "The Nerve of Ed Robinson." *Baseball Digest,* VII (August 1948), 29–31.

49748. Schneider, Russell. "Eddie Robinson: 'Lou, You Can Have My Glove and My Uniform, too — I'm Quitting.'" In: his *The Boys of the Summer of '48.* Champaign, IL: Sports Publishing, 1998. Pp. 104–111.

William Henry ("Bill") Robinson, Jr.

OF-1B. (B: June 26, 1943, McKeesport, PA). Atlanta (NL), 1966; New York (AL), 1967–1969; Philadelphia (NL), 1972–1974; Pittsburgh (NL), 1975–1982; Philadelphia (NL), 1982–1983. Remarks: Had 1,126 hits (I homers) In 1,472 games in 16 seasons; had three homers in one game, June 5, 1976; coach, New York (NL), 1984–1989.

49749. Fleischer, Victor. "Bill Robinson's Ball Game." *Buffalo, Magazine of the Buffalo News,* (October 11, 1992), 14–18.

49750. Kaplan, Jim. "He's an Irregular Regular." *Sports Illustrated,* XLVI (April 25, 1977), 62+.

49751. Smith, Sam. "Bill Robinson — in Search of Confidence." *Black Sports,* IV (September 1974), 22–25.

49752. Sparks, Barry. "For Bill Robinson, the Long Wait for Glory Was Worth It." *Baseball Digest,* XXXIX (March 1980), 72–77.

John Rocker

P. (B: October 17, 1974, Statesboro, GA). Atlanta (NL), 1998–2001; Cleveland (AL), 2001; Texas (AL), 2002; Tampa Bay (AL), 2003. Remarks: Through 2003, won 13 games and lost 22, with 88 "saves"; never able to live down hate-filled outburst in December 1999 *Sports Illustrated* interview.

49753. Abrams, Roger I. "Off his Rocker: Sports Discipline and Labor Arbitration." *Marquette Sports Law Review,* XI (Spring 2001), 167–174.

49754. Cannella, Stephen. "Rocking and Firing: A Mechanical Adjustment by John Rocker Could Spell Trouble for the Braves' Playoff Foes." *Sports Illustrated,* XCIIII (October 2, 2000), 120–121.

49755. Hoffer, Richard. "A Rocker, Sock 'Em Affair: The Long-Anticipated Showdown between John Rocker and New York Fans Fizzled, but the Braves and the Mets Provided Plenty of Fireworks on the Field." *Sports Illustrated,* XCIII (July 10, 2000), 36+.

49756. Jordan, Pat. "John Rocker." *George,* V (October 2000), 92+.

49757. Kurlantzick, Lewis. "John Rocker and Employee Discipline for Speech." *Marquette Sports Law Review,* XI (Spring 2001), 185–194.

49758. Le Batard, Dan. "Playing with Fire." *ESPN: The Magazine,* III (August 7, 2000), 56–55.

49759. Martinson, David L. "Freedom of Speech and John Rocker: A Window of Opportunity for High School Social Studies Teachers." *High School Journal,* LXXXV (October-November 2001), 30–31.

49760. Pearlman, Jeff. "At Full Blast: Shooting Outrageously from the Lip, Braves Closer John Rocker Bangs Away at His Favorite Targets: the Mets, Their Fans, Their City and Just About Everyone in It." *Sports Illustrated,* XCI (December 27, 1999), 60+.

Andre Rodgers *see* **Kenneth Andre Ian Rodgers**
Buck Rodgers *see* **Robert Leroy ("Buck" or "Bob") Rodgers**

Kenneth Andre Ian Rodgers

SS-1B-3B. (B: Dec. 2, 1934, Nassau, Bahamas-D: Dec. 13, 2004). New York (NL), 1957; San Francisco (NL), 1958–1960; Chicago (NL), 1961–1964; Pittsburgh (NL), 1965–1967. Remarks: In 11 seasons, had 628 hits (45 homers) and 22 stolen bases in 854 games; originally a cricket player from the Bahamas who paid his own way to a Giants tryout in 1954.

49761. Allison, Bob. "One More Time For and Re." *Sport,* XXVII (June 1959), 54–57.

49762. Wilson, Lyle K. "Andre Rodgers." *The Baseball Research Journal,* XXVIII (1999), 56–58.

Robert Leroy ("Buck" or "Bob") Rodgers

C-MGR. (B: Aug. 16, 1938, Delaware, OH). Los Angeles (AL) and California (AL), 1961–1969. Remarks. Obtained 704 hits (31 homers) in 932 games in big league nine playing years; coach, Minnesota (A.L), 1970–1974; minor league manager, 1975; coach, San Francisco (NL), 1976–1977; coach, Milwaukee (AL), 1978–1980; minor league manager, 1983–1984; manager, Milwaukee (AL), 1980–1982 (part), Montreal (NL), 1985–1991, and California (AL), 1991–1994, winning 784 games and losing 774 games (.503).

49763. Bryan, Mike. "Buck Rodgers." In: his *Baseball Lives.* New York: Pantheon Books, 1989. pp. 176–184.

49764. Fimrite, Ron. "Whitey, Buck and the Cowboy." *Sports Illustrated,* LXXVI (April 13, 1992), 60–68.

49765. Oates, Bob. "Bad Years Proved Good for Bob Rodgers." *Baseball Digest,* XXI (October-November 1962), 61–63.

49766. Reichler, Joseph L. "Buck Rodgers: Angel with a Dirty Face." In: Hershel Cohen, ed. *Willie Mays Baseball, 1963.* New York: Complete Sports, 1963. Pp. 22–27.

49767. Wendel, Tim. "A Tough Stretch." *USA Today Baseball Weekly,* I (March 11, 1992), 4–5.

Lester Rodney

WRITER. (B: 1911, Brooklyn, NY). Remarks: Sports reporter/editor, *Daily Worker,* 1936–1958, who eventually broke with the Communist Party, but not before helping launch a campaign to bring Blacks into MLB.

49768. Gallagher, T. "Lester Rodney, the *Daily Worker,* and the Integration of Baseball." *The National Pastime,* XIX (1999), 77–80.

49769. Klein, Robert. "Sports Reporting in New York City 1945–1960 by Two of the Era's Greatest and Most Influential Reporters — Arthur Daley and Lester Rodney." *Nine: A Journal of Baseball History and Social Policy Perspectives,* VI (Fall 1997), 15–30.

49770. Silber, Irwin. *Press Box Red: The Story of Lester Rodney, the Communist Who Helped Break the Color Line in American Sports.* Philadelphia, PA: Temple University Press, 2003. 248p.

Alexander Emmanuel ("A-Rod") Rodriguez

SS. (B: July 27, 1975, New York City). Seattle (AL), 1994–2000; Texas (AL), 2001–2003; New York (AL), 2004–. Remarks: Through 2004, has had 1,707 hits (381 homers) and 205 stolen bases in 1,430 games; led AL in doubles, 1996; AL batting champion, 1996; first Mariner to hit for the cycle in a nine-inning game, June 5, 1997; led AL in number of hits (213), 1998; had seven RBIs in one game, Sept. 30, 2000; had two homers in 2000 ALCS; 48 homers in 2001 a record for MLB shortstops; AL home run champion, 2001–2003; first $21 million per year player, Dec. 2000; AL RBI champion, 2002; AL MVP Award, 2003; had two homers in 2004 ALCS; has had 10 career grand slam homers; first $27 million per year player, 2005.

49771. Antonen, Mel. "Alex Rodriguez: Master of Baseball Arts." *Baseball Digest,* LIX (December 2000), 60–63.

49772. _____. "Mariners' Alex Rodriguez Has the Makings of Major Stardom." *Baseball Digest,* LV (October 1996), 48–51.

49773. Armentrout, David and Patricia. *Alex Rodriguez.* Vero Beach, FL: Rourke Pub., 2003. 32p.

49774. Berney, Louis. "Living His Dream." *Hispanic,* XV (April 2002), 34–35.

49775. Bradley, Jeff. "Lone Star." *ESPN: The Magazine,* IV (Fall 2001), 52–57. ARod

49776. Callahan, Gerry. "The Fairest of Them All." *Sports Illustrated,* LXXXV (July 8, 1996), 38–42.

49776a. Christensen, Joe. *Alex Rodriguez.* Awesome Athletes Series. Minneapolis, MN: Abdo Publishing, 2003. 32p. Juvenile.

49777. Emmons, Mark. "Setting Sail" *Beckett Focus on Future Stars,* IV, no. 38 (June 1994), 14–16.

49778. Fraley, Gerry. "The X Factor." *Inside Sports,* XVIII (September 1996), 24–27.

49779. Gallagher, Jim. *Alex Rodriguez.* Latinos in Baseball Series. Childs, MD: Mitchell Lane Publishers, 2000. 64p.

49780. Grant, Evan. "The A-Rod Era." *Baseball Digest,* LXI (March 2002), 24–29.

49781. "Great Expectations, Greater Results." In: Joe Hoppel, ed. *The Sporting News 1997 Baseball Yearbook.* St. Louis, MO: The Sporting News, 1997. Pp. 18–23.

49782. Hayes, Matt. "Focus on Alex Rodriguez." *Beckett Focus on Future Stars,* IV, no. 43 (November 1994), 76–79.

49783. Hickey, John. "Alex Rodriguez: Not a Typical Superstar." *Baseball Digest,* LIX (July 2000), 40–43.

49784. Kepner, Tyler. "Alex Rodriguez's Talent Has No Boundaries." *Baseball Digest,* LVIII (May 1999), 34–36.

49785. Kuenster, Bob. "Alex Rodriguez, *Baseball Digest's* 1996 Player of the Year." *Baseball Digest,* LVI (January 1997), 24–39.

49786. Kuenster, John. "A-Rod and [Derek] Jeter May Become Best Duo Ever on Left Side of Infield." *Baseball Digest,* LXIII (June 2004), 17–21.

49787. _____. "Alex Rodriguez Joined an Elite Group of Shortstops with His '96 Production." *Baseball Digest,* LV (December 1996), 17–19.

49788. Ladson, William. "Thinking Big." *Sport,* LXXXIX (June 1997), 65–67.

49789. Le Batard, Dan. "Heavy Hitter." *ESNP: The Magazine,* III (April 3, 2000), 72–75.

49790. Lockwood, Wayne. "Mariners' Alex Rodriguez: Standing Tall at Short." *Baseball Digest,* LVI (July 1997), 38–41.

49791. Menard, Valerie. "Alex Rodriguez." In: her *Careers in Sports.* Latinos at Work Series. Hockessen, DE: Mitchell Lane Publishers, 2002. Pp. 56–61.

49792. Nolan, Timothy. "Once in a Baseball Coach's Lifetime: An Interview." *Scholastic Coach & Athletic Director,* LXVI (February 1997), 46–54. Thoughts of Coach Rich Hofman regarding his best player.

49793. Noonan, D. "Baseball: A-Rod's Agent Guns for a Rich Deal." *Newsweek,* CXXXVI (2000), 57–59.

49794. Petersen, Eric. "Hot (A) Rod." *Beckett Baseball Card Monthly,* XVII (August 2000), 110–115.

49795. Raab, Scott. "Jackpot!" *Esquire,* CXXXV (April 2001), 100–109.

49795a. Rappoport, Ken. *Alex Rodriguez.* Super Sports Star Series. Hillside, NJ: Enslow, 2004. 48p.

49796. Ribowsky, Mark. "Alex Rodriguez." *Sport,* XCI (July 2000), 32–39.

49797. Rodriguez, Alex. "When I was a Kid: Interview." *Junior League Baseball,* no. 16 (July-August 1998), 10+; no. 33 (May-June 2001), 18+.

49798. _____., Greg Brown, and Doug Keith. *Hit a Grand Slam.* Dallas, TX: Taylor Pub. Co., 1998. 40p.

49799. _____., with Dan La Batard. "Earning My Stripes." *ESPN: The Magazine,* VII (April 12, 2004), 30+.

49800. Rolf, J. "A-Rod: $252M and Worth It." *Street & Smith's Sportsbusiness Journal,* III (December 18, 2000), 1, 45.

49801. Rosenthal, Ken. "Alex Rodriguez." In: his *Best of the Best, Baseball: 35 Major League Superstars.* Indianapolis, IN: Masters Press, 1998. Pp. 128–131.

49802. Schwarz, Alan. "Great Expectation$: Can Alex Rodriguez Prove He's Worth $252 Million?" *Sports Illustrated for Kids,* XIII (July 1, 2001), 29–36.

49803. _____. "Long at Short." *Inside Sports,* XIX (August 1997), 22–27.

49804. Shalin, Michael. *Alex Rodriguez: A+ Shortstop.* Champaign, IL: Sports Publishing, 1999. 81p.

49805. Stein, Joel. "Lord of the Swings." *Time,* CLXIII (April 5, 2004), 68–70.

49806. Stewart, Mark. *Alex Rodriguez: Gunning for Greatness.* Brookfield, CT: Millbrook Press, 1999. 43p.

49806. Stout, Glenn and Matt Christopher. *On the Field with — Alex Rodriguez.* Boston, MA: Little, Brown, 2002. 113p.

49807. Thornley, Stew. *Alex Rodriguez: Slugging Shortstop.* Minneapolis, MN: Lerner Publications Co., 1998. 64p.

49808. Tresniowski, Alex. "Golden Guy." *People Weekly,* LV (April 16, 2001), 83–84.

49809. Verducci, Tom. "Hello, New York!" *Sports Illustrated,* C (February 23, 2004), 36–38.

49810. _____. "The Lone Ranger: Alex Rodriguez." *Sports Illustrated,* XCVII (September 9, 2002), 34–40.

49811. _____. "Powerball: Alex Rodriguez Hit the Jackpot When the Rangers' Owner Offered Him $252 million and the City of Dallas." *Sports Illustrated,* XCIII (December 18, 2000), 102–106, 108, 110.

49812. _____. "Stumbling Start: Already Paying Dividends for the Rangers off the Field, Alex Rodriguez Tripped All Over Himself During His Debut with Texas." *Sports Illustrated,* XCIV (April 9, 2001), 46–59.

49813. _____. "Weekend Warrior." *Sports Illustrated,* XCIII (October 9, 2000), 74–77.

49814. Weber, Jennifer Funk, *et al.* "A-Rod by the Numbers." *Sports Illustrated for Kids,* XV (March 2003), 67–68.

49815. Whiteside, Kelly. "Alex Rodriguez." *Sports Illustrated,* LXXVIII (March 22, 1993), 74–75.

Antonio Hector ("Hec") Rodriguez

3B. (B: June 13, 1920, Villa Alguizar, Cuba). Chicago (AL), 1952. Remarks: Obtained 108 hits (one homer) and 17 stolen bases in 124 games in one major league season; named to Cuban Baseball Hall of Fame, 1974.

49816. Hoffman, John C. "Rodriguez New White Sox Senor." *Baseball Digest,* XI (May 1952), 71–74.

49817. _____. "Where's Hec?" *Sport Life,* V (October 1952), 54+.

Aurelio ("Leo") Rodriguez

3B-SS-2B. (B: Dec. 28, 1947, Cananea Sonora, Mexico-D: Sept. 30, 2000). California (AL), 1967–1970; Washington (AL), 1970; Detroit (AL), 1971–1979; San Diego (NL), 1980; New York (AL), 1980–1981; Chicago (AL), 1982–1983; Baltimore (AL), 1983. Remarks: Had 1,570 hits (124 homers) in 2,017 games in an 18-year major

league career; led AL 3B in fielding percentage, 1976, 1978; later a Mexican League manager; died the victim of an automobile accident.

49818. Flowers, Charles. "Aurelio Rodriguez, Born to Play Third." *Baseball Digest,* XXXI (December 1972), 28–31.

49819. Libby, Bill. "Aurelio Rodriguez." In: his *Heroes of the Hot Corner.* New York: Watts, 1972. Pp. 98–100.

Francisco ("Frank" or "Frankie") Rodriguez

P. (B: Dec. 11, 1972, Brooklyn, NY). Boston (AL) and Minnesota (AL), 1995; Minnesota (AL), 1996–1998; Seattle (AL), 1999–2000; Cincinnati (NL), 2001. Remarks: Obtained 29 victories, 39 defeats, and five "saves" in seven years.

49820. Cannella, Stephen and Luis Fernando Llosa. "Bienvenido, Nene Fran." *Sports Illustrated,* XCVII (November 18, 2002), 60–63.

49821. Epstein, Eddie. "Frank Rodriguez." In: STATS, Inc. *The STATS 1995 Minor League Scouting Notebook.* Skokie, IL: STATS Publishing, 1995. Pp. 140–141.

Gus Rodriguez

UMP. Remarks: PAC 10, WAC arbiter, 1976–date; president, Amateur Baseball Umpires Association, 2002–.

49822. "Interview: Gus Rodriguez." *Referee,* XXV (July 2000), 70–71.

Hec Rodriguez *see* **Antonio Hector ("Hec") Rodriguez**

Henry Rodriguez

OF. (B: Henry Anderson Rodriguez Lorenzo, Nov. 8, 1967, Santo Domingo, D.R.). Los Angeles (NL), 1992–1995; Montreal (NL), 1995–1997; Chicago (NL), 1998–2000; Florida (NL), 2000; New York (AL), 2001; Montreal (NL), 2002. Remarks: Through 2002, had 784 hits (160 homers) and 10 stolen bases in 950 games; had two grand-slam homers, May 7 and July 21, 1997; had seven RBIs in one game, May 14, 2000.

49823. Crasnick, Jerry. "Henry Rodriguez Enjoyed a Break-Through Year in '96." *Baseball Digest,* LVI (March 1997), 62–65.

49824. Johnson, Paul M. "Oh Henry." *Sport,* LXXXVIII (October 1996), 22–23.

49825. Koenig, Bill. "Found His Form." *USA Today Baseball Weekly,* II (July 22, 1992), 24–25.

Ivan ("I-Rod" or "Pudge") Rodriguez

C. (B: Ivan Rodriguez Torres, Nov. 27, 1971, Manati, P.R.). Texas (AL), 1991–2002; Florida (NL), 2003; Detroit (AL), 2004–. Remarks: Through 2004, has had 2,051 his (250 homers) and 97 stolen bases in 1,758 games; had nine RBIs in one game, April 13, 1999; had five hits in one game, Aug. 1, 1999; A. L. MVP Award, 1999; had one grand-slam homer, Aug. 18, 2001; had two homers in 2003 NLCS; MVP Award, NLCS, 2003; had two doubles in 2003 World Series.

49826. Barnas, Jo-Ann. "Born to Lead: Tigers Catcher Ivan Rodriguez." *Baseball Digest,* XLIII (December 2004), 52–57.

49827. Caldwell, Dave. "Ivan Rodriguez: His Pickoff Talents Keep Baserunners Honest." *Baseball Digest,* LVI (January 1997), 58–59.

49828. Chen, Albert. "Well-Healed." *Sports Illustrated,* XCIX (August 18, 2003), 79–80.

49829. Crothers, Tim. "Catch as Catch Can." *Sports Illustrated,* LXXXVI (May 19, 1997), 92, 96.

49830. DeMarco, Tony. *Ivan Rodriguez.* Latinos in Baseball Series. Childs, MD: Mitchell Lane Publishers, 2000. 64p.

49831. _____. "Ivan the Terrific." *Beckett Focus on Future Stars,* II, no. 15 (July 1992), 16–19.

49832. Edelson, Mat. "Ivan Rodriguez." *Sport,* LXXXIX (September 1998), 92–93.

49833. Gonzalez, Simon. "Ivan Rodriguez: Is He the Best Catcher Ever?" *Baseball Digest,* LX (July 2001), 32–33.

49834. _____. "Warning: This Guy is Armed." *USA Today Baseball Weekly,* VI (November 20, 1996), 16–17.

49835. Goss, David A. "Ivan (Torres) 'Pudge' Rodriguez." In: Vol. Q-Z of David L. Porter, ed. *Biographical Dictionary of American Sports: Baseball.* Rev. and enlarged ed. Westport, CT: Greenwood Press, 2000. Pp. 1307–1308.

49836. Grant, Evan. "The Backstop's Here." *Beckett Baseball Card Monthly,* XV (January 1998), 18–21.

49837. Hart, Stan. "Ivan Rodriguez." In: his *Scouting Reports: The Original Reviews of Baseball's Greatest Stars.* New York: Macmillan, 1995. Pp. 113–115.

49838. Howard, Johnette. "Pudge Factor." *Sports Illustrated,* LXXXVII (August 11, 1997), 40–44.

49839. Kosdrosky, Terry. "Pudge Factor." *Crain's Detroit Business,* XX (April 19, 2004), 1–2.

49840. Kuenster, John. "Ivan Rodriguez Earned Player of the Year Honors for Leading Marlins." *Baseball Digest,* LXIII (January 2004), 17–21.

49841. _____. "Texas Rangers Catcher Ivan Rodriguez, *Baseball Digest's* 1999 Player of the Year." *Baseball Digest,* LIX (January 2000), 19–23.

49842. Kurkjian, Tim. "Another Day at the Office." *Sports Illustrated,* LXXV (July 1, 1991), 53–55.

49843. Mayoral, Luis R. "Ivan Rodriguez of the Rangers Comes of Age as a Major League Star." *Baseball Digest,* LIII (December 1994), 55–57.

49844. Payne, Mike. "Ivan Rodriguez." *Beckett Baseball Card Monthly,* IX (February 1992), 13–14.

49845. "Pudge Takes on the Tigers." *ESPN: The Magazine,* VII (May 24, 2004), 30+.

49846. Reeves, Jim. "Lone Star All-Stars." *Yankees Magazine,* XIX (August 1998), 76–83. Rodriguez and Juan Gonzalez.

49847. Rodriguez, Ivan, with Joel Poiley. "How to Stop a Thief." *Sports Illustrated for Kids,* XV (June 1, 2003), 54+.

49848. Rogers, Phil "Ivan Rodriguez: Armed with Hall of Fame Tools." *Baseball Digest,* LVIII (December 1999), 48–51.

49849. Rosenthal, Ken. "Ivan Rodriguez." In: his *Best of the Best, Baseball: 35 Major League Superstars.* Indianapolis, IN: Masters Press, 1999. Pp. 132–135.

49850. Sandground, Grant. "Player's Choice: Ivan Rodriguez." *Beckett Baseball Card Monthly,* XVII (June 2000), 22–23.

49851. Sleppy, Rick. "Pudge' Rodriguez." *Beckett Focus on Future Stars,* I (September 1991), 10–13.

49852. Stewart, Mark. *Ivan Rodriguez, Armed and Dangerous.* New York: Children's Press, 1999. 48p.

49853. Tarrant, David. "Rangers' Ivan Rodriguez: The Majors' No. 1 All-Around Catcher." *Baseball Digest,* LVI (July 1997), 20–23.

49854. Verducci, Tom. "Catch This: The Incomparable Pudge Rodriguez Leads a Youthful Cast of Midseason All-Stars." *Sports Illustrated,* XCIII (July 17, 2000), 70–73.

49855. Zminda, Don. "Did Ivan's Arm Come Back, or Did He Just Get a Little More Help?" In: STATS, Inc. *STATS 1996 Baseball Scoreboard.* Skokie, IL: STATS Publishing, 1996. Pp. 190–192.

Tom Rodriguez
ARTIST

49856. Buckley, J., Jr. "An Artist's Field Day." *Sports Illustrated,* LXXIX (September 6, 1993), 8, 12.

Edwin Charles ("Preacher") Roe
P. (B. Feb. 26, 1915, Ashflat, AK). St. Louis (N.L), 1938; Pittsburgh (NL), 1944–1947; Brooklyn (NL), 1948–1954. Remarks: Won 127 games and lost 84, with 10 "saves," in 12 seasons; won Game Two of 1949 World Series; had 10-game winning streak, 1951; won Game Three of 1952 World Series and lost Game Two of 1953 World Series; admitted, after retirement, to having thrown the illegal spitter; elected to Missouri Sports Hall of Fame, 1997.

49857. Bjarkman, Peter C. "Elwin Charles 'Preacher' Roe." In: Vol. Q-Z of David L. Porter, ed. *Biographical Dictionary of American Sports: Baseball.* Rev. and enlarged ed. Westport, CT: Greenwood Press, 2000. Pp. 1308–1309.

49858. Burr, Harold C. "Roe-ing in Stride to Victory." *Baseball Digest,* X (May 1951), 19–21.

49859. Daley, Arthur. "Preacher Roe." in: his *Sports of The Times.* New York: E. P. Dutton, 1959. Pp. 110–113.

49860. Gross, Milton. "Preacher from the Ozarks." *Sport,* VIII (February 1950), 22–23+.

49861. Kahn, Roger. "The Road to Viola." In: his *The Boys of Summer.* New York: Harper & Row, 1972. Pp. 290–309. A pre-publication excerpt appeared in *Sport* LII (November 1971), 54–55+.

49862. Richman, Milton. "Roe After Roe After Roe." *Baseball Digest,* X (October 1951), 27–32.

49863. Rosenthal, Harold. "The Dodgers' Oddest Star." *Saturday Evening Post,* CCXXIII (February 3, 1951), 30+.

49864. _____. "Sermon on the Mound." In: his *The Artful Dodgers.* New York: A. S. Barnes, 1953. Pp. 155–167.

49865. Smith, Ira L. "Edwin Charles (Preacher) Roe." In: his *Baseball's Famous Pitchers.* New York: A. S. Barnes, 1954. Pp. 293–297.

49866. Stewart, Walter. "By Inch or Eye, Roe's $$ Shy." *Baseball Digest,* XI (April 1952), 19–21.

49867. Wilber, Cynthia J. "Preacher Roe." In: her *For the Love of the Game: Baseball Memories from the Men Who Were There.* New York: William Morrow, 1992. Pp. 293–302.

49868. Young, Dick. "Conversation Piece: Subject — Preacher Roe." *Sports Illustrated,* III (July 4. 1955), 18–21.

John ("Rockey") Roe
UMP.(B: ca. 1950). Remarks: AL arbiter, 1982–1994; elected to Eastern Michigan University Hall of Fame, 2002.

49869. Ehret, Scott. "Rocky Roe: Roe vs. Weight." *Referee,* XXII (June 1997), 38+.

Preacher Roe *see* **Edwin Charles ("Preacher") Roe**
Rocky Roe *see* **John ("Rocky") Roe**
Edward Jack ("Ed") Roebuck
P. (B: July 3, 1931, East Millsboro, PA). Brooklyn (NL), 1955–1957; Los Angeles (NL), 1958–1963; Washington (AL), 1963–1964; Philadelphia (NL), 1964–1966. Remarks: In 11 years, won 52 games and lost 31, with 62 "saves"; had 10-game winning streak, 1962.

49870. Laughlin, Bob, with Budd Theobald. *Ed Roebuck: Ace of the Bullpen Again.* Los Angeles, CA: Union Oil Company of California, 1960. 13p.

49871. Zimmerman, Paul B. "First Aid to Ed Roebuck's Pitching Arm." *Baseball Digest,* XIX (June 1960), 85–87.

Bullet Joe Rogan *see* **Wilber ("Bullet Joe") Rogan**
Wilber ("Bullet Joe") Rogan ★
OF. (B: July 28, 1889, Oklahoma City, OK-D: March 4, 1967). Kansas City Colored Giants, 1917; K.C. Monarchs, 1920–1938. Remarks: Obtained 106 victories and 44

losses, 1920–1930; also had .343 batting average; elected to National Baseball Hall of Fame in 1998, where his plaque reads: "A versatile performer who was equally superlative as a pitcher and hitter. Utilized a deceptively quick, no windup delivery to lead Kansas City to four Negro National League titles. Pitching repertoire included a forkball, curveball, and palmball, and featured a blazing fastball as an outpitch. Also played center field, hitting .343 as his club's cleanup hitter and .410 in World Series competition. Piloted the Monarchs in the dual role of player and manager for several seasons. Served as an umpire in the Negro Leagues following playing career.

49872. Holway, John B. *Bullet Joe Rogan and the Monarchs.* Washington, D.C.: Capital Press, 1984. 59p.

49873. Kleinknecht, Merl F. and John B. Holway. "Wilbur 'Bullet Joe' Rogan." In: Vol. Q-Z of David L. Porter, ed. *Biographical Dictionary of American Sports: Baseball.* Rev. and enlarged ed. Westport, CT: Greenwood Press, 2000. Pp. 1309–1310.

49874. Malloy, Jimmy. "Bullet Joe Rogan." In: John A. Garrity and Marsh C. Carries, eds. *American National Biography.* 24 vols. New York: Oxford University Press, 1999. XVIII, 747.

49875. Smith, Ron. "Joe Rogan." In: his *Heroes of the Hall: Baseball's Greatest Players.* New York: Contemporary Books, 2002. Pp. 396–397.

Billy Rogell see **William George ("Billy") Rogell**
William George ("Billy") Rogell
SS-3B-2B. (B: Nov.24, 1904, Springfield, IL-D: Aug. 9, 2003). Boston (AL), 1925–1928; Detroit (AL), 1930–1939; Chicago (NL), 1940. Remarks: In 14 years, had 1,375 hits (42 homers) and 82 stolen bases in 1,482 games; had four RBIs in Game Four of 1934 World Series; walked record seven times in a row, 1938.

49876. Bak, Richard. "Billy Rogell." In: his *Cobb Would Have Caught It: The Golden Age of Baseball in Detroit.* Detroit, MI: Wayne State University Press, 1991. Pp. 260–284.

49877. Frommer, Harvey and Frederick J. "Billy Rogell." In: their *Growing Up Baseball: An Oral History.* Dallas, TX: Taylor Publishing Co., 2001. Pp. 194–195.

49878. Grosshandler, Stanley. "Billy Rogell Looks Back on Glory Days with the Tigers." *Baseball Digest,* LII (December 1993), 70–72.

49879. Kelley, Brent P. "Bill Rogell: Infield of Dreams, 1925–1940." In: his *In the Shadow of the Babe: Baseball Players Who Played with or Against Babe Ruth.* Jefferson, NC: McFarland & Co., Inc., 1995. Pp. 15–26.

49880. Rogell, Bill, as told to Nick Wilson. "Major League Baseball was Tougher in the Old Days." *Baseball Digest,* LVII (November 1998), 78–83.

49881. Westcott, Rich. "Billy Rogell: Successful Players, Successful Politician." In: his *Masters of the Diamond.* Jefferson, NC: McFarland & Co., Inc., 1994. Pp. 97–106.

49882. Wilson, Nick. "Bill Rogell." In: his *Voices from the Pastime: Oral Histories of Surviving Major Leaguers, Negro Leaguers, Cuban Leaguers, and Writers, 1920–1934.* Jefferson, NC: McFarland & Co., Inc., 2000. Pp. 16–25.

Kenneth Scott ("Kenny") Rogers
P. (B: Nov. 10, 1964, Savannah, GA). Texas (AL), 1989–1995; New York (AL), 1996–1997; Oakland (A.L), 1998–1999; New York (NL), 1999; Texas (A.L), 2000–2002; Minnesota (AL), 2003; Texas (AL), 2004–. Remarks: Through 2004, has won 176 games and lost 123, with 28 "saves"; had perfect game, July 28, 1994; had 19-game home winning streak, 1997–2000.

49883. Buckley, James, Jr. "Kenny Rogers." In: his *Per-*

fect!: The Inside Story of Baseball's Sixteen Perfect Games. New York: Triumph Books, 2002. Pp. 196–211.

49884. Kurkjian, Tim. "As Good as It Gets." *Sports Illustrated,* LXXXI (August 8, 1994), 32–33. Perfect game.

Stephen Douglas ("Steve") Rogers
P. (B: Oct. 26, 1949, Jefferson City, MO). Montreal (NL), 1973–1985. Remarks: Won 158 games and lost 152, with two "saves," in 13 campaigns, becoming all-time winningest Expo pitcher; surrendered the 3,000th hit of Pete Rose (q.v.), May 5, 1978; also gave up crucial Game Five homer to Rick Monday (q.v.) in 1981 NLCS; consultant, then employee, MLBPA, 1987–.

49885. Carlson, Stan W. "Stephen Douglas 'Steve' Rogers." In: Vol. Q-Z of David L. Porter, ed. *Biographical Dictionary of American Sports: Baseball.* Rev. and enlarged ed. Westport, CT: Greenwood Press, 2000. Pp. 1310–1311.

49886. Elderkin, Phil "Steve Rogers: He Pitches as Though He's Falling Out of a Tree." *Baseball Digest,* XXXVIII (February 1979), 58–61.

49887. Fimrite, Ron. "This Rogers Isn't Very Jolly." *Sports Illustrated,* LVII (September 27, 1982), 42+.

49888. Glew, Kevin. "Curtain Calls: Former Pitcher Steve Rogers." *Baseball Digest,* LXIII (June 2004), 38–41.

49889. Kendall, Brian. "October 11, 1981: Steve Rogers Silences His Critics." In: his *Great Moments in Canadian Baseball.* Toronto, Ont.: Lester Publishing, 1995. Chapter 17.

49890. MacCarl, Neil "The Rookie Who Made Montreal a Contender." *Baseball Digest,* XXXIII (February 1974), 48–50.

49891. McKenzie, Mike. "Montreal Right-Hander Steve Rogers Deserves More Respect." *Baseball Digest,* XLI (July 1982), 40–42.

49892. Richman, Arthur. "The Amazing Case of the Hitless Pitcher." *Sport,* LXIX (October 1979), 46–47+.

49893. "Steve Rogers: The Expos' Complete Lanceur." In: Tommy Kay, ed. *Baseball Factbook.* Scottsdale, AZ: Jalart House, 1978. Pp. 96–99.

Saul Walter Rogovin
P. (B: Oct. 10, 1922, Brooklyn, NY-D: Jan. 23, 1995). Detroit (AL), 1949–1951; Chicago (AL), 1951–1953; Baltimore (AL), 1956; Philadelphia (NL), 1955–1957. Remarks: Won 48 games and lost 48 games, with two "saves," in 19 seasons; had one grand-slam homer, July 23, 1950.

49894. Burnes, Ed. "Chisox Cheer Rogovin, the Refugee from Brooklyn." *Baseball Magazine,* LXXX (July 1953), 22–23.

49895. Dexter, Charles. "Sudden Saul of the White Sox." *Baseball Digest,* XI (February 1952), 37–42.

49896. Ribalow, Harold U. "Saul Rogovin." In: his *Jew in American Sports.* New York: Bloch, 1959. Pp. 91–97.

49897. _____. and Meir Z. Ribalow. "Saul Rogovin: Power Pitcher." In: their *Jewish Baseball Stars.* New York: Hippocrene Books, 1984. Pp. 112–121.

49898. Richman, Milton. "Secret Weapons of the White Sox." *Sport,* XII (May 1952), 38–41.

George Anthony ("Whitey") Rohe
3B-2B-SS. (B: Sept.15, 1875, Cincinnati, OH-D: June 10, 1957). Baltimore (AL), 1901; Chicago (AL), 1905–1907. Remarks: In four big league seasons, had 197 hits (three homers) and 27 stolen bases in 269 games; had seven hits in 1906 World Series.

49899. Salant, Nathan. "George Rohe." In: his *Superstars, Stars, and Just Plain Heroes.* New York: Stein and Day, 1982. Pp. 233–235.

Whitey Rohe see **George ("Whitey") Rohe**

Daniel Jay ("Dan") Rohn
2B-SS. (B: Jan. 10, 1956, Alpena, MI). Chicago (NL), 1983–1984; Cleveland (AL), 1986. Remarks: Had 18 hits (one homer) in 54 games in three seasons.
49900. Bonkowski, Jerry. "Spring Training: Two Views." In: Bob Iback, ed, *Chicago Cubs Program Magazine*. Chicago, IL: Public Relations Department, Chicago Cubs, 1984. Pp. 16–19. Views of rookie Rohn and veteran Ron Cey.

Cookie Rojas *see* **Octavio Rivas ("Cookie") Rojas**

Mel Rojas
P. (B: Melquiades Rojas Medrano, Dec. 10, 1966, Haina, D.R.). Montreal (NL), 1990–1996; Chicago (NL) and New York (NL), 1997; New York (NL), 1998; Los Angeles (NL), Detroit (NL), and Montreal (NL), 1999. Remarks: In a decade, won 34 games and lost 31, with 126 "saves"; nephew of Felipe Alou, of Jesus Alou, of Matty Alou and cousin of Moises Alou, all q.v.
49901. Dewan, John and Don Zminda. "Was Mel Rojas Better Than the Eck Last Year?" In: STATS, Inc. *STATS 1993 Baseball Scoreboard*. New York: Harper Perennial, 1993. Pp. 182–184. Comparison with Dennis Eckersley (q.v.).

Minervino Alejandro Landin ("Minnie") Rojas
P. (B: Nov. 26, 1938, Remedios Las Villas, Cuba.). California (AL), 1966–1968. Remarks: Won 23 games and lost 16, with 43 "saves," in three year career ended by paralyzing automobile crash prior to Opening Day, 1969.
49902. Dexter, Charles. "Minnie Rojas, the Iron Angel." *Baseball Digest*, XXVII (June 1968), 23–27.
49903. Rumill, Ed. "Minnie Rojas: He Hardly Walks Anybody." *Baseball Digest*, XXVI (December 1967), 47–49.

Minnie Rojas *see* **Minervino Alejandro Landin ("Minnie") Rojas**

Octavio Rivas ("Cookie") Rojas
2B-OF-MGR. (B: March 6, 1930, Havana, Cuba). Cincinnati (NL), 1962; Philadelphia (NL), 1963–1969; St. Louis (NL), 1970; Kansas City (AL), 1970–1977. Remarks; Obtained 1,660 hits (54 homers) and 74 stolen bases in 1,822 games in 16 seasons; played eight positions early in career and, for the ninth, hurled one inning for the Phillies, June 30, 1967; coach, Chicago (NL), 1978–1981; manager, California (AL), 1988 and Florida (NL), 1996, winning 76 games and losing 79 (.490); coach, New York (NL), 1997–2000; Toronto (AL), 2001–2002; named to Cuban Baseball Hall of Fame, 1982.
49904. Berke, Art. "Cookie Rojas." In: his *Unsung Heroes of the Major Leagues*. New York: Random House, 1976. Pp. 63–76.
49905. Bryan, Mike. "Cookie Rojas." In: his *Baseball Lives*. New York: Pantheon Books, 1989. Pp. 74–79.
49906. Forbes, Gordon. "Here Comes Cook-ee!" *Baseball Digest*, XXIV (December 1965), 67–72.
49907. Hochman, Stan. "Cookie Rojas: Cookie Out of the Freezer." *Baseball Digest*, XXIII (August 1964), 66–67.
49908. McGuff, Joe. "Cookie Rojas, an Unheralded Star." *Baseball Digest*, XXXII (July 1973), 29–31.
49909. Rojas, Octavio R. ("Cookie"). "The Game I'll Never Forget." *Baseball Digest*, XXXVIII (November 1979), 73–75.
49910. Rumill, Ed. "This Cookie Doesn't Crumble." *Baseball Digest*, XXX (October 1971), 78–80.
49911. Vecsey, George. "The Cookie Rojas Beat." *Sport*, XL (October 1965), 34–35+.

Scott Bruce Rolen
3B. (B: April 4, 1975, Evansville, IN). Philadelphia (NL),

1996–2002; St. Louis (NL), 2002–. Remarks: Through 2004, has had 1,254 hits (226 homers) and 91 stolen bases in 1,195 games; N. L. Rookie of the Year Award, 1997; had nine RBIs in a doubleheader, Aug. 20, 1998; highly regarded defensive 3B, who had three homers in 2004 NLCS.
49912. Crothers, Tim. "The Last Laugh." *Sports Illustrated*, LXXXIX (July 27, 1998), 68–69.
49913. Etkin, Jack. "Third Baseman Scott Rolen, a Budding Star for the Phillies." *Baseball Digest*, LVI (December 1997), 46–49.
49914. Hagen, Paul. "Great Scott: Phillies Have a Rising Star in Rolen." *Baseball Digest*, LVIII (January 1999), 40–43.
49915. Hummell, Rick. "Scott Rolen: Baseball's Best All-Around Third Baseman." *Baseball Digest*, LXIII (September 2004), 24–27.
49916. Rolen, Scott. "When I was a Kid: Interview." *Junior Baseball*, no. 31 (January-February 2001), 10+.
49917. Schwarz, Alan. "Heart of the Heartland." In: Richard Levin, ed. *2004 League Championship Series Official Program*. New York: Major League Baseball Properties Corp., 2004. Pp. 46–51.
49918. Salisbury, Jim. "Scott Rolen." *Sport*, XC (August 1999), 70–75.
49919. Sullivan, T.R. "Model Major Leaguer." *Boys' Life*, LXXXVIII (July 1998), 22–23.
49920. Verducci, Tom. "The Perfect Player." *Sports Illustrated*, CI (July 12, 2004), 56–63.

Red Rolfe *see* **Robert Abial ("Red") Rolfe**

Robert Abial ("Red") Rolfe
3B-MGR.-COACH. (B: Oct. 17, 1908, Penacook, NH-D: July 8, 1969). New York (AL), 1931, 1934–1942. Remarks: Had 1,394 hits (69 homers) and 44 stolen bases in 1,175 games in a decade; Yale University coach and athletic director, 1943–1945, 1954–1967; also coach, Toronto (NBA), 1946; coach, New York (AL), 1946; director of farm system, Detroit (A.L), 1947–1948 and manager of the Tigers, 1949–1952, for whom he had 278 piloting victories and 256 defeats (.521); Rolf Division of Ivy League named in his honor along with, in 1971, the Dartmouth College baseball field .
49921. Cohane, Tim. "Red Rolfe, the Heart of the Tiger: His Quiet, Courageous Battle with Poor Health Inspires His Team's Flag Fight." *Look*, XIV (September 26, 1950), 71–74.
49922. Dexter, Charles, "The Tigers Have a Quiet Ringmaster." *Baseball Digest*, VIII (May 1949), 53–57.
49923. Frey, Leonard H. "Robert Abial 'Red' Rolfe." In: Vol. Q-Z of David L. Porter, ed. *Biographical Dictionary of American Sports: Baseball*. Rev. and enlarged ed. Westport, CT: Greenwood Press, 2000. Pp. 1311–1312.
49924. Gallagher, Mark. "Red Rolfe." In: his *50 Years of Yankee All-Stars*. New York: Leisure Press, 1984. Pp. 174–175.
49925. Green, Jerry. "Red Rolfe: He was a Real Yankee." *Baseball Digest*, XXIX (February 1970), 76–79.
49926. Gross, Milton. "Rolfe's One Shortcoming." *Baseball Digest*, XI (September 1952), 71–73.
49927. Henry, Mike. "In the Red." *Yankees Magazine*, XX (August 1999), 84–89.
49928. Meany, Thomas. "No Alibis for Red, Manager of the Detroit Tigers." *Collier's*, CXXV (March 4, 1950), 32+.
49929. Robinson, Ray. "Red Rolfe: The Man from Dartmouth." In: his *Greatest Yankees of Them All*. New York: G.P. Putnam's Sons, 1969. Pp. 163–170.

49930. Rolfe, Robert A. ("Red"). "Do the Tigers Have a Winning Secret?" Edited by Stanley B. Frank. *Saturday Evening Post,* CCXXIII (September 23, 1950), 31+.

49931. _____. "More Than Base Hits." *Collier's,* CVI (August 17, 1940), 13–15.

49932. _____., with Pinky Higgins. *How to Play Third Base.* Chicago, IL: Dow Periodicals, 1941. 60p.

49933. Smith, Walter ("Red"). "Rolfe: An Unspectacular Great." *Baseball Digest,* VIII (February 1949), 39–41.

49934. Spoelstra, Watson. "24 Hours with Rolfe." *Sport,* XI (August 1951), 18–21.

49935. "Two Young Yankees from College: Robert Rolfe of Dartmouth and John Broaca of Yale Demonstrate That Some Collegians Can Solve Their Unemployment Problems in the Business World of Baseball." *Literary Digest,* CVII (June 30, 1934), 32–33.

James Calvin ("Jimmy") Rollins
SS. (B: Nov. 27, 1978, Oakland, CA). Philadelphia (NL), 2000–. Remarks: Through 2004, has had 708 hits (47 homers) and 130 stolen bases in 636 games; NL co-stolen base champion, 2001; led NL in triples, 2001–2002, 2004.

49936. Rollins, Jimmy, with Alan Schwarz. "Base Stealing with Jimmy Rollins." *Sports Illustrated for Kids,* XIV (July 2002), 42–43.

Richard John ("Rich" or "Red") Rollins
3B. (B: April 16, 1938, Pleasant, PA). Minnesota (AL), 1961–1968; Seattle (AL), 1969; Milwaukee (AL) and Cleveland (AL), 1970. Remarks: Had 887 hits (77 homers) and 17 stolen bases in 1,002 games in a decade; led AL in triples, 1964; filled in for the injured Harmon Killebrew (q. v.), 1965.

49937. Donnelly, Joe. "The Rich Rollins Surprise." *Sport,* XXXIV (October 1962), 24–27.

49938. Gordon, Dick. "Rich Rollins: In Bluege's Footsteps." *Baseball Digest,* XXI (September 1962), 5–9.

49939. Simons, Herbert. "Rollins Hit .400-Twice!" *Baseball Digest,* XXIII (April 1964), 57–59. Minor league achievements.

49940. "Who's on Third?" *Time,* LXXX (July 20, 1962), 62–63.

Edwin Americus ("Eddie") Rommel
P-UMP. (B: Sept. 13, 1897, Baltimore, MD-D- Aug. 26, 1970). Philadelphia (AL), 1920–1932. Remarks: Had 171 victories, 119 defeats, and 29 "saves" in 13 seasons, won one game in 1929 World Series; pitched 17 of 18 innings in a game won by A's, July 10, 1932; coach, Philadelphia (AL), 1933–1934; minor league umpire, 1935–1937; AL umpire, 1938–1959.

49941. Lane, Ferdinand C. "Eddie Rommel: The Wizard of the Knuckleball." *Baseball Magazine,* XXXI (July 1923), 345–347+.

49942. _____. "The Star Hurler of the Athletic Club." *Baseball Magazine,* XXXVII (September 1926), 437–439.

49943. Phelps, Frank V. "Edwin Americus 'Eddie' Rommel." In: Vol. Q-Z of David L. Porter, ed. *Biographical Dictionary of American Sports: Baseball.* Rev. and enlarged ed. Westport, CT: Greenwood Press, 2000. Pp. 1312–1313.

49944. Rommel, Ed. "The Fine Edge of Winning Form." *Baseball Magazine,* XLII (May 1929), 534–535.

49945. Rothe, Emil "This was the Most Bizarre Relief Job in the Majors." *Baseball Digest,* LI (June 1992), 72–75.

49946. Scully, Charley. "Overtime with No Pay." *Baseball Magazine,* LXXXIX (July-August 1952), 28–29. Rommel's 17-inning game.

49947. Sulecki, Jerry. "Eddie Rommel's Last Win." *The Baseball Research Journal,* XXVII (1998), 103–104.

John Romonosky
P. (B: July 7, 1929, Harrisburg, IL). St. Louis (NL), 1953; Washington (AL), 1958–1959. Remarks: In all or part of three big league seasons, won three games and lost four.

49948. Swank, Bill. "John Romonosky." In: his *Echoes from Lane Field: A History of the San Diego Padres 1936–1957.* Paducah, KY: Turner Publishing Company, 1997. Pp. 128–129.

Charles Henry ("Charlie" or "Chinskie") Root
P. (B: March 17, 1899, Middletown, OH-D: Nov. 5, 1970). St. Louis (AL), 1923; Chicago (NL), 1924–1941. Remarks: Won 201 games and lost 160, with 40 "saves" in 17 years; pitcher who gave up George Herman ("Babe") Ruth's alleged "called shot" in 1932 World Series; also played for Hollywood (PCL), 1942–1944 and Columbus (AA), 1945–1946; minor league coach/manager, 1948–1951, 1954; coach, Chicago (NL), 1951–1953, 1960 and Milwaukee (NL), 1956–1957.

49949. Blaisdell, Lowell L. Charles Henry 'Charlie,' 'Chinskie' Root." In: Vol. Q-Z of David L. Porter, ed. *Biographical Dictionary of American Sports: Baseball.* Rev. and enlarged ed. Westport, CT: Greenwood Press, 2000. Pp. 1313–1314.

49950. Root, Charles. "Putting 'Stuff' on the Ball." *Baseball Magazine,* XLII (March 1929), 435–436.

49951. Spalding, John E. "Charlie Root" In: his *Pacific Coast League Stars, Vol. II: Ninety Who Made It to the Majors, 1905–1957.* San Jose, CA: John E. Spalding, 1997. Pp. 71–72.

Warren Vincent ("Buddy") Rosar
C. (B: July 3, 1914, Buffalo, NY-D: March 13, 1994). New York (AL), 1939–1942; Cleveland (AL), 1943–1944; Philadelphia (A>L.), 1945–1949; Boston (AL), 1950–1951. Remarks: In 13 seasons, obtained 836 hits (18 homers) and 17 stolen bases in 988 games; hit for the cycle, July 19, 1940; had pinch hit in 1942 World Series; recorded 147 consecutive errorless games, 1946–1947; later a powerhouse engineer for the Ford Motor Stamping Plant.

49952. Collins, Bud. "Buddy Rosar." In: Danny Peary, ed. *Baseball's Finest: The Greats, the Flakes, the Weird and the Wonderful.* North Dighton, MA: The JG Press, 1990. Pp. 10–14.

Edward W. ("Rusty") Rose, 3rd
EXEC. (B: 1951, Texas). Remarks: Co-general partner, Texas (AL), 1989–date.

49953. Taylor, J. H. "Rusty the Mortician." *Forbes,* CXLIV (July 24, 1989), 60+.

Peter Edward ("Pete" or "Charlie Hustle") Rose
OF-3B-2B-1B-MGR. (B: April 14, 1941, Cincinnati, Ohio). Cincinnati (NL), 1963–1978; Philadelphia (NL), 1979–1983; Montreal (NL), 1984; Cincinnati (NL), 1984–1986. Remarks: Had 4,256 hits (160 homers) and 198 stolen bases in games in 24 playing years; NL Rookie of the Year award, 1963; had one grand slam homer, July 18, 1964; ran into catcher Ray Fosse (q.v.) in 1970 All-Star Game; had homer in Game Three of 1970 World Series and in Game Six of 1972 World Series; also had homer in Game One of 1973 NLCS; NL MVP award, 1973; N.L batting champion, 1968–1969, 1973; led NL in doubles, 1974–1976, 1978, 1980; had homer in Game Three of 1975 NLCS; World Series MVP award, 1975; had five hits in first two games of 1976 NLCS; had 44-game hitting streak, tying with Wee Willie Keeler (q.v.) for NL mark, 1978; obtained 23 game hitting streak, 1979; holds NL records for most games played (3,562), most singles (3,215), and most ABs (14,053) and has established or tied dozens of records, captured the all-time lead in hits from Ty Cobb (q.v.), Sept. 11, 1985; only player to play 500 games at five different positions; player-manager, Cincin-

nati (NL), 1984–1986 and manager, 1986–1989, winning 426 games and losing 388 (.523); banned from baseball for life for gambling activities in 1989; opened a web-site, Nov. 30, 1999; remains ineligible for an otherwise absolute certainty of enshrinement in the National Baseball Hall of Fame.

49954. Aaseng, Nathan. "Pete Rose." In: his *Record Breakers of Pro Sports.* Minneapolis, MN: Lerner Publications, 1987. Pp. 8–21.

49955. _____. *Pete Rose: Baseball's "Charlie Hustle."* Minneapolis, MN: Lerner Publications, 1981. 44p.

49956. Abrams, Roger I. "The Crimes of Baseball: Pete Rose." In: his *Legal Bases: Baseball and the Law.* Philadelphia, PA: Temple University Press, 1998. Pp. 151–172.

49957. Addie, Bob. "Rose's Run at Joe DiMaggio's Streak." In: Sam L Andre, ed. *Street and Smith's Official 1979 Baseball Yearbook.* New York: Conde Nast Publications, 1979. Pp. 4–15.

49958. Allen, Maury. "Peter Rose (1963–Present)." In: his *Baseball's 100.* New York: Galahad Books, 1981. Pp. 78–80.

49959. _____. "The Reds' Rose." *Sport,* XXXVII (June 1964), 33–35.

49960. Alm, R. "Rose's Run for the Record: Everybody's Cashing In." *U.S. News and World Report,* XCIX (September 2, 1985), 50–51.

49961. "Amazing Grace in Record Time." *America,* CLIII (September 28, 1985), 145–146.

49962. Anderson, Dave. "What Makes Pete Rose Run?" *Reader's Digest,* CVIII (May 1976), 263–264+.

49963. Asinof, Eliot. "Pete Rose Can't Lose." *Sport,* LXXX (April 1989), 54–56.

49964. Attner, Paul. "Pete Rose, Manager." In: Tom Barnidge, ed. *Best Sports Stories of 1988.* St. Louis, MO: The Sporting News, 1988. Pp. 251–259.

49965. Barnett, Jim. "Has the World Turned Upside Down for Pete Rose?" *Sport World,* XXIV (February 1985), 30–34+.

49966. Bass, Mike. "The Pete Rose Way." *Inside Sports,* XI (April 1989), 59–67.

49967. Berkow, Ira. "1985: 4,192 — Rose Breaks Cobb's Record." In: Charles Einstein, ed. *The Fourth Fireside Book of Baseball.* New York: Simon and Schuster, 1987. Pp. 37–38.

49968. Bissinger, Buzz. "A Darker Side of Pete Rose." *Vanity Fair,* no. 493 (September 2001), 306–326.

49969. Blandford, Pat. "Still Sweet." *Beckett Sports Collectibles,* X (May 2001), 110–114.

49970. Bloom, Barry. "Pete Rose: Banished But Still a Baseball Man at Heart." *Baseball Digest,* LII (May 1993), 36–39.

49971. Bodlay, Hal. "For Boyish Rose, It's All Fun." In: Edward Ehre, ed. *Best Sports Stories of 1982.* St. Louis: The Sporting, News, 1982. Pp. 191–196.

49972. Bossert, Bill. "Pete Rose: The Ultimate [Card] Checklist." *Baseball Cards,* III (Spring 1983), 37–41.

49973. Brandt, Keith. *Pete Rose: Mr. .300.* New York: G.P. Putnam, 1977. 123p.

49974. Branner, John K., *et al.* "Rose News From Abroad." *Spitball,* no. 16 (Winter 1985), 4–8.

49975. Broeg, Bob. "Charlie Hustle." In: his *My Baseball Scrapbook.* St. Louis, MO: River City Publishers, 1983. Pp. 181–183.

49976. Brosnan, Jim. "Pete Rose: Rookie of the Year, 1963." In: his *Great Rookies of the Major Leagues.* New York: Random House, 1966. Pp.151+.

49977. Buck, Ray. *Pete Rose, "Charlie Hustle."* Chicago, IL: Children's Press, 1983. 41p.

49978. Burchard, Marshall. *Sports Hero Pete Rose.* New York: G.P. Putnam, 1976. 96p.

49979. Burick, Si. "No Moon People for Rose." *Baseball Digest,* XXVII (May 1969), 63–65.

49980. _____. "Pete Raw: 200 Grounders a Day." *Baseball Digest,* XXIV (July 1965), 39–41.

49981. "By Any Other Name." *The New Republic,* CCI (July 17, 1989), 6–7.

49982. Callahan, Tom. "For Pete's Sake, He Cried." *Time,* CXXVI (September 23, 1985), 60–61.

49983. _____. "A Rose is a Rose is a Rose." *Time,* CXXVI (August 19, 1985), 46–49.

49984. _____. "Savoring the Extra Innings After 40." *Time,* CXX (July 26, 1982), 44–47.

49985. Chapin, Dwight. "Pete Rose, Alias 'Charlie Hustle.'" *Baseball Digest,* XXVII (May 1969), 51–53.

49986. Church, G. J. "Why Pick on Pete?" *Time,* CXXXIV (July 10, 1989), 16–21.

59987. Clary, Jack. "Pete Rose." In: his *Captains.* New York: Atheneum, 1978. Pp. 2–30.

59988. Cohen, Irwin. "Talkin' Baseball with Pete Rose." *Baseball Cards,* V (August 1985), 24–27.

59989. Cook, William A. *Pete Rose: Baseball's All-Time Hit King.* Jefferson, NC: McFarland & Co., Inc., 2004. 241p.

49990. Cutlip, Scott M. "A Public Relations Footnote to the Pete Rose Affair." *Public Relations Review,* XV (Winter 1989), 46–48.

49991. Davids, Bob, "83 Season Saw End of Three Long Playing Streaks." *Baseball Digest,* XLIII (February 1984), 40–45. Garvey, Toby Harrah, and Rose.

49992. Davidson, Donald. "Pete Rose: Destined to Be the Last Playing-Manager?" *Baseball Digest,* XLVII (November 1988), 59–64.

49993. Davis, Craig. "Pete Rose Is a Swinger with a Simple Style." *Baseball Digest,* XLII (July 1983), 70–76.

49994. Deane, Bill. "Pete Rose: He's Also a Winner on Defense." *Baseball Digest,* XLI (March 1982), 42–45.

49995. Devaney, John. "Pete Rose: The Man Who Sparks the Reds." *Sport,* LIV (September 1967), 62–73.

49996. Director, Roger. "The Devil and 'Charlie Hustle.'" *Inside Sports,* IV (May 1982), 26–35.

49997. Dolson, Frank. "How Pete Rose Helped Nudge Mike Schmidt to Greatness." *Baseball Digest,* LIV (May 1995), 61–62.

49998. _____. and Bob Broeg. "Does Pete Rose Deserve a Spot in the Hall of Fame?" *Baseball Digest,* XLVIII (December 1989), 32–37.

49999. Dowd, John M. *The Dowd Report: Report to the Commissioner in the Matter of Peter Edward Rose, Manager, Cincinnati Reds Baseball Club.* New York: Office of the Commissioner of Baseball, 1989. 225p. On Rose's alleged gambling.

50000. _____. "The Dowd Report." *Mississippi Law Journal,* LXVIII, no. 3 (1999), 889–1051.

50001. Drury, Bob. "Pete Rose, Manager." *Sport,* LXXVI (June 1985), 80–82+.

50002. Duda, Marty. "Rose and Reds Dive Headfirst into Fitness." *The Physician and Sportsmedicine,* XVII (April 1989), 188–191.

50003. Erardi, John. "Desire Sustains Pete Rose in His Drive for New Hit Record." *Baseball Digest,* XLIV (August 1985), 23–28.

50004. _____. and Bob Rathgeber. *Pete Rose, 4192.* Cincinnati, OH: *Cincinnati Enquirer,* 1985. 96p.

50005. Fabbri, Helen and Larry D. Names, eds. *Dear Pete: The Life of Pete Rose.* Cincinnati, OH: Laranmark Press, 1985. 276p.

50006. Field, Jenniffer L. "The Power of One: The Effect of One Athlete's Behavior on a Sport." Unpublished MA thesis, Rowan University, 2000. 52p. Rose, Mike Tyson and Tonya Harding.

50007. Fimrite, Ron. "Past 3,000 and Still Counting." *Sports Illustrated*, XLVII (May 15, 1970), 26–28+.

50008. _____. "Pete's Out to Prove He Can Pull His Weight." *Sports Illustrated*, LX (February 13, 1984), 42–44, 47.

50009. _____. "Pete Rose." *Sports Illustrated*, LXXXI (September 19, 1994), 15–16.

50010. _____. "Sportsman of the Year." *Sports Illustrated*, XLII (December 22, 1975), 44–46+.

50011. Fitzgerald, M. "Sportswriters' Dilemma." *Editor and Publisher*, CXXIV (February 9, 1991), 35+.

50012. Fitzgerald, Ray. "Pete Rose: The Modern Ty Cobb." *Baseball Digest*, XXXVI (February 1977), 66–68.

50013. "For Pete's Sake, Pete." *Sports Illustrated*, LXXXIII (August 7, 1995), 18–19. Las Vegas radio show.

50014. Friedman, Jack. "As Pete Rose Chases Ty Cobb, Everyone from His Ex-Wife to Cobb Himself Offers an Opinion." *People Weekly*, XXIV (September 2, 1985), 28–31.

50015. Friend, Dave. "Pete Rose Goes for It." *Life*, VIII (May 1985), 115–120.

50016. Gammons, Peter. "A Threat Unveiled: After Finishing Second Thrice, the Reds' Pete Rose Can't Be a Bridesmaid Again." *Sports Illustrated*, LXVIII (April 10, 1988), 44–48.

50017. Gilbert, Thomas W. *Baseball Legends: Pete Rose.* New York: Chelsea House, 1995. 64p.

50018. Gillespie, Mark. "Baseball Fans Want Pete Rose in Hall of Fame, but Say No to Shoeless Joe." *The Gallup Poll Monthly*, (July 1999), 28–29.

50019. Gleason, Dan. "Last of the Big Time Hustlers." *Sport*, LVI (October 1973), 119–133.

50020. Goodman, Mark S. "Pete Rose Longs to Rise Again." *People Weekly*, XXXVI (September 2, 1991), 47–51.

50021. Graybar, Lloyd J. "Peter Edward 'Charlie Hustle' Rose." In: Vol. Q–Z of David L. Porter, ed. *Biographical Dictionary of American Sports: Baseball.* Rev. and enlarged ed. Westport, CT: Greenwood Press, 2000. Pp. 1314–1317.

50022. Gross, Milton. "Pete Rose: One of a Kind." *Baseball Digest*, XXIX (June 1970), 72–75.

50023. Grove, Wayne. "Player's Choice: Pete Rose." *Beckett Sports Collectibles*, X (May 2001), 12–13.

50024. "Guilty!" *Sports Illustrated*, LXXII (April 30, 1990), 13–14.

50025. Gutman, Bill. "Pete Rose." In: his *New Breed Heroes to Pro Baseball.* New York: Julian Messner, 1974. Pp. 163–175.

50026. _____. "Pete Rose." In: his *Superstars of the Sports World.* New York: Julian Messner, 1979. Pp. 77–91.

50027. Haltom, Bill. "The Trial of Pete Rose... a Very Bad Legal Precedent." *Tennessee Bar Journal*, XXXIX (September 2003), 41, 44.

50028. Harris, Mark J. "Tragedy as Pleasure: Giamatti and Rose." *Michigan Quarterly Review*, XXIX (Summer 1990), 335–346.

50029. Heffron, J. "They Can Ban Him from the Game, Bar Him from the Hall, But Pete Rose Will Always Be One of Us." *Cincinnati Magazine*, XXXVI (July 2003), 58–61, 129.

50030. Hemphill, Paul. "'Charlie Hustle,' Superstar." *Sport*, LVII (June 1974), 52–61.

50031. Henderson, Joe. "Pete Rose's Final Image: One

of Greatness or Fading Skills?" *Baseball Digest*, XLV (June 1986), 29–31.

50032. Herrera, Mitsuko and Greg Fox. *Pete Rose.* San Diego, CA: Revolutionary Comics, 1992. 30p.

50033. Hersh, Phil "In the End, Rose No Bigger Than Baseball." In: Gregory Wiley, ed. *Best Sports Stories of 1990.* St. Louis, MO: *The Sporting News*, 1990. Pp. 235–239.

50034. Hertzel, Bob. "The Parallels Between Pete Rose and Ty Cobb." *Baseball Digest*. XXXVII (May 1976), 26–29.

50035. _____. "Pete Gets 3,000th Amid Riverfront Standing Ovation: Reprinted from the *Cincinnati Register*, May 6, 1978." *Congressional Record*, CXXIV (May 8, 1978), 12922.

50036. _____. "Pete Rose: He's Still 'Charlie Hustle.'" *Baseball Digest*, XXXII (July 1973),18–22. Reprinted in John Kuenster, ed. *From Cobb to Catfish* (Chicago: Rand McNally, 1975), pp. 41–43.

50037. Higgins, George V. "Fields of Broken Dreams." *American Scholar*, LIX (Spring 1990), 199–210.

50038. "The Hit King Compromise: How Athletes Pay for Their Crimes." *Sports Illustrated*, LXXXVII (September 22, 1997), 15–16.

50039. Hochman, Stan. "Like an Elegant Clock, Pete Rose Keeps on Ticking." *Baseball Digest*, XL (November 1981), 20–25.

50040. _____. "A Love Triangle: Pete Rose, Joe Morgan, and Baseball." *Baseball Digest*, XLII (May 1983), 62–66.

50041. Hoffman, Frank W. and William G. Bailey. "The Pete Rose Gambling Scandal." In: their *Sports and Recreation Fads.* Binghampton, NY: Haworth, 1991. Pp. 311–314.

50042. Hollander, Zander. *Official Pete Rose Scrapbook.* New York: New American Library, 1978. 128p.

50043. Holtzman, Jerome. "Pete Rose: 4,000 Hits and Still Counting." *Baseball Digest*, XLIII (July 1984), 79–83.

50044. Honig, Donald. "Pete Rose." In: his *Baseball America: the Heroes of the Game and the Times of Their Glory.* New York: Macmillan, 1985. Pp. 331–333.

50045. _____. "Pete Rose." In: his *Up From the Minor Leagues.* New York: Cowles, 1970. Pp. 73–85.

50046. Hughes, Joseph J., Jr. "Two Great Hitters." *Beckett Baseball Card Monthly*, III (September 1989), 16–17. Rose and Cobb.

50047. Isle, Stan. "3,000 Hits, 44-Game Streak All in Year's Work for Rose." In: John Dittrich ed. *Baseball '78.* St. Petersburg, FL: National Association of Professional Baseball Leagues, 1978. Pp. 9–12.

50048. Johnson, William O. "The Greenbacking of Pete Rose." *Sports Illustrated*, L (January 22, 1979), 38+.

50048a. Jordan, David. *Pete Rose: A Biography.* Baseball's All-Time Greatest Hitters Series. Westport, CT: Greenwood Press, 2004. 208p.

50049. Jordan, Pat. "'Charlie Hustle' is 39." *Sport*, LXXII (January 1981), 52–55.

50050. _____. "War of the Roses." GQ -*Gentlemen's Quarterly*, LIX (April 1989), 274–279+.

50051. Kahn, Roger. "A Rose by Another Name." *Playboy*, XXXVIII (December 1991), 174+.

50052. Kaplan, Jim. "Is the Bloom Off the Rose?" *Sports Illustrated*, LVIII (June 27, 1983), 66+.

50053. _____. "Pete Rose." *Sport*, LXXVII (December 1986), 125, 143.

50054. _____. and Steve Wulf. "They're Playing the Sweet Music of the '40's." *Sports Illustrated*, LVII (July 19, 1982), 18–21.

50055. Keith, Larry. "Doing Much...." *Sports Illustrated*, XLIX (August 7, 1978), 12+.

50056. Kelly, Robert E. "Cobb vs. Rose: A Closer Look." In: his *Baseball For the Hot Stove League.* Jefferson, NC: McFarland & Co., Inc., 1989. Pp. 82–90.

50057. Kindred, Dave. "Pete Rose." In: his *Heroes, Fools, and Other Dreamers.* Marietta, GA: Longstreet Press, 1989. Pp. 178–180.

50058. Klein, Michael. "Rose is Black, Black Sox are Blue: A Comparison of 'Rose v. Giamatti' and the 1921 Black Sox Trial." *Hastings Communications and Entertainment Law Journal.*, XIII (Spring 1991), 551–588.

50059. Klemesrud, J. "Will Pete Rose Ever Grow Up?" *Esquire,* LXXXII (October 1974), 211+.

50060. Kobman, Randy. "Always Fourteen." In: David Cataneo. *Hornsby Hit One Over My Head: A Fans' Oral History of Baseball.* New York: Harcourt, Brace & Co., 1997. Pp. 226–232.

50061. Kowet, Don. "The Players Pick Baseball's Greatest Competitor." *Sport,* LXI(March 1971), 42–43.

50062. Kurlantzick, L. "Pete Rose: The Fundamental Conflict." *For the Record,* XV (April–June 2004), 6–7.

50063. Kuenster, John. "Dowd Report Details Extensive Gambling on Baseball by Pete Rose." *Baseball Digest,* LIX (March 2000), 17–21.

50064. _____. "Pete Rose: He'll Even Use Deception to Beat You." *Baseball Digest,* XXXV (November 1976), 16–20.

50065. _____. "Pete Rose: 1973 Player of the Year." *Baseball Digest,* XXXII (December 1973), 4–8.

50066. _____. "Pete Rose's No. 1 Fan Can Whittle Him Down to Size.*" Baseball Digest,* XXXVIII (July 1979), 15–21.

50067. Kuenster, John. "Rose and Guerrero Suspensions in the NL Showed Lack of Even-Handed Justice." *Baseball Digest,* XLVII (September 1988), 15–17.

50068. _____. "Should Major League Baseball Take Steps to Reinstate Pete Rose?" *Baseball Digest,* LVII (January 1998), 15–19.

50069. Lawson, Earl. "Pete Rose Fans as Beauty Queen Throws a Curve." *Baseball Digest,* XXV (February 1966), 77–79.

50070. _____. "Pete Rose Recalls Career Highlights in Each Park." *Baseball Digest,* XXXVI (September 1977), 82–83.

50071. Leerhsen, Charles. "All is Not Lost in Cincinnati." *Newsweek,* CXVI (July 30, 1990), 61–62.

50072. _____. "All the Odds Against Him." *Newsweek,* CXIV (July 10, 1989), 74–75.

50073. _____. "Closing in on Charlie Hustle." *Newsweek,* CXIV (July 3, 1989), 23+.

50074. _____. "The End of the Affair." *Newsweek,* CXIV (September 4, 1989), 58–59.

50075. _____. "Waiting for the Final Chapter." *Newsweek,* CXIII (April 10, 1989), 71+.

50076. Leggett, William. "'Charlie Hustle' Gives Twelve Dimes on the Dollar." *Sports Illustrated,* XXVIII (May 27, 19"), 32–34+.

50077. _____. "They Never Promised a Rose Garden." *Sports Illustrated,* XXXIX (September 17, 1973), 40–41.

50078. Leifer, Neil and Peter Bonventre. "Pete Rose." In: their *Neil Leifer's Sports Stars.* Garden City, NY: Doubleday, 1986. Pp. 52–53.

50079. Leiker, Ken. "7–1980: Pete Rose Breaks Ty Cobb's All-Time Record for Hits." In: his *Major League Baseball Memorable Moments: The Most Memorable Moments in Major League Baseball History.* New York: Ballantine Books, 2002. Pp. 44–47.

50080. Levine, John. "Restoring the Rose." *Forbes,* CXLV (June 25, 1990), 146+.

50081. Lewis, Allen. "Phils Were Thorns to a Budding Pete Rose." *Baseball Digest,* XXXVIII (March 1979), 70–73.

50082. Levy, Maury Z. and Samantha Stevenson. "Interview: Pete Rose." *Playboy,* XXVI (September 1979), 77+.

50083. Libby, Bill. *Pete Rose: They Call Him Charlie Hustle.* New York: G.P. Putnam, 1972. 159p.

50084. Lieber, Jill. "The Case Against Pete Rose." *Sports Illustrated,* LXXI (July 3, 1989), 10–20, 25.

50085. _____. and Craig Neff. "Deeper and Deeper." *Sports Illustrated,* LXXII (February 12, 1990), 50+.

50086. _____. "An Idol Banned." *Sports Illustrated,* LXXI (September 4, 1989), 29–30.

50087. _____. and Steve Wulf. "Sad Ending for a Hero: Baseball Great Pete Rose was Given Five Months in Jail for Cheating on His Taxes." *Sports Illustrated,* LXXIII (July 30, 1990), 22–25.

50088. Lumb, Chuck, Dan Polzien, and Earl Molnar. *The Almost Complete Pete Rose Checklist: A Guide to Collecting Pete Rose Memorabilia.* Chicago, IL: Head First Press, 1996. Unpaged.

50089. Lupica, Mike. "Goooooood Morning, Cooperstown: Pete Rose May Be a Hit on the Radio, But He's Still Gambling with Reinstatement." *Esquire,* CXVIII (September 1992), 135, 138.

50090. Mahoney, Ed. "Solving the Pete Rose Dilemma." *Elysian Fields Quarterly,* XVIII (Winter 2001), 23–25.

50091. Mann, Jack. "Joe Hustle May Bring Flag to the Reds." *Sports Illustrated,* XXIII (September 20, 1965), 114–115.

50092. Marcus, Steve. "Baseball's Thorny Issue: Pete Rose's Reinstatement." *Baseball Digest,* LI (March 1992), 38–45.

50093. Masterson, Dave and Timm Boyle. "1973." In: their *Baseball's Best: The MVPs.* Chicago: Contemporary Books, 1985. Pp. 262–267.

50094. McClure, Bill. "Pete Rose — Enos Slaughter with Talent." *Countrywide Sports,* I (August 1970), 55–61.

50095. McMane, Fred. "Pete Rose." In: his *The 3,000 Hit Club.* Champaign, IL: Sports Publishing, 2000. Pp. 2–9.

50096. Mosher, S. D. "Fielding Our Dreams: Rounding Third in Dyersville." *Sociology of Sport Journal,* VIII (September 1991), 272–280.

50097. Neff, Craig. "Cutting a Hit Record." *Sports Illustrated,* LXIII (September 16, 1985), 18–21.

50098. _____. "Truly a Baseball Immortal." *Sports Illustrated,* LXIII (September 23, 1985), 60+. Reprinted in Jack Canfield and Mark Victor Hansen, eds., *Chicken Soup for the Sports Fan's Soul: 101 Stories of Insight, Inspiration, and Laughter from the World of Sports.* (Deerfield Beach, FL: Health Communications, Inc., 2000), pp. 83–87.

50099. _____. and Jill Lieber. "Rose's Grim Vigil" *Sports Illustrated,* LXX (April 3, 1989), 52–54, 56, 58–59.

50100. Newman, Bruce." He's the Phillie Fillip." *Sports Illustrated,* L (May 28, 1979), 20–23.

50101. Newton, Craig. "Pete Rose: Interview." *Baseball Cards,* X (January 1990), 118–125.

50102. Osborne, Tom. "Ageless Rose: Pete Rose Model Athlete." *Current Health 2,* XIII (September 1986), 26–27.

50103. Pachman, Matthew B. "Limits on the Discretionary Powers of Professional Sports Commissioners: A Historical and Legal Analysis of Issues Raised by the Pete Rose Controversy." *Virginia Law Review,* LXXVI (October 1990), 1409–1439.

50104. Palmer, Pete. "Rose: An Ordinary Player for an

Extraordinary Time." *The Baseball Research Journal,* XX (1991), 8–9.

50105. Pascarelli, Peter. "How Waite Hoyt Compares Ty Cobb and Pete Rose." *Baseball Digest,* XLII (January 1983), 77–80.

50106. Peebles, Dick. "This Was One Hit Pete Rose Didn't Get!" *Baseball Digest,* XXXVII (September 1978), 36–39.

50107. *Pete Rose.* Collection Sport. Montreal, Canada: Quebecor, 1984. 192p. In French.

50108. "Pete Rose." In: *Current Biography Yearbook, 1975.* New York: H.W. Wilson Co,, 1975. Pp. 361–363.

50109. "Pete Rose: Mr. Hustle is MVP." In: Tommy Kay, ed. *Tommy Kay's Big Book of Baseball.* Scottsdale, AZ: Jalart House, 1974. Pp. 110–113.

50110. "Pete Rose's 44-Game Hitting Streak, 1979." *Baseball Digest,* XXXIX (February 1980), 11–15.

50111. "Pete Rose's Impossible Dream." In: Zander Hollander, ed. *1980: The Complete Handbook of Baseball.* New York: New American Library, 1980. Pp. 10–11.

50112. "Pete Rose's Pitching Pinups." In: Zander Hollander, ed. *1979: The Complete Handbook of Baseball.* New York: New American Library, 1979. Pp. 22–33.

50113. "Playing Hardball: Is Pete Rose's Lifetime Ban from Baseball Off Base?— News Debate." *Current Events, a Weekly Reader Publication,* CII (January 10, 2003), 3–5.

50114. Raab, Scott. "The Hit King." *GQ— Gentlemen's Quarterly,* LXVII (July 1997), 150–158. Reprinted in Bill Littlefield, ed. *The Best American Sports Writing, 1998.* Boston, MA: Houghton, Mifflin, 1998. Pp. 318–331.

50115. Rasmussen, Larry . "Pete Rose: Baseball's Most Consistent Hitter." *Baseball Digest,* XXXVIII (September 1979), 40–41.

50116. Rathgeber, Bob. "When Hustle Won An All-Star Game: Pete Rose." In: his *Cincinnati Reds Scrapbook.* Virginia Beach, VA: J.C.P. Corp. of Virginia, 1982. Pp. 134–135.

50117. Reichler, Joseph L. "Pete Rose: The Unblushing Flower." In: Joseph L. Reichler, ed. *Major League Baseball 1985 All-Star Game Program.* New York: Major League Baseball Promotion Corp., 1985. Pp. 14–20.

50118. Reidenbaugh, Lowell. "Move Over Stan, for Pete's Sake." In: C.C. Johnson Spink, ed. *The Sporting News 1981 Baseball Yearbook.* St. Louis: The Sporting News, 1981. Pp. 72–75. Comparison of Rose with Stan Musial.

50119. Reilly, Rick. "On Deck for the Big Knock." *Sports Illustrated,* LXIII (August 19, 1985), 34–37, 40–46, 53.

50120. "A Rose is a Rose." *Sports Illustrated,* LXXIX (August 16, 1993), 30–36.

50121. Reston, James, Jr. *Collision at Home Plate: The Lives of Pete Rose and Bart Giamatti.* New York: Harper-Collins, 1991. 326p.

50122. Ribowsky, Mark. "Inside Interview: Pete Rose." *Sport,* LXXXIX (January 1999), 72–75.

50123. Richman, Milton. "Pete Rose Still Loves to Play the Game." *Baseball Digest,* XXXIX (May 1980), 69–71.

50124. Ritter, Lawrence and Donald Honig. "Pete Rose." In: their *The 100 Greatest Baseball Players of All Time.* New York: Crown Publishers, 1981. Pp. 1–3.

50125. Robinson, Ray. "Pete Rose." In: Ray Robinson, ed. *Baseball Stars of 1969.* New York: Pyramid Books, 1969. Pp. 80–85.

50126. Robson, Britt. "The Reds' Blues Turn to Rose." *Sport,* LXXIV (October 1984), 67+.

50127. Rose, Pete. "Doing What Comes Naturally." In: Vito Stellino, ed. *Sports All-Stars 1969 Baseball.* New York. Maco Publishing Co., 1969. Pp. 12–15.

50128. "Interview." Edited by Marty Bell. *Sport,* LXVIII (April 1979), 17+.

50129. "Memories of My Dad." *Sport,* LI (April 1971), 16, 18, 52–53.

50130. *My Prison without Bars.* New York: Rodale Press, 2004. 288p.

50131. *The Official Pete Rose Scrapbook.* New York: New American Library, 1985. 128p.

50132. *Pete Rose: My Life in Baseball.* Garden City, NY. Doubleday, 1979. 134p.

50133. *The Pete Rose Story: Autobiography.* Cleveland, OH: World Publishing Co., 1970. 202p.

50134. "Pete Speaks." *Sports Illustrated,* LXXI (November 20, 1989), 23–24.

50135. and Bob Hertzel. *Charlie Hustle.* Englewood Cliffs, NJ: Prentice Hall, 1976. p. 240.

50136. *Pete Rose's Winning Baseball.* Chicago, IL: Regnery, 1976. 186p. "Charley Hustle's" thoughts on technique.

50137. and Hal Bodley. *Countdown to Cobb: My Diary of the Record-Breaking 1985 Season.* St. Louis, MO: The Sporting News, 1985. 224p.

50138. and Jim Brosnan. "How I Hit." *Boy's Life,* LXVI (March 1976), 20–23.

50139. and Peter Golenbock. *Pete Rose on Hitting: How to Hit Better Than Anybody.* New York: Perigee Books, 1985. 96p.

50140. and Roger Kahn. *Pete Rose: My Story.* New York: Collier-Macmillan, 1989. 300p.

50141. as told to George Vass. "The Game I'll Never Forget." *Baseball Digest,* XXXI (June 1972), 39–41.

50142. "Rose, the Joy of Summer." *Time,* CXII (August 7, 1978), 70–71.

50143. "Rose was 1985's Brightest Star." In: Bob Sparks, ed. *Baseball '86.* St. Petersburg, FL: NAPBL Promotion Corporation, 1986. Pp. 49–51.

50144. Ruark, James E. "Shifting Images." *Reformed Journal,* XXXIX (September 1989), 5–6.

50146. Rubin, Bob. *Pete Rose.* New York: Random House, 1975.152p.

50147. Rychiak, Ronald J. "Pete Rose, Bart Giamatti, and the Dowd Report." *Mississippi Law Journal,* LVIII (Spring 1999), 889–1051. Includes text of the report.

50148. Saldt, Bus. "Pete Rose: Player of the Decade." *Baseball Magazine,* New Series IV (April 1980), 20–25.

50149. Schlossberg, Dan. "Pete Rose: The Hustlin' Man." In: Ray Robinson, ed. *Baseball Stars of 1973.* New York: Pyramid Books, 1973. Pp. 84–91.

50150. Seaver, Tom, with Marty Appel. "The Joy That was Pete Rose." In: his *Great Moments in Baseball: From the World Series of 1903 to the Modern Records of Nolan Ryan.* New York: Carol Communications, 1992. Pp. 289–294.

50151. Shannon, Mike. "Pete Rose." In: his *Tales from the Ballpark: More of the Greatest True Baseball Stories Ever Told.* Lincolnwood, IL: Contemporary Books, 1999. Pp. 171–172.

50152. "Pete Rose." In: his *Tales from the Dugout: The Greatest True Baseball Stories Ever Told.* Lincolnwood, IL: NTC/Contemporary Books, 1997. Pp. 169–174.

50153. *Pete Rose Agonistes.* Conover, NC: Third Lung Press, 1987. 15p. Poetry.

50154. Shehan, Thomas. "Monk Walks Out of Babe Ruth's Past." In: Dean A. Sullivan, ed. *Middle Innings: A Documentary History of Baseball, 1900–1948.* Lincoln, NE: University of Nebraska Press, 1998. Pp. 153–156. An interview with Brother Matthias; reprinted from the *Boston Evening Transcript,* Feb. 28, 1935.

50155. Siller, Phillip. "The Truth About Pete Rose: Why You'd Rather Have Minnie Minoso on Your Team." *The Baseball Research Journal,* XXX (2000), 90–95.

50156. Smith, James P. *Pete Rose.* Mankato, MN: Creative Education, 1977. 31p.

50157. Smith, Ron. "Pete Rose 25." In: his *The Sporting News Selects Baseball's 100 Greatest Players.* St. Louis, MO: *The Sporting News,* 1998. Pp. 58–59.

50158. Sokolove, Michael Y. *Hustle: The Myth, Life and Lies of Pete Rose.* New York: Simon and Schuster, 1990. 304p.

50159. _____. "A Rough in the Diamond." *Fame,* III (October 1990), 51+.

50160. Stainback, Berry. "Pete Rose: Travels with 'Charlie Hustle.'" *Sport,* LVI (August 1968), 12–15.

50161. Strout, Lawrence. "Say It Ain't So — Joe [Jackson] and Pete: Reporting on Fallen Idols." *Media History Digest,* XII (Fall-Winter 1992), 2–10.

50162. Sugar, Bert Randolph. "Pete Rose's Record-Breaking Game: Cincinnati Reds vs. San Diego Padres, September 11, 1985." In: his *Baseball's 50 Greatest Games.* Rev. ed. North Dighton, MA: The JG Press, 1994. Pp. 151–153.

50163. Summerall, Pat and Jim Moskovitz, with Craig Kubey. "Pete Rose." In: their *Pat Summerall's Sports in America: 32 Celebrated Sports Personalities Talk About Their Most Memorable Moments In and Out of the Sports Arena.* New York: HarperCollins, 1996. Pp. 237–252.

50164. Swift, E.M. "Rose Might Not Be Red Anymore." *Sports Illustrated,* XLIX (November 6, 1978), 34–36+.

50165. Tartaglione, John. *Pete Rose: His Incredible Baseball Career.* Halesite, NY: Masstar Creations, 1995. 31p.

50166. Thorn, John. "Pete Rose: 'Charlie Hustle.'" In: his *Baseball's Dream Team.* New York: Ace Tempo Books, 1982. Pp. 16–27.

50167. Towle, Mike. *Pete Rose: Baseball's Charlie Hustle.* Nashville, TN: Cumberland House, 2003. 227p.

50168. Tucker, David, ed. *4192! A Celebration of Pete Rose, Baseball's Record-Breaking Hitter.* Chicago, IL: Contemporary Books, Inc., 1985. 85p.

50169. Utz, S. G. "The Authority of the Rules of Baseball: The Commissioner as Judge." *Journal of the Philosophy of Sport,* XVI (1989), 89–99.

50170. Vecsey, George. "Fresh Young Rose." In: John L. Pratt, ed. *Baseball All-Stars.* Garden City, NY: Doubleday, 1967. Pp. 29–38.

50171. Verdi, Bob. "For Pete's Sake." In: Bob Verdi. *The Bob Verdi Collection.* Dallas, TX: Taylor Publishing Co., 1988. Pp. 26–28.

50172. Wheeler, Lonnie. "The Boy of Summer." *Ohio,* VIII (July 1985), 30+.

50173. _____. "Their Love is Like a Red, Red Rose." *Inside Sports,* VII (September 1985), 74–77.

50174. Will, George F. "The Collision Between Bart and Pete." In: his *Bunts: Curt Flood, Camden Yards, Pete Rose and Other Reflections on Baseball.* New York: Touchstone Books, 1998. Pp.192–202.

50175. Wulf, Steve. "For Pete's Sake Look Who's Back." *Sports Illustrated,* LXI (August 27, 1984), 16–22. Rose as Cincinnati manager.

50176. _____. "There'll Be No More Tie with Ty [Cobb]." *Sports Illustrated,* LI (October 1, 1979), 50+.

50177. _____. "30 Days." *Sports Illustrated,* LXVIII (May 9, 1988), 22–25. Rose suspension for altercation with umpire Dave Pallone.

50178. Ziegel, Vic. "The Pete Rose Formula." *Sport,* XL (December 1965), 60–61+.

Peter Edward ("Pete") Rose, Jr.

3B. (B: 1970). Cincinnati (NL), 1997. Remarks: Son of Pete Rose, Sr. (above), played in 11 big league games with two hits and a .143 batting average; has played with various minor league teams since 1989, including Chattanooga (SL), Winnipeg (Northern League), 2002 and Joliet (Northern League), 2003; Colorado Springs (PCL), 2004; in 1,404 minor league contests through 2003, has had a .264 batting average and 100 homers.

50179. Bradley, John Ed. "Honor Thy Father." *Sports Illustrated,* LXXXVII (August 11, 1997), 70–80, 82–83.

50180. Jordan, Pat. "War of the Roses." *GQ — Gentlemen's Quarterly,* LIV (April 1989), 274–283.

50181. Maisel, Ivan. "A Rose in the Bud." *Sports Illustrated,* LXIII (August 19, 1985), 66–67.

John H. ("Johnny") Roseboro

C. (B: May 13, 1933, Ashland, OH-D: Aug. 16, 2002). Brooklyn (NL) and Los Angeles (NL), 1957–1967; Minnesota (AL), 1968–1969; Washington (AL), 1970. Remarks: Had 1,206 hits (104 homers) and 67 stolen bases in 1,585 games in 14 seasons; noted fielding backstop, whose key hits won Game One of 1963 World Series and Game Three of 1965 fall classic; coach, Washington (AL), 1971 and California (AL), 1972; minor league instructor/coach, Los Angeles (NL) farm system, 1977–1978, 1988–1992.

50182. Brown, Robert J. "John Junior 'Johnny,' 'Gabby' Roseboro." In: Vol. Q-Z of David L. Porter, ed. *Biographical Dictionary of American Sports: Baseball.* Rev. and enlarged ed. Westport, CT: Greenwood Press, 2000. Pp. 1317–1318.

50183. Flora, Earl. "If He Can Blend Two Years." *Baseball Digest,* XIX (May 1960), 53–55.

50184. Furillo, Bud. "Roseboro's Biggest Hit." *Baseball Digest,* XXV (March 1966), 95–99.

50185. Herskowitz, Mickey. "The Unheralded Dodger." *Sport,* XXXVIII (September 1964), 44–45+.

50186. Laughlin, Bob, with Budd Theobald. *John Roseboro: The Boy Who Took Over for Campy.* Meet the Dodgers Series. Los Angeles, CA: Union Oil Company of California, 1960. 13p.

50187. _____. *John Roseboro: Hard-Working.* Meet the Dodgers Series. Los Angeles, CA: Union Oil Company of California, 1961. 14p.

50188. Mann, Jack. "Battle of San Francisco." *Sports Illustrated,* XXIII (August 30, 1965), 12–15.

50189. Oates, Bob. "John Roseboro: A Soft-voiced Take-Charge Guy." *Baseball Digest,* XX (August 1961), 68–71.

50190. "A Pitcher Goes to Bat Against the Catcher." *Life,* LIX (September 3, 1965), 34–35. Fight with Juan Marichal (q.v.).

50191. Roseboro, Johnny, with Bill Libby. *Glory Days with the Dodgers and Other Days with Others.* New York: Atheneum, 1978. 297p.

50192. Schultz, Randy. "John Roseboro and Manny Sanguillen: Where are They Now?" *Baseball Digest,* XLIX (January 1990), 59–62.

50193. Stann, Francis. "New Career for Johnny Roseboro." *Baseball Digest,* XXVII (May 1968), 73–75.

50194. Stevens, Bob. "Marichal Attacks Dodgers' Roseboro with Bat During Game." In: Dean A. Sullivan, ed. *Late Innings: A Documentary History of Baseball, 1945–1972.* Lincoln, NE: University of Nebraska Press, 2002. Pp. 197–199. Reprinted from the *San Francisco Chronicle,* Aug. 23, 1965.

50195. Westcott, Rich. "Johnny Roseboro: Stability Behind the Plate." In: his *Splendor on the Diamond: Interviews with 35 Stars of Baseball's Past*. Gainesville, FL: The University Press of Florida, 2000. Pp. 291–299.

50196. "Whatever Happened to Johnny Roseboro?" *Ebony*, XXXIV (January 1979), 68+.

Albert Leonard ("Al" or "Flip") Rosen
3B-EXEC. (B; Feb. 29, 1924, Spartanburg, SC). Cleveland (AL), 1947–1956. Remarks: Obtained 1,063 hits (192 homers) in 1,044 games in a decade; had four grand slam homers in one year, 1951; AL home run champion, 1950 and 1953; had seven RBIs in one game, April 29, 1952; A. L. RBI champion, 1952–1953; AL MVP Award, 1953; had two consecutive homers in 1954 All-Star Game at Cleveland; while playing for Kansas City (AA) in 1948, had five consecutive homers; vice president of Cleveland branch of Bache & Co., a brokerage firm, 1956–1976; part-owner, New York (AL), 1973–1980; (Yankees vice president then president, 1977–1980); president/GM, Houston (NL), 1980–1985; president/GM, San Francisco (NL), 1986–1992.

50197. "Al Rosen." *Pathfinder News Magazine*, LVII (September 6, 1950), 50+.

50198. "Albert (Al) Rosen." In: *Current Biography Yearbook, 1954*. New York: H.W. Wilson Co., 1954. Pp. 541–543.

50199. Cobbledick, Gordon. "They Love Al Rosen in Cleveland." *Sport*, XII (May 1952), 50–51+.

50200. _____. "They'll Follow Rosen Now." *Baseball Digest*, XIII (March 1954), 29–31.

50201. Cuddy, Don. "Big Chief Rosen." *Sport*, XVI (April 1954), 32–33+.

50202. _____. "The Game's the Thing." in: Bruce Jacobs, ed. *Baseball Stars of 1954*. New York; Lion Books, 1954. Pp. 110–116.

50203. Daley, Arthur. "Rosen Rises to 'Most' Past." *Baseball Digest*, IX (September 1950), 29–31.

50204. Dickey, Glenn. "Introducing Al Rosen." *Giants Magazine*, I, no. 1 (1986), 10–13.

50205. Dolgan, Bob. "Close But No Cigar: When Al Rosen Nearly Won the Triple Crown." *Baseball Digest*, LXI (March 2002), 76–79. In 1953.

50206. Frommer, Harvey and Frederick J. "Al Rosen." In: their *Growing Up Baseball: An Oral History*. Dallas, TX: Taylor Publishing Co., 2001. Pp. 195–198.

50207. Gibbons, Frank. "Injun Clubber." *Sport Life*, IV (September 1951), 48–50+.

50208. _____. "Rosen — Indians' Mr. America." *Baseball Digest*, XI (August 1952), 50–55.

50209. Giglio, James N. "Albert Leonard 'Al,' 'Flip' Rosen." In: Vol. Q–Z of David L. Porter, ed. *Biographical Dictionary of American Sports: Baseball*. Rev. and enlarged ed. Westport, CT: Greenwood Press, 2000. Pp. 1318–1319.

50210. Gross, Milton. "They All Get Butterflies." *Baseball Digest*, XI (January 1952), 75–77.

50211. Honig, Donald. "1953: Al Rosen." In: his *American League MVP's*. New York: Bantam Books, 1989. Pp. 49–50.

50212. Lebovitz, Hal. "How Rosen Rocks 'Em." *Collier's*, CXXXIII (May 28, 1954), 72–73.

50213. _____. "The Story Behind the Rosen Headlines." *Sport*, XXIII (February 1957), 22–23+.

50214. Lewis, Franklin. "Bat Title for Rosen?" *Baseball Digest*, X (May 1951), 57–59.

50215. Lynn, Erwin. "Al Rosen." In: his *The Jewish Baseball Hall of Fame*. New York: Shapolsky Publications, 1987. Pp. 166–167.

50216. Masterson, Dave and Timm Boyle. "1953." In: their *Baseball's Best: The MVPs*. Chicago, IL: Contemporary Books, 1985. Pp. 142–147.

50217. Matos, Fred. "Al Rosen —1953." In: *his Baseball's Top 100: The Best Individual Seasons of All Time*. Wilton, CT: Diamond Library, 1996. Pp. 141–143.

50218. Miller, Hub. "Cleveland's Big Find: Al Rosen." *Baseball Magazine*, LXXXV (October 1950), 387–389.

50219. Paxton, Henry T. "That Clouting Kid from Cleveland." *Saturday Evening Post*, CCXXIV (August 11, 1951), 25–26+.

50220. Ribalow, Harold U. "Al Rosen." In: his *Jew in American Sports*. New York: Bloch, 1959. Pp. 99–109.

50221. _____ and Meir Z. Ribalow. "Al Rosen: Indian Chief." In: their *Jewish Baseball Stars*. New York: Hippocrene Books, 1984. Pp. 122–136.

50222. Rosen, Al. "They Pay Off on Runs Batted In." *Sport*, XVII (October 1954), 16–17+.

50223. _____. "You Gotta Hustle." *Complete Baseball*, IV (September 1952), 18–19+.

50224. Rosen, Terry. "My Guy 'Flip.'" *Baseball Digest*, XIII (October 1954), 29–40.

50225. Schneider, Russell. "Al Rosen: 'We Were Like the Three Musketeers, You Know, One for All and All for One.'" In: his *The Boys of the Summer of '48*. Champaign, IL: Sports Publishing, 1998. Pp. 136–145.

50226. Slater, Robert. "Al Rosen: He Wanted to Be a Jew of Whom All Could Be Proud." In: his *Great Jews in Sports*. Middle Village, NY: Jonathan David Publishers, 1983. Pp. 172–174.

50227. Swank, Bill. "Al Rosen." In: his *Echoes from Lane Field: A History of the San Diego Padres 1936–1957*. Paducah, KY: Turner Publishing Company, 1997. Pp. 101–102.

50228. Vass, George. "Al Rosen." In: his *The Game I'll Never Forget*. Chicago, IL: Bonus Books, 1999. Pp. 225–229.

50229. Wilber, Cynthia J. "Al Rosen." In: her *For the Love of the Game: Baseball Memories from the Men Who Were There*. New York: William Morrow, 1992. Pp. 96–106.

Alan Rosen
BASEBALL CARD DEALER.
50230. Geringer, D. "Mr. Mint." *Sports Illustrated*, LXIX (July 4, 1988), 78–82+.

Goodwin George ("Goody") Rosen
OF. (B: Aug. 28, 1912, Toronto, Canada-D: April 6, 1994). Brooklyn (NL), 1937–1939, 1944–1946; New York (NL), 1946. Remarks: Had 557 hits (22 homers) in 561 games in a six-year big league career; first Canadian-born major leaguer to be named to an All-Star team (1945); also played for Toronto (IL), 1947; also played for Louisville (AA), 1936 and Syracuse (IL), 1940–1943; became Toronto restaurateur and noted local softball player who led his Toronto Levy Auto Parts team into losing NSC Championship game against a Lubbock, TX nine, 1948; elected to Canadian Baseball Hall of Fame in 1984.

50231. Kendall, Brian. "April 28, 1946: Goody Rosen Gets Even with the Brooklyn Dodgers." In: his *Great Moments in Canadian Baseball*. Toronto, Ont.: Lester Publishing, 1995. Chapter 6.

50232. Kirst, Sean Peter. "Feisty Center Fielder Sparked Great Team." In: his *The Ashes of Lou Gehrig and Other Baseball Essays*. Jefferson, NC: McFarland & Co., Inc., 2003. Pp. 151–152.

50233. Murphy, Edward T. "The Midget at Ebbets Field." *Baseball Digest*, IV (September 1945), 1–5.

50234. Ribalow, Harold U. "Goody Rosen: Canadian

Clubber." In: his *The Jew in American Sports.* New York: Bloch Publishing Co., 1948. Pp. 62–66.

50235. Shearon, Jim. "Rosen's Revenge Cost Dodgers 1946 Pennant." In: his *Canada's Baseball Legends: True Stories, Records and Photos of Canadian-born Players In Baseball's Major Leagues.* Kanata, Ontario: Malin Head Press, 1994. Pp. 69–71.

50236. Turner, Dan. "Goody Rosen." In: his *Heroes, Bums and Ordinary Men.* Toronto: Doubleday Canada Ltd., 1988. Pp. 92–101.

50237. Van Blair, Rick. "Goody Rosen." In: his *Dugout to Foxhole: Interviews With Baseball Players Whose Careers Were Affected by World War II.* Jefferson, NC: McFarland & Co., Inc., 1994. Pp. 171–179.

Goody Rosen *see* **Goodwin George ("Goody") Rosen**

Harold Rosenthal
WRITER. (B: March 11, 1914, New York City-D: 1999). Remarks: Writer/reporter New York Herald-Tribune, 1931–1966; PR director, Continental Football League, 1966–1970; PR director, American Football League, 1970–1974; PR director, New American Library, 1975–death.

50238. Wilson, Nick. "Harold Rosenthal." In: his *Voices from the Pastime: Oral Histories of Surviving Major Leaguers, Negro Leaguers, Cuban Leaguers, and Writers, 1920–1934.* Jefferson, NC: McFarland & Co., Inc., 2000. Pp. 171–181.

Allan Roth
STATISTICIAN. Remarks: Team statistician, Brooklyn (NL) and Los Angeles (NL), 1947–1964.

50239. Roth, Alan. "The Responsibilities of a Team Statistician." In: Harold Rosenberg, ed. *Baseball is Their Business.* New York: Random House, 1952. Pp. 134–144. Reprinted in Dean A. Sullivan, ed., *Late Innings: A Documentary History of Baseball, 1945–1972* (Lincoln, NE: University of Nebraska Press, 2002), pp. 56–58.

Frank Roth *see* **Robert Frank ("Braggo" or "Globetrotter") Roth**

Robert Frank ("Braggo" or "The Globetrotter") Roth
OF. (B: Aug. 28, 1892, Burlington, WI-D: Sept. 11, 1936). Chicago (AL), 1914–1915; Cleveland (AL), 1915–1918; Philadelphia (AL) and Boston AL), 1919; Washington (AL), 1920; New York (AL), 1921. Remarks: Obtained 804 hits (30 homers) and 189 stolen bases in 811 games for six different teams in eight years; with seven "taters" was 1915 AL home run champion; stole home plate, June 1, 1917; coach, New York (AL), 1921, Cleveland (AL), 1923–1925.

50240. Hoefer, W.R. "Slugging Braggo Roth." *Baseball Magazine,* XIX (May 1917), 229–230+.

50241. Suehsdorf, Adie D. "Irresistible Braggo Roth." *The Baseball Research Journal,* XX (1991), 43+.

Arnold ("Great Brain" or "The Big Bankroll") Rothstein
POLITICIAN-GANGSTER. (B: 1882, New York City-D: Nov. 6, 1928). Remarks: Gifted pool shark, loan shark, Tammy Hall insider, bootlegger, and unindicted mastermind of the 1919 Black Sox scandal; murdered.

50242. Pietrusza, David and Peter C. Whybrow. *Rothstein: The Life, Times and Murder of the Criminal Genius Who Fixed the 1919 World Series.* New York: Carroll and Graf, 2003. 464p.

Edd J. ("Eddie") Roush ★
OF. (B: May 8, 1893, Oakland City, IN-D: March 21, 1988). Chicago (AL), 1913; Indianapolis (F.L.), 1914–1915; Newark (NL), 1915; New York (NL), 1916; Cincinnati (NL), 1916–1926; New York (NL), 1927–1929; Cincinnati

(NL), 1931. Remarks: Had 2,376 hits (67 homers) and 268 stolen bases in 1,967 games in 18 seasons; NL batting champion, 1917 and 1919; led AL in doubles, 1923; led AL in triples, 1924; coach, Cincinnati (NL), 1938; named to Indiana Baseball Hall of Fame, 1979; elected to National Baseball Hall of Fame in 1962, where his plaque reads: "Leading NL batter in 1917 and 1919. Batted .352 in 1921, .352 in 1922, .351 in 1923, .348 in 1924. Batted over .300—12 seasons. Lifetime batting average of .323. Most outfield putouts, 410 in 1920. F.L., 1914–1915."

50243. Allen, Lee, and Thomas Meany. "Edd Roush." In: their *Kings of the Diamond.* New York: G.P. Putnam, 1966. Pp. 185–188.

50244. Dellinger, Susan. "A Shadow in the Night...The Graying of the White: Edd Roush and the 1919 World Series." In: Mark Stang and Dick Miller, eds. *Baseball in the Buckeye State.* Cleveland, OH: Society for American Baseball Research, 2004. Pp. 16–21.

50245. Goldberg, Hy. "Roush Spikes Legend He Was Converted Letty." *Baseball Digest,* XXII (October-November 1963), 52–53.

50246. Green, Paul M. "Baseball and Edd Roush." *Sports Collector's Digest,* X (July 8, 1983), 80+.

50247. Lane, Ferdinand C. "He Played a Lone Hand to the Limit." *Baseball Magazine,* XLVII (August 1931), 395–397.

50248. _____. "The Last of the Great Place Hitters." *Baseball Magazine,* XLIII (October 1929), 493–495.

50249. _____. "Where Originality Counts in Batting." *Baseball Magazine,* XXXIX (August 1927), 397–400.

50250. Miller, Hub. "Reminiscing with Roush." *Baseball Magazine,* LXXIV (February 1946), 301–303+.

50251. Murdock, Eugene. "Edd Roush: 'The Pride of Oakland City.'" In: his *Baseball Between The Wars: Memories of the Game by the Men Who Played It.* Westport, CT: Meckler Publishing, 1992. Pp. 115–155.

50252. Porter, David L. "Edd J. 'Eddie' Roush." In: Vol. Q-Z of David L. Porter, ed. *Biographical Dictionary of American Sports: Baseball.* Rev. and enlarged ed. Westport, CT: Greenwood Press, 2000. Pp. 1319–1321.

50253. Rathgeber, Bob. "A Mean Bat and a Mean Negotiator: Edd Roush." In: his *Cincinnati Reds Scrapbook.* Virginia Beach, VA: J.C.P. Corp. of Virginia, 1982. Pp. 48–51.

50254. Ritter, Lawrence S. "Edd Roush." In: his *Glory of Their Times.* New York: Macmillan, 1966. Pp. 202–214.

50255. _____. and Donald Honig. "Edd Roush." In: *The 100 Greatest Baseball Players of All Time.* New York: Crown Publishers, 1981. Pp. 210–211.

50256. Roush, Edd J. "Edd Roush Looks Back at the Black Sox Scandal: Interview." *World Series Illustrated Review,* I, no. 7 (1962), 24–30.

50257. _____. "How I Won the Batting Crown." *Baseball Magazine,* XXI (June 1918), 295–297.

50258. Sietschier, Steven P. "Edd J. Roush." In: John A. Garrity and Marsh C. Carries, eds. *American National Biography.* 24 vols. New York: Oxford University Press, 1999. XVIII, 955–956.

50259. Smith, Ron. "Edd Roush." In: his *Heroes of the Hall: Baseball's Greatest Players.* New York: Contemporary Books, 2002. Pp. 397–398.

50260. Wayman, Joseph M. "Roush's Ruled-Out Batting Title, 1918." *The Baseball Research Journal,* XXII (1993), 9–10.

50261. _____. "Roush's Ruled-Out Batting Title, 1918: Protested Games (Replayed), Included in Official Records." In: Joseph M. Wayman, ed. *Grandstand Baseball Annual,*

1986. Downey, CA: Joseph M. Wayman, 1986. Pp. 64–67. Reprinted on pp. 124–127 of 1989 *Grandstand Baseball Annual.*

50262. Zinsser, William K. "A Visit to Edd Roush." *American Scholar,* LVIII (Winter 1989), 113–116.

John Charles ("Jack") Rowe
C-MGR. (B: Dec. 8, 1856, Harrisburg, PA-D: April 25, 1911). Buffalo (NL), 1879–1885; Detroit (NL), 1886–1888; Pittsburgh (NL), 1889; Buffalo (P), 1890. Remarks: In 12 years, obtained 1,256 hits (28 homers) and 47 stolen bases in 1,044 games; also played for Lincoln (W.A.), 1891–1892 and Buffalo (EL), 1893; manager, Buffalo (P), 1890, winning 27 games and losing 72 (.273); manager, Buffalo (EL), 1896–1898.

50263. Voigt, David Quentin. "John Charles 'Jack' Rowe." In: Vol. Q-Z of David L. Porter, ed. *Biographical Dictionary of American Sports: Baseball.* Rev. and enlarged ed. Westport, CT: Greenwood Press, 2000. Pp. 1321–1322.

Lynwood Thomas ("Schoolboy") Rowe
P. (B: Jan. 11, 1910, Waco, TX-D: Jan. 8,1961). Detroit (AL), 1933–1942; Brooklyn (NL), 1942; Philadelphia (NL), 1943, 1946–1949. Remarks: In a 15-year pro career, had 158 victories (including 16-in-a-row in 1934), 101 defeats, and a dozen "saves"; lost Games One and Three and won Game Two of 1934 World Series; went 5-for-5 in one game, Aug. 14, 1935; lost Game One of 1935 World Series; had pinch hit grand slam homer, May 2, 1943; career .263 hitter often used in the pinch; coach, Detroit (AL), 1954–1955, and scout, Detroit (AL), 1956–1961.

50264. Bloodgood, Clifford. "Everybody Calls Him 'Schoolboy' Rowe." *Baseball Magazine,* LIII (September 1934), 445–447+.

50265. Davids, L. Robert. "Lynwood Thomas 'Schoolboy' Rowe." In: Vol. Q-Z of David L. Porter, ed. *Biographical Dictionary of American Sports: Baseball.* Rev. and enlarged ed. Westport, CT: Greenwood Press, 2000. Pp. 1322–1323.

50266. Davis, Mac. "Warning — Pitcher to be Murdered." In: his *The Lore and Legends of Baseball.* New York: Lantern Press, 1953. Pp. 196–197. 1934 World Series.

50267. Hofmann, Herbert J. "Schoolboy' Rowe and the 1934 Tigers." *The National Pastime,* XVII (1997), 62–66.

50268. Lane, Ferdinand C. "The Schoolboy Pitcher Who Made Good." *Baseball Magazine,* L (January 1933), 357–358+.

50269. Robinson, Murray. "Schoolie (Rowe) Was a Character." *Baseball Digest,* X (March 1961), 33–35.

50270. Smith, Ira L. "Lynwood Thomas (Schoolboy) Rowe." In: his *Baseball's Famous Pitchers.* New York: A.S. Barnes, 1954. Pp. 256–261.

50271. "Sweat on His Brow." *Time,* XLIX (May 26, 1947), 61–62.

50272. Ward, Charles P. "Anything Can Happen to Schoolboy Rowe." *Baseball Magazine,* LXV (August 1940), 393–395.

50273. _____. "Dean of the Tigers' Pitching Staff." *Baseball Magazine,* LXVII (August 1941), 393–395.

50274. Wolfe, Edgar Forest. "Hillbilly Boy." *Liberty,* XII (May 23, 1935), 63–66.

Schoolboy Rowe *see* **Lynwood Thomas ("Schoolboy") Rowe**

Clarence Henry ("Pants") Rowland
MGR-UMP-EXEC. (B: Feb. 12, 1879, Platteville, WI-D: May 17, 1969). Remarks: Minor league catcher who rose to manage Chicago (AL), 1915–1918, winning 339 games and losing 247 (.578); AL umpire, 1923–1927; scout for Cincinnati (NL), 1929–1930 and Chicago (NL),

1933–1941; minor league official, 1942–1953, including president of Pacific Coast League; vice president, Chicago (N.L), 1954–1955,1959.

50275. Carmichael, John P. "They Said He'd Lost 30 Days." *Baseball Digest,* XIV (March 1955), 95–97.

50276. Crichton, Kyle S. "The Coast Demands Long Pants." *Collier's,* CXX (August 16, 1947), 16–18.

50277. Lane, Ferdinand C. "'Pants' Rowland, the Bush League Manager Who Made Good." *Baseball Magazine,* XX (December 1917), 200–205.

50278. Matz, David S. "Clarence Henry 'Pants' Rowland." In: Vol. Q-Z of David L. Porter, ed. *Biographical Dictionary of American Sports: Baseball.* Rev. and enlarged ed. Westport, CT: Greenwood Press, 2000. Pp. 1323–1324.

50279. Murphy, Joseph P., Jr. "The Busher from Dubuque." *The Baseball Research Journal,* XXIV (1995), 17–22.

50280. Rowland, Clarence H. "How I Became the White Sox Leader." *Baseball Magazine,* XIX (August 1917), 413–415.

Pants Rowland *see* **Clarence H. ("Pants") Rowland**

Jerome Kennis ("Jerry") Royster
3B-2B-SS-OF-MGR. (B: October 18, 1952, Sacramento, CA). Los Angeles (NL), 1973–1975; Atlanta (NL), 1976–1984; San Diego (NL), 1985–1986; Chicago (AL) and New York (AL), 1987; Atlanta (NL), 1988. Remarks: In 16 years, had 1,049 hits (40 homers) and 95 stolen bases in 1,428 games; 1975 PCL Player of the Year; career utility player in big leagues; manager, Kissimmee (Gulf Coast League), 1989; Yakima (Northwest League), 1990; Vero Beach (Florida State League), 1991; and San Antonio (TL), 1992; coach, Colorado (NL), 1993; manager, Las Vegas (PCL), 1996–1998; baserunning and infield coordinator, Montreal (NL), 1999; coach, Milwaukee (NL), 2000–2001; manager, Milwaukee (NL), 2002, winning 53 games and losing 94 (.361); infield coordinator, Los Angeles (NL), 2003–2004; manager, Las Vegas (PCL), 2005–.

50281. Gomez, Paul. "More Than a Day at the [Vero] Beach." *Los Angeles Dodgers Magazine and Scorecard,* IV, no. 4 (1991), 68–69.

50282. Royster, Jerry; as told to George Vass. "The Game I'll Never Forget." *Baseball Digest,* XLIV (May 1985), 55–57.

Jerry Royster *see* **Jerone Kennis ("Jerry") Royster**

David Scott ("Dave") Rozema
P. (B: August 5, 1956, Grand Rapids, MI). Detroit (AL), 1977–1984; Texas (AL), 1985–1986. Remarks: Won 60 games and lost 53, with 17 "saves."

50283. Ludtke, Melissa. "The Rose Has Bloomed." *Sports Illustrated,* XLVII (August 29, 1977), 72–73.

George Napoleon ("Nap") Rucker
P. (B: Sept. 30, 1884, Crabapple, GA-D: Dec. 19, 1970). Brooklyn (NL), 1901–1916. Remarks: Won 135 games and lost 136 with 13 "saves" in a decade; struck out 16 batters in one game, July 22, 1909; pitched first game in Ebbets Field, April 13, 1913; had one no-hitter, Sept. 5, 1908; scout, Brooklyn (NL), 1919–1934, 1939–1940.

50284. Blaisdell , Lowell L. "George Napoleon 'Nap' Rucker." In: Vol. Q-Z of David L. Porter, ed. *Biographical Dictionary of American Sports: Baseball.* Rev. and enlarged ed. Westport, CT: Greenwood Press, 2000. Pp. 1324–1325.

50285. Grayson, Harry. "George (Nap) Rucker." In: his *They Played The Game.* New York: A. S. Barnes, 1944. Pp. 140–142.

50286. _____. "Nap Rucker a $600 Find." *Baseball Digest*, III (March 1944), 49–53.

50287. LeBey, Dave. "How Rucker Won Giants' Respect." *Baseball Digest*, XI (April 1952), 93–99.

50288. Rucker, George N. ("Nap"). "The Biggest Mistake of My Career." *Baseball Magazine*, XIX (June 1917), 314–316.

50289. Stack, C. P. "The Napoleon of Southpaw Pitchers." *Baseball Magazine*, XI (June 1913), 45+.

Nap Rucker *see* **George Napoleon ("Nap") Rucker**

Irving Rudd

WRITER. (B: Oct. 13, 1917, Brooklyn, NY). Remarks: Long-time boxing publicist, later confident of Jackie Robinson (q.v.) and other New York area big league stars; elected to International Boxing Hall of Fame in 1999.

50290. Rudd, Irving. *Sporting Life: The Duke and Jackie, Pee Wee, Razor Phil, Ali, Mushy Jackson, and Me.* New York: St. Martin's Press, 1990.

Joseph Oden ("Joe") Rudi

OF-1B. (B: Sept. 7, 1946, Modesto, CA). Kansas City (AL) and Oakland (AL), 1967–1976; California (AL), 1977–1980; Boston (AL), 1981. Remarks: Had 1,427 hits (174 homers) in 1,476 games in 15 seasons, remembered for homer and heroics in Game Two of the 1972 World Series, his nine hits in the 1973 World Series, and his game-winning homer in Game Seven of the 1974 World Series; hit homer in last AB, Oct. 3, 1982; coach, Oakland (AL), 1986–1987.

50291. Ames, Steve. "Joe Rudi: Oakland's Overlooked Hero." *Baseball Digest*, XXXII (March 1973), 25–29.

50292. Berke, Art. "Joe Rudi." In: his *Unsung Heroes of the Major Leagues*. New York: Random House, 1976. Pp. 11–23.

50293. Elderkin, Phil "Joe Rudi: Oakland's 'Mr. Nobody.'" *Baseball Digest*, XXXIII '(December 1974), 90–92.

50294. Fimrite, Ron. "The Man Who'd Never Bite a Dog." *Sports Illustrated*, XLI (September 2, 1974), 23–24.

50295. Gammons, Peter. "The A's Joe Rudi Underrated No Longer." *Baseball Digest*, XXXIV (September 1975), 29–31.

50296. Green, Paul M. "The A's Dynasty: Joe Rudi Tells All." *Baseball Cards*, VI (June 1986), 82–87.

50297. Hawkins, Jim. "Game No. 2: Rudi's Catch Rates with the Greatest." *Baseball Digest*, XXXII (January 1973), 33–35.

50298. Linderman, Lawrence. "Don't Tell Anyone, but Joe Rudi's Becoming a Star." *Sport*, LIV (October 1972), 72–73.

50299. Robinson, Ray. "Joe Rudi: Mr. Nice Guy." In: Ray Robinson, ed. *Baseball Stars of 1975*. New York: Pyramid Books, 1975. Pp. 99–105.

50300. Rosenberg, Victor. "Joseph Oden 'Joe' Rudi." In: Vol. Q-Z of David L. Porter, ed. *Biographical Dictionary of American Sports: Baseball*. Rev. and enlarged ed. Westport, CT: Greenwood Press, 2000. Pp. 1325–1326.

50301. Rudi, Joseph O., as told to George Vass. "The Game I'll Never Forget." *Baseball Digest*, XLII (August 1993), 62–64.

Dick Rudolph *see* **Richard ("Dick" or "Baldy") Rudolph**

Frederick Donald ("Don") Rudolph

P. (B: Aug. 16, 1931, Baltimore, MD-D: Sept. 12, 1968). Chicago (AL), 1957–1959; Cincinnati (NL), 1959; Cleveland (A.L), 1962; Washington (AL), 1962–1964. Remarks: Won 18 games and lost 32 in six years; married striptease artist Patti Waggon; died of injuries in a California automobile accident.

50302. Fox, Larry. "Game's Fastest Pitcher?: He's a Slow-Baller." *Baseball Digest*, XXII (May 1963), 35–39.

Richard ("Dick" or "Baldy") Rudolph

P. (B: August 25, 1887, New York City-D: Oct. 20, 1949). New York (NL), 1910–1911; Boston (NL), 1913–1923, 1927. Remarks: Won 121 games and lost 108, with eight "saves" in 13 years; spitball pitcher who won 27 regular season and two World Series contests for the 1914 "Miracle" Boston Braves; coach, Boston (NL), 1921–1927; upon retirement from baseball, became a mortician.

50303. Lane, Ferdinand C. "Dick Rudolph, Pennant Winner." *Baseball Magazine*, XIV (February 1915), 37–42.

50304. Rudolph, Dick. "Is Pitching a Regular Job?" *Baseball Magazine*, XXI (May 1918),159–160.

50305. Spatz, Lyle. "Richard 'Dick,' 'Baldy' Rudolph." In: Vol. Q-Z of David L. Porter, ed. *Biographical Dictionary of American Sports: Baseball*. Rev. and enlarged ed. Westport, CT: Greenwood Press, 2000. Pp. 1326–1327.

Harold Dominic ("Muddy") Ruel

C-MGR. (B: Feb. 20, 1896, St. Louis, MO-D: Nov. 13, 1963). St. Louis (AL), 1915; New York (AL), 1917–1920; Boston (AL), 1921–1922; Washington (AL), 1923–1930; Boston (AL), 1931; Detroit (AL), 1931–1932; St. Louis (AL), 1933; Chicago (AL), 1934. Remarks: Obtained 1,242 hits (four homers) and 61 stolen bases in 1,461 games in 19 seasons; battery mate of Walter Johnson (q.v.); scored winning run of 1924 World Series; became a lawyer; admitted to practice before the U.S. Supreme Court, 1929; asst. to Baseball Commission Albert B. ("Happy") Chandler (q.v.), 1946; manager, SL Louis (AL), 1947, winning 59 games and losing 95 (.383); coach, Chicago (AL), 1936–1945 and Cleveland (AL), 1948–1950; farm club director, Cleveland (AL) 1951 and Detroit (AL), 1952–1953; GM, Detroit (AL), 1954–1956.

50306. Hilton, George W. "Harold Dominic 'Muddy' Ruel." In: Vol. Q-Z of David L. Porter, ed. *Biographical Dictionary of American Sports: Baseball*. Rev. and enlarged ed. Westport, CT: Greenwood Press, 2000. Pp. 1327–1328.

50307. Hirshberg, Al. "Muddy Ruel." In: his *Baseball's Greatest Catchers*. New York: G. P. Putnam, 1969. Pp. 61–69.

50308. Lane, Ferdinand C. "The Extraordinary Career of Muddy Ruel." *Baseball Magazine*, XXXIII (July 1924), 359–361.

50309. Lewis, Franklin. "Tigers Under New Farm Ruel." *Baseball Digest*, XI (January 1962), 61–63. Ruel completed his career as director of the Detroit (AL), minor league system.

50310. _____. "Remade by Ruel." *Baseball Digest*, III (1944), 11–15.

50311. Ruel, Harold ("Muddy"). "Advice to a Young Hurler." *Baseball Digest*, IV (July 1945), 37–41.

50312. _____. "Muddy Ruel of Washington." *Baseball Magazine*, XXXVI (May 1926), 554–555.

50313. _____. "A Player Who Works in the Dark." *Baseball Magazine*, XLII (February 1929), 399–408.

50314. Simons, Herbert. "The First Ruel of Baseball." *Baseball Magazine*, LXIX (July 1942), 341–343.

50315. Stann, Francis, "Muddy — but Stylish." *Baseball Digest*, XXIII (February 1964), 57–59.

50316. Veech, Ellis J. "Ruel-ing the Browns." *Baseball Magazine*, LXXVIII (December 1946), 233–235.

Muddy Ruel *see* **Herold Dominic ("Muddy") Ruel**

Kirk Wesley Rueter

P. (B: December 1, 1970, Hoyleton, IL). Montreal (NL), 1993–1996; San Francisco (NL), 1996–. Remarks:

Through 2004, has won 128 games and lost 85; tied a MLB record by starting his career with 10 straight wins; won one game of 2002 NLCS.

50317. Peck, Burton L., 4th. "Rookie Report: Kirk Rueter." *Beckett Baseball Card Monthly,* XI, no. 106 (January 1994), 126–127.

Walter Henry ("Dutch") Reuther
P-MGR. (B: Sept. 13, 1893, Alameda, CA-D: May 16, 1970). Chicago (NL), 1917; Cincinnati (NL), 1917–1920; Brooklyn (NL), 1921–1924; Washington (AL), 1925–1926; New York (AL), 1926–1927. Remarks: Had 127 victories and 95 defeats, with eight "saves," in 11 years; won Game One of 1919 World Series.

50318. Matz, David S. "Walter Henry 'Dutch' Reuther." In: Vol. Q-Z of David L. Porter, ed. *Biographical Dictionary of American Sports: Baseball.* Rev. and enlarged ed. Westport, CT: Greenwood Press, 2000. Pp. 1328–1329.

Joseph ("Joe") Rue
UMP. (B: 1897–D: 1984). Remarks: AL arbiter, 1938–1947.

50319. Gerlach, Larry R. "Joe Rue." In: his *The Men in Blue: Conversations with Umpires.* New York: Viking Press, 1980. Pp. 51–74. Reprinted by the University of Nebraska Press in 1994.

Bruce Wayne Ruffin
P. (B: October 4, 1963, Lubbock, TX). Philadelphia(NL), 1986–1991; Milwaukee (AL), 1992; Colorado (NL), 1993–1997. Remarks: In 12 years, won 60 games and lost 82, with 63 "saves"; career plagued by wildness.

50320. Finocchiaro, Ray. "Phillies' Bruce Ruffin Wants to Prove '86 was for Real." *Baseball Digest,* XLVI (June 1987), 27–30.

Charles Herbert ("Red") Ruffing ★
P. (B: May 3, 1904, Granville, IL-D: Feb. 17, 1986). Boston (AL), 1924–1930; New York (AL), 1930–1941, 1945–1946; Chicago (AL), 1947. Remarks: Had 273 victories, 225 defeats, and 16 "saves" in a 22-year playing career; led AL in losses, 1928–1929; between 1932 and 1942, won seven World Series games and lost two; pitched 52 shutouts; but also gave up Ted Williams' first major league hit; good batsman with career total 36 homers and 521 hits; minor league instructor/coach/scout, Chicago (AL), Cleveland (AL), and New York (NL), 1948–1973; elected to National Baseball Hall of Fame in 1967, where his plaque reads: "Winner of 273 games. Won 20 or more games in each of four consecutive seasons. Led in complete games 1929. Tied in shutouts 1938–1939. Won 7 out of 9 World Series decisions. Selected for All-Star teams 1937–1939–1939."

50321. Allen, Maury. "Red Ruffing (1924–1947)." In: his *Baseball's 100.* New York: Galahad Books, 1981. Pp. 259–261.

50322. Bulkley, George. "The Master Slinger." *Baseball Magazine,* LXII (March 1939), 463–465+.

50323. Davis, Mac. "The Lost Four Toes." In: his *The Lore and Legends of Baseball.* New York: Lantern Press, 1953. Pp. 133–134.

50324. Green, Paul M. "Red Ruffing." *Sports Collector's Digest,* XI (September 28, 1984), 114–116.

50325. Hickey, David and Kerry Keene. "Red Ruffing." In: their *The Proudest Yankees of All: From the Bronx to Cooperstown.* Lanham, MD: Taylor Trade Pub., dist. by National Book Network, 2003. Chapter 23.

50326. Klima, John. "Don't Forget the Duel: Red Ruffing vs. Thornton Lee (July 13, 1941)." In: his *Pitched Battle: 35 of Baseball's Greatest Duels from the Mound.* Jefferson, NC: McFarland & Co., Inc., 2002. Pp. 68–71.

50327. Lebovitz, Hal "A Trip Down Memory Lane with Red Ruffing." *Baseball Digest,* XLII (February 1963), 79–84.

50328. McAuley, Ed. "'Cold' Ruffing a 'Warm' Coach." *Baseball Digest,* X (June 1951), 62–63.

50329. McMillan, Ken. "Red Ruffing." In: his *Tales from the Yankee Dugout: A Collection of the Greatest Yankee Stories Ever Told.* Champaign, IL: Sports Publishing, Inc., 2001. Pp. 155–156.

50330. Miller, William J. "Red Ruffing." In: John A. Garrity and Marsh C. Carries, eds. *American National Biography.* 24 vols. New York: Oxford University Press, 1999. XIX, 46–47.

50331. Richman, Milton. "Red Ruffing was a Winner on the Mound and at Bat." *Baseball Digest,* XLV (August 1986), 75–78.

50332. Robinson, Ray. "Red Ruffing: The Pitcher Who Could Hit." In: his *Greatest Yankees of Them All.* New York: G.P. Putnam's Sons, 1969. Pp. 39–50.

50333. Shane, Ted. "Big Red." *American Magazine,* CXXVIII (August 1939), 44–47.

50334. Shecter, Leonard. "Ruffing Reveals He Won 273 with Sore Arm." *Baseball Digest,* XXI (August 1962), 33–35.

50335. Simpson, Douglas G. "Charles Herbert 'Red' Ruffing." In: Vol. Q-Z of David L. Porter, ed. *Biographical Dictionary of American Sports: Baseball.* Rev. and enlarged ed. Westport, CT: Greenwood Press, 2000. Pp. 1329–1330.

50336. Smith, Ira L. "Charles Herbert (Red) Ruffing." In: his *Baseball's Famous Pitchers.* New York: A.S. Barnes, 1954. Pp. 182–186.

50337. Smith, Ron. "Red Ruffing." In: his *Heroes of the Hall: Baseball's Greatest Players.* New York: Contemporary Books, 2002. Pp. 399–400.

50338. Stanley, Frank. "As Good as He Has to Be: The Story of Red Ruffing, Pinch Pitcher." *Saturday Evening Post,* CCXII (March 16, 1940), 37–43.

Red Ruffing *see* **Charles Herbert ("Red") Ruffing**
Chico Ruiz *see* **Hiraldo Sablon ("Chico") Ruiz**
Hiraldo Sablon ("Chico") Ruiz
2B-3B-SS-1B. (B: Dec. 12, 1938, Santo Domingo, Cuba-D: Feb. 9, 1972). Cincinnati (NL), 1964–1969, California (AL), 1970–1971. Remarks: Had 276 hits (two homers) and 34 stolen bases in 566 games in eight utility years, killed in automobile accident in San Diego.

50339. Katz, Fred. "Chico's Starring Role." *Sport,* XLIV (November 1967), 10–11.

50340. Ronberg, Gary. "The Bottom Part of the Lineup." *Sports Illustrated,* XXXI (August 25, 1969), 30–32+.

50341. Smith, Gary. "Don't Do It, Chico! No, No!: Red's Chico Ruiz Stuns Phillies by Stealing Home." *Sports Illustrated,* XCI (November 29, 1999), 94–95. On September 21, 1964.

50342. Stainback, Berry. "Oh, to Steal First." *Sport,* XXXVII (August 1964), 6–7.

Edward ("Ed") Runchey
UMP. Remarks: NCAA college umpire and regional umpire evaluator; international baseball umpire.

50343. Runchey, Dick. "Interview." *Referee,* XIX (April 1994), 72+.

Edward ("Ed") Runge
UMP (B: 1918–D: July 25, 2002). Remarks: AL arbiter, 1954–1970; right field umpire for Don Larsen's perfect game in 1956 World Series.

50344. Richman, Arthur. "Confessions of an Umpire:

Ed Runge." In: Zander Hollander, ed. *Baseball Yearbook, 1964.* New York: Popular Library, 1964. Pp. 8–9+.

50345. _____. "It's Top Rung for Runge." *Baseball Digest,* XXIII (February 1964), 43–45.

50346. Skipper, John C. "Ed Runge." In: his *Umpires: Classic Stories from the Men Who Made the Calls.* Jefferson, NC: McFarland & Co., Inc., 1997. Pp. 103–107.

James Edward ("Pete") Runnels
1B-2B-SS-MGR. (B: Jan. 28, 1929, Lufkin, TX-D: May 20, 1991). Washington (AL), 1951–1957; Boston (AL), 1958–1962; Houston (NL), 1963–1964. Remarks. Obtained 1,854 hits (49 homers) and 37 stolen bases in 1,799 games in 14 years; walked twice in the same inning, Aug. 14, 1959; had nine hits in a doubleheader, Aug. 30, 1960; AL batting champion, 1960 and 1962; had homer in 1962 All Star Game; coach, Boston (AL), 1965–1966 and interim manager, Boston (AL), 1966, winning eight games and losing eight (.500); elected to Texas Sports Hall of Fame, 1982; named to Boston Red Sox Hall of Fame, Nov. 2004.

50347. Evers, John L. "James Edward 'Pete' Runnels." In: Vol. Q-Z of David L. Porter, ed. *Biographical Dictionary of American Sports: Baseball.* Rev. and enlarged ed. Westport, CT: Greenwood Press, 2000. Pp. 1331–1332.

50348. Greene, Paul M. "Pete Runnels: Interview." *Sports Collector's Digest,* XII (August 16, 1985), 112–113, 117, 120–134.

50349. Greene, Sam. "Pete Runnels, the Champion Nobody Knows." *Baseball Digest,* XXII (February 1963), 31–35.

50350. Hirshberg, Al. "Pete Runnels: The Champ Nobody Wanted." In: Ray Robinson, ed. *Baseball Stars of 1963.* New York: Pyramid Books, 1963. Pp. 10–15.

50351. _____. "Secrets of a Batting Champion." *Saturday Evening Post,* CCXXXIV (April 22, 1961), 30, 113–114.

50352. Hurwitz, Hy. "Pete Runnels: He Sets the Table for the Red Sox." *Baseball Digest,* XVII (September 1958), 53–57.

50353. Kamm, Herb. "Pete Runnels." In: Jack Orr, ed. *Baseball's Greatest Players Today.* New York: Watts, 1963. pp. 137–143.

50354. Klein, Larry. "The Rap Against Runnels." *Sport,* XXXI (June 1961), 44–48.

50355. Linthicum, Jim. "Pete Runnels: The Inside Story." *Baseball Magazine,* LXXXI (June 1955), 16–17+.

50356. Povich, Shirley. "Singular Cleanup Hitter." *Baseball Digest,,* XII (February 1963), 13–15.

50357. _____. "The Runnels Kid." *Complete Baseball,* V (July 1953), 48–49+.

50358. Robinson, Ray. "Pete Runnels: Bosox Bat Champ." In: Ray Robinson, ed. *Baseball Stars of 1961.* New York: Pyramid Books, 1961. Pp. 81–86.

50359. Runnels, James L ("Pete"), as told to Al Hirshberg. "Secrets of a Batting Champion." *Saturday Evening Post,* CCXXXIV (April 22, 1961), 30+.

50360. Whittlesey, Merrell. "Runnels Still Has That Base-Hit Stroke." *Baseball Digest,* XXI (November-December 1962), 63–67.

Alfred Damon Runyon
WRITER. (B: Oct. 3, 1880, Manhattan, KA-D: Dec. 10, 1946). Remarks: Noted literary figure who covered New York (NL) for the *New York American,* 1911–1920; friend of Christy Mathewson (q.v.) and George Herman ("Babe") Ruth (q.v.); J. G. Taylor Spink Award, 1967.

50361. Breslin, Jimmy. *Damon Runyon.* New York: Ticknor & Fields, 1991.

50362. Clark, Tom. *The World of Damon Runyon.* New York: Harper & Row, 1978.

50363. Grant, Thomas. "Damon Runyon." In: Stanley Trachtenberg, ed. *Dictionary of Literary Biography, Volume 11: American Humorists, 1800–1950.* A Bruccoli Clark Layman Book. Detroit, MI: The Gale Group, 1982. Pp. 419–429.

50364. Runyan, Damon. "One Down, 713 to Go." In: Jeff Silverman, ed. *Classic Baseball Stories.* Guilford, CT: Lyons Press, 2003. Chapter 14.

50365. Runyon, Damon, Jr. *Father's Footsteps.* New York: Random House, 1954.

50366. Sandin, Paul J. "Damon Runyon." In: Richard Orodenker, ed. *Dictionary of Literary Biography, Volume 171: Twentieth-Century American Sportswriters.* A Bruccoli Clark Layman Book. Detroit, MI: The Gale Group, 1996. Pp. 293–303.

50367. Schwarz, Daniel R. *Broadway Boogie Woogie: Damon Runyon and the Making of New York City Culture.* New York: Palgrave Macmillan, 2003. 346p.

50368. Szuberla, Guy. "Damon Runyon." In: Bobby Ellen Kimbel, ed. *Dictionary of Literary Biography, Volume 86: American Short-Story Writers, 1910–1945, First Series.* A Bruccoli Clark Layman Book. Detroit, MI: The Gale Group, 1989. Pp. 234–251.

50369. Weiner, Ed. *The Damon Runyon Story.* New York, London & Toronto: Longmans, Green, 1948.

Jacob ("Jake" or "Colonel") Ruppert, Jr.
EXEC. (B: Aug. 5, 1867, New York City-D: Jan. 13, 1939). Remarks: President, New York (AL), 1915–1939.

50370. Crepeau, Richard C. "Jacob Ruppert." In: John A. Garrity and Marsh C. Carries, eds. *American National Biography.* 24 vols. New York: Oxford University Press, 1999. XIX, 70–71.

50371. Jones, Robert E. "Jacob 'Colonel' Rupert, Jr." In: Vol. Q-Z of David L. Porter, ed. *Biographical Dictionary of American Sports: Baseball.* Rev. and enlarged ed. Westport, CT: Greenwood Press, 2000. Pp. 1334–1335.

50372. Ruppert, Jacob ("Jake"). "Building a Winning Baseball Club." In: Sidney Offit, ed. *Best of Baseball.* New York: G.P. Putnam, 1956. Pp. 42–49. Reprinted from the June 1918 issue of *Baseball Magazine.*

Bob Rush see **Robert Ransom ("Bob") Rush**
Robert Ransom ("Bob") Rush
P. (B: Dec. 25, 1925, Battle Creek, MI). Chicago (NL), 1948–1957; Milwaukee (NL), 1958–1960; Chicago (AL), 1960. Remarks: Won 127 games and lost 152 in 13 campaigns; in 1952, had seven-game winning streak and was winning pitcher of the All-Star Game.

50373. Bloodgood, Clifford. "Rush of the Cubs." *Baseball Magazine,* LXXXIII November 1949), 415–417.

50374. Munzel, Edgar. "Windy City Win-Mill." In: Bruce Jacobs, ed. *Baseball Stars of 1953.* New York: Lion Books, 1953. Pp. 59–64.

50375. Westcott, Rich. "Bob Rush: Few Were Tougher or More Durable." In: his *Splendor on the Diamond: Interviews with 35 Stars of Baseball's Past.* Gainesville, FL: The University Press of Florida, 2000. Pp. 246–254.

50376. Wilbert, Warren and William Hageman. "Bob Rush—1952." In: their *Chicago Cubs: Seasons at the Summit, the 50 Greatest Individual Seasons.* Champaign, IL: Sagamore Publishing, 1997. Pp. 99–102.

Amos Wilson ("The Hoosier Thunderbolt") Rusie★
P. (B: May 30, 1871, Mooresville, IN-D: Dec. 6, 1942). Indianapolis (NL), 1889; New York (NL), 1890–1898; Cincinnati (NL), 1901. Remarks: Had 243 victories, 160 defeats, and five "saves" in a decade, giving up 1,716 walks in the process; had one no hitter, July 31, 1891; good hitter with 427 hits (eight homers) and 25 stolen bases,

served as superintendent of the Polo Grounds in New York, 1921–1928; named to Indiana Baseball Hall of Fame, 1979; elected to National Baseball Hall of Fame in 1977, where his plaque reads: "Generally considered fireball king of Nineteenth-Century moundsmen. Notched better than 240 victories in ten-year career. Achieved 30-victory mark four years in row and won 20 or more games eight successive times. Led league in strikeouts five years and led or tied for most shutouts five times."

50377. Eichmann, J. K. "Amos Rusie: The Hoosier Thunderbolt." *Sports Scoup*, II (June 1974), 10+. Ralph Berger's profile is a number in the online SABR Biography Project < http://bioproj.sabr.org/bioproj.cfm?a=v&v=l&bid=497&pid=12333>.

50378. Hawkins, Burton. "Rusie Was Daddy of Fireballers." *Baseball Digest*, II (March 1943), 17–19. Reprinted in John Kuenster, ed., *From Cobb to Catfish* (Chicago, IL: Rand McNally, 1975), p. 142.

50379. Johnson, Rich. "Amos Rusie — The World's Greatest Pitcher: Reprinted from the *Indianapolis Star-Magazine*, October 21, 1973." *Congressional Record*, CXIX (November 12, 1973), 36657–36660.

50380. Linthurst, Randy. "When Rusie Opposed Kid Nichols." *The Baseball Research Journal*, V (1976), 112–114.

50381. Merrell, David B. "Amos Wilson 'The Hoosier Thunderbolt' Rusie." In: Vol. Q–Z of David L. Porter, ed. *Biographical Dictionary of American Sports: Baseball.* Rev. and enlarged ed. Westport, CT: Greenwood Press, 2000. Pp. 1333–1335.

50382. Puff, Richard. "Amos Wilson Rusie." In: Frederick Ivor-Campbell, ed. *Baseball's First Stars.* Cleveland, OH: Society for American Baseball Research, 1996. Pp. 143–144.

50383. Salsinger, H.G. "All This — and Rusie-for $75,000." *Baseball Digest*, III (July 1944), 7–9.

50384. Seiken, Jeff. "Amos Wilson Rusie." In: John A. Garrity and Marsh C. Carries, eds. *American National Biography.* 24 vols. New York: Oxford University Press, 1999. XIX, 80–81.

50385. Smith, Ira L. "Amos Wilson Rusie." In: his *Baseball's Famous Pitchers.* New York: A.S. Barnes, 1954. Pp. 14–18.

50386. Smith, Robert H. "Amos Wilson Rusie: The Indiana Thunderbolt." In: his *Heroes of Baseball.* Cleveland, OH: World Publishing Co., 1952. Pp. 161–165.

50387. Wayman, Joseph M. "Amos Wilson Rusie: 19th-Century Fireball Ace." In: Joseph M. Wayman, ed. *Grandstand Baseball Annual, 1994.* Downey, CA: Joseph M. Wayman, 1994. Pp. 48–50.

50388. _____. "Amos Wilson Rusie: 19th Century Pitching Ace." In: Joseph M. Wayman, ed. *Grandstand Baseball Annual Pitching W-L Records NL 1890–1899.* Downey, CA: Joseph M. Wayman, 1996. Pp. 41–43.

Allen H. Russell
EXEC. (B: 1911–D: 1991). Remarks: Executive/owner, Milwaukee (NL), St. Louis (NL), Houston (TL), Beaumont (TL), Austin (TL), Dallas (TL), Beaumont (TL) and Fort Worth (TL).

50389. Russell, Allen H. *Touching All Bases!: The Autobiography of Allen H. Russell.* Houston, TX: Gulf Publishing Co., 1990. 105p.

Bill Russell *see* **William Ellis ("Bill") Russell**
Ewell Albert ("Reb") Russell
P–OF. (B: April 12, 1889, Jackson, MS–D: Sept. 30, 1973). Chicago (AL), 1913–1919; Pittsburgh (NL), 1922–1923. Remarks: In his nine pro years, Russell pitched for the White Sox and played outfield for the Pirates; as a

pitcher, won 74 games and lost 60 with 15 "saves" and as a hitter obtained 262 career hits (21 homers) in 417 games; out of baseball 1920–1921.

50390. Russell, Ewell A. ("Reb"). "How I Got My Chance." *Baseball Magazine*, XX (December 1917), 223–224.

Frederick ("Fred") Russell
WRITER. (B: 1906, Nashville, TN). Remarks: Reporter/sports editor, *Nashville Banner*, 1929–1998.

50391. Wilson, Nick. "Fred Russell." In: his *Voices from the Pastime: Oral Histories of Surviving Major Leaguers, Negro Leaguers, Cuban Leaguers, and Writers, 1920–1934.* Jefferson, NC: McFarland & Co., Inc., 2000. Pp. 167–170.

Jack Erwin Russell
P. (B: Oct. 24, 1905, Paris, TX–D: Nov. 3, 1990). Boston (AL), 1926–1932; Cleveland (AL), 1932; Washington (AL), 1933–1936; Boston (AL), 1936; Detroit (A.L), 1937; Chicago (NL), 1938–1939; St. Louis (NL), 1940. Remarks: In 15 years, won 85 games and lost 141, with 38 "saves"; first AL relief pitcher named to an All-Star team.

50392. Westcott, Rich. "Jack Russell — Standout Relief Pitcher." In: his *Diamond Greats.* Westport, CT: Meckler Books, 1988. Pp. 111–115.

Reb Russell *see* **Ewell Albert ("Reb") Russell**
William Ellis ("Bill" or "Ropes") Russell
SS–OF. (B: Oct. 21, 1948, Pittsburgh, KS). Los Angeles (NL), 1969–1986. Remarks: Had 1,926 hits (46 homers) and 167 stolen bases in 2,181 games in 18 seasons; coach, Los Angeles (NL), 1986–1991, 1994–1996; manager, Albuquerque (PCL), 1992–1993; manager, Los Angeles (NL), 1996–1998, winning 173 games and losing 149 (.537); coach, Tampa Bay (AL), 2000–.

50393. Bennett, Gaymon L. "William Ellis 'Bill,' 'Ropes' Russell." In: Vol. Q–Z of David L. Porter, ed. *Biographical Dictionary of American Sports: Baseball.* Rev. and enlarged ed. Westport, CT: Greenwood Press, 2000. Pp. 1335–1336.

50394. Delliquanti, Dom. "Bill Russell." In: his *Baseball: The New Champions.* New York: Platt & Munk, 1973. Pp. 30–33.

50395. Hill, Terry. "Bill Russell: 'A Dodger for 16 Years.'" In: his *Batting a Thousand.* Nashville, TN: Thomas Nelson, 1987. Pp. 50–53.

50396. Holmes, Tot. "Russell Did Exceptional Job." *Dodgers Dugout*, XI (October 15, 1996), 13–14.

50397. Malamud, Alan. "How a Crucial Error Turned It Around for Bill Russell." *Baseball Digest*, XXXVI (July 1977), 54–55.

50398. Reid, Jason. "The Pressure's On." *Dodgers Dugout*, XIII (May 30, 1998), 3–4.

50399. Russell, William E. ("Bill"), as told to George Vass. "The Game I'll Never Forget." *Baseball Digest*, XLIII (August 1984), 83–86.

50400. Zwikel, Tony. "Bill Russell: A Year of Firsts." In: Bill Shumard, ed. *1981 Los Angeles Dodgers Yearbook.* Anaheim, CA" Rotary Off-Set Printers, 1981. p. 47.

Jim Russo
SCOUT. (B: 1923–D: February 8, 2004). Remarks: Scout, St. Louis (AL), 1952–1954; scout, Baltimore (AL), 1954–1987.

50401. Russo, Jim, with Bob Hammel. *Super Scout: 35 Years of Major League Scouting with the Baltimore Orioles.* Chicago, IL: Bonus Books, 192. 230p.

Marius Ugo ("Lefty") Russo
P. (B: July 19, 1914, Brooklyn, NY–D: March 26, 2005). New York (AL), 1939–1943, 1946. Remarks: Won 45 games and lost 34, with five "saves"; had greatest successes in World Series of 1941 and 1943.

50402. Gallagher, Mark. "Marius Russo." In: his *50 Years of Yankee All-Stars*. New York: Leisure Press, 1984. Pp. 181–182.

50403. Russo, Marius. "How to Pitch." *Look*, VI (May 5, 1942), 62–65.

Arthur ("Art") Rust, Jr.
WRITER. Remarks: Sportscaster and sports historian, columnist for Amsterdam News and New York Daily News; broadcaster for NBC-TV and WMCA and WINS radio; host of 10-year *Sportstalk* show on WABC, 1980s; author of numerous sports books and articles, many of which are cited herein.

50404. Rust, Art, Jr. *Recollections of a Baseball Junkie*. New York: William Morrow, 1984. 168p. The then-host of WABC's *Sports Talk* show comments on baseball stars, power brokers, and eccentric fans.

George Herman ("Babe" or "The Bambino" or "The Sultan of Swat") Ruth, Jr. ★
P-OF. (B: Feb. 6, 1895, Baltimore, MD-D: Aug. 16, 1948). Boston (AL), 1914–1919; New York (AL), 1920–1934; Boston (NL), 1935. Remarks: The most famous athlete of his era or perhaps any, had 2,873 hits (714 homers-long first, but now second in total after Henry Aaron), 506 doubles, 136 triples, scored 2,174 runs, was walked 2,056 times, had 2,204 RBI's, a career batting average of .342, the highest slugging pct. ever, .490 — and struck out 1,330 times; pitched 1121.1 Innings (163 games) in ten years, winning 94 contests and losing 46 with four "saves"; had 29 consecutive scoreless innings in his Boston World Series appearances, winning the 14-inning Game Four in 1916 (a record for the longest World Series complete game which still stands) and Games One and Four of the 1918 classic; played for Providence (IL), 1914; won 23 games in 1916 and 24 in 1917; had four consecutive homers in a game, June 25, 1918; led AL in strikeouts, 1918, 1923–1924, 1927–1928; had four grand slam homers in one year, 1919; starred in a motion picture, *Heading Home*, which opened on Sept. 19, 1920; first player to hit 30+ homers (54) in a season, 1920; suspended first six weeks of 1922 season by Commissioner Kenesaw Mountain Landis (q.v.) for participation in an illegal barnstorming tour; AL MVP award, 1923; AL home run champion, 1918 (tie), 1921, 1923–1924, 1926–1931 (tie); first player to receive a $50,000 annual salary, March 1922; AL batting champion, 1924; AL RBI champion, 1919–1921, 1923, 1926, and 1928 (tie); caught stealing to end 1926 World Series; first batter to hit four homers in a World Series, 1926; stole home plate, June 19, 1927; hit grand slam homers in consecutive games twice, Sept. 27 and 29, 1927 and Aug. 6–7, 1929; first big league player to hit 60 homers in a season, 1927; hit first homer in All Star Game competition, 1934; coach, Brooklyn (NL), 1938; had 16 career grand slam homers; also established dozens of other records, many of which still stand (for a full list, *see* the latest edition of *The Sporting News Official Record Book*); largely responsible for taking the game out of the "dead ball" era and almost single-handedly making it truly a national pastime, Ruth coached for Brooklyn (NL) in 1938 and died ten years later, a victim of cancer; first baseball player on a U.S. postage stamp, May 1998; elected to the National Baseball Hall of Fame in 1936, where his plaque reads: "Greatest drawing card in history of baseball. Holder of many home run and other batting records. Gathered 714 home runs in addition to fifteen in World Series."

50405. Addle, Bob. "Babe Ruth's Home Run on an Infield Fly." *Baseball Digest*, XVII (June 1958), 89–91.

50406. Addington, L.H. "We Shall Not *See* His Like Again." *Baseball Magazine*, LXXIX (October 1947), 381–382.

50407. Adomites, Paul and Saul Wisnia. *Babe Ruth: His Life and Times*. Lincolnwood, IL: Publications International, Ltd., 1995. 240p.

50408. Ahern, Matyt. "Pride of the Party Boat." *Outdoor Life*, CXCIV (December 1994), 70–72. Meeting between L. Gehrig and B. Ruth while cod fishing off Sea Bright, NJ

50409. Akasaka, Kaneo. *Babe Ruth*. Tokyo, Japan: Popurasha, 1969. 174p. In Japanese.

50410. Albelli, A.A. "Babe Ruth's Home Run Secrets." *Popular Mechanics*, LXIX (March 1928), 370–374.

50411. Alcorn, Sam. "The Sultan of Swat." *Travel-Holiday*, CLXIX (February 1988), 102+.

50412. Allen, Bob, with Bill Gilbert. "Babe Ruth: The Greatest of Them All?" In: their *The 500 Home Run Club: Baseball's 15 Greatest Hitters from Aaron to Williams*. Champaign, IL: Sports Publishing, 1999. Pp. 213–231.

50413. Allen, Lee. *Babe Ruth: His Story in Baseball*. New York: G.P. Putnam, 1966. 189p.

50414. _____. "The Untold Story of Babe Ruth's Early Life." *Baseball Digest*, XI (May 1962), 36–42.

50415. _____. and Thomas Meany. "Babe Ruth." In: their *Kings of the Diamond*. New York: G.P. Putnam, 1965. Pp. 201–207.

50416. Altman, L.K. "The Babe's Other Record: Cancer Pioneer." *The New York Times Biographical Service*, XXIX (December 1998), 2120–2122.

50417. *Aramco World*, editors of. "Please Babe, One More." *Baseball Digest*, XVIII (August 1959), 51–55.

50418. Ardolino, Frank. "Babe's Banyan Tree Grows in Hawaii." *The National Pastime*, XVIII (1998), 62–63.

50419. _____. "Born is the Savior of Baseball: Babe Ruth as Christ-Figure in *The Babe Ruth Story."* *Aethlon: The Journal of Sport Literature*, XII (Spring 1995), 87–93.

50420. _____. "From Christ-Like Folk Hero to Bumbling Bacchus: Filmic Images of Babe Ruth, 1920–1992." In: Stephen C. Wood and J. David Pincus, eds. *Reel Baseball: Essays and Interviews on the National Pastime, Hollywood, and American Culture* (Jefferson, NC: McFarland & Co., Inc., 2003. Pp. 107–119.

50421. Aron, Paul. "Did the Babe Call His Shot?" In: his *Unsolved Mysteries of American History: An Eye-Opening Journey Through 500 years of Discoveries, Disappearances, and Baffling Events*. New York : John Wiley, 1997. Chapter 20.

50422. Babbitt, John S. "Babe Ruth is Still Popular with Topical Collectors." *Stamps*, CCLI (April 1, 1995), 1–2. On the postage stamp issued February 6, 1995 to mark his 100th birthday.

50423. "The Babe, Even at 100, is Still a Major Draw." *The New York Times Biographical Service*, XXVI (February 1995), 186–187.

50424. "Babe Ruth." In: *Current Biography Yearbook, 1944*. New York. H.W. Wilson Co., 1944. Pp. 571–575.

50425. *Babe Ruth*. North Mankato, MN: Capstone Press, 1989. 48p.

50426. *Babe Ruth*. West Haven, CT: Academic Industries, 1984. 54p. Written for adult literacy programs.

50427. "Babe Ruth." In: Joseph J. Vecchione, ed. *The New York Times Book of Sports Legends*. New York: Times Books, 1991. Pp. 288–305.

50428. "Babe Ruth is Supernormal, Hence the Homers." *Literary Digest*, LXX (October 1, 1921), 40–43.

50429. "Babe" Ruth Star of Century of Progress Game." *Newsweek*, I (July 15, 1933), 17–18.

50430. "The Babe Ruth Story." *Life*, LII (August 31, 1948), 46+. Illustrated.

50431. "Babe Ruth: 'The Sultan of Swat' was the Greatest Baseball Player Who Ever Lived." *Sports Illustrated for Kids*, XI (January 1, 1999), 58+.

50432. "Babe Ruth's Batting Record as a Pitcher." *Baseball Digest*, XXXIX (August 1980), 15.

50433. "Babe Ruth's 44-hp [horse-power] Swats, as Analyzed by Science." *Literary Digest*, LX (March 8, 1919), 88–93.

50434. "Babe Ruth's 60 Homers: The Record with Pictures." *Baseball Magazine*, LXXXIX (September 1952), 26–28.

50435. "Babe Ruth's 100th Anniversary." In: Gregg Mazzola, ed. *Yankees 1995 Yearbook*. New York: *Yankees Magazine*, 1995. Pp. 16–29.

50436. "Babe Ruth's $210,000 for Three Years of Swat." *Literary Digest*, XCII (March 19, 1927), 61–64.

50437. "The Babe's Big Effort to Come Back." *Literary Digest*, XC (July 31, 1926), 46–49.

50438. Baines, Rae. *Babe Ruth*. Mahawk, NJ: Troll Associates, 1985. 32p.

50439. Barrow, Edward G. "The Babe I Knew Was Like This." Edited by J.M. Kahn. *Collier's*, CXXV (June 10, 1950), 26–27+.

50440. *Baseball's Immortals: The Story of Babe Ruth*. Baseball's Immortals Series. Cooperstown, NY: The Home Plate Press, 1953. 26p.

50441. Beim, George, with Julia Ruth Stevens. *Babe Ruth: A Daughter's Portrait*. Dallas, TX: Taylor Publishing Co., 1998. 179p.

50442. Bell, Dan. "Did He Really Call His Shot?" *The National Pastime*, IX (1990), 15–16. Reprinted as "Did the Babe Call His Shot: Part II," in: Mark Alvarez, ed. *The Perfect Game* (New York: Barnes & Noble Books, 1995), pp. 241–244.

50443. Berke, Art. *Babe Ruth*. New York: Watts, 1988. 112p.

50444. Bernstein, Sam ("Leaden"). "I Hit Babe Ruth with a Peanut." In: David Cataneo. *Hornsby Hit One Over My Head: A Fans' Oral History of Baseball*. New York: Harcourt, Brace & Co., 1997. Pp. 48–54.

50445. "Big Leaguer for 20 Years, but Still Hanging On." *Newsweek*, IV (July 14, 1934), 16–17.

50446. Bikhazi, Nadim B., Alan M. Kramer, and Mark I. Singer. "Babe Ruth's Illness and Its Impact on Medical History." *The Laryngoscope*, CIX (January 1999), 1+.

50447. Bisher, Furman. "Babe Ruth and Hank Aaron." In: Sam E. Andre, ed. *Street and Smith's Official 1974 Baseball Yearbook*. New York: Conde Nast Publications, 1974. Pp. 10–21. A comparison.

50448. _____. "He Hit One 618 Feet." *Baseball Digest*, XII (July 1951), 85–87.

50449. Bloodgood, Clifford. "Babe Ruth's Long Battle to Keep Fit." *Baseball Magazine*, L (April 1953), 387–388.

50450. _____. "The Yankees' No. 3." *Baseball Magazine*, LVI (April 1936), 493–495.

50451. Bonner, Mary G. "Babe Ruth." In: her *Baseball Rookies Who Made Good*. New York: Alfred A. Knopf, 1954. Pp. 27–36.

50452. Boswell, Thomas. "Everyman and Superman." *Inside Sports*, XVII (May 1995), 60–64.

50453. Bradley, Hugh. "The Babe Had Homer Hunches." *Baseball Digest*, XX (November 1961), 73–75.

50454. Broeg, Bob. "Babe Ruth." In: his *Super Stars of Baseball*. St. Louis: *The Sporting News*, 1971. Pp. 209–216.

50455. Brother Gilbert, C.F.X. *Young Babe Ruth: His Early Life in Baseball from the Memoirs of a Xaverian Brother*. Edited by Harry Rothgerber. Jefferson, NC: McFarland & Co., Inc., 1999. 204p. Ruth at Baltimore's St. Mary's Industrial School.

50456. Broun, Heywood H. "The Babe." In: George Mayberry, ed. *Little Treasury of American Verse*. New York: Scribner's, 1949. Pp. 789–791.

50457. _____. "Ruth Comes into His Own with Two Homers." In: Nicholas Dawidoff, ed. *Baseball: A Literary Anthology*. New York: The Library of America, 2002. Pp. 108–113. In the World Series on October 10, 1921; reprinted from the October 12, 1923 issue of the *New York World*.

50458. Brown, Chip. "Gabo, the Babe and the Mid-Ocean Club." *Men's Journal*, I (May-June 1992), 92–101.

50459. Brown, Hugh. "Ruth Would Be Worth $500,000 a Year Now." *Baseball Digest*, XXVI (May 1967), 43–45.

50460. Bryson, Bill. "The Baseball Writer: My Father, Babe Ruth, and Me." *The New Yorker*, LXXVII (April 9, 2001), 44–49.

50461. _____. "'Real' Ruth Story Decries, Plants Half-Truths." *Baseball Digest*, XVIII (May 1959), 21–25.

50462. _____. "When the Babe Hit 64 in 162 Games." *Baseball Digest*, XXI (April 1962), 13–15.

50463. Buege, Bob. "Babe Ruth in Milwaukee." In: SABR. *Baseball in the Badger State*. Cleveland, OH: The Society for American Baseball Research, 2001. Pp. 23–25. Vaudeville.

50464. _____. "Best of the Babe." *Oldtyme Baseball News*, III, no. 3 (1991), 12–13.

50465. Bulger, Bozeman. "And Along Came Ruth." *Saturday Evening Post*, CCIV (November 28–December 19, 1931), 6–7+, 16–17+, 28+, 16–17+.

50466. Burchard, S.H. "Babe Ruth." In: his *Book of Baseball Greats*. New York: Harcourt, Brace, Jovanovich, 1983. Pp. 16–19.

50467. Burkholder, Ed. "Babe Ruth." In: his *Baseball Immortals*. New York: Christopher House, 1955. Pp. 16–22.

50468. Burleigh, Robert. *Home Run: The Story of Babe Ruth*. Minneapolis, MN: Voyager Press, 2003. 32p. Juvenile.

50469. Burns, Robert L. "Ruth's Record Homer was Unscreened." *Baseball Digest*, XIV (April 1955), 59–61.

50470. Cahill, J. J. "The Babe Ruth Museum and Birthplace." *Journal of Sport History*, XXIV (Summer 1997), 203–205.

50471. Camerer, Dave. "The Squabble That Made Ruth Quit Baseball" *Baseball Digest*, XIII (January 1954), 13–17.

50472. _____. "36 Years a Yankee." *Baseball Digest*, XVI (July 1957), 27–39.

50473. Canter, Len. *Babe Ruth*. New York: Baronet Books, 1996. 239p.

50474. Caple, Jim. "The Five Athletes Who Changed America: No. 4, Babe Ruth." *Sport*, XC (December 1999), 50–51.

50475. Carmichael, John P., *et al.* "Babe Ruth." In: John P. Carmichael, ed. *My Greatest Day in Baseball*. New York: A. S. Barnes, 1945. Pp. 1–5. First published in the *Chicago Dally News*.

50476. Caroulis, Jon. "Turn Back the Clock: Babe Ruth Pitches His Final Big League Game." *Baseball Digest*, LIX (August 2000), 78–80. October 1, 1933.

50477. Castle, George. "The Babe Myth: The Call That Was Never Made." *Sport*, LXXXIII (October 1992), 16, 19.

50478. Chapin, Dwight. "Ruth's [Baltimore] Shrine Forgotten in Grimy Ghetto." *Baseball Digest,* XXVIII (August 1960), 71–73.

50479. Chapman, Lou. "'Ruth's 714 Within Reach' Says [Hank] Aaron." *Baseball Digest,* XXVII (February 1989), 57–59.

50480. Chartier, Michael. "Babe Ruth." *Beckett Baseball Card Monthly,* V (November 1988), 4–6.

50481. Chastain, Bill. "This Was Babe Ruth's Longest Homer Against a Major League Foe." *Baseball Digest,* XLIII (March 1984), 71–72.

50482. Chen, Theo. "Babe Ruth." *Beckett Baseball Card Monthly,* VIII (June 1991), 7–8.

50483. Christopher, Matt. "May 25, 1935: Babe Ruth, 'That's All for Me Today.'" In: his *Matt Christopher's Great Moments in Baseball History.* Boston, MA: Little, Brown & Co., 1996. Pp. 13–21.

50484. Colver, J. Newton. "Who Was the Greatest Batter of All Time!" *Baseball Magazine,* XXXIX (September 1927), 453–454.

50485. Condon, David. "An Expert Analyzes Ruth and Aaron." *Baseball Digest,* XXXIII (July 1974), 44–47.

50486. Condon, Robert J. "Babe Ruth." In: his *The 50 Greatest Athletes of the 20th Century: A Worldwide Reference.* Jefferson, NC: McFarland & Co., Inc., 1990. Pp. 53–59.

50487. Connolly, Will. "The 'Inside' Story of Ruth's Shift to the Outfield." *Baseball Digest,* XIII (May 1954), 63–65.

50488. Considine, Bob. "A Ghost Goes to Rest." In: Editors of *True. Anthology of True.* New York: Nelson, 1962. Pp. 136–137.

50489. Cosell, Howard. "Great Moments in *Sports*: A Last Big Day for the Babe." *Sport,* XLI (February 1966), 8+. Fan appreciation day in 1948.

50490. Cosentino, Tom. "The Brooklyn Babe." *Beckett Sports Collectibles,* VII (April 1998), 20–33.

50491. Cottrell, Robert. C. *Blackball, the Black Sox, and the Babe: Baseball's Crucial 1920 Season.* Jefferson, NC: McFarland and Co., Inc., 2002. 321p.

50492. Craig, Michael. "The Boston Red Sox's Sale of Babe Ruth to the New York Yankees." In: his *The 50 Best (and Worst) Business Deals of All Time.* Franklin Lakes, NJ: Career Press, 2000. Pp. 46–48.

50493. Creamer, Robert W. "And Along Came Ruth." *Sports Illustrated,* XL (March 18–April 1, 1974), 74–78+, 40–44+, 40–44+.

50494. _____. "The Babe Goes to Hollywood." *Sports Illustrated,* LXXV (September 30, 1991), 44–49.

50495. _____. *Babe: The Legend Comes to Life.* New York: Simon and Schuster, 1974. 452p. Reprinted in a 443-page "Collector's Edition" by the Norwalk, CT, firm of Easton Press in 1998.

50496. _____. "Departure from Boston: Sold Down the River." In: Dan Riley, ed. *The Red Sox Reader.* Rev. ed. Boston, MA: Mariner Books, 1999. Pp. 17–25.

50497. _____. "George Ruth's First Day as a Professional." In: Al Silverman and Brian Silverman, eds. *The Twentieth Century Treasury of Sports.* New York: Viking Press, 1992. Pp. 104–110.

50498. _____. "The Left-Handed Genius: Best Pitcher in Baseball — Guess Who." In: Charles Einstein, ed. *The Fourth Fireside Book of Baseball.* New York: Simon and Schuster, 1988. Pp. 88–93.

50499. _____. "The Magnificent Moment: The Called-Shot Home Run." In: Brandt Aymar, ed. *Men in Sports: Great Sport Stories of All Time from the Greek Olympics to the American World Series.* New York: Crown Publishers, 1994. Pp. 84–91.

50500. _____. "The Personality of The Babe." In: George Plimpton, ed. *Home Run.* San Diego, CA: Harcourt, 2001. Chapter 6.

50501. _____. "Revolution in Baseball: Ruth Reaches New York." In: Barbara H. Solomon, ed. *Ain't We Got Fun: Essays, Lyrics and Stories of the Twenties.* New York: New American Library, 1980. Pp. 133–141.

50502. _____. "Ruth?: He is Still in the Spotlight, Still Going Strong." *Smithsonian,* XXV (February 1995), 68–70+. Abridged in *Reader's Digest,* CXLVI (June 1995), 71–75, under the title "Forever 'The Babe" and published in *Reader's Digest,* Editors of, *Reader's Digest Winner's Circle* (Hicksville, NY: Reader's Digest Association, 1996), pp. 18–23.

50503. Crepeau, Richard C. "Babe Ruth and the Feature Film: The Muddling of the Myth." In: Stephen C. Wood and J. David Pincus, eds. *Reel Baseball: Essays and Interviews on the National Pastime, Hollywood, and American Culture* (Jefferson, NC: McFarland & Co., Inc., 2003. Pp. 134–145.

50504. _____. "Tensions of the 20's: Lindbergh, Ford and Ruth." In: *Proceedings of the 5th Annual Convention of the North American Society for Sport History.* University Park, PA: North American Society for Sport History. 1977. p. 51+.

50505. Crothers, Tim. "Babe Ruth." In: his *Greatest Athletes of the 20th Century.* New York: Total Sports Illustrated, 2000. Pp. 28–33.

50506. Cummiskey, Joe, and Thomas Meany. "The Babe and Walter [Johnson] — Dressing Room Vignettes." *Baseball Digest,* I (November 1942), 39–42.

50507. "Da Babe." *Skybox,* IV (Spring 1993), 42–45.

50508. Daley, Arthur. "Babe Ruth." In: his *All the Home Run Kings.* New York: G.P. Putnam, 1972. Pp. 9–40.

50509. _____. "Babe Ruth." In: his *Kings of the Home Run.* New York: G.P. Putnam, 1962. Pp. 33–46.

50510. _____. "Babe Ruth." In: his *Sports of The Times.* New York: E. P. Dutton, 1959. Pp. 34–43.

50511. _____. "Down Memory Lane with the Babe." In: James Tuite, ed. *Sports of the Times: The Arthur Daley Years.* New York: Quadrangle Books, 1975. Pp. 57–61.

50512. _____. "Last Out for the Babe." In: James Tuite, ed. *Sports of the Times: The Arthur Daley Years.* New York: Quadrangle Books, 1975. Pp. 53–56. 1948 tribute-death.

50513. _____. "A New Slant on the Babe." *Baseball Digest,* XXIV (July 1965), 81–83.

50514. _____. "Still More on the Babe." In: James Tuite, ed. *Sports of the Times: The Arthur Daley Years.* New York: Quadrangle Books, 1975. Pp. 62–65.

50515. _____. "Why We Worship the Babe Ruths." *The New York Times Magazine,* (April 16, 1950), 19+.

50516. Daniel, Daniel M. "Babe Ruth Greatest Player — A Golden Figure in a Golden Era." *Baseball Magazine,* LXXXI (October 1948), 363–365+.

50517. _____. *Babe Ruth, Idol of the American Boy.* New York: Whitman Publishing Co., 1930. 108p.

50518. _____. *Real Babe Ruth.* St. Louis, MO: C. C. Spink, 1948. 161p. *See* comments by Bill Bryson, above.

50519. _____. "Ruth, [Hack] Wilson, and DiMaggio Records are Safe." In: Sam E. Andre, ed. *Street and Smith's Official 1972 Baseball Yearbook.* New York: Conde Nast Publications, 1972. Pp. 14–24.

50520. _____. and H. G. Salsinger. *Real Babe Ruth* [and] *I Remember Ruth.* 2nd ed. St. Louis: The Sporting News, 1963. 162p.

50521. Deedy, John. "The Day I Collected Babe Ruth's Autograph." *Baseball Digest,* LVI (February 1997), 56–60.

50522. Dell, John. "The Babe Could Pull Outside Pitch." *Baseball Digest,* X November 1961), 76–77.

50523. De Marco, Mario. "The King of Baseball: Baseball Collector's Treasure — The Babe." *Antiques and Collecting Hobbies,* XCVI (December 1991), 56+.

50524. Dolgan, Bob. "Major Leaguers Who Hit 60 Home Runs: Babe Ruth — He Set the Standard for Today's Sluggers." *Baseball Digest,* LVII (December 1998), 48–53.

50525. Donaldson, Norman, and Betty. "Babe Ruth." In: their *How Did They Die?* New York: St. Martin's Press, 1980. Pp. 323–324.

50526. "Dope for Babe Ruth Notebooks." *Literary Digest,* CXI (November 28, 1931), 31–32.

50527. Doyle, Ed ("Dutch"). *The Only One: A Fan Looks at the Babe.* Chicago, IL: Adams Press, 1974. 116p.

50528. Drebinger, John. "Babe Ruth and the Kids." *Baseball Magazine,* LXXIX (June 1947), 223–225.

50529. Drooz, Alan. "The Legend That Ruth Built." *Beckett Baseball Card Monthly,* XII, no. 119 (February 1995), 6–7.

50530. _____. "Sultan of $uccess." *Beckett Baseball Card Monthly,* XII, no. 119 (February 1995), 8–10. Curtis Management Group, owners to the rights to the player's name.

50531. Dunne, Michael. "Postwar Cultural Construction in *The Babe Ruth Story.*" *Studies in Popular Culture,* XIX, no. 1 (1996), 1+.

50532. Eaton, Paul W. "Baseball's Latest, the Super Home Run." *Baseball Magazine,* XXVII (October 1921), 491–493.

50533. Eichmann, J. K. "The Sultan of Swat: Babe Ruth." *Sports Scoup,* II (May 1974), 10+.

50534. Eisenberg, Lisa. *The Story of Babe Ruth: Baseball's Greatest Legend.* New York: Dell-Yearling, 1990. 92p.

50535. Eldridge, Larry. "The Master Showman." In: Joseph L. Reichler, ed. *1983 All-Star Game Program.* New York: Major League Baseball Promotion Corp., 1983. Pp. 78–84. Ruth hit the first All-Star Game homer.

50536. Elias, Al Munro. "Babe Ruth Comes Through for Number 500." *Baseball Magazine,* XLIII (October 1943), 495–497.

50537. _____. "Ruth's Sensational Role in the Grand Drama of Circuit Clouts." *Baseball Magazine,* XXXVIII (December 1926), 315–317.

50538. Epstein, Sam, and Beryl. "Babe Ruth." In: their *Stories of Champions.* Champaign, IL: Garrard, 1965. Pp. 79–96.

50539. "The Famous Dual Between the Babe and Columbia Lou [Gehrig]." *Great Moments in Sport,* III (September 1962), 34–39.

50540. Farrell, James T. "The King is Dead." *Sport,* LVII (May 1974), 56–61.

50541. Father Ted, S.S.P. *"The King Of Swat."* Canfield, OH: Pious Society of St. Paul, 1948. 47p.

50542. Fein, L.A. "The Babe's Last Moment of Glory." *Sports Illustrated,* XV (August 14, 1961), E3–E4.

50543. Figueredo, Jorge. "The Day [Cristobal] Torriente Outclassed Ruth." *The Baseball Research Journal,* XI (1982), 130–132.

50544. Fitzpatrick, James K. "George Herman Ruth, the Babe." In: his *Builders of the American Dream.* New Rochelle, NY: Arlington House, 1977. Pp. 252–275.

50545. Fleming, Thomas. "The Day I Saw Them All." *American Heritage,* XLI (November 1990), 30+. At Wrigley Field in 1932.

50546. Fuchs, Alfred H. "Psychology and the Babe." *Journal of the History of the Behavioral Sciences,* XXXIV (1998), 153–168.

50547. Fuller, Samuel. "Babe Ruth." In: Danny Peary, ed. *Baseball's Finest: The Greats, the Flakes, the Weird and the Wonderful.* North Dighton, MA: The JG Press, 1990. Pp. 127–130.

50548. Furlong, William B. "Babe Ruth Would Hit More Than 60!" *Baseball Digest,* XVII (December 1958), 12–13.

50549. _____ "The 60th Home Run." *The New York Times Magazine,* (August 20, 1961), 53+.

50550. Gallagher, Jack. "Bullet Joe Bush Remembers the Babe." *Baseball Digest,* XXXI (September 1972), 66–69.

50551. Gallico, Paul W. "The Babe." In: E. A. Walter, ed. *Essay Annual, 1933.* New York: Scott, 1933. Pp. 244–250. Reprinted in Editors of *Vanity Fair, Vanity Fair* (New York; Viking Press, 1960), pp. 204–205.

50552. _____ "Babe Ruth." In: his *The Golden People.* Garden City, N.Y: Doubleday, 1945. Pp. 31–48.

50553. _____. "His Majesty the King." In: his *Farewell to Sport.* New York: Alfred A. Knopf, 1938. Pp. 30–43. Reprinted in Ruth M. Stauffer, *et at,* eds., *Adventures in Modern Literature.* 3rd ed. New York: Harcourt, 1951, pp. 260–269 and in Chapter 5 of George Plimpton, ed. *Home Run* (San Diego, CA: Harcourt, 2001).

50554. _____. "Farewell to the Babe," In: John McCarthy, comp. *After The Game: Collection Of Best Sports Writing.* New York: Dodd, Mead, 1972. Chapter 13.

50555. _____. "The Word of Babe Ruth." *Saturday Evening Post,* CCXXVI (February 13, 1954), 21+.

50556. Garner, Joe and Bob Costas. "Babe Ruth Calls His Short." In: their *And the Crowd Goes Wild: Relive the Most Celebrated Sporting Events Ever Broadcast.* Naperville, IL: Sourcebooks, 1999. Chapter 1. The work also includes two sound CDs, with the Ruth homer recorded on the first.

50557. Gault, Clare and Frank. *The Home Run Kings: Babe Ruth, Henry Aaron.* New York: Walker, 1974. 79p.

50558. Gery, John. "Lie #5: That Babe Ruth Pointed Out That Famous Homer." *War, Literature & the Arts: An International Journal of the Humanities,* X, no. 1 (1998), 201–202.

50559. Gesker, Mike. "Babe Ruth Birthplace: Shrine to a Legend." *Maryland,* XIII (Spring 1981), 10–15.

50560. Gibbons, Frank. "Ruth Greater Than Cobb!" *Baseball Digest,* XIX (May 1960), 51–53.

50561. Gilbert, Thomas. *The Soaring Twenties: Babe Ruth & the Home-Run Decade.* New York: Franklin Watts, 1996. 160p.

50562. Gleeson; Bill. "This is the Majors' Most Unbeatable Slugging Record.*"Baseball Digest,* XXXVIII (February 1979), 26–29. Ruth's .847 in 1920.

50563. Gold, Eddie. "Babe Ruth Still the Champ in Home Run Frequency." *Baseball Digest,* LIII (March 1994), 82–83.

50564. Goldaper, Sam. "Flashback: When the Babe Hit No. 714." In: Clyde Hirt, ed. *Sports Quarterly Presents Baseball, 1973.* New York: Counterpoint, Inc., 1973. Pp. 26–29.

50565. Gonzalez, Raymond. "Still the Greatest One-Two Punch." *The Baseball Research Journal,* VI (1977), 98–100. Ruth and Gehrig.

50566. Gould, John. "The Day Babe Ruth (Sssh!) Pitched a Strikeout Record, but Lost a Double-Header." *Down East,* XXVIII (July 1982), 96–97.

50567. Graham, Frank. "The Babe Struck Out, Too!" *Baseball Digest*, XVII (December 1958), 57–58.

50568. _____. "Friendliness." *American Magazine*, XII (August 1931), 71+.

50569. _____. "More About George Herman Ruth." *Baseball Magazine*, LXXXI (November 1948), 415–417.

50570. _____. "Tell Me About Babe Ruth." *Sport*, XVII (October 1964), 50–60.

50571. _____. "The Year Babe Hit His 60." *Baseball Digest*, XXI (March 1962), 35–39.

50572. Graham, Frank, Jr. "Babe Ruth." In: his *Great Hitters of the Major Leagues*. New York: Random House, 1969. Pp. 17–31.

50573. Grayson, Harry. "Babe Ruth." In: his *They Played the Game: The Story of Baseball Greats*. New York: A. S. Barnes, 1944. Pp. 8–9.

50574. Greene, Lee. "Ruth's Ten Greatest Days." *Sport*, XXXVI (September 1963), 32–33.

50575. Greenfield, James. "Year of the God." *Sports Illustrated*, III (November 14, 1955), 57+. Ruth's 1934 visit to Japan.

50576. Gunfoile, Bill. "Babe Ruth Had the Best RBI-per-At-Bat Ratio in the Majors." *Baseball Digest*, XXXIX (May 1980), 79–80.

50577. _____. "Uniform No. 3. Most Popular Among Hall of Famers." *Baseball Digest*, XXXVIII (July 1979), 56–60.

50578. Gutman, Bill. "Babe Ruth." In: his *Famous Baseball Stars*. New York: Dodd, Mead, 1973. Pp. 61–72.

50579. Hahn, James, and Lynn. *Babe: The Sports Career of George Herman Ruth*. Edited by Howard Schroeder. Mankato, MN: Crestwood House, 1981. 47p.

50580. Hamilton, Neil A. "Babe Ruth." In: his *Lifetimes: The Great War to the Stock Market Crash — American History Through Biography and Primary Documents*. Westport, CT: Greenwood Press, 2002. Chapter 51.

50581. Hano, Arnold. "The Man Behind the Power." *Sport*, XXXVI (September 1963), 34–39.

50582. Haskins, James. *Babe Ruth and Henry Aaron: The Home Run Kings*. New York: Lothrop, Lee and Shepard, 1974. 123p.

50583. Heinz, W. C. "Down Memory Lane with the Babe." In: his *What a Time It Was: the Best of W.C. Heinz on Sports*. San Francisco, CA: Da Capo Press, 2001. Pp. 265–267.

50584. Herzog, Brad. "Babe Ruth." In: his *The 20 Greatest Athletes of the 20th Century*. New York: Rosen Pub. Group, 2003. Chapter 18.

50585. Hess, Jack D. "The First Time I Met Babe Ruth." *Baseball Digest*, XLVI (January 1987), 39–41.

50586. Heuman, William. "Babe Ruth." In: his *Famous American Athletes*. New York: Dodd, Mead, 1963. Pp. 43–57.

50587. Hirshberg, Al. "Baba Ruth." In: his *Greatest American Leaguers*. New York: G.P. Putnam, 1970. pp. 43–57.

50588. Hoff, Sy. *Mighty Babe Ruth*. New York: Scholastic Book Services, 1980. 32p.

50589. Hoffman, Frank W. and William G. Bailey. "Babe Ruth Calls His Shot." In: their *Sports and Recreations Fads*. Binghampton, NY: Haworth, 1991. Pp. 315–318. Compare with George Castle's article.

50590. Holland, Gerald. "The Babe Ruth Papers." *Sports Illustrated*, XI (December 21, 1959), 111–117. Reproductions of documents and letters.

50591. Holtzman, Jerome. "Babe Ruth's Last Stand Still a Vivid Memory." *Baseball Digest*, LI (August 1992), 63–65.

50592. Honig, Donald. "Babe Ruth." In: his *Baseball America: the Heroes of the Game and the Times of Their Glory*. New York: Macmillan, 1985. Pp. 120–139.

50593. _____. "Babe Ruth." In: his *The Power Hitters*. St. Louis, MO: *The Sporting News*, 1989. Pp. 8–23.

50594. Hopkins, E. "Where They Lived: Babe Ruth." *New York*, XVI (March 7, 1983), 48+.

50595. Hore, T. "'God, We Liked That Big Son of a Bitch': Babe Ruth, Still a Legend at 100." *Dugout*, III (April-May 1995), 21–24.

50596. Horgan, Tim. "Kumquats, Mr. Allen's Nobody Beats the Babe." *Baseball Digest*, XLI (March 1982), 93+.

50597. Howell, Colin. "The Man Who Taught the Bambino." In: William Humber and John St. James, eds. *All I Thought About was Baseball: Writings on a Canadian Pastime*. Toronto and Buffalo, NY: University of Toronto Press, 1996. Pp. 149–152. Brother Matthias.

50598. Hoyt, Waite. *Babe Ruth as I Knew Him*. New York: Dell Publishing Co., 1948. 50p.

50599. _____. "The Babe Ruth Known as 'Giggs.'" *Baseball Digest*, VI (August 1947), 7–9. Reprinted in *Baseball Digest*, XX (August 1961) and in John Kuenster, ed. *From Cobb to Catfish* (Chicago, IL: Rand McNally, 1975), p. 178.

50600. _____. as told to Ritter Collet. "Hoyt's First Meeting with Ruth — Strikingly Impressive' [and) 'New York Move Made Ruth' [and) 'Ruth Forced Showdown': Reprinted from the *Dayton Journal Herald*, September 1973." *Congressional Record*, CXIX (September 18, 1973), 30233–30235.

50601. Humber, William ("Bill"). "The Canuck of Clout." *Dugout*, III (August 1995), 30–33.

50602. "An In-depth Look at the Home Run Hitting of Babe Ruth." *Yankees Magazine*, V (June 7, 1984), 44+.

50603. Inabinett, Mark. "Babe Ruth." In: his *Grantland Rice and His Heroes: The Sportswriter as Mythmaker in the 1920s*. Knoxville, TN: University of Tennessee Press, 1994. Pp. 37–49.

50603. Jackendoff, Ray. "Babe Ruth Homered His Way into the Hearts of America." *Syntax and Semantics*, XXVI (1992), 155+.

50604. Jarvis, Robert M. "Babe Ruth as Legal Hero." *Florida State University Law Review*, XXII (Spring 1995), 885–897.

50605. Jenkinson, William J. "The Power and the Glory of the Babe." *USA Today Baseball Weekly*, IV (January 25, 1994), 16–17.

50606. Johnson, Walter. "What I Throw to Babe Ruth and Why." *Baseball Magazine*, XXV (September 1920), 478–491.

50607. Johnston, Charles H.L. "George Herman ('Babe) Ruth." In: his *Famous American Athletes of Today*. 1st Series. New York. Page, 1928. Pp. 97–124.

50608. Kahn, Roger. "Babe Ruth: A Look Behind the Legend." *Reader's Digest*, CV (August 1974), 136–140.

50609. _____. "The Real Babe Ruth." *Baseball Digest*, XVIII (October 1959), 23–32. Reprinted from *Esquire* and reprinted in Editors *of Esquire, Great Men and Moments in Sports* (New York: Harper, 1962), pp. 45–52.

50610. Kammer, David J. "A Matter of Timing: Babe Ruth and the Heroic Image in the Golden Age of Baseball." Unpublished M.A. Thesis, City University of New York, 1975. 63p.

50611. Keene, Kerry, Raymond Sinbaldi, and David Hickey. *The Babe in Red Stockings: An In-Depth Chronicle of Babe Ruth with the Boston Red Sox, 1914–1919*. Champagne, IL: Sagamore Publications, 1997. 307p.

50612. Keillor, Garrison. "The Babe." In: George Plimpton, ed. *Home Run*. San Diego, CA: Harcourt, 2001. Chapter 7.

50613. Kendall, Brian. "September 5, 1914: The Babe Goes Deep for the First Time." In: his *Great Moments in Canadian Baseball*. Toronto, Ont.: Lester Publishing, 1995. Chapter 4.

50614. Kermisch, Al. "The Babe Ruth Beginning." *The Baseball Research Journal*, IV (1975), 45–51.

50615. _____. "Ruth Makes War on Warhop." *The Baseball Research Journal*, II (1973), 19–21. Jack Warhop, Yankee pitcher, 1908–1915.

50616. Ketchum, R.M. "Faces from the Past: Babe Ruth." *American Heritage*, XVI (August 1965), 97+.

50617. Kirst, Sean Peter. "The Memory That Ruth Built," "Babe was a Smash in Syracuse," "A Baseball Lesson." In: his *The Ashes of Lou Gehrig and Other Baseball Essays*. Jefferson, NC: McFarland & Co., Inc., 2003. Pp. 20–26.

50618. Klima, John. "A Ruthian Duel: Sherry Smith vs. Babe Ruth (October 9, 1916)." In: his *Pitched Battle: 35 of Baseball's Greatest Duels from the Mound*. Jefferson, NC: McFarland & Co., Inc., 2002. Pp. 33–37.

50619. Kofoed, J.C. "Who Is the Greatest, Cobb or Ruth?" *Baseball Magazine*, XXXV (July 1925), 353–355.

50620. Koontz, Bill. "Baseball's Superstar." *Baseball Magazine*, XLIII (August 1929), 410–411+.

50621. Kronstadt, Norman. "Babe Ruth's Last Day." *Sport*, XXXI (February 1961), 78–87.

50622. Kuechle, Oliver E. "Ruth's Targets 232 Feet Farther." *Baseball Digest*, XVII (December 1968), 13–15.

50623. Kuenster, John. "Ruth Top Vote-Getter in Poll on 50 Greatest Players of Century." *Baseball Digest*, LVIII (December 1999), 19–29.

50624. Kunitz, Alfred. "I Was Babe Ruth's Batboy." *Baseball Digest*, XII (August 1953), 33–40.

50625. Lane, Ferdinand C. "After Babe Ruth, What?" *Baseball Magazine*, LII (January 1934), 339–341.

50626. _____. "Baseball's Big Question Mark — Will the Babe Come Back?" *Baseball Magazine*, XXX (April 1923), 483–485.

50627. _____. "Babe Ruth and Frenzied Finance." *Baseball Magazine*, XXXVIII (January 1927), 343–346. This account of the Bambino's salary problems was reprinted in Sidney Offit, ed., *Best of Baseball* (New York. G.P. Putnam, 1956), pp. 78–86.

50628. _____. "Babe Ruth Loses His Slugging Crown." *Baseball Magazine*, LXXXVI (May 1926), 551–552.

50629. _____. "Can Babe Ruth Repeat?" *Baseball Magazine*, XXVI (May 1921), 555–558.

50630. _____. "A Glimpse of Babe Ruth's Locker." *Baseball Magazine*, LI (June 1933), 293–294.

50631. _____. "The Greatest Record of a Baseball Generation." *Baseball Magazine*, XL (January 1928), 351–353.

50632. _____. "The Home Run Champion of 1923." *Baseball Magazine*, XXXIII (January 1924), 339–341.

50633. _____. "How Babe Ruth Became the Home Run King." *Baseball Magazine*, XXIV (April 1920), 611–614.

50634. _____. "How Babe Ruth Wins for the New York Yankees." *Baseball Magazine*, XXVII (June 1921), 291–294.

50635. _____. "An Insoluble Problem: What to Pitch to Babe Ruth." *Baseball Magazine*, XLI (July 1928), 339–341.

50636. _____. "The Man Who Gave the Yankees Their First Pennant." *Baseball Magazine*, XXVIII (December 1921), 593–594+.

50637. _____. "The Season's Sensation." *Baseball Magazine*, XXI (October 1918), 471–473+.

50638. _____. "Why Babe Ruth Has Become a National Idol." *Baseball Magazine*, XXVII (October 1921), 483–485.

50639. Lardner, Rex. "Babe Ruth: Home Run King." In: his *Ten Heroes of the '20's*. New York: G. P. Putnam, 1966. Pp. 15–45.

50640. Lardner, Ring W. "Pluck and Luck; or, The Rise of a Home Run King." *Collier's*, LXXXIII (March 16, 1929), 13+. Reprinted in Thomas Meany, ed., *Collier's Greatest Sports Stories* (New York: A.S. Barnes, 1955), pp. 104–107.

50641. Lawler, Joe. "The Babe Wins Boston Marathon." *Sox Fan News*, I (August 1986), 16–17. 1916 World Series game.

50642. _____. "Baker Bowl was the Site of Babe Ruth's Last Game." *Phillies Report*, V (February 16, 1989), 14–15.

50643. _____. "Today's Battery: Ruth and [Joe] Glenn." *The Baseball Research Journal*, XII (1983), 52–55.

50644. "Legends: Babe Ruth." *Sports Illustrated for Kids*, XI (March 1999), 58–59.

50645. Leiker, Ken. "18–1920: Babe Ruth Leaves the Red Sox for the Yankees." In: his *Major League Baseball Memorable Moments: The Most Memorable Moments in Major League Baseball History*. New York: Ballantine Books, 2002. Pp. 96–102.

50646. Liebowitz, Herbert. "The Babe Ruth Syndrome." *Parnassus: Poetry in Review*, XVII, no. 2 (1992), 9+.

50647. Leipold, L. Edmond. "Babe Ruth." In: his *Famous American Athletes*. Minneapolis, MN: Denison, 1969. Chapter 3.

50648. Leisman, Louis J. ("Fats"). *"I Was with Babe Ruth at St. Mary's."* Aberdeen, MD: Self-published, 1956. 36p.

50649. Levine, Peter. "Babe Ruth: My Magnificent Obsession." *Nine: A Journal of Baseball History and Social Policy Perspectives*, VI (Fall 1997), 69–80.

50650. Lewis, Allen. "Ruth's Impact on the Game More Than Just Records." *Baseball Digest*, XXXVII (June 1978), 79–80.

50651. Libby, Bill. "Babe Ruth." In: his *Baseball's Greatest Sluggers*. New York: Random House, 1973. Pp. 11–37.

50652. Lieb, Frederick G. "The Babe's First Homer." *Sport*, XXIII (May 1957), 72–75.

50653. _____. "Babe Ruth." In: his *Comedians and Pranksters of Baseball*. St. Louis: The Sporting News, 1958. Pp. 55–61.

50654. _____. "The Life Story of Babe Ruth." In: J.G. Taylor Spink, ed. *Baseball Register, 1948*. St. Louis: The Sporting News, 1948. pp. 2–32. Reprinted from the April 23, 1947 issue of *The Sporting News*.

50655. Limon, J. "Beautiful Failing: Franz Kafka and the Curse of the Bambino." *Yale Journal of Criticism*, XIV (Fall 2001), 415–429.

50656. Lipsyte, Robert and Peter. Levine. "Babe Ruth." In: their *Idols of the Game: A Sporting History of the American Century*. Kansas City, MO: Andrews and McMeel, 1995. Chapter 5.

50657. Lloyd, F.R. "The Home Run King." *Journal of Popular Culture*, IX (Spring 1976), 983–995. Reprinted in Christopher D. Geist and Jack Nachbar, eds. *The Popular Culture Reader* (Bowling Green, OH: Bowling Green State University Press, 1983), pp. 217–228.

50658. Locke, Barry. "The Babe: What Would It Be Like if Babe Ruth Played Today?" *Sport*, LXXXIII (May 1992), 30–37.

50659. Longstreet, Stephen. "Babe Ruth." In: Danny Peary, ed. *Baseball's Finest: The Greats, the Flakes, the Weird* *and the Wonderful.* North Dighton, MA: The JG Press, 1990. Pp. 131–135.

50660. Lorenz, Stacy L. "Bowing Down to Babe Ruth: Major League Baseball and Canadian Popular Culture, 1920–1929." *Canadian Journal of the History of Sport and Physical Education,* XXVI (May 1995), 22–39.

50661. MacCambridge, Michael. "Babe Ruth." In: his *ESPN Sports Century.* New York: Hyperion, 1999. Chapter 4.

50662. Macht, Norman L. "'The Babe Didn't Point,' Says Woody English." *Baseball Digest,* LI (February 1992), 61–63.

50663. _____. *Baseball Legend: Babe Ruth.* New York: Chelsea House, 1991. 64p.

50664. _____. "Cheap Shot Homer." *Beckett Baseball Card Monthly,* VI (July 1989), 79–80.

50665. Mann, Arthur. "Baseball vs. Big Babe Ruth." *Baseball Magazine,* XXXVII (October 1926), 505–507.

50666. Maris, Roger E. "What the Babe Means to Baseball Today." *Sport,* XXXVI (September 1963), 28–29.

50667. Mazumdar, Partha. "The Babe Ruth Stories." In: *North American Society for Sport History Proceedings and Newsletter.* University Park, PA: North American Society for Sport History, 1994. Pp. 53–54.

50668. McAuley, Ed. "Ruth Distances Still Sacred." *Baseball Digest,* VIII (August 1949), 13–15.

50669. _____. "Ruth's Liners, Too, Left Their Mark." *Baseball Digest,* V (July 1946), 7–9.

50670. _____. "They Walked [Yankee Shortstop Mark] Koenig to Pitch to Ruth." *Baseball Digest,* IX (August 1950), 26–27.

50671. McGeehan, W. O. "Ruth Breaks Own Home Run Record." In: Dean A. Sullivan, ed. *Middle Innings: A Documentary History of Baseball, 1900–1948.* Lincoln, NE: University of Nebraska Press, 1998. Pp. 127–129. Reprinted from the *New York Herald Tribune,* Oct. 2, 1927.

50672. McGovern, Arthur A. "Babe Ruth—'If I Can Come Back, Anybody Can.'" *Literary Digest,* XCIII (April 9, 1927), 54–60.

50673. McGovern, John T. "George Herman Ruth." In: his *Diogenes Discovers Us.* New York: Dial Press, 1933. Pp. 73–88.

50674. McGowen, Roscoe. "And There Stood the Babe." In: Sam E. Andre, ed. *Street and Smith's Official 1955 Baseball Yearbook.* New York: Street and Smith Publications, 1955. pp. 58–61.

50675. McGuire, B. "Babe Ruth." *New York Folklore,* I (January-February 1975), 97–107.

50676. McLinn, Stoney. "That Strange Affliction: The Ruth Complex." *Baseball Magazine,* XLVII (August 1931), 401–402+.

50676. McMillan, Ken. "Babe Ruth." In: his *Tales from the Yankee Dugout: A Collection of the Greatest Yankee Stories Ever Told.* Champaign, IL: Sports Publishing, Inc., 2001. Pp. 156–173.

50677. Meany, Thomas. "Babe Ruth." In: his *Baseball's Greatest Hitters.* New York: A. S. Barnes, 1950. Pp. 151–163.

50678. _____. "Babe Ruth." In: his *Baseball's Greatest Players.* New York: Grosset and Dunlap, 1953. Pp. 205–218.

50679. _____. "The Babe Ruth I Remember." *Sport,* XII (March 1952), 52–62.

50680. _____. *Babe Ruth: The Big Moments of the Big Fellow.* New York: A. S. Barnes, 1947. 180 p.

50681. _____. "How [Eddie] Mathews Compares to Ruth." *Baseball Digest,* XIII (June 1954), 13–24.

50682. _____and Tommy Holmes. "Babe Ruth." In: their *Baseball's Best.* New York: Watts, 1964. Pp. 187–196.

50683. Mercurio, John A. *Babe Ruth's Incredible Records and the 44 Players Who Broke Them.* New York: S. P. I. Books, 1993. 217p.

50684. Miller, Ernestine Gichner. *The Babe Book: George Herman Ruth Baseball Player.* Kansas City, MO: Andrews McMeel, 2000. 211p.

50685. _____. "The Babe's Called Shot." In: Richard Levin, ed. *2002 World Series Official Program.* New York: Major League Baseball Promotion Corp., 2002. Pp. 180–182.

50686. Moberly, M. R. "Babe's Sister." *People Weekly,* XXIV (September 16, 1985), 76–78.

50687. Mulvey, D.F. "Souvenir of the Babe." *American Heritage,* LI (October 2000), 26–27.

50688. Murnane, Timothy H. "Ruth Leads Red Sox to Victory, 1914." In: Glenn Stout, ed. *Impossible Dreams: A Red Sox Collection.* Boston, MA: Mariner Books, 2003. Pp. 64–66.

50689. Murphy, Charles W. "The Best Known, Best Loved Man in Baseball." *Baseball Magazine,* XXVII (June 1921), 315–316+.

50690. Nack, William. "The Colossus: Babe Ruth's 60-Homer Season in 1927." *Sports Illustrated,* LXXXIX (August 24 1998), 58–66, 68–70.

50691. Nason, Jerry. "Babe Ruth's Greatest Year." *Baseball Digest,* XXI (June 1962), 49–51.

50692. _____. "But ... Babe Ruth's 60 Weren't Off Aces." *Baseball Digest,* V (September 1956), 41–43.

50693. Nealon, Clark. "Ruth's Homer Cleared Two Rows of Houses." *Baseball Digest,* XXIV (August 1965), 57–59.

50694. "The New Hero of the Great American Game at Close Range." *Current Opinion,* LXIX (October 1920), 477–478.

50695. Newcombe, Jack. "*Sport's* Hall of Fame: The Mighty Bambino." *Sport,* XXX (October 1960), 24–25+.

50696. Nicholson, Lois. "Babe Ruth." In: his *From Maryland to Cooperstown: Seven Maryland Natives in Baseball's Hall of Fame.* Centreville, MD: Tidewater Publishers, 1999. Chapter 1.

50697. _____. *Babe Ruth: Sultan of Swat.* Westport, CT: Greenwood Press, 1994. 119p.

50698. Nissenson, H. "Babe Ruth, Savior of Baseball." In: Associated Press. *Sports Immortals.* Englewood Cliffs, NJ: Prentice-Hall, 1974. Pp. 42–47.

50699. Norris, R.B. "Babe Ruth—Pitcher." *The New York Times Magazine,* (August 10, 1958), 51+.

50700. Obojski, Robert. "Babe Ruth: Beats Whole American League in Home Run Production." In: his *Baseball's Strangest Moments.* New York: Sterling Publishing Co., 1988. Pp. 83–84.

50701. O'Day, Marie. "They Reared Babe Ruth." *Catholic Digest,* III (September 1938), 20+.

50702. "One Real Babe Ruth." *Literary Digest,* LXXXIII (October 4, 1924), 58–62.

50703. Ostrow, Rick. "The Legend Babe Ruth Created is Still Awesome." *Baseball Digest,* XLIV (September 1985), 64–68.

50704. Pacini, Le. "Fond Memories of Ty Cobb and Babe Ruth." *Baseball Digest,* XXIX (July 1970), 43–47.

50705. Palmer, Stetson. "What Club Will Ruth Manage, If Any?" *Baseball Magazine,* LII (April 1934), 503–505.

50706. _____. "What the Polo Grounds Mean to Ruth." *Baseball Magazine,* LV (June 1935), 311–313.

50707. Patterson, Ted. "Susan Luery's Statue 'Baltimore's Babe' a Work of Art." *Orioles Gazette,* III (May 7, 1993), 12–13.

50708. Pippen, Rodger H. "The Best Picker in Baseball." *McClure's Magazine,* LVIII (June 1927), 22–25.

50709. Pirone, Dorothy Ruth and Chris Martens. *My Dad the Babe: Growing Up with an American Hero.* Boston, MA: Quinlan Press, 1988. 250p.

50710. Pope, Edwin. "Babe Ruth, Always the No.1 Yankee for Mickey Mantle." *Baseball Digest,* XLIII (October 1984), 25–28.

50711. Poutasse, E.J. "Lighting the Babe's Way." *Yankee,* LXII (August 1998), 78–79.

50712. Povich, Shirley. "What Would Ruth Get Now?" *Baseball Digest,* VII (March 1948), 19–21.

50713. Powers, Jimmy. "Babe Ruth." In: his *Baseball Personalities.* Chicago: Field, 1949. Pp. 106–130.

50714. Puma, Mike. "Who was the Greatest?" *Yankees Magazine,* XXII (June 2001), 24–31.

50715. Rader, Benjamin G. "Compensatory Sport Heroes: Ruth, Grange, and Dempsey." *Journal Of Popular Culture,* XVI (Spring 1982),11–22.

50716. Rambeck, Richard. *Babe Ruth.* Mankato, MN: Child's World, 1993. 31p.

50717. Rathgeber, Bob. "When Babe Was Almost a Manager." In: his *Cincinnati Reds Scrapbook.* Virginia Beach, VA: J.C.P. Corp. of Virginia, 1982. Pp. 72–73.

50718. Reilly, Edward J. "Baseball Haiku: Basho, the Babe, and the Great Japanese-American Trade." In: William Simons, ed. *The Cooperstown Symposium on Baseball and American Culture, 2001.* Jefferson, NC: McFarland & Co., Inc., 2002. Pp. 246–259.

50719. Reisler, Jim. *Babe Ruth: Launching the Legend.* New York: McGraw-Hill 2004. 274p.

50720. Rhoades, A. D. "Uncle Abner and the Babe." *Sports Illustrated,* XVI (May 28, 1962), E5–E7.

50721. Rice, Grantland. "The Babe Gets His Revenge." In: his *Sportslights of 1923.* New York: G.P. Putnam's Sons, 1924. Pp. 123–130. 1923 World Series performance.

50722. _____. "The Big Fellow, Babe Ruth." In: Dave Camerer, ed. *The Best of Grantland Rice.* New York: Watts, 1963. Pp. 76–88. Also published as Chapter 8 in John McCarthy, ed., *After the Game: A Collection of the Best Sports Writing* (New York: Dodd, Mead, 1973).

50723. _____. "Game Called." In: David Halberstam, ed. *The Best American Sports Writing of the Century.* Boston, MA: Houghton, Mifflin, 1999. Pp. 140–143. Ruth's death.

50724. _____. "Ruth is Stranger Than Fiction—Wherein the Home-Run Kings Makes a Big Advance Over the Works of Horatio Alger, Jr." *Vanity Fair,* XVI (April 1921), 65–66.\par

50725. _____. "Setting the Pace: Babe Ruth Dies." In: Dean A. Sullivan, ed. *Middle Innings: A Documentary History of Baseball, 1900–1948.* Lincoln, NE: University of Nebraska Press, 1998. Pp. 218–220. Reprinted from the *New York Sun,* Aug. 18, 1948.

50726. _____. "What Happened to the Babe?" *Sport,* III (November 1947), 32–33. 1922 World Series slump; reprinted from a *New York Tribune* article of October 9, 1922.

50727. Richards, Kenneth. *Babe Ruth.* Chicago, IL: Children's Press, 1967. 95p

50728. Ritter, Laurence S. and Mark Rucker. *The Babe: A Life in Pictures.* New York: Ticknor and Fields, 1988. 282p.

50729. _____. *The Babe: The Game That Ruth Built.* New York: Total Sports, 1997. 296p.

50730. Robertson, John G. *The Babe Chases 60: That Fabulous 1927 Season, Home Run by Home Run.* Jefferson, NC: McFarland & Co., Inc., 1999. 178p.

50731. Robinson, Arthur. "My Friend Babe Ruth." *Collier's,* LXXIV (September 20,1924), 7–8.

50732. Robinson, Ray. "Babe Ruth." In: his *The Greatest Yankees of Them All.* New York: Putnam, 1969. Pp. 51+.

50733. Roeder, Bill. "Babe Ruth." In: Zander Hollander, ed. *Great American Athletes of the 20th Century.* New York: Random House, 1966. Pp. 136–139.

50734. Rogers, Terence. "Who is This Man Babe Ruth?" In: Richard Levin, ed. *World Series 1988 Program.* New York: Major League Baseball Promotion Corp., 1988. Pp. 16–21.

50735. Rothe, Emil H. "Babe Ruth's Last Game." In: Dick Wimmer, ed. *The Home Run Game.* Short Hills, NJ: Burford Books, 1999. Chapter 1.

50736. _____. "Babe Ruth's Last Major League Game." *Baseball Digest,* XXXI (November 1972), 38–39. Reprinted in John Kuenster, ed., *From Cobb to Catfish* (Chicago, IL: Rand McNally, 1975), pp. 105–106.

50737. Royal, Chip. "Babe's Day as a Manager." *Sport,* XVIII, (June 1955), 64–73.

50738. Rubin, Bob. "More on the Babe." *Sport,* XLVIII (August 1969), 8–9. As Brooklyn Dodgers coach, 1938.

50739. _____. "One-Time Yankee Teammate [Waite Hoyt] Recalls Babe Ruth." *Baseball Digest,* XXXVIII (May 1979), 90+.

50740. Rubin, L. D. "Babe Ruth's Ghost." *The Sewanee Review,* CI (Spring 1993), 240–247.

50741. Ruiz, Yuyo. *The Bambino Visits Cuba 1920: Unedited Notes Regarding the Visit of Babe Ruth to Cuba in 1920.* Puerto Rico: Priv. Print., 1996. 68p.

50742. Rumill, Ed. "Hall of Famers Pay Tribute to Ruth." *Baseball Digest,* XXVIII (November 1969), 20–24.

50743. "Runs Scored by Babe Ruth." *Literary Digest,* LXIV (February 14, 1920), 125–127.

50744. Runyan, Damon. "Damon Runyan Reports Babe Ruth's First Home Run." In: Dean A. Sullivan, ed. *Middle Innings: A Documentary History of Baseball, 1900–1948.* Lincoln, NE: University of Nebraska Press, 1998. Pp. 71–74. Reprinted from the *New York American,* May 7, 1915.

50745. Ruppert, Jacob. "Prominent Baseball Men and Their Opinion of Babe Ruth." *Baseball Magazine,* XXIV (April 1920), 617–618.

50746. Rushefsky, Nick. "Babe Ruth: A Philatelic Remembrance." *Journal of Sports Philately,* XXXVII (July-August 1999), 16–20.

50747. Russell, Fred. "When Babe Ruth Hit His Last Home Run." *Baseball Digest,* XXVIII (August 1969), 70–71.

50748. Ruth, Claire, with Bill Slocum. *The Babe and I.* Englewood Cliffs, NJ: Prentice-Hall, 1959. 215p. Abridged in *Saturday Evening Post,* CCXXXI (March 7, 1959), 24–25+.

50749. Ruth, George H, ("Babe"). *Babe Ruth's Baseball Book for 1932.* Edited by Christy Walsh. New York: Syndicate Publishing Co., 1932. All writings attributed to Ruth were ghostwritten, most by Walsh.

50750. _____. *Babe Ruth's Baseball Advice.* Chicago, IL: Rand McNally & Co., 1936. 32p. Ghostwritten tips in a booklet noteworthy for the full page photos of Ruth in action.

50751. _____. *Babe Ruth's Big Book of Baseball.* Akron, OH: The Quaker Oats Co., 1935. 63p. Ghostwritten book of tips; includes the Babe's lifetime record.

50752. _____. "Babe Ruth's Favorite Stories." *Baseball Digest,* XXIV (April 1965), 54–57.

50753. _____. *Babe Ruth's Own Book of Baseball.* New York: G.P. Putnam, 1928. 301p. Reprinted, with a new introduction by Jerome Holtzman, by the University of Nebraska Press in 1992.

50754. _____. "Bat It Out." *Rotarian,* LVII (July 1940), 12–14.

50755. _____. *How to Play Baseball.* Introduction by Christy Walsh. New York: Cosmopolitan Book Co., 1930–1933. Ghostwritten tips on technique by position, coaching and signaling.

50756. _____. *How to Play Baseball.* San Francisco, CA: Sports Classics Press, 1977. 48p. Condensation of edition first published in 1931.

50757. _____. "I Was a Bad Kid." In: Charles Einstein, ed. *The Second Fireside Book of Baseball.* New York: Simon and Schuster, 1958. Pp. 307–312.

50758. _____. "Kids Can't Take It If We Don't Give It." In: Norman V. Peale, ed. *Faith Made Them Champions.* Englewood Cliffs, NJ: Prentice-Hall, 1955. Pp. 45–48.

50759. _____. "My Greatest Baseball Experiences So Far." *Baseball Magazine,* XXV (November 1920), 597–668+.

50760. _____. "My Greatest Day in Baseball." In: Eliot Cohen, ed. *My Greatest Day in Baseball.* New York: Little Simon, 1991. Pp. 95–98.

50761. _____. *Quaker Oats Instructional Series: Baseball.* 4 vols. Akron, OH: Quaker Oats Co., 1939. Four ghostwritten booklets: 1) *How to Knock Home Runs*; 2) *How to Play the Outfield*; 3) *How to Play the Infield*; 4) *How to Throw Curves.*

50762. _____. "The Secret of My Heavy Hitting." *Baseball Magazine,* XXV (August 1920), 419–422.

50763. _____. "Things Which I Believe Have Been Responsible for My Successful Batting." *Baseball Magazine,* XXIV (April 1920), 618–621+.

50764. _____. "Voices from the Past: 'How It Feels to Be a Has-Been.'" *Sport,* XLIII (February 1967), 42–45.

50765. _____. "Why a Pitcher Should Hit." *Baseball Magazine,* XX (February 1918), 336–337. Ghostwritten.

50766. _____. "Why I Hate to Walk." *Collier's,* LXVI (July 10, 1920), 11.

50767. _____. and Bob Considine. *The Babe Ruth Story.* New York: E.P. Dutton, 1948, 250p.

50768. Salsinger, H.G. "The Day Ruth Thought He Was Tarzan." *Baseball Digest,* XII (October 1953), 79–81.

50769. _____. "Which Was the Greatest?: Ty Cobb or Babe Ruth?" In: J. G. Taylor Spink, ed. *Baseball Register, 1951.* St. Louis, MO: The Sporting News, 1951. Pp. 2–51. Author chooses Cobb.

50770. Sanborn, Irving E. "How Ruth Became Baseball's Most Famous Star." *Baseball Magazine,* XXXII (December 1923), 301–304.

50771. Sanford, William R. and Carl R. Green. *Babe Ruth.* Sports Immortals Series. New York: Crestwood House, 1992. 48p.

50772. Savage, Jeff. "Babe Ruth." In: his *Home Run Kings.* New York: Raintree Steck-Vaughn Publishers, 1999. Pp. 8–15.

50773. Sawyer, C. Ford. "The Man Who Gave Babe Ruth His Start." *Baseball Magazine,* XXIV (April 1920), 640–641+.

50774. Scahill, Edward M. "Did Babe Ruth Have a Comparative Advantage as a Pitcher?" *Journal of Economic Education,* XXI (Fall 1990), 402–410.

50775. Schalk, Ray. "Why Outguessing Ruth is Baseball's Toughest Problem." *Baseball Magazine,* XXV (October 1920), 519–521.

50776. Schonauer, David. "Babe's Last Blow." *American Photo,* XIII (March/April 2002), 68–69. Discusses newly discovered 1948 Ralph Morse photograph of Babe Ruth's farewell to Yankee Stadium in New York in 1948.

50777. Schott, Arthur O. "The Babe's First Big Box Score." *The Baseball Research Journal,* I (1972), 38–39.

50778. _____. "They've Now Dimmed Ruth Splurge." *The Baseball Research Journal,* IV (1975), 102–104.

50779. Schreiber, Le Anne. "Saviors : Babe Ruth, Jackie Robinson, Larry Bird, Magic Johnson, Pete Rozelle, Tiger Woods." In: Jay Lovinger, ed. *The Gospel According to ESPN: Saints, Saviors & Sinners.* New York : Hyperion, 2002. Chapter 3.

50780. Scully, Charley. "Babe Ruth-Pitcher." *Baseball Magazine,* LXXXVII (October 1951), 16–18.

50781. Seaver, Tom, with Marty Appel. "The Called-Shot Home Run." In: his *Great Moments in Baseball: From the World Series of 1903 to the Modern Records of Nolan Ryan.* New York: Carol Communications, 1992. Pp. 101–106.

50782. Seehorst, Mary. "PM People: Babe Ruth." *Popular Mechanics,* CLXXX (June 2003), 56, 58.

50783. Shannon, Paul H. "New York Clubs Gives $125,000 for Battering Babe, 1920." In: Glenn Stout, ed. *Impossible Dreams: A Red Sox Collection.* Boston, MA: Mariner Books, 2003. Pp. 95–104.

50784. Shapiro, Herb. *Babe Ruth.* San Diego, CA: Revolutionary Comics, 1992. 30p.

50785. Shapiro, Milton J. "Babe. Ruth." In: his *Champions at the Bat.* New York: Julian Messner, 1968. Pp. 21–31.

50786. Shaughnessy, Dan. "Babe Ruth: He Popularized the Home Run." *Baseball Digest,* LVIII (July 1999), 34–37.

50787. _____. *The Curse of the Bambino.* New York: Dutton, 1990. 210p.

50788. Shein, Arn. "Mom and the Babe." *Modern Maturity,* XXXIII (April-May 1990), 62–65.

50789. Sher, Jack. "The Babe Ruth You Never Knew." *Sport,* II (January 1947), 58–68. Reprinted in Editors of *Spot, Twelve Sports Immortals.* New York: Bartholomew House, 1959. Pp. 280–304.

50790. _____. "The Sultan of Swat." In: Editors of *Reader's Digest. Great Lives, Great Deeds.* Hicksville, NY: Reader's Digest Association, 1964. Pp. 474–479.

50791. _____. "What Baseball Owes to Babe Ruth." *Reader's Digest,* L (April 1947), 1–5.

50792. Shipp, Cameron. "Babe Ruth Speaking." *Sport,* V (September 1948), 10–11+.

50793. Shocker, Urban. "Pitching to Babe Ruth." *Baseball Magazine,* XXXI (November 1923), 540+.

50794. Shoemaker, Robert H. "Babe Ruth." In: his *Best in Baseball.* New York: Crowell, 1959. Pp. 169–185.

50795. Silverman, Al "Babe Ruth." In: his *Sports Titans of the 20th Century.* New York: G.P. Putnam, 1968. Pp. 29–50.

50796. Simons, Herbert. "The Babe's Phantom 155th Game." *Baseball Digest,* XV (October 1956), 35–37. Reprinted in *Baseball Digest,* XXX (January 1971), 69–74.

50797. Slevin, R.L. "The Babe Bows Out." In: Editors of *Sports Illustrated. Yesterday In Sports.* New York: A.S. Barnes, 1956. Pp. 109–110. Also published as "Roaring Tribute of the Unbelieving Fans was a Gratifying Sound," in Philip Dunaway and George DeKay, eds., *Turning Point* (New York: Random House, 1959) pp. 280–281.

50798. Sloate, Susan. "Babe Ruth." In: her *Hotshots:*

Baseball Greats of the Game When They Were Kids. Boston, MA: Little, Brown, 1991. Pp. 4–9.

50799. Smelser, Marshall. "The Babe on Balance." *American Scholar,* XLIV (April 1975), 299–304.

50800. _____. *Life That Ruth Built: A Biography.* New York: Quadrangle Books, 1975. 592p.

50801. Smith, Ira L. "George Herman (Babe) Ruth." In: his *Baseball's Famous Outfielders.* New York: A.S. Barnes, 1954. Pp. 139–144.

50802. Smith, Leverett T, Jr. "The Changing Style of Play: Cobb vs. Ruth." In: John E. Dreifort, ed. *Baseball History from Outside the Lines: a Reader.* Lincoln, NE: University of Nebraska Press, 2001. Chapter 8.

50803. _____. "Ty Cobb, Babe Ruth and the Changing Image of the Athletic Hero." In: Ray Broadus Browne, comp. *Heroes of Popular Culture.* Bowling Green, OH: Bowling Green University Popular Press, 1972. Chapter 7.

50804. Smith, Robert M. "Babe Ruth." In: his *Heroes of Baseball.* Cleveland: World Publishing Co., 1952. Pp. 196–205.

50805. _____. *Babe Ruth's America.* New York: Crowell, 1974. 309p.

50806. _____. "Babe: The One and Only." *Baseball Magazine,* XLVIII (August 1956), 34–41.

50807. _____. "One of a Kind." *The New York Times Magazine,* (September 16, 1973), 43–44+.

50808. Smith, Ron. "Babe Ruth." In: his *Heroes of the Hall: Baseball's Greatest Players.* New York: Contemporary Books, 2002. Pp. 402–406.

50809. _____. "Babe Ruth-1." In: his *The Sporting News Selects Baseball's 100 Greatest Players.* St. Louis, MO: The Sporting News, 1998. Pp. 10–12.

50810. _____. "Hammerin' Hank and the Babe." In: his *The Sporting News Selects Baseball's 25 Greatest Moments.* New York: McGraw-Hill, 1999. Pp. 40–45.

50811. Smith, Walter ("Red"). "Connie Mack Passed Up Babe Ruth." *Baseball Digest,* III (March 1944), 19–21.

50812. _____. "One of a Kind." In: Dan Riley and Miro Weinberger, eds. *The Yankees Reader.* New York: Mariner Books, 1999. Pp. 110–119 and in David Halberstam, ed. *The Best American Sports Writing of the Century* (Boston, MA: Houghton, Mifflin, 1999), pp. 156–161.

50813. Snider, Edwin D. ("Duke"). "We'll Never Break Ruth's Record." *Baseball Digest,* XVI (October-November 1957), 61–76.

50814. Sobol, Ken. *Babe Ruth and the American Dream.* New York: Random House, 1974. 309p.

50815. _____. "The True Story of Babe Ruth's Visit to Ailing Youth." *Baseball Digest,* XLV (March 1986), 81–84.

50816. "Speaking of Pictures: Discovery of Old Film with Babe as Homer-Hitting Iceman Adds to Ruth Legend." *Life,* XXIX (August 28,1960), 14–16.

50817. Stann, Francis. "The Babe Could Really Pitch." *Baseball Digest,* XVII (March 1969), 48–51.

50818. _____. "Ruth Deal Still Game's Top Steal." *Baseball Digest,* XXVI (March 1967), 49–51.

50819. Steadman, John F. "The Day Ruth Broke In." *Baseball Digest,* XXIII (July 1964), 47–51.

50820. _____. "Dolph Camilli: Old-Time National League Star Recalls The Babe." *Baseball Digest,* LVI (June 1997), 78–81.

50821. _____. "Lab Tests Proved That Babe Ruth was Indeed Superior." *Baseball Digest,* LI (October 1992), 57–59.

50822. _____. "[Waite] Hoyt Separates Fact, Fiction About Ruth." *Baseball Digest,* XXVII (May 1960), 62–65.

50823. Stevens, Julia Ruth, with Bill Gilbert. *Major League Dad: A Daughter's Cherished Memories.* New York: Benchmark Press, 2001. 128p. Also simultaneously published in a 117-page edition by the Chicago, IL, firm of Triumph Books.

50824. Stockton, J. Roy. "Baseball's Most Picturesque Player." *Baseball Magazine,* XXIX (June 1922), 302–303.

50825. Stoler, Peter. "The King of Swing." *Time,* CIV (August 26, 1974), 76+.

50826. Stuller, J. "Legends That Will Not Die." *Saturday Evening Post,* CCLVII (July-August 1985), 42–49.

50827. Sugar, Bert Randolph. "Babe Ruth's Last Hurrah: Pittsburgh Pirates vs. Boston Braves, May 25, 1935." In: his *Baseball's 50 Greatest Games.* Rev. ed. North Dighton, MA: The JG Press, 1994. Pp. 173–176.

50828. _____. "Babe Ruth's 60th Home Run: New York Yankees vs. Washington Senators, September 30, 1927." In: his *Baseball's 50 Greatest Games.* Rev. ed. North Dighton, MA: The JG Press, 1994. Pp. 138–140.

50829. Sullivan, George. "Babe Ruth." In: his *Great Lives: Sports.* New York: Scribner's, 1988. Pp. 227–235.

50830. Sumner, John L. "Babe Ruth's North Carolina Spring: The Tar Heel Perspective." *Maryland Historical Magazine,* LXXXVI (Spring 1991), 80–89.

50831. _____. "Jim Thorpe and Babe Ruth: Sports Legends." *Tar Heel Junior Historian,* (Spring 2000), 22–25.

50832. Susman, Warren. "Piety, Profits, and Play: The 1920s – Bruce Barton, Henry Ford, Babe Ruth." In: Vol. 2 of Howard H. Quint and Milton Cantor, eds. *Men, Women, and Issues in American History.* Homewood, IL: Dorsey Press, 1974. Chapter 11.

50833. Thomas, Chet. "Babe Ruth: the Super Player." *Baseball Magazine,* XXV (November 1920), 586–597+.

50834. Thomas, R. J. and J. D. Cantwell. "Tobacco, Alcohol and Cancer." *JAMA: Journal of the American Medical Association,* CCLVIII (October 16, 1987), 2062; CCLIX (February 12, 1988), 840–841.

50835. Thompson, Larry. "Let's Hear It Again: Ruth's 1920 Best Ever." *The Baseball Research Journal,* XIV (1985), 41–43. Reprinted as "The Best Year Any Player Ever Had," in: Mark Alvarez, ed. *The Perfect Game* (New York: Barnes & Noble Books, 1995), pp. 1–7.

50836. Torres, John Albert. "Babe Ruth." In: his *Top 10 Baseball Legends.* Berkeley Heights, NJ: Enslow Publishers, 2001. Pp. 34–37.

50837. Trachtenberg, Leo. "The Babe's Last Stand." *Yankees Magazine,* XIX (February 1999), 80–87. Final pitching appearance.

50838. Trimble, Patrick. "Babe Ruth and American Baseball: The Media Construction of a 1920s Sport Personality." *Colby Quarterly,* XXXII (March 1996), 45–57.

50839. _____. "Persistence of Vision: A Study of Babe Ruth in *Headin' Home.*" In: Stephen C. Wood and J. David Pincus, eds. *Reel Baseball: Essays and Interviews on the National Pastime, Hollywood, and American Culture* (Jefferson, NC: McFarland & Co., Inc., 2003. Pp. 120–133.

50840. Turley, Bob. "A Babe in the Woods: A Boy Who Caddied for Babe Ruth Remembers." *Yankee,* LVII (June 1993), 92+.

50841. "25 Years Ago in Life." *Life,* LXXII (May 12, 1972), 30–31.

50842. Urban, Mychael. "I Would Have Liked to Have Played with the Babe: Major Leaguers Choose Stars with Whom They'd Like to Have Performed With." *Baseball Digest,* LXIII (July 2004), 67–69.

50843. Valenti, Dan. "Babe Ruth." In: his *Clout!* New York: Stephen Greene Press, 1989. Pp. 40–47.

50844. Van Loon, N. "Babe Ruth Comes to Pickle River." In: William Humber and John St. James, eds. *All I Thought About was Baseball: Writings on a Canadian Pastime.* North York, Ont.: University of Toronto Press, 1996. Pp. 292–303.

50845. Van Ripper, Guernsey. *Babe Ruth, Baseball Boy.* Indianapolis: Bobbs-Merrill, 1954. 192p. History of Ruth's boyhood. Reissued in 1959, and in 1983, with the title *Babe Ruth, One of Baseball's Greatest.*

50846. Vecsey, George. "George Vecsey on Babe Ruth." In: *The Baseball Hall of Fame 50th Anniversary Book.* New York: Prentice-Hall, 1988. Pp. 136–154.

50847. Verrall, Charles S. "Babe Ruth." In: his *Mighty Men of Baseball.* New York; Aladdin Books, 1955. Pp. 97–106.

50848. ____. *Babe Ruth, "Sultan of Swat."* Champaign, IL: Garrard, 1976. 96p.

50849. Voigt, David Quentin. "Babe Ruth." In: John A. Garrity and Marsh C. Carries, eds. *American National Biography.* 24 vols. New York: Oxford University Press, 1999. XIX, 121–124.

50850. ____. "George Herman 'Babe,' 'Sultan of Swat,' 'The Bambino' Ruth, Jr." In: Vol. Q-Z of David L. Porter, ed. *Biographical Dictionary of American Sports: Baseball.* Rev. and enlarged ed. Westport, CT: Greenwood Press, 2000. Pp. 1336–1338.

50851. ____. "George Herman ('Babe') Ruth." In: Supplement 4 of John A. Garrity, ed. *The Dictionary of American Biography.* New York: Scribner, 1974. Pp. 709–712.

50852. Wagenheim, Kal. *Babe Ruth: His Life and Legend.* New York: Praeger, 1974. 274p. Reprinted by the Maplewood, NJ firm of Waterfront Press in 1990 and by the Kingston, RI, firm of Olmstead Press in 2001.

50853. Walker, Martin. "Babe Ruth and American Sports." In: his *America Reborn: A 20th Century Narrative in 26 Lives.* Westminster, MD: Alfred A. Knopf, 2000. Pp. 75–89.

50854. Wallace, Irving, *et al.* "Babe Ruth." In: their *Intimate Sex Lives of Famous People.* Now York: Delacorte, 1981. Pp. 561–563.

50855. Wallop, Douglas. "The Babe." In: Tom Seaver, ed. *How I Would Pitch to Babe Ruth.* Chicago: Playboy Press, 1974. Pp. 4–12.

50856. Walsh, John Evangelist. "Babe Ruth and the Legend of the Called Shot." *Wisconsin Magazine of History,* LXXVII (Summer 1994), 243–265.

50857. Ward, G. C. "Papa, Satchmo, and the Babe." *American Heritage,* XL (May-June 1989), 14+.

50858. Ward, Geoffrey C. and Ken Burns. "The Sultan of Swat." *U.S. News & World Report,* CXVII (August 29, 1994), 75–78+.

50859. Ward, John J. "The Coming Southpaw." *Baseball Magazine,* XVII (July 1916), 43–46.

50860. ____. "Records and Near-Records of Big Babe Ruth." *Baseball Magazine,* XXXVII (September 1926), 455–456+.

50861. ____, "A Red-Letter Day in the Babe's Career." *Baseball Magazine,* XXVII (August 1921), 402–403.

50862. ____. "A Revival for Babe Ruth?" *Baseball Magazine,* XXIX (July 1922), 349–351.

50863. ____. "They Call Him Baseball's Wealthiest Ballplayer." *Baseball Magazine,* XLIII (September 1929), 454–455.

50864. "Wedding Bells — and a Home Run." *Literary Digest,* CI (May 4, 1929), 66–69.

50865. Weiss, Peter. "Babe Ruth." In: his *Baseball's All-Time Goats: As Chosen by America's Top Sportswriters.* Holbrook, MA: Bob Adams, Inc, 1992. Pp. 144–147.

50866. Weldon, Martin. *Babe Ruth.* New York: Crowell, 1948. 280p.

50867. Werber, Bill, with Paul Rogers. "The Babe Ruth I Remember." *Elysian Fields Quarterly,* XVI (Winter 1999), 34–42. Also published in Werber's *Memories of a Ballplayer: Bill Werber and Baseball in the 1930s* (Cleveland, OH: The Society for American Baseball Research, 2001), pp. 11–20.

50868. West, Gary P. "Where and When the Babe Poled His First Homer." In: Clyde Hirt, ed. *Sports Quarterly Presents Baseball, 1971.* New York: Counterpoint, Inc., 1971. Pp. 7–8+.

50869. West, Richard. "The Babe Saves the Game." *Beckett Baseball Card Monthly,* IV (January-February 1987), 31–66.

50870. "What Babe Ruth is Worth to the Yankees." *Literary Digest,* CIV (March 29, 1930), 38–42.

50871. "When 'Babe Ruth Hit No. 60." *The New York Times Magazine,* (September 10, 1961), 104+.

50872. Will, George F. "Babe Ruth, Replacement Player." In: his *Bunts: Curt Flood, Camden Yards, Pete Rose and Other Reflections on Baseball.* New York: Touchstone Books, 1998. Pp. 253–255.

50873. Williams, Joe. "Babe Ruth." In: Christy Walsh, ed. *Baseball's Greatest Lineup.* New York: A.S. Barnes, 1962. Pp. 31–44.

50874. Williams, Pete. "Did the Babe Call His Shot?: Sportswriters and the Creation of Myth." *The Baseball Research Journal,* XVI (1987), 62–64. Reprinted as "Did the Babe Call His Shot: Part I," in: Mark Alvarez, ed. *The Perfect Game* (New York: Barnes & Noble Books, 1995), pp. 234–240.

50875. Williamson, Toni and Gary Rees. "Babe Ruth." In: their *Twenty Names in Sport.* New York : Marshall Cavendish, 1988. Chapter 1.

50876. Wolf: Al. "Good Low Change-Up Babe Ruth's Weakness." *Baseball Digest,* X (October 1961), 4–5.

50877. Wolf, Bob. "Many Parallels in Careers of Aaron and Ruth." *Baseball Digest,* XXXIV (July 1975), 37–40.

50878. Wolff, C.G. "Innocents at Home." *Massachusetts Review,* XVI (Summer 1975), 591–598.

50879. Wood, Allan. *1918: Babe Ruth and the World Champion Boston Red Sox.* San Jose, CA : Writers Club Press, 2000. 420p.

50880. "Yankee Doodle Dandy!" *Outlook,* CXXXV (October 24, 1923), 293–294.

50881. "Yankees Sign Babe Ruth." In: Dean A. Sullivan, ed. *Middle Innings: A Documentary History of Baseball, 1900–1948.* Lincoln, NE: University of Nebraska Press, 1998. Pp. 91–92. Reprinted from the *New York Herald,* Jan. 6, 1920.

50882. Zacharias, George. "My Life with the Babe." *Sport,* III (October 1947), 50–56+.

50883. Ziegel, Vic. "The Babe." *Life,* XV (April 1992), 40–51.

50884. Zeigler, Earle F. "Babe Ruth and Lou Gehrig: A United States Dilemma." *The Physical Educator,* XLIV (Spring 1987), 325–329.

50885. Zureick, Perry A. "Home Run Revolution." *Sports History,* III (September 1989), 30–35.

Richard David ("Dick") Ruthven
P. (B: March 27, 1951, Sacramento, CA). Philadelphia (NL), 1973–1975; Atlanta (NL), 1976–1978; Philadelphia (NL), 1978–1983; Chicago (NL), 1983–1986. Remarks: Won 123 games and lost 127 in 14 summer campaigns; won deciding Game Five of 1980 NLCS.

50886. Fimrite, Ron. "So Far, So Good, So Fast." *Sports Illustrated,* XXXVIII (April 30, 1973), 56+.

Blondy Ryan *see* **John Collins ("Blondy") Ryan**
Connie Ryan *see* **Cornelius ("Connie") Ryan**
Cornelius Joseph ("Connie") Ryan
2B-3B-MGR. Remarks: stole home in a game, July 7, 1950, had one grand slam homer, May 23, 1951, and went six-for-six in a game, April 16, 1953; interim manager, Atlanta (NL), 1975 and Texas (AL), 1977, winning 11 games and losing 22 (.333).

50887. Kelley, Brent P. "Connie Ryan: A Brave in Three Cities." In: his *The Early All-Stars: Conversations with Standout Baseball Players in the 1930s and 1940s.* Jefferson, NC: McFarland & Co., Inc., 1997. Pp. 145–152.

James Edward ("Jimmy") Ryan
OF-P. (B: Feb. 11, 1863, Clinton, MA-D: Oct. 26, 1923). Chicago (NL), 1885–1889; Chicago (P.), 1890; Chicago (NL), 1891–1900; Washington (AL), 1902–1903. Remarks: Had 2,531 hits (118 homers) and 408 stolen bases in 2,012 games in 18 seasons; as a pitcher, won five and lost one of 24 games involved in; hit for the cycle twice, July 28, 1888 and July 1, 1891; led NL in singles and doubles, 1888; scored six runs in one game, July 25, 1894; had career total of 20 lead-off homers; minor league manager, 1904; resided in Chicago post baseball career, becoming a deputy sheriff.

50877a. Ahrens, Arthur R. "An Assist for Jimmy Ryan." *The Baseball Research Journal,* XII (1983), 66–70.

50888. Kush, Raymond D. "James Edward 'Jimmy' Ryan." In: Vol. Q-Z of David L. Porter, ed. *Biographical Dictionary of American Sports: Baseball.* Rev. and enlarged ed. Westport, CT: Greenwood Press, 2000. Pp. 1338–1339.

50889. Tattersall, John C. "Hitting Leadoff Homers." *The Baseball Research Journal,* III (1973), 12–18.

50890. Wilbert, Warren and William Hageman. "Jimmy Ryan—1888." In: their *Chicago Cubs: Seasons at the Summit, the 50 Greatest Individual Seasons.* Champaign, IL: Sagamore Publishing, 1997. Pp. 183–186.

Jimmy Ryan *see* **James F. ("Jimmy") Ryan**
John Collins ("Blondy") Ryan
SS-3B. (B: Jan. 4, 1908, Lynn, MA-D: Nov. 28, 1959). Chicago (AL), 1930; New York (NL), 1933–1934; Philadelphia (NL) and New York (AL), 1935; New York (NL), 1937–1938. Remarks: Obtained 318 hits (eight homers) in 386 games in six big league seasons; tied a MLB record by turning five double plays in one game, April 21, 1935.

50891. Burkholder, Ed. "Blondy Ryan." In his *Baseball Immortals.* New York: Christopher, 1955. Pp. 104–105.

Lynn Nolan Ryan★
P. (B: Jan. 31, 1947, Refugio, TX). New York (NL), 1966–1971; California (AL), 1972–1979 Houston 1980–1988; Texas (AL), 1989–1993. Remarks: Had 324 victories and 292 defeats in 28 years; established various records including the modern ones for most seasons with 300 or more strikeouts, most strikeouts (5,714), most walks (2,795), and most no-hitters; pitched seven no-hitters (May 15 and July 15, 1973, Sept. 28, 1974, June 1, 1975, Sept. 26, 1981, June 11, 1990, and May 1, 1991); had 19 strikeouts in an 11 inning game, Aug. 20, 1974; had 19 strikeouts in a 10 inning game, June 8, 1977; and had 18 strikeouts in one nine inning game, Sept. 10, 1976; first player to receive a $1 million annual salary, Nov. 19, 1979; post baseball career, a rancher, television spokesman for a pain reliever, and asst. to the pres. of the Texas (AL) club; named to Texas Sports Hall of Fame, 1985; elected to the National Baseball Hall of Fame in 1999, where his plaque

reads: "A fierce competitor and one of baseball's most intimidating figures on the pitching mound for four decades. His overpowering fastball and unparalleled longevity produced 324 victories and a host of major league records. Lifetime benchmarks include 5,714 strikeouts, seven no-hitters and 12 one-hitters in 27 seasons pitched. Led league in strikeouts 11 times and fanned 300 batters in a season on six occasions, including a record 383 in 1973. Strikeout victims totaled 1,176 different players. A Texas legend whose widespread popularity extended far beyond his native state."

50892. Aaseng, Nathan. "Nolan Ryan." In: his *Record Breakers of Pro Sports.* Minneapolis, MN: Lerner Publications, 1987. Pp. 56–67.

50893. Allee-Walsh, Brian. "Nolan Ryan Belongs in a Higher League." *Baseball Digest,* XLI (January 1982), 26–30.

50894. Allen, Maury. "Nolan Ryan (1966–Present)." In: his *Baseball's 100.* New York: Galahad Books, 1981. Pp. 244–246.

50895. _____. "When Nolan Ryan Almost Quit the Game." *Baseball Digest,* XXXIX (March 1980), 68–71.

50896. Anderson, Dave. "The Ryan Express Races for the Records." *Sport,* LXVII August 1978), 66–69+.

50897. Anderson, John. "Sales Pitcher." *Texas Monthly,* XIX (September 1991), 96–97. Souvenir marketing of Ryan.

50898. Anderson, Ken. *Nolan Ryan: Texas Fastball to Cooperstown.* Austin, TX: Eakin Press, 2000. 158p.

50899. Axthelm, Pete. "Ryan's Fast-Ball Express." *Newsweek,* CVI (July 22, 1985), 67+.

50900. Baig, E. C. "Investing in Nolan Ryan." *U.S. News and World Report,* CXI (August 12, 1991), 50–52.

50901. *Beckett Tribute to Nolan Ryan.* Dallas, TX: Beckett Publications, 1993. 80p.

50902. Benson, John. "Nolan Ryan—1977." In: his *Baseball's Top 100: The Best Individual Seasons of All Time.* Wilton, CT: Diamond Library, 1996. Pp. 233–235.

50903. Blair, Sam. "Nolan Ryan: Strikeout King." *Boy's Life,* LXXXI (April 1991), 18–22.

50904. Blake, John, ed. *The Life and Times of Nolan Ryan.* Arlington, TX: Public Relations Department, Texas Rangers, 1991. 64p.

50905. _____. *Ryan 34: The Retirement of Nolan Ryan's Uniform Number.* Arlington, TX: Public Relations Department, Texas Rangers, 1996. 132p.

50906. Brewster, Tom. "The Care and Feeding of Baseball's Greatest Arm." *Life,* XII (May 1989), 86–87.

50907. Brill, Bob. "Nolan Ryan: National Hero and Businessman." *Sports Collector's Digest,* XXI (April 15, 1994), 60–61.

50908. Brody, Robert. "Ryan's Hope: At 44, Nolan Ryan Wants a Few More Good Seasons—Given How Hard He Works to Stay in Shape, We Wouldn't Bet Against Him." *Men's Health,* VI (August 1991), 72–75.

50909. "Brine for Nolan Ryan." *Life,* LXIV (May 31, 1968), 77–78.

50910. Buckley, James, Jr. "The Ryan Express." In: his *DK Readers: MLB Strikeout Kings.* New York: DK Pub Merchandise, 2001. Pp. 40–45.

50911. Burka, Paul. "Savoring the Private Ryan." *Texas Monthly,* XXVII (April 1999), 102–105+.

50912. Castleberry, Bruce. "A Closer Look: Nolan Ryan." *Beckett Baseball Card Monthly,* VI (October 1989), 6–7.

50913. Cernock, Larry. "Ryan Checklist." *Baseball Cards,* X (August 1990), 86–105.

50914. Chass, Murray. "Ryan Going to Astros for $4 Million: Reprinted from *The New York Times*, November 16, 1979." In: Gene Brown, ed. *The New York Times Encyclopedia of Sports, Vol. 15: Update.* New York: Arno Press, 1980. Pp. 50–51.

50915. "A Closer Look: Nolan Ryan." *Beckett Baseball Card Monthly,* IX (January 1992), 6–7.

50916. Compton, Eric. "A Sixth No-Hitter for Nolan Ryan?" In: Zander Hollander, ed. *1982 The Complete Handbook Of Baseball.* New York: New American Library, 1982. Pp. 32–39.

50917. Corliss, Richard. "An Old-Timer for All Seasons." *Time,* CXXXV (June 25, 1990), 68+.

50918. D'Aniello, Joe. "The 10,000 Careers of Nolan Ryan: A Computer Simulation Clarifies His Long Career." *The Baseball Research Journal,* XXX (2000), 54–57.

50919. Debs, Victor Jr. "Nolan's Near No-Hitters." In: his *Missed It by That Much: Baseball Players Who Challenged the Record Book.* Jefferson, NC: McFarland & Co., Inc., 1998. Pp. 160–175.

50920. DeFresne, Jim. "Nolan Ryan." In: his *Baseball's Hottest Hurlers.* [SL] : Willowisp Press, 1984. Chapter 1.

50921. DeMarco, Tony. "Nolan Ryan: The Eternal Flame." In: *Petersen's Baseball: 1992 Pro Preview.* Los Angeles, CA: Petersen's, 1992. Pp. 64–65.

50922. Dewan, John and Don Zminda. "Can Anyone Hit Nolan Ryan-Now or Ever?" In: STATS, Inc. *STATS 1992 Baseball Scoreboard.* Chicago, IL: STATS Publishing, 1992. Pp. 158–160.

50923. Dickey, Roger F. and Clyde E. *Nolan Ryan: Texas Rangers Hall of Fame Legend.* Richardson, TX : Crest Publications, 2000. 80p.

50924. DiPace, Tom. "Superstar Gallery: Nolan Ryan." *Beckett Baseball Card Monthly,* VII (January 1990), 82–83.

50925. Dowling, Tom. "Nolan Ryan: When He's Good, He's Great..." *Sport,* L September 1970), 50–53.

50926. Durslag, Melvin. "How Nolan Ryan Compares to [Sandy] Koufax." *Baseball Digest,* XXXIII (February 1974), 29–31.

50927. Fimrite, Ron. "Bringer of the Big Heat." *Sports Illustrated,* XLII (June 16, 1975), 32–33.

50928. _____. "A Great Hand with Old Cowhide." *Sports Illustrated,* LXV (September 29, 1986), 84–88.

50929. _____."Speed Trap for an Angel." *Sports Illustrated,* XLI (September 16, 1974), 98+.

50930. "Final Look: Nolan Ryan." *Beckett Baseball Card Monthly,* XI, no. 106 (January 1994), 105–106.

50931. "Forever Baseball's Strikeout King." In: *1991 Spring Training: Grapefruit and Cactus League Yearbook, Vol. IV.* Chapel Hill, NC: Vanguard Sports Publications, 1991. Pp. 10–12.

50932. Frommer, Harvey and Frederick J. "Nolan Ryan." In: their *Growing Up Baseball: An Oral History.* Dallas, TX: Taylor Publishing Co., 2001. Pp. 199–203.

50933. Furlong, William B. "Baseball's Best-Paid Pitcher Comes Along." *Sport,* LXX (April 1980), 66–69.

50934. Galloway, Randy. "Beers with Nolan Ryan." *Sport,* LXXXI (April 1990), 21–22.

50935. Gammons, Peter. "Nolan Ryan: Still a Gem Among His Pitching Peers." *Baseball Digest,* L (November 1991), 80–83.

50936. Gergen, Joe. "Nolan Ryan: The Greatest Strikeout Pitcher Ever." *Baseball Digest,* XLVIII (August 1989), 16–23.

50937. Givens, Robert. "Throwing Old Gracefully." *Newsweek,* CXIV (August 28, 1989), 65+.

50938. Gluck, Herb. "Nolan Ryan: A Season of Strike-

outs." In: his *Baseball's Great Moments.* New York: Random House, 1975. Pp. 47–56.

50939. Greenberg, Keith Eliot and Dick Smolinski. *Nolan Ryan, Ageless Superstar.* Vero Beach, FL: Rourke Enterprises, 1993. 48p.

50940. Greer, Jim. "Ryan Makes Winning Pitch for Rural Bank." *Houston Business Journal,* XX (June 18, 1990), 1–2. Danbury (TX) State Bank.

50941. _____. "Ryan Signs Multi-Faceted Deal with Astros." *Houston Business Journal,* XLIV (February 24, 2004), 1–2.

50942. Grove, Wayne. "Player's Choice: Nolan Ryan." *Beckett Sports Collectibles,* X (July 2001), 98–101.

50943. Gutman, Bill. "Nolan Ryan." In: his *More Modern Baseball Superstars.* New York: Dodd, Mead, 1978. Pp. 67–85.

50944. _____. "Nolan Ryan." In: his *New Breed Heroes in Pro Baseball.* New York: Julian Messner, 1974. Pp. 47–56.

50945. _____. "Nolan Ryan." In: his *Pro Sports Champions.* New York: Pocket Books, 1990. Chapter 7.

50946. Hano, Arnold. "Nolan Ryan: Stri-k-k-k-e in The Night!" In: Ray Robinson, ed. *Baseball Stars of 1974.* New York: Pyramid Books, 1974. Pp. 91–97.

50947. _____. "Nolan Ryan: The Natural." In: Ray Robinson, ed. *Baseball Stars of 1975.* New York: Pyramid Books, 1975. Pp. 106–110.

50948. _____. "Nolan Ryan: The Untouchable." In: Ray Robinson, ed. *Baseball Stars of 1973.* New York: Pyramid Books, 1973. Pp. 92–96.

50949. _____. "Warning: Nolan Ryan's Smoke is Dangerous to a Batter's Health." *Sport,* LV (June 1973), 36–41.

50950. Harper, James W. "Lynn Nolan Ryan." In: Vol. Q-Z of David L. Porter, ed. *Biographical Dictionary of American Sports: Baseball.* Rev. and enlarged ed. Westport, CT: Greenwood Press, 2000. Pp. 1339–1341.

50951. Henry, P. "Nolan Ryan and the Cy Young Award." *Nine: A Journal of Baseball History and Social Policy Perspective,* VII (Spring 1999), 102–115.

50952. Herrera, Mitsuko. *Nolan Ryan.* San Diego, CA: Revolutionary Comics, 1992. 30p.

50953. Herskowitz, Mickey. "Baseball Without Nolan Ryan." In: John Blake, *et al. Texas Rangers Official 1994 Yearbook.* Arlington, TX: Public Relations Dept., Texas Rangers, 1994. Pp. 50–54.

50954. _____. "Farewell to Nolan Ryan: He was a Baseball Treasure." *Baseball Digest,* LIII (February 1994), 38–43.

50955. Hillman, John. "The Fastest Pitch." *Boys' Quest,* (June-July 2000), 12–13.

50956. Hoffer, Richard. "Armed and Still Dangerous." *GQ-Gentlemen's Quarterly,* LVIII (May 1988), 246–249.

50957. Hohfeld, Neil "Knockout Punch: Fastball Helped Blaze Way for Nolan Ryan to Set Strikeout Mark." *Baseball Digest,* LX (January 2001), 50–53.

50958. _____. "Strikeout King Nolan Ryan Still a Power Pitcher at Age 38." *Baseball Digest,* XLIV (July 1985), 29–32.

50959. Holtzman, Jerome. "Nolan Ryan Legend Grew From 'a Little White Lie.'" *Baseball Digest,* L (August 1991), 34–37.

50960. _____. "Nolan Ryan: Past His Prime, But Still a Cut Above." *Baseball Digest,* XLVII (May 1988), 19–21.

50961. Iverson, Kurt. "A Deeper Look: Nolan Ryan." *Beckett Baseball Card Monthly,* IX, no. 88 (July 1992), 110–114.

50962. _____. "May Day Alert: Ryan Unhittable." In:

John Blake, *et al. Texas Rangers Official 1996 Yearbook.* Arlington, TX: Public Relations Dept., Texas Rangers, 1996. Pp. 41–47. Seventh no-hitter on May 1, 1991.

50963. "K." *Sports Illustrated,* LXXI (August 28, 1989), 30–33. List of all of Ryan's 4,994 strikeouts to time of publication.

50964. Kaplan, Jim. "For Ryan, It Was a Very Special X." *Sports Illustrated,* LVIII (May 9, 1983), 34–36+. When surpassed Walter Johnson's all-time strikeout mark.

50965. _____. "Ryan's Back on the Track." *Sports Illustrated,* XLIII (September 8, 1975), 73+.

50966. Keith, Larry. "It's Fishing Season for Free Agents: Nolan Ryan." *Sports Illustrated,* LI (November 19, 1979), 34–35.

50967. _____. "Whiff of Spring in Houston." *Sports Illustrated,* LII (April 21, 1980), 34–36.

50968. Kelley, Brent P. "Nolan Ryan?: In My Bullpen." *The Baseball Research Journal,* XXI (1992), 49–52.

50969. Kelnhofer, Scott. "Ryan is on Cooperstown's Doorstep." *Sports Collector's Digest,* XXV (November 27, 1998), 72–73.

50970. Kelley, Brent P. "Nolan Ryan Could Probably Pitch for Me." *The Baseball Research Journal,* XXI (1992), 49–52.

50971. Kerrane, Kevin. "Stuff." *The Show,* II, no. 1 (1991), 15–20.

50972. Kirst, Sean Peter. "After 27 Summers, Suddenly It Will Become Fall." In: his *The Ashes of Lou Gehrig and Other Baseball Essays.* Jefferson, NC: McFarland & Co., Inc., 2003. Pp. 115–116.

50973. Klein, Moss. "Tanana/Ryan: Best Lefty-Righty Duo Since Koufax/Drysdale?" *Baseball Digest,* XXXVI (August 1977), 30–37.

50974. Klima, John. "Duel of Lessons: Nolan Ryan vs. Randy Johnson (September 27, 1992)." In: his *Pitched Battle: 35 of Baseball's Greatest Duels from the Mound.* Jefferson, NC: McFarland & Co., Inc., 2002. Pp. 162–167.

50975. _____. "One versus Deuce: Nolan Ryan vs. Bert Blyleven (September 20, 1976)." In: his *Pitched Battle: 35 of Baseball's Greatest Duels from the Mound.* Jefferson, NC: McFarland & Co., Inc., 2002. Pp. 130–135.

50976. Kreuz, Jim. "High School Coach Recalls Nolan Ryan as a Young Pitcher." *Baseball Digest,* LV (March 1996), 60–64.

50977. Kuenster, Bob. "Baseball's Dramatic Moments: Nolan Ryan Establishes a New Strikeout Record." *Baseball Digest,* LIV (August 1995), 41–42.

50978. Kuenster, John. "Special Career Targets Stimulate Nolan Ryan and Rickey Henderson." *Baseball Digest,* XLIX (July 1990), 17–19.

50979. Kurkijan, Tim. "The Heart of Texas." *Sports Illustrated,* LXXIII (October 8, 1990), 103+.

50980. _____. "Nolan Ryan." *Sports Illustrated,* LXXIX (October 4, 1993), 46–47. Career ends with elbow injury.

50981. _____. "Nolan Ryan." *Sports Illustrated,* LXXXI (September 19, 1994), 132–133.

50982. Lace, William W. *Sports Great Nolan Ryan.* Hillsdale, NJ: Enslow, 1993. 64p. Reprinted in 1999.

50983. Lang, Jack. "The Mets' Worst Deal Ever: Trading Nolan Ryan in '71." *Baseball Digest,* XLVIII (December 1989), 72–73.

50984. Lapin,, Jackie. "Nolan Ryan, the Pitcher Batters Hate to Face." *Baseball Digest,* XXXIII (December 1974), 40–43. Reprinted in John Kuenster, ed., *From Cobb to Catfish* (Chicago: Rand McNally, 1975), pp. 73–74.

50985. Leerhsen, Charles. "Everything Old is Almost New Again — the Nolan Ryan Lesson: Move it or Lose it." *Newsweek,* CXVII (May 13, 1991), 61–62.

50986. Leggett, William. "The Angel Who Makes Turnstiles Sing." *Sports Illustrated,* XXXVIII (May 14, 1973), 26–27.

50987. Leiker, Ken. "10–1991: Nolan Ryan Pitches His Seventh No-Hitter, Three More Than Anyone Else." In: his *Major League Baseball Memorable Moments: The Most Memorable Moments in Major League Baseball History.* New York: Ballantine Books, 2002. Pp. 58–71.

50988. Levine, David. "A Play in Five Acts." In: *Major League Baseball Official 1991 Preview.* New York: Hachette Magazines, 1991. Pp. 90–92.

50989. Libby, Bill. *Nolan Ryan, Fireballer.* New York: G.P. Putnam, 1975. 160p.

50990. Lopresti, Mike. "Ryan Strikes Milestone." In: Gregory Wiley, ed. *Best Sport Stories of 1990.* St. Louis, MO: The Sporting News, 1990. Pp. 206–207.

50991. Lundgren, Hal. "Interview: Nolan Ryan." *Inside Sports,* X (April 1988), 20–25.

50992. Mackey, Thomas. "It's Nolan Ryan!: A Historiography Teaching Technique." *History Teacher,* XXXIV (May 1991), 353–356.

50993. Maher, Charles. "Nolan Ryan: Fastest Gun in the West." *Baseball Digest,* XXXI (October 1972), 41–50.

50994. Mangano, Joe. "Nolan Ryan: Tough Luck Great?" *The Baseball Research Journal,* XXI (1992), 46–48.

50995. McKay, Joe. "Nolan Ryan: Mr. No-Hitter." In: his *The Great Shutout Pitchers: 20 Profiles of a Vanishing Breed.* Jefferson, NC: McFarland & Co., Inc., 2004. Pp. 86–97.

50996. McLemore, Ivy. "Nolan Ryan's Long Career Built on Strong Work Ethic." *Baseball Digest,* LII (August 1993), 38–39.

50997. _____. "Strikeout King Nolan Ryan: He's One of a Kind." *Baseball Digest,* XLVI (August 1987), 70–74.

50998. Merry, Don. "Ryan's Records and Others." In: Sam E. Andre, ed. *Street and Smith's Official 1974 Baseball Yearbook.* New York: Conde Nast Publications, 1974. Pp. 64–67.

50999. _____. Miller, Dick. "Nolan Ryan: Next 30-Game Winner?" *Baseball Digest,* XXXII (May 1973), 16–21.

51000. _____. "Nolan Ryan Reveals What Really Happened to Him in '75." *Baseball Digest,* XXXV (April 1976), 109–113.

51001. Montville, Leigh. "Citizen Ryan: Down Home in Alvin, Texas, Nolan Ryan is an Old-Fashioned Cowboy." *Sports Illustrated,* LXXIV (April 15, 1991), 120–130. Reprinted in Thomas McGuane, ed., *The Best American Sports Writing, 1992.* (Boston, MA: Houghton, Mifflin, 1992), pp. 264–280.

51002. Moran, Neal. "No-Hitter Lollapaloozas." *The Baseball Research Journal,* XXII (1993), 93–94.

51003. Mulgannon, Tom. "The Nolan Ryan Scrapbook." *Sport,* LXXXV (October 1993), 66–69.

51004. Munson, Ed. "Nolan Ryan Entering His Prime as Power Pitcher." *Baseball Digest,* XXXIV (May 1975), 32–34.

51005. Nash, Bruce and Allan Zullo. "Nolan Ryan." In: their *Little Big Leaguers: Amazing Boyhood Stories of Today's Baseball Stars.* New York: Little Simon, 1990. Pp. 40–41.

51006. Neff, Craig. "King of the Ks." *Sports Illustrated,* LXXI (August 28, 1989), 12–14.

51007. _____. "No Dough, Yet." *Sports Illustrated,* LXX (May 1, 1989), 11–12.

51008. Newman, Bruce. "Hat's Off to You, Nolan Ryan: One-Hitter Against the Yankees." *Sports Illustrated,* LI (July 23, 1979), 12–17.

51009. Newton, Craig. "Nolan Ryan: Interview." *Baseball Cards,* X (August 1990), 78–85.

51010. Nicholson, Lois P. *Nolan Ryan.* Baseball Legends series. Philadelphia, PA: Chelsea House, 1995. 64p.

51011. "Nolan Ryan." *KidSports,* IV, no. 2 (1992), 12–17.

51012. "Nolan Ryan." In: *Current Biography Yearbook, 1970.* New York: H.W. Wilson Co., 1970. Pp. 367–369.

51013. "Nolan Ryan." In: *Good Sports : Athletes Your Kids Can Look Up To.* Dallas, TX: Beckett Publications, 1999. Chapter 24.

51014. Obojski, Robert. "Nolan Ryan: King of Zing." In: his *Baseball's Strangest Moments.* New York: Sterling Publishing Co., 1988. Pp. 70–71.

51015. _____. "Nolan Ryan: Superman on the Mound." *Spitball,* no. 32 (Winter 1989), 26–31.

51016. Pagel, Mike. "Big TX." *Beckett Sports Collectibles,* VII (March 1998), 106–109.

51017. Patoski, J. N. "A Farewell to Arm." *Texas Monthly,* XXI (May 1993), 114–115+.

51018. Perry, Patrick. "Nolan Ryan: Staying Ahead of the Game." *Saturday Evening Post,* CCLXXIII (July 2001), 36–39, 94–95.

51019. Pingel, D. Kent, ed. *Nolan Ryan: The Authorized Pictorial History.* New York: Summit Group, 1991. 215p.

51020. Pozer, Richard. "Nolan Ryan: Baseball's No. I Strikeout Artist." *Baseball Digest,* XXXVIII (September 1979), 20–23.

51021. Rains, Rob, ed. *Nolan Ryan: From Alvin to Cooperstown.* Champaign, IL: Sports Publishing, 1999. 164p.

51022. Rappoport, Ken. *Nolan Ryan: The Ryan Express.* New York: Dillon Press, 1992. 64p.

51023. Reeves, Jim. "Nolan Ryan: A Man for All Reasons to Esteem." In: George Leonard, ed. *Athlon's Baseball '91.* Nashville, TN: Athlon Sports Communications, 1991. Pp. 166–169.

51024. Reichler, Joseph. "1981: Houston Astros 5, Los Angeles Dodgers 0 — Nolan Ryan's Record Fifth No-Hitter." In: Charles Einstein, ed. *The Fourth Fireside Book of Baseball.* New York: Simon and Schuster, 1987. Pp. 302–303.

51025. Reiser, Howard. *Nolan Ryan: Strikeout King.* Chicago, IL: Children's Press, 1993. 48p.

51026. Ritter, Lawrence and Donald Honig. "Nolan Ryan." In: their *The 100 Greatest Baseball Players of All Time.* New York: Crown Publishers, 1986. Pp. 64–65.

51027. Roberts, Jack. *Nolan Ryan.* New York: Scholastic, 1992. 50p.

51028. Rolfe, John. *Nolan Ryan.* Boston, MA: Little, Brown, 1992. 124p.

51028. Romano, Vince. "Nolan Ryan Chases the Strikeout Record of 'The Big Train.'" *Baseball Digest,* XLI (May 1982), 20–21+.

51029. Rushin, Steve. "As Big as All Texas." *Sports Illustrated,* LXXIII (August 13, 1990), 18–21.

51030. Ryan, Michael. "First, Respect Yourself." *Parade Magazine,* (April 16, 1992), 4–5.

51031. Ryan, Nolan. "My Greatest Day in Baseball." In: Eliot Cohen, ed. *My Greatest Day in Baseball.* New York: Little Simon, 1991. Pp. 99–101.

51032. _____. and Harvey Frommer. *Throwing Heat: The Autobiography of Nolan Ryan.* Garden City, NY: Doubleday, 1988. 236p.; New York: Avon Books, 1990. 249p.

51033. _____. and Joe Torre, with Joel Cohen. *Pitching and Hitting.* Englewood Cliffs, NJ: Prentice-Hall, 1977. 213p.

51034. _____. and Tom House, with Jim Rosenthal. *Nolan Ryan's Pitcher's Bible: The Ultimate Guide to Power, Precision and Long-Term Performance.* New York: Simon and Schuster, 1991. 224p.

51035. _____. "What Contributed to Nolan Ryan's 95 mph Fastball, 6 No-hitters, 23 Seasons in the Major Leagues and 4,700 innings?: A Solid Program of Weight Training!" *Muscle & Fitness,* LII (July 1991), 82–87. An excerpt from the previous entry.

51036. _____., with Bill Libby. *The Other Gang.* Waco, TX: Word Books, 1977. 216p.

51037. _____., with Jerry Jenkins. *Miracle Man: The Autobiography of Nolan Ryan.* Dallas, TX: Word Books, 1992. 272p. A large text edition was published by the Boston, MA, firm of G. K. Hall in 1993.

51038. _____., with Mickey Herskowitz. *Kings of the Hill: An Irreverent Look at the Men on the Mound.* New York: HarperCollins, 1992. 243p.

51039. _____. with Steve Jacobson. *Nolan Ryan, Strikeout King.* New York: Scholastic Book Service, 1975. 69p.

51040. _____., with T.R. Sullivan and Mickey Herskowitz. *Nolan Ryan: The Road to Cooperstown.* Lenexa, KS: Addax Publishing, 1999. 112p.

51041. Ryan, Ruth. *Covering Home: My Life with Nolan Ryan.* Dallas, TX: Word Publishing, 1995. 266p.

51042. Seaver, Tom, with Marty Appel. "Only the Nolan." In: his *Great Moments in Baseball: From the World Series of 1903 to the Modern Records of Nolan Ryan.* New York: Carol Communications, 1992. Pp. 313–318.

51043. Schleicher, Paul. *Nolan Ryan: Sports Personalities.* Massapequa, NY; Personality Comics, 1991. 27p.

51044. Shannon, Mike. "Nolan Ryan." In: his *Tales from the Dugout: The Greatest True Baseball Stories Ever Told.* Lincolnwood, IL: NTC/Contemporary Books, 1997. Pp. 175–179.

51045. Shapiro, Herb. *Nolan Ryan: All American Athlete.* San Diego, CA: Revolutionary Comics, 1991. 30p.

51046. Sloate, Susan. "Nolan Ryan." In: her *Hotshots: Baseball Greats of the Game When They Were Kids.* Boston, MA: Little, Brown, 1991. Pp. 94–98.

51047. Smith, Ron. "Nolan Ryan." In: his *Heroes of the Hall: Baseball's Greatest Players.* New York: Contemporary Books, 2002. Pp. 406–409.

51048. _____. "Nolan Ryan 41." In: his *The Sporting News Selects Baseball's 100 Greatest Players.* St. Louis, MO: The Sporting News, 1998. Pp. 92–93.

51049. Texas Rangers. Public Relations Department. *The Life and Times of Nolan Ryan: A Historic Journey of Excellence.* 4 pts. Irving, TX: Printed for the Texas Rangers by Tarrant Printing, 1991. The four parts are: "Nolan: the Alvin Years," by Ken Sins and Ted Davidson, with photography by Debbie Wilson; "Nolan: Mets & Angels," by Jack Lang and Ross Newhan, with photography courtesy of the New York Mets, California Angels, National Baseball Hall of Fame, and The Topps Company; "Nolan : Astros & Rangers," by Neil Hohlfeld and Steve Pate, with photography by Linda Kaye, Brad Newton, Dennis Murphy (Wrangler), and the Houston Astros; and "Nolan : the Road to Cooperstown," by Larry Kelly, with photography by Bill Baptist, Brad Newton, and Linda Kaye.

51050. Thompson, Jim. "Express Delivery." *Beckett Baseball Card Monthly,* XVI (March 1999), 98–101.

51051. "Throwing Smoke." *Time,* CV (June 2, 1975), 37–38.

51052. Torres, John Albert. "Nolan Ryan." In: his *Top 10 Baseball Legends.* Berkeley Heights, NJ: Enslow Publishers, 2001. Pp. 38–41.

51053. Trujillo, Nick. "Hegemonic Masculinity on the Mound: Media Representations of Nolan Ryan and American Sports Culture." *Critical Studies in Mass Communication,* VIII (September 1991), 290–309. Reprinted as Chapter 1 in Susan Birrell and Mary G. McDonald, eds. *Reading Sport: Critical Essays on Power and Representation* (Boston, MA: Northeastern University Press, 2000).

51054. _____. "The Meaning of Nolan Ryan." In: Alvin L. Hall, ed. *Cooperstown Symposium on Baseball and the American Society (1990).* Baseball and American Society, no. 18. Westport, CT: Meckler, 1991. Pp. 109–143.

51055. _____. *The Meaning of Nolan Ryan.* College Station, TX: Texas A & M University Press, 1994. 163p.

51056. _____. "Remembering Nolan." In: *Texas is Baseball Country.* Cleveland, OH: Society For American Baseball Research, 1994. Pp. 15–16.

51057. Van Overloop, Mark E. "Nolan Ryan: the King of K." In: *Baseball Illustrated.* New York: Lexington Library, Inc., 1990. Pp. 55–59.

51058. Westcott, Rich. "Nolan Ryan: Strikeout Specialist." In: his *Winningest Pitchers: Baseball's 300-Game Winners.* Philadelphia, PA: Temple University Press, 2002. Pp. 177–186.

51059. Wulf, Steve. "Heaven for Seven." *Sports Illustrated,* LXXIV (May 13, 1991), 42–44.

Nolan Ryan *see* **Lynn Nolan Ryan**
Dominic Joseph ("Mike") Ryba
P. (B: June 9, 1903, DeLancey, PA-D: Dec. 13, 1971). St. Louis (NL), 1935–1938; Boston (AL), 1941–1946. Remarks: Won 51 games and lost 47 with 19 "saves" in a decade; also employed as substitute catcher and was the first man to play both positions in a World Series (1946); coach, St. Louis (NL), 1951–1954; died as result of injuries sustained in a fall from a home ladder.

51060. Broeg, Bob. "Mike Ryba-One-Man Team." *Baseball Digest,* II (February 1943), 61–63.

51061. Considine, Bob. "One-Man Team." *Collier's,* CVII (June 21, 1941), 50–52.

51062. Povich, Shirley. "Warms Up as Pitcher — Then Catches." *Baseball Digest,* XIII (June 1954), 89–90.

Mike Ryba *see* **Dominic Joseph ("Mike") Ryba**
Eugene Rudolph ("Gene" or "Half-Pint") Rye
OF. (B: Nov. 15, 1906, Chicago, IL-D: Jan. 21, 1980.). Boston (AL), 1931. Remarks: Had seven hits in ten major league games; while playing for Waco (T.L), had three homers in one (18-run) inning, Aug. 6, 1930.

51063. McConnell, Robert. "Three Shots of Rye." *The Baseball Research Journal,* IX (1980), 80–82.

51064. McGuire, Mark and Michael Sean Gormley. "Gene Rye." In: their *Moments in the Sun: Baseball's Briefly Famous.* Jefferson, NC: McFarland & Co., Inc., 2001. Pp. 82–85.

Kirk Craig Saarloos
P. (B: May 23, 1979, Long Beach, CA). Houston (NL), 2002–2003; Oakland (AL), 2004. Remarks: Through 2004, has had 10 victories and nine defeats.

51065. Pearlman, Jeff. "Hello, Houston!" *Sports Illustrated,* XCVII (August 19, 2002), 78–79.

Bret William ("Sabes") Saberhagen
P. (B: April 11, 1964, Chicago Heights, IL). Kansas City (AL), 1984–1991; New York Mets (NL), 1992–1995; Colorado (NL), 1995; Boston (AL), 1996–2001. Remarks: In 16 years, obtained 167 victories, 117 defeats, and one "save"; won Game Three of 1985 ALCS; won Game Three and Game Seven of 1985 World Series; World Series MVP Award, 1985; AL Cy Young Award, 1985, 1989; had one

no-hitter, Aug. 26, 1991; asst. then head baseball coach, Calabasas High School ,California, 2002-.

51066. Abramson, Dan. "A Second Look: Bret Saberhagen." *Beckett Baseball Card Monthly,* VII (March 1990), 73–77.

51067. Bowman, Marc "Bret Saberhagen—1989." In: his *Baseball's Top 100: The Best Individual Seasons of All Time.* Wilton, CT: Diamond Library, 1996. Pp. 271–272.

51068. "Bret Saberhagen: An Unbelievable Season." In: Owen C. Shaw, ed. *Petersen's 1986 Pro Baseball Annual.* Los Angeles, CA: Petersen's, 1986. Pp. 54–55.

51069. "Bret Saberhagen: He Has the World at His Feet." In: Tom Barnidge, ed. *The Sporting News 1986 Baseball Yearbook.* St. Louis, MO: *The Sporting News,* 1986. Pp. 4–11.

51070. Carlson, Stan W. "Bret William Saberhagen." In: Vol. Q-Z of David L. Porter, ed. *Biographical Dictionary of American Sports: Baseball.* Rev. and enlarged ed. Westport, CT: Greenwood Press, 2000. Pp. 1343–1344.

51071. Cohen, Irwin. "Baseball Beat: Bret Saberhagen." *Baseball Cards,* X (May 1990), 150–151.

51072. Etkin, Jack. "Bret Saberhagen: A New Member of the Majors' Pitching Elite." *Baseball Digest,* XLIV (December 1985), 67–72.

51073. Gammons, Peter. "Return of the Royal Nonesuch." *Sports Illustrated,* LXVI (June 8, 1987), 28–29.

51074. Gutman, Bill. "Bret Saberhagen." In: his *Baseball's Hot New Stars.* New York: G. P. Putnam, 1988. Pp. 119–134.

51075. Lewis, Gregory. "Bret Saberhagen." In: Ken Collier, ed. *The Baseball Book, 1986.* Scottsdale, AZ: Jalart House, 1986. pp. 14–15.

51076. McBride, M. "The SABeRhagen Syndrome: Pitching Streaks of a Special Kind." *The Baseball Research Journal,* XXIV (1995), 34–38.

51077. McGee, Todd. "Sabes' First Spring Start a Success, Sort Of...." *New York Mets Inside Pitch,* XII (May 1994), 5–6.

51078. Nash, Bruce and Allan Zullo. "Bret Saberhagen." In: their *More Little Big Leaguers: Amazing Boyhood Stories of Today's Baseball Stars.* New York: Little Simon, 1991. Pp. 80–81.

51079. Nightengale, Bob. "How They Spent Their Winter Vacation: Did Success Spoil Saberhagen?" *Sport,* LXXVIII (March 1987), 27–28.

51080. Noble, Marty. "A Deeper Look: Bret Saberhagen." *Beckett Baseball Card Monthly,* XII, no. 123 (June 1995), 22–23.

51081. Poses, Jonathan. "Saberhagen: 'I Have Something to Prove." *Inside Sports,* IX (September 1987), 74–77.

51082. Ringolsby, Tracy. "Interview: Bret Saberhagen." *Inside Sports,* XII (June 1990), 22–30.

51083. Rudeen, L. "Home Run." *Motor Boating & Sailing,* CLXXVIII (October 1996), 52–55+.

51084. Saberhagen, Bret. "When I was a Kid': Interview." *Junior League Baseball,* no. 2 (December 1996), 10+.

51085. Swift, E. M. "Attaboy, Bret." *Sports Illustrated,* LXIII (November 11, 1985), 80–84+.

Chris Andrew ("Spuds") Sabo
3B. (B: January 19, 1962, Detroit, MI). Cincinnati (NL), 1988–1993; Baltimore (AL), 1994; Chicago (AL) and St. Louis (NL), 1995; Cincinnati (NL), 1996. Remarks: Had 898 hits (116 homers) and 120 stolen bases in 911 games in nine years; had 11 assists in one game, April 7, 1988; NL Rookie of the Year Award, 1988; had two homers in Game Three of 1990 World Series; dir. of base-

ball operations, Florence (Frontier League), 2003; coach, Billings (Pioneer League), 2004; coach, Dayton (Midwest League), 2005-.

51086. Blanchino, Jim. "Chris Sabo: A New 'Charlie Hustle' in the Making?" *Baseball Digest,* XLVII (November 1988), 47–54.

51087. Crasnick, Jerry. "Sabo's A Spark in Piniella's New Big Red Machine Assembly." In: George Leonard, ed. *Athlon's Baseball '91.* Nashville, TN: Athlon Sports Communications, 1991. Pp. 62–67.

51088. Hart, Stan. "Chris Sabo." In: his *Scouting Reports: The Original Reviews Of Baseball's Greatest Stars.* New York: Macmillan, 1995. Pp. 116–118.

51089. Honig, Donald. "1988: Chris Sabo." In: his *National League Rookies of the Year.* New York: Bantam Books, 1989. Pp. 107–109.

51090. Kuenster, John. "Chris Sabo Personified Spirit of World Champion [Cincinnati] Reds." *Baseball Digest,* L (February 1991), 15–17.

51091. Nash, Bruce and Allan Zullo. "Chris Sabo." In: their *More Little Big Leaguers: Amazing Boyhood Stories of Today's Baseball Stars.* New York: Little Simon, 1991. Pp. 78–79.

51091. Shannon, Mike. "Chris Sabo." In: his *Tales from the Ballpark: More of the Greatest True Baseball Stories Ever Told.* Lincolnwood, IL: Contemporary Books, 1999. Pp. 175–178.

Raymond Michael ("Ray") Sadecki
P. (B: Dec. 26, 1940, Kansas City, MO). St. Louis (NL), 1960–1966; San Francisco (NL), 1966–1969; New York (NL), 1970–1974; St. Louis (NL) and Atlanta (NL), 1975; Kansas City (AL), 1975–1976; Milwaukee (AL), 1976; New York (NL), 1977. Remarks: Had 135 victories, 131 defeats, and seven "saves" in 18 seasons; won Game One of 1964 World Series.

51092. Fox, Tom. "The Court Martial That Made Ray Sadecki:— Though Known For His Model Behavior, Ray Well Remembers When He Was Fined and Banished To the Minors. It Was Probably the Turning Point of His Career." *Sport,* XXXIX (February 1965), 56–59.

51093. Jupiter, Harry. "Project Sadocki." *Baseball Digest,* XXVI (May 1967), 87–89.

51094. Mandel, Mike. "Ray Sadecki." In: his *The San Francisco Giants: An Oral History.* Santa Cruz, CA: Priv. print., 1979. Pp. 154–158.

51095. Mann, Jack. "It's Not Bad to Be Going Good." *Sports Illustrated,* XXIV (May 23, 1966), 30–31.

51096. Merchant, Larry. "Ray Sadecki: Man Out of the Doghouse." *Baseball Digest,* XXII (June 1963), 31–33.

Michael ("Mike") Sadek
C. (B: May 30, 1946, Minneapolis, MN). San Francisco (NL), 1973, 1975–1981. Remarks: Had 184 hits (five homers) in 383 games in eight seasons; backup catcher.

51097. Mandel, Mike. "Mike Sadek." In: his *The San Francisco Giants: An Oral History.* Santa Cruz, CA: Priv. Print., 1979. Pp. 216–218.

Donnie Sadler
2B-SS. (B: June 17, 1975, Gohlson, TX). Boston (AL), 1998–2000; Cincinnati (NL) and Kansas City (AL), 2001; Kansas City (AL), 2002–2003; Texas (AL), 2003; Arizona (NL), 2004-. Remarks: Through 2004, has had 155 hits (six homers) and 25 stolen bases in 417 games; utility man.

51098. O'Rourke, Larry. "Short but Sweet: After a Month in Center, Donnie Sadler is Back at Short." *Boston Baseball,* VII (July 1996), 38–39.

51099/51100. Schulz, Todd. "Speedy Sadler is Battle Cats' Catalyst." *Boston Baseball,* VI (June 1995), 36–37.

51101. Wood, Rodger. "No Challenge Too Big for Sadler." *Boston Baseball,* VII (May 1996), 32–33.

Bob Sadowski *see* **Robert P. ("Bob") Sadowski**
Robert P. ("Bob") Sadowski
P. (B: Feb. 19, 1938, Pittsburgh, PA). Milwaukee' (NL), 1963–1965; Boston (AL), 1966. Remarks: Won 20 games and lost 27 with eight "saves," in a four year big league career; won final Milwaukee (NL) Braves home opener, April 15, 1965.

51102. Walfoort, Cleon, "Bob Sadowski: A Bargain for the Braves." *Baseball Digest,* XXII (December 1963), 51–56.

Victor Sylvester ("Vic") Saier
1B. (B: May 4, 1891, Lansing, MI-D: May 14, 1967.). Chicago (NL), 1911–1917; Pittsburgh (NL), 1918. Remarks: Had 774 hits (55 homers) and 121 stolen bases in 864 games in eight seasons; led NL in triples, 1913.

51103. Gonzalez, Raymond. "Hitting Homers Off Christy Mathewson." *The Baseball Research Journal,* VIII (1980), 116–119. Saier's five most surrendered by the Hall of Famer to any one player.

51104. Stock, C.P. "The Hardest Hitter in Baseball." *Baseball Magazine,* XIII (October 1914), 60–61.

John Franklin ("Johnny") Sain
P. (B: Sept. 25, 1917. Havana, AK). Boston (NL), 1942, 1946–1951; New York (AL), 1951–1955; Kansas City (AL), 1955. Remarks: Had 139 victories, 116 defeats, and 51 "saves" in 11 seasons; coach, Kansas City (AL), 1959, New York (AL), 1961–1963, Minnesota (AL), 1965–1966, Detroit (AL), 1967–1949, California (AL), 1970, Chicago (AL), 1971–1974, Atlanta (NL), 1977, 1985–1986.

51105. Bethel, Dell. "Developing Your Pitcher." *Scholastic Coach,* XXXIX (March 1970), 40–43. Sain instructional.

51106. _____. "Johnny Sain On Pitching." *Scholastic Coach,* XXXVII (March 1968), 8–11.

51107. Birtwell, Roger. "Did Braves Trade Sain for Flag?" *Baseball Digest,* VIII (October 19,49), 24–27.

51108. Cairns, Bob. "Johnny Sain." In: his *Pen Men: Baseball's Greatest Bullpen Stories told by the Men who Brought the Game Relief.* New York: St. Martin's Press, 1992. Pp. 56–66.

51109. Deford, Frank. "Coochee Coos Another Tune." *Sports Illustrated,* XXVIII (April 8, 1968), 56–64. Sain and Jim "Mudcat" Grant.

51110. Dexter, Charles . "Pitchers Should Work Their Own Games'— Johnny Sain." *Baseball Digest,* XI (September 1952), 43–47.

51111. Fagen, Herb. "Johnny Said . . . and Pray For Rain." *Oldtyme Baseball News,* V, no. 3 (1993), 18–21.

51112. _____. "Johnny Sain Did It His Way . . . as a Pitcher and a Coach." *Baseball Digest,* LII (December 1993), 76–82.

51113. Figone, Albert J. "John Franklin 'Johnny' Sain." In: Vol. Q-Z of David L. Porter, ed. *Biographical Dictionary of American Sports: Baseball.* Rev. and enlarged ed. Westport, CT: Greenwood Press, 2000. Pp. 1344–1345.

51114. Forker, Dom. "Johnny Sain." In: his *The Men Of Autumn.* Dallas, TX: Taylor Publishing Co., 1989. Pp. 79–90.

51115. Jordan,, Pat. "In a World of Windmills." *Sports Illustrated,* XXXVI (May 8, 1972), 34–36+. Reprinted in Editors of *Sports Illustrated, Best of Sports Illustrated* (Boston, MA: Little, Brown, 1973), pp. 115–118 and in his *The Suitors Of Spring.* (New York: Dodd, Mead & Co., 1973), pp. 181–211.

51116. "Jug-Handle Johnny." *Time,* LIII (April 11, 1949), 83–84.

51117. Kahn, Roger. "The Pope of Pitching" In: his *The Head Game: Baseball Seen from the Pitcher's Mound.* Boston, MA: Harcourt, 2000. Pp. 277–286.

51118. Keene, Harold. "So This is Sain." *Sport,* VI (January 1949), 40–43.

51119. Masin, Herman L. "Gurus: New and Old. . . ." *Scholastic Coach,* LXI (January 1992), 12–13. Sain and Jim Kaat.

51120. _____. "Positively Saln." *Senior Scholastic,* LXXXIII (October 4, 1963), 40–49.

51121. Mortenson, Tom. "Johnny Sain: Winning Respect for Baseball Coaches." *Sports Collectors Digest,* XVIII (February 8, 1991), 90–91.

51122. Olszewski, Joe. "Developing a Pitching Staff." *Scholastic Coach,* XXXIV (February 1965), 12–15.

51123. Patterson, Ted. "Spahn and Sain: They Train Them To Win." *Baseball Digest,* XXXI (December 1972), 52–55.

51124. Rumill, Ed. "He's Sain — But Batters Aren't." *Baseball Digest,* V (November 1946), 35–39.

51125. _____. "Yanks Letting Him Go Wasn't Sain Move." *Baseball Digest,* XXIV (September 1965), 77–79.

51126. "A Safe and Sain John." *Scholastic Coach,* XXXIII (February 1964), 5–6.

51127. Sain, Johnny. "Developing Rotation and Breaking Pitches." *Scholastic Coach,* XXXIII (February 1964), 7–9+.

51128. _____. "Johnny Sain on Pitching." *Scholastic Coach,* XXXVII (March 1968), 8–9+.

51129. _____. "Johnny Sain Talks Pitching." *Scholastic Coach,* LIX (March 1990), 66–69.

51130. _____. "Pitch Like a Pro; Yankee Coach's Ball-on-a-Stick Teaches You How." *Popular Science,* CLXXXIII (October 1963), 100–101.

51131. _____. "Three Keys to Success in Pitching." *Boy's Life,* LXVI (August 1976), 30–33.

51132. _____. and J. R. Andrews. "Proper Pitching Techniques." In: B. Zarins, et al., eds. *Injuries to the Throwing Arm.* Philadelphia, PA: W. B. Saunders, 1985. Pp. 30–37.

51133. Skipper, John C. "Johnny Sain: On the Mound When Jackie Robinson First Came to Bat." In: his *Inside Pitch: A Closer Look at Classic Baseball Moments.* Jefferson, N.C.: McFarland & Company, Inc., 1996. Pp. 50–53.

51134. Smith, Marshall. "The Twins' Miracle Coach: Old Pitcher Johnny Sain Teaches Minnesota How to Win." *Life,* LIX (September 10, 1965), 83–86.

51135. Surface, Bill. "Johnny Sain Teaches the Power of Positive Pitching." *The New York Times Magazine,* (April 20, 1969), 48–59.

51136. Tourangeau, Dixie. "Spahn, Sain, and the '48 Braves." *The National Pastime,* XVIII (1998), 17–20.

51137. Turner, Ken C. "Johnny Sain: Will Johnny Ever Gain Enough Hall of Fame Support?" *Vintage & Classic Baseball Collector,* no. 8 (September 1996), 30–31.

51138. Waldman, Frank. "John Franklin (Johnny) Sain, Jr.: 'Twenty-Game Winner for Three Consecutive Years." In: his *Famous American Athletes of Today.* 11th Series. New York: Page, 1949. Pp. 259–278.

51139. Watts, Lew. "Watch Out: Curve Ahead." *Scholastic Coach,* XLI (February 1972), 18–30. Pitching instructional from Sain on Curveballs.

51140. Weiskopf, Donald C. "Pitching Coach Johnny Sain." *Athletic Journal,* LVI (March 1966), 8–15.

51141. Westcott, Rich. "Johnny Sain: Outstanding Pitcher and Coach." In: his *Masters of the Diamond.* Jefferson, NC: McFarland & Co., Inc., 1994. Pp. 107–116.

Helen Callaghan Candaele ("Cally") St. Aubin
P. (B: March 13, 1929, Vancouver, Canada-D: Dec. 8, 1992). Minneapolis Millerettes (All American Girls Professional Baseball League); 1944; , Fort Wayne Daisies (AAGPBL), 1945–1946; 1948; Kinosha Giants (AAGPBL), 1949. Remarks: Known as the "Ted Williams of Women's Baseball"; obtained 449 hits and 419 stolen bases in 495 games in six years; AAGPBL batting champion, 1945.

51142. Candaele, Kelly. "Gas Money." *Elysian Fields Quarterly,* XIX (Summer 2002), 24–33.

51143. Crawford, Scott A. G. M. "Helen Callaghan Candaele 'Cally' St. Aubin." In: Vol. Q-Z of David L. Porter, ed. *Biographical Dictionary of American Sports: Baseball.* Rev. and enlarged ed. Westport, CT: Greenwood Press, 2000. Pp. 1345–1347.

51144. St. Aubin, Helen. "This Mother Could Hit!" Edited by Todd Gold. *People Weekly,* XXVIII (August 17, 1987), 77–78+.

Alexander J. ("Al") Salerno
UMP. Remarks: AL arbiter, 1961–1968.

51145. Marguiles, Al. "Al Salerno: The Pink Slip." *Referee,* XVII (March 1992), 44+.

Harry Franklin ("Slim") Sallee
P. (B: Feb. 3, 1886, Higginsport, OH-D: March 22, 1950). St. Louis (NL), 1908–1916; New York (NL), 1917–1918; Cincinnati (NL), 1919–1920; New York (NL), 1920–1921. Remarks: Had 172 victories, 143 defeats, and 36 "saves" in a 14-year major league career; after playing years, operated "Slim's Café" in Higginsport.

51146. Lane, Ferdinand C. "Slim' Sallee, the Man Whose Luck Has Lasted for 12 Years." *Baseball Magazine,* XXIV (April 1920), 627–629.

51147. Lyons, M.Y.B. "Slim' Harry Sallee and His Marvelous Control.*" Baseball Magazine,* X (February 1913), 55–59.

51148. Matz, David S. "Harry Franklin 'Slim' Salee." In: Vol. Q-Z of David L. Porter, ed. *Biographical Dictionary of American Sports: Baseball.* Rev. and enlarged ed. Westport, CT: Greenwood Press, 2000. Pp. 1347–1348.

51149. Sallee, Harry F. "Can a Pitcher Still Work at His Trade?" *Baseball Magazine,* XXV (August 1924), 435–436. Hurling in light of new rules.

51150. Sallee, Paul and Eric. "Sallee Day, 1919." In: Mark Stang and Dick Miller, eds. *Baseball in the Buckeye State.* Cleveland, OH: Society for American Baseball Research, 2004. Pp. 14–15.

51151. Suehsdorf, Adie D. And Richard J. Thompson. "Slim Sallee's Extraordinary Year." *The Baseball Research Journal,* XIX (1990), 10–14. 20-game winner in 1919.

51152. "Two Pitchers Who Have Grudges Against the New Rules." *Literary Digest,* LXVI (September 18, 1920), 88–91. Salee and Hod Eller and the abolition of the spitball.

51153. Uzarowski, Leon. "Southpaw Supremacy: a One-Year Wonder." *Baseball Digest,* XXXIV (March 1975), 22–23.

Harry ("Beans") Salmon
P-OF. (B: May 30, 1895, Warrior, AL-D: July 1983). Birmingham Black Barons, 1920, 1923, 1925–1932; Pittsburgh Keystones, 1921–1922; Memphis Red Sox, 1924, 1930; Detroit Wolves, 1932; Homestead Grays, 1933–1935. Remarks: Well-regarded hurler who worked off-seasons in the Pennsylvania coal mines through 1929.

51154. Holway, John B. "Harry Salmon — Black Diamond of the Coal Mines." *Black Sports,* IV (November 1974), 52–53.

Timothy James ("Tim") Salmon
OF. (B: August 24, 1968, Long Beach, CA). California (AL), 1992–1996; Anaheim (AL), 1997-. Remarks: Through 2004, has had 1,618 hits (290 homers) and 48 stolen bases in 1,596 games; A. L. Rookie of the Year Award, 1993; had five hits in one game, May 13, 1994; had two homers in 2002 World Series.

51155. Bianchine, Jim. "Tim Salmon: There's Nothing Fishy About His Leadership." *Baseball Digest,* LVII (August 1998), 40–45.

51156. Cannella, Stephen. "Redeemed Angel: Tim Salmon." *Sports Illustrated,* XCVI (May 27, 2002), 95–96.

51157. Delaney, Maureen. "Keeping It Real." *Yankees Magazine,* XIX (April 1998), 64–71.

51158. Dewan, John and Don Zminda. "Can a Salmon Swim Up a Fence?" In: STATS, Inc. *STATS Baseball Scoreboard 1994.* New York: HarperPerennial, 1994. Pp. 86–88.

51159. Marazzi, Rich. "Superstar Salmon Awaits 1st All-Star Nod: Three-time Angels MVP Has Battled Nagging Injuries." *Sports Collector's Digest,* XXVI (January 1, 1999), 70–71.

51160. Rausch, Gary. "Focus on Tim Salmon." *Beckett Focus on Future Stars,* III, no. 26 (June 1993), 12–14.

51161. _____. "Headed Upstream." *Beckett Focus on Future Stars,* II, no. 17 (September 1992), 10–13.

51162. Towle, Mike. "Tim Salmon." In: his *True Champions: The Good Guys in American Sports Speak Out.* Ft. Worth, TX: The Summit Group, 1994. Pp. 62–69.

Stephanie Salter
FAN-WRITER. (B: 1950, Vincennes, IN). Remarks: Researcher, *Sports Illustrated,* 1971–1975; reporter/op-ed page columnist, *The San Francisco Chronicle,* 1976–2002; feature writer, *The San Francisco Chronicle,* 2003-.

51163. Salter, Stephanie. "Baseball Memories." In: Ron Fimrite, ed. *Birth of a Fan.* New York: Macmillan, 1993. Pp. 166–177.

Jack Salveson
P. (B: Jan. 5, 1914, Fullerton, CA-D: Dec. 28, 1974). New York (NL), 1933–1934; Pittsburgh (NL) and Chicago (AL), 1935; Cleveland (AL), 1945. Remarks: Won nine games and lost nine, with four "saves," in four big league years; also played for Los Angeles (PCL), 1936–1938; Oakland (PCL), 1939–1944; Portland (PCL), 1946; Sacramento (PCL), 1947; Oakland (PCL), 1948; altogether in 16 PCL years, won 204 games; had a bit part in the movie *Pride of the Yankees.*

51164. Spalding, John. "Jack Salveson." In: *Pacific Coast League Stars: One Hundred of the Best, 1903–1957.* San Jose, CA: John E. Spalding, 1994. Pp. 104–105.

Gyp Salvo *see* **Manny ("Gyp") Salvo**
Manny ("Gyp") Salvo
P. (B: June 30, 1912, Sacramento, CA-D: Feb. 7, 1997). New York (NL), 1939; Boston (NL), 1940–1943; Philadelphia (NL) and Boston (NL), 1943. Remarks: Won 33 games and lost 50 in five big league seasons; career minor leaguer whose nickname was short for gypsy; began PCL career in 1932 with Sacramento, for whom he performed for four years; also played for San Diego (PCL), 1938, 1944–1947.

51165. Spalding, John. "Manny Salvo." In: his *Pacific Coast League Stars: One Hundred of the Best, 1903–1957.* San Jose, CA: John E. Spalding, 1994. Pp. 84–85.

Joseph Charles ("Joe") Sambito
P. (B: June 28, 1952, Brooklyn, NY). Houston (NL), 1976–1984; New York (NL), 1985; Boston (AL), 1986–1987. Remarks: Won 37 games and lost 38, with 84 "saves," in 12 seasons; career largely derailed by elbow injury.

51166. "The Road Is Long." In: Mike Ryan, ed. *1984 Astros Official Yearbook.* Houston, TX: Houston Sports Association, Inc., 1984. Pp. 18–22.

51167. Wulf, Steve. "His Style is Perfect for Hairy Situations." *Sports Illustrated,* LVI (April 12,1982), 58+.

Billy Sample *see* **William Amos ("Billy") Sample**
William Amos ("Billy") Sample
OF-BROADCASTER. (B: April 2, 1955, Roanoke, VA). Texas (AL), 1978–1984; New York (NL), 1985; Atlanta (NL), 1986. Remarks: In nine seasons, had 684 hits (46 homers) and 98 stolen bases in 826 games; while playing for Tucson (PCL), scored 141 runs, 1978; broadcaster, California (AL) and Atlanta (NL), 1987–2000; broadcaster, MLB.com-Radio, 2001-.

51168. Debs, Victor, Jr. "Billy Sample." In: his *"That Was Part of Baseball Then": Interviews with 24 Former Major League Baseball Players, Coaches, and Managers.* Jefferson, NC: McFarland & Co., Inc., 2002. Pp. 98–110.

Doris ("Sammye") Sams
P-OF. (B: Feb. 2, 1927, Knoxville, TN). Muskegon Lassies (All-American Girls Professional Baseball League), 1946–1949; Kalamazoo Lassies (AAGPBL), 1950–1953. Remarks: As a pitcher, won 40 games, including a perfect game on Aug. 18, 1947, and lost 24; as a batter, obtained a .290 batting average, 22 homers, and 286 RBIs; AAGPBL MVP Award, 1947, 1949; AAGPBL home run champion, 1952; elected to Tennessee Sports Hall of Fame, 1970.

51169. Crawford, Scott A. G. M. "Doris 'Sammye' Sams." In: Vol. Q-Z of David L. Porter, ed. *Biographical Dictionary of American Sports: Baseball.* Rev. and enlarged ed. Westport, CT: Greenwood Press, 2000. Pp. 1348–1349.

Juan Milton ("Sammy") Samuel
2B. (B: Dec. 9, 1990, San Pedro do Macaris, Dominican Republic). Philadelphia (NL), 1983–1989; New York (NL), 1989; Los Angeles (NL), 1990–1992; Kansas City (AL), 1992; Cincinnati (NL), 1993; Detroit (AL), 1994–1995; Kansas City (AL), 1995; Toronto (AL), 1996–1998. Remarks: Had 1,578 hits (161 homers) and 396 stolen bases in 1,720 games in 16 seasons; only MLB player to achieve double figures in doubles, triples, home runs, and stolen bases in each of his first four big league seasons; coach, Detroit (AL), 1999-.

51170. Elderkin, Phil. "Juan Samuel: A Top Rookie for the Phillies." *Baseball Digest,* XLIII (September 1984), 73–77.

51171. Finocchiaro, Ray. "Sky's the Limit for Phils' Juan Samuel." *Baseball Digest,* XLVII (June 1988), 23–25.

51172. Henderson, Joe. "Going For the Ring; Samuel Content to Be Backup in Exchange For Shot at Championship." *Reds Report,* VI (April 1993), 23–24.

51173. Kurkjian, Tim. "Back from the Dead." *Sports Illustrated,* LXXIV (June 24, 1991), 66+.

51174. Maisel, Ivan. "Phillies New Whiz" *Sports Illustrated,* LX (April 30,1984), 62–63.

51175. Norris, Annette. "Dodger of the Month: Juan Samuel." *Los Angeles Dodgers Magazine and Scorecard,* IV, no. 3 (1991), 41–44.

51176. Porter, David L. "Juan Milton Samuel." In: Vol. Q-Z of David L. Porter, ed. *Biographical Dictionary of American Sports: Baseball.* Rev. and enlarged ed. Westport, CT: Greenwood Press, 2000. Pp. 1349–1350.

51177. Sokolove, Michael. "See Sammy Run." *Philadelphia Inquirer Magazine,* (September 2, 1984), 10–16.

51178. Stark, Jayson and Rick Hummel. "Is Juan Samuel a Danger at Second Base?: No-Yes." *Sport,* LXXVI (April 1985), 41–42.

51179. Williams, Pete." Samuel Gets Extended Tryout." *USA Today Baseball Weekly,* II (August 12, 1992), 11–12.

Ryne Dee ("Ryno") Sandberg★
2B-SS. (B: Sept. 18, 1959, Spokane, WA). Philadelphia (NL), 1981; Chicago (NL), 1982–1997. Remarks: Had 2,386 hits (282 homers) and 344 stolen bases in 2,164 games in 17 years; led NL in triples, 1984; NL MVP award, 1984; homered in 1989 NLCS; NL home run champion, 1990; first player granted a $7.1 million annual salary, March 2, 1992; first 2B to win nine Gold Glove Awards; holds MLB record for consecutive errorless games (123); highest career fielding percentage for 2B (.989); instructor, Chicago (NL), 1998-; elected to National Baseball Hall of Fame, January 2005.

51180. Abramson, Dan. "A Closer Look: Ryne Sandberg." *Beckett Baseball Card Monthly,* VII (August 1990), 6–7.

51181. Bagnato, Andrew. "Ryne Sandberg: Majors' Most Productive Second Baseman." *Baseball Digest,* XLIX (October 1990), 38–40.

51182. Beaton, Rod. "Simply the Best: Ryne Sandberg Is Without Question the Best Player in the Game Today." *Fantasy Baseball,* II (July 1991), 70–71.

51183. Brosnan, Jim. "Ryne Sandberg: They Call Him 'Kid Natural." *Boys' Life,* LXXV (August, 1985), 12–15.

51184. Castle, George. "Passing Up the Buck." *Sport,* LXXXIII (December 1992), 12+.

51185. Cohen, Eliot. "Ryne Sandberg." In: his *My Greatest Day in Baseball.* New York: Little Simon, 1991. Pp. 102–104.

51186. Cohen, Irwin. "Baseball Beat: Ryne Sandberg." *Baseball Cards,* VII (August 1987), 24–29.

51187. Daily, Bob. "Robocub." *Chicago,* XLII (April 1993), 76–80.

51188. "Final Look: Ryne Sandberg." *Beckett Baseball Card Monthly,* XI, no. 113 (August 1994), 105–106.

51189. George, Daniel P. "Ryne Sandberg; the Strong, Silent Type." *Boys' Life,* LXXXIII (June 1993), 8–10.

51190. Grigsby, Richard. "Second to Home: Ryne Sandberg Opens Up." *Nine: A Journal of Baseball History and Social Policy Perspectives,* IV (Spring 1996), 315–317.

51191. Habermas, John. *Ryne Sandberg.* San Diego, CA: Revolutionary Comics, 1992. 30p.

51192. Hart, Stan. "Ryne Sandberg. "In: his *Scouting Reports: The Original Reviews Of Baseball's Greatest Stars.* New York: Macmillan, 1995. Pp. 119–122.

51193. Honig, Donald. "1984: Ryne Sandberg." In: his *National League MVP's.* New York: Bantam, 1989. Pp. 111–112.

51194. Huzinec, Mary. "Family Portrait: Home Base." *Ladies' Home Journal,* CVI (September 1989), 130–132. Sandberg, his wife Cindy and his children Lindsey and Justin.

51195. Kuenster, John. "Ryne Sandberg Gets the Call as 1990 Player of the Year." *Baseball Digest,* L (January 1991), 17–19.

51196. _____. "Ryne Sandberg of the Cubs: *Baseball Digest's* 1984 Player of the Year." *Baseball Digest,* XLIV (January 1985), 13–16.

51197. Kurkjian, Tim. "Rolling a 7." *Sports Illustrated,* LXXVI (March 16, 1992), 16–21.

51198. Lawes, Rick. "Sandberg Hits the Jackpot: Cubs Make Star Baseball's First $7 Million Man." *USA Today Baseball Weekly,* I (March 4, 1992), 3–4.

51199. Leo, John. "New Boys for the Old Game." *Time,* CXXIV (September 24,1984), 64–66.

51200. Looney, Douglas S. "They'd [Chicago Cubs] Be Dyin' Without Ryne." *Sports Illustrated,* LX (May 20, 1984), 62–64.

51201. Lundgren, Hal. *Ryne Sandberg: The Triple Threat.* Chicago, IL: Childrens Press, 1986. 43p.

51202. Masterson, Dave and Tim Boyle. "1984: Ryne Sandberg." In: their *Baseball's Best: The MVPs.* Chicago, IL: Contemporary Books, Inc., 1985. Pp. 329–333.

51203. McGregor, Ed. "Ryne Sandberg: the Majors' Premier Second Baseman." *Baseball Digest,* XLVIII (December 1989), 46–50.

51204. McLemore, Ivy. "Second To None." In: *Street & Smith's Official 1991 Baseball Yearbook.* New York: Conde Nast Publications, 1991. Pp. 48, 50.

51205. Mitchell, Fred. "The Cubs' Ryne Sandberg: He's Going to Get Even Better." *Baseball Digest,* XLIII (June 1984), 42–45.

51206. Muskat, Carrie. "Second to None." *Topps Magazine,* (Summer 1992), 24–29.

51207. Neyer, Bob. "Chicago Cubs: Will Ryno Be Able to Come Back?" In:" *STATS 1996 Baseball Scoreboard.* Skokie, IL: STATS Publishing, 1996. Pp. 51–52.

51208. Newton, Craig. "Ryne Sandberg." *Baseball Cards,* X (December 1990), 118–125.

51209. Novak, Robert. "Quiet Ryne Sandberg Leads the Chicago Cubs Out of the Doldrums and Into a Pennant Race." *People Weekly,* XXII (August 27, 1984), 92–94.

51210. Rains, Bob. "I Can Do What I Want To Do': Ryne Sandberg Has No Regrets About Walking Away." *USA Today Baseball Weekly,* IV (August 24, 1994), 4–5.

51211. _____. And Carrie Muskat. "Competitive Fire Fueled Sandberg's Career." *USA Today Baseball Weekly,* IV (June 15, 1994), 6–7.

51212. Ringolsby, Tracy. "Ryne Sandberg Has Achieved It All . . . except for the [World Series] Ring." *Baseball Digest,* LII (March 1993), 30–31.

51213. Rosenbloom, Steve. "Mr. Cub, 90's Style." *Sport,* LXXXII (June 1991), 67–71.

51214. Roth, Ernie. *Ryne Sandberg Day Special Commemorative.* Chicago, IL: Chicago Cubs, 1997. 16p

51215. "Ryne Sandberg." In: *Current Biography Yearbook, 1994.* New York: H.W. Wilson Co., 1994. Pp. 516–519.

51216. "Ryne Sandberg." In: Carrie Muskat, ed. *Banks to Sandberg to Grace: Five Decades of Love and Frustration with the Chicago Cubs.* Chicago, IL: Contemporary Books, 2001. Pp. 191–194.

51217. "Ryne Sandberg: The Cubs' Golden Boy." In: Tom Barnidge, ed. *The Sporting News 1985 Baseball Yearbook.* St. Louis, MO: *The Sporting News,* 1985. Pp. 27–31.

51218. Sandberg, Ryne. "My Greatest Day in Baseball." In: Eliot Cohen, ed. *My Greatest Day in Baseball.* New York: Little, Simon, 1991. Pp. 102–104.

51219. _____., with Barry Rozner. *Second To Home: Ryne Sandberg Opens Up.* Chicago, IL: Bonus Books, 1995. 313p.

51230. _____., with Fred Mitchell. *Ryno!* Chicago, IL: Contemporary Books, 1985. 79p.

51231. _____. as told to George Vass. "The Game I'll Never Forget." *Baseball Digest,* LII (February 1993), 77–78. 1984 pennant race.

51232. Schulian, John. "Ryne Sandberg: A Budding Star in the Cubs' Youth Corps." *Baseball Digest,* XLI (December 1982), 43–45.

51233. Smith, Duane A. "Ryne Dee 'Ryno' Sandberg." In: Vol. Q-Z of David L. Porter, ed. *Biographical Dictionary of American Sports: Baseball.* Rev. and enlarged ed. Westport, CT: Greenwood Press, 2000. Pp. 1350–1351.

51234. Solomon, Alan. "Sandberg Is a Nonpareil But Cub Pitching Must Bear Up." In: George Leonard, ed. *Athlon's Baseball '91.* Nashville, TN: Athlon Sports Communications, 1991. Pp. 12–15.

51235. Sorci, Rick. "A Second Look: Ryne Sandberg." *Beckett Baseball Card Monthly,* VI (December 1989), 73–77.

51236. "Superstar Gallery: Ryne Sandberg." *Beckett Baseball Card Monthly,* IX, no. 88 (July 1992), 10–14.

51237. Thornton, K. D. "Ryne Sandberg." In: Ken Collier, ed. *The Baseball Book, 1985.* Scottsdale, AZ: Jalart House, 1985. Pp. 5–6.

51238. Van Dyke, Dave. "Farewell to Ryne Sandberg: A Class Act to the End." *Baseball Digest,* LIII (November 1994), 44–46.

51239. Verducci, Tom. "Second Time Around." *Sports Illustrated,* LXXXIV (March 11, 1996), 34–41.

51240. Weiskopf, Don. "Making the Double Play." *Athletic Journal,* LXVII (January 1987), 26–32. As demonstrated by Sandberg.

51241. Wilbert, Warren and William Hageman "Ryne Sandberg—1984." In: their *Chicago Cubs: Seasons at the Summit, the 50 Greatest Individual Seasons.* Champaign, IL: Sagamore Publishing, 1997. Pp. 27–30.

51242. Wood, Robert O. "Ryne Sandberg—1990." In: his *Baseball's Top 100: The Best Individual Seasons of All Time.* Wilton, CT: Diamond Library, 1996. Pp. 273–275.

Alexander Bennett ("Ben" or "Big Ben") Sanders
P. (B: Feb. 16, 1865, Catharpen, VA–D: Aug. 29, 1930). Philadelphia (NL), 1888–1889; Philadelphia (P), 1890; Philadelphia (AA), 1891; Louisville (NL), 1892. Remarks: Won 80 games and lost 70 in five seasons; had one no-hitter, Aug. 22, 1892.

51243. Ziegler, John H. "Alexander Bennett 'Ben,' 'Big Ben' Sanders." In: Vol. Q–Z of David L. Porter, ed. *Biographical Dictionary of American Sports: Baseball.* Rev. and enlarged ed. Westport, CT: Greenwood Press, 2000. Pp. 1351–1352.

Ben Sanders *see* **Alexander Bennett ("Ben" or "Big Ben" Sanders**

Deion Luwynn ("Prime Time" or "Neon") Sanders
OF. (B: August 9, 1967, Fort Myers, FL). New York (AL), 1989–1990; Atlanta (NL), 1991–1994; Cincinnati (NL), 1994–1995; San Francisco (NL), 1995; Cincinnati (NL), 1997, 2001. Remarks: In nine big league seasons, obtained 558 hits (39 homers) and 186 stolen bases in 641 games; had one inside-the-park homer, July 15, 1990; also played for Atlanta (N.F.L.), 1989–1993; San Francisco (N.F.L.), 1994; Dallas (N.F.L.), 1995–1999; and Washington (N.F.L.), 2000.

51244. Adelson, Bruce. "Deion Sanders." *Beckett Focus on Future Stars,* I (August 1991), 26–29.

51245. Bell, Jarrett. "Primed for a Switch." *USA Today Baseball Weekly,* IV (August 31, 1994), 24–25.

51246. Callahan, Gerry. "Running Start." *Sports Illustrated,* LXXXVI (May 19, 1997), 58–62.

51247. Chadwick, Bruce. *Deion Sanders.* Philadelphia, PA: Chelsea House, 1996. 64p.

51248. Chastain, Bill. "Beers With Deion Sanders." *Sport,* LXXXI (October 1990), 25–28.

51249. Cook, Kevin. "*Playboy* Interview: Deion Sanders." *Playboy,* XLI (August 1994), 51–62.

51250. "Deion Sanders." In: *Current Biography Yearbook, 1994.* New York: H. W. Wilson Co., 1995. Pp. 504–508.

51251. "Deion Sanders." In: Laurie L. Harris, ed. *Biography Today, 1996: Profiles of People of Interest to Young Readers.* Detroit, MI: Omnigraphics, 1996. pp. 145–154.

51252. Hannon, Kent. "Prime Time!" *Sports Illustrated for Kids.* VI (August 1994), 34–40.

51253. Harvey, Miles. *Deion Sanders: Prime Time.* Chicago, IL: Children's Press, 1996. 48p.

51254. Hemmer, Andy. "When Reds Signed Deion, City Got Major-League Endorser." *Cincinnati Business Courier,* XLI (July 11, 1994), 3–4.

51255. Hinton, Ed. "One Thing [Baseball] or the Other [Football]." *Sports Illustrated,* LXXVI (April 27, 1992), 38–45.

51256. King, Peter. "Time for a Game Plan." *Sports Illustrated,* LXXVII (August 24, 1992), 20–23.

51257. Kirkpatrick, Curry. "Deion Sanders: 'They Don't Pay Nobody to Be Humble.'" *Sports Illustrated,* LXXI (November 13, 1989), 52–56+.

51258. Klein, Aaron. *Deion Sanders.* New York: Walker, 1995. 149p.

51259. Ladson, William. "The *Sport* Q&A: Deion Sanders." *Sport,* LXXXVI (February 1995), 32–36.

51260. Lupica, Mike. "The Neon Nineties." *Esquire,* CXVII (June 1992), 59–60.

51261. Macnow, Glen. *Sports Great Deion Sanders.* Springfield, NJ: Enslow Publishers, 1999. 64p.

51262. McCoy, Hal. "Sanders Rolls Up His Baseball Sleeves." *USA Today Baseball Weekly,* VII (April 16, 1997), 8–9.

51263. "No Passing Zone." *Sports Illustrated for Kids,* IX (October 1997), 38–47.

51264. Pomerantz, Gary. "Interview: Deion Sanders." *Inside Sports,* XIII (September 1991), 18–23.

51265. _____. "The Marketing of Deion Sanders." *Football Digest,* XIX (April 1990), 60–67. Also applies to baseball.

51266. "Prime Time." *Sports Illustrated for Kids,* VI (August 1994), 34–41.

51267. Rains, Rob. "Showtime for Prime Time: Deion Out to Prove Baseball Can Be Fun." *USA Today Baseball Weekly,* IV (March 30, 1994), 8–10.

51268. Rosenberg, I.J. "A Closer Look: Deion Sanders." *Beckett Baseball Card Monthly,* IX, no. 88 (July 1992), 6–9.

51269. Rushin, Steve. "Catch-21." *Sports Illustrated,* LXXXIII (July 31, 1995), 54–59.

51270. Sanders, Deion, with Jim Nelson Black. *Power, Money & Sex: How Success Almost Ruined My Life.* Nashville, TN: Word Publishing, 1998. 194p.

51271. Savage, Jeff. *Deion Sanders: Star Athlete.* Springfield, NJ: Enslow, 1996. 104p.

51272. Scheiber, Dave. "Decisions, Decisions." *Sports Illustrated,* LXXI (July 3, 1989), 30–32+.

51273. Thornley, Stew. *Deion Sanders: Prime Time Player.* Minneapolis, MN: Lerner, 1997. 64p.

51274. "Two-Sport Phenom Sanders Ponders Quitting Baseball." *Jet,* LXXXVIII (October 2, 1995), 46–47.

51275. Von Borries, Philip. "Turn Out the Lights, Please, As You Leave." In: Joseph M. Wayman, ed. *Grandstand Baseball Annual, 1998.* Downey, CA: Joseph M. Wayman, 1998. Pp. 106–107.

51276. Weinberg, Rick. "The *Sport* Q & A: Deion Sanders." *Sport,* LXXXV (July 1994), 68–69+.

Kenneth George ("Ken" or "Daffy") Sanders
P. (B: July 8, 1941, St. Louis, MO). Kansas City (AL), 1964; Boston (AL) and Kansas City (AL), 1966; Oakland (AL), 1969; Milwaukee (AL), 1970–1972; Minnesota (AL), 1973; Cleveland (AL), 1973–1974; California (AL), 1974; New York (NL), 1975–1976; Kansas City (AL), 1976. Remarks: Won 29 games and lost 43, with 66 "saves," in a

decade; hurled for nine different teams and had but one start in 408 games.

51277. Schaap, Dick. "It's All Wrong, But It's All Right." *Sport,* XL (August 1966), 34–36+.

Reginald Laverne ("Reggie") Sanders
OF. (B: Dec. 1, 1967, Florence, SC). Cincinnati (NL), 1991–1998; San Diego (NL), 1999; Atlanta (NL), 2000; Arizona (NL), 2001; San Francisco (NL), 2002; Pittsburgh (NL), 2003; St. Louis (NL), 2004-. Remarks: Through 2004, has had 1,483 hits (271 homers) and 283 stolen bases in 1,572 games; had three homers in one game, Aug. 15, 1995; had two homers in 2002 World Series; first player to hit 20-plus home runs for six clubs.

51278. Ballew, Bill. "Reggie Sanders — Maybe Not the Next Eric Davis, But Reds-Ready Anyway." *Fantasy Baseball,* II (November 1991), 34–35.

51279. Crasnick, Jerry. "Prime Time Talent." *Beckett Focus on Future Stars,* II, no. 13 (May 1992), 18–19.

51280. Kurkjian, Tim. "Red-Faced." *Sports Illustrated,* LXXXIII (October 23, 1995), 41–42.

51281. Menendez, Tony. "Sanders Enjoying Security." *USA Today Baseball Weekly,* I (January 15, 1992), 12–13.

Scott Douglas Sanderson
P. (B: July 22, 1956, Dearborn, MI). Montreal (NL), 1978–1983; Chicago (NL), 1984–1989; Oakland (AL), 1990; New York (AL), 1991–1992; California (AL) and San Francisco (NL), 1994; Chicago (AL), 1994; California (AL), 1995–1996. Remarks: Obtained 163 victories, 143 defeats, and five "saves"; defeated all 26 MLB teams at least once during his career.

51282. Evers, John L. "Scott Douglas Sanderson." In: Vol. Q-Z of David L. Porter, ed. *Biographical Dictionary of American Sports: Baseball.* Rev. and enlarged ed. Westport, CT: Greenwood Press, 2000. Pp. 1352–1353.

Michael Joseph ("Mike") Sandlock
C-3B-SS-2B. (B: Oct. 17, 1915, Old Greenwich, CT). Boston (NL), 1942, 1944; Brooklyn (NL), 1942–1956; Pittsburgh (NL), 1953. Remarks: Had 107 hits (two homers) and two stolen bases in 195 major league games.

51283. Fehler, Gene. "Mike Sandlock." In: his *Tales from Baseball's Golden Age.* Champaign, IL: Sports Publishing Co., 2000. Chpt. 43.

Frederick ("Fred") Sanford
P. (B: Aug. 19, 1919, Garfield, UT). St. Louis (AL), 1943, 1946–1948; New York (AL), 1949–1951; Washington (AL) and St. Louis (AL), 1951. Remarks: Won 37 games and lost 55, with six "saves," in seven years.

51284. Ison, Jim. "Fred Sanford." In: his *Mormons in the Major Leagues.* Cincinnati, OH: Action Sports, 1991. Pp. 166–170.

Jack Sanford *see* **John Stanley ("Jack") Sanford**
John Stanley ("Jack") Sanford
P (B: May 18, 1929, Wellesley Hills, MA). Philadelphia (NL), 1956–1958; San Francisco (NL), 1959–1966; California (AL), 1966–1967; Kansas City (AL), 1967. Remarks: Had 137 victories, 101 defeats, and 11 "saves" in a dozen summer campaigns; NL Rookie of the Year award, 1957; won 16 consecutive games In 1962; coach, Cleveland (AL), 1968–1969; scout, Baltimore (AL), 1977–1987.

51285. Brown, Hugh. "The Phils' Newest Meal Ticket." *Sport,* XXIV (December 1957), 36–37+.

51286. Honig, Donald. "1957: Jack Sanford. "In: his *National League Rookies of the Year.* " New York: Bantam Books, 1989. Pp. 25–26.

51287. Libby, Bill. "Jack Sanford's Grim World." *Sport,* XXXV (March 1963), 26–28.

51288. Mandel, Mike. "Jack Sanford." In: his *The San Francisco Giants: An Oral History.* Santa Cruz, Ca: Mike Mandel, 1979. Pp. 112–115.

51289. McCormick, Bob. "Jack Sanford and Juan Marichal." In: his *Baseball's Greatest Players Today.* New York: Franklin Watts, 1963. Pp. 129–137.

51290. Paxton, Henry T. "Baseball's Oldest Youngster." *Saturday Evening Post,* CCXXX (March 29, 1968), 27, 74–76.

51291. Porter, David L. "John Stanley 'Jack' Sanford." In: Vol. Q-Z of David L. Porter, ed. *Biographical Dictionary of American Sports: Baseball.* Rev. and enlarged ed. Westport, CT: Greenwood Press, 2000. Pp. 1353–1354.

51292. Robinson, Ray. "Jack Sanford (National League Rookie of the Year)." In: Bruce Jacobs, ed. *Baseball Stars of 1958.* New York: Lion Books, 1958. Pp. 149–156.

51293. Stevens, Bob. "The Giants' Two Jack Sanfords." *Baseball Digest,* XVIII (July 1959), 67–71.

51294. "Thrower." *Newsweek,* L (September 2,1967), 84–85.

51295. Weiskopf, Don. "The Fifth Infielder." *Athletic Journal,* XLIV (January 1964), 14–26. Sanford demonstrates fielding by pitchers.

51296. Williams, Edgar. "Jack Sanford: Old Hothead's Hot Head Man Now." *Baseball Digest,* XVII (June 1958), 49–54.

51297. Zanger, Jack. "Jack Sanford." In: Ray Robinson, ed. *Baseball Stars of 1963.* New York: Pyramid Books, 1963. Pp. 37–42.

Manuel Dejesus ("Manny") Sanguillen
C-OF-1B. (B: March 21, 1944, Colon, Panama). Pittsburgh (NL), 1967, 1969–1976; Oakland (AL), 1977; Pittsburgh (N.L), 1978–1980. Remarks: Had 1,500 hits (65 homers) in 1,448 games In 13 seasons; often compared to Johnny Bench (q.v.); traded (with $100,000) for manager Chuck Tanner (q.v.), Nov. 5, 1976; had winning hit in Game Two of 1979 World Series.

51298. Abrams, Al. "Super Stardom Ahead for Sanguillen?" *Baseball Digest,* XXIX (June 1970), 42–46.

51299. Blount, Roy, Jr. "Now Playing Right: Manny Sanguillen." *Sports Illustrated,* XXXVIII (March 18, 1973), 28–29.

51300. Cohen, Joel H. *Manny Sanguillen, Jolly Pirate.* New York: G.P. Putnam, 1975. 127p.

51301. Ellison, James." An Outfielder in Disguise." *Sport,* LI (March 1971), 50–51.

51302. Fimrite, Ron. "Two Captains Cut from Royal Cloth: Johnny Beach and Manny Sanguillen." *Sports Illustrated,* XXXVI (June 26, 1972), 30–32+.

51303. Kuenster, John. "Majors' Two Best Catchers: Bench and Sarrguillen. " *Baseball Digest,* XXXI (September 1972), 4–8.

51304. Holden, William G. "Manny Sanguillen: Bucs' Free-Swinger." *Black Sports Magazine,* IV (September 1974), 44–51.

51305. Lenoir, Bob. "Manny Sanguillen Out from Clemente's Shadow." *Baseball Digest,* XXXIV (July 1975), 46–48.

51306. "Manny's Task." *Newsweek,* LXXXI (April 2, 1973), 55, 57.

51307. Porter, David L. "Manuel de Jesus (Magan) 'Manny' Sanguillen." In: Vol. Q-Z of David L. Porter, ed. *Biographical Dictionary of American Sports: Baseball.* Rev. and enlarged ed. Westport, CT: Greenwood Press, 2000. Pp. 1355–1356.

51308. Schultz, Randy. "John Roseboro and Manny Sanguillen: Where are They Now?" *Baseball Digest,* XLIX (January 1990), 59–62.

Benjamin Turner ("Ben") Sankey
SS-2B. (B: Sept. 2, 1907, Nauvoo, AL-D: March 12, 2001). Pittsburgh (NL), 1929–1931. Remarks: In all or parts of three big league seasons, obtained 36 hits in 72 games.
51309. Wilson, Nick. "Ben Sankey." In: his *Voices from the Pastime: Oral Histories of Surviving Major Leaguers, Negro Leaguers, Cuban Leaguers, and Writers, 1920–1934.* Jefferson, NC: McFarland & Co., Inc., 2000. Pp. 91–95.

Johan Santana
P. (B: March 13, 1979, Tovar Merida, Venezuela). Minnesota (AL), 2000-. Remarks: Through 2004, has won 43 games and lost 18, with one "save"; AL ERA leader, 2004.
51310. Antonen, Mel. "Twins' Johan Santana Thriving in His Role as a Starter." *Baseball Digest,* LXIII (November 2004), 40–43.

Benito Rivea ("Benny") Santiago
C. (B: Benito Santiago Rivera, March 9, 1965 in Ponce, P.R.). San Diego (NL), 1986–1992; Florida (NL), 1993–1994; Cincinnati (NL), 1995; Philadelphia (NL), 1996; Toronto (AL), 1997–1998; Chicago (NL), 1999; Cincinnati (NL), 2000; San Francisco (NL), 2001–2003; Kansas City (AL), 2004; Pittsburgh (NL), 2005-. Remarks: Through 2003, has had 1,824 hits (217 homers) and 91 stolen bases in 1,972 games; had 34-game hitting streak, 1987; NL Rookie of the Year Award, 1987; had three consecutive homers and six RBIs in one game and a fourth in a row in the next contest, Sept. 15–16, 1996; had two homers in 2002 NLCS.
51311. Davids, Bob. "In 1987, Majors Produced Two 30-Game Hitting Streaks." *Baseball Digest,* XLVII (April 1988), 82–87. One of which belonged to Santiago.
51312. Friend, Tom. "The Honeymoon's Over." *Sport,* LXXXIII (August 1992), 49–50+.
51313. Hedin, Mark. "Santiago se Une a Los Giants." *El Mensajero,* XIV (6 de April 2001), 28+.
51314. Honig, Donald. "1987: Benito Santiago." In: his *National League Rookies of the Year.* New York: Bantam Books, 1989. Pp. 105–106.
51315. Keown, Tim. "Game Face." *ESPN: The Magazine,* XI (May 2003), 40–47.
51316. Lidz, Franz. "Benito Finito at 34 Games." *Sports Illustrated,* LXVII (October 12, 1987), 26–27.
51317. Newman, Bruce. "The Man with the Golden Gun." *Sports Illustrated,* LXXIV (February 11, 1991), 60–62, 64–65.
51318. Pearlman, Jeff. "Giant Steps: Batting Behind Barry Bonds, 37-Year Old Benito Santiago Delivered Some of the Big Hits That Helped San Francisco Win Its First Pennant in 13 Years." *Sports Illustrated,* XCVII (October 21, 2002), 56–57.
51319. Peters, Nick. "Armed Behind the Plate." *Baseball Digest,* LXII (September 2003), 52–55.
51320. Porter, David L. "Benito (Rivea) 'Benny' Santiago." In: Vol. Q-Z of David L. Porter, ed. *Biographical Dictionary of American Sports: Baseball.* Rev. and enlarged ed. Westport, CT: Greenwood Press, 2000. Pp. 1356–1357.
51321. Reinman, T. R. "Maybe They Ought to Call Him 'Shotgun Santiago." *Baseball Digest,* XLVII (December 1988), 41–43.

Bailey Santistevan
COACH. Remarks: Coach of Bingham Canyon boys baseball teams, Eskimo Pie League, in Utah, 1928–1954.
51322. Schulian, John. "Bailey's Boys." *Sports Illustrated,* XCI (July 5, 1999), 66–72+.

Ronald Edward ("Ron") Santo
3B-BROADCASTER. (B: Feb. 26, 1940, Seattle, WA).

Chicago (NL), 1960–1973; Chicago (AL), 1974. RemaM: Obtained 2,254 hits (342 homers) in 2,243 games in 15 seasons; led NL in triples, 1964; had 28-game hitting streak, 1966; established various NL marks in fielding for third baseman as contemporary counterpart of AL's Brooks Robinson (q.v.); oil trucking company executive, 1975–1991; broadcaster, Chicago (NL), 1990-; lost part of right leg to diabetes, 2001.
51323. Blaisdell, Lowell L. "Ronald Edward 'Ron' Santo." In: Vol. Q-Z of David L. Porter, ed. *Biographical Dictionary of American Sports: Baseball.* Rev. and enlarged ed. Westport, CT: Greenwood Press, 2000. Pp. 1357–1358.
51324. Brosnan, Jim. "Ron Santo Comes of Age." *Sport,* LVI (September 1973), 70–73.
51325. _____. "Hot Hand at the Hot Corner." *Boy's Life,* LIX (April 1961)), 20+.
51326. _____. *Ron Santo, 3rd Baseman.* New York: G.P. Putnam, 1974. 143p.
51327. Condon, David. "Don't Take Ron Santo for Granted." *Baseball Digest,* XXXII (August 1973), 59–62.
51328. Dozer, Dick. "How the Cubs Are Cashing in on Ron Santo's $100,000 Error." *Super Sports,* II (March 1969), 34–37.
51329. Dray, Bill. "Ron Santo: A Hall of Fame Plaque in His Future?" *Baseball Digest,* LI (July 1992), 66–69.
51330. Frommer, Harvey and Frederick J. "Ron Santo." In: their *Growing Up Baseball: An Oral History.* Dallas, TX: Taylor Publishing Co., 2001. Pp. 204–206.
51331. Furlong, William B. ("Bill"). "Ron Santo: The Antihero in Chicago." In: Ray Robinson, ed. *Baseball Stars of 1970.* New York: Pyramid Books, 1970. Pp. 103–110.
51332. _____. "Ron Santo: Big Breeze in Windy City." In: Ray Robinson, ed. *Baseball Stars of 1967.* New York: Pyramid Books, 1967. Pp. 53–61.
51333. _____. "Ron Santo's Enemy." *Sport,* XL (August 1965), 36–39.
51334. Gallagher, Jack. "Ron Santo a Winner Among Losers." *Baseball Digest,* XXV (November 1966), 73–75.
51335. Hochman, Stan. "Ron Santo-Pull Isn't Always Needed for a Raise." *Baseball Digest,* XXII (December 1963), 79–83.
51336. Holtzman, Jerome. "No Wonder Cubs Believe in Santo." *Baseball Digest,* XX (August 1961), 13–21.
51337. Katz, Fred. "Ron Santo and His Million-Dollar Education." *Sport,* XLIII (May 1967), 62–68.
51338. Libby, Bill "Ron Santo." In: his *Heroes of the Hot Corner.* New York: Watts, 1972. Pp. 25–35.
51339. Phalen, Rick. "Ron Santo." In: his *Our Chicago Cubs.* South Bend, IN: Diamond Communications, 1992. Pp. 161–164.
51340. Pratt, John L. "Ron Santo." In: his *Baseball's All-Stars.* Garden City, N.Y.: Doubleday, 1967. Pp. 119–120.
51341. "Ron Santo." In: Carrie Muskat, ed. *Banks to Sandberg to Grace: Five Decades of Love and Frustration with the Chicago Cubs.* Chicago, IL: Contemporary Books, 2001. Pp. 95–100.
51342. "The Ron Santo Surge." In: Al Silverman, ed. *Inside Baseball, 1965.* New York: Maefadden-Bartell Corp., 1965. Pp. 36–39.
51343. Rosenthal, Herbert. "What Lippy [Leo Durocher] Taught Ron Santo." *All-Star Sports,* III (April 1969), 24–27.
51344. Santo, Ronald E. . "Ron Santo and Diabetes: 'Accept It, Live a Full Life." *Physician and Sports Medicine,* II (June 1974), 61–62.

51345. _____., as told to George Vass. "The Game I'll Never Forget." *Baseball Digest,* XXXI (July 1972), 55–58.

51346. _____., with Randy Minhoff. *Ron Santo — For Love of Ivy: The Autobiography of Ron Santo.* Chicago, IL: Bonus Books, 1993. 224p.

51347. Schneider, Armand. "Ron Santo's 12-Year Secret." *Baseball Digest,* XXX (October 1971), 42–45. Reprinted in John Kuenster, ed., *From Cobb to Catfish* (Chicago, IL: Rand McNally, 1975), pp. 61–62.

51348. Stern, Chris. "Ron Santo." In: his *Where Have They Gone?* New York: Tempo Books, 1979. Pp. 52–54.

51349. Watson, Emmett. "A Boy and a Dream." *Sport,* XXXIV (July 1962), 20–21+.

51350. Wilbert, Warren and William Hageman. "Ronald Edward Santo —1966." In: their *Chicago Cubs: Seasons at the Summit, the 50 Greatest Individual Seasons.* Champaign, IL: Sagamore Publishing, 1997. Pp. 15–18.

Louis ("Top" or "Big Bertha") Santop

C-OF-MGR. (B: Louis Santop Loftin, Jan. 17, 1890, Tyler-TX-D: Jan. 6, 1942). Fort Worth Wonders and Oklahoma Monarchs, 1909; Philadelphia Giants, 1909–1910; New York Lincoln Giants, 1911–1914, 1918; Brooklyn Royal Giants, 1914–1919; Chicago American Giants, 1915–1916; Hilldale Daisies, 1917–1926. Remarks: Powerful homerunning hitting catcher who became fan favorite.

51351. Holway, John B. "Louis Santop: The Big Bertha." *The Baseball Research Journal,* IX (1979), 93–97.

51352. _____. "Louis Loftin 'Top,' 'Big Bertha' Santop." In: Vol. Q–Z of David L. Porter, ed. *Biographical Dictionary of American Sports: Baseball.* Rev. and enlarged ed. Westport, CT: Greenwood Press, 2000. Pp. 1358– 1359.

Kazuhiro Sasaki

P. (B: Feb. 22, 1968, Sendai City, Japan). Seattle (AL), 2000–2003. Remarks: Through 2003, won seven U.S. big league games and lost 16, while "saving" 129 more.; AL Rookie of the Year Award, 2000; lost one game of 2002 ALCS; also played for Yokohama Taiyo Whales, 1990–1992 and Yokohama BayStars, 1993–1999, winning 42 games and losing 33, with 229 "saves"; returned to the BayStars in 2004.

51353. "New King in Town: Although Ace Reliever Sasaki's Season is Over, 'Kazmania' is Only Just Beginning." *Time International,* CLVI (October 30, 2000), 59+.

51354. Stone, Larry. "Closing in Seattle: Kazuhiro Sasaki's Exotic Pitch Finishes Off Foes." *Baseball Digest,* LX (February 2001), 48–51.

Gina Satriano

P. (B: Dec. 27, 1965, North Hollywood, CA). Remarks: first girl to play in California's Little League system; first woman to try-out with a college men's baseball team; played with Colorado Silver Bullets, 1994–1995 and Los Angeles Legends (California Ladies League), 1996–1997; later, deputy district attorney, County of Los Angeles, CA., remembered as the prosecutor in the case of comedienne Paul Poundstone.

51355. Lopiano, Donna. "Gina Satriano." In: her *Great Women in Sports.* Detroit, MI: Visible Ink, 1996. Pp. 420–422.

Kevin Andrew ("Hot Sauce") Saucier

P. (B: Aug. 9, 1936, Pensacola, FL). Philadelphia (NL), 1978–1980; Detroit (AL), 1981. Remarks: Won 12 games and lost ten, with 14 "saves," in four years.

51356. Kennedy, Ray. "Picking Up the Pieces." *Sports Illustrated,* LIX (August 29,1983), 42–47.

Hank Sauer *see* **Henry John ("Hammering Hank" or "Hank") Sauer**

Henry John ("Hammering Hank" or "Hank") Sauer

OF-1B. (B: March 17, 1917, Pittsburgh, PA-D: Aug. 24, 2001). Cincinnati (NL), 1941–1942, 1945, 1948–1949; Chicago (NL), 1949–1955; St. Louis (NL), 1956; New York (NL) and San Francisco (NL), 1957–1959. Remarks: Obtained 1,278 hits (288 homers) in 1,399 games in 15 seasons; had three homers in one game thrice; NL MVP award, 1952; NL home run champion (tie), 1952; NL RBI champion, 1952; coach, San Francisco (NL), 1959 and Giants minor league manager/ scout, 1960–1962; hit 50 homers with Syracuse (IL), 1947; elected to Illinois Sports Hall of Fame.

51357. Bitker, Steve. "Hank Sauer." In: his *The Original San Francisco Giants: The Giants of '58.* Champaign, IL: Sports Publishing, Inc., 1998. Pp. 73–80.

51358. Burnes, Ed. "The Sweet Sauer Man." *Baseball Magazine,* LXXXIX (September 1952), 8–10.

51359. Fagen, Herb. "The Mayor of Wrigley Field." *Oldtyme Baseball News,* IV, no. 1 (1992), 26–27.

51360. "Hank Sauer." In: Carrie Muskat, ed. *Banks to Sandberg to Grace: Five Decades of Love and Frustration with the Chicago Cubs.* Chicago, IL: Contemporary Books, 2001. Pp. 27–29.

51361. Hoffman, John C. *Hank Sauer.* New York: A.S. Barnes, 1953. 182p.

51362. _____. and Ed McAuley. "Hank Sauer's M.V. Award Legit?: Sauer Choice [and] Sauer Grapes." *Baseball Digest,* XII (February 1953), 30–37.

51363. Holtzman, Jerome. "Do You Remember ... When Hank Sauer was The Mayor of Wrigley Field." *Baseball Digest,* LX (December 2001), 64–67.

51364. Honig, Donald. "1952: Hank Sauer." In: his *National League MVP's.* New York: Bantam Books, 1989. Pp. 47–48.

51365. Mandel, Mike. "Hank Sauer." In: his *The San Francisco Giants: An Oral History.* Santa Cruz, CA: Mike Mandel, 1979. Pp. 28–30.

51366. Masterson, Dave And Timm Boyle. "1952." In: their *Baseball's Best: The MVPs.* Chicago, IL: Contemporary Books, 1985. Pp. 136–141.

51367. Munzel, Edgar. "Bruin Blockbuster." *Sport Life,* V (October 1952), 24–25+.

51368. _____. "Rags to Riches." In: Bruce Jacobs, ed. *Baseball Stars of 1953.* New York: Lion Books, 1953. Pp. 145–150.

51369. Obojski, Robert. "Former NL Slugger Hank Sauer Interviewed." *Sports Collectors Digest,* XXI (April 22, 1994), 131+.

51370. Phalen, Rick. "Hank Sauer." In: his *Our Chicago Cubs.* South Bend, IN: Diamond Communications, 1992. Pp. 30–41.

51371. Richman, Milton. "Homers Are His Specialty." In: Bruce Jacobs, ed. *Baseball Stars of 1955.* New York: Lion Books, 1955. Pp. 113–118.

51372. _____. "The Sauer Surprise." *Sport,* XIII (October 1952), 36–37+.

51373. _____. "The Strange Riddle of Hank Sauer." *Sport Life,* VI (June 1953), 31–35.

51374. Rumill, Ed. "That Red Menace Hank Sauer." *Baseball Magazine,* LXXXI (October 1948), 365–367+.

51375. Sargent, Jim. "Hank Sauer, Power Hitter." *Oldtyme Baseball News,* VIII, no. 2 (1996), 8–10.

51376. Sauer, Hank. "How I Pull the Ball." *Sport,* XIV (February 1953), 88+.

51377. Sexauer, Chuck. "Old Man Sauer." *Sport,* XXV (May 1958), 38–39.

51378. _____. "Sauer Sings a Home Run Tune." In: Al

Silverman, ed. *True's 1953 Baseball Yearbook*. Greenwich, CT: Fawcett Publications, 1953. Pp. 34–35+.

51379. Smith, Duane A. "Henry John 'Hammering Hank,' 'Hank' Sauer." In: Vol. Q–Z of David L. Porter, ed. *Biographical Dictionary of American Sports: Baseball*. Rev. and enlarged ed. Westport, CT: Greenwood Press, 2000. Pp. 1359–1360.

51380. Stump, Al. "Sauer Can't Win." *Sport*, XIV (June 1953), 28–29+.

51381. Swope, Tom. "Cincy's Sweet on Sauer." *Baseball Digest*, VII (October 1948), 17–23.

51382. Wilbert, Warren and William Hageman. "Henry "Hank" John Sauer–1952." In: their *Chicago Cubs: Seasons at the Summit, the 50 Greatest Individual Seasons*. Champaign, IL: Sagamore Publishing, 1997. Pp. 165–169.

Bob Savage *see* **John Robert ("Bob") Savage**

John Robert ("Bob") Savage

P. (B: Dec. 21, 1921, Manchester, NH). Philadelphia (AL), 1942, 1946–1948; St. Louis (AL), 1949. Remarks: Won 16 games and lost 27, with nine "saves," in five big league seasons; also played for San Diego (PCL), 1947, 1950; San Francisco (PCL), 1951–1952; worked for Wilson Sporting Goods Co., 1953–1968; baseball coach, Gorham High School (NH), 1969–1983; Gorham Clerk of the Probate Court, 1983–1986.

51383. Swank, Bill. "Bob Savage." In: his *Echoes from Lane Field; A History of The San Diego Padres 1936–1957*. Paducah, KY: Turner Publishing Company, 1997. Pp. 102–103. Savage's autobiography appears on the website of the Philadelphia Athletics Historical Society < http://www.philadelphiaathletics.org/a8.html>.

Edwin Milby ("Eddie") Sawyer

MGR. (B: Sept. 10, 1910, Westerly, RI–D: Sept. 22, 1997.). Remarks: Minor league player and manager, 1934–1948; manager, Philadelphia (NL), 1948–1952, 1958–1960, winning 390 games and losing 425 (.479).

51384. "Baseball: 'A Good Guy." *Newsweek*, XXXIV (July 18, 1949), 64–65.

51385. Baumgartner, Stan. "The Brains Behind the Phillies." *Sport*, X (January 1951), 16–19.

51386. Bloodgood, Clifford. "Eddie Sawyer, a Baseball Educator." *Baseball Magazine*, LXXXI (October 1948), 377–379.

51387. Cohane, Tim. "Eddie Sawyer: Boss of the Huckleberry Phils." *Look*, XV (January 30, 1951), 76–81.

51388. "Eddie Sawyer." In: *Current Biography Yearbook, 1950*. New York: H. W. Wilson Co., 1950. Pp. 516–518.

51389. Honig, Donald. "Eddie Sawyer." In: his *The Man in the Dugout*. Chicago, IL: Follett Publishing, 1977. Pp. 59–80.

51390. "My Boys." *Time*, LV (May 29, 1950), 43–44.

51391. Sawyer, Eddie. "Shepherding the Flock: The Manager." In: *Baseball is Their Business*. New York: Random House, 1952. Pp. 163–180.

51392. Yeutter, Frank. "Sawyer Has a Way with Him." *Baseball Digest*, IX (January 1950), 40–45.

Stephen Louis ("Steve") Sax

2B–BROADCASTER. (B: Jan. 20, 1960, Sacramento, CA). Los Angeles (NL), 1981–1988; New York (AL), 1989–1991; Chicago (AL), 1992–1993; Oakland (AL), 1994. Remarks: Had 1,949 hits (54 homers) and 444 stolen bases in 1,769 games in 14 years; NL Rookie of the Year award, 1982; stole home plate in a game, June 29, 1984; had six hits in 1985 NLCS; had 25-game hitting streak, 1986; had eight hits in 1988 NLCS and six in 1988 World Series; holder of two martial arts Black Belts and broadcast analyst for Fox Sports.

51393. Brody, Robert. "You'll Hear No Wailing from Steve Sax." *Men's Health*, V (June 1990), 54–58.

51394. Burns, Bob. "Dodgers' Steve Sax Traveled the Comeback Trail in '86." *Baseball Digest*, XLVI (January 1987), 42–45.

51395. Coffey, Wayne. "Baseball's Baby Boom." *Sport*, LXXIII (September 1982), 54–59+.

51395. Delsohn, Steve. "Steve Sax is Back with a Vengeance." In: Owen C. Shaw, ed. *Petersen's 1987 Pro Baseball Annual*. Los Angeles, CA: Petersen's, 1987. Pp. 68–73.

51396. Elderkin, Phil. "Steve Sax: Another Top Rookie for the Dodgers." *Baseball Digest*, XLI (April 1982), 31–33.

51397. Honig, Donald. "1982: Steve Sax." In: his *National League Rookies of the Year*. New York: Bantam Books, 1989. Pp. 92–93.

51398. Knobler, Danny. "Baseball's Best Leadoff Batters." *Sport*, LXXXI (July 1990), 40–45.

51399. Martinez, M. "Taking a Defensive Stand." *The New York Times Biographical Service* (May 1990), 440–441.

51400. Nash, Bruce and Allan Zullo. "Steve Sax." In: their *Little Big Leaguers: Amazing Boyhood Stories of Today's Baseball Stars*. New York: Little Simon, 1990. Pp. 10–11.

51401. Porter, David L. "Stephen Louis 'Steve' Sax." In: Vol. Q-Z of David L. Porter, ed. *Biographical Dictionary of American Sports: Baseball*. Rev. and enlarged ed. Westport, CT: Greenwood Press, 2000. Pp. 1360–1361.

51402. Sax, Steve. *Sax!* Chicago, IL: Contemporary Books, 1986. 95p.

51403. Shannon, Mike. "Steve Sax." In: his *Tales from the Dugout: The Greatest True Baseball Stories Ever Told*. Lincolnwood, IL: NTC/Contemporary Books, 1997. Pp. 185–186.

51404. Steinberg, Alan. "At the Crack of the Bat." *Inside Sports*, XI (October 1989), 84–91.

51405. _____. "L.A.'s Comic Dodger." *Inside Sports*, IX (October 1987), 79–85.

51406. Totoraitis, Joe. "A Second Look: Steve Sax." *Beckett Baseball Card Monthly*, VIII (April 1991), 89–93.

51407. Waldman, Alan Bennett. *My Steve Sax Connections: How a Hero Led an Abused Boy to Manhood*. Encino, CA: Astor Street Publishing Co., 1990. 272p.

John Thomas Sayles

WRITER/MOTION PICTURE DIRECTOR (B: Sept. 28, 1950, Schenectady, NY). Remarks: Remembered for, among other accomplishments, his directorship of the motion picture *Matewan* (1987) and the film version of Eliot Asinof's Black Sox history, *Eight Men Out* (1988).

51408. Johnson, Dick. "SABR Interviews John Sayles." *SABR Review of Books*, IV (1988), 96–101.

George Walter ("Tubby") Scales

2B-3B-1B-SS-OF-MGR. (B: Aug. 16, 1900, Talladega, AL-D: April 1976). Montgomery Grey Sox, 1919–1920; St. Louis Giants, 1921; St. Louis Stars, 1922; New York Lincoln Giants, 1923–1924; Homestead Grays, 1925–1926; Newark Stars, 1926; New York Lincoln Giants, 1927–1929; Homestead Grays, 1929–1931; New York Black Yankees, 1932–1934; Homestead Grays, 1935; New York Black Yankees, 1936; Santo Domingo Estrellas Orientales, 1937; Baltimore Elite Giants, 1938; New York Black Yankees, 1939–1940; Philadelphia Stars, 1940; Baltimore Elite Giants, 1940–1944; New York Black Yankees, 1945; Baltimore Elite Giants, 1946–1948; Birmingham Black Barons, 1952. Remarks: Noted Negro Leagues infielder, managing, at one time or another, the Black Yankees, Elite Giants, and Black Barons, as well as winter teams at Ponce and Santurce, PR.

51409. "George Scales : the Rifle Arm of Negro Professional Baseball." *Black Sports,* II (May 1973), 32–33.

51410. Kleinknecht, Merl F. "George Walter Scales." In: Vol. Q–Z of David L. Porter, ed. *Biographical Dictionary of American Sports: Baseball.* Rev. and enlarged ed. Westport, CT: Greenwood Press, 2000. Pp. 1361–1362.

Ray Wilson ("Rae") Scarborough
P. (B: July 23, 1917, Mt. Gilead, NC-D: July 1, 1982). Washington (AL), 1942–1943, 1946–1950; Chicago (AL), 1950; Boston (AL), 1951–1952; New York (AL), 1952–1953; Detroit (AL), 1953. Remarks: Won 80 games and lost 85, with 12 "saves," in 10 big league seasons; Mount Olive (N.C.) oil and supply company owner, 1954–1960; scout, Baltimore (AL), California (AL) and Milwaukee (AL), 1960–1982.

51411. Hirshberg, Al. "Will Scarborough Make the Difference?" *Sport,* X (April 1951), 16–20.

51412. Povich, Shirley. "Ray Scarborough." In: *My Greatest Baseball Game.* New York: A.S. Barnes And Co., 1950. Pp. 155–159.

Russ Scarritt *see* **Stephen Russell ("Russ") Scarritt**
Stephen Russell ("Russ") Scarritt
OF. (B: Jan. 14, 1903, Pensacola, FL-D: Dec. 4, 1994). Boston (AL), 1929–1931; Philadelphia (NL), 1932 Remarks: Obtained 296 hits (three homers) and 17 stolen bases in 285 games in four years; established a Red Sox rookie season record with 17 triples.

51413. Kelley, Brent P. "Russ Scarritt: The Rapid Red Sox Rookie, 1929–1932." In: his *In The Shadow Of The Babe: Baseball Players Who Played with or Against Babe Ruth.* Jefferson, NC: McFarland & Co., Inc., 1995. Pp. 69–72.

Lester ("Les") Scarsella
1B. (B: Nov. 23, 1913, Santa Cruz, CA-D: Dec. 17, 1958). Cincinnati (NL), 1935–1937, 1939; Boston (NL), 1940. Remarks: Had 255 hits (six homers) and 13 stolen bases in 265 games in five big league seasons; had NL high nine pinch hits in 1937; also played for Wilmington (Piedmont League), 1934–1935; Toronto (IL), 1936; Newark (IL), 1939; 1937, Cincinnati, National League; 1939, Newark, International League; 1939, Seattle (PCL), 1941–1942; Oakland (PCL), part of 1943–1944–1945; also a bowling enthusiast.

51414. Milne, Robert C. "He Packs Dynamite in Winter." *Baseball Magazine,* LVIII (March 1937), 467–468.

51415. Spalding, John. "Les Scarsella." In: his *Pacific Coast League Stars: One Hundred of the Best, 1903–1957.* San Jose, CA: John E. Spalding, 1994. Pp. 105–106.

Dick Schaap *see* **Richard Jay ("Dick") Schaap**
Richard Jay ("Dick") Schaap
WRITER-BROADCASTER. (B: Sept. 27, 1934, New York City-D: Dec. 21, 2001). Remarks: Successively sports editor, general editor, and senior editor, *Newsweek,* 1956–1963; city editor, then columnist, *New York Herald Tribune,* 1964–1966; columnist, *New York World Journal Tribune,* 1966–1967; sportscaster, WNBC-TV, 1971–1978; sportscaster, NBC-TV, 1978–1980 and ABC-TV, 1980–2001; also host of ESPN's *The Sports Reporters,* 1988–2001.

51416. Schaap, Dick. *Dick Schaap, as told to Dick Schaap: 50 Years of Headlines, Deadlines and Punchlines.* New York: HarperCollins, 2001. 400p.

51417. _____. "Magazine Memories." *Sport,* LXXXVII (September 1996), 77–78+.

Alexander ("Al" or "The Clown Prince of Baseball") Schacht
P. (B: Nov. 11, 1892, New York City-D: July 14, 1984.). Washington (AL), 1919–1921. Remarks: Won 14 games

and lost ten with two "saves" in three big league years; coach, Washington (AL), 1921–1924 and Boston (AL), 1935–1936 during which time he developed entertainment act which he took on the road to minor- and major-league parks and military facilities, later in company with ex-Senators pitcher, Nick Altrock (q.v.).

51418. "Al(exander) Schacht." In: *Current Biography Yearbook, 1946.* New York: H.W. Wilson Co., 1946. Pp. 534–537.

51419. Amman, Larry. "The Clown Prince of Baseball." *The Baseball Research Journal,* XI (1982), 119–126.

51420. Burr, Harold C. "It's the Gypsy in Him." *Baseball Magazine,* LXVIII (April 1942), 515–517.

51421. Cunningham, Bill. "Clown Prince." *Collier's,* C (September 4, 1937), 24–26.

51422. Lieb, Frederick G. "Al Schacht: Master of Pantomime." In: his *Comedians and Pranksters of Baseball.* St. Louis: *The Sporting News,* 1950. Pp. 16–18.

51423. Menke, Frank G. "Clowning Through Baseball In: his *Sports Tales and Anecdotes.* New York: A.S. Barnes, 1953. Pp. 50–51.

51424. Marazzi, Rich. "Al Schacht: 'The Clown Prince of Baseball." *Baseball History,* I (Winter 1986), 34–45.

51425. Powers, Jimmy. "Al Schacht." In: *Baseball Personalities.* New York: Rudolph Field, 1949. Pp. 25–41.

51426. Ribalow, Harold U. "Al Schacht: Clown Prince of Baseball." In: his *Jew In American Sports.* New York: Bloch, 1959. Pp. 119–124.

51427. _____. and Z. Meir. "Al Schacht: Clown Prince Of Baseball." In: their *Jewish Baseball Stars.* New York: Hippocrene Books, 1984. Pp. 138–145.

51428. Schacht, Al. *Clowning Through Baseball.* New York. A.S. Barnes, 1941. 189p.

51429. _____. *G.I. Had Fun.* New York: G. P. Putnam, 1945. 136p. World War II years.

51430. _____. *My Own Particular Screwball: An Informal Autobiography.* Edited by Ed Keyes. Garden City, N.Y.: Doubleday, 1955. 254p. Excerpted in *Sports Illustrated,* II (March 21, 1955), 30–32+.

51431. _____. "Who's Killing Minor League Baseball?" *American Mercury,* LXXIX (September 1954), 15–19. Fans, women and wives

51432. Schacht, Mike. *Mudville Diaries: A Book of Baseball Memories.* New York: Avon Books, 1996. 208p.

51433. Smith, Walter ("Red"). "When an Ump Got 'Hip' to Schacht." *Baseball Digest,* XII (August 1953), 77–79.

Germany Schaefer *see* **Herman A. ("Germany") Schaefer**
Herman A. ("Germany") Schaefer
2B- IB-3B-SS-OF-P. (B: Feb. 4, 1878, Chicago, IIL-D: May 16, 1919). Chicago (NL), 1901–1902; Detroit (AL), 1905–1909; Washington (AL), 1909–1914; Newark (F.L.), 1915; New York (AL), 1916; Cleveland (AL), 1918. Remarks: Had 972 hits (nine homers) and 201 stolen bases in 1,143 games in 15 MLB campaigns; zestful player who sometimes rattled opposing pitchers by stealing second base — and then running back to first; first to use hidden ball trick in a fall classic, Game One of the 1907 World Series; one of his vaudeville acts inspiration for Gene Kelly/Frank Sinatra musical *Take Me Out to the Ball Game;* scout, New York (NL), 1919; died of heart attack while on Canadian recruiting trip.

51434. Bingay, Malcolm. "Baseball's Troubadour: the Saga of Germany Schaefer." *Saturday Evening Post,* CCXII (January 27, 1940), 16–20.

51435. _____. "Troubadour: The Saga of Germany Schaefer." *Baseball Digest,* IV (February 1945), 5–8.

51436. Davis, Mac. "A Gay Troubadour." In: his *The Lore and Legends of Baseball.* New York: Lantern Press, 1953. Pp. 69–71.

51437. Drebinger, John. "They Guffawed Over Herman's High Jinks." In: J.G. Taylor Spink, ed. *Baseball Register, 1954.* St. Louis, MO: The Sporting, News, 1954. Pp. 21–24.

51438. Eisen, Bob. "White Sox 6, Giants 4 — In Garden City, L.I." *The Baseball Research Journal,* XXII (1993), 27–29.

51439. Fullerton, Hugh S. "The Extra Money Game." *Liberty,* V (September 15, 1928), 83–84.

51440. Horowitz, Harold H., and Ralph Tolleris. "Germany Schaefer." In: their *Big-Time Baseball.* New York: Hart, 1950. Pp. 110–112.

51441. Jones, David J. ("Kangaroo"). "Hurry, Schaefer." In: Charles Einstein, ed. *The Fourth Fireside Book of Baseball.* New York; Simon and Schuster, 1987. Pp. 181–186.

51442. Kavanagh, Jack. "Germany Schaefer: There Was Method to His Madness." *The Baseball Research Journal,* XIV (1985), 80–82.

51443. Lieb, Frederick G. "Germany Schaefer: Fun-Loving Exhibitionist." In: his *Comedians and Pranksters of Baseball.* St. Louis, MO: The Sporting News, 1958. Pp. 10–14.

51444. Menke, Frank G. "The Steal That Changed the Rules." In: his *Sports Tales and Anecdotes.* New York: A.S. Barnes, 1953. Pp. 21–22. Schaefer's "steal" of first base

51445. Robinson, John R. "Schaefer — Champion Grass Puller." *Baseball Magazine,* I (July 1908), 49–50.

51446. "Schaefer, the Grand Comedian of the Diamond." *Baseball Magazine,* XIII (July 1919), 166–167.

51447. Williams, Pete. "Apollo and Dionysius: Divisions." In: his *The Sports Immortals: Deifying the American Athlete.* Bowling Green, OH: Bowling Green State University Popular Press, 1994. Pp. 87–94.

51448. _____. "Stealing First and Fielding with Your Head: Germany Schaefer And Babe Herman as Fools." *The Baseball Research Journal,* XIX (1990), 39–44.

Raymond William ("Ray" or "Cracker") Schalk★
C-MGR. (B. Aug. 12,1892, Harvell, IL-D: May 19, 1970). Chicago (AL), 1912–1928; New York (N.LJ, 1929. Remarks: Obtained 1,345 hits (12 homers) and 176 stolen bases in 1,760 games in an 18-year major league career; noted fielding backstop; hit for the cycle, June 27, 1922; caught a ball dropped the 460' from the top of Chicago's Tribune Tower, May 11, 1925; manager, Chicago (AL), 1927–1928, winning 102 games and losing 125 (.449); coach, Chicago (NL), 1930–1931 as well as various minor league teams, 1932–1940 and 1950; assistant baseball coach, Purdue University, 1951–1968; elected to National Baseball Hall of Fame in 1965, where his plaque reads: "Holder of major league record for most years leading catcher in fielding — eight years; most putouts, nine years; most assists in one major league (1810); most chances accepted (8966). Caught four no-hit games including perfect game in 1922."

51449. Allen, Lee, and Thomas Meany. "Ray Schalk." In: their *Kings of the Diamond.* New York: G. P. Putnam, 1985. Pp. 89–90.

51450. Evers, John L. "Raymond William 'Ray,' 'Cracker' Schalk." In: Vol. Q-Z of David L. Porter, ed. *Biographical Dictionary of American Sports: Baseball.* Rev. and enlarged ed. Westport, CT: Greenwood Press, 2000. Pp. 1362–1363.

51451. Hirshberg, Al. "Ray Schalk." In: his *Baseball's*

Greatest Catchers. New York: G.P. Putnam, 1967. Pp. 37–44.

51452. Honig, Donald. "Ray Schalk." In: his *The Greatest Catchers of All Time.* Dubuque, IA: Wm. C. Brown Publishers, 1991. Pp. 14–19.

51453. Kalish, Stanley. "How Ray Schalk Got His Start." *Baseball Magazine,* XXXVI (June 1926), 315–317.

51454. Kuenster, John. "Ray Schalk Set an Example." *Baseball Digest,* XXIX (September 1970), 4–8.

51455. Lane, Ferdinand C. "The Man Who Breaks a Record at Every Game." *Baseball Magazine,* XXXVI (March 1926), 445–446.

51456. Povich, Shirley. "He Made a Play at Every Base." *Baseball Digest,* XIV (January-February 1955), 39–41.

51457. Ryan, Jack. "Schalk's Sucker Special." *Baseball Digest,* IV (September 1945), 53–54.

51458. Schalk, Ray. "Where Modern Pitching Is Wrong." *Baseball Magazine,* XXIII (August 1919), 203–205.

51459. _____., as told to Lloyd Lewis. "My Greatest Day In Baseball." In: John P. Carmichael, ed. *My Greatest Day in Baseball.* New York: A. S. Barnes, 1945. pp. 184–187. First published in the *Chicago Daily News.*

51460. Ward, John J. "The American League's Premier Catcher." *Baseball Magazine,* XVIII (November 1916), 31–35.

51461. _____. "Why Ray Schalk Is Baseball's Greatest Catcher." *Baseball Magazine,* XXXI (August 1923), 408–410+.

Arthur ("Art") Schallock
P. (April 25, 1924, Mill Valley, CA). New York (AL), 1951–1955; Baltimore (AL), 1955. Remarks: Won six games and lost seven in parts of five big league seasons; also played for Hollywood Stars (PCL), 1949–1950.

51462. Suehsdorf, Adie. D. "A Nice Little Career." *The National Pastime,* XVIII (1998), 32–35. .

Wally Schang *see* **Walter Henry ("Wally") Schang**
Walter Henry ("Wally") Schang
C-OF-3B. (B. Aug. 22, 1889, South Wales, NY-D: March 6, 1965). Philadelphia (AL), 1913–1917; Boston (AL), 1918–1920; New York (AL), 1921–1925; St. Louis (AL), 1926–1929; Philadelphia (AL), 1930; Detroit (AL), 1931. Remarks: Had 1,506 hits (69 homers) and 122 stolen bases in 1,840 games in 19 seasons; threw out AL record six runners attempting to steal in one game, May 12, 1915; first big league player to slug switch hit homers in the same game, Sept. 16, 1916; had an AL record eight assists in one game, May 12, 1920; only player to appear with three different World Series championship clubs; holds AL career mark for most errors by a catcher (218); manager, Joplin (W.A.), 1935, Muskogee (W.A.), 1936, Three Rivers (Prairie League), 1940, and Owensboro (Kentucky League), 1942.

51463. Borst, William A. ("Bill"). "Walter Herny 'Wally' Schang." In: Vol. Q-Z of David L. Porter, ed. *Biographical Dictionary of American Sports: Baseball.* Rev. and enlarged ed. Westport, CT: Greenwood Press, 2000. Pp. 1363–1365.

51464. Grayson, Harry. "Farmboy Schang Was a City Slicker Behind the Plate." *Baseball Digest,* III (September 1944), 23–25.

51465. Hirshberg, Al. "Wally Schang." In: his *Baseball's Greatest Catchers.* New York: G. P. Putnam, 1967. Pp. 54–60.

51466. Schang, Walter H. ("Wally"). "A Thumping, Clouting Backstop (Schang) and His Picturesque Career." *Baseball Magazine,* XXXIX (October 1927), 499–501+.

Bob Scheffing *see* **Robert Roden ("Bob") Scheffing**

Robert Roden ("Bob") Scheffing
C-MGR-EXEC. (B: April 11, 1915, Overland, MI-D: Oct. 26, 1985). Chicago (NL), 1941–1942, 1946–1950; Cincinnati (NL), 1950–1951; St. Louis (NL), 1961. Remarks: Obtained 357 hits (20 homers) in 517 games in eight playing seasons; had four RBIs in one game, May 11, 1947; minor league manager, 1939, 1965–1956; coach, St. Louis (AL), 1952–1953, Chicago (NL), 1954–1955, and Milwaukee (NL), 1960; manager, Los Angeles (PCL), 1955–1956, Chicago (NL), 1957–1959 and Detroit (AL), 1961–1963, winning 418 big league games and losing 427 (.495); scout, New York (NL), 1963 and Detroit (AL), 1964; director of player development, GM/VP New York (NL), 1965–1975.
51467. Spoelstra, Watson. "Bob Scheffing: He's a Player's Manager." *Baseball Digest,* XX (September 1961), 62–66.

Carl Scheib
P. (B: Jan. 1, 1927, Gratz, PA). Philadelphia (AL), 1943–1945, 1947–1954; St. Louis (NL), 1954. Remarks: Obtained 45 victories, 65 defeats, and 17 "saves" in nine seasons; youngest AL player at debut (16 years, eight months); had career BA of .250, with five homers.
51468. Appel, Marty. "Carl Scheib." In: his *Yesterday's Heroes: Revisiting the Old-Time Baseball Stars.* New York: William Morrow, 1988. Pp. 194–198.
51469. Fehler, Gene. "Carl Scheib." In: his *Tales from Baseball's Golden Age.* Champaign, IL: Sports Publishing Co., 2000. Chpt. 44.
51470. Kelley, Brent P. "Carl Scheib: A Major League Minor (1943–1954)." In: his *The Pastime in Turbulence: Interviews with Baseball Players of the 1940s.* Jefferson, NC: McFarland & Co., Inc., 2002. Pp. 133–144.
51471. McGuire, Mark and Michael Sean Gormley. "Carl Scheib." In: their *Moments in the Sun: Baseball's Briefly Famous.* Jefferson, NC: McFarland & Co., Inc., 2001. Pp. 39–42.

Richard Alan ("Richie") Scheinblum
OF. (B: Nov. 5, 1942, New York City). Cleveland (AL), 1965–1969; Washington (AL), 1971; Kansas City (AL), 1972; Cincinnati (NL), 1973; California (AL), 1973–1974; Kansas City (AL), 1974. Remarks: In an eight-year big league career, had 320 hits (13 homers) in 462 games; won 1971 AA batting and RBI titles while with the Denver Bears.
51472. Allen, Maury. "Richie Scheinblum Finally a Star." *Baseball Digest,* XXXI (November 1972), 67–69.

Richie Scheinblum *see* **Richard Alan ("Richie") Scheinblum**

Charles Thomas ("Chuck") Schilling
2B. (B: Oct. 25, 1937, Brooklyn, NY). Boston (AL), 1961–1965. Remarks: Obtained 470 hits (23 homers) in 541 Red Sox games in five years; retired rather than be traded.
51473. Brennan, Eamon. "Dressed For Sport: Chuck Schilling." *Sport,* XXXIV (July 1962), 46–49.
51474. "Chuck Schilling, Keystone of the Boston Red Sox." *Look,* XXVI (July 31, 1962), 38–40.
51475. Hirshberg, Al. "Don Schwall and Chuck Schilling: Kids with a Future ." In: Ray Robinson, ed. *Baseball Stars of 1962.* New York: Pyramid Books, 1962. Pp. 95–101.

Curt Schilling *see* **Curtis Montague ("Curt") Schilling**

Curtis Montague ("Curt") Schilling
P. (B: Nov. 14, 1966, Anchorage, AK) Baltimore (AL),

1988–1990; Houston (NL), 1991); Philadelphia (NL), 1992–1999; Arizona (NL), 2000–2003; Boston (AL), 2004–. Remarks: Through 2004, has won 184 games and lost 123, with 13 "saves"; 1993 NLCS MVP Award; lost Game One, but won Game Five of 1993 World Series; won Game Three of 2001 NLCS; won Game One of 2001 World Series; 2001 World Series MVP Award (tie); Branch Rickey Award, 2001; led A.L in victories (21) in 2004; won Game Six of 2004 ALCS and Game Two of 2004 World Series.
51476. Bandler, Michael J. "The Heart of Curt Schilling." *America West Airlines Magazine,* XVII (August 2002), 24–25, 50.
51477. Boeck, Greg. "Stronger Than Ever." *Baseball Digest,* LX (November 2001), 28–33.
51478. Cannella, Stephen. "Fast and in Your Face." *Sports Illustrated,* LXXXVIII (February 2, 1998), 78–82.
51479. _____. "Man of the Moment: In a Thrilling Series That Would Come Down to the Diamondbacks' Final At Bat, Curt Schilling Stepped Forward and Stifled St. Louis [in National League Playoffs]." *Sports Illustrated,* XCV (November 7, 2001), 46+.
51480. "Curt Schilling." In: *Current Biography Yearbook, 2001.* New York: H. W. Wilson, 2001. Pp. 482–484.
51481. Edes, Gordon. "Curt Schilling: Just a 'Regular Guy' Pitching in the Majors." *Baseball Digest,* LXIII (June 2004), 32–37.
51482. Farber, M. "More Heat in Arizona: Curt Schilling Joins Randy Johnson to Give the Diamondbacks a Daunting Fireballing Duo." *Sports Illustrated,* XCIII (August 14, 2000), 75–76.
51483. Hagen, Paul. *Curt Schilling: Phillie Phire!* Champaign, IL: Sports Publishing, 1999 . 82p.
51484. Henderson, John. "In '97, Curt Schilling Joined Ranks of Top Whiff Artists." *Baseball Digest,* LVI (December 1997), 64–65.
51485. Jerome, Richard. "Pitching Through Pain: Dazzling Even Under Personal Stress, World Series Hurler Curt Schilling Throws Heart and Soul into His Game." *People Weekly,* LVI (November 5, 2001), 73–74.
51486. Jordan, Pat. "The Odd Couple: Pitchers Curt Schilling and Randy Johnson." *The New York Times Magazine,* (September 29, 2002), 52–55.
51487. Keown, Tim. "2 Much: Are Curt Schilling and Randy Johnson the Best One-Two Punch Ever?—Just Ask NL Hitters." *ESPN: The Magazine,* IV (October 15, 2001), 46–51.
51488. Kuenster, John. "Schilling and [Mike] Mussina: Experts at Keeping Runners Off Basepaths." *Baseball Digest,* LII (May 1993), 17–21.
51489. Manoloff, Dennis. "Q & A: Interview with Curt Schilling." *Baseball Digest,* LXII (August 2003), 58–63.
51490. Massarotti, Tony. "Pitcher of the Year: Curt Schilling." *Baseball Digest,* LXIV (January-February 2005), 52–54.
51491. McCarver, Tim, with Danny Pear. "Curt Schilling." In: his *The Perfect Season: Why 1998 Was Baseball's Greatest Year.* New York: Villard Books, 1999. Pp. 191–195.
51492. Orens, Geoff. "Curt Schilling." *Current Biography,* LXII (October 2001), 60–64.
51493. Pickard, Chuck. "Phillies' Curt Schilling: No. 1 in Power Pitching Proficiency." *Baseball Digest,* LVII (March 1998), 26–29.
51494. Porter, David L. "Curtis Montague 'Curt' Schilling." In: Vol. Q-Z of David L. Porter, ed. *Biographical Dictionary of American Sports: Baseball.* Rev. and en-

larged ed. Westport, CT: Greenwood Press, 2000. Pp. 1365–1366.

51495. Rosenstein, Johnny. "The Big Game Pitcher: With Back-to-Back 20-Win Seasons, Curt Schilling of the Diamondbacks Has Become One of the Most Productive Starters Over the Last Two Years." *Baseball Digest,* LXI (November 2002), 52–55.

51496. Schilling, Shonda, with Diane Umansky. "I Didn't Think Skin Cancer was Real." *Good Housekeeping,* CCXXXV (August 2002), 61–63. The hurler's wife reveals her brush with melanoma.

51497. Schwarz, Alan. "Seeing the Light: Curt Schilling of the Arizona Diamondbacks has Learned to Make the Most of His Talent." *Sports Illustrated for Kids,* XIV (July 1, 2002), 29–36.

51497a. Stout, Glenn. *On the Mound with Curt Schilling.* Matt Christopher Sports Biographies. Boston, MA: Little, Brown, 2004. 112p.

51498. Tresniowski, Alex. "Quitting Time: Phillies' Pitcher Curt Schilling Kicks Smokeless Tobacco Habit." *People Weekly,* XLIX (June 1, 1998), 73–74.

51499. Tyler, Scott. "Coming Up Aces." *Diamondbacks Magazine,* III (September–October 2000), 28–32.

51500. Verducci, Tom. "The Power of Two: Sportsmen of the Year, Randy Johnson and Curt Schilling." *Sports Illustrated,* XCV (December 17, 2001), 112–124.

Jason David Schmidt

P. (B: Jan. 29, 1973, Lewiston, ID). Atlanta (NL), 1995–1996; Pittsburgh (NL), 1996–2001; San Francisco (NL), 2001–. Remarks: Through 2004, has won 104 games and lost 74; won one game in both the 2000 NLCS and 2000 World Series; 2.34 ERA led NL in 2003.

51501. Habib, Daniel G. "He Must Be Kidding." *Sports Illustrated,* CI (July 26, 2004), 54–57.

Michael Jack ("Mike") Schmidt★

3B. (B: Sept. 27, 1949, Dayton, OH). Philadelphia (NL), 1972–1989. Remarks: Obtained 2,234 hits (548 homers) and 174 stolen bases in 2,404 games in 18 seasons; first MLB player granted a $500,000 annual salary, Jan. 11, 1977; NL home run champion, 1974–1976, 1980–1981, 1983–1984 (tie), 1986; established major league record for most homers by a 3B; NL RBI champion, 1980–1981, 1984 (tie), 1986; NL MVP award, 1980–1981, 1986; had two homers in 1980 World Series; World Series MVP award, 1980; elected to the National Baseball Hall of Fame in 1995, where his plaque reads: "Unprecedented combination of power and defense with unusual mixture of strength, coordination and speed made him one of the game's greatest third basemen. 7th on all-time list with 548 homers. His 8 homerun titles (1 tie) bettered only by Babe Ruth. Belted 40 or more on 3 occasions and topped 30 ten other times. 48 homers in 1980 most ever by third baseman. Hit 4 in one game in 1976. 3-time MVP with 10 gold gloves for fielding excellence."

51502. Alexson, Bill. "Mike Schmidt, Philadelphia Phillies. "In: his *Batting a Thousand, Book 2.* Nashville, TN: Thomas Nelson Publishers, 1990. Pp. 28–32.

51503. Allen, Bob with Bill Gilbert. Mike Schmidt: The Impossible Dream? In: their *The 500 Home Run Club: Baseball's 15 Greatest Home Run Hitters from Aaron to Williams.* Champaign, IL: Sports Publishing, Inc., 1999. Pp. 232–246.

51504. Blengino, Tony. "Mike Schmidt: 1980." In: his *Baseball's Top 100: The Best Individual Seasons of All Time.* Wilton, CT: Diamond Library, 1996. Pp. 243–244.

51505. Bodly, Hal. "A Powerful Man in Philadelphia." In: C. C. Johnson Spink, ed. *The Sporting News 1981 Base-*

ball Yearbook. St. Louis, MO: *The Sporting News,* 1981. Pp. 8–11.

51506. Boswell, Thomas. "The Best Of All Time." In: his *Why Time Begins On Opening Day.* New York: Penguin, 1984. Pp. 215–222. Schmidt and Robin Yount.

51507. Burick, Si. "Mike Schmidt: The Complete Ballplayer." *Baseball Digest,* XXXVI (September 1977), 20–23.

51508. Cohen, Eliot. "Mike Schmidt." In: his *My Greatest Day In Baseball.* New York: Little Simon, 1991. Pp. 105–110.

51509. Cox, Jack. and Theo Chen. "A Final Look: Mike Schmidt." *Beckett Baseball Card Monthly,* VI (September 1989), 94–95.

51510. Dolson, Frank. "Mike Schmidt of the Phillies: Player of the '80's." *Baseball Digest,* XLI (May 1982), 59–63.

51511. Dunn, Jay. "The Rise of Mike Schmidt." *Baseball Quarterly,* I (Winter 1977), 8–11.

51512. Eldridge, Larry. "Mike Schmidt Would Rather Be Considered." *Baseball Digest,* XXXV (September 1976), 62–65.

51513. Fimrite, Ron. "Image in Sharper Focus." *Sports Illustrated,* LVI (May 31, 1982), 66–70+.

51514. "Final Look: Mike Schmidt." *Beckett Baseball Card Monthly,* XI, no. 111 (June 1994), 105–106.

51515. Fleishman, Bill. "Interview: Mike Schmidt." *Inside Sports,* IX (June 1987), 18–22.

51516. _____. "The Weight of Philly is on His Shoulders." *Inside Sports,* VI (June 1984), 22–29.

51517. Gutman, Bill. "Mike Schmidt." In: his *Baseball's Belters.* New York: Grosset and Dunlap, 1981. Pp. 67–117.

51518. _____. "Mike Schmidt." In: his *Great MVPs.* Tarrytown, NY: Angle Entertainment, Inc., 1989. Pp. 41–47.

51519. Herbert, Mike. *Mike Schmidt, the Human Vacuum Cleaner.* Chicago, IL: Childrens Press, 1983. 44p.

51520. Hochman, Stan. *Mike Schmidt: Baseball's King of the Swing.* New York: Random House, 1983. 131p.

51521. Holtzman, Jerome. "Mike Schmidt Joins Elite Hall of Fame Vote Leaders." *Baseball Digest,* LIV (April 1995), 21–23.

51522. Honig, Donald. "Mike Schmidt: The Late Bloomer." In: his *The Power Hitters.* St. Louis, MO: *The Sporting News,* 1989. Pp. 228–236.

51523. _____. "1980, 1981, 1986: Mike Schmidt." In: his *National League MVP's.* New York: Bantam Books, 1989. Pp. 104–106, 115–116.

51524. Hood, Robert E. "Mike Schmidt: No. 1 at Third." *Boys' Life,* LXXIX (March 1989), 20–23.

51525. Jablow, Paul. "Mike Schmidt: Not-so-Futile Philly." In: Ray Robinson, ed. *Baseball Stars of 1975.* New York: Pyramid Books, 1975. Pp. 111–117.

51526. James, Robert. "Mike Schmidt." In: Ken Collier, ed. *The Baseball Book, 1987.* Scottsdale, AZ: Jalart House, 1987. Pp. 34–35.

51527. Kashatus, William C. *Mike Schmidt: Philadelphia's Hall of Fame Third Baseman.* Jefferson, NC: McFarland & Co., Inc., 2000. 165p.

51528. Kausler, Don, Jr. "Schmidt and Luzinski: The Phils' 1–2 Punch." *Baseball Digest,* XXXIX (September 1980), 52–56.

51529. Kelly, Robert E. "Mike Schmidt." In: his *Baseball's Best: Hall of Fame Pretenders Active in the Eighties.* Jefferson, N.C.: McFarland & Co., Inc., 1988. Pp. 74–77.

51530. Kuenster, John. "Farewell to Mike Schmidt,

One of the Game's All-Time Great Third Basemen." *Baseball Digest,* XLVIII (September 1989), 15–17.

51531. _____. "Mike Schmidt of the Phils 1981 Player of the Year." *Baseball Digest,* XL (December 1981), 15–19.

51532. Lax, Eric. "Hanging Their Hopes High on Mike Schmidt." *Sport,* LXIX (September 1979), 80–83.

51533. Levy, Joe H. "This Was the Hardest Hit Single in the Major Leagues." *Baseball Digest,* XLV (May 1986), 37–38. Schmidt at the Astrodome.

51534. Levy, Maury Z. "The Phillies Find a Slugger." *Sport,* LVIII (December 1974), 84–87.

51535. Masterson, Dave and Timm Boyle. "1980 [and] 1981." In: their *Baseball's Best: The MVPs.* Chicago, IL: Contemporary Books, Inc., 1985. Pp. 305–316.

51536. McCoy, Hal. "Mike Schmidt: A Power Hitter Blossoms in Philly." *Baseball Digest,* XXXIII (September 1974), 45–47.

51537. Myslenski, Skip. "Mike Schmidt: The Struggle for Hitting Consistency." *Baseball Digest,* XXXVIII (October 1979), 64–67.

51538. Obojski, Robert. "Retired Phillies Great Mike Schmidt Interviewed." *Sports Collector's Digest,* XXI (July 22, 1994), 100–101.

51539. Palmer, Pete. "Sport Stats: Why Mike Schmidt is Better Than Ty Cobb." *Sport,* LXXV (April 1984), 52+.

51540. Platt, Larry. "Unloved Mike Schmidt." *Philadelphia Magazine,* LXXXVI (September 1995), 52–60.

51541. Rasmussen, Larry F. "Mike Schmidt Climbs to No. 2 on Home Run Title Chart." *Baseball Digest,* XLVI (March 1987), 22–23.

51542. Resciniti, Angelo G. "Mike Schmidt." In: his *Stars of the Diamond.* Mississauga, Ontario: School Book Fairs, Inc., 1981. Pp. 49–59.

51543. Ritter, Lawrence And Donald Honig. "Mike Schmidt." In: their *The 100 Greatest Baseball Players Of All Time.* New York: Crown Publishers, 1981. Pp. 34–35.

51544. Rossi, John P. "Michael Jack 'Mike' Schmidt." In: Vol. Q-Z of David L. Porter, ed. *Biographical Dictionary of American Sports: Baseball.* Rev. and enlarged ed. Westport, CT: Greenwood Press, 2000. Pp. 1366–1367.

51545. Rust, Art, with Michael Marley. "Mike Schmidt." In: his *Legends: Conversations with Baseball Greats.* New York: McGraw-Hill, 1989. Pp. 172–180.

51546. Schmidt, Michael J. ("Mike"). "Interview." *Scholastic Coach,* LII (April 1983), 44–46+.

51547. _____. "My Greatest Day in Baseball." In: Eliot Cohen, ed. *My Greatest Day in Baseball.* New York: Little Simon, 1991. Pp. 105–110.

51548. _____. and Barbara Walder. *Always on the Offense.* New York: Atheneum, 1981. 191p.

51549. _____. and Rob Ellis. *The Mike Schmidt Study: Building a Hitting Foundation.* Atlanta, GA: McGriff & Bell, 1993.160p. Instructional.

51550. _____. *The Mike Schmidt Study: Hitting Theory, Skills and Technique.* Atlanta: McGriff & Bell, Inc., 1994. 159p.

51551. _____., as told to George Vass. "The Game I'll Never Forget." *Baseball Digest,* XLV (December 1986), 43–47.

51552. _____., with Joe O'Loughlin. "Mike Schmidt Interview." *Baseball Digest,* LX (March 2001), 60–63.

51553. _____, with Rob Ellis. *The Mike Schmidt Study: Building a Hitting Foundation.* Atlanta, GA: McGriff & Bell, 1994. 78p. Emphasis on technique.

51554. Seaver, Tom, with Marty Appel. "Four for Mike Schmidt." In: his *Great Moments in Baseball: From the World Series of 1903 to the Modern Records of Nolan Ryan.* New York: Carol Communications, 1992. Pp. 259–264.

51555. Smith, Ron. "Mike Schmidt 28." In: his *The Sporting News Selects Baseball's 100 Greatest Players.* St. Louis, MO: The Sporting News, 1998. Pp. 66–67.

51556. Stevens, Richard. "The Nightmare Finaly Ended for Mike Schmidt." *Sports World,* XXIII (August 1984), 26–27.

51557. Sullivan, George. "Mike Schmidt." In: his *Glovemen: Twenty-Seven of Baseball's Greatest.* New York: Atheneum, 1996. Pp. 18–19.

51558. _____. "Mike Schmidt." In: his *Sluggers: Twenty Seven Of Baseball's Greatest.* New York: Atheneum, 1991. Pp. 14–15.

51559. Waggoner, Glen. "Master of Swat." *Esquire,* CVII (May 1987), 139–144.

51560. Washburn, Jim. "Mike Schmidt Checklist." *Baseball Cards,* VII (June 1987), 70–77.

51561. Westcott, Rich. *Baseball Legends: Mike Schmidt.* New York: Chelsea House, 1995. 64p.

51562. Whitford, David. "Mike Schmidt Loves Baseball Seriously." *Sport,* LXXVII (July 1986), 56–58.

51563. _____. "The Unhappiness of Mike Schmidt." *GQ — Gentlemen's Quarterly,* LXII (July 1992), 62, 66+.

51564. "Will Another MVP Season Satisfy Mike Schmidt?" In: Bob Sparks, ed. *Baseball '81.* St. Petersburg, FL: National Association of Professional Baseball Leagues, 1981. Pp. 33–34.

51565. Wright, Jim. *Mike Schmidt: Baseball's Young Lion.* New York: G. P. Putnam, 1979. 187p.

Walter Joseph Schmidt

C. (B: March 20, 1887, Cost Hill, AK-D: July 4, 1973). Pittsburgh (NL), 1916–1924; St. Louis (NL), 1925. Remarks: Had 619 hits (three homers) and 57 stolen bases in 769 games in a decade; also played for San Francisco (PCL), 1915.

51566. Ward, John J. *Walter Schmidt, an Unrecognized Catching Star." *Baseball Magazine,* XXVI (March 1921), 469–471.

John Albert ("Johnny" or "Bear Tracks*) Schmitz

P. (B: Nov. 27, 1930, Wausau, WI). Chicago (NL), 1941–1942, 1946–1951; Brooklyn (NL), 1951–1952; New York (AL) and Cincinnati (NL), 1952; New York (AL), 1953; Washington (AL), 1953–1955; Boston (AL) and Baltimore (AL), 1956. Remarks: Won 93 games and lost 114, with 19 "saves," in 13 seasons; won first game after throwing just one pitch in 9th inning, Sept. 10, 1941.

51567. Condon, David. "Johnny Schmitz — Dodger Killer." *Sport,* VI (June 1949), 24–27.

51568. Macht, Norman L. "Johnny Schmitz: Old Brooklyn Dodgers Were 'Patsies' for Him." *Baseball Digest,* LV (September 1996), 77–81.

51569. Rumill, Ed. "That Chicago Southpaw, Johnny Schmitz." *Baseball Magazine,* LXXIX (September 1947), 343–345.

51570. Wilbert, Warren and William Hageman. "John Albert Schmitz — 1948." In: their *Chicago Cubs: Seasons at the Summit, the 50 Greatest Individual Seasons.* Champaign, IL; Sagamore Publishing, 1997. Pp. 137–140.

Albert Fred ("Red") Schoendienst★

2B-OF-MGR. (B: Feb. 2, 1923, Germantown, Ill.). St. Louis (NL), 1945–1956; New York (NL), 1956–1957; Milwaukee (NL), 1957–1960; St. Louis (NL), 1961–1963. Remarks: In 19 playing years, obtained 2,449 hits (84 homers) and 89 stolen bases in 2,216 games; had game-winning homer in 1950 All-Star Game; holder of various major and NL records, including IL MVP Award, 1943;

coach, St. Louis (NL), 1962–1964 and Cardinals manager, 1964–1976, 1980, 1990, winning 1,041 and losing 955 (.521); coach, Oakland (AL), 1977–1978; coach, St. Louis (NL), 1979–1995; named to Missouri Sports Hall of Fame, 1987; elected to the National Baseball Hall of Fame in 1989, where his plaque reads: "Roomate Stan Musical credited him with 'Greatest Pair of Hands I've Ever Seen.' Sleek, far-ranging second baseman for 18 seasons. Led NL in fielding and hit .300 or better seven times. When elected in 1989 had worn major league uniform 45 consecutive seasons as player, coach and manager, piloting Redbirds to World Series in 1967 and 1968. 14th inning homer won 1950 All-Star Game for NL."

51571. Astor, Gavin. "Red Schoendienst, The Prime Cardinal." *Look,* XXXII (July 9, 1968), M10+.

51572. Bingham, Walter. "A Good Man Gets Bad News." *Sports Illustrated,* IX (December 1, 1958), 32–33. Discovery of TB, which caused him to miss much of 1959 season.

51573. Borst, William A. ("Bill") and Frank J. Olmsted. "Albert Fred 'Red' Schoendienst." In: Vol. Q–Z of David L. Porter, ed. *Biographical Dictionary of American Sports: Baseball.* Rev. and enlarged ed. Westport, CT: Greenwood Press, 2000. Pp. 1367–1368.

51574. Broeg, Bob. "Huck Finn in Flannels." In: his *My Baseball Scrapbook.* St. Louis, MO: River City Publishers, 1983. Pp. 113–116.

51575. _____. "The Natural." In: Bruce Jacobs, ed. *Baseball Stars of 1954.* New York. Lion Books, 1954. Pp. 116–122.

51576. _____. "Red Loves to Take Charge." *Saturday Evening Post,* CCXXIII (July 22, 1950), 223–228.

51577. _____. "Who's More Valuable Than Schoendienst?" *Baseball Magazine,* LXXX (October 1953), 16–17+.

51578. Burnes, Robert L. "The Way Schoendienst Does It." *Baseball Digest,* XXVII (October 1968), 23–25. Managerial style.

51579. Butler, Hal. "Red Schoendienst: From Hospital Bed to Baseball Diamond." In: his *Sports Heroes Who Wouldn't Quit.* New York: Julian, Messner, 1973. Pp. 55–67.

51580. Cohane, Tim. "The Glue That Made Milwaukee Famous." *Look,* XXII (September 2, 1958), 74–78.

51581. Craft, David And Tom Owens. "Red Schoendienst: Returned By An Unbroken Promise." In: their *Redbirds Revisited.* Chicago, IL: Bonus Books, 1990. Pp. 190–200.

51582. Devaney, John. "The Redhead." In: *The Greatest Cardinals of Them All.* New York: G.P. Putnam's Sons, 1968. Pp. 162–172.

51583. Hawkins, Burton. "Schoendienst's Best Play." *Baseball Digest,* XVII (December 1958), 23–25.

51584. Hirshberg, Al. *The Man Who Fought Back: Red Schoendienst.* New York: Julian Messner, 1961. 192p.

51585. Holland, Gerald. "Herr 'Beautiful Service.' *Sports Illustrated,* VII (September 30, 1957), 58–64.

51586. Kaplan, Jim and Dick Perez. "Red Schoendienst." In: their *The 2nd Official Baseball Hall of Fame Book of Superstars.* New York: Little Simon, 1990. Pp. 22–23.

51587. Kuenster, John. "Red Schoendienst Lives Up to His Surname as a Baseball 'Lifer.' *Baseball Digest,* LV (March 1996), 15–17.

51588. Langford, Walter. "Red Schoendienst: One of Baseball's 'Lifers.' *Baseball Digest,* XLVIII (January 1989), 62–64.

51589. Leggett, William. "Manager of the Money Men." *Sports Illustrated,* XXIX (October 7, 1968), 36–42.

51590. Molter, Harry. "Albert Fred (Red) Schoendienst: Versatile Star of the St. Louis Cardinals." In: *Famous American Athletes of Today.* 13th Series. New York: Page, 1953. Pp. 263–278.

51591. "Moses in Milwaukee." *Time,* LXX (September 2, 1957), 70–71.

51592. Murray, Jim. "The Return of the Red Head." *Sports Illustrated,* XII (June 6, 1960), 34–40.

51593. Newcombe, Jack. "Red Can Play — Anywhere." *Sport,* XIII (August 1952), 32–33+.

51594. Schoendienst, Albert F. ("Red"). *Fine Points of Infield Play.* Los Angeles: Union Oil Co., 1958. 11p. Instructional pamphlet.

51595. _____. "It Pays to Switch Hit." *Sport,* XVI (January 1954), 57–63.

51596. _____, as told to George Vass. "The Game I'll Never Forget." *Baseball Digest,* XXXIV (July 1975), 94–96. Reprinted in George Vass, ed. *The Game I'll Never Forget* (Chicago: Bonus Books, 1999), pp. 231–235.

51597. _____., with Rob Rains. *Red: A Baseball Life.* Champaign, IL: Sports Publishing, 1998. 218p.

51598. _____., with Gene Schoor. *Red Schoendienst Story.* New York: G. P. Putnam, 1961. 192p.

51599. Schoor, Gene. "They Called Him Red: Red Schoendienst." In: his *Courage Makes the Champion.* Princeton, NJ: Van Nostrand, 1967. Pp. 114–123.

51600. Silverman, Al. "Red Schoendienst." In: Ray Robinson, ed. *Baseball Stars of 1958.* New York: Lion Books, 1958. Pp. 95–101.

51601. Stockton, J. Roy. "The Wonderful Schoendienst Story." *Sport,* VII (September 1949), 54–55+.

51602. Terrell, Roy. "How to Win Without Red." *Sports Illustrated,* X (June 8, 1959), 46–51.

51603. Terry, Dickson. "Red Schoendienst's Road Back." *Sport,* XXVIII (December 1959), 30–33.

51604. Twombly, Wells. "Schoendienst Finds He Only Half-Won." *Baseball Digest,* XXVII (February 1968), 58–61.

51605. Vass, George. "The Softer Tones of Red." *Baseball Digest,* XXVI (October 1967), 83–87.

51606. Veech, Ellis J. "He Made the Boss Sit Down." *Baseball Digest,* XII (February 1953), 43–47.

51607. Westcott, Rich. "Red Schoendienst: A True Pro in Whatever He Did." In: his *Splendor on the Diamond: Interviews with 35 Stars of Baseball's Past.* Gainesville, FL: The University Press of Florida, 2000. Pp. 87–94.

51608. Wilber, Cynthia J. "Red Schoendienst." In: her *For the Love of the Game: Baseball Memories from the Men Who Were There.* New York: William Morrow, 1992. Pp. 287–291.

51609. Zachotsky, Dan. "Red Schoendienst." In: his *Idols of the Spring: Baseball Interviews About Spring Training.* Jefferson, NC: McFarland & Co., Inc., 2001. Pp. 201–208.

Red Schoendienst *see* **Albert Fred ("Red") Schoendienst**

Richard Craig ("Dick") Schofield

SS. (B: Nov. 21, 1962, Springfield, IL) California (AL), 1983–1992; New York (NL), 1992; Toronto (AL), 1993–1994; Los Angeles (NL), 1995; California (AL), 1995–1996. Remarks: In 14 seasons, obtained 989 hits (56 homers) and 120 stolen bases in 1,368 games; had one grand slam homer, Aug. 29, 1986; also played for Danville (Midwest League), 1982; manager, Springfield (Frontier League), 2001; South Bend (Midwest League), 2002.

51610. Schmuck, Peter. "Dick Schofield: The Angels' 'Kid' Shortstop Comes of Age." *Baseball Digest,* XLVI (March 1987), 64–69.

Margaret Unnewehr ("Marge") Schott

EXEC. (B: August 18, 1928, Cincinnati, OH-D: March 2, 2004). Remarks: Owner, pres/CEO, Schottco Corp., 1968-; part owner, Cincinnati (NL), 1981–1984; owner, pres/CEO, Cincinnati (NL), 1984–1999.

51611. Bass, Mike. *Marge Schott: Unleashed.* Champagne, IL: Sagamore Pub. Co., 1993. 309p.

51612. Capouya, Jim. "Queen of the Riverfront : Marge Schott Loves Her Reds, Her Dogs and Cincinnati — Everything Else Should Get Out of Her Way. ." *Sport,* LXXIX (July 1988), 28–32+.

51613. Cole, W. "To Each Her Own." *Time Special Edition,* CXXXVI (Fall 1990), 46–49.

51614. "Departing Schott." *Sports Illustrated,* LXXXIV (June 24, 1996), 20, 22.

51615. Kirshenbaum, Jerry. "Block That Schott." *Sports Illustrated,* LXXVII (November 30, 1992), 13–14.

51616. Kurkijan, Tim. "Dog Days." *Sports Illustrated,* LXXVII (October 19, 1992), 28–30.

51617. Loewenheim, Francis L. "Major League Woman: Marge Schott." *Harper's Bazaar,* CXVIII (September 1985), 288–289.

51618. Nuwer, Hank. "Marge Schott: Queen of Diamonds." *Modern Maturity,* XXIX (June-July 1986), 40–43.

51619. O'Brien, Richard. "Block That Schott (Con't)." *Sports Illustrated,* LXXVII (December 7, 1992), 15–16.

51620. Pappas, Doug. "Marge Schott Suspension." *Boston Baseball,* VII (August 1996), 20+.

51621. Plummer, William and Civia Tamarkin. "Big Red Embarrassment." *People Weekly,* XXXVIII (December 14, 1992), 79, 82.

51622. Reilly, Rick. "Heaven Help Marge Schott." *Sports Illustrated,* LXXXIV (May 20, 1996), 72–78, 80, 83–84, 87. Reprinted in George Plimpton, ed., *The Best American Sports Writing, 1997* (Boston, MA: Houghton, Mifflin, 1997), pp. 164–178.

51623. Schlossberg, Dan. "Nasty Does It!!" In: *Petersen's Pro Review—1991.* Los Angeles, CA: Petersen Publishing Co., 1991. Pp. 29–33.

51624. "Schott Out of the Park." *Time,* CXLI (February 15, 1993), 18–19. Racial comments.

51625. Shannon, Mike. "Marge Schott." In: his *Tales from the Ballpark: More of the Greatest True Baseball Stories Ever Told.* Lincolnwood, IL: Contemporary Books, 1999. Pp. 179–181.

51626. _____. "Marge Schott." In: his *Tales from the Dugout: The Greatest True Baseball Stories Ever Told.* Lincolnwood, IL: NTC/Contemporary Books, 1997. Pp. 187–188.

51627. Sheehy, Sandy G. "Lady in Red." *Town & Country,* CXLI (July 1987), 130–135.

51628. _____. "Not One of the Boys." *Ohio,* XI (April 1988), 11+.

51629. Stathoplos, Demmie. "Marge Has Them Eating Out of Her Hand." *Sports Illustrated,* LXIII (July 15, 1985), 42–44+.

51630. Tate, Skip. "Marge in Charge." *Cincinnati Business Courier,* VIII (April 6, 1992), 1–2.

51631. Van Biema, David. "A Millionairess Named Marge Proves a Schott in the Arm for the Dogged Cincinnati Reds." *People Weekly,* XXIV (July 22, 1985), 99–100+.

51632. Verducci, Tom. "Who's the Boss?" *Sports Illustrated,* LXXXIII (September 18, 1995), 46–48, 50.

51633. "Will Alleged 'Nigger' Slur by White Owner of Cincinnati Reds Hurt Baseball?" *Jet,* LXXXIII (December 21, 1992), 52–55.

Ossee Freeman Schreckengost

C-1B. (B: April 11, 1875, New Bethlehem, PA-D: July 9, 1914). Louisville (NL), 1897; Cleveland (NL), 1898; St. Louis (NL) and Cleveland (N.L), 1899; Boston (AL), 1901; Cleveland (AL), 1902; Philadelphia (AL), 1902–1908; Chicago (AL), 1908. Remarks: Had 828 hits (nine homers) and 52 stolen bases in 893 games in 11 years; noted comedian of the diamond.

51634. Esch, Harold. "[Rube] Waddell and Schreck in College." *The Baseball Research Journal,* X (1980), 144–145.

51635. Lieb, Frederick G. "Ossee Schreckengost." In: his *Comedians and Pranksters of Baseball.* St. Louis, MO: The Sporting News, 1958. Pp. 9–10.

Paul Frederick ("Von") Schreiber

P. (B: Oct. 8, 1902, Jacksonville, FL-D: Jan. 28, 1982). Brooklyn (NL), 1922–1923; New York (AL), 1945. Remarks: Saved one game in three widely-separated big league seasons.

51636. Richman, Arthur. "He Liked to Get Batted Around." *Baseball Digest,* XII (March 1953), 85–87.

Dorothy ("Dottie") Schroeder

SS. (B: April 11, 1928, Champaign, IL-D: Dec. 8, 1996). South Bend Blue Sox, 1943–1945; Kenosha Comets, 1945–1947; Fort Wayne Daisies, 1947–1952; Kalamazoo Lassies, 1953–1954. Remarks: Obtained 870 hits (42 homers) in 1,249 games in all 12 years of the All-American Girls Professional Baseball League, the only player to continue through the league's entire history; thereafter, toured four years with Bill Allington's All-Americans and worked 36 years for the Collegiate Cap & Gown Company in Champaign.

51637. Clark, Dennis S. "Dorothy 'Dottie' Schroeder." In: Vol. Q-Z of David L. Porter, ed. *Biographical Dictionary of American Sports: Baseball.* Rev. and enlarged ed. Westport, CT: Greenwood Press, 2000. Pp. 1368–1370.

51638. Sargent, Jim. "Dottie Schroeder." *Sports Collector's Digest,* XXIV (April 25, 1997), 180–181.

John Boland Schuerholz, Jr.

EXEC. (B: Oct. 1, 1940, Baltimore, MD). Remarks: adminstrv. asst., Baltimore (A.L), 1966–1968 and Kansas City (AL), 1968–1970; asst. farm dir., Kansas City (AL), 1970–1975; dir. scouting and player devel., Kansas City (AL), , 1976–1979; v.p. player personnel, Kansas City (AL), 1979–1981; exec. v.p., GM, Kansas City (AL), 1981–1990; exec. v.p., GM, Atlanta Braves, 1990-.

51639. Cattau, Daniel. "Boss of the Braves: Atlanta's John Schuerholz Talks Baseball." *The Lutheran,* VII (August 1994), 8+.

Joseph Charles ("Joe" or "Dode") Schultz, Jr.

C-MGR. (B: Aug. 29, 1918, Chicago, IL-D: Jan. 10, 1996.). Pittsburgh (NL), 1930–1941; St. Louis (AL), 1943–1948. Remarks: Obtained 85 hits (one homer) in 240 games in nine playing years; coach, St. Louis (NL), 1963–1968; manager, Seattle (AL), 1969 and Detroit (AL), 1973, winning 73 games and losing 112 (.411).

51640. Bouton, Jim. "Joe Schultz: The Manager Who Wasn't." In: Jim Bouton, ed. *"I Managed Good, But Boy Did They Play Bad."* Chicago, IL: Playboy Press, 1973. Pp. 298–303.

51641. Burnes, Robert L. "30 Seconds and Schultz Jumped." *Baseball Digest,* XXVII (February 1969), 47–49.

Harold Henry ("Prince Hal") Schumacher

P. (B: Nov. 23, 1910, Hinckley, NY-D: April 21, 1993.). New York (N.L), 1931–1942, 1946. Remarks: Had 158 victories and 121 defeats, plus 15 homers, in 13 seasons; won 11 consecutive games, 1935; helped found Adirondack Bat

Company in 1946, where he served until his 1967 retirement.

51642. Schumacher, Hal. *Hal Schumacher's Baseball Strategy.* Leonia, NJ: Wells Publishing Co., 1949. 29p.

51643. _____. "Pitching." *Scholastic Coach,* XVIII (March 1949), 8–15.

51644. Speer, Renwick W. *The Giants are Coming and So is Schuey: One Day in the Life of a Rookie Pitcher.* Lake Wales, FL: Renwick Speer, 1986. 19p. Excerpted, as "Schuey's Big Day," in *The Baseball Research Journal,* XVII (1988), 82.

51645. Stein, Fred. "Harold Henry 'Prince Hal' Schumacher." In: Vol. Q-Z of David L. Porter, ed. *Biographical Dictionary of American Sports: Baseball.* Rev. and enlarged ed. Westport, CT: Greenwood Press, 2000. P. 1371.

51646. Van Blair, Rick. "When [in 1935] the Majors Almost Suffered Second Fatality." *Baseball Digest,* LII (November 1993), 73–74. Heat prostration on July 25.

Ferdie Schupp *see* **Ferdinand Maurice ("Ferdie") Schupp**

Ferdinand Maurice ("Ferdie") Schupp

P. (B: Jan. 16, 1891, Louisville, KY-D: Dec. 16, 1971). New York (NL), 1913–1919; St. Louis (NL), 1919–1921; Brooklyn (N.L.), 1921; Chicago (AL), 1922. Remarks: Had 62 victories, 39 defeats, and five "saves" in a decade; success came despite a constant sore arm; lost Game Two of 1917 World Series, but won Game Four.

51647. Grayson, Harry. "Schupp Had Only Two Good Years, but They're Still in the Records." *Baseball Digest,* II (October 1943), 41–49.

51648. Ward, John J. "A Big League Pitcher Who Came Back." *Baseball Magazine,* XXV (August 1920), 428–429.

51649. _____. "The Most Effective Pitcher." *Baseball Magazine,* XIX (July 1917), 368–369+.

Donald ("Don") Schwall

P. (B: March 2, 1936, Wilkes-Barre, PA). Boston (AL), 1961–1962; Pittsburgh (NL), 1963–1966; Atlanta (NL), 1966–1967. Remarks: Won 49 games and lost 48, with four "saves," in seven summer seasons; A. L. Rookie of the Year Award, 1961; also played for Minneapolis (AA), 1960 and Seattle (PCL), 1961; won first big league game played in Atlanta.

51650. Hirshberg, Al. "Don Schwall and Chuck Schilling: Kids with a Future." In: Ray Robinson, ed. *Baseball Stars of 1962.* New York: Pyramid Books, 1962. Pp. 95–102.

51651. Honig, Donald. "1961: Don Schwall." In: his *American League Rookies of the Year.* New York: Bantam Books, 1989. Pp. 31–32.

Clay Schwartz

C-COACH. (B: 1972, Fond du Lac, WI). Remarks: University of Wisconsin at Milwaukee graduate and NCAA Division I-A all-time hit-by-pitch leader (70); catcher, Sheboygan A's (semi-pro) of Wisconsin State League, 1994–2003; asst. baseball coach, Marian College, 2002-.

51652. "Battered, But on Base." *Sports Illustrated,* LXVI (May 12, 1997), 23+. Holds NCAA record for being the most-hit batter.

Delmore David Schwartz

WRITER. (B: Dec. 8, 1913, Brooklyn, NY-D: July 11, 1966). Remarks: Poet, essayist, and associate editor, *Partisan Review,* 1943–1955; poetry editor, *The National Review,* 1955–1957; visiting professor, various universities, 1957–1966.

51653. Solomon, Eric. "A Portrait of the Artist as a Young Baseball Fan: Delmore Schwartz." *Aethlon: The Journal of Sport Literature,* XV (Fall 1998), 143–154.

Michael Lorrie ("Mike") Scioscia

C-MGR. (B: Nov. 27, 1958, Upper Darby, PA). Los Angeles (NL), 1982–1990. Remarks: In 13 big league seasons, obtained 1,131 hits (68 homers) and 29 stolen bases in 1,441 games; hit game tying homer, Game Four, 1988 NLCS; manager, Anaheim (AL), 2000-; through 2004, has won 425 games and lost 385 (.525).

51654/51655. Anderson, Bruce. "Just No Getting Around Him." *Sports Illustrated,* LXIII (October 7, 1985), 62–64+.

51656. Elderkin, Phil. "Mike Scioscia: The Dodgers' 'Iron Man' Behind the Mask." *Baseball Digest,* XLIX (August 1990), 20–24.

51657. Frommer, Harvey and Frederick J. "Mike Scioscia." In: their *Growing Up Baseball: An Oral History.* Dallas, TX: Taylor Publishing Co., 2001. Pp. 207–208.

51658. Moore, David L. "Mike Scioscia, Rising Dodger Star." In: Bill Shumard, ed. *1981 Los Angeles Dodgers Yearbook.* CA: Rotary Off-Set Printers, 1981. P. 48.

51659. O'Loughlin, Joe. "Angels' Mike Scioscia: An Interview." *Baseball Digest,* LXII (April 2003), 60–65.

51660. Scioscia, Mike and Peter Gammons. "Calling a Game." *Sports Illustrated,* LXX (April 9, 1989), 34–40.

51661. _____., as told to George Vass. "The Game I'll Never Forget." *Baseball Digest,* LIII (January 1994), 61–62.

Herbert Jude ("Herb") Score

P-BROADCASTER. (B: June 7, 1933, Rosedale, NY). Cleveland (AL), 19551959; Chicago (AL), 1960–1962. Remarks: Had 55 victories and 46 defeats in eight years; AL Rookie of the Year award, 1955; victim of one of the great playing tragedies in baseball history when league-leading strikeout artist of 1955–1956 was hit by line drive off bat of Gil McDougald (q.v.) on May 7, 1957; never fully recovered and quit the game; Indians broadcaster, 1963–1997.

51662. Benson, John. "Herb Score —1956." In: his *Baseball's Top 100: The Best Individual Seasons of All Time.* Wilton, CT: Diamond Library, 1996. Pp. 156–157.

51663. Brosnan, Jim. "Herb Score: Rookie of the Year —1955 — American League." In: his *Great Rookies of the Major Leagues.* New York: Random House, 1966. Pp. 61–79.

51664. Cobbledick, Gordon. "Herb Score is Back." *Sport,* XXVI (July 1958), 52–63.

51665. _____. "Herb Score Seriously Injured by Line Drive." In: Dean A. Sullivan, ed. *Late Innings: A Documentary History of Baseball, 1945–1972.* Lincoln, NE: university of Nebraska Press, 2002. Pp. 107–109. Reprinted from the *Cleveland Plain Dealer,* May 8, 1957.

51666. _____. "What's the Score on Herb?" *Sport,* XX (August 1966), 14–15+.

51667. _____. "Why Indians Traded Colavito, Score." *Baseball Digest,* XIX (June 1960), 69–72.

51668. _____. "You Can't Tell Score's Speed — Yet." *Baseball Digest,* XIV (July 1955), 41–43.

51669. Cohane, Tim. "Herb Score: Million-Dollar Pitcher." *Look* , XXI (May 28, 1957), 139–142.

51670. _____. "Herb Score Walks the Long Comeback Trail." *Look,* XXVI (March 13, 1962), 47–49.

51671. Creamer, Robert W. "Two Hot Young Pitchers Named Score and Turley." *Sports Illustrated,* II (May 30,1955), 39–41.

51672. Dolgan, Bob. "How Line Drive Damaged the Career of Herb Score." *Baseball Digest,* LVI (September 1997), 80–83.

51673. "Faster Than Feller." *Newsweek,* XLV (March 21, 1955), 94–95.

51674. Fitzgerald, Ed. "Herb Score." In: his *More Champions in Sports and Spirit.* New York. Farrar, Straus, 1959. Pp. 169–190.

51675. Furlong, William B. "The Rebuilding of Herb Score." *Sport,* XXXI (January 1961), 44–45.

51676. Gifford, Frank, with Charles Mangel. "Herb Score." In: his *Gifford on Courage.* New York: Evans, 1976. Pp. 4–25. Reprinted in: Charles Einstein, ed. *The Fourth Fireside Book of Baseball.* (New York: Simon and Schuster, 1987), pp. 135–142.

51677. "Herb Score: Million-Dollar Pitcher." *Look,* XXI (May 29, 1957), 139–142.

51678. "Herb Score Walks the Long Comeback Trail." *Look,* XXVI (March 13, 1060), 47–48.

51679. Honig, Donald. "Herb Score." In: his *Baseball Between the Lines: Baseball in the Forties and Fifties as Told By the Men Who Played It.* Lincoln, NB: University of Nebraska Press, 1976. Pp. 214–220.

51680. _____. "1955: Herb Score." In: his *American League Rookies of the Year.* New York: Bantam Books, 1989. Pp. 16–18.

51681. Jacobs, Bruce. "He Also Won Twenty: Herb Score." In: Bruce Jacobs, ed. *Baseball Stars of 1957.* New York: Lion Books, 1957. Pp. 126–131.

51682. _____. "Southpaw Sensation: Herb Score." In: Bruce Jacobs, ed. *Baseball Stars of 1956.* New York: Lion Books, 1956. Pp. 87–92.

51683. _____. "Herb, Score: Left-Handed Bob Feller." *Baseball Magazine,* XLVIII (July 1956), 40–54.

51684. Koelling, Les. "Here's the Score on Herb Score." *Baseball Digest,* XIV (April 1955), 21–26.

51685. Lebovitz, Hal. "Cleveland's Left-Handed Lightning." *Saturday Evening Post,* CCXXIX (May 11, 1957), 42–45.

51686. _____. "Score and Colavito: Mutual-Admiration Society." *Sport,* XXIV (August 1957), 20–21+.

51687. Lewis, Franklin. "Score Shouldn't Be Gun-Shy." *Baseball Digest,* XVI (August 1957), 39–41.

51688. _____. "Score Walks in Feller's Path." *Baseball Digest,* XIV (October 1955), 59–61.

51689. Linkugel, Wil A. and Edward J. Pappas. "Cleveland's Fireballer: Herb Score." In: their *They Tasted Glory: Among the Missing at the Baseball Hall of Fame.* Jefferson, NC: McFarland & Co., Inc., 1998. Pp. 40–50.

51690. Liston, Robert A. "Herb Score." In: his *The Pros.* New York: Platt and Munk, 1968. Pp. 249–272.

51691. Newcombe, Jack. "Fastball Backfire." In: his *Fireballers.* New York: G.P. Putnam, 1964. Pp. 92–94.

51692. Olsen, Jimmy. "The Private Ordeal of Herb Score." *Sports Illustrated,* XV (August 7, 1961), 25–27.

51693. Pepe, Phil. "Herb Score: 'Courage is Not the Exclusive Property of Winners." In: his *Winners Never Quit.* Englewood Cliffs, NJ: Prentice-Hall, 1968. Pp. 254–273.

51694. Ritter, Lawrence and Donald Honig. "Herb Score." In: their *The 100 Greatest Baseball Players Of All Time.* New York: Crown Publishers, 1981. Pp. 94–95.

51695. Santa Maria, Michael and James Costello. "St. Jude's Boy." In: their *In the Shadows of the Diamond.* Dubuque, IA: The Elysian Fields Press, 1992. Pp. 225–234.

51696. Score, Herbert J., with Tim Cohane. "Things I Saw in the Darkness." *Look,* XXX (August 20, 1957), 23–25.

51697. Skipper, James K., Jr. "Herbert Jude 'Herb' Score." In: Vol. Q-Z of David L. Porter, ed. *Biographical Dictionary of American Sports: Baseball.* Rev. and enlarged ed. Westport, CT: Greenwood Press, 2000. Pp. 1371–1372.

51698. Stump, Al. "Everything Happens to Herb." *True,* XXXIX (April 1958), 50–55.

51699. Sudyk, Bob. "The Line Drive That Changed Herb Score's Career." *Baseball Digest,* XXXVI (September 1977), 72–76.

51700. Vanderberg, Bob. "Herb Score: The Comeback Attempt that Failed." In: his *Sox — From Lane and Fain to Zisk and Fisk.* Chicago, IL: Chicago Review Press, 1982. Pp. 233–237.

51701. Zimmerman, John G. "The Man with a Million Fans." *Sports Illustrated,* VIII (May 26, 1968), 18–22. A pictorial.

Deacon Scott *see* **Lewis Everett ("Deacon") Scott**
Everett Scott *see* **Lewis Everett ("Deacon") Scott**
Gary Thomas Scott
3B. (B: August 22, 1968 New Rochelle, NY). Chicago (NL), 1991–1992. Remarks: In two big league seasons, had 28 hits (three homers) in 67 games.

51702. Struby, Tim. "Thrown a Curve: There's Always Tomorrow for Cubs Fans, There's Always Yesterday for Gary Scott." *ESPN: The Magazine,* VI (November 10, 2003), 106–111.

George Charles ("Great" or "Boomer") Scott
1B-3B-COACH. (B: March 23, 1944, Greenville, MN). Boston (AL), 1966–1971; Milwaukee (AL), 1972–1976; Boston (AL), 1977–1979; Kansas City (AL) and New York (AL), 1979. Remarks: Obtained 1,992 hits (271 homers) and 69 stolen bases In 2,034 games in 14-year big league career; won triple crown while playing for Pittsfield (EL), 1965; AL home run champion, 1975 (tie); AL RBI champion, 1975; minor league coach, 1980–1981; baseball coach, Foxbury (MA) Community College, 1982–1986; manager, Massachusetts Mad Dogs (Independent Northwest League), 1996-.

51703. Blount, Roy, Jr. "Sometimes the Ball Takes a Funny Bounce." *Esquire,* LXXXVIII (August 1977), 17–18.

51704. Crehan, Herbert F. and James W. Ryan. "George Scott." In: their *Lightning in a Bottle: The Sox of '67.* Boston, MA: Branden Publishing Co., 1992. Pp. 61–76.

51705. Dexter, Charles. "Great Scott." *Baseball Digest,* XXV (September 1966), 67–71.

51706. Elderkin, Phil. . "George Scott Learns the K Zone." *Baseball Digest,* XVII (March 1968), 52–56.

51707. Klein, Dave. "George Scott." In: his *On the Way Up: What It's Like in the Minor Leagues.* New York: Julian Messner, 1977. Pp. 99–106.

51708. Lautier, Jack. "George Scott." In: his *Fenway Voices.* Camden, ME: Yankee Books, 1990. Pp. 113–116.

51709. Libby, Bill. "George Scott." In: his *Heroes of the Hot Corner.* New York: Watts, 1972. Pp. 105–106.

51710. Mack, William. "George Scott Is Alive and Well and Playing in Mexico City." *Sports Illustrated,* LV (August 17,1981), 42+.

51711. McMurray, John. "Where are They Now?: Former Slugger George Scott." *Baseball Digest,* LVIII (November 1999), 66–69.

51712. Porter, David L. "George Charles 'Boomer,' 'Peatuck' Scott." In: Vol. Q-Z of David L. Porter, ed. *Biographical Dictionary of American Sports: Baseball.* Rev. and enlarged ed. Westport, CT: Greenwood Press, 2000. Pp. 1372–1374.

51713. Post, Paul. "The Boomer." *Sports Collector's Digest,* XXIV (August 1, 1977), 96+.

51714. Ribowsky, Mark. "Keep 'Em Happy George! Scott Is Doing Just That in Boston These Days. But the Yankees and Orioles Aren't Laughing." *Black Sports,* VII (September 1977), 17–22.

51715. Shecter, Leonard. "The Great Scott Puzzle." *Sport*, XLII (October 1966), 50–53.

Jack Scott *see* **John William ("Jack") Scott**

John William ("Jack") Scott
P. (B: April 18, 1892, Ridgeway, NC–D: Nov. 30, 1959.). Pittsburgh (NL), 1916; Boston (NL), 1917–1921; Cincinnati (NL), 1922; New York (NL), 1922–1923; 1925–1926; Philadelphia (NL), 1927; New York (NL), 1928–1929. Remarks: Had 103 victories, 149 defeats, and 19 "saves" in a dozen summer campaigns; had career .275 batting average and went four-for-four in one game, Sept. 23, 1922; also pitched both ends of a doubleheader, June 19, 1927.

51716. Graham, Frank. "The Drama of Jack Scott." *Baseball Digest*, V (July 1946), 34–37.

51717. "Jack Scott, Baseball's 'Broken Blossom' That 'Came Back." *Literary Digest*, LXXV (October 28, 1922), 40–42.

51718. Lane, Ferdinand C. "The Most Sensational Comeback on Record." *Baseball Magazine*, XXX (December 1922), 299–301.

Lewis Everett ("Deacon" or "Scotty") Scott
SS. (B: Nov. 19, 1892, Bluffton, IN–D: Nov. 2, 1960). Boston (AL), 1914–1921; Now York (AL), 1922–1925; Washington (AL), 1925; Chicago (AL) and Cincinnati (NL), 1926. Remarks: Obtained 1,455 hits (20 homers) and 69 stolen bases in 1,654 games in 13 seasons; played in 1,307 consecutive games (June 20, 1916 through May 5, 1920) — a record streak which ended less then one month before Lou Gehrig (q.v.) began pursuit of his famous consecutive game playing achievement; later minor league player and Fort Wayne bowling alley operator.

51719. Cava, Peter J. "Lewis Everett 'Deacon,' 'Scotty' Scott." In: Vol. Q–Z of David L. Porter, ed. *Biographical Dictionary of American Sports: Baseball*. Rev. and enlarged ed. Westport, CT: Greenwood Press, 2000. Pp. 1374–1375.

51720. Fullerton, Hugh S. "Eight Years with a Day Off." *Liberty*, I (June 21, 1924), 61–62.

51721. Lane, Ferdinand C. "The Man Who Never Fails." *Baseball Magazine*, XXIX (July 1922), 361–363.

51722. "Mr. Scott's Gold Medal for Perfect Attendance." *Literary Digest*, LXXVII (May 19, 1923), 62–64.

51723. "More Records Smashed." *New Republic*, XXXV (May 30, 1923), 5–6.

51724. Obojski, Robert. "Scott Sets Consecutive Game Record Before Being Benched for Weak Hitting." In: his *Baseball's Strangest Moments*. New York: Sterling Publishing Co., 1988. Pp. 102–103.

51725. Scott, Lewis E. "Everett Scott's Bid for Fame." *Baseball Magazine*, XXXIII (November 1924), 557–558.

51726. _____. "Recollections of a Veteran Shortstop." *Baseball Magazine*, XXXVII (August 1926), 401–403+.

51727. Trachtenberg, Leo. "The Durable Deacon." *Yankee Magazine*, LVIII (December 1992), 38–39, 41.

Michael Warren ("Mike") Scott
P. (B: April 26, 1955, Santa Monica, CA). New York (NL), 1979–1982; Houston (NL), 1983–1991. Remarks: In 13 years, won 124 games and lost 108, with three "saves"; had one no-hitter, Sept. 25, 1986; won two games of 1986 NLCS; NLCS MVP Award, 1986; NL Cy Young Award, 1986.

51728. Collier, Ken. "Mike Scott." In: Ken Collier, ed. *The Baseball Book, 1987*. Scottsdale, AZ: Jalart House, 1987. Pp. 8–10.

51729. Fimrite, Ron. "No Wonder He's Hot." *Sports Illustrated*, LXVI (January 12, 1987), 92–96, 98–102.

51730. Goss, David A. "Michael Warren 'Mike' Scott."

In: Vol. Q–Z of David L. Porter, ed. *Biographical Dictionary of American Sports: Baseball*. Rev. and enlarged ed. Westport, CT: Greenwood Press, 2000. Pp. 1376–1377.

51731. Granger, Dave. "The Anatomy of an At-Bat." *Sport*, LXXVIII (July 1987), 26–29. Scott vs. Dave Parker.

51732. Jordan, Pat. "Mike Scott Got a Grip on the Split-Fingered Fastball and Threw His Career a Nice Curve." *People Weekly*, XXVIII (July 6, 1987), 45–47.

51733. Klima, John. "Worse Than Fear: Mike Scott vs. Dwight Gooden (October 8, 1986)." In: his *Pitched Battle: 35 of Baseball's Greatest Duels from the Mound*. Jefferson, NC: McFarland & Co., Inc., 2002. Pp. 136–140.

51734. Kuenster, John. "Mike Scott Topped List of 'Stingiest' Pitchers in Majors in '86." *Baseball Digest*, XLVI (March 1987), 15–17.

51735. McKinley, L. "Mike Scott." *Inside Sports*, IX (April 1987), 18–22.

51736. Moran, M. "Unlikely Star Makes His Mark on Baseball." *The New York Times Biographical Service*, XVII (October 1986), 1253–1254.

51737. Pool, Chuck. "Mike Scott: a Day to Remember." *Houston Astros Magazine*, IV, no. 6 (1991), 12–22.

51738. Rasmussen, Larry F. "Mike Scott of the Astros: Oldest Pitcher to Fan 300 in a Season." *Baseball Digest*, XLVI (February 1987), 27–29.

51739. Scott, Mike, as told to George Vass. "The Game I'll Never Forget." *Baseball Digest*, XLIX (May 1990), 53–55.

51740. "With NL's Top Hurler Waiting in the Wings, Astros Just Missed Chance for Pennant." In: George Leonard, ed. *Athlon Baseball, 1995*. Nashville, TN: Athlon, 1995. Pp. 100–101.

Raymond ("Ray") Scott
BROADCASTER. (B: 1918, Johnstown, PA). Remarks: Although primarily remembered as a football commentator, also broadcast for Minnesota (AL), 1961–1967, Washington (AL), 1969–1970, Minnesota (AL), 1973, 1975, and Milwaukee (AL), 1976.

51741. Fimrite, Ron. "Ray Scott Redux: Return of a Golden Oldie." *Sports Illustrated*, LXIX (September 12, 1988), 10–11.

51742. Noverr, Douglas A. "Raymond 'Ray' Scott." In: David L. Porter, ed. *Biographical Dictionary of American Sports: 1992–1995 Supplement for Baseball, Football, Basketball and Other Sports*. Westport, CT: Greenwood Press, 1995. Pp. 358–359.

Vincent Edward ("Vin") Scully
BROADCASTER. (B: Nov. 29, 1927, Bronx, N.Y.). Remarks: Broadcaster, Brooklyn (NL), 1950–1957; Los Angeles (NL), 1957-, for CBS-TV, 1975–1982, and NBC-TV, 1983–1989; Ford C. Frick Award, 1982; on July 6th, 2000, The American Sportscasters Association named Scully as the No. One sportscaster of the 20th century.

51743. Creamer, Robert W. "The Transistor Kid." *Sports Illustrated*, XX (May 4, 1964), 96–103.

51744. Hodges, Jim. "Vin Scully Nears Half Century." In: Zander Hollander, ed. *The Complete Book of Baseball '97*. New York: Signet, 1997. Pp. 24–31.

51745. Laughlin, Bob with Budd Theobald. *The Dodger Broadcasters: Vin Scully and Jerry Doggett*. Los Angeles, CA: Union Oil Company of California, 1960. 13p.

51746. Luria, Rod. "Vin Scully: Call Him Mr. Blue." *Los Angeles Magazine*, XXXV (July 1990), 94–95.

51747. Rubin; Bob. "A Voice of Subtle Eloquence." *Inside Sports*, V (November 1983), 10–12.

51748. Scully, Vin. "Next Year Comes to Brooklyn." In: Maury Allen. *Voices of Sport*. New York: Grosset & Dunlap, 1971. Pp. 24–35. Interview

51749. Stump, Al. "Vin Scully: 'Call Me Mr. Blue.'" *Los Angeles Magazine,* XXIX (September 1984), 194–200.

51750. "Vin Scully: Voice of the Bums." *Look,* XX (July 10, 1956), 46–47.

John ("Ziggy") Sears
UMPIRE. Remarks: NL arbiter, 1934–1945.

51751. Lieb, Frederick G. "Profile of a Young Umpire." In: Dean A. Sullivan, ed. *Middle Innings: A Documentary History of Baseball, 1900–1948.* Lincoln, NE: University of Nebraska Press, 1998. Pp. 160–162. Reprinted from *The Sporting News,* Aug. 29, 1935.

George Thomas ("Tom" or "Tom Terrific") Seaver★
P-BROADCASTER. (B: Nov. 17, 1944, Fresno, CA). New York (NL), 1967–1977; Cincinnati (NL), 1977–1982; New York (NL), 1982–1983; Chicago (AL), 1984–1986; Boston (AL), 1986. Remarks: Won 311 games and lost 205 in 20 seasons; NL Rookie of the Year award, 1967: NL Cy Young Award, 1969, 1973, and 1975; had 19 strikeouts in one game, April 22, 1970; pitched no-hitter, June 16, 1978; established or tied various records; none are so vividly recalled as the 25 victories which led the 1969 "Miracle Mets" to the World Championship; TV analyst for New York (AL), 1992–1993, and New York (NL), 1993–; elected to National Baseball Hall of Fame in 1992, where his plaque reads: "Franchise power pitcher who transformed Mets from lovable losers into formidable foes. Won 311 games over 20 seasons. Set NL career record for strikeouts by RHP (3,272) and modern record for lowest ERA (2.73). Whiffed 200 or more NL record 10 times (19 in a single game). NL Rookie of Year 1967 and 3-time Cy Young Awardee. No-hit Cards in 1978."

51752. Allen, Maury. "The Two Sides of Tom Seaver." In: Zandell Hollander, ed. *Grand Slam 1972 Baseball Annual.* New York: Popular Library, 1972. Pp. 29–33

51753. ____. "Tom Seaver." In: his *Baseball's 100.* New York: Galahad Books, 1981. Pp. 109–112.

51754. Appel, Marty. "Almost There in Chicago." In: his *Great Moments in Baseball.* New York: Carol Publishing Group, 1992. Pp. 283–288.

51755. Attner, Paul. "Tom's Still Terrific." In: Tom Barnidge, ed. *Best Sports Stories of 1986.* St. Louis, MO: The Sporting News, 1986. Pp. 163–169.

51756. Belsky, Dick. *Tom Seaver, Baseball's Superstar.* New York: Walck, 1977. 54p.

51757. Bennett, Gaymon L. "George Thomas 'Tom,' 'Tom Terrific' Seaver." In: Vol. Q-Z of David L. Porter, ed. *Biographical Dictionary of American Sports: Baseball.* Rev. and enlarged ed. Westport, CT: Greenwood Press, 2000. Pp. 1377–1379.

51758. Broeg, Bob. "Tom Terrific." In: his *My Baseball Scrapbook.* St. Louis, MO: River City Publishers, 1973. Pp. 174–177.

51759. Brosnan, Jim. "Torn Seaver and the Art of Power Pitching." *Boy's Life,* LXVII (September 1977), 20+.

51760. Burchard, Sue, and Marshall. *Sports Star: Tom Seaver.* New York: Harcourt, Brace, Jovanovich, 1974. 64p.

51761. Burke, Phil "Can Seaver Reach Magic 300 Plateau?" In: Clyde Hirt, ed. *Sports Quarterly Presents Baseball, 1972.* New York: Counterpoint, Inc., 1972. Pp. 22–23+.

51762. Butler, Hal. "Tom Seaver." In: his *Baseball's Champion Pitchers.* New York: Julian Messner, 1974. Pp. 79–80.

51763. Chase, Murray. "New York's Best Pitcher: Seaver or Catfish [Hunter]?" *Baseball Digest,* XXXIV (December 1975), 28–31.

51764. Cohen, Irwin. "Talkin' Baseball with Tom Seaver." *Baseball Cards,* VI (April 1986), 18–23.

51765. Cohen, Joel H., ed. *Inside Corner: Talks with Tom Seaver.* New York: Atheneum, 1974. 246p.

51766. Cohen, Linda J. "Seaver's Bad Pitch." *Inside Sports,* XV (July 1993), 8, 12. Broadcasting difficulties.

51767. Condon, David. "Tom Seaver Next 30-Game Winner?" *Baseball Digest,* XXIX (June 1970), 27–31.

51768. Daniels, Paul. "Inside Tom Seaver's Struggle to Prove 'I'm the Best Ever.'" *Sport,* LXVII (August 1978), 16–17+.

51769. Davis, Mac. "Tom Seaver." In: his *The Greatest in Baseball.* New York: Scholastic Book Services, 1977. Pp. 109–111.

51770. Deegan, Paul J. *Tom Seaver: Superstar.* Chicago, IL: Childrens Press, 1974. 32p.

51771. Deford, Frank. "Behind the Fence." *Sports Illustrated,* LV (July 27, 1981), 50–54+.

51772. Devaney, John. *Tom Seaver: An Intimate Portrait.* New York: Popular Library, 1974. 254p.

51773. DiTrani, Vinny. "Tom Seaver Still Thrives as a Major League Winner." *Baseball Digest,* XLI (April 1982), 50–52+.

51774. Drucker, Maika, with Tom Seaver. *Tom Seaver: Portrait of a Pitcher.* New York: Holiday House, 1978. 160p.

51775. Durso, Joseph. "The Ordeal of George Thomas Seaver." *Saturday Review,* II (April, 19, 1975), 12–13.

51776. ____. "Tom Seaver's Goal: Pitching Perfection." *Baseball Digest,* XXXV (May 1976), 34–38.

51777. ____, ed. "Pitchman: An Interview." *Saturday Evening Post,* CCL (April 1979), 22–24.

51778. Fimrite, Ron. "Kings of the Hill Again: Tom Seaver and Jim Palmer." *Sports Illustrated,* XLIIII (July 21, 1975), 14–17.

51779. Friedman, Jack. "300!" *People Weekly,* XXIV (August 19, 1985), 41–42.

51780. Furlong, William B. "Portrait of an Artist with an Aging Arm." *Sport,* LXXII (February 1981), 48–50+.

51781. Gergen, Joe. "The Tom Seaver Legend Is Born." In: Clyde Hirt, ed. *Sports Quarterly Presents Baseball Extra, Summer 1971.* New York: Counterpoint, Inc., 1971. Pp. 16–19.

51782. Giamatti, A. Bartlett. "Tom Seaver's Farewell." *Harper's,* CCLV (September 1977), 93–94+.

51783. Goldaper, Sam. "The Real Tom Seaver." In: Clyde Hirt, ed. *Sports Quarterly Presents Baseball Extra, Summer 1971.* New York: Counterpoint, Inc., 1970. Pp. 14–16.

51784. Good, Paul. "The Year the Mets Lost the Franchise." *Sport,* LXV (November 1977), 71–79. Seaver goes to Cincinnati.

51785. Gutman, Bill. "Torn Seaver." In: his *Modern Baseball Superstars.* New York: Dodd, Need, 1973. Pp. 69–76.

51786. ____. "Tom Seaver." In: his *New Breed Heroes in Pro Baseball.* New. York: Julian Messner, 1974. Pp. 177–190.

51787. Harrelson, Derrell M. ("Bud"). "The Real Tom Seaver." *Sport,* LIV (August 1972), 34–37.

51788. Hart, Stan. "Tom Seaver." In: his *Scouting Reports: The Original Reviews of Baseball's Greatest Stars.* New York: Macmillan, 1995. Pp. 123–130.

51789. Herman, Jack. "Who's Better: Seaver or Palmer?" *Baseball Digest,* XXXVI (July 1977), 28–31.

51790. Honig, Donald. "Tom Seaver." In: his *National League Rookies of the Year.* New York: Bantam, 1989. Pp. 49–51.

51791. _____. "Tom Seaver." In: his *The Greatest Pitchers of All Times*. New York: Crown Publishers, 1988. Pp. 146–152.

51792. _____. "Tom Seaver." In: his *The October Heroes*. New York: Simon and Schuster, 1979. Pp. 103–113.

51793. _____. "Tom Seaver." In: his *Up from the Minor Leagues*. New York: Cowles, 1970. Pp. 39–51.

51794. Jares, Joe. "The Mets Find a Young Phenom." *Sports Illustrated*, XXVI (June 26, 1967), 64–66.

51795. Jordan, Pat. "Tom Seaver: To Fly Like the Gulls." In: his *The Suitors of Spring*. New York: Dodd, Mead, 1973. Pp, 133–151.

51796. _____. "Tom Terrific and His Mystic Talent." *Sports Illustrated*, XXXVII (July 24, 1972), 23–24+.

51797. Keese, Parton. "Tom Seaver." In: his *Measures of Greatness*. Englewood Cliffs, N.J.: Prentice-Hall, 1981.pp. 123–134.

51798. Keith, Larry. "Tom Seaver Arms the Red Arsenal." *Sports Illustrated*, XLVI (June 27, 1977), 22–24+.

51799. Kelly, Robert E. "Tom Seaver." In: his *Baseball's Best: Hall of Fame Pretenders Active in the Eighties*. Jefferson, N.C.: McFarland & Co., Inc., 1988. Pp. 154–157.

51800. Kiley, Mike. "300th Career Victory Added to the Tom Seaver Legend." *Baseball Digest*, XLIV (November 1985), 59–65.

51801. Klaff, Harry. "Can Tom Seaver Come Back?" *Countrywide Sports*, I (April 1971), 32–37.

51802. Klein, Dave. *Tom Seaver, Dave McNally, Ferguson Jenkins, Mickey Lolich: Great Pitchers*. New York: Tempo Books, 1972. 117p.

51803. Klima, John. "Duel of Upside-Down Days: Mike Cuellar vs. Tom Seaver (October 15, 1969)." In: his *Pitched Battle: 35 of Baseball's Greatest Duels from the Mound*. Jefferson, NC: McFarland & Co., Inc., 2002. Pp. 120–125.

51804. Lang, Jack. *Tom Seaver: Countdown to Glory*. West Point, N.Y.: Leisure Press, 1983. 224p.

51805. _____. "Tom Seaver Picks His Ten Most Memorable Games." *Baseball Digest*, XLVII (November 1988), 18–20. Reprinted from *The New York Daily News*.

51806. Leggett, William. "Sportsman of the Year." Sports Illustrated, XXXI (December 22, 1969), 33–34+.

51807. Libby, Bill. "Tom Seaver." In: his *Star Pitchers of the Major Leagues*. New York: Random House, 1971. Pp. 3–19.

51808. Linn, Ed. "Tom Seaver: Steady Anchor, Full Sail." *Sport*, XLIX (May 1970), 52–61.

51809. Macht, Norman. *Tom Seaver*. New York: Chelsea House Publishers, 1994. 61p.

51810. Mauro, James. "Mound Olympus: A Heroic Conversation with Tom Seaver." *Psychology Today*, XXV (July-August 1992), 22–23.

51811. McEwen, Tom. "Tom Seaver: Baseball's 'Professor of Pitching." *Baseball Digest*, XLI (May 1970), 34–36.

51812. McKay, Joe. "Tom Seaver: The Franchise." In: his *The Great Shutout Pitchers: 20 Profiles of a Vanishing Breed*. Jefferson, NC: McFarland & Co., Inc., 2004. Pp. 74–85.

51813. Mentus, Ron. "Some Quips and Tips from Tom Seaver." *Baseball Digest*, XLII (July 1983), 37–39.

51814. Mueller, Rob. "Final Look: Tom Seaver." *Beckett Baseball Card Monthly*, IX, no. 89 (August 1992), 126–127.

51815. Munves, Jim. "Tom Seaver: Mainly with Heart." In: Ray Robinson, ed. *Baseball Stars of 1974*. New York: Pyramid Books, 1974. Pp. 98–105.

51816. Murphy, Jim. "Pitcher: Tom Seaver." In: his *Baseball's All-Time All-Stars*. New York: Clarion Books, 1984. Pp. 54–58.

51817. Neff, Craig. "Tom Takes a Giant Step." *Sports Illustrated*, LXIII (August 12, 1985), 14–18. 300th victory.

51818. Noble, Marty. "Pitching as an Art': An Interview with Tom Seaver." *Baseball Digest*, LXII (July 2003), 52–55.

51819. Nunziata, Joe, 3rd. "Tom Seaver, 1969." In: *Baseball's Top 100: The Best Individual Seasons of All Time*. Wilton, CT: Diamond Library, 1996. Pp. 209–210.

51820. Parr, Jeanne. "A Hell of a Good Pitcher." In: her *The Superwives: Life with the Giant Jocks*. New York: Coward, McCann & Geoghegan, 1976. Pp. 103–110. Focuses on Nancy Seaver.

51821. Parr, Willis. "Seaver's Million-Dollar Contract Demand." *Countrywide Sports*, I (October 1970), 46–51.

51822. Pepe, Phil. "Tom Was Terrific in a Lost [1981] Season." In: Dick Kaegel, ed. *The Sporting News 1982 Baseball Yearbook*. St. Louis, MO: The Sporting News, 1982. Pp. 87–92.

51823. Pickard, Chuck. "These Pitchers Allowed Fewest Base Runners per Nine Innings." *Baseball Digest*, XLV (May 1986), 22–24. Seaver and Addie Joss.

51824. Poses, Jonathan W. "Still Amazin." *Inside Sports*, VII (July 1985), 24–32.

51825. Rathgeber, Bob. "The Man is Terrific: Tom Seaver." In: his *Cincinnati Reds Scrapbook*. Virginia Beach, VA: J. C. P. Corp. of Virginia, 1982. Pp. 148–149.

51826. Reilly, Sidney. "A Final Look: Tom Seaver." *Beckett Baseball Card Monthly*, VII (February 1990), 94–95.

51827. Ritter, Lawrence and Donald Honig. "Tom Seaver." In: their *The 100 Greatest Baseball Plays of All Time*. New York: Crown Publishers, 1981. Pp. 74–75.

51828. Robinson, Ray. "Tom Seaver: Education of a Pitcher." In: Ray Robinson, ed. *Baseball Stars of 1972*. New York: Pyramid Books, 1972. Pp. 94–99.

51829. _____. "Tom Seaver: New Kind of Met." In: Ray Robinson, ed. *Baseball Stars of 1968*. New York: Pyramid Books, 1968. Pp. 71–76.

51830. _____. "Tom Seaver: The Hero in Metville." In: Ray Robinson, ed. *Baseball Stars of 1970*. New York: Pyramid Books, 1970. Pp. 11–19.

51831. Rumill, Ed. "The New Robin Roberts." *Baseball Digest*, XXVI (August 1967), 59–61.

51832. Sabin, Lou. "Tom Seaver: The 10-K Streak of 'Tom Terrific." In: his *Record Breakers of the Major Leagues*. New York: Random House, 1974. Pp. 127–136.

51833. Schaap, Dick. "Tom Seaver Paints a Picture of the Perfect Pitcher." *Sport*, LXII (May 1976), 24–27.

51834. Schlossberg, Dan. "Tom Seaver: Perfection was His Goal as a Pitcher." *Baseball Digest*, LVIII (March 1999), 72–75.

51835. _____. and Steve Ascher. "Terrific: The Mets' Most Wonderful Pitcher, Profiled and Checklisted." *Baseball Cards*, XII (July 1992), 62–66.

51836. Schneider, Howard. "The Many Faces of Tom Seaver." *Baseball Digest*, XXII (June 1973), 65–71.

51837. Schoor, Gene. *Seaver: A Biography*. Chicago, IL: Contemporary Books, 1986. 344p.

51838. Seaver, Tom. "A Conversation with Hall of Famer Tom Seaver." In: John J. Ralph, ed. *The National Baseball Hall of Fame and Museum 1999 Yearbook*. Pittsburgh, PA: Geyer Printing Co., 1999. Pp. 16–19.

51839. _____. with Marty Appel. "The Miracle of '69, and I was There." In: his *Great Moments in Baseball: From the World Series of 1903 to the Modern Records of Nolan Ryan.* New York: Carol Communications, 1992. Pp. 239–244.

51840. _____. "My Greatest Day in Baseball." In: Eliot Cohen, ed. *My Greatest Day in Baseball.* New York: Little Simon, 1991. Pp. 111–115.

51841. _____. "Tom Seaver's Absolutes of the Pitching Mechanics (from Windup to Follow-through)." *Scholastic Coach,* LIV (April 1985), 18–21+.

51842. _____., as told to George Vass. "The Game I'll Never Forget." In: John Kuenster, ed. *From Cobb to Catfish* (Chicago: Rand McNally, 1975). Pp. 181–182 and George Vass, ed. *The Game I'll Never Forget* (Chicago: Bonus Books, 1999), pp. 236–241. This account of Seaver's 1969 one-hitter against the Cubs was reprinted from the November 1974 issue of Baseball Digest.

51843. _____., with Alice Siegel and Margo McLoone-Basta. *Tom Seaver's Baseball Card Book.* New York: Julian Messner, 1985. 187p.

51844. _____, with Dick Schaap. *Perfect Game: Tom Seaver and the Mets.* New York: E.P. Dutton, 1970. 189p. Autobiographical account of the 1969 season.

51845. _____, with Lee Lowenfish. *Art of Pitching.* New York: Hearst Books; dist. by William Morrow, 1984. 224p. Text and action photos provide tips from Seaver, Nolan Ryan, Steve Rogers, Mario Soto, and Steve Carlton. A 224-page rev. ed. was published in 1994.

51846. _____., with Marty Appel. "The Miracle of '69 — and I was There." In: Marty Appel, ed. *Great Moments in Baseball.* New York: Carol Publishing Group, 1992. Pp. 239–244.

51847. _____, with Norman Lewis Smith. *How I Would Pitch to Babe Ruth: Seaver vs. the Sluggers.* Chicago: Playboy Press, 1974. 268p.

51848. _____., with Steve Jacobson. *Baseball is My Life.* New York: Scholastic Book Services, 1973. 127p.

51849. _____. *Pitching with Tom Seaver.* Englewood Cliffs, N.J.: Prentice-Hall, 1973. 125p.

51850. Sloate, Susan. "Tom Seaver." In: her *Hotshots: Baseball Greats of the Game When They Were Kids.* Boston, MA: Little, Brown, 1991. pp. 86–91.

51851. Smith, Ron. "Tom Seaver 32." In: his *The Sporting News Selects Baseball's 100 Greatest Players.* St. Louis, MO: The Sporting News, 1998. Pp. 74–75.

51852. Sullivan, George E. *Tom Seaver of the Mets.* New York: G.P. Putnam, 1971. 156p.

51853. Surface, Bill. "Seaver Prepares to Strike." *The New York Times Magazine* (April 5, 1970), 37+.

51854. Thorn, John. "Tom Seaver: Tom Terrific." In: his *Baseball's Dream Team.* New York: Ace Tempo Books, 1982. Pp. 106–117.

51855. "Tom Seaver." In: *Current Biography Yearbook, 1970.* New York: H.W. Wilson Co., 1970. Pp. 384–386.

51856. "Tom Seaver." *Parade Magazine,* (August 31, 1969), 12 +.

51857. Weiskopf, Don. "Pitching with Tom Seaver." *Athletic Journal,* L (April 1970), 60–66.

51858. Westcott, Rich. "Tom Seaver: Artist on the Mound." In: his *Winningest Pitchers: Baseball's 300-Game Winners.* Philadelphia, PA: Temple University Press, 2002. Pp. 147–156.

51859. Wilner, Barry. "Tom Seaver and the Cincinnati Reds: A Winning Combination." In: *Baseball Forecast, 1978.* New York: Lexington Library, 1978. Pp. 52–55.

51860. Wulf, Steve. "It Was a Terrible Homecoming." *Sports Illustrated,* LVIII (April 18, 1983), 36–39.

51861. Young, Ken. "Tom Seaver: Leading a Franchise

to the Top." In: his *Cy Young Award Winners.* New York: Walker, 1994. Pp. 44–58.

James Patrick ("Pat") Seerey

OF. (B: March 17, 1923, Wilburton, OK-D: April 28, 1986). Cleveland (AL), 1943–1948; Chicago (AL), 1948–1949. Remarks: Obtained 406 hits (86 homers) in 561 games in seven years; had four homers in one game, July 18, 1948.

51862. Dittmar, Joe. "Seerey Slugs Four: July 18, 1948." In: his *Box Scores.* Fairview Village, PA: Priv. Print., 1988. Pp. 53–54.

51863. "1948 — a Year To Remember." *Oldtyme Baseball News,* VI, no. 1 (1992), 16–19.

Kal Hill Segrist

2B-3B. (B: April 14, 1931, Greenville, TX). New York (AL), 1952; Baltimore (AL), 1955. Remarks: Had four hits in 20 big league games.

51864. Rives, Hill. "Kal Segrist, Portrait of a Yankee Rookie." *Baseball Digest,* XI (April 1952), 101+.

Harry ("Socks") Seibold

P. (B: May 31, 1896, Philadelphia, PA-D: Sept. 21, 1965). Philadelphia (AL), 1915–1919; Boston (AL), 1929–1933. Remarks: Had 48 victories, 86 defeats, and five "saves" in nine big league years; surrendered two grand slam homers in one game, May 26, 1929.

51865. Lane, Ferdinand C. "The Uncommon Career of Socks Seibold." *Baseball Magazine,* XLIX (June 1932), 311–313.

Kevin Lee Seitzer

3B. (B: March 26, 1962, Springfield, IL). Kansas City (AL), 1986–1991; Milwaukee (AL), 1992–1996; Cleveland (AL), 1996–1997. Remarks: Obtained 1,447 hits (74 homers) and 80 stolen bases in 1,429 games in 12 years, went six-for-six with seven RBIs in one game, Aug. 2, 1987; first AL. rookie to have 200 hits in a season; currently operates an indoor baseball facility in Kansas.

51866. Herrick, Steve. "New Kids in Town." In: Cleveland Indians. *1996 Central Division Champion Indians.* Cleveland, OH: Cleveland Indians, 1996. Pp. 64–71. Seitzer and Jose Vizcaino.

51867. Kiley, Mike. "Kevin Seitzer: The Royals' Versatile Rookie." *Baseball Digest,* XLVI (September 1987), 83–85.

51868. Krause, Kent M. "Kevin Lee Seitzer." In: Vol. Q-Z of David L. Porter, ed. *Biographical Dictionary of American Sports: Baseball.* Rev. and enlarged ed. Westport, CT: Greenwood Press, 2000. Pp. 1379–1380.

51869. Nash, Bruce and Allan Zullo. "Kevin Seitzer." In: their *More Little Big Leaguers : Amazing Boyhood Stories of Today's Baseball Stars.* New York: Little Simon, 1991. Pp. 8–9.

51870. Seitzer, Kevin. "Fear Strikes Back: An All-Star Player Describes the Horror of Being Hit in the Head by a Big League Fastball." *Sports Illustrated,* LXXXIII (July 24, 1995), 118+.

51871. Weiner, Darren. "Kevin Seitzer: Interview." *Baseball Cards,* VIII (January 1988), 36–41.

Albert Karl ("Kip") Selbach

OF. (B: March 24, 1872, Columbus, OH-D: Feb. 17, 1956). Washington (NL), 1894–1898; Cincinnati (NL), 1899; New York (NL), 1900–1901; Washington (AL), 1903–1904; Boston (AL), 1904–1905. Remarks: Had 1,816 hits (44 homers) and 335 stolen bases in 1,608 games in 13 seasons; went 6-for-7 in one game, June 9, 1896; also played for Harrisburg (Tri-State League), 1907–1910.

51872. Graber, Ralph S. "Albert Karl 'Kip' Selbach." In: Vol. Q-Z of David L. Porter, ed. *Biographical Dictio-*

nary of American Sports: Baseball. Rev. and enlarged ed. Westport, CT: Greenwood Press, 2000. Pp. 1380–1381.

Kip Selbach *see* **Albert Karl ("Kip") Selbach**

Frank Gibson Selee★

MGR. (B: Oct. 26, 1859, Amherst, N.H.-D: July 5, 1909). Remarks: Manager, Boston (NL), 1890–1901 and Chicago (NL), 1902–1905, winning 1,284 games and losing 862 games in 16 piloting sessions; elected to the National Baseball Hall of Fame in 1999, where his plaque reads: "A master strategist and an impeccable judge of talent who became one of the game's most successful field managers. Guided the National League's Boston Beaneaters and Chicago Cubs, Compiling 1,284 victories over 16 seasons. His exceptional winning percentage of .598 is fourth highest all-time. Assembled Chicago's renowned double play combination of Tinkers, Evers and Chance, and laid the foundation for the Cubs' three successive pennants from 1906–1908. A courteous and mild-mannered leader, he captured five pennants and managed 12 future Hall of Famers."

51873. Fleitz, David L. "Frank Selee." In: his *Ghosts in the Gallery at Cooperstown: Sixteen Little-Known Members of the Hall of Fame.* Jefferson, NC: McFarland & Co., Inc., 2004. Pp. 202–215.

51874. Honig, Donald. "Heading for Greatness." In: his *The Chicago Cubs: An Illustrated History.* New York: Prentice Hall Press, 1991. Pp. 16–27.

51875. Murnane, Timothy H. "Tribute to a Great Leader." *Baseball Magazine,* II (August 1909), 59–61.

51876. Powers, Francis J. "A Salaam for Selee." *Baseball Digest,* V (August 1946), 48–49.

51877. Selee, Frank G. "21 Years in Baseball." *Baseball Magazine,* I (May 1908), 23–28. Reprinted in *Baseball Magazine,* VIII (December 1911), 63–57.

51878. Suehsdorf, Adie D. "Frank Gibson Selee." In: Vol. Q-Z of David L. Porter, ed. *Biographical Dictionary of American Sports: Baseball.* Rev. and enlarged ed. Westport, CT: Greenwood Press, 2000. Pp. 1381–1383.

51879. _____. "Frank Selee: Dynasty Builder." *The National Pastime,* IV (Winter 1985), 35–41. Reprinted in John Thorn, ed. *The National Pastime* (New York: Bell Publishing Co., 1987), pp. 326–338.

51880. _____. and Richard J. Thompson. "Slim Selee's Extraordinary Year." *The Baseball Research Journal,* XIX (1990), 10–14. 1890.

51881. Williams, Frank J. "Frank Selee, Manager: Pennants 1890s." In: *Grandstand Baseball Annual Pitching W-L Records NL, 1890–1899.* Downey, CA: Joseph M. Wayman, 1996. Pp. 38–39.

Allan H. ("Bud") Selig

EXEC. (B: July 30, 1934, Milwaukee, WI). Remarks: Owner, pres./CEO, Milwaukee (AL), 1970–1990; Interim Commissioner, Major League Baseball, 1991–1998; Commissioner, Major League Baseball, 1998-.

51882. Angell, Roger. "Hard Ball." *The New Yorker,* LXX (October 17, 1994), 65–76.

51883. Batistick, Mike. "Bud Selig." *Current Biography,* LX (January 1999), 46–49.

51884. "Bud Selig." In: Louise Mooney Collins and Gert J. Speace, eds. *Newsmakers, 1995: The People Behind the Headlines.* Detroit, MI: Gale Research, 1995. Pp. 466–469.

51885. "The Buddy System." *Sports Illustrated,* LXXXIV (May 6, 1996), 22+.

51886. Chaplin, Paul. "Audience with the Emperor." *Elysian Fields Quarterly,* XVI (Summer 1999), 5–8.

51887. _____. "Bud Selig, Renaissance Man?" *Elysian Fields Quarterly,* XV (Summer 1998), 9–11.

51888. Deford, Frank. "Suicide Squeeze: Bud Selig Has Put His Legacy on the Line by Tightening the Screws on the Players' Union — If There's a Strike This Season, He'll be the One Who Takes the Fall." *Sports Illustrated,* XCVII (July 8, 2002), 66+.

51889. Hoffman, Gregg. "Bud Brings 'Em Home." In: Michael J. McCormick, ed. *2002 All Star Game Official Program.* New York: Major League Baseball Promotion Corp., 2002. Pp. 125–129.

51890. "Interview with Allan H. "Bud" Selig, President of the MLB Executive Council." *World Baseball Magazine,* III (1996), 8–11.

51891. King, Bill. "A Conversation with … Bud Selig." *Baltimore Business Journal,* XVI (April 2, 1999), 20–21.

51892. Olmsted, Frank J. "Harold H. 'Bud' Selig." In: Vol. Q-Z of David L. Porter, ed. *Biographical Dictionary of American Sports: Baseball.* Rev. and enlarged ed. Westport, CT: Greenwood Press, 2000. Pp. 1383–1385.

51893. Sheehan, Joe. "Bud Selig: Commissioner Extraordinaire." *Elysian Fields Quarterly,* XIX (Winter 2002), 4–6.

51894. Verducci, Tom. "Brushback." *Sports Illustrated,* LXXXII (April 10, 1995), 60–62, 67.

51895. _____. "Making Small Talk: How Small Market Teams Led by a Car Dealer Got Control of Baseball and Drove It to a Strike." *Sports Illustrated,* LXXXI (September 26, 1994), 20, 22–24.

51896. _____. "So What Can You Do, Bud?: Interview." *Sports Illustrated,* C (March 15, 2004), 40–43.

51897. Whiteside, Kelly. "This, Bud, is for You." *Sports Illustrated,* LXXXII (May 8, 1995), 24+.

Bud Selig *see* **Alan H. ("Bud") Selig**

George Alexander ("Twinkletoes") Selkirk

C-OF-EXEC. (B: Jan. 4, 1908, Huntsville, Canada-D: Jan. 19, 1987). New York (AL), 1934–1942. Remarks: Obtained 810 hits (108 homers) and 49 stolen bases in 846 games in nine seasons; succeeded George Herman ("Babe") Ruth (q.v.) on August 12, 1934 and was assigned his No. 3 uniform number by the Yankees for the remainder of his career; managed minor league teams, 1946–1955; supervisor of player personnel, Kansas City (AL), 1956–1961; GM, Washington (AL), 1962–1969; scout, New York (AL), 1970–1977; elected to Canadian Baseball Hall of Fame, 1983.

51898. Akin, William E. "George Alexander 'Twinkletoes' Selkirk." In: Vol. Q-Z of David L. Porter, ed. *Biographical Dictionary of American Sports: Baseball.* Rev. and enlarged ed. Westport, CT: Greenwood Press, 2000. Pp. 1385–1386.

51899. Gallagher, Mark. "George Selkirk." In: his *50 Years of Yankee All-Stars.* New York: Leisure Press, 1984, Pp. 190–191.

51900. Schultz, Randy. "George Selkirk Recalls the Yankees of Old." *Baseball Digest,* XLI (September 1982), 65–66+.

51901. Shearon, Jim. "George Selkirk, the Man Who Replaced Babe Ruth." In: *Canada's Baseball Legends.* Kanata, Ontario: Malin Head Press, 1994. Pp. 51–54.

51902. Whittlesey, Merrell. "The Big Wait: Selkirk Starts War on Bringing in Pinch Hitters from Bullpen." *Baseball Digest,* XXIV (July 1965), 65–66.

Anita Selvaggio

2B. (B: 1962, Chicago, IL). Chicago Blue Notes (Great Lakes Women's Baseball League), 1996; Chicago TV reporter.

51903. Perkins, Cy. "Just Play Because You Love the Game': A Conversation with Anita Selvaggio of the

Chicago Blue Notes Baseball Team." *Elysian Fields Quarterly,* XV (Spring 1998), 68–73.

Andrew Wasil ("Andy" or "Watsie") Seminick
C. (B: Sept. 12, 1920, Pierce, WV-D: Feb, 22, 2004). Philadelphia (NL), 1943–1951; Cincinnati (NL), 1952–1955; Philadelphia (NL), 1955–1957. Remarks: Obtained 953 hits (164 homers) and 23 stolen bases in 1,304 games in 15 years; had two homers in one inning, June 2, 1949; coach, Philadelphia (NL), 1957–1958, 1967–1969; minor league manager for the Phillies, 1959–1966, 1970–1972 and minor league instructor/scout, 1983–1985; first active Russian Orthodox Church member in MLB.

51904. Ashburn, Rich. "The Day Seminick Wiped Out the Giants' Infield." *Baseball Digest,* XXXIII (August 1974), 7640. Reprinted in John Kuenster, ed., *From Cobb to Catfish* (Chicago, IL. Rand McNally, 1975), P. 251.

51905. Dexter, Charles. "Seminick, Phils' Key Man." *Baseball Digest,* IX (November 1960), 21–27.

51906. Marazzi, Rich. "Interview with a Whiz Kid: Andy Seminick." *Sports Collector's Digest,* XXV (July 31 and August 7, 1998), 80–81, 80–81. Conducted before the subject's death.

51907. Newcombe, Jack. "The Old Man of the Phillies." *Sport,* X (April 1951), 40–44.

51908. Paxton, Henry T. "The Ballplayer Nobody Wanted." *Saturday Evening Post,* CCXXIH (June 30, 1951), 30+.

51909. Rogers, C. Paul, 3rd. "The Day the Phillies Came of Age: June 2, 1949 — Andy Seminick Gets Things Started." *The National Pastime,* XIX (1999), 31–33.

51910. Rossi, John P. "Andrew Wasil 'Andy' Seminick." In: Vol. Q-Z of David L. Porter, ed. *Biographical Dictionary of American Sports: Baseball.* Rev. and enlarged ed. Westport, CT: Greenwood Press, 2000. Pp. 1386–1387.

51911. Yeutter, Frank. "Papa Seminick's Son, Andy." *Baseball Magazine,* LXXIX (June 1947), 237–239.

Ray Semproch *see* **Roman Anthony ("Ray" or "Baby") Semproch**
Roman Anthony ("Ray" or "Baby") Semproch
P. (B: Jan. 7, 1931, Cleveland, OH). Philadelphia (NL), 1958–1959; Detroit (AL), 1960; Los Angeles (AL), 1961. Remarks: Won 19 games and lost 21 in four seasons always troubled by asthma.

51912. Graham, Frank, Jr. "Where Semproch Came From." *Sport,* XXVI (November 1958), 6–7.

51913. Williams, Edgar. "Roman Semproch, the Phillies' Roman Candle." *Baseball Digest,* XVII (September 1968), 27–32.

Bill Serena *see* **William Robert ("Bill") Serena**
William Robert ("Bill") Serena
3B-SCOUT. (B: Oct. 2, 1924, Alameda, CA-D: April 17, 1996). Chicago (NL), 1949–1954. Remarks: Had 311 hits (48 homers) in 408 games in six years; had 190 RBIs plus 57 regular season homers and 13 "taters" in the postseason (70 overall) in 1947 while playing for Lubbock (West Texas — New Mexico League); scout for Cleveland (AL), Atlanta (NL) and Florida (NL), 1955–1996.

51914. Bloodgood, Clifford. "The Score on Bill Serena." *Baseball Magazine,* LXXXV (October 1950), 377–379+.

William C. ("Bonnie") Serrell
2B. (B: March 9, 1922, Dallas, TX). Kansas City Monarchs, 1942–1944; Tampico (Mexican League), 1945–1951; Yakima (Western International League) and San Francisco (PCL), 1951; Nuevo Laredo (Mexican League), 1952–1957; Nogales-Juarez (Arizona-Mexican League), 1958. Remarks: Highly regarded Negro League keystoner; Jackie

Robinson (q.v.) signed by Monarchs as his replacement in 1945.

51915. Wright, Jerry J. "William C. 'Bonnie' Serrell." In: Vol. Q-Z of David L. Porter, ed. *Biographical Dictionary of American Sports: Baseball.* Rev. and enlarged ed. Westport, CT: Greenwood Press, 2000. Pp. 1387–1388.

William ("Wild Bill") Setley
P-UMP. Remarks: Colorful late 19th Century/early 20th Century minor league player and umpire.

51916. Kissel, Tony and Scott Fiesthumel. *The Legend of Wild Bill Setley.* Kearney, NE : Morris Publishing, 2002. 130p.

Henry Lavai ("Hank") Severeid
C-SCOUT. (B: June 1, 1891, Story City, IA-D: Dec. 17, 1968). Cincinnati (NL), 1911–1913; Louisville (AA), 1914; St. Louis (AL), 1915–1925; New York (AL), 1926. Remarks: Obtained 1,245 hits (17 homers) and 35 stolen bases in 1,390 games in 16 years; caught a career total of 2,357 big league games; also played for Sacramento (PCL) and Hollywood (PCL), 1937–1931; manager, San Antonio (TL), 1932–1937; coach, Syracuse (IL), 1938; scout, Cincinnati (NL), 1938–1940, Chicago (NL), 1942, and Boston (AL), 1943–1968.

51917. Phelps, Frank V. "Henry Leval 'Hank' Severeid." In: Vol. Q-Z of David L. Porter, ed. *Biographical Dictionary of American Sports: Baseball.* Rev. and enlarged ed. Westport, CT: Greenwood Press, 2000. Pp. 1388–1389.

Frank Martin Seward
P. (B: April 7, 1921, Pennsauken, NJ). Newport News (Virginia League), 1942; New York (NL), 1943–1944; San Francisco (PCL), 1945–1947; Hollywood (PCL), 1947; Syracuse (IL), 1948–1949. Remarks: In parts of two big league seasons, won four games and lost seven; in minor league play, had 62 victories and 64 defeats.

51918. Kelley, Brent P. "Frank Seward." In: his *The San Francisco Seals, 1946–1957: Interviews with 25 Former Baseballers.* Jefferson, NC: McFarland & Co., Inc., 2002. Pp. 28–34.

James Luther ("Luke" or "Lucious Luke") Sewell
C-MGR. (B: Jan. 5, 1901, Titus, Ala.-D: May 14, 1987). Cleveland (AL), 1921–1932; Washington (AL .), 1933–1934; Chicago (AL), 1935–1938; Cleveland (AL), 1939; St. Louis (AL), 1942. Remarks: Had 1,393 hits (20 homers) and 65 stolen bases in 1,630 in two decades; had three hits in 1933 World Series; caught three no-hitters; 20 years an active catcher, the AL record; manager, St. Louis 1941–1942 and Cincinnati (NL), 1949–1952, winning 606 games and losing 644 (.485); brother of Joe Sewell (below), cousin of Truett Banks ("Rip") Sewell (below).

51919. Bloodgood, Clifford. "Professor Sewell." *Baseball Magazine,* LXXXII (January 1949), 269–271.

51920. Carinichael, John P. "Top of the Moanin' for Luke." *Baseball Digest,* IX (April 1950), 78–79.

51921. "Coz Luke and Coz Rip [Sewell]." *Newsweek,* XXII (August 2, 1943), 74–6.

51922. Crusinberry, James. "Cincinnati's New Manager." *Baseball Magazine,* LXXXIV (January 1960), 255–257.

51923. Daniel, Daniel M. "Luke Sewell's Inspirational Leadership Paramount on Browns." *Baseball Magazine,* LXXIII (October 1940), 369–371.

51924. Givens, Horace R. "James Luther 'Luke' Sewell." In: Vol. Q-Z of David L. Porter, ed. *Biographical Dictionary of American Sports: Baseball.* Rev. and enlarged ed. Westport, CT: Greenwood Press, 2000. Pp. 1389–1391.

51925. _____. "Luke Sewell Recalls an Earlier Era of Baseball." *Baseball Digest,* XLI (July 1982), 69–75.

51926. Honig, Donald. "Luke Sewell." In: his *The Man in the Dugout.* Chicago, IL: Publishing Co., 1977. Pp. 256–273.

51927. "Luke Sewell." In: *Current Biography Yearbook, 1944.* New York: H.W. Wilson 1944. Pp. 606–609.

51928. Lundquist, Carl. "The Manager Who Used Nine Pitchers in One Game." *Baseball Digest,* LI (June 1992), 58–61.

51929. McAuley, Ed. "Sewell Ungloves Iron Hand." *Baseball Digest,* IV (November 1945), 52–53.

51930. Murdock, Eugene. "Joe and Luke: The Sewell Story." In: Peter Levine, ed. *Baseball History.* Westport, CT: Meckler, 1989. Pp. 37–48.

51931. _____. "The Tuscaloosa Twosome: Joe and Luke Sewell." In: his *Baseball Players and Their Times: Oral Histories of the Game, 1920–1940.* Westport, Ct: Meckler Publishing, 1991. Pp. 142–160.

51932. Peterson, Cy. "The Athletics' Big Star." *Baseball Magazine,* LXIV (December 1939), 307+.

51933. Ryan, Jack. "Luscious Luke's' One Brag." *Baseball Digest,* II (August 1943), 3–5.

51934. Sewell, James L. ("Luke"). "How Brother Luke Made Good." *Baseball Magazine,* XXXIX (August 1927), 396–397.

51935. _____. *How to Play Baseball.* New York: Esquire Magazine, 1945. Booklet of tips.

51936. _____. "I Was Beaned." Edited by John R. Tunis. *Collier's,* CVIII (August 1941), 19+. Reprinted in *Baseball Digest,* Ill (February 1944), 15–18.

51937. _____. "They Made Me a Cinderella: Inside Story of How a One-Time Catcher Became a Manager and How a Big-League Pennant Was Won." As told to Ralph Cannon. *Esquire,* XXIV (July 1945), 86–89. Reprinted in *Baseball Digest,* IV (July 1945), 5–8 as, "They Made Me a Cinderella."

51938. Tunis, John R. "Who's Catching?" *Atlantic Monthly,* CLXIV (July 1939), 85–90.

51939. "Up Sewell." *Newsweek ,* XX (September 21, 1942), 91–92.

Joseph Wheeler ("Joe") Sewell★
SS-3B-SCOUT-COACH. (B: Oct. 9, 1898, Titus, Ala.-D: March 6, 1990.). Cleveland (AL), 1920–1930; New York (AL), 1931–1933. Remarks: Obtained 2,226 hits (49 homers) and 74 stolen bases In 1,902 games in a 14-year big league career; made debut as replacement for Ray Chapman (q.v.); had four hits in 1920 World Series and five in 1932 World Series; led AL in doubles, 1924; recorded most putouts by a SS in four straight years, 1924–1927; recorded fewest strikeouts in major league history (114 in 7,132 games); used bat named *Black Betsy* and also played in 1,103 consecutive games, 1922–1930; noted fielder; coach, New York (AL), 1934–1935; scout for Cleveland (AL), 1952–1962 and New York (NL), 1963; coach, University of Alabama, 1964–1970, winning Southeast Conference baseball crown in 1968; brother of Luke Sewell (above); cousin of Truett Banks ("Rip") Sewell, below; elected to National Baseball Hall of Fame in 1977, where his plaque reads: "Posted lifetime .312 batting average, topping .300 in ten of 14 years. Most difficult man to strike out in game's history. Created records with: fewest career strikeouts (114), four seasons of four whiffs or less in 500 at-bats and 115 games in row without fanning. Led AL shortstops in fielding twice and In putouts and assists four times."

51940. August, Bob. "Joe Sewell: He Was the Toughest Strikeout-Ever." *Baseball Digest,* XXXIV (December 1975), 51–54.

51941. Bloodgood, Clifford. "Joe Sewell, Once Star Player, Now Conscientious Coach." *Baseball Magazine,* LIV (February 1935), 411–412.

51942. Carmichael, John P. "Sewell Really Finished 'Em." *Baseball Digest,* IV (July 1946), 5–7.

51943. Davids, L. Robert. "Sewell Was a Real Fox at the Plate." *The Baseball Research Journal,* V (1976), 123–127.

51944. Eichmann, J. L. "Was Joe Sewell the AL's Greatest Shortstop?" *Sports Scoup,* I (August-September 1973), 5+.

51945. Givens, Horace R. "Joseph Wheeler 'Joe' Sewell." In: Vol. Q-Z of David L. Porter, ed. *Biographical Dictionary of American Sports: Baseball.* Rev. and enlarged ed. Westport, CT: Greenwood Press, 2000. Pp. 1391–1392.

51946. Green, Paul M. "Baseball and Joe Sewell." *Sports Collector's Digest,* X (April 15, 1083), 82+.

51947. _____. "Joe Sewell." In: his *Forgotten Fields.* Waupaca, WI: Parker Publications, 1984. Pp. 66–78.

51948. Hickey, David and Kerry Keene. "Joe Sewell." In: their *The Proudest Yankees of All: From the Bronx to Cooperstown.* Lanham, MD: Taylor Trade Pub., dist. by National Book Network, 2003. Chpt. 13.

51949. Honig, Donald. "Joe Sewell." In: his *The October Heroes.* New York: Simon and Schuster, 1979. Pp. 230–253.

51950. Hurt, Cecil. "Hall of Famer Joe Sewell." *Bama* (April 1981), 24–25.

51951. Lane, Ferdinand C. "The Greatest Shortstop on the Diamond." *Baseball Magazine,* XL (January 1928), 345–346+.

51952. _____. "Never Go After a Bad Ball!" *Baseball Magazine,* XLV (June 1930), 299–300.

51953. Langford, Walter M. "Joe Sewell: The Mighty Mite Who Almost Never Struck Out." *Baseball Digest,* XLIII (May 1984), 73–81.

51954. Milne, Robert. "The Use of the Bat on the Third Strike." *Baseball Magazine,* VIII (June 1934), 315–316.

51955. Murdock, Eugene. "Joe and Luke: The Sewell Story." In: Peter Levine, ed. *Baseball History.* Westport, CT: Meckler, 1989. Pp. 37–48.

51956. _____. "The Tuscaloosa Twosome: Joe and Luke Sewell." In: his *Baseball Players and Their Times: Oral Histories of the Game, 1920–1940.* Westport, Ct: Meckler Publishing, 1991. Pp. 142–160.

51957. Obojski, Robert. "Joe Sewell: 'Iron Man,' A Tough Batter to Strike Out." In: his *Baseball's Strangest Moments.* New York: Sterling Publishing Co., 1988. Pp. 79–81.

51958. Peters, Nick. "Little Joe Sewell: He was the Best Contact Hitter Ever." *Baseball Digest,* XLV (December 1986), 40–42.

51959. Ritter, Lawrence and Donald Honig. "Joe Sewell." In: their *The 100 Greatest Baseball Players of All Time.* New York: Crown Publishers, 1981. Pp. 260–261.

51960. Russell, Fred. "Joe Sewell: The Best Contact Hitter Ever." *Baseball Digest,* XXXVI (September 1977), 84–86.

51961. Sewell, Joseph W. "The Man [Sewell] Who Never Strikes Out." *Baseball. Magazine,* XXXVIII (February 1927), 389–390+.

51962. Turner, Ken C. "Joe Sewell: An American Success Story." *Vintage & Classic Baseball Collector,* I (June and September 1995), 14–17, 38–41.

51963. Voigt, David Quentin. "Joe Sewell." In: John

A. Garrity and Marsh C. Carries, eds. *American National Biography.* 24 vols. New York: Oxford University Press, 1999. XIX, 682–683.

51964. Ward, John J. "Baseball's Hardest Hitting Shortstop." *Baseball Magazine,* XXXII (February 1924), 405–406.

51965. _____. "Joe Sewell, Steady and Dependable." *Baseball Magazine,* XLIX (November 1932), 551–553.

Luke Sewell *see* **James Luther ("Luke" or "Lucious Luke") Sewell**

Rip Sewell *see* **Truett Banks ("Rip") Sewell**

Truett Banks ("Rip") Sewell
P. (B. May 11, 1907, Decatur, AL-D: Sept. 3, 1989). Detroit (AL), 1932; Pittsburgh (NL), 1938–1949. Remarks: Had 143 victories, 97 defeats, and 15 "saves" in 13 seasons; led NL in losses, 1941; had 11 consecutive victories during and led AL in victories, 1943; coach, Pittsburgh (NL), 1948; minor league manager, 1950–1955; coach, Kansas City (AL), 1956; hurled a high arching change-up which he called the "eephus pitch," one of which was homered by Ted Williams (q.v.) in the 1946 All Star Game; cousin of James ("Luke") Sewell and Joe Sewell (above).

51966. "Balloon Bell: Sewell Demonstrates How He Throws the 'Eephus Ball." *Life,* XV (August 16, 1943), 76–78+. Pictorial.

51967. "Coz Luke [Sewell] and Coz Rip." *Newsweek,* XXII (August 2, 1943), 74–6.

51968. Falls, Joe. "Remember Rip Sewell and the 'Eephus Ball'?" *Baseball Digest,* XXXIV (July 1975), 73–81.

51969. Hernon, Jack. "Rip Sewell Finds He's a Forgotten Man." *Baseball Digest,* XIII (June 1954), 67–69.

51970. Honig, Donald. "Rip Sewell." In: his *Baseball When the Grass was Real.* New York: Coward, McCann, Geoghegan, 1975. Pp. 249–251.

51971. Newcombe, Jack. "When Ted Williams Met the 'Eephus." *Sport,* LXXI (July 1980), 61–63. 1946 All-Star Game.

51972. Rubin, Bob. "It Floats Through the Air...." *Sport,* XLVIII (July 1969), 5–6.

51973. Skidmore, Arden. "Rip Sewell 'Parachutes' to Victory." *Baseball Digest,* II (September. 1943), 27–29.

51974. Smith, Chester L. "Rip Sewell Finds Seat of Trouble." *Baseball Digest,* V (May 1946), 18–19.

51975. Smith, Elston. *The Blooper Man: The Rip Sewell Story.* Bellvue, PA: Pohl Associates, 1981. 106p.

51976. Spoehr, Luther W. "Truett Banks 'Rip' Sewell." In: Vol. Q-Z of David L. Porter, ed. *Biographical Dictionary of American Sports: Baseball.* Rev. and enlarged ed. Westport, CT: Greenwood Press, 2000. Pp. 1392–1393.

51977. Westcot, Rich. "Rip Sewell: Father of the Blooper Pitch." In: his *Masters of the Diamond: Interviews With Players Who Began Their Careers More Than 50 Years Ago.* Jefferson, NC: McFarland & Co., Inc., 1994, Pp. 117–126.

Richie Sexson *see* **Richmond Lockwood ("Richie") Sexson**

Richmond Lockwood ("Richie") Sexson
1B-OF. (B: Dec. 29, 1974, Portland, OR). Cleveland (AL), 1997–2000; Milwaukee (NL), 2000–2003; Arizona (NL), 2004; Seattle (AL), 2005-. Remarks: Through 2004, has had 832 hits (200 homers) and 10 stolen bases in 836 games; had four homers in three days, Aug. 1998; hit first homer at Miller Park, April 6, 2001; had seven RBIs in one game, April 18, 2002; commanding figure at 6'7."

51978. McMurray, John. "Milwaukee's Richie Sexson: Big Man on a Mission." *Baseball Digest,* LX (September 2001), 64–67.

51979. Murphy, Dan. "Walk Tall and Carry a Big Stick." In: Michael J. McCormick, ed. *2002 All Star Game Official Program.* New York: Major League Baseball Promotion Corp., 2002. Pp. 130–135.

51980. Sorci, Rick. "Baseball Profile: Brewers Slugger Richie Sexson." *Baseball Digest,* LIX (December 2000), 26–27.

Ralph Orlando ("Socks") Seybold
OF-1B. (B: Nov. 23, 1870, Washingtonville, OH-D: Dec. 22, 1921). Cincinnati (NL), 1899; Philadelphia (AL), 1901–1908. Remarks: Obtained 1,085 hits (51 homers) in 997 games in nine big league seasons; had 16 homers in 1902, a record not broken until Babe Ruth's 29 in 1919; led AL in doubles, 1903; had two hits in 1905 World Series.

51981. Van Atta, Robert B. "Ralph Orlando 'Socks' Seybold." In: Vol. Q-Z of David L. Porter, ed. *Biographical Dictionary of American Sports: Baseball.* Rev. and enlarged ed. Westport, CT: Greenwood Press, 2000. Pp. 1393–1394.

Socks Seybold *see* **Ralph Orlando ("Socks") Seybold**

Cy Seymour *see* **James Bentley ("Cy") Seymour**

Harold Seymour
WRITER-HISTORIAN. (B: June 2, 1910-D: 1992). Remarks: Noted historian of the game; batboy for Brooklyn (NL) in 1920s; works written in silent partnership with Dorothy Jane Mills.

51982. Burke, Michael. "Baseball's Biographer: Dr. Harold Seymour." *The National Pastime,* X (1990), 65–68.

51983. Grella, George. "Harold Seymour (1920–1992)." *The National Pastime,* XVII (1997), 128–130.

51984. Mills, Dorothy Jane. "Ghost Writing for Baseball Historian Harold Seymour." *Nine: A Journal of Baseball History and Culture,* XI (Fall 2002), 49–59.

51985. _____. *A Woman's Work: Writing Baseball History with Harold Seymour.* Jefferson, NC: McFarland & Co., Inc., 2004. 304p.

51986. Riess, Steven A. "The Lead-off Batter who Slugged Home Runs: Harold Seymour and the Making of the History of Baseball." *Journal of Sport History,* XXIX (Spring 2002), 135–144.

51987. Seymour, Harold. "Big League Batboy." *Sports Heritage,* II (Spring 1988), 13–24.

James Bentley ("Cy") Seymour
OF-P. (B: Dec. 9, 1872, Albany, NY-D: Sept. 20, 1919). New York (NL), 1896–1900; Baltimore (AL), 1901–1902; Cincinnati (NL), 1902–1906; New York (NL), 1906–1910; Boston (NL), 1913. Remarks: As a pitcher, won 25 games and lost 19, with one "save"; as a batter, obtained 1,723 hits (six homers) and 24 stolen bases in 1,528 games in 16 seasons; set never-topped mark of four sacrifice flies in one game, July 25, 1902; 1905 NL batting champion, who also led NL in doubles, triples, and RBIs; also played for Worcester Farmers (EL), 1900–1901; following his big league career, played in the IL until 1916; retiring to New York, he was allowed to practice with the Giants until shortly before his death.

51988. Kirwin, Bill. "Cy Seymour: Only Babe Ruth was More Versatile." *The Baseball Research Journal,* XXIX (2000), 3–13.

51989. Rathgeber, Bob. "When Hitting Became a Science: Cy Seymour." In: his *Cincinnati Reds Scrapbook.* Virginia Beach, VA: J.C.P. Corp. of Virginia, 1982. Pp. 36–37.

51990. Spoehr, Luther W. "James Bentley 'Cy' Seymour." In: Vol. Q-Z of David L. Porter, ed. *Biographical Dictionary of American Sports: Baseball.* Rev. and enlarged ed. Westport, CT: Greenwood Press, 2000. Pp. 1394–1395.

Freddy Sez
FAN. (B: New York City, 1922). Remarks: Long-time Yankee fan famous for his various signs and plackards displayed at home games; has opened his own web-page showing some of the signs, http://www.freddysez.com.
51991. Doughty, Jim. "Why Do We Cheer?" *Yankees Magazine,* XX (September 1999), 58–67.

Arthur Shafer
EXEC.
51992. Mansfield, Rhea. "The Man Who Made Baseball in Japan." *Baseball Magazine,* IX (July 1912), 26–30.

Mike Shannon *see* **Thomas Michael ("Moonman") Shannon**

Thomas Michael ("Moonman") Shannon
OF-3B-BROADCASTER. (B: July 15, 1939, St. Louis, MO). St. Louis (NL), 1962–1970. Remarks: In nine big league seasons, obtained 710 hits (68 homers) and 19 stolen bases in 882 games; homered in Game One of 1964 World Series, in Game Three of 1967 World Series, and in Game Seven of 1968 World Series; broadcaster, St. Louis (NL), 1972-.
51993. Shannon, Mike, as told to Al Doyle. "The Game I'll Never Forget." *Baseball Digest,* LXII (December 2003), 78–81. 1964 World Series homer.

Bobby Shantz *see* **Robert Clayton ("Bobby") Shantz**
Robert Clayton ("Bobby") Shantz
P. (B: Sept. 26, 1925, Pottstown, PA). Philadelphia (AL) and Kansas City (AL), 1949–1956; New York (A.L), 1957–1960; Pittsburgh (NL), 1961; Houston (NL), 1962; St. Louis (N.L), 1962–1964; Chicago (NL), 1964. Remarks: Won 119 games, lost 99 and had 48 "saves" in 16 years; AL MVP award, 1952; lost Game Two of 1957 World Series; noted fielder, who had one career homer.
51994. Bernstein, Ralph. "Philadelphia's Little [5'6"] Miracle." In: Bruce Jacobs, ed. *Baseball Stars of 1953.* New York: Lion Books, 1953. Pp. 11–20.
51995. Biederman, Lester J. "Wee Shantz Pitched Big: He Loomed Large as a Fielder, Too." *Baseball Digest,* XXIV (March 1965), 91–93.
51996. Bonner, Mary G. "Bobby Shantz." In: her *Baseball Rookies Who Made Good.* New York: Alfred A. Knopt, 1964. Pp. 6–8.
51997. Carmichael, John P. "Why the Yankees Took a Shantz." *Baseball Digest,* XVI (May 1957), 49–51.
51998. "The Comeback." *Sports Illustrated,* II (May 16, 1955),15–17.
51999. Delaney, Ed. *Bobby Shantz.* New York: A.S. Barnes, 1953. 141p.
52000. Forker, Dom. "Bobby Schantz." In*: Sweet Seasons: Recollections of the 55–64 New York Yankees.* Dallas, TX: Taylor Publishing Co., 1989. Pp. 99–103.
52001. Gallagher, Mark. "Bobby Shantz." In: his *50 Years of Yankee All-Stars.* New York: Leisure Press, 1984. Pp. 192–193.
52002. Honig, Donald. "Bobby Shantz." In *his Baseball Between the Lines: Baseball in the Forties And Fifties as Told By the Men Who Played It.* New York: Coward, McCann & Geoghegan, 1976. Pp. 145–153.
52003. _____. "1952: Bobby Shantz." In: his *American League MVP's.* New York: Bantam Books, 1989. Pp. 47–48.
52004. Kiersh, Edward. "Bobby Shantz." In: his *Where Have You Gone, Vince DiMaggio?* New York: Bantam Books, 1983. Pp. 296–301.
52005. "The Little Left-Hander." *Time,* LIX (June 23, 1952), 57–58.
52006. "Little Pitcher with Big Wins: Bobby Shantz Leads Big Leagues." *Life,* XLIX (July 21, 1952), 40–50+.

52007. Lundquist, Carl. "He's the A's Fancy Shantz." *Baseball Digest,* XI (August 1952), 13–17.
52008. Marazzi, Rich. "Bobby Shantz Proves a Popular Autograph Guest at Sports Fest '98." *Sports Collector's Digest,* XXV (July 17, 1998), 110–111.
52009. Masterson, Dave And Timm Boyle. "1952." In: their *Baseball's Best: The MVPs.* Chicago, IL: Contemporary Books, 1985. Pp. 136–141.
52010. McAnulla, Chuck. "Bobby Shants: 1952 AL MVP Collects Memories." *Sports Collector's Digest,* XXV (April 3, 1998), 161–167.
52011. Merkle, Ray and Bobby Shantz. *Concentrated Baseball.* Philadelphia, PA: Whitmore Publishing Co., 1967.168p. Instructional.
52012. Molter, Harry. "Bobby Shantz: 'The Little Samson of the Mound." In: his *Famous American Athletes of Today.* 13th Series. New York. Page, 1953. Pp. 281–298.
52013. Obojski, Robert. "Bobby Shantz: 1952 AL MVP Interviewed." *Sports Collector's Digest,* XXI (August 19, 1994), 154+.
52014. O'Connell, T. S. "Bobby Shantz Discusses Memorable Career." *Sports Collector's Digest,* XVIII (May 17, 1991), Pp. 110–112.
52015. Olmsted, Frank J. "Robert Clayton 'Bobby' Shantz." In: Vol. Q-Z of David L. Porter, ed. *Biographical Dictionary of American Sports: Baseball.* Rev. and enlarged ed. Westport, CT: Greenwood Press, 2000. Pp. 1995–1997.
52016. "Robert Clayton Shantz." In: *Current Biography Yearbook, 1953.* New York: H.W. Wilson Co., 1953. Pp. 567–569.
52017. Ross, John M. "Might Mite of the A's." *Sport,* XII (July 1952), 26–27+.
52018. Rumill, Ed. "Shantz Pitching Dyna-MITE." *Baseball Digest,* LXXXIX (September 1952.), 12–14.
52019. Shantz, Robert C., as told to Ralph Bernstein. *Story of Bobby Shantz.* Philadelphia, PA: Lippincott, 1953. 190p. Reprinted by the same firm in 1998.
52020. Sullivan, George. "Bobby Shantz." In: his *Glovemen: Twenty-Seven of Baseball's Greatest.* New York: Atheneum, 1996. Pp. 42–43.
52021. Wilks, Ed. "Bobby Shantz: Still Great in the Clutch." *Baseball Digest,* XXII (October-November 1963), 81–83.
52022. Williams, Edgar. "Biggest Little Man in Baseball." *Saturday Evening Post,* CCXXV (July 26,1952), 25–29.
52023. _____. "Bobby Shantz: Biggest Little Man Once More." *Baseball Digest,* XVII (September 1957), 45–51.
52024. _____. "Shantz Shoots Up Fast!" *Baseball Digest,* IX (June 1950), 41–43.
52025. Westcott, Rich. "Bobby Shantz — Elfin Southpaw Was Spectacular in 1952." In: his *Diamond Greats.* Westport, CT: Meckler Books, 1988. Pp. 164–168.

Daniel ("Dan") Shaughnessy
WRITER. (B: 1953, Groton, MA). Remarks: Writer/reporter, *Baltimore Evening Sun* and *Washington Star,* 1975–1980 and *Boston Globe,* 1981-date; seven-time winner, Massachusetts Sportswriter of the Year Award.
52026. Shannon, Miek. "Dan Shaughnessy." In: his *Baseball: The Writer's Game.* 2nd ed. Dulles, VA: Brassy's, Inc., 2002. Pp. 225–244.

Francis Joseph ("Shag") Shaughnessy
OF. (B: April 8, 1883, Amboy, IL-D: May 15, 1969). Washington (AL), 1905; Philadelphia (AL), 1908. Remarks: In parts of two big league seasons, obtained nine hits and three stolen bases in nine games; later with the Montreal Royals.

52027. Shaughnessy, Frank J. ("Shag"). *Baseball: The Game of Games.* Montreal, Canada: The Canada Starch Co., 1936. 32p. Instructional from the Montreal Royals.

Shag Shaughnessy *see* **Francis Joseph ("Shag") Shaughnessy**

Joseph Benjamin ("Joe" or "Lefty") Shaute
P. (B: Aug. 1, 1899, Peckville, PA-D: Feb. 21, 1970). Cleveland (AL), 1922–1930; Brooklyn (NL), 1931–1933; Cincinnati (NL), 1934. Remarks: Won 99 games and lost 109 with 18 "saves" in 13 seasons; noted for enviable success in striking out George Herman ("Babe") Ruth (q.v.) over 30 times.

52028. Shaute, Joseph B. "A Young Coal Miner [Shaute] Who Has Become a Winning Pitcher." *Baseball Magazine,* XXXIV (May 1923), 549–550+.

Bob Shaw *see* **Robert John ("Bob") Shaw**

Robert John ("Bob") Shaw
P. (B: June 29, 1933, New York City.). Detroit (A. L.), 1957–1958; Chicago (AL), 1958–1961; Kansas City (AL), 1961; Milwaukee (NL), 1962–1963; San Francisco (NL), 1964–1966; New York (NL), 1966–1967; Chicago (NL), 1967. Remarks. Won 108 games and last 98, with 32 "saves," for seven big league teams in 11 years; set one-game balk record with five, May 4, 1963; coach, Los Angeles (NL), 1969–1973. .

52029. Allen, Maury. "Bob Shaw vs. the World." *Sport,* XLIII (June 1967), 28–32.

52030. Herskowitz, Mickwj. "Rob Shaw: He Quells Trouble On and Off the Mound." *Baseball Digest,* XXII (December 1963), 95–97.

52031. Hines, Rick. "Bob Shaw Was Big Man For '59 Chisox." *Sports Collector's Digest,* XVIII (March 8, 1991), 170–171.

52032. Middlesworth, Hal. "Bob Shaw Sins on Own Balk." *Baseball Digest,* VIII (October 1959), 75–81.

52033. Shaw, Bob. *Pitching: The Basic Fundamentals and Mechanics Of Successful Pitching.* New York; Viking Press, 1972. 208p.

52034. Shaw, Bob. *Pitching.* New York: Viking Press, 1972. 201p. Instructional.

52035. Vanderberg, Bob. "Bob Shaw: Ray Berres' Disciple." In: his *Sox—From Lane and Fain to Zisk and Fisk.* Chicago, IL: Chicago Review Press, 1982. Pp. 209–217.

Bob Shawkey *see* **James Robert ("Bob" or "Sailor Bob") Shawkey James Robert ("Bob" or "Sailor Bob" or "Sailor Bob") Shawkey**
P-MGR-COACH. (B: Dec. 4, 1890, Brookville, PA-D: Dec. 31, 1980). Philadelphia (AL), 1913–1915; New York (AL), 1915–1927. Remarks: In 15 seasons, had 198 victories, 150 defeats, and 28 "saves"; pitched the first game ever played at Yankee Stadium, 1923; coach, New York (AL), 1929; manager, New York (AL), 1930, winning 86 games and losing 68 (.558); minor league manager, 1931–1949; farm system pitching coach/baseball coach, Dartmouth College, 1952 to 1956; elected to Greater Syracuse Sports Hall of Fame, 1991.

52036. Diddlebock, Bob. "Bob Shawkey: An Old-Time Hero Recalls the Past." *Baseball Digest,* XXXVII (August 1978), 71–76.

52037. Honig, Donald. "Bob Shawkey." In: his *The Man in the Dugout.* Chicago, IL: Follet Publishing Co., 1977. Pp. 166–179.

52038. Murdock, Eugene. "Where's The Fire?': Bob Shawkey." In: his *Baseball Players and Their Times: Oral Histories of the Game, 1920–1940.* Westport, CT: Meckler Publishing, 1991. Pp. 24–40.

52039. Shawkey, James R. ("Bob"). "The Veteran

[Shawkey] of the Yankees' Pitching Staff." *Baseball Magazine,* XXXVII (July 1926), 349–351.

52040. Suehsdorf, Adie D. "James Robert 'Sailor Bob,' 'Bob the Gob' Shawkey." In: Vol. Q–Z of David L. Porter, ed. *Biographical Dictionary of American Sports: Baseball.* Rev. and enlarged ed. Westport, CT: Greenwood Press, 2000. Pp. 1397–1398.

Frank Joseph ("Spec" or "The Naugatuck Nugget") Shea
P. (B: Oct. 2, 1920, Naugatuck, CT-D: July 19, 2002). New York (A.L), 1947–1949, 1951; Washington (AL), 1952–1955. Remarks: Had 56 victories, 46 defeats, and five "saves" in eight pro years; winning pitcher, 1947 All-Star Game, who also won two games in 1947 World Series; nicknamed for his freckles.

52041. Forker, Dom. "Frank Shea." In: his *The Men of Autumn.* Dallas, TX: Taylor Publishing Co., 1989. Pp. 53–63.

52042. Gallagher, Mark. "Spec' Shea. In: his *50 Years of Yankee All-Stars.* New York: Leisure Press, 1984. Pp. 194–195.

52043. Gross, Milton. "Rookie of the Year." *Saturday Evening Post,* CCXX (July 26, 1947), 24–25+.

52044. Hawkins, Burton. "Shea, Mister!" *Baseball Digest,* XI (July 1952), 67–69.

52045. Parker, Dan. "Shea was Tough—Even to Scout." *Baseball Digest,* VII (July 1948), 23–25.

52046. Povich, Shirley. "The Senators Vote for Shea." *Sport,* XIV (March 1953), 26–27+.

52047. _____. "Shea's a Right-Handed Gomez." *Baseball Digest,* VI (September 1947), 47–49.

Spec Shea *see* **Frank Joseph ("Spec" or "The Naugatuck Nugget") Shea**

Thomas ("Tom") Shea
WRITER

52048. Thompson, D. "Tom Shea: This Little-Known SABR Founder was Baseball's Greatest Biographical Researcher." *The National Pastime,* XVIII (1998), 94–102.

Jim Sheckard *see* **Samuel James Tilden ("Jim" or Jimmy") Sheckard**

Samuel James Tilden ("Jim" or Jimmy") Sheckard
OF. (B: Nov. 23, 1878, Upper Chanceford, PA-D: Jan. 15, 1947). Brooklyn (NL), 1897–1898; Baltimore (NL), 1899; Brooklyn (NL), 1900–1901; Baltimore (NL), 1902; Brooklyn (NL), 1902–1905; Chicago (NL), 1905–1912; St. Louis (NL) and Cincinnati (NL), 1913. Remarks: Had 2,091 hits (56 homers) and 465 stolen bases in 2,121 games in 17 seasons; had three triples in one game, April 18, 1901; had grand slam homers in two consecutive games, Sept. 23–24, 1901; NL home run champion, 1903; NL stolen base champion, 1899 and 1903 (tie); had 147 walks in 1911, setting a seasonal mark which stood until 1945; minor league manager, 1914; coach, Chicago (NL), 1917; lost his life savings in the Stock Market crash of 1929 and worked as day laborer/gas station attendant until killed by a speeding automobile.

52049. Blaisdell, Lowell L. "Samuel James Tilden 'Jimmy' Sheckard." In: Vol. Q–Z of David L. Porter, ed. *Biographical Dictionary of American Sports: Baseball.* Rev. and enlarged ed. Westport, CT: Greenwood Press, 2000. Pp. 1398–1399.

52050. Dubbs, Gregg. "Jim Sheckard in the Dead Ball Era." *The Baseball Research Journal,* IX (1980), 134–139.

52051. Smith, Ira L. "Jimmy Sheckard." In: his *Baseball's Famous Outfielders.* New York: A. S. Barnes, 1954. Pp. 63–68.

Peter ("Pete") Sheehy
EXEC. New York (AL), 1927–1977. Remarks: Yankee

Stadium fixture who finished as clubhouse manager, 1968–1977.

52052. Trachtenberg, Leo. "Pete Sheehy: A Last Interview." *Baseball History,* I (Winter 1986), 28–33.

Earl Homer ("Whitey") Sheely

1B. (B: Feb. 12, 1893, Bushnell, IL-D: Sept. 16, 1952). Chicago (AL), 1921–1927; Pittsburgh (NL), 1929; Boston (NL), 1931. Remarks: In nine big league seasons, obtained 1,340 hits (48 homers) and 33 stolen bases in 1,234 games; had seven consecutive extra base hits (six doubles and a homer) in two games in two days, May 20–21, 1926; held White Sox record for games played at 1B for 70 years.

52053. Fitzsimmons, David. "Earl Homer 'Whitey' Sheely." In: Vol. Q-Z of David L. Porter, ed. *Biographical Dictionary of American Sports: Baseball.* Rev. and enlarged ed. Westport, CT: Greenwood Press, 2000. Pp. 1399–1400.

Whitey Sheely *see* **Earl Homer ("Whitey") Sheely**

Ben Sheets

P. (B: July 18, 1978, St. Amant, LA). Milwaukee (NL), 2001-date. Remarks: Through 2004, has won 45 games and lost 53; gained national attention in 2000 Olympics; led NL in losses, 2002; had 18 strikeouts in one game, May 16, 2004.

52054. Farber, Michael. "Smoking Cubans." *Sports Illustrated,* XCIII (October 9, 2000), 62–63.

52055. Haudricourt, Tom. "Ben Sheets' Success Burned Batters with Surprising Heat." *Baseball Digest,* XLIII (December 2004), 36–39.

52056. Shemanske, Susan. "Then and Now: Four Years Ago, Current Milwaukee Ace Ben Sheets Led the U.S. to Victory at the Sydney Olympics." In: Richard Levin, ed. *2004 World Series Official Program.* New York: Major League Baseball Properties Corp., 2004. Pp. 38–40.

Larry Kent Sheets

OF. (B. Dec. 6, 1959, Staughton, VA) Baltimore, 1984–1989; Detroit (AL), 1990; Taiyo Whales (Japan League), 1992; Seattle (AL), 1993. Remarks: Obtained 607 hits (94 homers) and 18 stolen bases in 748 games in eight U.S. big league seasons; had one grand slam homer, Aug. 6, 1986; earlier, was Appalachian League home run champion with Bluefield, 1980 and SL home run champion (tie) with Charlotte, 1983.

52057. Alexson, Bill. "Larry Sheets, Detroit Tigers." In: his *Batting a Thousand, Book 2.* Nashville, TN: Thomas Nelson Publishers, 1990. Pp. 94–97.

52058. Cohen, Irwin. "Baseball Beat: Larry Sheets." *Baseball Cards,* VIII (July 1988), 82–89.

52059. Wolff, Alexander. "He's Safe at Home." *Sports Illustrated,* LIV (June 15, 1981), 55–56+.

Gary Antonian Sheffield

SS. (B: Nov. 18, 1968, Tampa, FL). Milwaukee (AL), 1988–1991; San Diego (NL), 1992–1993; Florida (AL), 1993–1998; Los Angeles (NL), 1998–2001; Atlanta (NL), 2002–2003; New York (AL), 2004-. Remarks: Through 2004, has had 2,175 hits (415 homers) and 205 stolen bases in 2,036 games; had eight consecutive hits in two games, Sept. 17–18, 1995; had 11 homers in one month, May 1996; homered in both the 1997 NLCS and 1997 World Series; first big league player to win three 1–0 games with homers in a season, 2001; nephew of Dwight Gooden (q.v.); had 10 hits in 2004 ALCS; second player in MLB history to hit at least 30 home runs in a season for five different teams; first big league player (since RBIs became an official statistic in 1920) to drive in 100 runs with five different teams; first player to represent five different teams in the All-Star Game (San Diego, Florida, Los Angeles, Atlanta and the Yankees).

52060. Beaton, Rod. "Star-Gazing: Is Gary Sheffield a Rising Star — Or Just a Shot in the Dark?" *Fantasy Baseball,* IV (May 1993), 30–32.

52061. Cannella, Stephen. "Take That, You Mets!" *Sports Illustrated,* XCVI (January 28, 2002), 78–79.

52062. Chappell, K. "Gary Sheffield's Coast-to-Coast Mansions." *Ebony,* LIV (June 1999), 104–106+.

52063. Cohen, Irwin. "Baseball Beat: Gary Sheffield." *Baseball Cards,* X (November 190), 126+.

52064. Friend, Tom. "Higher Power." *ESPN: The Magazine,* IV (May 14, 2001), 46–55.

52065. Gammons, Peter. "Street Smarts." *Sports Illustrated,* LXX (April 1, 1989), 92–96.

52066. Johnson, Chuck. "Gary Sheffield: Growing into Major League Stardom." *Baseball Digest,* LX (March 2001), 56–59.

52067. Kitkowski, Dan "What's With Sheff? Is Gary Sheffield the Fantasy Player of the Future — Or Just Another Spoiled Talent?" *Fantasy Baseball,* II (March 1991), 86–88.

52068. Koenig, Bill. "Main Marlin." *USA Today Baseball Weekly,* (March 25, 1997), 10–12.

52069. Kurkjian, Tim. "A Blessing for the Padres." *Sports Illustrated,* LXXVI (April 27, 1992), 13–14.

52070. Martin, Bruce. "A Closer Look: Gary Sheffield." *Beckett Baseball Card Monthly,* IX, no. 91 (October 1992), 6–7.

52071. Olmsted, Frank J. "Gary Antonian Sheffield." In: Vol. Q-Z of David L. Porter, ed. *Biographical Dictionary of American Sports: Baseball.* Rev. and enlarged ed. Westport, CT: Greenwood Press, 2000. Pp. 1400–1401.

52072. Pearlman, Jeff. "Power of Love." *Sports Illustrated,* XCIII (August 14, 2000), 58–62.

52073. Poiley, Joel. "Brave New World." *Sports Illustrated for Kids,* XIV (June 2002), 37+.

52074. Reilly, Rick. "Can't Take Nothin' Off Nobody." *Sports Illustrated,* LXXVII (September 14, 1992), 54–56, 59–61.

52075. Rosenthal, Ken. "Gary Sheffield." In: his *Best of the Best, Baseball: 35 Major League Superstars.* Indianapolis, IN: Masters Press, 1998. Pp. 136–139.

52076. Schlossberg, Dan. "From Bum to Hero." *Topps Magazine,* (Fall 1992), 22–27.

52077. "Sheffield Tops List of 10 Highest-Paid Black Baseball Players for 1998 Season." *Jet,* XCV (December 14, 1998), 49–50.

52078. Stinson, Thomas. "Gary Sheffield: He Wants It All in Atlanta." *Baseball Digest,* XLI (July 2002), 56–61.

52079. "Too Good to Be True." In: Joe Hoppel, ed. *The Sporting News 1993 Baseball Yearbook.* St. Louis, MO: The Sporting News, 1993. Pp. 2–9.

52080. Topkin, Marc. "Gary Sheffield Sets His Sights on a Banner Year." *Baseball Digest,* LVI (June 1997), 66–67.

52081. Verducci, Tom. "Part of the Crowd." *Sports Illustrated,* LXXXIV (May 27, 1996), 68–70, 72.

52082. _____. "Swinging Away." *Sports Illustrated,* CI (October 11, 2004), 54–59.

52083. Zachotsky, Dan. "Gary Sheffield." In: his *Idols of the Spring: Baseball Interviews About Spring Training.* Jefferson, NC: McFarland & Co., Inc., 2001. Pp. 109–115.

52084. Zminda, Don. "Florida Marlins: What Kind of Career Will Sheffield Have?" In: STATS, Inc. *STATS 1996 Baseball Scoreboard.* Skokie, IL: STATS Publishing, 1996. Pp. 58–59.

Roland Frank ("Rollie") Sheldon

P. (B: Dec. 17, 1936, Putnam, CT). New York (AL),

1961–1962, 1964–1965; Kansas City (AL), 1965–1966; Boston (AL), 1966. Remarks: Had 38 wins, 36 defeats, and two "saves," in six years; earlier a star basketball player for the University of Connecticut.

52085. Forker, Dom. "Rollie Sheldon." In: his *Sweet Seasons: Recollections of the 55–64 New York Yankees.* Dallas, TX: Taylor Publishing Co., 1989. Pp. 161–165.

52086. McMillan, Ken. "Rollie Sheldon." In: his *Tales from the Yankee Dugout: A Collection of the Greatest Yankee Stories Ever Told.* Champaign, IL: Sports Publishing, Inc., 2001. Pp. 174–175.

Frank Victor ("Shelly") Shellenback
P-SCOUT. (B: Dec. 16, 1898, Joplin, MO-D: Aug. 17, 1969). Chicago (AL), 1918–1919. Remarks: Won 10 games and lost 15 in two big league seasons; career minor league pitcher who, in 20 years with the PCL, compiled a record of 295–178; noted spitball pitcher (spitter allowed in minors for some years after banned in majors) who managed Hollywood/San Diego (PCL), 1935–1938; pitching coach, St. Louis (AL), 1939, Boston (AL), 1940–1944, and Detroit (AL), 1946–1947; coach, New York (NL), 1948–1955; scout, New York (NL)/San Francisco (NL), 1956–1969.

52087. Dille, Russ. "300 Wins in the Minor Leagues: Frank Shellenback." *Sports Scoup,* II (June 1974), 10+.

52088. Smith, James D., 3rd. "Frank Victor 'Shelly' Shellenback." In: Vol. Q–Z of David L. Porter, ed. *Biographical Dictionary of American Sports: Baseball.* Rev. and enlarged ed. Westport, CT: Greenwood Press, 2000. Pp. 1401–1402.

52089. Spalding, John E. "Frank Shellenback." In: his *Pacific Coast League Stars: One Hundred of the Best, 1903–1957.* San Jose, CA: John E. Spalding, 1994. Pp. 53–54.

Shelly Shellenback *see* **Frank Victor ("Shelly") Shellenback**

Bert Robert Shepard
P. (B: June 28, 1920, Dana, IN). Washington (AL), 1945. Remarks: Minor league hurler whose fighter plane crashed in Germany during WWII; following leg amputation, was able to rehabilitate himself as pitcher with an artificial limb; became Senators pitching coach and threw five innings in one big league game, Aug. 4, 1945.

52090. Holway, John B. "Bert Shepard: The Man Who Pitched on One Leg." *Baseball Digest,* XLV (July 1986), 67–68.

52091. LoBello, Steven G. "Bert Shepard: Amputee War Hero and Major League Pitcher." *Nine: A Journal of Baseball History and Social Policy Perspectives,* II (Fall 1993), 29–39.

52092. McGuire, Mark and Michael Sean Gormley. "Bert Shepard." In: their *Moments in the Sun: Baseball's Briefly Famous.* Jefferson, NC: McFarland & Co., Inc., 2001. Pp. 7–13.

52093. Naiman, Joe. "Bert Shepard: One-Legged Baseball Player Also a War Hero." *The National Pastime,* XIX (1999), 75–76.

52094. Skipper, John C. "Bert Shepard: His One Appearance Remains a Remarkable Achievement." In: his *Inside Pitch: A Closer Look at Classic Baseball Moments.* Jefferson, NC: McFarland & Co., Inc., 1996. Pp. 148–152.

52095. Snelling, Dennis. "Bert Shepard, Pitcher, 1945 Washington Senators." In: his *A Glimpse of Fame: Brilliant But Fleeting Major League Careers.* Jefferson, NC: McFarland & Co., Inc., 1993. Pp. 115–135.

52096. Tellis, Richard. "Robert Earl 'Bert' Shepard, Washington Nationals, 1945." In: his *Once Around the Bases.* Chicago, IL: Triumph Books, 1998. Pp. 107–121.

Jack Leroy Shephard
C. (B: May 13, 1931, Clovis, CA-D: Dec. 31, 1994). Pittsburgh (NL), 1953–1956. Remarks: Obtained 195 hits (12 homers) in 278 games in four big league seasons; with three Stanford University degrees, turned to a business career after his short time in "the show."

52097. Nash, Ogden. "The Big Brain." *Life,* XXXIX (September 5, 1955), 90–91

Bob Sheppard
BROADCASTER Remarks: Public address announcer, New York (AL), 1951–2002; speech professor, St. John's University, 1979-; played himself in Billy Crystal's HBO motion picture *61*.*

52098. Grayson, Robert. "The Voice of Yankee Stadium." *Yankees Magazine,* XIX (January 1999), 62–67.

52099. Schefter, Art. "Q & A with Bob Sheppard." *Baseball Digest,* LXIII (November 2004), 54–56.

52100. "Yan-kee Ac-Cent." *The New Yorker,* LXIX (October 4, 1993), 69–70.

Bill Sherdel *see* **William Henry ("Bill" or "Wee Willie") Sherdel**

William Henry ("Bill" or "Wee Willie") Sherdel
P. (B, Aug. 15, 1896, McSherrytown, PA.-D: Nov. 14, 1968). St. Louis (NL), 1918–1930; Boston (NL), 1930–1932; St. Louis (NL), 1932. Remarks: Won 165 games and lost 146, with 26 "saves" and nine homers, in 15 years; noted for pitching a slow-ball and losing games in both the 1926 and 1928 World Series.

52101. Burnes, Robert L. "Bill Sherdel was Mr. 'Tough Luck." *Baseball Digest,* XII (January 1953), 95+.

52102. Olmsted, Frank J. "William Henry 'Wee Willie,' 'Sherry' Sherdel." In: Vol. Q–Z of David L. Porter, ed. *Biographical Dictionary of American Sports: Baseball.* Rev. and enlarged ed. Westport, CT: Greenwood Press, 2000. Pp. 1402–1404.

John F. ("Jack") Sheridan
UMP-SCOUT. (B: 1852, Decatur, IL-D: Nov. 2, 1914). NL umpire, 1892, 1896–1897 and AL arbiter, 1901–1914; awarded first forfeit in MLB history, May 31, 1901, Detroit (AL) to Baltimore (AL); retired due to sunstroke, becoming first MLB umpire scout, then chief AL umpire scout; the tutor of Hall of Fame umpire Billy Evans (q.v.).

52103. Gerlach, Larry R. "John F. Sheridan." In: Vol. Q–Z of David L. Porter, ed. *Biographical Dictionary of American Sports: Baseball.* Rev. and enlarged ed. Westport, CT: Greenwood Press, 2000. Pp. 1404–1405.

52104. Sheridan, John F. ("Jack"). *Baseball for Beginners.* New York: American Sports Publishing Co., 1920–1927. Includes basic rules, techniques, etc.; two further editions of this booklet were authored by John B. Foster and published by the same firm in 1930 and 1935.

52105. _____. "Umpiring in the Big Leagues." *Baseball Magazine,* I (May 1908), 9–12.

Neill Rawlins ("Wild Horse") Sheridan
OF. (B: Nov. 20, 1921, Sacramento, CA). San Francisco (PCL) and Chattanooga (SA), 1944; San Francisco (PCL), 1945–1947; Seattle (PCL) and Boston (AL), 1948; Seattle (PCL), 1949; San Francisco (PCL), 1950–1951; Minneapolis (AA), 1951; Toronto (IL) and San Antonio (TL), 1952; Oakland (PCL) and San Francisco (PCL), 1953; San Francisco (PCL), 1954. Remarks: In 11 minor league campaigns, obtained 1,424 hits and 118 homers in 1,446 games.

52106. Kelley, Brent P. "Neill Rawlins ('Wild Horse') Sheridan." In: his *The San Francisco Seals, 1946–1957: Interviews with 25 Former Baseballers.* Jefferson, NC: McFarland & Co., Inc., 2002. Pp. 67–74.

Larry Sherry *see* **Lawrence ("Larry") Sherry**

Lawrence ("Larry") Sherry
P. (B: July 25, 1935, Los Angeles, CA). Los Angeles (NL), 1958–1963; Detroit (AL), 1964–1967; Houston (NL), 1967; California (AL), 1968. Remarks: Had 53 victories, 44 defeats, and 82 "saves" in an 11-year career; minor league instructor; coach, California/Anaheim (AL), 1969–1981; won Games Four and Six of 1959 while saving Games Two and Three; World Series MVP award, 1959; brother and sometimes-battery-mate of Norman Sherry (below).

52107. Anderson, Dave. "The Dangers of Being a World Series Hero." *Sport,* XL (November 1965), 28–32.

52108. Cairns, Bob. "Larry Sherry." In: his *Pen Men: Baseball's Greatest Bullpen Stories told by the Men who Brought the Game Relief.* New York: St. Martin's Press, 1992. Pp. 199–211.

52109. Carroll, Bob. "Legitimizing the Fireman." *Oldtyme Baseball News,* II, no. 6 (1990), Pp. 1, 3.

52110. Falls, Joe. "Children's Hour: It's When Tiger Pitcher Take Private Batting Practice." *Baseball Digest,* XXIV (July 1965), 61–62.

52111. Gross, Milton. "The Dodgers' Precocious Pitcher." *Saturday Evening Post,* CCXXXII (March 12, 1960), 31+.

52112. Hano, Larry. "Larry Sherry: A Star is Born." In: Ray Robinson, ed. *Baseball Stars of 1960.* New York: Pyramid Books, 1960. pp. 11–18.

52113. Heiling, Joe. "Larry Sherry: Bullseye in the Bullpen." *Baseball Digest,* XXVI (December 1967), 34–35.

52114. Laughlin, Bob, with Budd Theobald. *Larry Sherry: King of the Dodger Bullpen.* Los Angeles, CA: Union Oil Company of California, 1961. 14p.

52115. _____. *Larry Sherry: World Series Hero.* Los Angeles, CA: Union Oil Company of California, 1960.13p.

52116. Ribalow, Harold W. and Meir. "Larry Sherry: Hero for a Season." In: their *Jewish Baseball Stars.* New York: Hippocrene Books, 1984. Pp. 172–180.

52117. Schlossberg, Dan. "How a Rookie Pitcher Rallied Dodgers to Title in '59." *Baseball Digest,* LII (November 1993), 42–43.

52118. Sherry, Lawrence. "Everybody Loves the Series Star." *Sport,* XXX (October 1960), 22–24.

52119. Simons, Herbert. "The Sherry Flip." *Baseball Digest,* XVIII (December 1959), 9–12.

52120. Slater, Robert. "Lawrence Sherry: The Pitcher Who Was Born with Two Club-Feet." In: his *Great Jews in Sports.* Middle Village, NY: Jonathan David Publishers, 1983. Pp. 205–206.

52121. Stainback, Berry. "Remember Larry Sherry." *Sport,* XXXVII (August 1964), 5–7.

52122. Terrell, Roy. "No Relief for Larry." *Sports Illustrated,* XII (March 28, 1960), 62–64.

52123. Waldmeir, Pete. "What Vintage is Sherry?" *Baseball Digest,* XXV (July 1966), 55–57.

Norman Burt ("Norm") Sherry
C-MGR. (B: July 16, 1931, New York City). Los Angeles (NL), 1959–1962; New York (NL), 1963. Remarks: Had 107 hits (18 homers) and one stolen base in 194 games in five big league seasons; manager, California (AL), 1976–1977, winning 76 games and losing 71 (.517); brother and sometimes-battery-mate of Larry Sherry (above).

52124. *Norm Sherry: Hard-Working Dodger Backstop.* Los Angeles: Union Oil Company of California, 1961. 14p.

52125. Shannon, Mike. "Norm Sherry." In: his *Tales from the Ballpark: More of the Greatest True Baseball Stories Ever Told.* Lincolnwood, Ill: Contemporary Books, 1999. Pp. 185–186.

52126. Wilber, Cynthia J. "Norm Sherry." In: her *For the Love of the Game: Baseball Memories from the Men Who Were There.* New York: William Morrow And Company, Inc., 1992. Pp. 168–176.

Benjamin Franklin ("Ben") Shibe
EXEC. (B: Jan. 23, 1838, Philadelphia, PA-D: Jan. 14, 1922.). Remarks: Inventor of cork-center baseball and partner of baseball equipment/publisher Alfred J. Reach; president, Philadelphia (AL), 1901–1922.

52127. Gietschier, Steven P. "Benjamin Franklin Shibe." In: John A. Garrity and Marsh C. Carries, eds. *American National Biography.* 24 vols. New York: Oxford University Press, 1999. XIX, 836.

52128. Lane, Ferdinand C. "Benjamin Shibe: Founder of the World Champions." *Baseball Magazine,* IX (May 1912), 7–9.

52129. Rossi, John P. "Benjamin Franklin 'Ben' Shibe." In: Vol. Q-Z of David L. Porter, ed. *Biographical Dictionary of American Sports: Baseball.* Rev. and enlarged ed. Westport, CT: Greenwood Press, 2000. P. 1405.

Billy Shindle *see* **William ("Billy") Shindle**
William ("Billy") Shindle
3B. (B: Dec. 5, 1860, Gloucester, NJ-D: June 3, 1936). Detroit (NL), 1886–1887; Baltimore (AA), 1888–1889; Philadelphia (P), 1890; Philadelphia (NL), 1891; Baltimore (NL), 1892–1893; Brooklyn (NL), 1894–1898. Remarks: Obtained 1,561 hits and 318 stolen bases in 1,442 games in 13 big league seasons; also played for Hartford (EL), 1899–1901, serving as player-manager, 1900–1901; elected to Gloucester Sports Hall of Fame, 1977.

52130. Phelps, Frank V. "William 'Billy' Shindle." In: Vol. Q-Z of David L. Porter, ed. *Biographical Dictionary of American Sports: Baseball.* Rev. and enlarged ed. Westport, CT: Greenwood Press, 2000. Pp. 1405–1406.

Craig Shipley
SS-2B. (B: Jan. 7, 1963, Parramatta, Australia). Los Angeles (NL), 1986–1987; New York (NL), 1989; San Diego (NL), 1991–1994; Houston (NL), 1995; San Diego (NL), 1996–1997; Anaheim (AL), 1998. Remarks: During 11 U.S. big league seasons, obtained 364 hits (20 homers) and 33 stolen bases in 582 games; first Australian baseball player signed to a modern era MLB contract; scout, San Diego (NL), 1999–2002; dir. player development, Boston (AL), 2003–.

52131. McDonald, John. "A Craig of All Trades." *Baseball Australia,* V (March 1993), 6–7.

52132. _____. "Signings of the Time." *Baseball Australia,* V (March 1993), 4–5.

Joseph Clark ("Joe" or "Moses") Shipley
P. (B: May 9, 1935, Morristown, TN). San Francisco (NL), 1959–1960; Chicago (AL), 1963. Remarks: Won no games and lost one of the 29 involved in during four big league years.

52133. Skardon, J.A. "Bus League: Road to the Big League." *Coronet,* XLII (May 1957), 44–53.

Charles Arthur ("Art" or "Art The Great") Shires
1B. (B: Aug. 13, 1907, Italy, TX-D: July 13, 1967). Chicago (AL), 1928–1930; Washington (AL), 1930; Boston (NL), 1932. Remarks: Had 287 hits (11 homers) and eight stolen bases in 290 games in four big league seasons; had four hits in first game, Aug. 20, 1928; short-lived boxing career ended by ruling of Commissioner Landis (q.v.), Jan. 20, 1930.

52134. Bulger, Bozeman. "The Diamond Drill." *Saturday Evening Post,* CCIV (March 26, 1932), 10–15. Spring training with Shire and John McGraw.

52135. Gold, Eddie. "Art Shires." *Oldtyme Baseball News,* VI, no. 6 (1995), 8–9.

52136. Lane, Ferdinand C. "Art Shires, Publicity Getter Extraordinary!" *Baseball Magazine,* XLVI (February 1931), 399–400.

52137. McGuire, Mark and Michael Sean Gormley. "Art Shires." In: their *Moments in the Sun: Baseball's Briefly Famous.* Jefferson, NC: McFarland & Co., Inc., 2001. Pp. 119–123.

Twila Shively

1B-OF. (B: March 22, 1922, Decatur, IL-D: Nov. 30, 1999). Grand Rapids Chicks (All-American Girls Professional Baseball League), 1945–1947; Chicago Colleens (AAGPBL), 1948; Peoria Redwings (AAGPBL), 1949–1950. Remarks: Obtained 429 hits (two homers) and 255 stolen bases in 614 games in six years; had one grand slam homer, 1950; career shortened by ankle injury; served as teacher in South Bend, IN, for 30 years; elected to Chicago Baseball Hall of Fame.

52138. Crawford, Scott A. G. M. "Twila Shively." In: Vol. Q-Z of David L. Porter, ed. *Biographical Dictionary of American Sports: Baseball.* Rev. and enlarged ed. Westport, CT: Greenwood Press, 2000. Pp. 1406–1407.

Leo C. ("Muscle") Shoals

1B. (B: Parkersburg, WV, 1916-D: Feb. 1999) Johnson City (Appalachian League), 1937–1939; Kingsport (Appalachian League), 1946–1948; Reidsville (Carolina League), 1949; Columbia (South Atlantic League) and Reidsville (Carolina League), 1950; Kingsport (Appalachian League), 1951–1955. Remarks: Career minor leaguer who obtained a .337 batting average, 362 home runs, and 1,529 RBIs (the homer record still stands in the Appy League); shot and seriously wounded in a dispute with a Johnson City bartender, 1939; powerful home run hitter who slugged a Carolina League record 55 "taters" while playing for the Reidsville Luckies in 1949; won Appalachian League triple crown (the first in that league's history), 1951; later served as volunteer baseball coach at Patrick Henry High School in Emory, VA.

52139. Hufford, Tom. "Leo 'Muscle' Shoals." *The Baseball Research Journal,* II (1974), 83–87. A press release from the Appalachian League detailing Shoals' life has been posted on the league website, http://www.appyleague.com/releases/022802c.html>.

52140. Shoals, Leo ("Muscle"), with George Stone. *Muscle: A Minor League Legend.* Haverford, PA: Infinity Books, 2003. 335p.

Urban James Shocker

P. (B: Urbain Jacques Shockcor, Aug. 22, 1890, Cleveland, OH-D: Sept. 9, 1928). New York (AL), 1916–1917; St. Louis (AL), 1918–1924; New York (AL), 1925–1928. Remarks, Had 188 victories, 117 defeats, and 25 "saves" in 13 campaigns; had nine game winning streak, 1921; one of last legal spitball pitchers, who won two games in one day, Sept. 6, 1924; lost Game Two of 1926 World Series; died of heart disease.

52141. Lane, Ferdinand C. "Urban Shocker, One of the Greatest Pitchers of 1920." *Baseball Magazine,* XXVI (January 1921), 381–382+.

52142. Steinberg, Steve L. "Back Where I Belong." *Nine: A Journal of Baseball History and Culture,* XI (Spring 2003), 162–168.

52143. _____. "Free Agency in 1923?" *The National Pastime, XIX* (2000), Pp. 121–123.

52144. Suehsdorf, Adie D. "Urban James Shocker." In: Vol. Q-Z of David L. Porter, ed. *Biographical Dictionary of American Sports: Baseball.* Rev. and enlarged ed. Westport, CT: Greenwood Press, 2000. Pp. 1407–1409.

Fern ("Shelly") Shollenberger

OF-3B. (B: May 18, 1923, Harrisburg, PA-June 12, 1977).

Kenosha Giants (All-American Girls Professional Baseball League), 1946–1951; Kalamazoo Lassies (AAGPBL), 1952–1954. Remarks: In nine years, obtained 725 hits (10 homers) and 167 stolen bases; killed with her father in automobile accident.

52145. Crawford, Scott A. G. M. "Fern 'Shelly' Shollenberger." In: Vol. Q-Z of David L. Porter, ed. *Biographical Dictionary of American Sports: Baseball.* Rev. and enlarged ed. Westport, CT: Greenwood Press, 2000. P. 1409.

Shelly Shollenberger *see* **Fern ("Shelly") Shollenberger**

Ernest Grady ("Ernie") Shore

P. (B: March 24, 1891, East Bend, N.C.-D: Sept. 24, 1980). New York (NL), 1912; Boston (AL), 1914–1917; New York (AL), 1919–1920. Remarks: Won 63 games and lost 42 in seven big league years; relieved George Herman ("Babe") Ruth (q.v.) in game of June 23, 1917 and went on to retire 26 men in a row after man on first put out in a failed steal, elected Sheriff of Forsyth County, NC and served from 1921–1954.

52146. Goldberg, Hy. "Sent in to Pitch inning, He Pitches Perfect Game." *Baseball Digest,* XXII (June 1963), 79–83.

52147. Honig, Donald. "Ernie Shore." In: his *The October Heroes.* New York: Simon and Schuster, 1979. Pp. 17–34.

52148. Lane, Ferdinand C. "Inside Dope from a Player's Hands." *Baseball Magazine,* XXI (July 1918), 270–278.

52149. Mayer, Ronald A. "Ernie Shore." In: his *Perfect: Biographies and Lifetime Statistics of 14 Pitchers of "Perfect" Baseball Games, With Summaries and Boxscores.* Jefferson, N.C.: McFarland & Co., Inc., 1991. Pp. 67–79.

52150. Seaver, Tom, with Marty Appel. "The Ultimate Relief Stint." In: his *Great Moments in Baseball: From the World Series of 1903 to the Modern Records of Nolan Ryan.* New York: Carol Communications, 1992. Pp. 47–51.

52151. Shore, Ernest. "A Pitcher's Day Dreams." *Baseball Magazine,* XIX (September 1917), 497–498. Fastballs.

52152. Stone, Christian. "No Hits, But No History." *Sports Illustrated,* LXXVII (October 5, 1992), 8–9.

Billy Short *see* **William Ross ("Billy") Short**

Christopher Joseph ("Chris") Short

P. (B: Sept. 19, 1937, Milford, DE-D: Aug. 1, 1991). Philadelphia (NL), 1959–1972; Milwaukee (AL), 1973. Remarks: Had 135 victories, 132 defeats, and 18 "saves" in a 15-year major league career; had 18 strikeouts in 15-inning called game, Oct. 2, 1965.

52153. Forbes, Gordon. "Chris Short Between Two Worlds." *Sport,* XLI (June 1966), 36–39.

52154. _____. "The Dodgers Aren't Champs to Chris Short." *Baseball Digest,* XXV (February 1966), 67–72.

52155. Hochman, Stan. "Chris Short, Philatelist on the Mound." *Baseball Digest,* XXII (December 1963), 93–95.

52156. _____. "Chris Short: The Farm Boy Grows Up." *Baseball Digest,* XXVII (June 1968), 32–35.

52157. Kelly, Ray. "Chris Short: King of the Broken Bats." *Baseball Digest,* XXIV (May 1965), 59–61.

Robert Earl Short

EXEC. (B: July 20, 1917, Minneapolis, Minn.-D: Nov. 20, 1982). Remarks: Owner, Washington (AL)/Texas (AL), January 1969 through May 1974.

52158. Fimrite, Ron. "A Bad Case of the Short Shorts." *Sports Illustrated,* XXXV (August 9, l971), 20–22+.

William Ross ("Billy") Short

P. (B: Nov. 27, 1937, Kingston, NY). New York (A.L), 1960; Baltimore (AL), 1962 and 1966; Boston (AL), 1966; Pittsburgh (NL), 1967; New York (NL), 1968; Cincinnati

(NL), 1969. Remarks: Won five games and lost 11, with two "saves," for six teams in six years.

52159. Dexter, Charles. "Billy Short: In the Manner of Lopat and. Ford." *Baseball Digest,* XIX (July 1960), 5–10.

Burton Edwin ("Burt" or "Barney") Shotton

OF-MGR. (B. Oct. 18, 1884, Brownhelm, OH-D: July 29, 1962). St Louis (AL), 1909, 1911–1917; Washington (AL), 1918; St. Louis (NL), 1919–1924. Remarks: In 14 playing years, had 1,338 hits (nine homers) and 294 stolen bases in 1,388 games; manager (in street clothes), Philadelphia (NL), 1928–1933, Cincinnati (NL), 1934, and Brooklyn (NL), 1947–1950, winning 697 games and losing 764 (.477).

52160. Gough, David. *Burt Shotton, Dodgers Manager: A Baseball Biography.* Jefferson, NC: McFarland & Co., Inc., 1994. 141p.

52161. _____. "A Tribute to Burt Shotton: One of Baseball's Unique Heroes." *The National Pastime,* XIV (1994), 99–101.

52162. Goven, Herb. "Burt Shotton: Felt-Hatted Pilot." *Baseball Digest,* VI (July, 1947), 3–5.

52163. McGowen, Roscoe. "Boss of the Bums, but Not a Bum Boss." *Baseball Magazine,* LXXIX (August 1947), 307–309.

52164. Shotton, Burt. "The Art of Working the Pitcher." *Baseball Magazine,* XXII (December 1918), 93–96.

52165. Young, Dick. "Inside Burt Shotton." *Baseball Digest,* IX (November 1950), 45–47.

Eric Vaughn Show

P. (B. May 19, 1956, Riverside, CA-D: March 16, 1994). San Diego (NL), 1981–1990; Oakland (AL), 1991. Remarks: Won 101 games and lost 89, with seven "saves," in 11 seasons; surrendered record-setting 4,192nd hit of Pete Rose (q.v.), Sept. 11, 1985; highly regarded amateur musician who owned a San Diego record store and whose death was connected to substance abuse.

52166. Jordan, Pat. "The Last Inning." *Los Angeles,* XL (June 1993), 88–96+.

52167. Lidz, Franz. "All's Right with His World." *Sports Illustrated,* LXI (August 6, 1984), 76+.

52168. "A Troubled Soul." *Sports Illustrated,* LXXX (March 28, 1994), 9–10.

52169. Show, Eric. "Interview." *Sport,* LXXV (October 1984), 23–33.

Buck Showalter *see* **William Nathaniel ("Buck") Showalter**

William Nathaniel ("Buck") Showalter

MGR-BROADCASTER. (B: May 23, 1956, DeFuniack Springs, FL). Remarks: Manager, New York (AL), 1992–1995 and Arizona (NL), 1996–2000, analyst, ESPN, 2001–2002; manager, Texas (AL), 2003-; through 2004, has won 723 games and lost 668 (.520); earlier, had served as manager, Fort Lauderdale (SL), 1983, 1987–1988; Oneonta (New York-Penn League), 1985–1986 and Albany (IL), 1989; coach, New York (AL), 1990–1991.

52170. Cannella, Stephen. "D-Backsliding: If Arizona Misses the Playoffs, Showalter Could Be Shown the Door." *Sports Illustrated,* XCIII (September 25, 2000), 104–105.

52171. Nolan, Timothy. "Another Day, Another Buck." *Coach & Athletic Director,* LXV (March 1996), 50–56.

52172. Pierce, Charles. "Southern Yankee: Buck Showalter." *The New York Times Magazine,* (July 10, 1994), 24–27.

52173. Price, Ed. "'Bucking' the Odds: Showalter's Bases-Full IBB." In: Mike Holden, ed. *Mining Towns to Major Leagues: A History of Arizona Baseball.* Cleveland,

OH: The Society for American Baseball Research, 1999. Pp. 62–63. Intentional Walk to Barry Bonds on May 28, 1997.

52174. Slimak, Kelly. "Bank One Signs New TV Pitchman." *Bank Advertising News,* XXI (March 23, 1998), 4–5.

52175. Verducci, Tom. "Bucking Up the Yanks." *Sports Illustrated,* LXXX (May 16, 1994), 48–50+.

52176. _____. "One Lucky Buck." *Sports Illustrated,* LXXXV (July 1, 1996), 50–54.

George Thomas ("Shotgun") Shuba

OF. (B: Dec. 13, 1924, Youngstown, OH). Brooklyn (NL), 1948–1955. Remarks: In seven big league seasons, obtained 211 hits (24 homers) and five stolen bases in 814 games; had pinch-hit homer in Game One of 1953 World Series.

52177. Kahn, Roger. "The Bishop's Brother." In: Charles Einstein, ed. *The Fourth Fireside Book of Baseball.* New York: Simon and Schuster, 1987. Pp. 191–197.

Norman Leroy ("Norm") Siebern

1B-OF. (B: July 26, 1933, St. Louis, MO). New York (A.L), 1956–1959; Kansas City (AL), 1960–1963; Baltimore (AL), 1964–1965; California (AL), 1966; San Francisco (NL), 1967, Boston (AL), 1967–1968. Remarks: Obtained 1,217 hits (132 homers) and 18 stolen bases in 1,408 games in a dozen years; had two five-hit games in one month, July 1958; had two errors in Game Four of the 1958 World Series; served as scouting supervisor for the Kansas City (AL) club in the 1970s and has also been a scout for Atlanta (NL).

52178. Dexter, Charles. "Norm Siebern: The Yankees' 'Kustom-Kut' Kid." *Baseball Digest,* XVII (October 1958), 75–81.

52179. Forker, Dom. "Norm Siebern." In: his *Sweet Seasons: Recollections of the 55–64 New York Yankees.* Dallas, TX: Taylor Publishing Co., 1989. Pp. 57–60.

52180. McCormick, Robert. "Norm Siebern." In: Jack Orr, ed. *Baseball's Greatest Players Today.* New York: Watts, 1963. Pp.105–112.

52181. Robinson, Ray. "Norm Siebern: Refugee from Left Field ." In: Ray Robinson, ed. *Baseball Stars of 1963.* New York: Pyramid Books, 1963. Pp. 133–137.

52182. Sendier, Dave. "Norm Siebern: Inconspicuous and Indispensable." *Sport,* XXXVIII (October 1964), 68–71.

52183. Terrell, Roy. "Somebody's Gotta Play Left." *Sports Illustrated,* XII (May 16, 1960), 70–73.

52184. Weir, Robert B. "Norman Leroy 'Norm' Siebern." In: Vol. Q-Z of David L. Porter, ed. *Biographical Dictionary of American Sports: Baseball.* Rev. and enlarged ed. Westport, CT: Greenwood Press, 2000. Pp. 1409–1411.

Dick Siebert *see* **Richard Walter ("Dick" or "The Chief") Siebert**

Richard Walter ("Dick" or "The Chief") Siebert

1B-BROADCASTER-COACH. (B: Feb. 19, 1912, Fall River, MA-D: Nov. 9, 1978). Brooklyn (NL), 1932–1936; St. Louis (NL), 1937–1939; Philadelphia (AL), 1938–1945. Remarks. Had 1,104 hits (32 homers) and 30 stolen bases in 1,055 games in 11 seasons; broadcaster, WTCN Radio, 1946; University of Minnesota baseball coach, 1948–1978, winning three NCAA national baseball titles (1956, 1960, 1964); Golden Gophers baseball field named in his honor.

52185. Bloodgood, Clifford. "How Siebert Serves." *Baseball Magazine,* LXVII (July 1941), 353–354.

52186. Carlson, Stan W. "Richard Walter 'Dick,' 'The Chief' Siebert." In: Vol. Q-Z of David L. Porter, ed. *Biographical Dictionary of American Sports: Baseball.* Rev. and enlarged ed. Westport, CT: Greenwood Press, 2000. Pp. 1411–1412.

52187. Kohler, Michael. "College Baseball: America's Greatest College Baseball Coach." In: his *America's Greatest Coaches.* Champaign, IL: Leisure Press, 1990. Pp. 12–19. Includes Siebert.

52188. Milne, Robert C. "The First Baseman of the A's." *Baseball Magazine,* LX (March 1938), 464–465+.

52189. Shama, Dave. "Dick Siebert." *University of Minnesota Alumni News,* LXX (March 1971), 23–25; LXXI (May 1972), 19–20.

52190. Siebert, Dick. *Learning How ... Baseball.* Mankato, Minn.: Creative Educational Society, 1961. 240 p. Instructional covers pitching, catching, batting, bunting, fielding, throwing, baserunning, etc.

52191. _____. and Otto Vogel. *Baseball.* New York: Sterling, 1965. 158p. Rev. and enl. edition of *How to Improve Your Baseball,* below; a 160-page edition published by the same firm in 1960.

52192. _____. and Otto Vogel. *How to Improve Your Baseball.* Chicago, IL: Athletic Institute, 1952. 94p. Brings together a series of seven pamphlets on hitting, fielding, pitching, etc. published by the Athletic Institute in 1948.

Sonny Siebert *see* **Wilfred Charles ("Sonny") Siebert**

Wilfred Charles ("Sonny") Siebert, 3rd

P. (B: Jan. 14, 1937, St. Mary's, MO). Cleveland (AL), 1964–1969; Boston (AL), 1969–1973; Texas (AL), 1973; St. Louis (NL), 1974; San Diego (NL), and Oakland (AL), 1975. Remarks: Had 140 victories, 114 defeats, and 16 "saves" in a dozen campaigns, along with 12 homers; pitched no-hitter, June 10, 1966; minor league coach, San Diego (NL), 1984–1993; pitching coach, San Diego (NL), 1994–1995, and Colorado (NL), 1996–2000.

52193. Herron, Gary. "Sonny Seibert Was Almost a Two-Sport Player." *Sport Collector's Digest,* XXIV (July 18, 1997), 132–133. Drafted by St. Louis Hawks (NBA).

52194. Olmsted, Frank J. "Wilfred Charles 'Sonny' Siebert, 3rd." In: Vol. Q-Z of David L. Porter, ed. *Biographical Dictionary of American Sports: Baseball.* Rev. and enlarged ed. Westport, CT: Greenwood Press, 2000. Pp. 1412–1414.

52195. Russo, Neal. "Sonny Siebert: Dad's Frown Kept Him from Mound Until He Was 23." *Baseball Digest,* XXIV (October 1965), 47–51.

52196. Shannon, Mike. "Sonny Siebert." In: his *Tales from the Ballpark: More of the Greatest True Baseball Stories Ever Told.* Lincolnwood, IL: Contemporary Books, 1999. Pp. 188–191.

52197. Siebert, Wilfred C. ("Sonny"). "Pitching — Little Things Count." *Athletic Journal,* LXIV (November 1983), 30–31, 53–54.

52198. Spiritosanto, Rick. "Sonny Siebert Recalls When He Put an End to Marathon Game." *Baseball Digest,* XLVI (February 1987), 31–32.

52199. Sudyk, Bob. "Sonny Siebert's Fight to Stop the Clock." *Sport,* XUV (July 1967), 26–29.

Ruben Angel ("Garcia") Sierra

OF. (B: Oct. 6, 1965, Rio Piedras, PR). Texas (AL), 1986–1992; Oakland (AL), 1992–1995; New York (AL), 1995–1996; Detroit (AL), 1996; Toronto (AL) and Cincinnati (NL), 1997; Chicago (AL), 1998; Texas (AL), 2000–2001; Seattle (AL), 2002; Texas (AL) and New York (AL), 2003; New York (AL), 2004-. Remarks: Through 2004, has obtained 2,108 hits (302 homers) and 142 stolen bases in 2,111 games; AL RBI champion, 1989; led AL in triples, 1989; traded three times in one year, 1996; had seven hits in 2004 ALCS.

52200. Barthel, Thomas H. "Ruben Angel (Garcia) Sierra." In: Vol. Q-Z of David L. Porter, ed. *Biographical Dictionary of American Sports: Baseball.* Rev. and enlarged ed. Westport, CT: Greenwood Press, 2000. Pp. 1414–1415.

52201. Castleberry, Bruce. "A Closer Look: Ruben Sierra." *Beckett Baseball Card Monthly,* VII (January 1990), 6–7.

52202. DeMarco, Tony. "A Second Look: Ruben Sierra." *Beckett Baseball Card Monthly,* IX, no. 87 (June 1992), 105–106.

52203. Jamail, Milton. "Who is Ruben Sierra?" *Hispanic,* (April 1990), 26–28.

52204. Moore, Sherrie. "Ruben Sierra: Is He Another Clemente in the Making?" *Baseball Digest,* XLIX (February 1990), 28–30.

52205. Murphy, Austin. "Rising to the Top of the Game." *Sports Illustrated,* LXXII (April 16, 1990), 60–63.

52206. "The Next Clemente?" In: Tom Barnidge, ed. *The Sporting News 1990 Baseball Yearbook.* St. Louis, MO: The Sporting News, 1990. Pp. 24–33.

52207. Ringolsby, Tracy. "Best Years are Ahead for Rangers' Ruben Sierra." *Baseball Digest,* XLVI (December 1987), 42–46.

52208. Verducci, Tom. "Hi, Sierra." *Sports Illustrated,* XCVI (May 6, 2002), 58–62.

52209. Weinberg, Rick. "Texas Terror." *Sport,* LXXXIII (May 1992), 38–40.

Roy Edward ("Squirrel") Sievers

1B-OF. (B: Nov. 18, 1926, St. Louis, MO). St. Louis (A.L), 1949–1953; Washington (AL), 1954–1959; Chicago (AL), 1960–1961; Philadelphia (NL), 1962–1964; Washington (AL), 1964–1965. Remarks: Obtained 1,703 hits (318 homers) and 14 stolen bases in 1,887 games in 17 seasons; AL Rookie of the Year award, 1949; homered in six consecutive games, July-Aug., 1957; AL home run champion, 1957; one of only two players to pinch hit grand slam homers in both AL and NL; AL RBI champion, 1957; had 21 game hitting streak, 1960; coach, Cincinnati (NL), 1966; manager, Williamsport (EL), 1967, Memphis (SL), 1968, and Burlington (Midwest League), 1969–1970.

52210. Addie, Bob. "Roy Sievers: From Junk Heap to Homer King." *Baseball Digest,* XVI (December 1957), 63–66.

52211. _____. "Steady Is the Word for Sievers." *Sport,* XXIV (August 1957), 34–35+.

52212. "The Big Brown Squirrel." *Baseball Digest,* IX (May 1950), 69–73.

52213. Borst, William A. ("Bill"). "Roy Edward 'Squirrel' Sievers." In: Vol. Q-Z of David L. Porter, ed. *Biographical Dictionary of American Sports: Baseball.* Rev. and enlarged ed. Westport, CT: Greenwood Press, 2000. Pp. 1415–1416.

52214. Boswell, Thomas. "My Hero." In: his *Game Day: Sports Writings 1970–1990.* New York: Penguin Books, 1990. Pp. 337–340.

52215. _____. "Roy Sievers." In: Danny Peary, ed. *Cult Baseball Players.* New York: Simon and Schuster, 1990. Pp. 53–57.

52216. _____. "Roy Sievers." In: Danny Peary, ed. *Baseball's Finest: The Greats, the Flakes, the Weird and the Wonderful.* North Digton, MA: The JG Press, 1990. Pp. 53–57. Both Peary books are identical.

52217. Brosnan, Jim. "Roy Sievers." In: his *Great Rookies of the Major Leagues.* New York: Random House, 1966. Pp. 41–51.

52218. Burick, Si. "Bad Deals for the Good Sievers." *Baseball Digest,* XXV (June 1966), 85–87.

52219. Cohn, Howard. "Pearson and Sievers. "In: Ray Robinson, ed. *Baseball Stars of 1959*. New York: Pyramid Books, 1959. Pp. 125–130.

52220. _____. "Roy Seivers." In: Ray Robinson, ed. *Baseball Stars of 1958*. New York: Lion Books, 1958. Pp. 102–109.

52221. Hawkins, Burton. "Roy Sievers: He Proves He's First Division Guy." *Baseball Digest*, XIX (November-December 1960), 13–18.

52222. Heiman, Lee. "Roy Sievers." In: his *When the Cheering Stops*. New York: Macmillan, 1990. pp. 186–198.

52223. Gillespie, Ray. "Roy Sievers." In: his *My Greatest Baseball Game*. New York: A.S. Barnes and Co., 1950. Pp. 175–161.

52224. Heiman, Lee, Dave Weiner And Bill Gutman. "Roy Sievers." In: their *When The Cheering Stops*. New York: Macmillan Publishing Co., 1990. Pp. 186–198.

52225. Honig, Donald. "1949: Roy Sievers." In: his *American League Rookies of the Year*. New York: Bantam Books, 1989. Pp. 3–4.

52226. Macht, Norman L. "Roy Sievers: A Forgotten Power Hitter of the 1950s." *Baseball Digest*, XLIX (July 1990), 56–58.

52227. Merchant, Larry. "Roy Sievers' Mission: Long a Leading Slugger in the American League, Roy Is Being Counted on to Keep It Up with the Philadelphia Phillies. Around His New Ballclub, He Is Regarded as the Possible Salvation of the Phillies. But There Are Lots of Problems." *Sport*, XXXIII (June 1962), 56–60.

52228. Moffi, Larry. "Roy Sievers: 'You Can't Describe It to the Average Person.'" In: his *This Side of Cooperstown*. Iowa City, IA: University of Iowa Press, 1996. Pp. 168–179.

52229. Povich, Shirley. "The Littlest Big Leaguer." *Saturday Evening Post*, CCXXXI (May 16, 1959), 34–36.

52230. _____. "Roy Sievers: Outfielder with a Caddy." *Baseball Digest*, XIII (June 1954), 63–65.

52231. Sievers, Roy as told to Robert Creamer. "Roy Sievers on the Art of Hitting." *Sports Illustrated*, VIII (March 31, 1958), 35–43.

52232. Stann, Francis "Is the Party Over for Sievers?" *Baseball Digest*, XXI (March 1962), 59–61.

52233. Stern, Chris. "Roy Sievers." In: his *Where Have They Gone?* New York: Tempo Books, 1979. Pp. 46–48.

52234. Vanderberg, Bob. "Roy Sievers: The Man Bill Veeck Had to Have." In: his *Sox — From Lane and Fain to Zisk and Fisk* .Chicago, IL: Chicago Review Press, 1982. Pp. 225–232.

52235. Westcott, Rich. "Roy Sievers: From Top Rookie to Top Home Run Hitter." In: his *Splendor on the Diamond: Interviews with 35 Stars of Baseball's Past*. Gainesville, FL: The University Press of Florida, 2000. Pp. 300–308.

Charles ("Charlie" or "Swede") Silvera
C. (B: Oct. 13, 1924, San Francisco, CA). New York (AL), 1948–1956; Chicago (NL), 1957. Remarks: Obtained 136 hits (one homer) and two stolen bases in 227 games in 10 years; third-string Yankee catcher during the late glory years.

52236. Fehler, Gene. "Charlie Silvera." In: his *Tales from Baseball's Golden Age*. Champaign, IL: Sports Publishing Co., 2000. Chpt. 45.

52237. Forker, Dom. "Charlie Silvera." In: his *The Men of Autumn*. Dallas: Taylor Publishing Co., 1989. Pp. 144–150.

Aloysius Harry ("Al" or "Bucketfoot Al") Simmons★
OF. (B: May 22, 1902, Milwaukee, WI-D: May 26,

1956). Philadelphia (A.L), 1924–1932; Chicago (A.L), 1933–1935; Detroit (AL), 1936; Washington (AL), 1937–1938; Boston, (NL) and Cincinnati (K.L.), 1939; Philadelphia (AL), 1940–1941; Boston (AL), 1943; Philadelphia (AL), 1944. Remarks: In two decades, obtained 2,927 hits (307 homers) and 87 stolen bases in 2,215 games; AL MVP award, 1920; had four grand slam homers, May 12, 1925, June 15, 1927, May 30, 1930, and June 11, 1935; had key homer in Game Four of 1929 World Series and another in Game One of the 1930 World Series; AL batting champion, 1930–1931; AL RBI champion, 1929; during big league career, had five homers on the date of his birth; coach, Philadelphia (AL), 1940–1942, 1945–1949 and Cleveland (AL), 1950; died of a heart attack while walking down a Milwaukee street; elected to National Baseball Hall of Fame in 1953, where his plaque reads: "Played with 7 major league clubs 1924–1944, Star with Phila. (AL). Batted .308 to .392 from 1924 to 1934. Leading batter .381 in 1930, .300 In 1931. Most hits by AL right-handed batter with 2831. Led league runs batted in, runs scored, hits and total bases several seasons. Hit 3 home runs, July 15, 1932. Lifetime batting average .334."

52238. Allen, Lee, and Thomas Meany. "Al Simmons." In: their *Kings of the Diamond* New York: G.P. Putnam, 1965. Pp. 170–171.

52239. Allen, Maury. "Al Simmons (1924–1944)." In: his *Baseball's 100*. New York: Galahad Books, 1981. Pp. 122–124.

52240. Bloodgood, Clifford. "Al Simmons' Amazing Career." *Baseball Magazine*, LXXIII (August 1944), 313–315+.

52241. Broeg, Bob. "Al Simmons." In: his *Super Stars of Baseball*. St. Louis, MO: The Sporting News, 1971. Pp. 217–224.

52242. Daley, Arthur. "King Aloysius: Al Simmons." In: his *Kings of the Home Run*. New York: G.P. Putnam, 1962. Pp. 197–203.

52243. Doyle, Ed ("Dutch"). *Al Simmons, The Best: A Fan Looks at Al the Milwaukee Pole*. Chicago, IL: Adams Press, 1979. 76p.

52244. Duncan, C. William. "Al Simmons — the Best Hitter the Athletics Ever Had." *Baseball Magazine*, XXXIX (September 1927), 453–455.

52245. Honig, Donald. "Al Simmons." In: his *Baseball America*. New York: Macmillan, 1985. pp. 173–174.

52246. Karnes, Thomas L. "Aloysius Harry 'Al,' 'Bucketfoot Al' Simmons." In: Vol. Q-Z of David L. Porter, ed. *Biographical Dictionary of American Sports: Baseball*. Rev. and enlarged ed. Westport, CT: Greenwood Press, 2000. Pp. 1416–1418.

52247. Lake, Austin. "Al Simmons: A Boy Who Scaled the Batting Heights." In: his *Famous American Athletes of Today*. 3rd Series. Boston, MA: L.C. Page, 1932. Pp. 199–225.

52248. Lane, Ferdinand C. "Al Simmons Goes to Chicago." *Baseball Magazine*, L (March 1933), 453–454.

52249. _____. "The Batting Champion of 1930." *Baseball Magazine*, XLVI (May 1931), 537–539.

52250. _____. "The Batting Champion of 1931." *Baseball Magazine*, XLVIII (May 1932), 543–544.

52251. _____. "The Greatest Player in the American League." *Baseball Magazine*, XLIV (April 1930), 483–486.

52252. _____. "The Hardest Batter to Pitch To." *Baseball Magazine*, XLVIII (May 1932), 547–549.

52253. _____. "The Sensational Simmons." *Baseball Magazine*, XLIII (November 1929), 553–554+.

52254. _____. "Simmons: A Candidate for Babe Ruth's

Crown." *Baseball Magazine,* LII (February 1934), 391–393.

52255. _____. "Simmons, the Superstar." *Baseball Magazine,* XLVI (December 1930), 299–301+.

52256. _____. "The Strong-Arm Slugger of the Fighting Athletics." *Baseball Magazine,* XLIII (September 1929), 435–496.

52257. _____. "The Veteran Mainstay of the White Box." *Baseball Magazine,* LV (September 1935), 449–451.

52258. _____. "Will He Prove a Second Tris Speaker?" *Baseball Magazine,* XXXVI (January 1926), 351–353.

52259. Levy, Sam. "Simmons' First Stop to Hall [of Fame]." *Baseball Digest,* II (April 1943), 25–29.

52260. McKinney, Gordon B. "Aloysius Harry Simmons (Szymanski)." In: Supplement 6 of John A. Gerrity, ed. *Dictionary of American Biography.* New York: Scribner's, 1980. Pp. 581–582.

52261. McLinn, Stoney. "Smiling Al Put Florida on the Baseball Map." *Baseball Magazine,* XXXVI (May 1926), 555–556.

52262. Meany, Thomas. "One Foot Free—Aloysius Harry Simmons." In: his *Baseball's Greatest Hitters.* New York: A.S. Barnes, 1960. Pp. 165–174.

52263. Phelps, Frank V. "Al Simmons." In: John A. Garrity and Marsh C. Carries, eds. *American National Biography.* 24 vols. New York: Oxford University Press, 1999. XIX, 944–945.

52264. Povich, Shirley. "Simmons Is Hall Worthy." *Baseball Digest,* XI (March 1952), 35–37.

52265. Reidenbaugh, Lowell. "Al Simmons." In: his *Cooperstown: Where Legends Live Forever.* St. Louis, MO: *The Sporting News,* 1983. Pp. 231–232.

52266. Salant, Nathan. "Al Simmons." In: his *Superstars, Stars, And Just Plain Heroes.* New York: Stein And Day, 1982. Pp. 57–63.

52267. Salsinger, H.G. "Nine Times Up—and a Title at Stake." In: Mitchell V. Charnley, ed. *Play the Game: The Book of Sports.* New York: Viking, 1931. Pp. 70–84. Simmons vs. Harry Heilmann for 1929 AL batting crown.

52268. Shoemaker, Robert H. "Bucket Foot Al." In: his *Best in Baseball.* New York: Crowell, 1966. pp. 1–24.

52269. Simmons, Al. "Climbing the Baseball Ladder." *Country Gentleman,* XCI (May 1926), 38–39.

52270. _____. "He [Simmons] Lost the Decision in the Last Round." *Baseball Magazine,* XL (March 1924), 435–437.

52271. _____. "Hints on Hitting." *Baseball Magazine,* LXI (September 1938), 466–467.

52272. _____. "Tips from a Master." *Baseball Magazine,* LXII (January 1939), 366–367.

52273. _____. "Will Simmons Keep the Terrific Pace He Has Set?" *Baseball Magazine,* XXXVII (October 1926), 500–501.

52274. _____. with John P. Carmichael, ed. "My Clutch 'n' Crutch Homer." *Baseball Digest,* V (February 1946), 34–37. Reprinted in *Baseball Digest,* XV (August 1956), 34–37.

52275. _____. "My Greatest Day in Baseball: Philadelphia Athletics 7, 8, Washington Senators 6, 7." In: John P. Carmichael, ed. My Greatest Day in Baseball. New York: A. S. Barnes, 1945. Pp. 69–72. First published in the *Chicago Daily News* and later reprinted in Charles Einstein, ed, *The Second Fireside Book of Baseball* (New York: Simon and Schuster, 1968), pp, 333–334. 1930 pennant chase.

52276. Smith, Ira L. "Al Simmons." In: his *Baseball's Famous Outfielders.* New York: A.S. Barnes, 1954. Pp. 189–194.

52277. Smith, Ron. "Al Simmons 43." In: his *The Sporting News Selects Baseball's Greatest Top 100 Players.* St. Louis, MO: The Sporting News, 1998. Pp. 96–97.

52278. Smith, Walter ("Red"). "The Duke of Milwaukee." In: his *To Absent Friends.* New York: New American Library, 1986. Pp. 471–473. Reprinted from the *New York Herald-Tribune,* May 28, 1956; also published in Charles Einstein, ed. *The Fourth Fireside Book of Baseball.* (New York: Simon and Schuster, 1987), pp. 359–360.

52279. Ward, John J. "That Fading Star Al Simmons." *Baseball Magazine,* LXXX (March 1937), 453–455.

52280. Williams, Dick. "Spare the Rod and Spoil a Star." *Liberty,* XI (July 7, 1934), 44–46.

Curtis Thomas ("Curt") Simmons

P. (B: May 19, 1929, Egypt, PA). Philadelphia (NL), 1947–1950, 1952–1960; St. Louis (NL), 1960–1966; Chicago (NL), 1966–1967; California (AL), 1967. Remarks: Had 193 victories, 183 defeats, and five "saves" in two decades; $65,000 bonus baby; first MLB player inducted into the U.S. Army for Korean War service; lost Game Six on 1964 World Series.

52281. Breslin, Jimmy. "A Pitcher's Arm Has Got to GO." *Sport,* XXII (September 1956), 24–25+.

52282. Broeg, Bob. "Season's Biggest Dollar's Worth." *Baseball Digest,* XXI (July 1962), 13–15.

52283. Brown, Hugh. "The Bonus Baby Who Made Good." *Sport,* XIII (October 1952), 18–19+.

52284. _____. "Is Kindness Killing Curt Simmons?" *Sport,* XX (September 1955), 24–25+.

52285. Kelley, Brent P. "Curt Simmons: Youngest of the 1950 Whiz Kids." *Sports Collectors Digest,* XVIII (July 5, 1991), 174–176.

52286. McHugh, Roy. "Curt Simmons: A Lucky Unlucky Guy." *Sport,* XXXVII (February 1964), 38–39+.

52287. Olmsted, Frank J. "Curtis Thomas 'Curt' Simmons." In: Vol. Q-Z of David L. Porter, ed. *Biographical Dictionary of American Sports: Baseball.* Rev. and enlarged ed. Westport, CT: Greenwood Press, 2000. Pp. 1418–1419.

52288. "The Phillies' Pitching Pals." *Sport,* XV (October 1953), 22–23+. Simmons and Roberts.

52289. Richman, Milton, "From Castoff to All-Star." *Sport,* XV (October 1953), 20–21+.

52290. Strohmeyer, John. "The Phillies' Prize Rookie." *American Legion Magazine,* XLIV (April 1948), 22–25.

52291. Terrell, Roy. "A Pitcher's Comeback." *Sports Illustrated,* V (August 27, 1958), 40–42.

52292. Williams, Edger. "Half a Comeback to Come." *Baseball Digest,* XII (February 1963), 5–14.

Ted Lyle ("Simba") Simmons

C-SCOUT. (B: Aug. 9, 1949, Highland Park, MI). St. Louis (NL), 1968–1980; Milwaukee (AL), 1981–1985; Atlanta (NL), 1986–1988. Remarks: Had 2,472 hits (248 homers) and 21 stolen bases in 2,456 games; had key homer in Game Three of 1981 ALCS; homered in Games One and Two of 1982 World Series; dir. player development, St. Louis (NL), 1989–1992; GM, Pittsburgh (NL), 1992–1993; special assignment scout, Cleveland (AL), 1994–1999; VP scouting/player development, San Diego (NL), 1999-.

52293. Broeg, Bob. "A Batting Title in Store for Ted Simmons?" *Baseball Digest,* XXXVII (May 1978), 38–41.

52294. _____. "Ted Simmons: 'Losing Drives Me Crazy.'" *Baseball Digest,* XXXII (June 1973), 21–25.

52295. Brosnan, Jim. "Ted Simmons: Power at the Plate." *Boys' Life,* LXV (March 1975), 34–37.

52296. _____. *Ted Simmons' Story.* New York: G. P. Putnam, 1977. 157p.

52297. Fimrite, Ron."He's Some Piece of Work." *Sports Illustrated,* XLVIII (June 5, 1978), 36–39.

52298. Gilligan, Vic. "Ted Simmons: 'I'm the Best Catcher in Baseball.'" *Sport,* LXVII (July 1978), 42–43+.

52299. Hoffman, Mac. "Ted Simmons: Finally Out of the Shadows." *Sport World,* XVIII (August 1979), 16, 80.

52300. Jozwik, Thomas D. "Ted Lyle 'Simba' Simmons." In: Vol. Q-Z of David L. Porter, ed. *Biographical Dictionary of American Sports: Baseball.* Rev. and enlarged ed. Westport, CT: Greenwood Press, 2000. Pp. 1419–1420.

52301. Koster, Rich. "Ted Simmons Talks About the Challenges of Hitting." *Baseball Digest,* XLII (March 1983), 75–77.

52302. Murray, Jim. "Ted Simmons: The National League's 'Other Catcher.'" *Baseball Digest,* XXXVI (October 1977), 28–29.

52303. Simmons, Ted. "The Game I'll Never Forget." *Baseball Digest,* XXXVIII (July 1979), 61–67.

52304. Smith, Jim. "The Best Hitting Catcher in National League History: Ted Simmons?" *Baseball Quarterly,* I (Winter 1977), 38–41.

Tex Simone
EXEC. (B: 1928). Remarks: CEO, Syracuse (IL), 1970–.

52305. Kirst, Sean Peter. "Simone Sees His Dream." In: his *The Ashes of Lou Gehrig and Other Baseball Essays.* Jefferson, NC: McFarland & Co., Inc., 2003. Pp. 156–157.

Dick Simpson *see* **Richard Charles ("Dick") Simpson**
Harry Leon ("Suitcase") Simpson
OF-P. (B: Dec. 3, 1925, Atlanta, GA-D: April 3, 1979). Philadelphia Stars, 1946–1948; Wilkes-Barre (EL), 1949; San Diego (P.C. L.), 1950; Cleveland (AL), 1951–1953; Indianapolis (AA), 1954; Kansas City (AL), 1955–1957; New York (AL), 1957–1958; Kansas City (AL), 1958–1959; Chicago (AL) and Pittsburgh (NL), 1959; Indianapolis (AA), 1960–1962; Mexico City (Mexican League), 1963–1964. Remarks: Obtained 752 hits (73 homers) and 17 stolen bases in 888 games in eight big league seasons.

52306. Moffi, Larry and Jonathan Kronstadt. "Harry Leon Simpson." In: their *Crossing the Line; Black Major Leaguers, 1947–1959.* Jefferson, N.C.: McFarland & Co., Inc., 1994. Pp. 65–67.

52307. Spalding, John E. "Harry Simpson." In: *his Pacific Coast League Stars, Vol. II: Ninety Who Made it to the Majors, 1905–1957.* San Jose, Ca: John E. Spalding, 1997. Pp. 147–148.

Richard Charles ("Dick") Simpson
OF. (B: July 28, 1943, Washington, D.C.). Los Angeles (NL), 1962, 1964; California (AL), 1965; Cincinnati (NL), 1966–1967; St. Louis (NL) and Houston (NL), 1968; New York (AL) and Seattle (AL), 1969. Remarks: Obtained 107 hits (15 homers) and 10 stolen bases in 299 games for seven teams in seven years.

52308. Broeg, Bob. "A New Card with Three Plays." *Baseball Digest,* XXVII (July 1969), 43–46.

Duane ("Duke") Sims
C. (B: June 5, 1941, Salt Lake City, UT). Cleveland (AL), 1964–1970; Los Angeles (NL), 1970–1971; Detroit (AL), 1972–1973; New York (AL), 1973–1974; Texas (AL), 1974. Remarks: Had 580 hits (100 homers) and six stolen bases in 843 games in 11 years; had two homers on Opening Day, 1968.

52309. Mentus, Ron. "Here Are Some Tips on Big League Catching Strategy." *Baseball Digest,* XLVII (May 1988), 35–37.

Duke Sims *see* **Duane ("Duke") Sims**
Harry Ford Sinclair
EXEC. (B: July 6, 1876, Wheeling, WV-D: Nov. 10,

1956). Remarks: Oil bam who owned the Newark (F.L.) club in 1915.

52310. Lane, Ferdinand C. "Harry Sinclair: The Live Wire of the Federal League." *Baseball Magazine,* XV (August 1915), 28–32.

Elmer ("Smokey") Singleton
P. (B: June 26, 1918, Ogden, Utah-D: Jan. 5, 1996). Boston (NL), 1945–1946; Pittsburgh (NL), 1947–1948; Washngton (AL), 1950; Chicago (NL), 1957–1959. Remarks: Obtained 11 victories and 17 defeats, plus four "saves," in parts of eight big league seasons.

52311. Ison, Jim. "Elmer Singleton." In: his *Mormons in the Major Leagues.* Cincinnati, OH: Action Sports, 1991. Pp. 170–175.

Kenneth Wayne ("Ken") Singleton
OF-BROADCASTER. (B: June 10, 1947, New York City). New York (NL), 1970–1971; Montreal (NL), 1972–1974; Baltimore (AL), 1975–1984. Remarks: Obtained 2,029 hits (246 homers) and 21 stolen bases in 2,081 games in 15 seasons; was a 100 RBI-in-a-season man in both the NL and AL; had 10 hits in 1979 World Series; broadcaster for Montreal (NL), 1985–1996 and New York (AL), 1997–.

52312. Burke, Tim. "Ken Singleton: NL's Most Improved Power Hitter." *Baseball Digest,* XXXII (December 1973), 94–87.

52313. Calabria, Pat. "Ken Singleton: A Hitter Comes of Age." *Baseball Digest,* XXXVI (November 1977), 44–46.

52314. Collier, Ken. "Ken Singleton." In: Tommy Kay, ed. *Tommy Kay's 1980 Baseball Factbook.* Scottsdale, AZ: Jalart House, 1980. Pp. 91–95.

52315. Holder, William G. "Singleton's the Man in Expo-Land." *Black Sports,* IV (October 1974), 36–38.

52316. Keith, Larry. "Beat Feet, but Eyes Right." *Sports Illustrated,* XLVII (July 25, 1977), 38+.

52317. Middleton, Charles R. "Kenneth Wayne 'Ken' Singleton." In: Vol. Q-Z of David L. Porter, ed. *Biographical Dictionary of American Sports: Baseball.* Rev. and enlarged ed. Westport, CT: Greenwood Press, 2000. Pp. 1420–1421.

52318. Piestez, Joel. "Ken Singleton: The Orioles' Unsung Batting Hero." *Baseball Dlgest,* XXXVIII (November 1979), 41–43.

52319. Siegel, Eric. "Ken Singleton: He Tries to Get on Base Any Way He Can." *Baseball Digest,* XXXVIII (February 1979), 42–44+.

52320. Singleton, Ken, as told to George Vass. "The Game I'll Never Forget." *Baseball Digest,* XLVIII (January 1989), 29–31.

Dick Sipek *see* **Richard Francis ("Dick") Sipek**
Richard Francis ("Dick") Sipek
OF. (B: Jan. 16, 1923, Watsonville, CA–D: July 17, 2005). Cincinnati (NL), 1945. Remarks: Had 38 hits in 82 games in one big league season.

52321. Newman, Zipp. "Sipek Conquers Nature's Handicap." *Baseball Digest,* III (October 1944), 19–21.

Douglas Randall ("Doug") Sisk
P. (B: Sept. 26, 1957, Renton, WA). New York (NL), 1982–1987; Baltimore (AL), 1988; Atlanta (NL), 1990–1991. Remarks: Won 22 games and lost 20, with 33 "saves," in 10 years; hurled all of 1986 season without surrendering a single homer.

52322. Durso, Joseph. "[Jesse} Orosco and [Doug} Sisk. Double-Relief for the Mets." *Baseball Digest,* XLIII (October 1984), 62–64.

David ("Dave") Sisler
P. (B: Oct. 16, 1931, St. Louis, MO). Boston (AL),

1958–1959; Detroit (AL), 1959–1960; Washington (AL), 1961; Cincinnati (NL), 1962). Remarks: Won 38 games and lost 44, with 29 "saves," in five big league seasons; son of Hall of Famer George Sisler (below).

52323. Mann, Arthur. "Baseball's Amazing Sislers." *Saturday Evening Post,* CCXXV (February 14, 1953), 36–40.

Dick Sisler *see* **Richard Allan ("Dick") Sisler**

George Harold ("Gorgeous George") Sisler★

P-1B-MGR-SCOUT. (B: March 24, 1893, Manchester, OH-D: March 26, 1973). St. Louis (AL), 1915–1927; Washington (A.L), 1928, Boston (NL), 1928–1930. Remarks: Had 2,812 hits (99 homers) and 375 stolen bases in 2,055 games in 15 seasons; won inaugural AL MVP award, 1922; AL stolen base champion, 1918, 1921–1922, 1927; hit for the cycle twice, Aug. 8, 1920 and Aug. 13, 1921; established major league record for most base hits in one season (257), 1920, eclipsed 84 years later by Ichiro Suzuki [q.v.] on October 1, 2004); led AL in triples, 1921–1922; obtained six hits in one game, Aug. 9, 1921; hit safely in 41 consecutive games, July 27 through Sept. 17, 1922; also had 34 game hitting streak, 1925; as a pitcher, won five and lost six of the 24 games involved during 1915–1916; noted as one of the two best defensive first basemen (with Hal Chase [q.v.]) in game's history; AL batting champion, 1920 and 1922 (had .407 batting average in 1920 and .420 in 1922); manager, St. Louis (AL), 1924–1926, winning 218 games and losing 241 (.475); minor league manager and big league scout, 1932, 1946–1956, 1962–1972; batting instructor for Brooklyn (NL), 1943, 1946–1950 and Pittsburgh (NL), 1951–1966, whose 1954 book on batting technique is still employed; father of Dave Sisler (above) and Dick Sisler (below); named to Missouri Sports Hall of Fame, 1965; elected to National Baseball Hall of Fame in 1939, where his plaque reads, "Holds two American League records, making 267 hits in 1920 and batting .41979 in 1922. Retired with major league average of .341. Credited with being one of the best two fielding first basemen in history of game."

52324. Allen, Lee, and Thomas Meany. "George Sisler." In: their *Kings of the Diamond.* New York: G.P. Putnam, 1965. Pp. 103–105.

52325. Allen, Maury. "George Sisler (1915–1930)." In: his *Baseball's 100.* New York: Galahad Books, 1981. Pp. 50–52.

52326. Barber, Walter ("Red"). "The Batter." In: his *Walk in the Spirit.* New York: Dial Press, 1969. Pp. 71–775.

52327. Baumgartner, Stan. "Like Sisler, Like Son [Dick]." *Sport,* IX (October 1950), 42–46.

52328. Bell, Floyd L. "George Sister is a .400 Hitter." *Baseball Magazine,* XXV (September 1920), 474–475.

52329. Blaisdell, Lowell L. "George Harold 'Gorgeous George' Sisler." In: Vol. Q-Z of David L. Porter, ed. *Biographical Dictionary of American Sports: Baseball.* Rev. and enlarged ed. Westport, CT: Greenwood Press, 2000. Pp.1421–1423.

52330. Borst, William A. ("Bill"). "George Sisler." In: John A. Garrity and Marsh C. Carries, eds. *American National Biography.* 24 vols. New York: Oxford University Press, 1999. XX, 49–50.

52331. Broeg, Bob. "George Sisler." In: his *Super Stars of Baseball.* St. Louis, MO: *The Sporting News,* 1971. Pp. 225–230.

52332. _____. "Poetry in Motion." In: his *My Baseball Scrapbook* St. Louis: River City Publishers, 1983. Pp. 42–44.

52333. Burick, Si. "'You Will Be Hit Again!'—George Sisler." *Baseball Digest,* XIX (August 1960), 61–63.

52334. Burkholder, Ed. "George Sisler." In: his *Baseball Immortals.* New York. Christopher, 1955. Pp. 57–59.

52335. Burnes, Robert L. "Who Was the All-Time Greatest First Baseman?" *Baseball Digest,* XXIX (April 1970), 32–37.

52336. Davis, Mac. "George Harold Sisler." In: *The Greatest in Baseball.* New York: Scholastic Book Services, 1977. Pp. 10–11.

52337. Dexter, Charles. "Sizzler Sisler." *Baseball Digest,* XXIV (July 1965), 67–72.

52338. "George Sisler: The Pitcher." *The Baseball Research Journal,* VI (1977), 94–97.

52339. Gordon, David. "George Sisler—1920." In: his *Baseball's Top 100: The Best Individual Seasons of All Time.* Wilton, CT: Diamond Library, 1996. Pp. 59–60.

52340. Graham, Frank. "Baseball's Greatest First Baseman." *Baseball Magazine,* XLV (November 1930), 547–549.

52341. _____. "The Greatest First Baseman." *Baseball Digest,* VI (August 1947), 34–37.

52342. Grayson, Harry. "George Harold Sisler." In: his *They Played The Game.* New York: A.S. Barnes, 1944. Pp. 137–139.

52343. _____. "Sisler Could Have Been a 30-Win Pitcher." *Baseball Digest,* III (May 1944), 47–52.

52344. Greene, Lee. "*Sport's* Hall of Fame. George Sisler, 'Picture Player." *Sport,* XXXV (March 1963), 50–51+.

52345. Hirshberg, Al. "George Sisler: First Base." In: his *The Greatest American Leaguers.* New York: G.P. Putnam's Sons, 1970. Pp. 61–70.

52346. Honig, Donald. "George Sisler." In: his *The Greatest First Basemen of All Time.* Chicago, IL: Follett Publishing Co., 1988. Pp. 20–27.

52347. Huhn, Rick. *The Sizzler: George Sisler, Baseball's Forgotten Great.* Columbia, MO: University of Missouri Press, 2004. 328p.

52348. Jennings, Hugh. "Will George Sisler Equal Ty Cobb?" *Baseball Magazine,* XXVI (March 1921), 468–469.

52349. Keener, Sid. "'Twas a Break for Sisler." *Baseball Digest,* VII (May 1948), 75–77. His conversion to an outfielder.

52350. Lane, Ferdinand C. "The Dazzling Record of George Sisler." *Baseball Magazine,* XXVI (March 1921), 465–468.

52351. _____. "George Sisler, Ty Cobb's Probable Sucessor." *Baseball Magazine,* XX (April 1919), 450–455.

52352. _____. "George Sisler Wins the American League Batting Record. *"Baseball Magazine,* XXX (March 1923), 443–445.

52353. _____. "George Sider's Pet Ambition." *Baseball Magazine,* XXIX (September 1922), 435–437.

52354. _____. "Who is the Greatest Player in Baseball?" *Baseball Magazine,* XXXI (June 1923), 291–293.

52355. Lewis, Allen. "George Sisler's 257 Hits in One Season: An Unbeatable Record?" *Baseball Digest,* xliv (December 1985), 94–96.

52356. Liebman, Ronald G. "George Sisler, the Pitcher." *The Baseball Research Journal,* VI (1977), 94–97.

52357. Lindberg, James Oscar. "At First Base for the Boston Braves ... George Sisler." In: Mark Kanter, ed. *The Northern Game and Beyond: Baseball in New England and Eastern Canada.* Cleveland, OH: The Society for American Baseball Research, 2002. Pp. 27–28.

52358. Losada, Luis A. "George Sisler, Manolin's Age, and Hemingway's Use of Baseball." *The Hemingway Review,* XIV (Fall 1994), 79+.

52359. Mann, Arthur. "Baseball's Amazing Sislers." *Saturday Evening Post,* CCXXV (February 14, 1953), 36–40.

52360. Maule, Tex. "The Thinking Hitter." *Sports Illustrated,* XIV (June 5, 1961), 56+.

52361. Meany, Thomas. "The Picture Player — George Harold Sisler." In: his *Baseball's Greatest Hitters.* New York: A.S. Barnes, 1950. Pp. 177–199.

52362. _____. "George Sisler." In: his *Baseball's Greatest Players.* New York: Grosset and Dunlap, 1953. Pp. 219–232.

52363. Reidenbaugh, Lowell. "George Sisler." In: his *Cooperstown: Where Legends Live Forever.* St. Louis, MO: *The Sporting News,* 1983. Pp. 233–234.

52364. Rickey, Branch; with Robert Riger. "George Sisler." In: his *The American Diamond: A Documentary of the Game of Baseball.* New York: Simon and Shuster, 1965. Pp. 14–17.

52365. Ritter, Lawrence and Donald Honig. "George Sisler." In: their *The 100 Greatest Baseball Players Of All Time.* New York: Crown Publishers, 1981. Pp. 78–79.

52366. Rumill, Ed. "The George Sisler of '22." *Baseball Magazine,* LXXIV (January 1945), 273–275.

52367. Salant, Nathan. "George Sisler." In: his *Superstars, Stars, and Just Plain Heroes.* New York: Stein & Day, 1982. Pp. 35–40.

52368. Santa Maria, Michael and James Costello. "Peerless." In: their *In the Shadows of the Diamond.* Dubuque, IA: The Elysian Fields Press, 1992. Pp. 208–214.

52369. Sisler, George. "Around the Infield with: George Sisler." *Scholastic Coach,* XVII (April 1948), 24+.

52370. _____. "Batting Averages Are Cockeyed." *Collier's,* CVI (July 6,1940), 23+.

52371. _____. "Breaking a Big League Record." *American Legion Weekly,* V (August 10, 1923), 21+.

52372. _____. "The First Baseman [Sisler] Who Outpitched Walter Johnson." *Baseball Digest,* XXIV (September 1965), 67–71. Reprinted in John Kuenster, ed, *From Cobb to Catfish* (Chicago, IL: Rand McNally, 1975), pp. 239–240.

52373. _____. "How the Star Player Must 'Live' Baseball." *Baseball Magazine,* XXXV (June 1925), 303–305.

52374. _____. "The Inside Story of Sisler's Comeback." *Baseball Magazine,* XXXIII (August 1924), 391–393+.

52375. _____. "Is It Good 'Dope' to Guess the Pitcher?" *Baseball Magazine,* XXXIX (August 1927), 401–403.

52376. _____. *The Knack of Batting.* Louisville, KY: Hillerich & Bradsby Co., 1934. 33p. Instructional pamphlet.

52377. _____. "My Best Season So Far." *Baseball Magazine,* XX (April 1918), 460–462; XXVI (March 1921), 461–464.

52378. _____. "My Greatest Day in Baseball." In: Eliot Cohen, ed. *My Greatest Day in Baseball.* New York: Little Simon, 1991. Pp. 116–120.

52379. _____. "Playing First Base." *Scholastic Coach,* XXV (March 1956), 46–47.

52380. _____. *Sisler on Baseball: A Manuel for Players and Coaches.* New York: David McKay, 1954. 226p. Still one of the most helpful of instructionals; includes personal recollections of play.

52381. _____. "A .350 Batting Average." *Baseball Magazine,* XIX (October 1917), 543–544.

52382. _____. "Why I Enlisted in the Army." *Baseball Magazine,* XXII (March 1919), 265–268.

52383. _____., as told to Lyall Smith. "My Greatest Day in Baseball." In: John P. Carmichael, ed. *My Greatest Day in Baseball.* New York: A. S. Barnes, 1945. Pp. 157–162. First published In the *Chicago Daily News.*

52384. Smith, Ira L. "George Harold Sisler." In: his *Baseball's Famous First Basemen.* New York: A.S. Barnes, 1956. Pp. 139–148.

52385. Smith, Ron. "George Sisler 33." In: his *The Sporting News Selects Baseball's 100 Greatest Players.* St. Louis, MO: *The Sporting News,* 1998. Pp. 76–77.

52386. Stockton, J, Roy. "George Sisler (First Base)." In: Christy Walsh, ed. *Baseball's Greatest Lineup.* New York: A.S. Barnes, 1952. Pp. 75–87.

52387. Sullivan, George. "George Sisler." In: his *Glovemen: Twenty-Seven of Baseball's Greatest.* New York: Atheneum, 1996. Pp. 56–57.

52388. Warburton, Paul. "George Sisler: 'If There is Anything He Cannot Do in the National Pastime, I Would Like to See It." *The National Pastime,* XX (2000), 93–97.

52389. Ward, John J. "The Famous Sisler Case." *Baseball Magazine,* XVII (October 1916), 36–38.

Richard Allan ("Dick") Sisler
1B-OF-MGR. (B: Nov. 2, 1920, St. Louis, MO-D: Nov. 20, 1998). St. Louis (N.L), 1946–1947; Philadelphia (NL), 1948–1951; Cincinnati, (NL), 1952; St. Louis (NL), 1952–1953. Remarks; Had 720 hits (55 homers) in 799 games in an eight-year playing career; had eight consecutive hits in two games in two days, May 4–5, 1950; hit pennant-clinching 10th inning homer, Oct. 1, 1950; coach, Cincinnati (NL), 1961–1964, then Reds manager, 1964–1965, wining 121 games and losing 94 (.563); coach, St. Louis (NL), 1966–1970; coach, San Diego (NL), 1975–1976; minor league batting instructor, New York (AL) farm system; coach, New York (NL), 1979–1980; son of George Sisler (above).

52390. Ashburn, Rich. "When Dick Sisler Had His Moment in the Spotlight." *Baseball Digest,* XXXIV (September 1975), 60–63.

52391. Baumgartner, Stan. "Like Sisler, Like Son." *Sport,* IX (October 1950), 42–46.

52392. Burick, Si. "How [Dick] Sisler Will Run [Cincinnati] Reds." *Baseball Digest,* XXIV (February 1965), 84–87. Managerial style.

52393. Kelley, Brent P. "Dick Sisler: The Whiz Kids' Biggest Hit." In: his *The Early All-Stars: Conversations with Standout Baseball Players of the 1930s and 1940s.* Jefferson, NC: McFarland & Co., Inc., 1997. Pp. 153–161.

52394. Lawson, Earl. "The Man Who Took Over Hutch's Team." *Sport,* XL (November 1965), 60–61.

52395. Mann, Arthur. "Baseball's Amazing Sislers." *Saturday Evening Post,* CCXXV (February 14, 1953), 36–40.

52396. Miller, Hub. "Dick Sisler, Son of George." *Baseball Magazine,* LXXXVI (January 1951), 279–281.

52397. Swank, Bill. "Dick Sisler." In: his *Echoes from Lane Field; A History of The San Diego Padres 1936-1957.* Paducah, KY: Turner Publishing Company, 1997. Pp. 131–132.

52398. Taylor, Sec. "Being Sisler Jr. Hurts, Helps." *Baseball Digest,* VI (July 1946), 57–59. Article concerns son Dick, not brother George Jr., who became President of the International League.

52399. Valenti, Dan. "Dick Sisler." In: his *Clout!* New York: Stephen Greene Press, 1989. pp. 80–88.

52400. Westcott, Rich. "Dick Sisler: Dramatic Home Run Won a Pennant." In: his *Splendor on the Diamond: Interviews with 35 Stars of Baseball's Past.* Gainesville, FL: The University Press of Florida, 2000. Pp. 164–172.

Sebastian Daniel ("Sibby") Sisti
2B-3B-SS-OF. (B: July 26, 1920, Buffalo, NY). Boston (NL), 1939–1942, 1946–1952; Milwaukee (NL), 1953–1954. Remarks: Had 732 hits (27 homers) and 30 stolen

bases in 1,016 major league games; top utilityman who also played for Indianapolis (AA), 1946; had small role in Robert Redford motion picture *The Natural.*

52401. Fehler, Gene. "Sibby Sisti." In: his *Tales from Baseball's Golden Age.* Champaign, IL: Sports Publishing Co., 2000. Chpt. 46.

Sibby Sisti *see* **Sebastian Daniel ("Sibby") Sisti**
Ted Crawford Sizemore
2B-SS (B: April 15, 1946, Gadsden, AL). Los Angeles (NL), 1969–1970; St. Louis (NL), 1971–1975; Los Angeles (NL), 1976; Philadelphia (NL), 1977–1978; Cincinnati (NL), 1979; Boston (AL), 1979–1980. Remarks: Obtained 1,311 hits (23 homers) and 69 stolen bases in 1,411 games in a dozen seasons; NL Rookie of the Year award, 1969; had one inside-the-park homer, August 7, 1972.

52402. Claire, Fred. "Sizemore Doesn't Believe in Sophomore Jinx." *Baseball Digest,* XXIX (March 1970), 60–64.

52403. Honig, Donald. "1969: Ted Sizemore." In: his *National League Rookies of the Year.* New York: Bantam Books, 1989. Pp. 56–57.

52404. Selman, Jim. "Ted Sizemore, 'Born Again' at Second Base." *Baseball Digest,* XXXVII (July 1974), 42–43.

Robert Roe ("Cotton") Skidmore
OF. (B: Oct. 30, 1945, Decatur, IL). Chicago (NL), 1970. Remarks: Had one hit — a homer — in one big league at bat.

52405. Holtzman, Jerome. "Roe Skidmore: He Finished with a 1.000 Batting Average." *Baseball Digest,* xlv (June 1986), 93–94.

Roe Skidmore *see* **Robert Roe ("Cotton") Skidmore**
Bob Skinner *see* **Robert Ralph ("Bob") Skinner**
Robert Ralph ("Bob") Skinner
OF-MGR. (B: Oct. 3, 1931, La Jolla, CA). Pittsburgh (NL), 1954, 1956–1963; Cincinnati (NL), 1963–1964; St. Louis (NL), 1964–1966. Remarks: Had 1,198 hits (103 homers) and 67 stolen bases in 1,381 games in 12 playing years; led NL with 54 pinch-hit appearances, 1956; had grand slam homer, May 31, 1959; had two pinch hits, 1964 World Series; manager, San Diego (PCL), 1967–1968; coach, San Diego (NL), 1970–1975; manager, Philadelphia (NL), 1968–1969 and San Diego (NL), 1977, winning 93 games and losing 123 (.431); coach, California (AL), 1978, Pittsburgh (NL), 1979–1985, and Atlanta (NL), 1986–1988.

52406. Grady, Sandy. "Bob Skinner's Relaxed Management." *Baseball Digest,* XXVII (December 1968), 49–51.

52407. McConnell, Mickey. "Let Flexibility Be Your Guide." *Scholastic Coach,* XXXVIII (March 1969), 12–14.

52408. Murphy, Joel. "Skinner's Business is Hitting." *Baseball Digest,* XXVII (December 1969), 49–51.

52409. Watts, Lew. "The Hitting Action." *Scholastic Coach,* XXX (February 1961), 10–15.

Bill Skowron *see* **William Joseph ("Bill" or "Moose") Skowron**
Moose Skowron *see* **William Joseph ("Bill" or "Moose") Skowron**
William Joseph ("Bill" or "Moose") Skowron
1B. (B: Dec.18, 1934, Chicago, IL). New York (AL), 1954–1962; Los Angeles (NL), 1963; Washington (AL), 1964; Chicago (AL), 1964–1967; California (AL), 1967. Remarks: Obtained 1,566 hits (211 homers) in 1,658 games in 14 seasons; had four hits and a homer in the 1955 World Series; a homer in the 1956 fall classic; seven hits and two homers in the 1958 World Series; 12 hits and two homers in the 1960 World Series; six hits and a homer

in the 1961 fall classic; four hits and a triple in the 1962 World Series; and five hits and a homer in the 1963 World Series; noted fielder with several other batting records to his credit, including first to have two grand slam homers in one season, 1957; currently does pr work for Chicago (AL).

52410. Bingham, Walter. "Miseries of the 'Moose.'" *Sports Illustrated,* XII (March 21, 1960), 62–63. Troubled by back problems throughout career.

52411. Devaney, John. "Bill Skowron." In: his *Where Are They Today? Great Sports Stars of Yesteryear.* New York: Crown Publishers, 1985. Pp. 177–180.

52412. _____. "Moose's' Life with the Also-Rans." *Sport,* XXXVIII (August 1964), 54–55+.

52413. Dexter, Charles. "The 'Moose' the Yankees Hunted 16 Years." *Baseball Digest,* XIV (July 1956), 5–10.

52414. _____. "Watch Out for the 'Moose.'" *Baseball Digest,* XXII (March 1963), 55–61.

52415. Forker, Dom. "Bill Skowron." In: his *Sweet Seasons: Recollections of the 55–64 New York Yankees.* Dallas, TX: Taylor Publishing Co., 1989. Pp. 18–25.

52416. Gallagher, Mark. "Bill Skowron." In: his *50 Years of Yankee All-Stars.* New York: Leisure Press, 1984, Pp. 196–198.

52417. Goddard, Joe. "Slugger Bill Skowron Looks Back on a Storied Big League Career." *Baseball Digest,* LXII (August 2003), 74–78.

52418. Gottehrer, Barry. "The 'Moose' Comes Through." In: William A. Wise, ed. *Cavalier's 1961 Major League Baseball.* Greenwich, CT: Fawcett Publications, 1961. Pp. 27–28+.

52419. Jozwik, Thomas D. "William Joseph 'Moose,' 'Bill' Skowron." In: Vol. Q-Z of David L. Porter, ed. *Biographical Dictionary of American Sports: Baseball.* Rev. and enlarged ed. Westport, CT: Greenwood Press, 2000. Pp. 1423–1424.

52420. Leiser, Bill. "Old 'Moose' Showed 'Em." *Baseball Digest,* XXII (December 1963), 21–23.

52421. Linn, Ed. "Bill Skowron's Fingers are Crossed." *Sport,* XXX (September 1960), 54–64.

52422. Prell, Ed. "Big Blond 'Moose.'" *Baseball Digest,* XVIII (September 1959), 44–47.

52423. Shecter, Leonard. "The Mild 'Moose.'" *Sport,* XXVIII (July 1959), 44–46.

52424. Skowron, William J. ("Moose"), as told to George Vass. "The Game I'll Never Forget." *Baseball Digest,* XXX (May 1971), 32–35.

52425. _____., with Bill Shaw. "Memories of a Moose." *People Weekly,* XXVIII (September 14, 1987), 82–86+.

52426. Vanderberg, Bob. "Bill Skowron: 'The Moose' Finally Came Home." In: his *Sox — From Lane and Fain to Zisk and Fisk.* Chicago, IL: Chicago Review Press, 1982. Pp. 282–290.

Donald Martin ("Don" or "Sluggo") Slaught
C. (B: Sept. 11, 1958, Long Beach, CA). Kansas City (AL), 1982–1984; Texas (AL), 1985–1987; New York (AL), 1988–1989; Pittsburgh (NL), 1990–1995; California (AL) and Chicago (AL), 1996; San Diego (NL), 1997. Remarks: Obtained 1,151 hits (77 homers) in 1,327 games in 16 years; had five hits in one game, July 7, 1994.

52427. Nash, Bruce and Allan Zullo. "Don Slaught." In: their *More Little Big Leaguers: Amazing Boyhood Stories of Today's Baseball Stars.* New York: Little Simon, 1991. Pp. 58–59.

52428. Towle, Mike. "Don Slaught." In: his *True Champions: The Good Guys in American Sports Speak Out.* Ft. Worth, TX: The Summit Group, 1994. Pp. 114–123.

Enos Bradsher ("Country") Slaughter★
OF-COACH. (B: April 27, 1916, Roxboro, NC-D: Aug. 12, 2002). St. Louis (NL), 1938–1942, 1946–1953; New York (AL), 1954–1955; Kansas City (AL), 1955–1956; New York (AL), 1956–1959; Milwaukee (NL), 1959. Remarks: Had 2,383 hits (169 homers) and 71 stolen bases in 2,380 games in a 19-year major league career; led NL in doubles, 1939; led NL in triples, 1942, 1949; NL RBI champion, 1948; hero of 1946 World Series; manager, Houston (AA) and Raleigh (Carolina League), 1961; retired to farm in North Carolina and helped coach Duke University baseball team, 1971–1977; elected to North Carolina Sports Hall of Fame, 1977; named to Missouri Sports Hall of Fame, 1999; elected to National Baseball Hall of Fame in 1985, where his plaque reads: "Hard-nosed, hustling performer who played the game with intensity and determination. Flat, level swing made him a lifetime .300 hitter who invariably came through in clutch situations. Excellent outfielder with strong arm. Daring baserunner famous for his mad dash home to win 1946 World Series. For Cardinals, batted .291 in 5 World Series."

52429. Appel, Marty. "Enos Slaughter." In: his *Yesterday's Heroes: Revisiting the Old-Time Baseball Stars.* New York: The Dial Press, 1988. Pp. 200–203.

52430. Ballew, Bill. "Enos 'Country' Slaughter: Hofer Was the Original 'Charlie Hustle." *Sports Collector's Digest,* XVIII (May 3, 1991), 90–93.

52431. Barber, Walter ("Red"). "The Hustler." In: his *Walk in the Spirit.* New York: Dial Press, 1969. Pp. 105–110.

52432. Bloodgood, Clifford. "Slaughter of the Cardinals." *Baseball Magazine,* LXIII (October 1939), 604–605.

52433. Breslin, Jimmy. "Enos Slaughter: Last of the Old Pros." *True,* XXXIX (August 1958), 22–28.

52434. Broeg, Bob. "Country." In: his *My Baseball Scrapbook.* St. Louis, MO: River City Publishers, 1983. Pp. 102–105.

52435. _____. "Country Boy Leads the Cards." In: Bruce Jacobs, ed. *Baseball Stars of 1950.* New York: Lion Books, 1950. Pp. 170–183.

52436. _____. "Slaughter Old Pro with the College Try." *Baseball Magazine,* LXXXIX (October 1952), 8–10.

52437. Burnes, Robert L. "St. Louis and the Slaughter Deal: It Figures — But Card Fans Resent It ." *Baseball Digest,* XIII (June 1954), 83–85.

52438. Carmichael, John P. "The One Time He Didn't Slaughter Them." *Baseball Digest,* XXIII (June 1964), 77–79.

52439. Cobbledick, Gordon. "Slaughter in a Hurry." *Baseball Digest,* V (November 1949), 47–49.

52440. Craft, David and Tom Owens. "Enos Slaughter: The Country Boy Could Run ... And Hit ... And Field." In: their *Redbirds Revisited.* Chicago, IL: Bonus Books, 1990. Pp. 216–222.

52441. Daley, Arthur. "A Take-Charge Guy." *Baseball Digest,* VI (May 1947), 50–61.

52442. Devaney, John. "Country." In: his *The Greatest Cardinals of Them All.* New York: G.P. Putnam's Sons, 1968. Pp. 134–144.

52443. DiMeglio, John E. "Enos Bradsher 'Country' Slaughter." In: Vol. Q-Z of David L. Porter, ed. *Biographical Dictionary of American Sports: Baseball.* Rev. and enlarged ed. Westport, CT: Greenwood Press, 2000. Pp. 1424–1425.

52444. Drees, Jack. "Enos Bradher Slaughter: The Country Boy Who Loved to Run." In: his *Where Is He Now?* Middle Village, NY: Jonathan David Publishers, 1973. Pp. 81–85.

52445. Eisenbath, Mike. "Enos Slaughter: He Set the Standard For Hustle." *Baseball Digest ,* LI (September 1992), 56–58.

52446. Fitzgeraldi Ed. "Enos Slaughter: Country Boy of the Cards." *Sport,* VI (May 1949), 52–65.

52447. Forker, Dom. "Enos Slaughter." In: his *Sweet Seasons: Recollections of the 55–64 New York Yankees.* Dallas, TX: Taylor Publishing Co., 1989. Pp. 93–98.

52448. Goldberg, Hy. "Enos Slaughter: 21 Years Running." *Baseball Digest,* XVI (May 1957), 73–75.

52449. Graham, Frank. "The Cardinals' Country Boy." *Sport,* XI (September 1951), 16–19.

52450. _____. "Enos Slaughter." In: his *Baseball Extra.* New York: A. S. Barnes, 1954. Pp. 100–108.

52451. Green, Paul M. "Baseball and Enos Slaughter." *Sports Collector's Digest,* X (October 14, 1983), 64+.

52452. Harmon, Pat. "Enos Slaughter Set Pattern for Pete Rose." *Baseball Digest,* XXVIII (August 1969), 69–70.

52453. Hickey, David and Kerry Keene. "Enos Slaughter." In: their *The Proudest Yankees of All: From the Bronx to Cooperstown.* Lanham, MD: Taylor Trade Pub., dist. by National Book Network, 2003. Chpt. 10.

52454. Hirshberg, Al and Joe McKenney. "Enos Bradsher Slaughter: 'He Stole a World Series.'" In: *Famous American Athletes of Today.* 10th Series. Boston, MA: L.C. Page, 1947. Pp. 303–317.

52455. Hochman, Stan. "Why Isn't Enos Slaughter in the Hall of Fame?" *Baseball Digest,* XLIII (October 1984), 28–32.

52456. Honig, Donald. "Enos Slaughter." In: his *Baseball Between the Lines: Baseball in the Forties and Fifties as Told By the Men Who Played It.* Lincoln, NE: University of Nebraska Press, 1976. Pp. 154–170.

52457. Johnson, George. "Country Comes Back." *Complete Baseball,* IV (November 1952), 40–50.

52458. _____. "He Never Went Away." In: Bruce Jacobs, ed. *Baseball Stars of 1953.* New York: Lion Books, 1953. Pp. 38–43.

52459. Knight, Ray. "Country Keynotes the Cardinals." *Saturday Evening Post,* CCXIX (May 17, 1947), 23+.

52460. Lieb, Frederick G. "He's Still a Country Boy." *Sport,* II (June 1947), 31–31+.

52461. Linn, Ed. "Last of the Old Breed." *Sport,* XXVI (August 1958), 20–23+.

52462. Murray, Arch. "Drivingest Guy — That's Slaughter." *Baseball Digest,* I (October 1947), 23–33.

52463. Richman, Milton. "Does a Ballplayer Know When He's Through?" *Sport,* XI (July 1951), 12–13+.

52464. Sargent, Jim. "Enos Country Slaughter." *Oldtyme Baseball News,* VIII, no 8 (1996), 6–8.

52465. Schwalberg, Bob. "They'll Have to Cut the Uniform Off Enos." *Sport,* XV (November 1953), 28–31.

52466. Slaughter, Enos, as told to Lyall Smith. "My Greatest Day in Baseball." In: John P. Carmichael, ed. *My Greatest Day In Baseball.* New York: A.S. Barnes And Co., 1945. Pp. 213–217.

52467. _____. with Kevin Reid. *Country Hardball: The Autobiography of Enos "Country" Slaughter.* Greensboro, NC: Tudor Publishers Inc., 1991. 208p.

52468. _____. "How to Stay Young in the Majors." In: At Silverman, ed. *True's 1953 Baseball Yearbook.* Greenwich, CT: Fawcett Publications, 1953. Pp. 8–9+.

52469. Smith, Ira L. "Enos Bradsher (Country) Slaughter." In: his *Baseball's Famous Outfielders.* New York: A.S. Barnes, 1964. Pp. 275–281.

52470. Stern, Chris. "Enos Slaughter." In: his *Where Have They Gone?* New York: Tempo, 1979. Pp. 153–156.

52471. Twombly, Wells. "Slaughter of the Innocents." *Baseball Digest,* XXVII (May 1968), 52–55.

52472. Veech, Ellis J. "Slaughter the Sparkler." *Baseball Magazine,* LXXXI (August 1948), 309–311.

52473. _____. "Slaughter's Still Slaying 'Em." *Baseball Digest,* XII (May 1953), 49–54.

52474. Westcott, Rich. "Enos Slaughter — Nobody Played The Game Any Harder." In: his *Diamond Greats.* Westport, CT: Meckler Books, 1988. Pp. 53–57.

52475. Wicker, Tom. "Player: Enos Slaughter, On His Toes." In: his *The Ultimate Baseball Book.* Boston, MA: Houghton Mifflin Co., 1979. Pp. 231–245. Reprinted in Charles Einstein, ed., *The Fourth Fireside Book of Baseball* (New York: Simon and Schuster, 1987), pp. 417–423.

Forrest Herbert ("Steve") Slayton
P. (B: April 26, 1902, Barre, VT-D: Dec. 20, 1984). Boston (AL), 1928. Remarks: Appeared in three big league games with no decisions.

52476. Mackay, Jim and Tom Simon. "Steve Slayton." In: Tom Simon, ed. *Green Mountain Boys of Summer: Vermonters in the Major Leagues, 1882–1993.* Shelburne, VT: The New England Press, 2000. Pp. 125–127.

Steve Slayton *see* **Forrest Herbert ("Steve") Slayton**
Roy Frederick Smalley III
SS-2B-BROADCASTER. (B: Oct. 25, 1952, Los Angeles, CA). Texas (AL), 1975–1976; Minnesota (AL), 1976–1982; New York (AL), 1982–1984; Chicago (AL), 1984; Minnesota (AL), 1985–1987. Remarks: Obtained 1,454 hits (163 homers) in 1,653 games in 13 seasons; color analyst for Minnesota (AL) in 1995 and ESPN in 1997.

52477. Elderkin, Phil. "Roy Smalley: 'Good Field, Good Hit' Shortstop." *Baseball Digest,* XXXVIII (September 1979), 50–53.

52478. Figone, Albert J. "Roy Frederick Smalley 3rd." In: Vol. Q-Z of David L. Porter, ed. *Biographical Dictionary of American Sports: Baseball.* Rev. and enlarged ed. Westport, CT: Greenwood Press, 2000. Pp. 1425–1426.

52479. Kaplan, Jim. "Shortstop Who's Long on Smarts." *Sports Illustrated,* L (May 14, 1979), 50+.

52480. Kuenster, John. "Roy Smalley Making His Mark as One of the Best All-Around Shortstops." *Baseball Digest,* XXXVIII (August 1979), 17–18.

52481. "Roy Smalley: Versatile Powerhouse." *Yankees Magazine,* V (June 28, 1984), 17–15.

John Patrick Smiley
P. (B: March 17, 1965, Phoenixville, PA). Pittsburgh (NL), 1986–1991; Minnesota (AL), 1992; Cincinnati (NL), 1995–1997; Cleveland (AL), 1997–1998. Remarks: Won 126 games and lost 103, with four "saves" in 12 years.

52482. Evers, John L. "John Patrick Smiley." In: Vol. Q-Z of David L. Porter, ed. *Biographical Dictionary of American Sports: Baseball.* Rev. and enlarged ed. Westport, CT: Greenwood Press, 2000. Pp. 1226–1427.

Al Smith (1) *see* **Alfred John ("Al") Smith**
Al Smith (2) *see* **Alphonse Eugene ("Al" or *Fuzzy")
Smith**
Alfred John ("Al") Smith
P. (B: Oct. 12, 1907, Belleville, IL-D: April 28, 1977). New York (NL), 1934–1937; Philadelphia (NL), 1938–1939; Cleveland (AL), 1940–1945. Remarks: Had 99 victories, 101 defeats, and 17 "saves" in a dozen campaigns; with Jim Bagby, Jr. (q.v.), stopped Joe DiMaggio's (q.v.) hitting streak at 56 games (July 17, 1941); also played for Sacramento (PCL), 1947.

52483. Appel, Marty. "Al Smith." In: his *Yesterday's Heroes: Revisiting the Old-Time Baseball Stars.* New York: William Morrow, 1988. Pp. 204–207.

52484. Casey, Larry. "Al Smith Recalls the Glory Years." *Baseball Digest,* XXXIV (January 1975), 76–80.

52485. Heiman, Lee. "Al Smith." In: his *When the Cheering Stops.* New York: Macmillan, 1990. Pp. 63–78.

Alphonse Eugene ("Al" or "Fuzzy") Smith
OF-3B. (B: Feb. 7, 1928, Kirkwood, MO-D: Jan. 3, 2002). Cleveland Buckeyes, 1948; Wilkes-Barre (EL), 1948–1949; San Diego (PCL), 1950–1952; Indianapolis (AA), 1952; Cleveland (AL), 1953–1957; Chicago (AL), 1958–1962; Baltimore (AL), 1963; Cleveland (A:L) and Boston (AL), 1964. Remarks: Had 1,468 hits (164 homers) and 67 stolen bases In 1,517 games in 12 seasons; had four hits and four RBIs in one game, Sept. 4, 1961; director, Chicago Parks Department baseball program, 1966–1981; elected to Ohio Baseball Hall of Fame in 1993.

52486. "Al Smith, White Sox Outfielder." *Ebony,* XV (October 1960), 85–88.

52487. Furlong, William B, "Minnie Minoso and Al Smith." In: Ray Robinson, ed. *Baseball Stars of 1961.* New York: Pyramid Books, 1961. Pp. 106–113.

52488. Kleinknecht, Merl F. "Alphonse Eugene 'Al,' 'Fuzzy' Smith." In: Vol. Q-Z of David L. Porter, ed. *Biographical Dictionary of American Sports: Baseball.* Rev. and enlarged ed. Westport, CT: Greenwood Press, 2000. Pp. 1427–1428.

52489. Lebovitz, Hal. "Al Smith: Leaning Tower of Cleveland." *Baseball Digest,* XIV (August 1955), 41–50.

52490. Marazzi, Rich. "Al Smith was the Consummate Lead Off Man for the Indians and White Sox." *Sport Collector's Digest,* XXII (November 17, 1995), 160–162.

Bob Smith *see* **Robert Ashley ("Bob") Smith**
Bryn Nelson Smith
P. (B: Aug. 11, 1965, Marietta, GA). Montreal (NL), 1982–1989; St. Louis (NL), 1990–1992; Colorado (NL), 1993. Remarks: Won 108 games and lost 94, with six "saves," in 12 years; opening day pitcher for expansion Rockies, April 9, 1993; coach, Allen Hancock College (CA), 1994–2000; coach, Carolina (SL), 2001–2002; coach, Salt Lake City (PCL), 2005-.

52491. Kaplan, Jim. "It's Tough to Tee Off on This Guy." *Sports Illustrated,* LX (May 7, 1984), 82–83.

Carl Reginald ("Reggie") Smith
OF-COACH. (B: April 2, 1945, Shreveport, LA). Boston (AL), 1966–1973; St. Louis (NL), 1974–1976; Los Angeles (NL), 1976–1981; San Francisco (NL), 1982; Tokyo Giants (Japan League), 1983. Remarks: Obtained 2,020 hits (314 homers) and 137 stolen bases in 1,987 games in 17 years; led NL in doubles, 1968, 1971; homer total second only to Mickey Mantle (q.v.) for switch-hitters; only player to homer from both sides of the plate in a game twice in both the NL and AL; only switch-hitter with 100 HR in both leagues; had a homer in 1967 World Series and three homers in 1977 World Series; had 21-game hitting streak, 1969; minor league instructor, Los Angeles (NL), 1989–1993; coach, Los Angeles (NL), 1994–1998; established youth baseball training facility, Reggie Smith Baseball Centers, at Encino, CA.; asst. coach, U.S. Pan American Team, 1999 and hitting coach, U.S. Olympic Baseball Team, 2000; named to Boston Red Sox Hall of Fame, May 2000.

52492. Broeg, Bob. "It's a New Deal for Reggie Smith." *Baseball Digest,* XXXIII (June 1974), 48–53.

52493. Brown, Robert J. "Carl Reginald 'Reggie' Smith." In: Vol. Q-Z of David L. Porter, ed. *Biographical Dictionary of American Sports: Baseball.* Rev. and enlarged ed. Westport, CT: Greenwood Press, 2000. Pp. 1428–1430.

52494. Crehan, Herbert F. and James W. Ryan. "Reggie Smith." In: their *Lightning in a Bottle: The Sox of '67.* Boston, MA: Branden Publishing Co., 1992. Pp. 171–196.

52495. Fimrite, Ron. "His Old-Self is on the Shelf." *Sports Illustrated,* XLIX (October 2, 1978), 38–43.

52496. Furillo, Bud. "Reggie Smith: Best Rightfielder in L.A. History." In: Bill Shumard, ed. *1981 Los Angeles Dodgers Yearbook.* Anaheim, CA: Rotary Off-Set Printers, 1981. Pp. 49–50.

52497. Grow, Doug, and Joe Valerio. "New Guns in Town Wanted-Reggie Smith of the Cardinals." *Sport,* LVIII (September 1974), 89–98.

52498. Halberstam, David. "The Education of Reggie Smith." *Playboy,* XXXI (October 1984), 100+.

52499. Hirshberg, Al. "A Carbon Copy of Yaz?" *Sport,* XLV (April 1968), 44–48.

52500. Honig, Donald. "Reggie Smith." In: his *Up from the Minor Leagues.* New York: Cowles, 1970. Pp. 53–71.

52501. Kaese, Harold. "Reggie Smith: New Leader for the Red Sox?" *Baseball Digest,* XXXI (July 1972), 43–47.

52502. Murray, Jim. "The Two Faces of Reggie Smith." *Baseball Digest,* XXXVI (December 1977), 40–43.

52503. Rumill, Ed. "Reggie Smith, Red Sox Insurance Policy." *Baseball Digest,* XXVII (September 1968), 6–7.

52504. Shaw, David. "Reggie Smith: 'Nobody Intimidates My Team.'" *Sport,* LXVI (January 1978), 44–47.

52505. Xanthakos, Harry. "Smith's Bat Keeps Cards in Contention." *Black Sports,* (September 1974), 26, 28, 38.

Charles ("Charlie" or Chino) Smith

OF-2B. (B: 1901, Greenwood, SC-D: Jan. 16, 1932). Philadelphia Giants, 1924; Pennsylvania Red Caps of New York, 1925; Brooklyn Royal Giants, 1925–1927; New York Lincolns, 1929–1930; Brooklyn Royal Giants, 1931. Remarks: According to Satchel Paige, one of the two best hitters in Black baseball; 1929 Negro American League batting and home run champion; career .423 hitter; died of unknown disease, suspected of being yellow fever.

52506. Holway, John B. "Charlie 'Chino' Smith." *The Baseball Research Journal,* VII (1978), 63–67.

52507. Riley, James A. "Charles 'Chino' Smith." In: Vol. Q-Z of David L. Porter, ed. *Biographical Dictionary of American Sports: Baseball.* Rev. and enlarged ed. Westport, CT: Greenwood Press, 2000. P. 1430.

David Stanley ("Dave") Smith, Jr.

P. (B: Jan. 21, 1955, Richmond, CA). Houston (NL), 1980–1990; Chicago (NL), 1991–1992. Remarks: Won 53 games and lost 53, with 216 "saves," in 13 years; surrendered Lenny Dykstra's (q.v.) homer in Game Three of the 1986 NLCS; pitching coach, Las Vegas (PCL), 1998 and San Diego (NL), 1999–2001.

52508. Hillman, John. "David Stanley 'Dave' Smith, Jr." In: Vol. Q-Z of David L. Porter, ed. *Biographical Dictionary of American Sports: Baseball.* Rev. and enlarged ed. Westport, CT: Greenwood Press, 2000. Pp. 1430–1431.

52509. Keteyian, Armen. "Flight 45 from Houston Has Arrived." *Sports Illustrated,* LXIV (June 23, 1986), 70+.

52510. _____. "Inside Stuff: Padres Pitching Coach Dave Smith." *Sport,* XC (April 1999), 30–31.

52511. _____. "Tossed on the Waves." *Sports Illustrated,* LXVII (December 14, 1987), 36+.

Earl Sutton ("Oil") Smith

C. (B, Feb. 14, 1897, Sheridan, AK-D: June 9, 1963). New York (NL), 1919–1923; Boston (NL), 1923–1924; Pittsburgh (NL), 1924–1928; St. Louis (NL), 1928–1930. Remarks: Had 686 hits (46 homers) in 860 games in 12 seasons; managed in minor leagues, 1935, 1938–1940; re-

membered as player. who was "robbed" by Sam Rice's (q.v.) famous catch in 1925 World Series.

52512. Smith, Earl S. "Oil Smith, the Pirates' Colorful Catcher." *Baseball Magazine,* XXXIX (June 1927), 311–313.

Eddie Smith *see* **Edgar ("Eddie") Smith**

Edgar ("Eddie") Smith

P. (B: Dec. 14, 1913, Mansfield, NJ-D: Jan. 2, 1994). Philadelphia (AL), 1936–1939; Chicago (AL), 1939–1947. Remarks: In 10 big league years, won 73 games and lost 113, with 12 "saves."

52513. Klima, John. "The Price of Myth: Eddie Smith vs. Bob Feller (April 15, 1940)." In: his *Pitched Battle: 35 of Baseball's Greatest Duels from the Mound.* Jefferson, NC: McFarland & Co., Inc., 2002. Pp. 63–67.

Edward Mayo Smith

OF-MGR. (B: Jan. 17, 1915, New London, CT-D: Nov. 24, 1977). Philadelphia (AL), 1945. Remarks: Had 43 hits in 73 games in one big league year; minor league player and manager, 1946–1954; manager, Philadelphia (NL), 1955–1958, Cincinnati (NL), 1959, and Detroit (AL), 1967–1970, winning 662 games and losing 611(.571).

52514. Burick, Si. "Adversity Molded Mayo Smith as a Manager." *Baseball Digest,* XVIII (February 1959), 67–71.

52515. Honig, Donald. "Mayo Smith." In: his *The Man In the Dugout.* Chicago: Follett Publishing Co., 1977. Pp. 230–240.

52516. Leggett, William. "Detroit's Refrain is Mayo and [Johnny] Sain." *Sports Illustrated,* XXV (April 3, 1967), 26–27.

52517. Tassinari, Edward J. "Edward Mayo Smith." In: Vol. Q-Z of David L. Porter, ed. *Biographical Dictionary of American Sports: Baseball.* Rev. and enlarged ed. Westport, CT: Greenwood Press, 2000. Pp. 1431–1432.

52518. Williams, Edgar. "Here's Who is Mayo Smith." *Baseball Digest,* XIV (April 1955), 31–38.

52519. Young, Dick. "Mayo Smith Eases Tension." *Baseball Digest.* XXVII (December 1968), 35–37.

Elmer Ellsworth ("Mike") Smith

P-OF. (B: March 23, 1868, Pittsburgh, PA-D: Nov. 3, 1945). Cincinnati (AA), 1886–1889; Pittsburgh (NL), 1892–1897; Cincinnati (NL), 1898–1900; New York (NL), 1900; Pittsburgh (NL) and Boston (NL), 1901. Remarks: As a hurler, won 75 games and lost 57; as a batter, obtained 1,462 hits (37 homers) and 243 stolen bases in 1,233 games in 14 seasons; had 30-game hitting streak, 1898; also played for Kansas City (W.A.), 1890–1891, Kansas City (AA), 1902, Minneapolis (AA), 1903, Kansas City (AA) and Ilion (New York State League), 1904; Scranton (New York State League), 1905.

52520. Kush, Raymond D. "Elmer Ellsworth 'Mike' Smith." In: Vol. Q-Z of David L. Porter, ed. *Biographical Dictionary of American Sports: Baseball.* Rev. and enlarged ed. Westport, CT: Greenwood Press, 2000. Pp. 1432–1433.

Frank Elmer ("Piano Mover") Smith

P. (B: Frank Elmer Schmidt, Oct. 28, 1879, Pittsburgh, PA-D: Nov. 3, 1952). Chicago (AL), 1904–1910; Boston (AL), 1910–1911; Cincinnati (NL), 1911–1912; Baltimore (F.L.), 1914–1915; Brooklyn (F.L.), 1915. Remarks: Won 138 games and lost 113, with seven "saves," in 12 seasons; had two no-hitters, Sept. 6, 1905 and Sept. 20, 1908.

52521. Hilton, George W. "Frank Elmer Smith." In: Vol. Q-Z of David L. Porter, ed. *Biographical Dictionary of American Sports: Baseball.* Rev. and enlarged ed. Westport, CT: Greenwood Press, 2000. Pp. 1433–1434.

Gary Smith

WRITER. Remarks: Senior writer for *Sports Illustrated.*

52522. Smith, Gary. *Beyond the Game: The Collected Sports Writing of Gary Smith.* New York: Atlantic Monthly Press, 2000. 320p.

Hal Smith (1) *see* **Harold Raymond ("Hal") Smith**
Hal Smith (2) *see* **Harold Wayne ("Hal") Smith**
Harold Raymond ("Hal") Smith

C-SCOUT (B: June 1, 1931, Barling, AK). St. Louis (NL), 1956–1961; Pittsburgh (NL), 1965. Remarks: Had 437 hits (23 homers) in 570 games in seven years; forced out of the game by heart attack, but came back briefly in 1965; coach, St. Louis (NL), 1962 and Pittsburgh (NL), 1966; later scout with St. Louis (NL).

52523. Herman, Jack. "Hal Smith. Hillbilly Tunesmith in Catcher's Mask." *Baseball Digest,* XVIII (July 1959), 74–77.

Harold Wayne ("Hal") Smith

C-3B-SCOUT. (B: Dec. 7, 1930, West Frankfort, IL). Baltimore (AL), 1955–1956, Kansas City (AL), 1956–1959; Pittsburgh (NL), 1960–1961; Houston (NL), 1962–1963; Cincinnati (NL), 1964–1965. Remarks: Obtained 715 hits (58 homers) in 879 games in a decade; had pinch-hit homer in Game Seven of 1960 World Series; minor league manager, 1966; coach, Pittsburgh (NL), 1967 and Cincinnati (NL), 1968–1969; scout, St. Louis (NL), 1970–1975, 1978–1980s.

52524. McHugh, Roy. "Pittsburgh's Pair of Catchers." *Sport,* XXX (November 1960), 32–34. Smith and Smokey Burgess.

52525. Povich, Shirley. "Hal Smith: Catcher at Third Base." *Baseball Digest,* XVIII (June 1959), 61–63.

52526. Richman, Milton. "Everybody's Watching Baltimore's Rookie Catcher." *Sport,* XVIII (June 1955), 30–31+.

52527. Steadman, John. F. "Lion-Hearted Oriole." *Baseball Digest,* XIV (July 1955), 55–60.

Hilton Lee Smith★

P. (B: Feb. 27, 1912, Giddings, TX-D: Nov. 18, 1983). Monroe Monarchs, 1932–1935; New Orleans Black Creoles and New Orleans Crescents, 1933; Kansas City Monarchs, 1936–1948. Remarks: Noted Negro League pitcher with an unofficial 161–32 record with the Monarchs, 1937–1948; later coach and teacher and employee of Armco Steel in Kansas City to 1978; associate scout, Chicago (NL), 1978 to death; elected to National Baseball Hall of Fame in 2001, where his plaque reads: "A quiet but confident righthander whose devastating fastball complemented what many regard as the best sweeping curveball in Negro Leagues history. After beginning his career with the Monroe Monarchs, was credited with 20 or more wins in each of 12 seasons with the Kansas City Monarchs, including a dominating record of 93–11 from 1939 to 1942. The six-time All-Star pitched a no hitter versus the powerful Chicago American Giants in 1937 and posted a near-perfect 25–1 mark in 1941. Played on seven pennant winners and one World Series championship team."

52528. Baxter, Terry A. "Hilton Lee Smith." In: Vol. Q-Z of David L. Porter, ed. *Biographical Dictionary of American Sports: Baseball.* Rev. and enlarged ed. Westport, CT: Greenwood Press, 2000. Pp. 1434–1435. Ralph Berger's Smith profile is a number in the online SABR Biography Project http://bioproj.sabr.org/bioproj.cfm?a=v&v= l&bid=539&pid=13243.

52529. Holway, John. "Hilton Smith." In: his *Voices from the Great Black Baseball Leagues.* New York: Da Capo Press, 1992. Pp. 280–297.

52530. Lester, Larry. "Hilton Smith." In: John A. Garrity and Marsh C. Carries, eds. *American National Biog-*

raphy. 24 vols. New York: Oxford University Press, 1999. XX, 203–204.

Janet Marie Smith

EXEC. (B: Dec. 13, 1957, Jackson, MS). Remarks: Coord. architecture and design, Battery Park City Authority, N.Y.C., 1982–1984; pres., chief exec. officer, Pershing Sq. Mgmt. Assn., L.A., 1985–1989; v.p. stadium planning and devel., Balt. Orioles Oriole Park at Camden Yard, 1989–1994; v.p. planning and devel., Atlanta Braves, 1994; v.p. sports facilities, Turner Properties, Atlanta, 1994–1997; pres., TBSSports Devel., Inc., 1997–2000; Struever Brothers, Eccles & Rouse, Inc., Balt., 2000–.

52531. Masello, D. "Playing the Field." *Architectural Record,* CLXXVIII (October 1990), 45–46.

John Ford ("Teniente" or "Geronimo") Smith

P. (B: Jan. 9, 1919, Phoenix, AZ-D: Feb.26, 1983). Chicago American Giants, 1939; Chicago Crawfords, 1940; Kansas City Monarchs, 1941, 1946–1948; Jersey City (IL), 1949–1950; Drummondville (Provincial League), 1951; Phoenix (Arizona-Texas League), 1952–1953; El Paso (Arizona-Texas League), 1954. Remarks: Had 21–7 record with Monarchs and went 46 and 40 with U.S. and Canadian minor league teams.

52532. Skinner, David. "John Ford Smith: Arizona's Black Baseball Pioneer." In: his *Mining Towns to Major Leagues: A History of Arizona Baseball.* Cleveland, OH: Society for American Baseball Research, 1999. Pp.11–13.

Lee Arthur Smith, Jr.

P. (B: Dec. 4, 1957, Jamestown, LA). Chicago (NL), 1980–1987; Boston (AL), 1988–1990; St. Louis (NL), 1990–1993; New York (AL), 1993; Baltimore (AL), 1994; California (AL), 1995–1996; Cincinnati (NL), 1996; Montreal (NL), 1997. Remarks: Obtained 71 victories, 93 defeats, and 478 "saves" in 18 years; surrendered Steve Garvey's (q.v.) homer in Game Four of the 1984 NLCS; first NL hurler to post 30+ saves in four consecutive seasons and owner of MLB record for most career saves and the mark for most game finishes (802); minor league pitching coach, San Francisco (NL), 2000-.

52533. Berney, Louis. "All-Time Saves Leader Lee Smith Wanted to Play in the NBA." *Orioles Gazette,* IV (March 1994), 11–12.

52534. Dewan, John and Dom Zminda. "Did Lee Smith Take a Short Cut to the Save Crown?" In: STATS, Inc. *STATS 1992 Baseball Scoreboard.* Chicago, IL: STATS Publishing, 1992. Pp. 164–167.

52535. Eisenbath, Mike. "Cards Hold Ace in Lee Smith But Reshuffling Necessary." In: George Leonard, ed. *Athlon's Baseball '91.* Nashville, TN: Athlon Sports Communications, 1991. Pp. 34–39.

52536. Hummel, Rick. "Lee Smith: The Pitcher with an Identity Crisis." *Baseball Digest,* LI (June 1992), 38–40.

52537. Kurkjian, Tim. "Case Closed?: California's Closer Quandary." *Sports Illustrated,* LXXXIV (May 6, 1996), 71+.

52538. _____. "What a Relief." *Sports Illustrated,* LXXII (may 14, 1990), 93–94.

52539. Ladson, William. "The Intimidator: The Cardinals' Lee Smith Commands Respect With His Huge Presence and Overpowering Fastball." *Sport,* LXXXIII (June 1992), 48–52.

52540. "Lee Smith." In: Carrie Muskat, ed. *Banks to Sandberg to Grace: Five Decades of Love and Frustration with the Chicago Cubs.* Chicago, IL: Contemporary Books, 2001. Pp. 183–184.

52541. O'Neill, Dan. "New Pitch Makes Cardinals' Lee Smith Even Tougher." *Baseball Digest,* L (August 1991), 58–60.

52542. Pierce, Charles P. "Railroaded." *Boston,* LXXXII (August 1990), 57–61.

52543. Ringolsby, Tracy. "No Hits, No Hype—Lee Smith, a Dominant Reliever for the Last 10 Years, Could Make the Hall of Fame Without Making a Splash." *Inside Sports,* XIV (September 1992), 74–77.

52544. Smith, Duane A. "Lee Arthur Smith, Jr." In: Vol. Q-Z of David L. Porter, ed. *Biographical Dictionary of American Sports: Baseball.* Rev. and enlarged ed. Westport, CT: Greenwood Press, 2000. Pp. 1436–1437.

52545. Wendel, Tim. "Fingers-Snapping: But Someday Smith Might Pass Reardon." *USA Today Baseball Weekly,* II (May 27, 1992), 4–5.

52546. Wilbert, Warren and William Hageman. "Lee Arthur Smith—1983." In: their *Chicago Cubs: Seasons at the Summit, the 50 Greatest Individual Seasons.* Champaign, IL: Sagamore Publishing, 1997. Pp. 107–110.

Leo Smith *see* **Lionel H. ("Leo") Smith**

Lionel H. ("Leo") Smith

SS. (B: May 13, 1859, Brooklyn, NY-D: Aug. 30, 1935). Rochester (AA), 1890. Remarks: In one big league season, had 21 hits and a stolen base in 35 games.

52547. Linthurst, Randolph. *Journal of Leo Smith.* Chicago, IL: Adams Press, 1976. 55p.

Lonnie ("Skates") Smith

OF. (B: Dec. 22, 1955, Chicago, IL). Philadelphia (NL), 1978–1981; St. Louis (NL), 1982–1985; Kansas City (AL), 1985–1987; Atlanta (NL), 1988–1992; Pittsburgh (NL), 1993; Baltimore (AL), 1993–1994. Remarks: Had 1,488 hits (98 homers) and 370 stolen bases in 1,613 games in 17 seasons; tied NL record for most stolen bases in a game (1982); had grand slam homer in Gave Five of 1992 World Series; also played for Richmond (IL), 1987.

52548. Berney, Louis. "World Series Veteran Lonnie Smith Hopes to Help O's Down the Stretch." *Orioles Gazette,* III (September 24, 1993), 18–19.

52549. Falkner, David. "The Comeback of Lonnie Smith." *The New York Times Biographical Service,* XX (July 1989), 700–701.

52550. Granville, John. "Lonnie Smith: He's a Catalyst for the Cardinals." *Baseball Digest,* XLI (September 1982), 75–76+.

52551. Gutman, Dan. "Lonnie Smith: Faked Out of the World Series." In: his *Baseball's Biggest Bloopers: The Games That Got Away.* New York: Puffin, 1995. Pp. 132–141.

52552. Hummel, Rick. "The Amazing Smiths of St. Louis." In: Dick Kaegel, ed. *The Sporting News 1983 Baseball Yearbook.* St. Louis, MO: The. Sporting News, 1983. Pp. 12–18. Lonnie and Ozzie.

52553. Kerrigan, Vince. "Lonnie and Ozzie: The Cardinals' Talented Smiths." *Baseball Digest,* XLI (December 1982), 18–21.

52554. Nash, Bruce and Allan Zullo. "Lonnie Smith." In: their *More Little Big Leaguers: Amazing Boyhood Stories of Today's Baseball Stars.* New York: Little Simon, 1991. Pp. 48–49.

52555. Olmsted, Frank J. "Lonnie 'Skates' Smith." In: Vol. Q-Z of David L. Porter, ed. *Biographical Dictionary of American Sports: Baseball.* Rev. and enlarged ed. Westport, CT: Greenwood Press, 2000. Pp. 1437–1438.

52556. Smith, Lonnie, as told to George Vass. "The Game I'll Never Forget." *Baseball Digest,* XLIX (November 1990), 31–32.

Mark Edward Smith

OF. (B: May 7, 1970, Pasadena, CA). Baltimore (AL), 1994–1996; Pittsburgh (NL), 1997–1998; Florida (NL), 2000; Montreal (NL) 2001; Milwaukee (NL), 2003. Re-

marks: Obtained 233 hits (32 homers) and 15 stolen bases in 414 games.

52557. Krapf, Christine. "A Relaxed Mark Smith, Orioles Top Pick, Climbing the Ladder." *Orioles Gazette,* II (May 18, 1992), 31–32.

52558. Snyder, Deron and Bob Nightengale. "A Mark of Futility." *USA Today Baseball Weekly,* VIII (May 27, 1998), 3+.

Mayo Smith *see* **Edward Mayo Smith**

Mike Smith *see* **Elmer Ellsworth ("Mike") Smith**

Oil Smith *see* **Earl Sutton ("Oil") Smith**

Osborne Earl ("Ozzie" or "Wizard") Smith★

SS-BROADCASTER. (B: Dec. 26, 1954, Mobile, AL). San Diego (NL), 1978–1981; St. Louis (NL), 1982–1996. Remarks: Had 2,460 hits (28 homers) and 560 stolen bases in 2,573 games in 19 years; famous defensive infielder remembered for back-flips and base-stealing; hit homer in Game Five of 1985 NLCS; NLCS MVP award, 1985; broadcaster, St. Louis (NL), 1997–1999; named to Missouri Sports Hall of Fame, 1997; elected to National Baseball Hall of Fame in January 2002, where his plaque reads: "Revolutionized defensive play at shortstop with his acrobatic fielding and artistic turning of double plays. The 13-time Gold Glove winner set six major league fielding records among shortstops, including most assists, double plays and chances accepted. An effective offensive player, he accumulated 2,460 hits and stole 580 bases. Named to 15 All-Star Teams. His relentless pursuit of perfection helped lead the Cardinals to three World Series, including a 1982 championship. His congenial personality, consummate professionalism and trademark back flip made "The Wizard" a fan favorite.

52559. Armstrong, Larry. "St. Louis' Wizard Named Oz is the Slickest-Fielding Shortstop in Baseball." *People Weekly,* XI (June 20, 1983), 119–120.

52560. Austin, Carl. "Ozzie Smith." In: Tommy Kay, ed. *Tommy Kay's Big Book of Baseball.* Scottsdale, AZ: Jalart House, 1979. Pp. 82–89.

52561. Berger, Dan. "Padres Shortstop Ozzie Smith: A Future Star." *Baseball Digest,* XXXVII (September, 1978), 78–80.

52562. Boswell, Thomas. "The Wizardry of Ozzie." *GQ—Gentlemen's Quarterly,* LVIII (April 1988), 246–249.

52563. Bove, Vincent. "Ozzie Smith." In: his *Playing His Game.* South Plainfield, NJ: Bridge Publishing, 1984. Pp. 215–217.

52564. Brosnan, Jim. "The Man with the Million Dollar Glove." *Boys' Life,* LXXIV (March 1984), 13–16.

52565. Burger, Dan. "Padres' Shortstop Ozzie Smith a Future Star." *Baseball Digest,* XXXVII (September 1978), 78–80.

52566. Coplan, Jeff. "Ozzie Smith: 'The Secret of My New Success.'" *Sport,* LXXVIII (November 1987), 50–51+.

52567. Davis, Craig. "Ozzie Smith: Baseball's Most-Graceful Fielder of Them All." *Baseball Digest,* XLII (July 1983), 80–83.

52568. Doyle, Al. "Defense Opened the Door—Ozzie Smith: Hall of Famer with a Steady Glove and a Whole Lot More." *Baseball Digest,* LXI (April 2002), 72–76.

52569. Eisenbath, Mike. "Cardinal Teammates Bid a Fond Farewell to Ozzie Smith." *Baseball Digest,* LV (October 1996), 52–55.

52570. Feldman, Loren. "A Cardinal in Peacock's Plume." *GQ—Gentlemen's Quarterly,* LVIII (April 1988), 249–251.

52571. Fimrite, Ron. "No. 1 in His Field." *Sports Illustrated,* LXVII (September 28, 1987), 60–69.

52572. Fresina, Michael J. "Catching Up with Ozzie Smith." In: D. Scott Smith, ed. *Street & Smith 2003 Baseball Yearbook.* Charlotte, NC: Street and Smith Sport Group Publications, 2003. Pp. 38–41.

52573. Grayson, Robert. "An SCD Interview with Ozzie Smith." *Sport Collector's Digest,* XXV (December 25, 1998), 30+.

52574. Honig, Donald. "Ozzie Smith." In: his *The Greatest Shortstops of All Time.* Dubuque, IA: Wm. C. Brown Publishers, 1992. Pp. 98–103.

52575. Hultman, Tom. "Smith Still the Wizard of Oz." *Sport Collector's Digest,* XXIV (July 11, 1997), 130–131.

52576. Hummel, Rick. "The Amazing Smiths of St. Louis." In: Dick Kaegel, ed. *The Sporting News 1983 Baseball Yearbook.* St. Louis, MO: *The Sporting News,* 1983. Pp. 12–18. Ozzie and Lonnie.

52577. Jacobs, Barry. "The Wizardry of Ozzie Smith." *Saturday Evening Post,* CCLV (May–June 1983), 64–65+.

52578. James, Bill. "Ozzie Smith, St. Louis." In: his *The Bill James Baseball Abstract 1983.* New York: Ballantine Books, 1983. Pp. 172–174.

52579. Kelley, Brent P. "Ozzie Smith Checklist." *Baseball Cards,* IX (March 1989), 78+.

52580. Kerrigan, Vince. "Lonnie and Ozzie: The Cardinals' Talented Smiths." *Baseball Digest,* XLI (December 1982), 18–21.

52581. Kuenster, John. "Ozzie Smith Reinforces Sentiment to Honor Game's Defensive Stars." *Baseball Digest,* LXI (October 2002), 19–21.

52582. Miller, Gary S. "A Closer Look: Ozzie Smith." *Beckett Baseball Card Monthly,* V (December 1988), 4–6.

52583. Mitchell, Jerry. "The Great Shortstop Swap." *Sport,* LXXIII (August 1982), 62–66. Smith for Garry Templeton.

52584. Murray, Jim. "Ozzie Smith: Baryshnikov in Cleats." In: Charles Einstein, ed. *The Fourth Fireside Book of Baseball.* New York: Simon and Schuster, 1987. pp. 263–264.

52585. Nash, Bruce and Allan Zullo. "Ozzie Smith." In: their *Little Big Leaguers: Amazing Boyhood Stories of Today's Baseball Stars.* New York: Little Simon, 1990. Pp. 28–29.

52586. Neft, David S. "Is Ozzie Smith Worth $2,000,000 a Season?" *The Baseball Research Journal,* XV (1986), 43–48. Reprinted in John Thorn, ed. *The National Pastime* (New York: Bell Publishing Co., 1987), pp. 131–149.

52587. Olmsted, Frank J. "Osborne Earl 'Ozzie,' 'Wizard,' 'The Oz' Smith." In: Vol. Q–Z of David L. Porter, ed. *Biographical Dictionary of American Sports: Baseball.* Rev. and enlarged ed. Westport, CT: Greenwood Press, 2000. Pp. 1438–1440.

52588. Smith, Ozzie. "My Greatest Day in Baseball." In: Eliot Cohen, ed. *My Greatest Day in Baseball.* New York: Little Simon, 1991. Pp. 121–123.

52589. _____., as told to George Vass. "The Game I'll Never Forget." *Baseball Digest,* LI (June 1992), 69–71.

52590. _____. with Rob Rains. *Wizard.* Chicago, IL: Contemporary Books, Inc., 1988. 187p.

52591. Smith, Ron. "Ozzie Smith-87." In: his *The Sporting News Selects Baseball's 100 Greatest Players.* St. Louis, MO: *The Sporting News,* 1998. Pp. 188–189.

52592. *Sports Illustrated. Ozzie Smith in The Kid Who Could.* New York: DC Comics, 1992. 16p.

52593. Stein, Herbert. "Ozzie Smith: 'I Could've Made It a Few Years Earlier.'" *Sport,* LXVIII (March 1979), 60–61.

52594. Sullivan, George. "Ozzie Smith." In: his *Glovemen: Twenty-Seven of Baseball's Greatest.* New York: Atheneum, 1996. Pp. 10–11.

52595. Topkin, Marc. "Deeper Look: Ozzie Smith." *Beckett Baseball Card Monthly,* XII, no. 124 (July 1995), 114–115.

52596. Whicker, Mark. "Ozzie Smith: The Cardinals' Magician on Defense." *Baseball Digest,* XLI (November 1982), 38–41.

Peter John ("Pete") Smith
P. (B: Feb. 27, 1966, Abington, MA). Atlanta (NL), 1987–1993; New York (NL), 1994; Cincinnati (NL), 1995; San Diego (NL), 1997–1998; Baltimore (AL), 1998. Remarks: Won 47 games and lost 71, with one "save," in 11 seasons.

52597. Clyne, Felice. "Former Rivals Now Fast Friends." *Beckett Focus on Future Stars,* I (November 1991), 14–15. Smith and Tom Glavine.

Randy Smith
EXEC. (B: 1963). Remarks: GM, San Diego (NL), 1993–1995; Detroit (AL), 1996–2002.

52598. Kurkjian, Tim, ed. "Pray for the New Padre." *Sports Illustrated,* LXXVIII (June 21, 1993), 58–59.

52599. Olney, Buster. "The Trading Game: A Behind-the-Scenes Look at the Road to Baseball Glory or Financial Bust." In: George Leonard, ed. *Athlon Baseball, 1995.* Nashville, TN: Athlon Publishing Co., 1995. Pp. 145–149.

Red Smith *see* **Walter Wellesley ("Red") Smith**
Reggie Smith *see* **Carl Reginald ("Reggie") Smith**
Riverboat Smith *see* **Robert Walkup ("R.W." or "Riverboat") Smith**
Robert Ashley ("Bob") Smith
P. (B: July 20, 1890, Woodbury, VT-D: Dec. 27, 1965). Chicago (AL), 1913; Buffalo (F.L.), 1914–1915. Remarks: In three big league seasons, neither won nor lost any games, but "saved" three.

52600. Thompson, Dick. "Bob Smith." In: Tom Simon, ed. *Green Mountain Boys of Summer: Vermonters in the Major Leagues, 1882–1993.* Shelburne, VT: The New England Press, 2000. Pp. 98–99.

Robert Walkup ("R.W." or "Riverboat") Smith
P. (B: May 13, 1927, Clarence, MO-D: June 23, 2003). Boston (AL), 1958; Chicago (NL) and Cleveland (AL), 1959. Remarks: In all or parts of two big league seasons, won four games and lost four; also played for, among others, San Francisco (PCL) and San Diego (PCL)

52601. Kelley, Brent P. "Riverboat Smith." In: his *The San Francisco Seals, 1946–1957: Interviews with 25 Former Baseballers.* Jefferson, NC: McFarland & Co., Inc., 2002. Pp. 247–253.

Sherrod Monroe ("Sherry") Smith
P. (B: Feb. 18, 1891, Monticello, GA-D: Sept. 12, 1949). Pittsburgh (NL), 1911–1912; Brooklyn (NL), 1915–1917, 1919–1922; Cleveland (AL), 1922–1927. Remarks: Obtained 114 victories, 118 defeats, and 21 "saves" in 14 seasons; lost Game Two of 1916 World Series to George Herman ("Babe") Ruth (q.v.); went 22–1 in 1925 while giving up a league-leading 296 hits.

52602. Grillo, Jerry. "The Hardluck Ace: Sherry Smith." *Oldtyme Baseball News,* III, no. 1 (1991), 6–7.

52603. Klima, John. "A Ruthian Duel: Sherry Smith vs. Babe Ruth (October 9, 1916)." In: his *Pitched Battle: 35 of Baseball's Greatest Duels from the Mound.* Jefferson, NC: McFarland & Co., Inc., 2002. Pp. 33–37.

52604. Ward, John J. "Brooklyn's Star Player of the [1916 World] Series." *Baseball Magazine,* XVIII (December 1916), 61–62.

Walter Wellesley ("Red") Smith

WRITER. (B: Sept. 25, 1905, Green Bay, WI-D: Jan. 15, 1982). Milwaukee *Sentinel* and *St. Louis Star*, 1927–1935; *Philadelphia Record*, 1936–1945; *New York Herald-Tribune/*Tribune syndicate, 1945–1971; *The New York Times*, 1971–1981. Remarks: Pulitzer prize winner, 1976; J. G. Taylor Spink Award, 1976; best known U.S. sportswriter after Grantland Rice (q.v.).

52605. Baldassaro, Lawrence. "Walter W(ellesley) Smith." In: Richard Orodenker, ed. *Dictionary of Literary Biography, Volume 171: Twentieth-Century American Sportswriters*. Detroit, MI: The Gale Group, 1996. Pp. 308–317.

52606. Bass, S. M. W. "Walter W(ellesley) Smith." In Perry J. Ashley, ed. *Dictionary of Literary Biography, Volume 29: American Newspaper Journalists, 1926–1950*. Detroit, MI: The Gale Group, 1984. Pp. 329–334.

52607. Berkow, Ira. *Red: A Biography of Red Smith*. New York: Times Books, 1986. 302 p.

52608. _____. "A Writer Called Red Smith." *The New York Times Magazine*, (March 2, 1986), 40–42.

52609. Galligan, E. L. "Red Smith: Essayist." *Midwest Quarterly*, XXVII (Spring 1986), 327–340.

52610. Kern, John L. "Red Smith in the Final Innings: An Interview." *Writer's Digest*, LXII (June 1982), 20–26.

52611. "Red Smith." In: Joseph J. Vecchione, ed. *The New York Times Book of Sports Legends*. New York: Times Books, 1991. Pp. 312–318.

52612. Smith, Walter ("Red"). *The Best of Red Smith*, Selected by Verna Reamer. New York: Watts, 1963. 184p. Columns originally written for the *New York Herald-Tribune*.

52613. _____. "Interview with John L. Kern." *Writer's Digest*, LXII (June 1982), 20–26.

52614. _____. *Press Box: Red Smith's Favorite Stories*. New York: W.W. Norton, 1976. 192p.

52615. _____. *Red Smith on Baseball: The Game's Greatest Writer on the Game's Greatest Years*. Foreword by Ira Berkow. Chicago, IL: Ivan R. Dee, 2000. 363p.

52616. _____., with Robert W. Creamer. *Rhubarb in the Catbird Seat*. Lincoln, NE: University of Nebraska Press, 1997. 338p. First published by the Garden City, NY, firm of Doubleday in 1968.

52617. _____. *Strawberries in the Winter: The Sporting World of Red Smith*. New York: Quadrangle Books, 1974. 340p.

52618. Stein, Herbert. "Sportswriting's Poet Laureate: Red Smith." *Sport*, LXVI (March 1978), 58–60, 63–64.

52619. Van Dijk, Ruid. "Walter 'Red' Smith." In: John A. Garrity and Marsh C. Carries, eds. *American National Biography*. 24 vols. New York: Oxford University Press, 1999. XX, 269–271.

Wendell Smith

WRITER. (B: June 27, 1914, Detroit, MI-D: Nov. 26, 1972). Remarks: Sportswriter, columnist, editor, *Pittsburgh Courier*, 1937–1947; sportswriter, *Chicago American*, 1947–1963; sports editor, WBBM-TV, 1964; reporter and sports writer, WGN-TV and *Chicago Sun-Times*, 1964–1972; ghostwriter of *Jackie Robinson: My Own Story*, by Jackie Robinson (q.v.); J. G. Taylor Spink Award, 1994; first Black writer so honored.

52620. Carroll, Brian. "Wendell Smith's Last Crusade: The Desegregation of Spring Training." In: William M. Simons, ed. *The Cooperstown Symposium on Baseball and American Culture, 2001*. Jefferson, NC: McFarland & Co., Inc., 2002. Pp. 123–138.

52621. Reisler, Jim. "Wendell Smith: The Best of His Generation." In: his *Black Writers/Black Baseball: An An-thology of Articles from Black Sportswriters Who Covered the Negro Leagues*. Jefferson, NC: McFarland & Co., Inc, 1994. Pp. 33–56.

52622. Schraf, Mark W. "Wendell Smith." In: Richard Orodenker, ed. *Dictionary of Literary Biography, Volume 171: Twentieth-Century American Sportswriters*. Detroit, MI: The Gale Group, 1996. Pp.318–325.

52623. Wiggins, David K. "Wendell Smith, the Pittsburgh Courier and the Campaign to Include Blacks in Organized Baseball, 1933–1945." *Journal of Sport History*, X (Summer 1983), 5–29.

Willie ("Wonderful Willie") Smith

OF-1B-P. (B: Feb. 11, 1939, Anniston, AL). Detroit (AL), 1963; Los Angeles (AL) and California (AL), 1964–1966; Cleveland (AL), 1967–1968; Chicago (NL), 1968–1970; Cincinnati (NL), 1971. Remarks: Obtained 410 hits (46 homers) in 691 games for five teams in nine seasons; as a pitcher, won two games and lost four of 29 contests involved in, with two "saves"; only black MLB player to appear in at least 20 big league games as a pitcher and 20 as a fielder.

52624. Libby, Bill. "Willie Smith: Amazing Transformation." *Baseball Digest*, XXIII (September 1964), 5–12.

Mike ("Billy Mike" or "Snuffy") Smithson

P. (B: Jan. 25, 1955, Centerville, TX). Texas (AL), 1982–1983; Minnesota (AL), 1984–1987; Boston (AL), 1988–1989. Remarks: Obtained 76 victories, 86 defeats, and two "saves" in eight big league seasons; 6'8" sinkerball specialist.

52625. Bennett, Bruce. "Mike Smithson: He Survives on Pitching Guile." *Baseball Digest*, XLV (May 1986), 66–68.

John Andrew ("Smoltzie") Smoltz

P. (B: May 15, 1967, Detroit, MI). Atlanta (NL), 1988-. Remarks: Through 2004, has had 163 wins, 121 losses, and 154 "saves"; led NL in wild pitches, 1990–1992; played in 1991 NLCS (2–0), 1992 NLCS (2–0), 1993 NLCS (0–1), 1995 NLCS (0–0), 1996 NLCS (2–0), 1997 NLCS (0–1), 1998 NLCS (0–0), 1999 NLCS (0–0), and 2001 NLCS (0–0); MVP Award, 1992; played in 1991–1992, 1995–1996, 1999 World Series (0–0); had 14-game winning streak, 1996; NL Cy Young Award, 1996; second cousin of Hall of Famer Charlie Gehringer (q.v.).

52626. Bowman, Mark. "Braves' Closer John Smoltz: Dominant in His New Role." *Baseball Digest*, LXI (December 2002), 58–61.

52627. Freeman, Scott. "Holy Smoltz." *Atlanta Magazine*, XLI (March 2002), 30, 32.

52628. Glier, Ray. "Smoltz Grabs Ace's Role: Majors' Best Starter Silences the Naysayers." *USA Today Baseball Weekly*, VI (May 22, 1996), 11+.

52629. Green, Jerry. "Trade for Smoltz Helped Turn Braves into Winners." *Baseball Digest*, LI (February 1992), 26–27.

52629. Johnson, Paul M. "Smoke Signals — the Message is Clear: Hard-Throwing John Smoltz Has at Last Reached His Prime." *Sport*, LXXXVII (November 1996), 74–77.

52630. Kaat, Jim. "Armed for Success." *Inside Sports*, XIX (March 1997), 40–51.

52631. Klima, John. "The Country Boy: Andy Pettitte vs. John Smoltz (October 24, 1996)." In: his *Pitched Battle: 35 of Baseball's Greatest Duels from the Mound*. Jefferson, NC: McFarland & Co., Inc., 2002. Pp. 175–179.

52632. _____. "Moment of Truth: John Smoltz vs. Jack Morris (October 27, 1991)." In: his *Pitched Battle: 35 of Baseball's Greatest Duels from the Mound*. Jefferson, NC: McFarland & Co., Inc., 2002. Pp. 157–161.

52633. Kuenster, Bob. "John Smoltz, *Baseball Digest's* 1996 Pitcher of the Year." *Baseball Digest,* LVI (January 1997), 24–39.

52634. Kuenster, John. "Why Braves' John Smoltz Ranks as a Top Gun Out of the Bullpen." *Baseball Digest,* LXII (August 2003), 17–19.

52635. Kurkjian, Tim. "In the Crosshairs: John Smoltz." *ESPN: The Magazine,* IV (December 24, 2001), 62–63.

52636. Plummer, William. "Faith Hurler: All-Star John Smoltz Has Finally Got a Game Plan." *People Weekly,* XLVI (July 15, 1996), 173–174.

52637. Rains, Rob. "Smoltz's Backyard Helps Barbecue Pirates." *USA Today Baseball Weekly,* II (October 14, 1992), 8–9.

52638. Rasmussen, Patty. "Restoration Project." In: Richard Levin, ed. *2002 World Series Official Program.* New York: Major League Baseball Promotion Corp., 2002. Pp. 114–119.

52639. Smoltz, John, with Jeff Bradley. "9th Life." *ESPN: The Magazine,* V (October 14, 2002), 58–63.

52640. Spoehr, Luther W. "John Andrew Smoltz." In: Vol. Q-Z of David L. Porter, ed. *Biographical Dictionary of American Sports: Baseball.* Rev. and enlarged ed. Westport, CT: Greenwood Press, 2000. Pp. 1440–1442.

52641. Verducci, Tom. "Atlanta's Endgame: Closer John Smoltz of the Braves." *Sports Illustrated,* XCVII (August 19, 2002), 50–52, 54.

52642. _____. "Eye-Opener." *Sports Illustrated,* LXXXIV (June 10, 1996), 46–48, 50, 55.

52643. Whiteside, Larry. "Braves' John Smoltz Making a Pitch for Cy Young Award." *Baseball Digest,* LV (October 1996), 22–25.

Jeffrey Smulyan
EXEC. (B: 1950) Remarks: Chmn. Bd., Emmis Broadcasting Corp., Indianapolis, IN; prin., owner, chmn., Seattle (AL), 1989–1991.

52644. Johnson, Douglas. "Mr. Radio Goes Major League." *Indiana Business Magazine,* XXXIII (October 1989), 8–12.

Edwin Donald ("Duke" or "The Silver Fox") Snider★
OF-SCOUT-BROADCASTER. (B: Sept. 19, 1926, Los Angeles, CA). Brooklyn (NL) and Los Angeles (NL), 1947–1962; New York (NL), 1963; San Francisco (NL), 1964. Remarks: In an 18-year major league career, obtained 2,116 hits (407 homers) and 99 stolen bases in 2,143 games; had four homers in 1952 World Series and four in the fall classic of 1955; had two grand slam homers in three days, Aug. 1953; NL RBI champion, 1955; had grand slam homer, May 13, 1956; NL home run champion, 1956; had first hit in Dodger Stadium, April 1962; established various other records; minor league manager and big league scout, 1965–1973; coach, Montreal (NL), 1974–1975; member, broadcasting team, Montreal (NL), 1973-; elected to National Baseball Hall of Fame in 1980, where his plaque reads: "Hit 407 career home runs and tied NL record with 40 or more roundtrippers five years in a row, 1953–1957. Batted .300 or better seven times in compiling .295 lifetime average. Topped league in slugging pct. twice and total bases three times. First to hit four homers in a World Series twice — in 1952 and 1955. Set NL record [since broken — MJS] for Series homers (11)."

52645. Allen, Maury. "Duke Snider (1947–1964)." In: his *Baseball's 100.* New York: Galahad Books, 1981. Pp. 256–258.

52646. Bjarkman, Peter C. *Baseball Legends: Duke Snider.* New York: Chelsea House Publishers, 1994. 61p.

52647. Borst, William A. ("Bill"). "Edwin Donald 'Duke,' 'Silver Fox' Snider." In: Vol. Q-Z of David L. Porter, ed. *Biographical Dictionary of American Sports: Baseball.* Rev. and enlarged ed. Westport, CT: Greenwood Press, 2000. Pp. 1442–1443.

52648. Breslin, Jimmy. "The Duke of Flatbush." In: Al Silverman, ed. *True's 1956 Baseball Yearbook.* Greenwich, CT: Fawcett Publications, 1956. Pp. 20–23.

52649. Burke, Tim. "Why No Crowning Touch for the Duke of Flatbush?" *Baseball Digest,* XXXIV (October 1975), 58–65.

52650. Burnham, Richard. "Duke Snider —1955." In: his *Baseball's Top 100: The Best Individual Seasons of All Time.* Wilton, CT: Diamond Library, 1996. Pp. 147–149.

52651. Burr, Harold C. "Episodes in a Duke's Past." *Baseball Digest,* XIII (September 1954), 58–61.

52652. Cohane, Tim. "Duke Snider: He Reaches for Greatness." *Look;* XIX (January 28, 1956), 107–110+.

52653. Daley, Arthur. "King Edwin: Edwin (Duke) Snider." In: his *All the Home Run Kings.* New York: G.P. Putnam, 1972. Pp. 81–93.

52654. _____. "Duke Snider." In: his *Kings of the Home Run.* New York: G.P. Putnam, 1962. Pp. 103–111.

52655. _____. "A Night for Duke Snider." In: his *Sports of The Times.* New York: E.P. Dutton,1959. Pp. 91–94.

52656. Dexter, Charles. "The Duke's a King Now." *Baseball Digest,* XI (November 1952), 5–9.

52657. Drees, Jack and James C. Mullen. "Duke Snider: The Duke of Brooklyn." In: their *Where Is He Now?* Middle Village, NY: Jonathan David Publishers, 1973. Pp. 132–136.

52658. "Duke Snider." In: *Current Biography Yearbook, 1956.* New York: H.W. Wilson Co., 1956. Pp. 590–591.

52659. "Duke Snider." *Sport Life,* IV (September 1951), 12+.

52660. "Duke Snider." *Sports Illustrated,* I (March 1953), 46+.

52661. Durslag, Melvin. "The Duke and His Miseries." *Sport,* XXVII (June 1950), 22–23+.

52662. Enders, Eric. "Legend: Three Future Hall of Famers Patrolled Center Field in New York During the 1950s and Duke Snider Might Have Been the Best of Them." In: Richard Levin, ed. *2004 World Series Official Program.* New York: Major League Baseball Properties Corp., 2004. Pp. 27–28.

52663. Goren, Herb. "The Duke of Dodgerdom." *Baseball Digest,* IX (July 1950), 71–75.

52664. Graham, Frank. "Why Don't They Stop Knocking the Duke?" *Sport,* XXIV (September 1951), 12–13+.

52665. Gross, Milton. "The Duke of the Dodgers." *Sport,* XI (July 1961), 20–21+.

52666. Guilfoile, Bill. "Snider and Kaline, Baseball's Newest Hall of Famers." In: Bill Shumard, ed. *1980 All-Star Game Program.* Los Angeles, CA: Public Relations Department, Los Angeles Dodgers, 1980. Pp. 82–83.

52667. Hano, Arnold. "The Duke of Los Angeles." *Sport,* XXIX (April 1960), 56–67.

52668. Hinckley, David. "Duke Snider." In: Danny Peary, ed. *Cult Baseball Players.* New York: Simon and Schuster, 1990. Pp. 32–37.

52669. _____. "Duke Snider." In: Danny Peary, ed. *Baseball's Finest: The Greats, the Flakes, the Weird and the Wonderful.* North Digton, MA: The JG Press, 1990. Pp. 32–37. Both Peary books are identical.

52670. Holmes, Tommy. "From Series Goat to Series Slugger." In: Bruce Jacobs, ed. *Baseball Stars of 1955.* New York: Lion Books, 1955. Pp. 119–124.

52671. Honig, Donald. "Duke Snider." In: his *Mays, Mantle, Snider: A Celebration.* New York: Macmillan, 1987. pp. 9–50.

52672. Jacobs, Bruce. "The Noblest Dodger: Duke Snider." In: Bruce Jacobs, ed. *Baseball Stars of 1956.* Now York: Lion Books, 1956. Pp. 82–86.

52673. Kahn, Roger. "The Duke of Fallbrook." In: his *The Boys Of Summer.* New York: Harper & Row, 1972. Pp. 374–385.

52674. Mann, Arthur. "The Dodgers' Problem-Child." *Saturday Evening Post,* CCXXVI (February 20, 1954), 27+.

52675. Meany, Tom. "The Iron Duke." In: his *The Artful Dodgers.* New York: A.S. Barnes, 1953. Pp. 56–66. Reprinted In 1954 edition; updated for 1958 and 1963 editions and reprinted in 1966.

52676. Park, Charlie. "Dulto Snider's Memory Book." *Baseball Digest,* XX (February 1961), 79–81.

52677. Reidenbaugh, Lowell. "Duke Snider." In: his *Cooperstown: Where Legends Live Forever.* St. Louis, MO: The Sporting News, 1983. Pp. 235–236.

52678. Ritter, Lawrence S. and Donald Honig. "Duke' Snider." In: their *The 100 Greatest Baseball Players of All Time.* New York: Crown Publishers, 1981. Pp. 16–17.

52679. Robinson, Murray. "Duke Snider: He Played 'Centipede." *Baseball Digest,* XXII (June 1963), 28–31.

52680. Rosenthal, Harold. "The Duke Grows Up." *Complete Baseball,* II (Fall 1950), 36–48.

52681. Salant, Nathan. "Duke Snider." In: his *Superstars, Stars, and Just Plain Heroes.* New York: Stein and Day, 1982. Pp. 119–128.

52682. Slear, Tom. "Duke Snider Was from the Golden Era of Baseball, But His Story Says a Lot About Today's Players, Too." *Sports History,* II (November 1988), 52–53.

52683. Smith, Ron. "Duke Snider 83." In: his *The Sporting News Selects Baseball's 100 Greatest Players.* St. Louis, MO: The Sporting News, 1998. Pp. 180–181.

52684. Snider, Edwin ("Duke"). "Duke Snider's Play Ball Tips." *Ontario Physical and Health Education Association Bulletin,* (Spring 1989), 58–60, 63.

52685. _____. *Fine Points of Batting.* Los Angeles, CA: Union Oil Company, 1958. 9p. Instructional pamphlet.

52686. _____. as told to George Vass. "The Game I'll Never Forget." In: George Vass, ed. *The Game I'll Never Forget.* Chicago: Bonus Books, 1999. Pp. 243–247.

52687. _____. with Bill Gilbert. *The Duke of Flatbush.* New York: Zebra Books, 1988. 288p.

52688. _____. with Roger Kahn. "I Play Baseball for Money-Not Fun." *Collier's,* CXXXVII (May 25, 1956), 42–44+.

52689. Steinberg, Alan. "Reggie, Mickey, and the Duke." *Baseball History,* I (Fall 1986), 20–38.

52690. Stump, Al. "Did the [1962 World] Series Make the Duke?" *Sport,* XIV (March 1953), 32–33+.

52691. _____. "Duke Snider's Story." *Sport,* XX (September 1955), 48–56.

52692. Thompson, Michael. "Al Kaline and Duke Snider Had the Added Extra." *Baseball Digest,* XXXIX (March 1980), 53–57.

52693. Weber, Bill. "When the Duke was King." *Beckett Baseball Card Monthly,* IV (November 1987), 30–31.

52694. Winehouse, Irwin. *Duke Snider Story.* New York: Julian Messner, 1964. 191p.

52695. Whitmarsh, F. E. "Duke Snider: Brooklyn Bomber." In: his *Famous American Athletes of Today.* 14th Series. Boston: L.C. Page, 1956. Pp. 221–232.

52696. Zimmerman, Paul. "The Duke." In: his *The Los Angeles Dodgers.* New York: Coward-McCann, 1960. Pp. 150–157.

Fred Carlisle ("Snow") Snodgrass
OF-1B. (B: Oct. 11, 1887, Ventura, CA-D: April 5, 1974.). New York (NL), 1908–1915; Boston (NL), 1915–1916. Remarks. Had 852 hits (11 homers) and 215 stolen bases in 945 games in nine years; committed memorable error ("$30,000 Muff") in Game Seven of 1912 World Series; years later, after playing days, served as mayor of Oxnard, Calif.

52697. Bell, Christopher. "Fred Snodgrass." In: his *Scapegoats: Baseballers Whose Careers are Marked by One Fateful Play.* Jefferson, NC: McFarland & Co., Inc., 2002. Pp. 21–30.

52698. Davis, Mac. "No Angel in the Outfield." In: his *The Lore and Legends of Baseball.* New York: Lantern Press, 1953. Pp. 96–97.

52699. Gutman, Dan. "The Snodgrass Muff." In: his *Baseball's Biggest Bloopers: The Games That Got Away.* New York: Puffin, 1995. Pp. 18–34.

52700. Hirshberg, Al. "No Goat Like Snodgrass." *Baseball Digest,* VIII (March 1949), 49–53.

52701. McGuire, Mark and Michael Sean Gormley. "Fred Snodgrass." In: their *Moments in the Sun: Baseball's Briefly Famous.* Jefferson, NC: McFarland & Co., Inc., 2001. Pp. 167–171.

52702. Pisano, Carmen. "The Truth Behind Snodgrass' Muff." *Oldtyme Baseball News,* III, no. 1 (1991), 8–9.

52703. Ritter, Lawrence S. "Fred Snodgrass." In: his *Glory of Their Times.* New York: Macmillan, 1966. Pp. 83–108. Excerpted in *Saturday Evening Post,* CCXXXIX (August 13,1966), 46–48.

52704. Santa Maria, Michael and James Costello. "Muff of a Lifetime." In: their *In the Shadows of the Diamond.* Dubuque, IA: The Elysian Fields Press, 1992. Pp. 11–17.

52705. Weiss, Peter. "Fred Snodgrass." In: his *Baseball's All-Time Goats: As Chosen by America's Top Sportswriters.* Holbrook, MA: Bob Adams, Inc, 1992. Pp. 152–155.

Jack Thomas ("J. T.") Snow
1B. (B: Feb. 26, 1968, Long Beach, CA). New York (AL), 1992; California (AL), 1993–1996; Florida (NL), 1997–2000; San Francisco (NL), 2001-. Remarks: Through 2004, has had 1,399 hits (185 homers) and 19 stolen bases in 1,560 games; obtained pinch-hit homer in Game Two of 2000 NLCS; had 11 hits and one homer (Game One) in 2002 World Series.

52706. Langill, Mark. "Rookie Report: J. T. Snow." *Beckett Baseball Card Monthly,* X, no. 101 (August 1993), 20–21.

52707. McCarthy, Charlie. "Prime Time Talent." *Beckett Focus on Future Stars,* III, no. 24 (April 1993), 16–17.

52708. Nightengale, Bob. "Heaven Sent." *Beckett Focus on Future Stars,* III, no. 28 (August 1993), 6–9.

52709. Stewart, Mark. *J. T. Snow.* New York: Children's Press, 1996. 48 p.

Cory Snyder see **James Cory Snyder**
James Cory Snyder
OF (B: Nov. 11, 1962, Inglewood, CA). Cleveland (AL), 1985–1990; Chicago (AL) and Toronto (AL), 1991; San Francisco (NL), 1992; Los Angeles (NL), 1993–1994. Remarks: Obtained 902 hits (149 homers) in 1,068 games in 10 years; had one grand slam homer, April 22, 1988 and became one of eight major league players to hit three homers in one game in both the NL and AL; also played on 1984 U.S. Olympic Baseball Team; coach, Seattle (AL), 1998; a coach in inaugural Toledo (IL) fantasy camp, Aug. 2002.

52710. Cohen, Irwin. "Baseball Beat: Cory Snyder." *Baseball Cards,* VII (July 1987), 24–29.

52711. Fimrite, Ron. "Pow! Wow!" *Sports Illustrated,* LXVI (April 6, 1987), 74–76+.

52712. Haynes, Paul. "Cory Snyder: A Budding Star Survives Transition Year." *Baseball Digest,* XLVII (January 1988), 40–41.

52713. Ison, Jim. "Cory Snyder." In: his *Mormons in the Major Leagues.* Cincinnati, OH: Action Sports, 1991. Pp. 180–183.

52714. Kuenster, John. "Cory Snyder of Indians Ready to Put It All Together in '89." *Baseball Digest,* XLVIII (May 1989), 13–14.

52715. Macnow, George. "The Erie Sensation." *Sport,* LXXVIII (May 1987), 37–43.

Russel Henry ("Russ") Snyder

OF (B: June 22, 1934, Oak, NE). Cleveland (AL), 1959–1960; Baltimore (AL), 1961–1967; Chicago (AL) and Cleveland (AL), 1968; Cleveland (AL), 1969; Milwaukee (AL), 1970. Remarks: Had 984 hits (42 homers) and 58 stolen bases in 1,365 games in 12 years; pinch hit safely twice in one inning, April 29, 1962; 3rd out in a triple play, July 30, 1968.

52716. Beard, Gordon. "Orioles Surge and '4–3' Plays Revive Memories of O's Pennants and 'Snydered Out' Grounders." *Orioles Gazette,* III (July 8, 1993), 14–15.

Albert Henry ("Hank") Soar

UMP. (B: Aug. 17, 1914, Alton, RI). Remarks: AL arbiter, 1950–1972; AL assistant supervisor of umpires, 1973.

52717. Fandell, Todd E. "For the Umps, It's a, Long, Long Season." In: John Kuenster, ed. *From Cobb to Catfish* (Chicago, IL: Rand McNally, 1975). Pp. 192–194.

Hank Soar *see* **Albert Henry ("Hank") Soar**

Louis Francis ("Chief") Sockalexis

OF. (B: Oct, 24, 1871, Old Town, ME-D: Dec. 24, 1913). Cleveland (N.L), 1897–1899. Remarks: Had 116 hits (three homers) and 16 stolen bases In 94 games in three major league seasons; first full-blooded Native American (Penobscot) to play big league ball; also played for Hartford (EL), 1899; later returned to Indian Island (ME), where he worked at a logging camp and coached boys' baseball teams; died from overexposure to "firewater"; supposedly honored in 1915 when Cleveland fans voted to rename their AL franchise the "Indians."

52718. Davis, Mac. "Frank Merriwell in Person." In: his *The Lore and Legends of Baseball.* New York: Lantern Press, 1953. Pp. 35–37. Suggests that Sockalexis was the model for juvenile writer Gilbert Patten's character Frank Merriwell.

52719. Feldman, Jay. "The Rise and Fall of Louis Sockalexis." *The Baseball Research Journal,* XV (1986), 39–42. Reprinted in Mark Alvarez, ed., *The Perfect Game: A Classic Collection of Facts, Figures, Stories and Characters from the Society for American Baseball Research* (New York: Barnes & Noble Books, 1995), pp. 106–112.

52720. Fleitz, David L. *Louis Sockalexis: The First Cleveland Indian.* Jefferson, NC: McFarland & Co., Inc., 2002. 229p.

52721. Gagnon, Richard ("Cappy"). "Louis M. 'Chief' Sockalexis." In: Vol. Q-Z of David L. Porter, ed. *Biographical Dictionary of American Sports: Baseball.* Rev. and enlarged ed. Westport, CT: Greenwood Press, 2000. Pp. 1443–1444.

52722. Kirst, Sean Peter. "Imagine Life as a Cartoon's Descendant." In: his *The Ashes of Lou Gehrig and Other Baseball Essays.* Jefferson, NC: McFarland & Co., Inc., 2003. Pp. 85–86.

52723. McDonald, Brian. *Indian Summer: The Tragic Story of Louis Francis Sockalexis, the First Native American in Major League Baseball.* New York: Rodale Press, 2003. 256p.

52724. McGuire, Mark and Michael Sean Gormley. "Chief Sockalexis." In: their *Moments in the Sun: Baseball's Briefly Famous.* Jefferson, NC: McFarland & Co., Inc., 2001. Pp. 43–49.

52725. Phillips, John. *Chief Sockalexis and the 1897 Cleveland Indians.* Cabin John, MD: Capital Publishing Co., 1991. 77 p.

52726. Rice, Ed. *Baseball's First Indian: Louis Sockalexis — Penobscot Legend, Cleveland Indian.* Windsor, CT: Tidemark Press, 2003. 207p.

52727. Salsinger, H.G. "The Facts About Sockalexis." *Baseball Digest,* XIII (June 1954), 54–57.

52728. Rice, Ed. "The Incomparable Indian Ballplayer from Maine." *Yankee,* LIII (October 1989), 66–67.

52729. Smith, Robert M. "Louis Sockalexis." In: his *Heroes of Baseball.* Cleveland, OH: World Publishing Co., 1952. Pp. 166–170.

52730. Staurowsky, Ellen J. "An Act of Honor or Exploitation?: The Cleveland Indians' Use of the Louis Francis Sockalexis Story." *Sociology of Sport Journal,* XV (December 1998), 299–316.

52731. _____. "The Cleveland 'Indians': A Case Study in American Indian Cultural Dispossession." *Sociology of Sport Journal,* XVII (December 2000), 307–330.

52732. _____. "Searching for Sockalexis: Exploring the Myth at the Core of Cleveland's 'Indian' Image." In: Thomas L. Altherr, ed. *The Cooperstown Symposium on Baseball and American Culture, 1998.* Jefferson, NC: McFarland & Co., Inc., 2002. Pp. 138–153.

52733. _____. "Sockalexis and the Making of the Myth at the Core of Cleveland's 'Indian' Image." In: Vine Deloria, Jr., ed. *Team Spirits: The Native American Mascots Controversy.* Lincoln, NE: University of Nebraska Press, 2001. Pp 82–108.

52734. Thompson, Stephen I. "The American Indian in the Major Leagues." *The Baseball Research Journal,* XII (1983), 1–7.

52735. Wilson, John R. M. "Louis M. Sockalexis." In: Paul Betz and Mark C. Carnes, eds. *American National Biography: Supplement I.* New York: Oxford University Press, 2002. Pp. 587–588.

Arthur Henry Soden

EXEC. (B: April 23, 1843, Framingham, MA-D: Aug. 13, 1925). Remarks: Owner, Boston (NL), 1876–1906 and originator of the "reserve clause."

52736. Laughlin, Brian L. "Arthur Henry Soden." In: Vol. Q-Z of David L. Porter, ed. *Biographical Dictionary of American Sports: Baseball.* Rev. and enlarged ed. Westport, CT: Greenwood Press, 2000. Pp. 1445–1446.

Luis Bettran Sojo

2B-SS-OF. (B: Jan. 3, 1965, Caracas, Venezuela). Toronto (AL), 1990; California (AL), 1991–1992; California (AL), 1993; Seattle (AL), 1994–1996; New York (AL), 1996–1999; Pittsburgh (NL), 2000; New York (AL), 2000-. Remarks: Through 2003, has had 671 hits (36 homers) and 28 stolen bases in 848 games; had winning hit in Game Five of 2000 World Series.

52737. Henry, Mike. "Amigo de Todos." *Yankees Magazine,* XIX (August 1998), 48–55.

Jimmie Lee Solomon

EXEC. (B: 1957, Thompsons, TX). Remarks: Exec. Dir., MLB Minor League Operations, 1991–2000; senior VP, MLB Baseball Operations, 2001-.

52738. Geffner, Michael P. "Major Minor." *Texas Monthly,* XXIV (August 1997), 68–71.

52739. Lombardo, John. "Jimmie Lee Solomon: He's Majoring in Minor League Baseball and Plans to Move Up." *Washington Business Journal,* XIII (October 14, 1994), 22–23.

Moe Solomon *see* **Morris H. ("Mose" or "Moe" or "The Rabbi of Swat") Solomon**

Morris H. ("Moses" or "Moe" or "The Rabbi Of Swat") Solomon

OF. (B: Dec. 8, 1900, New York City-D: June 25, 1966). New York (NL), 1923. Remarks: Had three hits in two major league games; nickname came from the fact that Solomon had hit 49 homers in 108 Southwestern League games — Giants' hopes for a "Jewish Babe Ruth" fizzled when his fielding deficiencies forced his return to the minors.

52740. Hertzel, Bob. "Moe Solomon: 'The Rabbi of Swat." *The Minneapolis Review of Baseball,* III (Spring-Fall 1963–30–32, 3–4–36, 36–37; IV (Winter 1984), 22–23.

52741. Lavelle, Howard. "Moses Solomon" 'The Rabbi of Swat." *The Baseball Research Journal,* V (1976), 90–92.

Charles W. Somers

EXEC. (B: Oct. 13, 1868, Newark, OH-D: June 29, 1934). Remarks: Founder/owner Cleveland (AL), 1900–1916; also investor in Philadelphia (AL), Chicago (AL), and Boston (AL), serving with the latter as president, 1901–1904; owner, New Orleans (SA), 1913–1934; VP, AL, 1901–1916.

52742. Matz, David S. "Charles W. Somers." In: Vol. Q–Z of David L. Porter, ed. *Biographical Dictionary of American Sports: Baseball.* Rev. and enlarged ed. Westport, CT: Greenwood Press, 2000. P. 1446.

Lary Sorensen

P-BROADCASTER(B: Oct. 4, 1955, Detroit, MI). Milwaukee (AL), 1977–1980; St. Louis (NL), 1981; Cleveland (AL), 1982–1983; Oakland (AL), 1984; Chicago (NL), 1985; Montreal (NL), 1987; San Francisco (NL), 1988. Remarks: Obtained 93 victories, 103 defeats, and six "saves" in 11 seasons; broadcaster, Detroit (AL), 1989–1997.

52743. Smithley, Al. "Anatomy of a Pitcher: An Interview." *Oldtyme Baseball News,* IV, no. 2 (1992), 8–9.

Alfonso Guilleard Soriano

2B. (B: San Pedro de Marco, P.R.). New York (AL), 1999–2003; Texas (AL), 2004-. Remarks: Through 2003, has had 741 hits (126 homers) and 139 stolen bases in 646 games; had homer in Game Three of 2001 ALCS; homered in Game Seven of 2001 World Series; AL stolen base champion, 2002; first big league 2B to hit 30 homers and steal 30 bases in the same season, 2002; had homer in Game Two of 2002 ALCS; 2004 All Star Game MVP award; went 6-for-6 in one game, May 8, 2004; also played for Hiroshima Toyo Carp (Japan League), 1996–1997.

52744. Heyman, Jon. "Yankees' Alfonso Soriano Hitting His Way to Stardom." *Baseball Digest,* LXII (August 2003), 44–45.

52745. Lucas, Ed and Paul Post. "Second Baseman Alfonso Soriano." *Baseball Digest,* LXI (October 2002), 46–50.

52746. Monk, Cody. *Alfonso Soriano: The Dominican Dream Come True.* Chicago, IL: Sports Publishing, 2003. 160p.

52747. Munz, Clemson Smith. "Profile." In: Richard Levin, ed. *2002 World Series Official Program.* New York: Major League Baseball Promotion Corp., 2002. Pp. 33–34.

52748. Pearlman, Jeff. "He's Arrived." *Sports Illustrated,* XCVII (August 26, 2002), 40–44.

52749. Schwarz, Alan. "Second to None." *Sports Illustrated for Kids,* XIV (October 2002), 50–52.

Victor Garland ("Vic") Sorrell

P-SCOUT. (B: April 9, 1901, Morrisville, N.C.-D: May 4, 1972). Detroit (AL), 1928–1937. Remarks. Won 92 games and lost 10, with 10 "saves," in a decade; minor league manager and Detroit (AL) scout, 1938–1944; baseball coach, North Carolina State University, 1945–1966; elected to North Carolina Sports Hall of Fame, 1999.

52750. Lane, Ferdinand C. "Vic Sorrell's Struggle with Defective Eyesight." *Baseball Magazine,* LI (June 1933), 311–312.

52751. Ward, John J. "Vic Sorrell of the Detroit Tigers." *Baseball Magazine,* XLV (July 1930), 356–357.

Paul Anthony Sorrento

OF. (B: Nov. 17, 1985, Somerville, MA). Minnesota (AL), 1989–1991; Cleveland (AL), 1992–1995; Seattle (AL), 1996–1997; Tampa Bay (AL), 1998–1999. Remarks: Had 876 hits (166 homers) and eight stolen bases in 1,093 games in 11 years; had two homers in one game, Aug. 18, 1996; had five hits and four RBIs in one game, April 15, 1997.

52752. Melia, Terry. "Making a Name for Himself: Paul Sorrento Is No Longer Tino's Replacement — He's the Genuine Article." *Mariners Magazine,* VII, no. 3 (1996), 45–46.

Samuel Peralta ("Sammy") Sosa

OF. (B: Nov. 12, 1968, San Pedro de Macoris, Dominican Republic). Texas (AL), 1989; Chicago (AL), 1989–1991; Chicago (NL), 1992–2004; Baltimore (AL), 2005-. Remarks: Through 2004, has had 2,220 hits (574 homers) and 233 stolen bases in 2,138 games; went 6-for-6 in one game, July 2, 1993; hit grand slam homers in consecutive games, July 27–28, 1998; N. L. MVP Award, 1998; first player to hit 60 homers in two consecutive big league seasons, 1998–1999; NL home run champion, 2000, 2002; NL RBI champion, 1998, 2001; had eight hits and two homers in 2003 NLCS.

52753. Angell, Roger. "Sammy's Sin." *The New Yorker,* LXXIX (June 30, 2003), 33–34.

52754. Bamberger, Michael. "Sammy Sosa Showed He's Indeed the Man — Even When He and the Cubs are Struggling." *Sports Illustrated,* LXXXIX (September 28, 1998), 46–51.

52755. Beaton, Rod. "Sosa Watch." *USA Today Baseball Weekly,* I (February 12, 1992), 15–16.

52756. Bolio, Roberto Velazquez. "McGwire y Sosa, en su Carrera por Romper el Record de Mas Cuadrangulares, dan Neuva Vida al Beisbol en Estados Unidos." *Proceso,* no. 1139 (30 de Agosto 1998), 77–78.

52757. Broome, Tol. "Chicago's Hope." *Beckett Baseball Card Monthly,* XVI (January 1999), 16–23.

52758. Burke, Rick. *Sammy Sosa.* Chicago, IL: Heinemann Library, 2001. 32p.

52759. Cannella, Stephen. "Better Than Ever." *Sports Illustrated,* XCV (August 27, 2001), 72–74.

52760. _____. "Bottom Line is the Bottom Line: Sosa Isn't Smiling." *Sports Illustrated,* XCII (June 29, 2000), 75, 78.

52761. Castle, George. "Cubs' Sammy Sosa: Ready to Fulfill His Potential?" *Baseball Digest,* LIII (April 1994), 74–76.

52762. _____. *Sammy Sosa: Clearing the Vines.* Champaign, IL: Sports Publishing, 1998. 223p.

52763. _____. *Slammin' Sammy Sosa: The Race for the Record.* Tulsa, OK: Trade Life Books, 1998. 159p.

52764. Christopher, Matt. *At the Plate with ... Sammy Sosa.* Boston, MA: Little, Brown and Co., 1999. 128p.

52765. Dougherty, Terri. *Sammy Sosa.* Minneapolis, MN: Abdo, 1999. 32p. Juvenile.

52766. Duncan, Patricia J. *Sosa! Baseball's Home Run Hero.* New York: Simon and Schuster, 1998. 220p. Text in English and Spanish, back to back and inverted.

52767. Etkin, Jack. "Major Leaguers Who Hit 60 Home Runs: Sammy Sosal — One of the Game's Most Exciting Players." *Baseball Digest,* LVII (December 1998), 64–67.

52768. Fisher, David. *Sammy Sosa.* Kansas City, MO: Andrews McMeel Publishing, 1999. 73p.

52769. Flynn, Gabriel. *Sammy Sosa.* [Chanhassen, MN] : Child's World, 2000. 24p.

52770. Gaines, Ann. *Sammy Sosa.* Overcoming Adversity Series. Philadelphia, PA: Chelsea House Publishers, 2001. 107p.

52771. Gergen, Joe. "Sosa Ties the Mark." In: Dick Wimmer, ed. *The Home Run Game.* Short Hills, NJ: Burford Books, 1999. Chpt. 16.

52772. Gin, Willie. "Sammy Sosa." *Current Biography,* LX (May 1999), 43–47.

52773. Ginnetti, Toni. "Sammy Sosa of the Cubs: From Star to Superstar." *Baseball Digest,* LVII (September 1998), 34–37.

52774. Gomez, Pedro. "Masters of the Universe." In: Richard Levin, ed. *1998 World Series Program.* New York: Major League Baseball Promotion Corp., 1998. Pp. 50–59. Sosa and McGwire.

52775. Greenstein, Teddy. "Sammy Sosa: Evolution of a Big League Hitter — an Interview." *Baseball Digest,* LXI (June 2002), 36–39.

52776. Gutman, Bill. *Sammy Sosa: Home Run Hero!* New York: Pocket Books, 1998. 294p. Text in English and Spanish, paged separately, back to back and inverted.

52777. Hagen, Paul. "Sammy Sosa Enjoys His Climb to Stardom." *Baseball Digest,* LVIII (December 1999), 54–57.

52778. Hedin, Mark. "Sosa con el Campeonato en la Mira, a Pesar de la Carrera de los Jonroneros." *El Mensajero,* XII (23 de Setiembre 1998), 24–25.

52779. Heuer, R. "Sammy Sosa, Home-Run Hitter with Heart." *Americas,* LI (March-April 1999), 14–21.

52780. Holtzman, Jerome. "Cubs' Sammy Sosa Destined to Join Game's Hitting Elite." *Baseball Digest,* LV (October 1996), 46–47.

52781. Hunt, Steve. "Sam I Am." *Beckett Sports Collectibles,* VII (October 1998), 6–9.

52782. Isaacson, Melissa. "Sammy Sosa: A Budding Star for the White Sox." *Baseball Digest,* XLIX (August 1990), 39–41.

52783. Jerome, Richard. "Sam I Am: Sammy Sosa Hits 62nd Home Run." *People Weekly,* L (September 28, 1998), 115–116.

52784. _____., et al. "Sammy Sosa, el Alma de un Heroe." *People en Espanol,* (Noviembre 1998), 28–30.

52785. Kennedy, Kostya and Mark Bechtel. "Much Ado about Corking." *Sports Illustrated,* XCVIII (June 16, 2003), 22–23.

52786. Kiley, Mike. "Better Than Ever: Sammy Sosa, Cub's Star Focuses on Team Play." *Baseball Digest,* LX (October 2001), 26–29.

52787. Kirkpatrick, Rob. *Sammy Sosa: Home-Run Hitter.* New York : PowerKids Press, 2000. 24p.

52788. Korman, Susan. *Sammy Sosa.* Lations in the Limelight. Philadelphia, PA: Chelsea House Publishers, 2002. 64p.

52789. Kuenster, John. "Sammy Sosa: A Narrow Winner Over Mark McGwire as 1998 Player of the Year." *Baseball Digest,* LVII (December 1998), 17–21.

52790. Le Batard, Dan. "What Next?" *ESPN: The Magazine,* III (July 10, 2000), 44–49.

52791. Leiker, Ken. "4–1998: Mark McGwire and Sammy Sosa Engage in a Record-Setting Home Run Race." In: his *Major League Baseball Memorable Moments: The Most Memorable Moments in Major League Baseball History.* New York: Ballantine Books, 2002. Pp. 28–32.

52792. Lopresti, Mike. "You Can't Slam Sammy: Sosa Makes His Mark on Many Fields." *USA Today Baseball Weekly,* VIII (October 28, 1998), 27–28.

52793. Lorenz, Patrick J. "Slamin' Sammy Sosa: Home Runs and Kisses." *You,* (May 1999), 14–15.

52794. McCarver, Tim, with Danny Peary. "Mark McGwire and Sammy Sosa." In: his *The Perfect Season: Why 1998 was Baseball's Greatest Year.* New York: Villard Books, 1999. Pp. 3–20.

52795. Maclean, Caleb. *Sammy Sosa, Cubs Clubber.* New York: Children's Press, 1999.48p.

52796. Mitchell, Fred. "Profile: Sammy Sosa." In: Michael J. McCormick, ed. *2002 All Star Game Official Program.* New York: Major League Baseball Promotion Corp., 2002. Pp. 80–81.

52797. "Much Ado About Corking." *Sports Illustrated,* XCVIII (June 16, 2003), 22+.

52798. Muskat, Carrie. "No Limit: From Humble Beginnings, Sammy Sosa Has Developed into a Star." *Cubs Quarterly,* XV (September 1996), 132–134.

52799. _____. *Sammy Sosa.* Childs, MD: Mitchell Lane Publishers, 1999. 64p.

52800. Noden, Merrell. *Home Run Heroes: Mark McGwire, Sammy Sosa, and a Season for the Ages.* New York: Simon and Schuster, 1998. 96p.

52801. Porter, David L. "Samuel Peralta 'Sammy' Sosa." In: Vol. Q-Z of David L. Porter, ed. *Biographical Dictionary of American Sports: Baseball.* Rev. and enlarged ed. Westport, CT: Greenwood Press, 2000. Pp. 1447–1448.

52802. Porter, Russell. *McGwire and Sosa: Baseball's Greatest Home Run Story.* New York: Welcome Rain Publishers, 1998. 128p.

52803. Preller, James. *McGwire & Sosa: A Season to Remember.* New York: Aladdin Paperbacks, 1998. 32p.

52804. Rogers, Phil. "The Hidden Profit Behind a Deal: The Cubs' Trade of Rafael Palmeiro to Texas in 1988 Remains Unpopular with Chicago Fans, But it Led to the Acquiring of Sammy Sosa." *Baseball Digest,* LXI (September 2002), 60–63.

52805. _____. "Sammy Sosa: 500 Homers and Beyond." *Baseball Digest,* LXII (June 2003), 26–28.

52806. Rushin, Steve. "Sam the Ham." *Sports Illustrated,* LXXXIX (September 14, 1998), 34–35.

52807. "Sammy Sosa." In: Carrie Muskat, ed. *Banks to Sandberg to Grace: Five Decades of Love and Frustration with the Chicago Cubs.* Chicago, IL: Contemporary Books, 2001. Pp. 257–258.

52808. "Sammy Sosa." In: *Current Biography Yearbook, 1999.* New York: H. W. Wilson, 1999. Pp. 541–544.

52809. *Sammy's Season.* Chicago, IL: Contemporary Books, 1998. 105p.

52810. "Sam's Club: With Less Than 1,000 Cards to Choose from, Sammy Sosa's Comprehensive Checklist is Both Short and Sweet." *Beckett Baseball Card Monthly,* XVI (January 1999), 100–103.

52811. Savage, Jeff. *Sammy Sosa, Home Run Hero.* Minneapolis, MN: Lerner Publications, 1999. 64p.

52812. _____. "Sammy Sosa." In: his *Home Run Kings.*

New York: Raintree Steck-Vaughn Publishers, 1999. Pp. 30–35.

52813. Schwarz, Alan. "Dominators of 1998: Sammy Sosa." *Sport,* XC (January 1999), 34–35.

52814. _____. "Sammy Sosa! Our Readers Chose Slammin' Sammy Sosa ... by a Smile!" *Sports Illustrated for Kids,* XI (December 1, 1999), 24+. As 1999 Athlete of the Year.

52815. _____. Slammin' Sammy: Sammy Sosa is Very Happy to be One of Baseball's Most Powerful and Popular Sluggers." *Sports Illustrated for Kids,* XI (July 1, 1999), 38+.

52816. *Slammin' Sammy Sosa: The Race for the Record.* Tulsa, OK: Trade Life Books, 1998. 159p.

52817. Smith, Gary. "Heaven and Hell: Sammy Sosa's Dream Season was a Nightmare for the Man Who Taught Him Baseball, But Had to Follow the Home Run Race from a Snake Pit of a Prison in the Dominican Republic." *Sports Illustrated,* LXXIX (December 21, 1998), 84–93. Hector Peguero.

52818. Sonnenberg, Jim. "Major Errors Not Confined to Field." *Crain's Chicago Business,* XXVI (June 9, 2003), 5–5. Sosa's corked bat.

52819. Sorci, Rick. "Baseball Profile: Outfielder Sammy Sosa." *Baseball Digest,* LVI (December 1997), 44–45.

52820. Sosa, Sammy, with Marcos Breton. *Sosa: An Autobiography.* New York: Warner Books, 2000. 209p. Excerpted in *Scholastic Scope,* XLIX (October 2, 2000), 17–19, under the title "A Hero's Beginnings."

52821. Stein, Joel. "Grand Sam: An Interview." *Time,* CLII (September 28, 1998), 76–77.

52822. Stewart, Mark and Mike Kennedy. *Home Run Heroes: Mark McGwire, Sammy Sosa and a Season for the Ages.* Brookfield, CT: The Millbrook Press, 1999. 64p.

52823. "Storm Center." *Sports Illustrated,* XCII (June 26, 2000), 66+. Contract negotiations.

52824. Thompson, Jim. "Double Mint: 1998 Beckett Man of the Year." *Beckett Baseball Card Monthly,* XV (December 1998), 16–23. With McGwire.

52825. Torres, John Albert. *Sports Great Sammy Sosa.* Hillside, NJ: Enslow Publishers, 2003. 64p.

52826. Van Schouwen, Daryl. "Sammy Sosa Produces But Still Has His Critics." *Baseball Digest,* LIV (December 1995), 49–51.

52827. Verdi, Bob. *They Went Yard: McGwire and Sosa, an Awesome Home Run Season.* Chicago, IL: Bonus Books, 1998. 160p.

52828. Verducci, Tom. "The Education of Sammy Sosa." *Sports Illustrated,* LXXXVIII (June 29, 1998), 26–29.

52829. _____. "The 500 Crowd: Sammy Sosa is the Latest to Hit His 500th Home Run." *Sports Illustrated,* XCVIII (April 14, 2003), 56+.

52830. _____. Power Couple: In a Reunion at Wrigley, Sammy Sosa Still Had a Hot Bat and an Infectious Grin While Mark McGwire Tried to Find Relief from an Infected Toe and a Voracious Public." *Sports Illustrated,* XC (June 7, 1999), 44–49.

52831. _____. "Sammy's Second Season." *Sports Illustrated,* XCIX (August 25, 2003), 38–41.

52832. _____. "Storm Center: By Angling for a Rich New Contract, Cubs Slugger Sammy Sosa Stirred Up a Hurricane That May Blow Him Clear Out of the Windy City — But to Where?" *Sports Illustrated,* XCII (June 26, 2000), 66–70.

Allen Sutton ("Dixie") Sothoron
P-MGR. (B: April 29, 1893, Laura, OH-D: June 17, 1939). St. Louis (AL), 1914–1915, 1917–1921; Boston (AL),

1921; Cleveland (AL), 1921–1922; St. Louis (NL), 1924–1926. Remarks: Had 92 victories, 100 defeats, and nine "saves," in 11 seasons; also played for Portland (PCL), 1916; coach, St. Louis (NL), 1927–1928; interim manager, St. Louis (AL), 1933, winning two games and losing six (.250).

52833. Burkholder, Ed. "Allen Sothoron." In: his *Baseball Immortals.* New York: Christopher, 1955. Pp. 97–100.

52834. Spalding, John E. "Allen Sothoron." In: his *Pacific Coast League Stars, Vol. II: Ninety Who Made It to the Majors, 1905–1957.* San Jose, CA: John E. Spalding, 1997. Pp. 33–35.

Dixie Sothoron *see* **Allen Sutton ("Dixie") Sothoron**
Mario Melvin Soto
P. (B: July 12, 1966, Bani, Dominican Republic). Cincinnati (NL), 1977–1988. Remarks: Had 100 victories and 92 defeats, with four "saves," in 12 years; struck out 15 batters in a game twice, Sept. 19, 1980 and Aug. 17, 1982; Reds' opening day pitcher, 1982–1986, 1988; career largely ended by injuries.

52835. Coplon, Jeff. "Mario Soto: The Year of Living Dangerously." *Sport,* LXXV (October 1984), 62–72.

52836. Kaplan, Jim. "Soto Isn't So-So Anymore." *Sports Illustrated,* LVII (July 5, 1982), 50–61.

52837. Kuenster, John. "Mario Soto Allowed Fewest Base Runners Per Game in 1982." *Baseball Digest,* XLII (February 1983), 15–21.

52838. Wulf, Steve. "His Bad Reputation Is a Bad Rap." *Sports Illustrated,* LXI (July 23, 1984), 28–31.

Sonia Sotomayor
EXEC-JUDGE. (B: June 25, 1954). Remarks: Asst. district attorney, Office of the New York (NY) County District Attorney, 1984–1987; associate then partner, Pavia and Harcourt, 1988–1992; district judge, U.S. District Court for the Southern District of NY, 1992–1998; circuit judge, U.S. Court of Appeals for The Second Circuit, 1998-.

52839. Abrams, Roger I. "Baseball's Labor Wars of the 1990s: Sonia Sotomayor." In: his *Legal Bases: Baseball and the Law.* Philadelphia, PA: Temple University Press, 1998. Pp. 173–200.

Stephen ("Steve" or "Bud") Souchock
OF-1B. (B: March 3, 1919, Yatesboro, PA-D: July 28, 2002). New York (AL), 1946–1948; Chicago (AL), 1949; Detroit (AL), 1951–1956. Remarks: In an eight-year pro utilityman career, had 313 hits (50 homers) in 473 games; decorated veteran of the Battle of the Bulge; earlier, in 1942, received EL MVP Award.

52840. Bisher, Furman. "Souchock Crashes Through." *Sport,* XXII (August 1956), 21–24.

52841. Feldman, Chic. "Another [Sam] Crawford for the Tigers." *Baseball Digest,* XII (January 1953), 65–67.

52842. Kelley, Brent P. "An SCD Interview with Steve Souchock." *Sports Collector's Digest,* XVIII (August 9, 1991), 230–231.

52843. _____. "Steve Souchock: A Career of Bad Brakes." In: his *They Too Wore Pinstripes: Interviews with 20 Glory-Days New York Yankees.* Jefferson, NC: McFarland & Co., 1998. Pp. 171–179.

52844. Trimble, Joe. "Souchock: Twelfth in Gehrig Quest." *Baseball Digest,* V (November 1944), 51–53.

Steve Souchock *see* **Stephen ("Steve" or "Bud") Souchock**
Billy Southworth *see* **William Harrison ("Billy") Southworth**
William Harrison ("Billy") Southworth
OF-MGR. (B: March 9, 1903, Harvard, NE-D: Nov.

15, 1969). Cleveland (AL), 1913, 1915; Pittsburgh (NL), 1918–1920; Boston (NL), 1921–1923; Now York (NL),1924–1926; St. Louis (NL), 1926–1927, 1929. Remarks: Obtained 1,296 hits (52 homers) and 138 stolen bases in 1,192 games in 13 playing years; led NL in triples, 1919; had three doubles and a homer in one game, Aug. 4, 1921; had key homer in Game Two of 1926 World Series; manager, St. Louis (NL), 1929, 1940–1945 and Boston (NL), 1946–1951, winning 1,815 games and losing 1,064 (.593); manager, Rochester (IL), 1928, 1929–1931; coach, New York (NL), 1933; minor league manager and scout in Braves' organization, 1951–1966.

52845. Baumgartner, Stan. "They'd Rather Hit Triples; Baseball's Perfectionist, Billy Southworth, Cures His Cards of the Inevitable Slumps by Reminding Them How They Play at Their Best." *Esquire,* XXIII (May 1945), 59–63.

52846. Bennett, Brian A. "Rochester, 1928." *The National Pastime,* XVII (1997), 50–53. Southworth and the Rochester Red Wings.

52847. "Billy Southworth." In: *Current Biography Yearbook, 1944.* New York: H.W. Wilson Co., 1944. Pp. 641–644.

52848. "Billy Southworth." *Liberty Magazine,* XXI (October 1944), 24–25+.

52849. "Billy the Brave." *Time,* XLVI (November 19, 1945), 68–69.

52850. Byrer, Lew. "Meet 'Billy the Kid' Southworth." *Baseball Digest,* I (December 1942), 37–41.

52851. Cannon, Jimmy. "This is Billy Southworth." *Baseball Digest,* VIII (May 1949), 43–48.

52852. Carmichael, John P. "A Lesson for Southworth." *Baseball Digest,* VI (September 1947), 28–29.

52853. Cleveland, Charles B. "You Can't Beat the Percentages." In: his *The Great Baseball Managers.* New York: Thomas Y. Crowell Co., 1950. Pp. 177–196.

52854. Dexter, Charles. "Baseball's 'Billy the Kid.'" *Collier's,* CXII (October 9, 1943), 21–23.

52855. Fischer, E. G. "Billy Southworth's St. Louis Swifties: 1942 St. Louis Cardinals World Champions." In: *St. Louis's Favorite Sport.* Cleveland: Society for American Baseball Research, 1992. Pp. 3–10.

52856. Graham, Frank. "The Comeback of Billy Southworth." *Sport,* Ill (September 1947), 34–35+.

52857. "Highlights In the Career of Billy Southworth." In: William H. Sullivan, ed. *Boston Braves 1947 Sketchbook.* Boston, MA: Public Relations Department, Boston Braves, 1947. Pp. 11–14.

52858. Holmes, Tommy. "What's Ahead for Southworth?" *Baseball Digest,* VIII (October 1949), 43–45.

52859. Hooey, Bob. "Life Story of 'Billy the Kid' Southworth." In: J.G. Taylor Spink, ed. *Baseball Register, 1945.* St. Louis, MO: *The Sporting News,* 1945. Pp. 5–19.

52860. Miller, Hub. "Southworth Speaks." *Baseball Magazine,* LXXVI (January 1946), 263–265.

52861. "Old Scout," pseud. "75 G's for Southworth?" *Baseball Digest,* V (April 1949), 56–57.

52862. Pope, Edwin. "William Harrison Southworth." In: his *Baseball's Greatest Managers.* Garden City, N.Y.: Doubleday, 1960. Pp. 234–246.

52863. Sampson, Arthur. "Billy Southworth, the Pennant Man." *Look,* XIII (May 24, 1949), 80–84.

62864. Smith, Walter ("Red"). "What Southworth Said on Those Trips to the Mound." *Baseball Digest,* III (November 1944), 7–9.

52865. Southworth, Billy. "The Greatest Ball Club an Earth: The Cardinals." *Saturday Evening Post,* CCXV (June 5,1943), 19+.

52866. _____. "Some Useful Hints on Playing the Outfield." *Baseball Magazine,* XXXVI (March 1926), 449–451.

52867. _____, as told to Bob Hooey. "My Greatest Day in Baseball." In: John P. Carmichael, ed. *My Greatest Day in Baseball.* New York: A.S. Barnes, 1945. Pp. 180–183. First published in the *Chicago Daily News.*

52868. Stockton, J. Roy. "The Red Birds Fly Again: Billy Southworth Comes Back with His Cardinals." *Saturday Evening Post,* CCIV (August 9, 1941), 18–19+.

52869. Walsh, Edward J. "William Harrison 'Billy' Southworth." In: Vol. Q-Z of David L. Porter, ed. *Biographical Dictionary of American Sports: Baseball.* Rev. and enlarged ed. Westport, CT: Greenwood Press, 2000. Pp. 1439–1440.

Warren Edward Spahn ★

P-SCOUT. (B: April 23, 1921, Buffalo, NY-D: Nov. 24, 2003). Boston (NL) and Milwaukee (NL), 1942, 1946–1964; New York (NL) and San Francisco (NL), 1965; Mexican League, 1966. Remarks: Had 363 victories, 245 defeats, and 29 "saves" in 21 seasons; had 18 strikeouts in a 15 inning game, June 14, 1952; NL Cy Young award, 1957; pitched two no-hitters, Sept. 16, 1960 and April 28, 1961; surrendered the first career homer of Willie Mays (q.v.), May 28, 1951; as a hitter, obtained 363 hits and 35 homers; established NL mark for most career home runs by a pitcher (35); and still holds several pitching records, including most wins by a "southpaw"; also played for Hartford (EL), 1942; minor league coach-manager and big league scout, 1967–1971, 1978–1981; coach, New York (NL), 1965 and Cleveland (AL), 1972–1973; named to Oklahoma Sports Hall of Fame, 1988; Turner Field plaza statue dedicated in his honor, Aug. 2003; elected to National Baseball Hall of Fame in 1973, where his plaque reads: "Became fifth biggest winner in majors' history with 363 victories. Most victories for a left-hander. Won 20 or more games 13 seasons, six in a row. Set all-time records for years leading league in victories (8) and complete games (9). Also NL career highs with 665 games started; 5,264 innings; 2,853 strikeouts. Pitched no-hitter in 1960. Another in 1961."

52870. Ajemian, Bob. "Warren Spahn." In: his *My Greatest Baseball Game.* New York: A.S. Barnes And Co., 1950. Pp. 181–187.

52871. Allen, Maury. "Warren Spahn (1942–1965)." In: his *Baseball's 100.* New York: Galahad Books, 1981. Pp. 84–86.

52872. Barrouquere, Peter. "Hall of Famer Warren Spahn Still Favors a Four-Man Pitching Rotation." *Baseball Digest,* XLIII (September 1984), 43–46.

52873. Barry, Jack. "Spahn-taneous Combustion." *Baseball Digest,* VII (February 1948), 9–12.

52874. Bjarkman, Peter C. *Baseball Legends: Warren Spahn.* New York: Chelsea House Publishers, 1995. 61p.

52875. Bonner, Mary G. "Warren Spahn." In: her *Baseball Rookies Who Made Good.* New York. Alfred A. Knopf, 1954. Pp. 57–58.

52876. Broeg, Bob." Hall of Fame Duel: How Musial Fared Against Spahn.*" Baseball Digest* , L (December, 1991), 76–77.

52877. _____. "The Mostest Lefty." In: his *My Baseball Scrapbook* . St. Louis, MO: River City Publishers, 1983. Pp. 130–133.

52878. _____. "Warren Spahn." In: his *Super Stars of Baseball.* St. Louis, MO: *The Sporting News,* 1971. Pp. 231–238.

52879. Brosnan, Jim. "Warren Edward Spahn." in: his

Great Baseball Pitchers. New York: Random House, 1965. Pp. 125–137.

52880. Bryson, Bill. "Goals for Spahn and Musial at 42." *Baseball Digest,* XII (August 1963), 55–57.

52881. Buege, Bob. "Spahn's First 'Loss' Wasn't." *The Baseball Research Journal,* XXVIII (1999), 62–63.

52882. Burick, Si. "Must Be Clutch Pitch to 'Own' It"— Warren Spahn." *Baseball Digest,* XXIII (June 1963), 49–51.

52883. Cohen, Hashell. "Spahn Has Got to Be the Greatest." *Baseball Monthly,* I (August 1962), 20+.

52884. Condon, Robert J. "Warren Edward Spahn." In: his *The Fifty Finest Athletes of the 20th Century.* Jefferson, NC: McFarland & Co., Inc., 1990. Pp. 124–126.

52885. Cope, Myron. "El Spahnie of Los Tigres." *Sports Illustrated,* XXV (July 4, 1966), 26–28+.

52886. Cosell, Howard. "Great Moments in *Sport:* Spahn Goes for No. 300." *Sport,* XLVII (June 1969), 82–91.

52887. Cutter, Robert A. *Warren Spahn.* Bronx, NY: JKW Sports Publications, 1964. 22p.

52888. Daley, Arthur. "Warren Spahn." In: his *All the Home Run Kings.* New York: G.P. Putnam, 1972. Pp. 80–87.

52889. Davis, Mac. "Warren Spahn." In: his *The Greatest in Baseball.* New York: Scholastic Book Services, 1977. Pp. 103–106.

52890. _____. "Warren Spahn: The Winningest Southpaw of All." In: his *Pacemakers in Baseball.* Cleveland, OH: World Publishing Company, 1968. Pp. 91–94.

52891. Dray, Bill. "A Final Look: Warren Spahn." *Beckett Baseball Card Monthly,* IX (March 1992), 118–119.

52892. Evers, John L. "Warren Edward Spahn." In: Vol. Q–Z of David L. Porter, ed. *Biographical Dictionary of American Sports: Baseball.* Rev. and enlarged ed. Westport, CT: Greenwood Press, 2000. Pp. 1449–1451.

52893. Felser, Larry. "Warren Spahn Still Reigns as King of Left-Handers." *Baseball Digest,* LI (May 1992), 67–68.

52894. Gray, Bill. "Warren Spahn —1958." In: his *Baseball's Top 100: The Best Individual Seasons of All Time.* Wilton, CT: Diamond Library, 1996. Pp. 164–165.

52895. Hern, Garry. "Spahn Just Plain Folks on the Mound." *Baseball Digest,* XII (May 1953), 47–49.

52896. Hirshberg, Al. "Milwaukee's Mr. Strikeout." *Sport,* XV (August 1953), 28–31.

52897. Honig, Donald. "Warren Spahn." In: his *The Greatest Pitchers of All Time.* New York: Crown Publishers, 1988. Pp. 96–101.

52898. Hornung, Paul. "When Willie Mays Stole Twice in Row on Spahn." *Baseball Digest,* XVII (February 1958), 96–97.

52899. Jacobs, Bruce. "The Last Man." In: Bruce Jacobs, ed. *Baseball Stars of 1955.* New York: Lion Books, 1955. Pp. 124–128.

52900. _____. "One-Two Punch: Warren Spahn and Lew Burdette." In: Bruce Jacobs, ed. *Baseball Stars of 1957.* New York: Lion Books, 1957. Pp. 111–120.

52901. Jupiter, Harry. "Marichal Bets Spahn in 16-Inning Pitching Duel." In: Dean A. Sullivan, ed. *Late Innings: A Documentary History of Baseball, 1945–1972.* Lincoln, NE: University of Nebraska Press, 2002. Pp. 177–179. On July 3, 1963; reprinted from the *San Francisco Examiner,* July 3, 1963.

52902. Kahn, Roger. "The Art of Warren Spahn." *Sport,* XXV (June 1959), 56–67.

52903. _____. "Spahnie" In: his *The Head Game: Baseball Seen from the Pitcher's Mound.* Boston, MA: Harcourt, 2000. Pp. 159–180.

52904. Kaplan, Dave. "Warren Spahn: Twelve to Go." In: Ray Robinson, ed. *Baseball Stars of 1961.* New York: Pyramid Books, 1961. Pp. 59–65.

52905. _____. and Dick Perez. "Warren Spahn." In: their *The 2nd Official Baseball Hall of Fame Book of Superstars.* New York: Little Simon, 1990. Pp. 35–36.

52906. Kiersh, Edward. "Warren Spahn: At War with General [George S.] Patton." In: his *Where Have You Gone, Vince DiMaggio?* New York: Bantam Books, 1983. Pp. 25–31.

52907. Klima, John. "Human Enough to Lose: Warren Spahn vs. Juan Marichal (July 2, 1963)." In: his *Pitched Battle: 35 of Baseball's Greatest Duels from the Mound.* Jefferson, NC: McFarland & Co., Inc., 2002. Pp. 102–109.

52908. Kuechle, Oliver E. "The Day Spahn Won His 300th." *Baseball Digest,* XX (October 1961), 15–18.

52909. Larson, Lloyd. "Spahn, Antonelli Study in Contrasts." *Baseball Digest,* XXI (April 1962), 10–11.

52910. _____. "Spahn's Greatness Grows with the Years." *Baseball Digest,* XXIX (February 1970), 39–41.

52911. Marren, Joe. "Spahn in the Bushes: The Great Lefty's First Year in Professional Baseball." *The National Pastime,* VIII (1998), 116–119. Playing for the Bradford (PA) Bees.

52912. Maule, Tex. "Masterpiece in Milwaukee." *Sports Illustrated,* XIV (May 8, 1961), 24–27.

52913. McKay, Joe. "Warren Spahn: The Greatest Left-Hander Ever." In: his *The Great Shutout Pitchers: 20 Profiles of a Vanishing Breed.* Jefferson, NC: McFarland & Co., Inc., 2004. Pp. 62–73.

52914. Meany, Thomas. "Big Chief of the Braves." *Baseball Digest,* XIII (July 1954), 31–38.

52915. _____. "The Chief (Warren Spahn)." In: his *Milwaukee's Miracle Braves.* New York: A.S. Barnes & Co., 1954. Pp. 82–96.

52916. _____. and Tommy Holmes. "Warren Spahn: 'Mr. Consistency.'" In: their *Baseball's Best.* New York: Watts, 1964. Pp. 72–79.

52917. Merritt, Ted. "This Southpaw's No Screwball." In: Bruce Jacobs, ed. *Baseball Stars of 1954.* New York: Lion Books, 1954. Pp. 122–124.

52918. Molter, Harry. "Warren Spahn: The Braves' Outstanding Southpaw." In: his *Famous American Athletes of Today.* 13th Series. New York: Page, 1953. Pp. 301–317.

52919. Oates, Bob. "Hall of Famer Warren Spahn Was Not the Retiring Sort." *Baseball Digest,* XLVIII (September 1989), 74–78.

52920. O'Neil, Paul. "Rousing Bravo for a Brave Brave." *Life,* LI (September 1, 1961), 13–14.

52921. Pratt, John L. "Warren Spahn." In: his *More Sport, Sport, Sport.* New York: Watts, 1962. Pp. 17–34.

52922. Reichler, Joseph L. "Is Warren Spahn the Best Ever?" *Sport,* XXXVII (May 1964), 50–51+.

52923. Reidenbaugh, Lowell. "Warren Spahn." In: his *Cooperstown: Where Legends Live Forever.* St. Louis: The Sporting News, 1983. Pp. 237–238.

52924. Ritter, Lawrence and Donald Honig. "Warren Spahn." In: their *The 100 Greatest Baseball Players of All Time.* New York: Crown Publishers, 1981. Pp. 132–133.

52925. Robinson, Ray. "Spahn and Burdette." In: Ray Robinson, ed. *Baseball Stars of 1958.* New York: Lion Books, 1958. Pp. 7–13.

52926. Rumill, Ed. "The Master of the Change-Up." *Baseball Magazine,* LXXIX (November 1947), 401–403.

52927. Rust, Art, with Michael Marley. "Warren Spahn." In: his *Legends: Conversations with Baseball Greats.* New York: McGraw-Hill, 1989. Pp. 66–80.

52928. Salsinger, H. G. "Spahn's 'Plus 16' Tops Pitchers." *Baseball Digest,* XIII (January 1954), 69–71.

52929. Schlossberg, Dan. "Did Boston Stay Separate Spahn from 400 Wins?" In: Mark Kanter, ed. *The Northern Game and Beyond: Baseball in New England and Eastern Canada.* Cleveland, OH: The Society for American Baseball Research, 2002. Pp. 3–4.

52930. Scott, Gene. "Spahn Wants to Win Them All." In: Lee Greene, ed. *True's 1961 Baseball Yearbook.* Greenwich, CT: Fawcett Publications, 1961. Pp. 34–37.

52931. Shapiro, Milton J. "Warren Spahn." In: his *Baseball's Greatest Pitchers.* New York: Julian Messner, 1969. Pp. 66–79.

52932. _____. *The Warren Spahn Story.* New York: Julian Messner, 1958. 192p. This biography was subject to a lawsuit, which alleged invasion of his privacy by Spahn, that made it all the way to the New York Supreme Court, which ruled on it in 1964 in its 15-page decision "Warren E. Spahn v. Julian Messner Inc. *et al.*"

52933. Shoemaker, Robert H. "Warren Spahn: The Pride of Milwaukee." In: his *Best in Baseball.* New York: Crowell, 1959. Pp. 127–136.

52934. Silverman, Al. "Warren Spahn." In: his *More Sports Titans of the 20th Century.* New York: G. P. Putnam, 1969. Pp. 203–221.

52935. _____. "Warren Spahn." In: Ray Robinson, ed. *Baseball Stars of 1959.* New York: Pyramid Books, 1959. Pp. 18–24.

52936. _____. "Warren Spahn: A Southpaw to Remember." In: Ray Robinson, ed. *Baseball Stars of 1962.* New York: Pyramid Books, 1962. Pp. 57–62.

52937. _____. "Warren Spahn: All-Time Lefty." In: Ray Robinson, ed. *Baseball Stars of 1964.* New York: Pyramid Books, 1964. Pp. 102–108.

52938. _____. *Warren Spahn, Immortal Southpaw.* New York: Bartholomew House, 1961. 158p.

52939. Simons, Herbert. "Will Wynn or Spahn Reach 300 First?" *Baseball Digest,* XIX (May 1960), 18–21.

52940. Smith, Ron. "Warren Spahn 21." In: his *The Sporting News Selects Baseball's 100 Greatest Players.* St. Louis, MO: *The Sporting News,* 1998. Pp. 50–51.

52941. "Southpaw." *Time,* XLIX (June 1947), 67–68.

52942. Spahn, Warren. "Advice to Pitchers." In: *Boy's Life,* Editors of *Baseball as We Played It.* New York: G.P. Putnam, 1969. Pp. 110–120.

52943. _____. "Deadly Six Inches." *Baseball Digest,* XV (January–February 1956), 21–30.

52944. _____. *The Fine Points of Pitching.* Englewood Cliffs, NJ: Prentice-Hall, 1959. 13p. Instructional pamphlet.

52945. _____. "How I Pick Off Base Runners." *Sport,* XI (August 1951), 93+.

52946. _____. and Neal Russo. *How to Pitch.* St. Louis, MO: Rawlings Manufacturing Co., 1964. Promotional booklet first published in 1962 giving tips on how to throw various pitches.

52947. _____. "I Can Still Win." *Sport,* XXXIX (February 1965), 30–33.

52948. _____. "You Can Fool Some of the Hitters All the Time." Edited by William C. Fay. *Collier's,* CXXXVI (July 22, 1955), 62–65.

52949. _____., as told to Neal Russo. *How To Pitch.* St. Louis: Rawlings Sporting Goods Co., 1962. 16p. Instructional pamphlet.

52950. Stann, Francis. "Is Spahn All Done at 44?" *Baseball Magazine,* XCV (March 1965), 18–21.

52951. _____. "Spahn Sees 20-Winner on Way Out." *Baseball Digest,* XX (June 1961), 33–35.

52952. Tourangeau, Dixie. "Spahn, Sain, and the '48 Braves." *The National Pastime,* XVIII (1998), 17–20.

52953. Van Blair, Rick. "Warren 'Lefty' Spahn." In: his *Dugout to Foxhole: Interviews With Baseball Players Whose Careers Were Affected by World War II.* Jefferson, NC: McFarland & Co., Inc., 1994. Pp. 180–190.

52954. Walfoort, Cleon. "The Marvelous Mr. Spahn." *Baseball Digest,* XXIII (July 1964), 57–61.

52955. _____. "Spahn: Better Now Than Ten Years Ago!" *Baseball Digest,* XIX (December 1960), 33–35.

52956. _____. "Spahn Hopes for 347th Win in '63." *Baseball Digest,* XXI (December 1962), 29–31.

52957. _____. "Warren Spahn — 'What It Takes to Be a 20-Win Pitcher.'" *Baseball Digest,* XVII (July 1958), 5–10.

52958. "Warren (Edward) Spahn." In: *Current Biography Yearbook, 1962.* New York: H.W. Wilson Co., 1962. Pp. 400–402.

52959. "Warren Spahn, King of the Hill." *Look,* XXVII (April 23, 1963), 67–70.

52960. Westcott, Rich. "Warren Spahn: The Complete Package." In: his *Winningest Pitchers: Baseball's 300-Game Winners.* Philadelphia, PA: Temple University Press, 2002. Pp. 107–116.

52961. _____. "Warren Spahn: The Finest Lefthanded Pitcher." In: his *Splendor on the Diamond: Interviews with 35 Stars of Baseball's Past.* Gainesville, FL: The University Press of Florida, 2000. Pp. 95–105.

52962. White, Eric Marshall. "Warren Spahn: Strong Down the Stretch." *The Baseball Research Journal,* XXXII (2003), 85–88.

52963. Wilber, Cynthia J. "Warren Spahn." In: her *For the Love of the Game: Baseball Memories from the Men Who Were There.* New York: William Morrow, 1992. Pp. 317–324.

52964. Wolf, Bob. "Spahn's Goal: 384 NL Wins." *Baseball Digest,* XXIV (February 1965), 63–65.

52965. _____. "Spahn's No Hitters Came Too Late, But They Were Welcome." *Baseball Digest,* XXXVIII (December 1979), 90+.

Albert Goodwill Spalding ★
P-1B-OF-MGR-EXEC. (B: Sept. 2, 1850, Byron, IL-D: Sept. 9, 1915). Boston Red Stockings (National Association), 1871–1875; Chicago (NL), 1876–1878. Remarks: Won 255 games (became game's first 200-game winner with 207 victories by 1875) and lost 69; pitched the first professional one-hitter (June 27, 1871); had 56 victories (24 in a row) in 1875; as a batter, obtained 462 hits in eight years; manager, Chicago (NL), 1876–1877, winning 78 games and losing 47 (.624); president, Chicago (NL), 1882–1891; helped draft NL constitution in 1875 and founded A.G. Spalding & Bros. sporting goods company the same year; organized the first baseball world tour in 1888; American commissioner for Paris Olympic Games, 1900; wrote (ghosted?) classic history, *America's National Game,* in 1911; elected to National Baseball Hall of Fame in 1939, where his plaque reads: "Organizational genius of baseball's pioneer days. Star pitcher of Forest City club in late 1860's, 4-year champion Boston's 1871–1875 and manager-pitcher of champion Chicago's in National League's first year. Chicago president for 10 years. Organizer of baseball first round-the-world tour in 1888."

52966. "Albert G. Spalding." In: *Tycoons and Entrepreneurs.* New York: Macmillan Library Reference USA, 1998. Pp. 221–222.

52967. "Albert G. Spalding's Round-the-World Tour Stops in London (1889)." In: Dean A. Sullivan, ed. *Early*

Innings: A Documentary History of Baseball, 1825–1908. Lincoln, NE: University of Nebraska Press, 1995. Pp. 173–174. Reprinted from the *London Times,* March 13, 1889.

52968. Bartlett, Arthur C. *Baseball and Mr. Spalding.* New York: Farrar, Straus, 1951. 295p.

52969. Brathain, Michelle. "Albert Goodwill Spalding." In: John A. Garrity and Marsh C. Carries, eds. *American National Biography.* 24 vols. New York: Oxford University Press, 1999. XX, 404–406.

52970. Carroll, P. "Spalding's Tourists in Bristol: Base Ball in Graceland." *The National Pastime,* XXI (2001), 64–66.

52971. "Celebration of the Conclusion of the Great Tour (1889)." In: Dean A. Sullivan, ed. *Early Innings: A Documentary History of Baseball, 1825–1908.* Lincoln, NE: University of Nebraska Press, 1995. Pp. 175–178. Reprinted from the *New York Clipper,* April 13, 1889.

52972. Chadwick, Henry. "The Albert G. Spalding I Knew." *Baseball Magazine,* II (March 1909), 13–15.

52973. Day, Bernard J. *Lost for a Hundred Years.* Nunthorpe, England: Bernard J. Day, [1996]. 216p. Stats, rosters, box/line scores, and photos from the first Around the World tour.

52974. Kiernan, John. "Albert Goodwill Spalding." In: . Vo. 9 of Dumas Malone, ed. *The Dictionary of American Biography.* New York: Scribners, 1936. Pp. 420–421.

52975. Levine, Peter. *A. G. Spalding and the Rise of Baseball: The Promise of American Sport.* New York: Oxford University Press, 1986. 184p.

52976. _____. "A. G. Spalding: Baseball's Barnum." *Timeline,* II (August–September 1985), 10+.

52977. McMahon, William E. "Al Spalding." In: Frederick Ivor-Campbell, ed. *Baseball's First Stars.* Cleveland, OH: The Society for American Baseball Research, 1996. Pp. 154–155. McMahon's Spalding profile is a number in the online SABR Biography Project http://bioproj.sabr.org/bioproj.cfm?a=v&v=l&bid=732&pid=13395.

52978. Peterson, Richard and Eliot Asinof. "Spalding, Spink, and the First Standard History of Baseball." In: their *Extra Innings: Writing on Baseball.* Sport and Society Series. Urbanna, IL: University of Illinois Press, 2001. Pp. 39–54.

52979. Sherman, Ardis L. *Reflects, Byron, Illinois, 1835–1976.* Byron, IL: Village of Byron, 1976. 93p. Much of the work is taken up with a biography of AG Spalding.

52980. Smith, Duane A. "Albert Goodwill 'Al' Spalding." In: Vol. Q–Z of David L. Porter, ed. *Biographical Dictionary of American Sports: Baseball.* Rev. and enlarged ed. Westport, CT: Greenwood Press, 2000. Pp. 1451–1453.

52981. Spalding, Albert C. *America's National Game: Historic Facts Covering the Beginning, Evolution, Development, and Popularity of Baseball, with Personal Reminiscences of Its Vicissitudes, Its Victories, and Its Votaries.* New York: American Sports Publishing Co., 1911. 542p. Reprinted in a 550-p. paperback edition by the University of Nebraska Press in 1992.

52982. _____. *America's National Game.* Edited By Samm Coombs and Bob West. San Francisco, CA: Halo Books, 1991. 364p. Heavily condensed version of 1911 original.

52983. _____. "How I Tried to Get Into the Polo Grounds." *Baseball Magazine,* I (December 1908), 7–10.

52984. Tax, J. "A Tribute to Albert G. Spalding and His Lifetime Love Affair with Baseball." *Sports Illustrated,* LXII (April 15, 1985), 12–13.

Arthur ("Art") Spander
WRITER. (B: August 30, 1938, Los Angeles, CA). Remarks: UPI reporter, 1960–1962; *Santa Monica Evening Outlook* reporter, 1963–1965; *San Francisco Chronicle* reporter, 1965–1979; *San Francisco Examiner* columnist, 1979–.

52985. Spander, Art. *The Art Spander Collection.* Dallas, TX: Taylor Publishing Co., 1988. 288p.

Bob Speake *see* **Robert Charles ("Bob" or "Spook") Speake**

Robert Charles ("Bob" or "Spook") Speake
OF-1B. (B: Aug. 22, 1930, Springfield, MO). Chicago (NL), 1955, 1957; San Francisco (NL), 1958–1959. Remarks: Had 601 hits (61 homers) and eight stolen bases in 872 games in four years; had 10 homers in June 1955.

52986. Bitker, Steve. "Bob Speake." In: his *The Original San Francisco Giants: The Giants of '58.* Champaign, IL: Sports Publishing, 1998. Pp. 198–202.

Tristram E ("Tris" or "The Gray Eagle" or "Spoke") Speaker★
OF-MGR-BROADCASTER. (B: April 4, 1880, Hubbard, TX-D: Dec. 8, 1958). Boston (AL), 1907–1915; Cleveland (AL),1918–1926; Washington (AL), 1927; Philadelphia (AL), 1928. Remarks: Obtained 3,515 hits (117 homers) and 433 stolen bases in 2,789 games in 22 seasons; in 1912, had two 20-game hitting streaks and a 30-game hitting streak, the latter in 1912; hit for the cycle, June 9, 1912; set MLB mark (which would stand until 1998) with 50 doubles and 50 steals in a year, 1912; in Game Seven of 1912 World Series, made only unassisted double play ever by an outfielder in a fall classic; 1912 AL Chalmers award; AL batting champion, 1916; AL RBI champion, 1923 (tie); led AL in doubles, 1912, 1914, 1916, 1918, 1920–1923; holds AL record for most doubles (793), most lifetime putouts by an outfielder (6,706), assists (449-major league record), and chances accepted (7,196); made two unassisted double plays in 1918 season and had 11 hits in succession (July 8, 9, 10, 1920); had grand slam homer, May 20, 1922; played briefly with Houston (TL), 1907 and Little Rock (SL), 1908; manager, Cleveland (AL), mid-1919 through 1926, winning 616 games and losing 520 (.542); minor league manager, 1929–1930; pioneer radio play-by-play broadcaster; president of the short-lived National Professional Indoor Baseball League, 1939; named to Texas Sports Hall of Fame, 1951; elected to National Baseball Hall of Fame in 1937, where his plaque reads: "Greatest centerfielder of his day. Lifetime major league batting average of .344. Manager in 1920 when Cleveland won its first pennant and World Championship."

52987. Allen, Lee, and Thomas Meany. "Tris Speaker." In: their *Kings of the Diamond.* New York: G.P. Putnam, 1965. Pp. 181–183.

52988. Allen, Maury. "Tris Speaker (1907–1928)." In: his *Baseball's 100.* New York: Galahad Books, 1981. Pp. 44–46.

52989. Alvarez, Mark. "'Say It Ain't So, Ty': The Cobb-Speaker Scandal." *The National Pastime,* XIV (1994), 21–28. Over the outcome of a questionable 1919 game.

52990. Bang, Ed. "Tris Speaker." In: Christy Walsh, ed. *Baseball's Greatest Lineup.* New York. A.S. Barnes, 1952. Pp. 47–59.

52991. Bang, Ed. "Tris Speaker (Centerfield)." In: Christy Walsh, ed. *Baseball's Greatest Lineup.* New York: A.S. Barnes, 1952. Pp. 47–59.

52992. Barton, Jerry. "Tristram E. (Spoke) Speaker." In: his *A Treasure Chest of the Hall of Fame.* Boston, MA: The Wilson-Hill Co., 1952. Pp. 20–21.

52992a. Blaisdell, Lowell L. "The [Ty] Cobb-Speaker

Scandal: Exonerated But Probably Guilty." *Nine: A Journal of Baseball History and Social Policy Perspective,* XIII (Spring 2005), 54–70.

52993. Bodayla, Stephen D. "Tris E Speaker." In: Supplement 6 of John A., Gaftity, ed. *The Dictionary of American Biography.* New York: Scribners, 1980. Pp. 588–590.

52994. Broeg, Bob. "Tris Speaker." In: his *Super Stars of Baseball.* St. Louis, MO: *The Sporting News,* 1971. Pp. 239–244.

52995. Carr, Bob. "A Letter From the Attic." *The National Pastime,* XI (1992), 23–24. Speaker and the Cleveland Indians; 1916

52996. Clark, Ellery H., Jr. "Tristram E. 'Tris,' 'The Gray Eagle,' 'Spoke' Speaker." In: Vol. Q-Z of David L. Porter, ed. *Biographical Dictionary of American Sports: Baseball.* Rev. and enlarged ed. Westport, CT: Greenwood Press, 2000. Pp. 1453–1454.

52997. Cobbledick, Gordon. "The Gray Eagle' Sights Blue Skies." *Baseball Digest,* XVI (December 1950), 69–72.

52998. _____ "Records Prove It's Speaker Over DiMaggio." *Baseball Digest,* XVII (October 1958), 61–63.

52999. _____. "Speaker Almost was a NL Star." *Baseball Digest,* III (May 1944), 59–61.

53000. _____. "Tris Speaker: 'The Gray Eagle.'" *Sport,* XII (July 1952), 34–37.

53001. Crichton, Kyle S. "Center-Field Lightning." *Collier's,* CI (March 26, 1938), 17–19.

53002. Davis, Mac. "Tristram (Spoke) Speaker." In: his *The Greatest in Baseball.* New York: Scholastic Book Services, 1977. Pp. 53–55.

53003. Fullerton, Hugh. "Are Baseball Games Framed?: The Story of 'Spoke' and Smoky Joe [Wood]." *Liberty,* III (April 2, 1927), 83–86.

53004. Gajus, Greg. "Tris Speaker—1912." In: his *Baseball's Top 100: The Best Individual Seasons of All Time.* Wilton, CT: Diamond Library, 1996. Pp. 44–45.

53005. Gettleson, Leonard. "Trip Speaker's Grand Career." *Baseball Magazine,* XXXVI (June 1926), 311–312+.

53006. Girsch, George. "When the A's Left Speaker Speechless." *Baseball Digest,* XIII (January 1954), 85–87. When traded him to Cleveland in 1916.

53007. Graham, Frank. "On Seeing Tris Speaker Again." *Baseball Digest,* XIII (November–December 1954), 93–96.

53008. Greene, Lee. "Sport's Hall of Fame: 'The Gray Eagle.'" *Sport,* XXX (August 1960), 34–38.

53009. Gutman, Bill. "Trio Speaker: The 'Gray Eagle' [1888–1958]." In: his *Famous Baseball Stars.* New York: Dodd, Mead, 1973. Pp. 50–60.

53010. Hirshberg, Al. "Tris Speaker: Outfield." In: his *The Greatest American Leaguers.* New York: G.P. Putnam's Sons, 1970. Pp. 40–49.

53011. Hoefer, W.R. "Tris of Texas." *Baseball Magazine,* XVIII (March 1917), 125–127.

53012. Karst, Gene. "Those Master Craftsmen: Ty [Cobb] and Tris." *Baseball Magazine,* XLIII (September 1929), 441–442+.

53013. Kermisch, Al. "Six Unassisted Outfield DPs For Speaker." *The Baseball Research Journal,* XIII (1984), 49–50.

53014. Kofoed, J.C. "Speaker in the Records." *Baseball Magazine,* XVIII (March 1917), 103–107.

53015. Lane, Ferdinand C. "Does Max Carey Compare with Tris Speaker?" *Baseball Magazine,* XXIX (September 1922), 447–450.

53016. _____. "The King of Outfielders." *Baseball Magazine,* XVIII (March 1917), 113–118.

53017. _____. "Tris Speaker: King of Outfield." *Baseball Magazine,* XIII (July 1914), 47–57.

53018. _____. "Tris Speaker Traded!" *Baseball Magazine,* XVII (June 1916), 19–28.

53019. _____. "The Veteran Slugger of the Cleveland Ball Club." *Baseball Magazine,* XXXVII (October 1926), 491–493.

53020. Lebovitz, Hal. "How the Indians Acquired Tris Speaker." *Baseball Digest,* XXVIII (July 1969), 96–104.

53021. McMane, Fred. "Tris Speaker." In: his *The 3,000 Hit Club.* Champaign, IL: Sports Publishing, 2000. Pp. 36–44.

53022. Meany, Tom. "'The Gray Eagle'— Tristram E. Speaker." In: his *Baseball's Greatest Hitters.* New York: A.S. Barnes, 1950. Pp. 191–202.

53023. _____. "'The Gray Eagle' Was a Lion at Bat." *Baseball Digest,* XXX (January 1971), 56–61. First published in *Baseball Digest,* XVIII (February 1959), 21–27.

53024. _____. "Tris Speaker." In: his *Baseball's Greatest Players.* New York: Grosset AW Dunlap, 1953. Pp. 233–243.

53025. Menke, Frang G. "Speaker—Famed for Fielding." In: his *Sports Tales and Anecdotes.* New York: A.S. Barnes, 1953. Pp. 27–28.

53026. Porter, David L. "Tris Speaker." In: John A. Garrity and Marsh C. Carries, eds. *American National Biography.* 24 vols. New York: Oxford University Press, 1999. XX, 425–426.

53027. "Pulling Grass Is Tris Speaker's Baseball Barometer." *Literary Digest,* LXVII (December 11, 1920), 81–83.

53028. Reidenbaugh, Lowell. "Tris Speaker." In: his *Cooperstown: Where Legends Live Forever.* St. Louis, MO: *The Sporting News,* 1983. Pp. 240–241.

53029. Rice, Grantland. "Cobb, Speaker Named in Gambling Scandal." In: Dean A. Sullivan, ed. *Middle Innings: A Documentary History of Baseball, 1900–1948.* Lincoln, NE: University of Nebraska Press, 1998. Pp. 124–126. Reprinted from *The Sporting News,* Dec. 30, 1926.

53030. Ritter, Lawrence and Donald Honig. "Tris Speaker." In: their *The 100 Greatest Baseball Players of All Time.* New York: Crown Publishers, 1981. Pp. 208–209.

53031. Roth, Morton. "Best Center Fielder of All Time: How About Tris Speaker?" *Baseball Digest,* XLVI (July 1987), 65–71.

53032. Salant, Nathan. "Tris Speaker." In: his *Superstars, Stars, and Just Plain Heroes.* New York: Stein And Day, 1982. Pp. 47–56.

53033. Salsinger, H.G. "Speaking Up for Speaker." *Baseball Digest,* VIII (August 1949), 23–26.

53034. Shapiro, Milton J. "Tris Speaker." In: his *All Stars of the Outfield.* New York: Julian Messner, 1970. Pp. 186–192.

53035. Smith, Ira L "Tristram E. (Tris) Speaker." In: his *Baseball's Famous Outfielders.* New York: A.S. Barnes, 1954. Pp. 107–112.

53036. Smith, Ron. "Tris Speaker 27." In: his *The Sporting News Selects Baseball's 100 Greatest Players.* St. Louis, MO: *The Sporting News,* 1998. Pp. 64–65.

53037. Speaker, Tris. "The Art of Making Hard Plays Easy." *Baseball Magazine,* XLI (October 1928), 489–491.

53038. _____. "How I Spend My Annual Vacation." *Baseball Magazine,* XXX (March 1923), 455–456.

53039. _____. "The Ins and Outs of Batting." *Baseball. Magazine,* XXII (April 1919), 331–333.

53040. _____. "Is Base Running the Lost Art?" *Sport Life,* V (October 1952), 12–13+.

53041. _____. "Play It Safe in Baseball." In: Mitchel V. Charnley, ed. *Secrets of Baseball Told by Big League Players.* New York: D. Appleton and Co., 1927. Pp. 11–25.

53042. _____. "A Triple Play Unassisted." *American Legion Weekly,* V (August 10, 1923), 6–7. 1920 World Series.

53043. _____. "Tris Speaker Explains." In: Sidney Offit, ed. *The Best of Baseball.* New York: G.P. Putnam, 1956. Pp. 30–34. Reprinted from the September 1916 issue of *Baseball Magazine.*

53044. _____. "Tris Speaker Speaks." *Baseball Magazine,* XVII (September 1916), 29–31.

53045. _____. "Tris Speaker: The Star of the 1920 Baseball Season." *Baseball Magazine,* XXVI (December 1920), 317–319+.

53046. _____. "What I Have Learned from 20 Years in the Outfield." *Baseball Magazine,* XXXV (September 1925), 444–445+.

53047. _____. "When a Champion Batter Slumps Below .300." *Baseball Magazine,* XXV (June 1920), 318–319.

53048. _____. "Winning the Batting Championship." *Baseball Magazine,* XVIII (March 1917), 85–86.

53049. _____. as told to Francis J. Powers. "My Greatest Day in Baseball." In: John P. Carmichael, ed. *My Greatest Day in Baseball.* New York: A.S. Barnes, 1945. Pp. 63–68, First published in the *Chicago Daily News;* reprinted In 1951, 1963 and 1968 editions. Boston Red Sox 3, New York Giants 2 in 1912 World Series.

53050. Stockton, J. Roy. "Baseball's Most Versatile Athlete." *Baseball Magazine,* VI (December 1925), 309–310.

53051. Sullivan, George. "Tris Speaker." In: his *Glovemen: Twenty-Seven of Baseball's Greatest.* New York: Atheneum, 1996. Pp. 58–59.

53051. Verral, Charls S. "Tris Speaker." In: his *Mighty Men of Baseball.* New York: Aladdin Books, 1965. Pp. 107–124.

53052. Ward, John J. "Tris Speaker, King of the Two-Base Hitters." *Baseball Magazine,* XXXIII (July 1924), 355–366+.

53053. "When Ty Cobb and Tris Speaker March Back to the Diamond." *Literary Digest,* XCII (February 12, 1927), 76–80. Contains material originally printed in *The New York Herald-Tribune, The New York Times,* and *The New York World* relative to the Commissioner's Office ruling on their potential scandal.

Chris Edward Speier
SS. (B: June 28, 1950, Alameda, CA). San Francisco (NL), 1971–1977; Montreal (NL), 1977–1983; St. Louis (N.L) and Minnesota (AL), 1984; Chicago (NL), 1985–1986; San Francisco (NL), 1987–1989. Remarks: Obtained 1,759 hits (112 homers) and 42 stolen bases in 2,260 games in 19 seasons; hit for the cycle twice, July 20, 1978 and July 9, 1988; had two grand slam homers, May 5 and May 9, 1987; minor league instructor, 1990–1998; coach, Milwaukee (AL/NL), 1999–2000, Arizona (NL), 2001, Oakland (AL), 2002–2004; Chicago (NL), 2005-; father of Justin Speier (below).

53054. Arndt, Rick. "Chris Speier." In: *his Safe at Home: Ten Major League Baseball Players Discuss Their Careers and Their Christian Commitment.* St. Louis, Mo: Concordia Pub. House, 1979. 186p.

53055. Israelson, Chad. "Chris Edward Speier." In: Vol. Q-Z of David L. Porter, ed. *Biographical Dictionary of American Sports: Baseball.* Rev. and enlarged ed. Westport, CT: Greenwood Press, 2000. Pp. 1454–1455.

53056. Hunt, Tom. "Chris Speier: Key to Giants' Surge." *Baseball Digest,* XXX (August 1971), 61–67.

53057. Mandel, Mike. "Chris Speier." In: his *The San Francisco Giants: An Oral History.* Santa Cruz, CA: Mike Mandel, 1979. Pp. 193–196.

53058. McHugh, Roy. "The Giants' Surprise Rookie." *Sport,* LII (October 1971), 64–69.

53059. Powell, Larry. "Former All-Star Chris Speier Understands the Cyclical Nature of the Game — and of Life." *Sport Collector's Digest,* XXII (October 27, 1995), 156+.

53060. Speier, Chris. "The Game I'll Never Forget." *Baseball Digest,* XLII (October 1983), 92–95.

53061. Stewart, Wayne. "The Speiers." In: his *Fathers, Sons & Baseball: Our National Pastime and the Ties That Bind.* Guilford, CT: The Lyons Press, 2002. Pp. 125–138.

53062. Twombly, Wells. "Chris Speier: The Giants Find a New Hero." *Baseball Digest,* XXXI (November 1972), 63–67.

Justin Speier
P. (B: Nov. 6, 1973, Walnut Creek, CA). Chicago (NL) and Florida (NL), 1998; Atlanta (NL), 1999; Cleveland (AL), 2000–2001; Colorado (NL), 2001–2003; Toronto (AL), 2004-. Remarks: Through 2004, has won 22 games and lost 18, with 17 "saves"; son of Chris Speier (above).

53063. Stewart, Wayne. "The Speiers." In: his *Fathers, Sons & Baseball: Our National Pastime and the Ties That Bind.* Guilford, CT: The Lyons Press, 2002. Pp. 125–138.

Stanley Orvil ("Stan") Spence
OF. (B: March 20, 1915, South Portsmouth KY-D: Jan. 9, 1983). Boston (AL), 1940–1941; Washington (AL), 1942–1944, 1946–1947; Boston (AL), 1958–1949; St. Louis (AL), 1949. Remarks: Had 1,090 hits (95 homers) and 21 stolen bases in 1,112 games in nine years; went six-for-six in a game, June 1, 1944; later, founder-owner, Southern Equipment Co., Kinston, NC.

53064. Fitzgerald, Tommy. "Signed Between Putouts." *Baseball Digest,* VI (August 1947), 30+.

53065. Miller, William J. "Stanley Orvil 'Stan' Spence." In: Vol. Q-Z of David L. Porter, ed. *Biographical Dictionary of American Sports: Baseball.* Rev. and enlarged ed. Westport, CT: Greenwood Press, 2000. Pp. 1455–1457.

Daryl Dean ("Big Dee") Spencer
OF-2B-3B. (B: July 13, 1929, Wichita, KA). New York (NL), 1952–1953, 1956–1957; San Francisco (NL), 1958–1959; Hankyu Braves (Japan League), 1964–1968, 1971–1972. Remarks: Had 901 hits (105 homers) in 1,098 games in six Giant seasons; hit first homer in an official big league game in Seals Stadium, April 15, 1958; had two homers, a double, triple, and six RBIs in one game, May 13, 1958; the first *Gaijin* (foreign player) to employ hard baserunning techniques and the first baserunner to break up a double play in the Japan Leagues, where he also hit 152 homers; later managed semi-pro baseball teams.

53066. Appel, Marty. "Daryl Spencer." In: his *Yesterday's Heroes: Revisiting the Old-Time Baseball Stars.* New York: The Dial Press, 1988. Pp. 208–211.

53067. Bitker, Steve. "Daryl Spencer." In: his *The Original San Francisco Giants: The Giants of '58.* Champaign, Il: Sports Publishing, 1998. Pp. 166–176.

53068. *Daryl Spencer: New Dodger Adds Infield Strength.* New 1961 Dodger Family series. Los Angeles: Union Oil Company of California, 1961. 14p.

53069. Mandel, Mike. "Daryl Spencer." In: his *The San Francisco Giants: An Oral History.* Santa Cruz, CA: Mike Mandel, 1979. Pp. 50–54.

53070. Skipper, John C. "Daryl Spencer: His Homer Was a Milestone in Baseball's Westward Move." In: his *Inside Pitch: A Closer Look at Classic Baseball Moments.* Jefferson, NC: McFarland & Co., Inc., 1996. Pp. 176–178.

Edward Russell ("Tub" or "Tubby") Spencer
C. (B: Jan. 26, 1884, Oil City, PA-D: Feb. 1, 1945.). St. Louis (AL), 1905–1908; Boston (AL), 1909; Philadelphia (NL), 1911; Detroit (AL), 1916–1918. Remarks: Had 298 hits (two homers) and 13 stolen bases in 449 games in nine years; was a hobo out of OB, 1912–1915.
53071. Lane, Ferdinand C. "The Most Remarkable Comeback on Record." *Baseball Magazine,* XXI (July 1914), 263–267.

George Elwell Spencer
P. (B: July 7, 1926, Columbus, OH). New York (NL), 1950–1955; Detroit (AL), 1958 and 1960. Remarks: Won 16 games and lost 10, with nine "saves," in eight seasons; had 55 appearances in 1951.
53072. Flora, Earl. "He Pitches Best When He's Tired." *Baseball Digest,* XII (March 1953), 15–17.

Roy Hampton Spencer
C. (B: Feb. 22, 1900, Scranton, NC-D: Feb. 8, 1973). Pittsburgh (NL), 1925–1927; Washington (AL), 1929–1932; Cleveland (AL), 1933–1934; New York (NL), 1936; Brooklyn (NL), 1937–1938. Remarks: Obtained 448 hits (three homers) and four stolen bases in 636 games in a dozen summer campaigns; had one fruitless AB in 1927 World Series.
53073. Bloodgood, Clifford. "Cleveland's Peppy Backstop." *Baseball Magazine,* LII (January 1934), 360–361.

Shane Spencer
OF. (B: Feb. 20, 1972, Key West, CA). New York (AL), 1998–2002; Cleveland (AL) and Texas (AL), 2003, New York (NL), 2004; Hanshin Tigers (Japan League), 2005- . Remarks: Through 2004, has had 438 hits (59 homers) and 13 stolen bases in 538 games; had four hits and one homer in 2001 World Series.
53074. Caldera, Pete and Stephanie J. Geosits. "Faces of the Future." *Yankee Magazine,* XIX (January 1999), 20–31. Spencer and Rickey Ledee.
53075. McCarver, Tim, with Danny Peary. "Shane Spencer." In: his *The Perfect Season: Why 1998 Was Baseball's Greatest Year.* New York: Villard Books, 1999. Pp. 207–210.

Tubby Spencer *see* **Edward Russell ("Tub" or "Tubby") Spencer**

Edward Wayne Spiezio
3B. (B: Oct. 31, 1941, Joliet, IL). St. Louis (NL), 1964–1968; San Diego (NL), 1969–1972; Chicago (AL), 1972. Remarks: In nine pro seasons, had 367 hits (39 homers) and 16 stolen bases in 554 games; injury-plagued utility-man; father of Scott Spiezio (below).
53076. Stewart, Wayne. "The Spiezios." In: his *Fathers, Sons & Baseball: Our National Pastime and the Ties That Bind.* Guilford, CT: The Lyons Press, 2002. Pp. 105–124.

Scott Edward Spiezio
2B-3B. (B: Sept. 21, 1972, Joliet, IL). Oakland (AL), 1996–1998; Anaheim (AL), 1999–2003; Seattle (AL), 2004-. Remarks: Through 2004, has obtained 858 hits (101 homers) and 32 stolen bases in 1,044 games; had six hits (2 doubles) in 2002 ALCS and six hits (one double, one triple) in 2002 World Series; son of Ed Spiezio (above).
53077. Stewart, Wayne. "The Speiers." In: his *Fathers, Sons & Baseball: Our National Pastime and the Ties That Bind.* Guilford, CT: The Lyons Press, 2002. Pp. 125–138.

Charlie Spikes *see* **Leslie Charles ("Charlie" or "The Bogalusa Bomber") Spikes**
Leslie Charles ("Charlie" or "The Bogalusa Bomber") Spikes
OF. (B: Jan. 23, 1951, Bogalusa, LA). New York (AL),

1972; Cleveland (AL), 1973–1977; Detroit (AL), 1978; Atlanta (NL), 1979–1980; Chunichi (Japan League), 1981. Remarks: Had 502 hits (65 homers) and 27 stolen bases in 670 games in nine U.S. big league seasons; had two hits in MLB debut, Sept. 1, 1972.
53078. Edwards, Dick. "Charlie Spikes: 'The Bogalusa Bomber.'" *Black Sports,* II (January 1973), 30–31.
53079. Rumill, Ed. "Charlie Spikes: New Hope for the Indians?" *Baseball Digest,* XXXIII (June 1973), 33–35.
53080. Sudyk, Bob. "Cleveland Dealt Itself Two Aces: George Hendrick and Charlie Spikes." *Sport,* LVIII (November 1974), 86–91.

Harry Spilman *see* **William Harry Spilman**
William Harry Spilman
1B. (B: July 18, 1954, Albany, GA). Cincinnati (NL), 1978–1981; Houston (NL), 1981–1985; Detroit (AL), 1986; San Francisco (NL), 1986–1988; Houston (NL), 1988–1989. Remarks: Obtained 192 hits (18 homers) and one stolen base in 583 games in 12 seasons; had homer in Game Three of 1987 NLCS: was EL MVP, 1977; minor league hitting instructor/manager, Cleveland (AL), 1990–1997; coach, Houston (NL), 1998-.
53081. "The Talk of the Town: Harry Spilman." *The New Yorker,* LXVII (May 20, 1991), 32–33.

Alfred Henry Spink
WRITER-EXEC. (B: Aug. 24, 1854, Canada-D: May 27, 1928). Remarks: brother of Charles Claude Spink (below) and uncle of J. G. Taylor Spink (below); sports editor of *Missouri Chronicle* and *St. Louis Chronicle* and founder-editor, *St. Louis World;* helped form American Association (AA) in 1882 and St. Louis Browns; founder-editor, in 1886, of *The Sporting News;* author, in 1910, of the first important baseball history, *The National Game,* which predates Albert G. Spalding's (q.v.) better-known *America's National Game* by a year.
53082. Brace, George Edward. "1886: A Very Important Year For Baseball." *Oldtyme Baseball News,* III, no. 3 (1991), 9+. Alfred and Charles Claude found TSN.
53083. Gietschier, Steve. "Before 'The Bible of Baseball': The First Quarter Century of *The Sporting News.*" In: his *St. Louis's Favorite Sport.* Cleveland, OH: Society For American Baseball Research, 1992. Pp. 31–34.
53084. Peterson, Richard and Eliot Asinof. "Spalding, Spink, and the First Standard History of Baseball." In: their *Extra Innings: Writing on Baseball.* Sport and Society Series. Urbanna, IL: University of Illinois Press, 2001. Pp. 39–54.

Charles Claude Spink
WRITER-EXEC. (B: Aug. 2, 1862, Isle of Orleans-D: April 22, 1914). Brother of Alfred H. Spink (above) and father of J. G. Taylor Spink (below); editor of TSN, 1888–1914.
53085. Brace, George Edward. "1886: a Very Important Year for Baseball." *Oldtyme Baseball News,* III, no. 3 (1991), 9+. Alfred and Charles Claude found TSN.
53086. Gietschier, Steve. "Before 'The Bible of Baseball': The First Quarter Century of *The Sporting News.*" In: his *St. Louis's Favorite Sport.* Cleveland, OH: Society for American Baseball Research, 1992. Pp. 31–34.

John George (J.G.) Taylor Spink
WRITER (B: Nov. 6, 1888, St. Louis, MO-D: Dec. 7, 1962). Nephew of Alfred H. Spink (above) and son of Charles C. Spink (above); editor, TSN, 1914–1962; honored by the National Baseball Hall of Fame in 1962 with a special award, subsequently BWAA annual meritorious service award named for him and made permanent, which recognizes journalists who have made outstanding contributions to baseball.

53087. Frank, Stanley B. "Bible of Baseball." *Saturday Evening Post,* CCXIV (June 20, 1942), 9–13. Reprinted in John E Drewry, ed. *More Post Biographies: Articles of Enduring Interest About Famous Journalists and Journals and Other Subjects Journalistic* (Athens, GA: University of Georgia Press, 1947), chpt. 20.

53087. Holland, Gerald. "Taylor Spink is First Class." *Sports Illustrated,* XIV (February 27, 1961), 58–67.

53088. "Mr. Baseball." *Time,* XLII (November 8, 1943), 74–75.

53089. Spink, C. C. Johnson. *Terrible-Tempered Taylor, The Soft-Hearted Spink.* St. Louis, MO: *The Sporting News,* 1973. 164p.

Ernest Lee ("Junior") Spivey, Jr.
2B-SS. (B: Jan. 28, 1975, Oklahoma City, OK). Arizona (NL), 2001–2003; Milwaukee (NL), 2004-. Remarks: Through 2004, has had 359 hits (41 homers) and 23 stolen bases in 380 games; lost much of 2003–2004 seasons to injury.

53090. Cannella, Stephen. "Junior Upstages His Seniors." *Sports Illustrated,* XCV (September 3, 2001), 82–83.

53091. _____. "Raising Arizona." *Sports Illustrated,* XCVII (August 26, 2002), 77–78.

Junior Spivey *see* **Ernest Lee ("Junior") Spivey, Jr.**

Paul William ("Splitt") Splittorff, Jr.
P. (B: Oct. 8, 1946, Evansville, IN). Kansas City (AL), 1970–1984. Remarks: Won 166 games and lost 143, with one "save," in 15 seasons.

53092. Olmsted, Frank J. "Paul William 'Splitt' Splittorff, Jr." In: Vol. Q-Z of David L. Porter, ed. *Biographical Dictionary of American Sports: Baseball.* Rev. and enlarged ed. Westport, CT: Greenwood Press, 2000. Pp. 1457–1458.

Alfred Ray Spohrer
C. (B: Dec. 3, 1902, Philadelphia, PA-D: July 17, 1972). New York (NL), 1928; Boston (N.L), 1928–1933. Remarks: Had 575 hits (six homers) and 13 stolen bases in 754 games in an eight-year major league career; threatened with banishment by Commissioner Landis if he continued in a second career as a boxer.

53093. Ward, John J. "That Sturdy Backstop Al Spohrer." *Baseball Magazine,* XLVIII (February 1932), 411–412+.

Karl Benjamin Spooner
P. (B: June 23, 1931, Oriskany Falls, NY). Brooklyn, 1954–1955. Remarks: In two big league seasons, won 10 games and lost six, with two "saves"; career ruined by arm problems.

53094. Silverberg, Robert. "Karl Spooner." In: Danny Peary, ed. *Cult Baseball Players.* New York: Simon and Schuster, 1990. Pp. 213–217.

53095. _____. "Karl Spooner." In: Danny Peary, ed. *Baseball's Finest: The Greats, the Flakes, the Weird and the Wonderful.* North Digton, MA: The JG Press, 1990. Pp. 213–217. Both Peary books are identical.

Edward Nelson ("Ed") Sprague, Jr.
3B-COACH. (B: July 25, 1967, Castro Valley, CA). Toronto (AL), 1991–1998; Oakland (AL), 1998; Pittsburgh (NL), 1999; San Diego (NL) and Boston (AL), 2000; Seattle (AL), 2001. Remarks: In 11 seasons, had 1,010 hits (152 homers) and six stolen bases in 1,203 games; homered in 1991 World Series; had four hits in Game One of 1993 ALCS; also played on 1988 U.S. Olympic Baseball Team; asst. coach, St. Mary's H.S. (CA), 2002; head coach, University of the Pacific, 2003-.

53096. Dvernichuk, S. "The Good Life on the Hot Corner." *Sports Canada Magazine,* (August 1993), 12–13.

53097. Milton, Steve. "Cleared for Takeoff." *Beckett Focus on Future Stars,* III, no. 24 (April 1993), 18–19.

53098. Montville, Leigh. "Home Alone, Two." *Sports Illustrated,* LXXVIII (January 11, 1993), 58–60, 64–66. Ed and his Olympic gold medal-winning wife Kristen Babb-Sprague.

Jack Russell Spring
P. (B: March 11, 1933, Spokane, WA). Philadelphia (NL), 1955; Boston (AL), 1957; Washington (AL), 1958; Los Angeles (AL), 1961–1964; Chicago (NL) and St. Louis (NL), 1964; Cleveland (AL), 1965. Remarks: Obtained 12 victories, five defeats, and eight "saves" in 11 seasons; made 57 appearances in 1962; also played for, among others, Syracuse (IL), Dallas (AA), and San Francisco (PCL).

53099. Kelley, Brent P. "Jack Spring." In: his *The San Francisco Seals, 1946–1957: Interviews with 25 Former Baseballers.* Jefferson, NC: McFarland & Co., Inc., 2002. Pp. 253–260.

53100. _____. "Jack Spring and the Evolution of 'Short' Relief." *Sports Collector's Digest,* XVIII (June 7, 1991), 100–102.

Martin J. ("Marty") Springstead
UMP. (B: 1937, New York City). AL umpire and supervisor of umpires, 1966–1985.

53101. Skipper, John C. "Marty Springstead." In: his *Umpires: Classic Baseball Stories From the Men Who Made the Calls.* Jefferson, N.C.: McFarland & Co., Inc., 1977. Pp. 77–81.

Marty Springstead *see* **Martin J. ("Marty") Springstead**

Joseph Conrad ("Joe" or "Mule") Sprintz
C. (B: Aug. 3, 1902, St. Louis, MO-D: Jan. 11, 1994). Cleveland (AL), 1930–1931; St. Louis (NL), 1933. Remarks: Had nine hits in 21 games in three years; remembered for an unsuccessful 1939 PR attempt, made while playing for San Dieog (PCL), to catch a ball dropped 800 feet down from a blimp.

53102. Hawks, Roger J. "Catching a Ball Dropped from a High Place." *The Baseball Research Journal,* XXVII (1998), 32–34. How Sprintz attempted without success to catch a baseball dropped from a blimp — and lost five teeth in the process.

53103. Macht, Norman. "From Golden Gate Park to the Big Leagues." In: his *Northern California Baseball History.* Cleveland, OH: Society for American Baseball Research, 1998. Pp. 59–60.

Eddie Stack *see* **William Edward ("Eddie" or "Smoke") Stack**

William Edward ("Eddie" or "Smoke") Stack
P. (B: Oct. 24, 1887, Chicago, IL-D: Aug. 28, 1958). Philadelphia (NL), 1910–1911; Brooklyn (NL), 1912–1913; Chicago (NL), 1913–1914. Remarks: Obtained 26 victories, 24 defeats, and two "saves" in five big league seasons; career affected by ptomaine poisoning from a lobster eaten during a rookie-year visit to Boston.

53104. Schmidt, Ray. "Eddie 'Smoke' Stack." *The National Pastime,* XVII (1997), 121–124.

Bill Stafford *see* **William Charles ("Bill") Stafford**

Heinie Stafford *see* **Henry Alexander ("Heinie") Stafford**

Henry Alexander ("Heinie") Stafford
PINCH RUNNER. (B: Nov. 1, 1891, Orleans, VT-D: Jan. 29, 1972). New York (NL), 1916. Remarks: Employed as a pinch runner in one game.

53105. Simon, Tom. "'Heinie' Stafford." In: Tom Simon, ed. *Green Mountain Boys of Summer: Vermonters in the Major Leagues, 1882–1993.* Shelburne, VT: The New England Press, 2000. Pp. 103–108.

William Charles ("Bill") Stafford
P. (B: Aug. 13, 1939, Catskill, NY-D: Sept. 19, 2001) New York (AL), 1960–1965; Kansas City (AL), 1966–1967. Remarks: Won 43 games and lost 40, with nine "saves," in eight seasons; career affected by April 1963 arm injury.
53106. Dexter, Charles. "Bill Stafford: He's Always Real Cool." *Baseball Digest,* XXI (June 1962), 67–72.

Charles Sylvester ("Chick") Stahl
OF-MGR. (B: Jan. 10, 1873, Avilla IN-D: March 28, 1907). Boston (NL), 1897–1900; Boston (AL), 1901–1906. Remarks: Had 1,552 hits (36 homers) and 173 stolen bases in 1,303 games in 10 years; only player to perform twice for Boston pennant winners in both leagues; manager, Boston final 40 games of 1906 season, winning 14 and losing 26 (.350); long troubled by depression, died a suicide.
53106a. Cava, Pete. "Requiem for a Ballplayer: Indiana's Chick Stahl." *Traces of Indiana and Midwestern History,* XVI (Summer 2004), 34–43.
53107. Christensen, Chris. "Chick Stahl: A Baseball Suicide." *Elysian Fields Quarterly,* XX (Spring 2003), 20–33.
53108. Suehsdorf, A. D. "Charles Syslvester 'Chick' Stahl." In: Vol. Q-Z of David L. Porter, ed. *Biographical Dictionary of American Sports: Baseball.* Rev. and enlarged ed. Westport, CT: Greenwood Press, 2000. Pp. 1458–1459.
53109. Thompson, Dick. "Chick and Jake Stahl: Were They Brothers? In: Joseph M. Wayman, ed. *Grandstand Baseball Annual, 1999.* Downey, CA: Joseph M. Wayman, 1999. Pp. 67–68. No.
53110. _____. "In Name Only." *The National Pastime,* XX (2000), 54–57.
53111. _____. "[Chick] Stahl's Suicide." *The Baseball Research Journal,* XXVIII (1999), 7–8.

Chick Stahl *see* **Charles Sylvester ("Chick") Stahl**
Garland Jake Stahl
OF-MGR. (B: April 13, 1879, Elkhart, IL-D: Sept. 18, 1922). Boston (AL), 1903; Washington (AL), 1904–1906; New York (AL), 1908; Boston (AL), 1908–1913. Remarks: Had 981 hits (31 homers) and 178 stolen bases in 981 games in 11 seasons; AL home run champion (10), 1910; player-manager, Washington (AL), 1905–1906; Boston (AL), 1912–1913, winning 263 games and losing 270 (.493).
53112. Thompson, Dick. "Chick and Jake Stahl: Were They Brothers? In: Joseph M. Wayman, ed. *Grandstand Baseball Annual, 1999.* Downey, CA: Joseph M. Wayman, 1999. Pp. 67–68. No.
53113. _____. "In Name Only." *The National Pastime,* XX (2000), 54–57.

Jake Stahl *see* **Garland Jake Stahl**
Scott Edmund Stahoviak
1B-3B-COACH. (B: March 6, 1970, Waukegan, IL). Minnesota (AL), 1993, 1995–1998. Remarks: Had 261 hits (27 homers) and 13 stolen bases in 344 games in five big league seasons; baseball coach, Carmel HS, Grayslake, IL., 2001-
53114. Bohen, Jim. "Student of the Game." *Twins Magazine,* IX (June 1996), 28–33.

Matthew Wade ("Matt") Stairs
OF. (B: Feb. 27, 1969, St. John, Canada). Montreal (NL), 1992–1993; Boston (AL), 1995; Oakland (AL), 1996–2000; Chicago (NL), 2001; Milwaukee (NL), 2002; Pittsburgh (NL), 2003; Kansas City (AL), 2004-. Remarks: Former NHL performer turned major leaguer; through 2004, has had 930 hits (194 homers) and 24 stolen bases in 1,172 games; tied MLB record with six RBIs in first inning of a game, July 5, 1996; hit two homers in a game twice within three days, Aug. 5–7, 2004.

53115. O'Shea, Joe. "Stairway to Boston?" *Boston Baseball,* VI (July 1995), 33–34.
53116. Otero, Salo. "Stairs Climbing Ladder to Majors." *USA Today Baseball Weekly,* I (January 15, 1992), 12–14. Montreal Canadiens hockey player.
53117. Sorci, Rick. "Baseball Profile: Matt Stairs." *Baseball Digest,* LIX (May 2000), 56–57.

Gerald Lee ("Gerry") Staley
P. (B: Aug. 21, 1920, Brush Prairie, WA). St. Louis (NL), 1947–1954; Cincinnati (NL), 1955; New York (AL), 1956–1956; Chicago (AL), 1956–1961; Kansas City (AL), 1961; Detroit (AL), 1961. Remarks: Had 134 victories, III defeats, and 61 "saves" in 15 years; won first night Opening Day game, April 18, 1950; surrendered the first homer of Ernie Banks (q.v.), Sept. 20, 1953; saved Chicago's pennant-clinching game, Sept. 22, 1959; post-baseball, served 17 years as the Clark County (Vancouver, WA.) superintendent of parks and recreation.
53118. Cohane, Tim. "The Old Pro in the Bullpen." *Look,* XXV (April 25, 1961), 85–86+.
53119. Hilton, George W. "Gerald Lee Staley." In: Vol. Q-Z of David L. Porter, ed. *Biographical Dictionary of American Sports: Baseball.* Rev. and enlarged ed. Westport, CT: Greenwood Press, 2000. Pp. 1459–1460.
53120. Silverman, Al. "What Makes Staley Win?" *Sport,* XIII (October 1952), 46–47+.
53121. Vanderberg, Bob. "Gerry Staley: A Sinker to Vic Power." *Sox — From Lane and Fain to Zisk and Fisk* . Chicago, IL: Chicago Review Press, 1982. Pp. 203–205.
53122. Veech, Ellis J. "Timber!: Look Out for Staley." *Baseball Digest,* XI (May 1952), 13–17.

Gerry Staley *see* **Gerald Lee ("Gerry") Staley**
Evan Tracy Stallard
P. (B, Aug. 31, 1937, Coeburn, VA). Boston (AL), 1960–1962; New York (NL), 1963–1964; St. Louis (NL), 1965–1966. Remarks: in a seven-year big league career, won 30 games and lost 57; remembered for serving up the pitch which Roger Maris (q.v.) slammed for his 61st home run, Oct. 1, 1961.
53123. Holway, John B. "For the Record: The Pitcher Who Has the Courage To Pitch To Maris." *Nine: A Journal of Baseball History and Social Policy Perspectives,* VIII (Fall 1999), 183–192.
53124. Santa Maria, Michael and James Costello. "Footnote to an Asterisk." In: their *In the Shadows of the Diamond.* Dubuque, IA: The Elysian Fields Press, 1992. Pp. 98–101.
53125. Shannon, Mike. "Tracy Stallard." In: his *Tales from the Ballpark: More of the Greatest True Baseball Stories Ever Told.* Lincolnwood, IL: Contemporary Books, 1999. Pp. 193–195.
53126. Shaughnessy, Dan. "Tracy Stallard: He Yielded No. 61 to Roger Maris." *Baseball Digest,* LI (January 1992), 59–60.
53127. Vecsey, George. "The Man Who Served Up 61." *Sport,* LVII (May 1974), 62–65.

Tracy Stallard *see* **Evan Tracy Stallard**
George Tweedy ("The Miracle Man") Stallings
C-OF-1B-MGR-EXEC. (B: Nov. 17, 1867, Augusta, GA-D: May 13, 1929). Brooklyn (NL), 1890; Philadelphia (NL), 1897–1898. Remarks: Had two hits In 20 at-bats in seven games in three big league playing years; manager, Philadelphia (NL), 1897–1898, Detroit (AL), 1901, New York (AL), 1909–1910, and Boston (NL), 1913–1920, winning 880 games and losing 900 (.494); also managed Kansas City (WL) and Nashville (SL), 1894, Nashville (SL), 1895, Detroit (WL), 1896, 1899–1900, Buffalo (IL),

1902–1906, 1911–1912, Rochester (IL), 1921–1927, and Montreal (IL), 1928; part-owner, Rochester (IL), 1924–1927; part owner-manager, Montreal (IL), 1928; this son of a Confederate officer and himself a plantation owner is remembered for his leadership of the cellar-dwelling Braves who rose in July 1914 and marched on to capture the NL pennant and defeat the powerful Philadelphia A's in that year's World Series.

53128. Brown, Warren. "George Stallings Introduced Platooning." *Baseball Digest,* XXX (February 1971), 76–80. Martin Kahoot's profile is a number in the online SABR Biography Project http://bioproj.sabr.org/bioproj.cfm?a=v&v=l&bid=884&pid=13501.

53129. Lane, Ferdinand C. "The Miracle Man." *Baseball Magazine,* XIV (February 1915), 57–66.

53130. Meany, Thomas. "The Miracle Man." In: Charles Einstein, ed. *The Fireside Book of Baseball.* New York, Simon and Schuster, 1956. Pp. 237–243. Reprinted in Jim Bouton, ed., *"I Managed Good, but Boy Did They Play Bad"* (Chicago, IL: Playboy Press, 1973), pp. 291–295 and in Charles Einstein, ed. *The New Baseball Reader: An All-Star Lineup from The Fireside Book of Baseball* (New York: Penguin Books, 1992), pp. 250–263.

53130. Pope, Edwin. "George Stallings." in: his *Baseball's Greatest Managers.* Garden City, N.Y.: Doubleday, 1960. Pp. 247–267.

53131. Stallings, George T. "The Miracle Man's Own Story." *Collier's,* LIV (November 28, 1914), 7–8.

53132. _____. "When I Was a Miracle-Man Myself." *Baseball Magazine,* XXIV (November 1919), 401–402.

53133. Stallings, George, Jr. "I Was Buddy-Buddy with the Rip-Roaring Players of My Dad's Team." *Baseball Digest,* XVI (July 1957), 79–92.

53134. Ziegler, John H. "George Tweedy 'The Miracle Man,' 'Chief,' 'The Edison of Baseball' Stallings." In: Vol. Q–Z of David L. Porter, ed. *Biographical Dictionary of American Sports: Baseball.* Rev. and enlarged ed. Westport, CT: Greenwood Press, 2000. Pp. 1460–1461.

Jack Stallings
COACH. (B: 1933, Durham, NC). Remarks: Asst. baseball coach, Wake Forest University and University of North Carolina, 1955–1958; head baseball coach and professor, Wake Forest University, 1958–1968, Florida State University, 1969–1975, and George Southern University, 1975–1999, with a record of 1,257 victories, 799 defeats and 10 ties (.612); author of two books, 17 instructional manuals, and 115+ articles; baseball coach and/or administrator for Pan American Games (1979, 1983, 1987) and Olympics (1984, 1988, 1992); elected to American Baseball Coaches Association Hall of Fame, 1988; elected to North Carolina Sports Hall of Fame, 2001; playing field at J.I. Clements Stadium, GSU, named in his honor, Feb. 19, 2005.

53135. Lawlor, Chris. "Georgia Southern Hospitality: Interview." *Scholastic Coach,* LXIV (November 1994), A20–A24.

53136. McDonald, T. "The King of Diamonds: Georgia Southern University's Own Legend, Jack Stallings." *The Reflector,* (September-October 2002), 9–11.

Oscar Harland Stanage
C. (B: March 17, 1883, Tulare, CA-D: Nov. 11, 1964). Cincinnati (NL), 1906; Detroit (AL), 1909–1920, 1925. Remarks: Obtained 819 hits (eight homers) and 30 stolen bases in 1,094 games in 14 seasons; noted fielding backstop, who, unhappily, once surrendered seven stolen bases in a game, Sept. 3, 1917.

53137. Smith, Lyall. "Caught Both Tiger No-Hitters." *Baseball Digest,* XI (August 1952), 93–95.

Burt L. Standish *see* **Gilbert Patten**
Albert Lee ("Stinger") Stange
P. (B: Oct. 27, 1936, Chicago, IL). Minnesota (AL), 1961–1964; Cleveland (AL), 1964–1966; Boston (AL), 1966–1970; Chicago (AL), 1970. Remarks: Had 62 victories, 61 defeats, and 21 "saves" in a decade; tied a MLB record with four strikeouts in an inning, Sept. 2, 1964; coach, Minnesota (AL), 1975 and Oakland (AL), 1977–1979.

53138. Elderkin, Phil. "The Strange Case of Lee Stange." *Baseball Digest,* XXVII (May 1968), 31–35.

53139. Lautier, Jack. "Lee Stange." *Fenway Voices.* Camden, ME: Yankee Books, 1990. Pp. 117–122.

53140. Stange, Lee. "The Science of Pitching." In: Deanne R. Peterson, ed. *1983 Official Red Sox Yearbook.* Boston, MA: Mark-Burton, 1983. Pp. 29–31.

Lee Stange *see* **Albert Lee Stange**
Joe Donald Stanka
P. (B: July 23, 1931, Hammon, OK). Chicago (AL), 1959; Nankai Hawks (Japan League), 1960–1965; Taiyo Whales (Japan League), 1966. Remarks: In a single U.S. big league season, won one game and lost none (1.000); won 100 games and lost 72 in Japan; also won 1964 Japan Pacific League MVP Award.

53141. Stanka, Joe and Jean Stanka. *Coping with Clouters, Culture, and Crisis.* Pasadena, CA: Dawn Publications, 1987. 176p.

53142. Trucks, Rob. "Joe Stanka." In: his *Cup of Coffee: The Very Short Careers of Eighteen Major League Pitchers.* New York: The Smallmouth Press Corporation, 2003. Chpt. 4.

Edward Raymond ("Eddie" or "The Brat" or "Muggsy") Stanky
2B-MGR-COACH. (B: Sept. 3, 1916, Philadelphia, PA-D: June 6, 1999). Chicago (NL), 1943–1944; Brooklyn (NL), 1944–1947; Boston (NL), 1948–1949; New York (NL), 1950–1954,; St. Louis (NL), 1952–1953. Remarks: In an 11-year playing career, had 1,164 hits (29 homers) and 48 stolen bases in 1,259 games; led NL in walks received, 1945–1946, 1950; had a double in both the World Series of 1947 and 1948; manager, St. Louis (NL), 1952–1955, Chicago, (AL), 1966–1968, and Texas (AL), 1977 (one game), winning 467 games and losing 435 (.518); coach, Cleveland (AL), 1957–1958; subject of Leo Durocher's (q.v.) inaccurately-remembered "nice guys finish last" remark; director of player development, New York (NL), 1963–1965 and baseball coach at University of South Alabama, 1969–1979, 1981–1983, compiling a record of 488–193; special assistant to president, University of South Alabama, 1982–1983; elected to Alabama Sports Hall of Fame; Stanky Field, University of South Alabama dedicated in his honor, March 8, 1980.

53143. Bisher, Furman. "First Year Wasn't Easy'—Stanky." *Baseball Digest,* XII March 1953), 26–29.

53144. "The Brat." *Time,* LIX (April 28, 1952), 60–64.

53145. "The 'Brat' Who Sparks the Giants; Eddie Stanky Can't Hit Much, But He Walks and Scores. He Isn't Fast, But He Makes the Key Defensive Plays." *Look,* XV (June 19, 1951), 52–53.

53146. "Brat's New World." *Time,* XC (July 7, 1967), 64–65.

53147. Broeg, Bob. "The Book on Manager Stanky." *Sport,* XVI (April 1954), 14–17.

53148. _____. "Stanky Tactical, but Not Tactful." *Baseball Digest,* XXVII (December 1960), 74–77.

53149. Brosnan, Jim. "Stanky and Durocher: A Player's Profile." *Chicago Tribune Magazine,* (April 3, 1966), *passim.*

53150. Cannon, Jimmy. "Stanky's Like DiMag[gio] This Way." *Baseball Digest,* VII (May 1948), 25–27.

53151. Davis, Mac. "You Can Be Wrong Twice." In: his *The Lore and Legends of Baseball.* New York: Lantern Press, 1953. Pp. 102–103.

53152. Dexter, Charles. *Eddie Stankey, Baseball Hero.* Greenwich, CT: Fawcett Publications, 1951. 35p. magazine format.

53153. "Eddie Stanky." In: *Current Biography Yearbook, 1951.* New York: H.W. Wilson Co, 1951. Pp. 604–606.

53154. Egan, Dave. "How Does Stanky Do It?" *Sport,* V (August 1948), 26–30.

53154a. Fimrite, Ron. "'The Brat' Is a Winner for Old USA: Baseball Coach Eddie Stanky." *Sports Illustrated,* XXXIV (May 3, 1971), 62–63.

53155. Findling, John E. "Edward Raymond 'The Brat,' 'Muggsy' Stanky." In: Vol. Q-Z of David L. Porter, ed. *Biographical Dictionary of American Sports: Baseball.* Rev. and enlarged ed. Westport, CT: Greenwood Press, 2000. Pp. 1461–1463.

53156. Fitzgerald, , Ed. "It's Gas House Stanky Now." *Sport,* XII (May 1952), 42–47.

53157. Furlong, William B. "Eddie Stanky: Genius or Jester?" *Sport,* XLIV (October 1967), 68–74.

53158. Graham, Frank. "He's Their Stanky Now." *Baseball Digest,* IX (September 1950), 25–27.

53159. _____. "The Storm over Stanky." *Sport,* XVIII (February 1955), 16–17.

53160. Hamill, Pete. "Eddie Stanky." In: Danny Peary, ed. *Cult Baseball Players.* New York: Simon and Schuster, 1990. Pp. 41–45.

53161. _____. "Eddie Stanky." In: Danny Peary, ed. *Baseball's Finest: The Greats, the Flakes, the Weird and the Wonderful.* North Digton, MA: The JG Press, 1990. Pp. 41–45. Both Peary books are identical.

53162. Katz, Fred. "Steady Eddie." *Sport,* XLIII (January 1967), 6+.

53163. Leggett, William. "Two Headliners Take Over Chicago." *Sports Illustrated,* XXIV (February 28, 1966), 26–34. Stankey with White Sox and Leo Durocher with Cubs.

53164. Lynch, Russell G. "The Cubs' Stanky." *Baseball Digest,* II (April 1943), 1–4.

53165. McCarthy, Colman. "The Brat Who Became a Father Figure: Reprinted from *The Washington Post,* May 15, 1977." *Congressional Record,* CXXIII (May 18, 1977), 15262–15263.

53166. McVay, Jim. "The Brewer, 'the Brat,' and the Cardinals." *Look,* XVIII (June 29, 1954), 70–74. Stanky's relationship with August A. Busch, Jr.

53167. Meany, Thomas. "The Brat's' a Giant." *Collier's,* CXXV (March 11, 1950), 28–30. Reprinted in his *Mostly Baseball* (New York: A.S. Barnes, 1958), pp. 123–134.

53168. Murphy, Edward T. "Stanky, the Stroller." *Baseball Digest,* IV (November 1945), 5–9.

53169. Parrot, Harold. "Stinky Stanky Drives Wild Men Wilder." *Saturday Evening Post,* CCXIX (February 1, 1947), 21+.

53170. Reichler, Joseph L. "The Gas House Gang Fuels Up." In: Bruce Jacobs, ed. *Baseball Stars of 1953.* New York: Lion Books, 1953. Pp. 119–125.

53171. Rust, Art, with Michael Marley. "Eddie Stanky." In: his *Legends: Conversations with Baseball Greats.* New York: McGraw-Hill, 1989. Pp. 81–90.

53172. Smith, Marshall. "Eddie's Cardinals May Be a Sleeper; the New, Milder Stanky Is Given Another Chance." *Life,* XXXVIII (April 4, 1955), 124–131.

53173. Smith, Walter ("Red"). "And the Hiring of Stanky." *Baseball Digest,* XI (February 1952), 47–50.

53174. Stanky, Edward R. ("Eddie"). "All Out for Beizbol." *Saturday Review,* XXXV (October 4, 1952), 24–25. The fiery manager's response to a Soviet assertion that U.S. baseball was a modified form of the Russian game *lapta.*

53175. _____.as told to Bob Broeg. "Managing Isn't So Tough!" *Saturday Evening Post,* CCXXV (March 7, 1953), 27+.

53176. _____. as told to Charles Dexter. "Just Call Me Stinky." *Sport,* X (March 1951), 46–47+.

53177. _____. as told to Tim Cohane. "Baseball Is a Tough Business." *Look,* XII (October 12, 1948), 80–84.

53178. _____. and William Leggett. "Better from the Neck Up." *Sports Illustrated,* XXVII (August 28, 1967), 18–23.

53179. Vanderberg, Bob "Eddie Stanky: He Locked the Door on Hubert Humphrey." In: his *Sox—From Lane and Fain to Zisk and Fisk.* Chicago, IL: Chicago Review Press, 1982. Pp. 90–98.

53180. Waldman, Frank. "Edward Raymond (Eddie) Stanky: Sparkplug of the Giants." *Famous American Athletes of Today.* 12th Series. Boston, MA: L.C. Page, 1951. Pp. 317–335.

53181. "The White Hat Mysteries." *Diamond Duds,* III (November 1993), 83–84.

53182. Wilson, John R. M. "Eddie Stanky." In: Paul Betz and Mark C. Carnes, eds. *American National Biography: Supplement I.* New York: Oxford University Press, 2002. Pp. 594–595.

53183. Young, Dick. "Separate 'Rules' for Stanky." *Baseball Digest,* VI (July 1947), 51–53.

Bob Stanley *see* **Robert William ("Bob" or "Big Foot" or "Steamer") Stanley**

Frederick Blair ("Fred" or "Chicken") Stanley
SS-2B. (B: August 13, 1947, Famhamville, IA). Seattle (AL), 1969; Milwaukee (AL), 1970; Cleveland (AL), 1971–1972; San Diego (NL), 1972; New York (AL), 1973–1980; Oakland (AL), 1981–1982. Remarks: Obtained 356 hits (10 homers) and 11 stolen bases in 815 games in 14 seasons; remembered as a durable late-inning defensive asset; minor league coach/exec, Milwaukee (AL/NL), 1983–1999; manager, Salem (Northwest League), 2000–2002; manager, Fresno (PCL), 2003-.

53184. Stanley, Fred and Lynn. *The Complete Instructional Baseball Manual: Professional Guidelines for Players and Coaches from the Youth Leagues to the Major Leagues.* 4th ed. Scottsdale, AZ: Stanley Co., 1988. 152p. First published in 1986.

Mickey Stanley *see* **Mitchell Jack ("Mickey") Stanley**
Mike Stanley *see* **Robert Michael ("Mike") Stanley**
Mitchell Jack ("Mickey") Stanley
SS-OF. (B: July 20, 1942, Grand Rapids, MI). Detroit (AL), 1964–1978. Remarks: In 15 seasons, had 1,243 hits (117 hits) and 44 stolen bases in 1,516 games; his 11 putouts tied AL record for most putouts in a game, July 13, 1973; upon retirement, formed the business "Mickey Stanley and Associates" at Brighton, MI, becoming housing developer in Livingston County.

53185. Falls, Joe. "With Stanley, It's No Gamble." *Sport,* XLVII (March 1969), 28–32.

53186. Flowers, Charles. "Mickey Stanley: The Kid Who Became a Star." *Baseball Digest,* XXXI (October 1972), 37–41.

53187. Green, Jerry. "Mickey Stanley: He Was the Complete Professional." *Baseball Digest,* XXXVIII (March 1979), 64–65.

53188. Hall, Donald. "How a Stopgap Shortstop Won a World Series." *Sports Illustrated,* LXIX (October 17, 1988), 18–20. 1968 World Series.

53189. _____. "October's Shortstop." In: his *The Ol' Ball Game.* Harrisburg, PA: Stackpole Books, 1990. Pp. 167–174.

Robert Michael ("Mike") Stanley

C. (B: June 25, 1963, Fort Lauderdale, FL). Texas (AL), 1986–1991; New York (AL), 1992–1995; Boston (AL), 1996–1997; New York (AL), 1997; Toronto (AL), 1998; Boston (AL), 1998–2000; Oakland (AL), 2000. Remarks: Had 1,138 hits (187 homers) and 13 stolen bases in 1,467 games in 15 years; had three homers and seven RBIs in one game, August 10, 1995; went 5-for-5 with five RBIs in one game, Sept. 4, 2000; coach, Boston (AL), 2002–2003

53190. Capezzuto, Tom. "Mike Stanley Made the Most of His Opportunity in '93." *Baseball Digest,* LIII (January 1994), 52–55.

53191. Lauber, Scott. "In the Opponent's Eyes: Mike Stanley." *Yankees Magazine,* XX (September 1999), 78–83.

Robert William ("Bob" or "Big Foot" or "Steamer") Stanley

P. (B: Nov. 10, 1954, Portland, ME). Boston (AL), 1977–1989. Remarks: Had 115 victories, 97 defeats, and 132 "saves" in eight seasons; a "goat" for wild pitch in the 1986 World Series; at his retirement, all-time Red Sox "saves" leader and only hurler to record 100 wins and 100 saves with the Boston team; coach, St. Lucie (Florida State League), 1997; coach, Binghampton (EL), 2000, Norwich (EL), 2004-; named to Boston Red Sox Hall of Fame, May 2000.

53192. Balf, Todd. "The Mouring After." *Sport,* LXXVIII (March 1987), 32–34.

53193. Gentile, Richard H. "Robert William 'Bob,' 'Steamer,' 'Bigfoot' Stanley." In: Vol. Q-Z of David L. Porter, ed. *Biographical Dictionary of American Sports: Baseball.* Rev. and enlarged ed. Westport, CT: Greenwood Press, 2000. Pp. 1463–1464.

53194. Kaplan, Jim. "Stanley Has the Steam." *Sports Illustrated,* LVIII (April 25, 1983), 66+.

53195. Wilkie, Curtis. "Another Fine Mess, Stanley." *Boston Globe Magazine,* (October 25, 1987), 16+.

Mike Stanton *see* **William Michael ("Mike") Stanton**

William Michael ("Mike") Stanton

P. (B: Sept. 25, 1952, Phoenix City, AL). Atlanta (NL), 1989–1995; Boston (AL) 1995–1996; Texas (AL), 1996; New York (AL), 1997–2002; New York (NL), 2003–2004; New York (AL), 2004-. Remarks: Through 2004, has won 57 games and lost 50, with 76 "saves"; established MLB record of 552 consecutive relief appearances prior to first start on May 9, 1999.

53195. Chastain, Bill. "Bullpen Ace Mike Stanton Thrives in Closing Role." *Baseball Digest,* LII (August 1993), 40–41.

Victor Starfin

P. (B: May 1, 1916, Russia-D: Jan. 12, 1957). Yomiuri Giants (Japan League), 1936–1944; Pacific/Taiyo Robins, 1946–1947; Goldstar, 1948; Daiei Stars, 1949–1953; Takahashi/Tombo Unions, 1954–1955. Remarks: Son of Russian immigrants exempted from military service but held under house arrest during World War II due to Russian background; had 303 victories and 176 defeats in 19 years, including an unsurpassed JL single-season record of 42 victories in 1939 and career total 83 shutouts; first JL pitcher to win 300 games and only non-Japanese player inducted into the Japanese Baseball Hall of Fame.

53196. Puff, Richard. "The Amazing Story of Victor Starfin." *The National Pastime,* XII (1992), 17–19.

53197. Starfin, Natasha. *Hakkyu ni Eiko ti Yume o Nosete (Throw White Ball With Glory and Dream).* Tokyo: Baseball Magazine Co., 1979.

53198. _____. *Russia Kara Keita Ace (Ace From Russia).* Kyoto: PHP Co., 1986.

53199. Thompson, Stephen I. and Masaru Ikei. "Victor Starfin: The Blue-Eyed Japanese." *Baseball History,* II (Winter 1987–1988), 4–19.

Wilver Dornel ("Willie" or "Pops") Stargell★

OF-BROADCASTER. (B: March 6, 1940, Earlsboro, OK-D: April 9, 2001). Pittsburgh (NL), 1962–1982. Remarks: Obtained 2,232 hits (475 homers) and 17 stolen bases in 2,360 games in 21 seasons; hit for the cycle, July 22, 1964; had 11 homers in one month, April 1971; had grand slam homer, June 20, 1971; NL home run champion, 1971 and 1973; NL RBI champion, 1973; had grand slam homer, Sept. 30, 1978; NL MVP award, 1979 (tie); NLCS MVP award, 1979; had three homers in 1979 World Series; World Series MVP award, 1979; had 11 career grand slam homers; uniform no. retired, Sept. 6, 1982; Pirates broadcaster, 1983–1984; coach, Pittsburgh (NL), 1985 and Atlanta (NL), 1986–1988; named to Bay Area Sports Hall of Fame, 1989; special assistant, GM, Pittsburgh (NL), 1994-death; elected to National Baseball Hall of Fame in 1988, where his plaque reads: "Intimidating presence between the lines and charismatic patriarch in clubhouse and dugout. Crushed 475 homers, many of tape-measure variety and hit most by any player during 1970's. Like his round-trippers, his 1,540 RBI's also most ever by a Pirate. Batted .282 over 21 seasons, all with Pittsburgh. Shared NL MVP honors in 1979, and named MVP in '79 NL championship series and World Series."

53200. Adelman, Bob and Susan Hall. *Out of Left Field: Willie Stargell and the Pittsburgh Pirates.* New York: The Two Continents Publishing Group, 1976. 224p.

53201. Allen, Maury. "Willie Stargell (1962-Present)." In: his *Baseball's 100.* New York: Galahad Books, 1981. Pp. 207–209.

53202. Anderson, Dave. "Willie Stargell: Baseball's Peerless Pirate." *Reader's Digest,* CXVI (April 1980), 88–92.

53203. Asinof, Eliot "Willie Stargell —'Where I Come from and Where I Am Going.'" *Sport,* LXX (April 1980), 29–31.

53204. Banks, Lacy J. "Big Man, Big Bat, Big Heart: Willie Stargell Voices Concern for People as Well as Pennants" *Ebony,* XXVI (October 1971), 132–136.

53205. Blount, Roy, Jr. "This Big Man Is the Cool Man." *Sports Illustrated,* XXXIII (October 4, 1970), 16–18.

53206. Bobrow, Norm. "Willie Stargell: Hat Trick." In: Ray Robinson, ed. *Baseball Stars of 1967.* New York: Pyramid Books, 1967. Pp. 69–75.

53207. Breslin, Jimmy. "Hard Night for a Hit Man." *Sport,* LVI (September 1973), 54–58.

53208. Brosnan, Jim. "Big Man in Pittsburgh." *Boy's Life,* LXVII (March 1977), 28–29.

53209. _____. "Willie Stargell: Heart and Soul of the Pirates." *Boy's Life,* LXXI (March 1981), 6+.

53210. Chick, Bob. "Willie Stargell: A Star of Stars." In: Drew Sheiman, ed. *Baseball '79.* St. Petersburg, FL: National Association of Professional Baseball Leagues, 1979. Pp. 14–15.

53211. Collier, Ken. "A Tribute to 'Pops.'" In: Ken Collier, ed. *The Baseball Book, 1983.* Scottsdale, AZ: Jalart House, 1983. P. 131+.

53212. Cotton, Anthony. "Fine Like Good Wine." *Sports Illustrated,* LI (April 20, 1979), 49–50.

53213. Durslag, Melvin. "Willie Stargell Needs a Press Agent." *Baseball Digest,* XXXII (August 1973), 18–21.

53214. Eldridge, Larry. "Willie Stargell: Pirate Treasure." *Baseball Digest,* XXXIII (December 1974), 54–56.

53215. Evans, Howie. "Stargell Takes Another Roundtrip : ...Leads Pirates in Homeruns and RBIs." *Black Sports,* I (August 1971), 36–39.

53216. Feeney, Charlie. "Willie Stargell Puts It All Together." *Baseball Digest,* XXX (September 1971), 19–23.

53217. Fimrite, Ron. "Sportsmen of the Year: Willie Stargell and Terry Bradshaw." *Sports Illustrated,* LI (December 24, 1979), 38–43.

53219. Flowers, Kevin. "Baseball Says Farewell to Pirate Great Willie Stargell." *Baseball Digest,* LX (July 2001), 68–71.

53220. Gray, Bill. "Willie Stargell —1973." In: *his Baseball's Top 100: The Best Individual Seasons of All Time.* Wilton, CT: Diamond Library, 1996. Pp. 226–227.

53221. Green, Paul M. "Willie Stargell: His Cards and His Career." *Baseball Cards,* V (October 1985), 64–69.

53222. Grove, Wayne. "Paying Tribute." *Beckett Sports Collectibles,* X (June 2001), 102–103.

53223. Hall, Susan, and Bob Adelman. *Out of Left Field: Wilie Stargell's Turning Point Season.* New York: Proteus Publishing Co., 1980. 224p. First published by the New York firm of Two Continents In 1976 as *Out of Left Field: Willie Stargell and the Pittsburgh Pirates.*

53224. Hanks, Stephen. "Willie Stargell: The Making of an MVP." *Sport,* LXX (January 1980), 12+.

53225. Hano, Arnold. "Willie Stargell and the Beautiful Challenge." *Sport,* LXII (August 1971), 60–89.

53226. _____. "Willie Stargell: Some Man!" In: Ray Robinson, ed. *Baseball Stars of 1972.* New York: Pyramid Books, 1972. Pp. 100–106.

53227. Heiling, Joe. "Willie Stargell: He Learned to Go with the Pitch." *Baseball Digest,* XXV (November 1966), 47–49.

53228. Hirt, Clyde. "Closeup: Willie Stargell." In: Clyde Hirt, ed. *Sports Quarterly Presents Baseball Extra, Summer 1971.* New York: Counterpoint, Inc., 1971. Pp. 28–29+.

53229. Honig, Donald. "1979: Willie Stargell, Keith Hernandez." In: his *National League MVP's.* New York: Bantam, 1989. Pp. 101–103.

53230. _____. "Willie Stargell: A 'Family' Man." In: his *The Power Hitters.* St. Louis, MO: *The Sporting News,* 1989. Pp. 206–215.

53231. Libby, Bill. *Willie Stargell, Baseball Slugger.* New York: G.P. Putnam, 1973. 159p.

53232. Masterson, Dave and Timm Boyle. "1979." In: their *Baseball's Best: The MVPs.* Chicago: Contemporary Books, Inc., 1985. Pp. 298–304.

53233. McHugh, Roy. "On the Hill." *Sport,* XVIII (October 1964), 44–48.

53234. Musick, Phil. "Willie Stargell's 'All in the Family.'" In: Zander Hollander, ed. *1980: The Complete Handbook of Baseball.* New York: New American Library, 1980. Pp. 22–30.

53235. Nauer, Hank. "Willie Stargell: The Pride of Pittsburgh." *Saturday Evening Post,* VII (May-June 1980), 29–38.

53236. "Of Course 'Pops' is Getting Older." *People Weekly,* XII (December 24, 1979), 78–79.

53237. Reidenbaugh, Lowell. "Willie Stargell." In: his *Baseball's Hall of Fame: Cooperstown, Where Legends Live Forever.* New York: Arlington House, 1988. Pp. 331–332.

53238. Ritter, Lawrence and Donald Honig. "Willie

Stargell." In: *their The 100 Greatest Baseball Players of All Time.* New York: Crown Publishers, 1986. Pp. 158–159.

53239. Rodriguez-Mayoral, Luis. "Willie Stargell: A Special Man Merits Special Honor." *Baseball Digest,* XLVII (May 1988), 65–67.

53240. Rubin, Bob. "Mr. Stargell, It's Cooperstown Calling." *Inside Sports,* X (March 1988), 14+.

53241. Rumill, Ed. "Stargell at Last Emerges from the Shadows." *Baseball Digest,* XXVII (October 1969), 85–97.

53242. Schlossberg, Dan. "Willie Stargell: In Roberto's Footsteps." In: Ray Robinson, ed. *Baseball Stars of 1974.* New York: Pyramid Books, 1974. Pp. 106–116.

53243. Shannon, Mike. *Willie Stargell.* New York: Chelsea House Publishers, 1992. 61p.

53244. Shelley, Fred M. "Wilver Dornel 'Willie,' 'Pops' Stargell." In: Vol. Q-Z of David L. Porter, ed. *Biographical Dictionary of American Sports: Baseball.* Rev. and enlarged ed. Westport, CT: Greenwood Press, 2000. Pp. 1464–1465.

53245. Singer, Tom. "Willie Stargell Wins the Yardstick Award." *Baseball Digest,* XXVIII (December 1960), 55–60.

53246. Smith, Ron. "Willie Stargell 81." In: his *The Sporting News Selects Baseball's 100 Greatest Players.* St. Louis, MO: *The Sporting News,* 1998. Pp. 176–177.

53247. Stargell, Willie, as told to George Vass. "The Game I'll Never Forget." *Baseball Digest,* XXXII (December 1973), 42–45. Multiple homer games.

53248. _____. "A Matter of Life and Death." In: Fred Down, ed. *Baseball News, 1972.* New York: Cord Communications, 1972. Pp. 14–45.

53249. _____. and Tom Bird. *Willie Stargell: An Autobiography.* New York: Harper & Row, 1984. 247p.

53250. "Willie Stargell." In: *Current Biography Yearbook, 1980.* New York: H. W. Wilson Co., 1980. Pp. 375–378.

53251. Wilson, John R. M. "Willie Stargell." In: Paul Betz and Mark C. Carnes, eds. *American National Biography: Supplement I.* New York: Oxford University Press, 2002. Pp. 596–597.

Albert ("Dolly") Stark
UMP-BROADCASTER. (B: Nov. 4, 1897, New York City-D: Aug. 24, 1968). NL arbiter, 1928-1935, 1937-1942; Philadelphia (NL) broadcaster, 1935.

53252. Bloodgood, Clifford. "Bearing Down on Every Pitch." *Baseball Magazine,* XLIX (August 1932), 401–402, 430.

53253. Burr, Harold C. "Fate Hounds This Ump." *Baseball Magazine,* LXIX (June 1942), 309–310, 329.

53254. Gerlach, Larry R. "Albert 'Dolly' Stark." In: Vol. Q-Z of David L. Porter, ed. *Biographical Dictionary of American Sports: Baseball.* Rev. and enlarged ed. Westport, CT: Greenwood Press, 2000. Pp. 1465–1466.

53255. Ribalow, Harold U. "Dolly Stark: Man in Blue." In: his *The Jew in American Sports.* New York: Bloch Publishing Co., 1948. Pp. 75–80.

53256. _____. and Meir Z. "Dolly Stark: Man in Blue." In: their *Jewish Baseball Stars.* New York: Hippocrene Books, 1984. Pp. 104–111.

53257. Stark, Albert. "How to Get the Thumb." *Baseball Digest,* XI (November 1952), 11–14.

Dolly Stark *see* Albert ("Dolly") Stark

Raymond Francis ("Ray" or "Iron Man") Starr
P. (B: April 23, 1906, Nowata, OK-D: Feb. 9, 1963). St. Louis (NL), 1932; New York (NL) and Boston (NL), 1933; Cincinnati (NL)., 1941–1943; Pittsburgh (NL), 1944–1945; Chicago (NL), 1945. Remarks: Obtained 37 big league victories and 35 defeats, with four "saves"; ca-

reer minor leaguer who earned his nickname from pitching both ends of more than 40 minor league doubleheaders.

53258. Balter, Sam. "Starr of Stars; at 35, He's a Rookie! Fame Took Its Time, Now He's a Major-League Sensation." *Liberty,* XIX (September 5, 1942), 42–46.

53259. Starr, Bill. *Clearing the Bases: Baseball Then and Now.* New York: Michael Kesend, 1989.

Joseph ("Joe" or "Old Reliable") Start
1B. (B: Oct. 14, 1842, New York City-March 27, 1927). Enterprise Club, 1860–1861; Brooklyn Atlantics, 1862–1870; New York (N.A.), 1871–1875; New York (NL), 1876; Hartford (NL), 1877; Chicago (NL), 1878; Providence (NL), 1879–1885; Washington (NL), 1886. Remarks: In 11 NL years, obtained 1,031 hits (seven homers) in 798 games; a three-decade player in three eras.

53260. Rucker, Mark D. "Joseph 'Joe,' 'Old Reliable' Start." In: Vol. Q-Z of David L. Porter, ed. *Biographical Dictionary of American Sports: Baseball.* Rev. and enlarged ed. Westport, CT: Greenwood Press, 2000. Pp. 1466–1467.

Arnold John ("Jigger") Statz
OF. (B: Oct.20, 1897, Waukegan, IL-D: March 16, 1988). New York (NL), 1919–1920; Boston (AL), 1920; Chicago (NL), 1922–1925; Brooklyn (NL), 1927–1928. Remarks: Had 737 hits (17 homers) and 77 stolen bases in 683 games in an eight-year big league career; also played for Hollywood (PCL), 1926, 1929–1942, achieving league records for hits (3,356), doubles (595), triples (137), and runs scored (1,996) to finish with 4,093 career hits (fourth on the all-time OB list behind Rose, Cobb, and Aaron); played himself in 1929 motion picture *Fast Company,* based on the George M. Cohan and Ring Lardner (q.v.) stage play *Elmer the Great;* named to Pacific Coast League Hall of Fame.

53261. Crichton, Kyle. "Take It 'Jigger'!" *Collier's,* CVII (June 14, 1941), 19–21.

53262. Cronin, Ned. "After 24 Seasons in the Outfield, 'Jigger' Statz Hangs Up His Glove." *Baseball Digest,* I (December 1942), 42–45.

53263. Spalding, John E. "'Jigger' Statz." In: *his Pacific Coast League Stars: One Hundred of The Best, 1903–1957.* San Jose, CA: John E. Spalding, 1994. Pp. 85–86.

Jigger Statz *see* Arnold John ("Jigger") Statz
Daniel Joseph ("Rusty" or "Le Grande Orange") Staub
OF-1B-BROADCASTER. (B: April 1, 1944, New Orleans, LA). Houston (NL), 1963–1968; Montreal (NL), 1969–1971; New York (NL), 1972–1975; Detroit (AL), 1976–1979; Montreal (NL), 1979; Texas (AL), 1980; New York (AL), 1981–1985. Remarks: Obtained 2,716 hits (292 homers) and 47 stolen bases in 2,951 games in 16 seasons; $100,000 bonus baby in 1961; had homer and three doubles in one game, April 17, 1969; had grand slam homer, May 14, 1972; hit homer that won Game Four of 1973 World Series; had record-tying 25 pinch hits, 1983; only player to appear in 500 games for four teams; only player with 500 hits for four teams; restaurateur and broadcaster, New York (NL), 1986–1995; elected to Louisiana Sports Hall of Fame, 1989; uniform number retired by Montreal (NL), May 15, 1993.

53264. Allen, Maury. "Au Revoir to Rusty Staub." *Baseball Digest,* XXXV (March 1976), 66–69.

53265. Angell, Roger. "My Summer Vacation." *The New Yorker,* LX (May 7, 1984), 74–120.

53266. Berger, Phil. "Rusty Staub: The Thinking Man's Hitter." In: Gerald Kavanagh, ed. *Street and Smith's*

Official 1984 Baseball Yearbook. New York: Conde Nast Publications, 1984. Pp. 96–97.

53267. Bisher, Furman. "Rusty Staub: Budding Bat King." *Baseball Digest,* XXVI (December 1967), 84–87.

53268. Bruce, H. "Rusty Staub: The Making of a Muscular Millionaire." *Maclean's,* LXXXIII (July 1970), 42–47.

53269. Burick, Si. "Rusty Staub: Cleanup Man at 19." *Baseball Digest,* XXIII (July 1963), 27–29.

53270. Devaney, John. "Rusty Staub and Montral: Une Affaire d'Amour." *Sport,* XLIX (May 1970), 38–39+.

53271. Eldridge, Leslie. "Daniel Joseph 'Rusy' Staub." In: Vol. Q-Z of David L. Porter, ed. *Biographical Dictionary of American Sports: Baseball.* Rev. and enlarged ed. Westport, CT: Greenwood Press, 2000. Pp. 1467–1468.

53272. Finch, Frank. "Staub's a Real 'Swinger.'" *Baseball Digest,* XXVI (September 1967), 27–29.

53273. Herskowitz, Mickey. "Rusty Staub: A Star to Build a Team On." *Sport,* XLIV (December 1967), 52–55.

53274. Janoff, Murray. "Rusty a Gate-Swinger." In: Clyde Hirt, ed. *Sports Quarterly Presents Baseball Extra, Summer 1972.* New York: Counterpoint, Inc., 1972. Pp. 36–39.

53275. Lape, Bob. "Baseball to Bordeaux: Rusty Staub Makes His Mark in the Restaurant Business." *Ovation,* X (June 1989), 42–44.

53276. "Le Grand Orange." *New York,* LXIV (January 2, 1989), 18–19.

53277. Mulvoy, Mark. "In Montreal, They Love 'Le Grande Orange.'" *Sports Illustrated,* XXXIII (July 6, 1970), 38–39.

53278. Murray, Jim. "Rusty Staub: He Tries Harder." *Baseball Digest,* XXXIII (May 1974), 42–45.

53279. Robertson, John. *Rusty Staub of the Expos.* Scarborough, Ontario: Prentice Hall of Canada, 1971. 185p.

53280. Ronberg, Gary. "Houston's Boy is Now a Man." *Sports Illustrated,* XXVII (August 14, 1967), 54–58.

53281. Staub, Daniel ("Rusty"). "There's More to Fielding Than Catching the Ball." *Baseball Digest,* XXX (December 1971), 52–59.

53282. _____., as told to George Vass. "The Game I'll Never Forget." *Baseball Digest,* XXXV (January 1976), 74–79.

Dude Stearns *see* John Hardin ("Dude") Stearns
John Hardin ("Dude") Stearns
C-BROADCASTER. (B: Aug. 21, 1951, Denver, CO). Philadelphia (NL), 1974; New York (NL), 1975–1984. Remarks: Had 696 hits (46 homers) and 91 stolen bases in 810 games in 11 seasons; set NL season record for steals by a catcher, one which lasted from 1978 to 1998; scout, Milwaukee (AL), 1987; instructor, Houston (NL), 1988; coach, New York (AL), 1989; manager, Knoxville (SL), 1990–1991; broadcaster, ESPN, 1992; manager, Princeton (Appalachian League), 1992–1994; scout, Cincinnati (NL), 1995; scout, Baltimore (AL), 1996–1997; coach, Baltimore (AL), 1998; roving instructor, Baltimore (AL), 1999; coach, NY (NL), 2000–2001, scout, NY (NL), 2002, manager, Binghamton (EL), 2003; manager, Norfolk (IL), 2004–.

53283. Kapan, Jim. "Hard Catcher to Nab." *Sports Illustrated,* XLIX (September 25, 1978), 44+.

53284. Wilner, Barry. "John Stearns: Good and He's Getting Better." *Baseball Digest,* XXXVIII (August 1979), 76–81.

Norman Thomas ("Turkey") Stearnes★
OF-1B. (B: May 8, 1901, Nashville, TN-D: Sept. 4, 1979). Nashville Elite Giants, 1920; Montgomery Grey

Sox, 1921; Memphis Red Sox, 1922; Detroit Stars, 1923–1930; New York Lincoln Giants, 1930; Detroit Stars and Kansas City Monarchs, 1931; Cole's American Giants, 1932; Detroit Stars and Cole's American Giants, 1933; Kansas City Monarchs and Cole's American Giants, 1934; Cole's American Giants, 1935; Philadelphia Stars, 1936; Detroit Stars, 1937; Kansas City Monarchs, 1938–1941; Detroit Black Sox, 1942; Toledo Cubs, 1945. Remarks: Powerful slugger, with 185 homers and seven Negro League home run titles; elected to National Baseball Hall of Fame in 2000, where his plaque reads: "One of the Negro Leagues' most feared hitters, he hit better than .300 in 14 of 19 seasons, collecting six home run titles and led the league in triples four times. A graceful center fielder as well, he played in four East-West All-Star Games. Played 11 seasons for the Detroit Stars, also excelling with the New York Lincoln Giants, Kansas City Monarchs, Chicago American Giants, and Philadelphia Stars."

53285. Bak, Richard. *"Turkey" Stearnes and the Detroit Stars: The Negro Leagues In Detroit, 1919–1933.* Detroit: Wayne State University Press, 1994. 298p.

53286. Holway, John B "'I Never Counted My Homers Unless They Won Games;' 'Turkey' Stearnes Tells His Story." *Detroit News Sunday Magazine,* (August 15, 1971), 21+.

53287. _____. "Turkey Stearnes." In: John A. Garrity and Marsh C. Carries, eds. *American National Biography.* 24 vols. New York: Oxford University Press, 1999. XX, 587–588.

53288. _____. "'Turkey' Stearnes —'A Humdinger of a Hitter.'" *Black Sports,* V (April 1976), 48–50.

53289. Martin, Douglas D. "Norman 'Turkey' Stearnes." In: Vol. Q-Z of David L. Porter, ed. *Biographical Dictionary of American Sports: Baseball.* Rev. and enlarged ed. Westport, CT: Greenwood Press, 2000. Pp. 1468–1469.

53290. Riley, James A. "Turkey' Stearnes and the Detroit Stars." *Nine: A Journal of Baseball History and Social Policy Perspectives,* III (Spring 1995), 303–305.

Gene Stechschulte
P. (B: August 12, 1973, Lima, OH). St. Louis (NL), 2000–2002; Memphis (PCL), 2002–2003. Remarks: Ashland University star who won eight big league games and lost seven, with six "saves" in three year big league career; had pinch hit homer in first official MLB at bat.

53291. Beck, Jason. "Now Pitching." *Accent: Ashland University Magazine,* (Summer 2001), 6–8.

Bill Stein *see* **William Allen ("Bill") Stein**
William Allen ("Bill") Stein
3B-2B-1B. (B: Jan. 21, 1947, Battle Creek, MI). St. Louis (NL), 1972–1973; Chicago (AL), 1974–1976; Seattle (AL), 1977–1980; Texas (AL), 1981–1985. Remarks: Obtained 751 hits (44 homers) and 16 stolen bases in 959 games in 14 seasons; in 1981, established AL record for most consecutive hits in one season (seven) by a pinch hitter.

53292. Pickard, Chuck. "Let's Hear It for Little-Known Record-Holder Bill Stein." *Baseball Digest,* XLI (April 1982), 62–67.

Terry Lee Steinbach
C.(B: March 2, 1962, New Ulm, MN). Oakland (AL), 1986–1996; Minnesota (AL), 1997–1999. Remarks: Had 1,453 hits (162 homers) and 23 stolen bases in 1,546 games in 14 years; first big league AB a pinch-hit homer, Sept. 12, 1986; homered in 1986 All-Star Game; All-Star Game MVP award, 1988; had homer and five RBIs in 1989 ALCS; had seven RBIs in 1989 World Series; homered in Game One of 1992 ALCS; had 21-game hitting streak,

1996; named to Cape Cod League Hall of Fame, January 2002.

53293. Snyder, Deron. "A's Quiet Man Delivers Dramatic Sonic Boom." *USA Today Baseball Weekly,* II (October 14, 1992), 24–25.

53294. Steinbach, Terry, as told to George Vass. "The Game I'll Never Forget." *Baseball Digest,* L (December 1991), 85–87.

53295. Swift, E. M. "Cold Sweet Home." *Sports Illustrated,* LXXXVI (January 27, 1997), 56–58, 61.

53296. Worthington, A. R. "Terry Steinbach: Small-town Boy Makes Good." In: Rob Kelly, ed. *1990 Oakland Athletics Magazine.* Benicia, CA: Mariposa Press, 1990. Pp. 93–103.

George Michael Steinbrenner III
EXEC. (B: July 4, 1930, Rocky River, OH). Remarks: Assistant football coach at Northwestern University, 1955 and Purdue University, 1956–1967, who inherited shipbuilding empire, becoming board chairman of American Shipbuilding Company; principal owner, New York (AL), 1973-date; suspended from baseball by the office of the Commissioner, 1974–1975; VP, U.S. Olympic Committee, 1989-date; noted for outspoken involvement in the game, a record number of managerial hirings and firings, and appearances in television commercials.

53297. Allen, Maury. *All Roads Lead to October: Boss Steinbrenner's Reign in the Bronx.* New York: St. Martin's Press, 2000. 298p.

53298. Axhelm, Pete. "George's Rage to Win." *Newsweek,* XCIII (April 23, 1979), 60–61+.

53299. Brenner, Marie. "Boss Steinbrenner." *New York,* XIV (April 13, 1981), 24–29.

53300. Callahan, Tom. "The Many Woes of Baseball's 'Bad Boy.'" *U.S. News and World Report,* CIX (August 6, 1990), 48–49.

53301. Carlson, Stan W. "George Michael Steinbrenner, 3rd." In: Vol. Q-Z of David L. Porter, ed. *Biographical Dictionary of American Sports: Baseball.* Rev. and enlarged ed. Westport, CT: Greenwood Press, 2000. Pp. 1469–1471.

53302. Cassidy, John. "Yankee Imperialist." *The New Yorker,* LXXVIII (July 8, 2002), 40–53.

53303. Cerrone, Rick. "A Conversation with Steinbrenner." *Baseball Quarterly,* II (Spring 1978), 12–13.

53304. Coffey, Frank. *The Wit and Wisdom of George Steinbrenner.* New York: Penguin Books, USA, 1993. 210p.

53305. Downey, Mike. "Cleveland, By George! Let's Indulge in a Bit of Revisionist History For a Moment and Imagine That George Steinbrenner — Humble Ship Builder, Baseball Visionary, and Homeboy — Never Bought the Yankees, But Purchased the Fortunate Indians, Instead." *Inside Sports,* XIV (July 1992), 68–70.

53306. Durslag, Melvin. "Breaking Two Toilets and Shoving a Lady Weren't Quite Devilish Enough." *TV Guide,* XXX (January 30, 1982), 24–26.

53307. _____. "Unbearable!, Impossible!, and Naturally, the Winner!" *TV Guide,* XXXI (February 5, 1983), 50–51+.

53308. Fimrite, Ron. "Yankee Clipper: Owner George Steinbrenner." *Sports Illustrated,* XLVII (October 16, 1977), 122–126.

53309. Fins, A. N. "Stee-rike!: Steinbrenner Just Can't Get a Hit." *Business Week,* (April 23, 1990), 121–122.

53310. Fussman, C. "'What I've Learned': George Steinbrenner." *Esquire,* CXXXVII (January 2002), 56–57.

53311. "George Michael Steinbrenner, 3rd." In: *Current Biography Yearbook, 1979.* New York: H. W. Wilson Co., 1979. Pp. 367–370.

53312. Gergen, Joe. "Bulletin ... George Steinbrenner to Manage the Yankees." In: Zander Hollander, ed. *1983 Season: The Complete Handbook of Baseball.* New York: New American Library, 1983. Pp. 6–13.

53313. Greenfield, Jeff. "George Steinbrenner — Get Out of Town!" *New York,* X (August 15, 1977), 32–34.

53314. "Is It Time to Ax Steinbrenner?" In: Owen C. Shaw, ed. *Petersen's 1989 Pro Baseball Annual.* Los Angeles, CA: Petersen's, 1989. Pp. 64–69.

53315. Kahn, Roger. "He's a Yankee Doodle Dandy." *Sport,* LXXII (June 1981), 36–40.

53316. Kaplan, David A. "A Boss Deep in His Own Dirt." *Newsweek,* CXVI (July 30, 1990), 62+.

53317. _____. "The Most Hated Man in Baseball." *Newsweek,* CXVI (August 6, 1990), 52–56.

53318. Klein, Joe. "Going, Going, Gone?" *New York,* XXIII (August 6, 1990), 20–25.

53319. Kluger, Jeffrey. "George Steinbrenner: A Candid Conversation." *Playboy,* XXXVIII (May 1991), 63–78.

53320. Kornheiser, Tony. "That Demon Yankee." *The New York Times Magazine,* (April 9, 1978), 40+.

53321. Kowet, Don. "George Steinbrenner." In: his *Rich Who Own Sports.* New York: Random House, 1977. Pp. 244–255.

53322. Leggett, William. "Top Banana at Tampa Bay." *Sports Illustrated,* LIV (January 12, 1981), 35–36.

53323. Lieber, Jill. "Will 'The Boss' Behave Himself?" *Sports Illustrated,* LXXVIII (March 1, 1993), 18–21.

53324. Madden, Bill. "The Big Payback." *Sport,* LXXXIV (March 1993), 52–57.

53325. _____. and Moss Klein. *Damned Yankees: A No-Holds-Barred Account of Life with "Boss" Steinbrenner.* New York: Warner Books, 1991. 454p. First published in 1990 and updated here to include 1990 season.

53326. McMillan, Ken. "George Steinbrenner." In: his *Tales from the Yankee Dugout: A Collection of the Greatest Yankee Stories Ever Told.* Champaign, IL: Sports Publishing, Inc., 2001. Pp. 175–178.

53327. Neff, Craig. "The Steinbrenner Probe." *Sports Illustrated,* LXXIII (July 23, 1990), 17–18.

53328. _____. and Jill Lieber. "Bad Job, Baseball." *Sports Illustrated,* LXXIII (October 8, 1990), 34–36+.

53329. _____. "Behind the Scenes with George and Fay." *Sports Illustrated,* LXXIII (August 13, 1990), 13–14.

53330. _____. "A Man on the Spot." *Sports Illustrated,* LXXIII (July 30, 1990), 26–28+.

53331. Oboiski, Robert. "Owner Steinbrenner, Baseball's Dr. Jekyll and Mr. Hyde." In: his *Baseball's Strangest Moments.* New York: Sterling Publishing Co., 1988. Pp. 57–59.

53332. Olney, Buster. "What Will Make George Steinbrenner Happy; or, How the Boss Changed His Stripes." *The New York Times Magazine,* (September 27, 1998), 69–70, 77, 84, 98, 104.

53333. Pedulla, Tom. "Steinbrenner: Gone At Last?" In: Owen C. Shaw, ed. *Petersen's Pro Baseball Review — 1991.* Los Angeles, CA: Petersen Publishing Co., 1991. Pp. 58–61.

53334. Pooley, Eric. "Let Him Walk." *New York,* XXVIII (February 13, 1995), 82–87.

53335. Schaap, Dick. *Steinbrenner.* New York: G. P. Putnam's Sons, 1982. 314p. Reprinted by Avon Books as a 1983 320 page edition.

53336. Shannon, Mike. "George Steinbrenner." In: his *Tales from the Dugout: The Greatest True Baseball Stories Ever Told.* Lincolnwood, IL: NTC/Contemporary Books, 1997. Pp. 197–198.

53337. Shapiro, Walter. "The Artful Pickoff." *Time,* CXXXVI (August 13, 1990), 62–63.

53338. Smith, Larry. "The Shipbuilder Who Owns the Yankees." *Dunn's Review,* CII (June 1973), 53–55+.

53339. Steinbrenner, George M., 3rd. "Interview." Edited by Dave Anderson. *Sport,* LXIX (October 1979), 27–28+.

53340. Toropov, Brandon. *101 Reasons to Hate George Steinbrenner.* New York: Citadel Press, 1997. 170p.

53341. "The Trouble with George." *The New Yorker,* LXIX (August 2, 1993), 4–5.

53342. Verducci, Tom. "Mr. Softie." *Sports Illustrated,* C (May 10, 2004), 64–73.

53343. Weiss, Peter. "George Steinbrenner." In: his *Baseball's All-Time Goats: As Chosen by America's Top Sportswriters.* Holbrook, MA: Bob Adams, Inc, 1992. Pp. 156–159.

53344. Whitton, M. "Pandemonium in Pinstripes." *The New York Times Book Review,* LXIX (October 1987), 11–12.

53345. Will, George F. "George Steinbrenner, an Acquired Taste." In: his *Bunts: Curt Flood, Camden Yards, Pete Rose and Other Reflections on Baseball.* New York: Touchstone Books, 1998. Pp.134–140.

53346. _____. "The Most Hated Man in Baseball." *Newsweek,* CXVI (August 6, 1990), 52–59.

53347. Wulf, Steve. "A Good Man — Sometimes." *Sports Illustrated,* LXXIII (December 31, 1990), 69–70.

53348. _____. "This Time George Went Overboard!" *Sports Illustrated,* LVI (May 10, 1982), 40–42+.

53349. Ziegell Vic. "George and Dick [Howser]: Love at First Place." *New York,* XIII (July 28, 1980), 7–8.

Gus Steiner
UMP. Remarks: N.C.A.A., Olympic Games arbiter.

53350. Steiner, Gus. "Interview." *Referee,* XVII (May 1992), 28+.

Harry M. ("Steinie") Steinfeldt
2B-3B-SS. (B: Sept. 29, 1877, St. Louis, MO-D: Aug. 17, 1914). Cincinnati (NL), 1898–1905; Chicago (NL), 1906–1910; St. Paul (AA) and Boston (NL), 1911. Remarks: In 14 seasons, gathered 1,575 hits (27 homers) and 189 stolen bases in 1,645 big league games; NL RBI champion, 1906; drove in a record three runs with three sacrifice flies in one game, 1909; remembered as the third baseman in the Cubs' famous Tinker-to-Evers-to-Chance infield; died of a cerebral hemorrhage.

53351. Kush, Raymond D. "Harry M. 'Steinie' Steinfeldt." In: Vol. Q–Z of David L. Porter, ed. *Biographical Dictionary of American Sports: Baseball.* Rev. and enlarged ed. Westport, CT: Greenwood Press, 2000. Pp. 1471–1472. Tom Simon's profile of Steinfeldt appears as a number in the online SABR biography project < http://bioproj.sabr.org/bioproj.cfm?a=v&v=l&bid=916&pid=13585>.

Casey Stengel *see* **Charles Dillon ("Casey" or "The Old Perfesser") Stengel**

Charles Dillon ("Casey" or "The Old Perfesser") Stengel★
OF-MGR. (B. July 30, 1890, Kansas City, MO-D: Sept. 29, 1975). Brooklyn (NL), 1912–1917; Pittsburgh (NL), 1918–1919; Philadelphia (NL), 1920–1921; New York (NL), 1921–1923; Boston (NL), 1924–1925. Remarks: Obtained 1,219 hits (60 homers) and 131 stolen bases in 1,277 games in 14 playing years; went 4-for-4 in first big league game, Sept. 17, 1912; had three inside-the-park homers, April 5, 1913 (1) and May 1, 1913; won two 1923 World Series games with homers (including Game One's famous inside-the-park scramble); manager, Toledo (AA), 1925–1931; coach, Brooklyn (NL), 1932–1933; manager, Brooklyn (NL),

1934–1936; manager, Boston (NL), 1938–1943; manager, Milwaukee (AA), 1944–1945; manager, Kansas City (AA), 1945–1946; manager, Oakland (PCL), 1947–1948; manager, New York (A.L,), 1949–1960 and New York (NL), 1961–1965, winning a total of 1,926 big league games and losing 1,867 (.508); named to Missouri Sports Hall of Fame, 1952; executive scout, New York (NL), 1966–1975; as a pilot, Stengel was colorful (talked in "Stengelese") and successful, including more victories in World Series games (37) than any other manager; when released by New York (AL) in 1960, the millionaire settled as a bank director in Oakland, CA; uniform numbers later retired by both the Yankees and the Mets; elected to National Baseball Hall of Fame In 1966, where his plaque reads: "Manager New York Yankees 1949–1960. Won 10 pennants and 7 World Series with New York Yankees, only manager to win 3 consecutive World Series 1949–1953. Played outfield 1912–1925 with Brooklyn, Pittsburgh, Philadelphia, New York and Boston NL teams. Managed Brooklyn 1934–1936, Boston Braves 1938–1943, New York Mets 1962–1965."

53352. Allen, Maury. "Casey Stengel on the Road." *Sport,* XXXVIII (September 1964), 32–35.

53353. _____. "The Humor of Casey Stengel." *Baseball Digest,* XXIX (November 1970), 60–63. Reprinted In John Kuenster, ed., *From Cobb to Catfish* (Chicago: Rand McNally, 1975), Pp. 201–202.

53354. _____. "Stengel." *Baseball Magazine,* New Series IV (August 1980), 59+.

53355. _____.You Could Look It Up: The Life of Casey Stengel. New York: Times Book, 1979. 310p.

53356. Bak, Richard. *Casey Stengel: A Splendid Baseball Life.* Dallas, TX: Taylor Publishing Co., 1997. 198p.

53357. Berkow, Ira and Jim Kaplan. *The Gospel According to Casey.* New York: St. Martin's Press, 1992. 168p.

53358. Berrigan, Darrell. "The Truth About Casey." *Saturday Evening Post,* CCXXVII (July 3, 1954), 30+.

53359. Beverage, Richard E. "Casey Stengel and the 1948 Oakland Oaks." *The Baseball Research Journal,* XIX (1990), 85–88.

53360. Bisher, Furman. "Wherein or Case Outsmarts a Tableful." *Baseball Digest,* XIII (June 1954), 51–54.

53361. Bryson, Bill. "How Foes Once Saved Stengel." *Baseball Digest,* XVIII (October 1959), 81–86.

53362. "Casey Stengel." In: *Current Biography Yearbook, 1949.* New York: H.W. Wilson Co., 1949. Pp. 586–588.

53363. "Casey Stengel Ain't Talkin'—About TV." *TV Guide,* V (July 5, 1958), 6–7.

53364. Cataneo, David. *Casey Stengel: Baseball's Old Professor.* Great American Sports Legends. Nashville, TN: Cumberland House, 2003. 240p.

53365. Cleveland, Charles B. "Casey Stengel." In: his *Baseball's Greatest Managers.* New York: Crowell, 1960. Pp. 231–246.

53366. Cohane, Tim. "Casey Stengel." *Look,* XXIII (April 28, 1959), 26–32.

53367. Conerly, Wally. "Is Professor Stengel Slipping?" In: Al Silverman, ed. *True's 1960 Baseball Yearbook.* Greenwich, Conn.: Fawcett Publications, 1960. Pp. 8–9+.

53368. Cooper, John A. "Mr. Casey Stengel Goes on the Air." *Baseball Magazine,* LIII (September 1934), 467–468.

53369. Creamer, Robert W. "The Amazin' Life and Times of Casey Stengel." *Reader's Digest,* CXXV (October 1984), 199–202+.

53370. _____. "Casey Stengel: An Appreciation." *Sports Illustrated,* XLIII (October 13, 1975), 41+.

53371. _____. "Casey Took a Walk." *Sports Illustrated,* IV (May 7, 1956), 46–48.

53372. _____. *Stengel: His Life and Times.* New York: Simon and Schuster, 1984. 349p. Excerpted in Nicholas Dawidoff, ed., *Baseball: A Literary Anthology* (New York: The Library of America, 2002), pp. 543–551.

53373. Daley, Arthur. "Listening to Stengel." In: James Tuite, ed. *Sports of the Times: The Arthur Daley Years.* New York: Quadrangle Books, 1975. Pp. 81–84.

53374. _____ "The 'Ol Perfesser' Spins a Tale." *Baseball Digest,* IX (June 1950), 44–46.

53375. _____. "The Philosophy of Casey Stengel." *The New York Times Magazine,* (July 26, 1953), 14+.

53376. _____. "The Silent Mr. Stengel." In: Joe McCarthy, ed. *After the Game: A Collection of the Best Sports Writing.* New York: Dodd, Mead, 1972. Pp. 135–139.

53377. Daniel, Daniel M. "Casey's Last Year." *Sport,* XXIX (June 1960), 16–17+.

53378. _____. "Is Stengel Great or Is He Lucky?" *Sport,* XVI (July 1954), 16–17+.

53379. _____. "Jester to Genius: The Life, Laughs, and Laurels of Charles Dillon Stengel." In. J.G. Taylor Spink, ed. *Baseball Register, 1959.* St. Louis, MO: *The Sporting News,* 1959. Pp. 3–29.

53380. _____. "The Return of Casey Stengel." *Baseball Monthly,* I (March 1962), 20–21+.

53381. _____. "Stengel Hard to Imagine as a Martinet, but He Can Do It." *Baseball Magazine,* LXXXII (December 1948), 233–235.

53382. _____. "Stengel's Fine Sense of Humor, Great Coaches, Help His Success." *Baseball Magazine,* LXXXVI (June 1951), 219–221.

53383. Deford, Frank. *Casey on the Loose.* New York: Viking Press, 1989. 106p.

53384. Dexter, Charles. "Make Mine Casey." *Baseball Digest,* VII. (April 1948), 19–27.

53385. _____. "Stengel and the Yankees." *Baseball Digest,* VIII (March 1949), 40–45.

53386. Durslag, Melvin. "Casey Stengel and His Mets." *TV Guide,* X (August 3, 1963), 12–14.

53387. Durso, Joseph. *Casey & Mr. McGraw.* St. Louis, MO: The Sporting News, 1989. 367p.

53388. _____. *Casey: The Life and Legend of Charles Dillon Stengel.* Englewood Cliffs, NJ: Prentice-Hall, 1967. 211p.

53389. Elderkin, Phil. "Casey Stengel: The Greatest News Source Ever Invented." *Baseball Digest,* XXXIV (April 1975), 80–83.

53390. "Exit Casey." *Time,* LXXVI (October 31, 1960), 70–72.

53391. Falls, Joe. "Casey Stengel: He Was One of a Kind." *Baseball Digest,* XXXVIII (December 1979), 42–55.

53392. _____. "Even to Kids, Casey's Like a Living Legend." *Baseball Digest,* XV (February 1966), 47–49.

53393. Felker, Clay. *Casey Stengel's Secret.* New York: Walker, 1961. 124p.

53394. Ford, Edward C. ("Whitey") and Mickey Mantle. "Life with Casey Stengel." Edited by Joseph Durso. *Saturday Evening Post,* CCXLIV (May 1977), 44–45+.

53395. Frayne, Trent. "The Loveable Old Perfesser." *Maclean's,* CV (May 11, 1992), 50+.

53396. Frommer, Harvey. "Casey Stengel." In: his *Baseball's Greatest Managers.* New York: Watts, 1985. Pp. 216–229.

53397. Ghlo, Joanne Mary. "Stockton [Calif] is Casey's Mudville." *Baseball Digest,* XIX (May 1960), 92–95.

53398. Goldman, Steve. "Casey Stengel." *Yankees Magazine,* XIX (February 1999), 70–75.

53399. Graham, Frank. *Casey Stengel: His Half Century in Baseball.* New York: Day, 1958. 192p.

53400. _____. "Stengel: A Man of Experience?" *Baseball Digest,* XI (March 1952), 33–35.

53401. Gross, Milton. "The Job Ahead for Stengel." *Baseball Digest,* XX (November 1961), 8–11.

53402. Hahn, James and Lynn. *Casey: The Sports Career of Charles Stengel.* Mankato, MN: Crestwood House, 1981. 47p.

53403. Hano, Arnold. "Casey Stengel." *Sport,* XLII (September 1966), 34–35+.

53404. Herrera, Mitsi. *Casey Stengel.* San Diego, CA: Revolutionary Comics, 1993. 30p. Juvenile.

53405. Hern, Gerry. "The Difference in Stengel." *Baseball Digest,* XII (January 1953), 19–21.

53406. _____ "Stengel an Elder Statesman, Now." *Baseball Digest,* VIII (November 1949), 19–21.

53407. Heuman, William. "Casey Stengel." In: his *Famous Coaches.* New York: Dodd, Mead, 1968. Pp. 90–101.

53408. Hickey, David and Kerry Keene. "Casey Stengel." In: their *The Proudest Yankees of All: From the Bronx to Cooperstown.* Lanham, MD: Taylor Trade Pub., dist. by National Book Network, 2003. Chpt. 24.

53409. Holland, Gerald. "Down the Stretch with Casey Stengel." *Sports Illustrated,* V (October 1, 1956), 69–77.

53410. Holmes, Tontray. "The Picturesque Casey Stengel." *Baseball Magazine,* LII (May 1934), 553–554+.

53411. Howard, Elston G. "Baseball's Grand Old Man." *Baseball Digest,* XCI (October 1967), 185–188+.

53412. Hutchins, J.K. "Casey at the Bat." *Saturday Review of Literature,* L (April 15, 1967), 29+.

53413. Jacobson, Steve. "Despite His Image as a Comic, Casey Stengel was a Smart Manager." *Baseball Digest,* L (January 1991), 42–43.

53414. Kaplan, Jim. and Ira Berkow. *The Gospel According to Casey: Casey Stengel's Inimitable, Instructional, Historical Baseball Book.* New York: St. Martin's Press, 1992. 172p.

53415. Kindred, Dave. "Casey Stengel." In: his *Heroes, Fools and Other Dreamers.* Marietta, GA: Longstreet Press, 1989. Pp. 151–153.

53416. Klein, Moss. "Billy Martin Recalls His Favorite Manager." *Baseball Digest,* XLIII (June 1984), 62–66.

53417. Koppett, Leonard. "The Day Casey First Appeared." *Baseball Digest,* XXI (February 1962), 20–23.

53418. Kuenster, John. "Baseball's Grand Old Man: Casey Stengel." *Baseball Digest,* XXXUI (August 1974), 6–11.

53419. Lardner, John. "The Improbable Casey Stengel." *Sport,* V (December 1948), 51–52+.

53420. Leifer, Neil. and Peter Bonventre. "Casey Stengel." In: their *Neil Leifer's Sports Stars.* Garden City, N.Y.: Doubleday, 1986. Pp. 174–179.

53421. "Lend an Ear to an Old Case." *Life,* XXXIII (September 29, 1962), 106–108+.

53422. Lewis, Franklin. "Stengel Changes His Talk." *Baseball Digest,* XIV (June 1955), 85–87.

53423. Libby, Bill. "Casey Stengel." in: his *The Coaches.* Chicago: Regaery, 1972. Pp. 121–122.

53424. Lieb, Frederick G. "Casey Stengel." In: his *Comedians and Pranksters of Basball.* St. Louis, MO: *The Sporting News,* 1958. Pp. 19–21.

53425. Linn, Ed. "Casey Stengel Reveals His Inner Struggle." *Sport,* XXXIV (December 1962), 14–17.

53426. _____. "Casey Stengel: Showman of the Series." *Sport,* XXVIII (October 1959), 56–65.

53427. _____. "Last Angry Old Man: Stengel of the Mets." *Saturday Evening Post,* CCXXXVIII (July 31, 1965), 75–78. Reprinted in Jim Bouton, ed. *"I Managed Good, But Boy Did They Play Bad"* (Chicago, IL: Playboy Press, 1973), pp. 63–77.

53428. _____. "The Many Faces of Casey Stengel." *Sport,* XXII (December 1956), 26–27+.

53429. Liss, Howard. "Casey Stengel." In: his *Baseball's Zaniest Stars.* New York. Random House, 1971. Pp. 3–17.

53430. MacKenzie, Kyle. "Remembering Casey." *Yale Review,* LXXVI (Winter 1987), 214–220.

53431. MacLean, Norman. *Casey Stengel: A Biography.* New York: Drake Publishers, 1971. 188p.

53432. Maher, Charles. "Casey Stengel: He's Left a Legacy of Smiles." *Baseball Digest,* XXXV (January 1976), 36–41.

53433. Mahon, Jack. "Casey Keeps Them in Stitches." *Baseball Magazine,* LXXXIX (September 1952), 25–26.

53434. Martin, Alfred M. ("Billy"). "I Loved the Old Man." *Sport,* XXXI (March 1961), 26–29+.

53435. _____. and Mark Kram. "The Unforgettable Casey Stengel." *Reader's Digest,* CVIII (April 1976), 78–82.

53436. McClure, Arthur F. "Charles Dillon 'Casey,' 'Dutch,' 'The Old Professor' Stengel." In: Vol. Q-Z of David L. Porter, ed. *Biographical Dictionary of American Sports: Baseball.* Rev. and enlarged ed. Westport, CT: Greenwood Press, 2000. Pp. 1472–1474.

53437. McConlogue, Neil. "Casey's Comeback." *Baseball Magazine,* XXIX (June 1922), 319–320.

53438. McMillan, Ken. "Casey Stengel." In: his *Tales from the Yankee Dugout: A Collection of the Greatest Yankee Stories Ever Told.* Champaign, IL: Sports Publishing, Inc., 2001. Pp. 179–184.

53439. Meany, Thomas. "Casey Stengel." In: his *Mostly Baseball."* New York: A. S. Barnes, 1958. Pp. 105–122.

53440. _____. "Casey Off the Cuff." *Look,* XXV (June 6, 1961), 100–102+.

53441. _____. "Casey Stengel: Legend and Fact." *Baseball Digest,* XVII (December 1958), 5–11.

53442. _____. "The 'Ol' Perfesser." In: Thomas Meany, ed. *Magnificent Yankees.* New York: Grosset and Dunlap, 1957. Pp. 13–46.

53443. _____. "Stengel: The 'Ol Perfesser.'" *Baseball Digest,* XI (June 1952), 76–81.

53444. _____. "They Didn't Hire Him for Laughs." *Saturday Evening Post,* CCXXI (March 12, 1949), 29+.

53445. _____. and Tommy Holmes. "Casey Stengel." In: their *Baseball's Best.* New York: Franklin Watts, 1964. Pp. 1–8.

53446. _____., with Jerry Mitchell. "Stengel: The Man Who Laughed Last." *Sport,* VIII (April 1950), 16–26.

53447. Menke, Frank G. "Uncomfortable — for the Yankees." In: his *Sports Tales and Anecdotes.* New York: A.S. Barnes, 1953. Pp. 59–60. 1923 World Series performance.

53448. Millstein, Gilbert. "Musings of a Dugout Socrates." *The New York Times Magazine,* (August 26, 1962), 17+. Reprinted in Jim Bouton, ed. *"I Managed Good, But Boy Did They Play Bad"* (Chicago, IL: Playboy Press, 1973), pp. 53–62.

53449. Munzel, Edgar. "How Casey Got His Teeth into the Art of Bunting." *Baseball Digest,* XVI (January-February 1957), 87–89.

53450. Murphy, Jack. "Casey Was the Perfect Manager for the Old Mets." *Baseball Digest,* XXVIII (December 1969), 45–47.

53451. Nicholson, Lois P. *Casey Stengel.* New York: Chelsea House Publishers, 1995. 64p.

53452. "…One of Those Things." *Newsweek,* LVI (October 31, 1960), 85–86. Casey's firing.

53453. Nuwer, Hank. "Casey Stengel." In: his *Strategies of the Great Baseball Managers.* New York: Watts, 1988. Pp. 84–95.

53454. Parrott, Harold. "Casey the Comic." *Baseball Magazine,* LXI (June 1938), 305–307.

53455. Paxton, Henry T. "Casey the Indestructible." *Saturday Evening Post,* CCXXXV (April 7, 1962), 46+.

53456. Pollock, Ed. "Who'll Succeed Stengel?" *Baseball Digest,* XVIII (September 1959), 17–19.

53457. Pope, Edwin. "Casey Stengel." In: his *Baseball's Greatest Managers.* Garden City, N.Y.: Doubleday, 1960. Pp. 268–286.

53458. Povich, Shirley. "Sounds from Stengel's Latest LP Record." *Baseball Digest,* XIX (May 1960), 81–83.

53459. Powers, Jimmy. "Casey 'Stangel.'" In: his *Baseball Personalities.* Chicago, IL: Field, 1949. Pp. 96–105.

53460. Reichler, Joseph L. "Crazy Like a Fox." In: Bruce Jacobs, ed. *Baseball Stars of 1953.* New York: Lion Books, 1953. Pp. 31–37.

53461. _____. "What Makes Stengel Tick?" *Complete Baseball,* III (February 1953), 8–15.

53462. Richman, Milton. "Casey Stengel: The Loneliest Man in the Game." *Baseball Digest,* XVI (May 1967), 13–17.

53463. Robinson, Murray. "The Beatles Meet 'Ol Case.'" *Baseball Digest,* XXIII (May 1964), 25–27.

53464. Robinson, Ray. "Casey Stengel." In: his *Baseball's Most Colorful Managers.* New York: G. P. Putnam, 1970. Pp. 47–48.

53465. _____. "Casey Stengel." In: Ray Robinson, ed. *Baseball Stars of 1959.* New York: Pyramid Books, 1959. Pp. 151–155.

53466. Rosenthal, Harold. "Casey Stengel." In: his *Baseball's Best Managers.* New York: Nelson, 1961. Pp. 7–52.

53467. _____. "Casey Stengel, the Successful Manager." In: Herbert Wind, ed. *The Realm of Sport.* New York: Simon and Schuster, 1966. Pp. 80–88.

53468. _____. "Casey Stengel was Never at a Loss for Words." *Baseball Digest,* XXXVI (September 1976), 26–30.

53469. _____. "The Day They Locked Up Casey Stengel." In: Bob Sparks, ed. *Baseball '82.* St. Petersburg, FL: National Association of Professional Baseball Leagues, 1982. Pp. 6–10. For striking a photographer.

53470. _____. "When Stengel Put the Squeeze on [Bob] Lemon." *Baseball Digest,* XXII (March 1963), 33–35.

53471. Rumill, Ed. "Casey Stengel, Batting Professor." *Baseball Digest,* IV (March 1945), 57–59.

53472. _____. "The Little Professor." *Baseball Magazine,* LXXIX (June 1947), 219–221.

53473. Schoor, Gene. *Casey Stengel: Baseball's Greatest Manager.* New York: Julian Messner, 1953. 185p.

53474. Seaver, Tom, with Marty Appel. "When Casey Ran the Bases." In: his *Great Moments in Baseball: From the World Series of 1903 to the Modern Records of Nolan Ryan.* New York: Carol Communications, 1992. Pp. 69–74.

53475. Shannon, Mike. "Casey Stengel." In: his *Tales from the Dugout: The Greatest True Baseball Stories Ever Told.* Lincolnwood, IL: NTC/Contemporary Books, 1997. Pp. 199–202.

53476. Siegel, Arthur. "Casey First Turned Down Yankee Job." *Baseball Digest,* XIII (March 1954), 14–15.

53477. Silverman, Al. "Casey at the Bat." In: his *Heroes of the World Series.* New York: G.P. Putnam's Sons. 1964. Pp. 62–73.

53478. Small, Collie. "Is Casey Stengel Good — or Just Lucky?" *Collier's,* CXXXI (March 28, 1953), 26+.

53479. Smith, Ira L. "Casey Stengel." In: his *Baseball's Famous Outfielders.* New York: A. S. Barnes, 1954. Pp. 126–131.

53480. Smith, Lyall. "Why Stengel Nixed Detroit Job, Took Mets' Offer." *Baseball Digest,* XXI (March 1962), 61–63.

53481. Spinelli, Jerry. "Retrospect: A Tip of the Hat." In: Edward Ehre, ed. *Best Sports Stories of 1982.* St. Louis, MO: *The Sporting News,* 1982. Pp. 233–238.

53482. Stainback, Berry and Fred Katz. "Casey Stengel: Platoon Manager." *Sport,* XXXIII (May 1962), 44–45.

53483. Stann, Francis, and Tommy Holmes. "Stengel Talks On: .400 Hitters, Pick-off, Hidden Ball." *Baseball Digest,* XVIII (May 1959), 25–29. Casey on techniques.

53484. Stengel, Charles D. ("Dillon"). "Casey Stengel's Greatest Day." *Baseball Digest,* IX (April 1950), 6–9.

53485. _____. "Casey Stengel's Sensational Comeback." *Baseball Magazine,* XXIX (October 1922), 502–503.

53496. _____. "Confessions of a Left-Hander." *Baseball Magazine,* XX (February 1918), 341–343. Reprinted in *Baseball Magazine,* XCIV (November 1964), 22–25.

53497. _____. *Quotable Casey: The Wit, Wisdom, and Wacky Words of Casey Stengel, Baseball's "Old Perfesser" and Most Amazin' Manager.* Edited by Fred McMane. Nashville, TN: TowleHouse Pub., 2002. 133p.

53498. _____. "Why Barnstorming Is a Good Thing." *Baseball Magazine,* XXXIV (March 1925), 455–456.

53499. _____. as told to Henry T. Paxton. *Casey at the Bat: The Story of My Life in Baseball.* New York: Random House, 1962. 254p. Abridged in *Saturday Evening Post,* CCXXXIV (September 16-October 14, 1961), 29–34, 54–57+, 62–63+, 66–68+, 54+ as "My Own Story."

53500. _____. as told to John P. Carmichael. "My Greatest Day in Baseball." In: John P. Carmichael, ed. *My Greatest Day in Baseball.* New York: A. S. Barnes, 1945. Pp. 498–201.

53501. "Stengelese Sampler." *Sports Illustrated,* XLI (December 23, 1974), 54–55.

53502. Stevens, Bob. "The Real Turning Point for Stengel." *Baseball Digest,* XVII (May 1958), 59–61.

53503. Strausberg, Jack. "One for the 'Box' Score." *Baseball Digest,* XII (October 1953), 68–72.

53504. "The Ten [Pennant] Races of Casey." *Sports Illustrated,* IX (October 6, 1958), 24–25.

53505. "The Man." *Time,* LXVI (October 3, 1956), 58–62.

53506. Twombly, Wells. "There was Only One Casey." In: Irving T. Marsh and Edward Ehre, eds. *Best Sports Stories of 1976.* New York: E. P. Dutton, 1976. Pp. 37–41. Reprinted in David Halberstam, ed. *The Best American Sports Writing of the Century* (Boston, MA: Houghton, Mifflin, 1999), pp. 451–454.

53507. Vecsey, George. "Why Baseball Needs Casey Stengel." In: Zander Hollander, ed. *Baseball Yearbook, 1964.* New York: Popular Library, 1964. Pp. 10–14.

53508. Verral, Charles S. *Casey Stengel, Baseball's Greatest Manager.* Champaign, IL: Garrard, 1978. 93p.

53509. Voigt, David Quentin. "Casey Stengel." In: John A. Garrity and Marsh C. Carries, eds. *American National Biography.* 24 vols. New York: Oxford University Press, 1999. XX, 653–655.

53510. Will, George F. "Speaking Stengelese." In: his *Bunts: Curt Flood, Camden Yards, Pete Rose and Other Reflections on Baseball.* New York: Touchstone Books, 1998. Pp.59–60.

53511. Williams, Roger. "Goodbye, Casey, Goodbye." *Sports Illustrated,* XIII (October 31, 1960), 63–65. Firing by Yankees.

53512. Wright, Alfred. "Look Out!: Here Comes Casey." *Sports Illustrated,* I (March 14, 1955), 8–11.

David Rotchford ("Dave") Stenhouse

P-COACH. (B: Sept. 12, 1933, Westerly, RI). Washington (AL), 1962–1964. Remarks: Won 16 games and lost 28, with one "save," in a three-year big league career; later baseball coach, Brown University.

53513. Zanger, Jack. "Dave Stenhouse." In: Ray Robinson, ed. *Baseball Stars of 1963.* New York: Pyramid Books, 1963. Pp. 150–154.

Renaldo Antonio ("Rennie") Stennett

2B-SS. (B: April 5, 1951, Colon, Panama). Pittsburgh (NL), 1971–1979; San Francisco (NL), 1980–1981. Remarks: Obtained 1,239 hits (41 homers) and 75 stolen bases in 1,237 games in 11 years; on September 16, 1975, became the only 20th Century player to collect seven hits in a nine-inning game.

53514. Fitzpatrick, Tom. "The Day Rennie Stennett Became a Hero." *Baseball Digest,* XXXIV (December 1975), 84–86.

53515. Powell, Larry. "Rennie Stennett Recalls His 7-for-7 Game." *Baseball Digest,* LI (December 1992), 69–71.

53516. Stennett, Renaldo A. ("Rennie"). "The Game I'll Never Forgot." *Baseball Digest,* XXVIII (December 1979), 55–61.

Jacob Charles ("Jake") Stenzel

OF. (B: Jacob Charles Stelzle, June 24, 1867, Cincinnati, OH-D: Jan. 6, 1919). Chicago (NL), 1890; Pittsburgh (NL), 1892–1897; Baltimore (NL), 1897–1898; St. Louis (NL), 1898–1899; Cincinnati (NL), 1899. Remarks: Obtained 1,024 hits and 292 stolen bases in nine big league seasons; had two homers in one inning, June 6, 1894; first Pittsburgh player to have six hits in one game, May 4, 1896; also played for Wheeling (Tri-State League), 1887–1888; Springfield (Tri-State League), 1889; Galveston (TL), 1890; Spokane (Pacific Northwest League), 1891; Portland (PNL), 1892; operated Cincinnati restaurant/bar, 1912–1914 .

53517. Akin, William E. "Jacob Charles 'Jake' Stenzel." In: Vol. Q-Z of David L. Porter, ed. *Biographical Dictionary of American Sports: Baseball.* Rev. and enlarged ed. Westport, CT: Greenwood Press, 2000. Pp. 1474–1475. Akin has also prepared a Stenzel profile as part of the online SABR biography project < http://bioproj.sabr.org/bioproj.cfm?a=v&v=1&bid=806&pid=13597>.

53518. Felber, Bill. "Hit'er Up Against Boston!" *Baseball History,* II (Winter 1987–1988), 20–31.

Jake Stephens *see* **Paul ("Jake") Stephens**

Paul Eugene ("Jake" or "Country Jake") Stephens

SS-2B. (B: Feb. 10, 1900, Pleasureville, PA-D: Feb. 5, 1981). Hilldale Daisies, 1921–1929; Philadelphia Giants, 1924; Homestead Grays, 1929–1932; Pittsburgh Crawfords, 1932; Philadelphia Stars, 1933–1935; New York Black Yankees, 1936–1937. Remarks: Obtained 190 hits (one homer) and 20 stolen bases in 795 games.

53519. Holway, John B. "Country Jake: Paul ("Jake") Stephens." In: his *Black Diamonds: Life in the Negro Leagues From the Men Who Lived It.* Baseball and American Society, no. 4. Westport, CT: Meckler, 1989. Pp. 1–17.

Vernon Decatur ("Vern" or "Junior" or "Buster") Stephens, Jr.

SS (B: Oct. 23, 1920, McAlister, NM-D: Nov. 3, 1968). St. Louis (AL), 1941–1947; Boston (AL), 1948–1952; Chicago (AL) and St. Louis (AL), 1953; Baltimore (A.L), 1954–1955; Chicago (AL), 1955. Remarks: Had 1,859 hits (247 homers) in 1,720 games in 13 summer campaigns; AL home run champion, 1944; AL RBI champion, 1944, 1949–1950 (tie); noted fielder, who participated in five double plays in one game, May 5, 1948; went 4-for-4 in one game, Aug. 28, 1948; his 159 RBIs of 1949 set a mark not broken until 1999; had two grand slam homers, April 21 and Aug. 24, 1950; also played for Springfield (Three-I League) and Johnstown (Middle Atlantic League), 1938, Mayfield (Kitty League), 1939, San Antonio (TL), 1940, Toledo (AA), 1941, Seattle (PCL), 1955–1956; died of heart attack.

53520. Devine, Tommy. "Fugitive from Futility." In: Bruce Jacobs, ed. *Baseball Stars of 1950.* New York: Lion Books, 1950. Pp. 184–191. Mark Armour's profile is a number in the online SABR Biography Project http://bioproj.sabr.org/bioproj.cfm?a=v&v=1&bid=555&pid=13605.

53521. Frey, Leonard H. "Vernon Decatur 'Junior,' 'Buster' Stephens." In: Vol. Q-Z of David L. Porter, ed. *Biographical Dictionary of American Sports: Baseball.* Rev. and enlarged ed. Westport, CT: Greenwood Press, 2000. Pp. 1475–1476.

53522. Hirshberg, Al. "Vern Stephens: Junior Red Socker." *Sport,* VII (August 1949), 16–22.

53523. Kaese, Harold. "A Little Slug for the White Sox." *Sport,* IV (June 1948), 50+.

53524. Molter, Harry "Vernon Stephens." In: his *Famous American Athletes of Today.* 13th Series. New York: Page, 1953. Pp. 359–360.

53525. Moore, Gerry. "Vern Stephens." In: his *My Greatest Baseball Game.* New York: A.S. Barnes, 1950. Pp. 188–192.

53526. Walman, Frank. "Vernon Decatur (Vern) Stephens, Jr.: 'Little Slug' of the Boston Red Sox." In: his *Famous American Athletes of Today.* 11th Series. New York: Page, 1949. Pp. 279–299.

Garrett Charles Stephenson

P. (B: Jan. 2, 1972, Takoma Park, MD). Baltimore (AL), 1996; Philadelphia (NL), 1997–1998; St. Louis (NL), 1999–2000, 2002–2003. Remarks: Through 2003, had 39 victories and 39 defeats; struck out 12 batters in first Phillies game, including first five faced, May 13, 1997; led NL in homers allowed 2000, 2003.

53527. McCorvey, Paul. "Maryland-Born Garrett Stephenson Earned a Chance to Pitch in the Free State Next Season." *Orioles Gazette,* III (October 8, 1993), 23–24.

53528. Sparesus, Brad. "Versatile Marylander Garrett Stephenson Big Plus for [Albany] Polecats." *Orioles Gazette,* III (July 8, 1993), 57–58.

Henry/Holly Stephenson

SCHEDULERS. (B: 1944 Henry, 1948 Holly). Remarks: MLB's schedule makers, 1985.

53529. Kim, A. "Popes, Blizzards, and Walleyed Pike: All Have Had an Impact on the Baseball Schedules Fashioned by Henry and Holly Stephenson to Satisfy a Dizzying Myriad of Requirements." *Sports Illustrated,* LXXIV (April 8, 1991), 10–13.

Jackson Riggs ("Old Hoss") Stephenson

OF-2B. (B: Jan. 5, 1898, Akron, AL-D: Nov. 15, 1985). Cleveland (AL), 1921–1925; Chicago (NL), 1926–1934. Remarks: In 14 seasons, had 1,515 hits (63 homers) and 54 stolen bases in 1,310 games; weak fielder, but keen-eyed hitter who struck out only 247 times in 4,508 ABs; led NL in doubles, 1927; had six hits and a double in 1929 World Series and eight hits and a double in 1932 World Series; also played for Indianapolis (AA), 1935; player-manager,

Birmingham (SA), 1936–1937; manager, Helena (Cotton State League), 1938 and Montgomery (Southeastern League), 1939; named to Alabama Sports Hall of Fame, 1971; owns the highest lifetime batting average (.336) of any eligible ballplayer not in the National Baseball Hall of Fame.

53530. Eichmann, J. K. "Riggs Stephenson: One of the Greatest of Them All." *Sports Scoup,* I (December 1973), 10+.

53531. Givens, Horace R. "Jackson Riggs 'Old Hoss' Stephenson." In: Vol. Q–Z of David L. Porter, ed. *Biographical Dictionary of American Sports: Baseball.* Rev. and enlarged ed. Westport, CT: Greenwood Press, 2000. Pp. 1476–1477.

53532. _____. "Riggs Stephenson Belongs in the Hall of Fame." *Baseball Digest,* XXXIX (August 1980), 64–69.

53533. Green, Paul M. "Baseball and Riggs Stephenson." *Sports Collector's Digest,* X (June 10, 1983), 72+. Reprinted in his *Forgotten Fields* (Waupaca, WI: Parker Publications, 1984), pp. 79–89.

53534. Kiely, Laurie. "A Football Star Turned Baseball Pro." *Bama* (March 1983), 23–25.

53536. Lane, Ferdinand C. "Riggs Stephenson, Who Led the Cubs' Offense." *Baseball Magazine,* L (December 1932), 301–302+.

53537. Langford, Walter. "Reminiscing with Riggs Stephenson." In: Peter Levine, ed. *Baseball History.* Westport, Ct: Meckler Publishing, 1989. pp. 75–80.

53538. Murdock, Eugene. "'Riggs' Stephenson: Football Star." In: his *Baseball Between the Wars : Memories of the Game By the Men Who Played It.* Westport, CT: Meckler Publishing, 1992. Pp. 213–234.

53539. Stephenson, Jackson R. ("Riggs"). "The Big Stick Wins Out Once More." *Baseball Magazine,* XXXIX (July 1927), 348–349.

Riggs Stephenson *see*
Jackson Riggs ("Old Hoss") Stephenson
Charles Augustus ("Chuck") Stevens, Jr.
1B. (B: July 10, 1918, Van Houten, NM). St. Louis (AL), 1941, 1946, 1948. Remarks: In three big league seasons, had 184 hits (four homers) and six stolen bases in 211 games; also played for Williamston (Coastal Plains League), 1937; Johnstown (Middle Atlantic League), 1938; Springfield (Three-I League), 1939; San Antonio (TL), 1940); Toledo (AA), 1941–1942, 1947; Hollywood (PCL), 1948–1953; San Francisco (PCL), 1954–1955; manager, Amarillo (WL), 1956; player-coach, Sacramento (PCL), 1957; secretary, Association of Professional Ball Players of America, 1960–1998.

53540. Frommer, Harvey and Frederick J. "Chuck Stevens." In: their *Growing Up Baseball: An Oral History.* Dallas, TX: Taylor Publishing Co., 2001. Pp. 209–211. Mark Armour's profile of Stevens is a number in the on-line SABR biography project http://bioproj.sabr.org/bioproj.cfm?a=v&v=l&bid=561&pid=18620.

Chuck Stevens *see* **Charles Augustus ("Chuck") Stevens, Jr.**
Bill Stewart *see* **William J. ("Bill") Stewart**
David Keith ("Dave" or "Smoke") Stewart
P-AGENT. (B: Feb. 19, 1957, Oakland, CA). Los Angeles (NL), 1978, 1981–1983; Texas (AL), 1983–1985; Philadelphia (NL), 1985–1986; Oakland (AL), 1986–1992; Toronto (AL), 1993–1994; Oakland (A.L), 1995. Remarks: Obtained 168 victories and 129 defeats, with 19 "saves," in 16 years; only 1980s pitcher with three 20-win seasons; World Series MVP award, 1989; had one no-hitter, June 29, 1990; ALCS MVP awards, 1990, 1993; special assistant

to G.M., Oakland (AL), 1996 and San Diego (NL), 1997; coach, San Diego (NL)1998; asst. GM, Toronto (AL), 1998; director, player personnel, Toronto (AL), 1999–2001; coach, Milwaukee (NL), 2002; coach, USA Baseball Olympic Qualifying Team, 2003; San Diego-based baseball agent, 2004–; named to Bay Area Sports Hall of Fame, 2000.

53541. Axthelm, Pete. "Winning for the Neighborhood." *Newsweek,* CXI (May 30, 1988), 71+.

53542. Chapin, Dwight. "Throwing Smoke." *Street & Smith Baseball Magazine,* LI (1991), 30, 40.

53543. Colston, Chris. "Pride and Prejudice: Dave Stewart Shields His Eyes from Racial Inequity's Hard Glare." *USA Today Baseball Weekly,* IX (March 10, 1999), 18–20.

53544. Dickey, Glenn. "Interview: Dave Stewart." *Inside Sports,* XII (March 1990), 20–29.

53545. "Eckersley and Stewart: Born-Again A's." In: Tom Barnidge, ed. *The Sporting News 1989 Baseball Yearbook.* St. Louis, MO: *The Sporting News,* 1989. Pp. 50–55.

53546. Egan, Terry, Stan Friedmann, and Mike Levine. "Doing the Right Thing: Hometown Hero Dave Stewart and the Earthquake of '89." In: their *The Macmillan Book of Baseball Stories.* New York: Macmillan, 1992. Chpt. 4.

53547. Fimrite, Ron. "The A's New Stew Can Do." *Sports Illustrated,* LXVII (October 5, 1987), 69–70.

53548. Gammons, Peter. "The A's Ace of an Ace." *Sports Illustrated,* LXVIII (May 16, 1988), 30–31.

53549. _____. "A Hero Lives Here." *Sports Illustrated,* LXXI (November 6, 1989), 28–31.

53550. Johnson, P. "From the Dodgers to the Dome: Is Dave Stewart's Long Journey Over?" *Dugout,* II (October 1994), 8–10.

53551. Kleinknecht, Merl F. "David Keith Stewart." In: Vol. Q–Z of David L. Porter, ed. *Biographical Dictionary of American Sports: Baseball.* Rev. and enlarged ed. Westport, CT: Greenwood Press, 2000. Pp. 1477–1479.

53552. Mattimore, Hank. "A Deeper Look: Dave Stewart." *Beckett Baseball Card Monthly,* IX (February 1992), 112–117.

53553. Muyo, Jim. "Smoke." *Oakland Athletics Magazine,* VIII, no. 2 (1988), 87–94.

53554. Newton, Craig. "Dave Stewart: Interview." *Baseball Cards,* X (May 1990), 152–157.

53555. Newhouse, Dave. "Why Have Pitching Awards Eluded A's Dave Stewart?" *Baseball Digest,* L (March 1991), 45–46.

53556. Pearlman, Jeff. "Back to the Classroom: Dave Stewart Returns." *Sports Illustrated,* XCIII (August 21, 2000), 83–84.

53557. Polzer, Tim. "A Second Look: Dave Stewart." *Beckett Baseball Card Monthly,* VIII (January 1991), 73–74.

53558. Rogers, Bill. "Dave Stewart: The A's Durable Anchor Man." *Baseball Digest,* XLVIII (October 1989), 20–21.

53559. Spander, Art. "Dave Stewart: R.E.S.P.E.C.T at Last." *Show,* I (July 1990), 26–29.

53560. Stewart, Dave, as told to George Vass. "The Game I'll Never Forget." *Baseball Digest,* LII (December 1993), 49–50.

53561. Stier, Kit. "Dave Stewart." In: *Major League Baseball Official 1991 Preview.* New York: Hachette Magazines, 1991. Pp. 84–85.

53562. _____. "The Transformation of Dave Stewart." In: Zander Hollander, ed. *The Complete Handbook of Baseball '90.* New York: Signet Books, 1990. Pp. 28–35.

53563. Weider, Bob. "Dave Stewart: Heart & Soul."

In: Rob Kelly, ed. *1990 Oakland Athletics Magazine*. Benicia, CA: Mariposa Press, 1990. Pp. 48–56.

53564. Wulf, Steve. "Dave Stewart." *Sports Illustrated*, LXXIX (December 27, 1993), 80+.

Ernest ("Ernie") Stewart

UMP. Remarks: AL arbiter, 1941–1945; dismissed by league president after protesting his salary.

53565. Gerlach, Larry R. "Ernie Stewart." In: his *The Men in Blue: Conversations with Umpires*. New York: Viking Press, 1980. Pp. 93–128. Reprinted by the University of Nebraska Press in 1994.

Frank ("Stewy") Stewart

P. (B: Sept. 8, 1906, Minneapolis, MN). Chicago (AL), 1927. Remarks: Hurled four big league innings and was charged with a loss.

53566. Wilson, Nick. "Frank Stewart." In: his *Voices from the Pastime: Oral Histories of Surviving Major Leaguers, Negro Leaguers, Cuban Leaguers, and Writers, 1920–1934*. Jefferson, NC: McFarland & Co., Inc., 2000. Pp. 70–72.

Shannon Harold Stewart

OF. (B: Feb. 25, 1974, Cincinnati, OH). Toronto (AL), 1995–2003; Minnesota (AL), 2003-. Remarks: Through 2004, has obtained 1,242 hits (90 homers) and 172 stolen bases in 1,0122 games; had 26-game hitting streak, 1999; established MLB record with four doubles in one game, July 18, 2000; had 15 game hitting streak, 2001; had five hits in one game, Sept. 19, 2002; hobbled by ham-string injury, 2004.

53567. Epstein, Eddie. "Shannon Stewart." In: *The STATS 1995 Minor League Scouting Notebook*. Skokie, IL: STATS Publishing, 1995. Pp. 153–154.

53568. Stewart, Shannon. "When I Was a Kid: Interview." *Junior Baseball*, no. 42 (November–December 2002), 10+.

William J. ("Bill") Stewart

UMP. (B: 1896,Fitchburg, MA-D: Feb. 18, 1967). Remarks: NL arbiter, 1933–1954. An off-season hockey coach, Stewart coached in both the college and pro ranks, leading the 1937–38 Chicago Black Hawks to the Stanley Cup championship; he also served nine winters as an NHL referee.

53569. Cannon, Jimmy. "A Few Words with Bill Stewart." *Baseball Digest*, VII (June 1948), 52–55.

53570. Graham, Frank. "That Hard-Working Ump Bill Stewart." *Baseball Magazine*, LXIX (November 1937), 541–543.

53571. "Man of Reflexes." *New Yorker*, XXV (July 16, 1949), 13–14.

53572. Stewart, William J. ("Bill"). "Confessions of an Umpire." Edited by Tim Cohane. *Look*, XIX (April 19, 1955), 125–129.

53573. _____. "I Knew I Had Guts." *Baseball Digest*, XIV (June 1955), 39–48.

53574. _____. "The Loneliest Man in Town." *American Magazine*, CLIV (October 1952), 26–27+.

53575. _____., as told to Stanley Woodward. "'Sometimes We're Right': a Man of Many Baseball Woes Briskly Talks Back, and Defends His Calling." *Liberty*, XVI (April 22, 1939), 39–40.

David Andrew ("Dave" or "Sir David") Stieb

P. (B: July 22, 1957, Santa Ana, CA). Toronto (AL), 1979–1992; Chicago (AL), 1993; Toronto (AL), 1998. Remarks: Had 176 victories and 137 defeats, with three "saves," in 16 years; won Game One and lost Game Seven of 1985 ALCS; missed no hitters in three consecutive starts, 1988–1989; lost two games in 1989 ALCS; pitched

no-hitter against Cleveland (AL) on Sept. 2, 1990; also played for Sarasota (Florida State League) and Omaha (I.L), 1993 and Dunedin (Florida State League) and Syracuse (IL), 1998.

53576. Bjarkman, Peter C. "David Andrew 'Dave,' 'Sir David' Stieb." In: Vol. Q-Z of David L. Porter, ed. *Biographical Dictionary of American Sports: Baseball*. Rev. and enlarged ed. Westport, CT: Greenwood Press, 2000. Pp. 1479–1480.

53577. Cohen, Eliot. "Dave Stieb." In: his *My Greatest Day in Baseball*. New York: Little Simon, 1991. Pp. 124–127.

53578. Crothers, Tim. "Comeback for the Aged: Stieb's Last Fling." *Sports Illustrated*, LXXXVIII (April 27, 1998), 94, 97.

53579. DiPace, Tom. "Superstar Gallery: Dave Stieb." *Beckett Baseball Card Monthly*, VII (December 1990), 11–12.

53580. Elliot, Bob. "Stieb is Plotter of Blue Jays' Flight Plan." In: George Leonard, ed. *Athlon's Baseball '91*. Nashville, TN: Athlon Sports Communications, 1991. Pp. 112–115.

53581. Fimrite, Ron. "A Rare Bird: The Natural." *Sports Illustrated*, LVIII (May 16, 1983), 48–52.

53582. James, Robert. "Dave Stieb." In: Ken Collier, ed. *The Baseball Book, 1984*. Scottsdale, AZ: Jalart House, 1984. P. 128+.

53583. Kurkjian, Tim. "Finally." *Sports Illustrated*, LXXIII (September 10, 1990), 142–143. Stieb's first no-hitter.

53584. Stieb, Dave, as told to George Vass. "The Game I'll Never Forget." *Baseball Digest*, LII (March 1993), 77–78.

53585. _____., with Kevin Boland. *Tomorrow I'll Be Perfect*. Garden City, NY and Toronto: Doubleday Canada Ltd., 1986. 167p.

53586. Steinberg, H. "Interview: Dave Stieb." *Inside Sports*, VII (August 1985), 19–24.

53587. Turner, Dan. "Teasing the Gods." In: his *Heroes, Bums and Ordinary Men*. Toronto: Doubleday Canada Ltd., 1988. Pp. 12–17.

Richard Lewis ("Dick") Stigman

P. (B: Jan. 24, 1936, Nimrod, MN). Cleveland (AL), 1960–1961; Boston (AL), 1962–1965. Remarks: Obtained 46 victories and 54 defeats, with 16 "saves," in six seasons.

53588. Crocker, Mike. "Minnesota Southpaw." *Twins Magazine*, IX (June 1996), 86–87.

Kelly Lee Stinnett

C. (B: Feb. 14, 1970, Lawton, OK). New York (NL), 1994–1995; Milwaukee (AL), 1995–1997; Arizona (NL), 1998–2000; Cincinnati (NL), 2001–2003; Kansas City (AL), 2004; Tucson (PCL), 2005. Remarks: Through 2004, has had 412 hits (57 homers) and 10 stolen bases in 608 big league games; injured in June 2004.

53589. Adamek, Steve. "Surprise, Surprise: Kelly Stinnett Emerges from the Pack to Claim the Mets' Starting Catching Job." *New York Mets Inside Pitch*, XII (May 1994), 1–2.

George Henry ("Snuffy") Stirnweiss

2B-3B. (B: Oct. 26, 1918, New York City-D: Sept. 15, 1958). New York (AL), 1943–1950; St. Louis (AL), 1950; Cleveland (AL), 1951–1952. Remarks: Obtained 989 hits (29 homers) and 134 stolen bases in 1,028 games in a decade; led AL in doubles, 1944–1945; AL batting champion, 1945; scored five runs in one game, May 24, 1947; noted fielder; minor league manager, 1954–1955; died in a train disaster at Newark Bay.

53590. Boyer, Carl. "The Hit and Run." *Scholastic Coach,* XX (March 1951), 10–11. Demonstrated by "Snuffy" Stirnweiss.

53591. Chastain, Bill. "This Was the Closest Race Ever for a Batting Title." *Baseball Digest,* LII (December 1993), 62–64. Between Stirnweiss and Tony Cuccinello in 1945.

53592. Cohane, Tim. "Yankee Bandit: George Stirnweiss of the Yanks is Big-League Base-Stealing King ." *Baseball Digest,* IV (July 1945), 34–36.

53593. Dexter, Charles. "Bronx Express: Snuffy Stirnweiss." *Collier's,* CXII (July 17, 1943), 30–31. Reprinted in *Baseball Digest,* VII (January 1948), 3–9.

53594. Gallagher, Mark. "'Snuffy' Stirnweiss." In: his *50 Years of Yankee All-Stars.* New York: Leisure Press, 1984. Pp. 199–200.

53595. Goldberg, Hy. "The Yankees' Sternweiss." *Baseball Digest,* II (April 1943), 5–9.

53596. Lardner, John. "Grandstand Larceny." *Newsweek,* XXIV (July 3, 1944), 77–78.

53597. Spatz, Lyle. "During War, Stirnweiss was Top AL Weapon." *USA Today Baseball Weekly,* VI (June 5, 1996), 40+.

53598. _____. "Snuffy." *The National Pastime,* XIX (1999), 46–48.

53599. Sumner, Jim L. "George Henry 'Snuffy' Stirnweiss." In: Vol. Q-Z of David L. Porter, ed. *Biographical Dictionary of American Sports: Baseball.* Rev. and enlarged ed. Westport, CT: Greenwood Press, 2000. Pp. 1480–1481.

Snuffy Sternweiss *see* **George Henry ("Snuffy") Stirnweiss**

Jack Stivetts *see* **John Elmer ("Jack" or "Happy Jack") Stivetts**

John Elmer ("Jack" or "Happy Jack") Stivetts
P. (B: March 31, 1868, Ashland, PA-D: April 18, 1930). St. Louis (AA), 1889–1891; Boston (NL), 1892–1898; Cleveland (NL), 1899. Remarks: In 11 seasons, won 203 games and lost 132, with four "saves"; had one no hitter, Oct. 15, 1892; as a batter, had 592 hits (35 homers) and 31 stolen bases; hit two homers in a game thrice.

53600. Eichmann, J. K. "Jack Stivetts: A Pitcher Who Could Really Hit." *Sports Scoup,* II (July 1974), 10+.

53601. Lawler, Joseph. "John Elmer 'Jack,' 'Happy Jack' Stivetts." In: Vol. Q-Z of David L. Porter, ed. *Biographical Dictionary of American Sports: Baseball.* Rev. and enlarged ed. Westport, CT: Greenwood Press, 2000. Pp. 1481–1482.

Charles Klein ("Chuck") Stobbs
P. (B: July 2, 1929, Wheeling, WV). Boston (AL), 1947–1951; Chicago (AL), 1952; Washington (AL), 1953–1957; St. Louis (NL), 1958; Washington (AL) and Minnesota (AL), 1959–1961, Remarks: Won 107 games and lost 130, with 19 "saves," in 15 years; remembered for throwing the pitch that Mickey Mantle (q.v.) hit out of Griffith Stadium, April 7, 1953, for his famous 565-foot "tape measure" home run.

53602. Addis, Bob. "Chuck Stobbs: Senator Returned to Office." *Baseball Digest,* XV (November-December 1956), 34–37.

53603. Goldblatt, Abe and Robert W. Wentz. "Chuck Stobbs: The Home Run He'd Rather Forget." In: their *The Great and the Hear Great: A Century of Sports in Virginia.* Norfolk, VA: Donning Company, 1976. Pp. 21–22.

53604. Heiman, Lee, Dave Weiner and Bill Gutman. "Chuck Stobbs." In: their *When the Cheering Stops.* New York: Macmillan, 1990. Pp. 263–272.

53605. Povich, Shirley. "Portrait of a Loser." *Sport,* XXV (January 1958), 24–28.

53606. Siegel, Morris. "Here's the Inside Story on Mantle's Epic Homer in '53." *Baseball Digest,* LII (August 1993), 52–53.

Milton Joseph ("Milt") Stock
3B. (B: July 11, 1893, Chicago, IL-D: July 16, 1977). New York (NL), 1914; Philadelphia (NL), 1915–1918; St. Louis (NL), 1919–1923; Brooklyn (NL), 1924–1926. Remarks: In 16 years, obtained 1,806 hits (22 homers) and 155 stolen bases in 1,628 games; had four hits in four consecutive games, June-July 1925; player-manager, Mobile (SA), 1926–1928, Dallas (TL), 1929, Knoxville (SA), 1931, Beckley (Mid-Atlantic League), 1934, Monessen (Pennsylvania State League), 1935, Macon (SA), 1938–1942, and Portsmouth (Pilot League), 1943; president, Mobile (Southeastern League), 1932 and Quincy (Midwest League), 1933; coach, Chicago (NL), 1944–1948; father-in-law of Eddie Stanky (q.v.).

53607. Stock, Milton. "The Advantage of Playing Deep at Third." *Baseball Magazine,* XXXIII (June 1924), 308–309.

53608. Weir, Robert E. "Milton Joseph 'Milt' Stock." In: Vol. Q-Z of David L. Porter, ed. *Biographical Dictionary of American Sports: Baseball.* Rev. and enlarged ed. Westport, CT: Greenwood Press, 2000. Pp. 1484–1485.

Wesley Gay ("Wes") Stock
P. (B: Longview, WA). Baltimore (AL), 1959–1964; Kansas City (AL), 1964–1967. Remarks: Obtained 60 victories and 57 defeats, with five "saves," in nine seasons; suffered no defeats in 100 games entered between July 1962 and July 1964; won 12 consecutive games in relief, 1964; pitching coach Oakland (AL), 1973–1976, Seattle (AL), 1977–1981, and Oakland (AL), 1984–1986; named to State of Washington Sports Hall of Fame.

53609. Driver, David. "Whatever Happened to ... Wes Stock?" *Orioles Gazette,* IV (March 1994), 10–11.

53610. Stainback, Berry. "Stock Up in the Bullpen." *Sport,* XXXVII (September 1964), 6–7.

Dick Stockton
BROADCASTER. (B: Dick Stokovis, Nov. 22, 1942, Philadelphia, PA). Remarks: Broadcaster, Boston (AL), 1975–1976; reporter, CBS-Sports, 1980–1994; broadcaster, Oakland (AL), 1995–1997.

53611. Harper, James W. "Dick Stockton." In: David L. Porter, ed. *Biographical Dictionary of American Sports: 1992–1995 Supplement for Baseball, Football, Basketball and Other Sports.* Westport, CT: Greenwood Press, 1995. Pp. 360–361.

James Roy Stockton
WRITER. (B: Dec. 16, 1892, St. Louis, MO-D: Aug. 24, 1972). Columnist/sports editor, *St. Louis Post-Dispatch;* writer for *Saturday Evening Post* and *Look;* received J. G. Taylor Spink Award, 1972.

53612. Vlasich, James A. "J. Roy Stockton." In: Richard Orodenker, ed. *Dictionary of Literary Biography, Volume 241: American Sportswriters and Writers on Sport.* A Bruccoli Clark Layman Book. Detroit, MI: The Gale Group, 2001. Pp. 283–290.

George Robert ("Silent") Stone
OF. (B: Sept. 3, 1876, Lost Nation, IA-D: Jan. 5, 1945). Boston (AL), 1903; St. Louis (AL), 1905–1910. Remarks: Had 984 hits (23 homers) and 132 stolen bases in 848 games in seven years; AL batting champion, 1906; Coleridge, NE banker, 1917 though 1940; while playing for Milwaukee (AA), hit .405 in 1904 becoming only player to top .400 in that league.

53613. Burkholder, Ed. "George Stone." In: his *Baseball Immortals.* New York: Christopher, 1955. Pp. 68–69.

53614. Ziegler, John H. "George Robert 'Silent' Stone." In: Vol. Q-Z of David L. Porter, ed. *Biographical Dictionary of American Sports: Baseball.* Rev. and enlarged ed. Westport, CT: Greenwood Press, 2000. Pp. 1484–1485.
John Thomas ("Johnny" or "Rocky") Stone
OF. (B: Oct. 10, 1905, Lynchburg, TN-D: Nov. 30, 1955). Detroit (AL), 1928–1933; Washington (AL), 1934–1938. Remarks: Obtained 1,391 hits (77 homers) and 45 stolen bases in 1,199 games in 11 years; star player of the 1927–1928 Maryville College nines forced from the game by tuberculosis, from which he recovered; had 23-game hitting streak in 1930 and 25-game streak in 1931; first player to have six extra-base hits in a doubleheader without extra innings, May 30, 1933; noted for hitting 105 triples in his career, including 18 in 1935.
53615. Blaisdell, Lowell L. "John Thomas 'Johnny,' 'Rocky' Stone." In: Vol. Q-Z of David L. Porter, ed. *Biographical Dictionary of American Sports: Baseball.* Rev. and enlarged ed. Westport, CT: Greenwood Press, 2000. Pp. 1485–1486.
53616. Thorn, John. "John Stone's Batting Streak." *The Baseball Research Journal,* XXI (1992), 61–62.
Rocky Stone *see* **John Thomas ("Johnny" or "Rocky") Stone**
Stephen Michael ("Steve") Stone
P-BROADCASTER. (B: July 14, 1947, Cleveland, OH). San Francisco (NL), 1971–1972; Chicago (AL), 1973; Chicago (NL), 1974–1976; Chicago (AL), 1977–1978; Baltimore (AL), 1979–1982. Remarks: Won 107 games and lost 93. with one "save"; AL Cy Young Award, 1980; retired due to arm injury; restaurateur; broadcaster, ABC-TV, 1982 and Chicago (NL), 1983–2004.
53617. Donovan, M. "To Restaurant Owner, Bon Vivant, and Poet, Steve Stone May, Soon Add Baseball's Best Pitcher." *People Weekly,* XIV (August 25, 1980), 39–40.
63618. Hye, Allen E. "Stephen Michael 'Steve' Stone." In: Vol. Q-Z of David L. Porter, ed. *Biographical Dictionary of American Sports: Baseball.* Rev. and enlarged ed. Westport, CT: Greenwood Press, 2000. Pp. 1486–1487.
53619. Kennedy, Ray. "Hold the Twinkies Flambe." *Sports Illustrated,* LII (June 16, 1980), 47–48.
53620. Kuenster, John. "Steve Stone Thinks He Can Improve on His Cy Young Award Year." *Baseball Digest,* XL (June 1981), 15–17.
53621. Markus, Robert. "How Steve Stone Turned into a Big Winner." *Baseball Digest,* XXXIX (November 1980), 66–69.
53622. Montville, Leigh. "The First to Be Free." *Sports Illustrated,* LXXII (April 16, 1990), 98–108.
53623. Patterson, Ed. "Where Have You Gone Steve Stone?" *Orioles Gazette,* II (May 1, 1992), 19–20.
53624. Ribalow, Harold W. and Meir Z. "Steve Stone: To Stardom From Obscurity." In: their *Jewish Baseball Stars.* New York: Hippocrene Books, 1984. Pp. 264–291.
53625. Shah, David K. "Phenomenal Odd Couple." *Newsweek,* XCVI (September 1, 1980), 80–81.
53626. Slater, Robert. "Steve Stone: The 1980 Cy Young Award Winner." In: his *Great Jews in Sports.* Middle Village, NY: Jonathan David Publishers, 1983. Pp. 215–217.
53627. Stone, Steve. "Steve Stone Remembers Harry Caray and More." *Midwest Wine and Cigar Connection,* IV (April 1999), 1–2.
53628. _____., as told to George Vass. "The Game I'll Never Forget." *Baseball Digest,* XLII (March 1983), 91–94.
53629. _____., with Nolan Anglum. *Teach Yourself To Win: Cy Young Winner Steve Stone Tells What It Takes to Make Success A Habit.* Chicago, IL: Bonus Books, 1991. 201p.

53630. _____., with Barry Rozner. *Where's Harry? Steve Stone Remembers His Years with Harry Caray.* Dallas, TX: Taylor Publishing, 1999. 213p.
Toni Stone
2B. (B: Marcenia Lyle Alberga, Jan. 21, 1921, St. Paul, MN-D: Nov. 10, 1996). San Francisco Sea Lions (semipro), 1949; New Orleans Creoles, 1949–1952; Indianapolis Clowns, 1953; Kansas City Monarchs, 1954. Remarks: First woman to play in the Negro Leagues; honored by National Baseball Hall of Fame, 1991; elected to Women's Sports Hall of Fame, 1993.
53631. Berlage, Gai. "Toni Stone." In: her *Women In Baseball: The Forgotten History.* Westport, CT: Praeger Publishers, 1994. Pp. 126–129.
53632. Edelson, Paula. "Toni Stone." In: her *A to Z of American Women in Sports.* New York: Facts on File, 2002. Pp.220–222.
53633. "Female Player Remembered by Major League Baseball: Toni Stone." *Jet,* LXXXII (June 1, 1992), 50–51.
53644. Gregorich, Barbara. "1954: Toni Stone." *American Visions,* VIII (June-July 1993), 27+.
53645. _____. "Toni Stone." In: her *Women at Play: The Story of Women in Baseball.* New York: Harcourt, Brace, 1993. Pp. 169–176.
53646. Hickok, Ralph. "Toni Stone." In: his *A Who's Who of Sport Champions.* Boston, MA: Houghton Mifflin, 1995. Pp. 756–757.
53647. "Lady Ball Player: Toni Stone is First of Sex to Play with Professional Team." *Ebony,* VIII (July 1953), 48–52.
53648. Stouse, Karla Farmer. "The Story of Toni Stone: When Baseball Began to Be Truly the National Pastime." In: Peter Carino, ed. *Baseball/Literature/Culture: Essays, 1995–2001.* Jefferson, NC: McFarland & Co., Inc., 2003. Pp. 170–176.
Charles Stoneham
EXEC. (B: July 5, 1876, Jersey City, NJ-D: Jan. 6, 1936). Remarks: Owner/president, New York (NL), 1919–1936; father of Horace C. Stoneham (below).
53649. Asnen, Alan R. "Charles Stoneham." In: Vol. Q-Z of David L. Porter, ed. *Biographical Dictionary of American Sports: Baseball.* Rev. and enlarged ed. Westport, CT: Greenwood Press, 2000. P. 1487.
Horace Charles Stoneham
EXEC. (B. April 27, 1903, Newark, NJ-D: Jan. 7, 1990). Remarks: Owner and president of the New York (NL)/San Francisco (NL) Giants, 1936 to 1976; son of Charles Stoneham (above).
53650. Angell, Roger. "Companions of the Game: Horace C. Stoneham, Owner of the San Francisco Giants." *New Yorker,* LI (September 22, 1976), 96–106+.
53651. Asnen, Alan E. "Horace Stoneham." In: Vol. Q-Z of David L. Porter, ed. *Biographical Dictionary of American Sports: Baseball.* Rev. and enlarged ed. Westport, CT: Greenwood Press, 2000. Pp. 1487–1489.
53652. Dickey, Glenn. "Bill Veeck vs. Horace Stoneham." In: his *Champs and Chumps: An Insider's Look at America's Sports Heroes.* San Francisco, CA: Chronicle Books, 1976. Pp. 115–129.
53653. Janoff, Bruce L. "Horace Charles Stoneham." In: John A. Garrity and Marsh C. Carries, eds. *American National Biography.* 24 vols. New York: Oxford University Press, 1999. XX, 877–878.
53654. Nevard, Norm. "Stoneham, the Reluctant Dragin." *Baseball Digest,* XVI (August 1957), 29–31.
53655. *The New York Times.* "Horace Stoneham: A Profile." *Sports Illustrated,* VII (July 29, 1957), 50.

53656. Treder, Steve. "A Legacy of What-ifs: Horace Stoneham and the Integration of the Giants." *Nine: A Journal of Baseball History and Social Policy Perspective,* X (Spring 2002), 71–103.

53657. Veeck, William Jr., and Ed Linn. "For He's a Jolly Good Fellow." *Sports Illustrated,* XXII (May 31, 1965), 51–52+.

William Hambly ("Bill") Stoneman

P. (B: April 7, 1944, Oak Park, IL). Chicago (NL), 1967–1969; Montreal (NL), 1969–1973; California (AL), 1974. Remarks: Had 54 victories, 85 defeats, and five "saves" in an eight-year big league career, pitched two no-hitters, April 17, 1969 and Oct. 2, 1972; exec, Montreal (NL), 1984–1987; GM, Montreal (NL), 1987–1999; GM, Anaheim (AL), 1999-.

53658. Kirwin, Bill. "Interview with Bill Stoneman, General Manager, Anaheim Angels." *Nine: A Journal of Baseball History and Culture,* X (Spring 2002), 172–176.

53659. Rumill, Ed. "Bill Stoneman: He Thrives on Completion." *Baseball Digest,* XXXII (January 1973), 64–67.

Ulysses Simpson Grant ("Lil") Stoner

P. (B: Feb. 28, 1899, Bowie TX.-D: June 26, 1966.). Detroit (AL), 1922–1929; Pittsburgh (NL), 1930; Philadelphia (NL), 1931. Remarks: Won 50 games and lost 58 with 14 "saves" in nine years; also pitched in the TL during 1923, including a no-hitter.

53660. Lane, Ferdinand C. "His Name Was So Long They Called Him 'Lil.'" *Baseball Magazine,* XXXVIII (February 1927), 399–400+.

Hannah Storm

BROADCASTER. (B: 1962). Remarks: NBC-TV sportscaster, 1983–2002; co-host, *The CBS Early Show,* 2002-.

53661. Young, C. "Storm Watch." *TV Guide,* XLI (June 26, 1993), 24–27.

Melvin Leon ("Mel") Stottlemyre

P. (B: Nov. 13, 1941, Hazelton, MO).New York (AL), 1964–1974. Remarks: In 11 big league seasons, had 164 victories and 139 defeats; won Game One and Lost Game Seven of 1964 World Series; hit inside-the-park grand slam homer against Boston (AL), July 20, 1965; roving minor league coach, Seattle (AL),1977–1981; coach, New York (NL), 1984–1993; coach, Houston (NL), 1994–1995; coach, New York (AL), 1996–2004; father of Todd Stottlemyre (below); named to State of Washington Sports Hall of Fame; diagnosed with multiple myeloma (a cancer of the blood plasma), April 9, 2000 and temporarily left team on Sept. 11, 2000 for stem cell transplant.

53662. Burke, Phil. "Closeup: Mel Stottlemyre." In: Clyde Hirt, ed. *Sports Quarterly Presents Baseball Extra, Summer 1972.* New York: Counterpoint, Inc., 1972. Pp. 80–86.

53663. Caldera, Pete. "The Man Behind the Pitching Machine." *Yankees Magazine,* XIX (March 1999), 54–59.

53664. Deindorfer, Robert G. "Mel Stottlemyre: Cool Guy." In: Ray Robinson, ed. *Baseball Stars of 1966.* New York: Pyramid Books, 1966. Pp. 120–125.

53665. Dexter, Charles. "Young Mel of Mabton." *Baseball Digest,* XXIII (December 1964-January 1965), 85–90.

53666. Gallagher, Mark. "Mel Stottlemyre." In: his *50 Years of Yankee All-Stars.* New York: Leisure Press, 1984. Pp. 201–203.

53667. Jacobson, Steve. "Mel Stottlemyre: Last Link to Yankee Glory Years." *Baseball Digest,* XXXIII (September 1974), 48–52.

53668. Kiersh, Edward. "Mel Stottlemyre: Croquet,

Anyone?" In: his *Where Have You Gone, Vince DiMaggio?* New York: Bantam Books, 1983. Pp. 71–75.

53669. Klapish, Bob. "Survivor." *Yankees Magazine,* XXII (April 2001), 54–61.

53670. Miller, William J. "Melvin Leon 'Stott,' 'Mel' Stottlemyre, Sr." In: Vol. Q-Z of David L. Porter, ed. *Biographical Dictionary of American Sports: Baseball.* Rev. and enlarged ed. Westport, CT: Greenwood Press, 2000. Pp. 1489–1490.

53671. Rubin, Bob. "Mel Stottlemyre: A Guy You Don't Worry About." *Sport,* XLVII (February 1969), 32–36. .

53672. Rumill, Ed. "Mel Stottlemyre: Overhand and Under Pitch." *Baseball Digest,* XXIV (September 1965), 105–109.

53673. Salant, Nathan. "Mel Stottlemyre." In: his *Superstars, Stars, and Just Plain Heroes.* New York: Stein and Day, 1982. Pp. 223–230.

53674. Stottlemyre, Melvin L. ("Mel"), as told to George Vass. "The Game I'll Never Forget." *Baseball Digest,* XXXIV (January 1975), 62–66.

53675. _____. and Tom Capezzuto. "Mel Stottlemyre Recalls His Most Memorable Game." *Baseball Digest,* XLIV (September 1985), 74–77.

53676. _____. "Out of a Jam with DP's [Double Plays]." In: Sam E. Andre, ed. *Street and Smith's Official 1966 Baseball Yearbook.* New York: Conde -Nast Publications, 1966. Pp. 8–13.

Todd Vernon Stottlemyer

P. (B: May 20, 1965, Sunnyside, WA). Toronto (AL), 1998–1994; Oakland (AL), 1995; St. Louis (NL), 1996–1998; Texas (AL), 1998; Arizona (NL), 1999–2002. Remarks: Through 2002, won 138 games and lost 121, with one "save"; had two hits in one inning in one game, June 30, 1996; won Game Two of 1996 NLCS; received Branch Rickey Award, 2000; son of Mel Stottlemyer (above).

53677. Pearlman, Jeff. "Against All Odds." *Sports Illustrated,* XCII (February 28, 2000), 52–56. 61.

Carl E. Stotz

EXEC. (B: Feb. 20, 1910, Williamsport, PA-D: June 4, 1992). Remarks: Founder of Little League Baseball, Inc. and first Commissioner, 1939–1956.

53678. Dawidoff, Nicholas. "Little League's Shutout: Carl Stotz, the Game's Founder, Isn't in on Its 50th Anniversary." *Sports Illustrated,* LXXI (August 28, 1989), 84–88.

53679. Stotz, Carl E., with M. W. Baldwin. *At Bat with the Little League.* Philadelphia, PA: Macrae-Smith Co., 1952. 271p. Concerns the organization Little League Baseball, Inc., during the years 1939–1952; Stotz founded the Little League at Williamsport, Pennsylvania.

Firebrand Stovall *see* **George Thomas ("Firebrand") Stovall**

George Thomas ("Firebrand") Stovall

1B-MGR. (B: Nov. 23, 1878, Independence, MO-D: Nov. 5, 1961). Cleveland (AL), 1904–1911; St. Louis (AL), 1912–1913; Kansas City (F.L.), 1914–1915. Remarks: Obtained 1,381 hits (15 homers) and 142 stolen bases in 1,412 games in a dozen campaigns; had seven assists in one game, Aug. 7, 1912; first MLB player to jump to F.L., Nov. 2, 1913; famous for temper on and off the field (hence nickname); managed Cleveland (AL), 1911, St. Louis (AL), 1912–1913, and Kansas City (F.L.), 1914–1915, winning 313 games and losing 376 (.454).

53680. Lane, Ferdinand C. "The 'Firebrand' of the Federal League." *Baseball Magazine,* XIII (July 1914), 25–32.

53681. _____. "George Stovall: The Hero of 1911." *Baseball Magazine,* IX (September 1912), 57–66.

53682. _____. "George Stovall: The Sensation Among American League Managers." *Baseball Magazine,* VIII (November 1911), 73–74.

53683. Stovall, George. "A Manager's Troubles." *Baseball Magazine,* VII (October 1911), 11+.

George Washington Stovey
P-OF. (B: 1866, Williamsport, PA-D: March 22, 1936). Cuban Giants, 1886; minor leagues, 1886–1887; Cuban Giants, 1888–1891; New York Gorhams, 1891; Cuban Giants, 1893; Cuban X-Giants and Brooklyn Colored Giants, 1896. Remarks: Considered the best African American pitcher of the 19th century, Stovey had 60 wins and 40 losses in six seasons; refusal by Adrian ("Cap") Anson (q.v.) to permit his Chicago nine to play a minor league team for which Stovey hurled said to have lead to institution of MLB's infamous color line.

53684. Hunsinger, Lou, Jr. "George W. Stovey: A Pitcher in the Shadows." *The National Pastime,* XIV (1994), 80–82.

53685. _____. "George Washington Stovey." In: Vol. Q-Z of David L. Porter, ed. *Biographical Dictionary of American Sports: Baseball.* Rev. and enlarged ed. Westport, CT: Greenwood Press, 2000. Pp. 1490–1491.

Harry Duffield Stovey
P-1B. (B: Harry Duffield Stowe, Dec. 20, 1856, Philadelphia, PA-D: Sept. 20, 1937). Philadelphia Defiance, 1876–1877; New Bedford Clam-Eaters, 1878–1879; Worcester (NL), 1880–1882; Philadelphia (AA), 1883–1889; Boston (P), 1890; Boston (NL), 1891–1892; Baltimore (NL), 1892–1893; Brooklyn (NL), 1893; minor leagues, 1894–1895. Remarks: Had 1,771 hits (122 homers) and 509 stolen bases in 1,486 games in 14 MLB seasons; NL batting champion, 1884; NL RBI champion, 1889; NL home run champion, 1880, 1883–1886, 1889; first player to wear sliding pads; changed his name so that his mother, who disapproved of baseball, wouldn't see his name in the newspapers.

53686. Graber, Ralph S. "Harry Duffield Stovey." In: Vol. Q-Z of David L. Porter, ed. *Biographical Dictionary of American Sports: Baseball.* Rev. and enlarged ed. Westport, CT: Greenwood Press, 2000. Pp. 1491–1492.

53687. _____. "Harry Stovey." In: John A. Garrity and Marsh C. Carries, eds. *American National Biography.* 24 vols. New York: Oxford University Press, 1999. XX, 903–905.

53688. Lipset, Lew. "'Grandpa' was Harry Stovey." *The National Pastime,* IV (Winter 1985), 84–85.

Paul Edward Strand
P-OF. (B: Dec. 19, 1893, Carbonedo, WA-D: July 2, 1974). Boston (NL), 1913–1915; Philadelphia (AL), 1924. Remarks: Won seven games and lost three, with two "saves," for the Braves; as a batter, had 43 hits and three stolen bases in 115 games in four years, the last played as an A's outfielder; also played for Seattle (PCL), Salt Lake (PCL), and Portland (PCL), 1920–1923, 1926–1927; obtained 323 hits in 1923 while playing for Salt Lake City (PCL); named to PCL Hall of Fame, 2004.

53689. Hern, Gerry. "Strand's Story of a Record Flop." *Baseball Digest,* X September 1951), 83–86.

53690. Stann, Francis. "Strand-ed by Fate." *Baseball Digest,* XXIII (March 1964), 45–47.

Alan Cochran ("Inky") Strange
SS. (B: Nov. 7, 1906, Philadelphia, PA-D: June 27, 1994). St. Louis (AL), 1934–1935; Washington (AL), 1935; St. Louis (AL), 1940–1942. Remarks: Had 211 hits (one homer) and six stolen bass in 314 games in five seasons; worked as printer, thus gaining his nickname.

53691. Obojski, Robert. "The Strange Case of Alan 'Inky' Strange." In: his *Baseball's Strangest Moments.* New York: Sterling Publishing Co., 1988. Pp. 47–48.

Edward l. Stratemeyer
WRITER. (B: Oct. 4, 1862, Elizabeth, NJ-D: May 10, 1930). Remarks: Wrote children books under numerous pen names; as Lester Chadwick, he wrote the "Baseball Joe" series from 1912 to 1928

53692. Dizer, John T. *Tom Swift(r)& Company: "Boys' Books" by Stratemeyer and Others.* Jefferson, NC: McFarland & Co., Inc., 1982.

53693. Donelson, Ken. "Nancy, Tom, and Assorted Friends in the Stratemeyer Syndicate Then and Now." *Children's Literature,* VII (1978): 17–44.

53694. Prager, Arthur. "Bless My Collar Button, If It Isn't Tom Swift!" *American Heritage,* XXVIII (December 1976): 65–75.

53695. _____. "Edward Stratemeyer and his Book Machine." *Saturday Review,* 54 (10 July 1971): 15–17, 52–53.

53696. Taylor, Mary-Agnes. "Edward L. Stratemeyer." In Glenn E. Estes, ed. *Dictionary of Literary Biography, Volume 42: American Writers for Children Before 1900.* A Bruccoli Clark Layman Book. Detroit, MI: The Gale Group, 1985. Pp. 351–362.

Monty Franklin Pierce ("Gander") Stratton
P. (B: May 21, 1912, Celeste, TX-D: Sept. 29, 1982). Chicago (AL), 1934–1938. Remarks: Had 36 victories, 23 defeats, and two "saves" in five seasons; employed trick pitch, the "gander"; career ended by hunting accident; coach, Chicago (AL), 1940–1941; also won 18 games for Sherman (East Texas League), 1946; life story became the 1949 Jimmy Stewart motion picture, *The Monte Stratton Story;* elected to Texas Sports Hall of Fame, 1961.

53697. Addinglon, L.H. "Monty Stratton's Courageous Comeback" *Baseball Magazine,* LXXVII (August 1946), 317+.

53698. Birtwell, Roger. "The Monty Stratton Story." *Baseball Digest,* XXVII (February 1969), 84–87.

53699. Bowman, R. D. "Off to See the Wizard." *Dugout,* II (June 1994), 29–30.

53700. Davis, Mac. "A Motion Picture That Was Real." In: his *The Lore and Legends of Baseball.* New York: Lantern Press, 1953. Pp. 134–135.

53701. Molen, Sam. "Monty Stratton's Jinx Lived On." *Baseball Digest,* II (July 1943), 1–4. Reprinted in *Baseball Digest,* VIII (July 1949), 7–9 and XII (July 1953), 57–59.

53702. Palmer, Cap. "How a Movie Gets Made." *Collier's,* CXXIV (September 17, 1949), 22–27 *The Monty Stratton Story.*

53703. Pickard, Chuck. "Monty Stratton: He Was Someone Special." *Baseball Digest,* XLII (January 1963), 91+.

53704. _____. "Monty Stratton Remembers the Day He Became a Hitter." *Baseball Digest,* XXVIII (September 1969), 59–61.

53705. Santa Maria, Michael and James Costello. "A Leg to Stand On." *In the Shadows of the Diamond.* Dubuque, IA: The Elysian Fields Press, 1992. Pp. 222–224.

53706. Sheldon, Harold. "Finishing the Stratton Story." *Baseball Digest,* VIII (September 1949), 45–49.

Darryl Eugene ("Straw Man") Strawberry
OF. (B. March 12, 1962, Los Angeles, CA). New York (NL), 1982–1990; Los Angeles (NL), 1991–1994; San Francisco (NL), 1994; New York (AL), 1995–1999; San Diego (NL), 2000. Remarks: Had 1,401 hits (335 homers) and 221 stolen bases in 1,583 games in 19 seasons; NL Rookie

of the Year award, 1983; had five hits and two homers in 1986 NLCS and five hits and one homer in 1986 World Series; first NL player voted to the All-Star Game in each of his first four full seasons; NL home run champion, 1988; had nine hits and one homer in 1988 NLCS; had five hits and three homers in 1996 ALCS and three hits and one homer in 1996 World Series; powerful slugger who suffered substance abuse problems and survived colon cancer surgery in 1998; obtained two hits and one homer in 1999 ALCS and one hit in 1999 World Series; suspended from MLB, 2001; spent 2002–2003 at Phoenix House and Gainesville Correctional Institution; quite after three months as roving instructor, New York (AL), 2003.

53707. Abramson, Dan. "A Closer Look: Darryl Strawberry." *Beckett Baseball Card Monthly,* VIII (March 1991), 6–7.

53708. Alfano, Peter. "Kittle & Strawberry: Home Run Kings of the '80s." In: Zander Hollander, ed. *1984 Season: The Complete Handbook of Baseball.* New York: New American Library, 1984. Pp. 16–25.

53709. Ambrosius, Greg. "Free Agents: Darryl Strawberry Lead$ a $elect Group of Free Agent$ Into the Open Market." *Fantasy Baseball* , I (January 1991), 66–68.

53710. Augustin, Mike. "The Straw Man." In: *Saint Paul Saints 1997 Yearbook* . [St. Paul, MN]: St. Paul Saints, 1997. Pp. 13–14.

53711. Beaton, Rod. "Straw Dog? Before Darryl's Defection to L.A. Get You All Hot, Here Are a Few Things To Consider." *Fantasy Baseball,* II (March 1991), 20–22.

53712. Birth, Margaret. *Darryl Strawberry.* San Diego, CA: Revolutionary Comics, 1992. 30p.

53713. Brenner, Richard J. *Roger Clemens, Darryl Strawberry.* New York: Lynx Books, 1989. 82p.

53714. Bridges, H. "Carnegie's Hall and Strawberry's Walk." *Gourmet,* LI (March 1991), 44+.

53715. Brown, Robert J. "Darryl Eugene 'Straw' Strawberry." In: Vol. Q–Z of David L. Porter, ed. *Biographical Dictionary of American Sports: Baseball.* Rev. and enlarged ed. Westport, CT: Greenwood Press, 2000. Pp. 1492–1494.

53716. Celizic, Mike. "Did Met Fans Expect Too Much of Darryl Strawberry?" *Baseball Diges*t, L (March 1991), 87–88.

53717. Chass, Brennan. "Strawberry Blues." *Los Angeles Magazine,* XXXVI (April 1991), 70–76.

53718. Cohen, Irwin. "Baseball Beat: Darryl Strawberry." *Baseball Cards,* IX (May 1989), 84+.

53719. "Darryl Strawberry: Sinner or Saint?" In: Tom Barnidge, ed. *The Sporting News 1988 Baseball Yearbook.* St. Louis, MO: The Sporting News, 1988. Pp. 14–19.

53720. Feinstein, John. "No Big Apple Hype." *Inside Sports,* VI (March 1984), 26–31.

53721. Fimrite, Ron. "The Long Shot." *Sports Illustrated,* LXXXI (July 18, 1994), 34+.

53722. Gross, Jane. "Darryl Strawberry: The Man for the Season." *The New York Times Magazine,* (February 26, 1984), 16–21+.

53723. Gurnick, Ken. "Dodger Blue." *Fantasy Baseball,* II (May 1991), 24–25.

53724. Gutman, Bill. "Darryl Strawberry." In: his *Baseball's Hot New Stars.* New York: Pocket Books, 1988. pp. 71–87.

53725. Hirdt, Peter. "Would You Trade Darryl Strawberry?" *Sport,* LXXVIII (April 1987), 41+.

53726. Hoffer, Richard. "Try, Try Again." *Sports Illustrated,* LXXX (March 14, 1994), 38–40.

53727. Honig, Donald. "1983: Darryl Strawberry." In:

his *National League Rookies of the Year.* New York: Bantam Books, 1989. Pp. 94–97.

53728. Klapisch, Bob. "Back in the News." *Yankees Magazine,* XIX (July 1998), 54–63.

53729. _____. "Darryl Grows Up." *Inside Sports,* XI (March 1989), 48–51.

53730. _____. *High and Tight: The Rise and Fall of Dwight Gooden and Darryl Strawberry.* New York: Villard Books, 1996. 228p.

53731. _____. "The Straw That Stirs the Mets." *Inside Sports,* X (October 1988), 79–85.

53732. Klein, Joe. "A Star in the East and Unto the Mets a Savior Is Born." *Sport,* LXXIV (July 1983), 80+.

53733. Kuenster, John. "Darryl Strawberry May Be Headed for an MVP Year with the Mets." *Baseball Digest,* XLV (May 1986), 15–17.

53734. _____. "Darryl Strawberry Primed For a 'Career Year' in His Debut with Dodgers." *Baseball Digest,* L (May 1991), 15–17.

53735. Kurkjian, Tim. "A New Straw Stirs." *Sports Illustrated,* LXXXV (July 29, 1996), 102–103.

53736. Leavy, William. "Daryl Strawberry: The Juiciest Fruit in the Mets' Crop." *Ebony,* XXXIX (June 1984), 62–64.

53737. Lehman, Stephen. "The Straw Man." *Elysian Fields Quarterly,* XVI (Summer 1999), 2–4.

53738. Lewis, Gregory. "Darryl Strawberry." In: Ken Collier, ed. *The Baseball Book, 1984.* Scottsdale, AZ: Jalart House, 1984. Pp. 88–89.

53739. Lupica, Mike. "A Swing and a Prayer." *Esquire,* CXVI (October 1991), 69–70+.

53740. _____. "The Strawberry Statement." *Esquire,* CIX (April 1988), 65–69.

53741. Nack, William. "The Perils of Darryl." *Sports Illustrated,* LX (April 23, 1984), 32–39.

53742. Nash, Bruce and Allan Zullo, compiled by Tom Muldoon. "Darryl Strawberry." In: their *More Little Big Leaguers.* New York: Little Simon, 1991. Pp. 10–11.

53743. Newman, Howie. "Darryl Strawberry: A New Met Star is On His Way." *Baseball Digest,* XLIII (January 1984), 37–41.

53744. O'Connor, Ian. "They Did It for Darryl." *Yankees Magazine,* XIX (November 1998), 16–20. His inability to participate in 1998 postseason.

53745. Ostler, Scott. "Darryl Strawberry: 'I Fear Nothing on the Field, No Pitcher, No Man on this Earth.'" *Sport,* LXXXII (June 1991), 32–39.

53746. Richmond, Peter. "Doc [Gooden] & Darryl." *GQ — Gentlemen's Quarterly,* LXXI (July 2001), 162–167.

53747. Roberts, Jack. *Darryl Strawberry.* New York: Scholastic Book Service, 1992. 44p.

53748. Saxon, Walt. *Darryl Strawberry.* New York: Dell Publishing Co., 1985. 187p.

53749. Seaver, Tom, with Marty Appel. "When the Straw Stirred the Drink." In: his *Great Moments in Baseball: From the World Series of 1903 to the Modern Records of Nolan Ryan.* New York: Carol Communications, 1992. Pp. 265–270.

53750. Shyer, Brent. "The Promised Land." *Los Angeles Dodgers Magazine and Scorecard,* IV, no. 1 (1991), 6–11.

53751. Silverman, Jeff. "Guess Who's Back." *California,* XVI (April 1991), 56–62.

53752. Smith, C. S. "Free Darryl!" *New York,* XXXII (May 3, 1999), 34+.

53753. Sokolove, Michael. "The Last Straw." *The New York Times Magazine,* (April 15, 2001), 26–31.

53754. _____. *The Ticket Out: Daryl Strawberry and the*

Boys of Crenshaw [High School]. New York: Simon & Schuster, 2004. 352p.

53755. Spander, Art. "The Maturing of the Mets' Darryl Strawberry." *Baseball Digest,* XLVII (September 1988), 33–34.

53756. Starr, Mark. "One More Time at Bat." *Newsweek,* CXXVI (July 3, 1995), 60–61.

53757. Strawberry, Charisse and Darryl. *Recovering Life.* North Farmington, PA: Plough Publishing, 1999. 141p.

53758. _____., as told to N. Burleigh. "For Better or Worse." *Redbook,* CXCIV (December 1999), 75–76+.

53759. Strawberry, Darryl, as told to George Vass. "The Game I'll Never Forget." *Baseball Digest,* LII (May 1993), 61–62.

53760. _____., with Art Rust, Jr. *Darryl.* New York: Bantam Books, 1992. 342p.

53761. _____., with Dan Castellano. *Darryl.* Chicago, IL: Contemporary Books, 1986. 79p.

53762. _____., with Don Gold. *Hard Learnin.'* New York: Berkley Books, 1990. 227p.

53763. Thrift, Syd. "Darryl: Just How Good Is 'The Straw Man'?" In: *Major League Baseball Official 1991 Preview.* New York: Hachette Magazines, Inc., 1991. Pp. 12–13.

53764. Torres, John and Michael John Sullivan. *Sports Great: Darryl Strawberry.* Hillside, NJ: Enslow Publishers, 1990. 64p.

53765. Tresniowski, Alex. "Crunch Time: Darryl Strawberry Undergoes Surgery for Colon Cancer." *People Weekly,* L (October 19, 1998), 137–138.

53766. Vento, Lane. "Darryl The Complete Checklist." *Baseball Cards,* IX (May 1989), 30–41.

53767. Wiley, Ralph. "Doc and Darryl." *Sports Illustrated,* LXIX (July 11, 1988), 70–74+. Strawberry and Gooden.

Charles Evard ("Gabby" or "Old Sarge") Street

C-MGR-BROADCASTER. (B: Sept. 30, 1882, Huntsville, AL-D: Feb. 6, 1961). Cincinnati (NL), 1904–1905; Boston (NL), 1905; Washington (A.L), 1908–1911; New York (AL), 1912; St. Louis (N.L), 1931. Remarks: Had 312 hits (two homers) and 17 stolen bases in 503 games In eight seasons; caught a baseball dropped from the top of the Washington Monument, Aug. 28, 1908; player -manager, Nashville (SA), 1919, Suffolk (Virginia League), 1920–1921; Joplin (W.A.), 1922–1923; Muskogee (W.A.), 1924–1925; Augusta (South Atlantic League), 1926; Colombia (South Atlantic League), 1927; and Knoxville (South Atlantic League), 1928; coach, St. Louis (NL), 1929–1930; manager, St. Louis (NL), 1930–1933; manager, San Francisco (PCL), 1934–1935; St. Paul (AA), 1936–1937; coach, St. Louis (AL), 1937; manager, St. Louis (AL), 1938, winning combined 368 games and losing 339 (.524) in six piloting years; broadcaster, St. Louis (NL), 1945–1950; Gabby Street Park in Joplin, MO, dedicated in his honor, Jan. 19th, 1950; elected to Missouri Sports Hall of Fame, 1966.

53768. Cooper, John A. "'Gabby' Street Gets on the Air." *Baseball Magazine,* LX (February 1939), 421–422.

53769. Davis, Mac. "He Almost Caught a Grapefruit." In: his *The Lore and Legends of Baseball.* New York: Lantern Press, 1953. Pp. 59–63.

53770. "'Gabby' the Great." *Outlook and Independent,* CLVI (October 8, 1930), 217–218.

53771. Hawks, Roger J. "Catching a Ball Dropped from a High Place." *The Baseball Research Journal,* XXVII (1998), 32–34.

53772. Helfer, Harold. "'Gabby' Street's Monumental Catch." *Baseball Digest,* XVII (December 1958), 95–98. Once caught a ball dropped from the top of the Washington Monument.

53773. Hull, Sally S. "My Dad 'Gabby' Street." *Baseball Magazine,* XLVIII (June-August 1956), 34–39, 26–33, 46–54. Volume numbering in error.

53774. Lane, Ferdinand C. "How 'Gabby' Street Made Good." *Baseball Magazine,* XLVI (December 1930), 203–205.

53775. _____. "When 'Gabby' Street Forecast the Future." *Baseball Magazine,* XLVIII (January 1932), 361–362.

53776. Olmsted, Frank J. "Charles Evard 'Gabby,' 'Old Sarge' Street." In: Vol. Q-Z of David L. Porter, ed. *Biographical Dictionary of American Sports: Baseball.* Rev. and enlarged ed. Westport, CT: Greenwood Press, 2000. Pp. 1494–1495.

53777. Palmer, Stetson. "St. Louis' Managerial Miracle." *Baseball Magazine,* LX (May 1930), 561–563.

53778. Stann, Francis. "Street's Ironic [Washington] Monument." *Baseball Digest,* X (April 1951), 29–31.

Gabby Street *see* **Charles Evard ("Gabby" or *Old Sarge") Street**

Samuel ("Sam" or "Lefty") Streeter

P. (B: Sept. 17, 1900, New Market, AL-D: Aug. 9, 1985). Montgomery Grey Sox, 1920; Atlanta Black Crackers and Chicago American Giants, 1921; Atlantic City Bacharach Giants, 1922; New York Lincoln Giants, 1923; Birmingham Black Barons, 1924–1925; Birmingham Black Barons and Homestead Grays, 1926; Birmingham Black Barons, 1927–1928; Homestead Grays, 1928–1929; Birmingham Black Barons, Homestead Grays, and Baltimore Black Sox, 1930; Cleveland Cubs, 1931; Pittsburgh Crawfords, 1931–1936. Remarks: Well-traveled spitballer with a record of at least 76 victories and 46 defeats.

53779. Holway, John B. "Sam Streeter Smartest Pitcher in Negro Leagues." *The Baseball Research Journal,* XIII (1984), 71–72.

George Bevan ("Bo") Strickland

SS-MGR. (B: April 16, 1916, Aliquppa, PA). Pittsburgh (NL), 1950–1952; Cleveland (AL), 1952–1960. Remarks: Had 633 hits (36 homers) and 12 stolen bases in 971 games in 10 years; coach, Minnesota (AL), 1962, Cleveland (AL), 1963–1969; interim manager, Cleveland (AL), 1964, 1966, winning 48 games and losing 63 (.432); coach, Kansas City (AL), 1970–1972.

53780. Gibbons, Frank. "Playmaker StrickIand: Bargain of the Year." *Baseball Digest,* XII (September 1953), 5–10.

53781. Lebovitz, Hal. "Strickland Fooled Them All." *Sport,* XVII (September 1954), 42–43+.

Elmer Griffin Stricklett

P. (B: Aug. 29, 1876, Glasco, KA-D: June 7, 1964). Chicago (AL), 1904; Brooklyn (NL), 1905–1907. Remarks: Had 34 victories, 52 defeats, and six "saves" in four big league seasons; famed early proponent of the spitter, who later supported its banning, believing it too difficult to control and downright dangerous.

53782. Meany, P. A. "Who Invented the Spit Ball." *Baseball Magazine,* XI (May 1913), 59–60.

Jersey Joe Stripp *see* **Joseph Valentine ("Jersey Joe") Stripp**

Joseph Valentine ("Jersey Joe") Stripp

3B-1B-SS-OF. (B: Feb. 3, 1903, Harrison, NJ-D: June 10, 1989). Cincinnati (NL), 1928–1931; Brooklyn (NL), 1932–1937; St. Louis (NL) and Boston (NL), 1938. Remarks: In 11 big league seasons, obtained 1,238 hits (24 homers) and 50 stolen bases in 1,146 games; participated in fielding a triple play, Sept. 6, 1931; later operated Joe Stripp School of Baseball.

53783. Mason, Ward. "Joe Stripp, Brilliant but 'Brittle.'" *Baseball Magazine,* LVIII (February 1937), 405–406.

T. R. ("Ted") Strong

OF. (B: Jan. 2, 1917, South Bend, IN-D: 1951). Indianapolis ABCs, 1938; Kansas City Monarchs, 1937–1942, 1946–1947; Indianapolis Clowns, 1948; Minot (Mandak League); 1950; Chicago American Giants, 1951. Remarks: Highly regarded outfielder who was also a member of the original Harlem Globetrotters basketball team.

53784. Riley, James A. "T. R. 'Ted' Strong." In: Vol. Q-Z of David L. Porter, ed. *Biographical Dictionary of American Sports: Baseball.* Rev. and enlarged ed. Westport, CT: Greenwood Press, 2000. Pp. 1495–1496.

Amos Aaron ("Dutchie") Strunk

OF. (B: Jan. 22, 1889, Philadelphia, PA-D: July 22, 1979). Philadelphia (AL), 1908–1917; Boston (AL), 1918–1919; Philadelphia (AL), 1919–1920; Chicago (AL), 1920–1924; Philadelphia (AL), 1924. Remarks: Obtained 1,415 hits (15 homers) and 185 stolen bases in 1,507 games in 17 years; played in five World Series, 1910–1914, 1918, having five hits in the former and four in the latter; led AL in pinch hits, 1923.

53785. Phelps, Frank V. "Amos Aaron 'Dutchie' Strunk." In: Vol. Q-Z of David L. Porter, ed. *Biographical Dictionary of American Sports: Baseball.* Rev. and enlarged ed. Westport, CT: Greenwood Press, 2000. Pp. 1496–1497.

Dick Stuart *see* **Richard Lee ("Dick" or "Stu" or "Dr. Strangeglove") Stuart**

Richard Lee ("Dick" or "Stu" or "Dr. Strangeglove") Stuart

1B. (B: Nov. 7, 1932, San Francisco, CA-D: Dec. 15, 2002). Pittsburgh (NL), 1958–1962; Boston (AL), 1963–1964; Philadelphia (NL), 1965; New York (NL) and Los Angeles (NL), 1966; Taiyo Whales (Japan League), 1967–1968; California (AL), 1969. Remarks: Obtained 1,055 hits (228 homers) and two stolen bases in 1,112 U.S. big league games in a decade; AL RBI champion, 1963; noted for power (not fielding), having nine career grand slam homers; still, he is only 1B in MLB history to have three assists in one inning, June 23, 1963; hit 66 homers for Lincoln (WL), 1956.

53786. Bryson, Bill. "Dick Stuart: Home Run King Who Has Yet to Score." *Baseball Digest,* XV (October 1956), 24–27.

53787. _____. "They Remember Dick Stuart." *Baseball Digest,* XIX (July 1960), 33–35.

53788. Cope, Myron. "An Irrepressible Egotist." *Saturday Evening Post,* CCXXXV (April 28, 1962), 65–66+.

53789. Creamer, Robert W. "Old Stonefingers — Best Show Around Boston in Years." *Sports Illustrated,* XIX (September 2, 1963), 42+.

53790. Daley, Arthur. "Dick Stuart: The Pirates' Daredevil Dick." *Baseball Digest,* XVIII (May 1959), 13–15.

53791. Flowers, Kevin. "Dick Stuart: Teammates Remember 'Dr. Strangeglove." *Baseball Digest,* LXII (May 2003), 68–69.

53792. Grady, Sandy. "Dick Stuart: Kicked in His Ego." *Baseball Digest,* XXV (May 1966), 73–75.

53793. Hano, Arnold. "Dick Stuart: Man and Showman." *Sport,* XXXVII (June 1964), 56–67.

53794. Harris, Mark. "The Man Who Hits Too Many Home Runs." *Life,* XLIII (September 2, 1957), 85–86+.

53795. Kaplan, Dick. "Dick Stuart: 'Well, Shut My Mouth!'" In: Ray Robinson, ed. *Baseball Stars of 1965.* New York: Pyramid Books, 1965. Pp. 155–162.

53796. Liston, Bill. "Dick Stuart: 'The Pirates Held Me Back....'" *Sport,* XXXV (June 1963), 30–32+.

53797. Merchant, Larry. "The Impact of [Bo] Belinsky and Stuart on the Phillies." *Sport,* XXXIX (June 1965), 32–33+.

53798. _____. "What's Happening to Dick Stuart?" *Sport,* XXXIV (August 1962), 18–19+.

53799. Orr, Jack. "The Unabashed Dick Stuart." *Sport,* XXVIII (September 1959), 20–21+.

53800. Robinson, Ray. "Dick Stuart: Poor Man's Babe Ruth." In: Ray Robinson, ed. *Baseball Stars of 1964.* New York: Pyramid Books, 1964. Pp. 48–53.

53801. Sayles, John. "Dick Stuart." In: Danny Peary, ed. *Cult Baseball Players.* New York: Simon and Schuster, 1990. Pp. 6–9.

53802. _____. "Dick Stuart." In: Danny Peary, ed. *Baseball's Finest: The Greats, the Flakes, the Weird and the Wonderful.* North Digton, MA: The JG Press, 1990. Pp. 6–9.

53803. Spoehr, Luther W. "Richard Lee 'Dick,' 'Stu,' 'Dr. Strangeglove' Stuart." In: Vol. Q-Z of David L. Porter, ed. *Biographical Dictionary of American Sports: Baseball.* Rev. and enlarged ed. Westport, CT: Greenwood Press, 2000. Pp. 1497–1499.

53804. Stann, Francis. "Dick Stuart: The Latter-Day [Zeke] Bonura." *Baseball Digest,* XXII (December 1963), 44–47.

53805. "A Trip Out of Town If He Doesn't Hit." *Sports Illustrated,* XVIII (April 8, 1963), 74–75.

John Anton Stuper

P-COACH. (B: May 9, 1957, Butler, PA). St. Louis (NL), 1982–1984; Cincinnati (NL), 1985. Remarks: Won 32 games and lost 28, with one "save," in four years; won Game Six of 1982 World Series; after college, served as head baseball coach, Butler County Community College, 1989–1990; a minor league hitting instructor for St. Louis (N.L), 1991; and head baseball coach, Yale University, 1991-; through 2004, Stuper has won 237 Ivy League games and lost 261.

53806. Hummel, Rick. "John Stuper: Proving Last Year was No Fluke." *Baseball Digest,* XLII (September 1983), 64–67.

Thomas Virgil ("Tom" or "Snake") Sturdivant

P. (B: April 28, 1930, Gordon, KA). New York (AL), 1955–1959; Kansas City (AL), 1959; Boston (AL),1960; Washington (AL), 1961; Pittsburgh (NL), 1961–1963; Detroit (AL), 1963; Kansas City (AL),1963–1964; New York (NL), 1964. Remarks: Won 59 games and lost 51 with 17 "saves" in a decade; won Game Four of 1956 World Series.

53807. Dexter, Charles. "Tom Sturdivant: A Sturdy Right Arm." *Baseball Digest,* XV (October 1956), 29–34.

53808. Forker, Dom. "Tom Sturdivant." In: his *Sweet Seasons: Recollections of the 55–64 New York Yankees.* Dallas: Taylor Publishing Co., 1989. Pp. 118–122.

Bobby Sturgeon *see* **Robert Howard ("Bobby") Sturgeon**

Robert Howard ("Bobby") Sturgeon

SS-2B. (B: August 6, 1919, Clinton, IN). Chicago (NL), 1940–1942, 1946–1947; Boston (NL), 1948. Remarks: In six big league seasons, obtained 313 hits (one homer) and seven stolen bases in 420 games.

53809. Woody, Clay. "Former Cub Bobby Sturgeon Remembers Sharp Feuds of 1940s." *Baseball Digest,* LIX (June 2000), 66–73.

John Peter Joseph ("Johnny") Sturm

1B-SCOUT. (B: Jan. 23, 1916, St. Louis, MO-D: Oct.

8, 2004). New York (AL), 1941. Remarks: Obtained 125 hits (three homers) and three stolen bases in 124 big league games; big league career ended by military service and injury; player-manager, Joplin (W.A.), 1948–1949; gave try out to and alerted Yankees to future Hall of Famer Mickey Mantle (q.v.); later scout for Houston (NL), Cincinnati (NL) and Boston (AL).

53810. DeVries, Jack. "1941 was Good to Johnny Sturm, Too." *USA Today Baseball Weekly,* I (October 18, 1991), 44–45.

53811. Etkin, Jack. "Johnny Sturm." In: his *Innings Ago: Recollections of Kansas City Ballplayers of Their Days in the Game.* Marceline, MO: Walsworth Publishing Co., 1987. Pp. 106–117.

Johnny Sturm *see* **John Peter Joseph ("Johnny") Sturm**
Peter ("Pete" or "Pecky") Suder
2B-3B-SS. (B: Feb. 19, 1923, Fredericksburg, VA). Philadelphia (AL), 1941–1943, 1946–1954; Kansas City (AL), 1955. Remarks: Had 1,268 hits (49 homers) and 19 stolen bases in 1,421 games in 13 MLB seasons; highly regarded infielder.

53812. Smith, Walter ("Red"). "Suder — Solid Man of the Athletics: His Roommates Get Ahead." *Baseball Digest,* XIII (May 1954), 65–66.

Edward ("Ed") Sudol
UMP. (B: 1920). Remarks: NL arbiter, 1957–1977.

53813. Gerlach, Larry R. "Ed Sudol." In: his *The Men in Blue: Conversations with Umpires.* New York: Viking Press, 1980. Pp. 215–234. Reprinted by the University of Nebraska Press in 1994.

Joseph ("Joe") Sugden
P-SCOUT. (B: July 31, 1870, Kinston, NC-D: June 28, 1959). St. Louis (AL), 1902. Remarks: Had no decisions in one big league season; coach, St. Louis (NL), 1921–1925; also served as Cardinals scout up until his death.

53814. Yeutter, Frank. "He Ran for Connie Mack." *Baseball Digest,* XII (April 1963), 34–39.

August Richard ("Gus" or "Goose") Suhr
1B. (B: Jan. 3, 1906, San Francisco, CA-D: Jan. 15, 2004). Pittsburgh (NL), 1930–1939; Philadelphia (NL), 1939–1940. Remarks: Had 1,446 hits (84 homers) and 53 stolen bases in 1,435 games in 11 seasons; good fielder with an 822-game consecutive playing streak (ninth longest) on his record, Sept. 11, 1931-June 4, 1937; also had 51 homers for San Francisco (PCL), 1929.

53815. Kelley, Brent P. "Gus Suhr: National League Iron Horse, 1930–1940." *Sports Collector's Digest,* XXI (May 27, 1994), 210–211. Expanded in his *In The Shadow of the Babe: Baseball Players Who Played with or Against Babe Ruth* (Jefferson, NC: McFarland & Co., Inc., 1995), pp. 85–92.

53816. Pacini, Le. "Gus Suhr Recalls the 'Good Old Days.'" *Baseball Digest,* XLI (June 1982), 87–90.

53817. Spoehr, Luther W. "August Richard 'Gus,' 'Goose' Suhr. "In: Vol. Q-Z of David L. Porter, ed. *Biographical Dictionary of American Sports: Baseball.* Rev. and enlarged ed. Westport, CT: Greenwood Press, 2000. Pp. 1499–1500.

Gus Suhr *see* **August Richard ("Gus") Suhr**
Clyde Leroy ("Sukey") Sukeforth
C-MGR. (B: Nov. 34, 1901, Washington, ME-D: Sept. 3, 2000). Cincinnati (NL), 1926–1931; Brooklyn (NL), 1932–1934, 1945. Remarks: Obtained 326 hits (two homers) and a dozen stolen bases in a decade of big league play; managed one game for Brooklyn (NL) in 1947 and by wining it came to possess a 1.000 piloting percentage; long-time Dodger coach credited with first scouting Jackie Robinson (q.v.).

53818. Green, Paul M. "Clyde Sukeforth." In: his *Forgotten Fields.* Waupaca, WI: Parker Publications, 1984. Pp. 141–148.

53819. Honig, Donald. "Clyde Sukeforth." In: his *Baseball When the Grass was Real.* New York: Coward, McCann, Geoghegan, 1975. Pp. 178–191.

53820. Kelley, Brent P. "Clyde Sukeforth: Baseball History, 1926–1945." In: his *In The Shadow of the Babe: Baseball Players Who Played with or Against Babe Ruth.* Jefferson, NC: McFarland & Co., Inc., 1995. Pp. 35–43.

53821. Lincoln, C. E. "A Conversation with Clyde Sukeforth." *The Baseball Research Journal,* XVI (1987), 72–73.

53822. Marks, Bo, ed. *Era of Clyde Sukeforth.* Coopers Mills, ME: Catfish Press, 1995. 196p.

53823. Wilson, Nick. "Clyde Sukeforth." In: his *Voices from the Pastime: Oral Histories of Surviving Major Leaguers, Negro Leaguers, Cuban Leaguers, and Writers, 1920–1934.* Jefferson, NC: McFarland & Co., Inc., 2000. Pp. 32–42, 152.

Billy Sullivan *see* **William Joseph ("Billy") Sullivan**
Frank Sullivan *see* **Franklin Leal ("Frank") Sullivan**
Franklin Leal ("Frank") Sullivan
P. (B: Jan. 23, 1930, Hollywood, CA) Boston (AL), 1953–1960; Philadelphia (NL), 1961–1962; Minnesota (AL), 1962–1963. Remarks: Had 97 victories, 100 defeats, and 18 "saves" in 11 campaigns; at 6'6½" was long the AL's tallest hurler.

53824. Fehler, Gene. "Frank Sullivan." In: his *Tales from Baseball's Golden Age.* Champaign, IL: Sports Publishing Co., 2000. Chpt. 47.

53825. Hurwitz, Hy. "Up And Coming (Frank Sullivan)." In: his *The Boston Red Sox.* New York: A.S. Barnes, 1956. Pp. 84–106.

53826. Morgan, Mark. "Boston's Head Hurler." *Baseball Digest,* XIV (November-December 1955), 69–73.

53827. Richman, Arthur. "Seafarer Sullivan Out of Troubled Waters?" *Baseball Digest,* XX (May 1961), 23–25.

53828. Warshaw, Robin. "Surviving the City of Brotherly Love-Hate." *Advertising Age,* LII (September 28, 1981), S14-S15.

Haywood Cooper Sullivan
C-MGR. (B: Dec. 15, 1930, Donaldsonville, GA-D: February 12, 2003). Boston (AL), 1955, 1957–1960; Kansas City (AL), 1961–1963. Remarks: Had 192 hits (13 homers) in 312 games in eight seasons; did not achieve his first big league hit until he had been playing for five years, April 19, 1960; manager, Kansas City (AL), 1965, winning 54 games and losing 82 (.397); dir. of player personnel, Boston (AL), 1965–1978; part owner, GM, Boston (AL), 1978–1983; exec. Boston (AL), 1983–1993; operated marina, Ft. Myer, FL., 1993–2001; father of Marc Cooper Sullivan (below).

53829. "Pitcher's View from the Mound." *Sports Illustrated,* VI (March 25, 1957), 24–25.

John Lawrence Sullivan
P.-PUGILIST. (B: Oct. 15, 1868, Boston, MA-D: Feb. 2, 1918). Remarks: Gifted amateur semi-pro player offered professional baseball opportunity, but who chose to make a name in the boxing arena.

53830. "Heavyweight Champion John L. Sullivan Nearly Causes a Riot at a California League Game (1886)." In: Dean A. Sullivan, ed. *Early Innings: A Documentary History of Baseball, 1825-1908.* Lincoln, NE: University of Nebraska Press, 1995. Pp. 144–146. The *San Francisco Examiner* of November 15, 1886 reported his umpiring of a game between the Greenhood & Morans of Oakland and the San Francisco Pioneers.

53831. Sullivan, John L. "When I Played the Game." *Baseball Magazine,* III (May 1909), 9–13.

Marc Cooper Sullivan

C. (B: July 25, 1958, Quincy, MA). Boston (AL), 1982–1987. Remarks: Obtained 67 hits (five homers) in 137 big league games; son of Haywood Sullivan (above).

53832. McCallum, Jack. "Pop in His Bat, or In His Corner." *Sports Illustrated,* LXVI (March 23, 1987), 24–25.

Scott Sullivan *see* **William Scott Sullivan**

William Joseph ("Billy") Sullivan

3B-OF-1B. (B: Oct. 23, 1910, Sarasota, FL-D: Jan. 4, 1994). Chicago (AL), 1931–1933; Cincinnati (NL), 1935; Cleveland (AL), 1936–1937; St. Louis (AL), 1938–1939; Detroit (AL), 1940–1941; Brooklyn (NL), 1942; Pittsburgh (NL), 1947. Remarks: In 12 seasons, had 820 hits (29 homers) and 30 stolen bases in 962 games; had five hits in one game, May 27, 1926.

53833. Sullivan, Billy. "The Exaggerated Importance of Runs Batted In." *Baseball Magazine,* LXXX (January 1937), 354–355.

William Scott Sullivan

P. (B: May 13, 1971, Carrolton, AL). Cincinnati (NL), 1995–2003; Chicago (AL), 2003; Kansas City (AL), 2004-. Remarks: Through 2004, has had 40 victories, 28 defeats, and nine "saves"; injured late in the 2004 season.

53834. Epstein, Eddie. "Scott Sullivan." In: *The STATS 1995 Minor League Scouting Notebook.* Skokie, IL: STATS Publishing, 1995. Pp. 154–155.

Bill Summers *see* **William Reed ("Bill") Summers**

William Reed ("Bill") Summers

UMP. (B. Nov. 10, 1895, Harrison, NJ-D: Sept. 12, 1966). Remarks: AL arbiter, 1933–1960.

53835. Davis, Mac. "An Umpire Who Thought He Was Paul Revere." In: his *The Lore and Legends of Baseball.* New York: Lantern Press, 1953. Pp. 218–219.

53836. Gerlach, Larry R. "William Reed 'Bill' Summers." In: Vol. Q-Z of David L. Porter, ed. *Biographical Dictionary of American Sports: Baseball.* Rev. and enlarged ed. Westport, CT: Greenwood Press, 2000. Pp. 1500–1501.

53837. Simons, Herbert. "Life of an Ump." *Baseball Magazine,* XXXIV (April 1942), 156–162.

53838. Slocum, William. "The Series Star in the Dark Blue Suit." *Sports Illustrated,* III (October 3, 1955), 35–36, 57–58.

53839. Summers, William R. ("Bill"). "What I Didn't Tell During 27 Years of Umpiring." *Baseball Digest,* XIX (September 1960), 35–44.

53840. _____., with Tim Cohane. "Baseball Boors I Have Known." *Look,* XXIV (July 5, 1960), 65–71.

Carl Ringdahl ("Lefty") Sumner

OF. (B: Sept. 28, 1908, Cambridge, MA). Boston (AL), 1928. Remarks: Obtained eight hits in 16 big league games.

53841. Wilson, Nick. "Carl Sumner." In: his *Voices from the Pastime: Oral Histories of Surviving Major Leaguers, Negro Leaguers, Cuban Leaguers, and Writers, 1920–1934.* Jefferson, NC: McFarland & Co., Inc., 2000. Pp. 96–98.

Jan Sumner

Remarks: Member of the "Over-50" baseball club and batting practice hurler, Colorado (NL), 1993–1999.

53842. Sumner, Jan. *Fat Pitch : My Six Seasons with the Colorado Rockies.* Denver, CO: JaDan Publishing, 2000. 132p.

Billy Sunday *see* **William Ashley ("Billy" Or "Parson" or "The Baseball Evangelist") Sunday**

William Ashley ("Billy" or "Parson" or "The Baseball Evangelist") Sunday

OF. (B: Nov. 19, 1862, Ames, IA-D: Nov. 6, 1935).

Chicago (NL), 1883–1887; Pittsburgh (NL), 1888–1890; Philadelphia (NL), 1890. Remarks: Had 498 hits (12 homers) and 236 stolen bases in 449 games in eight years; on May 23, 1883, struck out the first four ABs of the season, setting a record which stood until 1966; had 84 stolen bases in 1890; became extremely popular fundamentalist preacher who employed his base-sliding techniques to make stage entrances; at the forefront of the Prohibition movement.

53843. Allen, Robert A. *Billy Sunday: Home Run to Heaven.* Milford, MI: Mott Media, 1985. 152p.

53844. Barton, Bruce. "Billy Sunday — Baseball Evangelist." *Collier's,* LI (July 26, 1913), 7–9.

53845. Brown, Elijah P. *The Real Billy Sunday: The Life and Work of Rev. William Ashley Sunday, the Baseball Evangelist.* New York: Fleming H. Revell, 1914. 285p. Simultaneously published by the Dayton, OH-based The Otterbein Press in a 288-page edition.

53846. Bruno, Guido. "Billy Sunday, Who Makes Religion Pay." *Pearson's Magazine* (American Edition), XXXVII (April 1917), 323–332.

53847. Bruns, Roger A. *Preacher: Billy Sunday and Big-Time American Evangelism.* New York: W. W. Norton, 1992. 306p.

53848. Coleman, W. L. "Billy Sunday: A Style Meant for His Time and Place." *Christianity Today,* XXI (December 17, 1976), 14–17.

53849. Davis, Mac. "The Outfielder Who Became a Healer." In: his *The Lore and Legends of Baseball.* New York: Lantern Press, 1953. Pp. 11–13.

53850. Denison, Lindsay. "The Rev. Billy Sunday and His War on the Devil. "*American Magazine,* LXIV (September 1907), 450–469.

53851. Dorsett, Lyle W. "Billy Sunday." In: John A. Garrity and Marsh C. Carries, eds. *American National Biography.* 24 vols. New York: Oxford University Press, 1999. XXI, 150–152.

53852. _____. *Billy Sunday and the Redemption of Urban America.* Grand Rapids, MI: Wm. B. Eerdmans Publishing Co., 1991. 207p.

53853. Ellis, William T. *Billy Sunday, the Man and His Message.* Philadelphia: Universal Book and Bible House, 1914. 451p.

53854. Frankenburg, Theodore T. *Billy Sunday, His Tabernacles and Sawdust Trails: A Biographical Sketch of the Famous Baseball Evangelist.* Columbus, OH: F.J. Herr Co., 1917. 224p.

53855. _____. *Spectacular Career of Rev. Billy Sunday, Famous Baseball Evangelist.* Columbus, OH: McClelland & Co., 1913. 228p.

53856. Geyer, Orel R. "Billy Sunday's First Prayer." *Baseball Magazine,* XV (May 1915), 79–82.

53857. Giffin, Frederick C. "Billy Sunday: The Evangelist as 'Patriot." *Social Science,* XLVIII (Autumn 1973), 216–221.

53858. Gough, David. "Billy Sunday: From the Basepaths to the Sawdust Trail." In: *Grandstand Baseball Annual, 1998.* Downey, CA: Joseph M. Wayman, 1998. Pp. 137–141.

53859. Grayson, Harry. "William Ashley (Billy) Sunday." In: his *They Played the Game.* New York: A.S. Barnes, 1944. Pp. 49–50.

53860. Kimmel, Michael S. "Baseball and the Reconstitution of American Masculinity, 1880–1920." In: *1989 Cooperstown Symposium on Baseball and the American Culture.* Westport, CT: Meckler Publishing, 1991. Pp. 281–297.

53861. Knickerbocker, Wendy. *Sunday at the Ballpark: Billy Sunday's Professional Baseball Careers, 1883–1890.* Lanham, MD: Rowman & Littlefield, 2000. 192p. Reprinted in a 195-page edition by Scarecrow Press in 2004.

53862. Lockerbie, D. Bruce. *Billy Sunday.* Waco, TX: Word Books, 1965. 64p.

53863. Lockley, Fred. "How Billy Sunday Became a Famous Ball Player." *Baseball Magazine,* XXV (June 1920), 319–321+.

53864. Marin, Robert F. "Billy Sunday and Christian Manliness." *The Historian,* LVIII (Summer 1996), 811–823.

53865. Martin, Robert Francis. *Hero of the Heartland: Billy Sunday and the Transformation of American Society, 1962–1935.* Bloomington, IN: Indiana University Press, 2002. 194p.

53866. McLoughlin, William G. *Billy Sunday Was His Real Name.* Chicago, IL: University of Chicago Press, 1955. 324p.

53867. Miller, Basil W. "Billy Sunday." In: his *Ten Famous Evangelists.* Grand Rapids, MI: Zondervan, 1949. Pp. 75–81.

53868. Muhlbaek, Robert. "Billy Sunday, Evangelist." *The Baseball Research Journal,* LX (1980), 5–6.

53869. Oboiski, Robert. "Billy Sunday Batted Best Against Booze." In: his *Baseball's Strangest Moments.* New York: Sterling Publishing Co., 1988. Pp. 44–46.

53870. _____. "From Big League Ball Player to Evangelist: 'Billy' Sunday." In: his *Baseball's Strangest Moments.* New York: Sterling Publishing Co., 1988. Pp. 41–44.

53871. _____. "Sunday Disdained Tobacco, Too, But was Pictured on Cigarette Cards." In: his *Baseball's Strangest Moments.* New York: Sterling Publishing Co., 1988. Pp. 46–47.

53872. Rodeheaver, Homer. *Twenty Years with Billy Sunday.* Nashville, TN: Cokesbury Press, 1936. 149p.

53873. Stocker, Fern Neal. *Billy Sunday, Baseball Preacher.* Chicago, IL: Moody Press, 1985. 141p.

53874. Sunday, Nellie ("Ma"). *"Ma" Sunday Still Speaks.* Winona Lake, MN: Winona Lake Christian Assembly, 1957. 55p. Wife of Billy Sunday.

53875. Sunday, William A. ("Billy"). *Burning Truths from Billy's Bat: A Graphic Description of the Remarkable Conversion of Rev. Billy Sunday.* Philadelphia, PA: Diamond Publishing Co., 1914. 103 p.

53876. Thomas, Lee. *The Billy Sunday Story: The Life and Times of William Ashley Sunday.* Grand Rapids, MI: Zondervan, 1961. 256p.

53877. Valentry, Duane. "That Sunday Pitch." *Sport,* L (September 1970), 18–19.

53878. Warnock, James. "Playing Centerfield in the Lord's Ball Club: Billy Sunday's 1914 Denver Campaign." *Nine: A Journal of Baseball History and Social Policy Perspectives,* IV (Fall 1995), 62–84.

53879. Weisberger, Bernard. "Billy Sunday." In: his *They Gathered at the River.* Boston, MA: Little, Brown, 1955. Pp. 220–265.

53880. Wright, Melton. *Giant for God: A Biography of the Life of William Ashley ("Billy") Sunday.* Boyce, VA: Carr Publishing Co., 1951. 168 p.

James Howard ("Jim" or "Sunny") Sundberg
C-BROADCASTER. (B. May 18, 1951, Galesburg, IL). Texas (AL), 1974–1983; Milwaukee (AL), 1984; Kansas City (AL), 1985–1986; Chicago (NL), 1987–1988; Texas (AL), 1988–1989. Remarks: Had 1,493 hits (95 homers) and 20 stolen bases in 1,962 games in 15 years; broadcaster, Texas (AL), 1990–1995.

53881. Anderson, Bruce. "Jim Sundberg: A Goldmine Behind the Plate." *Baseball Digest,* XXXIX (July 1980), 46–49.

53882. Circelli, Jerry. "Jim Sundberg Strikes Gold Behind the Plate." *Baseball Digest,* XLI (October 1982), 61–66.

53883. Elderkin, Phil. "Jim Sundberg: Does He Rate as the No. 1 Catcher?" *Baseball Digest,* XXXVII (November 1979), 88–91.

53884. Harvey, Randy. "Jim Sundberg Adds Hitting to His Skills on Defense." *Baseball Digest,* XXXVI (December 1977), 64–69.

53885. Hill, Terry. "Jim Sundberg: 'Six Gold Glove Awards and Three All-Star Games.'" In: his *Batting A Thousand.* Nashville, TN: Thomas Nelson, 1987. Pp. 60–64.

53886. Holtzman, Jerome. "Jim Sundberg Sets Sights on All-Time Catching Mark." *Baseball Digest,* XLV (November 1986), 30–32.

53887. Kush, Raymond D. "James Howard 'Jim,' 'Sunny' Sundberg." In: Vol. Q-Z of David L. Porter, ed. *Biographical Dictionary of American Sports: Baseball.* Rev. and enlarged ed. Westport, CT: Greenwood Press, 2000. Pp. 1501–1502.

53888. Nash, Bruce and Allan Zullo. "Jim Sundberg." In: their *Little Big Leaguers: Amazing Boyhood Stories of Today's Baseball Stars.* New York: Little Simon, 1990. Pp. 72–73.

53889. Nightengale, Bob. "Jim Sundberg: Forgotten Man in the Catching Derby." *Baseball Digest,* XLVII (December 1988), 80–82.

53890. Sundberg, Jim, as told to George Vass. "The Game I'll Never Forget." *Baseball Digest,* XLVII (August 1988), 43–45.

53891. "Sundberg: Catcher with a Cannon." *What's Brewing,* VIII (June 1984), 4–7.

Thomas Jacob ("Tom" or "Lefty" or "Long Tom") Sunkel
P.(B: Aug. 9, 1912, Paris, IL-D: April 6, 2002). St. Louis (NL), 1937, 1939; New York (NL), 1941–1943; Brooklyn (NL), 1944. Remarks: Won nine games and lost 15 in seven big league years; developed a non-operable cataract and lost all sight in his left eye in 1941, forcing him to pitch and bat with his head cocked to the side.

53892. Davis, Mac. "An Eye for Fame." In: his *The Lore and Legends of Baseball.* New York: Lantern Press, 1953. Pp. 130–131.

Jeffrey Scot ("Jeff") Suppan
P. (B: Jan. 2, 1975, Oklahoma City, OK). Boston (AL), 1995–1997; Arizona (NL), 1998; Kansas City (AL), 1998–2002; Pittsburgh (NL) and Boston (AL), 2003; St. Louis (NL), 2004-. Remarks: Through 2004, has won 78 games and lost 84; led AL in home runs allowed, 2000; won one game and lost one of 2004 NLCS; lost one game of 2004 World Series.

53893. O'Rourke, Larry. "Suppan's Ahead of His Time." *Boston Baseball,* VI (March 1996), 10–11.

53894. Rutstein, Michael. "Suppan Heads List of Boston's Top Prospects." *Boston Baseball,* VI (March 1996), 16–19.

B.J. Surhoff *see* **William James ("B.J.") Surhoff**
William James ("B.J.") Surhoff
OF-C. (B: August 4, 1964, Bronx, NY). Milwaukee (AL), 1987–1995; Baltimore (AL), 1996–2000; Atlanta (NL), 2000–2002; Baltimore (AL), 2003-. Remarks: Through 2004, has had 2,248 hits (183 homers) and 141 stolen bases in 2,222 games; had six RBIs in one game, May 11,

1997; had three hits and one homer (Game Two) in 2001 NLCS; had grand slam homer, Sept. 19, 2004; member of 1984 U.S. Olympic baseball team.

53895. Cohen, Irwin. "Baseball Beat: B. J. Surhoff." *Baseball Cards,* VIII (May 1988), 70–75.

53896. Doyle, Al. "B. J. Surhoff Gave the Brewers Their Money's Worth in '95." *Baseball Digest,* LV (February 1995), 41–45.

53897. Driver, David. "Better with Age." *Baseball Digest,* LIX (March 2000), 54–58.

53898. Hanlon, T. "B. J. Surhoff." *Sports Illustrated,* LXVII (July 13, 1987), 48+.

53899. Sorci, Rick. "Baseball Profile: Orioles' Outfielder B.J. Surhoff." *Baseball Digest,* LVII (September 1998), 32–33.

Matthew Constantine ("Max") Surkont
P. (B: June 16, 1922, Central Falls, RI–D: Oct. 8, 1986). Chicago (AL), 1949; Boston (NL) and Milwaukee (NL), 1950–1953; Pittsburgh (NL), 1954–1956; St. Louis (NL), 1956; New York (NL), 1956–1957. Remarks: Won 61 games and lost 76 with eight "saves" in nine seasons; struck out eight consecutive batters in one game, May 25, 1953; also played in PCL; cousin of Ted Kluzewski (q.v.).

53900. Dexter, Charles. "Surkont's 14 Lost Years." *Baseball Digest,* X, (August 1951), 67–71.

53901. Holbrook, Bob. "Boston's Matty." *Sport Life,* IV (September 1951), 26–27+.

Max Surkont *see* **Matthew Constantine ("Max") Surkont**

Richard Lee ("Rick") Sutcliffe
P-BROADCASTER. (B: June 21, 1956, Independence, MO). Los Angeles (NL), 1979–1981; Cleveland (A.L), 1982–1984; Chicago (NL), 1984–1991; Baltimore (AL), 1992–1993; St. Louis (NL), 1994. Remarks: Won 171 games and lost 139, with six "saves," in 16 years; homered off Tom Seaver (q.v.), May 25, 1979; NL Rookie of the Year award, 1979; won Game One, but lost Game Five, 1984 NLCS; NL Cy Young Award, 1984; minor league pitching coach, San Diego (NL), 1996; broadcaster, San Diego (NL), 1997-date.

53902. Didinger, Ray. "Rick Sutcliffe: He Gave the Cubs a Shot in the Arm." *Baseball Digest,* XLIII (November 1984), 29–31.

53903. Garrity, John. "The Trade That Made the Cubs." *Sports Illustrated,* LXI (September 2, 1984), 28–31.

53904. Hersh, F. "The Good Guys Always Win." *Inside Sports,* VII (May 1985), 24–32.

53905. Honig, Donald. "1979: Rick Sutcliffe." In: his *National League Rookies of the Year.* New York: Bantam Books, 1989. Pp. 82–83.

53906. James, Robert. "Rick Sutcliffe." In: Ken Collier, ed. *The Baseball Book, 1985.* Scottsdale, AZ: Jalart House, 1985. Pp. 94–95.

53907. McDonnell, Joe. "Rick Sutcliffe: Huge Turnaround." In: Bill Shumard, ed. *1981 Los Angola Dodgers Yearbook.* Anaheim, CA: Rotary Off-Set Printers, 1981. Pp. 51–52.

53908. Nash, Bruce and Allan Zullo. "Rick Sutcliffe." In: their *Little Big Leaguers: Amazing Boyhood Stories of Today's Baseball Stars.* New York: Little Simon, 1990. Pp. 18–19.

53909. Pluto, Terry. "Rick Sutcliffe." *The* (Cleveland) *Plain Dealer Magazine,* (April 15, 1984), 22–27.

53910. "Rick Sutcliffe." In: Carrie Muskat, ed. *Banks to Sandberg to Grace: Five Decades of Love and Frustration with the Chicago Cubs.* Chicago, IL: Contemporary Books, 2001. Pp. 205–211.

53911. Smith, Duane A. "Richard Lee 'Dick' Sutcliffe." In: Vol. Q-Z of David L. Porter, ed. *Biographical Dictionary of American Sports: Baseball.* Rev. and enlarged ed. Westport, CT: Greenwood Press, 2000. Pp. 1502–1503.

53912. Snyder, Joe. "Rick Sutcliffe: A Star Still Burning." *Orioles Gazette,* II (March 1992), 27–28.

53913. Sutcliffe, Rick, as told to George Vass. "The Game I'll Never Forget." *Baseball Digest,* LI (April 1992), 87–89.

53914. Topkin, Marc. "Rick Sutcliffe: Tough Competitor With a Big Heart." *Orioles Gazette,* III (April 1993), 20–21.

53915. Wulf, Steve. "Waiting on Deck for a Shipload of Money." *Sports Illustrated,* LXI (December 10, 1984), 28–30+.

Bruce Sutter *see* **Howard Bruce Sutter**
Howard Bruce Sutter
P. (B: Jan. 8, 1953, Lancaster, PA). Chicago (NL), 1976–1980; St. Louis (NL), 1981–19841; Atlanta (NL), 1985–1989. Remarks: Won 68 games and lost 71 with 300 "saves" in nine years; NL Cy Young Award, 1979; won one game of 1982 NLCS; saved Game Seven, 1982 World Series; tied Don Quisenberry (q.v.) for major league record of most "saves" in a season (1984); one of three pitchers to save 300+ games.

53916. "Bruce Sutter." In: Carrie Muskat, ed. *Banks to Sandberg to Grace: Five Decades of Love and Frustration with the Chicago Cubs.* Chicago, IL: Contemporary Books, 2001. Pp. 146–149.

53917. Cairns, Bob. "Bruce Sutter. "In: his *Pen Men: Baseball's Greatest Bullpen Stories Told by the Men Who Brought the Game Relief.* New York: St. Martin's Press, 1992. Pp. 326–332.

53918. Chass, Murray. "Sutter of Cubs is Awarded $700,000 Pact by Arbitrator: Reprinted from *The New York Times,* February 26, 1980." In: Gene Brown, ed. *The New York Times Encyclopedia of Sports, Vol. I5 Update.* New York: Arno Press, 1980. Pp. 54–55.

53919. Elderkin, Phil. "Bruce Sutter: Master of the Game's Best Split-Finger Fastball." *Baseball Digest,* XXXVIII (December 1979), 76–79.

53920. Fimrite, Ron. "This Pitch in Time Saves Nine." *Sports Illustrated,* LI (September 17, 1979), 36–39.

53921. Gleason, Bill. "Bruce Sutter: He Was Born for the Bullpen." *Baseball Digest,* XXXVI (July 1977), 46–49.

53922. Gray, Bill. "Bruce Sutter—1979." In: his *Baseball's Top 100: The Best Individual Seasons of All Time.* Wilton, CT: Diamond Library, 1996. Pp. 241–242.

53923. Kahn, Roger. "A Bullpen Named Bruce" In: his *The Head Game: Baseball Seen from the Pitcher's Mound.* Boston, MA: Harcourt, 2000. Pp. 241–258.

53924. Klawans, Harold L. "The 10th Inning: Bruce Sutter." In: his *Why Michael Couldn't Hit and Other Tales of the Neurology of Sports.* New York: W.H. Freeman, 1996. Chpt. 10.

53925. Kurkijan, Tim. "Bruce Sutter: Baseball's No. 1 Relief Pitcher." *Baseball Digest,* XLII (February 1983), 34–36.

53926. Markus, Robert. "The Cardinals' Bruce Sutter: He's Back in Control." *Baseball Digest,* XLIII (August 1984), 60–63.

53927. Newman, Charles. "The Arms, the Tutor, and Bruce Sutter." *Sport,* LXXV (June 1984), 85–92.

53928. Rothe, Emil H. "Howard Bruce Sutter." In: Vol. Q-Z of David L. Porter, ed. *Biographical Dictionary of American Sports: Baseball.* Rev. and enlarged ed. Westport, CT: Greenwood Press, 2000. Pp. 1503–1504.

53929. Schlossberg, Dan. "The Ultimate Relievers: Bruce Sutter and Dan Quisenberry." *Baseball Digest,* XLIV (July 1985), 49–58.

53930. Sutter, Howard B. "The Game I'll Never Forget." *Baseball Digest,* XL (January 1981), 35–39.

53931. Thorn, John. "Bruce Sutter: 'Split-Finger Flinger.'" In: his *Baseball's Dream Team.* New York: Ace Tempo Books, 1982. Pp. 129–137.

53932. Thornton, K. D. "Bruce Sutter." In: Ken Collier, ed. *The Baseball Book, 1985.* Scottsdale, AZ: Jalart House, 1985. Pp. 122–123.

53933. Weiskoff, Don. "Keep 'Em Close." *Athletic Journal,* LXIV (January 1984), 40–47. As demonstrated by Sutter.

53934. Wilbert, Warren and William Hageman. "Bruce Sutter—1977." In: their *Chicago Cubs: Seasons at the Summit, the 50 Greatest Individual Seasons.* Champaign, IL: Sagamore Publishing, 1997. Pp. 65–68.

George ("Mule") Suttles
1B-OF. (B: March 2, 1901, Brockton, LA-D: 1968). Birmingham Black Barons, 1922–1925; St. Louis Stars, 1926–1931; Detroit Wolves and Washington Pilots, 1932; Cole's American Giants, 1933–1935; Newark Eagles, 1936–1940, 1940–1944; Indianapolis ABCs, 1939; New York Black Yankees, 1941–1942. Remarks: Career .338 hitter known for his 50-oz. bat and huge homers.

53935. Lester, Larry. "George "Mule" Suttles." In: John A. Garrity and Marsh C. Carries, eds. *American National Biography.* 24 vols. New York: Oxford University Press, 1999. XXI, 170–171.

Donald Howard ("Don") Sutton★
P. (B: April 2, 1945, Clio, AL). Los Angeles (NL), 1966–1980; Houston (NL), 1981–1982; Milwaukee (AL), 1983–1984; Oakland (AL), 1985; California (AL), 1985–1987; Los Angeles (NL), 1988. Remarks: Won 324 games and lost 256, with five "saves," in 19 seasons; holds MLB record for most games lost to one club (Chicago [NL], 13—1966–1969); won Games One and Four of 1974 NLCS; won Game Two of 1974 World Series; All-Star Game MVP award, 1977; won Game Two of 1977 NLCS; won Game Four of 1977 World Series; won Game Three of 1982 ALCS; broadcaster, WTBS, 1989–; elected to National Baseball Hall of Fame in 1998, where his plaque reads: "A stalwart on the mound for 23 major league seasons, his impressive pitching record includes 324 victories, 3,574 strikeouts and a 3.26 ERA. Strikeout total is fifth best all-time, while win total ranks tied for 12th. Did not miss a turn in the starting rotation due to injury or illness. Consistency and model control led to 15 or more wins in 12 seasons and 100 or more strikeouts 21 times. The right hander pitched in four World Series and was named to four All-Star teams."

53936. Allen, Maury. "Don Sutton (1966-Present)." In: his *Baseball's 100.* New York: Galahad Books, 1981. Pp. 305–307.

53937. Arndt, Rick. "Don Sutton. *Safe at Home.* St. Louis, MO: Concordia Publishing House, 1979. Pp. 66–77.

53938. Ballew, Bill. "Sutton Eyes Hall After Successful Career." *Sports Collector's Digest,* XVIII (February 1, 1991), 100–106.

53939. Bell, Marty. "Don Sutton Does Not Bleed Dodger Blue." *Sport,* LXVI (June 1978), 80–92+.

53940. Cohen, Irwin. "Talkin' Baseball With Don Sutton." *Baseball Cards,* VI (June 1986), 24–27.

53941. Fimrite, Ron. "Blood on the Dodger Blue." *Sports Illustrated,* XLIX (September 4, 1978), 24–25. Both

the Bell and Fimrite entries deal with a Sutton-Steve Garvey feud.

53942. _____. "God May Be a Football Fan." *Sports Illustrated,* LVII (July 12, 1982), 64–68.

53943. Grayson, Robert. "Don Sutton: Cooperstown was Always the Goal." *Sports Collector's Digest,* XXV (August 7, 1998), 120–121.

53944. Herskowitz, Mickey. "Houston Bets a Fortune That Don Can Break the Jinx." *Sport,* LXXII (June 1981), 26–32.

53945. Hoard, Greg, "Lofty Goals Keep Don Button Bearing Down." *Baseball Digest,* XLI (August 1982), 27–30.

53946. Kuenster, Bob. "Hall of Fame Doors Finally Opened for Don Sutton." *Baseball Digest,* LVII (April 1998), 72–73.

53947. Lipton, Jack P. "Donald Howard 'Don' Sutton." In: Vol. Q-Z of David L. Porter, ed. *Biographical Dictionary of American Sports: Baseball.* Rev. and enlarged ed. Westport, CT: Greenwood Press, 2000. Pp. 1505–1507.

53948. Markus, Robert. "Don Sutton: Will He Be the Best Dodger Pitcher Ever?" *Baseball Digest,* XXXVI (May 1977), 34–37.

53949. McKay, Joe. "Don Sutton: The Quiet and Consistent Performer." In: his *The Great Shutout Pitchers: 20 Profiles of a Vanishing Breed.* Jefferson, NC: McFarland & Co., Inc., 2004. Pp. 110–122.

53950. Newhan, Ross. "Little D's Big Day." *Dodgers Dugout,* XIII (July 30, 1998), 3–4. Induction into National Baseball Hall of Fame.

53951. "Player Profile: Don Sutton." *What's Brewing,* VIII (April 1980), 20–21.

53952. Reilly, Sue. "Don and Patti Sutton Were Striking Out 'till They Got Help—and Now They're Safe at Home." *People Weekly,* XVII (April 5, 1982), 89–93.

53953. Shannon, Mike. "Don Sutton." In: his *Tales from the Ballpark: More of the Greatest True Baseball Stories Ever Told.* Lincolnwood, IL: Contemporary Books, 1999. Pp. 196–197.

53954. Sorci, Rick. "Baseball Profile: Former Pitcher Don Sutton." *Baseball Digest,* LIV (January 1995), 45–46.

53955. Sutton, Don. *How to Throw a Curveball.* Chicago, IL: Follett Publishing Co., 1977. 184p.

53956. Sutton, Don. "My Greatest Day in Baseball." In: Eliot Cohen, ed. *My Greatest Day in Baseball.* New York: Little Simon, 1991. Pp. 128–131.

53957. _____., as told to George Vass. "The Game I'll Never Forget." *Baseball Digest,* XLIII (November 1984), 25–27. 1977 All-Star Game.

53958. Verrell, Gordon. "Sutton Gets Call from the Hall; Winningest Dodger Pitcher Voted in on Fifth Try." *Dodgers Dugout,* XII (January 1998), 1–2.

53959. "A Very Special K for Don Sutton." *What's Brewing,* VII (July 1983), 4–11.

53960. Weider, Robert S. "Don Sutton: An Unsung Achiever Among Mound Elite." *Baseball Digest,* XLIV (September 1985), 31–34.

53961. Westcott, Rich. "Don Sutton: Never Missed a Turn." In: his *Winningest Pitchers: Baseball's 300-Game Winners.* Philadelphia, PA: Temple University Press, 2002. Pp. 167–176.

Ezra Ballou Sutton
3B. (B: Sept. 17, 1850, Palmyra, NY-D: June 20, 1907). Forest City (N.A.), 1871–1872; Philadelphia (N.A./NL), 1873–1876; Boston (NL), 1877–1888. Remarks: Obtained 1,574 hits (25 homers) in 1,263 games in 19 big league seasons; made error in first NL game, 1876; led NL in hits

(162), 1884; also played for Rochester (I.A.), 1888 and Milwaukee (W.A.), 1889.

53962. Ivor-Campbell, Frederick. "Ezra Ballou Sutton." In: Vol. Q-Z of David L. Porter, ed. *Biographical Dictionary of American Sports: Baseball.* Rev. and enlarged ed. Westport, CT: Greenwood Press, 2000. Pp. 1508–1509.

Lawrence ("Larry") Sutton
SCOUT. (B:1858-D: 1944). A semi-pro manager/umpire who became one of the first MLB full-time scouts in 1909; worked for Brooklyn (NL), Detroit (AL), Philadelphia (NL), and Cincinnati (NL), discovering 100 big league players, including Casey Stengel and Zack Wheat.

53963. Sutton, Larry, as told to Hugh Bradley. "I Have Bought $1,000,000 Worth of Men: A Big League Scout Tells How to Make Makes Stars in Baseball or Business." *American Magazine,* CXV (February 1933), 44–46.

Ichiro Suzuki
OF. (B: Oct. 22, 1973, Kasugai, Japan). Orix Blue Wave (Japan League), 1992-2000; Seattle (AL), 2001-. Remarks: In nine Japan League (J.L.) seasons, obtained 1,278 hits (118 homers) and 199 stolen bases in 951 games; J.L. batting champion, 1994–2000; J.L. stolen base champion, 1995; J.L. stolen base champion, 1995; through 2004, has had 924 hits (37 homers) and 157 stolen bases in 634 U.S. MLB games; A. L. MVP Award, 2001; AL batting and stolen base champion, 2001; AL batting champion, 2004; established record for multihit games (80), 2004; with 262, eclipsed George Sisler's (q.v.) 84-year old record for most hits in a single season, 2004.

53963a. Ballantine, Brett. "Ichiro Suzuki: King of the Hit." *Baseball Digest,* LXIV (April 2005), 63–66.

53964. Bradley, Jeff. "East2West." *ESNP: The Magazine,* IV (May 14, 2001), 70–77.

53965. _____. "The Flash." *ESPN: The Magazine,* V (May 27, 2002), 70–77.

53966. Cannella, Stephen. "Batting Practice: Pitchers Still Can't Solve the Riddle of How to Get Seattle's Ichiro Suzuki Out." *Sports Illustrated,* XCVI (June 10, 2002), 101–102.

53966a. Dougherty, Terri. *Ichiro Suzuki.* Let's Meet Biographies Series. Minneapolis, MN: Abdo Publishing, 2003. 32p. Juvenile.

53967. Etkin, Jack. "Ichiro Mania." *Baseball Digest,* LX (December 2001), 40–45.

53968. Farber, Michael. "Rising Son: The Defection of Ichiro Suzuki, a Career .353 Hitter, Isn't Seen as All Bad News in Japan, if He Becomes a Sensation with the Mariners and Brings Honor to His Country." *Sports Illustrated,* XCIII (December 4, 2000), 68–71, 73.

53969. Finnigan, Bob. "Hitting Machine." *Baseball Digest,* LXI (November 2002), 22–27.

53969a. Leigh, David S. *Ichiro Suzuki.* Sports Heroes and Legends Series. Minneapolis, MN: Lerner, 2004. 106p.

53970. Leiker, Ken. "29–2001: Inchiro Cross the Pacific, Wins Two Major Awards, and is the Fan's Top Choice for the All-Star Game." In: his *Major League Baseball Memorable Moments: The Most Memorable Moments in Major League Baseball History.* New York: Ballantine Books, 2002. Pp. 146–149.

53971. Lorton, Steven R. "Ichiro's Town: Uncovering Japanese Seattle." *Sunset,* CCVIII (April 2002), 43–44.

53972. Price, S. L. "The Ichiro Paradox." *Sports Illustrated,* XCVII (July 8, 2002), 50+.

53972a. Rappoport, Ken. *Ichiro Suzuki.* Super Sports Stars Series. Hillside, NJ: Enslow Publishers, 2004. 48p.

53973. Schwarz, Alan. "Ichiro Steals the Show." *Sports Illustrated for Kids,* XIII (August 1, 2001), 46–47.

53974. _____. "Inside Ichiro." *Sports Illustrated for Kids,* XIV (April 2002), 29–36.

53975. Sherwin, Bob and Yukiko Shimizu. *Ichiro: Meja o Shinkan Saseta Otoko.* Tokyo, Japan: Asahi Shinbunsha, 2002. 293p.

53976. Shields, David. "Being Ichiro." *The New York Times Magazine,* (September 16, 2001), 50–58.

53977. _____. , with Ichiro Suzuki. *Baseball is Just Baseball: The Understated Ichiro.* New York: TNI Books, 2001. 120p.

53978. Stern, Kate. "Ichiro Suzuki." *Current Biography,* LXIII (July 2002), 78–82. Reprinted in *Current Biography Yearbook, 2002.* New York: H. W. Wilson, 2002. Pp. 545–548.

53979. Stevens, Christopher A. "Orient Express." *Beckett Baseball Card Monthly,* XVIII (July 2001), 130+.

53980. Stewart, Mark. *Ichiro Suzuki: Best in the West.* Brookfield, CT: Millbrook Press, 2002. 48p.

53981. Stout, Glenn and Matt Christopher. *At the Plate with — Ichiro.* Boston, MA: Little, Brown, 2003. 95p.

53982. Suzuki, Ichiro. *Ichiro on Ichiro: Interviews with Narumi Komatsu.* Seattle, WA: Sasquatch Books, 2004. 256p.

53983. Thiel, Art. "No Angst in All-Star Ichiro." In: Rick Reilly, ed. *The Best American Sports Writing, 2002.* Boston, MA: Houghton, Mifflin, 2002. Pp. 141–145. Reprinted from the July 6, 2001 issue of the *Seattle Post-Intelligencer.*

53984. Van Dyck, Dave. "Hitting Sensation: Seattle's Ichiro Suzuki." *Baseball Digest,* XLIII (December 2004), 20–27.

53985. Whitehouse, Erin. "Ichiro." In: Richard Levin, ed. *2001 World Series Official Program.* New York: Major League Baseball Promotion Corp., 2001. Pp. 80–85.

53986. Whiting, Robert. "Around the Horn: *Time* Sent Author Robert Whiting to Find Out Seattle Mariner Ichiro Suzuki's Take on Japan's Player Drain, the Future of U.S. Baseball and His Own Hyped-up Image — An Interview. *Time International,* CLX (November 18, 2002), 48+.

53987. "Winners, Losers: Asia's Hottest New Sports Export, Ichiro Suzuki, is Proving a Spectacular Hit with Seattle Baseball Fans, But Journeying to West is Proving Less Easy for Some of the Region's Other Stars." *Far Eastern Economic Review,* CLXIV (2001), 66–69.

53988. Wonham, Linc. *Ichiro: the Making of an American Hero.* Chicago, IL: Triumph Books , 2002. 48p.

Dale Curtis Sveum
3B-2B-SS. (B: Nov. 23, 1963, Richmond, CA). Milwaukee (AL), 1986–1991; Philadelphia (NL) and Chicago (AL), 1992; Oakland (AL), 1993; Seattle (AL), 1994; Pittsburgh (NL), 1996–1997; New York (AL), 1998; Pittsburgh (NL), 1999. Remarks: In 12 big league seasons, obtained 597 hits (69 homers) and 10 stolen bases in 862 games; had three homers and six RBIs in one game, July 17, 1986.

53989. Beach, Jerry. "The Time of His Life." *Yankees Magazine,* XIX (August 1998), 30–35.

Craig Steven Swan
P. (B: Nov. 30, 1950, Van Nuys, CA). New York (NL), 1973–1984; California (AL), 1984. Remarks: Won 59 games and lost 72, with two "saves," in 12 years; career ended by injuries.

53990. Fimrite, Ron. "The Second Time Around." *Sports Illustrated,* LXX (January 9, 1989), 110–114+.

Karl Edward Swanson
2B. (B: Dec. 17, 1900, North Henderson, IL-D: April 3, 2002). Chicago (AL), 1928–1929. Remarks: In all or parts

of two big league seasons, obtained nine hits and three stolen bases in 24 games.

53991. Wilson, Nick. "Karl Swanson." In: his *Voices from the Pastime: Oral Histories of Surviving Major Leaguers, Negro Leaguers, Cuban Leaguers, and Writers, 1920–1934.* Jefferson, NC: McFarland & Co., Inc., 2000. Pp. 73–81.

George Alexander ("No Sweat") Sweatt
OF-2B-3B-1B-C. (B: Dec. 12, 1893, Humbolt, KA–D: July 19, 1983). Kansas City Monarchs, 1921–1925; Chicago American Giants, 1926–1928; Chicago Giants, 1928. Remarks: Career .200+ hitter; only regular player to appear in all four World Series between the Negro National League and the Eastern Colored League; joined Post Office in 1928, where he was employed until 1957.

53992. Holway, John B. "George Sweatt: 'No Sweat' Would Take Two Strikes, Then Tear Cover Off Ball." *Black Sports,* V (September 1975), 49–51.

Charles J. ("Charlie") Sweeney
P. (B: April 13, 1863, San Francisco, CA–D: April 4, 1902). Providence (NL), 1882–1884; St. Louis (U), 1884; Cleveland (NL), 1885–1887. Remarks: Won 64 games and lost 52 in six seasons. On June 7, 1884, struck out 19 batters, a MLB record for a nine-inning game not broken for 102 years (Clemens, April 29, 1986). Also that year (after winning 17 games), expelled from NL for leaving a game in the middle; signed by new Union Association and finished the season with 24 more victories for his new team; both Providence and St. Louis were helped to 1884 pennant's by Sweeney's hurling; convicted of an 1894 San Francisco saloon murder, Sweeney died in prison.

53993. Franks, Joel. "Sweeney of San Francisco: A Local Boy Makes Good, Then Not So Good." *Baseball History,* II (Winter 1987–1988), 52–62.

53994. Harshman, Jack E. "The Radbourn and Sweeney Saga." *The Baseball Research Journal,* XVIII (1990), 7–9.

53995. Ivor-Campbell, Frederick. "Charles Radbourn(e), Jr." In: his *Baseball's First Stars.* Cleveland, OH: Society for American Baseball Research, 1996. Pp. 131–132.

53996. _____. "Sweeney's Whiff Feat of 1884 Rates No. 1." *The Baseball Research Journal,* XIV (1985), 57–60.

53997. Kermish, Al. "Unusual Five-Inning No-hitter in 1884." *The Baseball Research Journal,* XII (1983), 49–50. Sweeney's suspended game.

53998. Tackach, James. "Hazards and Tips for Researchers." *The Baseball Research Journal,* XV (1986), 86–89. Researching Sweeney.

Michael John ("Mike") Sweeney
1B. (B: July 22, 1973, Orange, CA). Kansas City (AL), 1995–. Remarks: Through 2004, has had 1,132 hits (161 homers) and 45 stolen bases in 1,026 games; had 25-game hitting streak, 1999; AL hit by pitcher leader, 2000; injured much of 2004.

53999. Bradley, Jeff. "Blue Crush." *ESPN the Magazine,* VI (May 12, 2003), 84–88.

54000. Doyle, Al. "From Royal Blue to Solid Gold: Mike Sweeney Finds Stardom in K.C." *Baseball Digest,* LX (January 2001), 44–47.

54001. Kaegel, Dick. "Ready for Battle." *Baseball Digest,* LX (November 2001), 78–81.

54002. Pearlman, Jeff. "A Run of Luck." *Sports Illustrated,* XCIII (July 24, 2000), 50–52, 55.

Ricky Joe ("Rick") Sweet
C. (B: Sept. 7, 1952, Longview, WA). San Diego (NL), 1978; New York (NL) and Seattle (AL), 1982; Seattle (AL), 1983. Remarks: Had 172 hits (six hits) and six stolen bases in 272 games in three big league seasons; coach, Seattle (AL), 1984; manager, Bellingham (Northwest League), 1987; Wausau (Midwest League), 1988; Oseola (Florida State League), 1989; Columbus, 1990–1991; Tucson (PCL), 1993–1995; coach, Houston (NL), 1996; Binghampton, 1997; Harrisburg (EL), 1998; minor league field coordinator, Montreal (NL), 1999–2000; manager, Portland (P.C.L), 2001–2003; manager, Erie (EL), 2004-.

54003. Ballard, S. "Houston Astros Named Rick Sweet Manager of Osceola of the Florida State League." *Sports Illustrated,* LXIX (December 12, 1988), 88–89.

Bill Swift (1) *see* **William Charles ("Bill") Swift**
Bill Swift (2) *see* **William Vincent ("Bill") Swift**
Bob Swift *see* **Robert Virgil ("Bob") Swift**
Robert Virgil ("Bob") Swift
C-MGR. (B: March 6, 1915, Salina, KA–D: Oct. 7, 1966) Philadelphia (AL), 1942–1943; Detroit (AL), 1944–1953 Remarks: in 14 seasons, had 635 hits (14 homers) and 10 stolen bases; behind the plate on August 18, 1951 when St. Louis (AL) sent midget Eddie Gaedel (q.v.) to bat; later, coach Detroit (AL), 1953–1954, 1963–1966; Tigers interim manager, 1965–1966, winning 56 games and losing 43 (.566).

54004. Swift, Bob. "A Baseball Is a Projectile." *Science Illustrated,* I (August 1946), 6–7. Catchers' equipment demonstrated by Swift.

William Charles ("Bill") Swift
P. (B: Oct. 27, 1961, Portland, ME). Seattle (AL), 1985–1991; San Francisco (NL), 1992–1994; Colorado (NL), 1995–1997; Seattle (AL), 1998. Remarks: In 13 years, had 94 victories, 78 defeats, and 27 "saves"; also hurled for 1984 U.S. Olympic baseball team.

54005. Buckley, Steve. "A Deeper Look: Bill Swift." *Beckett Baseball Card Monthly,* IX, no. 89 (August 1992), 122–123.

William Vincent ("Bill") Swift
P. (B: Jan. 10, 1908, Elmira, NY–D: Feb. 23, 1969). Pittsburgh (NL), 1932–1939; Boston (N.L), 1940; Brooklyn (NL), 1941; Chicago (AL), 1943. Remarks: In an 11-year big league career, had 96 victories, 82 defeats, and 20 "saves"; relied on fastball thrown from the side.

54006. Bloodgood, Clifford. "His Speed Ball is as Swift as His Name." *Baseball Magazine,* XLIX (November 1932), 557–558.

Forest Gregory ("Greg") Swindell
P-COACH. (B: Jan. 2, 1965, Fort Worth, TX). Cleveland (AL), 1986–1991; Cincinnati (NL), 1992; Houston (NL), 1993–1996; Cleveland (AL), 1996; Minnesota (AL), 1997–1998; Boston (AL), 1998; Arizona (NL), 1999–2002. Remarks: Through 2002, won 123 games and lost 122, with seven "saves"; pitched for 1984 U.S. Olympic baseball team; struck out 15 batters in one game, May 10, 1987; volunteer asst. baseball coach, University of Texas, 2003.

54007. Dolgan, Bob. "The Indians' Greg Swindell Makes His Pitch." *Baseball Digest,* XLVII (September 1988), 28–32.

54008. Glassman, Brian. "Guaranteed." *Elysian Fields Quarterly,* XI (Spring 1992), 70–72.

Greg Swindell *see* **Forest Gregory ("Greg") Swindell**
Ronald Alan ("Ron" or "Rocky") Swoboda
OF-BROADCASTER. (B. June 30, 1944, Baltimore, MD). New York (NL), 1965–1970; Montreal (NL), 1971; New York (AL), 1971–1973. Remarks: Obtained 624 hits (73 homers) and 20 stolen bases in 927 games in nine years; had grand slam homer, Sept. 13, 1969; had six hits in 1969 World Series; also played for Buffalo (IL) and Williamsport (EL), 1964; local television sports commentator, New York, Milwaukee, and New Orleans, 1975-.

54009. Allen, Maury. "With Swoboda, Every Day's an Adventure." *Sport,* XL (September 1965), 54–45+.Len Pasculli's Swoboda profile is a number in the online SABR Biography Project http://bioproj.sabr.org/bioproj.cfm?a=v&v=l&bid=1103&pid=13929.

54010. Appel, Marty. "Ron Swoboda." In: his *Yesterday's Heroes: Revisiting the Old-Time Baseball Stars.* New York: William Morrow, 1988. pp. 212–216.

54011. Astor, Gerald. "Super Swatter." *Look,* XXXII (July 23,1968), M12-M14.

54012. Broeg, Bob. "Ron Swoboda: A Throwback to Marvelous Marv." *Baseball Digest,* XXVIII (December 1969), 42–45.

54013. Gallant, Bill. "Ron Swoboda: Can Talent Catch Up with Desire?" *All-Star Sports,* II (June 1968), 40–43.

54014. Leggett, William. "A Sultan of Swat from Sparrow's Point." *Sports Illustrated,* XXII (June 14, 1965), 70+.

54015. Robinson, Ray. "Ron Swoboda: Met Wunderkind." In: Ray Robinson, ed. *Baseball Stars of 1966.* New York: Pyramid Books, 1966. Pp. 126–131.

54016. Swoboda Ronald A. "Seaver, the Mets, and Me." *Sport,* LII (July 1971), 44–47.

Patrick Sean ("Pat") Tabler

1B-OF. (B: February 2, 1958, Hamilton, OH). Chicago (NL), 1981–1982; Cleveland (AL), 1983–1988; Kansas City (AL), 1988–1990; New York (NL), 1990; Toronto (AL), 1991–1992. In 12 big league seasons, obtained 1,101 hits (47 homers) and 16 stolen bases in 1,202 games; highly-regarded clutch hitter later employed by the Sports Network in Toronto.

54017. Glassman, Brian. "From the Inside (Looking Out)." *Minneapolis Review of Baseball,* VIII (January 1988), 9–10. Interview.

James Raubin ("Jim" or "Rawhide") Tabor

3B. (B: Nov. 5, 1913, Owens Crossroads, AL-D: Aug. 22, 1953) Boston (AL), 1938–1944; Philadelphia (NL), 1946–1947. Remarks: Obtained 1,021 hits (104 homers) and 69 stolen bases in 1,005 games in nine seasons; had two "grand slams" and plus a one-run homer in one game on July 4, 1939; only pitcher to hit three grand slams in one game, May 13, 1942; also played for Sacramento (PCL), 1948–1950.

54018. Dittmar, Joe. "Tabor's Slams Lead Hit Parade: July 4, 1939." In: his *Box Scores.* Fairview Village, PA: Joseph J. Dittmar, 1988. Pp. 44–45.

54019. Spatz, Lyle. "James Raubin 'Jim,' 'Rawhide' Tabor." In: Vol. Q-Z of David L. Porter, ed. *Biographical Dictionary of American Sports: Baseball.* Rev. and enlarged ed. Westport, CT: Greenwood Press, 2000. Pp. 1511–1512.

William Howard Taft

PRESIDENT-POLITICIAN-JUDGE. (B: Sept. 15, 1857, Cincinnati, OH-D: March 8, 1930). Remarks: Lawyer, politician, first civil governor of the Philippines, 1900–1904; Secretary of War, 1904–1908, president of the United States, 1909–1912; Yale professor, 1913–1921; U.S. chief justice, 1921–1930; inaugurated tradition of U.S. president throwing out first baseball of the MLB big league season, April 14, 1910.

54020. Curreri, Joe. "Presidential First Love." *Boys' Quest,* (December 1998-January 1999), 33–35.

54021. Murphy, Charles W. "Taft, the Fan." *Baseball Magazine,* IX (July 1912), 1–9.

Frank Daryl Tanana

P. (B: July 3, 1953, Detroit, MI). California (AL), 1973–1980; Boston (AL), 1981; Texas (AL), 1982–1985; Detroit (AL), 1985–1992; New York (NL) and New York (AL), 1993. Remarks: Won 240 games and lost 236 in 13 years; struck out 17 batters in one game, June 21, 1975; lost one game of 1987 ALCS; holds AL record for most career homers allowed (422) and most career wins without a 20-game victory season.

54022. Alexson, Bill. "Frank Tanana, Detroit Tigers." In: his *Batting a Thousand, Book 2.* Nashville, TN: Thomas Nelson Publishers, 1990. Pp. 52–56.

54023. Cerrone, Rick. "Tame Tanana." Baseball Quarterly, II (Winter 1978–1979), 32–37.

54024. Debs, Victor, Jr. "Frank Tanana." In: his *"That Was Part of Baseball Then": Interviews with 24 Former Major League Baseball Players, Coaches, and Managers.* Jefferson, NC: McFarland & Co., Inc., 2002. Pp. 171–176.

54025. Distel, Dave. "Frank Tanana: The Angels' Rapid Rookie" *Baseball Digest,* XXXIII (July 1974), 34–37.

54026. Fimrite, Ron. "Not Enough Pop to Come out on Top." *Sports Illustrated,* L (April 16, 1979), 50+.

54027. _____. "This Guy Tanana's No Second Banana." *Sports Illustrated,* XLVII (July 11, 1977), 38–43.

54028. Heisler, Mark. "Frank Tanana: The Man with the Not-So-Golden Arm.*" Baseball Digest,* XXXVIII (June 1979), 31–33.

54029. Hill, Terry. "Frank Tanana: 'All-Star Team, #1 In Strikeouts, #1 In ERA, Still Empty Inside!" In: his *Batting a Thousand.* Nashville, TN: Thomas Nelson, 1987. Pp. 72–76.

54030. Kay, Tommy. "Frank Tanana." In: Tommy Kay, ed. *Tommy Kay's Big Book of Baseball.* Scottsdale, AZ: Jalart House, 1979. Pp. 74–81.

54031. Klein, Moss. "Tanana-Ryan: Best Lefty-Righty Duo Since Koufax-Drysdale?" *Baseball Digest,* XXXVI (August 1977), 30–37.

54032. Klima, John. "Death of the Fastball: Jimmy Key vs. Frank Tanana (October 4, 1987)." In: his *Pitched Battle: 35 of Baseball's Greatest Duels from the Mound.* Jefferson, NC: McFarland & Co., Inc., 2002. Pp. 146–150.

54033. Lincoln, Eric. "How an Elbow Injury Refined Frank Tanana as a Pitcher." *Baseball Digest,* XXXVII (November 1974), 62–65.

54034. Miller, Dick. "Frank Tanana: A Lefty Headed Right for the Hall Of Fame." *Baseball Digest,* XXXVI (May 1977), 54–55.

54035. Shook, Richard. "A Deeper Look: Frank Tanana." *Beckett Baseball Card Monthly,* VIII (December 1991), 108–109.

54036. Spencer, Lyle. "Frank Tanana: Best of the Young Southpaws." *Baseball Digest,* XXXIV (December 1975), 82–84.

54037. Sutton, William A. and Robert S. Butcher. "Frank Daryl Tanana." In: Vol. Q-Z of David L. Porter, ed. *Biographical Dictionary of American Sports: Baseball.* Rev. and enlarged ed. Westport, CT: Greenwood Press, 2000. Pp. 1512–1513.

54038. Tanana, Frank, as told to George Vass. "The Game I'll Never Forget." *Baseball Diges*t, LII (July 1993), 55–56.

54039. Wischnia, Bob. "Faultless Frank." *Sport,* LXIV (May 1977), 32–35.

Jesse Niles Tannehill

P-UMP. (B: July 14, 1874, Dayton, KY-D: Sept. 22, 1956). Cincinnati (NL), 1894; Pittsburgh (NL), 1897–1902; New York (AL), 1903; Boston (AL), 1904–1908; Washington (AL), 1908–1909; Cincinnati (NL), 1911. In 15 big league seasons, won 194 games and lost 119, with eight "saves" and one no-hitter (Aug. 17, 1904); as a batter, had 361 hits (six homers) and 19 stolen bases; also played for Minneapolis (AA), 1910; Birmingham (SA) and Montgomery (SA), 1911; South Bend (Central League) and Chillicothe (Ohio State League), 1912; and St. Joseph (WL), 1913; manager, Portsmouth (Virginia League), 1914 and Topeka (Southwest League), 1923; umpire, Ohio State League, 1916, IL, 1917, and WL 1920.

54040. Merrell, David B. "Jesse Niles Tannehill." In: Vol. Q–Z of David L. Porter, ed. *Biographical Dictionary of American Sports: Baseball.* Rev. and enlarged ed. Westport, CT: Greenwood Press, 2000. Pp. 1513–1514.

Charles William ("Chuck") Tanner, Jr.

OF-MGR. (B: July 4, 1929, New Castle, PA). Milwaukee (NL), 1955–1957; Chicago (N.L), 1957–1958; Cleveland (AL), 1959–1960; Los Angeles (AL), 1961–1962. Remarks: Had 231 hits (21 homers) in 396 games in eight playing seasons; minor league manager, 1963–1970; manager, Chicago (AL), 1970–1975; Oakland (AL), 1976; Pittsburgh (NL), 1977–1985, and Atlanta (NL), 1986–1988, winning 1,352 games and losing 1,381 (.495); special asst./scout, Milwaukee (AL/NL), 1992-date.

54041. Feeney, Charlie. "Chuck Tanner: All-American Person." In: Bill Shumard, ed. *1980 All-Star Game Program.* Los Angeles, CA: Public Relations Department, Los Angeles Dodgers, 1980. Pp. 7–8.

54042. Jones, Robert F. "Hula, Moolah and No Blahs." *Sports Illustrated,* XXXIII (August 24, 1970), 40–41. Tanner and the Hawaii Islanders.

54043. O'Laughlin, Joe. "Where are They Now?: Former Manager Chuck Tanner." *Baseball Digest,* LXIII (November 2004), 72–75.

54044. Porter, David L. "Charles William 'Chuck' Tanner, Jr. "In: Vol. Q–Z of David L. Porter, ed. *Biographical Dictionary of American Sports: Baseball.* Rev. and enlarged ed. Westport, CT: Greenwood Press, 2000. Pp. 1514–1515.

54045. Tanner, Charles W. ("Chuck"), as told to George Vass. "The Game I'll Never Forget." *Baseball Digest,* XXXIX (November 1980), 50–55.

54046. _____. and Jim Enright, eds. *The Official Major League Playbook.* Englewood Cliffs, N.J.: Prentice-Hall, 1964. 160p. Revised as…

54047. _____. *Chuck Tanner's Baseball Playbook: Major League Strategy for the 1980s.* New York: Smith Publications, 1981. 158p. Advice with diagrams from the longtime manager of the Pittsburgh Pirates.

54048. Vanderberg, Bob. "Chuck Tanner: Richie Allen and Rose-Colored Glasses." In: his *Sox — From Lane and Fain to Zisk and Fisk.* Chicago, IL: Chicago Review Press, 1982. Pp. 99–110.

54049. Wade, Ed. "Tanner's Fortune Can't Be Measured in Dollars and Cents." In: Ed Wade, ed. *The Pirates' Official 1983 Yearbook.* Pittsburgh, PA: Geyer Printing Co., 1983. Pp. 2–4.

Edwin Tapia

SCOUT. Los Angeles (NL)

54050. DeVoss, David. "Edwin Tapia Gets His Chance with the Dodgers." In: Tom Barnidge, ed. *Best Sports Stories of 1987.* St. Louis, MO: *The Sporting News,* 1987. Pp. 20–29. Recruiting Latinos.

Elvin Walter ("El") Tappe

MGR. (B: May 21, 1927, Quincy, IL–D: Oct. 11, 2001). Remarks: Manager, Chicago (NL), 1961–1962, winning 46 games and losing 70 (.397); coach, Chicago (NL), 1958–1965; also played for Los Angeles (PCL), 1952–1957; scout, Chicago (NL), 1965–1975; local broadcaster, Quincy, IL, 1975–2000.

54051. Skipper, John C. "Vedie Himsl and Elvin Tappe:

Two Years without a Manager?" In: his *Inside Pitch: A Closer Look at Classic Baseball Moments.* Jefferson, NC: McFarland & Co., Inc., 1996. Pp. 42–45.

Anthony ("Tony") Tarasco

OF. (B: Dec. 9, 1970, New York City). Atlanta (NL), 1993–1994; Montreal (NL), 1995; Baltimore (AL), 1996–1997; Cincinnati (NL), 1998; New York (AL), 1999. Remarks: Obtained 217 hits (28 homers) and 37 stolen bases in 397 games for five teams in seven years; had one pinch grand slam homer, Sept. 21, 1998.

54052. Koenig, Bill. "Tarasco Going Like Gang-Busters: Gift with a Bat Gets Him Out of the 'Hood.'" *USA Today Baseball Weekly,* V (May 24, 1995), 4–5.

Tony Tarasco *see* **Anthony ("Tony") Tarasco**

Danilo Mora ("Danny" or "Bull") Tartabull

OF. (B: Oct. 30, 1963, San Juan, PR). Seattle (AL), 1984–1986; Kansas City (AL), 1987–1991; New York (AL), 1992–1995; Oakland (AL), 1995; Chicago (AL), 1996; Philadelphia (NL), 1997. Remarks: Had 1,366 hits (282 homers) and 37 stolen bases in 1,406 games in 14 seasons; also played for Calgary (PCL), had 40 homers and was that league's MVP, 1985; had two inside-the-park homers, Oct. 1987 and May 1988; first Royal to hit three homers in one game, July 6, 1991; went 5-for-5 with nine RBIs, Sept. 8, 1992; had 11 career grand slam homers; portrayed a Yankee player in "The Pledge Drive" episode of the TV comedy series *Seinfeld,* 2003; son of Jose Tartabull (below).

54053. Dewan, John and Don Zminda. "New York Yankees: Will Danny Get Hurt Again This Year?" In: STATS, Inc. *STATS 1993 Baseball Scoreboard.* New York: Harper Perennial, 1993. Pp. 28–30.

54054. English, John T. "Danilo Mora 'Danny,' 'Bull' Tartabull." In: Vol. Q–Z of David L. Porter, ed. *Biographical Dictionary of American Sports: Baseball.* Rev. and enlarged ed. Westport, CT: Greenwood Press, 2000. Pp. 1515–1516.

54055. Gergen, Joe. "Danny Tartabull: He Surpasses His Father." *Baseball Digest,* LI (June 1992), 42–43. Son of major leaguer Jose Tartabull.

54056. Green, Paul M. "Danny Tartabull: Interview." *Baseball Cards,* VIII (February 1988), 70–77.

54057. Kurkjian, Tim. "Raging Bull." *Sports Illustrated,* LXXV (August 5, 1991), 36–37.

54058. Newman, Bruce. "Bright Light, New City." *Sports Illustrated,* LXXVI (March 23, 1992), 56–59.

54059. Nightengale, Bob. "Danny Tartabull Spurred By Desire for Stardom." *Baseball Digest ,* XLVII (July 1988), 72–74.

54060. Shalen, Mike. "A Second Look: Danny Tartabull." *Beckett Baseball Card Monthly,* VIII (November 1991), 97–101.

54061. Strong, Tom. "Danny Tartabull: Mariner with a Bright Future." *Baseball Digest,* XLVI (February 1987), 35–36.

54062. Thornton, K. D. "Danny Tartabull." In: Ken Collier, ed. *The Baseball Book, 1987.* Scottsdale, AZ: Jalart House, 1987. Pp. 117–118.

54063. Weinberg, Rick. "One-on-One: Danny Tartabull." *Sport,* LXXXIII (May 1992), 18–20.

Danny Tartabull *see* **Danilo Mora ("Danny" or "Bull") Tartabull**

Jose Guzman Tartabull

OF. (B: Dec. 17, 1938, Cienfuegos, Cuba). Kansas City (AL), 1962–1966; Boston (AL), 1966–1968; Oakland (AL), 1969–1970. Remarks: Obtained 484 hits (two homers) and 81 stolen bases in 749 games in nine years; had two hits in 1967 World Series; named to Cuban Baseball Hall of Fame, 1997; father of Danny Tartabull (above).

54064. Gergen, Joe. "Danny Tartabull: He Surpasses His Father." *Baseball Digest,* LI (June 1992), 42–43.

Willie Tasby

OF. (B: March 18, 1932, Black Rock, AL). St. Louis (NL), 1958–1959. Remarks: Had 14 hits (one homer) in 51 games in two years; colorful character who, on one occasion, played center field in his bare feet, afraid that lightning would strike his metal cleats; had one grand slam homer, June 18, 1961.

54065. Moffi, Larry and Jonathan Kronstadt. "Willie Tasby." In: their *Crossing the Line: Black Major Leaguers, 1947–1959.* Jefferson, N.C.: McFarland & Co., Inc., 1994. Pp. 193–194.

Edward Kenneth ("Eddie") Taubensee

C. (B: Oct. 31, 1968, Beeville, TX). Cleveland (AL), 1991; Houston (NL), 1992–1994; Cincinnati (NL), 1994–2000; Cleveland (AL), 2001. Remarks: In 11 big league years, obtained 784 hits (94 homers) and 11 stolen bases in 975 games; had a hit in 1995 NLCS; also played for Colorado Springs (PCL) and Tucson (PCL).

54066. Ditchfield, Christin. "Right Where He Needs to Be." *Share the Victory,* XX (June-July 2002), 12–14.

Julian Tavarez

P. (B: Julian Tavarez Carmen, May 22, 1973, Santiago, Dominican Republic). Cleveland (AL), 1993–1996; San Francisco (NL), 1997–1999; Colorado (NL), 2000; Chicago (NL), 2001; Florida (NL), 2002; Pittsburgh (NL), 2003; St. Louis (NL), 2004–. Remarks: Through 2004, has won 70 games and lost 52, with 17 "saves" ; lost one game in both the 1995 ALCS and 2004 NLCS and 2004 World Series, but won two games in 2004 NLCS.

54067. Epstein, Eddie. "Julian Tavarez." In: STATS, Inc. *The STATS 1995 Minor League Scouting Notebook.* Skokie, IL: STATS Publishing, 1995. Pp. 157–158.

Antonio Sanchez ("Tony") Taylor

2B-3B. (B: Dec. 19, 1935, Central Alara, Cuba). Chicago (NL.), 1958–1960; Philadelphia (NL), 1960–1971; Detroit (AL), 1971–1973; Philadelphia (NL), 1974–1976. Remarks: Obtained 2,007 hits (75 homers) and 234 stolen bases in 2,195 games in 19 summer campaigns; stole home plate six times while playing for the Phillies; coach-instructor, Philadelphia (NL), 1970–1980, 1988–1989, San Francisco (NL), 1990–1992, and Florida (NL), 1999–2001, 2004–; named to Cuban Baseball Hall of Fame, 1981.

54068. Grady, Sandy. "Tony Taylor: The Flashy Phillie." *Sport,* XXXII (July 1961), 38–39+.

54069. Green, Lee. "Tony Taylor: Sparkplug in Philly." In: Ray Robinson, ed. *Baseball Stars of 1961.* New York: Pyramid Books, 1961. Pp. 144–151.

54070. Hochman, Stan. "Phils Claim Their Taylor Sews Up Second." *Baseball Digest,* XXIII (February 1964), 80–81.

54071. Kelly, Ray. "Life Begins at 40 for Tony Taylor." *Baseball Digest,* XXXV (May 1976), 31–33.

54072. Moffi, Larry and Jonathan Kronstadt. "Antonio Sanchez "Tony" Taylor." In: their *Crossing the Line; Black Major Leaguers, 1947–1959.* Jefferson, N.C.: McFarland & Co., Inc., 1994. Pp. 195–196.

54073. Rossi, John P. "Antonio Nemesio Sanchez 'Tony' Taylor." In: Vol. Q-Z of David L. Porter, ed. *Biographical Dictionary of American Sports: Baseball.* Rev. and enlarged ed. Westport, CT: Greenwood Press, 2000. Pp. 1516–1517.

54074. Williams, Edgar. "Tony Taylor: The All-Out Lad from Alara." *Baseball Digest,* XX (February 1961), 19–24.

Benjamin H. ("Ben") Taylor

P-1B-MGR-UMP. (B: July 1, 1888, Anderson, SC-D:

Jan. 24, 1953). Birmingham Giants, 1908–1909; West Baden Sprudels, 1910, 1913; St. Louis Giants, 1912; New York Lincoln Giants, 1912; Chicago American Giants, 1913–1914; Indianapolis ABCs, 1914–1918, 1920–1922; Hilldale Daisies and New York Bacharach Giants, 1919; Washington Potomacs, 1923–1924; Harrisburg Giants, 1925; Baltimore Black Sox, 1926–1928; Atlantic City Bacharach Giants, 1929; California Stars, 1930; Silver Moons, 1931. Remarks: Highly regarded outfielder, who managed teams after 1922 while still playing for them; Negro National League umpire, early 1930s; brother of Charles Isam ("C.I.") Taylor (below).

54075. Martin, Douglas S. "Benjamin H. 'Ben' Taylor." In: Vol. Q-Z of David L. Porter, ed. *Biographical Dictionary of American Sports: Baseball.* Rev. and enlarged ed. Westport, CT: Greenwood Press, 2000. Pp. 1517–1518.

Charles Isam ("C.I.") Taylor

2B-MGR-EXEC. (B: Jan. 20, 1875, SC-D: Feb. 23, 1922). Birmingham Giants, 1904–1909; West Baden Sprudels, 1910–1913; Indianapolis ABCs, 1914–1921. Remarks: One of two greatest Negro League managers (with Rube Foster), became player-manager in 1904, moving to West Baden, IN to take over the keystone position and managerial duties for the Sprudels; in 1914, transferred to the state capital to take over the team of the American Brewing Company; served as VP of the Negro National League from its foundation until his death; brother of Benjamin H. ("Ben") Taylor (above).

54076. Boulton, Todd. "C.I. Taylor." In: John A. Garrity and Marsh C. Carries, eds. *American National Biography.* 24 vols. New York: Oxford University Press, 1999. XXI, 360–361.

54077. Kleinknecht, Merl F. "Charles Isham 'C.I.' Taylor." In: Vol. Q-Z of David L. Porter, ed. *Biographical Dictionary of American Sports: Baseball.* Rev. and enlarged ed. Westport, CT: Greenwood Press, 2000. Pp. 1518–1519.

54078. Taylor, C. I. "The Future of Colored Baseball." *Competitor,* I (February 1920), 76–79.

Dummy Taylor *see* **Luther Haden ("Dummy") Taylor**

Frederick Winslow Taylor

EXEC. (B: March 20, 1856, Germantown, PA-D: March 21, 1915). Remarks: Engineer/inventor who pioneered and preached time study in industrial management.

54079. Kanigel, Robert. *One Best Way: Frederick Winslow Taylor and the Enigma of Efficiency.* Sloan Technology Series. New York: Viking Press, 1997. 656p.

54080. Risker, D. C. "Frederick Taylor's Use of the Baseball Team Metaphor: A Historical Perspective on Scientific Management and Baseball." *Nine: A Journal of Baseball History and Social Policy Perspective,* IV (Fall 1995), 1–10.

James Wren ("Zack") Taylor

C-MGR. (B: July 27, 1898, Yulee, FL-D: July 6, 1974). Brooklyn (NL), 1920–1925; Boston (NL), 1926–1927; New York (NL), 1927; Boston (NL), 1928–1929; Chicago (NL), 1929–1933; New York (AL), 1934; Brooklyn (NL), 1935. Remarks: In 16 playing years, had 748 hits (nine homers) and nine stolen bases in 918 games; coach, Brooklyn (NL), 1937; minor league player and manager, 1937–1940; coach, St. Louis (AL), 1941–1946 and Pittsburgh (NL), 1947; manager, St. Louis (AL), 1946, 1948–1951; minor league manager, 1952–1953; big league scout, 1954–1970; while managing Browns to 235 victories and 410 defeats (.364), Taylor (on orders from owner Bill Veeck) once allowed game strategy to be determined by a vote of the fans in the stands!

54081. Smith, Walter ("Red"). "'Career' Man Takes Over Browns." *Baseball Digest,* VIII (April 1949), 27–28.

54082. _____. "The Man without a Ball Club." *Sport,* IV (April 1948), 17+.

54083. Taylor, James W. ("Zack"). "A Sturdy Backstop with the 'Goods.'" *Baseball Magazine,* XXXVIII (March 1927), 451–452+.

Jack Taylor *see* **John W. ("Jack") Taylor**

John W. ("Jack") Taylor
P. (B. Sept. 13, 1873, Straightville, OH-D: March 4, 1938). Chicago (NL), 1898–1903; St. Louis (NL), 1904–1906; Chicago (NL), 1906–1907. Remarks: Had 150 victories and 139 defeats in a decade of pitching; completed 278 of 286 starts (97% rate highest in baseball history); hurled 187 complete games between June 20, 1901 and August 19, 1906, never once being relieved; tied MLB record for most consecutive games in a season (39), 1902; winner of first Chicago City Series (Chicago White Sox vs. Chicago Cubs), Oct. 1, 1903; as a batter, had 238 hits and two homers.

54084. Ahrens, Arthur R. "Jack Taylor: King of the Iron Men." *The Baseball Research Journal,* V (1976), 92–96.

54085. Blaisell, Lowell L. "John W. 'Jack' Taylor." In: Vol. Q-Z of David L. Porter, ed. *Biographical Dictionary of American Sports: Baseball.* Rev. and enlarged ed. Westport, CT: Greenwood Press, 2000. Pp. 1519–1520.

54086. _____. "Trouble and Jack Taylor." *The National Pastime,* XVI (1996), 132–136.

54087. Mancuso, Peter J., Jr. "Brewery Jack Taylor: Big Talent, Big Problem." In: Mark Stang and Dick Miller, eds. *Baseball in the Buckeye State.* Cleveland, OH: Society for American Baseball Research, 2004. Pp. 10–13.

54088. Wilbert, Warren and William Hageman. "Jack Taylor—1902." In: their *Chicago Cubs: Seasons at the Summit, the 50 Greatest Individual Seasons.* Champaign, IL Sagamore Publishing, 1997. Pp. 35–38.

John ("Johnny" or "Schoolboy") Taylor
P. (B: Hartford, CT, date unknown-D: date unknown). New York Cubans, 1935–1938, 1940, 1942, 1945); Pittsburgh Crawfords, 1938; Toledo Crawfords, 1939; Cordoba (Mexican League), 1939; Vera Cruz (Mexican League), 1940–1941, 1945–1946; Hartford (EL), 1949. Remarks: Highly regarded hurler who defeated Satchel Paige exhibition teams twice in 1938.

54089. Holway, John B. "The Kid Who Taught Satchel Paige a Lesson." *The Baseball Research Journal,* XVI (1987), 36–44.

Luther Haden ("Dummy") Taylor
P. (B: Feb. 21, 1815, Oskaloosa, KA-D: Aug. 22, 1958). New York (NL), 1900-1901; Cleveland (A.L), 1902; New York (N.L), 1902–1908 Remarks: Won 112 games and lost 166, with three "saves," in nine years; nickname came from being a deaf mute; joined staff of Illinois School for the Deaf after playing career.

54090. Moore, Matthew Scott and Robert F. Panara. "Luther 'Dummy' Taylor, 1875–1958." In: their *Great Deaf Americans.* 2nd ed. Rochester, NY: Deaf Life Press, 1996. Pp. 106–111. First published by the Silver Spring, MD. firm of T. J. Publishers in 1983.

54091. Smith, Ira L. "Luther Haden 'Dummy' Taylor." In: his *Baseball's Famous Pitchers.* New York: A.S. Barnes, 1954. Pp. 54–58.

Robert Dale ("Hawk") Taylor
C. (B: April 3, 1939, Metropolis, IL). Milwaukee (NL), 1957–1963; New York (N.L), 1964–1967; California (AL), 1967; Kansas City (AL), 1968–1970. Remarks: Obtained 168 hits (16 homers) in 394 games in 11 campaigns; originally signed as $100,000 bonus baby.

54092. Wolf, Bob. "Braves Toss Taylor Enigma to Mets." *Baseball Digest,* XXIII (February 1964), 85–87.

Ronald Wesley ("Ron") Taylor
P-PHYSICIAN. (B: Dec. 13, 1937, Toronto, Canada). Cleveland (AL), 1962; St: Louis (NL), 1963–1965; Houston (NL), 1965–1966, New York (NL), 1967–1971; San Diego (NL), 1972. Remarks: Had 45 victories and 43 defeats, with 72 "saves," in 11 seasons; won one game in 1969 NLCS; saved one game in the 1964 World Series and 1969 World Series; following his med school graduation in 1977, became team physician, Toronto (AL); elected to Canadian Baseball Hall of Fame, 1985.

54093. Forman, Ross. "Down Memory Lane: Whatever Became of Ron Taylor?" *Baseball Digest,* LIV (September 1995), 77–78.

54094. Kendall, Brian. "October 12, 1969: Ron Taylor Comes to the Rescue of the Amazing Mets." In: his *Great Moments in Canadian Baseball.* Toronto, Ont.: Lester Publishing, 1995. Chpt. 12.

54095. Shearon, Jim. "Dr. Ron Taylor, Unhittable in the World Series." In: his *Canada's Baseball Legends.* Kanata, Ontario: Malin Head Press, 1994. Pp. 151–156.

54096. Turner, Dan. "Ron Taylor." In: his *Heroes, Bums and Ordinary Men.* Toronto: Doubleday Canada Ltd., 1988. Pp. 102–112.

54097. Wilks, Ed. "Ron Taylor: His Contradictory Life." *Baseball Digest,* XXII (December 1963), 77–79.

Tony Taylor *see* **Antonio Sanchez ("Tony") Taylor**

Zack Taylor *see* **James Wren Taylor**

Birdie Tebbetts *see* **George Robert ("Birdie") Tebbetts**

George Robert ("Birdie") Tebbetts
C-MGR. (B: Nov. 10, 1912, Burlington, VT-D: March 24, 1999). Detroit (AL), 1936–1942, 1946–1947; Boston (AL), 1947–1950; Cleveland (AL), 1951–1952. Remarks: Obtained 1,000 hits, (38 homers) in 1,162 games in 14 seasons; manager, Cincinnati (NL), 1954–1958, Milwaukee (NL), 1961–1962, and Cleveland (AL), 1963–1966, winning 781 games and losing 744 (.512); played for New Bedford (New England League), 1934–1936; also VP, Milwaukee (NL), 1959–1961; manager, Indianapolis (AA), 1952–1953; minor league manger, and scout, New York (AL), 1975–1982, Cleveland (AL), 1983–1988, Baltimore (AL), 1989–1992; and Florida (NL), 1993.

54098. Bloodgood, Clifford. "Birdie, a Bird of a Backstop." *Baseball Magazine,* LXIII (July 1939), 357–358.

54099. Burick, Si. "How Birdie Made Rip Psyche Out." *Baseball Digest,* XIX (February 1960), 41–43.

54100. Carmichael, John P. "Birdie with a Velvet Fist." *Baseball Digest,* XIII (January 1954), 89–92.

54101. Creamer, Robert W. "The Birdie Chirps." *Sports Illustrated,* IV (May 21,1956), 44+.

54102. _____. "Conversation Piece: The Three Worlds of Birdie Tebbets." *Sports Illustrated,* VI (February 25, 1957), 61–67.

54103. Cunningham, Bill. "Birdie Tebbetts Talks Up." *Baseball Digest,* I (November 1942), 46–49.

54104. Daley, Arthur. "Birdie Tebbetts." In: his *Sports of The Times.* New York: E.P. Dutton, 1959. Pp. 32–34, 81–83, 115–118.

54105. _____. "Tebbetts and the Two Hos." *Baseball Digest,* XIII (July 1954), 71–73.

54106. "A Game of Inches." *Time,* LXX (July 8, 1957), 42–47.

54107. Hern, Gerry. "Tebbets a .400 Hitter!" *Baseball Digest,* IX (July 1950), 30–31.

54108. _____. "Tebbetts: Most Valuable Player." *Baseball Digest,* XI (February 1952), 14–17.

54109. _____.. "They'll Be Watching the Birdie." *Baseball Digest,* XII (February 1953), 54–57.

54110. Hirshberg, Al. "Birdie Tebbetts." In: his *Baseball's Greatest Catchers.* New York: G.P. Putnam, 1967. Pp. 117–125.

54111. Kaese, Harold. "Boston's Battling Backstop." In: Bruce Jacobs, ed. *Baseball Stars of 1950.* New York: Lion Books, 1950. Pp. 192–200.

54112. Kelly, Jack. "Watch the Birdie." *Sport,* VI (June 1949), 44–47.

54113. Linn, Ed. "The Man in the Dugout." *Sport,* XVII (September 1954), 50–61.

54114. Nason, Jerry. "Manager of the Year: Tebbets." *Baseball Digest,* XV (October 1956), 67–69.

54115. Obojski, Robert. "Tebbets Crowned by Basket of Tomatoes in 'Vegetable War.'" In: his *Baseball's Strangest Moments.* New York: Sterling Publishers, 1988. Pp. 18–21. Fan behavior during the October 1940 playoff game at Cleveland Municipal Stadium won by Floyd Giebel (q.v.).

54116. Paxton, Henry T. "Can He Lift the Redlegs Out of Their Rut?" *Saturday Evening Post,* CCXXVI (May 22, 1954), 31+.

54117. Porter, David L. "George Robert 'Bird,' 'Birdie' Tebbetts." In: Vol. Q-Z of David L. Porter, ed. *Biographical Dictionary of American Sports: Baseball.* Rev. and enlarged ed. Westport, CT: Greenwood Press, 2000. Pp. 1520–1521.

54118. Rumill, Ed. "Tebbets: A Talker and a Doer." *Baseball Magazine,* LXXXIV (February 1950), 305–307.

54119. Shannon, Mike. "Birdie Tebbetts." In: his *Tales from the Ballpark: More of the Greatest True Baseball Stories Ever Told.* Lincolnwood, IL: Contemporary Books, 1999. Pp. 198–199.

54120. Simon, Tom. "Birdie Tebbetts." In: Tom Simon, ed. *Green Mountain Boys of Summer: Vermonters in the Major Leagues, 1882–1993.* Shelburne, VT: The New England Press, 2000. Pp. 133–138.

54121. Smith, Walter ("Red"). "Strictly for Birdie." *Sports Illustrated,* I (September 6, 1954), 55+.

54122. Tebbetts, George R. ("Birdie"). "Birdie Tebbetts' Own Story." *Baseball Digest,* VIII (October 1949), 57–64.

54123. _____. "I'd Rather Catch." In: Charles Einstein, ed. *The Second Fireside Book of Baseball.* New York: Simon and Schuster, 1958. Pp. 353–357. First published in *Atlantic,* CLXXXIV (September 1949), 45–48.

54124. _____., with James Morrison. *Birdie: Confessions of a Baseball Nomad.* Chicago, IL: Triumph Books, 2002. 192p.

54125. _____., with Tim Cohane. "I Don't Care Who They Are — All Ball Players Are Afraid." *Look,* XXI (May 14, 1957), 141–146.

54126. "Vegetable Plate." *Time,* XXXVI (October 7, 1940), 47–48.

54127. Waldman, Frank. "George Robert ('Birdie') Tebbets: Veteran American League Catching Star ." In: his *Famous American Athletes of Today.* 12th Series. New York: Page, 1951. Pp. 339–359.

54128. Wilber, Cynthia J. "Birdie Tebbetts." In: her *For the Love of The Game.* New York: William Morrow & Co., 1992. Pp. 54–62.

54129. Wilson, John R. M. "Birdie Tebbetts." In: Paul Betz and Mark C. Carnes, eds. *American National Biography: Supplement I.* New York: Oxford University Press, 2002. Pp. 627–628.

54130. Wolf, David. "Big Leaguer Big in the Boondocks: Birdie Tebbetts Manages the Marion (Virginia) Mets of the Appalachian Rookie League." *Life,* LXIII (September 1, 1967), 28–31.

Oliver Wendell ("Pat" or "Patsy") Tebeau
1B-3B-MGR. (Bi Dec. 5, 1864, St. Louis, MO-D: May 16, 1918). Chicago (NL), 1887; Cleveland (NL), 1889; Cleveland (P), 1890; Cleveland (NL), 1891–1898; St. Louis (NL), 1899–1900. Remarks: Had 1,291 hits (27 homers) and 164 stolen bases in 1,167 games in 13 playing seasons; abrasive manager of Cleveland (P) 1890, Cleveland (NL), 1891–1898, and St. Louis (NL), 1899–1900, who won 732 games and lost 675 (.560); post-career, owned a saloon, where he died of a self-inflicted gunshot wound.

54131. Bennett, Gaymon L. "Oliver Wendell 'Pat,' 'Patsy' Tebeau." In: Vol. Q-Z of David L. Porter, ed. *Biographical Dictionary of American Sports: Baseball.* Rev. and enlarged ed. Westport, CT: Greenwood Press, 2000. Pp. 1521–1522.

54132. Smith, Ira L. "Oliver Wendell (Patsy) Tebeau." In: his *Baseball's Famous First Basemen.* New York: A.S. Barnes, 1956. Pp. 27–34.

Patsy Tebeau *see* **Oliver Wendell ("Pat" or "Patsy") Tebeau**

Miguel Tejada
SS. (B: Miguel Odalis Tejada Martinez, May 25, 1976, Bani, Dominican Republic). Oakland (AL), 1997–2003; Baltimore (AL) 2004-. Remarks: Through 2004, has had 1,171 hits (190 homers) and 53 stolen bases in 1,098 games; hit for the cycle, Sept. 29, 2001; AL MVP Award, 2002; with 150, AL RBI champion, 2004.

54133. Breton, Marcos and Jose Luis Villegas. *Away Games: The Life and Times of a Latin Baseball Player.* New York: Simon & Schuster, 1999. 272p.

54134. Schwarz, Alan. "Miguel Tejada." *ESPN: The Magazine,* VI (July 7, 2003), 56–57.

54135. Vecsey, Laura. "Miguel Tejada: Baltimore's Enthusiastic Leader." *Baseball Diges*t, LXIII (June 2004), 42–45.

Kenton Charles ("Kent") Tekulve
P-BROADCASTER-EXEC. (B: March 5, 1947, Cincinnati, OH). Pittsburgh (NL), 1974–1985; Philadelphia (NL), 1985–1988; Cincinnati (NL), 1989. Remarks: Won 94 games and lost 90, with 184 "saves," in 16 seasons; Marietta College graduate noted for submarine delivery; lost one game of 1979 World Series; first reliever to pitch 1,000 consecutive games without making a start; coach, Pittsburgh (NL), 1990–1992; color commentator, Philadelphia (NL), 1993–2000; operations dir., Washington Wild Things (Frontier League), 2001-.

54136. Forman, Ross. "Durability Was Key to Success for Reliever Kent Tekulve." *Baseball Digest,* LII (September 1993), 76–79.

54137. Ostler, Scott. "How Kent Tekulve Proved the Skeptics Wrong." *Baseball Digest,* XXXVII (December 1978), 25–27.

54138. Ottum, Bob. "Here it Comes, Special Delivery." *Sports Illustrated,* LII (May 5, 1980), 32–37.

54139. Tekulve, Kent, as told to George Vass. "The Game I'll Never Forget." *Baseball Digest,* XL (December 1981), 91–93.

54140. Van Atta, Robert B. "Kenton Charles 'Kent,' 'Teke' Tekulve." In: Vol. Q-Z of David L. Porter, ed. *Biographical Dictionary of American Sports: Baseball.* Rev. and enlarged ed. Westport, CT: Greenwood Press, 2000. Pp. 1522–1523.

John Ellis ("Johnny") Temple
2B-BROADCASTER. (B: Aug. 8, 1928, Lexington, NC-D: Jan. 11, 1994). Cincinnati (NL), 1952–1959; Cleveland (AL), 1960–1961; Baltimore (AL), 1962; Houston (NL), 1962–1963; Cincinnati (NL), 1964. Remarks: Obtained

1,484 hits (22 homers) and 140 stolen bases in 1,420 games in 13 campaigns; combative fielder; coach, Cincinnati (NL), 1964; sports director, KHOU-TV (Houston) for some years; died a cancer victim.

54141. Bingham, Walter. "Temple's Temper." *Sports Illustrated,* XII (April 18, 1960), 67–70.

65142. Bisher, Furman. "Roughneck at Second Base." *Sport,* XXIX (January 1960), 36–39.

54143. Silverman, Al. "A Lot Depends on Temple." *Sport,* XXIX (May 1960), 10–20.

54144. Sumner, Jim L. "John Ellis Temple." In: Vol. Q–Z of David L. Porter, ed. *Biographical Dictionary of American Sports: Baseball.* Rev. and enlarged ed. Westport, CT: Greenwood Press, 2000. Pp. 1523–1524.

54145. Twombly, Wells. "Voice from the Temple." *Baseball Digest,* XXV (March 1966), 63–65.

54146. Williams, Edgar. "The Temple in Cincinnati." *Baseball Digest,* XIII (July 1954), 53–60.

Garry Lewis ("Jump Steady") Templeton
SS. (B: March 24, 1936, Lockey, TX). St. Louis (NL), 1976–1981; San Diego (NL), 1982–1991; New York (NL), 1991. Remarks: Had 2,096 hits (70 homers) and 242 stolen bases in 1,128 games in 16 seasons; led NL in triples, 1977–1979; 1982 trade brought Hall of Famer Ozzie Smith (q.v.) to the Cardinals; had five hits in 1984 NLCS and six hits in 1984 World Series; first big league player to have 100 hits from each side of the plate in one season; manager, Cedar Rapids (Midwest League), 1998; Erie (EL), 1999; Edmonton (PCL), 2000; Salt Lake City (PCL), 2001; Gary (Independent), 2003.

54147. Cobbs, Chris. "How Gerry Templeton Emerged as Leader of the Padres." *Baseball Digest,* XLIV (July 1985), 37–39.

54148. Hersh, Phil. "Garry Templeton: The Cards' Talented Young Shortstop." *Baseball Digest,* XXXVII (June 1978), 28–31.

54149. Kaegel, Dick. "Garry Templeton: His Horizons Are Unlimited." *Baseball Digest,* XXXVI (September 1977), 46–49.

54150. Kaplan, Jim. "Short, But Not on Hits." *Sports Illustrated,* XLVII (October 3, 1977), 52–53.

54151. Mendelson, Abby. "A Funny Thing Happened to Garry Templeton on the Way to Cooperstown." *Baseball Quarterly,* II (Fall 1978), 30–35.

54152. Mitchell, Gregg. "The Great Shortstop Swap." *Sport,* LXXIII (August 1982), 62–66. Templeton for Ozzie Smith (q.v.).

54153. Olmsted, Frank J. "Garry Lewis Templeton." In: Vol. Q–Z of David L. Porter, ed. *Biographical Dictionary of American Sports: Baseball.* Rev. and enlarged ed. Westport, CT: Greenwood Press, 2000. Pp. 1524–1526.

54154. Wulf, Steve. "All My Padres." *Sports Illustrated,* LXX (April 5, 1989), 42–50.

54155. _____. "Bounce, the Bench, and the Boo-Birds." *Sports Illustrated,* LV (September 7, 1981), 28–31.

Fury Gene Tenace
C–1B. (B: Fiore Gino Tennaci, Oct. 10, 1946, Russellton, PA). Oakland (AL), 1969–1976; San Diego (NL), 1977–1980; St. Louis (NL), 1981–1982; Pittsburgh (NL), 1983. Remarks: Had 1,060 hits (201 homers) and 36 stolen bases in 1,555 games in 16 years; had deciding hit in Game Five of 1972 ALCS; first player to homer in first two World Series appearances, Game One, 1972; also homered in Games Four and Five and drove in two runs in Game Seven 1972 World Series; World Series MVP award, 1972; had four hits and a double in 1973 ALCS and three hits and a double in the 1974 World Series; led AL in walks,

1974, 1977; coach, Houston (NL), 1986–1987 and Toronto (AL), 1990–1997; minor league instructor, Boston (AL), 1999–2000; coach, Trenton (EL), 2001; roving minor league instructor, St. Louis (NL), 2002-.

54156. Fimrite, Ron. "Hero Finds There's No One for Tenace." *Sports Illustrated,* XXXVIII (April 2, 1973), 71–72, 75–76.

54157. Honig, Donald. "Gene Tenace." In: his *The October Heroes.* New York: Simon and Schuster, 1979. Pp. 45–67.

54158. Porter, David L. "In: Vol. Q–Z of David L. Porter, ed. *Biographical Dictionary of American Sports: Baseball.* Rev. and enlarged ed. Westport, CT: Greenwood Press, 2000. Pp. 1526–1527.

54159. Robinson, Ray. "Gene Tenace: Assassin's Target." In: Ray Robinson, ed. *Baseball Stars of 1973.* New York: Pyramid Books, 1973. Pp. 97–102.

54160. Sabin, Lou. "Gene Tenace: The Miracle [1972] Series of 'Gino the Great.'" In: his *Record Breakers of the Major Leagues.* New York: Random House, 1974. Pp. 21–29.

54161. Tenace, Gene, as told to George Vass. "The Game I'll Never Forget." *Baseball Digest,* XXXVII (September 1978), 68–70.

Gene Tenace *see* **Fury Gene Tenace**
John Kinley Tener
P-EXEC-POLITICIAN. (8: July 25, 1863, Tyrone County, Ireland-D: May 19, 1946). Baltimore (AA), 1885; Chicago (NL), 1887–1889; Pittsburgh (P.), 1890. Remarks: Won 25 games and lost 31 in a four-year big league career; NL umpire; Republican Congressman from Pittsburgh, 1909–1911; Governor of Pennsylvania, 1911–1915; pres., NL, 1913–1918; negotiated breakup of Federal League, but resigned NL presidency over controversial player assignment.

54162. Gallagher, Richard C. "John Tener's Brilliant Career." *The Baseball Research Journal,* XIX (1990), 36–38.

54163. "Governor (or President) Tener." *Baseball Magazine,* XII (January 1914), 10–12.

54164. Jones, Robert C. "John Kinley Tener." In: Vol. Q–Z of David L. Porter, ed. *Biographical Dictionary of American Sports: Baseball.* Rev. and enlarged ed. Westport, CT: Greenwood Press, 2000. Pp. 1527–1528.

54165. Lane, Ferdinand C. "Has President Tener Made Good?" *Baseball Magazine,* XVI (April 1916), 62–67.

54166. Tener, John K. "Blazing the Trail." *Baseball Magazine,* XX (March 1918), 401–403.

54167. _____. "When I Was a Ball Player." *Baseball Magazine,* XXI (June 1918), 216–217+.

54168. Trimble, W. F. "Historical Notes and Documents: The Baseball Letters of John Tener." *Western Pennsylvania Historical Magazine,* LXV (April 1982), 167–177.

Frederick ("Fred") Tenney
1B-C-MGR-WRITER. (B: Nov. 26, 1871, Georgetown, MD-D: July 3, 1952). Boston (NL), 1904–1907; New York (NL), 1908–1909; Boston (NL), 1911. Remarks: Obtained 2,239 hits (22 homers) and 285 stolen bases in 1,994 games in a dozen years; 1894 Brown University graduate one of first to jump directly from college ranks to pros; one of the game's few left-handed catchers, holds major league record for most years leading league first baseman In assists (eight); established MLB record for seasonal assists (152 in 1905, a mark which stood until 1986; manager, Boston (NL), 1905–1907, 1911, winning 202 games and losing 404; manager, Newark (IL), 1916; part-time, then full-time correspondent/writer for the Boston *Sunday Post, Baseball Magazine,* and *The New York Times,* 1901-.

54169. Evers, John L. "Frederick 'Fred' Tenney." In: Vol. Q–Z of David L. Porter, ed. *Biographical Dictionary of American Sports: Baseball.* Rev. and enlarged ed. Westport, CT: Greenwood Press, 2000. Pp. 1528–1529. Mark Sternman's profile of Tenney appears as a number in SABR's online baseball biography project, http://bioproj.sabr.org/bioproj.cfm?a=v&v=l&bid=878&pid=14059.

54170. Fox, Stephen. "The Great Un-American Pastime." *Brown Alumni Monthly,* VII (April 1996), 16–20.

54171. Morse, Jacob C. "The Problem of a Trailender." *Baseball Magazine,* VII (August 1911), 47–48.

54172. Smith, Ira L. "Fred Tenney." In: his *Baseball's Famous First Basemen.* New York: A.S. Barnes, 1956. Pp. 45–52.

54173. Stann, Francis. "Tennet's Legacy: The Reverse D.P. [Double Play]." *Baseball Digest,* XI (September 1952), 26–29.

54174. Tenney, Fred. "The Crazy Artist." *Baseball Magazine,* I (July 1908), 53–55.

Jerry Wayne Terrell
SS-3B. (B: July 13, 1946, Waseca, MN). Minnesota (AL), 1973–1977; Kansas City (AL), 1978–1980. Remarks: Had 412 hits (four homers) and 50 stolen bases in 657 games in eight seasons; played every position save catcher; manager, Ft. Myers (Florida State League), 1987; Winston-Salem (Carolina League), 1999, and Burlington (Midwest League), 2000.

54175. Arndt, Rick. "Jerry Terrell." In: his *Safe at Home.* St. Louis, MO: Concordia Publishing House, 1979. Pp. 34–43.

54176. Fish, Mike. "Advance Scouts Travel Far in Seeking 'Edge." *Baseball Digest,* XLV (September 1986), 62–66.

54177. Peterson, Keith. "Making It to the Top with Twins Terrell." *Minnesota Sports Fan,* II (June 1973), 16–18.

Adonis Terry *see* **William H. ("Adonis") Terry**
Bill Terry *see* **William Harold ("Bill" or Memphis Bill") Terry**

Lancelot Yank Terry
P. (B: Feb. 11, 1911, Bedford, IN-D: Nov. 4, 1979). Boston (AL), 1940, 1942–1945. Remarks: Won 20 games and lost 28 in five seasons; began with Terre Haute (Three-I League), 1935; won 26 games for San Diego (PCL), 1941 winning that year's PCL MVP award.

54178. Swank, Bill. "Yank Terry." In: his *Echoes from Lane Field: A History of the San Diego Padres, 1936–1957.* Paducah, KY: Turner Publishing Company, 1997. Pp. 47–48.

Ralph Willard Terry
P. (B: Jan. 9, 1936, Big Cabin, OK). New York (AL), 1956–1957; Kansas City (AL), 1957–1959; New York (AL), 1959–1964; Cleveland (AL), 1965; Kansas City (AL), 1966; New York (NL), 1966–1967. Remarks. Had 107 victories, 99 defeats, and 11 "saves" in 12 summer campaigns; lost Game Four of 1960 World Series and was also charged with giving up Bill Mazeroski's (q.v.) home run in Game Seven; lost Game Two of 1961 World Series; lost Game Two of 1962 World Series, but won Games Five and Seven; World Series MVP award, 1962; after playing career became a golf pro.

54179. Dexter, Charles. "Ralph Terry: Brain, Sain, and a Slider." *Baseball Digest,* XXI (December 1962), 5–11.

54180. Ferdini, Til. "Ralph Terry: He's Terry the Barber Now." *Baseball Digest,* XXIII (September 1964), 79–81.

54181. Gallagher, Mark. "Ralph Terry." In: his *50 Years of Yankee All-Stars.* New York: Leisure Press, 1984. Pp. 204–205.

54182. Klink, Bill. "World Series Flashback II: In '62, Ralph Terry Got a Chance to Redeem Himself." *Baseball Digest,* LI (October 1992), 30–34.

54183. O'Shea, Marty. "Ralph Terry." In: Jack Orr, ed. *Baseball's Greatest Players Today.* New York: Watts, 1963. Pp. 38–43.

54184. Rosenthal, Harold. "Ralph Terry: Hero by Inches." In: Ray Robinson, ed. *Baseball Stars of 1963.* New York: Pyramid Books, 1963. Pp. 17–21.

54185. Santa Maria, Michael and James Costello. "A Game of Redemption." In: their *In the Shadows of the Diamond.* Dubuque, IA: The Elysian Fields Press, 1992. Pp. 91–97.

54186. Shecter, Leonard. "The Maturing of Ralph Terry." *Sport,* XXXVI (July 1963), 52–56.

54187. Silverman, Al. "A Matter of Half-Inches." *Heroes of the World Series.* New York: G.P. Putnam's Sons, 1964. Pp. 11–17.

54188. Stern, Chris. "Ralph Terry." In: his *Where Have They Gone?* New York: Tempo Books, 1979. Pp. 55–58.

54189. Weiss, Peter. "Ralph Terry." In: his *Baseball's All-Time Goats: As Chosen by America's Top Sportswriters.* Holbrook, MA: Bob Adams, Inc, 1992. Pp. 160–163.

William H. ("Adonis") Terry
P-OF. (B: Aug. 7, 1864, Westfield, MA-D: Feb. 24, 1915). Brooklyn (AA/NL), 1884–1891; Pittsburgh (NL), 1892–1893; Chicago (NL), 1894–1897. Remarks: Won 197 games and lost 196 in 14 big league seasons; also played for Milwaukee (WL), 1897.

54190. Voigt, David Quentin. "William H. 'Adonis' Terry." In: Vol. Q–Z of David L. Porter, ed. *Biographical Dictionary of American Sports: Baseball.* Rev. and enlarged ed. Westport, CT: Greenwood Press, 2000. Pp. 1529–1530.

William Harold ("Bill" or Memphis Bill") Terry★
1B-MGR. (B: Oct. 30, 1898, Atlanta, GA-D: Jan. 9, 1989). New York (NL), 1923–1936. Remarks. Had 2,193 hits (154 homers) and 56 stolen bases in 1,721 games in 14 playing years; had six hits, a triple, and a homer in 1924 World Series; hit for the cycle, May 29, 1928; had nine hits and six RBIs in a doubleheader, June 18, 1929; NL MVP award, 1930; NL batting champion, 1930; last NL player to hit .400 mark (.401), 1930; NL record (tied with Frank O'Doul) for most hits in a season (254), 1930; led NL in triples, 1931; hit six homers in four consecutive games, April 19–22, 1932; played 468 straight games, April 15, 1930— April 23, 1933; had six hits, a double and a homer in 1933 World Series; top vote-getter, first All-Star Game, summer 1933; had six hits in 1936 World Series; manager, New York (NL), 1932 through 1941, winning 823 games and losing 661 (.555); nickname derived from 1918–1922 stint with the semi-pro team sponsored by Standard Oil Company in Memphis, TN; post baseball, owned automobile dealerships in Memphis and Jacksonville; elected to National Baseball Hall of Fame in 1964, where his plaque reads: "Batted .401 and tied NL record for base hits with 254 in 1930. Made 200 or more hits in six seasons. Retired with lifetime batting average of .341, a modern NL record for left-handed batters. Most Valuable Player in 1930. Succeeded John McGraw as manager in 1932 and won pennants in 1933-38-37."

54191. Allen, Lee, and Thomas Meany. "Bill Terry." In: their *Kings of the Diamond.* New York: G.P. Putnam, 1965. Pp. 109–111.

54192. Allen, Maury. "Bill Terry (1923–1936)." In: his *Baseball's 100.* New York: Galahad Books, 1981. Pp. 189–191.

54193. Barber, Walter ("Red"). "Bill Terry Recalls Days with [John] McGraw." *Baseball Digest,* XXX (November 1971), 78–81.

54194. "A Baseball Manager Gives Sports Writers a Lecture." *Literary Digest,* CXXV (February 19, 1938), 20–21.

54195. Broeg, Bob. "Bill Terry." In: his *Super Stars of Baseball.* St. Louis, MO: *The Sporting News,* 1971. Pp. 245–252.

54196. _____. "Boss Man." In: his *My Baseball Scrapbook.* St. Louis, MO: River City Publishers, 1983. Pp. 58–60.

54197. Carmichael, John P. "Terry Almost 'Owns' the Pirates." *Baseball Digest,* XII (July 1953), 60–71.

54198. Cooper, John A. "Mr. Terry Gets on the Air." *Baseball Magazine,* LI (November 1933), 55–57.

54199. Daley, Arthur. "The Rajah, Frisch, and Terry." *Baseball Digest,* VII (February 1948), 52–55.

54200. Debs, Victor Jr. "Terry Ties." In: his *Missed It by That Much: Baseball Players Who Challenged the Record Book.* Jefferson, NC: McFarland & Co., Inc., 1998. Pp. 3–23.

54201. Drebinger, John. "The Much-Misunderstood Bill Terry." *Baseball Magazine,* LX (February 1938), 390–392+.

54202. Eichmann, J. K. "Memphis Bill Terry." *Sports Scoup,* II (July 1974), 10+.

54203. Forbes, Gordon. "Bill Terry: The Strong-Willed Giant." *Sport,* XXXIX (May 1965), 66–69.

54204. Graham, Frank." A Prodigy Grows Up." *Baseball Magazine,* XLIX (September 1932), 451–452.

54205. _____. "The Reluctant Hero." *Sport,* XVI (May 1954), 22–25.

54206. Hano, Arnold. "Sweet William." In: his *Greatest Giants of Them All.* New York: G.P. Putnam's Sons, 1967. Pp. 124–144.

54207. Honig, Donald. "Bill Terry." In: his *The Greatest First Basemen of All Time.* Chicago, IL: Follett Publishing Co., 1988. Pp. 42–51.

54208. Johnston, Charles H. L. "Bill Terry:" Able First-Baseman of the New York Giants and Scintillating Manager." In: his *Famous American Athletes of Today.* 4th Series. New York: Page, 1934. Pp. 179–191.

54209. Lane, Ferdinand C. "The Batting Champion of 1930." *Baseball Magazine,* LVI (May 1931), 537–539.

54210. _____. "The Greatest Player in the National League." *Baseball Magazine,* XLVI (April 1931), 495–497.

54211. _____. "John McGraw's Capable Successor." *Baseball Magazine,* LI (October 1933), 487–489.

54212. _____. "The Terrible Terry." *Baseball Magazine,* XLIV (April 1930), 495–497.

54213. Lewis, Jerry D. "The Master of the Giants." *Baseball Magazine,* LI (November 1933), 530–540+.

54214. Macht, Norman. L. "The Manager Who Succeeded Giants' Legendary John McGraw." *Baseball Digest,* XLV (May 1986), 74–76.

54215. McConnell, Robert C. "Bill Terry as Pitcher." *The Baseball Research Journal,* XVIII (1989), 53–54. For Standard Oil's semi-pro team.

54216. Meany, Thomas. "The Midas Touch — William Harold Terry." In: his *Baseball's Greatest Hitters.* New York: A.S. Barnes, 1950. Pp. 203–215.

54217. Murphy, Jim. "First Base: Bill Terry." In: his *Baseball's All-Time All-Stars.* New York: Clarion Books, 1984. Pp. 8–11.

54218. Pacini, Lee. "Bill Terry." In: *The Hall of Fame Giants: In Commemoration of Willie McCovey's Induction, Summer 1986.* San Francisco, CA: Woodford Publishing, 1986. Pp. 34–36.

54219. Reidenbaugh, Lowell. "Bill Terry." In: his *Cooperstown: Where Legends Live Forever.* St. Louis, MO: *The Sporting News,* 1983. Pp. 244–245.

54220. Rennie, Red. "Bill Terry Insults Dodgers." In: Dean A. Sullivan, ed. *Middle Innings: A Documentary History of Baseball, 1900–1948.* Lincoln, NE: University of Nebraska Press, 1998. Pp. 150–151. Reprinted from the *New York Herald-Tribune,* Jan. 25, 1934.

54221. Ritter, Lawrence and Donald Honig. "Bill Terry." In: their *The 100 Greatest Baseball Players of All Time.* New York: Crown Publishers, 1981. Pp. 8–9.

54222. Robert, Harry. "Baseball's Only .400 Hitter." *Baseball Magazine,* XLIV (January 1930), 341–343.

54223. Salisbury, Luke. "Bill Terry: Baseball Memory and Mere Excellence." *Nine: A Journal of Baseball History and Social Policy Perspectives,* III (Fall 1994), 122–125.

54224. Smith, Chester L. "Terry: Forever Blunt-He Enters Hall of Fame in Character." *Baseball Digest,* XIII (April 1954), 55–56.

54225. Smith, Ira L. "William Harold Terry." In: his *Baseball's Famous First Basemen.* New York: A.S. Barnes, 1956. Pp. 190–198.

54226. Smith, Lyall. "He Used Only Two Bats to Hit .400." *Baseball Digest,* XVI (December 1957), 10–11.

54227. Smith, Ron. "Bill Terry 59." In: his *The Sporting News Selects Baseball's 100 Greatest Players.* St. Louis, MO: *The Sporting News,* 1998. Pp. 130–131.

54228. Stein, Fred. "Bill Terry." In: John A. Garrity and Marsh C. Carries, eds. *American National Biography.* 24 vols. New York: Oxford University Press, 1999. XXI, 459–460.

54229. _____. "William Harold 'Bill,' 'Memphis Bill' Terry." In: Vol. Q-Z of David L. Porter, ed. *Biographical Dictionary of American Sports: Baseball.* Rev. and enlarged ed. Westport, CT: Greenwood Press, 2000. Pp. 1530–1531.

54230. Stockton, J. Roy. "Bill Likes Terry's Judgement." In: his *The Gashouse Gang and a Couple of Other Guys.* New York: A.S. Barnes, 1945. Pp. 104–118.

54231. Terry, William. "Fly by Night." *Collier's,* CV (April 20, 1940), 23–26.

54232. _____. "Headaches of a Big-League Manager." *Liberty,* XIV (March 13, 1937), 57–60.

54233. _____. "The Terrible Terry." Edited by Arthur Mann. *Saturday Evening Post,* CCX (January 29, 1939), 5–7+.

54234. Van Overloop, Mark. ".303 in 1930." In: his *The Ol' Ball Game.* Harrisburg, PA: Stackpole Books, 1990. Pp. 81–85.

54235. Ward, John J. "The Man Who Shoved George ('Highpockets') Kelly Off First Base." *Baseball Magazine,* XXXVI (February 1926), 409–410+.

54236. Williams, Peter. *When the Giants Were Giants: Bill Terry and the Golden Age of New York Baseball.* Chapel Hill, NC: Algonquin Books of Chapel Hill, 1994. 331p.

54237. Working, Paul. "The Manager Nobody Knows; Bill Terry Doesn't Give a Damn About Baseball as a Sport — Every Crack of the Bat Mean Money in the Cash Box." *Esquire,* IX (June 1938), 51–54.

Yank Terry *see* **Lancelot Yank Terry**

Wayne ("Twig") Terwilliger

2B. (B: June 27, 1925, Clare, MI). Chicago (NL), 1949–1951; Brooklyn (NL), 1951; Washington (AL), 1953–1954; New York (NL), 1955–1956; Kansas City (AL), 1959–1960. Remarks: Obtained 501 hits (22 homers) and 31 stolen bases in 666 games in nine seasons; Western Michigan University graduate collected eight consecutive hits in 1949; also played for Des Moines (WL), 1948,

Los Angeles (PCL), 1949; St. Paul (AA), 1952; Minneapolis (AA), 1956–1957; Charleston (AA), 1958; Richmond (IL), 1960; manager, Greensboro (Carolina League), 1961; Pensacola (Florida-Alabama League), 1962, Wisconsin Rapids (Midwest League), 1963, Geneva (New York-Penn League), 1964–1965; Burlington (Midwest League), 1966, Hawaii (PCL), 1967, Buffalo (IL), 1968; coach, Washington (AL), 1969–1971, Texas (AL), 1971; manager, Columbus (SL), 1973, Lynchburg (Carolina League), 1975, Asheville (Western Carolinas League), 1976–1979, and Tulsa (TL), 1980; coach, Texas (AL), 1981–1985, Minnesota (AL), 1985–1995, St. Paul (Northern League), 1995–2002, and Fort Worth (Central League), 2003–2004; friend Nancy Peterson has established a website for Twig at http://www.wayneterwilliger.com.

54238. Augustin, Mike. "Twig." In: *St. Paul Saints Souvenir Program, 1995.* St. Paul, MN: St. Paul Saints, 1995. Pp. 33–34.

54239. Fehler, Gene. "Wayne Terwilliger." In: his *Tales from Baseball's Golden Age.* Champaign, IL: Sports Publishing Co., 2000. Chpt. 48.

54240. "50 Years of Twig." In: *St. Paul Saints 1998 Yearbook.* St. Paul, MN: St. Paul Saints, 1998. Pp. 13–14.

54241. Kelley, Brent P. "Wayne Terwilliger: 40 Years to the Top (1949–1960)." In: his *The Pastime in Turbulence: Interviews with Baseball Players of the 1940s.* Jefferson, NC: McFarland & Co., Inc., 2002. Pp. 307–316.

54242. Levy, Paul. "Portrait: Twig." *Minnesota Monthly,* XXVIII (August 1994), 16–17.

54243. Mellskog, Pam. "Twig Skill Calls the Shots on First." *Get Up and Go!* (May 1999), 6–7.

Charles Monroe ("Jeff") Tesreau

P-COACH. (B: March 5, 1889, Ironton, MO-D: Sept. 24, 1946). New York (NL), 1912–1918. Remarks: Won 118 games and lost 72 with eight "saves" in seven years; pitched no-hitter, Sept. 6, 1912; lost Games One and Four, but won Game Seven of 1912 World Series; lost one game in 1913 World Series; came within two outs of a second no-hitter, May 16, 1914; retired to become baseball coach at Dartmouth College, 1919–1946 and served a summer (1928) as coach, Chicago (AL); also hurled for Galveston (TL), San Antonio (TL), and Houston (TL), 1909, Shreveport (TL), 1910, and Toronto (EL), 1911; died of a stroke.

54244. Cunningham, Bill. "Pitch Man, Jeff Tesreau." *Collier's,* XCVII (June 20,1936), 26+.

54245. Stein, Fred. "Charles Monroe 'Jeff' Tesreau." In: Vol. Q-Z of David L. Porter, ed. *Biographical Dictionary of American Sports: Baseball.* Rev. and enlarged ed. Westport, CT: Greenwood Press, 2000. Pp. 1531–1532.

54246. Ward, John J. "Jeff Tesreau: The New Master of the Spitball." *Baseball Magazine,* XI (May 1913), 33–40.

Jeff Tesreau *see* **Charles Monroe ("Jeff") Tesreau**

Nicholas ("Nick") Testa

C. (B: June 29, 1929, New York City). San Francisco (NL), 1958. Remarks: minor league backstop, 1946–1957; had no hits in one big league game, after which he finished the year as a Giants coach; returned to minors, 1959–1963; also caught in Japan; player-manager, Granby (Quebec Provincial League), 1966–1968; thereafter semi-pro catcher for New Rochelle Robins and strength/conditioning coach, New York (AL).

54247. Libby, Bill. "Portrait of a Baseball Failure." In: Editors of *Sport. World of Sport.* New York. Holt, Rinehart and Winston, 1962. Pp. 123–133.

Mickey Lee ("Fruit Loopes") Tettleton

C. (B: Sept. 16, 1960, Oklahoma City, OK). Oakland (AL), 1984–1987; Baltimore (AL), 1988–1990; Detroit (AL), 1991–1994; Texas (AL), 1995–1997. Remarks: Obtained 1,132 hits (245 homers) and 23 stolen bases in 1,485 games in 14 seasons; hit two homers out of Tiger stadium in four days, June 1991; led AL in walks, 1992; nickname based on a love for a certain breakfast cereal.

54248. Capezutto, Tom. "Mickey Tettleton Plays a Big Role in Orioles' Revival." *Baseball Digest,* XLVIII (September 1989), 63–64.

54249. Nash, Bruce and Allan Zullo. "Mickey Tettleton." In: their *More Little Big Leaguers: Amazing Boyhood Stories of Today's Baseball Stars.* New York: Little Simon, 1991.Pp. 34–35.

54250. Porter, David L. "Mickey Lee Tettleton." In: Vol. Q-Z of David L. Porter, ed. *Biographical Dictionary of American Sports: Baseball.* Rev. and enlarged ed. Westport, CT: Greenwood Press, 2000. Pp. 1532–1533.

54251. Rushin, Steve. "Cereal Killer at Large." *Sports Illustrated,* LXX (June 12, 1989), 82+.

54252. Wendel, Tim. "Comeback Trail Leads to Pennant Contention — Tettleton's Bat Roaring After Trade To Detroit." *USA Today Baseball Weekly,* I (August 9, 1991), 37–38.

54253. "You Are What You Eat." *Sports Illustrated,* LXXIII (September 10, 1990), 26–27. Tettleton's love of Fruit Loops.

Bob Tewksbury *see* **Robert Alan ("Bob") Tewksbury**

Robert Alan ("Bob") Tewksbury

P-BROADCASTER. (B: Nov. 30, 1960, Concord, NH). New York (AL), 1986–1987; Chicago (NL), 1987–1988; St. Louis (AL), 1989–1994; Texas (AL), 1995; San Diego (NL), 1996; Minnesota (AL), 1997–1998. Remarks: In 13 years, won 110 games and lost 102, with one "save"; also played for Ft. Lauderdale (Florida State League), 1982; had 76-pitch complete game, Aug. 29, 1990; minor league consultant, Boston (AL), 1999–2002; pre-game analyst, Boston (AL), 2002-.

54254. Frommer, Harvey and Frederick J. "Bob Tewksbury." In: their *Growing Up Baseball: An Oral History.* Dallas, TX: Taylor Publishing Co., 2001. Pp. 212–214.

Ernest Lawrence Thayer

WRITER (B: Aug. 14, 1863, Lawrence, MA-D: Aug. 21, 1940). Remarks: Author of the ballad *Casey at the Bat.* The actor DeWolf Hopper (March 30, 1858-Sept. 23, 1935), who was the husband of actress Hedda Hopper, began reciting the poem in 1892 and is credited with having performed it 10,000 times!

54255. Berrigan, Darrell. "The Truth About Casey." *Saturday Evening Post,* CCXXVII (July 3, 1954), 30–33.

54256. "DeWolf Hopper." *Vaudeville Times,* I, no. 3 (1999), 10+.

54257. Gardner, Martin. *Casey at the Bat.* 2nd ed. Chicago: University of Chicago Press, 1984.

54258. _____. "The Harvard Man Who Put the Ease in Casey's Manner." *Sports Illustrated,* XXIII (August 2, 1965), M3-M4.

54259. Hall, Donald. "Casey at the Bat: A Ballad of the Republic." In: John Thorn, ed. *Total Baseball.* 4th ed. New York: Viking, 1995. Pp. 621–625. Reprinted in 1997 edition

54260. _____. "In Mudville, Hope Springs Eternal: Mighty Casey's 100th Season." The *New York Times Book Review,* (June 5, 1988), 16–22.

54261. Isaacs, Benno. "Casey Hits 100." *Saturday Evening Post,* CCLX (May 1988), 20–21.

54262. Regan, Scott F. "The Mighty Casey: Enduring Folk Hero of Failure." *Journal of Popular Culture,* XXI (Summer 1997), 91–109.

Thomas ("Tommy") Thevenow
2B-SS-3B. (B: Sept. 6, 1903, Madison, IN-D: July 29, 1957). St. Louis (NL), 1924–1928; Philadelphia (NL), 1929–1930; Pittsburgh (NL), 1931–1935; Cincinnati (NL), 1936; Boston (NL), 1937; Pittsburgh (NL), 1938. Remarks: Obtained 1,030 hits (two homers) and 23 stolen bases in 1,229 games in 15 years; had two inside-the-park homers in six days, Sept. 22 and Sept. 27, 1936; in Game Two of 1936 World Series, scored on a third made possible by a George Herman ("Babe") Ruth (q.v.) fielding muff; the three 1926 inside jobs were his only big league round-trippers; named to Indiana Baseball Hall of Fame, 2001.
54263. Schott, Arthur O. "Thevenow Dimmed Ruth Splurge." *The Baseball Research Journal,* II (1975), 102–103.
Bert Thiel *see* **Maynard Bert Thiel**
Maynard Bert Thiel
P. (B: May 4, 1926, Marion, WI). Eau Claire (Northern League), 1947; Jackson (S.E.), 1948; Hartford (EL), 1949–1950; Milwaukee (AA), 1951; Boston (NL) and Milwaukee (AA), 1952; Toledo (AA), 1953–1955; Dallas (TL), 1956; San Francisco (PCL), 1957; Minneapolis (AA), 1958; New Orleans (SA) and Corpus Christi (TL), 1959; Corpus Christi (TL), 1960; and Pocatello (Pioneer League), 1961. Remarks: Won one game and lost one for the '52 Braves; as a career minor league hurler, obtained 143 victories and suffered 108 defeats.
54264. Kelley, Brent P. "Bert Thiel." In: his *The San Francisco Seals, 1946–1957: Interviews with 25 Former Baseballers.* Jefferson, NC: McFarland & Co., Inc., 2002. Pp. 260–267.
54265. Thiel, Bert. *The Road to Successful Pitching.* Washington, D.C.: Public Relations Department, Washington Senators, 1960. 20p.
Bobby Thigpen *see* **Robert Thomas ("Bobby") Thigpen**
Robert Thomas ("Bobby") Thigpen
P-COACH. (B: July 17, 1963, Tallahassee, FL). Chicago (AL), 1986–1993; Philadelphia (NL), 1993; Seattle (AL), 1994; Fukuoka Daiei Hawks (Japan League), 1994–1995. Remarks: Won 31 games and lost 36, with 201 "saves," in nine U.S. big league seasons, including a record 57 in 1990; also pitched for the Peninsula Oilers (Alaska Baseball League), 1984 and Indianapolis (AA), 1996; coach at Shorecrest Preparatory School, FL., 1997-.
54266. Castle, George. "Beers with … Bobby Thigpen." *Sport,* LXXXII (March 1991), 25–26.
54267. Garlick, Dave. "Bobby Thigpen: A Prized Stopper for White Sox." *Baseball Digest,* XLVIII (May 1989), 66–68.
54269. Myslenski, Skip. "Bobby Thigpen." In: Edward Ehre, ed. *The Sporting News 1991 Baseball Yearbook.* St. Louis, mo: *The Sporting News,* 1991. Pp. 43–45.
54270. Nash, Bruce and Allan Zullo, Compiled by Tom Muldoon. "Bobby Thigpen." In: their *More Little Big Leaguers: Amazing Boyhood Stories of Today's Baseball Stars.* New York: Little Simon, 1991. Pp. 50–51.
54271. Porter, David L. "Robert Thomas 'Bobby' Thigpen." In: Vol. Q-Z of David L. Porter, ed. *Biographical Dictionary of American Sports: Baseball.* Rev. and enlarged ed. Westport, CT: Greenwood Press, 2000. Pp. 1533–1534.
54272. Sherman, Ed. "Bobby Thigpen: He's Got a Great Arm and the Heart of a True Winner." *Chicago Sports Profiles Quarterly,* I (Fall 1988), 44–47.
54273. Van Dyck, Dave. "Thigpen Mends White Sox for New Comiskey Debut." In: George Leonard, ed.

Athlon's Baseball '91. Nashville, TN: Athlon Sports Communications, 1991. Pp. 154–157.
54274. Winston, Lisa. "Off to Japan." *USA Today Baseball Weekly,* IV (June 1, 1994), 6+. To play for the Fukuoka Daiei Hawks.
Bill Thomas *see* **William ("Bill") Thomas**
Chester David ("Pinch") Thomas
C. (B: Jan. 24, 1888, Camp Point, IL-D: Dec. 24, 1953). Boston (AL), 1912–1917; Cleveland (AL), 1919–1921. Remarks: Obtained 245 hits (two homers) and 12 stolen bases in 476 games in a decade; went 13 for 31 in the pinch-batter role (.417), 1913–1918; while in Boston, often backstopped George Herman ("Babe") Ruth (q.v.).
54275. Sawyer, C. Ford. "Baseball's Greatest Pinch Hitter." *Baseball Magazine,* XXII (April 1919), 327–330.
Clinton Cyrus ("Clint" or "Hawk") Thomas
OF-2B. (B: Nov. 25, 1896, Greenup, KY-D: Dec. 3, 1990). Brooklyn Royal Giants, 1920; Columbus Buckeyes, 1921; Detroit Stars, 1922; Hilldale Daisies, 1923–1928; Atlantic City Bacharach Giants, 1928–1929; New York Lincoln Giants, 1930; New York Harlem Stars, 1931; Indianapolis ABCs, 1932; New York Black Yankees, 1932–1935, 1937–1938; Newark Eagles, 1936. Remarks: Called the "Black Joe DiMaggio," known for power and defensive skills; a lifetime .300 hitter.
54276. Baxter, Terry A. "Clinton Cyrus 'Clint,' 'Hawk' Thomas." In: Vol. Q-Z of David L. Porter, ed. *Biographical Dictionary of American Sports: Baseball.* Rev. and enlarged ed. Westport, CT: Greenwood Press, 2000. Pp. 1534–1535.
Derrel Osbon Thomas
2B-OF-SS. (B: Jan. 14, 1951, Los Angeles, CA). Houston (NL), 1971; San Diego (NL), 1972–1974; San Francisco (NL), 1975–1977; San Diego (NL), 1978; Los Angeles (NL), 1979–1983; Montreal (NL) and California (AL), 1984; Philadelphia (NL), 1985. Remarks: Had 1,163 hits (43 homers) and 140 stolen bases in 1,597 games in 15 seasons; at the major league level, played every position except pitcher at least once; jailed for 47 days in 1992 on cocaine-related charges, currently works with disadvantaged youth in CA.
54277. Johnson, Tarry. "Derrel Thomas: Baseball's Best Utilityman." In: Bill Shumard, ed. *1981 Los Angeles Dodgers Yearbook.* Anaheim, CA: Rotary Off-Set Printers, 1981. Pp. 52–53.
54278. Palmer, Joe. "A Utility Man Dodger Fans Love to Hate." *Los Angeles,* XXVI (May 1981), 138–141.
Fay Wesley ("Scow") Thomas
P. (B: Oct. 10, 1904, Holyrood, KS-D: Aug. 16, 1990). New York (NL), 1927; Cleveland (AL), 1931; Brooklyn (NL), 1932; St. Louis (AL), 1935. Remarks: Career minor leaguer who, in four big league seasons, won nine games and lost 20, with one "save"; also hurled for the PCL teams at Sacramento, Oakland, Los Angeles, Portland, and Hollywood, 1930–1934, 1936–1941, and 1943; portrayed Christy Mathewson (q.v.) in 1942 movie *Pride of the Yankees;* this early proponent of the forkball was named to the PCL Hall of Fame, 2004.
54279. Spalding, John E. "Fay Thomas." In: his *Pacific Coast League Stars: One Hundred of the Best, 1903–1957.* San Jose, CA: John E. Spalding, 1994. Pp. 86–87.
Frank Edward ("The Big Hurt") Thomas, Jr.
1B. (B: May 27, 1968, Columbus, GA). Chicago (AL), 1990-. Remarks: Through 2004, has had 2,113 hits (436 homers) and 32 stolen bases in 1,925 games; led AL in walks, 1991–1992, 1994–1995; had five hits in one game, Sept. 16, 1992; led AL in doubles, 1992; had six hits and

one homer in 1993 ALCS; AL MVP award, 1993–1994; had six RBIs in one game, May 15, 1996; reached base safely 15 consecutive times, May 1997; AL batting champion, 1997; had one grand slam homer, July 31, 1998; injured most of 2004; White Sox all-time leader in home runs, RBI, extra-base hits, walks, total bases, slugging and on-base percentage.

54280. Ambrosius, Greg. "MVP — From Rookie Star to Superstar, There's No Mistaking Frank Thomas as *Fantasy Baseball's* Player of the Year." *Fantasy Baseball*, III (January 1992), 22–25.

54281. Aschenburner, Steve. "Frank Thomas of the White Sox Puts the 'Big Hurt' on Opposing Pitchers." *Baseball Digest*, LII (December 1993), 34–37.

54282. Ballew, Bill. "Frank Thomas." *Baseball Cards*, X (December 1990), 76–79.

54283. Beckett, James. *Beckett Tribute: Frank Thomas.* Dallas, TX: Beckett Publications, 1997. 64p.

54284. Buckley, Dan. "White Sox Slugger Frank Thomas Remains Unspoiled by Success." *Baseball Digest*, LIII (June 1994), 27–29.

54285. Chen, Albert. "Doubting Thomas?" *Sports Illustrated*, XCVIII (March 11, 2003), 80–81.

54286. Coburn, Marcia Froelke. "Talk Softly and Carry a Big Stick." *Chicago*, XLVII (April 1998), 68–75.

54287. Collett, Ritter. "I Never Aim at Fences'— Frank Thomas." *Baseball Digest*, XVIU (June 1950), 79–81.

54288. Cox, Ted. *Frank Thomas: The Big Hurt.* Chicago, IL: Children's Press, 1994. 48p.

54289. Deane, Bill. *Sports Greats: Frank Thomas.* Springfield, NJ: Enslow, 2000. 64p.

54290. Dunn, Stephen. "Tower of Power." *Sports Illustrated for Kids*, VIII (May 1996), 56–61.

54291. Foltman, Bob. "Frank Thomas: Offensive Numbers Rank Him Among Game's Elite Hitters." *Baseball Digest*, LXIII (June 2004), 50–53.

54292. "Frank Thomas and the Chicago White Sox are Big Contenders for Post Season." *Jet*, XCVIII (October 2, 2000), 51–52.

54293. "Frank Thomas: By the Numbers, Already an All-Time Great." In: Joe Hoppel, ed. *The Sporting News 1998 Baseball Yearbook.* St. Louis, MO: The Sporting News, 1998. Pp. 18–23.

54294. George, Daniel P. "Big Man on Base." *Boy's Life*, LXXXIV (July 1994), 16–18.

54295. Graham, Tim. "Talkin' with Frank Thomas." *Beckett Baseball Card Monthly*, XII, no. 124 (July 1995), 22–23.

54296. Gutman, Bill. *Frank Thomas, Power Hitter.* Brookfield, CT: Millbrook Press, 1996. 48p.

54297. Hotzman, Jerome. "Frank Thomas of the White Sox Debunks Sophomore Jinx Theory." *Baseball Digest*, LII (January 1993), 29–31.

54298. Howard, Johnette. "Frankly Speaking." *Sport*, LXXXIII (April 1992), 41–47.

54299. "Hurt So Good: Looking to Prove His Miserable 1998 was a Fluke, a Rededicated Frank Thomas Got Off to a Smoking Start — but Even He Couldn't Get Hot Enough to Make Winners of the Callow White Sox." *Sports Illustrated*, XC (April 19, 1999), 60+.

54300. "Hurtin': After Struggling for Two Years at the Plate, Frank Thomas is Trying to Reclaim His Place as One of the Game's Premier Hitters." *Sports Illustrated*, XCII (March 13, 2000), 64+.

54301. Keegan, Tom. "The Big Hurt." *Sport*, LXXXV (May 1994), 54–57.

54302. Korch, Jody. "A Closer Look: Frank Thomas." *Beckett Baseball Card Monthly*, VIII (October 1991), 6–7.

54303. Korman, Ken. "The Making of "Big Hurt Baseball." *Sports Illustrated for Kids*, VII (June 1995), 54–55. Personal involvement in design of a computer game.

54304. Kornacki, Steve. "Frank Thomas: A Big Hit in the City of Big Shoulders." *Baseball Digest*, L (December 1991), 32–35.

54305. Ladewski, Paul. "Big Hurt." *Inside Sports*, XIV (March 1992), 46–51.

54306. _____. "Big Hurt Puts Up Big Numbers." *Baseball Digest*, LIX (December 2000), 56–59.

54307. Landsverk, Rocky. "The Responsibilities of a Hero." *Sports Collector's Digest*, XXIII (October 4, 1996), 24–25.

54308. Muskat, Carrie. *Frank Thomas.* Philadelphia, PA: Chelsea House, 1997. 64p.

54309. _____. "Frankly Speaking." *Topps Magazine*, (Spring 1992), 34–36.

54310. Nack, William. "Hurtin': After Struggling for Two Years at the Plate, Frank Thomas is Trying to Reclaim His Place as One of the Game's Premier Hitters." *Sports Illustrated*, XCII (March 13, 2000), 64–72, 74–75.

54311. Olmstead, Frank J. "Frank Edward 'The Big Hurt' Thomas, Jr." In: Vol. Q-Z of David L. Porter, ed. *Biographical Dictionary of American Sports: Baseball.* Rev. and enlarged ed. Westport, CT: Greenwood Press, 2000. Pp. 1535–1536.

54312. Payne, Mike. "The Big Hurt." *Beckett Baseball Card Monthly*, XI, no. 116 (November 1994), 10–15.

54313. Perrotto, John. "Frank Thomas." *Beckett Focus on Future Stars*, I (June 1991), 6–9.

54314. Platta, Dave. "Doubting Thomas." *Baseball Cards*, XI (August 1991), 126–137.

54315. Reilly, Rick. "The Big Heart." *Sports Illustrated*, LXXXI (August 8, 1994), 16–22.

54316. Robbins, Liz. "Frank Thomas of the White Sox Piling Up Hall of Fame Statistics." *Baseball Digest*, LVI (September 1997), 44–47.

54317. Rolfe, John. *Head to Head: Ken Griffey, Jr. and Frank Thomas.* New York: Sports Illustrated for Kids, 1996. 144p.

54318. _____. "Tower of Power." *Sports Illustrated for Kids*, VIII (May 1996), 56–59.

54319. Ruda, Mark. "Closer Look: Frank Thomas." *Beckett Baseball Card Monthly*, X, no. 100 (July 1993), 6–9.

54320. Rushin, Steve. "No Doubting Thomas." *Sports Illustrated*, LXXV (September 16, 1991), 30–35.

54321. Schnert, Chris W. *Frank Thomas, MVP.* Edina, MN: Abdo & Daughters, 1996. 31p.

54322. Solomon, Alan. "Young and Restless." In: George Leonard, ed. *Athlon's 1992 Pro Baseball.* Nashville, TN: Athlon's, 1992. pp. 76–78.

54323. Spiros, Dean. *Frank Thomas: Star First Baseman.* Springfield, NJ: Enslow, 1996. 104p.

54324. Stewart, Mark. *Frank Thomas.* New York: Children's Press, 1996. 48p.

54325. "Superstar Gallery: Frank Thomas." *Beckett Baseball Card Monthly*, X, no. 94 (January 1993), 21–22.

54326. Thomas, Frank, as told to George Vass. "The Game I'll Never Forget." *Baseball Digest*, XLVIII (June 1989), 45–48.

54327. Thornley, Stew. *Frank Thomas: Baseball's Big Hitter.* Minneapolis, MN: Lerner Publications, 1997. 64p.

54328. Wulf, Steve. "The 'Big Hurt.'" *Sports Illustrated*, LXXIX (September 13, 1993), 40–43.

Frank Joseph Thomas, Jr.

OF-3B. (B: June 11, 1929, Pittsburgh, PA). Pittsburgh (NL), 1951–1958; Cincinnati (NL), 1959; Chicago (NL), 1960–1961; Milwaukee (NL), 1961; New York (NL), 1962–1964; Philadelphia (NL), 1964–1965; Houston (NL) and Milwaukee (NL), 1965; Chicago (NL), 1966. Remarks. In a 16-year big league career, had 1,671 hits (286 homers) in 1,766 games; had seven consecutive hits in a doubleheader, May 2, 1954; hit six consecutive homers in three straight games,1962; IBM School of Business recruiter, 1967–1984.

54329. Appel, Marty. "Frank Thomas." In: his *Yesterday's Heroes: Revisiting the Old-Time Baseball Stars.* New York: William Morrow, 1988. Pp. 218–221.

54330. Biederman, Lester J. "The 'Old' Frank Thomas Will Do." *Baseball Digest,* XIII (June 1964), 81–83.

54331. Cope, Myron. "The Cubs are Counting on Frank Thomas." *Sport,* XXIX (June 1960), 44–46.

54332. Grady, Sandy. "Frank Thomas: Pop Goes the Needle." *Baseball Digest,* XXIV (September 1965), 87–89.

54333. Fehler, Gene. "Frank Thomas." In: his *Tales from Baseball's Golden Age.* Champaign, IL: Sports Publishing Co., 2000. Chpt. 49

54334. Hano, Arnold. "Mazeroski and Thomas." In: Ray Robinson, ed. *Baseball Stars of 1959.* New York: Pyramid Books, 1969. Pp. 61–74.

54335. Hecht, Henry. "Frank Thomas: The Mets' Homer Champ Bows Out." *Baseball Digest,* XXXV (January 1976), 72–73.

54336. Hernon, Jack. "Frank Thomas Is Big League Baseball in Pittsburgh." *Sport,* XVIII (March 1955), 42–43+.

54337. Jacobs, Bruce. "Pittsburgh's Sandlot Special." In: Bruce Jacobs, ed. *Baseball Stars of 1955.* New York: Lion Books, 1955. Pp. 124–131.

54338. Spoehr, Luther W. "Frank Joseph Thomas, Jr." In: Vol. Q-Z of David L. Porter, ed. *Biographical Dictionary of American Sports: Baseball.* Rev. and enlarged ed. Westport, CT: Greenwood Press, 2000. Pp. 1536–1537.

54339. Terrell, Roy. "The Unknown Home Run Hitter." *Sports Illustrated,* IX (July 28, 1958), 38–41.

Gorman Thomas *see* **James Gorman ("Stormin Gorman") Thomas III**

Ira Felix Thomas

C. (B: Jan. 22, 1881, Balston Spa, NY-D: Oct. 11, 1958). New York (AL), 1906–1907; Detroit (AL), 1908; Philadelphia (AL), 1909–1915. Remarks: Obtained 327 hits (three homers) and 20 stolen bases in 481 games in a decade; had the first World Series pinch hit in Game One of the 1908 Fall Classic; had three hits in 1910 World Series and one in 1911 World Series.

54340. Kennedy, F. J. "Ira Thomas, One of Connie Mack's Trump Cards." *Baseball Magazine,* XII (May 1913), 45–50.

James Gorman ("Stormin Gorman") Thomas III

OF. (B. Dec. 12, 1950, Charleston, SC). Milwaukee (AL), 1973–1983; Cleveland (AL), 1983; Seattle (AL), 1984–1986; Milwaukee (AL), 1986. Remarks: Had 1,051 hits (268 homers) and 50 stolen bases in 1,435 games in 14 years; first player chosen by Seattle Pilots in June 1969 draft; had one grand slam homer, April 8, 1978; AL home run champion, 1979 and 1982 (tie); only big leaguer to have a double and homer in the same inning twice; had three homers in one game, April 22, 1985; also hit 51 homers for Sacramento (PCL), 1974.

54341. Cotton, Anthony. "Gorman is Always Stormin." *Sports Illustrated,* LI (September 10, 1979), 90+.

54342. Hanks, Stephen. "Gorman Thomas: The Home Run King Nobody Knows." *Baseball Magazine,* New Series IV (April 1980), 22–28.

54343. Isenberg, Jerry. "The Brewers' Gorman Thomas Wins Recognition at Last." *Baseball Digest,* XXXVIII (June 1979), 34–37.

54344. Pavlick, Edward J. "James Gorman 'Stormin' Gorman' Thomas, 3rd." In: Vol. Q-Z of David L. Porter, ed. *Biographical Dictionary of American Sports: Baseball.* Rev. and enlarged ed. Westport, CT: Greenwood Press, 2000. Pp. 1537–1538.

James Leroy ("Lee") Thomas

OF-1B. (B: Feb. 6, 1936, Peoria, IL). New York (AL), 1961; Los Angeles (NL), 1961–1964; Boston (AL), 1964–1965; Atlanta (NL), 1966; Chicago (NL), 1966–1967; Houston (NL), 1968. Remarks: Obtained 847 hits (106 homers) in 1,027 games in eight seasons; had nine hits in a doubleheader, Sept. 5, 1961; participates in a record (tie) six double plays in one game, Aug. 23, 1963; played pro ball in Japan, 1969; coach, St. Louis (NL), 1971–1972, 1983; minor league manager in 1970's.

54345. Furillo, Bud. "Lee Thomas Would Rather Do It Himself." *Baseball Digest,* XXIII (June 1964), 75–77.

54346. Hano, Arnold. "Lee Thomas: On the Side of the Angels." In: Bruce Jacobs, ed. *Baseball Stars of 1962.* New York: Pyramid Books, 1962. Pp. 133–138.

Lee Thomas *see* **James Leroy ("Lee") Thomas**

Leo Raymond ("Tommy") Thomas

3B-SS. (B: July 26, 1923, Turlock, CA-D: March 5, 2001.) St. Louis (AL), 1950 and 1952; Chicago (AL), 1952. Remarks: Had 57 hits (one homer) and two stolen bases in 95 games in two years.

54347. Green, Paul M. "Baseball and 'Tommy' Thomas." *Sports Collector's Digest,* XI (August 17, 1984), 96+.

Pinch Thomas *see* **Chester David ("Pinch") Thomas**

Roy Allen Thomas

OF-COACH. (B: March 24, 1874, Norristown, PA-D: Nov. 20, 1959). Philadelphia (NL), 1899–1908; Pittsburgh (NL), 1908; Boston (NL), 1909; Philadelphia (NL), 1910–1911. Remarks: Obtained 1,539 hits (seven homers) and 251 stolen bases in 1,472 games in 13 big league seasons; led NL in walks, 1900–1904, 1906–1907; indirectly responsible for modern foul-ball rule; later, baseball coach at University of Pennsylvania and Haverford College.

54348. Lawler, Joseph. "Roy Thomas: A Master at Getting on Base." *Phillies Report,* IX (April 11, 1991), 20–21.

54349. Moses, Ralph C. "Roy Thomas." *The National Pastime,* XV (1995), 41–42.

54350. Rossi, John P. "Roy Allen Thomas." In: Vol. Q-Z of David L. Porter, ed. *Biographical Dictionary of American Sports: Baseball.* Rev. and enlarged ed. Westport, CT: Greenwood Press, 2000. Pp. 1538–1539.

Tommy Thomas *see* **Leo Raymond ("Tommy") Thomas**

Valmy Thomas

C. (B: Oct. 21, 1928, Santurce, PR). New York (NL), 1957; San Francisco (NL), 1958; Philadelphia (NL), 1959; Baltimore (AL), 1960; Cleveland (AL), 1961. Remarks: Obtained 144 hits (12 homers) and two stolen bases in 252 games for five teams in six years; title of first big leaguer from the Virgin Islands also claimed; also played for Minneapolis (AA), 1955 and Albuquerque (PCL), 1956, and long in the Puerto Rico leagues; consultant, St. Croix Bureau of Recreation, 1963–1969 and St. Croix Deputy Commissioner, Department of Conservation and Cultural Affairs, 1970-.

54351. Bitker, Steve. "Valmy Thomas." In: his *The Original San Francisco Giants: The Giants of '58.* Champaign, IL: Sports Publishing, 1998. Pp. 111–114.

William ("Bill") Thomas
P. (B: 1905). Remarks: Career minor leaguer, 1926–1952, who has the still-standing records of 383 victories and 346 defeats; he also allowed a record number of hits (6,709) and runs (3,092); for alleged Evangeline League gambling activities, was suspended from OB, 1947–1949.

54362. James, Bill. "Life Begins at Houma: Ten Grand on Thibodaux." In: Charles Einstein, ed. *The Fourth Fireside Book of Baseball.* New York: Simon and Schuster, 1987. Pp. 179–180. Thomas won 35 games for Houma (Evangeline League) in 1946.

James Howard ("Jim") Thome
1B-3B. (B: Aug. 27, 1970, Peoria, IL). Cleveland (AL), 1991–2002; Philadelphia (NL), 2003–. Remarks: Through 2004, has had 1,625 hits (423 homers) and 18 stolen bases in 1,679 games; had four hits and two homers in 1995 ALCS and four hits and one homer in 1995 World Series; had six RBIs in one game twice, Aug. 18, 1996 and July 6, 2001; had one hit in 1997 ALCS, but eight hits and one homer in 1997 World Series; obtained seven hits and four homers in 1998 ALCS; had one grand slam homer, Oct. 7, 1999; struck out five times in one game, April 9, 2000; had 39 RBIs in one month, July 2001; hit homers in seven consecutive games, June-July 2002; hit 52 homers in 2002; all-time Indians home run leader; hit a 2-run HR in four straight games, Aug. 15–19, 2003; NL home run champion, 2003.

54363. Ballew, Bill. "Jim Thome—the Indians May Have Struck Gold with This 13th-Round Overachiever." *Fantasy Baseball,* II (November 1991), 36–39.

54364. Bamberger, Michael. "The Pride of Peoria." *Sports Illustrated,* LXXXIX (July 13, 1998), 46–48, 53.

54365. Cannella, Stephen. "Hot Commodity: Jim Thome." *Sports Illustrated,* XCVII (July 29, 2002), 82–83.

54366. Dolgan, Bob: "Jim Thome: Hard Work Pays Off for Cleveland Slugger—Indians First Baseman Chips Away at Club Record Book with Every Mighty Swing: Interview." *Baseball Digest,* LXI (June 2002), 22–24.

54367. Graves, Gary. "Jim Thome: Blue-Collar Slugger Charming the Philly Faithful." *Baseball Digest,* LXIII (October 2004), 22–27.

54368. Hoynes, Paul. "Cleveland's Jim Thome Comes Through in the Clutch." *Baseball Digest,* LIX (June 2000), 44–45.

54369. Ingraham, Jim. "Thome's Heart's Tied to the Tribe, But 12-Year Affair Faces Unsure Future." *Crain's Cleveland Business,* XXIII (March 18, 2002), 15-16.

54370. Johnson, P. M. "The Throwback." *Sport,* LXXXVI (November 1995), 94+.

54371. Koenig, Bill. "Cleveland's Likeable First Baseman Has Turned the Indians Into ... Team Thome." *USA Today Baseball Weekly,* VIII (July 15, 1998), 28–30.

54372. Manoloff, Dennis. "Q & A: Interview with Jim Thome." *Baseball Digest,* LXII (May 2003), 30–35.

54373. "The Pride of Peoria." *Sports Illustrated,* LXXXIX (July 13, 1998), 46–49.

54374. "Return of the Old-Time Slugger." *ESPN: The Magazine,* VII (June 7, 2004), 30+.

54375. Rosewater, Amy. "Indians' Jim Thome Thrives on Overcoming Challenges." *Baseball Digest,* LVI (January 1997), 44–48.

54376. _____. *Jim Thome: Lefty Launcher.* SuperStar Series. Champaign, IL: Sports Publishing, 2000. 92p.

54377. Thome, Jim. "When I was a Kid: Interview." *Junior Baseball,* no. 21 (May-June 1999), 10+.

54378. Withers, Tom. "In the Opponent's Eyes: Jim Thome." *Yankees Magazine,* XX (July 1999), 104–114.

Bill Thompson *see* **William McLain ("Bill") Thompson**

Chuck Thompson
BROADCASTER. (B: June 10, 1921, Philadelphia, PA-D: March 6, 2005). Remarks: Broadcaster, Philadelphia (AL/NL), 1946–1948; Baltimore (IL), 1949–1953; Baltimore (AL), 1954–1956; Washington (AL), 1957–1961; 1962–1987, 1991; Ford C. Frick Award, 1993.

54379. Thompson, Chuck and Gordon Beard. *Ain't the Beer Cold!* South Bend, IN: Diamond Communications, 1996.181p.

Danny Leon Thompson
SS-3B. (B: Feb. 1, 1947, Wichita, KA-D: Dec. 10, 1976). Minnesota (AL), 19701976; Texas (AL), 1976. Remarks: Had 550 hits (15 homers) and eight stolen bases in 694 games in seven years; his .276 batting average was tops among all regular MLB shortstops, 1972; died of leukemia.

54380. Clark, Steve. "Danny Thompson." In: his *Fight Against Time: Five Athletes—A Legacy of Courage.* New York: Atheneum, 1979. Pp. 38–70.

54381. Thompson, Danny, with Bob Fowler. *E-6: The Diary of a Big League Shortstop.* Minneapolis, MN: Dillon, 1975. 248p.

Eugene Earl ("Gene" or "Junior") Thompson
P. (B: June 7, 1917, Latham, IL). Cincinnati (NL), 1939–1942; New York (NL), 1946–1947. Remarks: Obtained 47 victories, 35 defeats, and seven "saves" in six seasons; lost one game in both the 1939 and 1940 World Series; later managed in minor leagues.

54382. Kelley, Brent P. "Gene Thompson: A Missing Piece (1939–1947)." In: his *The Pastime in Turbulence: Interviews with Baseball Players of the 1940s.* Jefferson, NC: McFarland & Co., Inc., 2002. Pp. 9–19.

54383. Van Blair, Rick. "Junior Thompson." In: his *Dugout to Foxhole.* Jefferson, NC: McFarland & Co., 1994. Pp. 191–203.

Fresco Thompson *see* **Lafayette Fresco ("Tommy") Thompson**

Gene Thompson *see* **Eugene Earl ("Gene" or "Junior") Thompson**

Hank Thompson *see* **Henry Curtis ("Hank") Thompson**

Henry Curtis ("Hank") Thompson
3B-OF-2B. (B: Dec. 8, 1925, Oklahoma City, OK-D: Sept. 30, 1969). Kansas City Monarchs, 1943, 1945–1948; St. Louis (AL), 1947; New York (NL), 1949–1956. Remarks: In a nine-year MLB career, had 801 hits (129 homers) and 33 stolen bases in 933 games; one of first African Americans in majors, going to Browns from Kansas City Monarchs; first African American to play in both big leagues; long-term alcohol problem coupled with an arrest record (once exonerated of justifiable homicide), brought a 10-year prison sentence for a Texas armed robbery, 1963; after 1966 parole, worked with youth groups in Fresno, CA.

54384. Chapin, Dwight. "Henry Thompson Looks Back to Days of Glory." *Baseball Digest,* XXVIII (September 1969), 45–49.

54385. Dexter, Charles. "Second-Fiddle Youngblood." *Baseball Digest,* XII (April 1963), 67–71.

54386. Drebinger, John. "Hank Thompson: Handy Man of the Giants." *Baseball Digest,* XIV (July 1955), 69–78. Also published in his *The Incredible Giants* (New York: A. S. Barnes, 1955), pp. 121–137.

54387. Durocher, Leo. "Hank Thompson: My Pick for Stardom." *Our World,* V (September 1950), 55–57.

54388. Moffi, Larry and Jonathan Kronstadt. "Henry Curtis 'Hank' Thompson." In: their *Crossing the Line: Black Major Leaguers, 1947–1959.* Jefferson, N.C.: McFarland & Co., Inc., 1994. Pp. 23–26.

54389. Schwamb, Ralph. "An Open Letter to Hank Thompson." *Sport,* XLII (August 1966), 36–38.

54390. Tassinari, Edward J. "Henry Curtis 'Hank' Thompson." In: Vol. Q-Z of David L. Porter, ed. *Biographical Dictionary of American Sports: Baseball.* Rev. and enlarged ed. Westport, CT: Greenwood Press, 2000. Pp. 1539–1540.

54391. Thompson, Henry C. ("Hank"). "Ex-World Series Star in Jail: 'How I Wrecked My Life and How I Hope to Save It.'" *Sport,* XL (December 1965), 46–51.

James Alfred ("Shag") Thompson
OF. (B: April 29, 1890, Haw River, NC-D: Jan. 7, 1990). Philadelphia (AL), 1914–1916. Remarks: Obtained 16 hits in 48 games in three seasons.

54392. Green, Paul M. "Baseball and Shag Thompson." *Sports Collector's Digest,* I (March 2, 1984), 72+.

Jason Dolph Thompson
1B. (B: July 6, 1954, Hollywood, CA). Detroit (AL), 1976–1980; California (AL), 1980; Pittsburgh (NL), 1981–1985; Montreal (NL), 1986. Remarks: Had 1,253 hits (208 homers) and eight stolen bases in 1,418 games in 11 years; had 30-homer seasons in both the AL (Detroit, 1977) and NL (Pittsburgh, 1982) and also hit homers in every big league stadium standing in 1970s and 1980s; later played for Spokane (PCL).

54393. Ewald, Dan. "Jason Thompson: The Tigers' Quiet Killer." *Baseball Quarterly,* II (Fall 1978), 42–45.

54394. Green, Jerry. "Jason Thompson: The Struggle to Regain Acclaim." *Baseball Digest,* XXXIX (June 1980), 40–43.

54395. Klein, Moss. "Jason Thompson: He Adds Punch to the Tiger Offense." *Baseball Digest,* XXXVII (October 1978), 61–63.

54396. Porter, David L. "Jason Dolph Thompson." In: Vol. Q-Z of David L. Porter, ed. *Biographical Dictionary of American Sports: Baseball.* Rev. and enlarged ed. Westport, CT: Greenwood Press, 2000. P. 1541.

Junior Thompson *see* **Eugene ("Junior") Thompson**
Justin Willard Thompson
P. (B: March 8, 1973, San Antonio, TX). Detroit (AL), 1996–1999. Remarks: Won 36 games and lost 43; big league career ended by shoulder injury; played for Frisco (TL), 2001–2004.

54397. Crothers, Tim. "Griffey's Nemesis." *Sports Illustrated,* LXXXVI (June 23, 1997), 72, 74.

Lafayette Fresco ("Tommy") Thompson
2B-SS-EXEC. (B: June 6, 1902, Centreville, AL-D: Nov. 20, 1968). Pittsburgh (NL), 1925; New York (NL), 1926; Philadelphia (NL), 1927–1930; Brooklyn (NL), 1931–1932; New York NL), 1934. Remarks: Had 762 hits (13 homers) and 69 stolen bases in 669 games in nine seasons; also played for Grand Island (Nebraska State League), 1923 and Omaha (WL), 1924; Dodger scout, 1942, 1946–1947, farm director, 1949–1968, and VP-GM, 1968.

54398. Bloodgood, Clifford. "A Bright Spot in the Philly Infield." *Baseball Magazine,* XLI (August 1928), 408–409.

54399. Murray, James. "Coining Gold in the Cellar." *Sports Illustrated,* VIII (June 30, 1958), 28–32.

54400. Rosenthal, Harold. "Farm Boss with a Green Thumb." In: Irving T. Marsh and Edward Ehre, eds. *Best Sports Stories of 1955.* New York: E. P. Dutton, 1955. Pp. 86–95. First published in *Elks Magazine,* December 1955.

54401. Thompson, Fresco, with Cy Rice. *Every Dia-* *mond Doesn't Sparkle.* New York: David McKay Co., 1964. 238p. Published in a 223-page paperback edition the following year by the Los Angeles firm of Holloway House Publishing.

Robert Randall ("Robby") Thompson
OF. (B: May 10, 1962, West Palm Beach, FL). San Francisco (NL), 1986–1996. Remarks: Had 1,187 hits (119 homers) and 103 stolen bases in 1,304 games in 11 seasons; caught stealing a record four times in one game, June 27, 1986; had homer in Game Three of 1989 NLCS; hit for the cycle, April 22, 1991; hits two homers in a game twice in two days, June 23–24, 1993; coach, San Francisco (NL), 2000–2001, Cleveland (AL), 2002.

54402. Stone, Larry. "In '93, Robby Thompson Came of Age as a Clutch Hitter." *Baseball Digest,* LII (December 1993), 46–47.

Ryan Orlando Thompson
OF. (B: Nov. 4, 1967, Chestertown, MD). New York (NL), 1992–1995; Cleveland (AL), 1996; Houston (NL), 1999; New York (AL), 2000; Florida (NL), 2001; Milwaukee (NL), 2002. Remarks: Through 2002, had 305 hits (52 homers) and nine stolen bases in 416 games.

54403. Schwarz, Alan. "Rookie Report: Ryan Thompson." *Beckett Baseball Card Monthly,* X, no. 98 (May 1993), 100–102.

Samuel Luther ("Sam" or "Big Sam" or "The Marvel") Thompson★
OF. (B: March 5, 1860, Danville, IN-D: Nov. 7, 1922). Detroit (NL), 1885–1888; Philadelphia (NL), 1888–1898; Detroit (AL), 1906. Remarks: In 15 MLB seasons, obtained 1,979 hits (128 homers) and 235 stolen bases in 1,406 games; first big leaguer to hit two bases-loaded triples in same game, May 7, 1887; led NL in triples, 1887; NL home run champion, 1889 and 1895; NL RBI champion, 1887 and 1895; led NL in doubles, 1890, 1893; first big leaguer to hit two bases-loaded triples in same game, May 7, 1887; led NL in triples, 1887; hit for the cycle, Aug. 17, 1894; his career home run total remained a record until broken by George Herman ("Babe") Ruth (q.v.) in 1921; named to Indiana Baseball Hall of Fame, 1979; elected to National Baseball Hall of Fame in 1974, where his plaque reads: "One of the foremost sluggers of his day. Lifetime batting average .336. Batted better than .400 twice. Great clutch hitter. Collected 200 or more hits in a season three times. Toped NL in home runs and runs batted in twice."

54404. Appleton, Sheldon. "Samuel Thompson." In: John A. Garrity and Marsh C. Carries, eds. *American National Biography.* 24 vols. New York: Oxford University Press, 1999. XXI, 577–578.

54405. Caswell, Jerrold. "The Best Outfielder Ever?" *The Baseball Research Journal,* XXVII (1998), 3–7.

54406. Lawler, Joseph. "Sam Thompson: One of Baseball's First Power Hitters." *Phillies Report,* VII (June 1, 1989), 20–21.

54407. Papalas, Anthony J. "Samuel Luther 'Sam,' 'Big Sam,' 'The Marvel' Thompson." In: Vol. Q-Z of David L. Porter, ed. *Biographical Dictionary of American Sports: Baseball.* Rev. and enlarged ed. Westport, CT: Greenwood Press, 2000. Pp. 1541–1543.

Shag Thompson *see* **James Alfred ("Shag") Thompson**
Tommy Thompson *see* **Lafayette Fresco ("Tommy") Thompson**
William McLain ("Bill") Thompson
P. (B: Aug. 30, 1870, Pittsburgh, PA-D: June 9, 1962). Pittsburgh (NL), 1892. Remarks: Pitched three innings of one game and surrendered three hits.

54408. Kearney, S. "Bill Thompson, Pioneer." *The National Pastime*, XVI (1996), 67–68.

Bobby Thomson *see* **Robert Brown ("Bobby" or "The Staten Island Scot") Thomson**

Robert Brown ("Bobby" or "The Staten Island Scot") Thomson

OF. (B: Oct. 25, 1923, Glasgow, Scotland). New York (NL), 1946–1953; Milwaukee (NL), 1954–1957; New York (NL), 1957; Chicago (NL), 1958–1959; Boston (AL) and Baltimore (AL), 1960. Remarks: Obtained 1,706 hits (264 homers) and 38 stolen bases in 1,799 games in 15 campaigns; had inside-the-park grand slam homer, Sept. 27, 1950; went 5-for-5 in one game, Sept. 7, 1951; hit homers in Games One and Three (latter is "the shot heard round the world") winning pennant, for Giants in 1951 NL playoffs against Brooklyn Dodgers, Oct. 3, 1951; had five hits and a double in 1951 World Series; stole home plate, May 14, 1952; elected to the Sports Hall of Fame of New Jersey, 2000.

54409. Barber, Walter ("Red"). "The Miracle of Coogan's Bluff." In: George Plimpton, ed. *Home Run*. San Diego, CA: Harcourt, 2001. Chpt. 10.

54410. Berkow, Ira. "Thomson's 1950 Homer Still Going." *The New York Times Biographical Service*, XVIII (July 1987), 1213–1214.

54411. Burnes, Robert L. "Bobby Thomson: A Postscript to Fame." *Baseball Digest*, XXXV (December 1976), 76–79.

54412. Debs, Victor, Jr. "Bobby Thomson." In: his *"That Was Part of Baseball Then": Interviews with 24 Former Major League Baseball Players, Coaches, and Managers*. Jefferson, NC: McFarland & Co., Inc., 2002. Pp. 13–19.

54413. Denman, Elliott. "The Shot Still Heard." *New Jersey Monthly*, XXVI (October 2001), 25+.

54414. Devaney, John. "Bobby Thomson." In: his *Where Are They Today?: Great Sports Stars of Yesteryear*. New York: Crown Publishers, 1985. Pp. 185–188.

54415. _____. "Bobby Thomson and Ralph Branca Fifteen Years Later." *Sport*, XLII (October 1966), 44–48. Branca (above) gave up Thomson's famous homer.

54416. Drebinger, John. "Bobby Thomson, Scotland's Gift to Baseball." *Baseball Magazine*, LXXIX (October 1947), 379–381.

54417. Drees, Jack and James C. Mullen. "Robert Brown Thomson: The Home Run Heard 'Round-the-World." In: their *Where Is He Now?* Middle Village, NY: Jonathan David Publishers, 1973. Pp. 121–125.

54418. Fehler, Gene. "Bobby Thomson." In: his *Tales from Baseball's Golden Age*. Champaign, IL: Sports Publishing Co., 2000. Chpt. 50.

54419. Fimrite, Ron. "Side-by-Side." *Sports Illustrated*, LXXV (September 16, 1991), 66–77. Thomson and Ralph Branca.

54420. Frommer, Harvey and Frederick J. "Bobby Thomson." In: their *Growing Up Baseball: An Oral History*. Dallas, TX: Taylor Publishing Co., 2001. Pp. 215–219.

54421. Garner, Joe and Bob Costas. "Bobby Thomson Hits 'Shot Heard 'Round the World." In: their *And the Crowd Goes Wild: Relive the Most Celebrated Sporting Events Ever Broadcast*. Napervile, IL: Sourcebooks, 1999. Chpt. 5. The work also includes two sound CDs, with the Thomson homer recorded on the first.

54422. Green, Paul M. "Baseball and Bobby Thomson." *Sports Collector's Digest*, IX (December 24, 1982), 76+.

54423. _____. "Bobby Thomson." In: his *Forgotten Fields*. Waupaca, WI: Parker Publications, 1984. Pp. 201–207.

54424. Gutman, Bill. "The Shot Heard 'Round the World." In: his *Baseball's Greatest Games*. New York: Viking, 1994. Pp. 2–25.

54425. Heiman, Lee, Dave Weiner and Bill Gutman. "Bobby Thomson." In: their *When the Cheering Stops*. New York: Macmillan Publishing Co., 1990. Pp. 253–262.

54426. Holmes, Tommy. "Bobby Thomson Home Run Clinches Miracle Pennant for Giants." In: Dean A. Sullivan, ed. *Late Innings: A Documentary History of Baseball, 1945–1972*. Lincoln, NE: University of Nebraska Press, 2002. Pp. 54–56. Reprinted from the *Brooklyn Eagle,* Oct. 4, 1951.

54427. Huard, Kevin. "Bobby Thomson: His Dramatic Shot Will Be Remembered Forever." *Sports Collector's Digest*, XVIII (April 5, 1991), 90–92.

54428. Kaese, Harold. "Thomson's Homer: Baseball's Most Dramatic Hit." *Baseball Digest*, XXIX (September 1970), 68–73. Reprinted in John Kuenster, ed., *From Cobb to Catfish* (Chicago: Rand McNally, 1975), pp. 229–231.

54429. Kahn, Roger. "The Day Bobby Hit the Home Run." *Sports Illustrated*, XIII (October 10, 1960), 40–59. Reprinted in his *How the Weather Was (*New York: Harper & Row, 1973), pp. 24–33.

54430. Kelly, Steve. "After 50 Years, 'Shot Heard 'Round the World' Still a Defining Moment in Baseball." *Baseball Digest*, LX (October 2001), 58–61.

54431. King, Joe. "Bobby Thomson." In: his *My Greatest Baseball Game*. New York: A.S. Barnes, 1950. Pp. 194–199.

54432. _____. "The Flying Scot of the Giants." *Sport*, VIII (May 1950), 38–42.

54433. Kirby, Gene. "The Shot Heard Again." *Sports Heritage*, I (September 1987), 26–31.

54434. Kuenster, John. "Dodgers Crushed by the 'Shot Heard 'Round the World.'" In: his *Heartbreakers: Baseball's Most Agonizing Defeats*. Chicago, IL: Ivan R. Dee, Publisher, 2001. Pp. 3–8.

54435. Leiker, Ken. "14–1951: Bobby Thomson Connects for the 'Shot Heard 'Round the World.'" In: his *Major League Baseball Memorable Moments: The Most Memorable Moments in Major League Baseball History*. New York: Ballantine Books, 2002. Pp. 78–81.

54436. McCulley, Jim. "Thomson Hopes to Relive '47." *Baseball Digest*, IX (March 1950), 8–9.

54437. Meany, Thomas. The Flying Scot (Bobby Thomson)." In: his *Milwaukee's Miracle Braves*. New York: A.S. Barnes, 1954. Pp. 106–117.

54438. Molter, Harry. "Robert Brown (Bobby) Thomson: Who Hit the Greatest of All Home Runs." In: his *Famous American Athletes of Today*. 13th Series. Boston: L.C. Page, 1953. Pp. 319–337.

54439. Newcombe, Jack. "Bobby Thomson: The Unwilling Hero." *Sport*, XVIII (May 1955), 48–57.

54440. Oates, Bob. "Thomson's Homer Just a Single in L.A." *Baseball Digest*, XVIII (October 1959), 59–61.

54441. O'Connell, T. S. "The Man Who Fired 'The Shot Heard 'Round the World' Had an All-Star Career That Seems Largely Overlooked." *Sports Collector's Digest*, XXI (July 1994), 160–164.

54442. Orr, Jack. "The Unpredictable Bobby Thomson." *Sport*, XXV (June 1953), 20–21+.

54443. Powell, Cecil. "Of Willie Mays, Joe McCarthy, and Bobby Thomson." *Massachusetts Review*, XXXII (Spring 1991), 100–108.

54444. Reisler, Jim. "Bobby Thomson Recalls That 'Moment' in '51 Playoffs." *Baseball Digest*, L (September 1991), 26–28.

54445. Renick, Oren. "How Thomson's 'Shot Heard 'Round the World' Changed My Life and Made Me a Hero." In: William M. Simons, ed. *The Cooperstown Symposium on Baseball and American Culture, 2001.* Jefferson, NC: McFarland & Co., Inc., 2002. Pp. 30–50.

54446. Robinson, Ray. *Home Run Heard Round the World.* New York: HarperCollins, 1991. 244p.

54447. Roeder, Bill. "The Shot Heard 'Round the World." In: his *Phillies Presents Famous Sports Moments.* New York: Associated Features, 1959. Pp. 50–52.

54448. Sargent, Jim. "Bobby Thomson, Giant Hero; the Slugger Lives with Baseball's Great Postwar Era." *Old-tyme Baseball News,* VII, no. 6 (1996), pp. 8–9.

54449. Seaver, Tom, with Marty Appel. "The Shot Heard Round the World." In: his *Great Moments in Baseball: From the World Series of 1903 to the Modern Records of Nolan Ryan.* New York: Carol Communications, 1992. Pp. 164–169.

54450. Smith, Ron. "The Shot Heard 'Round the World." In: his *The Sporting News Selects Baseball's 25 Greatest Moments.* New York: McGraw-Hill, 1999. Pp. 10–19.

54451. Smith, Walter ("Red"). "Deals Strengthen Braves, Giants: Thomson Swap Good for Both Clubs." *Baseball Digest,* XIII (April 1954), 47–48.

54462. Stein, Fred. "Robert Brown 'Bobby,' 'Flying Scot' Thomson." In: Vol. Q–Z of David L. Porter, ed. *Biographical Dictionary of American Sports: Baseball.* Rev. and enlarged ed. Westport, CT: Greenwood Press, 2000. Pp. 1543–1544.

54463. Sugar, Bert Randolph. "Bobby Thomson's 'Shot Heard 'Round the World.'" In: his *Baseball's 50 Greatest Games.* Rev. ed. North Digton, MA: The JG Press, 1994. Pp. 9–14.

54464. Thomson, Robert B. "The Home Run Saved Me." *Sport,* XII (April 1952), 26–27+.

54465. _____. "I'll Always Remember." *Complete Baseball,* IV (July 1952), 30–33.

54466. _____., with Lee Heiman and Bill Gutman. "*The Giants Win the Pennant! The Giants Win the Pennant!*" New York: Zebra Books, 1991. 285p.

54467. Tygiel, Jules. "The Shot Heard 'Round the World: America at Mid-Century." In: Robert Elias, ed. *Baseball and the American Dream: Race, Class, Gender and the National Pastime.* New York: M. E. Sharpe, 2001. Pp. 170–186.

54468. Valenti, Dan. "Bobby Thomson." In: his *Clout!* New York: Stephen Greene Press, 1989. Pp. 10–19.

54469. Westcott, Rich. "Bobby Thomson — Baseball's Most Memorable Homer." In: his *Diamond Greats.* Westport, CT: Meckler Books, 1988. Pp. 205–211.

54470. Whiteside, Erin. "Forever Linked: With One Pitch and One Swing, the Lives of Ralph Branca and Bobby Thomson Became Eternally Entwined." In: Michael J. McCormick, ed. *2001 League Championship Series Official Program.* New York: Major League Baseball Promotion Corp., 2001. Pp. 56–59.

Dickie Thon *see* **Richard W. ("Dickie") Thon**

Richard W. ("Dickie") Thon
SS. (B: June 20, 1959, South Bend, IN). California (AL), 1979–1980; Houston (NL), 1981–1987; San Diego (NL), 1988; Philadelphia (NL), 1989–1991; Texas (AL), 1992; Milwaukee (AL), 1993. Remarks: Had 1,176 hits (71 homers) and 167 stolen bases in 1,387 games in 15 campaigns; led NL in triples, 1982; hit in the face by a wild pitch from New York (NL) pitcher Mike Torrez (q.v.) in

1984; homered in 1986 NLCS; later, a coach, Santurce Crabbers (Puerto Rican League).

54471. Canfield, Kevin. "Dickie Thon: One Pitch from Cooperstown." *Elysian Fields Quarterly,* XIX (Summer 2002), 74–76.

54472. Didinger, Ray. "A Long Road Back for the Astros' Dickie Thon." *Baseball Digest,* XLW (December 1984), 72–77.

54473. Fimrite, Ron. "You Can't Keep a Good Man Down." *Sports Illustrated,* LXXII (April 16, 1990), 86–89.

54474. Kaplan, Jim. "He's a Thon in Their Sides." *Sports Illustrated,* LIX (August 1, 1983), 54+.

54475. Shattuck, Harry. "Dickie Thon: The Astros' Bright, Young Hope for the Future." *Baseball Digest,* XLII (October 1983), 61–65.

54476. Sorci, Rick. "Dickie Thon and Bill Doran: Houston's Star Second Base Combo." *Baseball Digest,* XLIII (April 1984), 84–89.

John Thorn
WRITER (B: April 17, 1947, Stuttgart, Germany). Remarks: Well-known anthologist who founded and has edited *The National Pastime: A Review of Baseball History,* an annual title from the Society for American Baseball Research.

54477. Muskat, Carrie. "Trends: Sometimes the Numbers Do Lie." *Inside Sports,* XVII (August 1995), 10–11.

54478. Shannon, Mike. "John Thorn." In: his *Baseball: The Writer's Game.* 2nd ed. Dulles, VA: Brassy's, Inc., 2002. Pp. 245–258. First published in the 1992 McFarland & Co. original, pp. 227–243.

Stew Thornley
WRITER. (B: 1945, St. Louis Park, MN). Remarks: Minnesota Department of Health employee and long-time SABRE member and Minneapolis Millers historian; batboy for University of Minnesota baseball team, 1968–1969.

54479. Thornley, Stew. "How I Helped the Gophers Win the Big Ten Title and How I Almost Helped Them Lose It." In: Dave Anderson, ed. *Before the Dome: Baseball in Minnesota When the Grass Was Real.* Minneapolis, MN: Nodin Press, 1993. Pp. 170–173. Writer when a batboy.

Andre ("Thunder" or "Andy" or "Thor") Thornton
1B. (B: Aug. 13, 1949, Tuskagee, AL). Chicago (NL), 1973–1976; Montreal (NL), 1976; Cleveland (AL), 1977–1979, 1981–1987. Remarks: Had 1,342 hits (253 homers) and 48 stolen bases in 1,565 games in 14 major league years; hit for the cycle, April 22, 1978; had one grand slam homer, Aug. 23, 1979; became president/CEO of the Chagrin Falls, OH-based marketing services firm Global Promotions and Incentives; named to Ohio Baseball Hall of Fame.

54480. Doyle, Al. "Where are They Now?: Former Cleveland Indians Slugger Andre Thornton." *Baseball Digest,* LXI (September 2002), 72–77.

54481. Fitzgerald, Joe. "Born Again: The Incredible Comeback Story of Andre Thornton." *Baseball Quarterly,* III (August 1979), 50–51+.

54482. Kush, Raymond D. "Andre 'Andy,' 'Thor,' 'Thunder' Thornton." In: Vol. Q–Z of David L. Porter, ed. *Biographical Dictionary of American Sports: Baseball.* Rev. and enlarged ed. Westport, CT: Greenwood Press, 2000. Pp. 1544–1546.

54483. Singerman, Peter. "The Inner Strength of Andre Thornton." *Sport,* LXIX (August 1979), 90–94.

54484. Stewart, Wayne. "A Deeper Look: Andre Thornton." *Beckett Baseball Card Monthly,* VIII (November 1991), 106–108.

54485. Telander, Rick. "Thunder, but No Gray Sides." *Sports Illustrated,* VII (August 2, 1982), 46–47.

54486. Thornton, Andre, as told to Al Janssen. *Triumph Born of Tragedy.* Eugene, OR: Harvest House Publishers, 1983. 156p.

54487. _____., as told to George Vass. "The Game I'll Never Forget." *Baseball Digest,* XLV (August 1986), 79–81.

James ("Jim") Thorpe
OF. (B: May 28, 1887, Prague, OK-D: March 28, 1953). New York (NL), 1913–1915; Cincinnati (NL) and New York (NL), 1917; New York (NL), 1918–1919; Boston (NL), 1919; Akron (IL), 1920. Remarks: Obtained 176 hits (seven homers) and 122 stolen bases in 201 games in six years; far better known as an Olympic athlete, college football player at Carlisle Indian School, and star and early founder of the National Football League; elected both the College Football Hall of Fame and the Pro Football Hall of Fame, as well as the Oklahoma Sports Hall of Fame; for far more extensive bibliographies, see the author's *Professional Football: The Official Pro Football Hall of Fame Bibliography* (Westport, CT: Greenwood Press, 1993), pp. 321–322 and *The College Football Bibliography* (Westport, CT: Greenwood Press, 1994), pp. 799–803.

54488. Alexander, Charles C. "James Francis ("Jim") Thorpe." In: David L. Porter, ed. *Biographical Dictionary of American Sports: Football.* Westport, Conn.: Greenwood Press, 1987. Pp. 596–598.

54489. "Amateur." *Outlook* CIII (February 8,1913), 293–295.

54490. Benagh, Jim. "We Remember Jim Thorpe." *Sport,* XLII (December 1966), 44+.

54491. Bernstein, Ralph. "Jim Thorpe, Son of Triumph and Tragedy." In: Associated Press. *Sports Immortals.* Englewood Cliffs, N.J.: Prentice-Hall, 1974. Pp. 28–33.

54491. Crawford, Bill. *All-American: The Rise and Fall of Jim Thorpe.* New York: Wiley, 2004. 288p.

54492. Crothers, Tim. "Jim Thorpe." In: his *Greatest Athletes of the 20th Century.* New York: Total Sports Illustrated, 2000. Pp.86–91.

54493. Daley, Arthur J. "Jim Thorpe." In: his *Sports of The Times.* New York: E. P. Dutton, 1959. Pp. 174–179.

54494. De Meyer, T. A. "Honor Restored: Jim Thorpe's Olympic Medals." In: K. Schaffer, ed. *The Olympics at the Millennium: Power, Politics, and the Games.* Piscataway, NJ: Rutgers University Press, 2000. Pp. 38–50.

54495. Dockstader, Frederick J. "Jim Thorpe." In: *Great North American Indians.* New York: Van Nostrand Reinhold, 1977. Pp. 298–299.

54496. Gelman, Steve. "Jim Thorpe." In: Zander Hollander, ed. Great American Athletes of the 20th Century. New York: Random House, 1966. Pp. 143–146.

54497. Gobrecht, Wilbur J. *Jim Thorpe, Carlisle Indian.* Carlisle, Pa.: Cumberland County Historical Society and Hamilton Library Association, 1972.

54498. Graham, Frank, Jr. "The Saga of Jim Thorpe." *Sport,* XXVI (October 1958), 24–30. Reprinted in John L. Pratt, ed., *Sport! Sport! Sport!* (New York: Franklin Watts, 1960), pp, 87–102.

54499. Hahn, James and Lynn. *Thorpe!: The Sports Career of Jim Thorpe.* Edited by Howard Schroeder. Mankato, MN: Crestwood House, 1981. 47p.

54500. "James F. Thorpe." In: *Current Biography Yearbook, 1950.* New York: H. W. Wilson, 1951. Pp. 569–572.

54501. "Jim Thorpe Exposed as Professional." In: Dean A. Sullivan, ed. *Middle Innings: A Documentary History of Baseball, 1900–1948.* Lincoln, NE: University of Nebraska Press, 1998. Pp. 68–70. Reprinted from the *New York Evening Post,* Jan. 25, 1913.

54502. Koehler, Mike. "The Greatest Athlete of the 20th Century?" *Olympian,* (March-April 1999), 10–17.

54503. Leipold, L. Edmond. "Jim Thorpe." In: *Heroes of a Different Kind.* Minneapolis, Minn.: Dennison, 1973. Pp. 19–30.

54504. Lipsyte, Robert and Peter Levine. "Jim Thorpe." In: their *Idols of the Game: A Sporting History of the American Century.* Atlanta, GA: Turner Publishing, 1995. Pp. 55–76.

54505. Masin, Herman L. "Meet Jim Thorpe." *Senior Scholastic,* LX (May 7, 1952), 6–7.

54506. McCallum, John D. "Rebuilding a Legend." *Sports Illustrated,* LVII (October 25, 1992), 48–49+.

54507. Newcombe, Jack. *The Best of the Athletic Boys: The White Man's Impact on Jim Thorpe.* Garden City, N.Y.: Doubleday, 1975. 250p.

54508. Ohl, Pierre. *Dieu Sauvage.* Montreal, Que., Cda: Libre Expressions, 1980. 236p. French language biography.

54509. Paddock, Charley. "Chief Bright Path." *Collier's,* LXXXIV (October 5–26, 1929), 16–17+, 40+; 30+; 30+.

54510. Reising, Robert W. "Jim Thorpe: Multi-Cultural Hero." *Indian History,* VII (Fall 1974), 4–16.

54511. _____. *Jim Thorpe: Tar Heel.* Rocky Mount, NC: Communique, Inc., 1974. 34p. Concerns his time with the Rocky Mount team of the Eastern Carolina League, 1909–1910.

54512. _____. *Jim Thorpe: The Story of an American Indian.* Minneapolis, Minn.: Dillon Press, 1974. 58p.

54513. Sadler, Carl H. "Jim Thorpe's 100th Birthday: A Pictorial Tribute." *Chronicles of Oklahoma,* LXV (Spring 1987), 90–97.

54514. Schoor, Gene, with Henry Gilfond. *The Jim Thorpe Story: America's Greatest Athlete.* New York: Julian Messner, 1951. 186p.

54515. Smith, Walter ("Red"). "Jim and His Baubles." In: David Halberstam, ed. *The Best American Sports Writing of the Century.* Boston, MA: Houghton, Mifflin, 1999. Pp. 153–155.

54516. Snow, Donald Clifford. *Jim Thorpe.* By Thomas Fall, pseud. New York: Thomas Y. Crowell, 1970. 34p.

54517. Steckbeck, John S. *The Fabulous Redman.* Harrisburg, Pa.: J. Horace McFarland, 1951. 150p.

54518. Stump, Al. "Jim Thorpe: The Greatest of Them All." *Sport,* VII (December 1949), 30+. Reprinted in: Ernest V. Heyn, ed., 12 More Sports Immortals. (New York: Bartholomew House, 1951), pp. 281–303.

54519. Sullivan, George. *Jim Thorpe: All-Around Athlete.* Champaign, IL: Garrard, 1971. 96p.

54520. Sumner, John L. "Jim Thorpe and Babe Ruth: Sports Legends." *Tar Heel Junior Historian,* (Spring 2000), 22–25.

54521. Thorpe, Jim, as told to Irving Wallace. "It's Mister Umpire Now!" *American Legion Magazine,* XXVIII (April 1940), 18–22. Arbitrating amateurs.

54522. Van Riper, Guernsey. *Jim Thorpe: Indian Athlete.* Indianapolis, IN: Bobbs-Merrill, 1961. 200p. Revised and published by the same firm in 1983 under the title *Jim Thorpe: Olympic Champion.*

54523. Wheeler, Robert W. *Jim Thorpe: World's Greatest Athlete.* Rev. ed. Norman, OK: University of Oklahoma Press, 1979. 320p.

54524. _____. *Pathway to Glory.* New York: Carlton Press, Inc., 1975. 275p.

54525. Wismer, Harry. "Who is America's Greatest All-Around Athlete?" *Sport,* VI (April 1949), 30+.

54526. Wolfe, Louis. "Jim Thorpe." In: his *Indians Courageous*. New York: Dodd, Mead, 1956. Pp. 120–146.

Sydnor W. ("Syd") Thrift, Jr.

SCOUT-EXEC. (B: 1929). Remarks: Scout, New York (AL) and Pittsburgh (NL), 1953–1956; scouting supervisor, Pittsburgh (NL), 1957–1967; scout and director, Baseball Academy, Kansas City (AL), 1968–1975; real-estate agent/part-time scout, 1981–1984; SVP-GM, Pittsburgh (NL), 1985–1988; GM, New York (AL), 1989–1990; VP-baseball opns., Baltimore (AL), 1994–2002; consultant, Tampa Bay (AL), 2003–2004.

54527. Holmes, John. "Credited with the Save [of the Pirates] Is Thrift." *Insight*, IV (May 9, 1988), 60–61.

54528. Kiersh, Edward. "Ambition: The Thrift." *Regardie's Magazine*, X (May 1990), 56–65.

54529. Ladewski, Paul. "In Honor of Thrift." *Inside Sports*, X (May 1988), 50–55.

54530. Shapiro, Barry. "The Great Pirate Hunter: Pittsburgh GM Syd Thrift Is One Sharp Bird Dog When It Comes to Tracking Down Baseball Talent." *Sport*, LXXIX (May 1988), 62–66.

54531. Swift, E. M. "Up Against the Wall." *Sports Illustrated*, LXXIII (October 29, 1990), 74–78+.

54532. Thrift, Syd and Barry Shapiro. *The Game According to Syd: The Theories and Teachings of Baseball's Leading Innovators*. New York: Simon & Schuster, 1990. 304p. Excerpted in *Show*, I (July 1990), 35–38.

54533. Van Wyngarden, Bruce. "A Man for All Seasons." *Pittsburgh*, XIX (April 1988), 43+.

54534. Wiley, Ralph. "The Thrift Shop." *Sports Illustrated*, LXVIII (May 9, 1988), 76+.

Faye Throneberry *see* **Maynard Faye Throneberry**

Marvelous Marv Throneberry *see* **Marvin Eugene ("Marvelous Marv") Throneberry**

Marvin Eugene ("Marvelous Marv") Throneberry

1B-OF-BROADCASTER (B: Sept. 2, 1933, Colliverville, TN-D: June 23, 1994). New York (AL), 1955, 1958–1959; Kansas City (AL), 1960–1961; Baltimore (AL), 1961–1962; New York (NL), 1962–1963. Remarks: Had 281 hits (53 homers) and three stolen bases in 480 games in seven years; struck out in his one 1958 World Series appearance; broadcaster, Memphis Blues, 1970s; became on of the original commercial spokesmen for Miller Lite beer; elected to Tennessee Sports Hall of Fame, 1983; brother of Maynard Faye Throneberry (below).

54535. Buege, Bob. "Marvelous Marv' & the Mets." *Oldtyme Baseball News*, VII, no. 3 (1995), 10–11.

54536. Daley, Arthur. "Marvelous Marv." In: his *Sports of The Times*. New York: Quadrangle, 1975. Pp. 213–215.

54537. Isaacs, Stan. "Marvelous Marv." In: Irving T. Marsh and Edward Ehre, eds. *Best Sports Stories of 1963*. New York: E. P. Dutton, 1963. Pp. 83–85.

54538. Vecsey, George. "Marv Throneberry." In: Danny Peary, ed. *Cult Baseball Players*. New York: Simon and Schuster, 1990. Pp. 90–94.

54539. _____. "Marv Throneberry." In: Danny Peary, ed. *Baseball's Finest: The Greats, the Flakes, the Weird and the Wonderful*. North Digton, MA: The JG Press, 1990. Pp. 90–94. Both Peary books are identical.

Maynard Faye Throneberry

OF. (B: June 22, 1931, Memphis, TN). Boston (AL), 1952, 1957; Washington (AL), 1957–1960; Los Angeles (AL). Remarks: Had 307 hits (29 homers) and 23 stolen bases in 521 games in an eight-year big league career; hit two grand slams in 1952; brother of first baseman Marvin "Marv" Throneberry (above).

54540. Nason, Jerry. "The Red Sox Got a Ditch Digger." *Baseball Digest*, XIV (June 1965), 35–37.

Bill Thurston *see* **William ("Bill") Thurston**

Hollis John ("Sloppy") Thurston

P-SCOUT. (B. June 2, 1899, Fremont, NE-D: Sept. 14, 1973). St. Louis (AL), 1923; Chicago (AL), 1923–1926; Washington (AL), 1927; Brooklyn (NL), 1930–1933. Remarks: Nickname based on his fastidious off-field dress; won 89 games and lost 86 with 13 "saves" in nine big league years; struck out side on nine pitches in one inning in a game, Aug. 22, 1923; in 1924, won ten straight victories before losing on July 29 and finished with a 20–14 record; surrendered six homers in one game, Aug. 13, 1932; had career .270 batting average, with 175 hits and five homers; also hit 28 homers while playing for San Francisco (PCL), 1928; later, a scout for Chicago (AL).

54541. Lane, Ferdinand C. "Hollis Thurston, the Big League Gold Miner." *Baseball Magazine*, LI (July 1933), 361–363.

54542. Spalding, John. E. "Sloppy Thurston." In: his *Pacific Coast League Stars, Vol. II: Ninety Who Made It to the Majors, 1905–1957*. San Jose, CA: John E. Spalding. 1997. Pp. 72–75.

54543. Ward, John J. "Hollis Thurston's Great Record." *Baseball Magazine*, XXXIII (October 1924), 488–489.

Sloppy Thurston *see* **Hollis John ("Sloppy") Thurston**

William ("Bill") Thurston

COACH. Remarks: Head baseball coach, Amherst College, 1966–; through 2004, has won 706 games and lost 409, with nine ties; elected to Maine Baseball Hall of Fame, 1996 and American Baseball Coaches Association Hall of Fame, 1997; NCAA Baseball Rules Editor, 1987–2001.

54544. Coffey, Wayne. "Heavy Hitter." *Yankee*, LXVII (July-August 2003), 62–65.

54545. Thurston, Bill. *Coaching Youth Baseball: A Baffled Parents Guide*. Camden, ME: International Marine/Ragged Mountain Press, 2000. 160p.

Louis Clemente Vega ("Luis" or "Louie" or "El Tiante") Tiant, Jr.

P-COACH. (B: Nov. 23, 1940, Marianao, Cuba). Cleveland (AL), 1964–1969; Minnesota (A.L), 1970; Boston (AL), 1971–1978; New York (AL), 1979–1980; Pittsburgh (NL), 1981; California (AL), 1982. Remarks: Had 229 victories and 172 defeats in 19 campaigns; pitched four consecutive shutouts, May 28-May 12, 1968; struck out 19 batters in one game, July 3, 1968; won Games One and Four of 1975 World Series; third-winningest MLB Latin American pitcher; also played for Mexico City (Mexican League), 1959–1961, Charleston (EL), 1962, Burlington (Carolina League), 1963, Portland (PCL), 1964 (had Beaver no-hitter in May), Louisville (AA), 1972; scout or coach in New York (AL) minor league system, 1983–1992; coach, Los Angeles (NL), 1993–1996 and Chicago (AL), 1997–2000; coach, Nicraguan Olympic baseball team, 1996; pitching coach, Savannah College, 2001–2003; coach, Lowell (EL), 2004–; son of famous Negro League hurler Louis Tiante, Sr.; elected to Cuban Baseball Hall of Fame and Boston Red Sox Hall of Fame, 1997.

54546. Bailey, Arnold C. "Former Pitching Star Luis Tiant Profiled." *Sports Collector's Digest*, XXIV (October 17, 1997), 140–141. Mark Armour's profile is a number in the online SABR Biography Project http://bioproj.sabr.org/bioproj.cfm?a=v&v=l&bid=645&pid=14207.

54547. Bjarkman, Peter C. "Luis Clemente Vega 'Louie' Tiant, Jr." In: Vol. Q-Z of David L. Porter, ed. *Biograph-*

ical Dictionary of American Sports: Baseball. Rev. and enlarged ed. Westport, CT: Greenwood Press, 2000. Pp. 1546–1547.

54548. "Can El Tiante Come Back (Again)?" In: Tommy Kay, ed. *Baseball Factbook*. Scottsdale, AZ: Jalart House, 1978. Pp. 40–45.

54549. Cope, Myron. "Where There's Smoke, There's Luis." *Sports Illustrated*, XXXVIII (May 7, 1973), 43–44+.

54550. Dolgan, Bob. "Turn Back the Clock —1968: When the Tribe's Luis Tiant Threw Four Consecutive Shutouts." *Baseball Digest*, LXI (July 2002), 78–81.

54551. Fitzgerald, Joe. "Luis Tiant: He Was Special to Boston Red Sox Fans." *Baseball Digest*, XXXVIII (March 1979), 66–69.

54552. Fitzpatrick, Tom. "The Most Popular Indian." *Sport*, XLVI (September 1968), 30–33.

54553. Gammons, Peter. "Luis Tiant." In: Danny Peary, ed. *Cult Baseball Stars*. New York: Simon and Schuster, 1990. Pp. 284–289.

54554. ____. "Luis Tiant." In: Danny Peary, ed. *Baseball's Finest: The Greats, the Flakes, the Weird and the Wonderful*. North Digton, MA: The JG Press, 1990. Pp. 284–289. Both Peary books are identical.

54555. Holway, John B. "Best Pitcher in '68?: Figures Support Tiant." *Baseball Digest*, XXVIII (July 1969), 21–27.

54556. ____. "Will the Real Luis Tiant Please Stand Up." *Baseball Digest*, XXXV (February 1976), 74–79.

54557. Liston, Bill. "The Comeback Saga of Luis Tiant." *Baseball Digest*, XXXIV (July 1975), 40–43.

54558. "Luis Tiant." In: *Current Biography Yearbook, 1977*. New York, H.W. Wilson Co., 1977. Pp. 399–401.

54559. Olan, Ben. "Luis Tiant: The Man with 1,000 Pitching Moves." *Sports Today*, V (December 1974), 72+.

54560. Robinson, Ray. "Luis Tiant." In: Ray Robinson, ed. *Baseball Stars of 1969*. New York: Pyramid Books, 1969. pp. 74–79.

54561. Tiant, Louis C. ("Luis"), as told to George Vass. "The Game I'll Never Forget." *Baseball Digest*, XXXIX (June 1980), 62–64.

54562. ____, and Joe Fitzgereld. *El Tiante: The Luis Tiant Story*. Garden City, N.Y.: Doubleday, 1976. 226p.

54563. Xanthakos, Harry. "Luis Tiant Dreams of Family Reunion." *Black Sports Magazine*, V (August 1975), 42–47.

54564. Young, Dick. "The Comeback of Luis Tiant." *Baseball Digest*, XXXI (December 1972), 31–33.

Michael Joseph ("Mike" or "Silent Mike") Tiernan
OF. (B: Jan. 21, 1867, Trenton, NJ-D: Nov. 9, 1918). New York (NL), 1887–1899. Remarks: Obtained 1,834 hits (106 homers) and 428 stolen bases in 1,476 games in 13 years; set MLB record with five errors in one game, May 16, 1887; tied NL record by scoring six runs in one game, June 15, 1887; hit for the cycle, Aug. 25, 1888; NL home run champion, 1890–1891; became first player to homer from one ballpark into another, hitting a blast which flew out of the Polo Grounds and into adjacent Brotherhood Park, May 12, 1890.

54565. Linthurst, B. Randolph. "Michael Joseph 'Mike,' 'Silent Mike' Tiernan." In: Vol. Q-Z of David L. Porter, ed. *Biographical Dictionary of American Sports: Baseball*. Rev. And enlarged ed. Westport, CT: Greenwood Press, 2000. Pp. 1547–1548.

54566. ____. "Silent Mike' Tiernan Belongs in the Hall of Fame." *TriM*, (April 1975), 30–31.

Leslie William ("Les" or "Toots") Tietje
P. (B: Sept. 11, 1911, Sumner, IA-D: Oct. 2, 1996).

Chicago (AL), 1933–1936; St. Louis (AL), 1936–1938. Remarks: Won 22 games and lost 41 in six seasons; also played for Oakland (PCL), 1939.

54567. Smart, Steve. "Les Tietje." *The National Pastime*, III (1983), 81–83.

Jack Tighe *see* **John Thomas ("Jack") Tighe**
John Thomas ("Jack") Tighe
C-MGR. (B: Aug. 9, 1913, Kearny, NJ-D: Aug. 1, 2002). Remarks: Charleston (Appalachian League), 1936; player-manager, Muskegon (Michigan State League), 1940–1941; coach, Detroit (AL), 1942; manager, Buffalo (IL), 1952–1953; coach, Detroit (AL), 1954–1956; manager, Detroit (AL), 1957–1958, winning 99 games and losing 104 (.488); minor league team instructor/official, Detroit (AL), 1959–1967; manager, Toledo (IL), 1968; consultant, Detroit (AL), 1969–1990; named to Muskegon Area Sports Hall of Fame, 1988.

54568. Middlesworth, Hal. "Jack Tighe: Now They're the Tigh-ers." *Baseball Digest*, XV (November-December 1956), 87–90.

Eustace Tilley
EXEC. Remarks: Fictional General Superintendent, *The New Yorker* so named by Corey Ford in issue of August 1925; Tilley's phone number in the Manhattan directory reaches the private office the magazine's publisher Editor Harold Ross.

54569. Altherr, T. L. "Eustace Tilley Draws the Game: The Image of Baseball in *The New Yorker*, 1925 to the Present." *Nine: A Journal of Baseball History and Social Policy Perspective*, III (Fall 1994), 14–35.

Harold ("Hooks") Tinker
OF. (B: 1905, Birmingham, AL). Pittsburgh Crawfords, 1928–1931; later became minister; credited with "discovery" of Josh Gibson (q.v.).

54570. Ruck, Rob. "Harold Tinker: He Played with the Best on The Hill —A Baseball Legend Looks Back," *Pittsburgh*, (August 1991), 30+.

54571. Wilson, Nick. "Reverend Harold Tinker." In: his *Voices from the Pastime: Oral Histories of Surviving Major Leaguers, Negro Leaguers, Cuban Leaguers, and Writers, 1920–1934*. Jefferson, NC: McFarland & Co., Inc., 2000. Pp. 125–129

Joseph Bert ("Joe") Tinker★
SS-MGR. (B: July 27, 1890, Muscotah, KS-D: July 27, 1948). Chicago (NL), 1902–1912; Cincinnati (NL), 1913; Chicago (F.L.), 1914–1915; Chicago (NL), 1916. Remarks: Obtained 1,694 hits (31 homers) and 336 stolen bases in 1,804 games in 15 playing years; member of famed "Tinker to Evers to Chance" doubleplay combo and noted fielder; hit inside-the-park homer, July 17, 1908; first player to steal home plate twice in one game, July 28, 1910; stole home plate, Aug. 7, 1911; manager, Cincinnati (NL), 1913, Chicago (P.L.), 1914–1915, and Chicago (N.I.), 1916, winning 304 games and losing 308 (.497); president and manager, Columbus (A.A), 1917–1920 and Orlando (Florida State League), 1921–1923; elected to National Baseball Hall of Fame in 1946, where his plaque reads: "Famous as a member of one of baseball's greatest double play combinations —from Tinker to Evers to Chance. A big leaguer from 1902 through 1916 with the Chicago Cubs and Cincinnati Reds and the Chicago Feds. Manager Cincinnati 1913 and Chicago NL, 1916. Shortstop on Cubs' team that won pennants in 1906, '07, '08 and 1910."

54572. Ahrens, Arthur It. "Tinker vs. Matty: A Study in Rivalry." *The Baseball Research Journal*, III (1974), 14–19.

54573. Allen, Lee, and Thomas Meany. "Joe Tinker."

In: their *Kings of the Diamond.* New York: G.P. Putnam, 1946. Pp. 152–154.

54574. Asnen, Alan R. and John E. Findling. "Joseph Bert 'Joe' Tinker." In: Vol. Q-Z of David L. Porter, ed. *Biographical Dictionary of American Sports: Baseball.* Rev. and enlarged ed. Westport, CT: Greenwood Press, 2000. Pp. 1548–1550.

54575. Barton, Jerry. "Joseph B. Tinker." In: his *A Treasure Chest of the Hall of Fame.* Boston, MA: The Wilson-Hill Co., 1952. Pp. 88–89.

54576. Bogen, Gil. *Tinker, Evers, and Chance: A Triple Biography.* Jefferson, NC: McFarland & Co., Inc., 2003. 272p.

54577. Chester, Carl W. "A Plutocrat of the Diamond." *Baseball Magazine,* I (September 1908), 51–52. Tinker's $1,600 salary disputed.

54578. Collins, Thomas W., Jr. "Joe Tinker." In: Paul Betz and Mark C. Carnes, eds. *American National Biography: Supplement I.* New York: Oxford University Press, 2002. Pp. 631–632.

54579. Davis, Mac. "Over a Foolish Quarrel." In: his *The Lore and Legends of Baseball.* New York: Lantern Press, 1953. Pp. 36–37. Tinker-Evers feud.

54580. Enright, Jim. "Players: Tinker-Evers-Chance." In: his *Baseball's Great Teams: Chicago Cubs.* New York: Collier Books, 1975. Pp. 119–124.

54581. Graham, Prank. "Joe Tinker." In: his *Baseball Extra.* New York: A.S. Barnes, 1954. Pp. 3–15.

54582. _____. "One for the Book." *Sport,* VI (June 1949), 36–39. "Tinker to Evers to Chance."

54583. _____. "They Warred Over Tinker." *Baseball Digest,* VII (October 1948), 60–63. Cincinnati (NL) and Brooklyn (NL) in 1913.

54584. Grayson, Harry. "Tinker to Evers to Chance." In: his *They Played the Game.* New York: A.S. Barnes, 1944. Pp. 95–97.

54585. Holtzman, Jerome. "How Poem Helped Elect Infield Trio to Hall of Fame *Baseball Digest,* LII (March 1993), 70–72.

54586. Lane, Ferdinand C. "Joe Tinker, Shortstop-Manager and His Remarkable Career." *Baseball Magazine,* XI (July 1913), 42–55.

54587. Menke, Frank G. "Silent Partners." In: his *Sports Tales and Anecdotes.* New York: A.S. Barnes, 1953. Pp. 24–25. Tinker-Evers feud.

54588. "Pinch Hitter." *Literary Digest,* XLV (August 10, 1912), 238.

54589. Povich, Shirley. "Everybody is Out!" *Baseball Digest,* VI (May 1947), 6–7.

54590. _____. "Tinker and Grob: 35 Years Later." *Baseball Digest,* VII (June 1940), 19–21.

54591. Powers, Francis J. "Joe Tinker." In: his *My Greatest Day In Baseball.* New York: A.S. Barnes, 1945. Pp. 135–138.

54592. Tinker, Joseph B. "When I 'Murdered' Matty." *Baseball Digest,* IV (September 1946), 10–13. Hit .400 against Mathewson in 1908.

54593. _____., as told to Francis J. Powers. "My Greatest Day in Baseball." In: John P. Carmichael, ed. *My Greatest Day in Baseball.* New York: A. S. Barnes, 1945. Pp. 135–138. First published in the *Chicago Daily News.*

54594. "Tinker's Big Bet." *Literary Digest,* XLIV (February 24, 1912), 389.

54595. Wilbert, Warren and William Hageman. "Joseph Bert Tinker—1908." In: *Chicago Cubs: Seasons at the Summit, the 50 Greatest Individual Seasons.* Champaign, IL: Sagamore Publishing, 1997. Pp. 119–122.

John Franklin ("Silent John" or "Tight Pants") Titus
OF. (B: Feb. 21, 1876, St. Clair, PA-D: Jan. 8, 1943). Philadelphia (NL), 1903–1912; Boston (NL), 1913–1914. Remarks: Obtained 1,401 hits (38 homers) and 140 stolen bases in 1,402 games in 11 big league seasons; also played for Kansas City (AA), 1913–1914.

54596. Lawler, John. "John Titus: His Actions Spoke Louder Than His Words." *Phillies Report,* X (May 21, 1992), 20–21.

54597. Phelps, Frank V. "John Franklin 'Silent John,' 'Tight Pants' Titus." In: Vol. Q-Z of David L. Porter, ed. *Biographical Dictionary of American Sports: Baseball.* Rev. and enlarged ed. Westport, CT: Greenwood Press, 2000. Pp. 1550–1551.

Jack Tobin *see* **John Thomas ("Jack") Tobin**
James Anthony ("Jim" or "Abba Dabba") Tobin
P. (B: Dec. 27, 1912, Oakland, CA-D: May 19, 1969). Pittsburgh (NL), 19371939; Boston (NL), 1940–1945; Detroit (AL), 1945. Remarks: Had 105 victories, 112 defeats, and five "saves," in nine seasons; pitched two no hitters, April 27 and June 22, 1944; as a batter, had 17 career home runs, including six in 1942 — three of those in one game on May 13; also played for Oakland (PCL), 1946–1948, helping to win loop's championship for his team in the final year with a stellar relief pitching performance.

54598. Miller, Hub. "That Double-Barreled Threat, Jim Tobin." *Baseball Magazine,* LXXIII (July 1944), 260–271+.

54599. Nason, Jerry. "Successive No-Hitters Eluded Jim Tobin." *Baseball Digest,* XXVIII (August 1969), 80–82.

54600. Spalding, John E. "Jim Tobin." In: his *Pacific Coast League Stars, Vol. II: Ninety Who Made It to the Majors, 1905-1957.* San Jose, CA: John E. Spalding, 1997. Pp. 115–116.

John Thomas ("Jack") Tobin
OF. (B: May 4, 1892, St. Louis, MO-D: Dec. 10, 1969). St. Louis (F.L.), 1914–1915; St. Louis (AL), 1916, 1918–1925; Washington (AL) and Boston (AL), 1926; Boston (AL), 1927. Remarks: Obtained 1,908 hits (64 homers) and 147 stolen bases in 1,617 games in 12 seasons; led AL in triples, 1921; feared bunter who two grand slam homers, both off Walter Johnson (q.v.); manager, Bloomington (3-1 League); coach, St. Louis (AL), 1944–1951.

54601. Borst, William A. ("Bill"). "John Thomas 'Jack' Tobin." In: Vol. Q-Z of David L. Porter, ed. *Biographical Dictionary of American Sports: Baseball.* Rev. and enlarged ed. Westport, CT: Greenwood Press, 2000. P. 1551.

Bobby Tolan *see* **Robert ("Bobby") Tolan**
Robert ("Bobby") Tolan
OF-1B. (B: Nov. 19, 1945, Los Angeles, CA). St. Louis (NL), 1965–1968; Cincinnati (NL), 1969 –1973; San Diego (NL), 1974–1975; Philadelphia (NL), 1976–1977; Pittsburgh (NL), 1977; San Diego (NL), 1978; Nankai (Japan League), 1979. Remarks: Had 1,121 hits (86 homers)and 193 stolen bases in 1,282 games in 13 U.S. big league years; NL stolen base champion, 1970; homered in Game Two, 1970 NLCS; had four hits and one homer in 1970 World Series; had five hits and one double in 1972 NLCS and seven hits and a double in the 1972 World Series; coach, San Diego (NL), 1980–1983; coach, Seattle (AL), 1987; minor league coach, 1980's; manager, Nashua (Atlantic League), 1999.

54602. Donnelly, Joe. "Room at the Top for Tolan." *Sport,* XLIX (June 1970), 42–45.

54603. Rubin, Bob. "For Whom the Bells Tolan." *Sport,* XLVIII (August 1969), 4–5.

54604. Teter, John. "The Comeback of Bobby Tolan." *Baseball Digest,* XXXII (April 1973), 62–65.

54605. _____. and William Holden. "Bobby Tolan : A Superstar Blooms in Pete Rose's Garden." *Black Sports,* II (June 1973), 26–28.

Jimmy Wayne Tolleson
SS. (B: Nov. 22, 1955, Spartanburg, SC). Texas (AL), 1981–1985; Chicago (AL), 1986; New York (AL), 1986–1990. Remarks: In a decade, obtained 559 hits (nine homers) and 108 stolen bases in 863 big league games; fleet but a light hitter; also 1977 NCAA Pass Receiving Champion, Western Carolina University; played for Tulsa (TL), 1980; became VP of sales for SC-based Centerplate Catering.

54606. Hill, Terry. "Wayne Tolleson." In: his *Batting a Thousand.* Nashville, TN: Thomas Nelson, 1987. pp. 100–104.

Wayne Tolleson *see* **Jimmy Wayne Tolleson**
Frederick Arthur ("Fred") Toney
P. (B: Dec. 11, 1887, Nashville, TN-D: March 11, 1953). Chicago, (NL), 1911–1913; Cincinnati (NL), 1915–1918; New York (NL), 1918–1922; SL Louis (NL), 1923. Remarks: In a dozen big league seasons, won 137 games and lost 102, with 12 "saves"; won two complete games in a day, July 1, 1917; pitched no-hitter of 10 innings, May 2, 1917; retired to a farm outside "Music City," to be employed by the Davidson County sheriff.

54607. Klima, John. "Nine of Nothing: Fred Toney vs. Hippo Vaughn (May 2, 1917)." In: his *Pitched Battle: 35 of Baseball's Greatest Duels from the Mound.* Jefferson, NC: McFarland & Co., Inc., 2002. Pp. 38–42.

54608. Matz, David S. "Fred Toney." In: Vol. Q-Z of David L. Porter, ed. *Biographical Dictionary of American Sports: Baseball.* Rev. and enlarged ed. Westport, CT: Greenwood Press, 2000. P. 1552.

54609. Sugar, Bert Randolph. "Double No-Hitter: Vaughn vs. Toney—Cincinnati Reds vs. Chicago Cubs, May 2, 1917." In: his *Baseball's 50 Greatest Games.* Rev. ed. North Digton, MA: The JG Press, 1994. Pp. 74–76.

54610. Tarvin, A. H. "Toney's 10-Inning No-Hitter." *Baseball Digest,* IV (March 1945), 44–45.

54611. Toney, Frederick A. "How I Won That [10-Inning No-Hit] Game." *Baseball Magazine,* XIX (July 1917), 363–364.

54612. "Toney-Vaughan Double No-Hitter." In: Dean A. Sullivan, ed. *Middle Innings: A Documentary History of Baseball, 1900–1948.* Lincoln, NE: University of Nebraska Press, 1998. Pp. 82–84. Reprinted from the *Chicago Daily Tribune,* May 3, 1917.

Jim Toomey
EXEC. (B: 1918-D: March 24, 2002). Remarks: Public relations dir., asst. GM, St. Louis (NL), 1949–1983; consultant/official scorer, St. Louis (NL), 1984–2000; press box at Busch Stadium named in his honor.

54613. Bryan, Mike. "Jim Toomey." In: his *Baseball Lives.* New York: Pantheon Books, 1989. pp. 321–327.

George ("Specs") Toporcer
SS-2B-3B-WRITER. (B: Feb. 9, 1899, New York City-D: May 17, 1989). St. Louis (NL), 1921–1928. Remarks: Obtained 437 hits (nine homers) and 22 stolen bases in 546 games in eight big league seasons; first infielder to wear glasses in the majors; had one RBI in 1926 World Series; also player-manager, Rochester (IL), 1928–1934 and Syracuse (IL), 1935; IL MVP award, 1929–1930; lost his eyesight while managing Buffalo (IL) in 1951; became baseball writer/lecturer.

54614. Motomora, Mitchell. *Specs: The True Story of George Toporcer.* Milwaukee, WI: Raintree Publications, 1990. 23p.

54615. Ritter, Lawrence S. "'Specs' Toporcer." In: his *The Glory of Their Times.* New York: William Morrow And Co., 1984. Pp. 259–270.

54616. Ross, Sid and Ernest La France. "Baseball's Bravest Man: The Heart-Warming Story of 'Specs' Toporcer." *Parade Magazine,* (August 30, 1953), 6–7.

54617. Toporcer, George ("Specs"). "Base Running." *Scholastic Coach,* XXXVI (February-March 1967), 28+, 32+.

54618. _____. *Baseball, from Backyard to Big League.* New York: Sterling Publishing Co., 1954. 160p. Reprinted by the same firm in 1961, this work by a former major league player, manager, and coach examines technique, training, coaching, etc.; includes a glossary.

54619. _____. "Batting Order, Platooning." *Scholastic Coach,* XXXVII (March 1968), 7+.

54620. _____. "Bunting to Sacrifice ... To Get On." *Scholastic Coach,* XXXIV (February 1965), 10–11, 64–66.

54621. _____. "The Case for an Aggressive Running Game." *Scholastic Coach,* XXXVII (February 1968), 24+.

54622. _____. "Coaching on the Lines." *Scholastic Coach,* XXXV (March 1966), 32–33, 98–99.

54623. _____. "How to Commit Suicide (Squeeze) for Profit." *Baseball Digest,* XXIV (May 1965), 35–39.

54624. _____. "The Inside of Outfielding." *Baseball Digest,* XXV (June 1966), 55–64.

54625. _____. "It's Catching." *Scholastic Coach,* XXXI (February-March 1962), 10–11+, 20+.

54626. _____. "The Keystone Combination." *Scholastic Coach,* XXXI (April-May 1962), 36+, 40+.

54627. _____. "On the Picket Line. The Outfielder." *Scholastic Coach,* XXXV (February 1966), 18+.

54628. _____. "Pitcher-Handlings' Tougher Than Ever." *Baseball Digest,* XXVII (June 1968), 53–62.

54629. _____. "Playing the Hot Corner." *Scholastic Coach,* XXXIV (March-April 1965), 8–9+, 46+. Third base.

54630. _____. "What You Should Know About Base Stealing." *Baseball Digest,* XXVI (June 1967), 67–74.

Daniel Reid ("Dan") Topping, Sr.
EXEC. (B: June 11, 1912, Greenwich, CT-D: May 18, 1974). Remarks: Owner, New York (AL), 1949–1966.

54631. Healy, John David "Daniel Reid 'Dan' Topping, Jr." In: Vol. Q-Z of David L. Porter, ed. *Biographical Dictionary of American Sports: Baseball.* Rev. and enlarged ed. Westport, CT: Greenwood Press, 2000. Pp. 1552–1553.

Jeffrey Allen ("Jeff") Torborg
C-MGR. (B: Nov. 26, 1941, Plainfield, NJ). Atlanta (NL), 1964–1970; California (AL), 1971–1973. Remarks: Had 297 hits (eight homers) and three stolen bases in 574 games in a decade; received $100,000 signing bonus, 1963; caught Sandy Koufax's (q.v.) perfect game, Sept. 9, 1965, plus two other no-hitters; coach, Cleveland (AL), 1975–1977, New York (AL), 1979–1988; ; manager, Cleveland (AL), 1977–1979, Chicago (AL), 1989–1991; New York (NL), 1992–1993; Montreal (NL), 2001; Florida (NL), 2002–2003, winning 634 games and lost 718 (.469) through 2003; also coach, New York (AL), 1979–1988.

54632. Lucas, Ed and Paul Post. "Jeff Torborg: A Baseball 'Lifer' Still Enamored by The Game." *Baseball Digest,* LXI (February 2002), 66–71.

54633. "Manager Jeff Torborg." In: *White Sox: 1990 Game Program.* Chicago, IL: PR Department, Chicago White Sox, 1990. Pp. 9–10.

Clifford Earl ("The Earl of Snohomish" or "Torgy") Torgeson
1B. (B: Jan. 1, 1924, Snohomish, WA-D: Nov. 8, 1990).

Boston (NL), 1947–1952; Philadelphia (NL), 1953–1955; Detroit (AL), 1955–1957; Chicago (AL), 1957–1961, New York (AL), 1961. Remarks: Obtained 1,318 hits (140 homers) and 133 stolen In 1,668 games in 15 years; obtained seven hits (three doubles) in 1948 World Series; led NL with runs (120), 1950; had a grand slam homer and seven RBIs in one game, June 30, 1951; stole home plate, July 17, 1955; coach, New York (AL), 1961; named to State of Washington Sports Hall of Fame.

54634. Appleton, Sheldon L. "Clifford Earl 'The Earl of Snohomish' Torgeson." In: Vol. Q-Z of David L. Porter, ed. *Biographical Dictionary of American Sports: Baseball.* Rev. and enlarged ed. Westport, CT: Greenwood Press, 2000. Pp. 1553–1555.

54635. Kaese, Harold. "It's Now or Never for Torgeson." *Sport,* XII (May 1952), 34–35, 93–95.

54636. Kiersh, Edward. "Earl Torgeson: Shadow Boxing." In: his *Where Have You Gone, Vince DiMaggio?* New York: Bantam Books, 1983. Pp. 102–110.

54637. Paxton, Henry T. "The Jesting First Baseman of Boston." *Saturday Evening Post,* CCXXIII (May 26, 1951), 27–31.

54638. Stern, Chris. "Earl Torgeson." In: his *Where Have They Gone?* New York: Tempo, 1979. Pp. 91–94.

Earl Torgeson *see* **Clifford Earl ("The Earl of Snohomish" or "Torgy") Torgeson**

Anthony ("Nini") Tornay

C-1B. (B: Oct. 6, 1929, San Francisco, CA). Yakima (W.I.), 1948–1950; San Francisco (PCL), 1951–1957; Portland (PCL), 1958–1959; Columbus (IL), 1960. Remarks: In 13 minor league campaigns, obtained 667 hits and 29 homers in 920 games.

54639. Kelley, Brent P. "Nini Tornay." In: his *The San Francisco Seals, 1946–1957: Interviews with 25 Former Baseballers.* Jefferson, NC: McFarland & Co., Inc., 2002. Pp. 169–174.

Nini Tornay *see* **Anthony ("Nini") Tornay**

Frank Joseph Torre

1B. (B: Dec. 30, 1931, Brooklyn, NY). Milwaukee (NL), 1956–1960; Philadelphia (NL), 1962–1963. Remarks: Had 404 hits (13 homers) and four stolen bases in 714 games in seven big league seasons; tied MLB record by scoring six runs in one game, Sept. 2, 1957; brother of Joe Torre (below).

54640. Marazzi, Rich. "Frank Torre Remembers the Classic World Series of 1957–58." *Sports Collector's Digest,* XXIV (October 3, 1997), 110–111.

Joseph Paul ("Joe" or "The Godfather") Torre, Jr.

C-1B-3B-BROADCASTER-MGR. (B: July 18, 1940, Brooklyn, NY). Milwaukee (NL) and Atlanta (NL), 1960–1968; St. Louis (NL), 1969–1974; New York (NL), 1975–1977. Remarks: Had 2,342 hits (252 homers) in 2,209 games in 18 playing years; had two homers in 1965 All-Star Game; NL MVP award, 1971; NL . batting champion, 1971; NL RBI champion, 1971; hit for the cycle, June 27, 1973; grounded into four consecutive double plays in one game, July 21, 1975; manager, New York (NL), 1977–1981, Atlanta (NL), 1982–1984, St. Louis (NL), 1990–1995, and New York (AL), 1996-date; through 2004, has won 1,781 games and lost 1,570 (.531); broadcaster, California (AL), 1985–1989; survived operation for prostate cancer, 1999; brother of Frank Torre (above). .

54641. Allen, Maury. "How Joe Torre Became a Big Leaguer." *Sport,* XXXVII (April 1964), 54–55+.

54642. Borstein, Larry. "Joe Torre: A Weighty Problem." In: Ray Robinson, ed. *Baseball Stars of 1972.* New York: Pyramid Books, 1972. Pp. 107–113.

54643. Cope, Myron. "Torre: The Last of the Great Catchers." *Saturday Evening Post,* CCXXXIX (July 2, 1966), 84–86+.

54644. Devaney, John. "Joe Torre and The Look in the Mirror." *Sport,* LII (September 1971), 90–127.

54645. Gaven, Michael. "Braves Say He'll Be Torre-fic." *Baseball Digest,* XV (August 1966), 71–73.

54646. Gerlach, Larry R. "Joseph Paul 'Joe' Torre, Jr." In: Vol. Q-Z of David L. Porter, ed. *Biographical Dictionary of American Sports: Baseball.* Rev. and enlarged ed. Westport, CT: Greenwood Press, 2000. Pp. 1555–1556.

54647. Hecht, Henry. "The Nice Guy Who Runs the Lousy Mets." *New York* XII (April 30, 1979), 83–86.

54648. Hochman, Stan. "Torrid Torre's Thoughts at Bat." *Baseball Digest,* XXIV (August 1965), 39–40.

54649. Honig, Donald. "1971: Joe Torre." In: his *National League MVP's.* New York: Bantam Books, 1989. Pp. 85–86.

54650. Isenberg, Jerry. "Joe Torre and the Silver Spoon." *Sport,* XLI (June 1966), 65–78.

54651. Jerome, Richard. "Torre, Torre, Torre." *People Weekly,* XLVI (November 11, 1996), 52–55.

54652. "Joe Torre." In: *Current Biography Yearbook, 1972.* New York: H.W. Wilson Co., 1972. Pp. 430–433.

54653. Jordan, Pat. "The Patience of Joe." *The New York Times Magazine,* (September 15, 1996), 34–37.

54654. Klapish, Bob. "Back for Good." *Yankees Magazine,* XX (October 1999), 18–21. From prostate cancer.

54655. ____. "The Midas Touch." *Yankees Magazine,* XIX (November 1998), 58–60.

54656. ____. "No Breaks for This Bomber." *Yankees Magazine,* XIX (January 1999), 16–19.

54657. Kuenster, John. "Joe Torre: *Baseball Digest's* Player of the Year." *Baseball Digest,* XXX (December 1971), 4–8.

54658. Kurkijan, Tim. "Who's on First, Joe?" *Sports Illustrated,* LXXII (March 6, 1995), 44–46+.

54659. Libby, Bill. "Joe Torre." In: his *Heroes of the Hot Corner.* New York: Watts, 1972. Pp. 135–142.

54660. Lockwood, Wayne. "Joe Torre Swings a Fast Bat." *Baseball Digest,* XXX (October 1971), 76–78.

54661. McCarver, Tim with Danny Peary. "Joe Torre." In: his *The Perfect Season: Why 1998 Was Baseball's Greatest Year.* New York: Villard Books, 1999. Pp. 87–96.

54662. McMillan, Ken. "Joe Torre." In: his *Tales from the Yankee Dugout: A Collection of the Greatest Yankee Stories Ever Told.* Champaign, IL: Sports Publishing, Inc., 2001. Pp. 185–187.

54663. McVay, I. R. "Joe Torre: Atlanta's Baseball Quarterback." *Look,* XXXII (April 30, 1968), 84–88.

54664. Morey, Charles. "Joe Torre and Mickey Lolich: League Leading WeightWatchers." In: Bob Rubin, ed. *Baseball Sports Stars of 1971.* New York: Hewfred Publications, 1972. Pp. 42–47.

54665. Mulvoy, Mark. "Aesop is the Official Scorer [in the] National League Setting Championship Race: Willie Davis and Joe Torre." *Sports Illustrated,* XXXV (July 26,1971), 18–19.

54666. Nicholson, W. G. "Explosive Weekend by Torre Destroyed Pennant-Bound Phils." *The Baseball Research Journal,* XIII (1984), 73–74.

54667. Outlar, Jesse. "Say It Is So, Joe." In: Wayne Minshew, ed. *Braves Illustrated 83.* Atlanta: Public Relations Department, Atlanta Braves, 1983. Pp. 17–19.

54668. Parker, Rob. "Charmed." *Yankees Magazine,* XIX (October 1998), 36–47.

54669. Peters, Alexander. "Joe Torre." In: his *Heroes of* *the Major Leagues.* New York: Random House, 1967. Pp. 146–160.

54670. Pratt, John L. "Joe Torre." In: his *Baseball All-Stars.* Garden City, N.Y.: Doubleday, 1967. Pp. 105–107.

54671. Shapiro, Milton J. "Joe Torre." In: his *Heroes Behind the Mask.* New York: Julian Messner, 1968. Pp. 135–154.

54672. Smith, Loran. "Torre Aiming High." In: Wayne Minshew, ed. *Braves Illustrated '82.* Atlanta, GA: Public Relations Department, Atlanta Braves, 1982. Pp. 26–28.

54673. _____. "You Gotta Be Going Up." *Atlanta,* XXI (April 1982), 94–97.

54674. Torre, Ali and D. Joe Hanover. "Whatever We Have to Do, We'll Get Through It: Interview." *Good Housekeeping,* CCXXIX (October 1999), 132–134. Cancer.

54675. Torre, Frank J. "My Brother Joe." In: William A. Wise, ed. *True's 1972 Baseball Yearbook.* Greenwich, CT: Fawcett Publications, 1972. Pp. 20–21

54676. Torre, Joe. "Joe Torre on the Little Things That Make Great Hitters." *Scholastic Coach,* L (April 1981), 26–27, 67.

54677. _____., as told to J. Stein. "Winning and Winning Again: Interview." *Time,* CLIV (November 1, 1999), 88–89.

54678. _____, with Henry Dreher. *Joe Torrre's Ground Rules for Winners: 12 Keys to Managing Team Players, Tough Bosses, Setbacks and Success.* New York: Hyperion, 1999. 282p.

54679. _____., with Tom Verducci. *Chasing the Dream: My Lifelong Journey to the World Series.* New York: Bantam Books, 1997. 272p.

54680. _____. "The Game I'll Never Forget." *Baseball Digest,* XXXIX (July 1980), 84–87. Reprinted in George Vass, ed. *The Game I'll Never Forget* (Chicago, IL: Bonus Books, 1999), pp. 249–253.

54681. _____. "I've Finally Found a Home." In: Vito Stellino, ed. *1971 Baseball Guidebook.* New York: Maco Publishing Co., 1971. Pp. 62–67.

54682. _____. "A Manager's Lament — They Trying to Run Me Out of Town!" *Sports Illustrated,* XLI (September 24,1984), 58–59.

54683. Tuite, James. "Torre-Ador, Ole!" In: Clyde Hirt, ed. *Sports Quarterly Presents Baseball, 1972.* New York; Counterpoint, Inc, 1972. Pp. 8–9+.

54684. Useem, J. "A Manager for All Seasons." *Fortune,* CXLIII (April 30, 2001), 66–72. Torre

54685. Verducci, Tom. "Crowd Pleasers." *Sports Illustrated,* LXXXIX (November 2, 1998), 46–56.

54686. _____. "Regular Joe." *Sports Illustrated,* LXXXV (October 28, 1996), 40–44.

54687. Walfoort, Cleon. "Joe Torre: Best Young Catcher." *Baseball Digest,* X (November 1961), 19–24.

54688. Wilks, Ed. "Joe Torre: The Making of an MVP." In: Zander Hollander, ed. *Grand Slam 1972 Baseball Annual.* New York: Popular Library, 1972. Pp. 6–10.

54689. Wulf, Steve. "The Torre of Love." *Time,* CXLVIII (October 28, 1996), 115+.

54690. Zanger, Jack. "Joe Torre." In: his *Great Catchers of the Major Leagues.* New York: Random House, 1970. Pp. 152–170.

Yorvit Torrealba

C. (B: July 19, 1978, Caracas, Venezuela). San Francisco (NL), 2001-. Remarks: Through 2004, has had 131 hits (12 homers) and three stolen bases in 186 games; had grand slam homer, May 2, 2004.

54691. Peters, Nick. "Armed Behind the Plate." *Baseball Digest,* LXII (September 2003), 52–55.

Felix Sanchez Torres

3B. (B: May 1, 1932, Ponce, Puerto Rico). Los Angeles (AL), 1962–1964. Remarks: Had 302 hits (27 homers) in 365 games in three years.

54692. Durslag, Melvin. "Hot Sauce and the Angels' Hot Corner Star." *Baseball Digest,* XXI (December 1962), 61–63.

Hector Epitacio Torres

SS-2B. (B: Sept 16 1945 Monterrey, Mexico). Houston (NL),1968–1970; Chicago (NL), 1971; Montreal (NL), 1972; Houston (NL), 1973; San Diego (NL),1975–1976; Toronto (AL), 1977. Remarks: Obtained 375 hits (18 homers) and two stolen bases in 622 games in nine campaigns; tied a MLB record by starting four double plays in one game, Aug. 23, 1963; first Blue Jays player to hit a grand slam homer, June 27, 1977; coach, Toronto (AL) organization, 1978–2002, including manager, Florence (South Atlantic League), 1985–1986, 1993.

54693. Hirshberg, Al. "The Little League Hero Ten Years Later." *Sport,* XLVI (July 1968), 24–28.

54694. Rumill, Ed. "Graceful Torres." *Baseball Digest,* XXVII (December 1968), 51–53.

Rosendo ("Rusty") Torres

OF. (B: Sept. 30, 1948, Aguadillia, PR). New York (AL), 1971–1972; Cleveland (AL), 1973–1974; California (AL), 1976–1977; Chicago (AL), 1978–1979; Kansas City (AL), 1980. Remarks: Obtained 279 hits (35 homers) and 13 stolen bases in 854 games in nine seasons; a switch-hitter who later became head baseball instructor at PowerHouse Baseball, Inc. .

54695. Appel, Marty. "Rusty Torres." In: his *Yesterday's Heroes: Revisiting the Old-Time Baseball Stars.* New York: William Morrow, 1988. Pp. 222–226.

Rusty Torres *see* **Rosendo ("Rusty") Torres**
Michael Augustine ("Mike") Torrez

P. (B: Aug. 28, 1946, Topeka, KS). St. Louis (NL), 1967–1971; Montreal (NL), 1971–1974; Baltimore (AL), 1975; Oakland (AL), 1976–1977; New York (AL), 1977; Boston (AL), 1978–1982; New York (NL), 1983–1984; Oakland (AL), 1984. Remarks. Won 185 games and lost 160 in 18 seasons; won two games in 1977 World Series; remembered for his unpredictability and wild pitches, one of which was Bucky Dent's (q.v.) game winning homer in the one-game New York-Boston AL East playoff, Oct. 2, 1978 and another that hit Houston (NL) SS Dickie Thon (q.v.) in the eye, April 8, 1984.

54696. Bell, Christopher. "Mike Torrez." In: his *Scapegoats: Baseballers Whose Careers are Marked by One Fateful Play.* Jefferson, NC: McFarland & Co., Inc., 2002. Pp. 62–87.

54697. Smith, Lowell D. "Michael Augustine 'Mike' Torrez." In: Vol. Q-Z of David L. Porter, ed. *Biographical Dictionary of American Sports: Baseball.* Rev. and enlarged ed. Westport, CT: Greenwood Press, 2000. Pp. 1556–1557.

54698. Torrez, Danielle G., and Ken Lizotte. *High Inside: Memoirs of a Baseball Wife.* New York: G.P. Putnam, 1983. 238p. Fashion model and spouse, 1974–1980.

54699. Weiss, Peter. "Mike Torrez." In: his *Baseball's All-Time Goats: As Chosen by America's Top Sportswriters.* Holbrook, MA: Bob Adams, Inc, 1992. Pp. 168–171.

Christobal Torriente

OF-P. (B: 1895, Cuba-D: 1938). All Nations/Cuban Stars, 1913–1918; Chicago American Giants, 1918–1925; Kansas City Monarchs, 1926; Detroit Stars, 1927–1928; Gilkerson's Union Giants, 1930; Atlanta Black Crackers and Cleveland Cubs, 1932. Remarks: Cuba's greatest home-run hitter, who also had a 15–7 record as a pitcher, with a career Negro National League batting average of .333; NNL batting champion, 1920 and 1923; also a star in Cuba, Torriente, an alcoholic, died of tuberculosis in New York City, but was returned to his island home a hero and enshrined in the Cuban Baseball Hall of Fame in 1939.

54700. Burgos, Adrian, Jr. "Cristobal Torriente." In Luis Martinez-Fernandez, *et al.*, eds. *Cuba: An Illustrated Encyclopedia.* New York: Oryx Press, 2002. P. 400+.

54701. Holway, John B. "Cristobal Torriente." *Baseball Historical Review* (1981), 72–74.

54702. _____. "The One-Man Team — Cristobal Torriente." *The Baseball Research Journal,* III (1974), 42–47.

54703. Kleinknecht, Merl F. "Cristobal Torriente." In: Vol. Q–Z of David L. Porter, ed. *Biographical Dictionary of American Sports: Baseball.* Rev. and enlarged ed. Westport, CT: Greenwood Press, 2000. Pp. 1557–1558.

54704. Pacelle, Richard L., Jr. "Cristobal Torriente." In: John A. Garrity and Marsh C. Carries, eds. *American National Biography.* 24 vols. New York: Oxford University Press, 1999. XXI, 761–762.

Cesar Leonardo ("Pepito") Tovar
OF-3B-2B-SS. (B: July 3, 1940, Caracas, Venezuela-D: July 14, 1994). Minnesota (AL), 1965–1972; Philadelphia (NL), 1973; Texas (AL), 1974–1975; Oakland (AL), 1975–1976; New York (AL), 1976. Remarks: Had 1,546 hits (46 homers) and 226 stolen bases in 1,488 games in a dozen seasons, played every position, including pitcher, during one nine-inning game, Sept. 22, 1968; stole home plate, May 18, 1969; had five hits and a triple in 1970 ALCS; hit for the cycle, Sept. 19, 1972.

54705. Gordon, Dick. "Cesar Tovar: Letter-Man at Minnesota." *Baseball Digest,* XXVI (July 1967), 29–32.

54706. Markusen, Bruce. "When Cesar Tovar Played All Nine Positions in One Game." *Baseball Digest,* LVII (December 1998), 86–89.

54707. Rothe, Emil H. "When Cesar Tovar Played All Nine Positions." *Baseball Digest,* XXXII (February 1973), 50–53.

54708. Zanger, Jack. "…and One Vote for Cesar." *Sport,* XLV (June 1968), 48–53.

Kevin Towers
EXEC. (B: Nov. 11, 1961, Medford, OR). Remarks: pitcher, San Diego (NL), farm system, 1982–1988; pitching coach/scout, San Diego (NL) farm system, 1989–1991; ; regional cross-checker, then national cross-checker, Pittsburgh (NL), 1992–1993; scouting dir., San Diego (NL), 1993–1995; SVP/GM, San Diego (NL), 1995–.

54709. Nightengale, Bob. "Padres' GM Knows How to Work a Room." *USA Today Baseball Weekly,* VIII (July 9, 1998), 25–27.

Alan Stuart ("Tram") Trammell
SS-MGR. (B: Feb. 21, 1958, Garden Grove, CA). Detroit (AL), 1977–1996. Remarks: Had 2,365 hits (185 homers) and 236 stolen bases in 2,293 games in 20 seasons; noted fielder; obtained four hits in 1984 ALCS; had two homers and six RBI in 1984 World Series; World Series MVP award, 1984; had four hits in 1987 ALCS; had grand slam homer, June 21, 1988; asst., baseball operations dept., Detroit (AL), 1996–1997; coach, Detroit (AL), 1998–1999 and San Diego (NL), 2000–2002; manager, Detroit (AL), 2003–; through 2004, has won 115 games and lost 209 (.355); elected to Michigan Sports Hall of Fame, 2000.

54710. Appleton, Sheldon L. "Alan Stuart 'Tram' Trammell." In: Vol. Q–Z of David L. Porter, ed. *Biographical Dictionary of American Sports: Baseball.* Rev. and enlarged ed. Westport, CT: Greenwood Press, 2000. Pp. 1558–1559.

54711. Associated Press. "The Remarkable Mr. Trammell." In: Charles Einstein, ed. *The Third Fireside Book of Baseball.* New York: Simon and Schuster, 1968. P. 40. Looks at the future star while he was on the University of Florida team

54712. Center, Bill. "Alan Trammell: He's Good and Getting Better." *Baseball Digest,* XLI (July 1982), 60–63.

54713. Clary, Jack. "Trammell-Ripken-Yount: How They're Turning Back the Clock." *Sport World,* XXIII (October 1984), 28–31. Comparison with past shortstops.

54714. Dewan, John and Don Zminda. "Will the Real Alan Trammell Please Stand Up?" In: STATS, Inc. *STATS 1992 Baseball Scoreboard.* Chicago, IL: STATS Publishing, 1992. Pp. 140–142.

54715. DiGiovanna, Mike. "Alan Trammell Earned His Stripes on the Tigers." *Baseball Digest,* XLIV (January 1985), 66–69.

54716. Gage, Tom. "The Tiger' Alan Trammell Comes of Age as a Hitter." *Baseball Digest,* XLVI (November 1987), 27–29.

54717. Garrity, John. "Having a Monster of a Season." *Sports Illustrated,* LX (May 28, 1984), 46–53.

54718. Goldberg, Robert. "The Teeth of the Tigers." *Sport,* LXXV (July 1984), 64–66+.

54719. Green, Jerry. "The Prized Rookie Combo: Trammel and [Lou] Whitaker." *Baseball Digest,* XXXVII (November 1978), 60–61.

54720. Honig, Donald. "Alan Trammell." In: his *The Greatest Shortstops of All Time.* Dubuque, IA: Wm. C. Brown Publishers, 1992. Pp. 92–96.

54721. Janoff, Barry. *Alan Trammell: Tiger on the Prowl.* Chicago: Children's Press, 1985. 46p.

54722. Lee, Tim. "Alan Trammell." *Sports Collector's Digest,* XXIII (May 31, 1996), 162–163.

54723. Trammell, Alan, as told to George Vass. "The Game I'll Never Forget." *Baseball Digest,* LI (March 1992), 31–33.

George McNeal ("Red") Trautman
EXEC. (B: Jan. 11, 1890, Bucyrus, OH-D: June 24, 1963). Remarks: president, Columbus (AA), 1932–1935; president, AA, 1935–1945; executive VP/GM, Detroit (AL), 1946; president, National Association of Professional Baseball Leagues, 1946–1962.

54724. Emory, David. "Energy Career Man — Red Trautman." *Baseball Digest,* IV (February 1945), 38–41. Reprinted in *Baseball Digest,* VI (February 1947), 34–37.

54725. "George M(cNeal) Trautman." In: *Current Biography Yearbook, 1951.* New York: H. W. Wilson Co., 1951. Pp. 630–631.

54726. Lundquist, Carl. "George McNeal 'Red' Trautman." In: Vol. Q–Z of David L. Porter, ed. *Biographical Dictionary of American Sports: Baseball.* Rev. and enlarged ed. Westport, CT: Greenwood Press, 2000. Pp. 1559–1561.

Red Trautman *see* **George McNeal ("Red") Trautman**
Bill Travers *see* **William Edward ("Bill") Travers**
William Edward ("Bill" or "Stork") Travers
P. (B: Oct. 27, 1952, Norwood, MA). Milwaukee (AL), 1974–1980; California (AL), 1981–1983. Remarks: Had 65 victories and 71 defeats, plus one "save," in a decade; surrendered 14 runs in one game, August 14, 1977.

54727. Whiteside, Larry. "Bill Travers: The Brewers' Bionic Pitcher." *Baseball Digest,* XXXV (October 1976), 82–85.

Cecil Howell Travis
SS-3B. (B: Aug. 8, 1913, Riverdale, CA). Washington (AL), 1933–1941, 1945–1947. Remarks: Had 1,544 hits (27 homers) and 23 stolen bases in 1,328 games in a dozen

campaigns; made five consecutive hits in his first big league game, May 16, 1933; had 218 hits in one year, 1941; Battle of the Bulge-received frostbite impaired postwar career; obtained six consecutive hits in two games, May 5–6, 1946; also played for Chattanooga (SA), 1931–1932; scout, Washington (AL), 1948–1955

54728. Appel, Marty. "Cecil Travis." In: his *Yesterday's Heroes: Revisiting the Old-Time Baseball Stars*. New York: William Morrow, 1988. Pp. 228–231. Rob Kirkpatrick's profile is a number in the SABR Online Biography Project http://bioproj.sabr.org/bioproj.cfm?a=v&v=l&bid=597&pid=14327. His biography, *Cecil Travis of the Washington Senators: The Warn-Torn Career of an All-star Shortstop*, is anticipated from McFarland & Co. in 2005.

54729. Bloodgood, Clifford. "Cecil Travis: Coming into Favor." *Baseball Magazine,* LIII (August 1934), 402–403.

54730. Fimrite, Ron. "A Call to Arms." *Sports Illustrated,* LXXV (October 28, 1991), 98–108.

54731. Graber, Ralph S. "Cecil Howard Travis." In: Vol. Q-Z of David L. Porter, ed. *Biographical Dictionary of American Sports: Baseball.* Rev. and enlarged ed. Westport, CT: Greenwood Press, 2000. Pp. 1561–1562.

54732. Hillman, John. "The Amazing Season of Cecil Who?" *Boys' Quest,* (October-November 1996), 44–45.

54733. _____. "Making the Pitch for Cecil Travis in the Hall of Fame." *Sport Collector's Digest,* XXII (July 7, 1995), 166+.

54734. Holway, John B. "Does Cecil Travis Belong in the Hall of Fame?" *Baseball Digest,* LII (May 1993), 63–66.

54735. Lavin, Thomas S. "Cecil Travis: Forgotten Star of Another Era." *Baseball Digest,* XLII (November, 1983), 91+.

54736. Newville, Todd. "Remembering Cecil Travis." *Baseball Digest,* LXII (May 2003), 58–62.

Harold Joseph ("Pie") Traynor★
3B-MGR-BROADCASTER. (B: Nov. 11, 1899, Framingham, MA-D: March 16, 1972). Pittsburgh (NL), 1920–1937. Remarks: Obtained 2,416 hits (58 homers) and 158 stolen bases in 1,941 games in a 17-year big league career; hit for the cycle, July 7, 1923; noted fielder who holds NL record for most career putouts by a third baseman (2,288); manager, Pittsburgh (NL), 1934–1939, winning 456 games and losing 406 (.530); scout, Pittsburgh (NL), 1940–1972; sports commentator, WKQV, 1944–1965; elected to National Baseball Hall of Fame in 1948, where his plaque reads: "Rated among the great third basemen of all time, became a regular with the Pittsburgh NL team in 1922 and continued as a player until conclusion of 1937 season. Managed the Pirates from June 1934 through Sept. 1939. Holds several fielding records and compiled a lifetime batting mark of .320. One of few players ever to make 200 or more hits during a season, collecting 208 in 1923."

54737. Allen, Lee, and Thomas Meany. "Pie Traynor." In: their *Kings of the Diamond.* New York: G.P. Putnam, 1965. Pp. 137–139.

54738. Allen, Maury. "Pie Traynor (1920–1937)." In: his *Baseball's 100.* New York: Galahad Books, 1981. Pp. 268–270.

54739. Barton, Jerry. "Harold 'Pie' Traynor." In: his *A Treasure Chest of the Hall of Fame.* Boston, MA: The Wilson-Hill Co., 1952. Pp. 104–105.

54740. Biederman, Lester J. "Pie Traynor Walks for Pleasure Now." *Baseball Digest,* I (November 1942), 59–61.

54741. Birtwell, Roger. "Pie Traynor: Best of All Third Basemen." *Baseball Digest,* XXVIII (September 1969), 70–73.

54742. Bloodgood, Clifford. "Good News Traynor to Lead Pirates Again." *Baseball Magazine,* LXXX (January 1937), 359–360.

54743. Broeg,, Bob. "Pie Traynor." In: his *Super Stars of Baseball.* St. Louis, MO: *The Sporting News,* 1971. Pp. 263–268.

54744. Davis, Mac. "Harold Joseph (Pie) Traynor." In: his *The Greatest in Baseball.* New York: Scholastic Book Services, 1977. Pp. 32–33.

54745. _____. "Pie Traynor: Pie on the Hot Corner." In: his *Pacemakers in Baseball.* Cleveland, OH. : World Publishing Company, 1968. Pp. 104–106.

54746. Doyle, Charles J. "Pie Traynor." In: Christy Walsh, ed. *Baseball's Greatest Lineup.* New York: A.S. Barnes, 1952. Pp. 119–130.

54747. Drebtnger, John. "The Super Third Baseman." *Baseball Magazine,* LXII (February 1939), 397–399+.

54748. Gietschier, Steven P. "Pie Traynor." In: John A. Garrity and Marsh C. Carries, eds. *American National Biography.* 24 vols. New York: Oxford University Press, 1999. XXI, 811–812.

54749. Graham, Frank. "On Seeing Pie Traynor Again" *Baseball Digest,* XIII (October 1954), 79–81.

54750. Greene, Lee. "*Sport's* Hall of Fame: At Third Base, Pie Traynor." *Sport,* XXXIV (July 1962), 38–39+.

54751. Helfer, Harold. "Winning the Pennant Wasn't as Easy as Pie." *Baseball Digest,* XIII (April 1954), 41–43.

54752. Kaese, Harold. "Pie Traynor: Greatest of Third Basemen." *Baseball Digest,* XXXI (June 1972), 87–91. Reprinted In John Kuenster, ed., *From Cobb to Catfish* (Chicago: Rand McNally, 1975), pp. 188–189.

54753. Keck, Harry. "Stolen Bats Sweetest'— Traynor." *Baseball Digest,* IV (May 1945), 44–50.

54754. Lane, Ferdinand C. "Can Pie Traynor Rival Jimmy Collins?" *Baseball Magazine,* XXXVII (November 1926), 543–544.

54755. _____. "Pie Traynor: A Coming Baseball Star." *Baseball Magazine,* XXXI (July 1923), 349–351.

54756. Libby, Bill. "Pie Traynor." In: his *Heroes of the Hot Corner.* New York: Watts, 1972. Pp. 73–76.

54757. Meany, Thomas and Tommy Holmes, "Pie Traynor: A Mild-Mannered Hero." In: their *Baseball's Best.* New York: Watts, 1964. Pp. 169–176.

54758. Murphy, Jim. "Third Base: Pie Traynor." In: his *Baseball's All-Time All-Stars.* New York: Clarion Books, 1984. Pp. 20–23.

54759. Ritter, Lawrence and Donald Honig. "'Pie' Traynor." In: their *The 100 Greatest Baseball Players of All Time.* New York: Crown Publishers, 1981. Pp. 104–105.

54760. Salant, Nathan. "Pie' Traynor." In: his *Superstars, Stars, And Just Plain Heroes.* New York: Stein and Day, 1982. Pp. 41–45.

54761. Shoemaker, Robert H. "Pie Traynor: Pride of the Pirates." In: his *Best in Baseball.* New York: Crowell, 1956. Pp. 115–119. First published in 1949.

54762. Smith, Ron. "Pie Traynor 70." In: his *The Sporting News Selects Baseball's 100 Greatest Players.* St. Louis, MO: *The Sporting News,* 1998. Pp. 152–153.

54763. Spoehr, Luther W. "Harold Joseph 'Pie' Traynor." In: Vol. Q-Z of David L. Porter, ed. *Biographical Dictionary of American Sports: Baseball.* Rev. and enlarged ed. Westport, CT: Greenwood Press, 2000. Pp. 1562–1563.

54764. Sullivan, George. "Pie Traynor." In: his *Glovemen: Twenty-Seven of Baseball's Greatest.* New York: Atheneum, 1996. Pp. 54–55.

54765. Traynor, Harold J. ("Pie"). "Around the Infield

with: Pie Traynor." *Scholastic Coach,* XVII (April 1948), 26–27.

54766. _____. "Pie Traynor Tells How He Does It." *Baseball Magazine,* LIII (September 1934), 443–445+.

54767. _____. "Playing the Hot Corner." *Scholastic Coach,* XXV (April 1956), 30–31.

54768. _____. "Study Your Opponents." In: *Secrets of Baseball Told by Big League Players.* New York: D. Appleton and Co., 1927. Pp. 88–100.

54769. Verral, Charles S. "Ple Traynor." In: his *Mighty Men of Baseball.* New York: Aladdin Books, 1965. Pp. 71–86.

Carlton Overton Tremper
OF. (B: March 22, 1906, Brooklyn, NY-D: Jan. 9, 1996). Brooklyn (NL), 1927–1928. Remarks: In two big league seasons, had 20 hits in 36 games.

54770. Kelley, Brent P. "Overton Tremper: Dark-Age Dodger." In: his *In the Shadow of the Babe: Interviews with Baseball Players Who Played with or Against Babe Ruth.* Jefferson, NC: McFarland & Co., Inc., 1995. Pp. 63–68.

Overton Tremper *see* **Carlton Overton Tremper**

Theodore ("Ted" or "Highpockets" or "Big Florida") Trent
P. (B: Dec. 17, 1903, Jacksonville, FL-D: Jan. 10, 1944). St. Louis Stars, 1927–1931; Washington Pilots, Detroit Wolves, Homestead Grays, Baltimore Black Sox, and Kansas City Monarchs, 1932; New York Black Yankees and Cole's American Giants, 1933–1934; Cole's American Giants, 1935; Kansas City Monarchs, 1936; Chicago American Giants, 1936–1939. Remarks: Very tall curveballer who won 94 games and lost 49 in 13 seasons; died of tuberculosis.

54771. Lester, Larry. "Theodore 'Ted,' 'Highpockets,' 'Big Florida' Trent." In: Vol. Q-Z of David L. Porter, ed. *Biographical Dictionary of American Sports: Baseball.* Rev. and enlarged ed. Westport, CT: Greenwood Press, 2000. Pp. 1563–1564.

54772. Marasco, David. "Apocrypha in Pittsburgh." *The National Pastime,* XVII (1997), 134–137.

Michael ("Mike") Tresh
C. (B: Feb. 23, 1914, Hazelton, PA-D: Oct. 4, 1966). Chicago (AL), 1938–1948; Cleveland (AL), 1949. Remarks: Obtained 788 hits (two homers) and 19 stolen bases in 1,027 games in 12 years; went 787 games between his first homer (1940) and second (1948); father of Tom Tresh (below).

54773. Tresh, Thomas M. "Yes, My Dad [Mike] Helped Me." In. Sam E. Andre, ed. *Street and Smith's Official 1963 Baseball Yearbook.* New York: Conde Nast Publications, 1963. Pp. 6–10.

Thomas Michael ("Tom") Tresh
OF-SS-COACH. (B: Sept 20, 1937, Detroit, MI). New York (AL), 1961–1969; Detroit (AL), 1969. Remarks: Had 1,041 hits (153 homers) and 45 stolen bases in 1,192 games in nine years; homered in Game Four of 1962 World Series; AL Rookie of the Year award, 1962; had four homers (3–1) in a doubleheader, June 6, 1965; post-career; Central Michigan University graduate, administrator, and asst. baseball coach, 1971–1998, who invented a machine to teach proper sliding techniques; son of Mike Tresh (above).

54774. Brosnan, Jim. "Tom Tresh." In: his *Great Rookies of the Major Leagues.* New York: Random House, 1966. Pp. 137–148.

54775. Devaney, John. "Is There a Real Tom Tresh?" In: his *Official Baseball Annual.* Greenwich, CT: Fawcett Publications, 1963. Pp. 24–28.

54776. Dexter, Charles. "Tom Tresh: Born to the Majors." *Baseball Digest,* XXI (October-November 1962), 67–71.

54777. Elderkin, Phil. "How Yanks' Tresh Got In and Out of Bat Slump." *Baseball Digest,* XXV (September 1966), 17–20.

54778. Gallagher, Mark. "Tom Tresh." In: his *50 Years of Yankee All-Stars.* New York: Leisure Press, 1984. Pp. 206–207.

54779. Heiman, Lee, Dave Weiner and Bill Gutman. "Tom Tresh." In: their *When The Cheering Stops.* New York: Macmillan Publishing Co., 1990. Pp. 4–20.

54780. Honig, Donald. "1962: Tom Tresh." In: his *American League Rookies of the Year.* New York: Bantam Books, 1989. Pp. 33–34.

54781. McCormick, Bob. "Bobby Richardson and Tom Tresh. In: his *Baseball's Greatest Players Today.* New York: Franklin Watts, 1963. Pp. 75–81.

54782. Newville, Todd. "Former Yankee Tom Tresh Recalls Stellar Rookie Year." *Baseball Ink,* I (December 2000), *passim.*

54783. Pepe, Phil. "Tom Tresh: A Study in Versatility." *Sport,* XXXV (February 1963), 56–59.

54784. Rosenthal, Harold. "Tom Tresh: Rookie of the Year." In: Ray Robinson, ed. *Baseball Stars of 1963.* New York: Pyramid Books, 1963. Pp. 43–48.

54785. Sabaini, Dave. "Tom Tresh and His Baseball Legacy." *Sports Collector's Digest,* XVI (February 3, 1989), 158–161.

54786. Tassinari, Edward J. "Thomas Michael 'Tom' Tresh." In: Vol. Q-Z of David L. Porter, ed. *Biographical Dictionary of American Sports: Baseball.* Rev. and enlarged ed. Westport, CT: Greenwood Press, 2000. Pp. 1564–1565.

54787. Trimble, Joe. "Tom Tresh: Baseball's New Idol." *Baseball Monthly,* II (April 1963), 8–13.

54788. Ward, Gene. "A Sad Ending for Tom Tresh's Once-Bright Dream." *Baseball Digest,* XXIX (July 1970), 59–61.

Gus Constantine Triandos
C-COACH. (B: July 30, 1930, San Francisco, CA). New York (AL), 1953–1954; Baltimore (AL), 1955–1962; Detroit (AL), 1963; Philadelphia (AL), 1964–1966; Houston (NL), 1965. Remarks: Obtained 954 hits (167 homers) and one stolen base in 1,206 games in 13 campaigns; first player to catch no-hitters in both the AL and NL; holds MLB record of 1,206 consecutive games without being caught stealing; later assistant baseball coach, University of California.

54789. Fagen, Herb. "Gus Triandos Looks Back on His Catching Career." *Baseball Digest,* LVI (June 1997), 82–88.

54790. Maisel, Bob. "Stranger Than Fiction: Gus Triandos' Inside-the-Park Home Run." *Orioles Gazette,* II (June 5, 1992), 15–16.

54791. Marazzi, Rich. "Lumbering Gus Triandos was an All-Star Catcher for Some Top-Flight Clubs." *Sports Collector's Digest,* XXIV (April 4, 1997), 80–81.

54792. Miller, William J. "Gus Constantine Triandos." In: Vol. Q-Z of David L. Porter, ed. *Biographical Dictionary of American Sports: Baseball.* Rev. and enlarged ed. Westport, CT: Greenwood Press, 2000. Pp. 1565–1566.

54793. Patterson, Ted. "Gus Triandos, Where Are You Now?" *Orioles Gazette,* III (February 19, 1993), 15–16.

54794. Steadman, John F. "Gus Triandos: 'Perfectly' O.K. to Shake Him Off." *Baseball Digest,* XXIII (September 1964), 57–60.

Bob Trice *see* **Robert Lee ("Bob") Trice**
Robert Lee ("Bob") Trice
P-OF. (B: Aug. 28, 1926, Newton, GA-D: Sept. 16, 1988). Homestead Grays, 1948–1950; Farnham/St. Hyacinthe (Provincial League), 1950–1952; Ottawa (IL), 1952–1955; Philadelphia (AL), 1953–1954; Kansas City (AL), 1955; Mexico City Reds (Mexican League), 1956–1958. Remarks: Won nine games and lost nine in three up-and-down big league seasons; also won 67 and lost 41 as a career minor leaguer; first African American A's player.
54795. Moffi, Larry and Jonathan Kronstadt. "Robert Lee 'Bob' Trice." In: their *Crossing the Line: Black Major Leaguers, 1947–1959.* Jefferson, N.C.: McFarland & Co., Inc., 1994. Pp. 103–104.
Jesus Manuel Marcano ("Manny" or "Indio") Trillo
2B. (B: Dec. 25, 1950, Eda Monagas, Venezuela). Oakland (AL), 1973–1974; Chicago (NL), 1975–1978; Philadelphia (NL), 1979–1982; Cleveland (AL) and Montreal (NL), 1983; San Francisco (NL), 1984–1985; Chicago (NL), 1986–1988; Cincinnati (NL), 1989. Remarks: Had 1,562 hits (61 homers) and 56 stolen bases in 1,780 games in 17 years; 1980 NLCS MVP award; noted fielder and first player to start consecutive All-Star games in two major leagues; played 89 errorless games with 479 consecutive chances, 1982; coach, Williamsport (New York-Penn League), 1996; coach, Orlando (Florida State League), 1997; coach, Rockford (Midwest League), 1998; minor league infield coordinator, Philadelphia (NL), 1999; coach, Norwich (New York-Penn League), 2000–2001; coach, Huntsville (SL), 2002–2003; coach, Birmingham (SL), 2004; coach, Charlotte (IL), 2005–.
54796. Ashburn, Richie. "How the Phils Let Manny Trillo Got Away." *Baseball Digest,* XXXVII (April 1978), 84–89.
54797. Brady, Frank. "Manny Trillo: Setting the Style at Second." In: Gerald Kavanagh, ed. *Street and Smith's Official 1983 Baseball Yearbook.* New York: Conde Nast Publications, 1983. Pp. 42–46.
54798. Brosnan, Jim. "Manny Trillo Plays with Style." *Boy's Life,* LXXII (September 1982), 12–14.
54799. Cotton, Anthony. "He's Hot, but Not a Hot Dog." *Sports Illustrated,* LIII (September 8, 1980), 86+.
54800. Smith, Duane A. "Jesus Manuel Marcano 'Manny' Trillo." In: Vol. Q-Z of David L. Porter, ed. *Biographical Dictionary of American Sports: Baseball.* Rev. and enlarged ed. Westport, CT: Greenwood Press, 2000. Pp. 1566–1567.
54801. Stark, Jayson. "Manny Trillo of the Phils: He's Unsung, but Not Underrated." *Baseball Digest,* XL (June 1981), 22–27.
54802. Trillo, Manny, as told to George Vass. "The Game I'll Never Forget." *Baseball Digest,* XLV (September 1986), 78–83.
Manny Trillo *see* **Jesus Manuel ("Manny" or "Indio") Trillo**
Harold Arthur ("Hal") Trosky, Sr.
1B. (B: Harold Arthur Troyavesky, Nov. 11, 1912, Norway, IA-D: June 18, 1979). Cleveland (AL), 19331941; Chicago (AL), 1944 and 1946. Remarks: Had 1,561 hits (68 homers) and 28 stolen bases in 1,347 games in 11 big league seasons; had 28-game hitting streak, 1928; had three consecutive homers in one game, May 30, 1934; involved in fielding a triple play, Sept. 7, 1935; missed 1942–1943, and 1945 seasons due to Illness; AL RBI champion, 1936; led "Crybaby Indians" revolt against their manager, Oscar Vitt (q.v.), 1940; stole home plate, May 11, 1944; scout, Chicago (AL), 1947–1948.

54803. Bloodgood, Clifford. "Hal Trosky of Norway." *Baseball Magazine,* LIII (October 1934), 507–509.
54804. Daniel, Daniel M. "Hal Trosky: Prize Rookie of the Year." *Baseball Magazine,* LIV (December 1934), 293–295.
54805. Eichmann, J. K. "Hal Trosky, First Baseman." *Sports Scoup,* II (October 1974), 10+.
54806. Linkugel, Wil A. and Edward J. Pappas. "The Other Iowa Farm Boy: Hal Trosky." In: their *They Tasted Glory: Among the Missing at the Baseball Hall of Fame.* Jefferson, NC: McFarland & Co., Inc, 1998. Pp. 62–71.
54807. Odenkirk, Jim. "Not Tolstoy, Not Trotsky, but Harold "Hal" Trosky — the Rise and Fall of Hal Trosky." *Nine: A Journal of Baseball History and Social Policy Perspective,* XI (Fall 2002), 69–83.
54808. Smith, Ira L. "Hal Trosky." In: his *Baseball's Famous First Basemen.* New York: A.S. Barnes, 1956. Pp. 236–243.
54809. Solomon, Eric. "Harold Arthur 'Hal' Trosky, Sr." In: Vol. Q-Z of David L. Porter, ed. *Biographical Dictionary of American Sports: Baseball.* Rev. and enlarged ed. Westport, CT: Greenwood Press, 2000. Pp. 1567–1568.
54810. Ward, John J. "Hal Trosky's Great Comeback." *Baseball Magazine,* LXIX (June 1937), 315–316.
Quincy Thomas Trouppe
C-OF. (B: Dec. 25, 1912, Dublin, GA-D: Aug. 10, 1993). St. Louis Stars, 1930–1931; Detroit Wolves, Homestead Grays, and Kansas City Monarchs, 1932; Chicago American Giants and Bismarck (ND) Cubs, 1933; Kansas City Monarchs and Bismarck Cubs, 1934–1936; Indianapolis ABCs, 1938–1939; Detroit Wolves, 1939; Mexico City (Mexican League), 1939–1944; Cleveland Buckeyes, 1944–1947; Chicago American Giants, 1947; New York Cubans, 1949; Drummondville (Canadian Provincial League), 1949; Guadalajara (Mexican League), 1950–1951; Cleveland (AL) and Indianapolis (AA), 1952. Remarks: Noted Negro League player with a lifetime .311 average, who managed Cleveland Buckeyes to NAL championships in 1945 and 1947 and the 1945 Black World Series title; appeared for the Indians in six games and got one hit in 10 ABs; scout, St. Louis (NL), 1953–1962.
54811. Forman, Ross. "Quincy Trouppe: Former All-Star Catcher Just Missed Majors." *Sports Collector's Digest,* XVIII (June 21, 1991), 180–181.
54812. Kleinknecht, Merl F. "Quincy Thomas Trouppe." In: Vol. Q-Z of David L. Porter, ed. *Biographical Dictionary of American Sports: Baseball.* Rev. and enlarged ed. Westport, CT: Greenwood Press, 2000. Pp. 1568–1569.
54813. Moffi, Larry and Jonathan Kronstadt. "Quincy Thomas Trouppe." In: their *Crossing the Line; Black Major Leaguers, 1947–1959.* Jefferson, N.C.: McFarland & Co., Inc., 1994. Pp. 81–82.
54814. Troupe, Quincy T. "Quincy Troupe — Portrait of a Super Star Negro League Player." Edited by Jeffery M. Elliott. *Negro History Bulletin,* XLI (March 1978), 804–807.
54815. _____. *20 Years Too Soon.* Los Angeles, CA: S & S Enterprises, 1977. 285p.
54816. _____.*20 Years Too Soon: Prelude to Major-League Integrated Baseball.* St. Louis: Missouri Historical Society Press, 1995. 158p. Rev. of 1977 1st ed.
Dizzy Trout *see* **Paul Howard ("Dizzy") Trout**
Paul Howard ("Dizzy") Trout
P-BROADCASTER. (B: June 29, 1915, Sandcut, IN-D: Feb. 28, 1972). Detroit (AL), 1929–1952; Boston (AL),

1952; Baltimore (AL), 1957. Remarks: In 15 years, had 170 victories, 161 defeats, and 35 "saves"; won Game Four of 1945 World Series; had grand slam homer, July 28, 1949; Tiger broadcaster, 1953–1955; director of speakers-bureau, Chicago (A.L), 1959–1972; father of Steve Trout (below); enshrined in Indiana Baseball Hall of Fame, 2000.

54817. Amman, Larry. "[Hal] Newhouser and Trout in 1944." *The Baseball Research Journal,* XII (1983), 18–21. The two combined for 56 victories.

54818. Blaisdell, Lowell L. "Paul Howard 'Dizzy' Trout." In: Vol. Q-Z of David L. Porter, ed. *Biographical Dictionary of American Sports: Baseball.* Rev. and enlarged ed. Westport, CT: Greenwood Press, 2000. Pp. 1569–1570.

54819. Bloodgood, Clifford. "Tiger Trout." *Baseball Magazine,* LXV (July 1940), 370–371.

54820. Gold, Eddie. "Father-son Pitching Duos Topped by the Trouts." *Baseball Digest,* LII (March 1993), 74–75.

54821. Lardner, John. "Dizzy's Day." *Newsweek,* XXXVI (August 28, 1950), 73–74.

54822. Salsinger, H. G. "The 'Why' of Trout's Decline." *Baseball Digest,* IV (September 1945), 49–51.

54823. Smith, Ira L. "Dizzy Trout." In: his *Baseball's Famous Pitchers.* New York: A. S. Barnes, 1954. Pp. 288–292.

54824. Smith, Lyall. "Comeback to Continue' — Trout." *Baseball Digest,* X (March 1951), 47–50.

54825. _____. "The Trout Nobody Wanted." *Baseball Digest,* VII (May 1948), 59–61.

54826. Smith, Walter ("Red"). "Doghouse to Let: Apply Newhouser and Trout, Gold-Dust Twins of Detroit Baseball Fandom." *Saturday Evening Post,* CCXVII (March 31, 1945), 22–23+.

54827. Trout, Paul H. ("Dizzy"). "The Game I'll Never Forget." *Baseball Digest,* XXX (June 1971), 36–41.

54828. Trout, Steve. *Home Plate: The Journey of the Most Flamboyant Father and Son Pitching Combination in Major League History.* Murray, UT : E.B. Houchin Co., 2002. 164p.

54829. White, James P. "Touchy Tiger." *Life,* XIII (October 5, 1942), 132–133.

Steven Russell ("Steve" or "Rainbow") Trout
P. (B: July 30, 1957, Detroit, MI). Chicago (AL), 1978–1982; Chicago (NL), 1983–1987; New York (AL), 1987; Seattle (AL), 1988–1989. Remarks: Won 88 games and lost 92, with four "saves," in 13 seasons; won Game Two of 1984 NLCS; son of Paul "Dizzy" Trout (above); minor league coach in Canada, 2003–2004; coach, Windy City Thunderbolts (Independent), 2005-.

54830. Gold, Eddie. "Father-son Pitching Duos Topped by the Trouts." *Baseball Digest,* LII (March 1993), 74–75.

54831. Korn, Peter. "Losing It: Steve Trout Pitched For Nine Years, Suddenly Lost Sight of Home Plate, Then Found Himself About To Be Taken Out of the Game. Completely." *Sport,* LXXIX (July 1988), 48–52.

54832. Trout, Steve. *Home Plate: The Journey of the Most Flamboyant Father and Son Pitching Combination in Major League History.* Murray, UT : E.B. Houchin Co., 2002. 164p.

Donald ("Don" or "Jeep") Trower
2B. (B: Dec. 10, 1919, Hartman, CO). San Francisco (PCL), 1940–1943, 1946–1948; Phoenix (Arizona-Texas League), 1949–1950; Twin Falls (Pioneer League), 1951; Phoenix (Arizona-Texas League), 1952–1953. Remarks: In 12 minor league seasons, obtained 1,270 hits and 42 homers in 1,369 games.

54833. Kelley, Brent P. "Don 'Jeep' Trower." In: his *The San Francisco Seals, 1946–1957: Interviews with 25 Former Baseballers.* Jefferson, NC: McFarland & Co., Inc., 2002. Pp. 38–47.

Dasher Troy *see* **John Joseph ("Dasher") Troy**
John Joseph ("Dasher") Troy
2B-SS. (B: May 8, 1856, New York City-D: March 30, 1938). Detroit (NL), 1881–1882; Providence (NL), 1882; New York (NL), 1883; New York (AA), 1884–1885. Remarks: Had 274 hits (four homers) in 292 games in five seasons; set record for errors by a SS on opening day (five), May 1, 1883.

54834. Troy, John J. ("Dasher"). "Reminiscences of an Old Timer." *Baseball Magazine,* XIV (April 1915), 76–81; XV (June 1915), 93–95.

Virgil Oliver ("Fire") Trucks
P. (B: April 26, 1919, Birmingham, AL). Detroit (AL), 1941–1952; St. Louis (AL), 1953; Chicago (AL), 1953–1955; Detroit (AL), 1956; Kansas City (AL), 1957–1958; New York (AL), 1956. Remarks: In a 17-year major league career, had 177 victories, 135 defeats, and 30 "saves"; pitched two no-hitters in one season (May 10 and Aug. 25, 1952); earlier, while playing for Andalusia (Alabama-Florida League) in 1938, set an all-time OB seasonal mark of 418 strikeouts — which will last only until 1946; also played for Beaumont (TL), 1939–1940 and Miami (IL), 1957; won Game Two of 1945 World Series; won 1949 All-Star Game; coach, Pittsburgh (N.L), 1963; scout for Seattle (AL), 1969); scout and minor league instructor, Atlanta (NL), 1970–1972.

54835. Blaisdell, Lowell L. "Virgil Oliver 'Fire' Trucks." In: Vol. Q-Z of David L. Porter, ed. *Biographical Dictionary of American Sports: Baseball.* Rev. and enlarged ed. Westport, CT: Greenwood Press, 2000. Pp. 1570–1571.

54836. Debs, Victor, Jr. "Virgil Trucks." In: his *"That Was Part of Baseball Then": Interviews with 24 Former Major League Baseball Players, Coaches, and Managers.* Jefferson, NC: McFarland & Co., Inc., 2002. Pp. 166–170.

54837. Devine, Tommy. "If-Man in Tiger-Land." *Sport Life,* IV (September 1951), 58–59.

54838. Dow, Bill. "Turn Back the Clock: Pitcher Virgil Trucks." *Baseball Digest,* LXIII (June 2004), 72–75.

54839. Fehler, Gene. "Virgil Trucks." In: his *Tales from Baseball's Golden Age.* Champaign, IL: Sports Publishing Co., 2000. Chpt. 51.

54840. Hoffman, John C. "There's New Mileage in Old Trucks." *Baseball Digest,* XII (September 1953). 21–27.

54841. Moffi, Larry. "Virgil Trucks: 'I've Got over $700 in my Pocket and That's Gonna Take Care of Me for About Two Years as Far as I Can Figure It.'" In: his *This Side of Cooperstown: An Oral History of Major League Baseball in the 1950s.* Iowa City, IA: University of Iowa Press, 1996. Pp. 13–35.

54842. Salin, Tony. "One Colorful Character: Virgil Trucks." In: his *Baseball's Forgotten Heroes: One Fan's Search for the Game's Most Interesting Overlooked Players.* Chicago: Masters Press, 1999. Pp. 190–192.

54843. Sargent, Jim. "Virgil Trucks: Firing Fastballs and No-Hitters in the Golden Era." *Oldtyme Baseball News,* IX, no. 1 (1998), 12–15.

54844. Spoelstra, Watson. "Beware of 'Fire' Trucks." *Sport,* VIII (May 1950), 28–32.

54845. Stern, Chris. "Virgil Trucks." In: his *Where Have They Gone?* New York: Tempo, 1979. Pp. 147–149.

54846. Trucks, Virgil O., as told to Milton Richman. "I'd Rather Win 20." In: Bruce Jacobs, ed. *Baseball Stars of 1954.* New York: Lion Books, 1954. Pp. 124–129.

54847. Westcott, Rich. "Virgil Trucks: Two No-Hitters in One Season." In: his *Masters of the Diamond.* Jefferson, NC: McFarland & Co., Inc., 1994. Pp. 137–146.

Tim Tschida

UMP. (B: May 4, 1960, St. Paul, MN). Remarks: AL arbiter, 1986-.

54848. Galt, Margot F. "Vitae: St. Paul's Own Tim Tschida." *Minnesota Monthly,* XXIV (April 1990), 40+.

54849. Kaibel, Elizabeth. "At Lunch; Fairest of the Fair." *Mpls/St. Paul Magazine,* XXI (April 1993), 32–33.

54850. Tschida, Tim. "Interview." *Referee,* XXVI (June 2001), 72–73.

Kazuto Tsuroka

MGR. (B: July 27, 1916, Hiroshima, Japan). Nankai Hawks (Japan League), 1939, 1946–1952; won two JL MVP awards and finished with .268 career batting average; manager, Nankai Hawks (Japan League), 1946–1968; led Hawks to nine Pacific League pennants and two Japan Series titles, winning 1,807 games and obtaining a .609 winning percentage; elected to Japanese Baseball Hall of Fame, 1965.

54851. Tsuruoka, Kazuto. *Tsuruoka Kazuto no Eiko to Ketsurui no Puro Yakyu Shi.* Tokyo, 1977. 401p.

Foghorn Tucker *see* **Thomas Joseph ("Tommy" or "Foghorn" or "Noisy Tom") Tucker**

Thomas Joseph ("Tommy" or "Foghorn" or "Noisy Tom") Tucker

1B. (B: Oct. 28, 1863, Holyoke, MA-D: Oct. 22, 1935). Baltimore (AA), 1887–1889; Boston (NL), 1890–1896; Washington (NL), 1897; Brooklyn (NL) and St. Louis (NL), 1898; Cleveland (NL), 1899. Remarks: In 13 big league seasons, obtained 1,882 hits and 352 stolen bases; went 6-for-6 in one game, July 15, 1897; also played for Springfield (EL), 1900; New London (Connecticut State League), 1901 and Meriden (Connecticut State League), 1902.

54852. Kush, Raymond D. "Thomas Joseph 'Tommy,' 'Foghorn,' 'Noisy Tom' Tucker." In: Vol. Q-Z of David L. Porter, ed. *Biographical Dictionary of American Sports: Baseball.* Rev. and enlarged ed. Westport, CT: Greenwood Press, 2000. Pp. 1572–1573.

Thurman Lowell ("Joe E.") Tucker

OF. (B: Sept. 26, 1917, Gordon, TX-D: May 7, 1993). Chicago (AL), 1942–1947; Cleveland (AL), 1948–1951. Remarks: In nine big league seasons, obtained 570 hits (nine homers) and 77 stolen bases in 701 games; had one hit in 1948 World Series; nickname based on perceived resemblance to comedian Joe E. Brown.

54853. Dudley, J. Bruce. "Thurman Tucker." *The Baseball Research Journal,* XXII (1993), 87–88.

John Thomas ("Tute") Tudor

P. (B: Feb. 2, 1954, Schenectady, NY). Boston (AL), 1979–1983; Pittsburgh (NL), 1984; St. Louis (NL), 1985–1988; Los Angeles (NL), 1988–1989; St. Louis (NL), 1990. Remarks: Won 117 games and lost 72, with one "save," in 12 seasons; lost Game One, but won Game Four of 1985 NLCS; won Games One and Four, but lost Game Seven of 1985 World Series; lost Game Two of 1987 NLCS, but won Game Six; won Game Three of 1987 World Series; minor league pitching instructor for St. Louis (NL), 1991–1992, Philadelphia (NL), 1993–1994, and Texas (AL), 1995-.

54854. Fiffer, Steve. "John Tudor: Interview." *Inside Sports,* VIII (June 1986), 18+.

54855. Gammons, Peter. "How Long Will It Last?" *Sports Illustrated,* LXXII (May 21, 1990), 78–80+.

54856. _____. "John Tudor: His Competitive Fire Burned Brightly in '85." *Baseball Digest,* XLV (January 1986), 65–67.

54857. Henderson, Joe. "John Tudor: The Man and the Image." *Baseball Digest,* XLV (August 1986), 48–51.

54858. Olmsted, Frank J. "John Thomas 'Tute' Tudor." In: Vol. Q-Z of David L. Porter, ed. *Biographical Dictionary of American Sports: Baseball.* Rev. and enlarged ed. Westport, CT: Greenwood Press, 2000. Pp. 1573–1574.

54859. Swift, E. M. "Out to Show He's a Good Skate." *Sports Illustrated,* LXIII (November 25, 1985), 26–28, 33.

John Robert Tunis

WRITER. (B: Dec. 7, 1889, Boston, MA-D: Feb. 4, 1979). Remarks: Noted sports journalist and author of children' books, most with a sports theme.

54860. Allen, Mel R. "The Kid from Rowayton." *Yankee Magazine,* (December 1989), 77–81, 116–119.

54861. Bergen, Philip. "Roy Tucker, Not Roy Hobbs: The Books of John R. Tunis." *SABR Review of Books,* I (1986), 85–97.

54862. Epstein, John. "A Boy's Own Author." *Commentary,* LXXXIV (December 1987), 50–56.

54863. Hammer, Adam. "Kidsport: The Works of John T. [sic] Tunis." *Journal of Popular Culture,* XVII (Winter 1983), 146–149.

54864. Holtzman, Jerome. "John R. Tunis." In: his *No Cheering in the Press Box.* New York: Holt, Rinehart & Winston, 1974. Pp. 260–272.

54865. Robinson, Lillian S. "John R. Tunis." In: John A. Garrity and Marsh C. Carries, eds. *American National Biography.* 24 vols. New York: Oxford University Press, 1999. XXI, 929–930.

54866. Shereikis, Richard. "How You Play the Game: The Novels of John R. Tunis." *Horn Book,* LIII (December 1977), 642–648.

54867. Smith, Leverette T., JR. "John Robert Tunis." In: Richard Orodenker, ed. *Dictionary of Literary Biography, Volume 171: Twentieth-Century American Sportswriters.* A Bruccoli Clark Layman Book. Detroit, MI: The Gale Group, 1996. Pp. 326–336.

54868. _____. "John R. Tunis's American Epic; or, Bridging the Gap Between Juvenile and Adult Sports Fiction." In: Wiley Lee Umphlett, ed. *The Achievement of American Sport Literature: A Critical Appraisal.* Rutherford, N.J.: Fairleigh Dickinson University Press, 1991. Pp. 46–61.

54869. _____. "The Realism of Roy Tucker." *SABR Review of Books,* V (1990), 110–120.

54870. Tunis, John R. *This Writing Game.* New York: A. S. Barnes, 1941.

54871. Weidman, Jerome. "John R. Tunis." *Horn Book,* XLIII (February 1968), 48–50.

Bob Turley *see* **Robert Lee ("Bob" or "Bullet Bob") Turley**

Robert Lee ("Bob" or "Bullet Bob") Turley

P. (B. Sept. 19, 1930, Troy, IL). St. Louis (AL), 1951 and 1953; Baltimore (AL), 1954; New York (AL), 1955–1962; Los Angeles (AL) and Boston (AL), 1963. Remarks: In 12 years, had 101 victories, 85 defeats, and 12 "saves"; came within two outs of a no hitter in the first night game played at Baltimore's Memorial Stadium, April 21, 1954; led AL in walks issued, 1954–1955, 1958; lost Game Six of 1956 World Series; lost Game Two of 1958 World Series, but won Games Five and Seven; World Series MVP award, 1958; AL Cy Young Award, 1958; coach, Boston (AL), 1964; post baseball, worked in insurance, founding Primerica Financial Services in 1977.

54872. "As Fast as Feller?" *Time,* LXIII (May 24, 1954), 74–75.

54873. Barnett, C. Robert. "Robert Lee 'Bob,' 'Bullet Bob' Turley." In: Vol. Q-Z of David L. Porter, ed. *Biographical Dictionary of American Sports: Baseball*. Rev. and enlarged ed. Westport, CT: Greenwood Press, 2000. Pp. 1574–1575.

54874. "Bullets Are His Business." In: *Phillies Presents the Sports Sketch Book*. New York: Associated Features, 1959. Pp. 44–45.

54875. Burick, Si. "The Three Changes in Bob Turley." *Baseball Digest*, XVI (December 1951), 45–47.

54876. Cobbledick, Gordon. "Turley and Seven Hitters." *Baseball Digest*, XVII December 1968), 25–27.

54877. Creamer, Robert W. "Two Hot Young Pitchers Named Score and Turley." *Sports Illustrated*, II (May 30, 1955), 39–41.

54878. Devaney, John. "Bob Turley." In: his *Where Are They Today? Great Sports Stars of Yesteryear*. New York: Crown Publishers, 1985. Pp. 189–192.

54879. "Fastest Ball Since Feller's; But Turley Toils Without Support." *Life*, XXXVI (June 7, 1954), 133–135.

54880. Gallagher, Mark. "Bob Turley." In: his *50 Years of Yankee All-Stars*. New York: Leisure Press, 1984. Pp. 208–209.

54881. Isaacs, Stan. "Bullet of the Bombers." *Sport*, XXVI (October 1958), 22–26.

54882. Kaplan, Dave. "Bob Turley." In: Ray Robinson, ed. *Baseball Stars of 1959*. New York: Pyramid Books, 1959. Pp. 7–12.

54883. Kelley, Brent P. "Bob Turley: New York Finally Got Him." In: his *They Too Wore Pinstripes: Interviews with 20 Glory-Days New York Yankees*. Jefferson, NC: McFarland & Co., Inc., 1998. Pp. 181–193.

54884. Macht, Norman L. "Cy Young Award Winner in 1958 Bullet Bob Turley Looks Back on His Big League Career." *Baseball Digest*, LXI (August 2002), 68–74.

54885. McVay, I. R. "The Pitcher Who Throws Bullets … The Yankees' Bob Turley Has Baseball's Best Fast One Since Bob Feller's Prime." *Look*, XIX (July 26, 1955), 72–75.

54886. Meany, Thomas. "Turley's Fastball: 94.2 MPH." *Collier's*, CXXXIII (June 25, 1954), 42–43.

54887. Nichols, Edward J. "Turley's Finest Fanning Season." *Baseball Digest*, XIV (March 1954), 39–41.

54888. "The Pitcher Who Throws Bullets." *Look*, XIX (July 20, 1955), 73–75.

54889. Povich, Shirley. "Turley, Away ffrom Mound 20 Months, to Try Comeback: Arm O.K., Desire to Key Chances with Houston." *Baseball Digest*, XXIV (March 1965), 65–66.

54890. Richman, Milton. "Is Turley the New Feller?" *Sport*, XVII (September 1954), 10–14. .

54891. Schoor, Gene. *Bob Turley, Fastball Pitcher*. New York: G.P. Putnam, 1959. 192p.

54892. Steadman, John F. "Turley Became Forgotten Man So Quickly." *Baseball Digest*, XXI (February 1962), 23–25.

54893. Turley, Robert L. "Bob Turley's Own Story." *Baseball Digest*, XVII (August 1958), 51–58.

54894. _____. *Bob Turley's Pitching Secrets*. New York: G.P. Putnam's Sons, 1965. 95p.

54895. _____. "How I Know What Pitchers Will Throw." *Sports Illustrated*, XXI (July 20, 1964), 30–33.

54896. _____, with Tim Cohane. "With the Yanks, You Win or Else." *Look*, XX (May 29, 1956), 78–83.

54897. Williams, Edgar. "Turley to Rise." *Baseball Digest*, XIII (July 1954), 15–21.

James Riley ("Jim" or "Milkman Jim") Turner
P. (B: Aug. 6, 1903, Antioch, TN-Nov. 29, 1998). Boston

(NL), 1937–1939; Cincinnati (NL), 1940–1942; New York (AL), 1942–1945. Remarks: Won 69 games and lost 60, with 20 "saves," in nine years; lost Game One of 1940 World Series; minor league manager, 1946–1948, 1960; coach, New York (AL), 1949–1959, 1966–1973 and Cincinnati (NL), 1961–1965; noted pitching instructor, especially while with the Yankees; a veteran of 51 consecutive years in OB; elected to Tennessee Sports Hall of Fame, 1972.

54898. Appel, Marty. "Jim Turner." In: his *Yesterday's Heroes: Revisiting the Old-Time Baseball Stars*. New York: William Morrow, 1988. Pp. 232–236.

54899. Barber, Red. "The Milkman." In: his *Walk in the Spirit*. New York: Dial Press, 1969. Pp. 63–67.

54900. Honig, Donald. "1938: Cliff Melton, Lou Fette & Jim Turner." In: his *National League Rookies of the Year*. New York: Bantam Books, 1989. Pp. 118–119.

54901. Linthurst, Randy. "Turner and [Lou] Fette in 1937." *The Baseball Research Journal*, VII (1979), 6–8.

54902. Miller, William J. "James Riley 'Jim,' 'Milkman Jim' Turner." In: Vol. Q-Z of David L. Porter, ed. *Biographical Dictionary of American Sports: Baseball*. Rev. and enlarged ed. Westport, CT: Greenwood Press, 2000. Pp. 1575–1576.

Robert Edward ("Ted") Turner III
EXEC. (B: Nov. 19, 1938, Cincinnati, OH). Remarks: pres., chmn. Bd., Turner Broadcasting System, 1970–1996; vice chmn, Time Warner AOL, 1996–2002; principal owner, Atlanta (NL), 1976–1996.

54903. Bibb, Porter. *It Ain't As Easy As It Looks: Ted Turner's Amazing Story*. New York: Crown Publishers, 1993. 468p.

54904. _____. "Ted Turner's Wild Ride to the Top." *Success*, XL (November 1993), 35–39.

54905. Danberg, Jeff. "The Cable Visions of Ted Turner." In: Zander Hollander, ed. *1983 Season: The Complete Handbook of Baseball*. New York: New American Library, 1983. Pp. 32–40.

54906. Fields, Robert Ashley. *Take Me Out to the Crowd: Ted Turner and the Atlanta Braves*. Huntsville, AL: The Strode Publishers, 1977. 256p.

54907. Fimrite, Ron. "Big Wig Flips His Lid in Wigwam." *Sports Illustrated*, XLV (July 17, 1978), 24–26+.

54908. Fischer, David M. *Ted Turner*. Vero Beach, FL: Rourke, 1993. 109p.

54909. Flower, Joe "High-Risk Power." *Sport*, LXXIII (July 1982), 65–66.

54910. Goldberg, Robert and Gerald Jay. *Citizen Turner: The Wild Rise of an American Tycoon*. New York: Harcourt Brace & Co., 1995. 525p.

54911. Hannon, Kenneth. "Benched from the Bench." *Sports Illustrated*, XLVI (May 23, 1977), 67–68.

54912. Kindred, Dave. "Ted Turner." In: his *Heroes, Fools and Dreamers*. Marietta, GA: Longstreet Press, 1989. Pp. 168–174.

54913. Lamm, Marcy. "Turner Tosses Millions into Building Sports Empire." *Atlanta Business Chronicle*, XXI. (February 26, 1999), B-3–B4.

54914. Landrum, Gene N. "Ted Turner." In: his *Profiles of Genius: Thirteen Creative Men Who Changed the World*. Buffalo, N.Y.: Prometheus Books, 1993. Pp. 213–229.

54915. Macht, Norman L. "Ted Turner." In: his *Famous Financiers and Innovators*. Broomall, PA: Chelsea House, 2002. Pp. 21–25.

54916. McManus, John. "The Ted Offensive: Turner's Buying All the Sports He Can Get." *Sports Inc*, I (November 14, 1988), 38–39.

54917. Meyer, Michael A. "Ted Turner." In: his *The Alexander Complex: The Dreams That Drive the Great Businessmen.* New York: Times Books, 1989. Pp. 197–234.

54918. Oboiski, Robert. "Turner Manages His Braves for One Day." In: his *Baseball's Strangest Moments.* New York: Sterling Publishing Co., 1988. Pp. 64–66. In 1977.

54919. Painton, Priscilla. "The Taming of Ted Turner." *Time,* CXXXIX (January 6, 1992), 34–39.

54920. Smith, Gary. "What Makes Ted Run?" *Sports Illustrated,* LXIV (June 23, 1986), 74–78+.

54921. Steiner, Stephen. "'The Mouth of the South' Talks About Being Baseball's Biggest Loser." *Sport,* LXXI (August 1980), 14–16.

54922. "Ted Turner." In: *Current Biography Yearbook, 1979.* New York: H.W. Wilson Co., 1979. Pp. 408–411.

54923. Vaughan, Roger. *Ted Turner: The Man Behind the Mouth.* Boston, MA: Sail Books, 1978. 230p.

Ted Turner *see* **Robert Edward ("Ted") Turner III**
William Robert ("Bill") Tuttle
OF. (B: July 4, 1929, Elwood, IL-D: Aug. 1, 1998). Detroit (AL), 1952, 1954–1957; Kansas City (AL), 1958–1961; Minnesota (AL), 1961–1963. Remarks: Had 1,105 hits (67 homers) and 38 stolen bases in 1,270 games in 11 seasons; was not afraid of the number 13, wearing it on his uniform throughout his career; died a victim of oral cancer occasioned by chewing tobacco.

54924. Dexter, Charles. "Tuttle Only Looks Worried." *Baseball Digest,* XIII (August 1954), 41–44.

54925. Koppett, Leonard. "The National Spit Tobacco Education Program." *The Baseball Research Journal,* XXVIII (1999), 134–140.

George Albert ("Lefty") Tyler
P-UMP. (B: Dec. 14, 1889, Derry, NY-D: Sept. 29, 1953). Boston (NL), 1910–1917; Chicago (NL), 1918–1922. Remarks: Won 127 games and lost 118, with seven "saves"; won 21-inning complete game, July 17, 1918; won Game Two but Lost Game Six of 1918 World Series; umpire, New England League and EL, 1923–1932.

54926. Akin, William E. "George Albert 'Lefty' Tyler." In: Vol. Q-Z of David L. Porter, ed. *Biographical Dictionary of American Sports: Baseball.* Rev. and enlarged ed. Westport, CT: Greenwood Press, 2000. Pp. 1577–1578.

Lefty Tyler *see* **George Albert ("Lefty") Tyler**
Peter Victor Ueberroth
EXEC. (B: Sept. 2, 1937, Evanston, IL). Remarks: Pres./MD, Los Angeles Olympic Organizing Com., 1979–1984; Commissioner of Baseball, 1984–1989. Cochmn., Doubletree Hotels Corp., Phoenix, 1993–.

54927. Ajemian, Robert. "Master of the Games." *Time,* CXXV (January 7, 1985), 32–39. For his work with the 1984 summer Olympics, Ueberroth was voted "Man of the Year" by both *Time* and *The Sporting News.*

54928. Anderson, Dave. "Talking Sports with Peter Ueberroth." *The New York Times Magazine,* (August 6, 1985), 46+.

54929. Axtheim, Pete. "Now Pitching, Peter Ueberroth." *Newsweek,* CVI (August 19, 1985), 54–55.

54930. _____. "Ueberroth: 'Play Ball.'" *Newsweek,* CVI (August 5, 1985), 58–59.

54931. Behar, Robert. "Take That, Peter Ueberroth." *Forbes,* CXXXIX (February 9, 1987), 36–38.

54932. Callahan, Tom. "Commissioner on Deck." *Time,* CXXIII (March 12, 1984), 58+.

65933. Castro, J. "The Designated Hero." *Time,* CXXXIII (April 17, 1989), 44–46.

54934. Collins, N. "Hardball: Interview." *New York,* XIX (June 9, 1986), 52–57+.

54935. Cramer, Richard Ben. "Citizen Ueberroth." *Esquire,* CVII (February 1987), 69–81.

54936. Deford, Frank. "The Boss Takes His Cuts." *Sports Illustrated,* LXXII (April 15, 1985), 100–102+.

54937. Fimrite, Ron. "The Score After One: Some Hits, Some Errors." *Sports Illustrated,* LXIII (December 16, 1985), 38–40+.

54938. Holtzman, Jerome. "Peter Ueberroth." In: his *The Commissioners: Baseball's Midlife Crisis.* New York: Total Sports, 1998. Pp. 208–230.

54939. Kaplan, Jim. "A Promising Entry into a Tough New Arena." *Sports Illustrated,* LXI (October 22, 1984), 41+.

54940. _____. and Ivan Maisel. "The Commissioner Gets Tough." *Sports Illustrated,* LXII (May 20, 1985), 32–34+.

54941. Leerhsen, Charles. "Ueberroth at Bat." *Newsweek,* CV (January 1, 1985), 70–71+.

54942. Lupica, Mike. "The Balk Stops Here." *Esquire,* CX (August 1988), 43–44.

54943. Masin, Herman L. "Striking Out…." *Scholastic Coach,* LVII (August 1987), 14–15.

54944. McManus, John. "Peter's Ninth Inning Legacy: Ueberroth Will Cut a TV Deal, Change the Game, and Leave." *Sports Inc.,* I (October 10, 1988), 22–23.

54945. Okrent, Daniel. "On the Money; as Baseball's Commissioner, Peter Ueberroth Used His Uncanny Power of Public Relations to Generate Unprecedented Profits." *Sports Illustrated,* LXX (April 10, 1989), 41–44.

54946. "Peter Principles." *Sports Illustrated,* LXVI (April 27, 1987), 72–73.

54947. "Peter Ueberroth." In: *Current Biography Yearbook, 1985.* New York: H. W. Wilson, 1985. Pp. 421–425.

54948. Rappoport, Ken. "Peter Ueberroth: At Bat for Baseball." *Saturday Evening Post,* CCLVII (November 1985), 62–65.

54949. Reibstein, Lawrence. "The Ueberroth Touch." *Newsweek,* CXIII (April 17, 1989), 44–45.

54950. Reiss, Craig. "Cable Driving Baseball Deal: Ueberroth Will Change Dynamics of Game Coverage." *Sports Inc.,* I (October 10, 1988), 1–2.

54951. Smilgis, M. "Peter Ueberroth." *People Weekly,* XXII (December 24, 1984), 44+.

54952. Thomas, Evan. "A Win for the Fans; the Owners Balk, the Players Walk, Then Ueberroth Gets the Save." *Time,* CXXVI (August 19, 1985), 44–45.

54953. Ueberroth, Peter V. "The Game's Incoming Chief Picks Up the Ball: An Interview." *U.S. News and World Report,* XCVII (October 15, 1984), 78–79.

54954. _____. "Inside Baseball: Interview." *U.S. News and World Report,* XCIX (October 28, 1985), 68+.

54955. _____. with Richard Levin and Amy Quinn. *Made in America: His Own Story.* New York: William Morrow, 1985. 401p.

54956. "Ueberroth Says Baseball's Future is on Cable TV." *Broadcasting,* CXV (August 8, 1988), 22–23.

54957. Verdi, Bob. "Give the Man a Hand." In: Bob Verdi. *The Bob Verdi Collection.* Dallas, TX: Taylor Publishing Co., 1988. Pp. 29–31.

Bob Uecker *see* **Robert George ("Bob") Uecker**
Robert George ("Bob") Uecker
C-BROADCASTER-ACTOR. (B: Jan. 26, 1935, Milwaukee, WI). Milwaukee (NL), 1962–1963; St. Louis (NL), 1964–1965; Philadelphia (NL), 1966–1967; Atlanta (NL), 1967. Had 146 hits (14 homers) in 297 games in six years; broadcaster, Milwaukee (AL), 1971–; commentator, *ABC Monday Night Baseball,* 1976–82; commentator

playoff and World Series, NBC Baseball, 1994–98; noted humorist and television personality — "Mr. Baseball"; co-star TV series *Mr. Belvedere,* ABC-TV, 1985; films include: *Major League,* 1989, *Major League 2,* 1994, (voice over) *Homeward Bound II: Lost in San Francisco,* 1996, *Major League: Back to the Minors,* 1998, *Andre the Giant: Larger Than Life,* 1999; inducted into Wisconsin Sports Hall of Fame, 1998; Ford C. Frick Award, 2003.

54958. "Bob Uecker, Baseball's Funny Man." In: Tom Barnidge, ed. *The Sporting News 1985 Baseball Yearbook.* St. Louis, MO: The Sporting News, 1985. Pp. 135–137.

54959. Cairns, Bob. "Bob Uecker." In: his *Pen Men: Baseball's Greatest Bullpen Stories told by the Men Who Brought the Game Relief.* New York: St. Martin's Press, 1992. Pp. 228–232.

54960. Carlson, T. "The Laughs Come Faster Than the Hits." *TV Guide,* XXXV (July 25, 1987), 32–35.

54961. Davis, Gode. "Diamond Diamonds in the Rough: Bob Uecker is Just One of *Baseball Cards'* Hidden Gems, According to Gode Davis." *Baseball Cards,* XI (February 1991), 110–112.

54962. McCarver, Tim. "Bob Uecker." In: Danny Peary, ed. *Cult Baseball Players.* New York: Simon and Schuster, 1990. Pp. 328–337.

54963. _____. "Bob Uecker." In: Danny Peary, ed. *Baseball's Finest: The Greats, the Flakes, the Weird and the Wonderful.* North Digton, MA: The JG Press, 1990. Pp. 328–337. Both Peary books are identical.

54964. Rubin, Bob. "The Hilarious Ueck: These Fans, They Love Him." *Inside Sports,* IX (July 1987), 16+.

54965. Rumill, Ed. "Bobby Uecker No. 2 Too Long." *Baseball Digest,* XXV (June 1966), 39–41.

54966. Russo, Neal. "Bob Uecker: Swiss with Good Movement." *Baseball Digest,* XXIII (August 1964), 57–59.

54967. Uecker, Robert G. ("Bob"), with Mickey Herskowitz. *Catch .222.* New York: G. P. Putnam, 1992. 320p.

54968. _____. *Catcher in the Wry.* New York: G.P. Putnam, 1982. 192p.

54969. Verdi, Bob. "Bob Uecker: Baseball's 'Rodney Dangerfield.'" *Baseball Digest,* XXXIX (September 1980), 69–77.

54970. _____. "Uecker Laments Lost Riches." In: Bob Verdi. *The Bob Verdi Collection.* Dallas, TX: Taylor Publishing Co., 1988. Pp.2–4.

George Ernest ("The Bull") Uhle
P. (B: Sept. 18, 1898, Cleveland, OH-D: Feb. 19, 1985). Cleveland (AL), 1919–1928; Detroit (AL), 1929–1933; New York (NL), 1933; New York (AL), 1933–1934; Cleveland (AL), 1936. Remarks: In a 17-year big league career, had 200 victories, 166 defeats, and 25 "saves"; pitched 20 innings of a 21-inning game, May 24, 1929; one of the first pitchers to employ the slider; as a batter, had 393 hits (nine homers) in 723 games and drove in six runs in one game, April 28, 1921; holds record for most base hits made in a season by a pitcher (52), 1923; coach, Cleveland (AL), 1936–1937, Buffalo (IL), 1938–1939, Chicago (NL), 1940 and Washington (AL), 1944; scout for Brooklyn (NL), 1941–1942; thereafter, a salesman for the Arrow Aluminum Casting Company.

54971. Bak, Richard. "George Uhle." In: his *Cobb Would Have Caught It: The Golden Age Of Baseball In Detroit.* Detroit, MI: Wayne State University Press, 1991. Pp. 174–189.

54972. Bang, Ed. "Fastest for One Pitch: George Uhle." *Baseball Digest,* XI (April 1952), 77–79.

54973. Evers, John L. and Harry A. Jebsen, Jr. "George Ernest 'The Bull' Uhle." In: Vol. Q-Z of David L. Porter,

ed. *Biographical Dictionary of American Sports: Baseball.* Rev. and enlarged ed. Westport, CT: Greenwood Press, 2000. Pp. 1579–1580.

54974. Gettleson, Leonard. "Can Pitchers Hit?" *Baseball Magazine,* XLV (June 1930), 320–322.

54975. Givens, Horace H. "George Uhle: The Pitcher Who Pioneered the Slider." *Baseball Digest,* XLI (November 1982), 89+.

54976. Green, Paul M . "Baseball and George Uhle." *Sports Collector's Digest,* XI (March 16, 1984), 78+.

54977. Murdock, Eugene. "The Greatest Hitting Pitcher?: George Uhle." In: his *Baseball Players and Their Times: Oral Histories of the Game, 1920–1940.* Westport, CT: Meckler Publishing, 1991. Pp. 126–141.

54978. Ward, John J. "The Champion Pitcher of the Past Season." *Baseball Magazine,* XXXVIII (March 1927), 444–445+.

Thomas Mullen ("Tommy") Umphlett
OF (B: May 12, 1930, Scotland Neck, NC). Boston(AL), 1953; Washington (AL), 1954–1955: Remarks: Obtained 285 hits (six homers) in 361 games in three big league years; also played for Sacramento (PCL).

54979. Povich, Shirley. "Washington's 'Yes, Sir' Kid." *Baseball Digest,* XIII (April 1954), 35–38.

54980. Skipper, John C. "Tommy Umphlett: He Played in an Inning that Has Never Been Duplicated." In: his *Inside Pitch: A Closer Look at Classic Baseball Moments.* Jefferson, NC: McFarland & Co., 1996. Pp. 80–83.

Thomas Gerald ("Tom") Underwood
P. (B: Dec. 22, 1953, Kokomo, IN). Philadelphia (NL), 1974–1977; St. Louis (NL), 1977; Toronto (AL), 1978–1979; New York (AL), 1980–1981; Oakland (AL), 1981–1983; Baltimore (AL), 1984. Remarks. Won 86 games and lost 87, with 18 "saves," in 11 seasons; appeared in 1976 NLCS and 1980–1981 ALCS, all without a decision; also pitched for Reading Phillies (EL), 1974 and named to that team's hall of fame, 2004.

54981. Lyon, Bill. "Tom Underwood: A Super Pitcher in the Making." *Baseball Digest,* XXXIV (September 1973), 46–49.

Don Unferth
EXEC. Chicago (AL) media director, 1970's.

54982. Unferth, Don. "Reflections of a Front Office Favorite." In: Paul Jensen, ed. *Chicago White Sox 1985 Yearbook.* Chicago, IL: Public Relations Department, Chicago White Sox, 1985. Pp. 79–81.

Bob Unglaub *see* **Robert Alexander ("Bob") Unglaub**
Robert Alexander ("Bob") Unglaub
3B-SS-2B-MGR. (B: July 31, 1881, Baltimore, MD-D: Nov. 29, 1916). New York (AL), 1904; Boston (AL), 1904–1908; Washington (AL), 1908–1910. Remarks: In six big league seasons, obtained 554 hits (five homers) and 66 stolen bases in 595 games; had 31 putouts in one 20-inning game, July 4, 1905; interim manager, Boston (AL), winning nine games and losing 20 (.310); also played for Worcester (EL), 1900–1901, Sacramento (California State League), 1902, Milwaukee (AA), 1903, Williamsport (Tri-State League), 1906, Minneapolis (Northern League), 1912–1916; killed in an industrial accident.

54983. Unglaub, Robert A. "How to Play First Base." *Baseball Magazine,* II (March 1909), 41–43. Marty Payne's profile of Unglaub is a number in the online SABR biography project http://bioproj.sabr.org/bioproj.cfm?a=v&v=l&bid=16&pid=14457>.

Delvert Edward ("Del") Unser
OF-1B. (B. Dec. 9, 1944, Decatur, IL). Washington (AL), 1968–1971; Cleveland (AL), 1972; Philadelphia (NL),

1973–1974; New York (NL), 1975–1976; Montreal (NL), 1976–1978; Philadelphia (NL), 1979–1982. Remarks. Obtained 1,344 hits (97 homers) and 84 stolen bases in 1,799 games in. 15 seasons; led AL in triples, 1969; had three consecutive pinch-hit homers, June 30, July 5 and July 10, 1979; scored winning run in Game Five of 1980 NLCS and in Game Five of 1980 World Series; coach, Philadelphia (NL), 1985–1988; named to Mississippi Sports Hall of Fame, 1997.

54984. "Philly Gets a Trio to Cheer: Outfielders Greg Lusinski, Del Unser, and Bill Robinson." *Sports Illustrated,* XXXIX (July 30,1973), 40–41.

54985. Rumill, Ed. "Del Unser: New Senator from Illinois." *Baseball Digest,* XXVII (September 1968), 40–41.

54986. Taylor, Jim. "Del Unser Finds New Life in Philly." *Baseball Digest,* XXXII (November 1973), 35–39.

Willie Clay Upshaw
OF-IB. (B: April 27, 1957, Blanco, TX). Toronto (AL), 1978, 1980–1987; Cleveland (AL), 1988; Nankai Hawks (Japan League), 1988–1989. Remarks: Had 1,103 hits (123 homers) and 88 stolen bases in 1,264 games in 10 seasons; had at least one RBI in eight consecutive games, September 1983; had six hits (two doubles) in 1985 ALCS; roving instructor, Cleveland (AL), 1992–1996; coach, Toronto (AL), 1996–1997; manager, Bridgeport Bluefish (Atlantic League), 1997–2000 and Akron (EL), 2002; roving instructor, San Francisco (NL), 2002; coach, Norwich (EL), 2003–.

54987. Blanchine, Jim. "Willie Upshaw Helps the Blue Jays Take Flight." *Baseball Digest,* XLIII (October 1984), 55–58.

Billy Urbanski *see* **William Michael ("Billy") Urbanski**

William Michael ("Billy") Urbanski
SS. (Bi June 5, 1903, Staten Island, NY-D: July 12, 1973). Boston (NL), 1931–1937. Remarks: Had 791 hits (19 homers) in 763 games in seven years; on base for each of the last three homers of George H. ("Babe") Ruth, May 1935.

54988. Ward, John J. "Urbanski of the Braves." *Baseball Magazine,* LII (January 1934), 368–369+.

Ugueth Urtain Urbina
P. (B: Feb. 15, 1974, Caracas, Venezuela). Montreal (NL), 1995–2001; Boston (AL), 2001–2002; Texas (AL) and Florida (NL), 2003; Detroit (AL), 2004. Remarks: Through 2004, has won 39 games and lost 43, with 227 "saves" ; hurler's mother, Maura Villaroel, kidnapped from her home at Ocumare del Tuy, Venezuela, on Sept. 1, 2004 and not released as of Feb. 1, 2005.

54989. Cannella, Stephen. "Back in the Swim?: Urbina's Struggles." *Sports Illustrated,* XC (June 7, 1999), 122, 125.

Bob Usher *see* **Robert Royce ("Bob") Usher**

Robert Royce ("Bob") Usher
OF (B: March 1, 1925, San Diego, CA). Cincinnati (NL), 1946–1947, 1950–1951; Chicago (NL), 1952; Cleveland (AL) and Washington (AL), 1957. Remarks: Had 259 hits (18 homers) and nine stolen bases in 428 games in all or parts of six big league seasons; also played for San Diego (PCL), 1955–1956.

54990. Ison, Jim. "Bob Usher." In: his *Mormons in the Major Leagues.* Cincinnati: Action Sports, 1991. Pp. 184–187.

54991. Swank, Bill. "Bob Usher." In: his *Echoes from Lane Field: A History of The San Diego Padres 1936-1957.* Paducah, KY: Turner Publishing Company, 1997. Pp. 139–140.

Marc Christopher Valdes
P. (B: Dec. 20, 1971, Tampa, FL). Florida (NL),

1995–1996; Montreal (NL), 1997–1998; Houston (NL), 2000; Atlanta (NL), 2001; Hanshin Tigers (Japan League), 2002; Chunichi Dragons (Japan League), 2003–2004. Remarks: Won 11 games and lost 16, with four "saves," in six U.S. big league seasons; won five games and lost seven with 24 saves in Japan.

54992. Epstein, Eddie. "Marc Valdes." In: STATS, Inc. *The STATS 1995 Minor League Scouting Notebook.* Skokie, IL: STATS Publishing, 1995. Pp. 162–163.

Jose Martinez ("Joe") Valdivielso
SS. (B: Jose Martinez De Valdivielso Lopez, May 22, 1934, Matanzes, Cuba). Washington (AL), 1955–1956, 1959–1960; Minnesota (AL), 1961. Remarks: Obtained 213 hits (nine homers) and six stolen bases in 401 games in all or part of five major league seasons; strong fielder, light hitter.

54993. Appel, Mary. "Jose Valdivielso." In: his *Yesterday's Heroes: Revisiting the Old-Time Baseball Stars.* New York: The Dial Press, 1988. Pp. 238–241.

John William Valentin
SS-3B-2B. (B: Feb. 18, 1967, Mineola, NY). Boston (AL), 1992–2001; New York (NL), 2002. . Remarks: Through 2002, has had 1,093 hits (124 homers) and 47 stolen bases in 1,105 games; first homer a grand slam, Aug. 22, 1992; made history's 10th unassisted triple play, July 8, 1994; obtained a second grand slam homer, May 2, 1995; became first big league SS with 15 total bases in a game, June 2, 1995; hit for the cycle, June 6, 1996; career curtailed by knee injury.

54994. Rutstein, Michael. "Hard-Hitting John Valentin Could Be Boston's Next All-Star." *Boston Baseball,* VI (May 1995), 7+.

Bobby Valentine *see* **Robert John ("Bobby") Valentine**

Bubba Valentine *see* **Ellis Clarence ("Bubba") Valentine**

Ellis Clarence ("Bubba") Valentine
OF. (B: July 30, 1954, Helena, AK). Montreal (NL), 1975–1981; New York (NL), 1981–1982; California (AL), 1983; Texas (AL), 1985. Remarks: Had 881 hits (123 homers) in 894 games in a decade; had two inside-the-park homers in one year, 1977; after playing career, worked for a car rental firm and for the A.V. Light Foundation.

54995. Eskow, John. "One Stone Don't Tip No Mountain." *Sport,* LXIX (July 1979), 56–59+.

54996. Quinn, Hal. "Love Letters from Out in Right Field." *Macleans,* XCIV (March Z3, 1981), 40+.

Robert John ("Bobby") Valentine
SS-OF-28-3B-MGR-BROADCASTER. (B: May 13, 1950, Stamford, CT). Los Angeles (NL), 1969 and 1971–1972; California (AL), 1973–1975; San Diego (NL), 1975–1977; New York (NL), 1977–1978; Seattle (A. L.), 1979. Remarks: Obtained 441 hits (12 homers) and 27 stolen bases in 639 games in a decade; minor league instructor, San Diego (NL), 1980–1981; coach, New York (NL), 1983–1984; manager, Texas (AL), 1985–1992, coach, Cincinnati (NL), 1993; manager, Chiba Lotte Marines (Japan League), 1993–1995 (first former U.S. major league manager to lead a Japanese team); New York (NL), 1996–2002; as U.S. big league pilot, won 1,117 games and lost 1,072 (.510); received Branch Rickey Award, 2002; analyst, ESPN, 2003; manager, Chiba Lotte Marines (Japan League), 2004–.

54997. Claire, Fred. "Bobby Valentine: Another Top Rookie for the Dodgers." *Baseball Digest,* XXX (March 1971), 27–31.

54998. Esham, Robin. "The Bobby Valentine Story."

The Journal of the American Chamber of Commerce, XXXIII (March 1996), 34+.

54999. Herman, P. G. "Bobby Valentine." *Current Biography,* LXII (July 2001), 74–80.

55000. Jordan, Pat. "Now That His Texas Rangers Are Gunning for the Top, Nobody's Telling Bobby Valentine To Shut Up." *People Weekly,* XXVI (July 7, 1986), 119–123.

55001. Montville, Leigh. "The Great Survivor." *Sports Illustrated,* LXXVI (April 6, 1992), 42–47.

55002. Murray, Jim. "Bobby Valentine: An Angel with True Grit." *Baseball Digest,* XXXIII (August 1974), 72–76.

55003. Price, S. L. "Valentine's Day." *Sports Illustrated,* XCI (October 11, 1999), 68–72+.

55004. Rapoport, Ron. "Bobby Valentine: No Regrets for What Might Have Been-" *Baseball Digest,* XXXVIII (February 1979), 38–41.

55005. Rogers, Phil. "86 Poses Another Challenge for Rangers' Bobby Valentine." *Baseball Digest,* XLV (March 1986), 28–31.

55006. Shapiro, Bobby. "Beers with Bobby Valentine." *Sport,* LXXVIII (August 1987), 23–24.

55007. Starr, Mark. "Losing in a New Language." *Newsweek,* CXXV (May 22, 1995), 46+.

55008. Verducci, Tom. "Valentine Days." *Sports Illustrated,* LXXXVII (August 4, 1997), 30–33.

55009. Wischnia, Bob. "After the Crash: Bobby Valentine at 25." *Sport,* LXI (July 1975), 57–62.

Fernando ("El Toro") Valenzuela

P-BROADCASTER. (B: Nov. 1, 1960, Navajoa, Mexico). Los Angeles (NL), 1980–1990; California (AL), 1991; Baltimore (AL), 1993; Philadelphia (NL), 1994; San Diego (NL), 1995–1997; St. Louis (NL), 1997; Hermosillo (Mexican League), 1998–2002; Mexicali (Mexican League), 2004–. Remarks: Won 173 games and lost 153 in all or part of 17 U.S. big league seasons; won Game Four of 1981 NLCS; won Game Two of 1981 World Series; N.L Rookie of the Year award, 1981; NL Cy Young Award, 1981 (first pitcher to win both awards the same year); won Game Two of 1983 NLCS; Spanish language broadcaster, Los Angeles (NL), 2003–2004; joined Mexicali (Mexican League) late in 2004 winning two games and losing two.

55010. Archer, Jim. "Fernando vs. 'The Bird.'" *The Baseball Research Journal,* XI (1982), 16–17. Comparison of Valenzuela and Mark Fidrych.

55011. Axtheim, Pete. "Ole!: Fernando Shapes Up." *Newsweek,* XCIX (April 5, 1982), 80–81.

55012. Beezley, William H. "The Rise of Baseball in Mexico and the First Valenzuela." *Latin American Popular Culture,* IV (1985), 3–13.

55013. Beltran del Rio, Pascal. "Pese a su Mala Temporada, Valenzuela Rechaza Hablar del Retiro." *Proceso,* no. 1080 (Julio 13, 1997), 76–79.

55014. _____. "Valenzuela Abrio la Puerta, y Los Mexicanos Invaden las Grandes Ligas." *Proceso,* no. 1965 (Marzo 30, 1997), 64–67.

55015. Broeg, Bob. "Fernando Valenzuela Spurs Renewed Interest in the Screwball." *Baseball Digest,* XLI (March 1982), 68–71.

55016. Burchard, S.H. *Sports Star Fernando Valenzuela.* New York: Harcourt, Brace, Jovanovich, 1982. 64p.

55017. Castro, Tony. "Something Screwy Going on Here." *Sports Illustrated,* LXIII (July 8, 1985), 31–37.

55018. Click, Paul. "20 Years Ago, Fernando Valenzuela was King of the Hill." *Baseball Digest,* LX (July 2001), 62–66.

55019. Didinger, Ray. "Fernando Valenzuela: Pitcher with the Golden Arm." *Baseball Digest,* XL (August 1981), 26–31.

55020. Elderkin, Phil. "Fernando Valenzuela: Big-League Rhythm." In: Bill Shumard, ed. *1981 Los Angeles Dodgers Yearbook.* Anaheim, CA: Rotary off-Set Printers, 1981. p. 53.

55021. "Fernando Valenzuela." In: *Current Biography Yearbook, 1982.* Now York: H.W. Wilson Co., 1982. Pp. 423–427.

55022. Gloeckner, Carolyn. *Fernando Valenzuela.* Mankato, MN: Crestwood House, 1985. 48p.

55023. Gonzalez, John. "The Comeback Kid." *Hispanic,* VI (October 1993), 66–67.

55024. Gordon, Morris. "Has Fernando Rediscovered His Release Point?" *Sport World,* XXIII (August 1984), 12–13.

55025. Gurnick, K. "Valenzuela Masterly Amid Dodger Mishaps." *The New York Times Biographical Service,* XVII (August 1986), 1019–1021.

55026. Hedin, Mark. "El Beisbol Rompe una Barrera: Valenzuela Triunfa en 'La Premera Serie." *El Mensajero,* X (Agosto 21, 1996), 16–17.

55027. Heisler, Mark. "He Came, He Pitched, He Conquered." In: Dick Kaegel: ed. *The Sporting News 1982 Baseball Yearbook.* St. Louis, MO: *The Sporting News,* 1982. Pp. 4–10.

55028. Honig, Donald. "1981: Fernando Valenzuela." In: his *National League Rookies of the Year.* New York: Bantam Books, 1989. Pp. 88–91.

55029. Jenkins, Chris. "Fernando Valenzuela: He Takes Nothing for Granted." *Baseball Digest,* XLVI (February 1987), 37–43.

55030. Kaplan, Jim., "Epidemic of Fernando Fever." *Sports Illustrated,* LIV (May 18, 1981), 22–24+.

55031. Kurkjian, Tim. "Fernandomania II." *Sports Illustrated,* LXXIV (June 17, 1991), 74–76.

55032. LaFrance, David G. "A Mexican Popular Image of the United States Through the Baseball Hero, Fernando Valenzuela." *Latin American Popular Culture,* IV (1985), 14–23.

55033. Lanker, Brian. "Fernando's Hideaway." *Life,* V (February 1982), 86–89.

55034. Lewis, Gregory. "Fernando Valenzuela." In: Ken Collier, ed. *The Baseball Book, 1983.* Scottsdale, AZ: Jalart House, 1983. Pp. 39–41.

55035. Littwin, Mike. *Fernando!* New York: Bantam Books, 1981. 115p.

55036. _____. *Fernando Valenzuela, the Screwball Artist.* Chicago: Children's Press, 1983. 43p.

55037. _____. "The Life and Times of Fabulous Fernando." In: Zander Hollander, ed. *1982 Season: The Complete Handbook of Baseball.* New York: New American Library, 1982. Pp. 6–13.

55038. Llosa, Luis Fernando. "Mania Man." *Sports Illustrated,* XCVIII (June 30, 2003), 50–53.

55039. Paramo, Fernando. "Interview: Fernando Valenzuela." *Sport,* LXXVII (July 1986), 19–22.

55040. Pedulla, Tom. "Perseverance Paid Dividends for Fernando Valenzuela." *Baseball Digest,* LV (December 1996), 74–76.

55041. Perez, Pedro Chavez. "Un 'Toro' Rejuvenecido." *Deporte Internacional,* I (Setiembre 19, 1997), 72–77.

55042. Regalado, Samuel O. "Fernando Valenzuela." In: Vol. Q-Z of David L. Porter, ed. *Biographical Dictionary of American Sports: Baseball.* Rev. and enlarged ed. Westport, CT: Greenwood Press, 2000. Pp. 1581–1582.

55043. Rivera, Eddie. "In America, Only in the Land of Opportunity Could a Kid from Anywhere Go to Sleep a Pauper and Wake Up a Millionaire." *Inside Sports,* IX (June 1987), 45–47, 50–52.

55044. Shah, Diane K. "Same Old Bull." *ESPN: The Magazine,* IV (March 19, 2001), 64–66, 68.

55045. Sloate, Susan. "Fernando Valenzuela: South of the Border Sensation." In: her *Hotshots — Greats of the Game When They Were Kids.* Boston, MA: Little, Brown & Co., 1991. Pp. 99–105.

55046. Thorn, John. Fernando Valenzuela: 'Mondo Fernando." In: his *Baseball's Dream Team.* New York: Ace Tempo Books, 1982. Pp. 1–15.

55047. Topkin, Marc. "Fernando Valenzuela Makes Comeback Bid With Birds." *Orioles Gazette,* III (March 19, 1993), 14–15.

55048. Valenzuela, Fernando, as told to George Vass. "The Game I'll Never Forget." *Baseball Digest,* LIII (July 1994), 81–82.

55049. Wheeler, Mark. "The Cooling of Fernandomania." *Inside Sports,* VI (May 1984), 24–33.

55050. Wulf, Steve. "It's That Screwball Again." *Sports Illustrated,* LXXVIII (March 22, 1993), 37+.

55051. _____. "Keeping Close Watch on Fernando." *Sports Illustrated,* LVI (April 5, 1982), 57–59.

55052. _____. "No Hideaway for Fernando." *Sports Illustrated,* LIV (March 23, 1981), 26–29.

55053. _____. "Out of the Blue." *Sports Illustrated,* LXXIV (April 8, 1991), 15–16.

55054. Young, Ken. "Fernando Valenzuela: 'The Fever' Spreads." In: his *Cy Young Award Winners.* New York: Walker and Co., 1994. Pp. 104–117.

55055. Zwikel, Tony. "Ole!: Es Fernando El Magnifico." In: Bob Sparks, ed. *Baseball '82.* St. Petersburg, FL: National Association of Professional Baseball Leagues, 1982. Pp. 19–22.

David ("Dave") Valle

C. BROADCASTER. (B: Oct. 30, 1960, Queens, NY). Seattle (AL), 1984–1993; Boston (AL) and Milwaukee (AL), 1994; Texas (AL), 1995–1996. Remarks: Obtained 658 hits (77 homers) in 970 games in 12 seasons; also played for Bellingham and Alexandria (Northwest League); broadcaster, Seattle (AL), 1998–.

55056. Garrity, John. "A Ray of Hope: Catcher Dave Valle Isn't a Star, Unless You Consider His Good Works Outside Baseball." *Sports Illustrated,* LXXXVI (February 17, 1997), 40–43.

55057. Nash, Bruce and Allan Zullo. "Dave Valle." In: their *Little Big Leaguers: Amazing Boyhood Stories of Today's Baseball Stars.* New York: Little Simon, 1990. Pp. 24–25.

Elmer William Valo

OF. (B: March 5, 1921, Ribnik, Czechoslovakia-D: July 19, 1998). Philadelphia (AL), 1940–1943, 1946–1954; Kansas City (AL), 1955–1956; Philadelphia (AL), 1956; Brooklyn (NL), 1957; Los Angeles (NL), 1958; Cleveland (A.L), 1959; New York (AL) and Washington (AL), 1960; Minnesota (AL) and Philadelphia (NL), 1961. Remarks: First big league player from Czechoslovakia; obtained 1,420 hits (58 homers) and 110 stolen bases in 1,806 games in 20 seasons; first AL player to hit two bases-loaded triples, May 1, 1949; hit for the cycle, Aug. 2, 1950; coach and minor league manager, Cleveland (AL), 1962–1965; scout, Philadelphia (NL), 1966–1982.

55058. Appel, Marty. "Elmer Valo." In: his *Yesterday's Heroes: Revisiting the Old-Time Baseball Stars.* New York: The Dial Press, 1988. Pp. 242–245.

55059. Charlton, J. "Elmer Valo: Four-Decade Man?" *The National Pastime,* XXI (2001), 9–10

55060. Graber, Ralph S. "Elmer William Valo." In: Vol. Q-Z of David L. Porter, ed. *Biographical Dictionary of American Sports: Baseball.* Rev. and enlarged ed. Westport, CT: Greenwood Press, 2000. Pp. 1582–1583.

55061. Kelley, Brent P. "Elmer Valo: Hustle (1940–1961)." In: his *The Pastime in Turbulence: Interviews with Baseball Players of the 1940s.* Jefferson, NC: McFarland & Co., Inc., 2002. Pp. 51–59.

55062. Macht, Norman L. "Elmer Valo: *Baseball Digest's* First 'Cover Boy.'" *Baseball Digest,* XLVII (September 1988), 48–50.

55063. Marazzi, Rich. "Elmer Valo Hustled His Way to a 20-Year Career." *Sports Collectors Digest,* XXI (October 7, 1994), 140–141.

55064. Morrow, Art. "Elmer Valo." In: his *My Greatest Baseball Game.* New York: A.S. Barnes And Co., 1950. Pp. 200–206.

55065. Westcott, Rich. "Elmer Valo — Fearless Flychaser." In: his *Diamond Greats.* Westport, CT: Meckler Books, 1988. Pp. 376–382.

Russell ("Russ" or "Sheriff") Van Atta

P. (B: June 21, 1906, Augusta, NJ-D: Oct. 10, 1986). New York (AL), 1933–1935; St. Louis (AL), 1935–1939. Remarks: Had 33 victories, 41 defeats, and six "saves" in a seven-year major league career; went 4-for-4 and won his first big league game, April 25, 1933.

55066. Linthurst, Randy. "A Most Spectacular Debut." *The Baseball Research Journal,* IV (1975), 16–18.

George Edward Martin ("Rip") Van Haltren

OF-P-UMP. (B: March 30, 1866, St. Louis, MO-D: Sept. 29, 1945). Chicago (NL), 1887–1889; Brooklyn (P), 1890; Baltimore (AA), 1891–1892; Pittsburgh (NL), 1892–1893; New York (NL), 1894–1903. Remarks: In 17 big league seasons, obtained 2,432 hits (69 homers) and 564 stolen bases in 1,984 games; led NL in triples, 1896; led NL in stolen bases, 1900; as a pitcher, won 40 games (including a June 28, 1888 no-hitter) and lost 31, manager, Baltimore (AA), 1891–1892, winning one game and losing 10 (.091); also played for Seattle (PCL), 1904 and Oakland (PCL), 1905–1909, serving as player-manager of the second-named team; umpire, PCL), 1909 and Northwest League, 1912; scout, Pittsburgh (N.L), 1910–1911.

55067. Kush, Raymond D. "George Edward Martin 'Rip' Van Haltren." In: Vol. Q-Z of David L. Porter, ed. *Biographical Dictionary of American Sports: Baseball.* Rev. and enlarged ed. Westport, CT: Greenwood Press, 2000. Pp. 1585–1586.

Charles Emmett Van Loan

WRITER. (B: June 29, 1876, San Jose, CA-D: March 2, 1919). Remarks: Reporter, Los Angeles Morning Herald, 1904–1907; reporter, *Denver Post,* 1907–1908; sports reporter, *New York American,* 1909–1911; columnist, editor and story writer, *Saturday Evening Post,* 1913–1919; great friend of Damon Runyan (q.v.) and author of well received sports stories.

55068. Brignano, R. C. "Charles E. Van Loan." In: Richard Orodenker, ed. *Dictionary of Literary Biography: Volume 171: Twentieth-Century American Sportswriters.* A Bruccoli Clark Layman Book. Detroit, MI: Gale Research, 1996. Pp. 3437–341.

55069. Davis, Robert E. "The Late Charles E. Van Loan." *The Bookman: A Review of Books and Life,* XLIX (May 1919), 280–285.

55070. Van Loan, Charles E. "How I Broke into the Magazines." *American Magazine,* LXXXVI (December 1918), 39–40, 118–122.

Todd Matthew Van Poppel

P. (B: Dec. 9, 1971, Hillsdale, IL). Oakland (AL), 1991, 1993–1996; Detroit (AL) and Texas (AL), 1996; Pittsburgh (NL), 1998; Chicago (NL), 2000–2001; Texas (AL), 2002–2003; Cincinnati (NL), 2003–2004. Remarks:

Through 2004, has won 40 games and lost 52, with four "saves" ; led AL in walks surrendered, 1994.

55071. Cannella, Stephen. "Finding Relief in the Bullpen: Van Poppel's Comeback." *Sports Illustrated,* XCIII (July 31, 2000), 72, 74.

55072. Stier, Kit. "Focus on Todd van Poppel." *Beckett Focus on Future Stars,* II, no. 14 (June 1992), 18–21.

Andrew James ("Andy" or "Slick") Van Slyke
OF-BROADCASTER. (B: Dec. 21, 1960, Utica, NY). St. Louis (NL), 1983–1986; Pittsburgh (NL), 1987–1994; Baltimore (AL) and Philadelphia (NL), 1995. Remarks: During 13 years, obtained 1,562 hits (164 homers) and 245 stolen bases in 1,658 games; played in 1985 and 1990–1992 NLCS, having a combined total of 18 hits, including six doubles, two triples, and a homer, and 10 RBIs; had unassisted double play, July 7, 1992; went 8-for-9 in a doubleheader, May 8, 1994; ESPN analyst, 1997; spring training instructor, Pittsburgh (NL), 2001.

55073. "Andy Van Slyke: When He Talks, People Listen." In: Tom Barnidge, ed. *The Sporting News 1989 Baseball Yearbook.* St. Louis, MO: The Sporting News, 1989. Pp. 22–27.

55074. Branon, Dave and Lee Pellegrino. "Andy Van Slyke." In: their *Safe at Home.* Chicago, IL: Moody Press, 1992. Pp. 308–310.

55075. Chastain, Bill. "Andy Van Slyke: Pirates' Man of Many Talents." *Baseball Digest,* XLVII (July 1988), 42–45.

55076. _____. "Beers with Andy Van Slyke." *Sport,* LXXX (April 1989), 19–20.

55077. Fletcher, Christopher. "Angel of the Outfield." *Pittsburgh,* XXV (July 1994), 17+.

55078. Meyer, Paul. "Interview: Andy Van Slyke." *Inside Sports,* XVI (June 1994), 22–29.

55079. Perrotto, John. "Deeper Look: Andy Van Slyke." *Beckett Baseball Card Monthly,* X, no. 94 (January 1993), 108–109.

55080. Rushin, Steve. "Playing for Laughs." *Sports Illustrated,* LXXVII (September 21, 1992), 56–62, 64.

55081. Seabrook, J. "Diamond Stud." *Vogue,* CLXXIX (April 1989), 406–407+.

55082. Thackeray, Frank W. "Andrew James 'Andy,' 'Slick' Van Slyke." In: Vol. Q-Z of David L. Porter, ed. *Biographical Dictionary of American Sports: Baseball.* Rev. and enlarged ed. Westport, CT: Greenwood Press, 2000. Pp. 1586–1587.

55083. Wiley, Ralph. "'Slick' Can Play." *Sports Illustrated,* LXX (April 5, 1989), 56–58, 65–66.

55084. Will, George F. "Andy van Slyke and the Present Monetary Status of Baseball." In: his *Bunts: Curt Flood, Camden Yards, Pete Rose and Other Reflections on Baseball.* New York: Touchstone Books, 1998. Pp. 232–234.

Clarence Arthur ("Dazzy") Vance★
P. (B: March 4, 1891, Orient, LA-D: Feb. 16, 1961.). Pittsburgh (NL), 1915; New York (AL), 1915 and 1919; Brooklyn (NL), 1922–1932; St. Louis (NL), 19331934; Cincinnati (NL), 1934; Brooklyn (NL), 1935. Remarks: Won 197 games and lost 140, with 11 "saves," in 16 seasons; also played for Hastings (Nebraska State League) and St. Joseph (WL), 1914, 1916–1917; Sacramento (PCL) 1919 and New Orleans (SL), 1920–1921; did not win first major league game until age 31; came within one inning of a no-hitter, June 17, 1923; won 14 consecutive games, 1924; NL MVP award, 1924; pitched no-hitter, Sept. 13, 1925; holds N.L record for most years and most consecutive years leading league in strikeouts (seven), 1922–1928); retired to Florida to operate Homosassa Springs hunting/fishing business; elected to National Baseball Hall of Fame in 1955, where his plaque reads:. "First pitcher in NL to lead in strikeouts for 7 straight years, 1922 to 1928. Led league with 28 victories in 1924; 22 in 1925. Won 15 straight in 1924. Pitched no-hit game against Phillies, 1925. Most Valuable Player NL 1924."

55085. Allen, Lee, and Thomas Meany. "Dazzy Vance." In. their *Kings at the Diamond.* New York: G.P. Putnam, 1966. Pp. 69–71.

55086. Bisher, Furman. "$25 Bonus Made Vance Whiff King." *Baseball Digest,* XI (June 1952), 56–59.

55087. Blengino, Tony. "Dazzy Vance —1924." In: his *Baseball's Top 100: The Best Individual Seasons of All Time.* Wilton, CT: Diamond Library, 1996. Pp. 63–64.

55088. Cain, Cullen. "Dazzy Vance — From Farm To Diamond." *Country Gentleman,* XC (February 21, 1925), 5–6.

55089. Cardello, Joseph. "Dazzy Vance in 1930." *The Baseball Research Journal,* XXV (1996), 127–130.

55090. Deberry, Hank. "In the Long Shadow of Dazzy Vance." *Baseball Magazine,* XLIII (August 1929), 395–396+.

55091. Gaven, Michael. "His Curve Was the Most." *Baseball Digest,* XIV (April 1955), 45–49.

55092. Hickey, David and Kerry Keene. "Dazzy Vance." In: their *The Proudest Yankees of All: From the Bronx to Cooperstown.* Lanham, MD: Taylor Trade Pub., dist. by National Book Network, 2003. Chpt. 30.

55093. Honig, Donald. "Dazzy Vance." In: his *The Greatest Pitchers of All Time.* New York: Crown Publishers, 1988. Pp. 56–61.

55094. Hornsby, Rogers. "The Time Vance Got Me in a Hole." *American Legion Weekly,* V (August 10, 1923), 20–21. During 1922 season.

55095. Jebsen, Harry, Jr. "Clarence Arthur ('Dazzy') Vance." In: Supplement 7 of John A. Garrity, ed. *Dictionary of American Biography.* New York: Scribners, 1981. Pp. 751–752.

55096. _____. "Clarence Arthur 'Dazzy' Vance." In: Vol. Q-Z of David L. Porter, ed. *Biographical Dictionary of American Sports: Baseball.* Rev. and enlarged ed. Westport, CT: Greenwood Press, 2000. Pp. 1583–1585.

55097. _____. "Dazzy Vance." In: John A. Garrity and Marsh C. Carries, eds. *American National Biography.* 24 vols. New York: Oxford University Press, 1999. XXII, 162–163.

55098. Lane, Ferdinand C. "Dazzy Vance: The Pitching Sensation of 1923." *Baseball Magazine,* XXXI (October 1923), 495–497.

55099. _____. "The Philosophy of Dazzy Vance." *Baseball Magazine,* LI (August 1933), 397–399.

55100. _____. "A New Record for Dazzy." *Baseball Magazine,* XLIII (June 1929), 291–293.

55101. Lieb, Frederick G. "The Star of the National League." *Baseball Magazine,* XXXIV (January 1925), 349–351.

55102. McDonald, Jack. "When [Sammy] Bohne Cost Vance a No-Hitter." *Baseball Digest,* XXVI (February 1967), 81–83.

55103. Meany, Thomas. "The Dazzler." In: his *Baseball's Greatest Pitchers.* New York: A.S. Barnes, 1951. Pp. 235–245.

55104. _____. "They Remember Dazzy Vance." *Baseball Digest,* XX (May 1961), 61–67.

55105. _____. and Tommy Holmes. "Dazzy Vance: The Overaged Cyclone." In: their *Baseball's Best.* New York: Watts, 1964. Pp. 80–88.

55106. Munro, Neil. "Great Pitching Seasons — Dazzy

Vance 1924." In: *Grandstand Baseball Annual, 1993.* Downey, CA: Joseph M. Wayman, 1993. Pp. 71–79.

55107. Newcombe, Jack. "Dazzy in Brooklyn." In: his *The Fireballers.* New York. G.P. Putnam, 1964. Pp. 55–65.

55108. Powers, Jimmy. "Arthur ('Dazzy') Vance." In: his *Baseball Personalities.* Chicago. Field, 1949. Pp. 131–138.

55109. Ritter, Lawrence and Donald Honig. "Dazzy Vance." In: their *The 100 Greatest Baseball Players of All Time.* New York: Crown Publishers, 1981. Pp. 168–169.

55110. Russell, Fred. "'Pitching All Year Is Good'— [Clarence 'Dazzy'] Vance." *Baseball Digest,* VII (May 1948), 39–40.

55111. Smith, Ira L. "Arthur Charles ('Dazzy') Vance." In: his *Baseball's Famous Pitchers.* New York: A.S. Barnes, 1954. Pp. 161–165.

55112. Spalding, John E. "Dazzy Vance." In: his *Pacific Coast League Stars, Vol. II: Ninety Who Made it to the Majors, 1905–1957* San Jose, CA: John E. Spalding, 1997. Pp. 35–36.

55113. Sparks, Barry. "Dazzy Vance's Strikeout Feat Still Unsurpassed." *Baseball Digest,* XLI (January 1982), 87–88.

55114. Stockton, J. Roy. "'Look Out! No Good Curves Ahead'—Vance." *Baseball Digest,* XVIII (May 1959), 45–47.

55115. Temple, Herman. "Is Dazzy Vance Slipping?" *Baseball Magazine,* XL (March 1928), 444–445.

55116. Vance, Clarence ("Dazzy"). "Advantages and Disadvantages of Speed Pitching." *Baseball Magazine,* XXXVI (April 1926), 497–498.

55117. _____. "Dead Shot Dazzy Vance of Brooklyn." *Baseball Magazine,* XXXIII (January 1924), 361–363.

55118. _____. "A Dissertation on 'Guts.'" *Baseball Magazine,* XIV (June 1930), 291–293.

55119. _____. "How the Strike-Out King (Vance] Applies His Pitching 'K.O.'" *Baseball Magazine,* XLI (May 1928), 547–548.

55120. _____. "I'd Hate to Pitch Nowadays." Edited by Furman Bisher. *Saturday Evening Post,* CCXXVIII (August 20, 1955), 27+.

55121. _____. "A Letter from a Famous Big League Star." *Baseball Magazine,* XLIV (February 1930), 409–411.

55122. _____. "The Oddest Play I Ever Saw." *Baseball Magazine,* XL (March 1928), 460–461.

55123. _____. "The Secret of Control in Speed-Pitching." *Baseball Magazine,* XXXVIII (March 1927), 435–436.

55124. _____. "When I Was Broke in Florida." *Baseball Magazine,* XXXIII (July 1924), 347–349.

55125. _____. "Why I Bear Down on Every Ball." *Baseball Magazine,* XXXIV (January 1925), 339–341.

John Samuel ("Johnny" or "The Dutch Master" or "Double No-Hit") Vander Meer

P. (B: Nov. 2, 1914, Prospect Park, NJ-D: Oct. 6, 1997). Cincinnati (NL), 1937–1943, 1946–1949; Chicago (NL), 1950; Cleveland (AL), 1951. Remarks: Had 119 victories, 121 defeats, and two "saves" in 13 campaigns; pitched two consecutive no-hitters (June 11 and 15, 1938) and 15 of 19 innings in history's longest fie game, Sept. 11, 1946; won 1938 All-Star Game; led NL in strikeouts, 1941–1943; also played for Durham (Piedmont League), 1936 and Beaumont (TL), 1952, where he threw another no-hitter, July 15; career ended by arm problems.

55126. Bloodgood, Clifford. 'The New Red Menace: Johnny Vander Meer." *Baseball Magazine,* LXI (August 1938), 401–402+. Reprinted in Sidney Offit, ed. *Best of Baseball* (New York: G.P. Putnam, 1966), pp. 112–117.

55127. Campbell, Gordon "John S. Vander Meer: Dou-

ble No-Hit Johnny." In: his *Famous American Athletes of Today.* 9th Series. New York: Page, 1945. Pp. 275–298.

55128. Crosley, Clayton B. "A Conversation with Johnny Vander Meer." *The Baseball Research Journal,* XXVII (1998), 69–70.

55129. Daniel, Daniel M. "Vander Meer, Rookie of the Year." *Baseball Magazine,* LXI (August 1938), 389–391.

55130. Drebinger, John. "The Super Pitcher." *Baseball Magazine,* LXI (October 1938), 505–507+.

55131. Guback, Steve. "Vander Meer Treasures No-Hit Mementoes." *Baseball Digest,* XXVIII (November 1969), 39–41.

55132. Keller, David N. "Oh, Johnny: Forgotten Baseball Legend." *Timeline,* XVI (February 1999), 34+.

55133. Kermisch, Al. "Johnny Vander Meer's Breakthrough in 1938 Not Foretold by Previous Record." *The Baseball Research Journal,* XXXI (2001), 132–133.

55134. Kush, Raymond D. "John Samuel 'Johnny,' 'Double No-Hit,' 'The Dutch Master' Vander Meer." In: Vol. Q-Z of David L. Porter, ed. *Biographical Dictionary of American Sports: Baseball.* Rev. and enlarged ed. Westport, CT: Greenwood Press, 2000. Pp. 1587–1589.

55135. Lang, Jack. "Vander Meer Throws Historic Gem at Night." In: *Wrigley Field: Commemorating Wrigley Field's First Night Baseball Game.* Chicago, IL: Sherman Media Co., 1988. Chpt. 3.

55136. Langfort, Walter M. "Johnny Vander Meer Recalls His Consecutive No-Hitters." *Baseball Digest,* XLIV (June 1985), 63–69.

55137. _____. "Two No Hitters in Five Days." In: Peter Levine, ed. *Baseball History 2.* Westport, CT: Meckler, 1989. Pp. 86–91.

55138. Leiker, Ken. "24–1938: Johnny Vander Meer Pitches Two Consecutive No-Hitters." In: his *Major League Baseball Memorable Moments: The Most Memorable Moments in Major League Baseball History.* New York: Ballantine Books, 2002. Pp. 122–125.

55139. Levitt, Ed. "Vander Meer Recalls His Double No-Hitters." *Baseball Magazine,* XXX (October 1971), 68–75.

55140. McGowan, Roscoe. "40,000 See Vander Meer of Reds Hurl Second No-Hit, No-Run Game in Row: Reprinted from *The New York Times,* June 16, 1938." In: Gene Brown, ed. *The New York Times Encyclopedia of Sports: Vol. 2, Baseball.* New York: Arno Press, 1979. Pp. 62–63.

55141. Newcombe, Jack. "Johnny Vander Meer." In: his *Fireballers.* New York: G.P. Putnam, 1964. Pp. 119–131.

55142. Saccucci, Fluffy. "Former Reds Pitcher Johnny Vander Meer 'Dutch Master' Hurled Back-to-Back No-Hitters." *Sports Collector's Digest,* XXIII (November 29, 1996), 140–141.

55143. Seaver, Tom, with Marty Appel. "Vander Meer, Twice." In: his *Great Moments in Baseball: From the World Series of 1903 to the Modern Records of Nolan Ryan.* New York: Carol Communications, 1992. Pp. 125–130.

55144. Siegel, Jeff. "Vander Meer Pitches Double No-Hitter." *Boy's Life,* LXXVIII (May 1988), 12+.

55145. Sugar, Bert Randolph. "Johnny Vander Meer's Second No-Hitter, Cincinnati Reds vs. Brooklyn Dodgers, June 15, 1938." In: his *Baseball's 50 Greatest Games.* Rev. ed. North Digton, MA: The JG Press, 1994. Pp. 36–38.

55146. Sullivan, Tim. "Vander Meer's Legacy: A Feat for the Ages." In: Richard Levin, ed. *Major League Baseball 1988 All-Star Game Program.* East Rutherford, N.J.: Meehan Tooker, 1988. Pp. 58–64.

55147. Vander Meer, John S. "Two Games Don't Make

a Pitcher." Edited by George Kirksey. *Saturday Evening Post,* CCXI (August 27, 1938), 10–11+.

55148. _____.as told to Gabriel ("Gabe") Paul. "My Greatest Day in Baseball." In: John P. Carmichael, ed. *My Greatest Day in Baseball.* New York: A.S. Barnes, 1945. Pp. 144–147. First published in the *Chicago Daily News.*

55149. Wilson, John R. M. "Johnny Vander Meer." In: Paul Betz and Mark C. Carnes, eds. *American National Biography: Supplement I.* New York: Oxford University Press, 2002. Pp. 653–654.

55150. Woody, Clayton. "Johnny Vander Meer's No-Hitters Are Still Unique.*" Baseball Digest,* XXXIX (July 1980), 78–83.

Elam Russell Vangilder

P. (B: April 23, 1896, Cape Girardeau, MO-D: April 30, 1977). St. Louis (AL), 1919–1927; Detroit (AL), 1928–1929. Remarks: Won 99 games and lost 102 with 19 "saves" in 11 years; hurled more games (323) than any other Browns' pitcher; won three games in three days in relief In 1925.

55151. Lane, Frank C. "The Prosaic Career of Elam Russell Vangilder." *Baseball Magazine,* XI, (February 1928), 411–412+.

William Joseph Vanlandingham

P. (B: July 16, 1970, Columbia, TN). San Francisco (NL), 1994–1997. Remarks: In four big league seasons, won 27 games and lost 26; lost no-hitter to Kevin Brown (q.v.), June 10, 1997.

55152. Camps, Mark. "Rookie Report: William Vanlandingham." *Beckett Baseball Card Monthly,* XI, no. 117 (December 1994), 126–127.

Arky Vaughan *see* **Joseph Floyd ("Arky") Vaughan**
Joseph Floyd ("Arky") Vaughan★

SS-3B. (B: March 9, 1912, Clifty, AK-D: Aug. 30, 1952). Pittsburgh (NL), 1932I941; Brooklyn (NL), 1942–1943, 1947–1948. Remarks: Obtained 2,103 hits (96 homers) and 118 stolen bases in 1,817 games in a 14-year major league career; had grand slam homer, May 1, 1933; hit for the cycle twice, June 24, 1933 and July 19, 1939; led NL in triples, 1933; led NL in walks, 1934–1936; NL batting champion, 1935; NL stolen base champion, 1943; hit two homers in 1941 All-Star Game; died in swimming accident; elected to National Baseball Hall of Fame in 1985 where his plaque reads: "Among Hall of Fame shortstops, his .318 lifetime batting average is second only to Honus Wagner's .329. Led league with .385 in 1935. Homered twice in 1941 All-Star Game. Fanned only 276 times in 6622 career at-bats. Polished fielder and accomplished baserunner, leading NL with 20 stolen bases in 1943."

55153. Grosshandler, Stan. "Arky Vaughan: Baseball's Forgotten Hero." *Baseball Digest,* XXXV (May 1976), 39–41.

55154. Honig, Donald. "Arky Vaughan." In: his *The Greatest Shortstops of All Time.* Dubuque, IA: Wm. C. Brown Publishers, 1992. Pp. 40–45.

55155. Kelly, Edward H. "How About Ernie Lombardi and Arky Vaughan for the Hall of Fame?" *Baseball Digest,* XLHI (November 1984), 50–59.

55156. Lane, Frank C. "A New Batting King is Crowned." *Baseball Magazine,* LVI (December 1935), 291–293.

55157. Martin, Douglas D. "Joseph Floyd 'Arky' Vaughan." In: Vol. Q-Z of David L. Porter, ed. *Biographical Dictionary of American Sports: Baseball.* Rev. and enlarged ed. Westport, CT: Greenwood Press, 2000. Pp. 1589–1590.

55158. Smith, Mark Augustus. "Arky Vaughan." In:

John A. Garrity and Marsh C. Carries, eds. *American National Biography.* 24 vols. New York: Oxford University Press, 1999. XXII, 289.

Gregory Lamont ("Greg") Vaughn

OF. (B: July 3, 1965, Sacramento, CA). Milwaukee (AL), 1989–1996; San Diego (NL), 1996–1998; Cincinnati (NL), 1999; Tampa Bay (AL), 2000–2002; Colorado (NL), 2003–. Remarks: Through 2003, had 1,475 hits (355 homers) and 121 stolen bases in 1,731 games; slammed two homers in 1998 World Series.

55159. Doyle, Al. "Padres' Greg Vaughn Thrives on Everyday Duty." *Baseball Digest,* LVII (November 1998), 52–45.

55160. Haft, Chris. "Greg Vaughn Key to Reds' Success in 1999." *Baseball Digest,* LVIII (December 1999), 64–67.

Hippo Vaughn *see* **James Leslie ("Hippo") Vaughn**
James Leslie ("Hippo") Vaughn

P. (B: April 9, 1888, Weatherford, TX-D: May 29, 1966). New York (AL), 1908, 1910–1912; Washington (AL), 1912; Chicago (NL), 1913–1921. Remarks: Had 176 victories, 137 defeats, and six "saves" in 13 seasons; pitched 41 shutouts; pitched 9 1/3 innings of no-hit ball (May 2, 1917), but lost to Fred Toney (q.v.), who won the game as a no-hitter for Cincinnati (NL); lost Games One and Three, but won Game Five of 1918 World Series; also hurled for Temple (TL), 1906, Corsicana (North Texas League)/Hot Springs (Arkansas State League), 1907, Scranton (New York State League), 1908, Macon (South Atlantic League)/Louisville (AA), 1909 (had one no hitter for each 1909 team), Kansas City (AA), 1912–1913 (had no-hitter June 23, 1913); Beloit (Midwest League), 1921–1922.

55161. Klima, John. "Nine of Nothing: Fred Toney vs. Hippo Vaughn (May 2, 1917)." In: his *Pitched Battle: 35 of Baseball's Greatest Duels from the Mound.* Jefferson, NC: McFarland & Co., Inc., 2002. Pp. 38–42. Jan Finkel's profile of Vaughn is a number in the online SABR biography project http://bioproj.sabr.org/bioproj.cfm?a=v&v=l&bid=921&pid=14570.

55162. Suehsdorf, Adie D. "James Leslie 'Hippo' Vaughn." In: Vol. Q-Z of David L. Porter, ed. *Biographical Dictionary of American Sports: Baseball.* Rev. and enlarged ed. Westport, CT: Greenwood Press, 2000. Pp. 1590–1592.

55163. Sugar, Bert Randolph. "Double No-Hitter: Vaughn vs. Toney — Cincinnati Reds vs. Chicago Cubs, May 2, 1917." In: his *Baseball's 50 Greatest Games.* Rev. ed. North Digton, MA: The JG Press, 1994. Pp. 74–76.

55164. "Toney-Vaughan Double No-Hitter." In: Dean A. Sullivan, ed. *Middle Innings: A Documentary History of Baseball, 1900–1948.* Lincoln, NE: University of Nebraska Press, 1998. Pp. 82–84. Reprinted from the *Chicago Daily Tribune,* May 3, 1917.

55165. Vaughn, James ("Hippo"). "What It Seems to Lose a No-Hit Game.*" Baseball Magazine,* XIX (July 1917), 364–365.

55166. _____., with Hal Totten. "Vaughn Tells of Double No-Hitter." *Baseball Digest,* IV (February 1945), 14–17. Reprinted in *Baseball Digest,* XXV (September 1966), 81–83, and in John P. Carmichael, ed., *My Greatest Day in Baseball* (New York: A.S. Barnes, 1945), pp. 193–197.

55167. Wilbert, Warren and William Hageman. "James "Hippo" L. Vaughn —1918." In: their *Chicago Cubs: Seasons at the Summit, the 50 Greatest Individual Seasons.* Champaign, Il; Sagamore Publishing, 1997. Pp. 153–156.

Maurice Samuel ("Mo" or "Hit Dog") Vaughn

1B. (B: Dec. 15, 1967, Norwalk, CT). Boston (AL), 1991–1998; Anaheim (AL), 1999–2000; New York (NL),

2002–2003. Remarks: Through 2003, had 1,620 hits (328 homers) and 30 stolen bases in 1,512 games;; AL MVP Award, 1995; AL RBI champion, 1995; had two homers and seven RBIs in Game One of 1998 ALCS; had two homers and six RBIs in one game, June 24, 1999; went 5-for-5 in one game, May 24, 2000; had 10 career grand slam homers; also played for Pawtucket (IL), 1990; career ended by arthritic left knee.

55168. Arnold, Eric. *A Day in the Life of Baseball Player Mo Vaughn.* New York: Scholastic, 1996. Unpaged.

55169. Cafardo, Nick. "Closer Look: Mo Vaughn." *Beckett Baseball Card Monthly,* XII, no. 118 (January 1995), 6–9.

55170. _____. "Focus on Mo Vaughn." *Beckett Focus on Future Stars,* II (April 1992), 18–20.

55171. Callahan, Gerry. "Sox Appeal." *Sports Illustrated,* LXXXIII (October 2, 1995), 42–44, 47–48.

55172. Cannella, Stephen. "First Things First for Angels: Who'll Replace Mo Vaughn?" *Sports Illustrated,* XCIV (February 26, 2001), 56–57.

55173. Castle, George. "In the Opponents' Eyes: Mo Vaughn." *Yankees Magazine,* XX (May 1999), 70–73.

55174. Christopher, Matt. *At the Plate with ... Mo Vaughn.* Boston, MA: Little, Brown and Co., 1997. 113p.

55175. Dawidoff, Nicholas. "They're Hungry for Mo." *Sports Illustrated,* LXXIV (April 1, 1991), 51+.

55176. Dieffenbach, Dan. "Hitting It with Mo Vaughn." *Sport,* LXXXVII (May 1996), 86–87.

55177. _____. "Mo Vaughn's Prize." *Sport,* LXXVII (July 1996), 79–81.

55178. Evers, John L. "Maurice Samuel 'Mo' Vaughn." In: Vol. Q-Z of David L. Porter, ed. *Biographical Dictionary of American Sports: Baseball.* Rev. and enlarged ed. Westport, CT: Greenwood Press, 2000. Pp. 1592–1593.

55179. Fleming, David. "To Ward Off Another Late-season Collapse, the Angels Have Mo Power To 'em." *Sports Illustrated,* XC (March 29, 1999), 102–103.

55180. Folstad, Rick. "Mo Vaughn Sets His Sights on Career Consistency." *Baseball Digest,* LVII (September 1998), 56–57.

55181. Frommer, Harvey and Frederick J. "Mo Vaughn." In: their *Growing Up Baseball: An Oral History.* Dallas, TX: Taylor Publishing Co., 2001. Pp. 220–221.

55182. Mahoney, Michael J. "'Hit Dog' Becomes a Red Sox Team Leader." *Sports Collector's Digest,* XXIV (October 3, 1997), 144+.

55183. Maisel, Bob. "Mo Vaughn's Homer Recalls Babe's Famous Promise." *Orioles Gazette,* III (May 21, 1993), 11–12. Promise to hit one for a sick child.

55184. Massarotti, Tony. "Mo Vaughn 42: Boston's Silver Lining." *Boston Baseball,* VII (August 1996), 4–5.

55185. "Mo's Town." In: Joe Hoppel, ed. *The Sporting News 1995 Baseball Yearbook.* St. Louis, MO: The Sporting News, 1995. Pp. 32–35.

55186. Moir, A and D. Christy. "The Role Model." *Forbes,* CLIII (March 14, 1994), 58–62.

55187. Montville, Leigh. "Guardian Angel: Mo Vaughn's Spiritual Impact on the Anaheim Angels." *Sports Illustrated,* XC (April 19, 1999), 92–101.

55188. Pierce, Charles P "Mo (the 'Hit Dog' Explained)." *Boston,* LXXXVI (July 1994), 54–57.

55189. Ribowsky, Mark. "Inside Interview: Mo Vaughn." *Sport,* XC (July 1999), 34–37.

55190. Rosenthal, Ken. "Mo Vaughn." In: his *Best of the Best, Baseball: 35 Major League Superstars.* Indianapolis, IN: Masters Press, 1998. Pp. 144–147.

55191. Rutstein, Michael. "Mo Honors; Or 'Hit Dog' Will Win the AL MVP — You Read It Here First ." *Boston Baseball,* VI (September 1995), 4–5.

55192. Santella, Andrew. *Mo Vaughn.* New York: Children's Press, 1996. 48p.

55193. Shalin, Michael. *Mo Vaughn: Angel on a Mission.* Champaign, IL: Sports Publishing, 1999. 81p.

55194. "10 Questions for Mo Vaughn." *Sports Illustrated for Kids,* XI (August 1999), 28–29.

55195. Vaughn, Mo, with Greg Brown. *Follow Your Dreams.* Dallas: Taylor Publishing Co., 1996. 308p.

Mo Vaughn see **Maurice Samuel ("Mo" or "Hit Dog") Vaughn**

Ronald ("Ron") Vaughn

COACH-SCOUT. Remarks: Hitting coach, University of Southern California, 1981–1982; assistant coach, Anchorage Glacier Pilots, 1982; coach, Azusa Pacific University and scout, Oakland (AL), 1982–1999; mentor of Mark McGwire (q.v.).

55196. Verducci, Tom. "Stroke of Genius: Ron Vaughn Saw Potential of Mark McGwire While Coaching Him at USC." *Sports Illustrated,* LXXXIX (December 21, 1998), 44–48+.

Bobby Veach see **Robert Hayes ("Bobby") Veach**

Robert Hayes ("Bobby") Veach

OF. (B: June 29, 1888, Island, KY-D: Aug. 7, 1945). Detroit (AL), 1912–1923; Boston (AL), 1924–1925; New York (AL) and Washington (AL), 1925. Remarks: Obtained 2,063 hits (64 homers) and 195 stolen bases in 1,821 games in 12 big league years; led AL in doubles, 1915 and 1919; led AL in triples, 1919; AL RBI champion, 1915, 1917–1918; hit for the cycle, Sept. 17, 1920; had one RBI in 1925 World Series; played for Toledo (AA), 1926–1929 and Jersey City (IL), 1930.

55197. Grayston, Harry. "Robert (Bobby) Veach." In: his *They Played The Game.* New York: A.S. Barnes, 1944. Pp. 152–153.

55198. Matz, David S. and Luther W. Spoehr. "Robert Hayes 'Bobby' Veach." In: Vol. Q-Z of David L. Porter, ed. *Biographical Dictionary of American Sports: Baseball.* Rev. and enlarged ed. Westport, CT: Greenwood Press, 2000. Pp. 1593–1594.

55199. Ward, John J. "Robert Veach and the $100,000 Outfield." *Baseball Magazine,* XV (October 1915), 33–36.

Bob Veale see **Robert Andrew ("Bob") Veale**

Robert Andrew ("Bob") Veale, Jr.

P. (B: Oct. 28, 1935, Birmingham, AL). Pittsburgh (NL), 1962–1972; Boston (AL), 1972–1974. Remarks: Won 120 games and lost 95 with 21 "saves" in 13 seasons; struck out 16 batters in a game twice, Sept. 30, 1964 and June 1, 1965; also played for Columbus (AA), 1961–1962; minor league pitching coach, Atlanta (NL), 1974–1983 and New York (AL), 1984.

55200. Abrams, Al. "Bob Veale Discounts Wildness." *Baseball Digest,* XXIV (May 1965), 85–67.

55201. Heiman, Lee, Dave Weiner and Bill Gutman. "Bob Veale." In: their *When The Cheering Stops.* New York: Macmillan Publishing Co., 1990. Pp. 112–125.

55202. Rumill, Ed. "Bob Veale: Just Wild Enough to Keep Hitters Honest." *Baseball Digest,* XXIV (August 1965), 33–35.

55203. Shannon, Mike. "Bob Veale." In: his *Tales from the Dugout: The Greatest True Baseball Stories Ever Told.* Lincolnwood, IL: NTC/Contemporary Books, 1997. Pp. 219–220.

55204. Spoehr, Luther W. "Robert Andrew 'Bob' Veale, Jr." In: Vol. Q-Z of David L. Porter, ed. *Biographical Dictionary of American Sports: Baseball.* Rev. and enlarged ed. Westport, CT: Greenwood Press, 2000. Pp. 1594–1595.

55205. Westcott, Rich. "Bob Veale — An Imposing Sight." In: his *Diamond Greats.* Westport, CT: Meckler Books, 1988. Pp. 334–337.

George Spencer Vecsey
WRITER. (B: July 4, 1939, Jamaica, NY). Remarks: Sports writer/report, *Long Island Newsday,* 1956–1968; *The New York Times,* 1968–1970; sports columnist, 1971–date.

55206. Vecsey, George. *A Year in the Sun: The Games, the Players, the Pleasure of the Sports.* New York: Times Books, 1989. 334p.

Bill Veeck *see* **William ("Bill") Veeck, Jr.**

Michael ("Mike") Veeck
EXEC. (B: 1951). Remarks: President, Miami (Florida State League), 1989–1992; St. Paul (AA), 1993–2000; marketing director, Tampa Bay (AL), 1998–1999; owner/president, Charleston (South Atlantic League), 1996–; consultant, Detroit (AL), 2001–; son of Bill Veeck (below).

55207. Cohen, Charles E. "Baseball Oddball: Michael Veeck, Promoter for the Miracle in Florida." *People Weekly,* XXXV (June 10, 1991), 57–58.

55208. Richmond, Peter. "Veeck II: Meet Mr. Minors." *GQ — Gentlemen's Quarterly,* LXV (April 1995), 211+.

55209. Veeck, Mike and Jim Lucas. *Every Day is Opening Day: On Life, the Family Legacy and Why Fun is Good.* Lenexa, KS: Addax Publishing, 2002. 272p.

William ("Bill") Veeck, Jr.★
EXEC-BROADCASTER. (B: Feb. 9, 1914, Chicago, IL-D: Jan. 2, 1986). Remarks: Son of 1919–1933 Chicago Cubs owner Veeck, Sr.; owner of Milwaukee (AA), 1941–1945; lost leg due to World War II injury received while serving with U.S. Marine Corp; owner and president, Cleveland (AL), 1947–1949, where he brought Black players Larry Doby and Satchel Paige into the major leagues; owner, St. Louis (AL), 1951–1953 and Chicago (AL), 1959–1961, 1976 through 1980; colorful executive who tried various sensational ideas to increase baseball popularity with fans; broadcaster, NBC-TV, 1957–1958; father of Michael ("Mike") Veeck (above); elected to National Baseball Hall of Fame in 1991, where his plaque reads: "Owner of Indians, Browns, and White Sox. Created heightened fan interest at every stop with ingenious promotional schemes, fan participation, exploding scoreboard, outrageous door prizes, names on uniforms. Set M.L. attendance record with pennant-winner at Cleveland in 1948; won again with 'Go-Go' Sox in 1959. Signed AL's first Black player, Larry Doby in 1947 and oldest rookie, 42-year old Satchel Paige in 1948. A champion of the little guy."

55210. Allen, Lee. "Just Plain Bill." In: his *The American League Story.* New York: Hill & Wang, 1962. Pp. 172–182.

55211. Beck, Peggy. "Working in the Shadows of Rickey and Robinson: Bill Veeck, Larry Doby, and the Advancement of Black Players in Baseball." In: Peter M. Rutkoff, ed. *The Cooperstown Symposium on Baseball and American Culture, 1997 (Jackie Robinson).* Jefferson, NC: McFarland & Co., Inc., 2000. Pp. 109–122.

55212. "Bill Veeck." In: *Current Biography Yearbook, 1948.* New York: H.W. Wilson Co., 1948.

55213. Boudreau, Lou, with Ed Fitzgerald. "Bill Veeck and Me." *Sport,* VI (May 1949), 36–39.

55214. Brashler, William. "A Day in the Life of Bill Veeck: An Interview." *Esquire,* XCI (February 27, 1979), 82+.

55215. _____. "Veeck: The Wreck is Still Rambling." *Chicago,* XXVII (July 1978), 94–99.

55216. Broeg, Bob. "A Day a Midget Batted in the Ma-

jors." *Baseball Digest,* XXXI (March 1972), 35–37. Veeck employed 43-inch tell Edward Gaedel (q.v.) as a pinch-hitter during the second game of a double-header with Detroit (AL), Aug. 19, 1951.

55217. _____. "Veeck and the Midget." In: his *The Ol' Ball Game.* Harrisburg, PA: Stackpole Books, 1990. Pp. 134–142.

55218. Boxerman, Burton A. "Bill Veeck: The Populist." In: his *Ebbets to Veeck to Busch: Eight Owners Who Shaped Baseball.* Jefferson, NC: McFarland & Co., Inc., 2003. Pp. 124–151.

55219. Cerrone, Rick. "A Conversation with Bill Veeck." *Baseball Quarterly,* II (Fall 1978), 16–19.

55220. Cobbledick, Gordon. "Bill Veeck: Baseball's Greatest Showman." *Sport,* V (September 1948), 54–68.

55221. _____. "'No Idle Roomers': Veeck's Plan." *Baseball Digest,* VII (May 1948), 37–39.

55222. Cohane, Tim. "Bill Veeck: The Man Who Has Almost Everything." *Look,* XXVI (July 3, 1962), 95–96.

55223. Daniel, Daniel M. "32-Year Old Marine Bill Veeck a New Type of Major League Magnate." *Baseball Magazine,* LXXVII (September 1946), 331–333+.

55224. Dickey, Glenn. "Bill Veeck vs. Horace Stoneham." In: his *Champs and Chumps: An Insider's Look at America's Sports Heroes.* San Francisco, CA: Chronicle Books, 1976. Pp. 115–129.

55225. Dolgan, Bob. "When Bill Veeck Enlivened the Cleveland Baseball Scene." *Baseball Digest,* LVII (October 1998), 78–81.

55226. Enders, Eric. "His Way: If It Meant a Good Time for Loyal Fans, No Idea was Too Crzzy for Master Innovator Bill Veeck." In: Richard Levin, ed. *2004 League Championship Series Official Program.* New York: Major League Baseball Properties Corp., 2004. Pp. 69–71.

55227. Eskenazi, Gerald. *Bill Veeck: A Baseball Legend.* New York: McGraw-Hill Book Co., 1988. 182p.

55228. Evers, John L. "William Louis 'Bill' Veeck, Jr." In: Vol. Q-Z of David L. Porter, ed. *Biographical Dictionary of American Sports: Baseball.* Rev. and enlarged ed. Westport, CT: Greenwood Press, 2000. Pp. 1595–1597.

55229. Frank, Stanley B. "Bill Veeck." *Liberty Magazine,* XXIV (July 19, 1947), 132+.

55230. _____. "A Visit with Bill Veeck." *Saturday Evening Post,* CCXXXI (June 6, 1959), 31+.

55231. Furlong, William B. "Au Revoir to Bill Veeck." *Sports Illustrated,* XIV (June 19, 1961), 52+.

55232. _____. "Bill Veeck: Master of Illusion." *Sports Illustrated,* XIII (July 4, 1960), 54–60.

55233. _____. "A Day with Bill Veeck." *Sport,* XXVIII (August 1959), 22–23+.

55234. _____. "Uncorking Some Wild Pitches." *TV Guide,* XXIV (June 5, 1976), 14–16.

55235. _____. "The Veeck-Yankee Feud is for Real." *Sport,* XXIX (March 1960), 20–21+.

55236. Gibbons, Frank. "The No-Hitter That Cost Veeck $17,500." *Baseball Digest,* XVIII (March 1959), 55–57.

55237. Gietschier, Steven P. "Bill Veeck." In: John A. Garrity and Marsh C. Carries, eds. *American National Biography.* 24 vols. New York: Oxford University Press, 1999. XXII, 313–315.

55238. _____. "Bill Veeck, Indian Chief." *Timeline,* VII (April-May 1990), 28–39.

55239. Goodman, Mark. "If Baseball Is Poetry, Bill Veeck Must Be Shakespeare." *New Times,* VI (April 16, 1976), 50–60.

55240. Greenberg, Hank. "The Unforgettable Bill Veeck." *Reader's Digest,* CXXIX (July 1986), 67–72.

55241. Jordan, David, *et al.* "A Baseball Myth Exploded: Bill Veeck and the 1943 Sale of the Phillies." *The National Pastime,* XVII (1998), 3–13.

55242. Kahn, Roger. "William the Unconquerable." In: his *A Season in the Sun.* New York: Harper & Row, 1977. Pp. 127–146.

55243. Kindred, Dave. "Bill Veeck." In: his *Heroes, Fools and Other Dreamers.* Marietta, GA: Longstreet Press, 1989. Pp. 29–31.

55244. Lieb, Frederick G. "Bill Veeck." In: his *Comedians and Pranksters of Baseball.* St. Louis: *The Sporting News,* 1958. Pp. 38–40.

55245. Linn, Ed. "Veeck — as in White Sox." *Sport,* LXII (April 1976), 24–37.

55246. McAuley, Ed. "Tales of the One and Only Veeck." *Baseball Digest,* IX (February 1950), 51–55.

55247. Marshall, Charles. "The Wizard of White Sox Park." *Advertising Age,* L (August 27, 1979), S34–S35+.

55248. Obojski, Robert. "Bill Veeck: Baseball's Showman Extraordinaire." In: his *Baseball's Strangest Moments.* New York: Sterling Publishing Co., 1988. Pp. 59–62.

55249. Povich, Shirley. "Veeck Over Miami." *Baseball Digest,* XV (March 1956), 95–97.

55250. Rapoport, Ron. "Veeck Death Symbolizes End of an Era." In: Tom Barnidge, ed. *Best Sports Stories of 1986.* St. Louis, MO: *The Sporting News,* 1986. Pp. 144–146.

55251. Robson, Britt. "The Man Behind the Curtain; Stunt Man." *City Pages* (Minneapolis), XVII (August 9, 1995), 8–9+. Bill Veeck and Saints.

55252. Seaver, Tom, with Marty Appel. "Veeck Brings a Flag to Cleveland." In: his *Great Moments in Baseball: From the World Series of 1903 to the Modern Records of Nolan Ryan.* New York: Carol Communications, 1992. Pp. 157–163.

55253. "Selling a Bell Club to the Fans: Bill Veeck and the Cleveland Indians.*" Business Week,* (October 2, 1948), 52+.

55254. Shane, Ted. "Bill Veeck: Bad Boy of Basebrawl." *Reader's Digest,* LX (May 1952), 92–96.

55255. ____. "Veeck: The Barnum of Baseball." *Baseball Magazine,* LXXXVIII (April 1952), 8–10.

55256. Shannon, Mike. "Eddie Gaedel and Bill Veeck." In: his *Tales from the Ballpark: More of the Greatest True Baseball Stories Ever Told.* Lincolnwood, Il: Contemporary Books, 1999. Pp. 72–74.

55257. Smith, Walter ("Red"). "Challenge or Sentence?" *Baseball Digest,* X (September 1951), 97–99. Veeck takes over weak St. Louis Browns.

55258. Smith, Wendell. "Baseball Needs Bill Veeck." *Baseball Monthly,* II (April 1963), 50–55.

55259. Stein, Harry. "Role Models for Modern Times: Bill Veeck." *Esquire,* CIII (March 1985), 35–37.

55230. Tootle, Jim. "Bill Veeck and James Thurber: The Literary Origins of the Midget Pinch Hitter." *Nine: A Journal of History and Public Policy Perspective,* X (Spring 2002), 110–120.

55231. Veeck, William ("Bill"), Jr. "How I Didn't Buy a Ball Club." Edited by Ed Linn. *Saturday Evening Post,* CCXXXVI (September 7, 1963), 78–80.

55232. ____. "So You Want to Run a Ball Club." *Saturday Evening Post,* CCXXI (April 23, 1949), 32–33+.

55233. ____. "Veeck — as in Peck." *Sport,* XLVIII September 1969), 20–33.

55234. ____. "Veeck — as in Wreck: Interview." *Scholastic Coach,* LIII (December 1983), 32–34+.

55235. ____. *Veeck as in Wreck: The Autobiography of Bill Veeck.* Edited by Ed Linn. New York: G.P. Putnam, 1962. 380p. Reprinted in a 398-page edition by the New York firm of Simon and Schuster in 1989 and by the University of Chicago Press in 2001, the latter with a foreword by Bob Verdi; excerpted in Will Balliett and Tom Dyja, eds., *The Hard Way: Writing by the Rebels Who Changed Sports* (New York: Thunder's Mouth Press, 1999), pp. 23–34.

55236. ____. and Ed Linn. "Back Where I Belong." *Sports Illustrated,* XLIV (March 15, 1976), 73–77+. As owner of the Chicago White Sox.

55237. ____. "How They Booted Me Out of Baseball." *Look,* XXVI (June 19, 1962), 66+.

55238. ____. *The Hustler's Handbook.* New York G.P. Putnam, 1965. 344p. Excerpted in *Sports Illustrated,* XXII (May 17–June 14, 1965), 87–89+, 40–42+, 50–52+, 32–34+, 40–50+.

55239. ____. *Thirty Tons a Day.* New York: Viking Press, 1972. 296p.

55240. "Veeck — a New Bill for the White Sox." *Look,* XXIU (August 4, 1959), 92–96.

55241. "Veecksation." *Newsweek,* XXXII (August 16, l948), 70+.

55242. Williams, Pat and Michael Weinreb. *Marketing Your Dreams: Business and Life Lessons from Bill Veeck, Baseball's Marketing Genius.* Champaign, IL: Sports Publishing, Inc., 2001. 256p.

55243. Yoder, Robert M., and James. Kearns. "Boy Magnate: Bill Veeck and the Milwaukee Brewers." *Saturday Evening Post,* CCXVI (August 28, 1943), 19+.

55244. Young, Bill. "Bill Veeck." In: *Through the Years: Comiskey Park: A Commemorative Tribute to Comiskey Park, 1910–1990.* Chicago, IL : Sherman Media, 1990. Chpt. 4.

Robin Mark Ventura
3B. (B: July 14, 1967, Santa Maria, CA). Chicago (AL), 1989–1998; New York (NL), 1999–2001; New York (AL), 2002–2003; Los Angeles (NL), 2003–2004. Remarks: Through 2004, had 1,885 hits (294 homers) and 24 stolen bases in 2,079 games; had six RBIs in one game twice, July 19, 1991 and April 8, 2002; obtained four hits, one homer, and five RBIs in 1993 ALCS; became eighth MLB player to hit two grand slam homers in one game, Sept. 4, 1995; had three hits (one double, one homer) in both the 1999 and 2000 NLCS; hit grand slam homers in consecutive games (double-header), May 20, 1999; obtained three hits (including a double and a homer) in the 2000 World Series; had 18 career grand slam homers; also had 58-game hitting streak while an undergraduate at the University of Oklahoma.

55245. Bessone, L. T. "A Hollywood Homer." *Sports Illustrated,* LXXII (May 21, 1990), 97+.

55246. Cannella, Stephen. "New Harbinger of Mets' Spring: Robin Ventura's Rebirth." *Sports Illustrated,* XCIV (April 16, 2001), 73–74.

55247. Castle, George. "Rockin' Robin." *Yankees Magazine,* XIX (July 1998), 76–81.

55248. Condiff, Michael. "Chicago's Great Bright Hope." *Beckett Baseball Card Monthly,* VII (February 1990), 12–13.

55249. Holtzman, Jerome. "Robin Ventura Seeks a Repeat of His Productive '96 Season." *Baseball Digest,* LVI (April 1997), 74–75.

55250. Kuenster, Bob. "Why Mets Value Robin Ventura's Special Talents." *Baseball Digest,* LVIII (November 1999), 28–34.

55251. Newton, Craig. "Robin Ventura." *Baseball Cards,* X (December 1990), 62–64.

55252. Shannon, Mike. "Robin Ventura." In: his *Tales from the Ballpark: More of the Greatest True Baseball Stories Ever Told.* Lincolnwood, IL: Contemporary Books, 1999. Pp. 212–213.

55253. Sorci, Rick. "A Closer Look: Robin Ventura." *Beckett Baseball Card Monthly,* VIII (December 1991), 6–7.

55254. Thackeray, Frank W. "Robin Mark Ventura." In: Vol. Q–Z of David L. Porter, ed. *Biographical Dictionary of American Sports: Baseball.* Rev. and enlarged ed. Westport, CT: Greenwood Press, 2000. Pp. 1597–1598.

55255. Zachotsky, Dan. "Robin Ventura." In: his *Idols of the Spring: Baseball Interviews About Spring Training.* Jefferson, NC: McFarland & Co., Inc., 2001. Pp. 175–180.

Quilvio Alberto Veras

2B. (B: April 3, 1971, Santo Domingo, Dominican Republic). Florida (NL), 1995–1996; San Diego (NL), 1997–1999; Atlanta (NL), 2000–2001. Remarks: Has had 750 hits (32 homers) and 228 stolen bases in 696 games in seven big league seasons; NL stolen base champion, 1995; obtained six hits and one double in 1998 NLCS and three hits (two doubles) in 1998 World Series. .

55256. Epstein, Eddie. "Quilvio Veras." In: STATS, Inc. *The STATS 1995 Minor League Scouting Notebook.* Skokie, IL: STATS Publishing, 1995. Pp. 163–164.

Dutch Verban *see* **Emil Matthew ("Dutch" or "The Antelope") Verban**

Emil Matthew ("Dutch" or "The Antelope") Verban

2B. (B: Aug. 27, 1915, Lincoln, IL–D: June 8, 1968). St. Louis (NL), 1944–1946; Philadelphia (NL), 1946–1948; Chicago- (NL), 1948–1950; Boston (NL), 1950. Remarks. In a seven-year major league career, obtained 793 hits (one homer) in 853 games; had seven hits (including winning stroke in Game Six) and two RBIs in 1945 World Series.

55257. Drees, Donald H. "The Velvety Verban." *Baseball Digest,* V (September 1946), 21–27.

55258. Holmes, Tommy. "How Verban Gave It Away." *Baseball Digest,* VII (June 1948), 17–19.

55259. Yeutter, Frank. "That Exceedingly Pleasant Character." *Baseball Magazine,* LXXVII (September 1946), 333–335.

Gene Kermit ("Satchel") Verble

SS-2B. (B: June 29, 1928, Concord, NC). Washington (AL), 1951 and 1953. Remarks: Had 40 hits and a stolen base in 81 games in two seasons.

55260. Povich, Shirley. "Verble—in the Harris Mold?" *Baseball Digest,* X (June 1951), 47–50.

Robert William ("Bob") Verdi

WRITER. (B: August 31, 1946, Brooklyn, NY). Remarks: Sports columnist, *Chicago. Tribune,* 1967–date; received Sportswriter of Year for Illinois Award, National Sportscasters and Sportswriters Assn., 1975–78, 80–82, 84–87, 89–90.

55261. Verdi, Bob. *The Bob Verdi Collection.* Dallas, TX: Taylor Publishing Co., 1988. 269p.

Thomas Matthew ("Tom") Verducci

WRITER. (B: Oct. 23, 1960, East Orange, NJ). Remarks: Sports reporter, Newsday, 1983–1993; senior writer, Sports Illustrated, 1994–.

55260a. Verducci, Tom. "I Was a Blue Jay." *Sports Illustrated,* CII (March 14, 2005), 60–73. How, á la George Plimpton (q.v.), the writer spent five days as a full-fledged member of the Toronto (AL) club.

James Barton ("Mickey") Vernon

1B-MGR. (B: April 22, 1918, Marcus Hook, PA). Washington (AL), 1939–1943; 1946–1948; Cleveland (AL), 1949–1950; Washington (AL), 1950–1955; Boston (AL), 1956–1957; Cleveland (AL), 1958; Milwaukee (NL), 1959; Pittsburgh (NL), 1960. Remarks: Obtained 2,495 hits (172 homers) and 137 stolen bases in 2,409 games in two big league decades (career in four); hit for the cycle, May 19, 1946; made two unassisted doubleplays in one game, May 29, 1946; AL batting champion, 1946 and 1953; led AL in doubles, 1946, 1953–1954; had 20-game hitting streak, 1953; holds various other records, including AL record for lifetime putouts by a first baseman (19,754) and modern major league lifetime record for most games played at first base (2,237); coach, Pittsburgh (NL), 1960; manager, Washington (AL), 1961–1963, winning 135 games and losing 227 (.373); coach, Pittsburgh (N.L) and St. Louis (NL), 1964–1965, Montreal (NL), 1977–1978, and New York (AL), 1982; minor league manager, Vancouver (PCL), 1966–1968, Richmond (IL), 1969–1970, and Manchester (EL), 1971; batting instructor, Kansas City (AL), 1973–1974 and Los Angeles (NL), 1975–1976; scout, New York (AL), 1986–1987.

55262. Addle, Bob. "Mickey Vernon Slips Time a 'Mickey.'" *Baseball Digest,* XVII (July 1958), 49–51.

55263. Furlong, William B. "The Silent Senator." In: Bruce Jacobs, ed. *Baseball Stars of 1954,* Now York: Lion Books, 1954. Pp. 129–136.

55264. Harris, Will. "Vernon's Making Base Hits for Baby." *Baseball Magazine,* XC (September 1953), 19–20.

55265. Hawkins, Burton. "Mickey Vernon: Washington's Quiet Bang." *Baseball Digest,* XII (August 1953), 15–20.

55266. Hirshberg, Dan. "Flashback—Mickey Vernon: Twice He Led the AL in Hitting." *Baseball Digest,* LIV (January 1995), 56–62.

55267. Honig, Donald. "Mickey Vernon." In: his *Baseball Between the Lines: Baseball in the Forties and Fifties as Told By the Men Who Played It.* Lincoln, NB: University of Nebraska Press, 1976. Pp. 113–124.

55268. Lautier, Jack. "Mickey Vernon." In: his *Fenway Voices.* Camden, ME: Yankee Books, 1990. Pp. 75–80.

55269. Meany, Thomas. "Eternal Youth (Mickey Vernon)." In: his *The Boston Red Sox.* New York: A.S. Barnes, 1956. Pp. 73–83.

55270. _____. "Mickey Vernon: The Obscure Mr. Vernon." *Baseball Digest,* XVI (January-February 1967), 57–62.

55271. Povich, Shirley. "King Vernon's Crown's Awry." *Baseball Digest,* VI (August 1947), 39–41.

55272. _____. "The Oldest Batting Champion." *Baseball Digest,* XIII (March 1954). 23–25.

55273. _____. "Washington's New Mt. Vernon." *Baseball Digest,* V (August 1946), 13–15.

55274. Smith, Ira L. "James Barton ('Mickey') Vernon." In: his *Baseball's Famous First Basemen.* New York: A.S. Barnes, 1956. Pp. 280–297.

55275. Sullivan, George. "Mickey Vernon." In: his *Glovemen: Twenty-Seven of Baseball's Greatest.* New York: Atheneum, 1996. Pp. 46–47.

55276. Westcott, Rich. "Mickey Vernon—Bat Champ Who Fielded with a Velvet Touch." In: his *Diamond Greats.* Westport, CT: Meckler Books, 1988. Pp. 252–257.

Mickey Vernon *see* **James Barton ("Mickey") Vernon**

Zoilo Casanova ("Zorro") Versalles

SS. (B: Dec. 18, 1939, Vedado, Cuba). Washington (AL) and Minnesota (AL), 1959–1967; Los Angeles. (NL), 1968; Cleveland (AL) and Washington (AL), 1969; Atlanta (NL), 1971. Remarks: In 12 seasons, obtained 1,246 hits (95 homers) and 97 stolen bases in 1,400 games; led AL in triples, 1963–1965; led AL in doubles, 1965; had eight hits (including a double, triple, and homer) in 1965 World Series; AL MVP award, 1965; named to Cuban Baseball Hall of Fame, 1980.

55277. Honig, Donald. "1965: Zoilo Versalles." In: his *American League MVP's*. New York: Bantam Books, 1989. Pp. 74–75.

55278. Izenberg, Jerry. "The Exile." In: his *Great Latin Sports Figures*. Garden City, N.Y.: Doubleday, 1976. Pp. 73–89.

55279. _____. "Zoilo Versalles: How a Problem Child Becomes an MVP." *Sport*, XLI (March 1966), 70–85. Reprinted in Al Silverman, ed., *The Best of Sport, 1946–1971* (New York: Viking Press, 1971), pp. 383–395.

55280. Libby, Bill. "Versalles in Search of Himself." *Sport*, XXXVII (February 1964), 48–51.

55281. Pratt, J. Lowell. "Zoilo Versalles." In: his *Baseball's All-Stars*. Garden City, N.Y.: Doubleday, 1967. Pp. 113–114.

55282. Robinson, Ray. "Zoilo Versalles: Angriest Twin." In: Ray Robinson, ed. *Baseball Stars of 1966*. New York: Pyramid Books, 1966. Pp. 132–137.

55283. Shapiro, Milton J. "Zoilo Versalles." In: his *The Year They Won the MVP Award*. Now York: Julian Messner, 1966. Pp. 23–28.

55284. Stainback, Barry. "Baseball's Mr. Zero." *Sport*, XX (September 1963), 42–45.

55285. _____. "Zorro's Marks to Make." *Sport*, XXXV (June 1963), 8–9.

55286. Stann, Francis. "Erstwhile Moody Versalles Finally Wins Acceptance." *Baseball Digest*, XXIV (October 1965), 29–31.

55287. _____. "Zoilo Versalles: The New Mark of Zorro." *Baseball Digest*, XXII (June 1963), 41–43.

55288. Terzian, James P. *The Kid from Cuba: Zoilo Versalles*. Garden City, N.Y.: Doubleday, 1967. 142p.

55289. Vecsey, George. "Zoilo Versalles." In: his *Baseball's Most Valuable Players*. New York: Random House, 1966. Pp. 168–180.

Zorro Versalles *see* **Zoilo Casanova ("Zorro") Versalles**

Lee Viau *see* **Leon A. ("Lee") Viau**

Leon A. ("Lee") Viau
P. (B: July 5, 1866, Corinth, VT-D: Dec. 17, 1947). Cincinnati (NL), 1888–1890; Cleveland (NL), 1890–1892; Louisville (NL) and Boston (NL), 1892. Remarks: In five NL seasons, had 83 victories, 77 defeats, and one "save."

55290. Waterman, Guy. "Lee Viau." In: Tom Simon, ed. *Green Mountain Boys of Summer: Vermonters in the Major Leagues, 1882–1993*. Shelburne, VT: The New England Press, 2000. Pp. 15–18.

Harry Porter ("Rube") Vickers
P-C. (B: May 17, 1878, St. Mary's, Canada-D: Dec. 9, 1958). Cincinnati (NL), 1902; Brooklyn (NL), 1903; Philadelphia (NL), 1907–1909. Remarks: Won 23 games and lost 27, with three "saves," in all or part of five big league seasons; pressed into service as a catcher and had six passed balls in one game, Oct. 4, 1902; in a day-night doubleheader on October 5, 1907, Vickers won 15-inning first game after 12-innings of relief and then hurled a perfect game to take the nightcap; also played for Seattle (PCL), 1906–1907, winning 39 games in the latter year, a tie for the most ever in that loop.

55291. Kermisch, Al. "Vickers Set Modern Passed Ball Mark in Joke Game." *The Baseball Research Journal*, XI (1982), 68–69.

Rube Vickers *see* **Harry Porter ("Rube") Vickers**

Richards Vidmer
WRITER. (B: Oct. 7, 1898, Washington, DC-D: July 23, 1978). Remarks: Sportswriter, *Washington Herald*, 1921–1922; sports editor, *Washington Daily News*, 1922–1924; sportswriter, *The New York Times*, 1924–1929; sportswriter, *New York Morning Herald*, 1929; sportswriter/columnist, *New York Herald Tribune*, 1929–1951; golf pro, Barbados, 1951–1960s; editor, Dun and Bradstreet, 1960s to death.

55292. Crowley, Bernard J. "Richards Vidmer." In: Richard Orodenker, ed. *Dictionary of Literary Biography, Volume 241: American Sportswriters and Writers on Sport*. A Bruccoli Clark Layman Book. Detroit, MI: The Gale Group, 2001. Pp. 309–314.

55293. Holtzman, Jerome. "Richards Vidmer." In: Nicholas Dawidoff, ed. *Baseball: A Literary Anthology*. New York: The Library of America, 2002. Pp. 114–118. Reprinted from Holtzman's *No Cheering in the Press Box*, pp. 98–113.

Fernando Vina
2B-SS-3B. (B: April 16, 1969, Sacramento, CA). Seattle (AL), 1993; New York (NL), 1994; Milwaukee (AL/NL), 1995–1999; St. Louis (NL), 2000–2003; Detroit (AL), 2004–. Remarks: Through 2004, has had 1,196 hits (40 homers) and 116 stolen bases in 1,148 games; NL hit-by-pitch leader, 1994, 2000; had six hits in both the 2000 and 2002 NLCS; had nine-game hitting streak, 2003, plagued by hamstring problems.

55294. Eisenbath, Mike. "Hard Work Pushes Fernando Vina to Excel." Baseball Digest, LX (June 2001), 82–84.

55295. Sorci, Rick. "Baseball Profile: Cardinals' Infielder Fernando Vina." *Baseball Digest*, LX (October 2001), 66–67.

Jose Vidro
2B. (B: Jose Angel Vidro Cetty, Aug. 27, 1974, Mayaguez, P.R.). Montreal (NL), 1997–2004; Washington (NL), 2005–. Remarks: Through 2004, has had 1,061 hits (101 homers) and 20 stolen bases in 973 games; had 13-game hitting streak, July 2003; has had three career grand slam homers.

55296. Bianchine, Jim. "Rising Star: Montreal's Jose Vidro Ranks Among Top Second Basemen." *Baseball Digest*, XLI (July 2002), 64–67.

Francis Thomas ("Fay") Vincent, Jr.
EXEC. (B: May 29, 1938, Waterbury, CT). Deputy Commissioner of Baseball, 1989; Commissioner of Baseball, 1989–1992; chairman, New England Collegiate Baseball League, 1997–.

55297. Angell, Roger. "The Rules of the Game." *The New Yorker*, LXVIII (October 5, 1992), 178+.

55298. "Baseball Commissioner Fay Vincent Resigns." *Facts on File*, LII (September 10, 1992), 671–672.

55299. Brunning, Fred. "Baseball and Politics: Lessons in Hardball." *Maclean's*, CV (September 28, 1992), 13+.

55300. Callahan, Tom. "Baseball's Unlikely Champion: Fay Vincent Has Handled a Tough First Year with Grace." *U.S. News and World Report*, CIX (October 15, 1990), 97–98.

55301. Castle, George. "End Of Baseball As We Know It?" In: *Petersen's Baseball 1992 Pro Preview*. Los Angeles, CA: Petersen, 1992. Pp. 74–77.

55302. Cohen, Richard. "Nothing But Curve Balls." *The New York Times Magazine*, (June 3, 1990), 34, 56–58.

55303. Corliss, Ray. "Fay Vincent Gets Beaned." *Time*, CXL (September 14, 1992), 61–62.

55304. Demak, Richard. "Baseball Strikes Out." *Sports Illustrated*, LXXVII (September 14, 1992), 13+.

55305. "Fay Vincent." In: *Current Biography Yearbook, 1991*. New York: H. W. Wilson, 1991. Pp. 588–593.

55306. Gross, Kevin. "After the Death of Bart Giamatti, His Friend Fay Vincent Steps In as the Commissioner's Pinch Hitter." *People Weekly,* XXXII (September 18, 1989), 56–57.

55307. Hammer, Joshua, David A. Kaplan, and Todd Barrett. "Paradise Lost: Why Baseball's Economic Troubles May Force Fay Vincent Out of the Box." *Newsweek,* CXX (September 14, 1992), 72–74.

55308. Hoffer, Richard. "Take Care of the Game." *Sports Illustrated,* LXXVI (March 2, 1992), 46–48+.

55309. Holtzman, Jerome. "Fay Vincent." In: his *The Commissioners: Baseball's Midlife Crisis.* New York: Total Sports, 1998. Pp. 257–270.

55310. Kaplan, David A. "Take Him Out to a Ball Game: Does the Beleaguered Commissioner Need Relief?" *Newsweek,* CXX (July 20, 1992), 56+.

55311. "A League of Their Own: Baseball's Bosses are Back in Charge After Fay Vincent Resigns." *Time,* CXL (September 21, 1992), 20–21.

55312. Lupica, Mike. "Welcome to Hardball City." *Esquire,* CXV (June 1991), 38–40.

55313. Neff, Craig and Jill Lieber. "Behind the Scenes with George [Steinbrenner] and Fay." *Sports Illustrated,* LXXIII (August 13, 1990), 13–14.

55314. Sandomir, Richard. "Twists of Fate: His Career Began Traditionally, But Calls from Old Friends Landed Fay Vincent First in the Movies and Now in Baseball." *Sports Inc.,* II (February 27, 1989), 26–28.

55315. "Selig Wasn't Available." *Sports Illustrated,* LXXXVII (December 22, 1997), 24–25. New England Collegiate Baseball League chairmanship.

55316. Smith, Claire. "The State of the Game." *Inside Sports,* XIII (April 1991), 74–77.

55317. Verducci, Tom. "Have You Seen This Man?" *Sports Illustrated,* LXXIX (July 5, 1993), 38–41.

55318. Vincent, Francis T. ("Fay"), Jr. "An Agenda for the Most Original Game Ever Invented: Baseball in the 1990s." *Vital Speeches of the Day,* LVIII (June 15, 1992), 541+.

55319. _____. "Education and Baseball." *America,* CLXIV (April 6, 1991), 372–373.

55320. _____. *The Last Commissioner: A Baseball Valentine.* New York: Simon & Schuster, 2002. 304p.

55321. Voigt, David Quentin. "Francis Thomas 'Fay' Vincent, Jr." In: Vol. Q-Z of David L. Porter, ed. *Biographical Dictionary of American Sports: Baseball.* Rev. and enlarged ed. Westport, CT: Greenwood Press, 2000. Pp. 1599–1601.

55322. Wulf, Steve. "A Man in Command." *Sports Illustrated,* LXXI (October 30, 1989), 30–32.

Frank John ("Sweet Music") Viola, Jr.
P. (B: April 19, 1960, East Meadow, NY). Minnesota (AL), 1982–1989; New York (NL), 1989–1991; Boston (AL), 1992–1994; Cincinnati (NL), 1995; Toronto (AL), 1996. Remarks: Won 176 games and lost 150 in 15 seasons; won Game Four of 1987 ALCS; won Games One and Seven and lost Game Four of 1987 World Series; World Series MVP award, 1987; AL Cy Young award, 1988.

55323. Abramson, Dan. "A Closer Look: Frank Viola." *Beckett Baseball Card Monthly,* VII (July 1990), 6–7.

55324. Carpenter, Jerry and Steve DiMeglio, Edited By Paul J. Deegan. *Minnesota Twins: Frank Viola.* Minneapolis, MN: Abdo & Daughters, 1988. 32p.

55325. Cohen, Irwin. "Baseball Beat: Frank Viola." *Baseball Cards,* VIII (June 1988), 86+.

55326. Gammons, Peter. "Concerto for Viola and Twins." *Sports Illustrated,* LXVII (November 2, 1987), 32–33.

55327. _____. "Near Perfect Pitch." *Sports Illustrated,* LXIX (August 22, 1988), 44–46, 56, 58–59.

55328. Hart, Stan. "Frank Viola." In: his *Scouting Reports: The Original Reviews of Baseball's Greatest Stars.* New York: Macmillan, 1995. Pp. 133–135.

55329. Kuenster, John. "Frank Viola of Twins Was a Deserving World Series MVP." *Baseball Digest,* XLVII (February 1988), 13–15.

55330. _____. "Pitching Staff, Headed by Frank Viola, Fostered Twins' Surprise in '84." *Baseball Digest,* XLIV (March 1985), 17–19.

55331. Pate, Steve. "Frank Viola Pitching 'Sweet Music' Again for the Mets." *Baseball Digest,* XLIX (August 1990), 32–34.

55332. Pooley, Ed. "Sports: Frank Viola." *New York,* XXIII (September 10, 1990), 122–123.

55333. Porter, David L. "Frank John Viola, Jr." In: Vol. Q-Z of David L. Porter, ed. *Biographical Dictionary of American Sports: Baseball.* Rev. and enlarged ed. Westport, CT: Greenwood Press, 2000. Pp. 1601–1602.

55334. Powell, Larry. "Frank Viola Wants Another World Series Ring." *Sports Collector's Digest,* XXI (May 20, 1994), 190+.

55335. Rogers, Tom. "Viola Reaps His Rewards." *The New York Times Biographical Service,* XVIII (October 1987), 1132–1133.

55336. Russo, Joe. "The Greening of World Series MVP, Frank Viola." *Scholastic Coach,* LVII (May 1988), 44–47.

55337. Wulf, Steve. "The Best Man Wins." *Sports Illustrated,* LXVII (October 26, 1987), 41–42.

Bill Virdon *see* **William Charles ("Bill" or "Quail") Virdon**

William Charles ("Bill" or "Quail") Virdon
OF-MGR. (B: June 9, 1931, Royal Oak Township, MI). St. Louis (NL), 1955–1956; Pittsburgh (NL), 1956–1966 and 1968. Remarks: Had 1,596 hits (91 homers) in 1,583, games in a dozen seasons; NL Rookie of the Year award, 1955; hit bad-hop grounder in Game Seven of the 1960 World Series that caught Tony Kubek (q.v.) in the throat; minor league manager, 1966–1967; manager, Pittsburgh (NL), 1972–1973, New York (AL), 1974–1975, Houston (NL), 1976–1982; Montreal (NL), 1983–1984, winning 995 games and losing 921 in 14 piloting years; named to Missouri Sports Hall of Fame, 1983; scout/minor league instructor, Pittsburgh (NL), 1984–1995; coach, Houston (NL), 1997–2000.

55338. "Bill Virdon." *Coaching Review,* VI (May-June 1983), 8–14.

55339. Broeg, Bob. "How Good Is Bill Virdon?" *Sport,* XXV (April 1958), 42–43+.

55340. Fehler, Gene. "Bill Virdon." In: his *Tales from Baseball's Golden Age.* Champaign, IL: Sports Publishing Co., 2000. Chpt. 52.

55341. Greenwood, Chuck. "Virdon Has Lived the American Dream." *Sports Collector's Digest,* XXII (September 29, 1995), 160–161.

55342. Honig, Donald. "1955: Bill Virdon." In: his *National League Rookies of the Year.* New York: Bantam Books, 1989. Pp. 21–22.

55343. Horrigan, Jack. "Dividend on the Slaughter Deal." *Baseball Digest,* XIII (November-December 1954), 65–68.

55344. Jacobs, Bruce. "The Word is Confidence: Bill Virdon." In: Bruce Jacobs, ed. *Baseball Stars of 1957.* New York: Lion Books, 1957. Pp. 87–92.

55345. _____. "Yankee Mistake: Bill Virdon." In: Bruce

Jacobs, ed. *Baseball Stars of 1956.* New York: Lion Books, 1956. Pp. 129–133.

55346. Kappler, Brian. "Can Virdon Manage to Beat Whitey?" *Sport,* LXXIV (July 1983), 68–69.

55347. Langford, Walter. "Bill Virdon Will Always Remember '60 World Series." *Baseball Digest,* XLVII (October 1988), 39–44.

55348. Richman, Arthur. "Who's Best in Center?: Bucs Say Virdon." *Baseball Digest,* XX (May 1961), 57–59.

55349. Spoehr, Luther W. "William Charles 'Bill,' 'Quail' Virdon." In: Vol. Q-Z of David L. Porter, ed. *Biographical Dictionary of American Sports: Baseball.* Rev. and enlarged ed. Westport, CT: Greenwood Press, 2000. Pp. 1602–1604.

55350. Virdon, William C. "The Game I'll Never Forget." *Baseball Digest,* XXXV (December 1976), 87–94.

55351. _____. "Interview." *Coaching Review,* VI (May-June 1983), 8–14.

Ozzie Virgil
3B–SS. (B: Osvaldo Jose Virgil Sr., May 17, 1933, Monte Cristi, D.R.). New York (NL), 1956–1957; Detroit (AL), 1958, 1960–1961; Kansas City (AL), 1961; Baltimore (AL), 1962; Pittsburgh (NL), 1965; San Francisco (NL), 1966, 1969. Remarks: First big league player from the Dominican Republic; in nine big league seasons, obtained 174 hits (14 homers) and six stolen bases in 324 games; coach, San Francisco (NL), 1969–1972, 1974–1975, Montreal (NL), 1976–1981, San Diego (NL), 1982–1985, Seattle (AL), 1986–1988.

55352. Briley, Ronald F. "In the Tradition of Jackie Robinson: Ozzie Virgil and the Integration of the Detroit Tigers." In: William M. Simons, ed. *The Cooperstown Symposium on Baseball and American Culture 2002.* Jefferson, NC: McFarland & Co., Inc., 2003. Pp. 137–153.

Omar Enrique Visquel
SS (B: Omar Enrique Visquel Gonzalez, April 24, 1967, Caracas, Venezuela). Seattle (AL), 1989–1993; Cleveland (AL), 1994–2004; San Francisco (NL), 2005–. Remarks: Through 2004, has had 2,147 hits (66 homers) and 318 stolen bases in 2,138 games; had winning hits in Games Two and Four of 1997 ALCS; had seven hits (two doubles) in 1997 World Series; obtained 11 hits (one triple) in 1998 ALCS; had streak of 95 errorless games, Sept. 26, 1999–July 21, 2001; had three doubles in one game, May 5, 2002; won eight Golden Gloves; led AL in sacrifice hits, 1997, 1999, 2004.

55353. Call, Andy. "Omar!" *Crain's Cleveland Business,* XXIV (March 24, 2003), 14–15.

55354. Hoynes, Paul. "Omar Visquel of the Indians: He's an Artist at Shortstop." *Baseball Digest,* LVII (February 2002), 40–45.

55355. Kurkijan, Tim. "Playmaker." *Sports Illustrated,* LXXXIV (April 1, 1996), 68–72.

55356. Manoloff, Dennis. *Omar Vizquel: The Man with the Golden Glove.* SuperStar Series, no. 6. Champaign, Il: Sports Publishing, Inc., 1999. 85p.

55357. Pluto, Terry. "Omar Vizquel: Baseball's Best Defensive Shortstop." *Baseball Digest,* LVIII (February 1999), 26–27.

55358. Robbins, Liz. "Omar Visquel: His Smooth Glove Work Heartens the Indians." *Baseball Digest,* LIV (November 1995), 64–70.

55359. Stone, Larry. "Outstanding in His Field: With His Glove, Omar Visquel Ranks Among the Best." *Baseball Digest,* LX (June 2001), 62–65.

55360. Visquel, Omar and Bob Dyer. *Omar: My Life On and Off the Field.* New York: Gray and Company, 2002. 256p.

55361. Williams, Pete. "The Power of Glove." *USA Today Baseball Weekly,* VIII (August 12, 1998), 8–9.

Oscar Joseph ("Ossie") Vitt
3B-2B-OF-MGR. (B: Jan. 4, 1890, San Francisco, CA-D: Jan. 31, 1963). Detroit (AL), 1912–1918; Boston (AL), 1919–1921. Remarks: Had 894 hits (four homers) and 114 stolen bases in 506 games in a decade; led AL in sacrifice hits, 1915; set a 21-year record of 615 fielding chances in a season, 1916; also played for San Francisco (PCL), 1911 and Salt Lake City (PCL), 1923; manager, Oakland (PCL), 1935 and Newark (IL),1936–1937; manager, Cleveland (AL), 1938–1940; aggressive managerial tactics resisted by Indians players, who, in petitioning for his removal in 1940, became known as "The Crybabies."

55362. Spalding, John E. "Ossie Vitt." In: his *Pacific Coast League Stars, Vol. II: Ninety Who Made it to the Majors, 1905–1957.* San Jose, CA: John E. Spalding, 1997. Pp. 36–38.

Ossie Vitt *see* **Oscar Joseph ("Ossie") Vitt**
Jose Vizcaino
SS-2B-3B. (B: Jose Luis Vizcaino Pimental, March 26, 1968, San Cristobal, D.R.). Los Angeles (NL), 1989–1990; Chicago (NL), 1991–1993; New York (NL), 1994–1886; Cleveland (AL), 1996); San Francisco (NL), 1997; Los Angeles (NL), 1998–2000; New York (AL), 2000; Houston (NL), 2001–. Remarks: Through 2004, has had 1,276 hits (30 homers) and 71 stolen bases in 1,504 games.

55363. Herrick, Steve. "New Kids in Town." In: Cleveland Indians. *1996 Central Division Champion Indians.* Cleveland, OH: Cleveland Indians, 1996. Pp. 64–71. Vizcaino and Kevin Seitzer.

David Quentin Voigt
WRITER. (B: August 9, 1926, Reading, PA). Remarks: Professor, Albright College, 1964–2000; sociologist and baseball historian.

55364. Adelman, H. "Captain Voigt and American Baseball History." *Canadian Journal of History of Sport,* XX (May 1989), 69–85.

Jack Voigt *see* **John David ("Jack") Voigt**
John David ("Jack") Voigt
OF (B: May 17, 1968, Sarasota, FL). Baltimore (AL), 1992–1995; Texas (AL), 1995–1996; Milwaukee (AL), 1997; Oakland (AL), 1998. Remarks: Had 138 hits (20 homers) and seven stolen bases in 294 games in all or part of seven big league seasons; manager, Frederick Keys (Carolina League), 2001–2002; minor league roving baserunning and bunting coach, Atlanta (NL), 2003–2004; coach, Washington (NL), 2005–.

55365. Alatzas, Trif. "Red Wings' Versatile Jack Voigt Promoted to the Big Leagues." *Orioles Gazette,* III (May 7, 1993), 26–27.

55366. Berney, Louis. "Rookie Jack Voigt, a Man of Many Names, Loves to Talk." *Orioles Gazette,* III (September 24, 1993), 14–15.

Bill Voiselle *see* **William Symmes ("Bill" or "Big Bill" or "Ninety-Six") Voiselle**
William Symmes ("Bill" or "Big Bill" or "Ninety-Six") Voiselle
P. (B: Jan. 29, 1919, Greenwood, SC-D: Jan. 31, 2005). New York (NL), 1942–1947; Boston (NL), 1947–1949; Chicago (NL), 1950. Remarks: Won 74 games and lost 94 in nine seasons; lost Game Six of 1948 World Series; last rookie pitcher ever to pitch more than 300 innings in his first season; 6'4" hurler wore uniform number, 96, highest ever in the major leagues.

55367. Daniel, Daniel M. "Bill Voiselle: Giant Pitcher

Achieves Rookie of the Year Laurels for 1944 Season." *Baseball Magazine,* LXXIV (January 1945), 465–467.

55368. Dooly, Bill. "Rookie of the Year: Voiselle." *Baseball Digest,* III (November 1944), 61–62.

55369. Kelley, Brent P. "Bill Voiselle: No. 96." In: his *The Early All-Stars: Conversations with Standout Baseball Players of the 1930s and 1940s.* Jefferson, NC: McFarland & Co., Inc., 1997. Pp. 163–172.

55370. _____. "Bill Voiselle Was Key Member of '48 Braves." *Sports Collector's Digest,* XVIII (July 19, 1991), 100–101.

55371. Mayer, Bob. "Bill Voiselle and the $500 Pitch." *The Baseball Research Journal,* XXVI (1997), 136–138.

55372. Skipper, John C. "Bill Voiselle: The Number-Three Starter Behind Spahn and Sain." In: his *Inside Pitch: A Closer Look at Classic Baseball Moments.* Jefferson, NC: McFarland & Co., Inc., 1996. Pp. 46–49. '48 Boston (NL) team.

55373. Smith, Ken. "V for Vim, Victory, and Voiselle." *Baseball Magazine,* LXXIV (January 1945), 259–261.

55374. Westcott, Rich. "Bill Voiselle: Number 96, One of a Kind." In: his *Masters of the Diamond.* Jefferson, NC: McFarland & Co., 1994. Pp. 147–157.

Clyde Frederick Vollmer

OF. (B: Sept. 24, 1921, Cincinnati, OH). Cincinnati, (N.L), 1942, 1946–1948; Washington (AL), 1948–1950; Boston (AL), 1950–1953; Washington (AL),. 1953–1954. Remarks: Obtained 508 hits (69 homers) in 685 games in a decade; hit first pitch received in first big league game for homer, May 31, 1942; in the only such occurrence in MLB history, went to plate eight times in eight innings in one game, June 8, 1950; obtained grand slam homer, July 7, 1951; had three homers and six RBIs in one game, July 26, 1951; had 16th-inning grand slam homer, July 28, 1951.

55375. Burick, Si. "Vollmer the Embalmer." *Baseball Digest,* X (October 1951), 79–83.

55376. Miller, Hub. "The Darling of Fenway Park." *Baseball Magazine,* LXXXVII (October 1951), 10–12.

Christo Von Buffalo

CARTOONIST. Remarks: First cartoonist to draw baseball.

55377. Overfield, Joseph. "The First Baseball Cartoonist?" *The Baseball Research Journal,* X (1981), 147–149. Christo Von Buffalo.

Chris Von Der Ahe *see* **Christian Frederick Wilhelm ("Der Poss President") Von Der Ahe**

Christian Frederick Wilhelm ("Der Poss President") Chris Von Der Ahe

EXEC. (B: Oct. 7, 1851, Hille, Germany-D: June 7, 1913). Remarks: Brewer and owner, St. Louis (AA), 1882–1891 St. Louis (NL), 1892–1898.

55378. Borst, William A. ("Bill") "Christian Frederick Wilhelm 'Der Poss President' Von der Ahe." In: Vol. Q-Z of David L. Porter, ed. *Biographical Dictionary of American Sports: Baseball.* Rev. and enlarged ed. Westport, CT: Greenwood Press, 2000. Pp. 1604–1605.

55379. Bowman, Larry G. "Christian Von der Ahe, the St. Louis Browns, and the World's Championship Playoffs, 1885–1888." *Missouri Historical Review,* XCI (July 1997), 385–405.

55380. Egenriether, R. "Chris Von Der Ahe: Baseball's Pioneering Huckster." *Nine: A Journal of Baseball History and Social Policy Perspectives,* VII (Spring 1999), 14–39.

55381. Gietschier, Steven P. "Christian Frederick Wilhelm Von der Ahe." In: John A. Garrity and Marsh C. Carries, eds. *American National Biography.* 24 vols. New York: Oxford University Press, 1999. XXII, 396–397.

55382. Egenriether, Richard. "Chris Von der Ahe: Baseball's Pioneering Huckster." *The Baseball Research Journal,* XVIII (1989), 27–31.

55383. Rygelski, Jim. "Baseball's 'Boss President': Chris von der Ahe and the 19th Century St. Louis Browns." *Gateway Heritage,* XIII (Summer 1992), 42–53.

Bruce Frederick Von Hoff

P. (B. Nov. 17, 1943, Oakland, CA). Houston (NL), 1965 and 1967. Remarks: Won 0 and lost three of 13 big league games in which appeared.

55384. McKean, W. J. "Big Pitch for a Baseball Baby." *Look,* XXXI (June 27,1967), 53–58.

Joseph Franklin ("Joe") Vosmik

OF. (B: April 4, 1910, Cleveland, OH-D: Jan. 27, 1962). Cleveland (AL), 1930–1936; St. Louis (AL), 1937; Boston (AL), 1938–1939; Brooklyn (NL), 1940–1941; Washington (AL), 1944. Remarks: In 13 seasons, obtained 1,682 hits (65 homers) and 23 stolen bases in 1,414 games; had four hits in one game, Sept. 3, 1933; led AL in doubles and triples, 1935; led AL in hits (201), 1938; also played for Louisville (AA), 1941 and Minneapolis (AA), 1942–1943; manager, Tucson (Arizona-Texas League, 1947), Dayton (Central League), 1948; Oklahoma City (TL), 1949–1950; Batavia (Pony League), 1951; scout, Cleveland (AL), 1951–1952.

55385. Giglio, James N. "Joseph Franklin 'Joe' Vosmik." In: Vol. Q-Z of David L. Porter, ed. *Biographical Dictionary of American Sports: Baseball.* Rev. and enlarged ed. Westport, CT: Greenwood Press, 2000. Pp. 1605–1606.

Inrz ("Lefty") Voyce

1B-P. (B: Aug. 16, 1924, Rathbun, IA). South Bend Blue Sox (All-American Girls Professional Baseball League), 1946; Grand Rapids Chicks (AAGPBL), 1957–1953. Remarks: In eight years, obtained 68 homers and 168 stolen bases.

55386. Crawford, Scott A. G. M. "Inez 'Lefty' Voyce." In: Vol. Q-Z of David L. Porter, ed. *Biographical Dictionary of American Sports: Baseball.* Rev. and enlarged ed. Westport, CT: Greenwood Press, 2000. Pp. 1606–1607.

Peter Dennis ("Pete") Vuckovich

P-BROADCASTER. (B; Oct. 27, 1952, Johnstown, PA). Chicago (AL), 1975–1976; Toronto (AL), 1977; St. Louis (NL), 1978–1980; Milwaukee (AL), 1981–1986. Remarks: Won 93 games and lost 69, with 10 "saves," in a decade; lost Game Two of 1982 ALCS; lost Game Three of 1982 World Series; AL Cy Young Award, 1982; color analyst, Milwaukee (AL), 1983; coach/special GM assistant, Philadelphia (NL), 1998–2003.

55387. Gammons, Peter. "Pete Vuckovich: He Doesn't Look Pretty, but He Wins." *Baseball Digest,* XLII (April 1983), 26–28.

55388. Kausler, Don, Jr. "Pete Vuckovich of the Brewers Silences His Critics." *Baseball Digest,* XLI (May 1982), 51–53.

55389. Mehno, John. "Vuckovich: He Has Something to Prove in '84." *Baseball Digest,* XLIII (April 1984), 97–100.

55390. Olmsted, Frank J. "Peter Dennis 'Pete' Vuckovich." In: Vol. Q-Z of David L. Porter, ed. *Biographical Dictionary of American Sports: Baseball.* Rev. and enlarged ed. Westport, CT: Greenwood Press, 2000. Pp. 1607–1609.

55391. Sell, Dennis. "Pete Vuckovieh, 1982 Cy Young Award Winner." In: Tom Skibosh, ed. *Milwaukee Brewers 1983 Official Yearbook.* Waukesha, WI: Delzer Lithograph Corp., 1983. Pp. 18–19.

John Christopher Vukovich

3B-SS. (B: July 31, 1947, Sacramento, CA). Philadelphia

(NL), 1970–1971; Milwaukee (AL), 1973–1974; Chicago (NL), 1975; Philadelphia (NL), 1976–1981. Remarks: In all or parts of 12 big league seasons, obtained 90 hits (six homers) and four stolen bases in 277 games; coach, Chicago (NL), 1982–1987; interim manager, Chicago (NL), 1986 and Philadelphia (NL), 1988, winning six games and losing five (.545); had surgery to remove brain tumor, May 2001.

55392. "John Vukovich." In: Carrie Muskat, ed. *Banks to Sandberg to Grace: Five Decades of Love and Frustration with the Chicago Cubs.* Chicago, IL: Contemporary Books, 2001. Pp. 201–204.

George Edward ("Rube") Waddell★

P. (B. Oct. 12, 1876, Bradford, PA–D: April 1, 1914). Louisville (NL), 1897 and 1899; Pittsburgh (N.L), 1900–1901; Chicago (NL), 1901; Philadelphia (AL), 1902–1907; St. Louis (AL), 1908–1910. Remarks. In a 13-year major league career, had 193 victories, 142 defeats, and ten "saves"; had 34 complete games, 1903; holds AL record for most strikeouts in one season by a lefthander (349 in 1904); led NL in strikeouts, 1900; led AL in strikeouts, 1902–1908; very colorful — very eccentric as an actor on and off the field; died of tuberculosis in a sanatorium; elected to National Baseball Hall of Fame in 1946, where his plaque reads: "Colorful left-handed pitcher who was in both leagues, but who gained fame as a member of the Philadelphia AL team, Won more than 20 games in first four seasons with that club and compiled more than 200 victories during major league career. Was noted for his strikeout achievements."

55393. Akin, William "Rube Waddell." In: John A. Garrity and Marsh C. Carries, eds. *American National Biography.* 24 vols. New York: Oxford University Press, 1999. XXII, 429–430.

55394. Allen, Lee. "A Citizen Named Waddell." In: his *The American League Story.* New York: Hill & Wang, 1962. Pp. 36–42.

55395. _____. and Thomas Meany. "Rube Waddell." In: their *Kings of the Diamond.* New York: G.P. Putnam, 1965. Pp. 37–40.

55396. Barton, Jerry. "George Edward 'Rube' Waddell." In: his *A Treasure Chest of the Hall of Fame.* Boston: The Wilson-Hill Co., 1952. Pp. 90–91.

55397. Burkholder, Ed. "Rube Waddell." In: his *Baseball Immortals.* New York: Christopher, 1955. Pp. 36–39.

55398. Daley, Arthur. "The Day Before Yesterday: The Great Early Stars-Young, Waddell, Cobb, and Wagner." In: Herbert W. Wind, ed. *The Realm of Sport.* New York: Simon and Schuster, 1968. Pp. 30–36.

55399. _____. "Saga of a Screwball: Rube Waddell." In: his *Sports of The Times.* New York: E.P. Dutton, 1959. Pp. 49–53.

55400. Davis, Mac. "A Fool There Was." In: his *The Lore and Legends of Baseball.* New York: Lantern Press, 1953. Pp. 57–59.

55401. _____. "Rube Waddell: The Boy Who Never Grew Up." In: his *Pacemakers in Baseball.* Cleveland, OH: World Publishing Company, 1968. Pp. 19–22.

55402. Duchess, Eric D. *Rube Waddell: Butler's Outrageous Southpaw.* Old Stone House Series, v. 3. [Butler, PA: Priv. Print., 1998?] Unpaged.

55403. Esch, Harold "Waddell and Schreck in College." *The Baseball Research Journal,* IX (1980), 144–145. Ossee Schreckengost.

55404. Gordon, David. "Rube Waddell —1902." In: his *Baseball's Top 100: The Best Individual Seasons of All Time.* Wilton, CT: Diamond Library, 1996. Pp. 24–26.

55405. Grayson, Harry. "George Edward ('Rube') Waddell." In: his *They Played the Game.* New York: A.S. Barnes, 1944. Pp. 20–22.

55406. Honig, Donald. "Rube Waddell." In: his *Baseball America.* New York: Macmillan, 1985. pp. 40–49.

55407. _____. "Rube Waddell." In: his *The Greatest Pitchers of All Time.* New York: Crown Publishers, Inc., 1988. Pp. 6–11.

55408. Klima, John. "First to Perfection: Rube Waddell vs. Cy Young (May 5, 1904)." In: his *Pitched Battle: 35 of Baseball's Greatest Duels from the Mound.* Jefferson, NC: McFarland & Co., Inc., 2002. Pp. 3–7.

55409. Levy, Alan H. "The Right Myths at the Right Time: Myth Making and Hero Worship in Post-Frontier American Society-Rube Waddell vs. Christy Mathewson." In: William Simons, ed. *The Cooperstown Symposium on Baseball and American Culture, 2001.* Jefferson, NC: McFarland & Co., Inc., 2002. Pp. 51–65.

55410. _____. *Rube Waddell: The Zany, Brilliant Life of a Strikeout Artist* Jefferson, NC: McFarland &Co., Inc., 2000. 327p.

55411. Lewis, Allen. "Feller Only Tied Waddell!" *Baseball Digest,* V (November 1946), 29–31.

55412. Lieb, Frederick G. "Rube Waddell: He Answered Fire Bell in Middle of Game." In: his *Comedians and Pranksters of Baseball.* St. Louis, MO: The Sporting News, 1968. Pp. 6–9.

55413. Liss, Howard. "Rube Waddell." In: his *Baseball's Zaniest Stars.* New York: Random House, 1971. Pp. 35–53.

55414. Martin, Douglas D. "George Edward 'Rube' Waddell." In: Vol. Q-Z of David L. Porter, ed. *Biographical Dictionary of American Sports: Baseball.* Rev. and enlarged ed. Westport, CT: Greenwood Press, 2000. Pp. 1611–1613.

55415. McGillicuddy, Cornelius ("Connie Mack"). "Reminiscence of Rube Waddell." *Baseball Magazine,* VIII (February 1912), 73–75.

55416. _____. As told to Bill Dietrich. "The One and Only Rube." *Saturday Evening Post,* CCVIII (March 14, 1936), 12–17.

55417. Martin, Thornton ("Pete"). "Rube Waddell." In: his *Pete Martin Calls On.* New York: Simon and Schuster, 1962. Pp. 43–57.

55418. McKay, Joe. "Rube Waddell: The Man-Child of Major League Baseball." In: his *The Great Shutout Pitchers: 20 Profiles of a Vanishing Breed.* Jefferson, NC: McFarland & Co., Inc., 2004. Pp. 196–207.

55419. Meany, Thomas. "The Rube." In: his *Baseball's Greatest Pitchers.* New York: A.S. Barnes, 1951. Pp. 247–256.

55420. _____. "Rube Waddell." In: his *Baseball's Greatest Players.* New York: Grosset and Dunlap, 1953. Pp. 244–253.

55421. Menke, Frank G. "Waddell — the One and Only." In: his *Sports Tales and Anecdotes.* New York: A.S. Barnes, 1953. Pp. 12–16.

55422. Newcombe, Jack. "A Lefty Called Rube." In: his *The Fireballers.* New York: G.P. Putnam, 1964. Pp. 27–38.

55423. Palmer, Pete. "Rube Waddell in 1902." *The Baseball Research Journal,* VIII (1979), 98–100.

55424. Rankin, C.T. "Anecdotes of Rube Waddell." *Baseball Magazine,* IX (May 1912), 31–33.

55425. Ritter, Lawrence and Donald Honig. "Rube Waddell." In: their *The 100 Greatest Baseball Players of All Time.* New York: Crown Publishers, 1981. Pp. 108–111.

55426. Robinson, Ray. "Hey, Rube!" In: Charles Einstein, ed. *The Fireside Book of Baseball.* New York: Simon and Schuster, 1956. Pp. 274–277.

55427. Salsinger, H.G. "Greatest Pitcher?: Waddell." *Baseball Digest,* X (September 1951), 72–75.

55428. Scott, Joe. "The Rube Arrives." *The National Pastime,* X (1990), 72–74.

55429. Smith, Ira L. "George Edward ('Rube') Waddell." In: his *Baseball's Famous Pitchers.* New York: A.S. Barnes, 1954. Pp. 43–47.

55430. Smith, Robert M. "George Edward Waddell: The Original Rube." In: his *Heroes of Baseball.* Cleveland, OH: World Publishing Co., 1952. Pp. 178–184.

55431. Spink, J.G. Taylor. "Rube Waddell: His Life, Laughs, and Laurels." In: J.G. Taylor Spink, ed. *Baseball Register, 1944.* St. Louis, MO: The Sporting News, 1944. Pp. 4–21.

55432. Tarvin, A.H. "How a Straw Hat Kept Waddell Out of a World Series." *Baseball Digest,* II (November 1943), 1–3.

55433. _____. "More About Waddell." *Baseball Magazine,* LXXXI (July 1948), 270–271+.

55434. Thorn, John. "Rube Waddell: The Peter Pan of Baseball." *Elysian Fields Quarterly,* XI (Spring 1992), 76–81.

55435. Waddell, George L ("Rube"). "Reminiscences of Rube Waddell." *Baseball Magazine,* XII (January 1914), 43–49.

Hiawatha Terrell Wade
P. (B: Rembert, SC, Jan. 25, 1973). Atlanta (NL), 1995–1997; Tampa Bay (AL), 1998. Remarks: Won eight games and lost eight, with one "save," in four big league years; career ruined by shoulder injury.

55436. Epstein, Eddie. "Terrell Wade." In: STATS, Inc. *The STATS 1995 Minor League Scouting Notebook.* Skokie, IL: STATS Publishing, 1995. Pp. 165–166.

55437. Schwartz, Alan. "A Brave Named Hiawatha." *Beckett Focus on Future Stars,* IV, no. 34 (February 1994), 82–83.

Terrell Wade *see* **Hiawatha Terrell Wade**

Audrey Wagner
OF. (B: Dec. 27, 1927, Bensenville, IL). Kenosha Comets (All-American Girls Professional Baseball League, 1943–1949. Remarks: In 694 games, had 627 hits (20 homers) and 246 stolen bases; AAGPBL home run champion, 1946–1947; later became medical doctor.

55438. Clark, Dennis S. "Audrey Wagner." In: Vol. Q-Z of David L. Porter, ed. *Biographical Dictionary of American Sports: Baseball.* Rev. and enlarged ed. Westport, CT: Greenwood Press, 2000. P. 1613.

Billy Wagner *see* **William Edward ("Billy") Wagner**

Charles Thomas ("Charlie" or "Broadway") Wagner
P-EXEC. (B: Dec. 3, 1912, Reading, PA). Boston (AL), 1938–1942, 1946. Remarks: Won 32 games and lost 23 in six big league seasons; had seven one-run victories, June 7-August 15, 1942; later, Red Sox farm team director and scout; oldest surviving Sox player who lived to see the "Curse of the Bambino" lifted in 2004.

55439. Crissey, Kit. "A Man for All Seasons." *The National Pastime,* XIX (1999), 65–66.

55440. Lautier, Jack. "Charlie 'Broadway' Wagner." In: his *Fenway Voices.* Camden, ME: Yankee Books, 1990. Pp. 29–32.

Charles F ("Heinie") Wagner
SS-2B-MGR. (B: Sept. 23, 1880, New York City-D: March 20, 1943). New York (NL), 1902; Boston (AL), 1906–1916, 1918. Remarks: Obtained 834 hits (10 homers) and 144 stolen bases in 983 games in 13 big league seasons; coach, Boston (AL), 1927–1929; manager, Boston (AL), 1930, winning 52 games and losing 102 (.338).

55441. "Trials of a Big League Player: The Star's Career is Not a Rosy One." *Baseball Magazine,* VII (August 1911), 61–62.

Charlie Wagner *see* **Charles Thomas ("Charlie" or "Broadway") Wagner**

Hans Wagner *see* **Johnnes Peter ("Honus" or "Hans" or "The Flying Dutchman") Wagner**

Heinie Wagner *see* **Charles F ("Heinie") Wagner**

Honus Wagner *see* **Johnnes Peter ("Honus" or "Hans" or "The Flying Dutchman") Wagner**

Johnnes Peter ("Honus" or "Hans" or "The Flying Dutchman") Wagner★
SS-MGR-COACH. (B: Feb. 24, 1874, Carnegie, PA-D: Dec. 6, 1965). Louisville (NL), 1897–1899,- Pittsburgh (NL), 1900–1917. Remarks: In a 21-year playing career, obtained 3,430 hits (101 homers) and 722 stolen bases (tenth on all-time list) in 2,786 games; NL batting champion, 1900, 1903–1904, 1906–1909, 1911; led N. L. in triples, 1900, 1903, 1908; led NL in doubles, 1900, 1902, 1904, 1906–1909; NL stolen base champion, 1901–1902, 1904, 1907–1908; had six hits (one double) in 1903 World Series; first player to have his named branded into a Louisville Slugger baseball bat, 1905; NL RBI champion, 1907–1908; had eight hits (two doubles and a triple) in 1909 World Series; holds NL record for most triples (252) and while undoubtedly long the game's greatest shortstop, also the shortstop with the most errors lifetime (676) since 1900; managed five games for Pittsburgh (NL) in 1917, winning one and losing four; baseball coach, Carnegie-Mellon University, 1918–1932; coach, Pittsburgh (NL), 1933–1951; elected to National Baseball Hall of Fame in 1936, where his plaque reads: "The greatest shortstop in baseball history. Born Carnegie, Pa., Feb. 24, 1874. Known to fans as 'Honus,' 'Hans,' and 'The Flying Dutchman.' Retired in 1917, having scored more runs, made more hits, and stolen more bases than any other player in the history of his league."

55442. Abramson, Dan. "The Man Behind the Card." *Beckett Baseball Card Monthly,* VI (December 1989), 14–15.

55443. Adomites, Paul D. "Honus Wagner." In: John A. Garrity and Marsh C. Carries, eds. *American National Biography.* 24 vols. New York: Oxford University Press, 1999. XXII, 444–445.

55444. Allen, Lee, and Thomas Meany. "Honus Wagner." In: their *Kings of the Diamond.* New York: G.P. Putnam, 1965. Pp. 149–152.

55445. Barrow, Edward G. "The Dutchman — Greatest of Them All." Edited by J.M. Kahn. *Collier's,* CXXV (May 27, 1950), 18–19+.

55446. Barton, Jerry. "John Peter (Honus) Wagner." In: his *A Treasure Chest of the Hall of Fame.* Boston, MA: The Wilson-Hill Co., 1952. Pp. 10–11.

55447. *Baseball's Immortals: The Story of Honus Wagner.* Cooperstown, NY: The Home Plate Press, 1961. 30p. Pamphlet.

55448. Broeg, Bob. "The Flying Dutchman." In: his *My Baseball Scrapbook.* St. Louis, MO: River City Publishers, 1983. Pp. 5–8.

55449. _____. "Honus Wagner." In: his *Super Stars of Baseball.* SL Louis, MO: The Sporting News, 1971. Pp. 259–264.

55450. "Characteristic Anecdotes About Hans Wagner." *Baseball Magazine,* XIV (January 1915), 57–62.

55451. Condon, Robert J. "John Peter Wagner." In: his *The Fifty Finest Athletes of the 20th Century.* Jefferson (NC): McFarland & Co., Inc., 1990. Pp. 130–132.

55452. Daley, Arthur. "The Day Before Yesterday: The

Great Early Stars-Young, Waddell, Cobb, and Wagner." In: Herbert W. Wind, ed. *The Realm of Sport.* New York: Simon and Schuster, 1966. Pp. 30–36.

55453. _____. "The 'Dutchman' Retires." In: his *Sports of The Times.* New York. E.P. Dutton, 1959. Pp. 83–86.

55454. Davis, Mac. "Honus Wagner: 'The Flying Dutchman." In: his *Pacemakers in Baseball.* Cleveland, OH: World Publishing Company, 1968. Pp. 49–51.

55456. _____. "John Peter ('Honus') Wagner." In: his *The Greatest in Baseball.* New York: Scholastic Book Services, 1977. Pp. 36–38.

55457. DeMarco, Mario. "John Peter Wagner, Baseball." In: his *Great American Athletes.* Menlo Park, CA: Pacific Coast Publishers, 1962. Pp. 4–5.

55458. De Valeria, Dennis and Jeanne Burke De Valeria. *Honus Wagner: A Biography.* New York: Henry Holt and Co., 1996. 334p. Reprinted by the University of Pittsburgh Press in 1998.

55459. _____. "Honus Wagner's Major League Debut. In: *A Celebration of Louisville Baseball in the Major and Minor Leagues.* Cleveland, OH: The Society for American Baseball Research, 1997. Pp. 8–9.

55450. _____. "Honus Wagner's Tricks of the Trade." *The National Pastime,* XVI (1996), 11–13.

55451. Drebinger, John. "The Super Shortstop." *Baseball Magazine,* LXII (March 1939), 439–441+.

55452. Dreyfus, Barney. "Hans Wagner's Comeback." *Baseball Magazine,* XIX l August 1917), 432–433.

55453. "The Dutchman's Crown." *Literary Digest,* LIV (March 24,1917), 847–848.

55454. Enders, Eric. "Baseball Legend." In: Richard Levin, ed. *2000 World Series Official Program.* New York: Major League Baseball Promotion Corp., 2000. Pp. 38–39.

55455. Fullerton, Hugh S. "Wagner: Greatest Baseball Player in the World." *American Magazine,* LXIX (January 1910), 378–395.

55456. Gajus, Greg. "Honus Wagner—1908." In: his *Baseball's Top 100: The Best Individual Seasons of All Time.* Wilton, CT: Diamond Library, 1996. Pp. 33–35.

55457. Geyer, Orel R. "Hans,' 'Honus,' 'Dutch,' or Plain John Henry Wagner." *Baseball Magazine,* I (August 1908), 22–25.

55458. Graham, Frank. "*Sport's* Hall of Fame: The Flying Dutchman." *Sport,* XXIX (January 1960), 44–45+.

55459. Grayson, Harry. "John Honus ('The Flying Dutchman') Wagner." In: his *They Played the Game.* New York: A.S. Barnes, 1944. Pp. 6–7.

55460. Gutman, Bill. "John Peter (Honus) Wagner: 'The Dutchman' [1874–1955]." In: his *Famous Baseball Stars.* New York: Dodd, Mead, 1973. Pp. 1–11.

55461. Gutman, Dan. *Honus and Me: A Baseball Card Adventure.* New York: Avon Books, 1997. 140p.

55462. Hageman, William. *Honus: The Life and Times of a Baseball Hero.* Champaign, IL: Sagamore Publishing, 1996. 218p.

55463. "Hans Wagner's Debut." *Literary Digest,* XLVI (June 21, 1913), 1401+.

55464. Harrington, John. *Honus Wagner: "The Flying Dutchman."* San Diego, CA: Revolutionary Comics, 1992. 30p. Pamphlet.

55465. Hittner, Arthur D. *Honus Wagner: The Life of Baseball's "Flying Dutchman."* Jefferson, NC: McFarland & Co., Inc, 1996. 306p. Reprinted in 2003.

55466. Honig, Donald. "Honus Wagner." In: his *Baseball America.* New York: Macmillan, 1985. Pp. 57–60.

55467. _____. "Honus Wagner." In: his *The Greatest*

Shortstops of All Time. Dubuque, IA: Wm. C. Brown Communications, 1992. Pp. 2–10.

55468. "Honus or Bogus: Honus Wagner Baseball Cards." *Sports Illustrated,* LXXII (June 4, 1990), 18–19.

55469. "Honus Wagner." In: Joseph J. Vecchione, ed. *The New York Times Book of Sports Legends.* New York: Times Books, 1991. Pp. 352–356.

55470. Kaplan, Jim and Dick Perez. "Honus Wagner." In: their *The Official Baseball Hall of Fame Book of Superstars.* New York: Little Simon, 1989. Pp. 18–19.

55471. Kavanagh, Jack. *Honus Wagner.* New York: Chelsea House Publishers, 1994. 61p.

55472. Keck, Harry. "Hans Wagner (Shortstop)." In: Christy Walsh, ed. *Baseball's Greatest Lineup.* New York: A.S. Barnes, 1952. Pp. 105–117.

55473. Lane, Ferdinand C. "The Grand Old Man of Baseball." *Baseball Magazine,* IV (January 1915), 39–46.

55474. _____. "The Greatest of All Shortstops." *Baseball Magazine,* XI (October 1913), 47–58.

55475. Lieb, Frederick G. "Hans Wagner." *Baseball Magazine,* IV (December 1909), 53–57.

55476. McMane, Fred. "Honus Wagner." In: his *The 3,000 Hit Club.* Champaign, IL: Sports Publishing, 2000. Pp. 45–52.

55477. Meany, Ttomes. "The Flying Dutchman." In: Charles Einstein, ed. *The Third Fireside Book of Baseball.* New York: Simon and Schuster, 1968. Pp. 311–316.

55478. _____. "The Flying Dutchman': John Peter Wagner." In: his *Baseball's Greatest Hitters.* New York: A. S. Barnes, 1950. Pp. 215–225.

55479. _____and Tommy Holmes. "Honus Wagner." In: their *Baseball's Best.* New York. Watts, 1964. Pp. 151–159.

55480. Murphy, Jim. "Shortstop: Honus Wagner." In: his *Baseball's All-Time All-Stars.* New York: Clarion Books, 1984. Pp. 16–19.

55481. Parker, Dan. "Ed Barrow Reminisces About Honus Wagner." *Baseball Digest,* I (December 1942), 21–23.

55482. Phelon, William A. "Honus Wagner: A Unique Character." *Baseball Magazine,* XIV (January 1915), 51–56.

55483. Powers, Jimmy. "John Peter 'Honus' Wagner." In: his *Baseball Personalities.* New York: Rudolph Field, 1949. Pp. 43–51.

55484. Reidenbaugh, Lowell. "Honus Wagner." In: his *Cooperstown: Where Legends Live Forever.* St. Louis: The Sporting News, 1983. Pp. 251–252.

55485. Rice, Grantland. "Grand Old Dope." *Baseball Magazine,* XLV (May 1915), 36.

55486. Ritter, Lawrence and Donald Honig. "Honus Wagner." In: their *The 100 Greatest Baseball Players of All Time.* New York: Crown Publishers, 1981. Pp. 212–215.

55487. Royal, Chip. "Hans Wagner's Great Days." *Sport,* XXII (October 1956), 74–79.

55488. Salant, Nathan. "Honus Wagner." In: his *Superstars, Stars, and Just Plain Heroes.* New York: Stein & Day, 1982. Pp. 21–27.

55489. Sher, Jack. "Honus Wagner: The Flying Dutchman." *Sport,* VI (June 1949), 52–65. Reprinted in his *Twelve Sport Immortals* (New York: Bartholomew House, 1949), pp. 83–104.

55490. Smith, Lyall. "Old Honus Can Stretch the Truth Like He Stretched Hits." *Baseball Digest,* III (July 1944), 19–21.

55491. Smith, Ron. "Honus Wagner 13." In: his *The Sporting News Selects Baseball's 100 Greatest Players.* St. Louis, MO: The Sporting News, 1998. Pp. 34–35.

55492. Stann, Francis. "You Should Have Seen Old Hans." *Baseball Digest,* XV (January-February 1956), 66–67. Reprinted in John Kuenster, ed. *From Cobb to Catfish* (Chicago: Rand McNally, 1975), p. 87–88.

55493. Suehsdorf, Adie D. "Honus Wagner's Rookie Year." *The National Pastime,* VI (1987), 11–17.

55494. Sullivan, George. "Honus Wagner." In: his *Glovemen: Twenty-Seven of Baseball's Greatest.* New York: Atheneum, 1996. Pp. 62–63.

55495. Tarvin, A. H. "Another Wagner Tale." *Baseball Magazine,* LXXX (February 1948), 305–306.

55496. Vecchione, Joseph J. "Honus Wagner." In: his *The New York Times Book of Sports Legends.* New York: Random House, 1991. Pp. 352–356.

55497. Verral, Charles S. "Honus Wagner." In: his *Mighty Men of Baseball.* New York. Aladdin Books, 1955. Pp. 59–70.

55498. Wagner, John P. ("Honus"). *Baseball Grins.* Pittsburgh: Laurel House, 1933. 32p. Humorous reminiscences and anecdotes.

55499. _____. "A Few Facts About My Life." *Baseball Magazine,* XIV (January 1915), 33–39.

55500. _____. "Help! Help! Help! Help for the Pitchers." Edited by George Kirksey. *Saturday Evening Post,* CCXXIII (July 13,1940), 20–21+.

55501. _____. "Honus Wagner's First Contract." *Baseball Magazine,* XIV (January 1915), 56–57.

55502. _____. "I Never Get Tired of Playing." *Collier's,* XCIX (May 22, 1937), 20+. Reprinted in Tom Seaver, ed., *How I Would Pitch to Babe Ruth* (Chicago: Playboy Press, 1974), pp. 239–249.

55503. _____. "Interview with an Old Timer." *Baseball Magazine,* XXI (July 1918), 293–295+.

55504. _____. "Reminiscences of a Grand Old-Timer." *Baseball Magazine,* LIII (October 1934), 501–503+.

55505. _____. "21 Years in the Big Leagues." *Baseball Magazine,* XX (March 1918), 395–398+.

55506. _____. "When You're Out of It." *Baseball Magazine,* XVII (October 1916), 27–31. Reprinted in Sidney Offit, ed., *Best of Baseball* (New York: G.P. Putnam, 1956), pp. 37–42.

55507. _____. as told to Chet Smith. "My Greatest Day in Baseball." In: John P. Carmichael, ed. *My Greatest Day in Baseball.* New York: A.S. Barnes, 1946. Pp. 22–25. First published in the *Chicago Daily News.*

55508. _____., as told to Lester Biederman. "Play of the Shortstop." *Scholastic Coach,* XIX (April 1950), 12–15.

55509. Walsh, Edward J. "John Peter 'Honus,' 'Hans,' 'The Flying Dutchman' Wagner." In: Vol. Q-Z of David L. Porter, ed. *Biographical Dictionary of American Sports: Baseball.* Rev. and enlarged ed. Westport, CT: Greenwood Press, 2000. Pp. 1613–1615.

55510. Ward, John J. "Shortstop Extraordinary." *Baseball Magazine,* XIV (March 1915), 33–36.

Leon Lamar ("Daddy Wags") Wagner
OF-ACTOR. (B: May 13, 1934, Chattanooga, TN-D: Jan. 3, 2003). San Francisco (NL), 1958–1959; St. Louis (NL), 1960; Los Angeles (AL), 1961–1963; Cleveland (AL), 1964–1968; Chicago (AL), 1966; San Francisco (NL), 1969.' Remarks: In a dozen campaigns, had 1,202 hits (211 homers) and 54 stolen bases in 1,362 games; hit first homer in Candlestick Park, April 12, 1960; (2nd game) All-Star Game MVP award, 1962 (tie); post-baseball, an actor, whose films included *A Woman Under the Influence* and *The Bingo Long Traveling All-Stars and Motor Kings.*

55511. August, Bob. "Leon Wagner: The One-Handed Fielder." *Baseball Digest,* XXIV (May 1965), 31–33.

55512. Bitker, Steve. "Leon Wagner." In: his *The Original San Francisco Giants: The Giants of '58.* Champaign, IL: Sports Publishing, Inc., 1998. Pp. 120–129.

55513. Creamer, Robert W. "A Free-Swinging Angel Who Never Fears to Tread." *Sports Illustrated,* XIX (August 12, 1963), 40–41.

55514. Davis, George T. "Why the Angels Traded Wagner." *Baseball Digest,* XXIII (March 1964), 43–45.

55515. Graham, Frank. "The Making of an Outfielder." *Baseball Digest,* XXII (February 1963), 65–67.

55516. "The Has-Been Who Became a Star." *Ebony,* XVIII (October 1963), 103–104, 106–108.

55517. Kiersh, Edward. "Leon Wagner: Brooks Brothers, Pacino, or Hall of Fame." In: his *Where Have You Gone, Vince DiMaggio?* New York: Bantam Books, 1983. Pp. 32–37.

55518. Libby, Bill. "Swing Along With Wags." *Sport,* XXXV (January 1963), 24–30.

55519. Moffi, Larry and Jonathan Kronstadt. "Leon Lamar Wagner." In: their *Crossing the Line; Black Major Leaguers, 1947–1959.* Jefferson, N.C.: McFarland & Co., Inc., 1994. Pp. 197–198.

55520. Moss, Morton. "Leon Wagner: Power with a Spread-Grip." *Baseball Digest,* XXI (September 1962), 11–17.

55521. O'Shea, Marty. "Leon Wagner." In: Jack Orr, ed. *Baseball's Greatest Players Today.* New York: Watts, 1963. Pp. 44–49.

55522. Peebles, Dick. "Indians 'Steal' Wagner." *Baseball Digest,* XXIII (February 1964), 27–29.

55523. "Policeman of the Outhouse." *Time,* LXXXI (June 21, 1963), 74–75.

55524. Robinson, Jackie. "Leon Wagner." In: his *Baseball Has Done It.* Philadelphia, PA: Lippincott, 1964. Pp. 189–199.

55525. Tassinari, Edward J. "Leon Lamar 'Daddy Wags' Wagner." In: Vol. Q-Z of David L. Porter, ed. *Biographical Dictionary of American Sports: Baseball.* Rev. and enlarged ed. Westport, CT: Greenwood Press, 2000. Pp. 1615–1616.

55526. Zanger, Jack. "Leon Wagner: Cool Cucumber." In: Ray Robinson, ed. *Baseball Stars of 1963.* New York: Pyramid Books, 1963. Pp. 88–92.

William Edward ("Billy") Wagner
P. (July 25, 1971, Tannersville, VA). Houston (NL), 1995–. Remarks: Through 2004, has won 30 games and lost 29, with 246 "saves"; pitched one inning of a combined no-hitter, June 11, 2003; also led Midwest League with 204 strikeouts while playing for Quad City, 1994.

55527. Bamberger, Michael. "Astro Physics: To Understand How Houston Closer Billy Wager Can Throw a Baseball 100 mph, You've Got to Examine the Dynamics of His Rural Upbringing." *Sports Illustrated,* XCI (September 20, 1999), 68–72, 74–78.

55528. Doyle, Al. "Closer Billy Wagner Silences Hitters with His Dominating Fastball." *Baseball Digest,* LVIII (September 1999), 66–68.

55529. Kurkjian, Tim. "Billy Hits the Big Time." *Sports Illustrated,* LXXXV (August 19, 1995), 72–73.

55530. Schwarz, Alan. "A Day in the Life…." *Sports Illustrated for Kids,* XII (July 2000), 42–45.

55531. _____. "Smoke Screen." *Sport,* XC (March 1999), 58–63.

Betty Ann Wagoner
P-OF. (B: July 17, 1930, Lebanon, MO). Muskegan Lassies (All-American Girls Professional Baseball League), 1948; South Bend Blue Sox (AAGPBL), 1949–1954. Re-

marks: In seven years, obtained 609 hits, while also winning 13 games and losing 22; later, player-coach, South Bend Rockettes basketball team, which won national championships, 1954–1960.

55532. Crawford, Scott A. G. M. "Betty Ann Wagoner." In: Vol. Q-Z of David L. Porter, ed. *Biographical Dictionary of American Sports: Baseball.* Rev. and enlarged ed. Westport, CT: Greenwood Press, 2000. Pp. 1616–1617.

Kermit Emerson Wahl

3B. (B: Nov. 18, 1922, Columbia, SD-D: Sept. 16, 1987).Cincinnati (NL), 1944–1947; Philadelphia (AL) and St. Louis (AL), 1951. Remarks: Obtained 145 hits (three homers) and three stolen bases as a utility infielder in 231 big league games in five seasons; returned to SD to become scholastic umpire as well as football and basketball referee; elected to South Dakota Sports Hall of Fame.

55535. Cresap, Dick. "A's Find Wahl a Solid Third Baseman." *Baseball Digest,* IX (November 1950), 76–77.

Edward Stephen ("Eddie") Waitkus

1B. (B: Sept. 4, 1919, Cambridge, MA-D: Sept. 15, 1972). Chicago, (NL), 1941, 1946–1948; Philadelphia (NL), 1949–1953; Baltimore (AL), 1954–1955; Philadelphia (N L.), 1955. Remarks: Had 1,214 hits (24 homers) and 28 stolen bases in 1,140 games in an 11-year major league career; had inside the park homer, June 23, 1946; had inside the park grand slam homer, Aug. 24, 1947; victim of Chicago hotel shooting by a personally-unknown female fan (Ruth Steinhagen), June 15,1949 — this bizarre incident served as the real-life inspiration for the scene in Bernard Malamud's (q.v.) *The Natural* (no. 5578); had four hits (one double) in 1950 World Series; also played for Los Angeles (PCL), 1943; died a cancer victim.

55536. Alexander, Charles C. Eddie Waitkus and Bernard Malmud: Life Versus Art ." *Nine: A Journal of Baseball History and Social Policy Perspectives,* VI (Spring 1998), 15–24.

55537. Berkow, Ira. "Eddie Waitkus." In: Danny Peary, ed. *Cult Baseball Players.* New York: Simon and Schuster, 1990. Pp. 187–191.

55538. _____. "Eddie Waitkus." In: Danny Peary, ed. *Baseball's Finest: The Greats, the Flakes, the Weird and the Wonderful.* North Digton, MA: The JG Press, 1990. Pp. 187–191. Both Peary books are identical.

55539. Brumby, Bob. "Can Eddie Waitkus Come Back?" *Sport,* VIII (April 1950), 22–26.

55540. Burnes, Robert L. "Why the Waitkus Deal?" *Baseball Digest,* VIII (March 1949), 63–67.

55541. "The Fanatic Fan." *Newsweek,* XXXV (April 24, 1950), 49–50.

55542. Fay, William B. "They Woke the Busher Up." *Baseball Digest,* VI (May 1941), 39–41.

55543. "From *A Report to Felony Court: File No.—, the Behavior Clinic."* In: Charles Einstein, ed. *The New Baseball Reader: An All-Star Lineup from The Fireside Book of Baseball.* New York: Penguin Books, 1992. Pp. 124–132.

55544. McGuire, Mark and Michael Sean Gormley. "Eddie Waitkus." In: their *Moments in the Sun: Baseball's Briefly Famous.* Jefferson, NC: McFarland & Co., Inc., 2001. Pp. 101–107.

55545. "A Neurotic Fan with a Rifle." *Newsweek,* XXXIII (June 27, 1949), 27–28.

55546. "A Report to Felony Court." In: Charles Einstein, ed. *The Fireside Book of Baseball.* New York: Simon and Schuster, 1956. Pp. 118–122.

55547. Rumill, Ed. "The Only Cub Regular Who Hit .300 in 1946." *Baseball Magazine,* LXXVIII (March 1947), 329–331.

55548. Spalding, John E. "Eddie Waitkus." In: his *Pacific Coast League Stars, Vol. II: Ninety Who Made it to the Majors, 1905–1957.* San Jose, CA: John E. Spalding, 1997. Pp. 135–137.

55549. Theodore, John. *Baseball's Natural: The Story of Eddie Waitkus.* Carbondale, IL: Southern Illinois University Press, 2002. 176p.

55550. Visco, Ron and Bruce Markusen. "Fatal Attraction: The Girl Who Shot Eddie Waitkus." *Elysian Fields Quarterly,* XVI (Fall 1999), 28–31.

55551. Yeutter, Frank. "They Can't Bump Off Waitkus." *Baseball Digest,* XII (September 1953), 45–47.

Dick Wakefield *see* **Richard Cummings ("Dick") Wakefield**

Richard Cummings ("Dick") Wakefield

OF. (B: May 6, 1921, Chicago, IL-D: Aug. 26, 1985). Detroit (AL), 1941, 1943–1944, 1946–1949; New York (AL), 1950; New York (NL), 1952. Remarks: Obtained 625 hits (56 homers) and 10 stolen bases in 638 games in nine years; one of the first high-paid "bonus babies," who had severe contract problems; also played for Beaumont (TL), 1942 and Oakland (PCL), 1950–1951.

55552. Honig, Donald. "Dick Wakefield." In: his *Baseball Between the Lines: Baseball in the Forties and Fifties as Told by the Men Who Played It.* New York: Coward, Mc-Cann, Geoghegan, 1976. Pp. 79–88.

55553. Rice, Grantland. "Walloping Wakefield." *Baseball Digest,* III (October 1944), 7–9.

55554. Salsinger, H.G. "Dick Wakefield Will Vindicate Detroit's $52,500 Judgement." *Baseball Digest,* I (December 1942), 7–9.

55555. _____. "Wakefield." *Sport,* I (September 1946), 24, 84–85.

55556. Sheldon, Harold. "The Tigers' Wakefield." *Baseball Digest,* II (April 1943), 9–11.

55557. Smith, Lyall. "The New Dick Wakefield." *Baseball Digest,* VI (May 1947), 51–53.

55558. Talbot, Gayle. "The Wakefield Awakening." *Baseball Digest,* IX (March 1950), 77–80.

Timothy Stephen ("Tim") Wakefield

P. (B: Aug. 2, 1966, Melbourne, FL). Pittsburgh (NL), 1992–1993; Boston (AL), 1995–. Remarks: Through 2004, has won 128 games and lost 111, with 22 "saves"; won two games in 1992 NLCS; established 1990s records for most pitches thrown in a game (172-April 27, 1993) and most hits surrendered in a game (16-June 10, 1996); hurled most of 1995 for Buffalo (IL); won two games and but lost the 2003 ALCS when surrendered Aaron Boone's (q.v.) home in Game Seven; won a game in 2004 ALCS.

55559. Hartsock, John. "Tim Wakefield Frustrated Foes with His Knuckleball." *Baseball Digest,* LII (February 1993), 53–55.

55560. Never, Rob. "Boston Red Sox: How Many Games Will Wakefield Win?." In: STATS, Inc. *STATS 1996 Baseball Scoreboard.* Skokie, IL: STATS Publishing, 1996. Pp. 8–9.

George Elvin ("Rube") Walberg

P. (B: July 27, 1896, Pine City, MN-D: Oct. 27, 1978). New York (NL), 1923; Philadelphia (AL), 1923–1933; Boston (AL), 1934–1937. Remarks: Won 156 games and lost 141, with 32 "saves," in 15 years; lost Game Four of 1930 World Series; completed 140 of 307 career starts; scout, Philadelphia (A.L), 1938–1947; named to State of Washington Sports Hall of Fame.

55561. Spatz, Lyle. "George Elvin 'Rube' Walberg. "In: Vol. Q-Z of David L. Porter, ed. *Biographical Dictionary* *of American Sports: Baseball.* Rev. and enlarged ed. Westport, CT: Greenwood Press, 2000. Pp. 1617–1618,

Susyn Waldman

BROADCASTER. (B: 1950, Boston, MA). Remarks: Broadway entertainer, 1972–1987; first female broadcaster/talk show host, WFAN-All Sports Radio, 1987–1996; broadcaster, WPIX, MSG Network, and WNYW/FOX 5, 1997–2001; pre and post game reporter for the YES Network, 2002–; first woman to work on a nationally televised baseball broadcast and first woman to provide play by play for a major league team, New York (NL); NY Sportscaster of the Year Award from The National Sportscasters and Sportswriters, 1996; Star Award for Radio, from American Women in Radio and TV, 1999.

55562. Espinoza, Galina. "Woman on First: Suzyn Waldman Battled Sexism — and Breast Cancer — to Score as Baseball's Pioneer Female Broadcaster." *People Weekly,* LVI (October 8, 2001), 131–132.

55563. Viles, Peter. "First for Mets, WFAN: A Woman in the Booth — Waldman Does Color, Not Play-by-Play; Fans May Already Know Her Singing Voice." *Broadcasting & Cable,* (June 1993), 61+.

Bob Walk *See* **Robert Veron ("Bob" or "Whirlybird") Walk**

Robert Veron ("Bob" or "Whirlybird") Walk

P-BROADCASTER. (B: Nov. 26, 1956, Van Nuys, CA). Philadelphia (NL), 1980; Atlanta (NL), 1981–1983; Pittsburgh (NL), 1984–1993. Remarks: In 14 years, won 105 games and lost 81, with five "saves"; won Game One of 1980 World Series and Game Five of 1992 NLCS; broadcaster, WCWB-TV, FOX Sports Net Pittsburgh, and KDKA-Radio, 1994–.

55564. Walk, Bob, as told to George Vass. "The Game I'll Never Forget." *Baseball Digest,* LIV (March 1995), 50–53.

Albert Bluford ("Rube") Walker

C. (B: May 16, 1926, Lenoir, NC-D: Dec. 12, 1992). Chicago (NL), 1948–1951; Brooklyn (NL) and Los Angeles (NL), 1951–1958. Remarks: During 11 big league seasons, had 360 hits (35 homers) and three stolen bases in 608 games; had one grand slam homer, May 18, 1950; coach, Los Angeles (NL), 1958, minor league manager, 1959–1964, coach, Washington (AL), 1959–1964, New York (NL), 1968–1981, and Atlanta (NL), 1982–1984.

55565. Bingham, Walter. "Say It Again, Rube!" *Sports Illustrated,* XXXII (June 1, 1970), 10–13.

55566. Daley, Arthur. "The Rube Comes Out of the Shadows." *Baseball Digest,* XVII (May 1958), 35–38. Walker spent much of his career as backup to Roy Campanella (q.v.).

55567. Rumill, Ed. "Rube Walker Big Factor in Met Pitching." *Baseball Digest,* XXVII (October 1968), 43–45.

Clarence William ("Tilly") Walker

OF-UMP. (B: Sept. 4, 1887, Telford, TN-D: Sept. 20, 1959). Washington (AL), 1911; St. Louis (AL), 1912–1916; Boston (AL), 1916–1917; Philadelphia (AL), 1918–1923. Remarks: Had 1,423 (118 homers) and 130 stolen bases in 1,421 games in 10 years; had three hits (one triple) in 1916 World Series; AL home run champion (joint), 1918; had four homers in two days, July 1–2, 1922 and, with 37, two more for that season than George H. ("Babe") Ruth (q.v.); later, a minor league player and manager; Appalachian League umpire, 1928–1937; umpire, Appalachian League, 1938–1929; manager, Erwin (Appalachian League), 1940; Tennessee state trooper, 1940–1953.

55568. Billson, Marky. "Tilly Walker: Fine Bat, Great Arm, Mixed Career." *The National Pastime,* XX (2000), 105–108.

55569. Davids, L. Robert. "Clarence William 'Tilly' Walker." In: Vol. Q-Z of David L. Porter, ed. *Biographical Dictionary of American Sports: Baseball.* Rev. and enlarged ed. Westport, CT: Greenwood Press, 2000. Pp. 1620–1621.

55570. Lane, Ferdinand C. "One Reason Why the Browns are Winning." *Baseball Magazine,* XIII (September 1914), 73–76.

Curt Walker *see* **William Curtis ("Curt") Walker**

Dixie Walker *see* **Frederick E. ("Dixie" or "Fred" or "The Peepuls Cherce") Walker**

Fleet Walker *see* **Moses Fleetwood Walker**

Frederick E. ("Dixie" or "Fred" or "The Peepuls Cherce") Walker

OF. (B: Sept. 24, 1910, Villa Rica, GA-D: May 17, 1962). New York (AL), 1931–1936; Chicago (AL), 1936–1937; Detroit (AL), 1938–1939; Brooklyn (NL), 1939–1947; Pittsburgh (NL), 1948–1949. Remarks: Obtained 1,064 hits (105 homers) and 69 stolen bases in 1,905 games in 18 big league seasons; led AL in triples, 1937; had four hits (one double) in 1941 World Series; had inside-the-park homer, May 31, 1942; NL batting champion, 1944; NL RBI champion, 1945; obtained six hits (one double, one homer) in 1947 World Series; manager, Atlanta (SA), 1950–1952, Houston (TL), 1953–1954; Rochester (IL), 1955–1956, and Toronto (IL), 1957–1959; coach, St. Louis (NL), 1953, 1955; coach, Milwaukee (NL), 1963–1965; scout, Milwaukee (NL) and Atlanta (NL), 1960–1968; minor league instructor, Los Angeles (NL), 1968–1969; coach, Los Angeles (NL), 1970–1973; brother of Harry Walker (below); elected to Alabama Sports Hall of Fame.

55571. Bisher, Furman. "Dixie Walker, Manager." *Sport,* XIII (September 1962), 44–45+.

55572. Bloodgood, Clifford. "After Babe Ruth — Fred Walker." *Baseball Magazine,* LIII (June 1934), 307–308+.

55573. _____. "He Plugged the Weak Spot in the Yankee Lineup." *Baseball Magazine,* LI (September 1933), 461–462.

55574. Campbell, Gordon. "Fred ('Dixie') Walker: Major League Batting King." In: his *Famous American Athletes at Today.* 9th Series. New York: Page, 1945. Pp. 301–322.

55575. Danforth, Ed. "Lefties Finally Foil Dixie Walker." *Baseball Digest,* X (August 1951), 75–77.

55576. Frank, Stanley B. "Nobody Wanted Him but the Fans." *Saturday Evening Post,* CCXIV (February 14, 1942), 27+.

55577. Hurwitz, Hy. "Brotherly Love." *Baseball Digest,* VI (November 1947), 3–5. Walker had two major league brothers, Ernie and Harry.

55578. Kavanagh, Jack. "Dixie Walker: 'The Peepul's Cherce.'" *The Baseball Research Journal,* XXII (1993), 80–83.

55579. Lane, Ferdinand C. "Babe Ruth's Understudy." *Baseball Magazine,* LI (August 1933), 387–389.

55580. Lipton, Jack P. "Fred 'Dixie,' 'The People's Choice' Walker." In: Vol. Q-Z of David L. Porter, ed. *Biographical Dictionary of American Sports: Baseball.* Rev. and enlarged ed. Westport, CT: Greenwood Press, 2000. Pp. 1620–1621.

55581. Meany, Thomas. "Dixie Deal Strictly Business." *Baseball Digest,* VII (March 1948), 55–61.

55582. Powell, Larry. "Jackie Robinson and Dixie Walker: Myths of the Southern Baseball Player." *Southern Cultures,* VIII (Summer 2002), 56–71.

55583. Roth, Morton. "Dixie Walker: Farewell to a Boyhood Hero." *Baseball Digest,* XLII (February 1983), 38–42.

55584. Smith, Ira L. "Dixie Walker." In: his *Baseball's Famous Outfielders.* New York: A.S. Barnes, 1954. Pp. 246–251.

55585. Tiller, Guy. "Prospect[ing] for Majors: Dixie Walker." *Baseball Digest,* IX (October 1950), 85–87.

Gee Walker *see* **Gerald Holmes ("Geer) Walker**

Gerald Holmes ("Gee") Walker

OF. (B: March 19, 1908, Gulfport, MS-D: March 20, 1981). Detroit (AL), 1931–1937; Chicago (AL), 1938–1939; Washington (AL), 1940; Cleveland (A.L), 1941; Cincinnati (NL), 1942–1946. Remarks: Had 1,991 hits (124 homers) and 223 stolen bases in 1,783 games in 15 campaigns; only major league player ever to hit for the cycle on Opening Day, April 20, 1937; had 27-game hitting streak, May 1937; coach, Cincinnati (NL), 1946; minor league manager, 1947–1949, and later a real estate agent; elected to Mississippi Sports Hall of Fame, 1969.

55586. Abodaher, N.J. "Walker the Tiger Firebrand." *Baseball Magazine,* LV (August 1935), 413–415.

55587. Bloodgood, Clifford. "That Sensational Rookie, Gerald Walker." *Baseball Magazine,* XLIX (September 1932), 456–457+.

55588. Hilton, George W. "Gerald Holmes 'Gee' Walker." In: Vol. Q–Z of David L. Porter, ed. *Biographical Dictionary of American Sports: Baseball.* Rev. and enlarged ed. Westport, CT: Greenwood Press, 2000. Pp. 1621–1622.

55589. Smith, Ira L. "Gerald Holmes ('Gee') Walker." In: his *Baseball's Famous Outfielders.* New York: A.S. Barnes, 1954. Pp. 234–239.

Gregory Lee ("Greg") Walker

1B. (B: Oct. 6, 1959, Douglas, GA). Chicago (AL), 1982–1990; Baltimore (AL), 1990. Remarks: Obtained 746 hits (113 homers) and 19 stolen bases in 855 games in nine years; had pinch-hit single in first big league AB, Sept. 16, 1982; suffered life-threatening seizure, July 1988 which kept him off the field for a year; fantasy camp/instructional league coach, Chicago (AL), 2000–2001; coach, Charlotte (IL), 2002–2003, coach, Chicago (AL), 2003–.

55590. Newman, Bruce. "Just Happy to Be Here." *Sports Illustrated,* LXX (April 17, 1989), 34–36+.

Harry William ("The Hat") Walker

OF-IB-MGR-BROADCASTER. (B: Oct. 22, 1918, Pascagoula, MS-D: Aug. 8, 1999). St. Louis (NL), 1940–1943, 1946–1947; Philadelphia (NL), 1947–1948; Chicago (NL) and Cincinnati (NL), 1949, St. Louis (NL), 1950–1951, 1955. Remarks: Obtained 786 hits (10 homers) and 42 stolen bases in 807 games in 11 seasons; had seven hits (two doubles) in 1946 World Series; led NL in triples, 1947; NL batting champion, 1947; only player to win a NL batting title playing for two teams in the same season; also played for Tiffin (Ohio State League), 1936–1937; minor league manager, 1951–1958, 1963–1964; coach, St. Louis (NL), 1959–1962; batting instructor, Houston (N.L), 1967–1968 and St. Louis (NL), 1973; manager, St. Louis (NL), 1955, Pittsburgh (NL), 1965–1967, and Houston (NL), 1968–1972, winning 630 games and losing 604 (.511); broadcaster, St. Louis (NL), 1973; brother of Fred ("Dixie") Walker (above); head baseball coach (first), University of Alabama-Birmingham, 1978–1986; elected to Alabama Sports Hall of Fame.

55591. Appel, Marty. "Harry Walker." In: his *Yesterday's Heroes: Revisiting the Old-Time Baseball Stars.* New York: The Dial Press, 1988. Pp. 246–249.

55592. Baumgartner, Stan. "Harry Walker: The Hard Luck Kid." *Sport,* V (July 1948), 44+.

55593. Burick, Si. "Twas a Bounty on the Mutiny as Walker Walked the Plank." *Baseball Digest,* XXVI (September 1967), 29–31.

55594. Caestecker, Thomas E., Jr. "Harry Walker: He Played for Two Teams While Winning a Batting Title." *Baseball Digest,* LVIII (July 1999), 84–89.

55595. Craft, David and Tom Owens. "Harry Walker: Have Bat, Will Travel." In: their *Redbirds Revisited.* Chicago: Bonus Books, 1990. Pp. 231–240.

55596. "Harry the Hat." *Time,* L (August 18, 1947), 67.

55597. Horrigan, Jack. "Star-Maker Harry Walker." *Baseball Digest,* XIV (August 1956), 81–86.

55598. Hurwitz, Hy. "Brotherly Love." *Baseball Digest,* VI (November 1947), 3–5.

55599. Libby, Bill. "Harry 'The Hat' Walker." In: his *The Coaches.* Chicago, IL: Henry Regerny Co., 1972. Pp. 123–125.

55600. McDermott, Joe. "Harry the Hat." *Life,* LXII (April 7, 1967), 105–108+.

55601. Mann, Jack. "Voice of the Pirates." *Sports Illustrated,* XXV (September 5, 1966), 14–17.

55602. Miller, Hub. "Harry the Hat." *Baseball Magazine,* LXXX (January 1948), 265–267+.

55603. Powell, Larry. *"Bottom of the Ninth": An Oral History on the Life of Harry 'the Hat' Walker.* Cincinnati, OH: Writer's Showcase Press, 2000. 268p.

55604. Prato, Lou. "Harry Walker Sounds Off: 'Why There Should Be Twice as Many .300 Hitters.'" *Sport,* XLIII (April 1967), 22–27.

55605. Veech, Robert. "What I Know About Batting." *Baseball Magazine,* XX (January 1918), 265–266.

55606. _____. "The Hat' Talks About Batting." Edited by J.O. Herbold. *Scholastic Coach,* XXXVIII (April 1969), 12–13+. An excerpt from the next entry.

55607. Walker, Harry, with Thomas Meany. *How to Bat.* Illustrated By Albert Micale. New York: McGraw-Hill Book Co., 1963. 117p.

55608. Wilber, Cynthia J. "Harry Walker." In: her *For the Love of the Game: Baseball Memories from the Men Who Were There.* New York: William Morrow, 1992. Pp. 333–339.

55609. Wilson, John R. M. "Harry Walker." In: Paul Betz and Mark C. Carnes, eds. *American National Biography: Supplement I.* New York: Oxford University Press, 2002. Pp. 667–668.

Larry Kenneth Robert Walker

OF. (B: Dec. 1, 1966, Maple Ridge, British Columbia, Canada). Montreal (NL), 1989–1994; Colorado (NL), 1995–2004; St. Louis (NL), 2004-. Remarks: Through 2004, has had 2,069 hits (368 homers) and 228 stolen bases in 1,888 games; led NL in doubles, 1994; had six RBIs in one game, May 21, 1996; NL MVP award (first won by a Canadian), 1997; NL home run champion, 1997; NL batting champion, 1998–1999, 2001; had 20-game hitting streak, 1999; had five triples in one month, April 2003; became first Canadian-born player to obtain 2,000 hits, June 30, 2004; had seven hits (one double, one triple, two homers) in 2004 ALCS; had five hits (two doubles, two homers) in 2004 World Series; all time most prolific Canadian home run hitter.

55610. Boswell, Thomas. "Total Average 1997: Rocky Mountain High." *Inside Sports,* XX (February 1998), 60–67.

55611. Callahan, Gerry. "See It, Hit It." *Sports Illustrated,* LXXXVII (July 14, 1997), 40–49.

55612. Came, Barry. "The Homegrown Hero." *Maclean's,* CV (August 24, 1992), 56+.

55613. Cassoff, Derek. "Larry Walker of Expos Makes

Impact as a Canadian Big Leaguer." *Baseball Digest,* LI (October 1992), 52–57.

55614. Deacon, James. "Larry Walker." Maclean's, CXI (December 21, 1998), 68–69.

55615. DeMarco, Tony. *Larry Walker.* Philadelphia, PA: Chelsea House, 1999. 64p.

55616. _____. *Larry Walker: Canadian Rocky.* Champaign, IL: Sports Publishing, 1999. 89p.

55617. Finlayson, A. "The Dreams of Summer." *Maclean's,* XCIX (September 8, 1986), 6+.

55618. Henderson, John. "Canadian Clubber." *USA Today Baseball Weekly,* VII (April 23, 1997), 8–9.

55619. Hoffer, Richard. "Handy Man." *Sports Illustrated,* XCIV (June 11, 2001), 100–112.

55620. Joyce, Gare. "Yerrr Out!: Canada's Best Baseball Players Wants to Stay with Canada's Best Baseball Team, but the Expos are Probably Too Cheap to Keep Larry Walker." *Saturday Night,* CIX (October 1994), 71–74.

55621. Keown, Tim. "Higher Ground." *ESPN: The Magazine,* III (May 1, 2000), 52–56.

55622. Klis, Mike. "Historic Years by Griffey and Walker Make Them Mega Valuable Players: Walker Overcomes the Coors Prejudice." *USA Today Baseball Weekly,* VII (November 12, 1997), 21–22.

55623. Koenig, Bill. "Going for the Green: Top Free Agent Larry Walker Ponders Club Selection." *USA Today Baseball Weekly,* IV (March 8, 1995), 20–21.

55624. Kuenster, John. "1997 *Baseball Digest* Player of the Year: Larry Walker. Colorado Rockies Outfielder Last Season Turned in One of the Best All-Around Performances in Major League History." *Baseball Digest,* LVII (January 1998), 24–27.

55625. Montville, Leigh. "The Accidental Ballplayer." *Sports Illustrated,* LXXVIII (April 5, 1993), 78–80. Also published in *Sports Illustrated Canada,* I (April 5, 1993), 70–72, 75, under the title "Southern Exposure."

55626. Morrissey, Rick. "Rockies' Larry Walker: A Natural in Disguise." *Baseball Digest,* LVI (October 1997), 32–38.

55627. Munro, Neil. "Larry Walker's 1997 Campaign." In: Joseph M. Wayman, ed. *Grandstand Baseball Annual, 1998.* Downey, CA: Joseph M. Wayman, 1998. Pp. 91–98.

55628. O'Shei, Tim. "Larry Walker of Expos Chases Big-Time Stardom." *Baseball Digest,* LIII (August 1994), 31–36.

55629. Perrotto, John. "Second Look: Larry Walker." *Beckett Baseball Card Monthly,* X, no. 94 (January 1993), 97–98.

55630. Ringolsby, Tracy. "Giving It All He's Got: Larry Walker Strives for a Shot at the World Series." *Baseball Digest,* LXI (February 2002), 28–33.

55631. Robertson, John G. "Larry Kenneth Robert Walker, Jr." In: Vol. Q–Z of David L. Porter, ed. *Biographical Dictionary of American Sports: Baseball.* Rev. and enlarged ed. Westport, CT: Greenwood Press, 2000. Pp. 1622–1623.

55632. Rosenthal, Ken. "Larry Walker." In: his *Best of the Best, Baseball: 35 Major League Superstars.* Indianapolis, IN: Masters Press, 1998. Pp. 148–151.

55633. Rubin, Bob. "Expos' Larry Walker Climbing the Stairs to Stardom." *Baseball Digest ,* LII (July 1993), 29–30.

55634. Schwarz, Alan. "Serious Fun." *Sport,* XC (September 1999), 50–52.

55635. Shannon, Mike. "Larry Walker." In: his *Tales from the Dugout: The Greatest True Baseball Stories Ever Told.* Lincolnwood, IL: NTC/Contemporary Books, 1997. Pp. 221–222.

55636. Shearon, Jim. "Larry Walker, Probably the Best Canadian Ever." In: his *Canada's Baseball Legends.* Kanata, Ontario: Malin Head Press, 1994. Pp. 205–209.

55637. Sorci, Rick. "Baseball Profile: Colorado's Larry Walker." *Baseball Digest,* LXI (July 2002), 62–63.

55638. Stone, Larry. "Despite His Fame, Larry Walker Remembers Where He Came From." *Baseball Digest,* LVIII (October 1999), 52–55.

55639. Turner, Dan. "Larry Walker and Company." In: his *Heroes, Bums and Ordinary Men.* Toronto: Doubleday Canada Ltd., 1988. Pp. 64–70.

55640. Verducci, Tom. "MVP?" *Sports Illustrated,* LXXXVII (October 6, 1997), 43–48.

55641. "Walker's Run." *Beckett Baseball Card Monthly,* XV (August 1998), 100–102.

Moses Fleetwood ("Fleet") Walker

C-WRITER-POLITICIAN. (B: Oct. 7, 1857, Mt. Pleasant, OH-D: May 11, 1924). Toledo (Northwest League), 1883; Toledo (AA), 1884; Cleveland (WL), 1885; Waterbury (EL), 1885–1886; Newark (IL), 1887; Syracuse (IL), 1888–1889. Remarks: First African American major leaguer, who went 0–3 in his first big league game, May 1, 1884; during 1885 AA season, obtained 40 hits in 42 games; formed first black battery with George Stovey (q.v.) at Newark, 1887; regarded as a mediocre player, later became newspaper editor in Steubenville, OH, opera theater owner in Cadiz, OH, and African American political leader; older brother of Weldy Wilberforce Walker (below).

55642. Bowman, Larry. "Moses Fleetwood Walker: The First Black Major League Baseball Player." In: Peter Levine, ed. *Baseball History.* Westport, CT: Meckler, 1989. Pp. 61–74.

55643. Brewer, William A. "Barehanded Catcher." *Negro Digest,* IX (1951), 85–87.

55644. "Fleetwood Walker : The First Black Player in Major League Baseball." *Black Sports,* I (November 1971), 48–49.

55645. Gerlach, Larry R. "Moses Fleetwood Walker." In: John A. Garrity and Marsh C. Carries, eds. *American National Biography.* 24 vols. New York: Oxford University Press, 1999. XXII, 507–509.

55646. Giancaterino, Randy. "1884: Moses Fleetwood Walker." *American Visions,* VIII (June-July 1993), 25–26.

55647. Kirst, Sean Peter. "The Trials of Fleet Walker." In: his *The Ashes of Lou Gehrig and Other Baseball Essays.* Jefferson, NC: McFarland & Co., Inc., 2003. Pp. 76–81.

55648. Lowenfish, L. "Fleet Walker's Divided Heart: The Life of Baseball's First Black Major Leaguer." *Nine: A Journal of Baseball History and Social Policy Perspectives,* VII (Spring 1999), 121–125.

55649. Malloy, Jerry. "Out At Home." *The National Pastime,* II (1983), 14–28; IV (1985), 87–88.

55650. Matheney, Timothy Michael. "Heading for Home: Moses Fleetwood Walker's Encounter with Racism in America." Unpublished senior thesis, Princeton University, 1989.

55651. Nutt, A. "An All-But-Forgotten First: Long Before Jackie Robinson's Dodger Debut, Moses Walker Played Ball for Toledo." *Sports Illustrated,* LXXVI (June 15, 1992), 26+.

55652. "Prejudice Against an African-American Player in Louisville (1881)." In: Dean A. Sullivan, ed. *Early Innings: A Documentary History of Baseball, 1825–1908.* Lincoln, NE: University of Nebraska Press, 1995. Pp. 117–118. Reprinted from the *Louisville Courier Journal,* August 22, 1881.

55653. Von Borries, Philip. "Turn Out the Lights, Please, As You Leave." In: *Grandstand Baseball Annual, 1998*. Downey, CA: Joseph M. Wayman, 1998. Pp. 106–107.

55654. Walker, Moses Fleetwood. *Our Home Colony: A Treatise on the Past, Present and Future of the Negro Race in America*. Steubenville, OH: Herald Printing Co., ca. 1908.

55655. Wheeler, Lonnie. "Hounded Out of Baseball." *Ohio*, XVI (May 1993), 22+.

55656. Williams, Nadie E. "Footnote to Trivia: Moses Fleetwood Walker and the All-American Dream." *Journal of American Culture*, XI (Summer 1988), 65–72.

55657. Zang, David W. *Fleet Walker's Divided Heart: The Life of Baseball's First Black Major Leaguer*. Lincoln, NE: University of Nebraska Press, 1995.157p.

55658. _____. "Moses Fleetwood 'Fleet' Walker." In: Vol. Q-Z of David L. Porter, ed. *Biographical Dictionary of American Sports: Baseball*. Rev. and enlarged ed. Westport, CT: Greenwood Press, 2000. Pp. 1623–1624.

Rube Walker *see* **Albert Bluford ("Rube") Walker**
Tilly Walker *see* **Clarence William ("Tilly") Walker**
Walter S. ("Walt") Walker
Of-POLITICIAN. (B: March 12, 1860, Berlin, MI-D: Feb. 28, 1922). Detroit (NL), 1884; Baltimore (AA), 1885. Remarks: Played in one game in 1884 and two games in 1885.

55659. Morris, P. "One of Baseball's Odd Lives: Walter S. Walker, Ballplayer, Politician and Tragic Figure." *The National Pastime*, XV (1995), 97–99.

Weldy Wilberforce Walker
OF. (B: June 1859, Steubenville, OH-D: Nov. 23, 1937). Toledo (AA), 1884. Played five big league games, with two hits before being barred; younger brother of Moses Fleetwood Walker (above).

55660. Walker, Weldy Wilberforce. "Why Discriminate?" In: David K. Wiggins and Patrick B. Miller, eds. *The Unlevel Playing Field: A Documentary History of the African American Experience in Sport*. Champaign, IL: University of Illinois Press, 2003. Pp. 36–38. Reprinted from *The Sporting Life*, March 14, 1888.

William Curtis ("Curt") Walker
OF-JUDGE. (B: July 3, 1896, Beeville, TX-D: Dec. 9, 1955). New York (AL), 1919; New York (NL), 1920–1921; Philadelphia (AL), 1921–1924; Cincinnati (NL), 1924–1930. Remarks: Obtained 1,475 hits (64 homers) and 96 stolen bases in 1,359 games in 12 years; had two triples in one inning in one game, July 26, 1927; mortician by trade, who served as a Beeville Justice of the Peace, 1954–1955; named to Texas Baseball Hall of Fame, 2001.

55661. Hillman, John. "William Curtis 'Curt' Walker." In: Vol. Q-Z of David L. Porter, ed. *Biographical Dictionary of American Sports: Baseball*. Rev. and enlarged ed. Westport, CT: Greenwood Press, 2000. Pp. 1624–1625.

Bobby Wallace *see* **Roderick**
John ("Bobby" or "Rhody") Wallace Roderick John ("Bobby" or "Rhody") Wallace★
P-3B-SS-UMP-MGR. (B: Nov. 4, 1873, Pittsburgh, PA-D: Nov. 3, 1960). Cleveland (NL), 1894–1898; St. Louis (NL), 1899–1901; St. Louis (AL), 1902–1916; St. Louis (NL), 1917–1918. Remarks: Played a quarter of a century, obtaining 2,314 hits (35 homers) and 201 stolen bases in 2,386 games; as a pitcher, won 24 games and lost 22; manager, St. Louis (AL), 1911–1912 and Cincinnati (NL), 1937, winning 62 games and losing 154 (.287); AL umpire, 1915–1916; manager, Wichita (WL), 1917 and Muskogee (Southwest League), 1921; coach, Cincinnati (NL), 1926, 1928; scout for Chicago (NL), 1924, Cincinnati (NL),

1927–1937, 1938–1960; his $6,500 1912 salary was then the highest in baseball; elected to National Baseball Hall of Fame in 1953, where his plaque reads: "One of longest careers in major leagues. Over 60 years as pitcher, third-baseman, shortstop, manager, umpire and scout. Active as player for 25 years. Set AL record for chances in one game at shortstop, 17, June 10, 1902. Recognized as one of the greatest shortstops. Pitched for Cleveland in 1896 Temple Cup Series."

55662. Allen, Lee, and Thomas Meany. "Bobby Wallace." In: their *Kings of the Diamond*. New York: G.P. Putnam, 1965. Pp. 147–148.

55663. Borst, William A. ("Bill"). "Bobby Wallace." In: John A. Garrity and Marsh C. Carries, eds. *American National Biography*. 24 vols. New York: Oxford University Press, 1999. XXII, 527–528.

55664. Burkholder, Ed. "Bobby Wallace." In: his *Baseball Immortals*. New York: Christopher House, 1955. Pp. 68–69.

55665. Fleitz, David L. "Bobby Wallace." In: his *Ghosts in the Gallery at Cooperstown: Sixteen Little-Known Members of the Hall of Fame*. Jefferson, NC: McFarland & Co., Inc., 2004. Pp. 95–107.

55666. Olmsted, Frank J. "Roderick John 'Bobby,' 'Rhody' Wallace." In: Vol. Q-Z of David L. Porter, ed. *Biographical Dictionary of American Sports: Baseball*. Rev. and enlarged ed. Westport, CT: Greenwood Press, 2000. Pp. 1625–1626.

55667. Wallace, Roderick J. ("Bobby"). "Wallace Wants Time to Show Worth as a Manager; He Gives His Views on the Situation in St. Louis." *Baseball Magazine*, VII (May 1911), 77–78.

Timothy Charles ("Tim") Wallach
3B. (B: Sept. 14, 1957; Huntington Park, CA). Montreal (NL), 1980–1992; Los Angeles (NL), 1993–1995; California (AL) and Los Angeles (NL), 1996. Remarks: Had 2,085 hits (260 homers) and 51 stolen bases in 2,212 games in 17 seasons; obtained a home run in his first official big league at bat; had three homers in one game, May 4, 1987; led NL in doubles, 1987, 1989; also played for Alaska Goldpanners (Alaska League), 1978–1979; Alaska League MVP Award, 1978; manager, Rancho Cucamonga Quakes (California League) and Los Angeles (NL), 2004-.

55668. Carbray, Paul. "Tim Wallach: The Expos' Dedicated Run Producer." *Baseball Digest*, XLVI (November 1987), 42–43.

55669. Israelson, Chad. "Timothy Charles 'Tim' Wallach." In: Vol. Q-Z of David L. Porter, ed. *Biographical Dictionary of American Sports: Baseball*. Rev. and enlarged ed. Westport, CT: Greenwood Press, 2000. Pp. 1626–1627.

Douglass Wallop *see* **John Douglass Wallop III**
John Douglass Wallop III
WRITER. (B: March 8, 1920, Washington, DC-D: April 2, 1985). Remarks: American novelist remembered by baseball fans for his novel *The Year the Yankees Lost the Pennant* (no. 5694), turned musical, winner of the 1956 Tony Award.

55670. "Book Jinxes Yankees." *Sports Illustrated*, I (September 27, 1954), 21–22.

55671. Wallop, Douglass. *The Year the Yankees Lost the Pennant*. New York: Random House 1954.

55672. ____. with George Abbott. *Damn Yankees*. Random House, 1956. Musical based on novel; produced in New York at 46th St. Theatre, May 5, 1955.

Lee Walls *see* **Ray Lee Walls**
Ray Lee Walls
OF-3B-1B. (B: Jan. 6, 1933, San Diego, CA-D: Oct. 11,

1993). Pittsburgh (NL), 1952, 1956–1957; Chicago (NL), 1957–1959; Cincinnati (NL), 1960; Philadelphia (NL), 1960–1961; Los Angeles (NL), 1962–1964. Remarks: Had 670 hits (66 homers) and 21 stolen bases in 902 games in a decade; went 5-for-5 in one game, May 2, 1956; hit for the cycle in one game, July 2, 1957; obtained three homers in one game, Aug. 24, 1958; coach, Oakland (AL), 1979–1982, New York (AL), 1983; began involvement with baseball as a San Diego (PCL) batboy in 1940s.

55673. Greenfield, Josh. "Will the Real Lee Walls Please Stand Up?" *Sport,* LV (April 1973), 24–25. Playing in Japan.

55674. Spalding, John E. "Lee Walls." In: his *Pacific Coast League Stars, Vol. II: Ninety Who Made it to the Majors, 1905–1957.* San Jose, CA: John E. Spalding, 1997. Pp. 148–149.

Edward Augustine ("Ed" or "Big Ed") Walsh★
P-COACH (B: May 14, 1881, Plains, PA-D: May 26, 1959). Chicago (AL), 1904–1916; Boston (NL), 1917. Remarks: In 14 years, had 195 victories, 126 defeats, and 40 "saves"; pitched one no-hitter, Aug. 27, 1911; won two games in a day twice, Sept. 26, 1905 and Sept. 29, 1908; won Games Three and Five of 1906 World Series; noted spitball hurler who learned the pitch from a White Sox teammate; minor league manager, 1920; AL umpire, 1922; coach, Chicago (AL), 1923–1925, 1928–1930; University of Notre Dame baseball coach, 1926; elected to National Baseball Hall of Fame in 1946, where his plaque reads: "Outstanding right-handed pitcher of Chicago AL from 1904 through 1916. Won 40 games in 1908 and won two games in the 1906 World Series. Twice pitched and won two games in one day, allowing only one run in doubleheader against Boston on Sept. 29, 1908. Finished big league pitching career with Boston NL in 1917."

55675. Allen, Lee, and Thomas Meany. "Ed Walsh." In: their *Kings of the Diamond.* New York. G.P. Putnam, 1965. Pp. 54–56.

55676. Brown, Warren. "Ed Walsh: An Ironman of Yesteryear." *Baseball Digest,* XXXI (January 1972), 95–97.

55677. Cannon, Jimmy. "He Fanned 'Big 3' [Babe Ruth] on Nine Pitches." *Baseball Digest,* X (April 1951), 95–97.

55678. Farmer, Ted. "[Addie] Joss vs Walsh: October 2, 1908 — The Greatest Pitching Duel in Baseball History?" *The National Pastime,* XV (1995), 71–73.

55679. Farrell, James T. "Ed Walsh Pitches a No-Hitter." In: Ralph S. Graber, ed. *The Baseball Reader.* New York: A.S. Barnes, 1951. Pp. 25–31.

55680. Golenbock, Peter J. "Edward Augustine Walsh." In: Supplement 6 of John A. Garrity, ed. *Dictionary of American Biography.* New York: Scribners, 1980. Pp. 662–663.

55681. Hilton, George W. "Edward Augustine 'Ed,' 'Big Ed' Walsh." In: Vol. Q-Z of David L. Porter, ed. *Biographical Dictionary of American Sports: Baseball.* Rev. and enlarged ed. Westport, CT: Greenwood Press, 2000. Pp. 1627–1628.

55682. Klima, John. "The Spitballer and the Gentleman: Eddie Walsh vs. Addie Joss (October 2, 1908)." In: his *Pitched Battle: 35 of Baseball's Greatest Duels from the Mound.* Jefferson, NC: McFarland & Co., Inc., 2002. Pp. 21–24.

55683. Lane, Ferdinand C. "The Pitching Sensation of 1913." *Baseball Magazine,* XI (August 1913), 53–59.

55684. _____. "The Spitball King." *Baseball Magazine,* X (March 1913), 41–59.

55685. McKay, Joe. "Ed Walsh: King of the Spitballers."

In: his *The Great Shutout Pitchers: 20 Profiles of a Vanishing Breed.* Jefferson, NC: McFarland & Co., Inc., 2004. Pp. 123–134.

55686. Meany, Thomas. "Ed Walsh." In: his *Baseball's Greatest Players.* New York. Grosset and Dunlap, 1953. Pp. 265–273.

55687. _____. "Ed Walsh's Fabulous Week." *Baseball Digest,* XVIII (August 1959), 59–62.

55688. Rumill, Ed. "42 'Spitters' in One Game." *Baseball Digest,* VII (March 1948), 51–53.

55689. Schalk, Ray, and Lloyd Lewis. "When Walsh Burned Himself Out." *Baseball Digest,* IV (April 1945), 10–43.

55690. Sheen, Jim. "Big Ed Walsh: The Inside Story." *Baseball Magazine,* LXXX (November-December 1954), 11–12+.

55691. Smith, Ira L. "Ed Walsh." In: his *Baseball's Famous Pitchers.* New York: A.S. Barnes, 1954. Pp. 99–106.

55692. Smith, Ron. "Ed Walsh-82." In: his *The Sporting News Selects Baseball's 100 Greatest Players.* St. Louis, MO: *The Sporting News,* 1998. Pp. 178–179.

55693. Walsh, Edward A. ("Big Ed"). "The Advantages of Being Hard-Headed." *Baseball Magazine,* XX (April 1918), 459–460+.

55694. _____. "Big Ed Walsh's 1.82 ERA Tops Everyone." *Diamond Report,* V (May 1981), 23–28.

55695. _____, as told to Francis J. Powers. "The Day I Fanned [Napoleon] Lajoie." *Baseball Digest,* IV (March 1944), 10–14. Oct. 3, 1908. Reprinted in John P. Carmichael, ed., *My Greatest Day in Baseball* (New York. A.S. Barnes, 1945), pp. 78–82, and in John Kuenster, ed., *From Cobb to Catfish* (Chicago. Rand McNally, 1975), pp. 94–95.

55696. "Walsh's 1.82 ERA Tops Everybody." *Diamond Report,* V (May 1989), 23–28.

55697. Ward, John J. "The Spitball King Becomes an Umpire." *Baseball Magazine,* XXVIII (February 1922), 688–689.

Alfred John ("Roxy") Walters
C. (B: Nov. 5, 1892, San Francisco, CA-D: June 3, 1956). New York (AL), 1915–1918; Boston (AL), 1919–1923; Cleveland (AL), 1924–1925. Remarks: Had 317 hits and 13 stolen bases in 498 games in an 11-year major league career.

55698. Kofoed, J.C. "The Live-Wire of American League Catchers." *Baseball Magazine,* XVIII (January 1917), 63–66.

Bucky Walters *see* **William Henry ("Bucky") Walters, Jr.**

Roxy Walters *see* **Alfred John ("Roxy") Walters**
William Henry ("Bucky") Walters, Jr.
3B-P-MGR. (B: April 19, 1909, Philadelphia, PA-D: April 20, 1991). Boston (NL), 1931–1932; Boston (AL), 1933–1934; Philadelphia (NL), 1934–1938; Cincinnati (NL), 1938–1948; Boston (NL), 1950. Remarks: Had 198 victories, 160 defeats, and four "saves" after conversion into pitcher, including nine-game winning streak, 1940; lost two games in 1939 World Series, but won two in 1940 World Series; as batter, had 477 hits (23 homers) and 12 stolen bases in 713 games in 14 years; NL MVP award, 1939; manager, Cincinnati (NL), 1948–1949, winning 81 games and losing 123 (.397); coach, Boston (NL) and Milwaukee (NL), 1950–1955, New York (NL), 1957–1958; minor league manager-instructor, 1952 and 1958.

55699. Considine, Bob. "One-Two Punch: Bucky Walters and Pal Derringer, Pitching Pride of Cincinnati Reds." *Collier's,* CVI (September 28, 1940), 12+.

55700. Honig, Donald. "Bucky Walters, 1934–48, 1950." In: his *Baseball When the Grass was Real.* New York: Harcourt, Brace, Jovanovich, 1975. Pp. 87–99.

55701. _____. "1939: Bucky Walters." In: his *National League MVP's.* New York: Bantam Books, 1989. Pp. 21–22.

55702. Kirksey, George. "He Didn't Want to Pitch: The Strange Success of Bucky Walters, $200,000 Hurler Who Thinks Third Basemen Have the Most Fun." *Look,* IV (August 27, 1940), 44–47.

55703. Mamaux, Al. "What It Takes to Make a Pitcher." *Scholastic Coach,* X (April 1941), 12–15.

55704. Meany, Thomas. "Jack of All Trades." In: his *Baseball's Greatest Pitchers.* New York: A.S. Barnes, 1951. Pp. 269–276.

55705. "Mister Bucky." In: George S. Rosenthal, ed. *The Reds Official Souvenir Book, 1949.* Cincinnati, OH: G. S. Rosenthal, 1949. Pp. 25–32.

55706. Porter, David L. "William Henry 'Bucky' Walters, Jr." In: Vol. Q–Z of David L. Porter, ed. *Biographical Dictionary of American Sports: Baseball.* Rev. and enlarged ed. Westport, CT: Greenwood Press, 2000. Pp. 1629–1630.

55707. Rathgeber, Bob. "To the Mound by Way of Third: Bucky Walters." In: his *Cincinnati Reds Scrapbook.* Virginia Beach, VA: J.C.P. Corp. of Virginia, 1982. Pp. 90–91.

55708. Rumill, Ed. "Bucky Walters Will Try Again." *Baseball Magazine,* LXXXII (January 1949), 273–275.

55709. Spalding, John E. "Bucky Walters." In: his *Pacific Coast League Stars, Vol. II: Ninety Who Made It to the Majors, 1905–1957.* San Jose, CA: John E. Spalding, 1997. Pp. 116–117.

55710. Westcott, Rich. "Bucky Walters — Switch to the Mound Paid Off." In: his *Diamond Greats.* Westport, CT: Meckler Books, 1988. Pp. 169–174.

Daniel James ("Danny") Walton
OF-1B. (B: July 14, 1947, Los Angeles, CA). Houston (NL), 1968; Seattle (AL), 1969; Milwaukee (AL), 1970–1971; New York (AL), 1971; Minnesota (AL), 1973–1975; Los Angeles (NL), 1976; Houston (NL), 1977; Taiyo Whales (Japan League), 1978–1979; Texas (AL), 1980. Remarks: Obtained 174 hits (28 homers) and four stolen bases in 297 games in 10 U.S. big league seasons; also played for Syracuse (IL), 1972.

55711. Appel, Marty. "Danny Walton." In: his *Yesterday's Heroes: Revisiting the Old-Time Baseball Stars.* New York: The Dial Press, 1988. Pp. 250–253.

Jerome O'Terrell Walton
OF. (B: Newnan, GA, July 8, 1965). Chicago (NL), 1989–1992; California (AL), 1993; Cincinnati (NL), 1994–1996; Atlanta (NL), 1996; Baltimore (AL), 1997; Tampa Bay (AL), 1998. Remarks: Had 423 hits (25 homers) and 58 stolen bases in 598 games in a decade; had 30-game hitting streak, 1989; had eight hits in 1989 NLCS; NL Rookie of the Year Award, 1989.

55712. Walton, Jerome, with Jim Langford. *Rookie: The Story of a Season.* South Bend, IN: Diamond Communications, Inc., 1990. 162p.

55713. Whiteside, Larry. "Cubs' Jerome Walton: Top Man of the 1989 NL Rookie Class." *Baseball Digest,* XLIX (February 1990), 36–38.

William Adoph ("Bill") Wambsganss
2B-SS. (B: March 19, 1894, Garfield Heights, OH-D: Dec. 8, 1985). Cleveland (AL), 1914–1923; Boston (AL), 1924–1925; Philadelphia (AL), 1926. Remarks: Obtained 1,359 hits (7 homers) and 142 stolen bases in 1,492 games in 13 campaigns; in Game Five of the 1920 World Series, made the only unassisted triple play in the history of the fall classic; led AL in sacrifice hits, 1921–1922; participated in six other triple plays during career; also played for Kansas City (AA), 1929.

55714. Christopher, Matt. "October 10, 1920: Bill Wambsganss, the Man Who Was Ready." In: his *Matt Christopher's Great Moments in Baseball History.* Boston, MA: Little, Brown & Co., 1996. Pp. 3–12.

55715. Green, Paul M. "Baseball and Bill Wambsganss." *Sports Collector's Digest,* X (June 24, 1983), 94+. Reprinted in his *Forgotten Fields* (Waupaca, WI: Parker Publications, 1984), pp. 28–49.

55716. Holway, John B. "First and Only World Series Triple Play Recalled." *Baseball Digest,* LII (February 1993), 73–76.

55717. Lane, Ferdinand C. "The Man Who Made That Wonderful Triple Play." *Baseball Magazine,* XXVI (December 1920), 333–335+.

55718. McGuire, Mark and Michael Sean Gormley. "Bill Wambsganss." In: their *Moments in the Sun: Baseball's Briefly Famous.* Jefferson, NC: McFarland & Co., Inc., 2001. Pp. 189–192.

55719. Ritter, Lawrence S. "Bill Wambsganss." In: his *Glory of Their Times.* New York: Macmillan, 1966. Pp. 215–224.

Big Poison Waner *see* **Paul Glee ("Big Poison") Waner**

Little Poison Waner *see* **Lloyd James ("Little Poison") Waner**

Lloyd James ("Little Poison") Waner★
OF. (B: March 16, 1906, Harrah, OK-D: July 22, 1982). Pittsburgh (NL), 1927–1941; Boston (NL) and Cincinnati (NL), 1941; Philadelphia (NL), 1942; Brooklyn (NL), 1944; Pittsburgh (NL), 1944–1945. Remarks: Had 2,459 hits (28 homers) and 67 stolen bases in 1,992 games in 18 seasons, holds NL record for most singles in a season (198), 1927); had six hits (one double, one triple) in 1927 World Series; led NL in triples, 1929; scout, Pittsburgh (N.L), 1946–1949, and Baltimore (AL), 1955; brother of Paul ("Big Poison") Waner (below); named to Oklahoma Sports Hall of Fame, 1991; elected to National Baseball Hall of Fame in 1967, where his plaque reads: "Made 223 hits in 1927 first year with Pittsburgh including 198 singles, a modern major league record. Led NL in most singles 1927–1928–1929–1931. Life total of 2459 hits. Batting average .316. With brother Paul, 'Big Poison," starred in Pittsburgh outfield 1927–1940."

55720. Bloodgood, Clifford. "Lloyd Waner and His 223 Hits." *Baseball Magazine,* XL (January 1928), 365–367+.

55721. _____. "Lloyd Waner's Record Three Seasons." *Baseball Magazine,* XLV (July 1930), 357–358+.

55722. Brown, Phil. "Is Lloyd Waner the Worst Player in the Hall of Fame?" *Oldtyme Baseball News,* IV, no. 4 (1992), 12–13.

55723. Graham, Frank. "The Other Waner Had a Haul, Too." *Baseball Digest,* XI (April 1952), 33–35.

55724. Grisette, Felix A. "The Waner Brothers and Their Star Act." *Baseball Magazine,* XXXIX (July 1927), 361–362+.

55725. Honig, Donald. "Lloyd Waner." In: his *The October Heroes.* New York: Simon and Schuster, 1979. Pp. 114–129.

55726. Macht, Norman L. "Double Dose." *Beckett Baseball Card Monthly,* VIII (April 1991), 99–102. Lloyd and Paul Waner.

55727. Monahan, Kasper. "They Were Poison." *Baseball Digest,* VIII (June 1949), 20–28.

55728. Parker, Clifton Blue. *Big and Little Poison: Paul and Lloyd Waner, Baseball Brothers.* Jefferson, NC: McFarland & Co., Inc., 2003. 336p.

55729. Schott, Thomas E. "Pittsburgh Poison: The Waner Boys." In: Randy Roberts, ed. *Pittsburgh Sports: Stories from the Steel City.* Pittsburgh, PA: University of Pittsburgh Press, 2000. Pp. 76–92.

55730. Sutton, William A. "Lloyd James 'Little Poison' Waner." In: Vol. Q-Z of David L. Porter, ed. *Biographical Dictionary of American Sports: Baseball.* Rev. and enlarged ed. Westport, CT: Greenwood Press, 2000. Pp. 1630–1632.

Paul Glee ("Big Poison") Waner ★

OF. (B: April 16, 1903, Harrah, OK-D: Aug. 29, 1965). Pittsburgh (NL), 19261940; Brooklyn (NL), 1941; Boston (NL), 1941–1942; Brooklyn (NL), 1943–1944; New York (AL), 1944–1945.Remarks: Obtained 3,152 hits (112 homers) and 104 stolen bases in 2,549 games in two decades; had six hits in one game, Aug. 26, 1926; led NL in triples, 1926–1927; NL MVP award, 1927; NL batting champion, 1927, 1934, and 1936; NL RBI champion, 1927; had five hits (one double) in 1927 World Series; led NL in doubles, 1928, 1932; manager, Miami (IL), 1946; coach, Milwaukee (NL), 1957, St. Louis (NL), 1958–1959, and Philadelphia (NL), 1960, 1965 ; brother of Lloyd ("Little Poison") Waner (above); named to Oklahoma Sports Hall of Fame, 1991; elected to National Baseball Hall of Fame in 1952, where his plaque reads: "Left handed hitting outfielder batted .300 or better 14 times in National League. One of seven players ever to compile 3,000 or more hits. Set modem NL record by collecting 200 or more hits eight seasons. Most Valuable Player in 1921 and four times selected for All-Star Game."

55731. Abrams, Al. "Clemente Better Than Waner, Youngs?" *Baseball Digest,* XXVI (May 1966), 33–35. A comparison.

55732. _____. "Paul Waner's Furious Stretch Drive." *Baseball Digest,* XVIII (May 1969), 33–35.

55733. Addinglon, L.H. "Batting Champion of Organized Baseball for 1934." *Baseball Magazine,* LIV (March 1935), 461–462.

55734. Allen, Lee, and Thomas Meany. "Paul Waner." In: their *Kings at the Diamond.* New York: G.P. Putnam, 1965. Pp. 216–218.

55735. Allen, Maury. "Paul Waner (1926–1945)." In: his *Baseball's 100.* New York: Galahad Books, 1981. Pp. 125–127.

55736. Barton, Jerry. "Paul G. Waner." In: his *A Treasure Chest of the Hall of Fame.* Boston, MA: The Wilson-Hill Co., 1952. Pp. 118–119.

55737. Bloodgood, Clifford. "Paul Waner: One of the Truly Great Players of All Time." *Baseball Magazine,* LXXIV (January 1945), 255–257+.

55738. Broeg, Bob. "Paul Waner." In: his *Super Stars of Baseball.* St. Louis, MO: *The Sporting News,* 1971. Pp. 265–270.

55739. Brown, Warren. "Bill Klem, Paul Waner Were Genuine Characters." *Baseball Digest,* XXIX (November 1970), 52–56.

55740. Bursky, Herbert. "The Day Paul Waner Refused a Base Hit." *Baseball Digest,* XXX (August 1971), 68–70.

55741. Cashman, Joe. "How Waner Got His 3,000." *Baseball Digest,* XVII (June 1958), 9–11.

55742. Cohane, Tim. "Paul Waner — the Sharpest Eyes in Sport." *Baseball Digest,* IV (May 1945), 9–11.

55743. _____. "The Sharpest Eyes in Sport; They Belong to Paul Waner, One of Seven Major Leaguers Ever to Make 3,000 Hits." *Look,* IX (April 17, 1945), 61–64.

55744. Davis, Mac. "He Objected to a Hit." In: his *The Lore and Legends of Baseball.* New York: Lantern Press, 1953. Pp. 48–50.

55745. Drohan, John. "That Little Punk." In: Sidney Offit, ed. *Best of Baseball.* New York: G.P. Putnam, 1956. Pp. 168–176. Reprinted from the September 1942 issue of *Baseball Magazine.*

55746. Gammon, Wirt. "Want 3,100 Hits?: Swing Down on Ball, Says [Paul] Waner." *Baseball Digest,* XX (September 1961), 43–45.

55747. Gietschier, Steven P. "Paul Waner." In: John A. Garrity and Marsh C. Carries, eds. *American National Biography.* 24 vols. New York: Oxford University Press, 1999. XXII, 602–603.

55748. Grisette, Felix A. "The Waner Brothers and Their Star Act." *Baseball Magazine,* XXXIX (July 1927), 361–362+.

55749. Hickey, David and Kerry Keene. "Paul Waner." In: their *The Proudest Yankees of All: From the Bronx to Cooperstown.* Lanham, MD: Taylor Trade Pub., dist. by National Book Network, 2003. Chpt. 33.

55750. Holmes, Tommy. "Skullduggery by Waner." *Baseball Digest,* II (July 1943), 5–7.

55751. Howlett, Charles F. "Paul Glee Waner." In: Supplement 7 of John A. Garrity, ed. *Dictionary of American Biography.* New York: Scribners, 1981. Pp. 768–769.

55752. Lalire, Gregory. "Perspective: Asked by a Fan Why He was in the Yankee Outfield, Paul Waner Replied: 'Because Joe D Is in the Army!'" *World War II,* VIII (September 1993), 64+.

55753. Lane, Ferdinand C. "A Champion Batter Speaks: An Interview with Paul Waner." *Baseball Magazine,* XLIX (September 1932), 441–442.

55754. McMane, Fred. "Paul Waner." In: his *The 3,000 Hit Club.* Champaign, IL: Sports Publishing, 2000. Pp. 110–117.

55755. Meany, Thomas. "Big Poison." *Baseball Digest,* XXIV (May 1965), 52–58.

55756. _____. "Poison, Economy Size — Paul Glee Waner." In: his *Baseball's Greatest Hitters.* New York: A.S. Barnes, 1950. Pp. 227–238.

55757. Monahan, Kasper. "They Were Poison." *Baseball Digest,* VIII (June 1949), 20–28.

55758. Parker, Clifton Blue. *Big and Little Poison: Paul and Lloyd Waner, Baseball Brothers.* Jefferson, NC: McFarland & Co., Inc., 2003. 336p.

55759. "Paul Waner's Multiple Batting Streaks in 1927." *The Baseball Research Journal.* VII (1978), 104–106.

55760. Reidenbaugh, Lowell. "Paul Waner." In: his *Cooperstown: Where Legends Live Forever.* St. Louis: The Sporting News, 1983 Pp. 256–257.

55761. Ritter, Lawrence S. "Paul Waner." In: his *Glory of Their Times.* New York: Macmillan, 1966. Pp. 278–291.

55762. _____. and Donald Honig. "Paul Waner." In: their *The 100 Greatest Baseball Players of All Time.* New York: Crown Publishers, 1981. Pp. 230–233.

55763. Russell, Fred. "The Old Picture Hitter." In: Irving T. Marsh and Edward Ehre, eds. *The Best Sport Stories of 1960.* New York: E. P. Dutton, 1960. Pp. 95–97. Reprinted from an article which appeared in the *Nashville Banner* in 1959.

55764. Schott, Thomas E. "Pittsburgh Poison: The Waner Boys." In: Randy Roberts, ed. *Pittsburgh Sports: Stories from the Steel City.* Pittsburgh, PA: University of Pittsburgh Press, 2000. Pp. 76–92.

55765. Smith, Ira L. "Paul Glee ('Big Poison') Waner." In; his *Baseball's Famous Outfielders.* New York: A.S. Barnes, 1954. Pp. 200–204.

55766. Smith, Ron. "Paul Waner 62." In: his *The Sporting News Selects Baseball's 100 Greatest Players.* St. Louis, MO: The Sporting News, 1998. Pp. 136–137.

55767. Spalding, John E. "Paul Waner." In: his *Pacific Coast League Stars, Vol. II: Ninety Who Made It to the Majors, 1905–1957.* San Jose, CA: John E. Spalding, 1997. Pp. 75–76.

55768. Sutton, William A. "Paul Glee 'Big Poison' Waner." In: Vol. Q–Z of David L. Porter, ed. *Biographical Dictionary of American Sports: Baseball.* Rev. and enlarged ed. Westport, CT: Greenwood Press, 2000. Pp. 1632–1633.

55769. Waner, Paul G. "How to Bat." Edited by Sol Metzger. *Youth's Companion,* CIII (April 1929), 204–205.

55770. _____. "I Like to Be Good." In: Charles Einstein, ed. *The Fourth Fireside Book of Baseball.* New York: Simon and Schuster, 1987. Pp. 408–414.

55771. _____. *Paul Waner's Batting Secrets: An Aid to Good Hitting.* St. Petersburg, FL: Baseball Associates, 1962. 34p. Pamphlet.

Aaron Lee Ward
2B-3B. (B: Aug. 28, 1896, Boonesville, AK-D: Jan. 30, 1961). New York (AL), 1917–1926; Chicago (AL), 1927; Cleveland (AL), 1928. Remarks: Had 966 hits (60 homers) and 37 stolen bases In 1,059 games in a dozen years; played in 1921, 1922, and 1923, having a cumulative 18 hits (three homers — two homers in 1922 classic) and nine RBIs.

55772. Ward, Aaron L. "Big League Timber from Arkansas." *Baseball Magazine,* XXXVI (February 1926), 402–403+.

Archibald Burdette ("Arch") Ward
WRITER. (B: Dec. 27, 1896, Irwin, IL-D: July 9, 1955). Remarks: Sports editor, *Chicago Tribune,* 1929-death; noted sports promoter who, in 1933, was asked to devise a sports event to coincide with the Chicago Century of Progress Exposition. His response was an All-Star baseball game, which thereafter has been held annually.

55773. "Arch Ward: The Father of the All-Star Game Was An Enterprising Sportswriter." *Show,* I (July 1990), 47–48.

55774. Littlewood, Thoams B. *Arch: A Promoter, Not a Poet— the Story of Arch Ward.* Ames, IA: Iowa State University Press, 1990. 225p.

55775. Noverr, Douglas A. "Archibald Burdette 'Arch' Ward." In: John A. Garrity and Marsh C. Carries, eds. *American National Biography.* 24 vols. New York: Oxford University Press, 1999. XXII, 620–622.

55776. Rothe, Emil. "40 Years Ago — the First All-star Game." *Baseball Digest,* XXXII (July 1973), 44–50.

55778. Vogel, Mike. "Creative Sports Editor Arch Ward Was the Father of the All-Star Game." *Orioles Gazette,* III (July 8, 1993), 22–23.

Bryan Matthew Ward
P. (B: Jan. 28, 1972, Bristol, PA). Chicago (AL), 1998–1999; Philadelphia (NL) and Anaheim (AL), 2000. Remarks: In three big league seasons, won one game and lost three, with one "save"; has also played for Pawtucket (IL), 2001; Colorado Springs Sky Sox (PCL), 2002–2003; Camden (Atlantic League),2003–2004; Tacoma (PCL), 2004.

55778a. Ward, Amy. "A Life of Uncertainty: Trials and Tribulations of a Baseball Family." *Nine: A Journal of Baseball History and Social Policy Perspective,* XIII (Spring 2005), 110–115.

Duane Ward
P. (May 28, 1964, Park View, NM). Atlanta (NL), 1986; Toronto (AL), 1986–1995. Remarks: Obtained 32 victories, 37 defeats, and 121 "saves" in 10 years; won Game Three of 1992 World Series in relief; suffered shoulder injury. .

55779. Kurkijan, Tim. "Hanging on to One Man's Arm." *Sports Illustrated,* LXXX (April 4, 1994), 114+.

55780. _____. "Stuck in the Middle." *Sports Illustrated,* LXXIV (May 27, 1991), 70–73.

55781. Shelton, Gary. "Jays' Duane Ward Steps into 'Prime Time' as Reliever." *Baseball Digest,* LII (July 1993), 38–39.

Geoffrey Champion Ward
WRITER. (B: Nov. 30, 1940, Newark, OH). Remarks: Senior picture editor, *Encyclopedia Britannica,* 1964–1968; art director and writer in General Books Division, *Reader's Digest,* 1969–1970; freelance writer, 1973–1975; managing editor, *American Heritage,* 1976–1977; columnist, *American Heritage,* 1977–1982; freelance writer, 1982-date; collaborator with producer Ken Burns (q.v.) on numerous PBS documentary films .

55782. Ward, Geoffrey C. "Learning to Like Baseball: What Happened When a Historian Indifferent to the Subject Set Out to Write the Script for Ken Burn's Big New Documentary." *American Heritage,* XLV (October 1994), 86–91.

John Montgomery ("Monte") Ward★
SS-2B-P-OF-3B-MGR-EXEC. (B: March 3, 1860, Bellefonte, PA-D: March 4. 1925). Providence (NL), 1878–1882; New York (NL), 1883–1889; Brooklyn (P.), 1890; Brooklyn (NL), 1891–1892; New York (NL), 1893–1894. Remarks: Pitched from 1878–1884, winning 161 games (including a perfect game, June 11, 1880) and losing 101, with three "saves"; converted to infield and obtained (for career) a total of 2,123 hits (26 homers) and 504 stolen bases in 1,825 games over 17 campaigns; holds or tied for several records, including the pitching and winning of two games in one day, Aug. 9, 1878, the hurling of a no-hitter, June 17, 1880, and pitching and winning an 18-inning shutout, Aug. 17, 1882; NL stolen base champion, 1887, 1892; organizing force behind the creation of the baseball Brotherhood, which led to the creation of the ill-fated Players League of 1890; manager, Brooklyn (P.) and Brooklyn (NL), 1890–1894, winning 394 games and losing 397 (.562); president, Boston (NL), 1911–1912 and later NL attorney; married to popular actress Helen Deuvray; died of pneumonia on Georgia hunting trip; elected to National Baseball Hall of Fame in 1964, where his plaque reads: "Pitching pioneer who won 158, lost 102 games in seven years. Pitched perfect game for Providence of NL in 1880. Turned to shortstop and made 2,151 hits. Managed New York and Brooklyn in NL President of Brooklyn, NL, 1911–1912. Played important part in establishing modern organized baseball."

55783. Abrams, Roger I. "The Legal Process at the Birth of Baseball: John Montgomery Ward." In: his *Legal Bases: Baseball and the Law.* Philadelphia, PA: Temple University Press, 1998. Pp. 7–26.

55784. Allen, Lee and Thomas Meany. "John Montgomery Ward." In their *Kings of the Diamond.* New York: G. P. Putnam, 1965. Pp. 143–145.

55785. Alvarez, Mark. "John Montgomery Ward." In: Frederick Ivor-Campbell, ed. *Baseball's First Stars.* Cleveland, OH: Society for American Baseball Research, 1996. Pp. 167–168.

55786. Bass, Cynthia. "The Making of a Baseball Radical." *The National Pastime,* II (1982), 63–65.

55787. Bowman, L. G. "Baseball's Intriguing Couple: Helen Dauvray and John Montgomery Ward." *The Na-*

tional Pastime, XVIII (1998), 69–72. Monte's three- year marriage to the noted New York actress (1885–1888).

55788. _____. "A Celebrity Allegory: Fame, Indeed, for John Montgomery Ward." *The National Pastime,* XX (2000), 90–92.

55789. _____. "The Helen Dauvray Cup." *The National Pastime,* XVII (1997), 73–76. After the Giants won the postseason world championship in 1888, Ward arranged to have the team presented with the Dauvray Cup, the first world's series trophy.

55790. Buckley, James, Jr. "John M. Ward." In: his *Perfect!: The Inside Story of Baseball's Sixteen Perfect Games.* New York: Triumph Books, 2002. Pp. 18–27.

55791. Cochrane, Wayne C. "A Man and His Vision: John Montgomery Ward and the Players' League." Unpublished MA thesis, University of Idaho, 2003. 108p.

55792. Di Salvatore, Brian. *A Clever Base-Ballist : The Life and Times of John Montgomery Ward.* New York : Pantheon Books, 1999. 477p. Reprinted in paperback by Johns Hopkins University Press in 2000.

55793. Lowenfish, Lee E. "John Montgomery Ward." In: John A. Garrity and Marsh C. Carries, eds. *American National Biography.* 24 vols. New York: Oxford University Press, 1999. XXII, 636–637.

55794. _____. "The Latter Years of John Montgomery Ward." *The National Pastime,* II (1982), 66–69.

55795. Mayer, Ronald A. "John Montgomery Ward." In: his *Perfect! Biographies and Lifetime Statistics of 14 Pitchers of Perfect Game.* Jefferson, NC: McFarland & Co., Inc., 1991. Pp. 23–29.

55796. Smith, Robert M. "John Montgomery Ward: Undersized Giant." In: his *Heroes of Baseball.* Cleveland, OH: World Publishing Co., 1952. Pp. 81–88.

55797. Stevens, David. *Baseball's Radical for All Seasons: A Biography of John Montgomery Ward.* Lanham, MD: Scarecrow Press, 1998. 250p.

55798. Voigt, David Quentin. "John Montgomery Ward." In: Vol. Q-Z of David L. Porter, ed. *Biographical Dictionary of American Sports: Baseball.* Rev. and enlarged ed. Westport, CT: Greenwood Press, 2000. Pp. 1633–1635.

55799. Ward, John Montgomery. *Base-Ball: How To Become A Player with the Origin, History, and Explanation of the Game.* .Philadelphia, PA: The Athletic Publishing Co., 1888. 149p. Reprinted in a paperback edition at Cleveland in 1993 by the Society for American Baseball Research.

55800. _____. "Is the Base Ball Player a Chattel?" *Lippincott's Magazine,* XL (August 1887), 310–319.

55801. _____. "John Montgomery Ward Attacks the Reserve Clause (1887)." In: Dean A. Sullivan, ed. *Early Innings: A Documentary History of Baseball, 1825–1908.* Lincoln, NE: University of Nebraska Press, 1995. Pp. 161–170. A reprinting of the previous entry.

55802. _____. "John Ward Explains the Hit and Run Play (1896)." In: Dean A. Sullivan, ed. *Early Innings: A Documentary History of Baseball, 1825–1908.* Lincoln, NE: University of Nebraska Press, 1995. Pp. 235–236. Reprinted from pp. 89–90 of *Spalding's Official Base Ball Guide* (New York: A. G. Spalding, 1896), as reprinted by the St. Louis firm of Horton in 1989.

55803. _____. "Notes of a Base Ballist." *Lippincott's Monthly Magazine,* XXXVIII (1886), 212+.

Monte Ward *see* **John Montgomery ("Monte") Ward**

Peter Thomas ("Pete") Ward

3B-OF-1B. (B: July 26, 1939, Montreal, Canada). Baltimore (AL), 1962; Chicago (AL), 1963–1969; New York (AL), 1970. Remarks: Had 776 hits (98 homers) and 20

stolen bases in 973 games in nine years; had 18-game hitting streak, 1963; coach, Atlanta (NL), scout, New York (AL), manager, Portland (PCL), 1963–1982; salesman, Miller Brewing Company, 1982–1986; named to Oregon Sports Hall of Fame, 1985; founder/operator, Pete Ward Travel & Cruise Company, 1986-; elected to Canadian Baseball Hall of Fame, 1991.

55804. Allen, Maury. "Pete Ward: Rookie on the Rise." *Sport,* XXXXVI (October 1963), 40–42.

55805. Bryson, Bill. "Pete Ward: His Gripping Story." *Baseball Digest,* XXII (September 1963), 77–80.

55806. _____. "Pete Ward: Like a Refugee from the Rinkydinks." *Baseball Digest,* XXIV (September 1965), 39–41.

55807. Cope, Myron. "Mecca Lunch Kid." *Saturday Evening Post,* CCXXXVIII (August 14, 1965), 70+.

55808. Creamer, Robert W. "Boot a Few, Bat a Million." *Sports Illustrated,* XIX (July 15, 1963), 48–50.

55809. Furlong, Bill. "Gary Peters-Pete Ward: White Sox Wonder Boys." In: Bruce Jacobs, ed. *Baseball Stars of 1964.* New York: Pyramid Books, 1964. Pp. 138–144.

55810. Kendall, Brian. "April 9, 1963: Rookie Pete Ward Sparks the White Sox." In: his *Great Moments in Canadian Baseball.* Toronto, Ont.: Lester Publishing, 1995. Chpt. 9.

55811. McHugh, Roy. "Pete Ward: A Guy Like That is Good for Morale." *Sport,* XL (September 1965), 64–70.

55812. Shearon, Jim. "Pete Ward, Power Hitter and Pinch-Hit Champion." In: his *Canada's Baseball Legends.* Kanata, Ontario: Malin Head Press, 1994. Pp. 147–150.

55813. Vanderberg, Bob. "Pete Ward: The Pistol from Portland." In: his *Sox—From Lane and Fain to Zisk and Fisk.* Chicago, IL: Chicago Review Press, 1982. Pp. 252–260.

Robert B. Ward

EXEC. (D: 1915). Owner, Brooklyn (F.L.), 1914–1915. Remarks: The millionaire CEO of the Tip Top Bakery offered his players a profit-sharing plan and planned to introduce night games in 1916—but the "Tip Tops" made no profits and the whole Federal League failed a month after the magnate's death.

55814. Lane, Ferdinand C. "R. B. Ward, the Master Baker, Vice-President of the Feds." *Baseball Magazine,* XV (July 1915), 24–40.

Francis Xavier ("Frank" or "Weasel") Warfield

2B-MGR. (B: 1895, Indianapolis, IN-D: July 24, 1932). St. Louis Giants, 1914–1916; Indianapolis ABCs, 1915, 1917–1918; Bowser's ABCs, 1916; Dayton Marcos, 1919; Detroit Stars, 1919–1922; Kansas City Monarchs, 1921; Hilldale Daisies, 1923–1928; Baltimore Black Sox, 1929–1931; Washington Pilots, 1932. Remarks: Highly-regarded fielder, with lifetime .264 batting average; manager, Hilldale and Baltimore, who died of heart attack.

55815. Kleinknecht, Merl F. "Francis Xavier 'Frank,' 'Weasel' Warfield." In: Vol. Q-Z of David L. Porter, ed. *Biographical Dictionary of American Sports: Baseball.* Rev. and enlarged ed. Westport, CT: Greenwood Press, 2000. Pp. 1635–1636.

Frank Warfield *see* **Francis Xavier ("Frank" or "Weasel") Warfield**

John Milton ("Jack" or "Crab" or "Chief") Warhop

P. (B: July 4, 1884, Hinton, WV-D: Oct. 4, 1960). New York (AL), 1908–1915. Remarks: Had 63 victories, 94 defeats, and eight "saves" in an eight-year major league career; set AL record for most hit batters in one season (26), 1909); led AL in home runs surrendered, 1914–1915; served up the first two big league home runs of George Herman

("Babe") Ruth (q.v.), May 6 and June 2, 1915; also played for Freeport (Wisconsin-Illinois League), 1906–1907, Williamsport (Tri-State League, 1908, Salt Lake City (PCL) and Baltimore (IL), 1916; Toronto (IL), 1917–1918; later played semi-pro ball before joining Bridgeport (EL), 1927–1928.

55816. Kermisch, Al. "Ruth Makes War on Warhop." *The Baseball Research Journal,* II (1973), 19–21.

55817. Kofoed, J.C. "The Unluckiest Pitcher in the American League." *Baseball Magazine,* XV (August 1915), 51–54.

Lonnie ("Lon" or "The Arkansas Hummingbird") Warneke
P-UMP-JUDGE. (B: March 20, 1909, Mt. Ida, AK-D: June 23, 1976). Chicago (NL), 1930–1936; St. Louis (NL), 1937–1942; Chicago (NL), 1942–1943, 1946. Remarks: Won 193 games and lost 121 with 13 "saves" in 15 seasons; lost Game Two of the 1932 World Series; obtained the first hit by a NL batter in the first All-Star Game, 1933; won Games One and Five of the 1935 World Series; hurled no-hitter, Aug. 30, 1941; PCL umpire, 1946–1948 and NL umpire, 1949–1956; only person to have both played and umpired in an All-Star Game and a World Series; Garland County (AK) judge, 1963–1973.

55818. Drees, Jack and James C. Mullen. "Lon Warneke: 'The Arkansas Hummingbird.'" In: their *Where Is He Now?* Middle Village, NY: Jonathan David Publishers, 1973. Pp. 27–31.

55819. Kush, Raymond D. "Lonnie 'Lon,' 'The Arkansas Hummingbird' Warneke." In: Vol. Q-Z of David L. Porter, ed. *Biographical Dictionary of American Sports: Baseball.* Rev. and enlarged ed. Westport, CT: Greenwood Press, 2000. Pp. 1636–1637.

55820. Lane, Ferdinand C. "The Ace of the Cubs' Hurling Staff." *Baseball Magazine,* XLIX (November 1932), 550–551.

55821. Smith, Ira L. "Lonnie Warneke." In: his *Baseball's Greatest Pitchers.* New York: A.S, Barnes, 1954. Pp. 230–234.

55822. Wilbert, Warren and William Hageman. "Lon Warneke: 1933." In: their *Chicago Cubs: Seasons at the Summit, the 50 Greatest Individual Seasons.* Champaign, IL: Sagamore Publishing, 1997. Pp. 45–48.

Michael Bruce ("Mike") Warren
P. (B: March 26, 1961, Inglewood, CA). Oakland (AL), 1983–1985. Remarks: Won nine games and lost 13 in three seasons; pitched no-hitter against Chicago (AL), Sept. 29,1983.

55823. Asevedo, David. "Revenge of a Rookie." In: David Azevedo, ed *The Oakland Athletics 1984 Magazine.* Oakland, CA: Public Relations Department, Oakland Athletics, 1984. Pp. 108–116, 125.

Thomas Gentry ("Tommy" or "Wahoo Tommy") Warren
P. (B: July 5, 1920, Tula, OK-D: Jan. 2, 1968). Brooklyn (NL), 1944. Remarks: Won one game and lost four during his only major league season.

55824. Holmes, Tommy. "Wahoo Tommy Warren." *Baseball Digest,* III (May 1944), 15–17.

John Truman Wasdin
P. (B: Aug. 5, 1972, Fort Belvoir, VA). Oakland (AL), 1995–1996; Boston (AL), 1997–2000; Colorado (NL), 2000–2001; Baltimore (AL), 2001; Texas (AL), 2004. Remarks: Won 33 games and lost 34, with three "saves," in seven eight league seasons; had four-game winning streak, 1996; also played for Oklahoma (PCL), 2002–2003.

55825. Epstein, Eddie. "John Wasdin." In: STATS, Inc.

The STATS 1995 Minor League Scouting Notebook. Skokie, IL: STATS Publishing, 1995. Pp. 167–168.

Ray Clark Washburn
P-COACH. (B: May 11, 1938, Pasco, WA). St. Louis (NL), 1961–1969; Cincinnati (NL), 1970. Remarks: Obtained 72 victories, 64 defeats, and five "saves" in a decade; had one no-hitter, Sept. 18, 1968; won Game Three, but lost Game Six of 1968 World Series; asst. coach/head baseball coach and PE instructor, Bellevue Community College (WA), 1972–; named to Central Washington Sports Hall of Fame and State of Washington Sports Hall of Fame, 1999.

55826. Craft, David and Tom Owens. "Ray Washburn: A Moment of Glory." In: their *Redbirds Revisited.* Chicago, IL: Bonus Books, 1990. Pp. 241–246.

Chester L. ("Ches") Washington
WRITER. (B: 1902, Pittsburgh, PA-D: 1983). Remarks: Sports reporter, *Pittsburgh Courier,* 1925–1948; reporter/editor, *The Los Angeles Times,* 1948–1966; owner/publisher, Wave Newspaper chain, 1966-death.

55827. Reisler, Jim. "Chester L. Washington: From Writer to Millionaire." In: his *Black Writers/Black Baseball: An Anthology of Articles from Black Sportswriters Who Covered the Negro Leagues.* Jefferson, N.C.: McFarland & Co., Inc, 1994. Pp.93–112.

Claudell Washington
OF. (B: Aug. 31, 1954, Los Angeles, CA). Oakland (AL), 1974–1976; Texas (AL), 1977–1978; Chicago (AL), 1978–1980; New York (NL), 1980; Atlanta (NL), 1981–1986; New York (AL), 1986–1988; California (AL), 1989–1990; New York (AL), 1990. Remarks: Had 1,884 hits (164 homers) and 312 stolen bases in 1,912 games in 17 seasons; obtained three hits (one double) in both the 1974 and 1975 ALCS and four hits in the 1974 World Series; had three homers in a game twice, July 14, 1979 and June 22, 1980; hit 10,000th homer in New York Yankees history, April 20, 1988.

55828. "Braves Star Admits Coke Hurt His Playing Ability." *Jet,* LXVI (March 19, 1984), 47.

55829. Dickey, Glenn. "Think How Good Claudell Washington is Going to Be ... When He Learns How to Play Baseball." *Sport,* LXII (March 1976), 68–72.

55830. Elderkin, Phil. "Claudell Washington: A New Star in the Making for the A's." *Baseball Digest,* XXXIV (March 1975), 44–49.

55831. "Make Way for Washington." *Time,* CVI (July 21, 1975), 47–48.

55832. Oboiski, Robert. "Autograph Hunters Are Dangerous to a Player's Health!" In: his *Baseball's Strangest Moments.* New York: Sterling Publishing Co., 1988. Pp. 32–33.

55833. Porter, David L. "Claudell Washington." In: Vol. Q-Z of David L. Porter, ed. *Biographical Dictionary of American Sports: Baseball.* Rev. and enlarged ed. Westport, CT: Greenwood Press, 2000. Pp. 1638–1639.

55834. Scott, Jim. "Claudell ... Finley's Uneasy Housepet." *Black Sports,* V (October 1975), 50–52.

55835. Tucker, Tim. "Claudell Washington: He Beat the Rap." In: Wayne Minshew, ed. *Braves Illustrated '83.* Atlanta, GA: Public Relations Department, Atlanta Braves, 1982. Pp. 22–24.

55836. Washington, Claudell, as told to George Vass. "The Game I'll Never Forget." *Baseball Digest,* XLVIII (May 1989), 75–78.

Herbert ("Herb") Washington
PINCH RUNNER. (B: Nov. 16, 1950, Flint, Mich.). Oakland (AL), 1974–1975. Remarks: Employed exclu-

sively as a pinch runner, had 31 stolen bases and scored 30 runs in two years; became Boardman, OH, businessman and, in 1993, a member of the board of directors of the U.S. Federal Reserve Bank of New York; named to Flint Area Sports Hall of Fame, 1999.

55837. Gutman, Dan. "Herb Washington: Designated Pick-Off Victim." In: his *Baseball's Biggest Bloopers: The Games That Got Away.* New York: Puffin, 1995. Pp. 112–121.

55838. Lidz, Franz. "Whatever Happened to … Herb Washington." *Sports Illustrated,* LXXIX (July 19, 1993), 86+.

55839. Moore, Ken. "Elf Washington on the Bases." *Sports Illustrated,* XL (June 10, 1974), 69–72.

55840. Pitoniak, Scott. "Herb Washington." *The National Pastime,* XVII (1997), 95–97.

Stanley ("Stan") Wasiak

MGR. (B: 1919, Chicago, IL). Remarks: Infielder, Mobile (SA), 1943–1949; player-manager, Valdosta (Georgia-Florida League), 1950–1957; manager, Great Falls (Pioneer League), 1958–1959; Greenwood (South Atlantic League), Newport News (South Atlantic League), Mobile (South Atlantic League), Valdosta (Georgia-Florida League), Green Bay (Midwest League), Salem (Northwest League), and Lynchburg (Carolina League), 1960–1965; Fox Cities (Midwest League), 1966–1968; Evansville (SL), 1968–1969; Daytona (Florida State League), 1970–1972; Albuquerque (PCL), 1973–1976; Lodi (California State League), 1977–1979; Vero Beach (Florida State League), 1980–1985. By 1985, had achieved 2,497 victories, most ever by a minor league pilot, and 2,254 defeats; recipient, Minor League Baseball's King of Baseball plaque, 1986.

55841. Maisel, Ivan. "The Rarest Bird in the Bushes." *Sports Illustrated,* LXIII (August 26, 1985), 72+. Winningest minor league manager.

55842. "Stan Wasiak, King of the Minors." In: Bob Sparks, ed. *Baseball '86.* St. Petersburg, FL: NAPBL Promotion Corporation, 1986. Pp. 14–15.

55843. Wasiak, Stan. with Pat Jordan. "King of the Minors." *People Weekly,* XXIV (September 9, 1985), 75–76+.

Gary Lee ("Was") Waslewski

P. (B: July 21, 1941, Meridian, CT). Boston (AL), 1967–1968; St. Louis (NL), 1969; Montreal (NL), 1969–1970; New York (AL), 1970–1971; Oakland (AL), 1972. Remarks: Obtained 11 victories, 26 defeats, and five "saves" in five big league seasons; pitched 8.3 innings of decisionless ball in the 1967 World Series.

55844. Lautier, Jack. "Gary Waslewski." In: his *Fenway Voices.* Camden, ME: Yankee Books, 1990. Pp. 123–128.

Donald Watkins

EXEC. (B: Sept. 8, 1948, Parsons, KS). Remarks: Attorney and entrepreneur; ownership suitor of Montreal (NL), Tampa Bay (AL), Minnesota (AL), and Anaheim (AL); as of January 2005, his attempts to become the first black controlling owner of a major league baseball team have all failed.

55845. "Buying a MLB Team: A Profile of Donald Watkins." *Journal of Sport Management,* XVII (January 2003), 82–83.

Allen Kenneth Watson

P. (B: Nov. 18, 1970, Jamaica, NY). St. Louis (NL), 1993–1995; San Francisco (NL), 1996; Anaheim (A.L), 1997–1998; New York (NL), Seattle (AL), New York (AL), 1999; New York (AL), 2000. Remarks: Won 51 games and lost 55, with one "save," in eight years; led AL in homers allowed, 1997.

55846. Wheatley, Tom. "Rookie Report: Allen Watson."

Beckett Baseball Card Monthly, X, no. 105 (December 1993), 112–113.

Bob Watson *see* **Robert Jose ("Bob" or "Bull") Watson**

Robert Jose ("Bob" or "Bull") Watson

1B-OF-EXEC. (B. April 10, 1946, Los Angeles, CA). Houston (NL), 1966–1979; Boston (AL), 1979; New York (AL), 1980–1982; Atlanta (NL), 1982–1984. Remarks: Had 1,826 hits (184 homers) and 27 stolen bases in 1,832 games in 19 campaigns; had one grand slam homer, Sept. 7, 1970; scored 1,000,000th run in big league history, May 4, 1978; first to hit for cycle in both NL (June 24, 1977) and A.L (Sept. 15, 1979); minor league instructor, Oakland (AL), 1986–1988; asst. GM/GM, Houston (NL), 1989–1995, first Black GM; VP/GM, New York (AL), 1996–1998; VP-field operations, MLB, Feb. 21, 2002.

55847. Arndt, Rick. "Bob Watson." In: his *Safe at Home.* St. Louis, MO: Concordia Publishing House, 1979. Pp. 54–64.

55848. Connolly, Ed. "Bob Watson: He's More Than an Answer to a Trivia Question." *Baseball Digest,* XLVII (September 1988), 84–86.

55849. Geffner, Michael P. "Hardball: An Interview." *Texas Monthly,* XXV (April 1997), 48–50.

55850. Kaplan, Jim. "All-American, but Not an All-Star." *Sports Illustrated,* XLIII (July 14, 1975), 52–53.

55851. Olmsted, Frank J. "Robert Jose 'Bob,' 'Bull' Watson." In: Vol. Q–Z of David L. Porter, ed. *Biographical Dictionary of American Sports: Baseball.* Rev. and enlarged ed. Westport, CT: Greenwood Press, 2000. Pp. 1638–1640.

55852. Rumill, Ed. "Bob Watson: The Astros' Big Bopper." *Baseball Digest,* XXXII (August 1973), 49–52.

55853. Watson, Bob, as told to George Vass. "The Game I'll Never Forget." *Baseball Digest,* XLV (April 1986), 95–97.

55854. _____., with Russ Pate. *Survive to Win: The Inspiring Story of One Man Who Overcame Incredible Odds & Came Out a Champion.* Nashville, TN: Thomas Nelson Publishers, 1997. 240p.

55855. Wulf, Steve. "Bob Watson." *Sports Illustrated,* LXXIX (October 18, 1993), 74+. As a GM.

David T. Watson

PHYSICIAN.

55856. Duda, Marty. "Treating Big Leaguers: An Insider's View." *Physician and Sportsmedicine,* XIV (July 1986), 147–148, 153–154.

Evelyn ("Evie") Wawryshyn

2B. (B: Nov. 11, 1924, Tyndall, MN). Kenosha (All American Girls Professional Baseball League), 1946; Muskegon (AAAGPBL), 1946–1947; Springfield (AAGPBL), 1948; Fort Wayne (AAGPBL), 1949–1951. Remarks: In six seasons, obtained 275 hits (one homer) and 273 stolen bases in 554 games.

55857. Johnson, Susan E. ("Susie"). "Evelyn 'Evie' Wawryshyn." In: her *When Women Played Hardball: Professional Lives and Personal Stories From the All-American Girls Professional Baseball League, 1943–1954.* Seattle, WA: Seal Press, 1994. Pp. 237–266.

Cyril Roy ("Stormy") Weatherly

OF. (B: Feb. 25, 1915, Warren, TX-D: Sept. 19, 1991). Cleveland (AL), 1936–1942; New York (AL), 1943, 1946; New York (NL), 1950. Remarks: Had 794 hits (43 homers) and 42 stolen bases in 811 games in eight big league seasons; one of only three players to hit two triples in debut game; had 20-game hitting streak, 1936; first big leaguer to catch 10 fly balls in a game twice, April 28 and June 12, 1943.

55858. Sampson, Arthur. "The Day Ferrell Met Weatherly: It's an Oh, Oh Henry Story." *Baseball Digest,* XIII (May 1954), 55–56.

Roy ("Stormy") Weatherly *see* **Cyril Roy ("Stormy") Weatherly**

Big Jim Weaver *see* **James Dement ("Big Jim") Weaver**

Buck Weaver *see* **George Davis ("Buck") Weaver**

Earl Sidney Weaver★

MGR. (B: Aug. 14, 1930, St. Louis, MO). Remarks: Minor league player, 1948–1954; player-manager, Montgomery (South Atlantic League), 1955–1956 and Fitzgerald (Georgia-Florida League), 1957; manager, Dublin (Georgia-Florida League), 1958, Aberdeen (Northern League), 1959; Fox Cities (3I League), 1960–1961, Elmira (EL), 1962–1965, and Rochester (IL), 1966–1967; manager, Baltimore (AL), 1968–1982, 1985–1986 winning 1,480 games and losing 1,060 in 15 piloting seasons (.583); won 16 ALCS (most by any manager) games and lost seven and one of four World Series managed; elected to National Baseball Hall of Fame in 1996, where his plaque reads: "Managed Orioles with intensity, flair and acerbic wit for 17 seasons. .583 winning percentage (1480–1060) ranks fifth all-time among 20th century managers with 10 or more years service. 94.3 wins per seasons ranks first. Five 100-win seasons second on all-time list. Won six AL East titles, four pennants and 1970 World Series."

55859. "Baltimore's Soft-Shelled Crab: Manager Earl Weaver." *Time,* CXIV (July 23, 1979), 62–65.

55860. Barrett, Wayne M. "The Earl of Baltimore." *USA Today,* CXXV (July 1996), 65+.

55861. Boswell, Thomas. "Ballpark Wanderer." In: his *Why Time Begins on Opening Day.* New York: Penguin Books, 1984. Pp. 1–20.

55862. _____. "The Ultimate Oriole." *Inside Sports,* III (July 1981), 34–40.

55863. Brown, Bob. "Earl Weaver's a Happy Man." *Orioles Gazette,* II (August 3, 1992), 8–9.

55864. Cope, Myron. "Earl of Rasp." *Sports Illustrated,* XLIII (July 7, 1975), 58–62.

55865. Deford, Frank. "Mr. and Mrs. Earl Weaver." *Sports Illustrated,* LIII (June 30, 1980), 50–54+.

55866. Donovan, Dan. "Jim Palmer Looks Back on the Earl Weaver Regime." *Baseball Digest,* XLII (April 1983), 69–73.

55867. Durslag, Melvin. "Earl Weaver: Not Your Normal Field Leader." In: Bill Shumard, ed. *1980 All-Star Game Program.* Los Angeles, CA: Public Relations Department, Los Angeles Dodgers, 1980. Pp. 9–10.

55868. Dwyre, William. "Earl Weaver: An Insider's Look." *Referee,* VII (October 1982), 12.

55869. "The Earl of Switch." *Newsweek,* LXXX (August 14, 1972), 54+.

55870. "Earl Weaver." In: *Current Biography Yearbook, 1983.* New York: H.W. Wilson Co, 1983. Pp. 434–437.

55871. "Earl Weaver, Dick Williams, Dallas Green and Gene Mauch Discuss the Art of Managing." *Show,* I (July 1990), 40–45.

55872. Figone, Albert J. "Earl Sidney Weaver." In: Vol. Q-Z of David L. Porter, ed. *Biographical Dictionary of American Sports: Baseball.* Rev. and enlarged ed. Westport, CT: Greenwood Press, 2000. Pp. 1640–1641.

55873. Frommer, Harvey. "Earl Weaver." In: his *Baseball's Greatest Managers.* New York: Franklin Watts, 1985. Pp. 230–242.

55874. Grayson, Robert. "Wearing a Path to Cooperstown." *Sports Collector's Digest,* XXIII (August 9, 1996), 80–81.

55875. Henneman, Jim. "The Earl of Baltimore." In: Rick Kucner, ed. *Orioles Official 1982 Yearbook.* Baltimore. F.A.T.A., Inc., 1982. Pp. 5–7, 48.

55876. Hirshberg, Al. "The Ordeal of a World Series Manager." *Sport,* LIV (October 1972), 66–72.

55877. Kitkowski, Dan. "FB Talks to Earl Weaver About the Game He Knows Best." *Fantasy Baseball,* II (July 1991), 67–69.

55878. Klein, Moss. "When Earl Weaver Almost Called It Quits." *Baseball Digest,* XXXVI (October 1977), 30–32.

55879. Kuenster, John. "Earl Weaver Reveals Strategy He Used as a Winning Manager." *Baseball Digest,* XLIII (March 1984), 15–17.

55880. Linn, Ed. "The Earl of Baltimore: He's a Mouthful." *Sport,* LXXI (July 1980), 32–36.

55881. Looney, Douglas S. "Smile for the Birdies." *Sports Illustrated,* L (June 18,1979), 18–19.

55882. Lupica, Mike. "That's Earl, Folks." *Esquire,* CXI (May 1989), 53–54.

55883. Mitchell, Greg. "The Earl of Baltimore." *Quest,* V (September 1981), 18+.

55884. Neff, Craig. "A Weaver of Dreams Returns to Baltimore." *Sports Illustrated,* LXII (June 24, 1985), 26–29.

55885. Nigro, Ken. "Teacher, Motivator, Winner." *Coach and Athlete,* XLIII (April 1981), 12–15.

55886. Nuwer, Hank. "Earl Weaver: Lord Baltimore." In: his *Strategies of the Great Baseball Managers.* New York: Franklin Watts, 1988. Pp. 116–125.

55887. Palmer, Jim, and Jim Dale. *Together We Were Eleven Foot Nine: The Twenty-Year Friendship of Hall of Fame Pitcher Jim Palmer and Orioles Manager Earl Weaver.* Kansas City, MO: Andrews and McMeel, 1996. 169p.

55888. Pepe, Phil. "That's Earl Folks!" In: Clyde Hirt, ed. *Sports Quarterly Presents Baseball, 1972.* New York: Counterpoint, Inc., 1972. Pp. 10–11+.

55889. Pluto, Terry. *The Earl of Baltimore: The Story of Earl Weaver, Baltimore Orioles Manager.* Piscataway, N.J.: New Century Publishing Co., 1982. 207p.

55890. Seligman, Daniel. "Quantifying Earl." *Fortune,* CV (March 22, 1982), 47–48.

55891. Shafer, Kevin. *Earl Weaver: Hall of Fame Manager.* Berkeley, CA: Osborne McGraw-Hill, 1992. 490p.

55892. Shannon, Mike. "Earl Weaver." In: his *Tales from the Dugout: The Greatest True Baseball Stories Ever Told.* Lincolnwood, IL: NTC/Contemporary Books, 1997. Pp. 223–226.

55893. Ward, Robert. "Earl Weaver Gets No Garlands from Wayne Garland." *Sport,* LXIII (November 1976), 47–48.

55894. Weaver, Earl. "Managing Sure Does Beat Broadcasting." *TV Guide,* XXXIII (July 20, 1985), 32–34.

55895. _____. "World Series Strategy." *TV Guide,* XXXI (October 8, 1983), 15–18.

55896. _____. *Winning.* Edited by John Sammis. New York: William Morrow, 1972, 202p.

55897. _____. with Berry Stainback. *It's What You Learn After You Know It All That Counts.* Garden City, NY: Doubleday, 1982. 300p. Autobiography; updated by six pages in 1983 to reflect lessons of the 1982 season.

55898. _____., with Terry Pluto. *Weaver on Strategy.* New York: Collier Books, 1984. 187p. Pithy advice from the long-time manager of the Baltimore Orioles; updated by the Washington firm of Brassey's in 2002 into a 196-page edition under the title *Weaver on Strategy: The Classic Work on the Art of Managing a Baseball Team.*

55899. Will, George F. "The Earl." In: his *Bunts: Curt*

Flood, Camden Yards, Pete Rose and Other Reflections on Baseball. New York: Touchstone Books, 1998. Pp.51–53.

55900. Wilner, Barry. "The Earl of Baltimore." *Baseball Quarterly,* III (August 1979), 16–21.

55901. Wulf, Steve. "Hoping to Bring in One Last Big Harvest." *Sports Illustrated,* LVII (September 13, 1982), 24–26+.

55902. Youngman, Randy. "When the Stats Talk, Earl-Weaver Listens." *Baseball Digest,* XL (January 1991), 54–60.

George Daniel ("Buck" or "The Ginger Kid") Weaver
SS-3B. (B: Aug. 18, 1890, Stowe, PA–D: Jan. 31, 1950). Chicago (AL), 1912–1920. Remarks: Had 1,310 hits (21 homers) and 172 stolen bases in 1,254 games in nine seasons; led AL in sacrifice hits, 1915–1916; participated in one triple play, April 29, 1916; although had 11 hits in 1919 World Series, Weaver was one of the "Black Sox" banned from the game by Judge Landis; in his case, not for his participation, but for his failure to report his knowledge of plans for "fixing" that classic.

55903. Barton, George. "Weaver's Role in Fixed World Series." *Baseball Digest,* XV (April 1956), 49–51.

55904. Couch, Greg. "Buck Weaver: Wrong Man Out." *Baseball Digest,* LX (March 2001), 76–79.

55905. Farrell, James T. "Did Buck Weaver Get a Raw Deal?" *Baseball Digest,* XVI (August 1957), 69–78. This pro-Weaver piece was reprinted in Charles Einstein, ed., *The Second Fireside Book of Baseball* (New York: Simon and Schuster, 1968), pp. 127–132.

55906. Lane, Ferdinand C. "The Star of American League Third Basemen." *Baseball Magazine,* XXIV (November 1919), 405–407.

55907. Spalding, John E. "Buck Weaver." In: his *Pacific Coast League Stars, Vol. II: Ninety Who Made It to the Majors, 1905–1957* San Jose, CA: John E. Spalding, 1997. Pp. 38–39.

55908. Stein, Irving. "Buck Weaver: An Innocent Victim of 1919 Scandal." *Baseball Digest,* XLIX (March 1990), 87–93.

55909. _____. *"The Ginger Kid": The Buck Weaver Story.* Madison, WI: Elysian Fields Press, 1992. 368p.

55910. Suehsdorf, Adie D. "George Daniel 'Buck' Weaver." In: Vol. Q–Z of David L. Porter, ed. *Biographical Dictionary of American Sports: Baseball.* Rev. and enlarged ed. Westport, CT: Greenwood Press, 2000. Pp. 1641–1642.

55911. Weaver, George D. ("Buck"), as told to Hal Totten. "My Greatest Day in Baseball." In: John P. Carmichael, ed. *My Greatest Day in Baseball.* New York: A.S. Barnes, 1945. Pp. 42–47. First published in the *Chicago Daily News.*

James Dement ("Big Jim") Weaver
P. (B: Nov. 25, 1903, Obion Co., TN–D: Dec. 12, 1983). Washington (AL), 1938; New York (AL), 1931; St. Louis (AL) and Chicago (NL), 1934; Pittsburgh (NL), 1935–1937; St. Louis (AL), 1938; Cincinnati (NL), 1938–1939. Remarks: Obtained 57 victories, 36 defeats, and three "saves" in nine seasons; among the first to hurl the forkball and traded three times from teams which would win the NL pennant.

55912. Riley, James A. "Unlucky Hurler Missed Three Flags by a Year." *The Baseball Research Journal,* XIV (1985), 74–77.

Jeff Weaver
P. (B: August 22, 1976, Northridge, CA). Detroit (AL), 1999–2002; New York (AL), 2002–2003; Los Angeles (NL), 2004-. Remarks: Through 2004, has won 64 games

and lost 76, with two "saves" ; had three shutouts in 2002; lost Game Four of 2003 World Series.

55913. Spadafore, Jim. "Jeff Weaver's Competitive Spirit Drives Him to Succeed." *Baseball Digest,* LXI (August 2002), 52–54.

Joanne ("Jo" or "Jo the Jolter" or "The Little") Weaver
OF. (B: Dec. 19, 1935, Metropolis, IL). Fort Wayne Daisies (All-American Girls Professional Baseball League), 1950–1954. Remarks: In 329 games, had 438 hits (29 homers) and 79 stolen bases; AAGPBL MVP Award, 1954; AAGPBL batting champion, 1952–1954; had .429 batting average in 1954.

55914. Heaphy, Leslie. "Joanne 'Jo,' 'Jo the Jolter,' 'The Little' Weaver." In: Vol. Q–Z of David L. Porter, ed. *Biographical Dictionary of American Sports: Baseball.* Rev. enlarged ed. Westport, CT: Greenwood Press, 2000. Pp. 1642–1643.

Monte Weaver *see* **Montgomery Morton ("Monte" or "Prof") Weaver**

Montgomery Morton ("Monte" or "Prof") Weaver
P. (B: June 15, 1906, Helton, NC–D: June 14, 1994). Washington (AL), 1931–1938; Boston (AL), 1939. Remarks: Had 71 victories and 50 defeats, with four "saves," in nine seasons; lost Game Four of 1933 World Series; earned MS in Math and taught at Emory & Henry College, VA.

55915. Kelley, Brent P. "Monte Weaver: The Senators' Last Hurrah, 1931–1939." In: his *In the Shadow of The Babe: Baseball Players Who Played with or Against Babe Ruth.* Jefferson, NC: McFarland & Co., Inc., 1995. Pp. 119–121.

55916. Macht, Norman L. "Monte Weaver Recalls Pitching for the Old Senators." *Baseball Digest,* LI (May 1992), 53–57.

Brandon Webb
P. (B: May 9, 1979, Ashland, KY). Arizona (NL), 2003-. In two big league seasons through 2004, has won 17 games and lost 25; also played for El Paso (TL), 2002.

55917. Chen, Albert. "Quality Start." *Sports Illustrated,* XCIX (July 14, 2003), 118–119.

Del E. Webb
EXEC. (B: May 17, 1899, Fresno, CA–D: July 4, 1974). Remarks: Vice-president, New York (AL), 1945–1965 and Yankees part-owner, 1954–1964.

55918. Brown, Joe David. "The Webb of Mystery." *Sports Illustrated,* XII (February 29, 1960), 68–80.

55919. Carmichael, John P. "Caught in the Webb." *Baseball Digest,* IV (April 1945), 19–21.

55920. Povich, Shirley. "They Know Del Webb Now." *Baseball Digest,* VI (August 1947), 53–55.

Earl Webb *see* **William Earl Webb**

William Earl Webb
OF. (B: Sept. 17, 1897, Bon Air, TN–D: May 23, 1965). New York (NL), 1925; Chicago (NL), 1927–1928; Boston (AL), 1930–1932; Detroit (AL), 1932–1933; Chicago (AL), 1933. Remarks: Had 661 hits (56 homers) and eight stolen bases in 650 games in seven seasons; led AL in doubles, 1931.

55921. Bloodgood, Clifford. "A Big League Cast-Off Who Broke a Record." *Baseball Magazine,* XLVIII (May 1932), 555–557.

55922. Blount, Roy, Jr. "Plink-Rumba-Barumba-Boom." *Sports Illustrated,* LXXIX (August 9, 1993), 64–73.

55923. Glebe, Iris Webb. *Earl of Dublin: Major League Record Holder.* Ann Arbor, MI: McNaughton & Gunn, Inc., 1988. 62p.

55924. Holway, John B. "Earl Webb: His One-Season Doubles Mark Still Stands." *Baseball Digest,* LIII (December 1994), 80–83. Had 67 two-baggers in 1931.

Mitchell Dean ("Mitch") Webster
OF. (B: May 16, 1959, Larned, KS). Toronto (AL), 1983–1985; Montreal (NL), 1985–1988; Chicago (NL), 1988–1989; Cleveland (AL), 1990–1991; Pittsburgh (NL), 1991; Los Angeles (NL), 1991–1995. Remarks: Obtained 900 hits (70 homers) and 160 stolen bases in 1,265 games in 13 seasons; led N. L. in triples, 1986; scout, Los Angeles (NL), 1991–1993.

55925. Hill, Terry. "Mitch Webster: 'I Threw My Helmet and Had a Few Choice Words for the Umpire.'" In: his *Batting a Thousand.* Nashville, TN: Thomas Nelson, 1987. Pp. 96–99.

Elaine c. Weddington-Stewart
EXEC. (B: 1963, Flushing, NY). Remarks: Associate general counsel, Boston (AL), 1988–1990; VP, assistant GM, and general counsel, Boston (AL), January 26, 1990-date, the highest ranking black female executive in MLB.

55926. Turner, Renee D. "Introducing Elaine C. Weddington: First Woman Baseball Executive." *Ebony,* XLV (July 1990), 25–26.

Herman Ralph ("Herm" or "Hermie") Wehmeier
P. (B: Feb. 18, 1927, Cincinnati, OH-D: May 21, 1973). Cincinnati (NL), 1945, 1947–1954; Philadelphia (NL), 1954–1956; Detroit (AL), 1956; St. Louis (NL), 1956–1958. Remarks: Had 92 Victories, 108 defeats, and nine "saves" in 13 seasons; wildness allowed him to lead the NL in walks, 1949–1950, 1952 and hits batsmen, 1952; scout, Cincinnati (NL), 1959–1961; died of heart attack while testifying in court as a government witness in a theft case.

55927. Daley, Arthur. "He Had a Kick Coming." *Baseball Digest,* XVI (June 1957), 63–65.

55928. Harmon, Pat. "The $300,000 Wehmeier Mystery." *Baseball Digest,* XIII (August 1954), 51–53.

55929. Quinn, Joe. "Wehmeier Knows His Way." *Baseball Digest,* VII (August 1949), 59–61.

Dick Weik *see* **Richard Henry ("Legs") Weik**
Richard Henry ("Dick" Or "Legs") Weik
P. (B: Nov. 17, 1927, Waterloo, IA-D: April 21, 1991). Washington (AL), 1948–1950; Cleveland (AL), 1950 and 1953; Detroit (AL), 1054. Remarks: Won six games and lost 22, with one "save," in five years; walked 13 players in one game, 1949.

55930. Povich, Shirley. "The Senators Look to Weik." *Baseball Digest,* IX (May 1950), 57–59.

Sidney Weil
EXEC. (B: 1891-D: 1966). Remarks: Jewish owner, Cincinnati (NL), 1929–1933, forced by financial reversal to sell his team to Powel Crosley and financiers.

55931. Weil, Sidney. "Memoir." In: Mark Stang and Dick Miller, eds. *Baseball in the Buckeye State.* Cleveland, OH: Society for American Baseball Research, 2004. Pp. 29–32.

Carl Woolworth Weilenmann *see* **Carl Woolworth ("Zeke") Weilman**
Carl Woolworth ("Zeke") Weilman
P. (B: Nov. 29, 1889, Hamiton, OH-D: May 25, 1924). St. Louis (AL), 1912–1917; 1919–1920. Remarks: Extremely tall hurler born Weilenmann; won 85 games, lost 94, with nine "saves" in a career interrupted by World War I; first big league player to strike out six consecutive times in one game, July 25, 1913.

55932. Lane, Ferdinand C. "Long Carl Weilman, the Tiger Tamer." *Baseball Magazine,* XV (October 1915), 47–53.

Jacob ("Tornado Jake") Weimer
P-COACH. (B: Nov. 29, 1873, Ottumwa, IA-D: June 19, 1928). Chicago (NL), 1903–1905; Cincinnati (NL), 1906–1908; New York (NL), 1909. Remarks: Won 97 games and lost 69, with two "saves," in seven big league seasons; later, coach, Chicago Loyola Academy.

55933. Voigt, David Quentin. "Jacob 'Tornado Jake' Weimer." In: Vol. Q-Z of David L. Porter, ed. *Biographical Dictionary of American Sports: Baseball.* Rev. and enlarged ed. Westport, CT: Greenwood Press, 2000. Pp. 1644–1645.

Philip ("Phil" or "Mickey") Weintraub
OF-1B. (B: Oct. 2, 1907, Chicago, IL-D: June 21, 1987). New York (NL), 1933–1935, 1937; Cincinnati (NL), 1937; Philadelphia (NL), 1938; New York (NL), 1944–1945. Remarks: Obtained 925 hits (73 homers) and 61 stolen bases in 894 games in all or part of seven big league seasons; on April 30, 1944, drove in 11 runs, one short of the MLB record; had last hit in Baker Bowl at Philadelphia, June 30, 1938; while playing for Nashville, had first .400 season for any player in SA history, 1934.

55934. Buege, Bob. "Mayhem on a Sunday Afternoon." *Oldtyme Baseball News,* V, no. 1 (1993), 14–15.

55935. Gauthreaux, Jay. "Bats on Fire." In: his *Baseball in New York.* Cleveland, OH: Society for American Baseball Research, 1991. Pp. 23–24.

Albert John ("Al") Weis
2B-SS (B: April 2, 1938, Franklin Square, NY). Chicago (AL), 1962–1967; New York (NL), 1968–1971. Remarks: Had 346 hits (seven homers) and 55 stolen bases in 800 games in a decade; utility Infielder who had .455 batting average in 1969 World Series, including winning hit in Game Two and homer in Game Five.

55936. Heiman, Lee, Dave Weiner and Bill Gutman. "Al Weiss." In: their *When The Cheering Stops.* New York: Macmillan Publishing Co., 1990. Pp. 79–94.

55937. McGuire, Mark and Michael Sean Gormley. "Al Weiss." In: their *Moments in the Sun: Baseball's Briefly Famous.* Jefferson, NC: McFarland & Co., Inc., 2001. Pp. 182–188.

55938. Salant, Nathan. "Al Weiss." In: his *Superstars, Stars, and Just Plain Heroes.* New York: Stein and Day, 1982. Pp. 285–289.

55939. Vass, George. "Al Weis: An Improbable Hem." *Baseball Digest,* XXIX (January 1970), 13–18.

55940. Weis, Al, as told to George Vass. "The Game I'll Never Forget." *Baseball Digest,* L (March 1991), 51–52.

Alta Weiss
P. (B: 1890, Berlin, OH-D: 1964). Vermillion Independents (semi-pro), 1907; Weiss All Stars (semi-pro), 1908. Remarks: Played baseball on all-male semi-pro team, the Vermilion Independents, making debut on Sept. 7, 1907; her father purchased half interest in Cleveland-based semi-pro club in 1908; used funds earned to put herself through medical school at Starling College of Medicine (later Ohio State University Medical College); later practiced medicine at Norwalk, OH, and continued to pitch on men's teams into the 1920s; retired at Ragersville, OH.

55941. Gregorich, Barbara. "'You Can't Play in Skirts': Alta Weiss, Baseball Player." *Timeline,* XI (July 1994), 38+.

55942. Hopkinson, Deborah. *Girl Wonder: A Baseball Story in Nine Innings.* New York: Simon and Schuster Children, 2003. 40p. Fictionalized biography.

George Martin Weiss★
EXEC. (B: June 23, 1895, New Haven, CT-D: Aug. 13, 1972). Remarks: Manager, New York (AL) farm system,

1932–1947; GM, New York (AL), 1947–1960, who brought Casey Stengel (q.v.) in as Yankees manager; president, New York (NL), 1961–1966; advisor, New York (NL), 1966–1971; elected to National Baseball Hall of Fame in 1971, where his plaque reads: "Master builder of championship teams. Was club executive in minors and majors from 1919 to 1964. Developed best minor league chain in game as New York Yankee farm manager, 1932–1947. General Manager of the Yankees from 1947–1960 which won 10 pennants and 7 World Series during this period. President of the New York Mets 1961–1968."

55943. Alexander, Charles C. "George Martin Weiss." In: John A. Garrity and Marsh C. Carries, eds. *American National Biography.* 24 vols. New York: Oxford University Press, 1999. XXII, 910–911.

55944. "Baseball: The Unknown Yankee." *Newsweek,* L (July 15, 1957), 78–79.

55945. "Baseball: Weiss at the Plate." *Newsweek,* XXX (October 20, 1947), 78–79.

55946. Burr, Harold C. "The Wizardry of Weiss." *Baseball Magazine,* LXX (April 1943), 487–489+.

55947. Daniel, Daniel M. "Weiss Brought Varied Talents into General Managership of the Yankees." *Baseball Magazine,* LXXX (February 1944), 299–301.

55948. Forbes, Editors of. "The Champion Dollar Guy." *Baseball Digest,* X (October 1951), 61–76.

55949. Frank, Stanley B. "The Boss of the Yankees." *Saturday Evening Post,* CCXXI (April 16, 1960), 31+.

55950. _____. "Yankee Kingmaker." *Saturday Evening Post,* CCXXI (July 24, 1948), 23, 108–110+.

55951. Gross, Milton. "The Yankees: After Weiss and Stengel, What?" *Sport,* XXV (June 1958), 14–19.

55952. Hickey, David and Kerry Keene. "George Weiss." In: their *The Proudest Yankees of All: From the Bronx to Cooperstown.* Lanham, MD: Taylor Trade Pub., dist. by National Book Network, 2003. Chpt. 19.

55953. King, Joseph E. "George Martin Weiss." In: Vol. Q–Z of David L. Porter, ed. *Biographical Dictionary of American Sports: Baseball.* Rev. and enlarged ed. Westport, CT: Greenwood Press, 2000. Pp. 1644–1646.

55954. Lane, Frank ("Trader"). "Casey Stengel Was Wise, but Weiss was Wiser." *Collier's,* CXXXIII (May 14, 1954), 84–96+.

55955. Meany, Thomas. "George Weiss, Perfectionist." In: his *The Yankee Story.* New York: E.P. Dutton, 1960. Pp. 141–154.

55956. _____. "George Weiss: The Real Yankee Clipper." *Sport,* III (December 1947), 16–17+.

55957. "The Organization Men of Baseball: Tradition and George Weiss Shape Yankee Players and Team Success." *Life,* XLV (September 29, 1958), 94–101.

55958. Shaplen, Robert. "How to Build a Ball Club." *Sports Illustrated,* XVI (March 6, 1962), 37–39+.

55959. _____. "The Yankees' Real Boss." *Sports Illustrated,* I (September 20, 1954), 34–37.

55960. Weiss, George M. and Robert Shaplen. "The Man of Silence Speaks." *Sports Illustrated,* XIV (March 6–13, 1961), 45–52,28–39.

Walter William ("Walt") Weiss
SS. (b: Nov. 28, 1963, Tuxedo, TX). Oakland (AL), 1987–1992; florida (NL), 1993); Colorado (NL), 1994–1997; Atlanta (NL), 1998–2000. Remarks: Had 1,207 hits (25 homers) and 96 stolen bases in 1,495 games in 14 seasons; AL Rookie of the Year award, 1988; played in 13 post season series, obtaining five hits in 1988 ALCS and six in 1999 NLCS, but making a significant error in Game Four of 1988 World Series; coach, Colorado (NL), 2002–2003.

55961. Honig, Donald. "1988: Walt Weiss." In: his *American League Rookies of the Year.* New York: Bantam Books, 1989. Pp. 105–107.

55962. Kaplan, Jim. "The Education of a Shortstop: It Isn't as Easy as 6–4–3. Herewith the Freshman Course of the Athletics; Walt Weiss and the Mets' Kevin Elster." *Sport,* LXXIX (August 1988), 48–52.

55963. Schacht, John. "Walt Weiss: Off and Flying." In: A. R. Worthington, ed. *1989 Oakland Athletics Magazine.* Benicia, CA: Mariposa Press, 1989. Pp. 35–38.

55964. Zachotsky, Dan. "Walt Weiss." In: his *Idols of the Spring: Baseball Interviews About Spring Training.* Jefferson, NC: McFarland & Co., Inc., 2001. Pp. 23–32.

John Ludwig ("Johnny") Welaj
OF-EXEC. (B: May 27, 1914, Moss Creek, CA-D: Sept. 13, 2003). Washington (AL), 1939–1941, Philadelphia (AL), 1943. Remarks: Had 198 hits (four homers) and 36 stolen bases in four big league seasons; minor league manager, Washington (AL), 1954–1956; dir. of sales and promotions, Washington (AL), 1957–1971 and Texas (AL), 1972; dir. of stadium operations, Texas (AL), 1973–1984; spring training dir., Texas (AL), 1985–1999; continued to travel to spring training through 2001.

55965. Kelley, Brent P. "Johnny Welaj: Cobb Said He Could fly (1939–1943)." In: his *The Pastime in Turbulence: Interviews with Baseball Players of the 1940s.* Jefferson, NC: McFarland & Co., Inc., 2002. Pp. 29–40.

Bob Welch *see* **Robert Lynn ("Bob") Welch**
John Vernon ("Johnny") Welch
P. (B: Dec. 2, 1866, Washington, DC-D: Sept. 2, 1940). Chicago (NL), 1926–1931; Boston (NL), 1932–1936; Pittsburgh (NL), 1936. Remarks: Had 36 victories, 41 defeats, and six "saves" in nine years.

55966. Bloodgood, Clifford. "The Braves' Premier Pitcher of 1934." *Baseball Magazine,* LIV (February 1935), 407–409+.

Michael Francis ("Mickey" or "Smiling Mickey") Welch★
P. (B: July 4, 1859, Brooklyn, NY-D: July 30, 1941). Troy (NL), 1880–1882; New York (NL), 1883–1892. Remarks: Won 311 games and lost 207, with four "saves," in 13 seasons; as a hitter, obtained 492 hits (12 homers) and 10 stolen bases; won two games in a day, July 4, 1881; set still-standing MLB mark by striking out first nine hitters faced, Aug. 28, 1884; won 17 consecutive games, July 18-Sept. 4, 1885; strong drinker and strong hurler who won 47 games in 1885; began with Auburn and Holyoke (N.A.), 1878–1879; became first big league pinch hitter — and struck out, Sept. 18, 1889; elected to National Baseball Hall of Fame in 1973, where his plaque reads: "Credited with more than 300 victories during 13 seasons in majors. Won 17 games in a row in 1885 while compiling 44–11 record for league-leading .800 winning percentage. Topped 34-victory total in four years."

55967. Babcock, N. P. "The 'Pitcher' and His Methods." *Harper's Young People,* VI (September 29, 1885), 763–765.

55968. Bergman, Irv. "Michael Francis Welch." In: Frederick Ivor-Campbell, ed. *Baseball's First Stars.* Cleveland, OH: Society for American Baseball Research, 1996. Pp. 170–171.

55969. Bulkley, George. "Why Did Mickey Smile?" *The Baseball Research Journal,* XI (1982), 127–129.

55970. Evers, John L. "Michael Francis 'Mickey,' 'Smiling Mickey' Welch." In: Vol. Q–Z of David L. Porter, ed. *Biographical Dictionary of American Sports: Baseball.* Rev. and enlarged ed. Westport, CT: Greenwood Press, 2000. Pp. 1646–1647.

55971. Singletary, Wes. "Mickey Welch." In: John A. Garrity and Marsh C. Carries, eds. *American National Biography.* 24 vols. New York: Oxford University Press, 1999. XXII, 923–924.

55972. Westcott, Rich. "Mickey Welch: A Lot to Smile About." In: his *Winningest Pitchers: Baseball's 300-Game Winners.* Philadelphia, PA: Temple University Press, 2002. Pp. 17–24.

Robert Lynn ("Bob") Welch
P. (B: Nov. 3, 1956, Detroit, MI). Los Angeles (NL), 1978–1987; Oakland (A.L), 1987–1994. Remarks: Won 211 games and lost 146, with eight "saves," in 17 years; saved Game Two of 1978 World Series, but lost Game Four; last 20th century pitcher to homer in a 1–0 game, June 17, 1983; lost one game in both the 1983 and 1985 NLCS; won one game in both the 1989 and 1990 ALCS; AL Cy Young Award, 1990; coach, Arizona (NL), 2001.

55973. Bagnato, Andrew. "Bob Welch Finally Reached Top of His Game in 1990." *Baseball Digest,* L (January 1991), 26–29.

55974. Bennett, Gaymon L. "Robert Lynn 'Bob' Welch." In: Vol. Q-Z of David L. Porter, ed. *Biographical Dictionary of American Sports: Baseball.* Rev. and enlarged ed. Westport, CT: Greenwood Press, 2000. Pp. 1647–1648.

55975. Boatman, Kim. "Welch's World." In: Mike Nahrsted, ed. *The Sporting News 1991 Baseball Yearbook.* St. Louis, MO: *The Sporting News,* 1991. Pp. 5–10.

55976. Fimrite, Ron. "One Pitch at a Time." *Sports Illustrated,* LXXIII (September 17, 1990), 58–63.

55977. Gammons, Peter. "Ride of Terror." *Sports Illustrated,* LXXI (October 30, 1989), 28–29.

55978. McDonnell, Joe. "Bob Welch of Dodgers Sets Goals for '84 Season." *Baseball Digest,* XLIII (May 1984), 48–57.

55979. Mortensen, Chris. "Bob Welch: Intense and. Aggressive." In: Bill Shumard, ed. *1981 Los Angeles-Dodgers Yearbook.* Anaheim, CA: Rotary Off-Set Printers, 1981. p. 54.

55980. Schultz, Randy. "Armed & Ready: A Look at 1990's Cy Young Award Winners." In: *Baseball Preview.* New York: Lexington Library, 1991. Pp. 66–71.

55981. Vecsey, George. "Bob Welch: Young, Talented and an Alcoholic." *The New York Times Biographical Service,* XI (April 1980), 626–628.

55982. Welch, Robert L. "Final Season: For 12 Years, Our Summers Revolved Around Baseball Games Won and Lost, and as a Family, We Shared Them All." *Reader's Digest* (Canada), CLIII (July 1998), 97–98, 100+.

55983. _____., as told to George Vass. "The Game I'll Never Forget." *Baseball Digest,* L (September 1991), 29–31. 1978 World Series Game 2.

55984. _____. with George Vecsey. *Five O'Clock Comes Early: A Cy Young Award Winner Recounts His Greatest Victory.* New York: Fireside, 1991. 256p. Updates the next entry through the 1990 season; excerpted in *Reader's Digest,* CXXXIX (October 1991), 187–215, under the title "Bob Welch's Greatest Victory."

55985. _____. *Five O'Clock Comes Early: A Young Man's Battle with Alcoholism.* New York: William Morrow, 1982. 244p.

55986. Wilner, Barry. "Bob Welch, Doug Drabek Deserving Cy Young Winners." *Baseball World's Baseball '91,* I, no. 3 (1991), 10–11.

Timothy James ("Tim") Welke
UMP. (B: Aug. 23, 1957, Pontiac, MI). AL arbiter, 1984–.

55987. Welke, Tim. "Interview." *Referee,* XIX (July 1994), 72+.

Bob Wells *see* **Robert Lee ("Bob") Wells**
David Lee ("Boomer") Wells
P. (B: May 20, 1963, Torrance, CA). Toronto (AL), 1987–1992; Detroit (AL), 1993–1995; Cincinnati (NL), 1995; Baltimore (AL), 1996; New York (AL), 1997–1998; Toronto (AL), 1999–2001; New York (AL), 2002–2003; San Diego (NL), 2004; Boston (AL), 2005-. Remarks: Through 2004, has won 212 games and lost 136, with 13 "saves"; won both games of a doubleheader, July 17, 1989; won one game in 1996 and 2003 ALCS and two in 1998 ALCS; had 13th perfect game in modern MLB history, May 17, 1998; ALCS MVP Award, 1998; won one game of 1998 World Series.

55988. Antonen, Mel. "Yankees' David Wells: A Fan Favorite in New York." *Baseball Digest,* LVIII (January 1999), 22–23.

55989. Appel, Marty. "History Uncapped." *Beckett Sports Collectibles,* VII (August 1998), 28–32.

55990. Buckley, James, Jr. "David Wells." In: his *Perfect!: The Inside Story of Baseball's Sixteen Perfect Games.* New York: Triumph Books, 2002. Pp. 212–231.

55991. Farber, Michael. "A Doggone Red." *Sports Illustrated,* LXXXIII (October 16, 1995), 33+.

55992. Koenig, Bill. "Yankee with a Cause." *USA Today Baseball Weekly,* VIII (September 30, 1998), 9–10.

55993. Kuenster, John. "David Wells Created an Amazing Oddity in Pitching Perfect No-Hitter." *Baseball Digest,* LVII (September 1998), 17–21.

55994. Lane, Jon. "The One and Only." *Yankees Magazine,* XIX (June 1998), 52–65.

55995. Lidz, Franz. "The Unvarnished Ruth." *Sports Illustrated,* LXXXVII (September 8, 1997), 70–79.

55996. McCarver, Tim, with Danny Peary "David Wells." In: his *The Perfect Season: Why 1998 Was Baseball's Greatest Year.* New York: Villard Books, 1999. Pp. 52–58.

55997. McEvoy, Pat. "A Dream Come True." *Yankees Magazine,* XIX (June 1998), 42–51. Perfect game.

55998. McMillan, Ken. "David Wells." In: his *Tales from the Yankee Dugout: A Collection of the Greatest Yankee Stories Ever Told.* Champaign, IL.: Sports Publishing, Inc., 2001. Pp. 188–190.

55999. O'Neil, Michael. "Picture Perfect; Yes, Virginia, There is a Santa Claus ... and He's Got a Nasty Four-Seam Fastball: David Well's Perfect Game Was Among the Bountiful Gifts Delivered to Sports Fans This Year." *Sports Illustrated,* LXXXIX (December 28, 1998), 122–123.

56000. Pearlman, Jeff. "Heavy Duty: They Said He Wouldn't Last, but Toronto's Large-Livin' Lefthander, David Wells, Has Become Baseball's Most Reliable Pitcher — and a Clubhouse Wise Man to Boot." *Sports Illustrated,* XCIII (July 10, 2000), 42–45, 48.

56001. _____. "Roger Who?: In Tumultuous Toronto, Championship Hopes Are Alive and Wells." *Sports Illustrated,* XC (March 29, 1999), 84–85.

56002. "Pitcher Perfect." *Sports Illustrated,* LXXXVIII (May 25, 1998), 4–5.

56003. Shannon, Mike. "David Wells." In: his *Tales from the Ballpark: More of the Greatest True Baseball Stories Ever Told.* Lincolnwood, IL: Contemporary Books, 1999. Pp. 214–217.

56004. Verducci, Tom. "Hot Damn Yankee; David Wells Likes His Music Loud, His Drinks Cold, His Chin Hair — and, as He Showed Against the Indians, the Ball in His Hand When the Season's on the Line." *Sports Illustrated,* LXXXIX (October 19, 1998), 38–41.

56005. Wells, David, with Chris Kreski. *Perfect I'm Not: Boomer on Beer, Brawls, Backaches, and Baseball.* New York: William Morrow, 2003. 432p.

56006. Wertheim, L. Jon. "Perfection." *Sports Illustrated,* LXXXVIII (May 25, 1998), 52–53.

Ed Wells *see* **Edwin Lee ("Ed" or "Eddy") Wells**

Edwin Lee ("Ed" or "Eddy") Wells

P. (B: June , 7, 1900, Ashland, OH–D: May 1, 1986). Detroit (AL), 1923–1927; New York (AL), 1929–1932; St. Louis (AL), 1933–1934. Remarks: Won 68 games and lost 69, with 13 "saves," in 11 seasons; had 33-inning scoreless streak, 1926; also played for Ludington (Central League), 1922; Birmingham (SA), 1923, 1928.

56007. Bak, Richard. "Eddy Wells (1923–1934)." In: his *Cobb Would Have Caught It: The Golden Age of Baseball in Detroit.* Detroit, MI: Wayne State University Press, 1991. Pp. 151–165.

56008. Bloodgood, Clifford. "The Picturesque Ed Wells." *Baseball Magazine,* XLVII (June 1931), 305–306.

56009. Green, Paul M. "Baseball and Ed Wells." *Sports Collector's Digest,* XI (August 3,1984), 94+.

56010. Lane, Ferdinand C. "A Studious Young Man Who Mixes Brains with His Baseball." *Baseball Magazine,* XXXVIII (May 1927), 542–543+.

56011. Murdock, Eugene. "Ed Wells: 'Bethany's Best.'" In: his *Baseball Between the Wars: Memories Of The Game by the Men Who Played It.* Westport, CT: Meckler Publishing, 1992. Pp. 62–93.

Robert Lee ("Bob") Wells

P. (B: Nov. 1, 1966, Yakima, WA). Philadelphia (NL), 1994; Seattle (AL), 1994–1998; Minnesota (AL), 1999–2002. Remarks: Through 2002, won 40 games and lost 28, with 15 "saves"; reliever whose career ended by arm injury.

56012. Barron, Chris. "Armed Again: Bob Wells Rebounded from Major Elbow Surgery to Become a Mainstay in the Mariners Rotation." *Mariners Magazine,* VII, no. 3 (1996), 61–63.

Vernon Wells

OF. (B: Dec. 8, 1978, Shreveport, LA). Toronto (AL), 1999–. Remarks: Through 2004, has obtained 581 hits (81 homers) and 28 stolen bases in 511 games; led AL in doubles, 2003; also played for St. Catherine's (New York-Penn League), 1997, Hagerstown (South Atlantic League) and Sydney (Australian Baseball League), 1998, and Knoxville (SL) and Syracuse (IL), 1999.

56013. Kuenster, John. "Jays' Carlos Delgado, Vernon Wells Destined to Join Majors RBI Elite?" *Baseball Digest,* LXII (September 2003), 19, 21–23.

Willie James ("The Devil") Wells★

SS-2B-3B-MGR. (B: Aug. 10, 1905, Austin, TX–D: Jan. 22, 1989). San Antonio Black Aces, 1923; St. Louis Stars (1924–1931; Detroit Wolves, Homestead Grays, and Kansas City Monarchs, 1932; Cole's American Giants, 1933–1934; Kansas City Monarchs, 1934; Cole's American Giants, 1935; Newark Eagles, 1936–1939; Vera Cruz (Mexican League), 1940–1941; Newark Eagles, 1942; Tampico and Mexico City (Mexican League), 1943–1944; Chicago American Giants and Memphis Red Sox, 1944; New York Black Giants, 1945–1946; Baltimore Elite Giants, 1946; Indianapolis Clowns, 1947; Memphis Red Sox, 1948; Winnipeg (Canadian Leagues), 1949–1953; Birmingham Black Barons, 1954 Remarks: had lifetime .334 batting average, with reputation as best shortstop in Black baseball; elected to National Baseball Hall of Fame in 1995, where his plaque reads: "Combined superior batting skills, slick fielding and speed on the bases to become an eight-time All-Star in the Negro Leagues. A power hitting shortstop with great hands, ranks among the all-time Negro League leaders in doubles, triples, home runs and stolen bases. Played on three pennant-winning teams with the St. Louis Stars, one with the Chicago American Giants and one with the Newark Eagles. Overall he played for many Negro League clubs with stints in the Canadian, Mexican, and Cuban leagues. Player-manager in the Negro Leagues as well."

56014. Fleitz, David L. "Willie Wells." In: his *Ghosts in the Gallery at Cooperstown: Sixteen Little-Known Members of the Hall of Fame.* Jefferson, NC: McFarland & Co., Inc., 2004. Pp. 189–201.

56015. Holway, John B. "The Black Cal Ripken: Willie Wells." *Sports Collector's Digest,* XXIV (April 18, 1997), 134+.

56016. _____. "Willie Wells." In: his *Voices from the Great Black Baseball Leagues.* New York: Da Capo Press, 1992. Pp. 218–230.

56017. _____. "Willie Wells: A Devil of a Shortstop." *The Baseball Research Journal,* XVIII (1988), 50–54.

56018. Riley, James A. "The Devil." In: his *Dandy, Day and The Devil.* Cocoa, fl: TK Publishers, 1987. Pp. 103–146. Wells, Ray Dandridge, and Leon Day.

56019. Ruck, Robert L. "Willie 'El Diablo' Wells." In: Vol. Q-Z of David L. Porter, ed. *Biographical Dictionary of American Sports: Baseball.* Rev. and enlarged ed. Westport, CT: Greenwood Press, 2000. Pp. 1648–1649.

Steven John ("Turk") Wendell

P. (B: May 19, 1957, Pittsfield, MA). Chicago (NL), 1993–1997; New York (NL), 1997–2001; Philadelphia (NL), 2002–2003; Colorado (NL), 2004; Houston (NL), 2005-. Remarks: Through 2004, has won 36 games and lost 33, with 33 "saves"; won one game in both the 1999 and 2000 NLCS, but lost one game of 2000 World Series.

56020. Jordan, Pat. "What Makes Turk Tick?" *The New York Times Magazine,* (August 8, 1993), 36–39.

56021. Shannon, Mike. "Turk Wendell." In: his *Tales from the Ballpark: More of the Greatest True Baseball Stories Ever Told.* Lincolnwood, IL: Contemporary Books, 1999. Pp. 218–221.

Turk Wendell *see* **Steven John ("Turk") Wendell**

Harry Hunter Wendelstedt, Jr.

UMP. (B: July 27, 1938, Baltimore, MD). NL arbiter, 1966–1998; called four All-Star Games, five World Series, and first NLCS; most controversial call occurred during a Dodgers-Giants game on May 30, 1968, involving a pitch by Don Drysdale (q.v.); first president of Major League Umpires Association, 1970–1974; acquired Al Somers Umpire School in 1977, renaming it the Harry Wendelstedt School for Umpires.

56022. Allen, Maury. "Harry Wendelstedt." In: his *Baseball: The Lives Behind the Seams.* New York: Macmillan, 1990. Pp. 159–166.

56023. Gerlach, Larry R. "Harry Hunter Wendelstedt, Jr." In: Vol. Q-Z of David L. Porter, ed. *Biographical Dictionary of American Sports: Baseball.* Rev. and enlarged ed. Westport, CT: Greenwood Press, 2000. Pp. 1649–1650.

56024. "Harry Wendelstedt: 27 Year National League Umpire, Crew Chief." *Referee,* XVIII (August 1993), 72+.

56025. Krause, Steve. "He Touched All the Bases: Former NL Umpire Harry Wendelstedt." *Referee,* XXV (June 2000), 36–40.

56026. Mulvoy, Mark. "The Giants Find It Tough." *Sports Illustrated,* XXVI (June 10, 1968), 28–31.

56027. Wendelstedt, Harry. "Interview." *Referee,* X (May 1985), 16–19.

Bill Werber *see* **William Murray ("Bill") Werber**

William Murray ("Bill") Werber

38. (B: June 20, 1908, Berwyn, MD). New York (AL),

1930 and 1933; Boston (AL), 1933–1936; Philadelphia (AL), 1937–1938; Cincinnati (NL), 1939–1941; New York (NL), 1942. Remarks: Obtained 1,363 hits (78 homers) and 215 stolen bases in 1,295 games in an 11-year major league career; NL stolen base champion, 1934–1935, 1937 (tie); first to hit four consecutive doubles in one AL game, July 17, 1935, and in one NL contest, May 13, 1940, remaining only player to do so in both leagues; first MLB player to bat in a televised game, Aug. 26, 1939; insurance company owner, Hyattsburg, MD, 1942–1972, who was also the first All-American basketball player at Duke University.

56028. Graber, Ralph S. "William Murray 'Bill' Werber." In: Vol. Q–Z of David L. Porter, ed. *Biographical Dictionary of American Sports: Baseball.* Rev. and enlarged ed. Westport, CT: Greenwood Press, 2000. Pp. 1650–1652.

56029. Honig, Donald. "Bill Werber." In: his *Baseball Between the Lines: Baseball in the Forties And Fifties as Told By the Men Who Played It.* New York: Coward, McCann & Geoghegan, Inc., 1976. Pp. 134–144.

56030. Kelley, Brent P. "Bill Werber: The Reds' Winning Edge." *Sports Collector's Digest,* XXI (June 17, 1994), 184–187.

56031. _____. "Bill Werber: Tiger, 1930–1942." In: his *In the Shadow of the Babe: Baseball Players Who Played with or Against Babe Ruth.* Jefferson, NC: McFarland & Co., Inc., 1995. Pp. 101–218.

56032. Langford, Walter. "Bill Werber: Star of Another Era." *Baseball Digest,* XLVIII (March 1989), 77–84.

56033. Macht, Norman. "Bill Weber Recalls How It was in the 1930s." *Baseball Digest,* XLVI (November 1987), 87–89.

56034. Rathgeber, Bob. "A First-Class Player on Third: Bill Werber." In: his *Cincinnati Reds Scrapbook.* Virginia Beach, VA: J.C.P. Corp. of Virginia, 1982. Pp. 94–95.

56035. Werber, William M. *Circling the Bases.* N.p.: Priv. print., 1978. 214p. A Duke University English graduate, Werber did not employ a ghost writer to pen these recollections.

56036. _____. *Memories of a Ballplayer: Bill Werber and Baseball in the 1930s.* Cleveland, OH: The Society for American Baseball Research, 2001. 170p.

56037. _____. with Harold Parrott. "A Ballplayer Boos Back." *Saturday Evening Post,* CCXV (July 25, 1942), 23+.

56038. Westcott, Rich. "Bill Werber: Good Field, Good Hit Star of the 1930s." In: his *Masters of the Diamond: Interviews with Players Who Began Their Careers More Than 50 Years Ago.* Jefferson, NC: McFarland & Co., Inc., 1994. Pp. 159–169.

56039. Wilson, Nick. "Bill Werber." In: his *Voices from the Pastime: Oral Histories of Surviving Major Leaguers, Negro Leaguers, Cuban Leaguers, and Writers, 1920–1934.* Jefferson, NC: McFarland & Co., Inc., 2000. Pp. 99–103.

Percival Wheritt ("Perry" or "Moose") Werden

P-1B-UMP. (B: July 21, 1865, St. Louis, MO-D: Jan. 9, 1934). St. Louis (U.), 1884; Washington (NL), 1888; Toledo (AA), 1890; Baltimore (AA), 1891; St. Louis (NL), 1892–1893; Louisville (NL), 1897. Remarks: Won 12 games and lost one In 1884; career batting marks included 773 hits (26 homers) and 150 stolen bases in 893 games for five different big league teams in seven years; with Minneapolis (WL) in 1894–1895, hit 42 and 45 homers, respectively, becoming the only pro player to hit more than 29 in a year prior to 1921; minor league player, 1898–1906; minor league umpire (1907, 1913–1914, 1920–1922), coach (1908), and manager.

56040. Davids, L. Robert. "Percival Wherrit Werden." In: *Nineteenth Century Stars.* Kansas City, MO: Society for American Baseball Research, 1989. Pp. 133–134.

56041. Nemec, Raymond J. "The Performance and Personality of Perry Werden." *The Baseball Research Journal,* VI (1977), 127–131.

56042. Smith, James D., 3rd. "Percival Wherrit 'Perry,' 'Moose' Werden." In: Vol. Q–Z of David L. Porter, ed. *Biographical Dictionary of American Sports: Baseball.* Rev. and enlarged ed. Westport, CT: Greenwood Press, 2000. Pp. 1652–1653.

Perry Werden see **Percival Wheritt ("Perry" or "Moose") Werden**

Bill Werle see **William George ("Bill" or "Bugs") Werle**

William George ("Bill" or "Bugs") Werle

P. (B: Dec. 21, 1920, Oakland, CA). Pittsburgh (NL), 1949–1952; St. Louis (NL), 1952; Boston (AL), 1953–1954. Remarks: Obtained 29 victories, 39 losses, and 15 "saves" in five big league seasons; had played for San Francisco (PCL), 1943–1948 and later returned to the PCL, before becoming West Coast scout, Cleveland (AL), 1964-.

56043. Kelley, Brent P. "Bill Werle." In: his *The San Francisco Seals, 1946–1957: Interviews with 25 Former Baseballers.* Jefferson, NC: McFarland & Co., Inc., 2002. Pp. 85–98.

56044. Swank, Bill. "Bill Werle." In: his *Echoes from Lane Field: A History of the San Diego Padres 1936–1957.* Paducah, KY: Turner Publishing Company, 1997. Pp. 155–156.

Victor Woodrow ("Vic") Wertz

OF-1B. (B: Feb. 9, 1925, York, PA-D: July, 7, 1983). Detroit (A.L), 1941–1952; St. Louis (AL) and Baltimore (AL), 1952–1954; Cleveland (AL), 1954–1958; Boston (AL), 1959–1961; Detroit (AL), 1961–1963; Minnesota (AL), 1963. Remarks: Had 1,602 hits (266 homers) and nine stolen bases in 1,862 games in 17 campaigns; hit seven home runs in five consecutive games, July 27-Aug. 1, 1950; homered in 1951 All-Star Game; remembered as Indians player who hit the long drive in Game One of the 1954 World Series at the Polo Grounds that Willie Mays (q.v.) caught over his shoulder; had record-tying four doubles in one game, Sept. 26, 1956; had three grand slam homers, Aug. 14, 1959 and May 10 and Aug. 25, 1960.

56045. Buege, Bob. "Only in the Polo Grounds." *Old-tyme Baseball News,* III, no. 6 (1991), 14–15.

56046. Johnson, George. "Browns Hope for Wertz." *Complete Baseball,* V (September 1963- 30–31+.

56047. Klawans, Harold L. "A Break in the Action: Willie Mays, Vic Wertz, and Eddie Gaedel." In: his *Why Michael Couldn't Hit and Other Tales of the Neurology of Sports.* New York: W.H. Freeman, 1996. Chpt. 13.

56048. Lebovitz, Hal. "Vic Wertz Finds Out: Everybody Loves a Hero." *Sport,* XVIII (March 1955), 28–29.

56049. Newcombe, Jack. "Vic Wertz." In: Bruce Jacobs, ed. *Baseball Stars of 1958.* New York: Lion Books, 1958. Pp. 130–136.

56050. Skipper, James K., Jr. "Victor Woodrow 'Vic' Wertz." In: Vol. Q–Z of David L. Porter, ed. *Biographical Dictionary of American Sports: Baseball.* Rev. and enlarged ed. Westport, CT: Greenwood Press, 2000. Pp. 1653–1654.

56051. Smith, Lyall. "Tiger Tune Has New Wertz." *Baseball Digest,* VI (November 1947), 25–27.

56052. _____. "Wertz is a Workhorse." *Sport,* IX (September 1950), 22–25.

56053. Stern, Chris. "Vic Wertz." In: his *Where Have They Gone?* New York: Tempo, 1979. Pp. 168–171.

56054. Woody, Clay. "World Series Flashback 1: A Difference of 200 Feet Highlighted '54 Fall Classic." *Baseball Digest,* LI (October 1992), 24–30.

Joe West *see* **Joseph Henry ("Joe") West**

Joseph Henry ("Joe") West

UMP. (B: Oct. 31, 1952, Asheville, NC). Remarks: Umpired in Western Carolinas League, 1974; florida Instructional League, 1974–1976; Carolina League, 1975–1976; Southern League, 1976); American Association, 1976–1977; and Puerto Rican League; 1977; NL umpire, 1978–; country-western singer who has performed at the *Grand Ole Opry;* has patented hard shell chest protector for umpires; played an umpire in the motion picture *The Naked Gun;* named to South Atlantic League Hall of Fame, 2002.

56055. McCallum, Jack. "Eye in the Sky." *Sports Illustrated,* LXXIX (November 1, 1993), 13–14.

Max Edward West

OF. (B: Nov. 28, 1916, Dexter, MO-D: Dec. 31, 2003). Boston (NL), 1938–1942, 1946; Cincinnati (NL) and Pittsburgh (NL), 1948. Remarks: Had 681 hits (77 homers) and 19 stolen bases in 824 games in seven big league seasons; homered in 1940 All-Star Game; walked five times in one game, April 25, 1948; also played for San Diego (PCL), 1947, 1949–1950, hitting 43, 48, and 33 homers for the team in those three years, respectively, and Los Angeles (PCL), 1952–1954; named to Pacific Coast League Hall of Fame, 2002.

56056. Spalding, John E. "Max West." In: his *Pacific Coast League Stars: One Hundred of the Best, 1903–1957.* San Jose, CA: John E. Spalding, 1994. Pp. 108–109.

56057. Swank, Bill. "Max West." In: his *Echoes from Lane Field: A History of the San Diego Padres 1936–1957.* Paducah, KY: Turner Publishing Company, 1997. Pp. 79–80.

Samuel Filmore ("Sammy") West

OF. (B: Oct. 5, 1904, Longview, TX-D: Nov. 23, 1985). Washington (AL), 19271932; St. Louis (AL), 1933–1938; Washington (AL), 1938–1941; Chicago (AL), 1942. Remarks. Obtained 1,938 hits (75 homers) and 53 stolen bases in 1,753 games in 18 seasons; had six hits in one game, April 13, 1933; coach, Washington (AL), 1947–1949.

56058. Blaisdell, Lowell L. "Samuel Filmore 'Sammy' West." In: Vol. Q-Z of David L. Porter, ed. *Biographical Dictionary of American Sports: Baseball.* Rev. and enlarged ed. Westport, CT: Greenwood Press, 2000. Pp. 1654–1655.

56059. Bloodgood, Clifford. "Sammy West of the Hustling Washington Club." *Baseball Magazine,* XLIX (August 1932), 394–396.

56060. Green, Paul M. "Baseball and Sammy West." *Sports Collector's Digest,* XI (May 11, 1994), 82+.

56061. West, Sammy. "Instruction in Outfielding." *Baseball Magazine,* LXI (August 1938), 412–413.

James Patrick ("Jim") Westlake

1B. (B: July 3, 1930, Sacramento, CA-D: January 3, 2003). Salt Lake City (Pioneer League), 1948–1949; San Francisco (PCL), 1949–1950, 1954; Philadelphia (NL) and Syracuse (IL), 1955; Miami (IL) and Sacramento (PCL), 1956; Sacramento (PCL), 1957–1958; Portland (PCL), 1959. Remarks: In nine minor league seasons, obtained 1,076 hits and 39 homers in 1,172 games; appeared in one Phillies game; later worked half a century as a paper company salesman; brother of Wally Westlake (below).

56062. Kelley, Brent P. "Jim Westlake." In: his *The San Francisco Seals, 1946–1957: Interviews with 25 Former Baseballers.* Jefferson, NC: McFarland & Co., Inc., 2002. Pp. 195–200.

Waldon Thomas ("Wally") Westlake

OF. (B: Nov. 8, 1920, Gridley, CA). Pittsburgh (NL), 1947–1951; St. Louis (NL), 1951–1952; Cincinnati (NL), 1952; Cleveland (AL), 1952–1955. Remarks: Had 848 hits (127 homers) and 19 stolen bases in 958 games in nine big league seasons; also played for Oakland Oaks (PCL), 1941, 1946; hit for the cycle twice, July 30, 1948 and June 14, 1948; brother of Jim Westlake (above).

56063. Dudley, Bruce. "The Day The Indians Pocketed a Pennant." *The National Pastime,* XIV (1994), 72–73.

56064. Fehler, Gene. "Wally Westlake." In: his *Tales from Baseball's Golden Age.* Champaign, IL: Sports Publishing Co., 2000. Chpt. 53.

56065. Silverman, Al. "Westlake Packs a Wallop." *Sport,* XI (October 1951), 20–23.

Wesley Noreen ("Wes") Westrum

C-MGR. (B: Nov. 28, 1922, Clearbrook, MN-D: May 28, 2002). New York (NL), 1947–1957. Remarks: Had 503 hits (96 homers) and 10 stolen bases in 919 games in 11 seasons; coach, San Francisco (NL), 1958–1963, 1968–1973; involved in only MLB trade of coaches, going to New York (NL) in 1964 for Cookie Lavagetto (q.v.); manager, New York. (NL), 1965–1967 and San Francisco (NL), 1974–1975, winning 260 games and losing 366 (.415); died a cancer victim.

56066. Bitker, Steve. "Wes Westrum." In: his *The Original San Francisco Giants: The Giants of '58.* Champaign, IL: Sports Publishing, Inc., 1998. Pp. 236–239.

56067. Clausen, C. L. "From Small Town to Big Leagues: Clearbrook, Minnesota's Wes Westrum." *Minneapolis Review of Baseball,* V (April 1985), 6–8.

56068. Crocker, Mike. "From Coughan's Bluff to Clearbook." In: *Minneapolis Loons 1994 Souvenir Program — Inaugural Season.* Minneapolis, MN: Minneapolis Loons, 1994. Pp. 18–21. Wes Westrum Baseball Museum.

56069. Dexter, Charles. "Westrum: The Giant Viking." *Baseball Digest,* XI (July 1952), 27–31.

56070. Kelley, Brent. "Wes Westrum New York's Other Catcher." *Vintage & Classic Baseball Collector,* no. 6 (May 1996), 26–27.

56071. Mayer, Bob. "Turn Back the Clock: Former Catcher Wes Westrum Recalls Career with Giants." *Baseball Digest,* LX (November 2001), 82–87.

56072. McCulley, Jim. "Giants Go West-rum." *Baseball Digest,* IX (September 1950), 57–59.

56073. _____. "The Receiver (Wes Westrum)." In: his *The Incredible Giants.* New York: A.S. Barnes, 1955. Pp. 138–150.

56074. _____. "Westrum — Robot with a Brain." *Baseball Digest,* XIV (June 1965), 23–29.

56075. Smith, Ken. "A Pitcher's Catcher." *Baseball Magazine,* LXXXVI (May 1961), 411–413.

John Karl Wetteland

P. (B: August 21, 1966, San Mateo, CA). Los Angeles (NL), 1989–1991; Montreal (NL), 1992–1994; New York (AL), 1995–1996; Texas (AL), 1997–2000. Remarks: In 12 years, had 48 victories, 45 defeats, and 330 "saves"; saved four games in 1996 World Series; World Series MVP Award, 1996.

56076. Farber, Michael. "Going to Extremes." *Sports Illustrated,* LXXXI (July 4, 1994), 44–48+.

Lee H. Weyer

UMP. (B: 1937-D: July 4, 1988). Remarks: N. L. arbiter, 1961, 1963–1988; died of heart attack.

56077. Barber, F. "Remembering Lee." *Referee,* XIV (May 1989), 28–33. NL ump.

August ("Gus" or "Cannonball") Weyhing

P. (B: Sept. 29, 1866, Louisville, KY-D: Sept. 4, 1955).

Philadelphia (AA), 1887–1888; Brooklyn (P), 1890; Philadelphia (AA), 1891; Philadelphia (NL), 1892–1895; Pittsburgh (NL), 1895; Louisville (NL), 1895–1896; Washington (NL), 1898–1899; St. Louis (NL) and Brooklyn (NL), 1900; Cleveland (AL) and Cincinnati (NL), 1901. Remarks: Won 266 games and lost 229, with four "saves," in 13 years; also hurled for Grand Rapids (WL), 1901 and Memphis (SL), Atlanta (SL), and Little Rock (SL), 1902–1903; manager, Tulsa (TL), 1910.

56078. Olmsted, Frank J. "August 'Gus,' 'Cannonball' Weyhing." In: Vol. Q-Z of David L. Porter, ed. *Biographical Dictionary of American Sports: Baseball.* Rev. and enlarged ed. Westport, CT: Greenwood Press, 2000. Pp. 1655–1656.

Zacharlah Davis ("Zack" or "Buck") Wheat★
OF. (B: May 23, 1888, Hamilton, MO–D: March 11, 1972). Brooklyn (NL), 19091926; Philadelphia (AL), 1927. Remarks: In a 19-year major league career, had 2,884 hits (132 homers) and 205 stolen bases in 2,410 games; NL batting champion, 1918; had 26-game hitting streak, July 11–Aug. 7, 1918; still holds several Dodger records; also played for Minneapolis (AA), 1928; Kansas City (MO) police officer, 1930–1936; fishing camp operator, Versailles (MO), 1936–1951; named to Missouri Sports Hall of Fame, 1958; elected to National Baseball Hall of Fame in 1959, where his plaque reads: "Brooklyn outfielder for 18 years. Holds Brooklyn records for-games played 2,318, at bat 8,859, hits 2,804, singles 2,038, doubles 464, triples 171, total bases 4,003, extra base hits 766. Batted .375 (1923), .375 (1924), .359 (1925) league batting leader, .335 (1918). Lifetime batting average .317 with 2,884 hits. Played 2,406 games."

56079. Allen, Lee, and Thomas Meany. "Zack Wheat." In: their *Kings of the Diamond.* New York: G.P. Putnam, 1965. Pp. 168–170.

56080. Bergen, Phil. "Wheat in the Chaff." *The Baseball Research Journal,* XIV (1985), 61–62.

56081. Graham, Frank. "Only Thing Zack Wheat Didn't Have Was Color." *Baseball Digest,* XXIV (March 1965), 89–91.

56082. McClure, Arthur F. "Zach Wheat." In: John A. Garrity and Marsh C. Carries, eds. *American National Biography.* 24 vols. New York: Oxford University Press, 1999. XXIII, 120–121.

56083. _____. "Zachariah Davis 'Zach,' 'Buck' Wheat." In: Vol. Q-Z of David L. Porter, ed. *Biographical Dictionary of American Sports: Baseball.* Rev. and enlarged ed. Westport, CT: Greenwood Press, 2000. Pp. 1656–1657.

56084. Murphy, Charles W. "When Zack Wheat Was Called a Lemon." *Baseball Magazine,* XXV (August 1920), 436–437.

56085. Ward, John J. "The Brooklyn Clean-Up Slugger." *Baseball Magazine,* XV (July 1915), 47–52.

56086. _____. "Old Zack Wheat's Slugging Spree." *Baseball Magazine,* XXXI (August 1923), 401–402.

56087. Wheat, Zach. "Hitting in the Pinch." *Baseball Magazine,* XXXVII (September 1926), 457–458.

56088. _____. "The Strain of Breaking a Record." *Baseball Magazine,* XXII (March 1919), 279–280.

56089. _____. "A Veteran's Best Season." *Baseball Magazine,* XXXII (April 1924), 495–496.

56090. "Zack Wheat Most Graceful of Outfielders." *Baseball Magazine,* XVIII (January 1917), 49–51.

Louis Rodman ("Lou" or "Sweet Lou") Whitaker, Jr.
2B. (B: May 12, 1957, Brooklyn, NY). Detroit (AL), 1977–1995. Remarks. Had 2,369 hits (244 homers) and 143 stolen bases in 2,390 games in 19 big league seasons; AL Rookie of the Year award, 1978; had inside-the-park homer, July 13, 1984; had two hits in the 1984 ALCS and three in the 1987 ALCS (one a homer, in Game Two), plus five hits (two doubles) in the 1984 World Series; had a grand slam homer and seven RBIs in one game, May 4, 1994; also played for Lakeland (florida State League), 1975 and Montgomery (SL), 1976; special coach, Detroit (AL), 2003-.

56091. Appleton, Sheldon L. "Louis Rodman 'Sweet Lou' Whitaker, Jr." In: Vol. Q-Z of David L. Porter, ed. *Biographical Dictionary of American Sports: Baseball.* Rev. and enlarged ed. Westport, CT: Greenwood Press, 2000. Pp. 1657–1658.

56092. Goldberg, Robert. "The Teeth of the Tigers." *Sport,* LXXV (July 1984), 64–65+.

56093. Green, Jerry. "Prized Rookie Combo: Trammel and Whitaker." *Baseball Digest,* XXVII (November 1978), 60–61.

56094. Hammer, Lloyd. "Inside Lou Whitaker – the Diamond's Reluctant Superstar." *Sports World,* XXIII (August 1994), 25–26.

56095. Honig, Donald. "1978: Lou Whitaker." In: his *American League Rookies of the Year.* New York: Bantam Books, 1989. Pp. 77–80.

56097. Koenig, Bill. "Like Uncle, Like Nephew." *USA Today Baseball Weekly,* II (July 1, 1992), 20–21. Lou Whitaker and his nephew, Jeff, a minor leaguer with the Burlington Indians (Appalachian League).

56098. Shook, Richard. "Second Look: Lou Whitaker." *Beckett Baseball Card Monthly,* X, no. 93 (March 1993), 97–98.

Bill White *see* **William Dekova ("Bill") White**
Chaney ("Reindeer") White
OF. (B: Dallas, TX–D: 1965). Hilldale Daisies, 1919–1922, 1928, 1930–1932); Atlantic City Bacharach Giants, 1923–1929; Philadelphia Stars, 1933–1935; Baltimore Black Sox, 1932; New York Cubans, 1936. Remarks: Obtained .302 lifetime Negro Leagues batting average; noted for his speed and agility.

56099. Riley, James A. "Chaney 'Reindeer' White." In: Vol. Q-Z of David L. Porter, ed. *Biographical Dictionary of American Sports: Baseball.* Rev. and enlarged ed. Westport, CT: Greenwood Press, 2000. Pp. 1658–1659.

Charles ("Charlie") White
C-3B. (B: Aug. 12, 1928, Kingston, NC). Philadelphia Stars, 1950; Toronto (I.L), 1951–1952; San Antonio (IL), 1953; Milwaukee (NL), 1954–1955; Wichita (AA), 1956; Vancouver (PCL), 1957–1961, 1965; Hawaii (PCL), 1962–1963. Remarks: Career minor leaguer who began in the Negro leagues and enjoyed two major league seasons, during which he had 29 hits, including a home run.

56100. Moffi, Larry and Jonathan Kronstadt. "Charles ('Charlie') White." In: their *Crossing the Line: Black Major Leaguers, 1947–1959.* Jefferson, NC: McFarland & Co., Inc., 1994. Pp. 123–124.

Deacon White *see* **James Laurie ("Deacon") White**
Devon Markes White
OF. (B: Dec. 29, 1962, Kingston, Jamaica). California (AL), 1985–1991; Toronto (AL), 1991–1995; florida (NL), 1996–1997; Arizona (NL), 1998; Los Angeles (NL), 1999–2000. Remarks: Had 1,826 hits (194 homers) and 328 stolen bases in 1,815 games in 16 seasons; stole three bases (including home) in one inning, Sept. 9, 1989; had two grand slam homers in one week, May 10 and May 15, 2001; had 11 career grand slam homers; also played for Edmonton (PCL), 1986.

56101. Doll, M. "Devon White." *Sports Illustrated,* LXVII (July 13, 1987), 44+.

56102. Fainaru, Steve. "Devon White: A 'Classic Glove' in Center Field." *Baseball Digest, LI* (March 1992), 29–30.

56103. Kuenster, John. "Devon White's Catch a Turning Point in '92 World Series." *Baseball Digest, LII* (February 1993), 15–17.

56104. Porter, David L. "Devon Markes White." In: Vol. Q-Z of David L. Porter, ed. *Biographical Dictionary of American Sports: Baseball.* Rev. and enlarged ed. Westport, CT: Greenwood Press, 2000. Pp. 1659–1660.

56105. Toll, Matthew. "Devon White." *Sports Illustrated, LXVII* (July 13, 1987), 44–45.

Doc White *see* **Guy Harris ("Doc") White**

Ernest Daniel ("Ernie") White

P. (B: Sept. 5, 1916, Pacolet Mills, SC-D: May 22, 1974). St. Louis (NL), 1940–1943; Boston (NL), 1946–1948. Remarks: Had 30 victories, 21 defeats, and six "saves" in his seven-year big league career; won Game One of 1942 World Series.

56106. McConnell, Mickey. "The Pitcher's Fielding and Pickoff Moves." *Scholastic Coach,* XXXIV (April 1965), 62–66. Demonstrated by White.

Frank ("Academy Frank") White, Jr.

2B-SS. (B: Sept. 4, 1950, Greenville, MS). Kansas City (AL), 1973–1990. Remarks: Kansas City Baseball Academy graduate had 2,006 hits (160 homers) and 178 stolen bases in 2,324 games in 18 campaigns; hit for the cycle twice, Sept. 26, 1979 and Aug. 3, 1982; had six hits (one double and one homer) in 1980 ALCS; ALCS MVP award, 1980; had five hits in 1985 ALCS and seven hits (three doubles and a homer) in 1985 World Series; minor league manager, Boston (AL), 1991–1993; coach, Boston (AL), 1994–1996; named to Missouri Sports Hall of Fame, 1994; coach, Boston (AL), 1994–1996, Kansas City (AL), 1998–2001; manager, Wichita (TL), 2002-.

56107. Giffner, Michael. "Frank White: He Plays a Royal Second Base." *Baseball Digest,* XL (December 1981), 88–91.

56108. Nash, Bruce and Allan Zullo. "Frank White." In: their *More Little Big Leaguers: Amazing Boyhood Stories of Today's Baseball Stars.* New York: Little Simon, 1991. Pp. 28–29.

56109. Olmsted, Frank J. "Frank White, Jr." In: Vol. Q-Z of David L. Porter, ed. *Biographical Dictionary of American Sports: Baseball.* Rev. and enlarged ed. Westport, CT: Greenwood Press, 2000. Pp. 1660–1661.

56110. White, Frank, as told to Al Doyle. "The Game I'll Never Forget." *Baseball Digest,* LXII (May 2003), 58–53. Game 6, '85 World Series.

56111. _____., as told to George Vass. "The Game I'll Never Forget." *Baseball Digest,* XLVI (July 1987), 61–64.

56112. _____., with Matt Fulks. *Good as Gold: Techniques for Fundamental Baseball.* Chicago, IL: Sports Publishing, 2004. 162p.

Frederick ("Fred") White

BROADCASTER. Remarks: Broadcaster, Kansas City (AL), 1973–1998.

56113. Matthews, Denny, Fred White, and Matt Fulks. *Play by Play: 25 Years of Royals on Radio.* Lenexa and Kansas City, MO: Addax Pub. Group, dist. by Andrews McMeel Pub., 1999. 223p.

Guy Harris ("Doc") White

P. (B: April 9, 1879, Washington, DC-D: Feb. 17, 1969). Philadelphia (NL), 1901–1902; Chicago (AL), 1903–1913. Remarks: Had 189 victories, 156 defeats, and six "saves" in 13 years, pitched five shutouts in 19 days, Sept. 12–30, 1904; dental surgery graduate of Georgetown University (1902); gave up dentistry in 1906 to enter vaudeville;

owner, Dallas (TL), 1917–1918 and Waco (TL), 1919; later became college and high school coach in Washington, DC and traveling evangelist.

56114. Fuchs, Bill. "Why Doc White Jumped NL for $3,500." *Baseball Digest* XI (June 1962), 75–77.

56115. Grayson, Harry. "Remember Doc White?" *Baseball Digest,* II (November 1943), 39–41.

56116. Hilton, George W. "Guy Harris 'Doc' White." In: Vol. Q-Z of David L. Porter, ed. *Biographical Dictionary of American Sports: Baseball.* Rev. and enlarged ed. Westport, CT: Greenwood Press, 2000. Pp. 1661–1662.

56117. Smith, Ira L. "Guy Harris ('Doc') White." In: his *Baseball's Famous Pitchers.* New York: A.S. Barnes, 1954. Pp. 64–69.

James Laurie ("Deacon") White

3B-C-1B-OF-MGR. (B. Dec. 7, 1847, Caton, NY-D: July 7, 1939.). Chicago (NL), 1876; Boston (NL), 1877; Cincinnati (NL), 1878–1880; Buffalo (NL), 1881–1885; Detroit (NL), 1886–1888; Pittsburgh (NL), 1889; Buffalo, (P.), 1890. Remarks: Had 1,619 hits (18 homers) in 1,299 games in 15 seasons; interim manager, Cincinnati (NL), 1879, winning eight games and losing eight (.500); NL batting champion, 1877; first catcher to play his position directly behind the batter.

56118. Overfield, Joseph M. "James 'Deacon' White." *The Baseball Research Journal,* IV (1975), 1–11. A condensed bio appears in SABR's *Nineteenth Century Stars* (Kansas City, MO: Society for American Baseball Research, 1989), p. 135 and then in Vol. Q-Z of David L. Porter, ed. *Biographical Dictionary of American Sports: Baseball.* (Rev. and enlarged ed.; Westport, CT: Greenwood Press, 2000), pp. 1662–1664.

Joyner Michael ("Mike") White

OF-2B. (B: Dec. 18, 1938, Detroit, MI). Houston (NL), 1963–1965. Remarks: Had 78 hits in 100 games in three seasons.

56119. Thomy, Al. "Mike White: In a World of New York Cuts." *Baseball Digest,* XXIII (September 1964), 52–55.

Mike White *see* **Joyner Michael ("Mike") White**

Reindeer White *see* **Chaney ("Reindeer") White**

Rondell Bernard White

OF. (B: Feb. 23, 1972, Milledgeville, GA). Montreal (NL), 1993–2000; Chicago (AL), 2000–2001; New York (AL), 2002; San Diego (NL) and Kansas City (AL), 2003; Detroit (AL), 2004-. Remarks: Through 2004, has had 1,300 hits (175 homers) and 92 stolen bases in 1,240 games; had 16-game hitting streak, May–June 2003.

56120. Bianchine, Jim. "Building a Foundation." *Baseball Digest,* LIX (August 2000), 70–73.

56121. Zachotsky, Dan. "Rondell White." In: his *Idols of the Spring: Baseball Interviews About Spring Training.* Jefferson, NC: McFarland & Co., Inc., 2001. Pp. 181–185.

Roy Hilton White

OF. (B: Dec. 27, 1943, Los Angeles, CA). New York (AL), 1965–1979; Yorimuri Giants (Japan League), 1980–1982. Remarks: Obtained 1,803 hits (100 homers) and 232 stolen bases in 1,981 games in 15 U.S. big league seasons; hit home runs from both sides of the plate in the same game five times; had switch hit triples in a game, Sept. 8, 1970; led AL in walks, 1972; in 1975 fielded 1.000, becoming the first Yankee to play an errorless season; had five hits (three doubles) and walked five times in 1976 ALCS; had five hits (one homer) in 1978 ALCS and eight hits (one homer) in the 1978 World Series; coach, New York (AL), 1983–1984, 1986; minor league instructor, New York (AL), 1985, 1987–1998; coach, Sacramento (PCL), 1999–2003; elected to New Jersey Sports Hall of Fame.

56122. Devaney, John. "Roy White" In: his *Where Are They Today? Great Sports Stars of Yesteryear.* New York: Crown Publishers, 1985. Pp. 197–200.

56123. ____. "The Yankees Have a Cleanup Hitter Who Chokes the Bat!" *Sport,* LI (May 1971), 76–80.

56124. Dexter, Charles. "White's Clutch Hits Count for Yanks" *Baseball Digest,* XXVII (December 1969), 45–49.

56125. Gallagher, Mark. "Roy White." In: his *50 Years of Yankee All-Stars.* New York: Leisure Press, 1984. Pp. 210–212.

56126. Klein, Dave. "Roy White." In: his *On the Way Up: What Its Like in the Minor Leagues.* New York: Julian Messner, 1977. Pp. 37–47.

56127. Klein, Moss. "The Dependable Yankee." *Baseball Digest,* XXXV (June 1976), 32–35.

56128. ____. "A Special Kind of Yankee." *Baseball Digest,* XXXVIII (April 1979), 52–55

56129. Kleinknecht, Merl F. "Roy Hilton White." In: Vol. Q–Z of David L. Porter, ed. *Biographical Dictionary of American Sports: Baseball.* Rev. and enlarged ed. Westport, CT: Greenwood Press, 2000. Pp. 1665–1666.

56130. Pepe, Phil. "Look Who's Among the All-Time Yankee Greats." *Black Sports,* VI (December 1976), 29–31.

56131. White, Roy, as told to George Vass. "The Game I'll Never Forget." *Baseball Digest,* XLVI (March 1987), 84–87.

Samuel Charles ("Sammy") White

C. (B: July 7, 1928, Wenatchee, WA–D: Aug. 5, 1991). Boston (AL), 1951–1959; Milwaukee (NL), 1961; Philadelphia (NL), 1962. Remarks. Had 916 hits (66 homers) and 14 stolen bases in 1,043 games in an 11-year big league career; only 20th-century player to score three runs in one inning, June 18, 1953; honored with membership in the State of Washington Sports Hall of Fame.

56132. Dexter, Charles. "Red Sox Get a Dash of White." *Baseball Digest,* XI (September 1952), 61–64.

56133. Hern, Gerry. "The Pepper Pot (Sammy White)." In: his *The Boston Red Sox.* New York: A.S. Barnes, 1956. Pp. 61–72.

56134. ____. "Sammy White: The Most Unlikely Catcher." *Baseball Digest,* XV (October 1956), 71–77.

56135. Newcombe, Jack. "Boston's Cocky Catcher." *Sport,* XX (August 1955), 46–47+.

Solomon ("Sol") White

2B-SS-3B-MGR-EXEC-WRITER. (B: June 12, 1868, Bellaire, OH–D: Aug. 1955). Pittsburgh Keystones and Washington Capital Citys, 1887; New York Gorhams and Cuban Giants, 1889; Cuban Giants and Philadelphia Big Gorhams, 1891; Cuban Giants, 1893–1894; Pittsburgh Keystones and Page Fence Giants, 1895; Cuban X-Giants, 1896–1899; Columbia Giants, 1900; Cuban X-Giants, 1901; Philadelphia Giants, 1902–1909; Quaker Giants, 1909; Brooklyn Royal Giants, 1910; New York Lincoln Giants, 1911; Boston Giants, 1912; Columbus Buckeyes, 1920. Remarks: Joint founder, and player-manager, of Philadelphia Giants, later manager, Brooklyn Royal Giants. Best remembered for his 1907 chronicle of his own 1906 season experiences and of black baseball, White post baseball was a columnist for the *Amsterdam News.*

56136. Bernstein, David. "Solomon White." In: John A. Garrity and Marsh C. Carries, eds. *American National Biography.* 24 vols. New York: Oxford University Press, 1999. XXIII, 238–239.

56137. Holway, John B. "Sol White: White on Blackball." In: his *Blackball Stars.* Westport, CT: Meckler Corp., 1988. Pp. 1–7.

56138. Kleinknecht, Merl F. "King Solomon 'Sol' White." In: Vol. Q–Z of David L. Porter, ed. *Biographical Dictionary of American Sports: Baseball.* Rev. and enlarged ed. Westport, CT: Greenwood Press, 2000. Pp. 1664–1665.

56139. Malloy, Jerry. "Sol White and the Origin of African-American Baseball." In: John E. Dreifort, ed. *Baseball History from Outside the Lines: a Reader.* Lincoln, NE: University of Nebraska Press, 2001. Chpt. 5.

56140. ____. "The Strange Career of Sol White, Black Baseball's First Historian." *Nine: A Journal of Baseball History and Social Policy Perspective,* IV (Spring 1996), 217–236.

56141. White, Sol. *Sol White's Official Base Ball Guide.* Philadelphia, PA: H. Walter Schlichter, 1907. 128p.

56142. ____. *Sol White's Official Base Ball Guide.* Edited By H. Walter Schlichter. Columbia, SC: Camden House, Inc., 1984. 128p. Reprint of 1907 original, with an Introduction by Red Barber. Schlichter and White, in 1902, founded the Philadelphia Giants.

56143. ____. *Sol White's History of Colored Base Ball, With Other Documents on the Early Black Game 1886–1936.* Compiled and introduced by Jerry Malloy. Lincoln, NE: University of Nebraska Press, 1995. 187p. Includes the 1907 original, plus later writings through 1936.

William Dekova ("Bill") White

1B-OF-BROADCASTER-EXEC. (B: Jan. 28, 1934, Lakewood, FL). New York (NL) and San Francisco (NL), 1956 and 1958; St. Louis (NL), 1959–1965; Philadelphia (NL), 1966–1968; St. Louis (NL), 1969. Remarks: Obtained 1,706 hits (202 homers) and 103 stolen bases in 1,673 games In 13 seasons; homered in first big league game, May 6, 1956; hit for the cycle, Aug. 14, 1960; had 14 hits in consecutive doubleheaders, July 17–18, 1961; had three hits (one double) in 1964 World Series; broadcaster in St. Louis and Philadelphia, 1970 and for New York (AL), 1971–1989; Hiram College graduate was first black broadcaster of major league games; NL president, 1989–1994.

56144. "Bill White: The National League's New Boss." *Ebony,* XLIV (May 1989), 44+.

56145. Bitker, Steve. "Bill White." In: his *The Original San Francisco Giants: The Giants of '58.* Champaign, IL: Sports Publishing, Inc., 1998. Pp. 208–214.

56146. Broeg, Bob. "Bill White: Devine's Guidance." *Baseball Digest,* XIX (October-November 1960), 59–61.

56147. Burnes, Robert L. "Bill White Man of Class." *Baseball Digest,* XXV (February 1966), 59–61.

56148. Callahn, Tim. "Baseball Picks a Pioneer." *Time,* CXXXIII (February 13, 1989), 76.

56149. Dolson, Frank. "Bill White Clears the Last Hurdle." *Baseball Digest,* XVII (May 1968), 91–95.

56150. Edwards, Bill. "Bill White." *Baseball Magazine,* XCI (June 1955), 19–20.

56151. Gelman, Steve. "Bill White – 'A Man Must Say What He Thinks Is Right.'" *Sport,* XXXVIII (July 1964), 52–61.

56152. Gottehrer, Barry. "Bill White is a Hitter." *Sport,* XXX (September 1960), 46–47+.

56153. Herman, Jack. "Bill White: He Makes Cards Like That Deal." *Baseball Digest,* XVIII (September 1959), 31–35.

56154. ____. "Killer Instinct Is What Bill White Needs." *Baseball Digest,* XXI (August 1962), 67–71.

56155. Hochman, Stan. "Bill White Keeps His Promise." *Baseball Digest,* XXVII December 1968), 39–40.

56156. "It's Great to be Traded." *Ebony,* XIV (October 1959), 46–48.

56157. Masin, Herman L. "The Great White Hope …" *Scholastic Coach,* LVIII (April 1989), 12–13. As NL president.

56158. McConnell, Mickey. "The One-Way Stretch at First." *Scholastic Coach,* XXXV (February 1966), 8–9. As demonstrated by Bill White.

56159. Moffi, Larry and Jonathan Kronstadt. "William DeKova ('Bill') White." In: their *Crossing the Line; Black Major Leaguers, 1947–1959.* Jefferson, NC: McFarland & Co., Inc., 1994. Pp. 160–161.

56160. "The National League's New Boss: Bill White." *Ebony,* XLIV (May 1989), 44–45.

56161. Noverr, Douglas A. "William DeKova 'Bill' White." In: Vol. Q-Z of David L. Porter, ed. *Biographical Dictionary of American Sports: Baseball.* Rev. and enlarged ed. Westport, CT: Greenwood Press, 2000. Pp. 1666–1668.

56162. Peck, Ira. "Bill White: Hot Hand in St. Loo." In: Ray Robinson, ed. *Baseball Stars of 1964.* New York: Pyramid Books, 1964. Pp. 91–96.

56163. Phillips, Bob. "If At First You Do Succeed." *Scholastic Coach,* LVIII (April 1989), 24–25.

56164. Randolph, Laura B. "Bill White: National League President." *Ebony,* XLVII (August 1992), 52–53.

56165. "Rap with Bill White and Joe Garagiola On 'Professional' Sports Broadcasting." *Black Sports,* II (May 1972), 17–24.

56166. Robinson, Jackie. "Bill White." In: his *Baseball Has Done It.* Philadelphia, PA: Lippincott, 1964. Pp. 134–144.

56167. Smith, Claire. "National League President Bill White: Baseball's Angry Man." *The New York Times Magazine,* (October 13, 1991), 28–31, 53–56.

56168. Smith, Curt. "Baseball's Angry Man." *The New York Times Magazine,* (October 13, 1991), 28–31.

56169. Vecsey, George. "First Base: Bill White's Winning Code." In: John L. Pratt, ed. *Baseball's All-Stars.* Garden City, N.Y.: Doubleday, 1967. Pp. 21–28.

56170. White, Bill. "How to Play First Base." In: *Boy's Life,* Editors of. *Baseball as We Played It.* New York: G.P. Putnam, 1969. Pp. 96–109.

William Henry ("Will" or "Whoop-La") White
P-MGR. (B: Oct. 11, 1854, Canton, NY-D: Aug. 11, 1911). Boston (NL), 1877; Cincinnati (NL), 1878–1880; Detroit (NL), 1881; Cincinnati (AA), 1882–1886. Remarks: In a decade, won 229 games (including 40 in 1882) and lost 166; also hurled for Buffalo (IL), 1889.

56171. Overfield, Joseph M. "William Henry 'Will,' 'Whoop-La' White." In: Vol. Q-Z of David L. Porter, ed. *Biographical Dictionary of American Sports: Baseball.* Rev. and enlarged ed. Westport, CT: Greenwood Press, 2000. Pp. 1668–1669.

Burgess Urquhart ("Whitey") Whitehead
2B-3B. (B: June 29, 1910, Tarboro, NC-D: Nov. 25, 1993). St. Louis (NL), 1933–1935; New York (NL), 1936–1941; Pittsburgh (N.L), 1946. Remarks: Had 883 hits (17 homers) and 51 stolen bases in 924 games in nine years; had significant error in Game Five of 1937 World Series; missed all of 1938 season due to mental breakdown.

56172. Bloodgood, Clifford. "The Giants Get a Second Baseman." *Baseball Magazine,* LVI (February 1936), 407–408.

56173. Grosshandler, Stan. "Burgess Whitehead: Last of the Old St. Louis Cardinals' 'Gas House Gang.'" *Baseball Digest,* LI (June 1992), 66–68.

56174. Kelley, Brent P. "Burgess Whitehead: Gashouse Gang." In: his *The Early All-Stars: Conversations with Standout Baseball Players of the 1930s and 1940s.* Jefferson, NC: McFarland & Co., Inc., 1997. Pp. 173–178.

Whitey Whitehead *see* **Burgess Urquhart ("Whitey") Whitehead**

Earl Oliver ("The Earl") Whitehill
P. (B: Feb. 7, 1899, Cedar Rapids, IA-D: Oct. 22, 1954.). Detroit (AL), 1923–1932; Washington (AL), 1933–1936; Cleveland (AL), 1937–1938; Chicago (NL), 1939. Remarks: In 17 years, had 218 victories, 185 defeats, and 11 "saves"; won one game in the 1933 World Series; coach, Cleveland (AL), 1941, Philadelphia (NL), 1943, and Buffalo (IL), 1944; PR director, A.G. Spalding Co., 1944–1954, killed in an automobile accident.

56175. Paplas, Anthony J. "Earl Oliver 'The Earl' Whitehill." In: Vol. Q-Z of David L. Porter, ed. *Biographical Dictionary of American Sports: Baseball.* Rev. and enlarged ed. Westport, CT: Greenwood Press, 2000. Pp. 1669–1671.

56176. Whitehill, Earl. "The Pitching Ace of the Tiger Club." *Baseball Magazine,* XXXIV (May 1925), 545–547+.

Leonard Joseph ("Len" or "Whitey") Whitehouse
P-COACH. (B: Sept. 10, 1957, Burlington, VT). Texas (AL), 1981; Minnesota (AL), 1983–1985. Remarks: Won nine games and lost four, with four "saves," in all or parts of four big league years; pitching coach, St. Michael's College (VT), 2000-.

56177. Simon, Tom. "Len Whitehouse." In: Tom Simon, ed. *Green Mountain Boys of Summer: Vermonters in the Major Leagues, 1882–1993.* Shelburne, VT: The New England Press, 2000. Pp. 168–173.

56178. _____. "The Vulture: The Unlikely Career of Vermont's Len Whitehouse, in His Own Words." *The National Pastime,* XVIII (1998), 112–115.

George ("Lucky") Whiteman
OF. (B: Dec. 23, 1882, Peoria, IL-D: Feb. 10, 1947). Boston (AL), 1907; New York (AL), 1917; Boston (AL), 1918. Remarks: Had 70 hits (1 homer) and 11 stolen bases in 85 games in three big league seasons; defensive hero of 1918 World Series.

56179. Salant, Nathan. "George Whiteman." In: his *Superstars, Stars, and Just Plain Heroes.* New York: Stein and Day, 1982. Pp. 245–251.

Mark Anthony Whiten
OF-P. (B: Nov. 25, 1966, Pensacola, FL). Toronto (AL), 1990–1991; Cleveland (AL), 1991–1992; St. Louis (NL), 1993–1994; Boston (AL), 1995; Philadelphia (NL), 1995–1996; Atlanta (NL) and Seattle (AL), 1996; New York (AL), 1997; Cleveland (AL), 1998–2000. Remarks: Had 804 hits (105 homers) and 78 stolen bases in 940 games for nine teams in 11 seasons; had 12 RBIs and four homers in one game, Sept. 7, 1993; had five RBIs in one game, June 2, 1996; had one grand slam homer, Aug. 29, 1996; pitched two big league innings, July 31, 1998; had two hits (one double, one homer) in 1998 ALCS; coach, Spokane (Northwest League), 2005-.

56180. "Cardinals' Whiten Jolts 4 Homers, 12 RBI in Game." *Jet,* LXXXIV (September 27, 1993), 46+.

56181. Fimrite, Ron. "Mark Whiten." *Sports Illustrated,* LXXIX (September 20, 1993), 45+.

56182. Muskat, Carrie. "He's On the Road Again: Another Year, Another New Team for Whiten." *USA Today Baseball Weekly,* VII (May 14, 1997), 6+.

Fred Dwight ("Wingy") Whitfield
1B. (B: Jan. 7, 1938, Vandiver, AL). St. Louis (NL), 1962; Cleveland (AL), 1963–1967; Cincinnati (NL), 1968–1969; Montreal (NL), 1970. Remarks: Obtained 578 hits (108 homers) and seven stolen bases in 817 games in nine big

league seasons; had 93 homers in four years, 1963–1967; all-time top home run hitter and RBI champion for Keokuk (Midwest League), 1958.

56183. Bisher, Furman. "Fred Whitfield and the Happy Delusion." *Sport,* XLI (February 1966), 44–45.

Terry Bertland Whitfield

OF. (B: Jan. 12, 1953, Blythe, CA). New York (AL), 1974–1976; San Francisco (NL), 1977–1980; Seibu Lions (Japan League), 1981–1983; Los Angeles (NL), 1984–1986. Remarks: Had 537 hits (33 homers) and 18 stolen bases in 730 games in nine U.S. big league seasons; had 85 "taters" in Japan; also played for Syracuse (IL).

56184. Mandel, Mike. "Terry Whitfield." In: his *The San Francisco Giants: An Oral History.* Santa Cruz, CA: Mike Mandel, 1979. Pp. 246–248.

Robert Whiting

FAN-WRITER. (B: Oct. 24, 1942, Long Branch, NJ). Remarks: editor/project editor, *Encyclopedia Britannica* and Grolier International in Tokyo, 1969–1974; project director, Time Life Books in Tokyo, 1975–1976; president/co-owner, Creative Resources Group in Tokyo, 1977–; author of several books/articles on Japanese baseball.

56185. Whiting, Robert. "A Fan Reborn." In: Ron Fimrite, ed. *Birth of a Fan.* New York: Macmillan, 1993. Pp. 178–194.

Walt Whitman

WRITER. (B: West Hills, NY, May 31, 1819-D: March 26, 1892). Remarks: Noted American poet; the Whitman bibliography is extensive and is detailed in Folsom's *Dictionary of Literary Biography* entry.

56186. Folsom, Lowell Edwin. "America's 'Hurrah Game': Baseball and Walt Whitman." *The Iowa Review,* XI (Spring-Summer 1980), 68–80.

56187. _____. "'The Manly and Healthy Game': Walt Whitman and the Development of American Baseball." *Arete: the Journal of Sport Literature,* II (Fall 1984), 43–62.

56188. _____. "Walt Whitman." In: Kent P. Liungquist, ed. *Dictionary of Literary Biography, Volume 250: Antebellum Writers in New York, Second Series.* A Bruccoli Clark Layman Book. Detroit, MI: The Gale Group, 2001. Pp. 348–383.

56189. _____. *Walt Whitman's Native Representations.* New York: Cambridge University Press, 1997. 194p.

56190. Kaplan, Justin. *Walt Whitman: A Life.* New York: Simon and Schuster, 1980. 432p.

56191. Reef, Catherine. *Walt Whitman.* New York: Clarion, 1995.

56192. Reynolds, David S. *A Historical Guide to Walt Whitman.* Historical Guides to American Authors. New York: Oxford University Press, 1999. 280p.

56193. *Walt Whitman's America: A Cultural Biography.* New York: Alfred Knopf, 1995. 671p.

Arthur Carter ("Pinky") Whitney

3B-2B. (B: Jan. 2, 1905, San Antonio, TX-D: Sept. 1, 1987). Philadelphia (NL), 1928–1933; Boston (NL), 1933–1936; Philadelphia (NL), 1936–1939. Remarks. Obtained 1,701 hits (93 homers) and 56 stolen bases in 1,639 games in a dozen campaigns; had RBIs in 10 consecutive games, 1931; had one grand slam homer, May 22, 1936; elected to Texas Sports Hall of Fame, 1983.

56194. Graber, Ralph S. "Arthur Carter 'Pinky' Whitney." In: Vol. Q-Z of David L. Porter, ed. *Biographical Dictionary of American Sports: Baseball.* Rev. and enlarged ed. Westport, CT: Greenwood Press, 2000. Pp. 1671–1672.

56195. Langford, Walter. "Pinky Whitney: Philly Star from Another Era." *Baseball Digest,* XLVII (June 1988), 69–73.

56196. Ward, John J. "Highlights of Pinky Whitney's Career." *Baseball Digest,* LIII (August 1934), 405–406+.

Grasshopper Jim Whitney *see* **James Evans ("Grasshopper Jim") Whitney**

James Evans ("Grasshopper Jim") Whitney

P. (B: Nov. 10, 1857, Conklin, NY-D: May 21, 1891). Boston (NL), 1881–1885; Kansas City (NL), 1886; Washington (NL), 1887–1888; Indianapolis (NL), 1889; Philadelphia (AA), 1890. Remarks: Won 191 games and lost 204 in a decade; led NL in wins (31), 1881; led NL in "saves" (two), 1883; led NL in walks issued, 1883–1887; died of tuberculosis.

56197. Ivor-Campbell, Frederick. "James Evans 'Grasshopper Jim' Whitney." In: Vol. Q-Z of David L. Porter, ed. *Biographical Dictionary of American Sports: Baseball.* Rev. and enlarged ed. Westport, CT: Greenwood Press, 2000. Pp. 1672–1673.

Pinky Whitney *see* **Arthur Carter ("Pinky") Whitney**

Eddie Lee ("Ed") Whitson

P. (B: May 19, 1955, Johnson City, TN). Pittsburgh (NL), 1977–1979; San Francisco (NL), 1979–1981; Cleveland (AL), 1982; San Diego (NL), 1983–1984; New York (AL), 1985–1986; San Diego (NL), 1986–1991. Remarks: In 15 big league seasons, won 126 games and lost 123, with eight "saves"; won Game Three of 1984 NLCS.

56198. Shannon, Mike. "Ed Whitson." In: his *Tales from the Dugout: The Greatest True Baseball Stories Ever Told.* Lincolnwood, IL: NTC/Contemporary Books, 1997. Pp. 227–228.

Leo Ernest ("Ernie") Whitt

C. (B: June 13, 1952, Detroit, MI). Boston (AL), 1976; Toronto (AL), 1977–1978, 1980–1989; Atlanta (NL), 1990; Baltimore (AL), 1991. Remarks: Had 938 hits (134 homers) and 22 stolen bases in 1,328 games in 15 seasons; had three homers in one game, Sept. 14, 1987; coach/interim, Dunedin (florida State League) and Syracuse (IL), 1997; roving minor league instructor, Toronto (AL), 1997–1998, 2000–2003; manager, Baseball Canada, 1999 Pan Am Games and 2004 Olympic Games; coach, Toronto (AL), 2005-.

56199. Joyce, George. "Catching On." *MVP Magazine,* XIX (July-August 1987), 52–56.

56200. Kendall, Brian. "September 14, 1987: Ernie Whitt Leads Jays' Record Homer Barrage." In: his *Great Moments in Canadian Baseball.* Toronto, Ont.: Lester Publishing, 1995. Chpt. 20.

56201. MacCarl, Neil. "Ernie Whitt and Blue Jays Have Grown Up Together." *Baseball Digest,* XLVII (June 1988), 66–68.

56202. Whitt, Ernie and Greg Cable. *Catch: A Major League Life.* Toronto, Canada: McGraw-Hill Ryerson, 1989. 271 p.

56203. Zack, Bill. "Catching Up with Ernie." *Scorebook,* XIV (September 13, 1990), 40–41.

George Bostic ("Possum") Whitted

OF-3B-1B. (B: Feb. 4, 1890, Durham, NC-D: Oct. 16, 1962). SL Louis (NL), 1912–1914; Boston (NL), 1914; Philadelphia (NL), 1915–1919; Pittsburgh (NL), 1919–1021; Brooklyn (N.L), 1922. Remarks: Had 978 hits (23 homers) and 116 stolen bases in 1,021 games in 11 seasons; had three hits (one double) in 1914 World Series and one hit in 1915 World Series; traded once on Christmas Eve, Dec. 24, 1914.

56204. Kofoed, J.C. "The Most Improved Player in the Game." *Baseball Magazine,* XV (September 1915), 44–46.

Possum Whitted *see* **George Bostic ("Possum") Whitted**

David Clifford ("Dave" or "Wick") Wickersham
P. (Sept. 27, 1935, Erie, PA). Kansas City (AL), 1960–1963; Detroit (AL), 1964–1967; Pittsburgh (NL), 1968; Kansas City (AL), 1969. Remarks: Won 68 games and lost 57, with 18 "saves," in a decade; missed winning 20th game when ejected, Oct. 1, 1964.

56205. Hefley, James C. "Dave Wickersham: The Apple Pitcher Who Made the Big League." In: his *Play Ball.* Grand Rapids, MI: Zondervan Publishing House, 1964. Pp. 99–105.

Frank ("The Red Ant" or "Smokey") Wickware
P. (B: 1888, Coffeyville, KS-D: Nov. 2, 1967). Dallas Giants, 1909; Leland Giants, 1909–1910; Chicago American Giants, 1911–1912; Brooklyn Royal Giants, 1912–1914; Chicago American Giants, 1914–1918; Detroit Stars, 1919; Norfolk Stars and New York Lincoln Giants, 1920; Chicago American Giants, 1920–1921; Calgary (Canadian League), 1921; New York Lincoln Giants, 1925. Remarks: Negro League pitcher known for blazing fastball and who, in periods of barnstorming, won two of three exhibition games against Walter Johnson.

56206. Keetz, Frank. "When 'The Big Train' [Walter Johnson] Met 'The Red Ant.'" *The Baseball Research Journal,* XX (1991), 63–65. Three 1913–1914 exhibition game, two won by Wickware.

56207. Lester, Larry. "Frank 'Red Ant' Wickware." In: Vol. Q-Z of David L. Porter, ed. *Biographical Dictionary of American Sports: Baseball.* Rev. and enlarged ed. Westport, CT: Greenwood Press, 2000. Pp. 1673–1674.

Whitey Wietelmann *see* **William Frederick ("Whitey") Wietelmann**

William Frederick ("Whitey") Wietelmann
SS-2B-P-EXEC. (B: March 15, 1919, Zanesville, OH-D: March 26, 2002). Boston (NL), 1939–1946; Pittsburgh (NL), 1947. Remarks: Obtained 409 hits (seven homers) and 14 stolen bases in 580 games in eight big league seasons; also played for Sacramento (PCL), 1948 and San Diego (PCL), 1949–1952; won 21 games while hurling for Yuma (Arizona-Mexico League), 1955; coach, San Diego (PCL), 1960–1965; coach, Cincinnati (NL), 1966–1967; coach, San Diego (PCL), 1968; coach, San Diego (NL), 1969–1979; exec, San Diego (NL), 1980–1994; also invented a machine to clean baseballs and helped initiate the practice of charting pitches.

56208. Swand, Bill. "Whitey Wietelmann." In: his *Echoes From Lane Field: A History of The San Diego Padres 1936–1957.* Paducah, KY: Turner Publishing Company, 1997. Pp. 104–106.

Delbert Quentin ("Del" or "Babe") Wilber
C-MGR. (B: Feb. 24, 1919, Lincoln Park, MI-D: July 18, 2002). St. Louis (NL), 1946–1949; Philadelphia (NL), 1951–1952; Boston (AL), 1952–1954. Remarks: Had 174 hits (nine homers) and one stolen base in 299 games in eight years; hit three homers in one game, August 27, 1951; also played for Columbus (AA), 1946; coach, Chicago (AL), 1955–1956 and Washington (AL), 1970; manager, Denver (PCL), 1971–1972; manager, Spokane (PCL), 1973; interim manager, Texas (AL), 1973, winning one game and losing none (1.000); scout, Minnesota (AL), 1974–1989; noted for drawings done on baseballs given as presents.

56209. Wilber, Cynthia J. "Del Wilber." In: her *For the Love of the Game: Baseball Memories from the Men Who Were There.* New York: William Morrow And Company, 1992. Pp. 235–247.

56210. Wilber, Rick. "Aparicio's Glove and Other Gifts." *Elysian Fields Quarterly,* XVIII (Fall 2001), 13–20.

56211. _____. "Our Second Season." *Elysian Fields Quarterly,* XVI (Summer 1999), 13–16.

56212. Yeutter, Frank. "Phils' Wilber Masked Artist?" *Baseball Digest,* X (August 1951), 89–91.

Milton Edward ("Milt") Wilcox
P. (B: April 20, 1950, Honolulu, HI). Cincinnati (NL), 1970–1971; Cleveland (AL), 1972–1974; Chicago (NL), 1975; Detroit (AL), 1975–1985; Seattle (AL), 1986. Remarks: In 16 years, won 119 games and lost 113, with six "saves"; one out from perfect game when hit yielded, April 15, 1983; won Game Three of 1984 ALCS.

56213. Wilcox, Milt, as told to George Vass. "The Game I'll Never Forget." *Baseball Digest,* XLV (June 1986), 45–47.

Timothy ("Tim") Wiles
EXEC-WRITER. (B: 1964, Libertyville, IL). Remarks: Research director, National Baseball Hall of Fame and Museum, 1995-.

56214. Wilcox, Carol. "Let's Play Ball!" *Iowa Alumni Magazine,* LVI (April 2003), 24–25.

Hoyt Wilhelm *see* **James Hoyt Wilhelm**

James Hoyt Wilhelm ★
P. (B: My 26, 1923, Huntersvine, NC-D: Aug. 23, 2002). New York (NL), 1952–1956; St. Louis (NL), 1957; Cleveland (AL), 1957–1958; Baltimore (AL), 1958–1962; Chicago (AL), 1963–1968; California (AL), 1969, Atlanta (NL), 1960–1970; Chicago (NL), 1970; Atlanta (NL), 1971; Los Angeles (N.L), 1971–1972. Remarks: In 21 years, had 143 victories, 122 defeats, and 227 "saves"; won 124 games in relief for a major league record; other records include most. games pitched (1,070) and most innings pitched in relief (1,845); pitched no-hitter, Sept. 30, 1958; master of the knuckleball and a hero of the World War II Battle of the Bulge; saved one game in 1954 World Series; minor league instructor/coach New York (AL), 1973–1993; elected (first relief pitcher so honored) to National Baseball Hall of Fame in 1985, where his plaque reads: "Baseball's premier relief pitcher used knuckle ball to win 143 games (a record 124 in relief) and amassed 227 saves over 21-year career. No-hit Yankees on Sept. 20, 1958 in infrequent start for Orioles. Pitched in record 1070 games with lifetime ERA of 2.52."

56215. Baida, Peter. "Hoyt Wilhelm." In: Danny Peary, ed. *Cult Baseball Players.* New York: Simon and Schuster, 1990. Pp. 197–202.

56216. _____. "Hoyt Wilhelm." In: Danny Peary, ed. *Baseball's Finest: The Greats, the Flakes, the Weird and the Wonderful.* North Digton, MA: The JG Press, 1990. Pp. 197–202. Both Peary books are identical.

56217. Cairns, Bob. "Hoyt Wilhelm." In: his *Pen Men: Baseball's Greatest Bullpen Stories told by the Men who Brought the Game Relief.* New York: St. Martin's Press, 1992. Pp. 138–142.

56218. Dozer, Richard. "Sizing Up Old Hoyt Wilhelm." *Baseball Digest,* XXVI (October 1967), 17–21.

56219. Elderkin, Phil. "How to Win in Baseball Without Throwing Hard." *Baseball Digest,* XXXIII (December 1974), 44–46.

56220. Eldridge, Larry. "Hoyt Wilhelm Discusses Art of Knuckler, Relief Pitching." *Baseball Digest,* XLIV (August 1985), 59–61.

56221. Furlong, William ("Bill"). "The Next 900 Won't Be So Tough" *Sport,* XLVI (November 1968), 64–67.

56222. Greene, Lee. "Suddenly, Wilhelm's a Mystery." *Sport,* XXVIII (September 1959), 30–33.

56223. Horowitz, Paul. "I Caught Wilhelm's Knuckler." *Baseball Digest,* XII (September 1953), 49–51.

56224. "Hoyt Wilhelm." *This Week,* (August 16,1959), 15+.

56225. "James 'Hoyt' Wilhelm." In: *Current Biography Yearbook, 1971.* New York: H.W. Wilson Co., 1971. Pp. "441–443.

56226. Kuenster, John. "A Salute to Aaron and Wilhelm." *Baseball Digest,* XXIX (August 1970), 4–6.

56227. Lang, Marshall. "Behind the Hoyt Wilhelm Miracle." *Sport,* XXXII (October 1961), 32–35.

56228. Libby, Bill. "Hoyt Wilhelm." In: his *Star Pitchers of the Major Leagues.* New York: Random House, 1971. Pp. 94–108.

56229. Markus, Robert. "How Long Can Wilhelm Keep Fooling 'Em?" *Baseball Digest,* XXIX (May 1970), 58–63.

56230. Meany, Thomas, and Tommy Holmes. "James Hoyt Wilhelm — Relief Specialist." In: their *Baseball's Best.* New York: Watts, 1964. Pp. 89–94.

56231. Sabin, Lou. "Hoyt Wilhelm: The Supreme Reliever." In: his *Record Breakers of the Major Leagues.* New York: Random House, 1974. Pp. 114–120.

56232. Schaap, Dick. "Hoyt Wilhelm: Nothing But Knucklers." In: Ray Robinson, ed. *Baseball Stars of 1960.* New York: Pyramid Books, 1960. Pp. 54–60.

56233. Shapiro, Milton J. "Hoyt Wilhelm." In: his *Heroes at the Bullpen: Baseball's Greatest Relief Pitchers.* New York: Julian Messner, 1967. Pp. 89–102.

56234. Sheldon, Harold. "Wilhelm Just Knuckles Along." *Baseball Digest,* XI (October 1952), 45–50.

56235. Smith, Leverett T., Jr. "James Hoyt Wilhelm." In: Vol. Q-Z of David L. Porter, ed. *Biographical Dictionary of American Sports: Baseball.* Rev. and enlarged ed. Westport, CT: Greenwood Press, 2000. Pp. 1674–1675.

56236. Stainback, Berry. "Goodbye, Sweet Hoyt." *Sport,* XXXV (March 1963), 6–7.

56237. Steadman, John F. "The Knuckler Doesn't Grow Old." *Baseball Digest,* XXI (July 1962), 55–57.

56238. _____. "No-Hit: Wilhelm's Knuckler Just Isn't." *Baseball Digest,* XVII (December 1958), 86–87.

56239. Terrell, Ray. "Nobody Hits It." *Sports Illustrated,* X (June 29, 1959), 14–19.

56240. Thorn, John. "The Ten Best: Wilhelm." In: his *The Relief Pitcher.* New York: E.P. Dutton, 1979. Pp. 85–93.

56241. Trader, Hugh. "Hoyt Wilhelm: Prize Fingernails." *Baseball Digest,* XVIII (August 1959), 5–9.

56242. Uthoff, Harry. "Suddenly Wilhelm's a Mystery." *Sport,* XXVIII (September 1959), 33–34+.

56243. Vass, George. "Stars in the Twilight: Hoyt Wilhelm." *Baseball Digest,* XXVII (February 1969), 16–21.

56244. Welsh, Chris. "The Count Is 0–2- Now What?" *Thinking Pitcher,* I, no. 2 (1993), 3–4.

56245. Wilhelm, James Hoyt, as told to Stanley Frank. "So I Escaped from the Bullpen." *Saturday Evening Post,* CCXXXII (August 1, 1959), 25–27.

Joseph William ("Joe") Wilhoit
OF. (B: Dec. 20, 1885, Hiawatha, KS-D: Sept. 25, 1930). Boston (NL), 1916–1917; Pittsburgh (NL), 1917; New York (NL), 1917–1918; Boston (AL), 1919. Remarks: In four big league seasons, had 201 hits (three homers) and 28 stolen bases in 283 games; while playing for Wichita (W.A.) in 1920, had 69-game hitting streak, which remains the OB record.

56246. Rives, B. "Joe Wilhoit and Ken Guettler: Minor League Hitting Record-Setters." *The Baseball Research Journal,* XXIX (2000), 121–125.

James Leslie ("J. L.") Wilkinson
EXEC. (B: 1874, Perry, IA-D: Aug. 21, 1964). Remarks: Founder of Kansas City Monarchs and the only Caucasian owner in the Negro National League when it was organized in 1920; champion Monarchs first pro team (1930) to use portable lighting for night baseball.

56247. Holway, John B. "J. L. Wilkinson: The Gift of Light." In: his *Blackball Stars.* Westport, CT: Meckler Corp., 1988. Pp. 327–343.

56248. _____. and Merl F. Kleinknecht. "James Leslie Wilkinson." In: Vol. Q-Z of David L. Porter, ed. *Biographical Dictionary of American Sports: Baseball.* Rev. and enlarged ed. Westport, CT: Greenwood Press, 2000. Pp. 1675–1676.

James E. ("Jimmy" or "Seabiscuit") Wilkes
OF. (B: ?-D:?). Newark Eagles, 1946–1948; Houston Eagles, 1949–1950; Elmira (EL) and Three Rivers (Canadian-American League), 1950–1951; Great Falls (Pioneer League) and Indianapolis Clowns, 1952. Remarks: Remembered for his speed and attempt to enter OB in the early 1950s; also played for Brantford in Ontario's Intercounty Major Baseball League, 1954.

56249. Kirst, Sean Peter. "Baseball Celebrates; Something's Missing." In: his *The Ashes of Lou Gehrig and Other Baseball Essays.* Jefferson, NC: McFarland & Co., Inc., 2003. Pp. 94–97.

56250. Snider, Michael. "'God's Country': Jimmy Wilkes Played for Negro Leagues in Canada." *Maclean's,* CXIV (May 14, 2001), 37–40.

George Frederick Will
WRITER. (B: May 4, 1941, Champaign, IL). Remarks: Political science instructor, Michigan State University and Toronto University, 1967–1969; senatorial aide, 1970–1972; Washington editor, *National Review,* 1972–1976; columnist, *Washington Post,* 1974-date; contributing editor, *Newsweek,* 1976-date; won Pulitzer Prize, 1977; commentator, ABC-News, 1981-date; baseball historian.

56251. Friedman, Jack. "Turning from Politics, George Will Writes a Love Story About Men and Baseball." *People Weekly,* XXXIV (July 9, 1990), 45–46.

56252. "George Frederick Will." *Current Biography,* XLII (September 1981), 39–42.

56253. Kagan, Donald. "George Will's Baseball: A Conservative Critique." *The Public Interest,* (Fall 1990), 3–20.

56254. Kowet, Don. "Brainy Star at Heart a Baseball Nut." *Insight on the News,* VI (June 4, 1990), 46–48.

56255. Staggs, Sam. "George Will: Interview." *Publisher's Weekly,* CCXXXVII (March 16, 1990), 54–55.

56256. Strauber, Ira. "Take Me Out to the Polity: Baseball as a Synecdoche for Community in George F. Will's *Men at Work.*" *American Studies,* XXXVI (Fall 1995), 149-57.

56257. Will, George F. *Bunts: Curt Flood, Camden Yards, Pete Rose, and Other Reflections on Baseball.* New York: Scribner, 1998. 288p. Essays.

56258. _____. *Bunts: With an Update on the 1998 Season, "OK, Try to Top This."* New York: Simon and Schuster/Touchstone Books, 1999. 360p.

56259. Wright, William W. "Safe at Home for What?: George F. Will and the Republic of Baseball." *Diversity,* I (Spring 1993), 57+.

Carl Willey *see* **Carlton Francis ("Carl") Willey**
Carlton Francis ("Carl") Willey
P. (B: June 7, 1931, Cherryfield, ME). Minnesota (AL), 1958–1962; New York (NL), 1963–1965. Remarks: Won 38 games, but lost 58, with one "save," in seven big league seasons; had one grand slam homer, 1963.

56260. Schaap, Dick. "[Joey] Jay and Willey: Unlikely Roommates." *Sport,* XXVII (April 1959), 38–43.

Alberto [Desouza] ("Al") Williams
P. (B: May 6, 1954, Pearl Lagoon, Nicaragua). Minnesota (AL), 1980–1984. Remarks: Won 35 and lost 38, with two "saves," in five big league seasons; career ended by elbow injuries.
56261. Schertsten, Paul. "Profile: Al Williams." *Minneapolis Review of Baseball*, II (Late Summer 1982), 43–46.

Bernabe ("Bernie") Williams
OF. (B: Bernabe Williams Figueroa, Sept. 13, 1968, San Juan, PR). New York (AL), 1991-. Remarks: Through 2004, has had 2,097 hits (263 homers) and 144 stolen bases in 1,656 games; had eight RBIs in one game, Sept. 12, 1996; had nine hits (three doubles, two homers) in 1996 ALCS; 1996 ALCS MVP Award; had four hits (one homer), 1996 World Series; AL batting champion, 1998; obtained eight hits (one double) in 1998 ALCS and a homer in 1998 World Series; first player since Stan Musial (q.v.) to have 200 hits, 100 runs, 100 RBI, and 100 walks in a season, 1999; obtained five hits (one homer) in 1999 ALCS and three hits in the 1999 World Series; had 10 hits (one double, one homer) in 2000 ALCS and two hits (one homer) in 2000 World Series; had five RBIs in one game, Oct. 14, 2001; obtained four hits (three homers) in 2001 ALCS and five hits (one double) in 2001 World Series; had five hits in one game, Sept. 17, 2002; had five hits (one double) in 2003 ALCS and 10 hits (two doubles, two homers) in 2003 World Series; obtained 11 hits (three doubles, two homers) in 2004 ALCS; all-time postseason leader in homers and RBIs; accomplished guitarist who released album *The Journey Within,* 2003.
56262. Bodley, Hal. "Yankees' Bernie Williams: He Makes Sweet 'Music' at the Plate." *Baseball Digest,* LVI (January 1997), 53–57.
56263. Cannella, Stephen. "Real Scorchers in August." *Sports Illustrated,* XCVII (August 26, 2002), 77–78.
56264. Fine, Josh. "Bernie Williams Plays Jazz Clubs, Concert Halls, and Broadway Stages." *Biography,* II (April 1998), 86–89.
56265. Fischer, David. "A Yankee Doodle Dandy." *Sports Illustrated for Kids,* IX (April 1997), 24–27.
56266. Gmelch, George and J. J. Weiner. "Bernie and Waleska Williams, Center Fielder, New York Yankees, and Ball Player's Wife." In: their *In the Ballpark: The Working Lives of Baseball People.* Washington, D.C.: Smithsonian Institution Press, 1998. Pp. 78–91.
56267. Goldman, Steve. "Bernie Williams: How Good is He, Anyway?" *Yankees Magazine,* XX (May 1999), 54–69.
56268. Henry, Mike. "Welcome Back, Bernie." *Yankees Magazine,* XIX (December 1998), 22–29.
56269. Jordan, Pat. "The Music in a Yankee's Soul." *Reader's Digest,* CLVII (October 2000), 34–37.
56270. Kernan, Kevin. *Bernie Williams: Quiet Superstar.* Champaign, IL: Sports Publishing, 1999. 88p.
56271. Koenig, Bill. "Three of a Kind: Yanks' Modest Young Stars [Jeter, Williams, and Pettite] Have Plenty of Incentive to Pursue Second World Title." *USA Today Baseball Weekly,* VII (March 26, 1997), 8–10.
56272. Martin, Bruce. "Making an Impact." *Beckett Focus on Future Stars,* II (January 1992), 16–19.
56273. Muskat, Carrie. *Bernie Williams.* Latinos in Baseball Series. Childs, MD: Mitchell Lane Publishers, 2000. 64p.
56274. Pearlman, Jeff. "Hitting His Stride." *Sports Illustrated,* XCIV (June 25, 2001), 74–75.
56275. Poiley, Joe. "Yankee Doodle Dandy: Interview." *Boys' Life,* XCII (May 2002), 34–37.

56276. Rosenthal, Ken. "Bernie Williams." In: his *Best of the Best, Baseball: 35 Major League Superstars.* Indianapolis, IN: Masters Press, 1998. Pp. 152–155.
56277. Ryan, Jeff. "A Field of Dreams Deferred — No One Expects Him to Be Another Mickey Mantle, but Bernie Williams is Trying to End a Decade of Doldrums in Yankee Stadium's Center Field." *Inside Sports,* XV (June 1993), 58–61.
56278. _____. "In Tune with Greatness." *Sport,* LXXXIX (July 1997), 71–74.
56279. Smith, Daren. "Bernie Williams." *Beckett Baseball Card Monthly,* IX (February 1992), 11–12.
56280. Stewart, Mark. *Bernie Williams: Quiet Leader.* New York: Children's Press, 1998. 32p.
56281. Tringali, Rob, Jr. "Yankee Doodle Dandy." *Sports Illustrated for Kids,* IX (April 1997), 24–27.
56282. Tyler, Stanley C. "Bernie Williams: 'Batting Crown-Gold Glove-World Series Winner' Feat: Unique or Just Usually Rare?" In: Joseph M. Wayman, ed. *Grandstand Baseball Annual, 1999.* Downey, CA: Joseph M. Wayman, 1999. Pp. 183–184.
56283. Verducci, Tom. "Market Swing: Because He Lacks Power, Free Agent Bernie Williams Was Entertaining Few Offers in His Bid to Become the Major Leagues' Highest-Paid Player." *Sports Illustrated,* LXXXIX (November 30, 1998), 64–67.
56284. "Williams' Play in '95 Showcased a Multi-Talented Player." In: Arlys Warfield, ed. *1995 AL Division Series Scorebook and Souvenir Program.* New York: Professional Sports Publications, 1995. Pp. 38–43.

Bernard ("Bernie") Williams
OF. (B: Oct. 8, 1948, Alameda, CA). San Francisco (NL), 1970–1972; San Diego (NL), 1974. Remarks: In all or parts of four big league seasons, obtained 33 hits (four homers) and two stolen bases in 102 games.
56285. Snelling, Dennis. "Bernie Williams, Outfielder, 1970–72 Giants, 1974 San Diego Padres." In: his *A Glimpse of Fame.* Jefferson, NC: McFarland & Co., Inc., 1993. Pp. 201–216.

Bernie Williams *see* **Bernabe ("Bernie") Williams**
Bernie Williams *see* **Bernard ("Bernie") Williams**
Billy Leo ("Sweet Swinging") Williams★
OF-1B. (B: June 19, 1939, Whistler, AL). Chicago (NL), 1969–1974; Oakland (AL), 1975–1976. Remarks: Obtained 2 711 hits (426 homers) and 90 stolen bases in 2,488 games in 18 seasons; NL Rookie of the Year award, 1961; hit for the cycle, July 17, 1968; had five consecutive homers in two games, Sept. 8 and 10, 1968; had four consecutive doubles in one game, April 9, 1969; went 8-for-8 in a doubleheader, July 11, 1972; NL batting champion, 1972; holds several major league and NL records, including the then NL mark for most games played consecutively (11,117), Sept. 22, 1963 to Sept. 2, 1970; minor league instructor, Chicago (NL) and Oakland (AL), 1973–1985, 1988–1991; coach, Chicago (NL), 1986–1987; VP, MLPAA, 1992; coach, Chicago (NL), 1992–2001; elected to Alabama Sports Hall of Fame; elected to National Baseball Hall of Fame in 1987, where his plaque reads: "Soft-spoken, clutch performer was one of the most respected hitters of his day. Batted solid .290 over 18 seasons socking 426 home runs. Hit 20 or more homers 13 straight seasons. 1961 Rookie of the Year. 1972 NL batting champion with .333. Held NL record for consecutive games played with 1117."
56286. "Billy Williams." In: Carrie Muskat, ed. *Banks to Sandberg to Grace: Five Decades of Love and Frustration with the Chicago Cubs.* Chicago, IL: Contemporary Books, 2001. Pp. 77–81.

56287. "Billy Williams Joins His Friends in the Hall." *Jet,* LXXI (February 2, 1987), 46–47.

56288. "Billy Williams' Speech Fans Hall of Fame Fires." *Jet,* LXXII (August 10, 1987), 51+.

56289. Brosnan, Jim. "The Billy Williams Doll: Wind It Up and It Hits Line Drives." *Sport,* LV (May 1973), 44–47.

56290. Claassen, Harold W. "Billy Williams in Depth." In: Clyde Hirt, ed. *Sports Quarterly Presents Baseball, 1973.* New York: Counterpoint, Inc., 1973. Pp. 24–25+.

56291. Collett, Ritter. "Billy Williams: Proud of His Line Drive Complex." *Baseball Digest,* XXVII (August 1968), 25–27.

56292. Enright, Jim. "Billy Williams: Quiet Man Who Swings Fast Bat." *Baseball Digest,* XXVIII (September 1969), 21–25.

56293. Eubanks, Lou. "Billy Williams: The Streaking Ball Player." In: Alan Goldfarb, ed. *Baseball Illustrated, 1971.* New York: Complete Sports, 1971. P. 59+.

56294. Frommer, Harvey and Frederick J. "Billy Williams." In: their *Growing Up Baseball: An Oral History.* Dallas, TX: Taylor Publishing Co., 2001. Pp. 222–223.

56295. Furlong, William B. "Billy Williams: Hitter." *Sport,* XXXVIII (August 1964), 26–27+.

56296. Gleason, Bill. "Billy Williams: Baseball's No. 1 Hitter." *Baseball Digest,* XXXI (December 1972), 34–37.

56297. Gonzales, Raymond. "Billy Williams: A No-Hit Spoiler." *Baseball Digest,* XXXIII (July 1974), 38–40.

56298. Hano, Arnold. "Billy Williams: Professional." *Sport,* L (September 1970), 68–103.

56299. Hochman, Stan. "Quiet Man' Billy Williams Belongs in the Hall of Fame." *Baseball Digest,* XLIV (November 1985), 81–85.

56300. Kremenko, Barney. "Billy Williams: Above-Average Player." *Baseball Digest,* XXIII (October 1964), 84–87.

56301. Kuenster, John. "Billy Williams for MVP." *Baseball Digest,* XXIX (November 1970), 4–8.

56302. _____. "Hall of Famer Billy Williams Talks About the Fine Art of Hitting." *Baseball Digest,* LVI (July 1997), 17–19.

56303. _____. "How New Grip Helped Billy Williams." *Baseball Digest,* XXIX (December 1970), 4–8.

56304. Liorens, D. "Baseball's Gentle Iron Man." *Ebony,* XXII (July 1967), 50–52+.

56305. Mavrelis, Pete. "Billy Williams: The Heart of the Chicago Cubs." *Black Sports Magazine,* III (October 1973), 28–31.

56306. McDermott, Joe. "Bend an Ear to Billy's Music." *Sports Illustrated,* XXXIX (July 23, 1973), 27–28+.

56307. Payne, Dave. "Billy Williams Finds a New Career in Oakland." *Baseball Digest,* XXXIV (August 1975), 42–45.

56308. Schneider, Armand. "Billy Williams Remembers the Glory Years." *Baseball Digest,* XXXVI (February 1977), 74–76.

56309. Smith, Duane A. "Bill Leo 'Sweet Swinging' Williams." In: Vol. Q-Z of David L. Porter, ed. *Biographical Dictionary of American Sports: Baseball.* Rev. and enlarged ed. Westport, CT: Greenwood Press, 2000. Pp. 1676–1677.

56310. Westcott, Rich. "Billy Williams: Sweet-Swinger was a Hit in Chicago." In: his *Splendor on the Diamond: Interviews with 35 Stars of Baseball's Past.* Gainesville, fl: The University Press of florida, 2000. Pp. 106–116.

56311. Williams, Billy L. "My Greatest Day in Baseball." In: Eliot Cohen, ed. *My Greatest Day in Baseball.* New York: Little Simon, 1991. Pp. 136–140.

56312. _____. and Irv Haag. *Billy: The Classic Hitter.* Chicago, IL: Rand McNally, 1974. 207p.

56313. _____., as told to George Vass. "The Game I'll Never Forget." *Baseball Digest,* XXXIV (February 1975), 62–64.

56314. _____. with Rich Simon. *Iron Man.* Chicago, IL: Childrens Press, 1970. 64p.

Button Williams *see* **James Thomas ("Home Run" or "Button") Williams**

Charles Herman ("Charlie") Williams

UMP. (B: Dec. 20, 1943, Denver, CO–D: Sept. 15, 2005). Remarks: Umpire, California League, Texas League and Pacific Coast League; NL arbiter, 1978-date.

56315. Boga, Steve. "My Travels with Charlie." *Referee,* XII (June 1987), 28–33. NL ump.

Clarence ("Possum") Williams

AMATEUR. Remarks: Little League baseball player.

56316. Carothers, James B. "Playing Possum: 'All I Ever Said Was Way to Go and Nice Catch.'" In: Charles Einstein, ed. *The Fourth Fireside Book of Baseball.* New York: Simon and Schuster, 1987. Pp. 72–73.

Claude Preston ("Lefty") Williams

P. (B: March 9, 1903, Aurora, MO–D: Nov. 4, 1959). Detroit (AL), 1913–1914; Chicago (AL), 1916–1920. Remarks: Won 82 games and lost 48, with five "saves," in seven years; lost three games of 1919 World Series; banned by Judge Landis (q.v.) for alleged participation in Black Box scandal; purchased Shoeless Joe Jackson's (q.v.) Chicago pool hall for $1, becoming its owner-manager, Oct. 6, 1921.

56317. Findling, John E. "Claude Preston 'Lefty' Williams." In: Vol. Q-Z of David L. Porter, ed. *Biographical Dictionary of American Sports: Baseball.* Rev. and enlarged ed. Westport, CT: Greenwood Press, 2000. Pp. 1677–1678.

56318. flagler, J. M. "Requiem for a Southpaw." *New Yorker,* XXXV (December 5, 1959), 230+.

56319. Williams, Claude. "The Advantages of Being a Port-Sider." *Baseball Magazine,* XXIV (February 1920), 515–517. Pitching left-handed.

Cy Williams *see* **Fred ("Cy") Williams**

Dale Williams

UMP. Remarks: NCAA arbiter, Big West Conference

56320. Williams, Dale. "Interview." *Referee,* XV (August 1990), 20–23.

Davey Williams *see* **David Carlos ("Davey") Williams**

David Carlos ("Davey") Williams

2B. (B: Nov. 2, 1927, Dallas, TX). New York (NL), 1949, 1951–1955. Remarks: Had 450 hits (32 homers) and eight stolen bases in 517 games in six big league seasons; walked twice in 1954 World Series; coach, New York (NL), 1956–1957.

56321. Heiman, Lee, Dave Weiner and Bill Gutman. "Davey Williams." In: their *When the Cheering Stops.* New York: Macmillan Publishing Co., 1990. Pp. 214–226.

Dick Williams *see* **Richard Hirschfield ("Dick") Williams**

Earl Craig Williams, Jr.

C-1B-3B. (B: July 14, 1949, Newark, NJ). Atlanta (NL),1970–1972; Baltimore (AL), 1973–1974; Atlanta (NL), 1975–1976; Montreal (NL), 1976; Oakland (AL), 1977. Remarks: Had 756 hits (139 homers) and two stolen bases in 889 games in seven seasons; NL Rookie of the Year award, 1971; had five hits (two doubles, one homer) in

1973 ALCS; only Brave (other than Hank Aaron) to hit a ball into the upper deck at Atlanta — Fulton County Stadium.

56322. Cole, Robert. "Ball, Bat and Ad." *The Baseball Research Journal,* VIII (1979), 77–79.

56323. Hemphill, Paul. "Earl William: 'My Favorite Position Is Batter.'" *Sport,* LIV (August 1972), 46–47+.

56324. Honig, Donald. "1971: Earl Williams." In: his *National League Rookies of the Year.* New York: Bantam Books, 1989. Pp. 60–61.

56325. Schlossberg, Dan. "Cagey Rookie Makes It Big." *Black Sports,* II (July 1972), 56–59.

56326. _____. "Will the Sophomore Jinx Hobble Earl Williams?" *Baseball Digest,* XXXI (May 1972), 28–30.

Edward Bennet Williams

EXEC. (B: May 31, 1930, Hartford, CT-D: Aug. 13, 1988). Remarks: Noted attorney and owner/president, Baltimore (AL), 1979–1988.

56327. flower, Joe. "Well-Connected Power." *Sport,* LXXIII (July 1982), 86–167.

56328. Thomas, Evan. *The Man to See.* New York: Simon and Schuster, 1991. 587p.

Edward Laquan ("Eddie") Williams

1B-3B. (B: Nov. 1, 1964, Shreveport, LA). Cleveland (AL), 1986–1988; Chicago (AL), 1989; San Diego (NL), 1990, 1994–1995; Detroit (AL), 1996. Remarks: Had 288 hits (39 homers) and two stolen bases in 395 games in all or parts of eight big league seasons; badly hurt in 1993 automobile accident.

56329. Wakelee-Lynch, Joseph. "Pressure at the Plate." *Diabetes Forecast,* L (September 1997), 22–26.

Frank Williams

P. (B: Feb. 13, 1958, Seattle, WA). San Francisco (NL), 1984–1986; Cincinnati (NL), 1987–1988; Detroit (AL), 1989. Remarks: Had 24 wins, 14 losses, and eight "saves" in all or parts of six big league seasons; also pitched for San Francisco (PCL) and Phoenix (PCL), 1985–1986.

56330. Daly, Michael J. "Baseball's Statistics are This Local Player's Field of Dreams." In: *Grandstand Baseball Annual, 1994.* Downey, CA: Joseph M. Wayman, 1994. Pp. 80–81. Reprinted from the *Bridgeport Post,* October 7, 1990.

56331. Wayman, Joseph M. "GBA Correspondence Interview: Frank Williams." In: Joseph M. Wayman, ed. *Grandstand Baseball Annual, 1986.* Downey, CA: Joseph M. Wayman, 1986. Pp. 68–89.

Fred ("Cy") Williams

OF. (B: Dec. 21, 1887, Wadens, IN-D: April 23, 1974). Chicago (NL), 1912–1917; Philadelphia (NL), 1918–1930. Remarks: Obtained 1,991 hits (251 homers) and 115 stolen bases in 2,002 games in a 19-year major league career; NL home run champion, 1916 (tie), 1920, 1923, and 1927 (tie); stole three bases in one game, April 19, 1922; first NL player to hit over 200 career homers; career 11 pinch-hit homers a record until 1960; also had seven career grand slam homers and 12 inside-the-park round-trippers; post-baseball, the Notre Dame grad an architect in Eagle River, Wisconsin.

56332. Gagnon, Richard ("Cappy"). "Fred C. 'Cy' Williams." In: Vol. Q-Z of David L. Porter, ed. *Biographical Dictionary of American Sports: Baseball.* Rev. and enlarged ed. Westport, CT: Greenwood Press, 2000. Pp. 1678–1679.

56333. Lawler, Joseph. "Cy Williams: Home Run King of the 1920s." *Phillies Report,* VII (June 29, 1989), 10–11.

56334. Mason, Ward. "The Greatest Outfielder in the National League." *Baseball Magazine,* XVII (September 1916), 45–50.

56335. Williams, Fred ("Cy"). "Hitting Home Runs." *Country Gentleman,* XCI (May 1926), 38+.

Glenn Williams

2B. (B: 1978, New South Wales, Australia). Remarks: Australian Baseball League player signed by Atlanta (NL) in 1992 for $925,000; played for Macon (Carolina League), 1997 and Danville (Carolina League), 1998; returned to Australia in 1999 to play for Dunedin Blue Jays and participated on Australian Olympic Team, 2000; Syracuse (IL), 2001–2003; played for Australian Olympic Team, 2004.

56336. Crawley, P. "Fast Ball: Glenn Williams." *Sports Weekly (Australia),* (February 27, 1996), 28–29.

Home Run Williams *see* **James Thomas ("Home Run" or "Button") Williams**

James Francis ("Jimy") Williams

2B-SS-MGR. (B: Oct. 4, 1943, Santa Maria, CA). St. Louis (NL), 1966–1968; Cincinnati (NL), 1968; Montreal (NL), 1969–1971. Remarks: Had but three big league hits in 14 games; manager, Quad Cities (Midwest League), 1974; manager, El Paso (Texas League), 1975; manager, Salt Lake City (PCL), 1976–1977; manager, Springfield (AA), 1978; manager, Salt Lake City (PCL), 1979; coach, Toronto (AL), 1980–1986; manager, Toronto (AL), 1986–1989; coach, Atlanta (NL), 1990–1996; manager, Boston (AL), 1997–2001; manager, Houston (NL), 2002–2004, winning, through July 13, 2004, a total of 910 major league games while losing 790 (.535).

56337. Livinstone, Seth. "Is New Manager Jimy Williams the Man Who Clear Up the Disarray in Fenway?" *USA Today Baseball Weekly,* VI (November 27, 1996), 18–19.

56338. Macht, Norman L. "Jimy Williams Has 40 Years of Baseball Stories to Tell." *Orioles Gazette,* III (September 10, 1993), 17–18.

56339. Verducci, Tom. "Hubbub: Manager Jimy Williams." *Sports Illustrated,* XCV (July 2, 2001), 36–41.

James Thomas ("Home Run" or "Button") Williams

3B. (B: Dec. 20, 1876, St. Louis, MO-D: Jan. 16, 1965). Pittsburgh (NL), 1899–1900; Baltimore (AL), 1901–1902; New York (AL), 1903–1907; St. Louis (AL), 1908–1909. Remarks: Obtained 1,507 hits (49 homers) and 159 stolen bases in 1,457 games in 11 seasons; had 27-game hitting streak, 1899; had six hits in one game, Aug. 25, 1902; also played for Minneapolis (AA), 1910–1916; scout, Cincinnati (NL), 1930–1935.

56340. Miller, William J. "James Thomas 'Home Run,' 'Button' Williams." In: Vol. Q-Z of David L. Porter, ed. *Biographical Dictionary of American Sports: Baseball.* Rev. and enlarged ed. Westport, CT: Greenwood Press, 2000. Pp. 1679–1681.

Jimy Williams *see* **James Francis ("Jimy") Williams**

Joseph ("Joe") Williams

WRITER. (B: 1891-D: 1972). Remarks: Columnist, *New York World-Telegram* and *New York Sun,* 1927–1961.

56341. Williams, Joe, and Peter Williams. *The Joe Williams Baseball Reader.* Chapel Hill, N.C.: Algonquin Books, 1989. 205p. New York and Cleveland scribe.

56342. Williams, Peter. "Appendix, Baseball in '47: Racism and Scapegoats." In: *The Joe Williams Reader.* Chapel Hill, NC: Algonquin Books of Chapel Hill, 1989. Pp. 202–207.

56343. _____. "When Chipmunks Become Wolves: The Scapegoating of Sportswriter Joe Williams by His Peers." *Nine: A Journal of Baseball History and Social Policy Perspective,* IV (Fall 1995), 51–61.

Joseph ("Joe" or "Cyclone" or "Smokey Joe") Williams★

P. (B: April 6, 1886, Seguin, TX-D: March 12, 1946). San

Antonio Black Bronchos, 1907–1909; Chicago Giants, 1910; New York Lincoln Giants, 1911–1912; Newark Giants, 1913; Chicago American Giants, 1914; Atlantic City Bacharach Giants, 1916; Hilldale Daisies, 1917; New York Lincoln Giants, 1918–1923; Brooklyn Royal Giants, 1924; Homestead Grays, 1925–1932; Detroit Wolves, 1932. Remarks: Considered one of the two greatest Negro League pitchers, who compiled a 20–7 record in exhibition games against white major leaguers; elected to National Baseball Hall of Fame in 1999, where his plaque reads: "A star pitcher in the early days of the Negro Leagues, the lanky right-hander with the smooth, overhand delivery, was destined for greatness with his pinpoint control, effective change of pace pitch and fastball that traveled with exceptional velocity. Playing for several teams, the New York Lincoln Giants (1911–23) and the Homestead Grays (1925–32) were the primary beneficiaries of his accomplishments. The easy-going Texan routinely reached double-digits in strikeouts in a game and on August 7, 1930, he struck out 27 Monarchs in a 12-inning contest. Voted the top pitcher in Negro Leagues history in a 1952 poll conducted by the *Pittsburgh Courier.* "

56344. Bernstein, David. "Joe Williams." In: John A. Garrity and Marsh C. Carries, eds. *American National Biography.* 24 vols. New York: Oxford University Press, 1999. XXIII, 470–471.

56345. Coates, John M. "Smokey Joe Williams." *Baseball Historical Review,* (1981), 46–47.

56346. Holway, John B. "Joe Williams: Smokey Joe." In: his *Blackball Stars.* Westport, CT: Meckler Corp., 1988. Pp. 61–78.

56347. _____. *Smokey Joe and The Cannonball.* Washington: Capital Press, 1983. 38p. Williams and Dick Redding.

56348. Kleinknecht, Merl F. and John B. Holoway. "Joseph 'Joe,' 'Smoky Joe,' 'Cyclone' Williams." In: Vol. Q–Z of David L. Porter, ed. *Biographical Dictionary of American Sports: Baseball.* Rev. and enlarged ed. Westport, CT: Greenwood Press, 2000. Pp. 1681–1682.

56349. Lester, Larry. "Smokey and The Bandit." *The National Pastime,* XIV (1994), 18–20.

56350. McCord, Jeff. "Color Commentary: Joe Williams of the Negro Leagues Elected to Hall of Fame." *Texas Monthly,* XXVII (August 1999), 52+.

56351. "Smokey Joe Williams Fans 27 Players." In: Dean A. Sullivan, ed. *Middle Innings: A Documentary History of Baseball, 1900–1948.* Lincoln, NE: University of Nebraska Press, 1998. Pp. 143–144. Reprinted from the *Kansas City American,* Aug. 7, 1930.

Kenneth Roy ("Ken") Williams
OF. (B. June 28, 1890, Grant's Pass, OR–D: Jan. 22, 1959). Cincinnati (NL), 1915–1916; St. Louis (AL), 1918–1927; Boston (AL), 1928–1929; New York (AL), 1930. Remarks: Obtained 1,552 hits (196 homers) and 154 stolen bases in 1,397 games in 15 seasons; AL home run champion, 1922; AL RBI champion, 1922; hit six homers in six games, July 28–Aug. 2, 1922; first player to hit 30 homers, steal 30 bases and hit .300 in one season (1922); also played for Portland (PCL), 1930–1931.

56352. Alvarez, Mark. "Ruth's First Rival." In: his *The Ol' Ball Game: A Collection of Baseball Characters and Moments Worth Remembering.* Harrisburg, PA: Stackpole Books, 1990. Pp. 25–30.

56353. Erwin, Phillip P. "Kenneth Roy 'Ken' Williams." In: Vol. Q–Z of David L. Porter, ed. *Biographical Dictionary of American Sports: Baseball.* Rev. and enlarged ed. Westport, CT: Greenwood Press, 2000. Pp. 1682–1683.

56354. Ward, John J. "A Rival for Babe Ruth?" *Baseball Magazine,* XXIX (July 1922), 349–351.

Kennety Royal ("Kenny" or "Ken") Williams
OF–BROADCASTER–EXEC. (B: April 6, 1964, Berkeley, CA). Chicago (AL), 1985–1988; Detroit (AL), 1989–1990; Toronto (AL), 1990–1991; Montreal (NL), 1991. Remarks: In seven big league seasons, had 252 hits (27 homers) and 49 stolen bases in 451 games; named to Oregon Sports Hall of Fame, 1980; scout, Chicago (AL), 1992–1994; studio analyst, SportsChannel, 1995; special asst. to chairman, Chicago (AL), 1994–1996; dir., minor league opns., Chicago (AL), 1996–1997; VP–Player development, Chicago (AL), 1998–2000; GM, Chicago (AL), 2000– (first African American GM in Chicago sports history).

56355. "Ken Williams: Making a Big Statement in the Big Leagues." *Ebony,* LVI (April 2001), 48–50.

Lefty Williams *see* **Claude Preston ("Lefty") Williams**

Matthew Derrick ("Matt") Williams
SS–3B. (B: Nov. 28, 1965, Bishop, CA). San Francisco (NL), 1987–1996; Cleveland (AL), 1997; Arizona (NL), 1998–2003. Remarks: Through June 2003, had 1,878 hits (378 homers) and 53 stolen bases in 1,866 games; had six hits (one double, two homers) in 1989 NLCS and two hits (one homer) in 1989 World Series; NL home run champion, 1994; had six RBIs in one game, June 28, 1997 and six RBIs in one inning, Aug. 27, 1997; had five hits (one double) in 1997 ALCS and 10 hits (one double, one homer) in 1997 World Series; had one grand slam homer (a first for the Diamondbacks), April 14, 1998; had five hits (one double) in 2001 NLCS and seven hits (two doubles, one homer) in 2001 World Series; had 12 career grand slam homers; owns Chandler, AZ, construction company; consultant, Arizona (NL), 2005–.

56356. Ballew, Bill. "Giants' Matt Williams Comes of Age as a Power Hitter." *Baseball Digest,* XLIX (November 1990), 34–36.

56357. Fimrite, Ron. "The Strong Silent Type." *Sports Illustrated,* LXXXI (July 25, 1994), 30–32, 37.

56358. Gilbert, Steve. "Matt Williams' Four-Homer Night." In: SABR. *Mining Towns to Major Leagues: A History of Arizona Baseball.* Cleveland, OH: Society for American Baseball Research, 1999. Pp. 23–24.

56359. Gilmartin, Joe. "The Marine." *Diamondbacks Magazine,* III (April 2000), 24–29.

56360. Goldman, Michael. "Take the Field." *Boys' Life,* LXXXVII (August 1997), 22–25.

56361. Greule, Otto, Jr. "Superstar Gallery: Matt Williams." *Beckett Baseball Card Monthly,* VIII (January 1991), 16–17.

56362. Kaplan, Ben. "Get Into Baseball." *Sports Illustrated for Kids,* VII (April 1995), 22–27.

56363. Kuenster, John. "Matt Williams Building Credentials as Majors' Premier Third Baseman." *Baseball Digest,* LIII (August 1994), 17–19.

56364. Nightengale, Bob. "Inside the Matt Williams Trade: The Real Deal." *USA Today Baseball Weekly,* VII (December 10, 1997), 8–11.

56365. Pascarelli, Peter. "Watch the Door, Matt." *USA Today Baseball Weekly,* V (November 29, 1995), 5–6.

56366. Pearlman, Jeff and Stephen Cannella. "Desert Rebirth: After Dreary Debuts in Arizona, Diamondbacks Batting Stars Matt Williams and Jay Bell Are Living Up to Expectations." *Sports Illustrated,* XC (May 17, 1999), 75–76.

56367. Pluto, Terry. "Matt Williams Turns a New Page

as AL Power Hitter." *Baseball Digest,* LVI (June 1997), 34–36.

56368. Porter, David L. "Matthew Derrick 'Matt' Williams." In: Vol. Q-Z of David L. Porter, ed. *Biographical Dictionary of American Sports: Baseball.* Rev. and enlarged ed. Westport, CT: Greenwood Press, 2000. Pp. 1683–1684.

56369. Ratto, Ray. "Williams Takes Giant-Sized, If Muffled, Steps to Fame." In: George Leonard, ed. *Athlon's Baseball '91.* Nashville, TN: Athlon Sports Communications, 1991. Pp. 68–71.

56370. Rousch, Gary. "A Closer Look: Matt Williams." *Beckett Baseball Card Monthly,* VI (December 1989), 6–7.

56371. Snyder, Dron. "His Numbers Are Truly Giant But Matt Williams' Reputation is Not ... Yet." *USA Today Baseball Weekly,* IV (May 18, 1994), 8–9.

56372. Spander, Art. "Matt Williams: Roller Coaster to Stardom." *The Show,* II, no. 1 (1991), 86–89.

56373. Weinberg, Rick. "Lasting Impression: Giants' Slugger Matt Williams' Battles to be the Best." *Sport,* LXXXIII (September 1992), 64–67.

56374. Wendel, Tim. "Playing Through Pain: Cleveland's Matt Williams is Used to Overcoming Injuries, But This Year He's Healing a Broken Heart." *USA Today Baseball Weekly,* VII (September 24, 1997), 22–23.

56375. Whiteside, Kelly. "Big Matt Attack." *Sports Illustrated,* LXXXII (June 5, 1995), 32–35.

56376. Williams, Matt. "When I was a Kid: Interview." *Junior League Baseball,* no. 18 (November-December 1998), 10+.

Mitchell Steven ("Mitch" or "The Wild Thing") Williams

P. (B: Nov. 17, 1964, Santa Ana, CA). Texas (AL), 1986–1988; Chicago (NL), 1989–1990. Remarks: Won 45, lost 58, and saved 192 games in five big league seasons; coach, Atlantic City (Atlantic League), 2001–2002; manager, Atlantic City (Atlantic League), 2002–2003; identified with character in motion picture *Major League.*

56377. Bell, Christopher. "Mitch Williams." In: his *Scapegoats: Baseballers Whose Careers are Marked by One Fateful Play.* Jefferson, NC: McFarland & Co., Inc., 2002. Pp. 142–156.

56378. Cairns, Bob. "Mitch Williams." In: his *Pen Men: Baseball's Greatest Bullpen Stories told by the Men who Brought the Game Relief.* New York: St. Martin's Press, 1992. Pp. 380–384.

56379. Couch, Greg. "A Wiser Wild Thing: Mitch Williams Returns to the Game as a Pitching Coach." *Baseball Digest,* LX (July 2001), 72–75.

56380. Dewan, John and Don Zminda. "Why Did Mitch Love to Pitch Last August?" In: STATS, Inc. *STATS 1992 Baseball Scoreboard.* Chicago, IL: STATS Publishing, 1992. Pp. 40–42.

56381. Garcia, Dan. "Mitch Williams: The Cubs' New Bullpen Stopper." *Baseball Digest,* XLVIII (September 1989), 84–86.

56382. Kurkjian, Tim. "Relief at Last." *Sports Illustrated,* LXXX (June 13, 1994), 42–45.

56383. _____. "A Walk on the Wild Side." *Sports Illustrated,* LXXIX (November 1, 1993), 22–23.

56384. "Mitch Williams." In: Carrie Muskat, ed. *Banks to Sandberg to Grace: Five Decades of Love and Frustration with the Chicago Cubs.* Chicago, IL: Contemporary Books, 2001. Pp. 231–232.

56385. Plummer, William and Meg Grant. "Out of Control." *People Weekly,* XLI (May 9, 1994), 158–159.

56386. Rains, Bob. "Wild Thing Warms Up: Williams

Waits for a Call." *USA Today Baseball Weekly,* IV (November 16, 1994), 4–6.

56387. Reynolds, Gretchen. "Great Balls of Fire." *Chicago,* XXXIX, no. 4 (1990), 112–113.

56388. Telander, Rick. "Wild Thing — Mitch Williams, the Cubs' Ace Reliever, is as Unpredictable as the Movie Character He Idolizes. But Who Cares? It Works." *Sports Illustrated,* LXXI (August 28, 1989), 38–42.

56389. "The Unforgiven." In: Joe Hoppel, ed. *The Sporting News 1994 Baseball Yearbook.* St. Louis, MO: *The Sporting News,* 1994. Pp. 12–19.

56390. Verducci, Tom. "Mitch Williams." *Sports Illustrated,* LXXIX (December 13, 1993), 62–63.

Richard Hirschfield ("Dick") Williams

OF-3B-1B-2B-MGR. (B: May 7, 1928, St. Louis, MO). Brooklyn (NL), 1951–1954, 1956; Baltimore (AL), 1956–1959; Kansas City (AL), 1959–1960; Baltimore (AL), 1961–1962; Boston (AL), 1963–1964. Remarks: Had 768 hits (70 homers) and 12 stolen bases in 1,023 games in 13 playing years; obtained one hit in 1953 World Series; had grand slam homer, May 10, 1960; minor league manager, 1965–1966; manager, Boston (AL), 1967–1969, Oakland (A.L), 1971–1973, California (AL), 1974–1976, Montreal (NL), 1977–1981, and San Diego (NL), 1982–1986; Seattle (AL), 1986–1987, winning 1,571 games and losing 1,451 (.522) and becoming only the second manager after Bill McKechnie, (q.v.) to win pennants with three different teams; consultant, New York (AL), 1996-.

56391. Abel, Allen. "Dick Williams Can Remember Baseball's Angry Days." *Baseball Digest,* XXXIX (July 1980), 35–40.

56392. Berry, Henry. "Managers: Dick Williams." In: his *Baseball's Great Teams: Boston Red Sox.* New York: Collier Books, 1975. Pp. 128–132.

56393. Bouton, Jim. "Dick Williams: How Dick Williams Became the World Champion Manager." In: Jim Bouton, ed. *"I Managed Good, but Boy Did They Play Bad."* Chicago, IL: Playboy Press, 1973. Pp. 283–290.

56394. Burick, Si. "[1972 World Series] Game No. 4: Dick Williams Gambled and Got Away With It." *Baseball Digest,* XXXII (January 1973), 37–39.

56395. Crehan, Herbert F. and James W. Ryan. "Dick Williams." In: their *Lightning in a Bottle: The Sox of '67.* Boston, MA: Branden Publishing Co., 1992. Pp. 227–240.

56396. Debs, Victor, Jr. "Dick Williams." In: his *"That Was Part of Baseball Then": Interviews with 24 Former Major League Baseball Players, Coaches, and Managers.* Jefferson, NC: McFarland & Co., Inc., 2002. Pp. 195–200.

56397. Diaz, Jaime. "A Fresh Breeze Cools the Desert Air." *Sports Illustrated,* LXIV (March 10, 1986), 18–21.

56398. "Dick Williams." In: *Current Biography Yearbook, 1973.* New York: H.W. Wilson Co., 1973. Pp. 437–439.

56399. Elderkin, Phil. "Dick Williams Reflects Dodger Influence." *Baseball Digest,* XXVII (July 1968), 87–90.

56400. Ellis, James. "Dick Williams: He Isn't Afraid of Winning." *Baseball Digest,* XVI (June 1957), 7–11.

56401. Frey, Leonard H. "Richard Hirschfield 'Dick' Williams." In: Vol. Q-Z of David L. Porter, ed. *Biographical Dictionary of American Sports: Baseball.* Rev. and enlarged ed. Westport, CT: Greenwood Press, 2000. Pp. 1684–1686.

56402. Frommer, Harvey. "Dick Williams." In: his *Baseball's Greatest Managers.* New York: Franklin Watts, 1985. Pp. 243–253.

56403. Gammons, Peter. "Dick Williams: He's Mellowed, but He's Still a Winner." *Baseball Digest,* XLIII (November 1984), 31–37.

56404. Hirshberg, Al. Dick Williams' Second World Series [1972]: 'This Time the Heroes Wore Mustaches." *Sport,* LVI (October 1973), 96–103.

56405. Honig, Donald. "Dick Williams." In: his *The Man In the Dugout.* Chicago, IL: Follett Publishing Co., 1977. Pp. 198–212.

56406. Jares, Joe. "Slight Revival of Hope in Boston. Red Box Disciplined by Tough-Guy Manager." *Sports Illustrated,* XXVI (May 15, 1967), 66–68+.

56407. Kaplan, Jim. "The Padres' Persnickety Papa." *Sports Illustrated,* LVI (June 28, 1982), 22–24+.

56408. Lautier, Jack. "Dick Williams." In: his *Fenway Voices.* Camden, ME: Yankee Books, 1990. Pp. 97–100.

56409. Liston, Robert. "Dick Williams." In: his *The Pros.* New York: Platt & Munk, 1968. Pp. 153–170.

56410. Lorge, Barry. "Dick Williams: He Likes to Play 'Hardball." *Baseball Digest,* XLII (July 1983), 86–90.

56411. Mulvoy, Mark. "What a Difference a Day, Makes: Dick Williams, Manager of the California Angels." *Sports Illustrated,* XLI (July 15, 1974), 48+.

56412. Patterson, Ted. "Three-Time Oriole Dick Williams Hasn't Mellowed a Bit." *Orioles Gazette,* II (April 17, 1992), 17–18.

56413. Swift, E. M. "A Summer Winner in Montreal." *Sports Illustrated,* LI (July 16, 1979), 20–21.

56414. "Trying to Manage a Pennant." *Macleans,* XCII (July 23, 1979), 34–35.

56415. Williams, Richard H. ("Dick"). "The Game I'll Never Forget." *Baseball Digest,* XXX (January 1971), 29–32.

56416. _____. and Bill Plaschke. *No More Mr. Nice Guy: A Life of Hardball.* San Diego, CA: Harcourt Brace Jovanovich Publishers, 1990. 344p.

Smokey Joe Williams *see* **Joseph ("Smokey Joe") Williams**

Stanley Wilson ("Stan") Williams

P. (B: Sept. 14, 1939, Enfield, NH). Los Angeles (NL), 1958–1962; New York (AL), 1963–1964; Cleveland (AL), 1965, 1967–1969; Minnesota (AL), 1970–1971; St. Louis (NL), 1971; Boston (AL), 1972. Remarks: Had 109 victories, 94 defeats, and 43 saves in 14 big league seasons; won Game Two of 1959 NL playoffs; pitched five innings in 1959 and 1963 World Series and six innings in 1972 ALCS, all without a decision; minor league instructor and coach, Boston (AL), 1975–1976; coach, Chicago (AL), 1977–1978, New York (AL), 1980–1982, 1985, 1987–1988, Cincinnati (NL), 1984, 1989–1991, Seattle (AL), 1998–1999.

56417. Stone, Larry. "Reds' 'Nasty Boys' Took Cue from Their Pitching Coach." *Baseball Digest,* L (April 1991), 70–71.

Ted Williams *see* **Theodore Samuel ("Ted" or "The Kid" or "The Splendid Splinter" or "The Thumper") Williams ★**

Theodore Samuel ("Ted" or "The Kid" or "The Splendid Splinter" or "The Thumper") Williams ★

OF-MGR. (B: Aug. 30, 1918, San Diego, CA-D: July 5, 2002). Boston (AL), 1939–1942, 1946–1960. Remarks: Obtained 2,654 hits (521 homers) and 24 stolen bases in 2,292 games in 19 years; hit game-winning homer, 1941 All-Star Game; AL MVP award, 1946 and 1949 (lost to Joe DiMaggio (q.v.) by one point In 1941); AL Triple Crown Winner, 1942 and 1947; AL batting champion, 1941–1942, 1947–1948, 1957–1958; AL home run champion, 1941–1942, 1947, 1949; AL RBI champion,1939, 1942, 1947,

1949 (tie); led AL in walks, 1941–1942, 1946–1949, 1951, 1954; led AL in doubles, 1948–1949; hit two homers in 1946 All-Star Game, the second an "eephus pitch" hurled by Truett Banks ("Rip") Sewell (q.v.); hit pennant-clinching inside-the-park homer, Sept. 13, 1946; went 5-for-25 in 1946 World Series; first AL batter to face three pitchers in one inning, July 4, 1948; had 13 hits in a doubleheader, May 16, 1954; had four homers in four official ABs in four games, Sept. 1957; hit last homer in last AB, Sept. 28, 1960; made or tied numerous major league and AL records, including most consecutive years leading in runs scored (5), most consecutive years leading in walks received (6), obtained lifetime 2,019 walks, most All-Star Game homers (4), second to George Herman ("Babe") Ruth (q.v.); oldest player to win batting crown and last to hit .400 or better for a season (.406 in 1941); obtained 17 career grand slam homers; the first of only three big league players to steal a base in four decades; began with San Diego (PCL), 1936–1937 and Minneapolis (AA), 1938; flew 39 Korean War jet combat missions, 1952; manager, Washington (AL/Texas (AL), 1969–1972, winning 273 games and losing 364 (.429); presided over the opening of the Ted Williams Retrospective Museum and Library (Hernando, fl), Feb. 9, 1994; honored at 1999 All-Star Game; elected to National Baseball Hall of Fame in 1966, where his plaque reads: "Batted .406 in 1941. Led AL in batting 6 times; slugging percentage 9 times; total bases 6 times; runs scored 6 times; bases on balls 8 times. Total hits 2654 Included 521 home runs. Lifetime batting average .344. Lifetime slugging average .634. Most Valuable AL Player 1946 & 1949. Played in 18 AII-Star Games. Named Player of the Decade 1951–1960."

56418. Addle, Bob. "The 'Real' Ted Williams Sounds Off." *Baseball Digest,* XXIX (January 1970), 41–43.

56419. _____. "Ted Williams Sights Another Crown at 40." *Baseball Digest,* XVI (December 1957), 11–13.

56420. Allen, Lee. "The Splendid Splinter." In: his *The American League Story.* New York: Hill & Wang, 1962. Pp. 167–171.

56421. Allen, Mel, and Jim Britt. "Who is the World's Greatest Ballplayer: Joe DiMaggio-Ted Williams-What Do You Think?" *Sport,* V (September 1948), 19–29.

56422. Amory, Cleveland. "Young Ted Williams. 'I Wanna Be an Immortal.'" In: Editors of *Saturday Evening Post. Sport U.SA* New York: Nelson, 1961. Pp. 334–338.

56423. Ashby, Ted. "Ted Made 'Em Speak Up." *Baseball Digest,* VIII (September 1949), 66–69.

56424. Astor, Gerald. "The 'Splendid Splinter' Swings Again." *Look,* XXXIII (April 29, 1969), 88–90+.

56425. "A Baseball Immortal's Life and Times." *Sport,* XLI (February 1966), 58–63. Pictorial.

56426. Baldassaro, Lawrence. *Ted Williams: Reflections on a Splendid Life.* Boston, MA: Northeastern University Press, 2003. 250p.

56427. _____. "Ted Williams: The Reluctant Hero." *Journal of American Culture,* IV (Fail 1981), 66–74.

56428. _____., ed. *The Ted Williams Reader.* New York: Fireside, 1991. 299p.

56429. Bethel, Dell. "What I Learned About Hitting from Ted Williams." *Coach and Athletic Director,* LXXIV (January 2005), 24, 26–31.

56430. Bingham, Walter. "New Season-Old Ted." *Sports Illustrated,* XII (May 2, 1960), 14–17.

56431. Birtwell, Roger. "Ted Sees Fifth Title on .370." *Baseball Digest,* VIII (May 1949), 3–5.

56432. Bisher, Furman. "The Kid Grows Up." *Complete Baseball,* IV (September 1952), 34–36.

56433. _____. "The Splinter, Partner and Manager." In: Furman Bisher, ed. *The Furman Bisher Collection.* Dallas, TX: Taylor Publishing Co., 1989. Pp. 191–193. Reprinted from the February 17, 1969 issue of the *Atlanta Journal-Constitution.*

56434. Blandford, Peter. "The Last Time Up." *American Heritage,* XLI (April 1990), 30–31.

56435. Blood, Ted. *"Splendid Splinter": The Story of How the Sportswriters Tried to Chop Up "The Splinter" for Firewood.* Hicksville, N.Y.: Exposition Press, 1960. 92p.

56436. Bolin, Dan and Ed Diaz. "Ted Williams." In: their *The Winning Run and Other Life Lessons from Baseball.* New York: Navpress, 1999. Pp. 85–88.

56437. Brandt, M.J. "Theodore Goes Mild." *Baseball Magazine,* LXV (November 1940), 545–547.

56438. Broeg, Bob. "Ted Williams." In: his *Super Stars of Baseball.* St. Louis, MO: The Sporting News, 1971. Pp. 271–280.

56439. Brown, Warren. "'Fence Busters Make the Game' — Ted Williams." *Baseball. Digest,* XIX (September 1960), 32–33.

56440. _____. "What Might Have Been for Ted Williams." *Baseball Digest,* XXXI (March 1972), 82–85.

56441. Bryant, Nelson A. "Greatest Offensive Power-DiMaggio or Williams? "*Baseball Magazine,* LXXVI (March 1946), 341–343.

56442. Bryson, Bill. "Ted Needs .324 for Mark for 41-Year Olds." *Baseball Digest,* XVIII (May 1950, 11–13.

56443. _____. "Ted Williams On-Base Champ." *Baseball Digest,* XIX (April 1960), 36–37.

56444. _____. "Ted's H.R. [Home Run] Finish Outdid the Babe's." *Baseball Digest,* XX (June 1961), 57–58.

56445. _____. "Williams' Head Start." *Baseball Magazine,* LXVIII (February 1942), 407–408+.

56446. Burchard, S.H. "Ted Williams." In: his *Book of Baseball Greats.* New York: Harcourt, Brace, Jovanovich, 1983. Pp. 20–23.

56447. Chamberlain, John. "Ted Williams: Baseball's Foremost Problem Child." *Life,* XXI (September 23, 1946), 108–110+.

56448. Christopher, Matt. "September 28, 1960: Ted Williams, the Greatest Hitter's Last At-Bat." In: his *Matt Christopher's Great Moments in Baseball History.* Boston, MA: Little, Brown & Co., 1996. Pp. 42–55.

56449. Condon, Robert J. "Ted Williams." In: his *The 50 Greatest Athletes of the 20th Century: A Worldwide Reference.* Jefferson, N.C.: McFarland & Co., Inc., 1990. Pp. 63–66.

56450. Considine, Bob. "The 'Why' of Ted Williams." *Baseball Digest,* V (November 1946), 13–15.

56451. Corry, J. "The Return of Ted Williams." *HararHarpers,* CCXXXVIII (June 1949), 73–78.

56452. Cramer, Richard Ben. *What Do You Think of Ted Williams Now?: A Remembrance.* New York: Simon and Schuster, 2002. 128p. Expanded from the next entry.

56453. _____. "What Do You Think of Ted Williams, Now?" *Esquire,* CV (June 1986), 74–76. Reprinted in David Halberstam, ed. *The Best American Sports Writing of the Century* (Boston, MA: Houghton, Mifflin, 1999), pp. 58–89.

56454. _____. Mark Rucker and John Thorn. *Ted Williams: The Seasons of the Kid.* New York: Prentice Hall Press, 1991. 256p.

56455. Creamer, Robert W. "Ted Is Hope." *Sports Illustrated,* IV (March 12, 1956), 40–45.

56456. Crissy, Kit. "The Splendid Splinter's Splendid Finish." *The National Pastime,* XI (1992), 52–54.

56457. Crothers, Tim. "Ted Williams." In: his *Greatest Athletes of the 20th Century.* New York: Total Sports Illustrated, 2000. Pp. 92–97.

56458. Cunningham, Bill. "Royal Rookie." *Collier's,* CIII (June 24, 1939), 24+.

56459. _____. "Williams." *Sport,* I (September 1946), 25, 86–87.

56460. Daley, Arthur. "The Fabulous Career of Tempestuous, Terrific Ted." In: J. G. Taylor Spink, ed. *Baseball Register, 1961.* St. Louis: The Sporting News, 1961. Pp. 2–18.

56461. _____. "Feats at 38: Targets for Ted? *Baseball Digest,* XVI (May 1957), 75–77.

56462. _____. "A Prideful Man: Ted Williams." *Baseball Digest,* XV (August 1956), 58–61.

56463. _____. "Return of the Master." *Baseball Digest,* XIV (July 1955), 11–13.

56464. _____. "Ted Williams." In: his *All the Home Run Kings.* New York: G.P. Putnam, 1972. Pp. 47–57.

56465. _____. "Ted Williams." In: his *Kings of the Home Run.* New York: G.P. Putnam, 1962. Pp. 57–61.

56466. _____. "Ted Williams." In: his *Sports of The Times.* New York: E.P. Dutton,1959. Pp. 81–83, 268–270.

56467. _____. "That Williams Explosion." *Baseball Digest,* X (February 1951), 39–41.

56468. Daniel, Daniel M. "Ted Williams: Rookie of the Year." *Baseball Magazine,* LXIII (August 1939), 387–389+.

56469. Debs, Victor Jr. "Ted's Try for a Third Triple Crown." In: his *Missed It by That Much: Baseball Players Who Challenged the Record Book.* Jefferson, NC: McFarland & Co., 1998. Pp. 83–97.

56470. Devaney, John. "Ted Williams." In: his *Baseball's Youngest Big Leaguers.* New York: Holt, Rinehart and Winston, 1969. Pp. 1–26.

56471. Dreyspool, Joan P. "Conversation Piece — Subject-Ted Williams." *Sports illustrated,* III (August 1, 1955), 28–31.

56472. Durslag, Melvin. 'Will Anyone Hit .400 Again?" *TV Guide,* XXIX (April 4, 1981), 18–20.

56473. Egan, Dave ("The Colonel"). "Colonel Sends Word to Williams: 'Why Wait 'till '54 End? — Quit Now, 1954.'" In: Glenn Stout, ed. *Impossible Dreams: A Red Sox Collection.* Boston, MA: Mariner Books, 2003. Pp. 182–184.

56474. _____. "Slight to Ted Disgraceful." In: Glenn Stout, ed. *Impossible Dreams: A Red Sox Collection.* Boston, MA: Mariner Books, 2003. Pp. 189–191.

56475. Egan, Terry, Stan Friedmann, and Mike Levine. "Going to Bat for America: A Tip of the Cap to Ted Williams." In: their *The Macmillan Book of Baseball Stories.* New York: Macmillan, 1992. Chpt. 6.

56476. Enders, Eric. "Baseball Legend." In: Richard Levin, ed. *2002 World Series Official Program.* New York: Major League Baseball Promotion Corp., 2002. Pp. 39–40.

56477. Ferroli, Steve. *Hit Your Potential: Mastering the Ted Williams Approach.* Indianapolis, IN: Masters Press, 1998. 169p.

56478. Fitzgerald, Ed. "Two Guys Named Ted Williams." *Sport,* IV (April 1948), 59–69.

56479. Forman, Ross. "A Chat with the Best Hitter Who Ever Lived. "*Sports Collector's Digest,* XXII (June 30, 1995), 80–82.

56480. Freeburg, Dwight. "Batter Number One." In: Sidney Offit, ed. *Best of Baseball.* New York: G.P. Putnam, 1956. Pp. 176–182. Reprinted from the January 1942 issue of *Baseball Magazine.*

56481. French, Bob. "Ted Learned His Lesson." *Baseball Digest,* VII (July 1949), 39–42.

56482. Gagnon, Richard ("Cappy"). "The Greatest Batting Eye in History." In: Mark Alvarez, ed. *The Perfect Game: A Classic Collection of Facts, Figures, Stories and Characters from the Society for American Baseball Research.* New York: Barnes & Noble Books, 1995. Pp. 79–88.

56483. Garner, Joe and Bob Costas. "Ted Williams Finishes Career with Home Run" In: their *And the Crowd Goes Wild: Relive the Most Celebrated Sporting Events Ever Broadcast.* Napervile, IL: Sourcebooks, 1999. Chpt. 9. The work also includes two sound CDs, with the Williams deed recorded on the first.

56484. Gartner, Michael. *Ted Williams, Sam the Genius, and Other Sports Stories from The Wall Street Journal.* Princeton, N.J.: Dow Jones Books, 1970. 192p.

56485. Gerlach, Larry R. "Ted Williams Redivivus." *Nine: A Journal of Baseball History and Social Policy Perspectives,* II (Fall 1993), 112–119.

56486. _____. "Theodore Samuel 'Ted,' 'The Splendid Splinter,' 'The Thumper,' 'The Kid,' 'The Big Guy,' 'Teddy Ballgame' Williams." In: Vol. Q-Z of David L. Porter, ed. *Biographical Dictionary of American Sports: Baseball.* Rev. and enlarged ed. Westport, CT: Greenwood Press, 2000. Pp. 1686–1688.

56487. Gibbons, Frank. "Ted Williams: Rembrandt of the Rappers." *Baseball Digest,* XIX (November-December 1960), 19–22.

56488. Gillooly, Mike. "The Case FOR Ted Williams." *Baseball Digest,* XVII (May 1958), 5–14.

56489. _____. "How Ted Williams Became Popular." *Sport,* XXV (June 1958), 28–29+.

56490. Gold, Victor. "Last Hurrah: Washington was First in War, First in Peace, and Last in the American League — Until Ted Williams Arrived." *Washingtonian,* XXXV (May 2000), 37–42.

56491. Grady, Sandy. "Ted Williams: Fan Added Six Years to His Career." *Baseball Digest,* XXV (May 1966), 56–67.

56492. Graham, Frank. "Ted Williams." In: his *Baseball Extra.* New York: A.S. Barnes, 1964. Pp. 109–121

56493. _____. "Ted Williams." In: his *Greatest Hitters of the Major Leagues.* New York: Random House, 1969. Pp. 95–107.

56494. Green, Bob. "Ted Williams." In: his Ed Fitzgerald, ed. *Heroes of Sport.* New York: Bartholomew House, 1961. Pp. 98–107.

56495. Gutman, Bill. "Ted Williams." In: his *Famous Baseball Stars.* New York: Dodd, Mead, 1973. Pp. 112–113.

56496. Hannan, Jerry. "Ted Williams, Premier Batting Coach: Big Improvements for the '68 Senators." *The Baseball Research Journal,* XXIV (1995), 101–102.

56497. Hano, Arnold. "*Sport's* Hall of Fame: Ted Williams' Wild Career." *Sport,* XXXVIII (September 1964), 24–27.

56498. Hanvik, Bill. "Ted Williams — the Minneapolis [Millers] Beginning: The Boys of Summer of 1938." *Active Lifestyles,* VIII (September 1991), 24–25, 38.

56499. Hawkins, Burt. "Ted Williams, First Rangers Manager." In: John Blake, *et al. Texas Rangers Official 1994 Yearbook.* Arlington, TX: Public Relations Dept., Texas Rangers, 1994. Pp. 56–60.

56500. Hern, Gerry. "It's Williams' Last Year." *Baseball Digest,* XIII (March 1954), 69–71.

56501. _____. "Ted Sets Back Baseball Clock, 1950." In: Glenn Stout, ed. *Impossible Dreams: A Red Sox Collection.* Boston, MA: Mariner Books, 2003. Pp. 179–181.

56502. _____. "Ted Williams Fined $5,000 for Spit-

ting." In: Dean A. Sullivan, ed. *Late Innings: A Documentary History of Baseball, 1945–1972.* Lincoln, NE: University of Nebraska Press, 2002. Pp. 92–94. Reprinted from the *Boston Post,* Aug. 8, 1956.

56503. Hirshberg, Al. "Handsome Bad Boy of the Boston Red Sox." *Cosmopolitan,* CXLI (July 1056), 123–127.

56504. _____. "Ted Williams." In: his *Greatest American Leaguers.* New York: G.P. Putnam, 1970. Pp. 165–176.

56505. _____. "Who Says Ted Williams is Dumb?" *Sport,* XI (September 1951), 6–7+.

56506. _____. "Williams Can Win for Boston." *Sport,* XVI (April 1954), 34–35+.

56507. Hoffer, Richard. "We Kid You Not! Williams Tops .400: The Author Returns to Yesteryear to Report on the Splinter's Splendid Final-Weekend Drive to Preserve a Piece of Hitting History." *Sports Illustrated,* XCVII (July 17, 2002), 42–45.

56508. _____. "Williams Does It!: Bosox Slugger Ends Season with .406 Mark." *Sports Illustrated,* LXXIX (July 19, 1993), 25–26, 28.

56509. Holbrook, Bob. "When Ted Williams Batted in the Outfield." *Baseball Digest,* XIX (February 1960), 73–75.

56510. _____. "Williams Hits Homer, Covers Mouth Before 30,338." In: Glenn Stout, ed. *Impossible Dreams: A Red Sox Collection.* Boston, MA: Mariner Books, 2003. Pp. 185–188.

56511. Holtzman, Jerome. "Quickness, a Key to Good Hitting, Says Ted Williams." *Baseball Digest,* XLVI (May 1987), 27–29.

56512. _____. "Ted Williams: He's Still Connecting with Strong Views." *Baseball Digest,* LVI (June 1997), 54–55.

56513. Holway, John B. *The Last .400 Hitter: The Anatomy of a .400 Season.* Dubuque, IA: Wm. C. Brown Publishers, 1992. 360p.

56514. _____. "Ted Williams: His Missing Seasons Cost Him Titles." *Baseball Digest,* LVII (April 1998), 64–67.

56515. _____. "What Might Have Been for Williams, Feuer." *Baseball Digest,* XVI (September 1967), 77–84. If the two had not served in World War II.

56516. Honig, Donald. "Ted Williams." In: his *Baseball America.* New York: Macmillan, 1985. Pp. 228–243.

56517. _____. "Ted Williams." In: his *The Power Hitters.* St. Louis, MO: The Sporting News, 1989. pp. 78–91.

56518. Howard, Frank. "What It's Like to Play for Ted Williams." *Sport,* XLIX (March 1970), 22–23+.

56519. Hufford, Tim. "Ted Williams Pitching for the Red Sox." *The Baseball Research Journal,* VII (1978), 8–11. Threw two innings in a 1940 game, neither winning nor losing.

56520. Jacobs, Barry. "Few Belong to the .400 Club, but Ted Williams Holds the Door Open." *Baseball Digest,* XL (December 1981), 67–71.

56521. Jacobs, Bruce. "Ted Williams In: his *Baseball Stars of 1956.* New York: Lion Books, 1956. Pp. 98–147.

56522. Janoff, Murray. "Tolerant Ted Takes a New Tack." In Clyde Hirt, ed. *Sports Quarterly Presents Baseball Extra, Summer 1971.* New York: Counterpoint, Inc., 1971. Pp. 6–9.

56523. Johnson, Dick, ed. *Ted Williams: A Portrait in Words and Pictures.* New York: Walker and Company, 1991. 225p.

56524. Kaese, Harold. "Now That Williams Is Back." *Baseball Digest,* XIV (July 1955), 13–15.

56525. _____. "So You Think You Know Ted Williams." *Sport,* III (August 1947), 14–15+.

56526. _____. "Ted's Longest Homer Pierces Straw Hat on Head 450 Feet Away, 1946." In: Glenn Stout, ed. *Impossible Dreams: A Red Sox Collection.* Boston, MA: Mariner Books, 2003. Pp. 134–135.

56527. _____. "Why We [the Press] Pick on Ted Williams." *Sport,* VI (May 1949), 8–9+.

56528. _____. "Will Ted Williams Manage the Red Sox?" *Baseball Digest,* XVIII (September 1958), 19–21.

56528. _____.and Frederick G. Lieb. "Who's the Greatest Hitter in Baseball?: Musial vs. Williams." *Sport,* III (July 1947), 72–75+.

56529. Kelly, Edward H. "Ted William Best Ever at Reaching Base Safely." *Baseball Digest,* XXXIX (December 1980), 54–59.

56530. Kelly, Robert E. "Tribute to Ted." In: his *Baseball for the Hot Stove League.* Jefferson, NC: McFarland & Co., Inc., 1989. Pp. 145–154.

56531. Kindred, Dave. "A Hitter First, a Hitter Always." In: Dan Jenkins, ed. *The Best American Sports Writing, 1995.* Boston, MA: Houghton, Mifflin, 1995. Pp. 4–11.

56532. King, Joe. "Williams Wants to Make Good." *Complete Baseball,* IV (July 1962), 18–19+.

56533. Kirwin, B. "Ted Williams Ad Referendum." *Nine: A Journal of Baseball History and Social Policy Perspectives,* II (Fall 1993), 119–121.

56534. Krabbenhoft, Herm. "Ted Williams' OBPCG." *The Baseball Research Journal,* XXXII (2003), 41–46.

56535. Kunen, James S. "The Last of the .400 Hitters." *The New York Times Magazine,* (May 12, 1974), 22–25.

56536. Kuenster, John. "Why Ted Williams Called It Quits [as a Manager]." *Baseball Digest*, XXXII (January 1973), 4–8.

56537. Lake, Austen. "Ted Williams Blasts Boston, 1940." In: Glenn Stout, ed. *Impossible Dreams: A Red Sox Collection.* Boston, MA: Mariner Books, 2003. Pp. 175–178.

56538. _____. "The Other Ted Williams." *Baseball Digest,* XI (January 1952), 10–13.

56539. Leiker, Ken. "6–1941: Ted Williams Hits .406 — the Last Player to Achieve .400." In: his *Major League Baseball Memorable Moments: The Most Memorable Moments in Major League Baseball History.* New York: Ballantine Books, 2002. Pp. 38–43.

56540. Lewis, Allen. "Even Retired, Ted Awes Them." *Baseball Digest,* XX (May 1961), 59–61.

56541. Lewis, Jerry D. "Baby Ruth." *American Magazine,* CXXIX (June 1940), 57+.

56542. Libby, Bill. "Ted Williams." In: his *Baseball's Greatest Sluggers.* New York: Random House, 1973. Pp. 64–89.

56543. Linn, Ed. "Growing Up with Ted." *Sport,* XLI (February 1966), 56–51.

56544. _____. *Hitter: The Life and Turmoils of Ted Williams.* New York: Harcourt Brace Jovanovich & Co., 1993. 427p.

56545. _____. "The Kid's Last Game." *Sport,* XXXI (February 1961), 52–43. Reprinted In Editors of *Sport. World of Sport,* (New York: Holt, Rinehart and Winston, 1962), pp. 81–105 and Al Silverinan, ed., *Best of Sport, 1946–1971* (New York: Viking Press, 1971), pp. 186–212; Charles Einstein, ed., *The Third Fireside Book of Baseball* (New York: Simon and Schuster, 1968), pp. 272–284; in Al Silverman and Brian Silverman, eds., *The Twentieth Century Treasury of Sports* (New York: Viking Press, 1992), pp. 419–443; and in Glenn Stout, ed., *Impossible Dreams: A Red Sox Collection* (Boston, MA: Mariner Books, 2003), pp. 192–220.

56546. _____. The Last Summer of #9 and #6." *Sport,* XVIII (September 1959), 12–15.

56547. _____. "The Ted Williams Miracle." *Sport,* XXV (January 1958), 14–17.

56548. _____. *Ted Williams: The Eternal Kid.* New York: Bartholomew House, 1961. 175p.

56549. _____. "Ted Williams: The Kid Comes of Age." *Sport,* XVII (August 1954), 50–61.

56550. Liss, Howard. "Ted Williams." In: his *Triple Crown Winners.* New York: Julian Messner, 1969. Pp, 37–50.

56551. Maher, Charles. "Ted Williams Goes Back to Where It All Began." *Baseball Digest,* XXXVII (March 1978), 78–86.

56552. Malaney, Jack. "Ted Williams Hasn't Changed a Bit." *Baseball Digest,* V (April 1946), 23–25.

56553. _____. "Theodore: A .409 Thumper." *Baseball Magazine,* LXVIII (December 1941), 307–309.

56554. Maracin, Paul R. "Ted Williams Struggled in His First Year as a Pro." *Baseball Digest,* LIV (November 1995), 71–72.

56555. _____. "Ted Williams was Better Than His Record Shows." *Baseball Digest,* XLIV (December 1985), 81–84.

56556. Markusen, Bruce. *Ted Williams: A Biography.* Baseball's All-Time Greatest Hitters Series. Westport, CT: Greenwood Press, 2004. 168p.

56557. Masin, Herman L. "Mr. Hit: Ted Williams." *Scholastic,* XLVIII (September 16, 1946), 38–39.

56558. McAulay, Ed. "The Kid's in a Heck of a Fix." *Baseball Digest,* VIII (January 1949), 16–24.

56558a. McCormack, Shaun. *Ted Williams.* Baseball Hall of Famers Series New York: Rosen, 2004. 112p.

56559. McGinniss, Joe. "What Ted Williams is Like Today." *Sport,* XLVII (June 1969), 16–19.

56560. McGuff, Joe. "Williams' Theories on Hitting Charm Audience." *Baseball Digest,* XXVII (May 1969), 78–91.

56561. Meany, Thomas. "Ted Williams." In: his *Baseball's Greatest Hitters.* New York: A.S. Barnes, 1950. Pp. 239–250.

56562. _____. "Ted Williams." In: his *Baseball's Greatest Players.* New York: Grosset and Dunlap, 1953. Pp. 274–288.

56563. _____. "Ted Williams: Hitting Unlimited." *Baseball Digest,* XXV (March 1966), 85–94.

56564. _____. "Ted Williams: The Feudal Champion." *Baseball Digest,* XV (November-December 1966), 61–70.

56565. _____. *Theodore Samuel Williams: Hitting Unlimited.* New York: A.S. Barnes, 1951. 25p.

56566. _____. and Tommy Holmes. "Ted Williams." In: their *Baseball's Best.* New York, Watts, 1964. Pp. 216–229.

56567. Mentus, Ron. "The 'Splendid Splinter' Speaks Out on the Art of Hitting." *Baseball Digest,* XLV (May 1986), 47–54.

56568. Moderow, Gertrude. "Ted Williams." In: her *People to Remember.* New York: Scott, 1969. Pp. 51–56.

56569. Molen, Sam. "The Kid and Ty Cobb." *Baseball Digest,* III (July 1944), 59–61.

56570. Montville, Leigh. "Goodbye, Teddy Ballgame: A New Englander Reflects on a Half Century of Encounters with the Man and the Icon." *Sports Illustrated,* XCVII (July 15, 2002), 45–50, 52, 54, 56.

56571. _____. *Ted Williams: The Biography of an American Hero.* Garden City, NY: Doubleday, 2004. 528p.

56572. Morgan, Bill. *Ted Williams.* New York: Scholastic Books, 1993. 44p.

56573. Nason, Jerry. "A Change Comes Over Williams." *Baseball Digest,* III (March 1944), 47–49.

56574. Nowlin, Bill. "Good Eye Leads to Two More Walks for Ted." In: Mark Kanter, ed. *The Northern Game and Beyond: Baseball in New England and Eastern Canada.* Cleveland, OH: The Society for American Baseball Research, 2002. Pp. 2–3.

56574a. _____. *The Kid: Ted Williams in San Diego.* Cambridge, MA: Rounder Books, 2004. 320p.

56575. _____. "Ted and Jimmy: The Social Work of Ted Williams." *Nine: A Journal of Baseball History and Social Policy Perspectives,* VIII (Fall 1999), 31–53.

56576. _____. "Ted Williams and the Jimmy Fund." In: Mark Kanter, ed. *The Northern Game and Beyond: Baseball in New England and Eastern Canada.* Cleveland, OH: The Society for American Baseball Research, 2002. Pp. 18–19.

56577. _____. and Jime Prime. *Ted Williams: The Pursuit of Perfection.* Chicago, IL: Sports Publishing, 2002. 200p.

56578. Nunes, John L. "The Kid from San Diego." *Elysian Fields Quarterly,* XIX (Summer 2002), 10–13.

56579. O'Neil, Dan. "Ted Williams' .406 Still a Major Number 50 Years Later." *Baseball Digest,* L (May 1991), 58–61.

56580. Owen, Russell. "'It's All in Your Eyes and Timing': Ted Williams Tells How He Knocks Out Homers." *The New York Times Magazine,* (August 4, 1946), 20+.

56581. Pepe, Phil. "Ted Williams." In: his *Great Comebacks in Sports.* New York: Hawthorne Books, 1975. Pp. 84–91.

56582. Peterson, Dan. "The Kid Surprises a Kid: In a Train Station, Ted Williams Made a Young Fan's Day." *Sports Illustrated,* LXIX (April 4, 1988), 126–127.

56583. Pope, Edwin. *Ted Williams: The Golden Year* [1957] *Year.* Englewood Cliffs, N.J.: Prentice-Hall, 1970. 167p.

56584. Povich, Shirley. "Ted Couldn't Resist New Challenge." *Baseball Digest,* XXVII (May 1969), 75–78. Managing.

56585. _____. "Ted's Big Itch: To Outhit [Mickey] Mantle." *Baseball Digest,* XV (September 1956), 43–45.

56586. _____. "Was Williams Most Valuable?" *Baseball Digest,* VI (February 1947), 51–53.

56587. Powers, Jimmy. "How Would You Pitch to Ted Williams?" *Baseball Digest,* V (September 1946), 3–5.

56588. Price, S. L. "Rounding Third." *Sports Illustrated,* LXXXV (November 25, 1996), 92–96, 98, 100, 102–104, 106.

56589. _____. "Twilight of a God." *Sports Illustrated,* XCVII (July 17, 2002), 60+.

56590. Prime, Jim and Bill Nowlin. *Ted Williams: A Tribute.* Indianapolis, IN: Masters Press, 1997. 246p.

56591. _____. "Ted Williams: Interview." *Baseball Cards,* VIII (April 1988), 28–45.

56592. _____. "Ted Williams Talks About Hitters, Past and Present." *Baseball Digest,* XLVII (June 1988), 46–56.

56593. Reddy, John. "Ted Williams: A Legend Returns to Baseball." *Reader's Digest,* XCV (July 1969), 201–204+.

56594. Reichler, Joseph L. "The Williams I Know." *Sport,* XLI (February 1966), 64–65.

56595. Rice, Grantland. "Ott, Williams 'Most Valuable' in Rice's Book." *Baseball Digest,* I (December 1942), 9–11.

56596. Robinson, Murray. "Cronin Now Ted's Judge." *Baseball Digest,* XVIII (April 1959), 42–45.

56597. Robinson, Ray. *Ted Williams.* New York: G. P. Putnam, 1962. 191p.

56598. Rothe, Emil H. "Ted Williams' Last At Bat in the Majors." *Baseball Digest,* XXXII (April 1973), 75–79. Homer hit an Sept. 29, 1960; reprinted in John Kuenster, ed., *From Cobb to Catfish* (Chicago: Rand McNally, 1975), pp. 140–141.

56599. Rumill, Ed. "Ted Started Hitting Before He Got to the Plate." *Baseball Digest,* XXV (October 1966), 57–59.

56600. Russell, Fred. "Ted Williams: Baseball's Most Efficient Hitter." *Baseball Digest,* XXXI (October 1972), 35–37.

56601. _____. "Ted's .401 Gets Bigger and Bigger." *Baseball Digest,* XXV (August 1966), 37–39.

56602. Ryan, Steve. "Still Splendid." *Beckett Baseball Card Monthly,* X, no. 101 (August 1993), 108–110.

56603. Sabin, Lou. "Ted Williams." In: his *Record Breakers of the Major Leagues.* New York: Random House, 1974. Pp. 70–79.

56604. Sabino, David. "Figures of Greatness: No Matter How You Slice the Numbers, the Bottom Line is Clear: Williams Made His Mark on the Game He Loved." *Sports Illustrated,* XCVII (July 17, 2002), 40–41.

56605. Sampson, Arthur. "Early Weakness Behind Williams' Caution." *Baseball Digest,* IX (April 1950), 11–13.

56606. _____. *Ted Williams: A Biography of "The Kid."* New York: A.S. Barnes, 1950. 180p.

56607. Sarris, Andrew. "Ted Williams." In: Danny Peary, ed. *Cult Baseball Stars.* New York: Simon and Schuster, 1990. Pp. 271–275.

56608. _____. "Ted Williams." In: Danny Peary, ed. *Baseball's Finest: The Greats, the Flakes, the Weird and the Wonderful.* North Digton, MA: The JG Press, 1990. Pp. 271–275. Both Peary books are identical.

56609. Schlossberg, Dan. "Ted Williams: He Mastered the Strike Zone." *Baseball Digest,* LXI (March 2002), 80–87.

56610. Schoor, Gene, and Henry Guilfond. *Ted Williams Story.* New York: Julian Messner, 1954. 188p.

56611. Seaver, Tom, with Marty Appel. "Farewell to The Thumper." In: his *Great Moments in Baseball: From the World Series of 1903 to the Modern Records of Nolan Ryan.* New York: Carol Communications, 1992. Pp. 197–202.

56612. Sechrist, Darren. "On the Rocks: Friends and Family of a Recently Deceased Baseball Player are Squabbling Over His Son's Decision to Have the Corpse Frozen and Brought Back to Life Some Time in the Future." *Current Science,* LXXXVIII (November 22, 2002), 8–12.

56613. Seidel, Michael. *Ted Williams: A Baseball Life.* Chicago: Contemporary Books, 1991. 400p. Reprinted in a 202-page edition by the University of Nebraska Press in 2000.

56614. Shapiro, Herb. *Ted Williams.* San Diego, CA: Revolutionary Comics, 1992. 30p.

56615. Shapiro, Milton J. "Ted Williams." In: his *Champions of the Bat.* New York: Julian Messner, 1968. Pp. 71–83.

56616. Shaughnessey, Dan. "Opposing Pitcher [Jack Fisher] Recalls Ted Williams' Final Homer." *Baseball Digest,* LII (March 1993), 82–83.

56617. Shermack, Jeff. "Can Ted Williams Keep It Up?" *Countrywide Sports,* I (August 1970), 34–37.

56618. Shoemaker, Robert H. "Ted Williams." In: his *Best in Baseball.* New York: Crowell, 1956. Pp. 42–58.

56619. Silverman, Al. "Four Slants on Ted Williams." *Sport,* XXII (July 1956), 12–13+.

56620. Simms, J. "Ted Williams. Last of the .400 Hitters." In: Associated Press. *Sports Immortals.* Englewood Cliffs, N.J.: Prentice Hall, 1974. Pp. 174–179.

56621. Singer, Bart. "Line Drive." *American Heritage*, XLVIII (December 1997), 30–31. How a boy caught a line drive off the bat of Williams while in the outfield at a spring training practice session in Sarasota, florida, in the 1950's.

56622. Smith, Ira L. "Ted Williams." In: his *Baseball's Famous Outfielders*. New York: A.S. Barnes, 1954. Pp. 282–286.

56623. Smith, Lyall. "Williams Is 'Most Walked.'" *Baseball Digest*, VIII (March 1949), 5–7.

56624. Smith, Ron. "Ted Williams-8." In: his *The Sporting News Selects Baseball's 100 Greatest Players*. St. Louis, MO: *The Sporting News*, 1998. Pp. 24–25.

56625. Smith, Walter ("Red") "Ted Williams Spits." In: Dan Riley, ed. *The Red Sox Reader*. Rev. ed. Boston, MA: Mariner Books, 1999. Pp. 50–52.

56626. Stann, Francis. "Can Williams Come Back at 36?" *Baseball Digest*, IX (September 1953), 55–59.

56627. _____. "The Storybook Tale of Ted Williams." *Baseball Digest*, XXVII (February 1969), 79–82.

56628. Stewart, Walter. "The Broken Arm Breaks Myth." *Baseball Digest*, X (September 1950), 39–40.

56629. Storin, Eddie. "Ted Williams a 'Sleeper' at Bat King." *Baseball Digest*, XVII (February 1958), 7–9.

56630. Stout, Glenn. "Looking for Ted Williams, 2002." In: Glenn Stout, ed. *Impossible Dreams: A Red Sox Collection*. Boston, MA: Mariner Books, 2003. Pp. 385–389.

56631. _____. and Dick Johnson. *Ted Williams: A Portrait in Words and Pictures*. New York: Walker, 1991. 225p.

56632. Street, Jim. "Farewell to Ted Williams (August 30, 1918-July 5, 2002): A Baseball Legend and American Hero." *Baseball Digest*, LXI (October 2002), 22–29.

56633. Sullivan, George. "Ted Williams." In: his *Great Lives: Sports*. New York: Scribners, 1988. Pp. 254–261.

56634. Summerall, Pat and Jim Moskovitz, with Craig Kubey. "Ted Williams." In: their *Pat Summerall's Sports in America: 32 Celebrated Sports Personalities Talk About Their Most Memorable Moments In and Out of the Sports Arena*. New York: HarperCollins, 1996. Pp. 283–292.

56635. "Ted Williams." In: *Current Biography Yearbook, 1947*. New York: H.W. Wilson Co., 1947. Pp. 685–687.

56636. "Ted Williams Defies His Critics." *Sports Illustrated*, V (August 20, 1956), 22–25.

56638. Thomsen, Ian. "Boston Mourns Its Hero." *Sports Illustrated*, XCVII (July 17, 2002), 70–75.

56639. Tretter, Frank. "A Final Look: Ted Williams." *Beckett Baseball Card Monthly*, VII (July 1990), 94–95.

56640. Trimble, Joe. "Williams Feels the Shift." *Baseball Digest*, VI (August 1947), 57–60.

56641. Underwood, John. "Gone Fishing: His Baseball Days Behind Him, The Kid Took to the Waters off the Keys with a Boatload of Yarns, a Few Friends, and One Mission — Bring in the Big Ones." *Sports Illustrated*, XCVII (July 17, 2002), 46+. Reprinted from the original article, "Going Fishing with 'The Kid," in *Sports Illustrated*, XXVII (August 21, 1967), 60–70, which was reprinted in *Sports Illustrated*, LXXXI (July 4, 1994), 56–60+. Also republished as "Fishing with the Kid." In: Editors of *Sports Illustrated, The Boston Collection: the Best Boston Sports Stories from the Pages of SI* (Los Angeles, CA: Time, Inc., 1997), Chpt. 20.

56642. _____. "The Newest Senator in Town." *Sports Illustrated*, XXX (February 24, 1969), 20–21.

56643. _____. "Teaching Them Ted's Way." *Sports Illustrated*, XXX (May 17, 1969), 18–23.

56643. _____. "Ted Williams at Midstream." *Sports Illustrated*, LV (June 29,1981), 66–70+.

56644. _____. "Ted Williams: 'My Year.'" *Sports Illustrated*, XXXII (January 2 , 1970), 50–53+.

56645. Updike, John. "The Last Game of Ted Williams." *New Yorker*, XXXVI (October 22, 1960), 109–110+. Reprinted in Herbert W. Win, ed., *The Realm of Sport* (New York: Simon and Schuster, 1966), pp. 63–71; as Chpt. 9 in George Plimpton, ed., *Home Run* (San Diego, CA: Harcourt, 2001); in David Halberstam, ed., *The Best American Sports Writing of the Century* (Boston, MA: Houghton, Mifflin, 1999), pp. 304–317; In: Dan Riley, ed., *The Red Sox Reader*. (Rev. ed., Boston, MA: Mariner Books, 1999), pp. 53–72; in Nicholas Dawidoff, ed., *Baseball: A Literary Anthology* (New York: The Library of America, 2002), pp. 301–317; and as a freestanding 29-page monograph from the Northridge, California, firm of Lord John Press in 1977; all five reprints are entitled "Hub Fans Bid 'Kid' Adieu."

56646. _____. "Ted Williams." *Sport*, LXXVII (December 1986), 56–57.

56647. Verducci, Tom. "Splendor at the Plate: Over Two Brilliant Decades, Ted Williams Proved He was What He Always Wanted to Be — The Best Hitter Who Ever Lived." *Sports Illustrated*, XCVII (July 17, 2002), 10+.

56648. _____. "Triple Threats: Two-Time Triple Crown Winner Ted Williams Nearly Won It Five Times in Six Years." *Sports Illustrated*, LXXXV (July 1, 1996), 25–30, 32, 37.

56649. _____. "What Really Happened to Ted Williams." *Sports Illustrated*, XCIX (August 18, 2003), 66–70, 72–73.

56650. "Veterans Day Tribute: An Interview with Ted Williams, USMC Reservist, Baseball Legend." *Officer*, LXXV (November 1999), 24–26+.

56651. Washburn, Patrick S. "The Greatest Hitter Who Ever Lived': All Ted Williams Wanted to Be was the Best — Many Say He Achieved His Goal." *Boys' Life*, XCII (April 2002), 46–49.

56651. Watt, Richard. "Ted Williams: Interview." *Sport*, LXXXIX (November 1998), 122–123.

56652. Weiss, Peter. "Ted Williams." In: his *Baseball's All-Time Goats: As Chosen by America's Top Sportswriters*. Holbrook, MA: Bob Adams, Inc, 1992. Pp. 172–175.

56653. Wesson, Al. "Ted Williams: Evangelical Swatter." *Baseball Digest*, I (December 1942), 11–18.

56654. Williams, Ted. *Batting Tips from Ted*. Chicago: Sears, Roebuck, 1967. Instructional pamphlet.

56655. _____. "Hitting Was My Life." Edited by John Underwood. *Sports Illustrated*, XXVIII (June 10–17, 1968), 82–86+, 31–32+, 28–29+; XXIX (July 1–8, 1968– 40–47, 32–45.

56656. _____. *How to Be a Better Hitter*. Louisville, KY: Hillerich & Bradsby, 1957. Instructional pamphlet drawn from the next entry.

56657. _____. "How to Be a Better Hitter." *Scholastic Coach*, XXV (April 1956), 8–9+.

56658. _____. "My Baseball Memory Book." *Look*, XX (June 26, 1956), 136–140+.

56659. _____. "My Batting Tips for Little Leaguers." *Look*, XX (May 1, 1956), 57–61.

56660. _____. "The Splendid Splinter: Interview with Ted Williams." *The Officer*, LXXIX (July-August 2002), 8–10.

56661. _____. "Ted Williams Talks Hitting: Interview." *Coach and Athletic Director*, LXIX (September 2000), 11–17.

56662. _____. "A Visit with Hall of Famer Ted Williams." In: John J. Ralph, ed. *The National Baseball*

Hall of Fame and Museum 2000 Yearbook. Pittsburgh, PA: Geyer Printing Co., 2000. Pp. 16–24.

56663. _____. as told to Joseph L. Reichler. "This Is My Last Year." *Saturday Evening Post,* CCXXVI (April 10–24, 1954), 17–19+, 24–25+, 31+. No so!

56664. _____. with David Pietrusza. *Ted Williams: My Life in Pictures.* Kingston, NY: Total Sports Publishing, 2001. 224p.

56665. _____., with Don Sider. "A Slugger Goes Back to School." *People Weekly,* XLIII (March 13, 1995), 44–47.

56666. _____. with John Underwood. *My Turn at Bat: The Story of My Life.* New York: Simon and Schuster, 1969. 288p. A rev. 267-page paperback edition was published by the same firm in 1988.

56667. _____. *The Science of Hitting.* New York: Simon and Schuster, 1971. 95p.

56668. _____. *The Science of Hitting.* Rev. and Updated ed. New York: Simon and Schuster, 1986. 98p.

56669. _____. *The Ted Williams Reader.* New York: Fireside Books; dist. by Simon and Schuster, 1991. 299p.

56670. _____. "Ted Williams' Finest Moment." *50+,* XXVIII (May 1988), 76–78+.

56671. Will, George F. "I Can't Stand It, I'm So Good." In: his *Bunts: Curt Flood, Camden Yards, Pete Rose and Other Reflections on Baseball.* New York: Touchstone Books, 1998. Pp.184–187.

56672. "Williams of the Red Sox is Best Hitter." *Life,* XI (September 1, 1941), 43–44.

56673. Wimmer, Dick. "Some Ted Williams Homers." In: Dick Wimmer, ed. *The Home Run Game.* Short Hills, NJ: Burford Books, 1999. Chpt. 5.

56674. Wolff, Rick. *Baseball Legends: Ted Williams.* New York: Chelsea House Publishers, 1993. 61p.

Walter Allen ("Walt" or "No Neck") Williams

OF. (B: Dec. 19, 1943, Brownwood, TX). Houston (NL), 1964; Chicago (AL), 1967–1972; Cleveland (AL), 1973; New York (AL), 1974–1975. Remarks: Obtained 640 hits (33 homers) and 34 stolen bases in 842 games in a decade; had five hits and scored five runs in one game, May 31, 1970; coach, Chicago (AL), 1988.

56675. Downey, Mike. "Walt ('No Neck') Williams." In: Danny Peary, ed. *Cult Baseball Players.* New York: Simon and Schuster, 1990. Pp. 192–196.

56676. _____. "Walt ('No Neck') Williams." In: Danny Peary, ed. *Baseball's Finest: The Greats, the Flakes, the Weird and the Wonderful.* North Digton, MA: The JG Press, 1990. Pp. 192–196. Both Peary books are identical.

Edward Nagle ("Ned") Williamson

3B-SS-C-P. (B: Oct. 24, 1857, Philadelphia, PA-March 3, 1894). Indianapolis (NL), 1878; Chicago (NL), 1879–1891. Remarks: Obtained 1,159 hits (63 homers) and 75 stolen bases in 1,201 games in 14 seasons; as a hurler, one of 12 games pitched and lost one, with three "saves"; had three hits in one inning, Sept. 6, 1883; led NL in doubles, 1883; first big leaguer to hit three homers in one game, May 30, 1884; set 35-year MLB single-season homer record of 27, 1884; led NL in walks (75) and "saves" (two), 1885; Chicago saloon owner, 1891–1894.

56677. Akin, William E. "Edward Nagle 'Ned' Williamson." In: Vol. Q-Z of David L. Porter, ed. *Biographical Dictionary of American Sports: Baseball.* Rev. and enlarged ed. Westport, CT: Greenwood Press, 2000. Pp. 1688–1689.

56678. Stevens, D. "A Home Run King without a Headstone: Ned Williamson." *The National Pastime,* XXI (2001), 58–59.

56679. Wilbert, Warren and William Hageman. "Edward 'Ned' Nagle Williamson —1884." In: their *Chicago Cubs: Seasons at the Summit, the 50 Greatest Individual Seasons.* Champaign, IL: Sagamore Publishing, 1997. Pp. 129–132.

Ned Williamson see **Edward Nable ("Ned") Williamson**

Scott Ryan Williamson

P. (B: Feb. 17, 1976, Fort Polk, LA). Cincinnati (NL), 1999–2003; Boston (AL), 2003–2004; Chicago (NL), 2005-. Remarks: Through 2004, has won 25 games and lost 24, with 55 "saves"; NL Rookie of the Year award, 1999; injured much of 2004.

56680. Cannella, Stephen. "Armed and Dangerous: Williamson's Woes." *Sports Illustrated,* XCIV (April 23, 2001), 81, 84, 86.

56681. Forman, Ross. "Reds' Pitcher Williamson Loves Autograph Collecting: Winner of '99 NL Rookie of Year Award. "*Sports Collector's Digest,* XXVII (April 7, 2000), 110–111.

Carl Blake Willis

P. (B: Dec. 28, 1960, Danville, VA). Detroit (AL), 1984; Cincinnati (NL), 1984–1986; Chicago (AL), 1988; Minnesota (AL), 1990–1995. Remarks: Won 22 games, lost 16, and had 13 "saves" in nine seasons; threw only 12 big league innings between 1988–1991; had 25 scoreless-inning streak, July 1991; hurled 12.3 post-season innings in 1991 with neither decision or save; also played for Portland (PCL), 1991; coach, Watertown (New York-Penn League), 1997, Burlington (Carolina League), 1998, Columbus (American Association), 1999, Akron (EL), 2000, Buffalo (IL), 2001–2002, and Cleveland (AL), 2003-

56682. Wendel, Tim. "Willis Finds Himself in Middle of Big Victory." *USA Today Baseball Weekly,* I (October 11, 1991), 28–30.

Dontrelle Wayne Willis

P. (B: Jan. 12, 1982, Oakland, CA). Florida (NL), 2003-. Remarks: In his Rookie year, had 24 victories and 17 defeats; won eight games and lost 1 between May 25 and June 30, but lost one game of 2003 NLCS.

56683. Ballard, C. "The Kid with The Kick." *Sports Illustrated,* XCVIII (June 30, 2003), 40–45.

56684. Keown, Tim. "Kick Start." *ESPN: The Magazine,* VI (August 4, 2003), 50–54.

Victor Gazaway ("Vic") Willis★

P. (B: April 12, 1876, Wilmington, DE-D: Aug. 3, 1947). Boston (NL), 1898–1905; Pittsburgh (NL), 1906–1909; St. Louis (N.L.) 1910. Remarks: Had 248 victories, 208 defeats, and ten "saves" in 13 years; pitched no-hitter, Aug. 7, 1899; led NL in strikeouts, 1902; had 45 complete games (27 victories) in 1902 and 39 in 1904; elected to the National Baseball Hall of Fame in 1995, where his plaque reads: "Tall, graceful workhorse with sweeping curve that made him a strikeout artist. While compiling 249–205 record, posted 50 shutouts and 2.83 ERA and completed 388 of 471 starts. 45 complete games in 1902 are most in NL 20th century. Mainstay of Boston Beaneaters' staff before trade to Pittsburgh, where he averaged 22 wins a season."

56685. Bisher, Furmari. "Vic Willis: A Neglected Hero." *Baseball Digest,* XXX (May 1971), 80–85.

56686. Cunerd, Stephen. "Vic Willis: Turn-of-the-Century Great." *The Baseball Research Journal,* XVIII (1989), 55–57.

56687. Fleitz, David L. "Vic Willis." In: his *Ghosts in the Gallery at Cooperstown: Sixteen Little-Known Members of the Hall of Fame.* Jefferson, NC: McFarland & Co., Inc., 2004. Pp. 176–188.

56688. McKay, Joe. "Vic Willis: Ultimate Recognition at Long Last." In: his *The Great Shutout Pitchers: 20 Profiles of a Vanishing Breed.* Jefferson, NC: McFarland & Co., Inc., 2004. Pp. 208–215.

56689. Olmsted, Frank J. "Victor Gazaway 'Vic' Willis." In: Vol. Q-Z of David L. Porter, ed. *Biographical Dictionary of American Sports: Baseball.* Rev. and enlarged ed. Westport, CT: Greenwood Press, 2000. Pp. 1689–1691.

56690. Wayman, Joseph M. "Vic Willis, Standout Pitcher." In: *Grandstand Baseball Annual, 1992.* Downey, CA: Joseph M. Wayman, 1992. Pp. 49–50.

Bump Wills *see* **Elliott Taylor ("Bump") Wills**
Elliott Taylor ("Bump") Wills
2B. (B: July 27, 1952, Washington, DC). Texas (AL), 1977–1981; Chicago (NL), 1982. Remarks: Had 693 hits (30 homers) and 161 stolen bases in 703 games in five years; played for Hankyu Braves (Japan League), 1983–1984; manager, Hermosillo Orange Growers (Mexican Pacific League), 1988; son of Maury Wills (below).

56691. Gammons, Peter. "Bumper Crop of Boys from the Farm." *Sports Illustrated,* XLVI (March 28, 1977), 24–26.

56692. Scott, Jim. "Maury's Kid: Like Dad, Maybe Better." *Black Sports,* IV (September 1974), 14–16.

Maurice Morning ("Maury" or "The Mouse") Wills
SS-MGR-BROADCASTER. (B: Oct. 2, 1932, Washington, DC). Los Angeles (NL), 1959–1966; Pittsburgh (NL), 1967–1968; Montreal (NL), 1969; Los Angeles (NL), 1969–1972. Remarks: Obtained 2,134 hits (20 homers) and 586 stolen bases in 1,942 games in 14 seasons; had five hits in 1959 World Series; NL stolen base champion, 1960–1965, including MLB record 104 in 1962; hit two homers (one from each side of the plate) in one game, May 3, 1962; NL MVP award, 1962; All-Star Game MVP award, 1962 (tie); had two hits in 1963 World Series, 11 hits (four doubles) in 1965 World Series, and one hit in the 1966 World Series; had 24-game hitting streak, 1968; also played for Spokane (PCL), 1959; manager in off-season, Hermosilli (Mexican Pacific League), 1970–1972, minor league manager/instructor and NBC-TV commentator, 1973–1979; manager, Seattle (AL), 1980–1981, winning 26 games and losing 56 (.319); employed by community services department, Los Angeles (NL), 1982; minor league instructor for 15 major league organization and teams in Korea, 1983–1990; consultant, Hankyu Braves (Japan League); coach/broadcaster, Fargo-Morehead RedHawks (Northern League), 1996–2000; baserunning-bunting instructor, Los Angeles (NL), 2000-; present for 2001 opening of Maury Wills Museum at Fargo's Newman Field; named in a 2002 poll as the most exciting player in the 40 year history of Dodger Stadium; father of Elliott ("Bump") Wills (above).

56693. Allen, Maury. "Maury Wills (1959–1972)." In: his *Baseball's 100.* New York: Galahad Books, 1981. Pp. 180–182.

56694. *Boy's Life,* Editors of. "Baseball's Biggest Burglar: Maury Wills." In: their *Baseball as We Played It.* New York: G.P. Putnam, 1969. Pp. 152–165.

56695. Brody, T.C. "Snake-Sliding Dodger Tries to Steal the Pennant." *Sports Illustrated,* XVII (October 1, 1962), 22–23.

56696. Bryson, Bill. "The Big Giveaway." In: Irving T. Marsh and Edward Ehre, eds. *Best Sports Stories of 1963.* New York: E. P. Dutton, 1963. Pp. 68–70. Reprinted from a 1962 article in the *Des Moines Register.*

56697. _____. "Counting Wills Out." *Baseball Digest,* XXIV (September 1965), 23–26.

56698. _____. "Maury Wills Fooled by 1899 'Frisco Whirl." *Baseball Digest,* XXII (April 1963), 65–69.

56699. Devaney, John. "Maury Wills." In: his *Where Are They Today? Great Sports Stars of Yesteryear.* New York: Crown Publishers, 1985. Pp. 206–209.

56700. _____. "Maury Wills: A Revealing Look at a Man on the Go." *Sport,* XLI (May 1966), 72–78.

56701. Doyle, Al. "Where are They Now?: Former Speedster Maury Wills." *Baseball Digest,* LXI (October 2002), 58–61.

56702. Durslag, Melvin. "He'll Manage Without It." *TV Guide,* XXV (July 2, 1977), 15–16.

56703. _____. "Maury Wills Would Rather Be in the Dugout." *TV Guide,* XXI (July 7, 1973), 17–18.

56704. "Ex-Dodger Wills Talks About Life After Baseball, Drugs." *Jet,* LXXVII (March 12, 1990), 49+.

56705. Feeney, Charlie. "Baseball's No Game to Maury Wills." *All-Star Sports,* II (August 1968), 52–55.

56706. Fox, Larry. "Maury Wills." In: Jack Orr, ed. *Baseball's Greatest Players Today.* New York: Watts, 1963. Pp. 1–9.

56707. Furlong, William B. "Behind the Scenes in the Maury Wills Record Race." *Sport,* XXIV (October 1962), 59–61.

56708. _____. "Maury Wills." In: Ray Robinson, ed. *Baseball Stars of 1962.* New York: Pyramid Books, 1962. Pp. 22–29.

56709. _____. "Maury Wills: Ghost of Ty Cobb." In: Ray Robinson, ed. *Baseball Stars of 1963.* New York: Pyramid Books, 1963. Pp. 22–29.

56710. Grady, Sandy. "Wills Deal Hints Change in Dodgers' Style." *Baseball Digest,* XXVI (February 1967), 19–21.

56711. Green, Jerry. "Maury Wills: He's Stealing the Scene." *Baseball Digest,* XXIV (September 1965), 20–22.

56712. Greenwell, Paul M. "Maury Wills and the Stolen Base." *The Baseball Research Journal,* IX (1980), 120–127.

56713. Hochman, Start. "What There Is About Wills." *Baseball Digest,* XXIV (July 1965), 59–61.

56714. Honig, Donald. "1962: Maury Wills." In: his *National League MVP's.* New York: Bantam Books, 1989. Pp. 67–68.

56715. Libby, Bill. "Maury Wills: The Artful Dodger." In: Ray Robinson, ed. *Baseball Stars of 1966.* New York: Pyramid Books, 1966. Pp. 145–154.

56716. Landes, Stan. "Maury Wills Is Off Base Again." *Sport,* LX (January 1975), 60–63.

56717. Leggett, William. "The Mouse Who Builds the Mountains." *Sports Illustrated,* XXIII (July 12, 1965), 39–42.

56718. Lipton, Jack P. "Maurice Morning 'Maury,' 'The Mouse' Wills." In: Vol. Q-Z of David L. Porter, ed. *Biographical Dictionary of American Sports: Baseball.* Rev. and enlarged ed. Westport, CT: Greenwood Press, 2000. Pp. 1691–1693.

56719. Masterson, Dave and Timm Boyle. "1962: Maury Wills." In: their *Baseball's Best: The MVPs.* Chicago, IL: Contemporary Books, 1985. Pp. 196–101.

56720. "Maury Wills." in: *Current Biography Yearbook, 1966.* New York: H.W. Wilson Co., 1966. Pp. 447–449.

56721. *Maury Wills: Base-Running Buzz Saw.* Los Angeles, CA: Union Oil Company of California, 1961.14p. Pamphlet.

56722. "Maury Wills: Man of the Year." *Sport,* XXXV (February 1963), 24–29.

56723. McMane, Fred. "Where There's a Way, There's a Wills." *Baseball Quarterly,* II (Summer 1978), 44–47.

56724. Moffi, Larry and Jonathan Kronstadt "Maurice Morning 'Maury' Wills." In: their *Crossing the Line; Black Major Leaguers, 1947–1959.* Jefferson, N.C.: McFarland & Co., Inc., 1994. Pp. 222–224.

56725. Park, Charlie. "The Versatile Maury Wills." *Baseball Digest,* XXI (February 1962), 35–37.

56726. Patterson, Arthur F. ("Red"). "The Maury Wills Nobody Appreciates." In: Harold Rosenthal, ed. *1966 Baseball Guidebook.* New York: Maco Publishing Co., 1966. Pp. 12–16.

56727. Pepe, Phil. "The Case of the Missing Shortstop." In: Irving T. Marsh and Edward Ehre, eds. *Best Sports Stories of 1967.* New York: E. P. Dutton, 1966. Pp. 63–65. Reprinted from a 1966 article in the *New York World Journal Tribune.*

56728. _____. "Maury Wills: 'Go Back Home and Forget Major League Baseball. You're Just Too Little, Kid.'" In: his *Winners Never Quit.* Englewood Cliffs, NJ: Prentice-Hall, 1968. Pp. 110–130.

56729. "Rap with Maury Wills: Black Athlete and Broadcasting." *Black Sports,* V (April 1976), 24–27.

56730. Reichler, Joseph L. "Maury Wills: Greater Than Cobb?" *Baseball Monthly,* II (April 1963), 36–41.

56731. Ribowsky, Marty. "Where There's Wills, There's Controversy." *Black Sports Magazine,* VII (August 1977), 18–26.

56732. Robinson, Louie. "World's Greatest Diamond Thief: Maury Wills' 104 Base Steals Revives Old Art." *Ebony,* XVIII (May 1963), 35–36.

56733. Robinson, Ray. "Maury Wills." In: Ray Robinson, ed. *Baseball Stars of 1961.* New York: Pyramid Books, 1961. Pp. 155–156.

56734. _____. "Maury Wills: Base Larceny." In: his *Speed Kings of the Base Paths.* New York G.P. Putnam, 1964. Pp. 95–112.

56735. Rosenthal, Harold. "The Thief of Baghdad." In: his *The Artful Dodgers.* New York: Grosset & Dunlap, 1963. Pp. 187–190.

56736. Seaver, Tom, with Marty Appel. "Speed Returns to the Game." In: his *Great Moments in Baseball.* New York: Carol Publishing Group, 1992. Pp. 215–220.

56737. Sender, Dave. "Shortstop: Maury Wills a Go-Go." In: John L. Pratt, ed. *Baseball's All-Stars.* Garden City, N.Y: Doubleday, 1967. Pp. 39–48.

56738. Sheldon, Harold. "How Experts Compare Cobb and Wills." *Baseball Digest,* XXII (February 1963), 6–10.

56739. Smith, David. "Maury Wills and the Value of a Stolen Base." *The Baseball Research Journal,* IX (1980), 120–127.

56740. Stann, Francis. "Maury Wills: His First Job to Lose." *Baseball Digest,* XX (May 1961), 20–23.

56741. _____. "Maury Wills: What It's Like at 35." *Baseball Digest,* XXVII (June 1968), 50–53.

56742. _____. "Maury Wills: White Kangaroo Kid." *Baseball Digest,* XXII (June 1963), 50–53.

56743. Vecsey, George. "Maury Wills." In: his *Baseball's Most Valuable Players.* New York: Random House, 1966. Pp. 142–155.

56744. Weiskopf, Don and Ken Gimblin. "Base-Running with Maury Wills." *Athletic Journal,* XLVI (April 1966), 24–31.

56745. Whittlesey, Merrell. "Ex-Base King 'Cases' Wills." *Baseball Digest,* XXI (September 1962), 34–35+.

56746. Wills, Maurice ("Maury"). "The Great Stealer Tells Some Secrets." *Life,* LIII (September 28,1962), 50–52.

56747. _____. "How I Made Myself a Ballplayer." *Sport,* XXXV (June 1963), 12–13+.

56748. _____. "Stealing the Spotlight." In: Larry Fox, ed. *Little Men in Sport.* New York: W. W. Norton Co., 1969. Pp. 1–14.

56749. _____. as told to George Vass. "The Game I'll Never Forget." *Baseball Digest,* XXIX (November 1971), 40–43.

56750. _____. as told to Steve Gardner. *It Pays to Steal.* Englewood Cliffs, N.J.: Prentice Hall 1963. 862p.

56751. _____. with Don Freeman. *How to Steal a Pennant.* New York: G.P. Putnam, 1976. 252p.

56752. _____. with Mike Celizic. *On the Run: The Never Dull and Often Shocking Life of Maury Wills.* New York: Carroll & Graf Publishers, 1991. 334p.

56753. Zimmerman, Paul. "The Stitch in Time." In: his *The Los Angeles Dodgers.* New York: Coward-McCann, Inc., 1960. Pp. 138–143.

Artie Wilson *see* **Arthur Lee ("Artie") Wilson**

Arthur Lee ("Artie") Wilson

SS. (B: Oct. 28, 1920, Springville, AL). Birmingham Black Barons, 1944–1948; Oakland (PCL), 1949–1950; New York (NL), 1951; Seattle (PCL), Portland (PCL), Oakland (PCL), and Sacramento (PCL), 1952–1957; Portland (PCL) and Kennewick (Northwest League.), 1962. Remarks: Negro League player who transitioned to white minor leagues and spent part of 1951 with Giants, where he had four hits and two stolen bases in 19 games; also hit .402 in 1947 becoming the last man to hit over .400 for a major professional baseball league; named to Oregon Sports Hall of Fame, 1989; member, board of directors, Negro League Baseball Players Association; enshrined in PCL Hall of Fame, 2003.

56754. Moffi, Larry and Jonathan Kronstadt "Arthur Lee ('Artie') Wilson." In: their *Crossing the Line: Black Major Leaguers, 1947–1959.* Jefferson, N.C.: McFarland & Co., 1994. Pp. 68–69.

56755. Riley, James A. "Arthur Lee 'Artie' Wilson." In: Vol. Q–Z of David L. Porter, ed. *Biographical Dictionary of American Sports: Baseball.* Rev. and enlarged ed. Westport, CT: Greenwood Press, 2000. Pp. 1693–1694.

56756. Spalding, John. "Artie Wilson." In: his *Pacific Coast League Stars: One Hundred of the Best, 1903–1957.* San Jose, CA: John E. Spalding, 1994. Pp. 119–120.

56757. Swank, Bill. "Artie Wilson." In: his *Echoes from Lane Field: A History of the San Diego Padres 1936–1957.* Paducah, KY: Turner Publishing Company, 1997. Pp. 103–104.

August Wilson

WRITER. (B: Frederick August Kittell, April 27, 1945, Seattle, WA–D: Oct. 2, 2005). Remarks: Highly-regarded African American dramatist whose play *Fences* (no. 5700) depicts the travails of a Negro League player, a role made famous by James Earl Jones.

56758. Bogumi, Mary L. *Understanding August Wilson.* Columbia: University of South Carolina Press, 1998.

56759. Elkins, Marilyn, ed. *August Wilson: A Casebook.* New York: Garland, 1994.

56760. Little, Jonathan. "August Wilson." In: Christopher J. Wheatley, ed. *Dictionary of Literary Biography, Volume 228: Twentieth-Century American Dramatists, Second Series.* A Bruccoli Clark Layman Book. Detroit, MI: Gale Group, 2000. Pp. 289–302.

56761. O'Neill, Michael. "Interview with August Wilson." In: Philip C. Kolin, ed. *American Playwrights Since 1945: A Guide to Scholarship, Criticism, and Performance.* New York: Greenwood Press, 1989. Pp. 175–177.

56762. Pereira, Kim. *August Wilson and the African-American Odyssey.* Urbana, IL: University of Illinois Press, 1995.

56763. Shannon, Sandra G. *The Dramatic Vision of August Wilson.* Washington, DC: Howard University Press, 1995.

56764. Snodgrass, Mary Ellen. *August Wilson: A Literary Companion.* Jefferson, NC: McFarland & Co., Inc., 2004. 273p.

Bill Wilson *see* **William Donald ("Bill") Wilson**

Black Jack Wilson *see* **John Francis ("Jack" or "Black Jack") Wilson**

Boojum Wilson *see* **Ernest Judson ("Jud" or "Boojum") Wilson**

Chief Wilson *see* **John Owen ("Chief") Wilson**

Daniel Allen ("Dan") Wilson

C. (B: March 25, 1969, Arlington Heights, IL). Cincinnati (NL), 1992–1993; Seattle (AL), 1994–. Remarks: Through 2004, has had 1,092 hits (88 homers) and 23 stolen bases in 1,288 games; had two grand slam homers, April 16, 1996 and May 3, 1988, had a hit in 2000 ALCS and two in the 2002 ALCS.

56765. Anderson, Lars. "Dan Wilson." In: David Bauer, ed. *SI Presents Baseball 1997.* New York: Sports Illustrated, 1997. Pp. 142–145.

56766. Driver, David. "How Hard Work Paid Off for Mariners' Receiver Dan Wilson." *Baseball Digest,* LV (December 1996), 83–85.

Donald Edward ("Don") Wilson

P. (B. Feb. 12, 1946, Monroe, La.-D: Jan. 5, 1975). Houston (NL), 1966–1974. Remarks: Won 104 games and lost 92 in nine seasons; pitched two no-hitters, June 18, 1967 and May 1, 1969; had an 18-strikeout game, July 14, 1968; died a suicide.

56767. Bortstein, Larry. "The Pitcher Who Has Aaron's Number." *Baseball Digest,* XXXIII (June 1974), 70–71.

56768. Christine, Bill. "Don Wilson: the End Came Too Soon." *Baseball Digest,* XXIV (April 1975), 60–69.

Earl Lawrence ("Moose") Wilson

P. (B: Oct. 2, 1934, Ponchatoula, LA–D: April 23, 2005). Boston (AL), 1959–1960, 1962–1966; Detroit (AL), 1966–1970; San Diego (NL), 1970. Remarks: Won 121 games and lost 109 in 12 years; first Black player signed by Boston Red Sox; one of the greatest slugging pitchers who hit two homers in one game, August 16, 1965; had seven homers in a season twice; later founded Detroit-based Autotek Sealants and became third president of the non-profit Baseball Assistance Team; elected to Louisiana Sports Hall of Fame, 1996.

56769. Falls, Joe. "The Turning Point for Earl Wilson." *Sport,* XLIII (February 1967), 52–54.

56770. Moffi, Larry and Jonathan Kronstadt. "Earl Lawrence Wilson." In: their *Crossing the Line: Black Major Leaguers, 1947–1959.* Jefferson, N.C.: McFarland & Co., Inc., 1994. Pp. 225–227.

56771. Robinson, Ray. "Earl Wilson: Swinger from Ponochatoula." In: Ray Robinson, ed. *Baseball Stars of 1968.* New York: Pyramid Books, 1968. Pp. 77–81.

Ernest Judson ("Jud" or "Boojum") Wilson

3B-1B-MGR. (B: Feb. 28, 1899, Remington, VA-D: June 26, 1963). Baltimore Black Sox, 1922–1930; Homestead Grays, 1931–1932; Pittsburgh Crawfords, 1932; Philadelphia Stars, 1933–1939; Homestead Grays, 1940–1945. Remarks: Powerful, ill-tempered Negro League hitter with a .345 lifetime batting average; managed Stars, 1937–1939.

56772. Harris, Ed. "Our Jud." In: Jim Reiser, ed. *Black Writers-Black Baseball: An Anthology of Articles from Sportswriters Who Covered the Negro Leagues.* Jefferson, N.C.: McFarland & Co., Inc., 1994. Pp. 155–156. Reprinted from the *Philadelphia Tribune,* August 18, 1938.

56773. Holway, John B. "Jud ('Boojum') Wilson." In: his *Blackball Stars: Negro League Pioneers.* Westport, CT: Meckler Books, 1988. Pp. 50–51. Reprinted from the June 24, 1979 issue of the *Baltimore Sun Magazine.*

56774. Kleinknecht, Merl F. and John B. Holway. "Ernest Judson 'Jud' Wilson." In: Vol. Q-Z of David L. Porter, ed. *Biographical Dictionary of American Sports: Baseball.* Rev. and enlarged ed. Westport, CT: Greenwood Press, 2000. Pp. 1694–1695.

Glenn Dwight ("Tex") Wilson

OF-BROADCASTER. (B: Dec. 22, 1958, Baytown, TX). Detroit (AL), 1982–1983; Philadelphia (NL), 1984–1987; Seattle (AL), 1988; Pittsburgh (NL), 1988–1989; Houston (NL), 1989–1990; Pittsburgh (NL), 1993. Remarks: Obtained 1,098 hits (98 homers) and 27 stolen bases in 1,201 games in 10 years; manager, Amarillo (TL), 1995; analyst for FOX Sports Southwest, 1997–2003; baseball analyst for Comcast Sportsnet's *Phillies Post Game Live,* 2004–

56775. Nash, Bruce and Allan Zullo. "Glenn Wilson." In: their *Little Big Leaguers: Amazing Boyhood Stories of Today's Baseball Stars.* New York: Little Simon, 1990. Pp. 84–85.

Hack Wilson *see* **Lewis Robert ("Hack") Wilson**

Jack Wilson *see* **John Francis ("Jack" or "Black Jack") Wilson**

James ("Jimmie" or "Ace") Wilson

C-MGR. (B: July 21, 1900, Philadelphia PA-D: May 31, 1947). Philadelphia (NL), 1923–1928; St. Louis (NL), 1928–1933; Philadelphia (NL),1934–1938; Cincinnati (NL), 1939–1940. Remarks: Had 1,358 hits (32 homers) and 86 stolen bases in 1,526 games in 18 playing years; appeared in 1928, 1930–1931, and 1940 obtaining a combined 16 hits (two doubles); player-manager, Philadelphia (N.L), 1934–1939; player-coach for Cincinnati, (NL) in 1940 and hero of that year's fall classic; manager, Chicago (NL), 1941–1944, winning 493 games and losing 735 (.401); coach, Cincinnati (NL), 1944–1946.

56776. Hoffman, John C. "Jimmy Wilson Philosophizes." *Baseball Digest,* II (October 1943), 16–17. ,

56777. Kaese, Harold. "James Wilson: World Series Hero at Forty." In: *Famous American Athletes of Today.* 8th Series. Boston: L.C. Page, 1942. Pp. 297–315.

56778. Lane, Ferdinand C. "The Vindication of Jimmy Wilson." *Baseball Magazine,* LVIII (January 1937), 346–347+.

56779. Lawler, Joseph." Jimmie Wilson: One of the Philies' Finest Catchers." *Phillies Report,* VIII (October 25, 1990), 14–15.

56780. McLemore, Henry. "Jimmy Wilson: A Study in Cussedness." *Look,* V (May 20, 1944), 52–55.

56781. "On the Ball." *Newsweek,* XXIII (May 8, 1944), 89–90.

56782. Phelps, Frank V. "James 'Jimmie' Wilson." In: Vol. Q-Z of David L. Porter, ed. *Biographical Dictionary of American Sports: Baseball.* Rev. and enlarged ed. Westport, CT: Greenwood Press, 2000. Pp. 1695–1696.

56783. Rathgeber, Bob. "The Coach Who Caught the Series: Jimmie Wilson." In: his *Cincinnati Reds Scrapbook.* Virginia Beach, VA: J.C.P. Corp. of Virginia, 1982. Pp. 100–101.

56784. Wilson, James ("Jimmy"). "One Player Who Has Been Strong for the Phillies." *Baseball Magazine,* XXXIX (July 1927), 350–351.

56785. _____. as told to John P. Carmichael. "My Greatest Day in Baseball." In: John P. Carmichael, ed. *My Greatest Day in Baseball.* New York:, A.S. Barnes, 1945. Pp. 242–206. First published in the *Chicago Daily News.*

James Alger ("Jim") Wilson
P-EXEC. (B; Feb. 20, 1922, San Diego, CA). Boston , (A.L), 1945–1946; St. Louis (AL), 1948, Philadelphia (AL), 1949; Boston (NL) and Milwaukee (NL), 1950–1954; Baltimore (AL), 1955–1956; Chicago (AL), 1956–1958. Remarks: Won 84 games and lost 89 in a dozen campaigns; suffered broken skull (recovered) when hit by ball off bat of Hank Greenberg (q.v.), Aug. 8, 1945; pitched one no-hitter, June 12, 1954; scout, Houston (NL), 1963–1971; VP, Milwaukee (AL), 1972–1977.

56786. Dowling, Tom, Jr. "A Pitcher's Heart." *Baseball Magazine,* LXXX (November-December 1954), 15–16+.

56787. Sheldon, Harold. "Jim Wilson Fought On." *Baseball Digest,* XIII (August 1954), 61–64.

56788. Stevens, Bob. "Jim Wilson Fights On." *Baseball Digest,* IX (June 1950), 13–15.

John Francis ("Jack" or "Black Jack") Wilson
P. (B: April 12, 1912, Portland, OR-D: April 19, 1995). Philadelphia (AL), 1934; Boston (AL), 1935–1941; Detroit (AL) and Washington (AL), 1942. Remarks: In nine years, won 68 games and lost 72, with 20 "saves"; had two homers in one game, June 16, 1940; named to Oregon Sports Hall of Fame, 1994.

56789. Kelley, Brent P. "Jack Wilson: Red Sox Ace." In: his *In the Shadow of the Babe: Baseball Players Who Played with or Against Babe Ruth.* Jefferson, NC: McFarland & Co., Inc., 1995. Pp. 157–166.

John Owen ("Chief") Wilson
OF. (B: Aug. 21, 1883, Austin, TX-D: Feb. 22, 1954). Pittsburgh (NL), 1908–1913; St. Louis (NL), 1914–1916. Remarks: Obtained 1,246 hits (59 homers) and 98 stolen bases in 1,280 games in nine years; had four hits (one double) in 1909 World Series; hit three triples in one game, July 24, 1911; NL RBI champion, 1911; hit largest number of triples in a MLB season (36), 1912; also played for Austin/Fort Worth (TL), 1905–1906, Des Moines (WL), 1907, and San Antonio (TL), 1917.

56790. Bryson, Bill. "Triple Miracle." *Baseball Magazine,* LXXIII (August 1944), 308–310. Mark Armour's Wilson profile is a number in the online SABR Biography Project http://bioproj.sabr.org/bioproj.cfm?a=v&v=l&bid=903&pid=15320.

56791. Burtt, Richard L. "Triples, the Pirates and Forbes Field." *The Baseball Research Journal,* IX (1980), 106–111.

56792. Therminy, Charles. *Owen Wilson, Earl Webb, Roger Maris: An Empirical Survey.* Tucson, AZ: Bank Street Publishing, 1993. 136p.

Jud Wilson *see* **Ernest Judson ("Jud" or "Boojum") Wilson**

Lewis Robert ("Hack") Wilson★
OF. (B: April 26, 1900, Elwood City, PA-D: Nov. 23, 1945). New York (NL), 1923–1925; Chicago (NL), 1926–1931; Brooklyn (NL), 1922–1934; Philadelphia (NL), 1934. Remarks: Obtained 1,491 hits (244 homers) and 52 stolen bases in 1,348 games in a dozen seasons; obtained seven hits (one double) in 1924 World Series; hit two homers in one inning, July 10, 1925; NL home run champion, 1926, 1927 (tie), 1928 (tie), and 1930; had eight hits (one triple) in 1929 World Series; hit for the cycle, June 23, 1930; had seven RBIs in one game, Aug. 10, 1930; NL RBI champion, 1929–1930; had pinch inside-the-park grand slam homer, May 14, 1933; set major league record for most runs batted in during a season (191 in 1930) and NL records for most homers in a season, (56 in 1930 — exceeded by Sosa and McGwire in 1998) and most extra bases an long hits in a season (215 in 1930); forced from the game by alcoholism; elected to National Baseball Hall

of Fame in 1979, where his plaque reads: Established major league record of 190 runs batted in and National League high of 56 homers in 1930, Led or tied for NL homer title four times. Compiled lifetime .307 batting average and drove in 140 or more runs six years. Hit two homers in inning in 1925 and three in game in 1930."

56793. Bloodgood, Clifford. "Making Major League History in 1930." *Baseball Magazine,* XLVI (December 1930), 317–321.

56794. Boone, Robert S. "Hack Wilson: He Was One of a Kind." *Baseball Digest,* XXXIV (January 1979), 88+.

56795. _____. and Gerald Grunska. *Hack: The Meteoric Life of One of Baseball's First Superstars.* Chicago, IL: Follett Publishing Co., 1978. 149p.

56796. Broeg, Bob. "Hack." In: his *My Baseball Scrapbook.* St. Louis, MO: River City Publishers, 1983. Pp. 64–66.

56797. Brown, Warren. "Hack Wilson Know How to Live It Up." *Baseball Digest,* XXX (November 1971), 90–93.

56798. Carmichael, John P. "Mantle, Feats Add Luster to Hack's [RBI] Mark." *Baseball Digest,* XV (September 1956), 39–41.

56799. Daniel, Daniel M. "Hack Wilson." *Baseball Magazine,* XCI (June 1955), 25–26.

56800. _____. "Ruth, Wilson, and DiMaggio Records are Safe." In: Sam E. Andre, ed. *Street and Smith's Official 1972 Baseball Yearbook.* New York: Conde Nast Publications, 1972. Pp. 14–24.

56801. Debs, Victor, Jr. "Hack of Year." In: his *Still Standing After All These Years: 12 of Baseball's Longest-Standing Records.* Jefferson, NC: McFarland & Co., Inc., 1997. Pp. 108–151.

56802. Dolgan, Bob. "Former Teammates Recall Hack Wilson." *Baseball Digest,* XXXVII (March 1978), 64–72.

56803. Drooz, AL "But Memories of Hack Wilson Fade Away." *Baseball Digest,* XXXIII (October 1974), 56–60. Reprinted in John Kuenster, ed, *From Cobb to Cattish* (Chicago, IL: Rand McNally, 1975), pp. 219–220.

56804. Enright, Jim. "Players: Hack Wilson." In: his *Baseball's Great Teams: Chicago Cubs.* New York: Collier Books, 1975. Pp. 131–135.

56805. Findling, John E. "Hack Wilson." In: John A. Garrity and Marsh C. Carries, eds. *American National Biography.* 24 vols. New York: Oxford University Press, 1999. XXIII, 574–575.

56806. _____. "Lewis Robert 'Hack' Wilson." In: Vol. Q-Z of David L. Porter, ed. *Biographical Dictionary of American Sports: Baseball.* Rev. and enlarged ed. Westport, CT: Greenwood Press, 2000. Pp. 1696–1697.

56807. Gray, Bill. "Hack Wilson —1930." In: his *Baseball's Top 100: The Best Individual Seasons of All Time.* Wilton, CT: Diamond Library, 1996. Pp. 76–77.

56808. Gutman, Dan. "Hack Wilson: Out in the Sun Too Long." In: his *Baseball's Biggest Bloopers: The Games That Got Away.* New York: Puffin, 1995. Pp. 88–99.

56809. "Hack." *Time,* XIX (February 1, 1932), 44–45.

56810. "Hack Wilson Hits the Babe Ruth Trail." *Literary Digest,* CVI (September 13, 1930), 46–47.

56811. Holway, John B. "Hack Wilson Belted Homers and Hecklers with Equal Gusto." *Baseball Digest,* LV (June 1996), 78–84.

56812. Hughes, Joseph H., Jr. "A Forgotten Baseball Hero." *Beckett Baseball Card Monthly,* I (March 1985), 44+.

56813. Kram, Mark. "Hack Wilson: 'Why Ain't I in the Hall of Fame?'" *Sports Illustrated,* XLVI (April 11, 1977), 88–90+.

56814. _____. "A Tale of Two Men and One City." *Sports Illustrated,* XXXI (September 29, 1969), 78–82. Chicago's Wilson and Ernie Banks.

56815. Lane, Ferdinand C. "The Babe Ruth of the National League." *Baseball Magazine,* XLVI (February 1931), 387–390+.

56816. _____. "Cutting Straight to the Heart of the Baseball Dope." *Baseball Magazine,* XXXVIII (February 1927), 387–389.

56817. Nelson, Don. "A Tale of Two Sluggers: Roger Maris and Hack Wilson." *The National Pastime,* II (1982), 32–33. Reprinted in John Thorn, ed. *The National Pastime* (New York: Bell Publishing Co., 1987), pp. 261–264.

56818. Parker, Clifton Blue. *Fouled Away: The Baseball Tragedy of Hack Wilson.* Jefferson, NC: McFarland & Co., Inc., 2000. 232p.

56819. Rosenthal, Harold. "Hack Wilson: What the 190-RBI Man Was Like." *Baseball Digest,* XXII (August 1963), 13–17.

56820. Rothe, Emil H. "The Day Hack Wilson Set His RBI Mark." *Baseball Digest,* XXXU (Juno 1973), 80–85.

56821. Salin, Tony. "Remembering Hack: Les Munns." In: his *Baseball's Forgotten Heroes: One Fan's Search for the Game's Most Interesting Overlooked Players.* Chicago, IL: Masters Press, 1999. Pp. 189–191.

56822. Simons, Robert. "Hack Drove in Three of Every Ten Runners." *Baseball Digest,* XXII (October-November 1963), 67–71.

56823. _____. "The One Record They'll Never Break." *Baseball Digest,* XXII (July 1963), 5–9. Wilson's 191-RBI mark.

56824. Smith, Ira L. "Lewis Robert (Hack) Wilson." In: his *Baseball's Famous Outfielders.* New York: A.S. Barnes, 1954. Pp. 156–161.

56825. Steadman, John F. "The Sad Demise of Home Run King Hack Wilson." *Baseball Digest,* XLIX (February 1990), 65–67.

56826. Sullivan, George. "Lewis 'Hack' Wilson." In: his *Sluggers: Twenty Seven of Baseball's Greatest.* New York: Atheneum, 1991. Pp. 54–55.

56827. Weiss, Peter. "Hack Wilson." In: his *Baseball's All-Time Goats: As Chosen by America's Top Sportswriters.* Holbrook, MA: Bob Adams, Inc, 1992. Pp. 176–179.

56828. Wilbert, Warren and William Hageman. "Lewis 'Hack' Wilson — 1930." In: their *Chicago Cubs: Seasons at the Summit, the 50 Greatest Individual Seasons.* Champaign, IL: Sagamore Publishing, 1997. Pp. 103–106.

56829. Wilks, Ed. "The Year When Hack Wilson Put It All Together." *Baseball Digest,* XXXI (January 1972), 56–59. 1930.

56830. Wilson, Walt. "Hack Wilson in 1930: How to Drive in 191 Runs." *The Baseball Research Journal,* XXIX (2000), 27–29.

Mookie Wilson *see* **William Hayward ("Mookie") Wilson**

Nigel Edward Wilson
OF. (B: Jan. 12, 1970, Oshawa, Canada). Florida (NL), 1993, Cincinnati (NL), 1995, Cleveland (AL), 1996; Buffalo (IL), 1997; Nippon Ham Fighters (Japan League), 1997–2001; Osaka Kintetsu Buffaloes (Japan League), 2002. Remarks: Obtained three hits (two homers) in 22 U.S. big league games and 113 homes while playing in Japan.

56831. Giuliotti, Ed. "Expanding Opportunities: Nigel Wilson/Marlins." *Beckett Focus on Future Stars,* III, no. 24 (April 1993), 9–11.

Owen Wilson *see* **John Owen ("Chief") Wilson**

Paul Anthony Wilson
P. (B: March 28, 1973, Orlando, FL). New York (NL), 1996; Tampa Bay (AL), 2000–2002; Cincinnati (NL), 2003-. Remarks: Through 2004, has had 39 victories and 53 defeats; sinkerball specialist.

56832. Schwarz, Alan. "Fanning the Flames." *Beckett Focus on Future Stars,* IV, no. 41 (September 1994), 16–17.

Preston Wilson
OF. (B: July 19, 1974, Bamberg, SC). New York (NL), 1998; Florida (NL), 1998–2002; Colorado (NL), 2003-. Remarks: Through 2004, has obtained 774 hits (146 homers) and 104 stolen bases in 809 games; NL strikeout leader, 2000; NL RBI champion, 2003; stepson of William (Mookie) Wilson (below).

56833. Habib, Daniel G. "Altitude Adjustment." *Sports Illustrated,* XCVIII (April 28, 2003), 38–40.

Red Wilson *see* **Robert James ("Red") Wilson**

Robert James ("Red") Wilson
C. (B: March 7, 1929, Milwaukee, WI). Chicago (AL), 1951–1954; Detroit (AL), 1954–1960; Cleveland (AL), 1960. Remarks: Obtained 455 hits (24 homers) and 25 stolen bases in 602 games in a decade; battery mate of famed "Yankee Killer" Frank Lary (q.v.).

56834. Kelley, Brent P. "Yankee Killer Red Wilson Profiled." *Sports Collector's Digest,* XVIII (October 25, 1991), 120–121.

Stephen Douglas ("Steve") Wilson
P. (B: Dec. 13, 1964, Victoria, Canada). Texas (AL), 1988; Chicago (NL), 1989–1991; Los Angeles (NL), 1991–1993. Remarks: Won 13 games and lost 16, with six "saves," in six big league seasons; lost a game in 1989 NLCS.

56835. Shearon, Jim. "Steve Wilson, Out of the Bullpen into the Spotlight." In: his *Canada's Baseball Legends.* Kanata, Ontario: Malin Head Press, 1994. Pp. 218–220.

Steve Wilson *see* **Stephen Douglas ("Steve") Wilson**
Tex Wilson *see* **Glenn Dwight ("Tex") Wilson**
Trevor Kirk ("T-Dub") Wilson
P. (B: June 7, 1966, Torrance, CA). San Francisco (NL), 1988–1997; Anaheim (AL), 1998. Remarks: Injured in 1994, 1996–1997; in seven playing years, had 41 victories and 46 defeats.

56836. Dewan, John and Don Zminda. "Will it Be Dr. Trevor … Or Mr. Wilson?" In: STATS, Inc. *STATS 1992 Baseball Scoreboard.* Chicago, IL: STATS Publishing, 1992. Pp. 202–204.

W. Rollo Wilson
WRITER-EXEC. (B: 1891, Pittsburgh, PA-D: 1956). Remarks: 1914 graduate of the Pharmacy School, University of Pittsburgh; reporter, *Pittsburgh Courier,* 1920–1934; commissioner, Negro National League; reporter, *Philadelphia American,* 1936–1942; *Philadelphia Tribune,* 1943–1945.

56837. Reisler, Jim. "Dr. W. Rollo Wilson: The Red Smith of His Day." In: his *Black Writers/Black Baseball: An Anthology of Articles from Black Sportswriters Who Covered the Negro Leagues.* Jefferson, N.C.: McFarland & Co., Inc, 1994. Pp. 113–126.

William Donald ("Bill") Wilson
OF. (B: Nov. 6, 1928, Montgomery, AL). Chicago (AL), 1950, 1953–1954; Philadelphia (AL) and Kansas City (AL), 1954–1955. Remarks: Had 145 hits (32 homers) in 224 games in four seasons.

56838. Gazel, Neil R. "Foes Forewarned: Bill Wilson's Forearmed." *Baseball Digest,* XII (May 1953), 85–91.

William Hayward ("Mookie") Wilson
OF. (B: Feb. 9, 1956, Bamberg, SC). New York (NL), 1980–1989; Toronto (AL), 1989–1991. Remarks: Obtained

1,397 hits (67 homers) and 327 stolen bases in 1,403 games in 12 seasons; had three hits in 1986 NLCS and seven hits (one double) in 1986 World Series; remembered for winning hit in Game Six of the 1986 World Series that rolled through the legs of Bill Buckner (q.v.); had two hits in 1988 NLCS; also played in 1989 ALCS (five hits) and 1991 ALCS (two hits); coach, New York (NL), 1997–2002; stepfather of Preston Wilson (above).

56839. Greenwood, Chuck. "Wilson Is Known for More Than 'Mookie' Ball: A Mets Staffer for 10 Seasons, He Is Team's All-time Leader in Stolen Bases and Triples." *Sports Collector's Digest,* XXIV (October 3, 1997), 70–71.

56840. Milton, Steve. "Nuke 'Em, Mook!." In: Toronto Blue Jays. *Blue Jays Scorebook: ALCS '89 at Skydome.* Toronto, Canada: Toronto Blue Jays, 1989. Pp. 16–25.

56841. Rushin, Steve. "The Sky's the Limit." *Sports Illustrated,* LXXV (July 8, 1991), 36–39.

56842. Wilson, Mookie, as told to George Vass. "The Game I'll Never Forget." *Baseball Digest,* XLIX (January 1990), 63–64. Game Six of 1986 World Series.

Willie James Wilson
OF. (B: July 9, 1965, Montgomery, AL). Kansas City, (AL), 1976–1990; Oakland (AL), 1991–1992; Chicago (NL), 1993–1994. Remarks: Had 2,207 hits (41 homers) and 668 stolen bases in 2,154 games in 19 years; had one hit in 1978 ALCS; AL stolen base champion, 1979; obtained five inside-the-park homers in one season, 1979; had 32-consecutive steals, 1980; first player with 700 ABs in one season, 1980; had five-year record 184 singles, 1980; became 2nd MLB player to obtain 100 hits from both sides of the plate, 1980; had four hits (two doubles, one triple) in 1980 ALCS and four hits (one double) and two stolen bases in 1980 World Series, but also a record 12 strikeouts; AL batting champion, 1982; led AL in triples, 1980, 1982, 1985, 1987–1988; obtained two hits in 1984 ALCS; had 11 hits (one triple) and three stolen bases in 1985 World Series; had 325 chances in 147 consecutive errorless games, 1987; also appeared 1992 ALCS, where he had five hits (one double) and seven stolen bases; holder of MLB's highest lifetime percentage for stolen bases (.842); elected to Missouri Sports Hall of Fame, 2001, and the Sports Hall of Fame of New Jersey, 2002.

56843. Bennett, Gaymon L. "Willie James Wilson." In: Vol. Q-Z of David L. Porter, ed. *Biographical Dictionary of American Sports: Baseball.* Rev. and enlarged ed. Westport, CT: Greenwood Press, 2000. Pp. 1697–1699.

56844. Flaherty, Joe. "Wilson Making Every Hit Count." *The New York Times Biographical Service,* (August 1982), 1112–1114.

56845. Garrity, John. "They Taught Him How to Steal." *Sport,* LXXI (October 1980), 56–60.

56846. Hart, Stan. "Willie Wilson." In: his *Scouting Reports: The Original Reviews of Baseball's Greatest Stars.* New York: Macmillan, 1995. Pp. 136–139.

56847. James, Bill. "Willie Wilson, Kansas City." In: his *The Bill James Baseball Abstract 1983.* New York: Ballantine Books, 1983. Pp. 177–178.

56848. Kaplan, Jim. "K.C. Takes Off on Willie's Wings." *Sports Illustrated,* LI (September 10, 1979), 26–27.

56849. _____. "Will He Be Willie Again?" *Sports Illustrated,* LIV (February 9, 1981), 78–79.

56850. Looney, Douglas S. "Fleetest of the Royal Fleet." *Sports Illustrated,* XLVIII (April 24, 1978), 54–56.

56851. Remington, Pete. "Willie Wilson." In: Tommy Kay, ed. *Tommy Kay's 1980 Baseball Factbook.* Scottsdale, AZ: Jalart House, 1980. pp. 48–54.

56852. Richman, Milton. "Willie Wilson: Fastest Run-

ner of Them All." *Baseball Digest,* XXXIX (October 1980), 93+.

56853. Solomon, Alan. "Willie Wilson: Helping Win Games Keeps Him Going." *Baseball Digest ,* LII (June 1993), 36–37.

56854. Wilson, Willie, as told to George Vass. "The Game I'll Never Forget." *Baseball Digest,* L (January 1991), 53–54.

George Leroy ("Hooks") Wiltse
P. (B: Sept. 7, 1880, Hamilton, NY-D: Jan. 21, 1959). New York (NL), 1904–1914; Brooklyn (F.L.), 1915. Remarks: Obtained 138 victories and took 90 defeats, with 38 "saves," in 12 years; had one no-hitter, July 4, 1908; only pitcher in MLB history to strike out seven batters in two successive innings, 1908; also played 1B in Game Two of 1913 World Series; also played for Syracuse (IL), 1908; player-manager, Jersey City (IL), 1915; Albany (New York State League), 1916, Reading (New York State League), 1917; Buffalo (IL), 1918–1924, coach, New York (AL), 1925; player-manager, Reading (IL), 1926; Deputy Assessor of the City of Syracuse, 1943–1944; President of Syracuse Industrial Baseball League, 1944; elected to IL Baseball Hall of Fame, 1952; named to Greater Syracuse Sports Hall of Fame, 1990.

56855. Blaisdell, Lowell L. "George LeRoy 'Hooks' Wiltse." In: Vol. Q-Z of David L. Porter, ed. *Biographical Dictionary of American Sports: Baseball.* Rev. and enlarged ed. Westport, CT: Greenwood Press, 2000. Pp. 1699–1700.

Herbert Warren Wind
WRITER. (B: Aug. 11, 1916, Brockton, MA). Remarks: Columnist for *The New Yorker,* 1947–1989; although principally known for his work with golf, he was editor of several tomes containing baseball tales.

56856. Augustyn, Frederick J., Jr. "Herbert Warren Wind." In: David L. Porter, ed. *Biographical Dictionary of American Sports: 1992–1995 Supplement for Baseball, Football, Basketball and Other Sports.* Westport, CT: Greenwood Press, 1995. Pp. 360–361.

56857. Sanders, David. "Herbert Warren Wind." In: Richard Orodenker, ed. *Dictionary of Literary Biography: Volume 171, Twentieth-Century American Sportswriters.* A Bruccoli Clark Layman Book. Detroit, Mi: Gale Research, 1996. Pp. 342–348.

Bobby Wine *see* **Robert Paul ("Bobby" or "Wine-O") Wine**

Robert Paul ("Bobby" or "Wine-O") Wine
SS-3B-MGR. (B: Sept. 17, 1938, New York City). Philadelphia (NL), 1960, 1962–1968; Montreal (NL), 1969–1972. Remarks: Obtained 682 hits (30 homers) in 1,164 games in 12 playing seasons; participated in record 137 double plays, 1970; coach, Philadelphia (NL), 1972–1983; scout, Atlanta (NL), 1984, 1986; coach/interim manager, Atlanta (NL), 1985, winning 16 games and losing 25 (.390); coach, New York (NL), 1993–1996.

56858. Giampalmi, Joe. "Bobby Wine on Infielding." *Scholastic Coach,* XLIX (February 1980), 55–56.

David Mark ("Dave" or "The Rave") Winfield★
OF-1B. (B: Oct. 3, 1951, St. Paul, MN). San Diego (NL), 1973–1980; New York (AL), 1981–1988, 1990; California (AL), 1990–1991; Toronto (AL), 1992; Minnesota (A.L), 1993–1994; Cleveland (AL), 1995. Remarks: Had 3,110 hits (465 homers) and 223 stolen bases in 2,973 games in 22 years; NL RBI champion, 1975; had two hits (one double) in 1981 ALCS and one hit in 1981 World Series; had 20-game hitting streak, 1984; stole home plate, Sept. 7, 1985; hit for the cycle, June 24, 1991; first 40-year-old to

drive in 100 runs in a season, 1992; obtained six hits (two doubles, one homer) in 1992 ALCS and five hits (one double) in 1992 World Series; had 11 career grand slam homers; Branch Rickey Award, 1992; MVP of 1973 College World Series; founder/president, Winfield Foundation; named to Ted Williams' Hitters Hall of Fame, Feb. 18, 2001; VP, San Diego (NL), 2002-; uniform no. (31) retired by Padres, Aug. 20, 2004; elected to National Baseball Hall of Fame in 2001, where his plaque reads: "A complete player who intimidated the opposition with his immense stature, power, aggressive baserunning and dominant defense. Advanced directly from college to the major leagues. The 12-time All-Star compiled 3,110 hits, 465 home runs, 1,833 RBI and a .283 career average. The multitalented outfielder, renowned for long strides and a rocket arm, earned seven Gold Glove awards. Among all-time leaders in hits, RBI, games, doubles, extra base hits, total bases and putouts, his 11th inning, two-out double in Game Six clinched Toronto's 1992 World Series title."

56859. Allen, Maury. "Dave Winfield (1973-Present)." In: his *Baseball's 100.* New York: Galahad Books, 1981. Pp. 271–273.

56860. Ambrosius, Greg. "On Deck for Cooperstown: Dave Winfield: Dave Winfield Wants to Win a World Title for Toronto Before He Retires. Can He Do It?" *Baseball Cards,* XII (July 1992), 110–112.

56861. Banks, Don. "Dave Winfield Still Chasing a Title." *Baseball Digest,* LI (June 1992), 32–33.

56862. "Baseball Star Dave Winfield Says a Week in Rio With Ex-Lover [Sandra Renfro] Now Haunts Him." *Jet,* LXXIV (May 23, 1988), 48–50.

56863. Bennett, Gaymon L. "David Mark 'Dave' Winfield." In: Vol. Q-Z of David L. Porter, ed. *Biographical Dictionary of American Sports: Baseball.* Rev. and enlarged ed. Westport, CT: Greenwood Press, 2000. Pp. 1700–1702.

56864. Berentson, Jane. "Interview: Dave Winfield." *Worth,* X (February 2001), 25+.

56865. Berger, Phil. "The Yankees' $20 Million Gamble." *The New York Times Magazine,* (March 29, 1981), 26–40.

56866. Berkow, Ira. "Winfield Looks Back on Satisfying Season." *The New York Times Biographical Service,* (November 1981), 1609–1611.

56867. Bigelow, Barbara Carlisle." Dave Winfield." In: Vol. 5 of *Contemporary Black Biography.* Detroit, MI: Gale Group, 1994. Pp. 285–288.

56868. Caple, Jim. "Deeper Look: Dave Winfield." *Beckett Baseball Card Monthly,* XI, no. 117 (December 1994), 106–109.

56869. Chass, Murray. "The Hurt Pride of a Yankee." *Inside Sports,* VI (August 1984), 24–31.

56870. _____. "Prize of the Yankees." *Baseball Magazine,* New Series V (May 1981), 35–37+.

56871. Click, Paul. "Dave Winfield Zeroes in on Exclusive 3,000 Hit Club." *Baseball Digest,* LII (July 1993), 32–35.

56872. Collier, Ken. "Dave Winfield." In: Tommy Kay, ed. *Tommy Kay's 1980 Baseball Factbook.* Scottsdale, AZ: Jalart House, 1980. Pp. 30–34.

56873. "Dave Winfield." In: *Current Biography Yearbook.* New York: H.W. Wilson Co., 1984. Pp. 457–460.

56874. "Dave Winfield: 'A Winner Surrounded by Fiasco!'" In: Tommy Kay, ed. *Baseball Factbook.* Scottsdale, AZ: Jalart House, 1978. Pp. 91–95.

56875. "Dave Winfield's Jersey Retired, Will Go into Hall of Fame as a Padre." *Jet,* XCIX (April 30, 2001), 52–53.

56876. Dewan, John and Don Zminda. "How Will Winfield Do In '93?" In: STATS, Inc. *STATS 1993 Baseball Scoreboard.* New York: Harper Perennial, 1993. Pp. 156–158.

56877. Doctor, Ken, ed. *Dave Winfield: 3,000 and Counting.* Kansas City: Andrews & McMeel, 1993. 88p.

56878. Donoho, Ron. "Prodigal Son." *San Diego Magazine,* LIII (July 2001), 56+.

56879. Durso, Joe. "All-Round Athlete." *The New York Times Biographical Service,* (December 1980), 1832–1833.

56880. Enders, Eric. "Night and Day: 2001 Hall of Fame Inductees Kirby Puckett and Dave Winfield Had Little in Common — Until Now." In: Michael J. McCormick, ed. *2001 League Championship Series Official Program.* New York: Major League Baseball Promotion Corp., 2001. Pp. 32–43.

56881. Fimrite, Ron. "Good-Hitter, Better Man." *Sports Illustrated,* LI (July 9, 1979), 32–34.

56882. _____. "The Richest Kid on the Block." *Sports Illustrated,* LIV (January 5, 1981), 22–26.

56883. Freeman, Don. "Winfield's the Name, Hitting's the Game." *Sport,* LXI (December 1975), 68–71.

56884. Gallagher, Mark. "Dave Winfield." In: his *50 Years of Yankee All-Stars.* New York: Leisure Press, 1984. Pp. 213–214.

56885. Grayson, Robert. "Press Credentials." *Beckett Sports Collectibles,* X (July 2001), 14–17. Press coverage of the HOFer.

56886. "He's a Hall of Famer, George." *Sports Illustrated,* LXXXIV (February 19, 1996), 14–15.

56887. Hickey, David and Kerry Keene. "Dave Winfield." In: their *The Proudest Yankees of All: From the Bronx to Cooperstown.* Lanham, MD: Taylor Trade Pub., dist. by National Book Network, 2003. Chpt. 2.

56888. Kaplan, Jim. "Taking a Run at Monumental Success." *Sports Illustrated,* LIV (April 20, 1981), 42–44+.

56889. Kiersh, Edward. "Dave Winfield — Even After a Season of Heroics in Toronto, Baseball's Elder Stateman Still Has Some Chips on His Shoulder." *Inside Sports,* XV (February 1993), 24–28.

56890. Kuenster, John. "Dave Winfield, Yankees' Multi-Talented Threat, Puts It All Together." *Baseball Digest,* XLVII (August 1988), 17–19.

56891. _____. "Mickey Mantle Likes the Way Dave Winfield Plays the Game." *Baseball Digest,* XLII (September 1983), 17–20.

56892. Kurkjian, Tim. "Mr. Longevity." *Sports Illustrated,* LXXIX (September 27, 1993), 55+.

56893. _____. "This Old Man, He Plays Good." *Sports Illustrated,* LXXVII (November 2, 1992), 27+.

56894. Ladson, William. "The *Sport* Q & A: Dave Winfield." *Sport,* LXXXII (August 1991), 84–86.

56895. Liss, Howard. *Pictorial Story of Dave Winfield.* New York: Julian Messner, 1982. 47p.

56896. Ludtke, Melissa. "Nobody Knows the Doubles I've Creamed." *Sports Illustrated,* XLVII (July 11, 1977), 44–45+.

56897. McMane, Fred. "Dave Winfield." In: his *The 3,000 Hit Club.* Champaign, IL: Sports Publishing, 2000. Pp. 126–132.

56898. McMillan, Ken. "Dave Winfield." In: his *Tales from the Yankee Dugout: A Collection of the Greatest Yankee Stories Ever Told.* Champaign, IL: Sports Publishing, Inc., 2001. Pp. 191–194.

56899. Monroe, Judy. *Dave Winfield.* Sports Close-up Series. Mankato, MN: Crestwood House, 1988. 48p.

56900. Pepe, Phil. "By George, Winfield's Worth It."

In: C. C. Johnson Spink, ed. *The Sporting News 1981 Baseball Yearbook.* St. Louis, MO: *The Sporting News,* 1981. Pp. 79–81.

56901. Ragazzi, Reno. "Dave Winfield's Crucial Battle with Himself." *Sports World,* XXIII (August 1984), 35–36.

56902. Rains, Rob. "The Wisdom of Winfield." *USA Today Baseball Weekly,* IV (March 1, 1995), 20–22.

56903. Reilly, Rick. "Dave Winfield: 'I Feel a Whole Lot Better Now.'" *Sports Illustrated,* LXXVI (June 29, 1992), 56–60.

56904. Richman, Milton. "Dave Winfield: He Wants to Be Part of a Winner." *Baseball Digest,* XXXVI (April 1977), 72–75.

56905. Resciniti, Angelo G. "Dave Winfield." In: his *Stars of the Diamond.* Mississauga, Ontario: School Book Fairs, 1981. Pp. 80–89.

56906. Rust, Art, with Michael Marley. "Dave Winfield." In: his *Legends: Conversations with Baseball Greats.* New York: McGraw-Hill, 1989. Pp. 181–188.

56907. Saint Paul Pioneer Press and the Minnesota Twins, comps. *Dave Winfield, 3,000 and Counting.* Kansas City, MO: Andrews and McMeel, 1993. 88p.

56908. Sansevere, Bob. "Hall of Fame Election: Dave Winfield's All-Around Talent Places Him Among the Game's Best." *Baseball Digest,* LX (April 2001), 70–72.

56909. Schnakenberg, Bob. *Dave Winfield.* San Diego: Revolutionary Comics, 1993. 30p.

56910. Schoor, Gene. *Dave Winfield: The 23 Million Dollar Man.* Briarcliff Manor, N.Y.: Stein & Day, 1982. 184p.

56911. Shalin, Mike. "Diamond in the Rough." *Baseball Quarterly,* III (October 1979), 26–29.

56912. Shaw I David. "Dave Winfield: The Prince of the Padres." *Sport,* LXX (January 1980), 78–80+.

56913. "Slugger Dave Winfield Continues to Shine On and Off the Field." *Jet,* LXXXIV (September 27, 1993), 48+.

56914. Smith, Robert M. "Dave Winfield: The Best is Yet to Come." *Baseball Digest,* XXXVIII (February 1979), 34–35.

56915. Smith, Ron. "Dave Winfield 94." In: his *The Sporting News Selects Baseball's 100 Greatest Players.* St. Louis, MO: *The Sporting News,* 1998. Pp. 202–203.

56916. Souhan, Jim. "Hitting: A Constant Learning Process for Dave Winfield." *Baseball Digest,* LIII (January 1994), 32–35.

56917. "Superstar Gallery: Dave Winfield." *Beckett Baseball Card Monthly,* IX, no. 91 (October 1992), 12–13.

56918. Swift, E. M. "Yanked About by the Boss." *Sports Illustrated,* LXVIII (April 11, 1988), 36–39.

56919. Thorn, John. "Dave Winfield: 'The $23 Million Dollar Man.'" In: *Baseball's Dream Team.* New York: Ace Tempo Books, 1982. Pp. 93–105.

56920. Whitford, Don. "What Do You Think of Dave Winfield?" *Sport,* LXXVII (October 1986), 92–98.

56921. Winfield, Dave. *Ask Dave: Dave Winfield Answers Kids' Questions About Baseball and Life.* Kansas City, MO: Andrews and McMeel, 1994. 102p.

56922. _____. "My Greatest Day in Baseball." In: Eliot Cohen, ed. *My Greatest Day in Baseball.* New York: Little Simon, 1991. Pp. 141–143.

56923. _____., as told to George Vass. "The Game I'll Never Forget." *Baseball Digest,* LII (October 1993), 27–29. 11th inning, two-out double in Game Six of 1992 World Series.

56924. _____. with Eric Swenson. *The Complete Baseball Player.* New York: Avon Books, 1990. 212p.

56925. _____. *Turn It Around: There's No Room for Drugs.* New York: Paperjacks, Ltd., 1987. 120p.

56926. _____. with Tom Parker. *Winfield: A Player's Life.* New York: W.W. Norton & Co., 1988. 314p. A rev. 290-page paperback edition was published by the New York firm of Avon Books in 1989.

56927. "Winfield Hits 3,000 Mark; Becomes 19th Man to Do It." *Jet,* LXXXIV (October 4, 1993), 46+.

56928. "Winfield, Puckett Head Baseball's Class of 2001 Hall of Fame Inductees." *Jet,* C (August 20, 2001), 52–53.

56929. Wolff, C.T. "$24 Million Man Tells Why." *Sport,* LXXII (March 1981), 15–16+.

56930. Wulf, Steve. "And May the Best Man Win." *Sports Illustrated,* LXI (September 10, 1984), 20–22. The batting crown battle between Yankee teammates Winfield and Don Mattingly, won by the latter.

56931. "Yankee Dave Winfield Fans a Nasty Controversy with His Free-Swinging New Book [*Winfield: A Player's Life*]." *People Weekly,* XXIX (April 18, 1988), 50–51.

Bobby Winkles *see* **Robert Brooks ("Bobby") Winkles**

Robert Brooks ("Bobby") Winkles

COACH-MGR-BROADCASTER. (B: March 11, 1930, Tuckerman, AR). Remarks: Minor leaguer who won lasting fame as head baseball coach, Arizona State University, 1959–1971; coach, California (AL), 1971–1972; manager, California (AL), 1973–1974; coach, Oakland (AL), 1974–1975; coach, San Francisco (NL), 1976–1977; manager, Oakland (AL), 1977–1978, winning combined total of 170 games and losing 213 (.444); coach, Chicago (AL), 1979–1982; scouting and farm team dir., Chicago (AL), 1983–1985; coach, Montreal (NL), 1986–1988; broadcaster, Montreal (NL), 1992–1994; elected to American Baseball Coaches Association Hall of Fame, 1997; baseball field at Arizona State named in his honor.

56932. Carry, Peter. "Odd One for the Sun Devils." *Sports Illustrated,* XXX (June 30, 1969), 48–49.

56933. Gagnon, Richard ("Cappy"). "Bobby Brooks Winkles." In: Vol. Q-Z of David L. Porter, ed. *Biographical Dictionary of American Sports: Baseball.* Rev. and enlarged ed. Westport, CT: Greenwood Press, 2000. Pp. 1702–1703.

56934. Mann, Jack. "Red-Hot Baseball in the Valley of the Sun." *Sports Illustrated,* XXII (May 24, 1965), 66–70.

56935. Phillips, Bob. "Catching Up with 'Mr. Hurry-Up Baseball.'" *Scholastic Coach,* LVII (March 1988), 58–64.

56936. "Up From Academe." *Sports Illustrated,* XXXVI (January 3, 1972), 7–8.

Joanne Emily Winter

P. (B: Nov. 24, 1924, Chicago, IL-D: Sept. 22, 1996). Racine Belles (All-American Girls Professional Baseball League), 1943–1950; Chicago Admirals (Chicago National League), 1951–1954; Phoenix A-1 Queens, 1955–1958: Remarks: Won 133 AAGPBL games and lost 115; later, played golf on Ladies LPGA circuit, 1962–1965, later teaching golf for 30 years.

56937. Odenkirk, James E. "Joanne Emily Winter." In: Vol. Q-Z of David L. Porter, ed. *Biographical Dictionary of American Sports: Baseball.* Rev. and enlarged ed. Westport, CT: Greenwood Press, 2000. Pp. 1703–1704.

Jesse ("Nip") Winters

P. (B: 1899, Washington, DC-D: Dec. 1971). Norfolk Stars, 1919–1921; Baltimore Black Sox, 1921; Atlantic City Bacharach Giants, 1921–1922; Hilldale Daisies, 1922–1928; Homestead Grays, 1928; New York Lincoln Giants, 1928–1929; Baltimore Black Sox, 1929; Hilldale Daisies and Newark Browns, 1931; Atlantic City Bacharach Giants and Washington Pilots, 1932; Atlantic City Bacharach Giants and Philadelphia Stars, 1933. Remarks: Obtained at least 121 victories in 14 seasons; in two exhibition contests with the Babe Ruth All-Stars, defeated Lefty Grove (q.v.) once, but lost once.

56938. Bernstein, David "Jesse 'Nip' Winters." In: Vol. Q-Z of David L. Porter, ed. *Biographical Dictionary of American Sports: Baseball.* Rev. and enlarged ed. Westport, CT: Greenwood Press, 2000. Pp. 1704–1705.

56939. Winters, Jesse and John B. Holway. "Reminiscences of Jesse Winters: 'How I Struck Out Babe Ruth and Lefty Grove.'" *Records of the Columbia Society of Washington, D.C. 1971–1972,* XLVIII (1973), 752–757.

Nip Winters *see* **Jesse ("Nip") Winters**

Casey Wise *see* **Kendall Cole ("Casey") Wise**

Kendall Cole ("Casey") Wise
2B-SS (B: Sept. 8, 1932, Lafayette, IN). Chicago (NL), 1957; Milwaukee (NL), 1959–1959; Detroit (AL), 1960. Remarks: Obtained 56 hits (three homers) in 126 games in four seasons; had one appearance (strikeout) in 1958 World Series.

56940. Bryson, Bill. "Wondrous Wise." *Baseball Digest,* XVI (March 1957), 51–54.

Richard Charles ("Rick") Wise
P. (B: Sept. 13, 1945, Jackson, MS). Philadelphia (NL), 1964–1971; St. Louis (NL), 1972–1973; Boston (AL), 1974–1977; Cleveland (AL), 1978–1919; San Diego (NL), 1980–1982. Remarks: Had 188 victories, 181 defeats, and 0 "saves" in an 18-year major league career; pitched no-hitter, June 23, 1971; as a batter, had 130 hits (15 homers) in 668 at-bats (only big leaguer to ever pitch a no-hitter and hit two homers in the same game); had two homers in one game two months later, Aug. 28, 1971; pitching coach, Madison (Midwest League), 1985–1986, Sarasota (Gulf Coast League), 1987, Auburn (New York-Pennsylvania League), 1988–1989, New Britain (EL), 1991–1992, and Pawtucket (IL), 1993–1995; Long Island (Atlantic League), 1996–2002; Nashua (Atlantic League), 2003-; named to Oregon Sports Hall of Fame, 1987.

56941. Ballew, Bill. "Rick Wise." In: his *The Pastime in the Seventies: Oral Histories of 16 Major Leaguers.* Jefferson, NC: McFarland & Co., Inc., 2002. Pp. 27–36.

56942. Bisher, Furman. "Rick Wise: A 9th Bat in the Lineup." *Baseball Digest,* XXX (October 1971), 80–83.

56943. Elderkin, Phil. "What Wise Means to the Red Sox." *Baseball Digest,* XXXIII (June 1974), 58–59.

56944. Gergen, Joe. "Rick Wise Makes Waves — on the Mound." *Sport,* LVII (June 1974), 73–80.

56945. Glew, Kevin. "Curtain Calls: Former Pitcher Rick Wise." *Baseball Digest,* LXIII (July 2004), 50–51.

56947. Leggett, William. "Enter an All-Round Wise Guy." *Sports Illustrated,* XXXV (July 5, 1971), 40+.

56948. O'Loughlin, Joe. "Where are They Now?: Rick Wise." *Baseball Digest,* LX (September 2001), 76–80.

56949. Porter, David L. "Richard Charles 'Rick' Wise." In: Vol. Q-Z of David L. Porter, ed. *Biographical Dictionary of American Sports: Baseball.* Rev. and enlarged ed. Westport, CT: Greenwood Press, 2000. Pp. 1705–1707.

56950. Westcott, Rich. "Rick Wise: A No-Hitter Like No Other." In: his *Splendor on the Diamond: Interviews with 35 Stars of Baseball's Past.* Gainesville, FL: The University Press of Florida, 2000. Pp. 173–184.

Samuel Washington ("Sam" or "Modoc") Wise
SS-1B. (B: Aug. 18, 1857, Akron, OH-D: Jan. 22, 1910). Detroit (NL), 1881; Boston (NL), 1882–1888; Washington (NL), 1889; Buffalo (P), 1890; Baltimore (AA), 1891;

Washington (NL), 1893. Remarks: In 1,175 games, obtained 1,281 hits (49 homers) and 172 stolen bases in 12 years; led NL in strikeouts (104), 1884; also played for Rochester (EL) and Binghampton (EL), 1892.

56951. Ivor-Campbell, Frederick. "Samuel Washington 'Sam,' 'Modoc' Wise." In: Vol. Q-Z of David L. Porter, ed. *Biographical Dictionary of American Sports: Baseball.* Rev. and enlarged ed. Westport, CT: Greenwood Press, 2000. Pp. 1707–1708.

Mary Nesbitt ("Wish") Wisham
P-1B. (B: Feb. 1, 1925, Greenville, SC). Racine Belles (All-American Girls Professional Baseball League), 1943–1945; Peoria Redwings (AAGPBL), 1947–1948, 1950. Remarks: Obtained 419 hits (14 homers) as a batter, while winning 65 games and losing 49.

56952. Crawford, Scott A. G. M. "Mary Nesbitt 'Wish' Wisham." In: Vol. Q-Z of David L. Porter, ed. *Biographical Dictionary of American Sports: Baseball.* Rev. and enlarged ed. Westport, CT: Greenwood Press, 2000. Pp. 1708–1709.

Connie ("Iron Woman" or "Polish Rifle") Wisniewski
P. (B: Feb. 18, 1922, Detroit, MI-D: May 4, 1995). Milwaukee Chicks (All-American Girls Professional Baseball League), 1944; Grand Rapids Chicks (AAGPBL), 1945–1952. Remarks: In five years (1944–1949) as a hurler, won 107 games and lost 48; had .291 batting average; AAGPBL home run champion (seven), 1948.

56953. Heapy, Leslie. "Connie 'Iron Woman,' 'Polish Rifle' Wisniewski." In: Vol. Q-Z of David L. Porter, ed. *Biographical Dictionary of American Sports: Baseball.* Rev. and enlarged ed. Westport, CT: Greenwood Press, 2000. Pp. 1709–1710.

Lawton Walker ("Whitey") Witt
OF-SS. (B: Laislaw Waldemar Wittkowski, Sept. 28, 1895, Orange, MA-D: July 14, 1988). Philadelphia (AL), 1916–1917, 1919–1921; New York (AL), 1922–1925; Brooklyn (NL), 1926. Remarks: Obtained 1,195 hits (18 homers) and 78 stolen bases in 1,129 games in a decade; knocked out by a pop bottle thrown from the bleachers, Sept. 16, 1922; had four hits (one double, one triple) in 1922 World Series and six hits (two doubles) in 1923 World Series.

56954. Westcott, Rich. "Whitey Witt — A Rich Career Among the Greats." In: his *Diamond Greats.* Westport, CT: Meckler Books, 1988. Pp. 116–123.

Ladislaw Waldemar Wittkowski *see* **Lawton Walker ("Whitey") Witt**

Michael Atwater ("Mike") Witt
P. (B: July 20, 1960, Fullerton, CA). California (AL), 1981–1990; New York (AL), 1990–1991, 1993. Remarks: Obtained 117 victories, 116 defeats, and five "saves" in 12 years; 6'7" pitcher had 16 strikeouts in one game, July 23, 1984; hurled perfect game, Sept. 30, 1984; won Game One of 1986 ALCS; combined with Mark Langston (q.v.) for no-hitter, April 11, 1990.

56955. Anderson, Bruce. "Brevity is the Role of Witt." *Sports Illustrated,* LXII (April 22, 1985), 62+.

56956. Brown, Dennis. "Mike Witt of the Angels Has the 'Right Stuff.'" *Baseball Digest,* XLVI (July 1987), 22–23.

56957. Buckley, James, Jr. "Mike Witt." In: his *Perfect!: The Inside Story of Baseball's Sixteen Perfect Games.* New York: Triumph Books, 2002. Pp. 150–167.

56958. Mayer, Ronald A. "Mike Witt." In: his *Perfect! Biographies and Lifetime Statistics of 14 Pitchers of Perfect Game.* Jefferson, NC: McFarland & Co., Inc., 1991. Pp. 182–195.

56959. Nack, William. "Thrown for Heavy Losses."

Sports Illustrated, LXIV (March 24, 1986), 40–44. Poor financial investments.

56960. Sorci, Rick. "Mike Witt and Kirk McCaskill: Double Trouble for Angel Foes." *Baseball Digest,* XLV (November 1986), 74–77.

56961. Witt, Mike, as told to George Vass. "The Game I'll Never Forget." *Baseball Digest,* XLVII (December 1968), 55–57. 1–0 perfect vs. California.

Whitey Witt *see* **Lawton Walker ("Whitley") Witt**

Jerome Charles ("Jerry") Witte
1B. (B: July 30, 1915, St. Louis, MO-D: April 27, 2002). St. Louis (AL), 1946–1947. Remarks: In two big league seasons, obtained 28 hits (four homers) in 52 games.

56962. Witte, Jerry, with Bill McCordy. *A Kid from St. Louis: Jerry Witte's Life in Baseball.* Houston, TX: Pecan Park Eagle Press, 2003. 317p.

Jerry Witte *see* **Jerome Charles ("Jerry") Witte**

Mark Edward Wohlers
P. (B: Jan. 23, 1970, Holyoke, MA). Atlanta (NL), 1991–1999; Cincinnati (NL), 1999–2001; New York (AL), 2001; Cleveland (AL), 2002. Remarks: Through 2002, won 39 games and lost 29, with 119 "saves"; pitched two innings of a shared no hitter, Sept. 9, 1991; lost one game of 1993 NLCS, but won one game of 1995 NLCS; surrendered homer to Jim Leyritz (q.v.) in Game Four of 1996 World Series; retired voluntarily.

56963. Ballew, Bill. "Ball of Fire: The Hottest Prospect for Fantasy Owners is Atlanta's Mark Wohlers." *Fantasy Baseball,* III (May 1992), 40–41.

56964. Verducci, Tom. "Turning Up the Heat." *Sports Illustrated,* LXXXIII (October 9, 1995), 56, 61.

Jimmy Wolf *see* **William Van Winkle ("Chicken Wolf" or "Jimmy") Wolf**

Warner William Wolf
BROADCASTER. (B: Nov. 11, 1937, Washington, DC). Remarks: Sportscaster, ABC Sports and WABC, 1976–1980; sportscaster, CBS Sports and WCBS, 1980-date.

56965. Wolf, Warner, with William Taafe. *Gimme a Break!* New York: McGraw-Hill, 1983. 186p.

56966. _____., with Larry Weisman. *Let's Go to the Videotape: All the Plays — and Replays — from My Life in Sports.* New York: Warner Books, 2000. 302p.

William Van Winkle ("Chicken Wolf" or "Jimmy") Wolf
OF-MGR. (B: May 12, 1862, Louisville, KY-D: May 16, 1903). Louisville (AA), 1882–1891. Remarks: The only player to labor his entire big league career in the AA; obtained 1,438 hits (18 homers) and 163 stolen bases in 1,198 games; had two homers in one game, Aug. 22, 1886; Colonels' manager, 1889, winning 14 games and losing 51 (.215); A. A. batting champion, 1890; lowest-paid big leaguer in history ($9 per week); A. A. career leader in hits (1438), doubles (214), triples (109), total bases (1921) and games played (1195); also played for Syracuse (EL), 1892 and Buffalo (EL), 1893; Louisville fireman, 1894–1899.

56967. Mondore, Scot E. "William Van Winkle 'Chicken Wolf,' 'Jimmy' Wolf." In: Vol. Q-Z of David L. Porter, ed. *Biographical Dictionary of American Sports: Baseball.* Rev. and enlarged ed. Westport, CT: Greenwood Press, 2000. Pp. 1710–1711. Bob Bailey's profile of Wolf is a number in the online SABR Biography Project http://bioproj.sabr.org/bioproj.cfm?a=v&v=l&bid=19&pid=15454.

Bob Wolff *see* **Robert ("Bob") Wolff**

Miles Wolff
WRITER-BROADCASTER-EXEC. (B: Dec. 30, 1945, Baltimore, MD). Remarks: GM, Savannah (Carolina League), 1971–1973; GM Anderson (Carolina League), 1974; GM, Jacksonville, 1975; broadcaster, Richmond, 1977; president, Durham (Carolina League), 1980–1993; president, Utica Blue Sox, 1982; publisher, *Baseball America,* 1982-date; founder/Commissioner, Northern League, 1993–2001; Commissioner, Central League (formerly Texas-Louisiana League), 2001-date.

56968. Hersch, Hank. "His Life is a Movie." *Sports Illustrated,* LXIX (August 8, 1988), 67+.

Rick Wolff
COACH-WRITER. (B: 1951). Remarks: Played Detroit (AL) farm system, 1973–1974; head baseball coach, Mercy College, 1982–1990; team psychological counselor, Cleveland (AL), 1990–1995; authority on childrens' baseball.

56969. Wolff, Rick. "Triumphant Return: Writer and Former Minor Leaguer Plays a Few Games at South Bend for a Story." *Sports Illustrated,* LXXI (August 21, 1989), 10–13. Played 37 games with South Bend (Midwest League)

Robert ("Bob") Wolff
BROADCASTER. Remarks: Broadcaster, Washington (AL), 1947–1960 and Minnesota, 1961; NBC-TV *Game of the Week* broadcaster, 1962–1966; Madison Square Garden and New York City broadcaster, 1966–; Ford C. Frick Award, 1995.

56970. Allen, Maury and Bob Wolff. "The Perfect Game." In: Marv Albert and Maury Allen, eds. *Voices of Sport.* New York: Grosset & Dunlap, 1971. Pp. 194–205. Wolff called Don Larsen's 1956 World Series triumph.

56971. Wolff, Bob. *It's Not Who Won or Lost the Game, It's How You Sold the Beer.* South Bend, IN: Diamond Communications, 1996. 239p.

56972. _____. "The Perfect Game." In: Maury Allen. *Voices of Sport.* New York: Grosset & Dunlap, 1971. Pp. 194–205. Interview, 1956.

Harry Meigs Wolter
OF-1B-P. (B: July 11, 1884, Monterey, CA-D: July 7, 1970). Cincinnati (NL), Pittsburgh (NL), and St. Louis (NL), 1907; Boston (AL), 1909; New York (AL), 1910–1913; Chicago (NL), 1917. Remarks: Obtained 514 hits (12 homers) and 94 stolen bases in 587 games in 14 seasons; as a pitcher for Pittsburgh, St. Louis, and Boston, won four games and lost five, with a single "save"; also played for Sacramento (PCL), 1908.

56973. Spalding, John. "Harry Wolter." In: his *Pacific Coast League Stars: One Hundred of the Best, 1903-1957.* San Jose, CA: John E. Spalding, 1994. Pp. 34–35.

Harry Sterling Wolverton
3B-MGR. (B: Dec. 6, 1873, Mt. Vernon, OH-D: Feb. 4, 1937). Chicago (NL), 1898–1900; Philadelphia (NL), 1902–1904; Boston (NL), 1906; New York — (AL), 1912. Remarks: Had 833 hits (seven homers) and 83 stolen bases in 782 games in nine years; had three triples in one game, July 13, 1900; manager, Oakland (PCL), 1910–1911; manager, New York (AL), 1912, winning 50 games and losing 102 (.329).

56974. Chase, Hal. "My Opinion of Manager Wolverton." *Baseball Magazine,* IX (June 1912), 1–2.

56975. Jarrett, Scott A. "That Wolverton Rag." *Vintage & Classic Baseball Collector,* no. 4 (December 1995), 8–9.

56976. Jordan, H. H. "Harry, Wolverton, Manager and Man." *Baseball Magazine,* IX (June 1912), 19–21.

56977. Wolvertorn, Harry S. "How It Seems to Be a Major League Manager." *Baseball Magazine,* IX (June 1912), 17–19.

Dooley Womack *see* **Horace Guy ("Dooley") Womack**

Horace Guy ("Dooley") Womack

P. (B: Aug. 25, 1939, Columbia, SC). New York (AL), 1966–1968; Houston (NL) and Seattle (AL), 1969; Oakland (AL), 1970. Remarks: Obtained 19 victories, 18 defeats, and 24 "saves" in five big league seasons; torn rotator cuff ended his career.

56978. Kelley, Brent P. "Dooley Womack: The [1967] Yankee Saver." In: his *They Too Wore Pinstripes: Interviews with 20 Glory-Days New York Yankees.* Jefferson, NC: McFarland & Co., 1998. Pp. 194–207. Expanded from the next entry.

56979. _____. "Dooley Womack: The Yankee Saver." *Sports Collector's Digest,* XVIII (November 29, 1991), 250–252.

Howard Ellsworth ("Joe" or "Smokey Joe") Wood

P-OF-COACH. (B: Oct. 25, 1889, Kansas City, MO-D: July 27, 1985). Boston (AL), 1908–1915; Cleveland (AL), 1917, 1919–1920. Remarks: Won 116 games and lost 57, with 17 "saves," in 11 seasons before sore arm forced him to become an outfielder for five seasons, 1918–1924; in 14 total seasons as a batter, had 553 hits (23 homers) and 23 stolen bases in 695 games; pitched no-hitter, July 29, 1911; obtained 34 victories in 1912; won three games and lost one in 1912 World Series; retired from pro ball to become baseball coach at Yale University, 1923–1942; received LLD. Degree from Yale in 1984; named to Red Sox Hall of Fame, 1995.

56980. Alvarez, Mark. "An Interview with Smokey Joe Wood." *The Baseball Research Journal,* XVI (1987), 53–56.

56981. Angell, Roger. "Web of the Game." *New Yorker,* LVII (July 20, 1981), 96–102+.

56982. Clark, Ellery H., Jr. "Joe 'Smokey Joe' Wood." In: Vol. Q-Z of David L. Porter, ed. *Biographical Dictionary of American Sports: Baseball.* Rev. and enlarged ed. Westport, CT: Greenwood Press, 2000. Pp. 1711–1712.

56983. Dagaverian, Debra A., and Mark Rucker. "The Joe Wood Scrapbook." *The National Pastime,* II (1982), 39–47.

56984. Gershman, Michael. "Smokey Joe's Shining [1912] Season." *Sports Heritage,* I (September-October 1987), 42–50.

56985. Green, Paul M. "Baseball and Joe Wood." *Sports Collector's Digest,* IX (November 26, 1982), 28+.

56986. _____. "Joe Wood." In: his *Forgotten Fields.* Waupaca, WI: Parker Publications, 1984. Pp. 6–24.

56987. Holway, John B. *Smokey Joe and the Cannonball.* Washington, D.C.: Capital Press, 1985.

56988. Honig, Donald. "Smokey Joe Wood." In: his *Baseball America.* New York: Macmillan, 1985. Pp. 76–82.

56989. _____. "Joe Wood." In: his *The October Heroes.* New York: Simon and Schuster, 1979. Pp. 164–182.

56990. "Joe Wood, Pennant Winner." *Literary Digest,* XLV (September 21, 1912), 484.

56991. Klima, John. "Birth of Hope: Smokey Joe Wood vs. Walter Johnson (September 6, 1912)." In: his *Pitched Battle: 35 of Baseball's Greatest Duels from the Mound.* Jefferson, NC: McFarland & Co., Inc., 2002. Pp. 25–32.

56992. Lane, Ferdinand C. "The Extraordinary Career of Smokey Joe Wood." *Baseball Magazine,* XXVII (October 1921), 493–495+.

56993. _____. "Flashback — Smokey Joe Wood." *Baseball Magazine,* XC (August 1954), 19–20.

56994. _____. "Smokey Joe Wood." In: Sydney Offit, ed. *Best of Baseball.* New York: G.P. Putnam, 1956. pp. 61–67. Reprinted from the September 1926 issue of Baseball Magazine.

56995. Laney, Al. "34 Wins in One Year and Then…" *Baseball. Digest,* XIX (May 1960), 26–31.

56996. Linkugel, Wil A. and Edward J. Pappas. "The Kansas Cyclone: Smoky Joe Wood." In: their *They Tasted Glory: Among the Missing at the Baseball Hall of Fame.* Jefferson, NC: McFarland & Co., Inc., 1998. Pp. 9–23.

56997. Ritter, Lawrence S. "Smokey Joe Wood." In: his *Glory of Their Time.* New York: Macmillan, 1966. pp. 146–161. Excerpted in *Saturday Evening Post,* CCXXXIX (August 13, 1966), 48+.

56998. Roth, Emil H. "The Wood-Johnson Duel." *The Baseball Research Journal,* III (1974), 20–23.

56999. Salisbury, Luke. "Smokey Joe Wood." In: John A. Garrity and Marsh C. Carries, eds. *American National Biography.* 24 vols. New York: Oxford University Press, 1999. XXIII, 779–780.

57000. Ward, John J. "Joseph Wood, Esquire-Pitcher." *Baseball Magazine,* X (November 1912), 49–60.

57001. Whaley, Joan. "Smokey Joe Wood Looks Back on His Baseball Career." *Baseball Digest,* XL (May 1981), 40–59.

57002. Wood, "Smokey Joe." "Not Far from Slumgullion Gulch." In: Charles Einstein, ed. *The Third Fireside Book of Baseball.* New York: Simon and Schuster, 1968. Pp. 492–495.

Joe Wood *see* **Howard Ellsworth ("Joe" or "Smokey Joe") Wood**

Kerry Lee Wood

(B: June 16, 1977, Irving, TX). Chicago (NL), 1998–2002. Remarks: Through 2004, has won 67 games and lost 50; set still-standing MLB mark with 20 strikeouts in one game, May 6, 1998; despite injuries in 1998; NL Rookie of the Year Award, 1998; led NL in strikeouts (266), 2003; lost one game in 2003 NLCS.

57003. Crothers, Tim. "The Mystery of the Dead Arm: Wood Fatigue." *Sports Illustrated,* LXXXIX (August 24, 1998), 54, 56.

57004. Hunt, John. "Wood Using Kerry Be Foolish?" *USA Today Baseball Weekly,* VIII (April 22, 1998), 22–23.

57005. "Kerry Wood." In: Carrie Muskat, ed. *Banks to Sandberg to Grace: Five Decades of Love and Frustration with the Chicago Cubs.* Chicago, IL: Contemporary Books, 2001. Pp. 267–270.

57006. Kiley, Mike. "A Wiser Wood: Cubs' Right-Hander Prepares Himself for a Successful Season." *Baseball Digest,* LXI (May 2002), 50–53.

57007. Klima, John. "Then It Happened: Kerry Wood vs. Shane Reynolds (May 6, 1998)." In: his *Pitched Battle: 35 of Baseball's Greatest Duels from the Mound.* Jefferson, NC: McFarland & Co., Inc., 2002. Pp.180–184.

57008. Kuenster, John. "Strikeout Pitchers Like Cubs' Kerry Wood Help Fill the Seats." *Baseball Digest,* LVII (August 1998), 17–21.

57009. Latimer, Clay. "Natural Wood." *Beckett Baseball Card Monthly,* XV (August 1998), 96–99.

57010. McCarver, Tim with Danny Peary. "Kerry Wood." In: his *The Perfect Season: Why 1998 Was Baseball's Greatest Year.* New York: Villard Books, 1999. Pp. 36–43.

57011. Snyder, Deron. "Cubs Polishing Fine Wood: Hard-Throwing Rookie Gets High Marks Despite Living in the Spotlight." *USA Today Baseball Weekly,* VIII (May 6, 1998), 26–28.

57012. Van Dyck, Dave. "Kerry Wood's Goal for '99: Improve on Rookie Season." *Baseball Digest,* LVIII (February 1999), 60–63.

57013. Wendel, Tim. "In a Class by Themselves: Kerry Wood, Ben Grieve Receive Highest Marks as a Top Rookie Tandem." *USA Today Baseball Weekly,* VIII (November 11, 1998), 6–7.

57014. Wertheim, L. Jon. "Flame Thrower." *Sports Illustrated,* LXXXVIII (May 18, 1998), 48–50, 53, 56. .

57015. White, Paul and Carrie Muskat. "Was Wood's Injury Inevitable?" *USA Today Baseball Weekly,* VIII (March 24, 1999), 8–10.

57016. Wojciechowski, Gene. "Chicago Hope." *ESPN: The Magazine,* III (May 29, 2000), 94–99.

57017. Wood, Kerry. "When I Was a Kid: Interview." *Junior Baseball,* no. 30 (November-December 2000), 10+.

Smokey Joe Wood *see* **Howard Ellsworth ("Joe" or "Smokey Joe") Wood**

Wilbur Forrester ("Mr. Knuckles") Wood, Jr.

P. (B: Oct. 22, 1941, Cambridge, MA). Boston (AL), 1961–1964; Pittsburgh (N.L), 1964–1965; Chicago (AL), 1967–1979. Remarks: Had 164 victories, 156 defeats, and 57 "saves" in 17 years; the only great left-handed knuckleballer; save both ends of a doubleheader, June 24, 1969; won a suspended and full game in one day, May 28, 1973; started and lost both games of a doubleheader, July 20, 1973; in 1973, became first pitcher since Walter Johnson (1916) to both win and lose 20 games in same season; hit a record three consecutive batters, Sept. 10, 1977; also played for Columbus (IL), 1966.

57018. Elderkin, Phil. "How to Win in Baseball without Throwing Hard." *Baseball Digest,* XXXIII (December 1974), 44–46.

57019. Fimrite, Ron. "Wilbur's Knuckler Is Alive, and Well." *Sports Illustrated,* XXXVIII (June 4,1973), 24–29.

57020. Forman, Ross. "Knuckleballer Wilbur Wood Recalls How It Was in the '70s." *Baseball Digest,* LII (July 1993), 62–65.

57021. _____. "Wilbur Wood." *Sports Collector's Digest,* XXV (May 29, 1998), 170–171.

57022. Furlong, William B. "Wilbur Wood: All In the Knuckles." In: Ray Robinson, ed. *Baseball Stars of 1973.* New York: Pyramid Books, 1973. Pp. 117–124.

57023. _____. "Wilbur Wood: Iron Knuckles." In: Ray Robinson, ed. *Baseball Stars of 1972.* New York: Pyramid Books, 1972. Pp. 114–119.

57024. Hirshberg, Al. "Wilbur Wood and the Art of the Knuckleball." *Sport,* IV (August 1972), 54–57.

57025. Kiersh, Edward. "Wilbur Wood: Three Hundred Pounds of Clam Chowder." In: his *Where Have You Gone, Vince DiMaggio?* New York: Bantam Books, 1983. Pp. 208–211.

57026. Malamud, Allan. "Wilbur Wood: A Fluttering Success Story." *Baseball Digest,* XXXI (November 1972), 31–35.

57027. Olmstead, Frank J. "Wilbur Forrester 'Mr. Knuckles' Wood, Jr." In: Vol. Q-Z of David L. Porter, ed. *Biographical Dictionary of American Sports: Baseball.* Rev. and enlarged ed. Westport, CT: Greenwood Press, 2000. Pp. 1712–1714.

57028. Robinson, Ray. "Wilbur Wood: Easy Does It." In: Ray Robinson, ed. *Baseball Stars of 1974.* New York: Pyramid Books, 1974. Pp. 117–124.

57029. Ryerson, Bill. "Wilbur Wood; King of the Knucklers." *Baseball Digest,* XXXH (August 1973), 38–41.

57030. Talley, Rick. "When the White Box Almost Traded Wilbur Wood." *Baseball Digest,* XXXII (October 1972), 40–42.

57031. Vanderberg, Bob. "Wilbur Wood: Knuckling Down to Business." In: *his Sox—From Lane and Fain to Zisk and Fisk.* Chicago, IL: Chicago Review Press, 1982. Pp. 309–315.

57032. Wood, Wilbur. "Double-Plays Double Now." *Baseball Digest,* VIII (May 1949), 13–15.

57033. _____., as told to George Vass. "The Game I'll Never Forget." *Baseball Digest,* XXXV (April 1976), 120–123.

Harold Joseph ("Hal") Woodeshick

P. (B: Aug. 24, 1932, Wilkes-Barre, PA). Detroit (AL) and Cleveland (AL), 1958; Washington (AL), 1959–1961; Detroit (AL), 1961; Houston (NL), 1962–1965; St. Louis (NL), 1965–1967. Remarks: Obtained 44 victories, 62 defeats, and 61 "saves" in a decade; led NL with 24 "saves" in 1964.

57034. Stainback, Berry. "The Gravy Waltzer." *Sport,* XXXVI (October 1963), 7–8.

Eugene Richard ("Gene" or "Old Faithful") Woodling

OF. (B: Aug. 16, 1922, Akron, OH-D: June 2, 2001). Cleveland (AL), 1943, 1946; Pittsburgh (NL), 1947; New York (AL), 1949–1954; Baltimore (AL), 1955; Cleveland (AL), 1955–1957; Baltimore (AL), 1958–1960; Washington (AL), 1961–1962; New York (AL), 1962. Remarks: Obtained 1,585 hits (147 homers) and 29 stolen bases in 1,796 games in 17 seasons; appeared in five World Series (1949–1953) achieving a cumulative 27 hits (five doubles, two triples, three homers) and six RBIs; had two grand slam homers, July 27, 1959 and May 11, 1962; also played for San Francisco (PCL), 1948; coach, Baltimore (AL), 1964–1967; scout, Cleveland (AL), late 1970s and through the mid-1980s; remembered for efforts to obtain a big league pension plan.

57035. Birtwell, Roger. "Woodling Spared Goat's Horns." *Baseball Digest,* XI (January 1952), 47–50.

57036. Daniel, Daniel M. "Woodling Announces .300 Ambitions with Great Confidence." *Baseball Magazine,* LXXXVI (May 1951), 415–417.

57037. Darcey, Dick. "Woodling Will Be There Opening Day." *Baseball Monthly,* I (March 1962), 22–27.

57038. Fehler, Gene. "Gene Woodling." In: his *Tales from Baseball's Golden Age.* Champaign, IL: Sports Publishing Co., 2000. Chpt. 54.

57039. Forker, Dom. "Gene Woodling." In: his *The Men of Autumn.* Dallas, TX: Taylor Publishing Co., 1989. Pp. 174–181.

57040. "Gene Woodling's Little Leaguers." *Collier's,* CXXXI (May 9, 1953), 18–19. Woodling coached a team in Fair Lawn, N.J.

57041. Gottehrer, Barry. "Gene Woodling Fooled Them All." *Sport,* XXIX (June 1960),48–49+.

57042. Kiersh, Edward. "Gene Woodling: But Where's the Camel?" In: his *Where Have You Gone, Vince DiMaggio?* New York: Bantam Books, 1983. Pp. 65–70.

57043. Lewis, Franklin. "Woodling's 448-Foot Catch." *Baseball Digest,* XIII (July 1954), 73–75.

57044. Meany, Thomas. "The Gold Dust Twins (Hank Bauer—Gene Woodling." In: his *The Magnificent Yankees.* New York: A.S. Barnes & Co., 1952. Pp. 144–151.

57045. _____. "The Yankees' Gold Dust Twins: Bauer and Woodling." *Baseball Digest,* XII (March 1953), 21–26. Taken from the previous entry.

57046. Moffi, Larry. "Gene Woodling: 'I Wrote Hitting Books Too—That's Only for Money.'" In: his *This Side of Cooperstown: An Oral History Of Major League Baseball in the 1950s.* Iowa City, IA: University of Iowa Press, 1996. Pp. 49–60.

57047. Newcombe, Jack. "The Yankee They Take for Granted." *Sport,* XIV (February 1953), 26–27+.

57048. O'Neill, Steve. "Closed Stance Reopens the Door for Woodling." *Baseball Digest,* XIX (February 1960), 32–35.

57049. Richman, Milton. "Wait a Minute, Woodling." *Baseball Digest,* X (November 1951), 29–33.

57050. Sargent, Jim. "Where are They Now?: Former Outfielder Gene Woodling Recalls Career in Majors." *Baseball Digest,* LIX (February 2000), 68–77.

57051. Scanlon, Lee E. "Eugene Richard 'Gene,' 'Old Faithful' Woodling." In: Vol. Q–Z of David L. Porter, ed. *Biographical Dictionary of American Sports: Baseball.* Rev. and enlarged ed. Westport, CT: Greenwood Press, 2000. Pp. 1714–1715.

57052. "So You Want to Play Golf with Gene Woodling." *Sport,* VIII (April 1950), 64–67. Fashions.

57053. Spalding, John E. "Gene Woodling." In: *his Pacific Coast League Stars, Vol. II: Ninety Who Made It to the Majors, 1905–1957.* San Jose, CA: John E. Spalding, 1997. Pp. 137–138.

57054. Steadman, John P. "An 'Old Pro' Offers Tips on Batting." *Baseball Digest,* XXXVI (August 1977), 50–55. Advice from Gene Woodling.

57055. Stann, Francis. "Gene Woodling a Professional — Not a 'Pro.'" *Baseball Digest,* XX (June 1961), 61–63.

57056. Stern, Chris. "Gene Woodling." In: *his Where Have They Gone?* New York: Tempo, 1979. Pp. 175–177.

57058. Stevens, Bob. "Yankee Angry Man." In: Bruce Jacobs, ed. *Baseball Stars of 1954.* New York: Lion Books, 1954. Pp. 140–146.

57059. Terrell, Roy. "Somebody's Gotta Play Left." *Sports Illustrated,* XII (May 16, 1960), 70–73.

57060. Westcott, Rich. "Gene Woodling — A Certified Winner." In: *his Diamond Greats.* Westport, CT: Meckler Books, 1988. Pp. 383–388

57061. Woodling, Gene. *Gene Woodling's Secrets of Batting.* New York: G.P. Putnam's Sons, 1967. 94p.

Florence Irene ("Smokey") Woods
P. (B: 1899, Portland, ME–D: 1987). Portlanders semi-pro player, 1913–ca. 1916; later, nun, who taught local schoolchildren for 48 years; elected to Maine Baseball Hall of Fame, 1979.

57062. Lannin, Joanne. "Smokey was a Natural." *Yankee,* LVII (April 1993), 96–99.

Gary Lee Woods
OF. (B: July 20, 1954, Santa Barbara, CA). Oakland (AL), 1976; Toronto (AL), 1977–1978; Houston (NL), 1980–1981; Chicago (NL), 1982–1985. Remarks: Obtained 251 hits (13 homers) and 19 stolen bases in 525 games in nine big league seasons; obtained first Blue Jays' stolen base; obtained two hits and an RBI in the 1980 NLCS.

57063. Phalen, Rick. "Gary Woods." In: *his Our Chicago Cubs.* South Bend, IN: Diamond Communications, 1992. Pp. 171–180.

Parnell l. Woods
3B–MBR. (B: Feb. 26, 1912, Birmingham, AL–D: July 22, 1977). Birmingham Black Barons, 1922–1938, 1940; Jacksonville Red Caps, 1938, 1941; Cleveland Bears, 1939–1940; Cincinnati Buckeyes, 1942; Cleveland Buckeyes, 1943–1948; Oakland (PCL) and Louisville Buckeyes, 1949; Memphis Red Sox, 1950; Chicago American Giants, 1951. Remarks: Had career .316 batting average and was highly regarded as a fielder; manager, Cincinnati, 1942 and Cleveland, 1943–1944; business manager, Harlem Globetrotters basketball team, 1952–1977.

57064. Kleinknecht, Merl F. "Parnell L. Woods." In: Vol. Q–Z of David L. Porter, ed. *Biographical Dictionary of American Sports: Baseball.* Rev. and enlarged ed. Westport, CT: Greenwood Press, 2000. Pp. 1715–1716.

Rufus Stanley ("Stan") Woodward
WRITER. (B: June 5, 1895, Worcester, MA–D: Nov. 29, 1965). Remarks: Reporter, later editor, *Worcester Gazette,* 1920–1922; reporter, later sports editor, *Boston Herald,* 1922–1929; sports writer/editor, *New York Herald-Tribune,* 1930–1948; columnist, *New York Daily Compass,* 1949–1950; sports editor, *Miami News,* 1950–1955; writer, Newhouse newspaper chain, 1955–1959; sports editor, *New York Herald-Tribune,* 1959–1962.

57065. Rosenthal, Harold. "Stanley Woodward." In: Richard Orodenker, ed. *Dictionary of Literary Biography: Volume 171, Twentieth-Century American Sportswriters.* A Bruccoli Clark Layman Book. Detroit, Mi: Gale Research, 1996. Pp. 349–355.

57066. Ziegler, John H. "Rufus Stanley 'Stan' Woodward." In: David L. Porter, ed. *Biographical Dictionary of American Sports: 1992–1995 Supplement for Baseball, Football, Basketball and Other Sports.* Westport, CT: Greenwood Press, 1995. Pp. 362–363.

Stanley Woodward *see* **Rufus Stanley ("Stan") Woodward**

Todd Roland Worrell
P. (B: Sept. 28, 1959, Arcadia, CA). St. Louis (NL), 1985–1989, 1992; Los Angeles (NL), 1993–1997. Remarks: Obtained 50 victories, 52 defeats, and 258 "saves" in 11 big league seasons; injured 1990–1991; struck out six consecutive batters in Game Five of 1985 World Series; NL Rookie of the Year award, 1986; struck out 9th inning opposing side with nine pitches, Aug. 13, 1999; only MLB pitcher to record 30 saves in each of his first three full seasons; only Cardinal to have three 30-save seasons.

57067. Alexson, Bill. "Todd Worrell, St. Louis Cardinals." In: *his Batting a Thousand, Book 2.* Nashville, TN: Thomas Nelson Publishers, 1990. Pp. 34–37.

57068. Collier, Ken. "Todd Worrell." In: Ken Collier, ed. *The Baseball Book, 1987.* Scottsdale, AZ: Jalart House, 1987. Pp. 58–59.

57069. Honig, Donald. "1986: Todd Worrell." In: *his National League Rookies of the Year.* New York: Bantam Books, 1989. Pp. 103–104.

57070. Nash, Bruce and Allan Zullo. "Todd Worrell." In: *their Little Big Leaguers: Amazing Boyhood Stories of Today's Baseball Stars.* New York: Little Simon, 1990. Pp. 64–65.

57071. Rains, Rob. "Vince Coleman and Todd Worrell: All-Out Assault on Baseball's Record Book." In: Kip W. Ingle, ed. *St. Louis Cardinals 1989 Yearbook.* St. Louis, MO: Public Relations Department, St. Louis Cardinals, 1989. Pp. 6–9.

Allan Fulton ("Al" or "Red") Worthington
P. (B: Feb. 5, 1929, Birmingham, AL). New York (NL) and San Francisco (NL), 1953–1954, 1956–1959; Boston (AL), 1960; Chicago (AL), 1960; Cincinnati (NL), 1963–1964; Minnesota (AL), 1964–1969. Remarks: Won 75 games and lost 92, with 110 "saves," in 14 years; coach, Minnesota (AL), 1972–1973.

57072. Bitker, Steve. "Al Worthington." In: *his The Original San Francisco Giants: The Giants of '58.* Champaign, IL: Sports Publishing, Inc., 1998. Pp. 163–166.

57073. Devaney, John. "Al Worthington." In: *his Where Are They Today? Great Sports Stars of Yesteryear.* New York: Crown Publishers, 1985. Pp. 210–213.

57074. _____. "Bible in the Bullpen." *Saturday Evening Post,* CCXXXVII (May 2, 1964), 28–29.

57075. _____. "A Sundown Kind of Pitcher." *Sport,* XL (December 1965), 42–46.

57076. Gordon, Dick. "Control, Confidence, Conscience: Three C's Make Worthington Worth-a-ton to Twins." *Baseball Digest,* XXIV (April 1965), 67–70.

57077. Hefley, James C. "Al Worthington: The Fireman

with Faith." In: his *Play Ball.* Grand Rapids, MI: Zondervan Publishing House, 1964. Pp. 69–75.

57078. Mandel, Mike. "Al Worthington." In: his *The San Francisco Giants: An Oral History.* Santa Cruz, CA: Mike Mandel, 1979. Pp. 24–28.

57079. Schultz, Randy. "Where are They Now?: Al Worthington." *Baseball Digest,* XLV (March 1986), 67–70.

Bill Wright *see* **Burnis ("Bill" or "Wild Bill") Wright**
Buckshot Wright *see* **Forrest Glenn ("Buckshot") Wright**

Burnis ("Bill" or "Wild Bill") Wright
OF. (B: June 6, 1914, Milan, TN–D: Aug. 3, 1996). Nashville Elite Giants, 1932–1934; Columbus Elite Giants, 1935; Washington Elite Giants, 1936–1937; Baltimore Elite Giants, 1938–1939, 1942, 1945; Mexican League, 1940–1941, 1943–1944, 1946–1956. Remarks: Lifetime Negro League .361 batter, who enjoyed greatest fame in Mexico; opened restaurant in Aquascalienes, Mexico; elected to Mexican Baseball Hall of Fame, 1982.

57080. Craft, David. "'Wild Bill' Was the 'Wright' Man for the Job." *Sports Collectors Digest,* XVIII (June 21, 1991), 86–87.

57081. Kelley, Brent P. "'Wild Bill' Wright: 'The Black Joe DiMaggio.'" *Sports Collector's Digest,* XXIII (August 30, 1996), 140+.

57082. Klima, John. "Shutout the Whispers: Bill Wright vs. Satchel Paige (August 20, 1948)." In: his *Pitched Battle: 35 of Baseball's Greatest Duels from the Mound.* Jefferson, NC: McFarland & Co., Inc., 2002. Pp. 77–81.

57083. Riley, James A. "Burnis 'Bill,' 'Wild Bill' Wright." In: Vol. Q-Z of David L. Porter, ed. *Biographical Dictionary of American Sports: Baseball.* Rev. and enlarged ed. Westport, CT: Greenwood Press, 2000. Pp. 1716–1717.

57084. _____. "Wild Bill Wright: A Mexican League Legend Comes Home." *Oldtyme Baseball News,* III, no. 3 (1991), 17+. Attended Negro League reunion in 1990.

57085. Swank, Bill. "Bill Wright." In: his *Echoes from Lane Field: A History of the San Diego Padres 1936–1957.* Paducah, KY: Turner Publishing Company, 1997. Pp. 132–133.

Clyde ("Skeeter") Wright
(B: Feb. 20, 1941, Jefferson City, TN). California (AL), 1966–1973; Milwaukee (AL), 1974), Texas (AL), 1975. Remarks: Won 100 games, lost 111, and had three "saves"; hurled no-hitter, July 3, 1970; operates the year round Clyde Wright Pitching School in Anaheim, CA; father of Jaret Wright (below).

57086. Bell, Joseph N. "One Wrong Season Makes a Wright." *Sport,* LII (July 1971), 54–57.

57087. Stewart, Wayne. "The Wrights." In: his *Fathers, Sons & Baseball: Our National Pastime and the Ties That Bind.* Guilford, CT: The Lyons Press, 2002. Pp. 139–154.

Ed Wright *see* **Henderson Edward Wright**

Forrest Glenn ("Buckshot") Wright
SS. (B: Feb. 6, 1901, Archie, MO–D: April 7, 1984). Pittsburgh (NL), 1924–1928; Brooklyn (NL), 1929–1933; Chicago (AL), 1935. Remarks: Had, 1,219 hits (93 homers) in 1,119 games in an 11-year major league career; became an immortal by making an unassisted triple play, May 7, 1925; playing in 1925 and 1927 World Series, obtaining a cumulative seven hits (one double, one homer) and five RBIs; Boston (AL) farm team manager, 1937–1946; scout, 1947 into the 1970's; named to Missouri Sports Hall of Fame, 1976.

57088. Lane, Ferdinand C. "The Man Who Gave Pittsburgh Its Batting Punch." *Baseball Magazine,* XXXIII (November 1924), 536–537+.

57089. Langford, Walter. "An Interview with Glenn Wright." *The Baseball Research Journal,* XIX (1990), 71–76.

57090. Murdock, Eugene C. "Forest Glenn 'Buckshot' Wright." In: Vol. Q-Z of David L. Porter, ed. *Biographical Dictionary of American Sports: Baseball.* Rev. and enlarged ed. Westport, CT: Greenwood Press, 2000. Pp. 1717–1719.

57091. _____. "Glenn Wright: Last of the 1925 All-Stars." *The Baseball Research Journal,* VIII (1979), 109–112.

57092. _____. "That Easy Unassisted Triple Play: Glenn Wright." In: his *Baseball Players and Their Times: Oral Histories of the Game, 1920–1940.* Westport, CT: Meckler Publishing, 1991. Pp. 242–248.

57093. Ward, John J. "Has Pittsburgh Found a Worthy Successor to Hans Wagner?" *Baseball Magazine,* XXXV (November 1925), 538, 568.

57094. Wright, Forest Glenn "Glenn Wright's Sensational Comeback." *Baseball Magazine,* XLVI (January 1931), 351–352+.

George Wright ★
SS-2B-P-MGR. (B: Jan. 28, 1847, Yonkers, NY–D: Aug. 21, 1937). New York Gothams, Philadelphia Olympics, Morrisania Unions, Washington Nationals, and Cincinnati Red Stockings (all independents), 1864–1870; Boston (National Association) 1871–1875; Boston (NL), I 876–1878; Providence (NL), 1879; Boston (NL), 1880–1881; Providence (NL), 1892. Remarks: In seven NL playing years, had 383 hits (two homers) in 329 games; manager, Providence (NL), 1879, winning 59 games and losing 26 (.702); brother of Harry Wright (below); founder of Wright and Ditson Sporting Goods Co.; possible originator of phrase: "I'd rather be Wright than President"; chosen shortstop by Henry Chadwick, on the first All-Star team in 1868; introduced golf, hockey, and tennis to the U.S. sporting public; elected to National Baseball Hall of Fame in 1937, where his plaque reads: "Star of baseball's first professional team, the Cincinnati Red Stockings of 1869. Great shortstop and captain of champion Bostons in National Leagues pioneer years."

57095. Allen, Lee and Thomas Meany. "George Wright." In: their *Kings of the Diamond.* New York: G.P. Putnam, 1966. pp. 141–143.

57096. Brock, Darryl. "The Wright Way." *Sports Heritage,* I (March 1987), 35–43.

57097. Ivor-Campbell, Frederick. "George Wright." In: Vol. Q-Z of David L. Porter, ed. *Biographical Dictionary of American Sports: Baseball.* Rev. and enlarged ed. Westport, CT: Greenwood Press, 2000. Pp. 1719–1722.

57098. _____. "George Wright." In: John A. Garrity and Marsh C. Carries, eds. *American National Biography.* 24 vols. New York: Oxford University Press, 1999. XXIV, 20–21.

57099. Kaese, Harold. "George Wright." In: Supplement 2 of Robert L. Schuyler and Edward T. James, eds. *Dictionary of American Biography.* New York: Scribner's, 1958. p. 737.

57100. Smith, Robert. M. "George Wright." In: his *Heroes of Baseball.* Cleveland, OH: World Publishing Co., 1952. Pp. 31–37.

57101. Wright, George. "Sketch of the National Game of Baseball." *Columbia Historical Society Records,* XXIII (1920), 80–85.

57102. Wright, Jerry Jaye. "Brother Against Brother: Events and Final Days of Professional Baseball's 1879 Season." *Nine: A Journal of Baseball History and Social Policy Perspectives,* III (Spring 1995), 204–217.

Glenn Wright see **Forrest Glenn ("Buckshot") Wright**

Harry Wright see **William Henry ("Harry") Wright**

Henderson Edward ("Ed") Wright
P. (B: May 15, 1919, Dyersburg, TN-D: Nov. 19, 1995). Boston (NL), 1945–1948; Philadelphia (AL), 1952. Remarks: Had 25 victories and 16 losses, with one "save," in five major league seasons.

57103. Kelley, Brent P. "Ed Wright: 50 Years Too Soon (1945–1952)." In: his *The Pastime in Turbulence: Interviews with Baseball Players of the 1940s.* Jefferson, NC: McFarland & Co., Inc., 2002. Pp. 182–191.

Jaret Samuel Wright
P. (B: Dec. 29, 1975, Anaheim, CA). Cleveland (AL), 1997–2002; San Diego (NL), 2003; Atlanta (NL), 2004; New York (AL), 2005-. Remarks: Through 2004, has won 52 games and lost 45, with two "saves"; won one game in 1997 World Series, but lost one game in 1998 ALCS; also played for Portland (PCL), 2003; son of Clyde Wright (above).

57104. Cannella, Stephen. "Is Wright Finally Right?" *Sports Illustrated*, XCI (October 4, 1999), 105+.

57105. Howard, J. "Jaret Wright: The Audacious Indians Rookie Stood Firm While Veteran Pitchers Quaked." *Sports Illustrated*, LXXXVII (October 13, 1997), 46–47.

57106. Stewart, Wayne. "The Wrights." In: his *Fathers, Sons & Baseball: Our National Pastime and the Ties That Bind.* Guilford, CT: The Lyons Press, 2002. Pp. 139–154.

57107. Verducci, Tom. "Who You Calling a Headhunter?" *Sports Illustrated*, XC (June 14, 1999), 23+.

57108. Wendel, Tim. "Indians Pitcher Has the Wright Stuff." *USA Today Baseball Weekly*, VII (October 8, 1997), 22–23.

57109. Wright, Jaret. "When I was a Kid: Interview." *Junior League Baseball*, no. 15 (May-June 1998), 20+.

John Richard ("Johnny") Wright, Sr.
P. (B: Nov. 28, 1916, New Orleans, LA-D: May 10, 1990). Newark Eagles, 1937–1938; Atlanta Black Crackers and Pittsburgh Crawfords, 1938; Toledo Crawfords, 1939; Indianapolis Crawfords, 1940; Homestead Grays, 1941–1943, 1945; Montreal Royals (IL), 1946; Homestead Grays, 1947–1948. Remarks: Second Black after Jackie Robinson chosen to play in O.B.; well-regarded Negro leagues pitcher, who could not successfully transition.

57110. Bell, Dan. "The Wright Stuff." In: Tom Barnidge, ed. *Best Sports Stories of 1986.* St. Louis, MO: The Sporting News, 1986. Pp. 260–271. Black pitcher on minor league team.

Taft Shedron ("Taffy") Wright
OF. (B. Aug. 10, 1911, Tabor City, NC-D: Oct. 22, 1981). Washington (AL), 1938–1939; Chicago (AL), 1940–1942, 1946–1948; Philadelphia (AL), 1940. Remarks: Obtained 1,115 hits (38 homers) and 32 stolen bases in 1,029 games in nine years; had RBIs in 13 straight games, 1941; manager, Ottawa (IL), 1954, Amarillo (West Texas-New Mexico League), 1955, and Orlando (Florida State League), 1956; elected to North Carolina Sports Hall of Fame in 1992.

57111. Bloodgood, Clifford. "He Drives in Runs for Washington." *Baseball Magazine*, LXIV (January 1940), 367–368+.

57112. Sumner, Jim L. "Taft Shedron Wright." In: Vol. Q-Z of David L. Porter, ed. *Biographical Dictionary of American Sports: Baseball.* Rev. and enlarged ed. Westport, CT: Greenwood Press, 2000. P. 1722.

"Wild Bill" Wright see **Burnis ("Bill" or "Wild Bill") Wright**

William Henry ("Harry") Wright ★
P-OF-MGR. (B: Jan. 10, 1835, Sheffield, Eng.-D: Oct. 3, 1895). Remarks: Cricket player (who also played for New York Knickerbockers), 1858–1866; organized Cincinnati Red Stockings in July 1866, gave up cricket in 1869 when named Red Stockings manager (the first professional pilot, his annual salary was $1,200), and brought his brother George Wright (above) to team in 1869, making it the game's first pro nine; won 130 consecutive games, 1869 to June 14, 1870; obtained 222 hits (four homers) and nine stolen bases in 180 games, 1871–1877 and, as a hurler, won four games and lost four, with eight "saves," 1871–1874; manager, Boston (National Association) in 1871 and won pennants with that team in 1872–1873–1874–1875; became manager of Boston (NL), 1876, and won-pennants, in 1877–1880; manager Providence (NL), 1882–1883, and Philadelphia (NL), 1884–1893; in 18 NL campaigns as pilot, won 1,225 games and lost 885 (.581); became NL umpire-in-chief (an honorary post) in 1893; introduced the knickerbockers uniform and long host to replace pantaloons and other non-uniform clothes earlier worn and organized the first foreign baseball tour, which took his Red Stockings and the Athletics to England in 1874; elected to the National Baseball Hall of Fame in 1953 where his plaque reads: "Manager and centerfielder of famous Cincinnati Red Stockings. Undefeated in 69 games in 1869–1870. First manager to win four straight pennants with Boston National Association 1872–73–74–75. Brother of George Wright also in Hall of Fame. Sponsored first baseball tour to England in 1876 [1874 — MJS]. Introduced knicker. uniforms. Hit 7 home runs in game at Newport, Ky. in 1867."

57113. Allen, Lee, and Thomas Meany. "Harry Wright." In: their *Kings of the Diamond.* New York: G.P. Putnam, 1965. pp. 220–221.

57114. Alvarez, Mark. "William Henry Wright." In: Frederick Ivor-Campbell, ed. *Baseball's First Stars.* Cleveland, OH: Society for American Baseball Research, 1996. Pp. 177–178.

57115. Brock, Darryl. "The Wright Way." *Sports Heritage*, I (March 1987), 35–43.

57116. Casway, Jerrold. "A Monument for Harry Wright." *The National Pastime*, XVII (1997), 35–37.

57117. Devine, Christopher. *Harry Wright: The Father of Professional Baseball.* Jefferson, NC: McFarland & Co., Inc., 2003. 191p. Devine's profile is a number in the online SABR Biography Project http://bioproj.sabr.org/ bioproj.cfm?a=v&v=1 &bid=14&pid=15558.

57118. Kiernan, John. "Harry Wright." In: Vol, X of Dumas Malone, ed. *Dictionary of American Biography.* New York: Scribners, 1936. p. 554.

57119. *Newsfront*, Editors of. "Harry Wright." In: their *Fifty Great Pioneers of American Industry.* New York: Year, 1964. Pp. 59–63.

57120. Rathgeber, Bob. "The English Founder of the Pros: Harry Wright." In: his *Cincinnati Reds Scrapbook.* Virginia Beach, VA: J.C.P. Corp. of Virginia, 1982. Pp. 20–21.

57121. Seymour, Harold. "Baseball's First Professional Manager." *Ohio Historical Quarterly*, LXIV (October 1955), 406–423.

57122. Simmons, Harry. "Harry Wright: Baseball's Forgotten Immortal." *Baseball Magazine*, LXVII (November 1941), 555–557+.

57123. Sloate, Barry. "Harry Wright Scorebooks Chronicle Early Years of National League." *Vintage & Classic Baseball Collector*, II, no. 6 (May 1996), 10–12.

57124. Smith, Robert M. "Harry Wright." In: his *Heroes of Baseball*. Cleveland, OH: World Publishing Co., 1952. Pp. 24–30.

57125. ____. "William Henry (Harry) Wright, Father of Professional Baseball." In: his *Pioneers of Baseball*. Boston: Little, Brown, 1978. Pp. 9–17.

57126. Wright, Jerry Jaye. "Brother Against Brother: Events and Final Days of Professional Baseball's 1879 Season." *Nine: A Journal of Baseball History and Social Policy Perspectives*, III (Spring 1995), 204–217.

Bill Wrigley *see* **William ("Bill") Wrigley, Jr.**

Philip Knight ("Phil") Wrigley

EXEC. (B. Dec. 5, 1994, Chicago, IL-D: April 12, 1977). Remarks: Owner (from 1932) and president (from 1930) of Chicago (NL) team until death; founder of All-American Girls Professional Baseball League; son of William Wrigley, Jr. (below).

57127. Angle, Paul. *Philip Knight Wrigley: A Memoir of a Modest Man*. Chicago, IL: Rand McNally, 1975. 192p.

57128. "Baseball Advertises: Phil Wrigley Invokes for Cubs Same Force That Made Spearmint Famous." *Printer's Ink*, CLXX (January 17, 1935), 52–53.

57129. Blaisdell, Lowell L. "Philip Knight 'Phil' Wrigley." In: Vol. Q-Z of David L. Porter, ed. *Biographical Dictionary of American Sports: Baseball*. Rev. and enlarged ed. Westport, CT: Greenwood Press, 2000. Pp. 1722–1723.

57130. Boyle, Robert H. "Wrigley of Chicago." *Sports Illustrated*, VIII (April 14, 1958), 80–88.

57131. Brattain, Michelle. "Philip Knight Wrigley." In: John A. Garrity and Marsh C. Carries, eds. *American National Biography*. 24 vols. New York: Oxford University Press, 1999. XXIII, 68–69.

57132. Castle, George. "Philip K. Wrigley: The Contrarian Man and His Deputies." In: his *The Million-to-One Team: Why the Chicago Cubs Haven't Won a Pennant Since 1945*. South Bend, IN: Diamond Communications, 2000. Pp. 10–48.

57133. Diehl, Digby. "Philip Wrigley." In: his *Supertalk*. Garden City. N.Y.: Doubleday, 1974. Pp. 267–280.

57134. Hoffman, John C. "Wrigley and His Gummed-Up Cubs." *Baseball Digest*, XI (February 1952), 5–13.

57135. Holtzman, Jerome. "When Cubs Owner Phil Wrigley Revolutionized the Managerial System." *Baseball Digest*, LV (May 1996), 60–64.

57136. "Is Phil Wrigley Right in Refusing to Install Lights at Wrigley Field for Night Baseball?" *Sports Illustrated*, III (July 25, 1955), 6–7.

57137. Kowet, Don. "Philip Wrigley." In: his *Rich Who Own Sports*. New York: Random House, 1977. Pp. 11–25.

57138. "Philip K(night) Wrigley." In: *Current Biography Yearbook, 1975*. New York: H. W. Wilson, 1975. Pp. 449–452.

William ("Bill") Wrigley, Jr.

EXEC. (B: Sept. 30, 1861, Philadelphia, PA-D: Jan. 26, 1932). Remarks: Executive owner of Chicago (NL) team, 1919–1932, father of Philip Knight Wrigley (above).

57139. Otto, Wayne K. "William Wrigley: Baseball's Wealthiest Magnate." *Baseball Magazine*, XXIX (September 1922), 453–455.

57140. Wrigley, William, Jr. "Owning a Big League Ball Team." *Saturday Evening Post*, CCIII (September 13, 1930), 24–25+.

Steve Wulff

WRITER. Remarks: Well-known *Sports Illustrated* columnist, now executive editor of *ESPN: The Magazine*.

57141. Wulff, Steve. "Like Father, Like Son: A Dad, Jaded by Access to Baseball's Inner Most Sanctums, Views the Sport Anew, Thanks to His Young Boy." *Sports Illustrated*, LXXIV (April 15, 1991), 22+.

John Whitlow ("Whit") Wyatt

P. (B: Sept. 27, 1907, Kensington, GA.-D: July 16, 1998.). Detroit (AL), 1929–1933; Chicago (AL), 1933–1936; Cleveland (AL), 1937; Brooklyn (NL), 1939–1944; Philadelphia (NL), 1945. Remarks: Had 106 victories, 95 defeats, and 13 "saves" in 15 seasons; came within one out of a no-hitter, June 3, 1933; won Game Two and lost Game Five of 1941 World Series; also played for Milwaukee (AA), 1938 and Evansville (Three-I League), 1929; coach/manager, Atlanta (SA), 1950–1954; coach, Philadelphia (NL), 1955–1957, Milwaukee (NL), 1958–1965, and Atlanta (NL), 1966–1967.

57142. Cobbledick, Gordon. "Whit Wyatt's Strange Career." *Baseball Digest*, II (July 1943), 39–41.

57143. Dexter, Charles. "Pitching Is Mathematics." In: Charles Dexter, ed. *Dodgers Victory Book 1942*. New York. W. and H. Baseball Publishing Co., 1942. Pp. 45–46, 60.

57144. Graber, Ralph S. "John Whitlow 'Whit' Wyatt." In: Vol. Q-Z of David L. Porter, ed. *Biographical Dictionary of American Sports: Baseball*. Rev. and enlarged ed. Westport, CT: Greenwood Press, 2000. Pp. 1723–1725.

57145. Green, Paul M. "An Interview with Whitlow Wyatt." *Sport Collector's Digest*, XIII (March 28, 1986), 172–220.

57146. Kram, Mark. "He Sends in the Smoke for the Green Goose." *Sports Illustrated*, XX (June 22, 1964), 56–58.

57147. Liley, Thomas. "Whit Wyatt — The Dodgers' 1941 Ace." *The National Pastime*, XI (1992), 46–47.

Whit Wyatt *see* **John Whitlow ("Whit") Wyatt**

Butch Wynegar *see* **Harold Delano ("Butch") Wynegar**

Harold Delano ("Butch") Wynegar

C. (B: March 14, 1956, York, PA). Minnesota (AL), 1976–1982; New York (AL), 1982–1986; California (AL), 1987–1988. Remarks: Had 1,102 hits (65 homers) and 10 stolen bases in 1,301 games in 13 years; caught Dave Righetti's (q.v.) no-hitter; July 4, 1983; caught Phil Niekro's (q.v.) 300th victory, October 1, 1985; manager, Albany (South Atlantic League), 1994; minor league hitting instructor, Texas (AL), 1995–2002; coach, Milwaukee (NL), 2003-.

57148. Ballew, Bill. "Butch Wynegar." In: his *The Pastime in the Seventies: Oral Histories of 16 Major Leaguers*. Jefferson, NC: McFarland & Co., Inc., 2002. Pp. 155–163.

57149. Hawkins, Jim. "How the Tigers Missed Out in Drafting Butch Wynegar." *Baseball Digest*, XXXVI (November 1977), 47–50.

57150. Looney, Douglas S. "He's Catching on Real." *Sports Illustrated*, XLIV (June 21, 1976), 47–48.

57151. MacPeak, Walt. "Butch Wynegar: The Twins' Budding Star." *Baseball Digest*, XXXV (November 1978), 76–81.

57152. McMillan, Ken. "Butch Wynegar." In: his *Tales from the Yankee Dugout: A Collection of the Greatest Yankee Stories Ever Told*. Champaign, IL: Sports Publishing, Inc., 2001. Pp. 195–196.

57153. Sparks, Barry. "Butch Wynegar Enjoyed a Meteoric Rise to the Majors." *Baseball Digest*, LV (July 1996), 70–72.

Alexander Wynn

EXEC. Remarks: Owner, Lowell (MA) minor league team.

57154. Stokes, William M. "How Winn Won." *Baseball Magazine,* II (November 1908), 37–39.

Early ("Gus") Wynn, Jr. ★
P-BROADCASTER. (B: Jan. 6, 1920, Hartford, AL-D: April 9, 1999). Washington (AL), 1939–1944, 1946–1948; Cleveland (A.L), 1949–1957; Chicago (AL), 1958–1962; Cleveland (AL), 1963. Remarks: Won 300 games and lost 244, with 15 "saves," in 23 seasons; Cy Young Award winner, 1950; lost Game Four of 1954 World Series; won Game One of 1959 World Series, but lost Game Seven; also had 365 hits and 17 homers; coach, Cleveland (AL), 1964–1966 and Minnesota (AL), 1967–1969; minor league manager, 1970–1972; broadcaster, Toronto (AL), 1977–1981; holds major league record for most years pitched in big leagues and for the most walks issued lifetime (1,775); elected to Alabama Sports Hall of Fame; elected to National Baseball Hall of Fame in 1972, where his plaque reads: "Winner of 300 major league games. Set record by pitching 23 years in majors. Gained 20 or more victories five years and led AL in earned run average in 1950. Leader in innings pitched three seasons and in strikeouts twice. Tied for most victories with 23 in 1954 and led league with 22 wins at age 39 in 1959 to earn Cy Young Award."

57155. Breslin, Jimmy. "An Old Indian's Last Stand." *Life,* LIV (April 5, 1963), 118–119+.

57156. Brown, Warren. "Winning: The Only Goal for Early Wynn." *Baseball Digest,* XXXI (April 1972), 77–80.

57157. Buricki SI. "Early Wynn Recalls the 'Old Days.'" *Baseball Digest,* XXXV (September 1979), 47–53.

57158. Cobbledick, Gordon. "The Indians Bank on Wynn." *Sport,* X (May 1951), 22–29.

57159. Evers, John L. "Early 'Gus' Wynn, Jr." In: Vol. Q-Z of David L. Porter, ed. *Biographical Dictionary of American Sports: Baseball.* Rev. and enlarged ed. Westport, CT: Greenwood Press, 2000. Pp. 1725–1726.

57160. Furlong, William B. "Early Wynn." In: Ray Robinson, ed. *Baseball Stars of 1960.* New York: Pyramid Books, 1960. Pp. 18–24.

57161. Gordon, Jack. "Early Wynn: The Warrior." *Sport,* XXVIII (December 1959), 43–45.

57162. Herskowitz, Mickey. "He's 42, but His Arm is 20." *Baseball Digest,* XXI (August 1962), 52–55.

57163. Jones, Harry. "The Indian Bad Medicine Man." In: Bruce Jacobs, ed. *Baseball Stars of 1955.* New York: Lion Books, 1955. Pp. 131–136.

57164. _____. "Wynn Hates to Lose." *Complete Baseball,* V (Summer 1953), 40–43.

57165. "Just One More." *Newsweek,* LXII (July 1, 1963), 62–63.

57166. Kahn, Roger. "Early Wynn: The Story of a Hard Loser." *Sport,* XXI (March 1956), 52–61.

57167. _____. "Early Wynn's Struggle." *Sport,* XXIV (July 1962), 14–17.

57168. _____. "Golden Triumphs, Tarnished Dreams." *Sports Illustrated,* XLV (August 30, 1976), 32–35.

57169. Kuenster, John. "Hall of Famer Early Wynn: He was a Fierce Warrior But a Softy Off the Field." *Baseball Digest,* LVIII (July 1999), 15–19.

57170. _____. "Wynn, Berra Merit Place in Hall of Fame." *Baseball Digest,* XXX (March 1971), 4–8.

57171. Lewis, Franklin. "The Amply-Proportioned Alabaman: Early Wynn." *Baseball Digest,* XIII (August 1954), 29–31.

57172. _____. "Cleveland's Real Wynn-er." *Baseball Digest,* IX (November 1950), 71–73.

57173. Povioh, Shirley. "Why Wynn Belongs the Spoils." *Baseball Digest,* VII (April 1948), 75–77.

57174. Reidenbaugh, Lowell. "Early Wynn." In: his *Cooperstown: Where Legends Live Forever.* St. Louis, MO: The Sporting News, 1983. Pp. 268–269.

57175. Rosenbaum, Art. "How Early Wynn Made DiMaggio Quit." *Baseball Digest,* XXII (September 1963), 15–17.

57176. Rumill, Ed. "The Versatile Mr. Wynn." *Baseball Magazine,* LXXXI (August 1948), 303–305+.

57177. _____. "You Never Know Early." *Baseball Magazine,* LXXXVI (March 1951), 329–331.

57178. Simons, Herbert. "Will Wynn or Spahn Reach 300 First?" *Baseball Digest,* XIX (May 1960), 18–21.

57179. Smith, Ron. "Early Wynn 100." In: his *The Sporting News Selects Baseball's 100 Greatest Players.* St. Louis, MO: The Sporting News, 1998. Pp. 214–215.

57180. "*Sport* Visits: The Early Wynns." *Sport,* XXV (April 1958), 48–51.

57181. Stann, Francis. "Early Wynn Deserves Spot in the Hall of Fame." *Baseball Digest,* XXIX (May 1970), 29–32.

57182. Swanson, Pete. "The Biggest of Early's 300 Wynns." *Baseball Digest,* XXII (October-November 1963), 47–51.

57183. Westcott, Rich. "Early Wynn: Expert on Intimidation." In: his *Winningest Pitchers: Baseball's 300-Game Winners.* Philadelphia, PA: Temple University Press, 2002. Pp. 117–126.

57184. Wilson, John R. M. "Early Wynn." In: Paul Betz and Mark C. Carnes, eds. *American National Biography: Supplement I.* New York: Oxford University Press, 2002. Pp. 697–698.

57185. Wynn, Early. "A Ballplayer's Got to Look Out for Himself." *Sport,* XXW (May 1957), 14–17. Contract thoughts by a Hall of Fame pitcher.

57186. _____, as told to George Vass. "The Game I'll Never Forget." *Baseball Digest,* XXX (April 1971), 64–67.

James Sherman ("Jimmy" or "The Toy Cannon") Wynn
OF. (B: March 12, 1942, Cincinnati, OH). Houston (NL), 1963–1973; Los Angeles (NL), 1974–1975; Atlanta (NL), 1976; New York (AL) and Milwaukee (AL), 1977. Remarks: Had 1,665 hits (291 homers) and 225 stolen bases in 1,920 games in 15 campaigns; led NL in walks, 1969; almost killed when stabbed in abdomen during a December 1970 domestic dispute; had grand slam homer, Sept. 15, 1974; had two doubles in 1974 NLCS and three hits (one double, one homer) in the 1974 World Series; hit 100th All-Star Game homer in the 1975 Milwaukee classic.

57187. Grow, Doug, and Joe Valerio. "New Guns in Town: Reggie Smith of the Cardinals [and] Jimmy Wynn of the Dodgers." *Sport,* LVIII (September 1974), 89–98.

57188. Herskowitz, Mickey. "Jimmy Wynn: 'Toy, Cannon." *Sport,* XLIV (November 1967), 54–55+.

57189. Lipton, Jack P. and Susan M. Lipton. "James Sherman 'Jimmie,' 'The Toy Cannon' Wynn." In: Vol. Q-Z of David L. Porter, ed. *Biographical Dictionary of American Sports: Baseball.* Rev. and enlarged ed. Westport, CT: Greenwood Press, 2000. Pp. 1726–1727.

57190. Mulvoy, Mark. "Big Blasts from a 'Toy Cannon.'" *Sports Illustrated,* XXX (June 9, 1969), 76+.

57191. Murray, Jim. "The Rise and Fall of Jimmy Wynn." *Baseball Digest,* XXXV (March 1976), 49–54.

57192. Olan, Ben. "Jim Wynn: Can He Lead the Dodgers Out of the Wilderness?" *Pro Sports,* X (November 1974), 18–21.

57193. Peebles, Dick. "Better Days Ahead for Jimmy Wynn." *Baseball Digest,* XXXI (June 1972), 59–61.

57194. Wynn, Jimmy, as told to Al Doyle. "The Game I'll Never Forget." *Baseball Digest,* LXII (March 2003), 74–77. Entire career.

57196. Xanthakos, Harry. "Jim Wynn: Dodgers' Winning Ticket." *Black Sports Magazine,* IV (November 1974), 22–27.

Jimmy Wynn *see* James Sherman ("Jimmy" or "The Toy Cannon") Wynn

John Barney ("Johnny") Wyrostek

OF. (B: July 12, 1919, Fairmont City, IL-D: Dec. 12, 1986). Pittsburgh (NL), 1942–1943; Philadelphia (NL), 1946–1947; Cincinnati (NL), 1948–1952; Philadelphia (NL), 1952–1954. Remarks: Obtained 1,149 hits (58 homers) and 33 stolen bases in 1,221 games in 11 years; had eight RBIs in one game, Sept. 4, 1950.

57197. Johnson, George. "Everybody Underrates Wyrostek." *Sport,* XII (April 1962), 28–29+.

Hank Wyse *see* Henry Washington ("Hank" or "Hooks") Wyse

Henry Washington ("Hank" or "Hooks") Wyse

P. (B: March 1, 1918, Lunsford, AK-D: Oct. 23, 2000). Chicago (NL), 1942–1947; Philadelphia (NL), 1950–1951; Washington (AL), 1951. Remarks: In eight big league seasons, had 79 victories, 70 defeats, and eight "saves"; lost Game Two of 1945 World Series.

57198. "Hank Wyse." In: Carrie Muskat, ed. *Banks to Sandberg to Grace: Five Decades of Love and Frustration with the Chicago Cubs.* Chicago, IL: Contemporary Books, 2001. Pp. 15–16.

57199. Phalen, Rick. "Hank Wyse." In: his *Our Chicago Cubs.* South Bend, IN: Diamond Communications, 1992. Pp. 13–18.

Jonathan Yardley

WRITER. (B: Oct. 27, 1939, Pittsburgh, PA). Remarks: James Reston's assistant at *The New York Times,* 1961–1962; writer, "News of the Week in Review," 1962–1964; editorial writer and book editor, *Greensboro Daily News,* 1964–1974; book editor and viewpoint editor, *Miami Herald,* 1974–1981; contributing editor, *Sports Illustrated,* 1974–1981; columnist/book editor, *The Washington Post,* 1981-; won Pulitzer Prize for Distinguished Criticism, 1981.

57200. Yardley, Jonathan. "Stuck for Life." In: Ron Fimrite, ed. *Birth of a Fan.* New York: Macmillan, 1993. Pp. 195–208.

Ed Yarnall

P. (B: Dec. 4, 1975, Lima, PA). New York (AL), 1999–2000. Remarks: Pitched 20 innings, winning one game and losing none.

57201. Frommer, Harvey and Frederick J. "Ed Yarnall." In: their *Growing Up Baseball: An Oral History.* Dallas, TX: Taylor Publishing Co., 2001. Pp. 224–225.

Carl Michael ("Yaz") Yastrzemski★

OF-1B. (B: Aug. 22, 1939, Southampton, NY). Boston (AL), 1961–1983. Remarks: Had 3,419 hits (452 homers) and 168 stolen bases in 3,308 games in 23 Red Sox seasons; hit for the cycle, April 14, 1965; AL MVP award, 1967; AL Triple Crown, 1967 established major league lifetime record for most games played (3,308) and A.L records for most at-bats (11,980, most plate appearances (13,990), most intentional walks received (190) and many other marks, including distinction of being the only AL player with 3,000 hits and 400 homers; AL batting champion, 1963, 1967–1968; led AL in doubles, 1963, 1965–1966; AL home run champion, 1967 (tie); AL RBI champion, 1967; had 10 hits (two doubles, three homers) in 1967 World Series; had grand slam homer, April 26, 1969; All-Star Game MVP award, 1970; had five hits (one double, one homer)

in 1975 ALCS and nine hits in 1975 World Series; had five homers in two games, May 19–20, 1976; also played for Raleigh (Carolina League), 1959 and Minneapolis (AA), 1960; hitting instructor, Boston (AL), 1984-; Boston uniform no. (8) retired, Aug. 6, 1989; elected to National Baseball of Fame in 1989 (first former Little Leaguer), where his plaque reads: "Succeeded Ted William's in Fenway's left field in 1961 and retired 23 years later as all-time Red Sox leader in 8 categories. Played with graceful intensity in record 3,308 AL games. Only AL player with 3,000 hits and 400 homers. 3-time batting champion. Won MVP and Triple Crown in 1967 as he led Red Sox to "impossible dream" pennant."

57202. Allen, Maur. "Carl Yastrzemski (1961-present). In: his *Baseball's 100.* New York: Galahad Books, 1981. Pp. 140–142.

57203. Benson, John. "Carl Yastrzemski —1967." In: his *Baseball's Top 100: The Best Individual Seasons of All Time.* Wilton, CT: Diamond Library, 1996. Pp. 194–196.

57204. Berno, Mike. "A Final Look: Carl Yastrzemski." *Beckett Baseball Card Monthly,* VIII (January 1991), 94–95.

57205. Berry, Henry. "Players: Carl Yastrzemski." In: his *Baseball's Great Teams: Boston Red Sox.* New York: Collier Books, 1975. Pp. 159–165.

57206. Bingham, Walter. "In Left Field for Boston." *Sports Illustrated,* XIV (April 3, 1961), 38+.

57207. Brenner, Marie. "Two Out in the Eighth, He Stepped! Up and…." Reprinted from the Boston *Herald-American,* September 13, 1979." *Congressional Record,* CXXV (September 14, 1979), 24621.

57208. Brosnan, Jim. "Carl Yastrzemski: The Reluctant Leader." In: his *Little League to Big League.* New York: Random House, 1968. Pp. 2–16.

57209. Bulkley, George. "Can Yaz Do It?" *Baseball Digest,* XXVII (July 1968), 35–39.

57210. "Carl Yastrzemski: Man of the Year." *Sport,* XLV (February 1968), 32–33.

57211. "Carl (Michael) Yastrzemski." In: *Current Biography Yearbook, 1968.* New York: H.W. Wilson Co., 1968. Pp. 445–447.

57212. "Catching Up With Yaz." In: Joe Hoppel, ed. *The Sporting News 1997 Baseball Yearbook.* St. Louis, MO: The Sporting News, 1997. Pp. 160–161.

57213. Claflin, Larry. "Yaz Sets His Sights on 3,000 Hits." *Baseball Digest,* XXXV (September 1976), 32–35.

57214. Clary, Jack T. "Yaz to Red Sox Kids: 'It's Time for a New Leader.'" *Pro Sports,* XI (November 1975), 14–17.

57215. Coffey, Wayne R. "Carl Yastrzemski." In: his *Superstars: Baseball's All-Time Greats.* Mahwah, NJ: Watermill Press, 1980. Pp. 113–123.

57216. Creamer, Robert W. "Boston's Razzmatazz." *Sports Illustrated,* XVIII (May 10, 1963), 63–64+.

57217. Crehan, Herbert F. and James W. Ryan. "Carl Yastrzemski." In: their *Lightning in a Bottle: The Sox of '67.* Boston, MA: Branden Publishing Co., 1992. Pp. 197–212.

57218. Daniel, Daniel M. "Carl Yastrzemski Faces His Biggest Threat." *All-Star Sports,* II (August 1968), 8–11.

57219. _____. "What Yaz Must Still Prove." *All-Star Sports,* III (April 1969), 41–49.

57220. Devaney, John. "Carl Yastrzemski." In: his *Baseball's Youngest Big Leaguers.* Now York: Holt, Rinehart and Winstono 1969. Pp. 116–139.

57221. Eskow, John. "Indian Summer of Carl Yastrzemski." *New Times,* XI (October 30, 1978), 50–57.

57222. Falk, Joe. "Yestrzemski Still No. 1." *Baseball Digest,* XXVII (February 1969), 72–74.

57223. Falkner, David. "For Yastrzemski, the Fire Still

Burns." *The New York Times Biographical Service,* XVII (October 1986), 1262–1263.

57224. Fine, Happy. "Don't Cry for Me: Carl Yastrzemski." *Inside Sports,* IV November 1982), 60–67.

57225. Fitzgerald, Joe. "Yaz-Aging Like a Fine Wine." *Baseball Quarterly,* I (Winter 1977), 28–33.

57226. Fitzgerald, Ray. "'Yaz Sir, That's My Baby': Carl Yastrzemski." In: his *Champions Remembered: Choice Picks from a Boston Sports Desk.* Brattleboro, VT: Stephen Greene Press, 1982. Pp. 25–40.

57227. Frey, Leonard H. "Carl Michael 'Yaz' Yastrzemski." In: Vol. Q-Z of David L. Porter, ed. *Biographical Dictionary of American Sports: Baseball.* Rev. and enlarged ed. Westport, CT: Greenwood Press, 2000. Pp. 1729–1730.

57228. Gammons, Peter. "Carl Yestrzemski Recalls His Most Memorable Games." *Baseball Digest,* XL (September 1981), 18–22.

57229. _____. "Last Was the Toughest." *Sports Illustrated,* LI (September 24, 1979), 46+.

57230. _____. "Yaz Has One Tough Out." *Sport,* LXXIII (October 1982), 67+.

57231. _____. "Yaz Hits 3,000: Reprinted from the *Boston Globe,* September 13, 1979." *Congressional Record,* CXXV (September 14, 1970), 24620–24621.

57232. Greene, J. R. "Yaz: The Checklist." *Baseball Cards,* V (August 1985), 72–77.

57233. Gross, Milton. "When Yastrzemski Almost Quit." *Baseball Digest,* XXXII (July 1973), 23–25.

57234. Gutman, Bill. "Carl Yastrzemski." In: his *Great MVPs.* Tarrytown, NY: Angle Entertainment, Inc., 1989. Pp. 29–33.

57235. Hirshberg, Al. "Carl Yastrzemski: Bosox Swat Champ." In: Ray Robinson, ed. *Baseball Stars of 1964.* New York: Pyramid Books, 1964. Pp. 109–113.

57236. _____. Carl Yastrzemski: Missing by a Whisker." In: Ray Robinson, ed. *Baseball Stars of 1971.* New York: Pyramid Books, 1971. Pp. 113–118.

57237. _____. Carl Yastrzemski: Super Hero — A Year Later." In: Ray Robinson, ed. *Baseball Stars of 1969.* New York: Pyramid Books, 1969. Pp. 56–59.

57238. _____. "Carl Yastrzemski: 'Yaz Sir, That's My Baby.'" In: Ray Robinson, ed. *Baseball Stars of 1968.* New York: Pyramid Books, 1968. Pp. 11–16.

57239. _____. "Don't Pout for Yaz." *Baseball Digest,* XXVII (May 1968), 35–37.

57240. _____. "How Yaz Shook Himself Up." *Sport,* XLI (January 1966), 40–42+.

57241. Hoard, Greg. "Few Recognized Carl Yastrzemski as a Special Player." *Baseball Digest,* XLII (December 1983), 50–55.

57242. Honig, Donald. "1967: Carl Yastrzemski." In: his *American League MVP's.* New York: Bantam Books, 1989. Pp. 78–79.

57243. "Its Been a Long Time, but Its the Same Old Yaz." In: Drew Sheinman, ed. *Baseball '79.* St. Petersburg, FL: National Association of Professional Baseball Leagues, 1979. Pp. 19–22.

57244. Jackson, Robert B. *"Let's Go Yaz": The Story of Carl Yastrzemski.* New York: Walck, 1968. 64p.

57245. Kaese, Harold. "Yaz Clutch Streak Has No Parallel, 1967." In: Glenn Stout, ed. *Impossible Dreams: A Red Sox Collection.* Boston, MA: Mariner Books, 2003. Pp. 238–240.

57246. Kaplan, Jim and Dick Perez. "Carl Yastrzemski." In: their *The 2nd Official Baseball Hall of Fame Book of Superstars.* New York: Little Simon, 1990. Pp. 39–40.

57247. _____. and Steve Wulf. "They're Playing the Swing Music of the '40's." *Sports Illustrated,* LVII (July 19, 1982),18–21.

57248. Kiester, Edward, Jr. "Is Yastrzemski Worth All That Money?" *Sport,* LII (July 1971), 34–37.

57249. Kimball, George. "Quotations from Chairman Carl." In: his *Baseball I Gave You All the Best Years of My Life.* Oakland, CA: North Atlantic Books, 1977. Pp. 314–315.

57250. Lautier, Jack. "Carl Yastrzemski." In: his *Fenway Voices.* Camden, ME: Yankee Books, 1990. Pp. 189–192.

57251. Lee, Bill, with Richard Lally. "Yaz: Indestructible Player." *Advertising Age,* LV (July 9, 1984), 18–19. An excerpt from Lee's book, *The Wrong Stuff.*

57252. Linn, Ed. "After the Storm: A Searching Look at Carl Yastrzernski." *Sport,* XLV (June 1968), 62–69.

57253. Liss, Howard, "Carl Yastrzemski." In: his *Triple-Crown Winners.* New York: Julian Messner, 1969. Pp. 74–84.

57254. Long, Shepard. *Baseball Legends: Carl Yastrzemski.* New York: Chelsea House Publishers, 1993. 61p.

57255. Mann, Jack. "Yastrzemski Arrives." *Sport,* XXXVI (September 1963), 24–27.

57256. Martin, Ned. "Yaz Remembers." In: Deanne R. Peterson, ed. *1983 Official Red Sox Yearbook.* Boston: Mark-Burton, Inc., 1983. Pp. 8–12.

57257. Masin, Herman L. "Bean Town Buster." *Senior Scholastic,* LXXVIII (April 26, 1961), 30+.

57258. Masterson, Dave and Timm Boyle. "1967 — Carl Yastrzemski." In: their *Baseball's Best: The MVPs.* Chicago, IL: Contemporary Books, 1985. Pp. 226–230.

57259. McMane, Fred. "Carl Yastrzemski." In: his *The 3,000 Hit Club.* Champaign, IL: Sports Publishing, 2000. Pp. 53–60.

57260. Obojski, Robert. "Still a Regular at 44 — Yaz Sets Mark for Long Career." In: his *Baseball's Strangest Moments.* New York: Sterling Publishing Co., 1988. Pp. 98–99.

57261. O'Neill, Thomas ("Tip"). "Finer Gentleman: Reprinted from the *Boston Herald-American,* September 14, 1979." *Congressional Record,* CXXV (September 14, 1979), 24621–24622.

57262. Orr, Jack. "Carl Michael Yastrzemski ." In: his *My Greatest Day in Baseball.* New York: Grosset & Dunlap, 1968. Pp. 179–183.

57263. Parr, Jeanne. "Mrs. Yaz." In: her *The Superwives: Life with the Giant Jocks.* New York: Coward, McCann & Geoghegan, 1976. Pp. 120–127. Carol Yastrzemski.

57264. Rapoport, Ron. "Like Old Man River, Carl Yastrzemski Keeps Rolling." *Baseball Digest,* XLI (August 1982), 34–37.

57265. Ribowsky, Mark. "Patron Saint of the Red Sox." *Sport,* LXVII (October 1978), 16–18+.

57266. Richman, Milton. "Yaz a Bad Influence?" *Baseball Digest,* XXVII (February 1968), 39–41.

57267. Ritter, Lawrence and Donald Honig. "Carl Yastrzemski." In: their *The 100 Greatest Baseball Players of All Time.* New York: Crown Publishers, 1981. Pp. 228–229.

57268. Rumill, Ed. "It's Yeah for Yaz in Boston." *Baseball Digest,* XXII (July 1963), 51–59.

57269. _____. "Yaz: A Winner Motivated by Fierce Pride." *Baseball Digest,* XXIX (December 1970), 32–36.

57270. _____. "Yaz Three Years from Peak." *Baseball Digest,* XXIII (June 1964), 21–29.

57271. Ryan, Bob. "Turn Back the Clock, 1967: Carl Yastrzemski Wins AL Triple Crown." *Baseball Digest,* LIX (November 2000), 70–73.

57272. Schlossberg, Dan. "When Carl Yastrzemski Became a Star." *Baseball Digest,* LXI (July 2002), 74–77. 1967.

57273. Shalin, Mike. "Rivals Found Yaz a Tough Opponent Between the Lines." *Baseball Digest,* XLVIII (November 1989), 42–43.

57274. Shaughnessy, Dan. "Triple Crown Season in '67 Marked High Point for Yaz." *Baseball Digest,* LI (August 1992), 66–68.

57275. Smith, Ron. "Carl Yastrzemski 72." In: his *The Sporting News Selects Baseball's 100 Greatest Players.* St. Louis, MO: *The Sporting News,* 1998. Pp. 156–157.

57276. Thornton, K. D. "The Curtain Call for Yaz." In: Ken Collier, ed. *The Baseball Book, 1983.* Scottsdale, AZ: Jalart House, 1983. Pp. 91–92.

57277. Tuite, James J. "Are Yaz's Days in Boston Numbered?." In: Clyde Hirt, ed. *Sports Quarterly Presents Baseball, Summer 1971.* New York: Counterpoint, W., 1971. Pp. 20–25.

57278. Wetmore, David. "Yaz." *The American Scholar,* LIII (Summer 1984), 396–400.

57279. Williams, Stephen. "Goodbye, Yaz." *Inside Sports,* VI (January 1984), 64–69.

57280. Yastrzemaki, Carl. "A Future Hall-of-Famer Contemplates His First Spring Without Baseball in 23 Years." *People Weekly,* XXI (April 23,1984), 113–114.

57281. _____. *Play Ball.* Columbus, Oh: Grow Ahead Press, 1971. 32p. Pamphlet.

57282. _____. *Winning Baseball.* Columbus, Oh: For Children, Inc., 1968. 32p.

57283. _____, as told to George Vass. "The Game I'll Never Forget." *Baseball Digest,* XXXIII (July 1974), 78–80. Reprinted in John Kuenster, ed., *From Cobb to Catfish* (Chicago: Rand McNally, 1975), pp. 209–210 and in George Vass, ed. *The Game I'll Never Forget* (Chicago: Bonus Books, 1999). pp. 262–265; concerns the game which clinched the 1967 pennant for Boston.

57284. _____. with Al Hirshberg. *Batting.* New York: The Viking Press, 1972. 118p.

57285. _____. *Yaz.* New York: Viking Press, 1968. 183p.

57286. _____., with Gerald Eskenazi. *Yaz: Baseball, The Wall, and Me.* Garden City, N.Y.: Doubleday & Co., 1990. 303p.

57287. Young, Dick. "Yaz Says Hands Key to Hitting." *Baseball Digest,* XXVIII (June 1969), 86–88. Opinion of Carl Yastrzemski.

Thomas Austin ("Tom") Yawkey★

EXEC. (B: Feb. 21, 1903, Detroit, MI-D: July 9, 1976). Remarks: Born Thomas Austin, then adopted; owner and president, Boston (AL), 1933–1976; first to have club travel by plane; vice president of AL, 1956–1973; elected to National Baseball Hall of Fame in 1980, whom his plaque reads: "Gave baseball more than four decades of dedicated service as owner-president of Boston Red Box from 1933 to 1976. Rated one of sport's finest benefactors. Set precedent for AL in 1936 as first to have team travel by plane. His club won pennants, in 1946, 1967, and 1975 — and narrowly missed in 1948, 1949, and 1972. Vice-president of AL from 1956 to 1973."

57288. Ashwell, Tim. "Tom Yawkey." In: John A. Garrity and Marsh C. Carries, eds. *American National Biography.* 24 vols. New York: Oxford University Press, 1999. XXIV, 118–119.

57289. Berry, Henry. "The Coming of Tom Yawkey: An Interview." In: his *Baseball's Great Teams: Boston Red Sox.* New York: Collier Books, 1975. Pp. 20–27.

57290. Cunningham, Bill "Starch for the Red Sox." *Collier's,* XCII (March 30, 1935), 25+.

57291. Daley, Arthur. "Super Fan." *Baseball Digest,* X (November 1961), 75–82.

57292. King, Joseph E. "Thomas Austin Yawkey." In: Vol. Q-Z of David L. Porter, ed. *Biographical Dictionary of American Sports: Baseball.* Rev. and enlarged ed. Westport, CT: Greenwood Press, 2000. Pp. 1731–1732.

57293. Kunen, James S. "The Man with the Greatest Job in Boston." *Boston,* LXVII (September 1975), 60–63, 97–102.

57294. Lane, Ferdinand C. "Thos. Yawkey Turns from 'Buying' to 'Building.'" *Baseball Magazine,* LXIX (July 1937), 339–341.

57295. McAuley, Ed. "What Will Superfan Do Now?" *Baseball Digest,* XIII (August 1954), 47–49.

57296. "Pennant at a Price: Yawkey of the Red Sox." *Literary Digest,* CXX (December 21, 1935), 35.

57297. Pierce, Charles P. "The Yawkey Way." *Sports Illustrated,* LXXVI (March 9, 1992), 18–19.

57298. Powers, Jimmy. "Buying a World's Championship Team." *Liberty,* XIII (March 14, 1936) 33–34.

57299. Sullivan, George E. "Tom Yawkey Enters the Hall of Fame." In: Deanne R. Peterson, ed. *Red Sox Official 1980 Yearbook.* Brookfield, MA: W.A. Krueger, 1980. Pp. 5–7.

57300. Yawkey, Thomas A. "You Can't Buy a Pennant … I Found Out." *Look,* III (August 1, 1939), 26–27.

Emil Ogden Yde

P. (B: Jan. 26, 1900, Great Lakes, IL-D: Dec. 5, 1968). Pittsburgh (NL), 1924–1927; Detroit (A. L.), 1929. Remarks: Submarine pitcher; won 49 games and lost 25 in five big league seasons; had double and triple in one game, June 25, 1924; lost Game Four of 1924 World Series.

57301. Lane, Ferdinand C. "The Season's Pitching Sensation." *Baseball Magazine,* XXXIV (February 1925), 401–402.

Stephen Wayne ("Steve") Yeager

C. (B: Nov. 24, 1949, Huntington, WV). Los Angeles (NL),1972-. Remarks: Had 816 hits (102 homers) and 14 stolen bases in 1,269 games In 15 seasons; introduced catchers' neck protector, 1976; hit game winning homer, Game Five, 1981 World Series; World Series MVP award, 1981 (tie); posed as a *Playgirl* centerfold; manager, San Bernardino (California League), 1999; manager, Long Beach Breakers (Western Baseball League), 2001–2002; coach, Jacksonville (SL), 2005-; nephew of retired USAF Brig. Gen. Chuck Yeager, first man to break the sound barrier.

57302. Elderkin, Phil. "Catching the Intangibles." *Dodgers Magazine,* XIII, no. 1 (2000), 71–73.

57303. Joy, Bill. "Steve Yeager Solid Dodger Favorite." In: Bill Shumard, ed. *1981 Los Angeles Dodgers Yearbook.* Anaheim, CA: Rotary Off-Set Printers, 1982. P. 56.

57304. Krikorian, Doug. "The Indispensable Dodger." *Baseball Digest,* XXXVII (July 1978), 37–41.

57305. Obojski, Robert. "Hit on Head By Bat While in On-Deck Circle." In: his *Baseball's Strangest Moments.* New York: Sterling Publishing Co., 1988. Pp. 33–34.

57306. Yeager, Steve, as told to George Vass. "The Game I'll Never Forget." *Baseball Digest,* XLV (May 1986), 77–83.

Mose J. ("Chief") Yellowhorse

P. (B: Jan. 28, 1898, Pawnee, OK-D: April 10, 1964). Pittsburgh (NL), 1921–1922. Remarks: In two big league seasons, this Native American (Pawnee) hurler won eight games and lost four, with one "save"; also pitched for Arkansas (SA), 1918–1920, Sacramento (PCL), 1923–1924; Fort Worth (TL), 1924; Sacramento (PCL), 1925; appeared in wild west shows, and served as a model for the character "Yellowpony" in his friend Chester Gould's *Dick Tracy* comic strip.

57307. Fuller, Marshall Todd. *60' 6" and Other Distances from Home: The (Baseball) Life of Mose Yellowhorse.* Duluth, MN: Holy Cow Books, 2001. 180p. Originally submitted as a 162-page 1999 PhD. Dissertation to Oklahoma State University under the title, "60 Feet 6 Inches and Other Distances from Home: A Creative Biography About Mose Yellowhorse, Baseball, Cartoons, and the Pawnee."

57308. Horowitz, Mikhail. "Wholly Mose." *Elysian Fields Quarterly,* XIX (Fall 2002), 77–80. Ralph Berger's profile of Yellowhorse appears as a number in the online SABR Biography Project < http://bioproj.sabr.org/bioproj.cfm?a=v&v=1 &bid=729&pid=15620>.

Wallace ("Wally" or "The Nisei Jackie Robinson") Yonamine

OF-MGR. (B: 1925, Honolulu, HI). Tokyo Yomiuri Giants, 1951–1961; Chunichi Dragons, 1962. Remarks: fifth foreigner (third American) and first after WWII to play in Japan; had 1,911 hits (82 homers) in 1,219 games in 12 years and lifetime .311 average; Japan League batting champion, 1954, 1956–1957; Japan League MVP award, 1957; scout, manager who, on October 23rd, 1974, became only non-Japanese manager ever to win the Japan Series when his Chunichi Dragons defeated the Lotte Orions; elected to Japanese Baseball Hall of Fame, 1990, the first American so honored; elected to Hawaii Sports Hall of Fame, 1997; Order of the Sacred Treasure, Gold Rays with Rosette (from Japanese government), 1998; special assistant to the Governor of Hawaii for Sports Promotion, 1998–.

57309. Ardolino, Frank. "Wally Yonamine: From Hawaiian Plantation to the Japanese Baseball Hall of Fame." *The National Pastime,* XIX (1999), 10–11.

57310. Franks, Joel S. "Pacific Crossings and Baseball: Comments on Hawaii and America's National Pastime and the Great Wally Yonamine." *Nine: A Journal of Baseball History and Social Policy Perspectives,* VIII (Fall 1999), 54–72.

Preston Rudolph ("Rudy" or "Chief") York

1B-C-MGR. (B: Aug. 17, 1913, Ragland, AL-D: Feb. 2, 1970). Detroit (AL), 1934, 1931–1945; Boston (AL), 1946–1947; Chicago (AL), 1947; Philadelphia (AL), 1948. Remarks: Obtained 1,621 hits (277 homers) in 1,621 games in a 13-year playing career; had four grand slam homers in one year (three in one month-May), 1938; had two homers each in two straight games, May 2–3, 1942; homered in 1942 All-Star Game; AL home run champion, 1943; AL RBI champion, 1943; held major league record for most home runs hit in one month (18), August 1937, broken by Sammy Sosa (q.v.) in 1998; set mark in 1945 for most assists by a first baseman (8); had 10 RBIs on two grand slam homers in one game — and made it into *Ripley's Believe It or Not* when the balls broke two different windows in the same car in the parking lot, July 27, 1946; had two homers in 1946 World Series, including the one which won Game One; had 12 career grand slam homers; also played for Union City (Kentucky-Illinois-Tennessee League), 1949–1950; player-manager, Oil City-New Castle (South Atlantic League), 1951— where he hit 34 homers with 107 RBI; coach, Boston (AL), 1959–1962, piloting — and losing — one Red Sox game in 1959; died victim of lunch cancer.

57311. Akin, William E. "Preston Rudolph 'Rudy,' 'Chief' York." In: Vol. Q-Z of David L. Porter, ed. *Biographical Dictionary of American Sports: Baseball.* Rev. and enlarged ed. Westport, CT: Greenwood Press, 2000. Pp. 1732–1734.

57312. Bisher, Furman. "The Cherokee Has No Regrets." *Baseball Digest,* XIII (July 1954), 47–51.

57313. _____. "Rudy York's Letter to His Son." *Baseball Digest,* XXIX (June 1970), 75–79. Also published in Charles Einstein, ed., *The Fireside Book of Baseball* (New York : Simon and Schuster, 1956). pp. 382–387.

57314. Crichton, Kyle S. "Rough and Rudy." *Collier's,* CII July 2, 1938), 19+.

57315. Hirshberg, Al, and Joe MeKenney. "Rudy York." In: their *Famous American Athletes of Today.* 10th Series. Boston: L.C. Page, 1947. Pp. 371–374.

57316. Hufford, Tom. "Rudy York: The Big Gun of August." *Baseball Digest,* XXXIV (August 1975), 31–23. Also published in *The Baseball Research Journal,* IV (1975), 12–15.

57317. Kaese, Harold. "Rudolph Preston York: Challenger of Ruth's Records." In: *Famous American Athletes of Today.* 6th Series. Boston, MA: L.C. Page, 1938. Pp. 361–391.

57318. Parker, Chantal. "Rudolph Preston "Rudy" York, Atco's Home Run King." *Cartersville Magazine,* III (Summer 2001), 4+.

57319. Smith, Ira L. "Rudolph Preston 'Rudy' York." In: his *Baseball's Famous First Basemen.* New York: A.S. Barnes, 1956. Pp. 255–262.

57320. Smith, Lyall. "How [Rudy] York Used Batting Science for Homer Mark." *Baseball Digest,* XXI (July 1962), 75–77.

57321. York, Rudy, as told to Furman Bisher. "A Letter to My Son." *Sport,* XVII (September 1954), 40–46. Also published in Charles Einstein, ed. *The Fireside Book of Baseball* (New York: Simon & Schuster, 1956), pp. 382–387.

Masato Yoshii

P. (B: April 20, 1965, Osaka, Japan). New York (NL), 1995–1999; Colorado (NL), 2000; Montreal (NL), 2001–2002; Orix Blue Wave (Japan League), 2003-. Remarks: In seven seasons, won 32 games and lost 47; lost one game of 1999 NLCS.

57322. Bechtel, Michael. "Rising Sons, Stealth Pitcher: With Little Fanfare, the Mets' Yoshii is Dominating Hitters." *Sports Illustrated,* LXXXVIII (June 8, 1998), 70, 73.

Edward Frederick ("Eddie" or "The Walking Man") Yost

3B. (B. Oct. 13, 1926, Brooklyn, NY). Washington (AL), 1944, 1946–1958; Detroit (AL), 1959–1964; Los Angeles (AL), 1961–1962. Remarks: Had 1,863 hits (139 homers) and 72 stolen bases in 2,109 games in 18 seasons; played in 838 consecutive games, July 6, 1949–May 12, 1955; led NL in doubles, 1951; led AL in walks, 1950, 1952–1953, 1956, 1959–1960; coach, Washington (AL), 1963–1967, New York (NL), 1968–1976, and Boston (AL), 1977–1986; earned BA and MA degrees from New York University; remembered for the many walks received (hence nickname), including 100+ per year, 1950–1954.

57323. Dexter, Charles. "Yost: Senator from New York." *Baseball Digest,* X (March 1951), 5–9.

57324. Frommer, Harvey and Frederick J. "Eddie Yost." In: their *Growing Up Baseball: An Oral History.* Dallas, TX: Taylor Publishing Co., 2001. Pp. 226–229.

57325. Graber, Ralph S. "Edward Fred Joseph 'Eddie,' 'The Walking Man' Yost." In: Vol. Q-Z of David L. Porter, ed. *Biographical Dictionary of American Sports: Baseball.* Rev. and enlarged ed. Westport, CT: Greenwood Press, 2000. Pp. 1734–1735.

57326. Heft, Herb. "Yost Now 'Walking Man.'" *Baseball Digest,* IX (October 1950), 49–50.

57327. Jacobs, Bruce. "He's the Most." In: Bruce Jacobs, ed. *Baseball Stars of 1955.* New York: Lion Books, 1955. Pp. 136–140.

57328. Kelley, Brent P. "An Interview with 'The Walking Man.'" *Sports Collector's Digest,* XVI (October 13, 1989), 190–192.

57329. Middlesworth, Hal. "Eddie Yost: 12 Years in the Wrong Park." *Baseball Digest* XVIII (December 1959), 67–74.

57330. _____. "Eddie Yost; 17 Years at Third Base." *Baseball Digest,* XIX (November-December 1960), 61–67.

57331. Povich, Shirley. "The 'Walking Man' Starts Swinging." *Baseball Digest,* XII (May 1953), 33–35.

57332. Richman, Milton. "Yost Bypasses All Farms." *Baseball Digest,* VIII (February 1949), 69–71.

57333. Smith, Lyall. "The Rules Made Him a Big Leaguer." *Baseball Digest,* VI (October 1947), 61–63.

57334. Stann, Francis. "Yost and the Unwashed Uniform." *Baseball Digest,* XIII (March 1954), 65–67

57335. Yost, Eddie. "How to Play the Hot Corner." *Sport,* XII (May 1952), 74–81.

Anthony Wayne Young

P. (B: Jan. 19, 1966, Houston, TX). New York (NL), 1991–1993; Chicago (NL), 1994–1995; Houston (NL), 1996. Remarks: In six years, won 15 games and lost 48, with 20 "saves"; lost 27 consecutive games, 1992–1993.

57336. Shannon, Mike. "Anthony Young." In: his *Tales from the Dugout: The Greatest True Baseball Stories Ever Told.* Chicago, IL: NTC/Contemporary Books, 1997. Pp. 229–230.

57337. Whiteside, Kelly. "Sigh Young." *Sports Illustrated,* LXXIX (July 5, 1993), 26–28. On the recording of his 24th straight loss.

Cy Young *see* **Denton True ("Cy") Young**

Denton True ("Cy") Young★

P-MGR. (B: March 29, 1867, Gilmore, OH-D: Nov. 1, 1955). Cleveland (NL), 1890–1898; St. Louis (NL), 1899–1900; Boston , (AL), 1901–1908; Cleveland (AL), 1909–1911; Boston (NL), 1911. Remarks: Had 511 victories, 313 defeats, and 17 "saves" in a 22-year big league career; won more games, lost more games, and pitched more innings (7,356) than any other hurler in major league history, including the most consecutive hitless innings (24 in 1904); throw three no-hitters in 906 games, including victories on Sept. 18, 1897, May 4, 1904 (perfect game), and June 30, 1908; as a batter, had 623 hits and 18 home runs (two in one game on April 20, 1899) in 2,960 at-bats; managed seven games for Boston (AL) in 1907, winning three and losing four; also played for Canton (Tri-State League), 1889; retired to farming in the Buckeye State upon the completion of his playing days; the top prize given to pitchers since 1956 has been named in his honor, the Cy Young Memorial Award; elected to National Baseball Hall of Fame in 1937, where his plaque reads: "Only pitcher in first hundred years of baseball to win 500 games. Among his 511 victories were 3 no-hit shutouts. Pitched perfect game, May 5, 1904, no opposing batsman reaching first base."

57338. Allen, Lee and Thomas Meany." Cy Young." In: their *Kings of the Diamond.* New York: G. P. Putnam, 1965. Pp. 32–35.

57339. Barton, Jerry. "Denton True Young." In: his *A Treasure Chest of the Hall of Fame.* Boston, MA: The Wilson-Hill Co., 1952. Pp. 22–23.

57340. Belanger, John Harvey. "Baseball's Premier Pitcher of All Time." *Baseball Magazine,* LI (September 1933), 441–443+.

57341. Broeg, Bob. "Cy Young." In: his *Super Stars of Baseball.* St. Louis, MO: The Sporting News, 1972. Pp. 281–286.

57342. _____. and William J. Miller, Jr. "What Cy Saw." In: their *Baseball from a Different Angle.* South Bend, IN: Diamond Communications, Inc., 1988. Pp. 243–260.

57343. Browning, Reed. *Cy Young: A Baseball Life.* Amherst, MA: University of Massachusetts Press, 2000. 283p.

57344. Buckley, James, Jr. "Cy Young." In: his *Perfect!: The Inside Story of Baseball's Sixteen Perfect Games.* New York: Triumph Books, 2002. Pp. 28–41.

57345. Clark, Ellery H., Jr. "Denton True 'Cy' Young." In: Vol. Q-Z of David L. Porter, ed. *Biographical Dictionary of American Sports: Baseball.* Rev. and enlarged ed. Westport, CT: Greenwood Press, 2000. Pp. 1735-1737.

57346. Cobbledick, Gordon. "Cy Young." In: Christy Marsh, ed. *Baseball's Greatest Lineup.* New York: A. S. Barnes, 1952. Pp. 281–294.

57347. Cooper, John A. "Old Cy Young Gets on the Air." *Baseball Magazine,* LXI (August 1938), 421–422.

57348. "Cy Young." In: Joseph J. Vecchione, ed. *The New York Times Book of Sports Legends.* New York: Random House, 1991. Pp. 357–360.

57349. "Cy Young's String of Hitless Innings." *The Baseball Research Journal,* VII (1978), 103–104.

57350. Daley, Arthur. "Cy Young." In: his *Sports of The Times.* New York: E. P. Dutton, 1959. Pp. 67–69.

57351. _____. "The Day Before Yesterday: The Great Early Stars — Young, Waddell, Cobb, and Wagner." In: Herbert W. Wind, ed. *The Realm of Sport.* New York: Simon and Schuster, 1966. Pp. 30–36.

57352. Davis, Mac. "Cy Young: The Master of All." In: his *Pacemakers in Baseball.* Cleveland, OH: World Publishing Company, 1968. Pp. 70–72.

57353. _____. "Denton True (Cy) Young." In: his *The Greatest in Baseball.* New York: Scholastic Book Services, 1977. Pp. 89–90.

57354. _____. "The Hayseed for a Ride." In: his *The Lore and Legends of Baseball.* New York: Lantern Press, 1953. Pp. 117–119.

57355. "Denton 'Cy' Young: The Most Remarkable Records in the Annals of Baseball." *Baseball Magazine,* VII (May 1911), 96–97.

57356. Doherty, Paul F. "Cy Young's Final Fling." *The Baseball Research Journal,* VIII (1979), 6–8. 1911 season.

57357. Duncan, C. William. "Baseball's Most Successful Hurler." *Baseball Magazine,* XLIII (August 1929), 407–408+.

57358. D'Vys, George W. "Old Cy Young." *Baseball Magazine,* I (August 1908), 32–33.

57359. Epstein, Sam, and Beryl. "Cy Young: The Canton Cyclone." In: Bennett Wayne, ed. *Big League Pitchers and Catchers.* Champaign, IL: Garrard, 1974. Pp. 9–27.

57360. "50th Anniversary of a Perfect Game." *Baseball Digest,* XIII (May 1954), 15–20.

57361. Gordon, David. "Cy Young — 1901." In: his *Baseball's Top 100: The Best Individual Seasons of All Time.* Wilton, CT: Diamond Library, 1996. Pp. 18–21.

57362. Grayson, Harry. "Denton Tecumseh (Cy) Young." In: his *They Played the Game.* New York: A.S. Barnes, 1944. Pp. 18–19.

57363. Hawkins, Burton. "A Chat with Cy Young." *Baseball Digest,* II (October 1943), 25–27. Reprinted in

John Kuenster, ed., *From Cobb to Catfish* (Chicago, IL: Rand McNally, 1975), pp. 20–21.

57364. Honig, Donald. "Cy Young." In: his *The Greatest Pitchers of All Time.* New York: Crown Publishers, 1988. Pp. 1–5.

57365. "Iron Man." *Time,* LXVI (November 14, 1955), 66–67.

57366. Kahn, Roger. "Cy Young, Ticket Salesman" In: his *The Head Game: Baseball Seen from the Pitcher's Mound.* Boston, MA: Harcourt, 2000. Pp. 73–86.

57367. Kaplan, Jim and Dick Perez. "Cy Young." In: their *The Official Baseball Hall of Fame Book of Superstars.* New York: Little Simon, 1989. Pp. 9–10.

57368. Kavanagh, Jack. "The Day [July 29, 1921] Cy Young Came Home." In*: Cleveland Indians 1984 Official Souvenir Program.* New York: Professional Sports Publications, 1984. Pp. 22, 40.

57369. Klima, John. "First to Perfection: Rube Waddell vs. Cy Young (May 5, 1904)." In: his *Pitched Battle: 35 of Baseball's Greatest Duels from the Mound.* Jefferson, NC: McFarland & Co., Inc., 2002. Pp. 3–7.

57370. Kofoed, J.C. "The Greatest Pitcher in Baseball History." *Baseball Magazine,* XXIX (October 1922), 499–501.

57371. Koppett, Leonard. "Greatest Pitcher of Them All." *Baseball Digest,* XXIV (February 1965), 35–42.

57372. Lawler, Joseph. "The Man Who Won 511 Major League Baseball Games." In: *Old Farmer's Almanac.* Special Canadian ed., 198th ed. Dublin, NH: Yankee Publishing, 1990. Pp. 118–121.

57373. Lewis, Franklin. "Was Cy Young Greatest?: We'll Never Know." *Baseball Digest,* XV (January-February 1956), 85–87.

57374. Macht, Norman. *Baseball Legends: Cy Young.* New York: Chelsea House Publishers, 1992. 61p.

57375. Mayer, Ronald A. "Cy Young." In: his *Perfect! Biographies and Lifetime Statistics of 14 Pitchers of Perfect Game.* Jefferson, NC: McFarland & Co., Inc., 1991. Pp. 40–55.

57376. McKay, Joe. "Cy Young: So Great They Named an Award After Him." In: his *The Great Shutout Pitchers: 20 Profiles of a Vanishing Breed.* Jefferson, NC: McFarland & Co., Inc., 2004. Pp. 39–50.

57377. Meany, Thomas. "Cy Young." In: his *Baseball's Greatest Pitchers.* New York: A.S. Barnes, 1951. Pp. 279–288.

57378. _____. "Cy Young." In: his *Baseball's Greatest Players.* New York: Grosset and Dunlap, 1963. Pp. 287–295.

57379. Menke, Frank G. "From 'Cy' to 'Cyclone.'" In: his *Sports Tales and Anecdotes.* New York: A.S. Barnes, 1953. Pp. 19–20.

57380. Morse, Jacob G. "The Story of Cy Young." *Baseball Magazine,* I (September 1908), 38–46.

57381. Peterjohn, Alvin. "The First Year of 'Cyclone' Young." *The Baseball Research Journal,* V (1976), 83–89.

57382. Pisetzner, Joel. "Cy Young: His Name Remains a Symbol of Greatness." *Baseball Digest,* XL (July 1981), 85–89.

57383. Porter, David L. "Cy Young." In: John A. Garrity and Marsh C. Carries, eds. *American National Biography.* 24 vols. New York: Oxford University Press, 1999. XXIV, 160–161.

57384. Reidenbaugh, Lowell. "Cy Young." In: his *Cooperstown: Where Legends Live Forever.* St. Louis, MO: *The Sporting News,* 1983. Pp. 271–272.

57385. Ritter, Lawrence and Donald Honig. "Cy Young." In: their *The 100 Greatest Baseball Players Of All Time.* New York: Crown Publishers, 1981. Pp. 226–227.

57386. Romig, Ralph H. *Cy Young, Baseball's Legendary Giant.* Philadelphia, PA: Dorrance, 1964. 127p.

57387. Shapiro, Milton J. "Cy Young." In: his *Baseball's Greatest Pitchers.* New York: Julian Messner, 1969. Pp. 164–173.

57388. Skelton, Bill. "Cy Young and His Records: They Never Grow Old." *Baseball Magazine,* XC (May 1953), 28–31.

57389. Smith, Ira L. "Denton True (Cy) Young." In: his *Baseball's Famous Pitchers.* New York: A.S. Barnes, 1964. Pp. 29–34.

57390. Smith, Ron. "Cy Young 14." In: his *The Sporting News Selects Baseball's 100 Greatest Players.* St. Louis, MO: *The Sporting News,* 1998. Pp. 36–37.

57391. Spink, Alfred H. "Discovering Cy Young." In: Jeff Silverman, ed. *Classic Baseball Stories.* Guilford, CT: Lyons Press, 2003. Chpt. 9.

57392. Tiemann, Robert L. "Denton True Young." In: Frederick Ivor-Campbell, ed. *Baseball's First Stars.* Cleveland, OH: Society for American Baseball Research, 1996. Pp. 179–180.

57393. Torres, John Albert. "Cy Young." In: his *Top 10 Baseball Legends.* Berkeley Heights, NJ: Enslow Publishers, 2001. Pp 42–45.

57394. Wayman, Joseph M. "[Old Hoss] Radbourn 1884 and Young 1900, Wins?." In: Joseph M. Wayman, ed. *Grandstand Baseball Annual, 1998.* Downey, CA: Joseph M. Wayman, 1998. Pp. 39–46.

57395. Westcott, Rich. "Cy Young: An Unappreciated Record." In: his *Winningest Pitchers: Baseball's 300-Game Winners.* Philadelphia, PA: Temple University Press, 2002. Pp. 49–58.

57396. Wilson, Brad. "The Love Story of the Legendary Cy Young." *Baseball Digest,* XXXIV (November 1975), 71–75.

57397. Young, Clarence. "Cy Young Offered $2,000 Bribe." *Baseball Digest,* IX (April 1950), 21–25.

57398. Young, Denton T. ("Cy"). "Cy Young's Baseball Epigrams, 1904." In: Glenn Stout, ed. *Impossible Dreams: A Red Sox Collection.* Boston, MA: Mariner Books, 2003. Pp. 44–45.

57399. _____. "First—Learn to Control the Ball!" *SABR Review of Books,* I (1986), 58–59. Remarks from Spalding's 1912 book *How to Pitch.*

57400. _____. "How I Learned to Pitch." *Baseball Magazine,* I (September 1908), 13–16.

57401. _____., as told to Francis J. Powers. "My Greatest Day in Baseball." In: John P. Carmichael, ed. *My Greatest Day in Baseball.* New York: A.S. Barnes, 1945. Pp. 104–107. This account of Young's May 5, 1904 perfect game was first published in the *Chicago Daily News* and later in Charles Einstein, ed., *The Third Fireside Book of Baseball* (New York: Simon and Schuster, 1968), pp. 496–497; Eliot Cohen, ed., *My Greatest Day in Baseball* (New York: Little Simon, 1991), pp. 144–147; and in Glenn Stout, ed., *Impossible Dreams: A Red Sox Collection.* (Boston, MA: Mariner Books, 2003), pp. 41–43.

Dick Young

WRITER. (B: 1917 [some sources say 1918], New York City-D: August 31, 1987). Remarks: Sportswriter, sports editor, *New York Daily News,* 1936–1981; *New York Post,* 1982–1987; columnist, *The Sporting News,* late 1950s to 1985; G. G. Taylor Spink Award, 1978.

57402. "Dick Young, RIP." *National Review,* XXXIV (September 25, 1987), 19–20.

57403. Noverr, Douglas A. "Dick Young." In: David L. Porter, ed. *Biographical Dictionary of American Sports: 1989–1992 Supplement for Baseball, Football, Basketball and Other Sports*. Westport, CT: Greenwood Press, 1992. Pp. 358–359.

57404. Rapoport, Ron. "Young's Views Never Shaded." In: Tom Barnidge, ed. *Best Sports Stories of 1988*. St. Louis, MO: *The Sporting News*, 1988. Pp. 62–63.

57405. "Voice of the People." *Newsweek*, LXXXI (May 21, 1973), 60, 65.

57406. Wetzsteon, Ross. "Dick Young's America." *Sport*, LXXVI (August 1985), 78–82.

57407. Young, Dick. "Being a Baseball Writer." *Baseball Digest*, XII (January 1953), 83–94.

57408. _____. "How I'd Shake Up Baseball." *Sport*, XLVI (November 1968), 40–44.

57409. Ziegler, Jack. "Dick Young." In: Richard Orodenker, ed. *Dictionary of Literary Biography, Volume 171: Twentieth-Century American Sportswriters*. A Bruccoli Clark Layman Book. Detroit, MI: The Gale Group, 1996. Pp. 356–364.

Eric Orlando Young
2B. (B: May 16, 1967, New Brunswick, NJ). Los Angeles (NL), 1992; Colorado (NL), 1993–1997; Atlanta (NL), 1997–1999; Chicago (NL), 1999–2001; Milwaukee (NL), 2002–2003; San Francisco (NL), 2003; Texas (AL), 2004- . Remarks: Through 2004, has had 1,664 hits (74 homers) and 450 stolen bases in 1,614 games; had five hits in one game, April 27, 1996; stole six bases in one game, June 30, 1996, and five in another, May 14, 2000; led NL in triples, 1995; NL stolen base champion, 1996.

57410. Acee, Kevin. "Its Great to Be Young and a Dodger." *Dodgers Dugout*, XII (August 30, 1997), 1–2.

57411. Dewan, John and Don Zminda. "Is He the Next Vince Coleman ... Or the Next Donell Nixon?" In: STATS, Inc. *STATS 1992 Baseball Scoreboard*. Chicago, IL: STATS Publishing, 1992. Pp. 119–121.

57412. Kurkjian, Tim. "Young and Gifted: Oh, to Be Young in Colorado." *Sports Illustrated*, LXXXV (July 1, 1996), 60+.

57413. Lowery, S. "Numbers in Strength: How Colorado Rockies Second Baseman Eric Young Rediscovered Weight Training, Revved Up His Stats, and Revived His Career." *Men's Fitness*, XIII (May 1997), 88–91.

57414. Reid, Jason. "Mets Want Young in [Any Bobby] Bonilla Trade." *Dodgers Dugout*, XIII (October 30, 1998), 1–2.

57415. Sorci, Rick. "Baseball Profile: Cubs' Eric Young." *Baseball Digest*, LX (June 2001), 38–39.

Ernest Wesley ("Ernie") Young
OF. (B: July 8, 1969, Chicago, IL). Oakland (AL), 1994–1997; Kansas City (AL), 1998; Atlanta (NL), 1999; Detroit (AL), 2003; Cleveland (AL), 2004. Remarks: Through 2004, has obtained 179 hits (27 homers) and 10 stolen bases in 288 games in six seasons; had six RBIs in one game, with four hits, including three homers, May 10, 1996; also played for Buffalo (IL), 2000–2002.

57416. Epstein, Eddie. "Ernie Young." In: STATS, Inc. *The STATS 1995 Minor League Scouting Notebook*. Skokie, IL: STATS Publishing, 1995. Pp. 174–175.

Frank A. ("Fay") Young
WRITER. (B: 1884, Chicago, IL-D: 1957). Remarks: Reporter, *Chicago Defender*, 1907–1928; managing editor, *Chicago Defender*, 1929–1934; managing editor, *The Kansas City Call*, 1934–1937; managing editor/columnist, *Chicago Defender*, 1937–1957.

57417. Reisler, Jim. "Frank A. Young: Chicago's Boss of the Sports World." In: his *Black Writers/Black Baseball: An Anthology of Articles from Black Sportswriters Who Covered the Negro Leagues*. Jefferson, N.C.: McFarland & Co., Inc, 1994. Pp. 57–74.

Kevin Stacey Young
3B-1B. (B: June 16, 1969, Alpena, MI). Pittsburgh (NL), 1992–1995; Kansas City (AL), 1996; Pittsburgh (NL), 1997–2003. Remarks: Through 2003, has had 1,007 hits (144 homers) and 83 stolen bases in 1,205 games; went 4-for-5 in one game, June 29, 1997 and 4-for-4 in another, Aug. 4, 1998; also played for Rochester (IL), 2003.

57418. Perrotto, John. "Rookie Report: Kevin Young." *Beckett Baseball Card Monthly*, X, no. 99 (June 1993), 20–21.

Lawrence ("Larry") Young
UMP. (B: Feb. 6, 1954, Dixon, IL). Remarks: Umpire, Midwest League, 1978; Florida Instructional League, 1978–1979; EL, 1979; and AA, 1980–1984; AL arbiter, 1985-date; National Association of Sports Officials (NASO) Gold Whistle Award, 2002.

57419. Jackel, Peter. "NASO Gold Whistle Award Winner Larry Young." *Referee*, XXVII (July 2002), 10+.

57420. Young, Larry. "Interview." *Referee*, XII (August 1987), 20–23.

Michael Darren ("Mike") Young
OF. (B: March 20, 1960, Oakland, CA). Baltimore (AL), 1982–1987; Milwaukee (AL) and Philadelphia (NL), 1988; Cleveland (AL), 1989; Hiroshima Carp (Japan League), 1990. Remarks: Had 454 hits (72 homers) and 22 stolen bases in 635 games in eight U.S. big league years; fifth major leaguer to hit two consecutive extra-inning homers in one game, May 28, 1987.

57421. Heller, Dick. "Mike Young: Another Power Switch-Hitter for Orioles." *Baseball Digest*, XLV (July 1986), 29–30.

Nicholas Emanuel Young
EXEC. (B: Sept. 12, 1840, Amsterdam, NY-D: Oct. 31, 1916). Remarks: Secretary, N.A., 1871–1875; secretary-treasurer, NL, 1876–1885; NL president, 1885–1901.

57422. Akin, William E. "Nicholas Emanuel Young." In: Vol. Q-Z of David L. Porter, ed. *Biographical Dictionary of American Sports: Baseball*. Rev. and enlarged ed. Westport, CT: Greenwood Press, 2000. Pp. 1737–1738.

Joel Randolph Youngblood III
OF-3B-2B. (B- Aug. 28, 1951, Houston, TX). Cincinnati (NL), 1976; St. Louis (NL), 1977; New York (NL), 1977–1982; San Francisco (NL), 1983–1988; Chicago (NL), 1989. Remarks: Had 969 hits (80 homers) in 1,408 games in 14 years; first big-leaguer ever to play for two different teams in two different cities on the same day, and had a hit in each game, August 4, 1982; hitting instructor, Baltimore (AL), 1991; manager, Kane County Cougars (Midwest League), 1992–1993; coach, Cincinnati (NL), 1994–1997; coach, Milwaukee (NL), 1998–1999; project manager for Arizona-based software development company, 2000–2001; manager, Newark Bears (Atlantic League), 2002-.

57423. McGee, Todd. "Plenty of Experience — New Coaches Joel Youngblood, Grant Jackson and Bob Boone Bring a Wealth of Experience to the Job." *Reds Report*, VII (January 1994), 16–17.

57424. Sullivan, Robert. "Star, Not a Starter." *Sports Illustrated*, LV (August 24, 1981), 82–83.

57425. Willhite, Lindsey. "Cougar's Youngblood Hopes Chess Skills Will Make Him a Better Manager." *Orioles Gazette*, II (May 1, 1992), 30–32. Manager, Kane County Cougars, 1992–93.

Ross Youngs *see* **Royce Middlebrook ("Ross" or "Pep") Youngs**

Royce Middlebrook ("Ross" or "Pep") Youngs★

OF. (B: April 10, 1897, Shiner, TX-D: Oct. 22, 1927). New York (NL), 1917–1926. Remarks: Obtained 1,491 hits (42 homers) and 153 stolen bases in 1,211 games in a decade; noted fielder whose career was ruined by Bright's disease; led NL in doubles, 1919; first player to have two hits in one World Series game, 1921; also played for Sherman (W.A.), 1916; named to Texas Sports Hall of Fame, 1983; elected to National Baseball Hall of Fame in 1972, where his plaque reads: "Star right fielder of champion Giants of 1921–22–23–24 when he batted .327,.331, .336 and .356. Compiled lifetime average of .322, topping .300 in nine of ten years. Twice made 200 or more hits in a season. Led league in doubles in 1919 and runs scored in 1923. Led NL outfielders in assists twice and tied once."

57426. Abrams, Al. "Clemente Better Than Waner, Youngs?" *Baseball Digest,* XXVI (May 1967), 33–35.

57427. Asnen, Alan R. "Ross Middlebrook 'Pep' Youngs." In: Vol. Q-Z of David L. Porter, ed. *Biographical Dictionary of American Sports: Baseball.* Rev. and enlarged ed. Westport, CT: Greenwood Press, 2000. Pp. 1738–1739.

57428. Blair, Sam. "Forgotten Tragedy: Despite Untimely Death, Ross Youngs' Story Often Overlooked." In: his *Texas Is Baseball Country.* Cleveland, OH: Society for American Baseball Research, 1994. Pp. 17–20.

57428. Graham, Frank. "The Saga of Ross Youngs." *Baseball Magazine,* LVI (February 1936), 391–392+.

57429. _____. "The Youngs McGraw Never Forgot." *Baseball Digest,* XIX (February 1960), 65–67.

57430. Hano, Arnold. "The Greatest Fighter." In: his *Greatest Giants of Them All.* New York: G.P. Putnam's Sons, 1967. Pp. 198–212.

57431. Lane, Ferdinand C. "How Ross Youngs Was Christened 'Pep.'" *Baseball Magazine,* XXV (July 1920), 377–379.

57432. Ritter, Lawrence and Donald Honig "Ross Youngs." In: their *The 100 Greatest Baseball Players of All Time.* New York: Crown Publishers, 1981. Pp. 170–171.

57433. Santa Maria, Michael and James Costello. "Striking His Stride." In: their *In the Shadows of the Diamond.* Dubuque, IA: The Elysian Fields Press, 1992. Pp. 160–163.

57434. Smith, James D., 3rd. "Bowing Out on Top." *The National Pastime,* II (1982), 73–81.

57435. Youngs, Ross ("Pip"). "The Right Fielder's Side of the Case." *Baseball Magazine,* XXXHI (June 1924), 307–308.

Robin R. Yount★

SS, (B: Sept. 16, 1955, Danville, IL). Milwaukee (AL), 1974–1993. Remarks: Had 3,142 hits (251 homers) and 271 stolen bases in 2,856 games in 20 seasons; led AL in doubles, 1980, 1982; AL MVP award, 1982, 1989; had four hits in 1982 ALCS and 12 hits (three doubles, one homer) in 1982 World Series; led AL in triples, 1983, 1988; hit for the cycle, June 12, 1988; (named to Ted William's Hitters Hall of Fame, Feb. 18, 2001; coach, Arizona (NL), 2002- ; elected to National Baseball Hall of Fame in 1999, where his plaque reads: "A prolific hitter with a stoic demeanor who was equally graceful at shortstop and in center field. One of three players to earn MVP honors at two positions. Produced 3,142 hits, 7th most in American League history. Hit .300 six times, 40 doubles four times, 20 HR four times and scored 100 runs five times. Exceptional conditioning and extraordinary work ethic made him a bastion of consistency and durability for 20 seasons. An every day major leaguer at age 18."

57436. Adelson, Bruce. "Robin Yount: He Has a Hall of Fame Approach to Baseball." *Baseball Digest,* LI (September 1992), 26–30.

57437. Aronson, Harvey. "The Once and Future Superstars: Milwaukee's Young Robin." *Sport,* LXI (September 1975), 48–53.

57438. Baldassaro, Larry. "The Robin Yount Countdown Diary, September 7–9, 1992." *Elysian Fields Quarterly,* XII (Spring 1993), 78–81.

57439. Benson, John. "Robin Yount—1982." In: his *Baseball's Top 100: The Best Individual Seasons of All Time.* Wilton, CT: Diamond Library, 1996. Pp. 247–248.

57440. Capezzuto, Tom. "Robin Yount Sets His Sights on 3,000 Career Hits in '92." *Baseball Digest,* L (September 1991), 32–34.

57441. Clary, Jack. "Trammell-Ripken-Yount: How They're Turning Back the Clock." *Sport World,* XXIII (October 1984), 28–31. Comparison with past shortstops.

57442. Cohen, Irwin. "Rappin' with Rockin' Robin." *Baseball Cards,* IV (June 1984), 22–23+.

57443. Creamer, Robert W. "This Robin is a Rare Bird." *Sports Illustrated,* LVII (September 27, 1982), 34+.

57444. Cryns, Jim. "Blue-Collar Hero." In: Michael J. McCormick, ed. *2002 All Star Game Official Program.* New York: Major League Baseball Promotion Corp., 2002. Pp. 155–156.

57445. Deane, Bill. "Robin Yount Joined Elite Group of Fielders in 1986." *Baseball Digest,* XLVI (April 1987), 90–91.

57446. Etkin, Jack. "Robin Yount: Next Player to Reach 3,000 Hits?" *Baseball Digest,* XLVIII (September 1989), 28–29.

57447. Flaherty, Tom. "1982 Was Yount's Miracle." In: Dick Kaegel, ed. *The Sporting News 1983 Baseball Yearbook.* St. Louis, MO: The Sporting News, 1983. Pp. 4–10.

57448. _____. "Rating Robin Yount Vs. All-Time Shortstops." In: Zander Hollander, ed. *1983 Season: The Complete Handbook of Baseball.* New York: New American Library, 1983. Pp. 14–23.

57449. _____. "Robin Yount: The American League's Best All-Around Shortstop." *Baseball Digest,* XLI (October 1982), 18–21.

57450. Gammons, Peter. "Forever a Kid: Robin Yount has MVP Talents Worth Millions, But Revels in High-Risk Fun with Very Big Toys." *Sports Illustrated,* LXXII (April 30, 1990), 76–80, 82–89.

57451. Gilligan, Vin. "Robin Yount Shifts Gears: A Shortstop Learns to Stop Short." *Sport,* LXIII (September 1976), 65–68.

57452. Gonring, Mike. "Molitor and Yount: Opposites Really Do Attract." *Baseball Quarterly,* III (June 1979), 50–57.

57453. Hart, Stan. "Robin Yount." In: his *Scouting Reports: The Original Reviews of Baseball's Greatest Stars.* New York: Macmillan, 1995. Pp. 140–143.

57454. Haudricourt, Tom. "Deeper Look: Robin Yount." *Beckett Baseball Card Monthly,* XI, no. 111 (June 1994), 126–127.

57455. _____. "Robin Yount was Admired for His Work Ethic." *Baseball Digest,* LVIII (November 1999), 70–75.

57456. Honig, Donald. "1982: Robin Yount." In: his *American League MVP's.* New York: Bantam Books, 1989. Pp. 108–109.

57457. _____. "Robin Yount." In: his *The Greatest Shortstops of All Time.* Dubuque, IA: Wm. C. Brown Publishers, 1992. Pp. 86–90.

57458. Korn, Peter. "The Brews Brothers." *Inside Sports,* IX (August 1987), 72–79. Yount and Paul Molitor.

57459. Kuenster, John. "Robin Yount: *Baseball Digest*'s 1982 Player of the Year." *Baseball Digest,* XLI (December 1982), 15–19.

57460. Kurkijan, Tim. "Make Room in Cooperstown." *Sports Illustrated,* LXXVII (September 21, 1992), 48–49.

57461. Libman, Gary. *Robin Yount.* Mankato, MN: Creative Education, 1983. 32p.

57462. McMane, Fred. "Robin Yount." In: his *The 3,000 Hit Club.* Champaign, IL: Sports Publishing, 2000. Pp. 118–125.

57463. Mortenson, Tom and Greg Ambrosius. "Robin Yount." *Baseball Cards,* X (September 1990), 70–77.

57464. Newton, Craig. "Robin Yount: Interview." *Baseball Cards,* X (September 1990), 78–85.

57465. Point, High. "Bat Man and Robin." *Beckett Baseball Card Monthly,* XV (September 1998), 94–97. Yount and George Brett.

57466. Prugh, Jeff. "Robin Yount: In Milwaukee, They Call Him Super Kid." *Baseball Digest,* XXXIII (November 1974), 28–33.

57467. "Robin Yount." In: *Current Biography Yearbook, 1993.* New York: H. W. Wilson, 1993. Pp. 615–619.

57468. Sell, Dennis. "1,000th Hit Comes Early for Robin." In: Tom Skibosh, ed. *Milwaukee Brewers 1981 Official Yearbook.* Waukesha, WI: Delzer Lithograph Corp., 1981. Pp. 35–36.

57469. _____. "Robin Yount, 1982 Most Valuable Player." In: Tom Skibosh, ed. *Milwaukee Brewers 1983 Official Yearbook.* Waukesha, WI: Delzer Lithograph Corp., 1983. Pp. 16–17.

57470. Sorci, Rick. "A Second Look: Rockin' Robin Yount." *Beckett Baseball Card Monthly,* VI (October 1989), 75–76.

57471. Stanton, Jack R. "Robin R. Yount." In: Vol. Q-Z of David L. Porter, ed. *Biographical Dictionary of American Sports: Baseball.* Rev. and enlarged ed. Westport, CT: Greenwood Press, 2000. Pp. 1739–1740.

57472. "Superstar Gallery: Robin Yount." *Beckett Baseball Card Monthly,* IX, no. 90 (September 1992), 14–15.

57473. Van Dyck, Dave. "Robin Yount: A Future Hall of Famer Bows Out Quietly." *Baseball Digest,* LIII (May 1994), 24–25.

57474. Verdi, Bob. "Memories of '82 Season Enrich Robin Yount." *Baseball Digest,* L (August 1991), 50–51.

57475. Verducci, Tom. "The Race for 3,000 Hits: George Brett vs. Robin Yount." *Baseball Digest,* L (July 1991), 28–31.

57476. "What's Brewing with Robin Yount." *What's Brewing,* VIII (April 1984), 10–13.

57477. Wulf, Steve. "Robin Yount." *Sports Illustrated,* LXXX (February 21, 1994), 74+. Retirement.

57478. Yount, Robin. "My Greatest Day in Baseball." In: Eliot Cohen, ed. *My Greatest Day in Baseball.* New York: Little Simon, 1991. pp. 148–150.

57479. _____., as told to Al Doyle. "The Game I'll Never Forget." *Baseball Digest,* LXII (September 2003), 70–73. Division-clinching 1982 game.

57480. _____., as told to George Vass. "The Game I'll Never Forget." *Baseball Digest,* XLV (July 1986), 31–35.

57481. "Yount Rides to MVP Honors." In: Bob Sparks, ed. *Baseball '83.* St. Petersburg, FL: National Association of Professional Baseball Leagues, 1983. Pp. 15–16.

Adrian Rodriguez Zabala

P. (B: Aug. 26, 1916, San Antonio, Cuba-D: Jan. 4, 2002). New York (NL), 1945; New York (NL), 1949. Re-

marks: Had four victories and seven defeats, with one "save," in two seasons; worked for Jacksonville, FL-based St. Regis Paper Company, 1961–1981; named to Cuban Baseball Hall of Fame, 1994.

57482. Kelley, Brent P. "Adrian Zabala: Done In by Durocher (1945–1949)." In: his *The Pastime in Turbulence: Interviews with Baseball Players of the 1940s.* Jefferson, NC: McFarland & Co., Inc., 2002. Pp. 226–236.

Jonathan Thompson Walton ("Tom") Zachery

P. (B: May 7, 1896, Graham, NC-D: Jan. 24, 1969). Philadelphia (AL), 1919; Washington (AL), 1919–1925; St. Louis (AL), 1926–1927; Washington (AL), 1927–1928; New York (NL), 1928–1930; Boston (NL), 1930–1934; Brooklyn (NL), 1934–1936; Philadelphia (NL), 1936. Remarks: Had 185 victories, 191 defeats, and 22 "saves" in 18 seasons; won Games Two and Six of the 1924 World Series and Game Three in 1928 fall classic; surrendered Tris Speaker's (q.v.) 3,000th hit, May 17, 1925; surrendered Ruth's 60th homer, Sept. 30, 1927. First major league relief pitcher to win as many as 12 games in a season without a defeat, 1929; named to North Carolina Sports Hall of Fame. Matz, David S. "Jonathan Thompson Walton 'Tom' Zachery." In: Vol. Q-Z of David L. Porter, ed. *Biographical Dictionary of American Sports: Baseball.* Rev. and enlarged ed. Westport, CT: Greenwood Press, 2000. Pp. 1741–1742.

57483. Sumner, Jim. "Tom Zachary's Perfect Season." In: *Baseball History 3: An Annual of Original Baseball Research.* Westport, CT: Meckler, Inc., 1990. Pp. 89–97.

Patrick Paul ("Pat") Zachry

P. (B: April 24, 1952, Richmond, TX). Cincinnati (NL), 1976–1977; New York (NL), 1977–1982; Los Angeles (NL), 1983–1984; Philadelphia (NL), 1985. Remarks: Obtained 69 wins, 67 losses, and three "saves" in a decade; won one game each in the 1976 NLCS and World Series.

57484. Honig, Donald. "1976: Pat Zachry, Butch Metzger." In: his *National League Rookies of the Year.* New York: Bantam Books, 1989. Pp. 71–74. Tie.

Tom Zachery *see* **Jonathan Thompson Walton ("Tom") Zachery**

Dominick Thomas ("Dom") Zanni

P. (B: March 1, 1932, Bronx, NY). San Francisco (NL), 1958–1959, 1961; Chicago (AL), 1962–1963; Cincinnati (NL), 1963, 1965–1968. Remarks: Had nine victories and six defeats, plus 10 "saves," in parts of eight big league seasons; came in to relieve in first inning of one game with no outs and finished, gaining credit for a victory but not a complete game, June 22, 1962.

57485. Bitker, Steve. "Dom Zanni." In: his *The Original San Francisco Giants: The Giants of '58.* Champaign, Il: Sports Publishing, Inc., 1998. Pp. 202–203.

Allen Lee ("Al" or "Zeke") Zarilla

OF. (B: May 1, 1919, Los Angeles, CA-D: Sept. 4, 1996). St. Louis (AL), 1943–1949; Boston (AL), 1949–1950; Chicago, (AL), 1951–1952; St. Louis (AL), 1952; Boston (AL), 1952–1953. Remarks: Had 975 hits (61 homers) and 33 stolen bases in 1,120 games in a decade; had one hit and one RBI in Game Three of the 1944 World Series; had two triples in one inning, July 13, 1946 and two doubles in one inning, June 8, 1950; coach, Texas (AL), 1972.

57486. Drees, Donald H. "Zealous Zeke Zarilla." *Baseball Digest,* VII (October 1948), 53–59.

57487. Fehler, Gene. "Al Zarilla." In: his *Tales from Baseball's Golden Age.* Champaign, IL: Sports Publishing Co., 2000. Chpt. 55.

57488. Kelley, Brent P. "Al Zarilla: Fournier's Find." In: his *The Early All-Stars: Conversations with Standout Base-*

ball Players, 1930–1940. Jefferson, NC: McFarland & Co., Inc., 1997. Pp. 179–190.

57489. Rumill, Ed. "Al Zarilla: One Player the Browns Didn't Trade." *Baseball Magazine,* LXXXI (September 1948), 345–347.

57490. Skipper, John C. "Al Zarilla: The Greatest Victory Margin Ever in One Game." In: his *Inside Pitch: A Closer Look at Classic Baseball Moments.* Jefferson, NC: McFarland & Co., Inc., 1996. Pp. 167–170.

57491. Swank, Bill. "Al Zarilla." In: his *Echoes from Lane Field; A History of the San Diego Padres 1936–1957.* Paducah, KY: Turner Publishing Company, 1997. Pp. 137–138.

57491. Westcot, Rich. "Al Zarilla: A Slugging Outfielder Who Always Played Hard." In: his *Masters of the Diamond.* Jefferson, NC: McFarland & Co., Inc., 1994. Pp. 171–180.

Gus Edward ("Ozark Ike") Zernial
OF-BROADCASTER. (B: June 27, 1923, Beaumont, TX). Chicago (AL), 1949–1951; Philadelphia (AL) and Kansas City (AL), 1951–1957; Detroit (AL), 1958–1959. Remarks: Obtained 1,093 hits (237 homers) and 15 stolen bases in 1,234 games in 11 years; had four homers (1–3) in a doubleheader, Oct. 1, 1950; had seven homers in four consecutive games, May 1951; had grand slam homer, June 2, 1951 and a second, the last in history of Philadelphia (AL) team, May 26, 1954; AL RBI champion, 1951; AL home run champion, 1951; had 10 career pinch-hit homers; also played for Hollywood (PCL), 1947–1948; broadcaster, CBS affiliate, Fresno, CA, 1960–1976.

57492. Etkin, Jack. "Gus Zernial." In: his *Innings Ago: Recollections of Kansas City Ballplayers of Their Days in the Game.* Marceline, MO: Walsworth Publishing Co., 1987. Pp. 86–99.

57493. Fagen, Herb. "Gus Zernial: The Forgotten Power Boy of the 1950s." *Oldtyme Baseball News,* VI, no. 6 (1994), 22–24.

57494. Fehler, Gene. "Gus Zernial." In: his *Tales from Baseball's Golden Age.* Champaign, IL: Sports Publishing Co., 2000. Chpt.56.

57495. Green, Paul M. "'I Could Always Handle the Stick': SCD Talks to Gus Zernial." *Sport Collector's Digest,* XV (December 30, 1988), 136–138.

57496. Hilton, George W. "Gus Edward Zernial." In: Vol. Q-Z of David L. Porter, ed. *Biographical Dictionary of American Sports: Baseball.* Rev. and enlarged ed. Westport, CT: Greenwood Press, 2000. Pp. 1742–1743.

57497. Hoffman, John C. "Gus Zernial." In: his *My Greatest Baseball Game.* New York: A.S. Barnes And Co., 1950. Pp. 213–219. Digested as "Gus Looks the Part," in *Baseball Digest,* IX (April 1950), 13–15.

57498. Kent, Ted. "Zernial Due to Get Lucky." *Baseball Magazine,* LXXXIX (June 1952), 22–24.

57499. Kiersh, Edward. "Gus Zernial: Money is the Best Revenge." In: his *Where Have You Gone, Vince DiMaggio?* New York: Bantam Books, 1983. Pp. 230–235.

57500. Marazzi, Rich. "Gus Zernial Smacked Seven Homers in Four Games." *Sports Collector's Digest,* XXV (October 9, 1998), 80–81.

57501. Richman, Milton. "Watch Gus Go." *Complete Baseball,* IV (September 1953), 20–21+.

57502. Skipper, John C. "Gus Zernial: He Wouldn't Take a Pay Cut to Play in the Majors." In: his *Inside Pitch: A Closer Look at Classic Baseball Moments.* Jefferson, NC: McFarland & Co., Inc., 1996. Pp. 112–114.

57503. Stump, Al. "'Ozark Ike' Lives to Hit." *Sport,* XII (April 1952), 32–33+.

57504. _____. "'Ozark Ike' Zernial" In: his *Champions Against Odds.* New York: Macrae Smith, 1952. Pp. 194–204.

57505. Westcott, Rich. "Gus Zernial: A Real-Life Ozark Ike." In: his *Splendor on the Diamond: Interviews with 35 Stars of Baseball's Past.* Gainesville, FL: The University Press of Florida, 2000. Pp. 309–318.

Todd Edward Zeile
3B. (B: Sept. 9, 1965, Van Nuys, CA). St. Louis (NL), 1989–1995; Chicago (NL), 1995; Philadelphia (NL) and Baltimore (AL), 1996; Los Angeles (NL), 1997–1998; Florida (NL), 1998; Texas (AL), 1998–1999; New York (NL), 2000–2001; Colorado (NL), 2002; New York (AL) and Montreal (NL), 2003; New York (NL), 2004-. Remarks: Through 2004, has had 2,004 hits (253 homers) and 53 stolen bases in 2,158 games; obtained eight hits (three homers) in 1996 ALCS, seven hits (three doubles, one homer) in 2000 NLCS, and eight hits (two doubles) in the 2000 World Series; much traveled infielder, who became first to homer for 11 major league teams, Sept. 5, 2003.

57506. Craft, David. "Todd Zeile." *Baseball Cards,* X (May 1990), 136–145.

57507. Frommer, Harvey and Frederick J. "Todd Zeile." In: their *Growing Up Baseball: An Oral History.* Dallas, TX: Taylor Publishing Co., 2001. Pp. 230–232.

57508. Wheatley, Tom. "A Closer Look: Todd Zeile." *Beckett Baseball Card Monthly,* VII (March 1990), 6–7.

57509. Zeile, Todd. "When I was a Kid: Interview." *Junior League Baseball,* no. 7 (May 1997), 10+.

Alma ("Gabby" or "Ziggy") Ziegler
2B-P. (B: Jan. 9, 1921, Chicago, IL). Milwaukee Chicks (All-American Girls Professional Baseball League), 1944; Grand Rapids Chicks (AAGPBL), 1945–1954. Remarks: As a batter, obtained 628 hits and 383 stolen bases; as a hurler, won 60 games and lost 34.

57510. Crawford, Scott A. G. M. "Alma 'Gabby,' 'Ziggy' Ziegler." In: Vol. Q-Z of David L. Porter, ed. *Biographical Dictionary of American Sports: Baseball.* Rev. and enlarged ed. Westport, CT: Greenwood Press, 2000. Pp. 1743–1744.

Charles Louis ("Chief") Zimmer
C-MGR. (B: Nov. 23, 1860, Marietta, OH-D: Aug. 22, 1949). Detroit (NL), 1884; New York (AA), 1886; Cleveland (AA/NL), 1887–1899; Louisville (NL), 1899; Pittsburgh (NL), 1900–1902. Remarks: Obtained 1,224 hits (26 homers) and 157 stolen bases in 1,280 games in 19 years; first backstop to catch 125 games in a season, 1899; president, Players' Protective Association, 1899; also played for Ironton (Ohio State League), 1881–1883; manager, Pittsburgh (NL), 1903, winning 49 games and losing 86 (.363); umpire in NL, 1904, EL, 1905, and SA, 1907; part-owner, Little Rock (SA), 1906.

57511. Ivor-Campbell, Frederick. "Charles Louis 'Chief' Zimmer." In: Vol. Q-Z of David L. Porter, ed. *Biographical Dictionary of American Sports: Baseball.* Rev. and enlarged ed. Westport, CT: Greenwood Press, 2000. Pp. 1744–1746.

Chief Zimmer *see* **Charles Louis ("Chief") Zimmer**
Donald William ("Don" or "Zim" or "Popeye") Zimmer
3B-2B-SS-MGR. (B: Jan. 17, 1931, Cincinnati, OH). Brooklyn (NL) and Los Angeles (NL), 1954–1959; Chicago (NL), 1960–1961; New York (NL) and Cincinnati (NL), 1962; Los Angeles (NL), 1963; Washington (AL), 1963–1965; Toei Flyers (Japan League), 1966. Remarks: Obtained 773 hits (91 homers) and 45 stolen bases in 1,495

games in a dozen campaigns; had two hits in 1955 World Series; also played for Cambridge (Eastern Shore League), 1950, Elmira (EL) and St. Paul (AA), 1951–1953; AA MVP award, 1953; minor league manager, 1967–1970; coach, Montreal (N.L) and San Diego (NL), 1971–1972; manager, San Diego (NL), 1972–1973, coach, Boston (AL), 1974–1975; coach, St. Louis (NL), 1976; manager, Boston (A.L), 1976–1980 and Texas (A.L), 1981–1982, coach, New York (AL), 1983, Chicago (NL), 1984–1986, New York (AL) and San Francisco (NL), 1987; manager, Chicago (NL), 1988–1991; coach, Boston (AL), 1992, Colorado (NL), 1993–1995. and New York (AL), 1996–2003; as a big league pilot, won 885 games and lost 858 (.508); senior advisor, Tampa Bay (AL), 2004-.

57512. Burr, Harold. "Zimmer Finds It's Target Time." *Baseball Digest,* XIII (July 1964), 69–71.

57513. Daley, Arthur. "Don Zimmer: Brash, Bouncy, and Determined." *Baseball Digest,* XVII (September 1958), 76–78.

57514. "Don Zimmer." In: Carrie Muskat, ed. *Banks to Sandberg to Grace: Five Decades of Love and Frustration with the Chicago Cubs.* Chicago, IL: Contemporary Books, 2001. Pp. 63–67.

57515. Fitzgerald, Joe. "Don Zimmer's Nightmare." *Baseball Quarterly,* III (October 1979), 30–33. Service as Red Sox manager.

57516. _____. "No Manager's Got a Better Job." *Boston Sunday Globe Magazine,* (August 14, 1977), 19+.

57517. Frommer, Harvey and Frederick J. "Don Zimmer." In: their *Growing Up Baseball: An Oral History.* Dallas, TX: Taylor Publishing Co., 2001. Pp. 233–236.

57518. Hano, Arnold. "Don Zimmer." In: Ray Robinson, ed. *Baseball Stars of 1959.* New York: Pyramid Books, 1959. Pp. 137–144.

57519. Holtzman, Jerome. "Don Zimmer: A 'Baseball Lifer' Says Goodbye to the Game He Loves." *Baseball Digest,* LIV (October 1995), 63–64.

57520. Hye, Allen E. "Donald William 'Don,' 'Popeye' Zimmer." In: Vol. Q-Z of David L. Porter, ed. *Biographical Dictionary of American Sports: Baseball.* Rev. and enlarged ed. Westport, CT: Greenwood Press, 2000. Pp. 1746–1747.

57521. Koenig, Bill. "Don Zimmer: A Baseball Life." *USA Today Baseball Weekly,* VIII (October 7, 1998), 16–18.

57522. Linn, Ed. "Don Zimmer and the Baseball Code." *Sport,* XL (July 1965), 47–49.

57523. _____. "The Meaning of the Game." *Sport,* LXV (July 1977), 79–82.

57524. Lomartire, Paul. "The Memories Live On." In: Bob lback, ed. *Chicago Cubs 1984 Program Magazine.* Chicago, IL: Public Relations Department, Chicago Cubs, 1984. Pp. 66–76.

57525. "Looking Back." *Sports Illustrated,* LXXVII (October 12, 1992), 2–3.

57526. Macht, Norman. "1949: When Don Zimmer Broke into Pro Baseball." *Baseball Digest,* LXI (May 2002), 74–75.

57527. Marazzi, Rich. "Don Zimmer: A Half Century as a Major Leaguer." *Sports Collector's Digest,* XXV (February 6, 1998), 142–144.

57528. _____. "Don Zimmer Remembers a Generation of Legendary Players." *Sports Collector's Digest,* XXV (February 20, 1998), 70–71.

57529. _____. "Manager of the Year Award in 1989 was a Highlight for Zimmer." *Sports Collector's Digest,* XXV (February 13, 1998), 80–81.

57530. McMillan, Ken. "Don Zimmer." In: his *Tales from the Yankee Dugout: A Collection of the Greatest Yankee Stories Ever Told.* Champaign, IL: Sports Publishing, Inc., 2001. Pp. 205–206.

57531. Montville, Leigh. "The Face of Genius." *Sports Illustrated,* LXXI (September 25, 1989), 58–64.

57532. Obojski, Robert. "'Popeye' Signs on as Yankees Coach for '96." *Sports Collector's Digest,* XXII (December 22, 1995), 100–101.

57533. Picarello, Robert. "Happy 50th Anniversary, Zim." *Yankees Magazine,* XIX (July 1998), 22–33.

57534. Raab, Scott. "Don Zimmer." *Esquire,* CXXXV (January 2001), 96–101.

57535. Rifkin, Alan. "Hangtime." *Los Angeles,* XL (May 1995), 32–35.

57536. Stainback, Berry. "If I Had the Wings." *Sport,* XL (July 1965), 7–8.

57537. Whiteside, Larry. "There's Plenty of Vim Still Left in Don Zimmer." *Baseball Digest,* LIII (July 1994), 36–38.

57538. Will, George F. "Don Zimmer's 52nd Season." *Newsweek,* CXXXV (April 3, 2000), 91–92.

57539. Wulf, Steve. "Meet the New Boss." *Sports Illustrated,* LXXIV (June 3, 1991), 66+.

57540. Zimmer, Don, with William C. ("Bill") Madden. *The Zen of Zim: Baseballs, Beanballs, and Bosses.* New York: St. Martin's Press, 2004. 288p.

57541. _____. *Zim: A Baseball Life.* New York: Total Sports, 2001. 304p.

Henry ("Heinie" or "The Great Zim") Zimmermann

3B-2B-SS-1B. (B: Feb. 9, 1987, New York City-D: March 14, 1969). Chicago (NL), 1907–1916; New York (NL), 1916–1919. Remarks: Obtained 1,566 hits (58 homers) and 175 stolen bases in 1,458 games in 12 years; had four hits (one double) in 1910 World Series; led NL in doubles, 1912; NL RBI champion, 1916–1917; obtained three hits (one triple) in the 1917 fall classic; remembered for supposed "boner" in Game Six of the 1917 World Series; abruptly suspended (with teammate Hal Chase) near end of the 1919 season for participation in alleged game fixing scheme; banned (with Chase) from baseball; later, allegedly affiliated with New York underworld and co-owner of a Big Apple speakeasy with Dutch Schultz in 1929–1930 who, thereafter, made a living as a steamfitter.

57542. Burnes, Robert L. "How Would You Score This Play?" *Baseball Digest,* XXXIII (October 1974), 46–47.

57543. Davis, Mac. "Nobody Wanted to Hear His Alibi." In: his *The Lore and Legends of Baseball.* New York: Lantern Press, 1953. Pp. 99–100. 1917 World Series bonehead play.

57544. Gutman, Dan. "Heinie Zimmermann's Dash to the Plate." In: his *Baseball's Biggest Bloopers: The Games That Got Away.* New York: Puffin, 1995. Pp. 68–77.

57545. Menke, Frank G. "Zimmerman's Real Boner." In: his *Sports Tales and Anecdotes.* New York: A.S. Barnes, 1953. Pp. 51–52.

57546. Santa Maria, Michael and James Costello. "Monkey Business." In: *their In the Shadows of the Diamond.* Dubuque, IA: The Elysian Fields Press, 1992. Pp. 18–23.

57547. Smith, Leverette T., Jr. "Henry 'Heinie,' 'The Great Zim' Zimmermann." In: Vol. Q-Z of David L. Porter, ed. *Biographical Dictionary of American Sports: Baseball.* Rev. and enlarged ed. Westport, CT: Greenwood Press, 2000. Pp. 1747–1748.

James Edward ("Jimmy") Zinn, Sr.

P. (B: Jan. 31, 1895, Benton, Ark.-D: Feb. 26, 1991). Philadelphia (NL), 1919; Pittsburgh (NL), 1920–1922;

Cleveland (AL), 1929. Remarks: Won 13 games and lost 16 in five big league seasons; enjoyed 22-year minor league career, where he was 295–198, including five 20-win seasons; also an occasional switch-hitting OF, with a .301 career average with Kansas City (AA) and San Francisco (PCL).

57548. Salin, Tony. "Fired for Striking Out the Babe: Jimmy Zinn, Sr." In: his *Baseball's Forgotten Heroes.* Chicago, IL: Masters Press, 1999. Pp. 198–199.

Richard Walter ("Richie") Zisk

OF. (B: Feb. 6, 1949, Brooklyn, NY). Pittsburgh(NL), 1971–1976; Chicago (AL), 1977; Texas (AL), 1978–1980; Seattle (AL), 1981–1983. Remarks: Had 1,477 hits (207 homers) and eight stolen bases in 1,453 games in 14 years; hit for the cycle, June 9, 1974; had three hits in 1974 NLCS and five hits (one double) in 1975 NLCS; earned BA degree, 1987; minor league instructor, Chicago (NL), 1987–1999; minor league hitting coordinator, Chicago (NL), 1999; manager, Daytona (Florida State League), 2000; minor league hitting coordinator, Chicago (NL), 2001–2003; coach, Daytona (Florida State League), 2004; manager, Dayton (Florida State League), 2005–.

57549. Devaney, John. "Chicago: It's Richie Zisk's Kinda Town." *Sport,* LXV (September 1977), 91–95.

57550. Gammons, Peter. "Old Uniforms, New Sox." *Sports Illustrated,* XLVI (May 16, 1977), 53–54.

57551. James, Bill. "Richie Zisk, Seattle." In: his *The Bill James Baseball Abstract 1983.* New York: Ballantine Books, 1983. Pp. 189–190.

57552. Ringolsby, Tracy. "Shipwrecked in Seattle." *Sport,* LXXV (March 1984), 61–71.

57553. Rumill, Ed "Here Comes the Pirates' Richie Zisk." *Baseball Digest,* XXXIII (October 1974), 34–37.

57554. Spoehr, Luther W. "Richard Walter 'Richie' Zisk." In: Vol. Q-Z of David L. Porter, ed. *Biographical Dictionary of American Sports: Baseball.* Rev. and enlarged ed. Westport, CT: Greenwood Press, 2000. Pp. 1748–1749.

57555. Swift, E.M. "At Home in the [King] Dome." *Sports Illustrated,* LIV (May 18,1981), 57–58.

Barry William Zito

P. (B: May 13, 1978, Las Vegas, NV). Oakland (AL), 2000-date. Remarks: Through 2003, has won 72 games and lost 40; AL 2002 Cy Young Award.

57556. Bradley, Jeff. "Smoke and Mirrors." *ESPN: The Magazine,* IV (April 2, 2001), 78–81.

57557. Jones, Chris. "He Came from Outer Space: Pitcher Barry Zito." *Esquire,* CXXXVII (June 2002), 48–54.

57558. Keown, Tim. "Perfect Pitch." *ESPN: The Magazine,* VI (February 17, 2003), 72–76.

57559. Pearlman, Jeff. "New Wave: Whether Riding His Surfboard or Conversing with His Precocious Left Arm, A's Phenom Barry Zito Follows His Own Eccentric Path." *Sports Illustrated,* XCIV (January 15, 2001), 44–48.

57560. Silver, Michael. "Inside Barry's Head." *Sports Illustrated,* C (June 21, 2004), 72–79.

57561. Schwarz, Alan. "Uncommon Dominator: Barry Zito of the Oakland A's is One of a Kind." *Sports Illustrated for Kids,* XV (April 1, 2003), 27+.

William Henry ("Bill" or "Goober") Zuber

P. (B: March 26, 1913, Middle Amana, IA-D: Nov. 2, 1982). Cleveland (AL), 1936, 1938–1940; Washington (AL), 1941–1942; New York (AL), 1943–1946; Boston (AL), 1946–1947. Remarks: In 11 years, won 43 big league games and lost 42, with six "saves"; after leaving the game, Zuber and his family operated Bill Zuber's Dugout Restaurant at Homestead, IA for the next 40 years.

57562. Trumpold, Cliff. *Now Pitching: Bill Zuber from Amana.* Middle Amana, IA: Lakeside Publishing Co., 1991. 141p.

Jerry Mike Zuvela

OF. (B: Sept. 21, 1929, San Pedro, CA-D: July 28, 1995). Yakima (W.I.), 1950–1952; San Francisco (PCL), 1953–1954; Seattle (PCL), Nashville (SA) and Wantachee (Northwest League), 1955; Fresno (California League), 1957. Remarks: In eight minor league campaigns, obtained 809 hits and 69 homers in 821 games.

57563. Kelley, Brent P. "Jerry Zuvela." In: his *The San Francisco Seals, 1946–1957: Interviews with 25 Former Baseballers.* Jefferson, NC: McFarland & Co., Inc., 2002. Pp. 175–181.

George Zuverink

P. (B: Aug. 20, 1924, Holland, MI). Cleveland (AL), 1951–1952; Cincinnati (NL), 1954; Detroit (AL), 1954–1955; Baltimore (AL), 1955–1959. Remarks: Obtained 32 victories, 36 defeats, and 40 "saves" in nine seasons; part of first "Z" battery when teamed with catcher Frank Zupo in 1957; also played for Oklahoma (PCL).

57564. Swank, Bill. "George Zuverink." In: his *Echoes from Lane Field: A History of the San Diego Padres 1936–1957.* Paducah, KY: Turner Publishing Company, 1997. Pp. 108–109.

Paul Zwaska

GROUNDSKEEPER Remarks: Head groundskeeper, Oriole Park and Camden Yards.

57565. Gmelch, George. "Paul Zwaska: Head Groundskeeper." *Nine: A Journal of Baseball History and Social Policy Perspectives,* VI (Fall 1997), 161–172.

Robert Zwissig

FAN. Remarks: San Francisco (PCL/NL) backer, 1948–.

57566. Kelley, Brent P. "Robert Zwissig." In: his *The San Francisco Seals, 1946–1957: Interviews with 25 Former Baseballers.* Jefferson, NC: McFarland & Co., Inc., 2002. Pp. 271–275.

JOURNALS, PERIODICALS AND MAGAZINES EXAMINED

Following are the titles of the 1,712 journals, periodicals, and magazines examined and from which one or more articles were taken for bibliographic listing in this bibliography. A total of 365 were referenced in the 1986 first edition of this work.

A+
AB Bookman's Weekly
ABA Journal
Aberdeen's Concrete Construction
Academy of Management Journal
Accent on Living
Across the Board
Actualite
Addiction Research & Theory
Adirondac
Administrative Science Quarterly
Advanced Materials & Processes
Advertising Age
Advocate: The National Gay & Lesbian Newsmagazine
Adweek's Marketing Week
Aethlon: The Journal of Sport Literature
Afro-Americans in New York Life and History
Against the Current
Aggressive Behavior
Air Conditioning, Heating and Refrigeration News
Airman
Akron Law Review
Alabama Law Review
Alaska
Albany Law Review
Alberta Report
All-Star Sports
America
America West Airlines Magazine
American Banker
American Boy
American Business Law Journal
American Cinematographer
American City

The American College
American Demographics
The American Economist
American Examiner: A Forum of Ideas
American Film
American Fitness Quarterly
American Health
American Heritage
American Heritage of Invention and Technology
American Historical Review
American History
American History Illustrated
American Indian Quarterly
American Jewish History
American Journal of Ophthalmology
American Journal of Physics
American Journal of Psychology
American Journal of Sociology
American Journal of Sports Medicine
American Journal of Trial Advocacy
American Law Review
American Legion Magazine
American Legion Weekly
American Libraries
American Literature: A Journal of Literary History, Criticism, and Bibliography
American Magazine
American Mathematical Monthly
American Medical News
American Mercury
The American Philatelist
American Photo
American Physical Education Review
American Poetry Review
American Profile

The American Prospect
American Quarterly
American Review of Public Administration
American Scholar
American Sociological Review
The American Spectator
American Speech
American Statistician
American Studies International
American Theater
American University International Law Review
American Visions
American Way
Americana
Americas
Amherst Graduate's Magazine
Amusement Business
Angels Halo Insider
Annals of Biomedical Engineering
Annals of Emergency Medicine
Annals of Iowa
Annals of Regional Science
Annals of the American Academy of Political and Social Science
Anthropological Linguistics
Antioch Review
Antiquarian Book Review
Antique Trader
Antiques and Collecting Magazine
Antitrust Bulletin
APG Quarterly
Appleton's Magazine
Applied Economics
Applied Economics Letters
Applied Mathematics and Computation

Applied Research in Coaching and Athletics Annual
Arete: The Journal of Sport Literature
Arbitration Journal
Archives of Suicide Research
Arena Review
Arithmetic Teacher
Arizona Highways
Arizona's Economy
Arkansas Historical Quarterly
Arkansas Law Notes
Arkansas Times
Army
Art Education
Art News
Artforum
Arthroscopy
ASEE Prism
Asian Journal of Physical Education
Association of the Bar of the City of New York Record
At the Yard
Athletic Business
Athletic Journal
Athletic Therapy
Atlanta
Atlanta Business Chronicle
Atlanta History: A Journal of Georgia and the South
Atlantic
Atlantic Advocate
Atlantic Economic Journal
Audubon
Aussie Sport Action
Australian Journal of Jewish Studies
Australian Leisure
Australian Magazine
Australian Society for Sports History Bulletin
Avante
Axis

Back Stage
Balls and Strikes
Baltimore Business Journal
Baltimore Magazine
Baltimore Sun Magazine
Bama
Barron's
Baseball America
Baseball Analyst
Baseball Australia
Baseball Cards
Baseball Digest
Baseball History
Baseball Magazine
Baseball Monthly
Baseball Parent
Baseball Quarterly
The Baseball Research Journal
Bay Sports Review
Baylor Law Review
BC Report
BE Radio

The Beaver
Beckett Baseball Card Monthly
Beckett Focus on Future Stars
Beckett Sports Collectibles
Beckett Vintage Sports
Beehive History
Behavioral Medicine
Behavior Modification
Behavioral Science
Bell Journal of Economics
Bellingham Business Journal
Bench & Bar of Minnesota
Berea Alumnus, The
Berkeley Express
Better Homes and Gardens
Biography
Biography for Beginners
Biological Cybernetics
Birmingham Business Journal
Black Enterprise
Black Issues Book Review
Black Issues in Higher Education
Black Scholar
Black Sports Magazine
Blair and Kitchum's Country Journal
Book
The Bookman: A Review of Books and Life
Boston Bar Journal
Boston Baseball
Boston Globe Magazine
Boston Magazine
Boston University Public Interest Law Journal
Boy's Quest
Boy's Life
Boy's Quest
Brandweek
Braves Banner
Braves Fan Magazine
Brill's Content
Broadcasting
Broadcasting and Cable
Brookings Review
Brown Alumni Monthly
Buffalo, Magazine of the Buffalo News
Buffalo Law Review
Buildings
Bulletin (Sydney)
Bulletin du Groupe de Recherche sur L'Histoire de L'Activite Physique (Quebec)
Bulletin of Economic Research
Bulletin of the Psychonomic Society
Bullpen
Bungei Shunju
Bureau Farmer
Business
Business Courier Serving Cincinnati — Northern Kentucky
Business Economics
Business First of Buffalo
Business First of Columbus
Business First of Louisville

Business Horizons
Business Insurance
The Business Journal — Milwaukee
The Business Journal of Tampa
The Business Journal Serving Charlotte and the Metropolitan Area
The Business Journal — Serving Phoenix & the Valley of the Sun
Business Mexico
Business Week
By the Numbers

CA Magazine
CabinetMaker
Cable Vision
California
California Lawyer
California Parks and Recreation
The Californians: The Magazine of California History
Callaboo
Campus Law Enforcement Journal
Canadian
Canadian Architect
Canadian Business
Canadian Courier
Canadian Geographic Magazine
Canadian Historical Review
Canadian Journal of History of Sport and Physical Education
Canadian Journal of Psychiatry
Canadian Literature
Canadian Living
Canadian Medical Association Journal
Canadian Science Digest
Canadian Sports Collector
Canadian Tax Journal
Canadian Workshop
Capital University Law Review
Cardozo Law Review
Career World
Carolina Comments
Carologue: A Bulletin of South Carolina History
Case Western Law Review
Catholic Digest
Catholic Library
Catholic University Law Review
CATO Journal
CDA
Centennial Review of Arts and Sciences
Centro: Journal del Centro de Estudios Puertorriquenos
Century Illustrated Magazine
CFO
Challenge
Chance
Changing Times
Channels
Charleston Gazette-Mail State Magazine
Chicago
Chicago History

Chicago Review
Chicago Times
Chicago Tribune Magazine
The Chicagoan
Child Life
Childhood Education
Children's Literature
Choice: Current Reviews for Academic
  Libraries
Christian Century
Christian Reader
Christianity Today
The Chronicle of Higher Education
Chronicle: The Quarterly Magazine of
  the Historical Society of Michigan
Chronicles of Oklahoma
Cincinnati Business Courier
Cincinnati Historical Society Bulletin
Cincinnati Magazine
Cineaction
CIO
Citius, Altius, Fortius
City Family
City Pages
City Paper
Civil Engineering
Civil Rights Digest
Civil War History
Civil War Times Illustrated
Civilization
Claridad
Clearing House
Cleveland
Cleveland-Marshall Law Review
[Cleveland] Plain Dealer Magazine
Cleveland State Law Review
Clinical Journal of Sport Medicine
Clinics in Sports Medicine
Coach and Athletic Director
Coaching Clinic
Coaching Review
Cobblestone
Coffin Corner, The
Colby Quarterly
Collection Management
College and Research Libraries News
College Board Review
The College Mathematics Journal
College of Wooster Magazine
Collegiate Baseball
Collier's
Color
Colorado Business Magazine
ColorLines
Colorado Heritage
Columbia
Columbia Historical Society Records
Columbia Journal of Law and Social
  Problems
Columbia Journalism Review
Columbia Law Review
Columbia-VLA Journal of Law & the
  Arts
Commonweal

Communication
Communication Research Trends
Communications News
Competitor
Complete Baseball
Composite Structures
Compressed Air Magazine
Compute
Computer
Computer Graphics World
Computer Life
Computerworld
Computers and Operations Research
Concrete International: Design and
  Construction
Confluencia
Congressional Record
Connecticut
Connecticut Historical Society Bulletin
Connecticut Law Practice
Connoisseur
Constitution
Contemporary American Issues
Contemporary Economic Policy
Contemporary Issues in Law
Contemporary Sociology
Contemporary Thought on Perfor-
  mance Enhancement
Contractor
Cornell Journal of Law and Public
  Policy
Coronet
Corporate Report—Minnesota
Cosmopolitan
Country Gentleman
Country Home
Country Living
Countrywide Sports
Crab Orchard Review
Crain's Chicago Business
Crain's Cleveland Business
Crain's Detroit Business
Crain's New York Business
Creative Nonfiction
Crickett
Crisis
Critical Studies in Mass Communica-
  tion
Critique: Studies in Contemporary
  Fiction
Crosscurrents
Cuba Update
Cubs Quarterly
Cue
Cultural Critique
Cultural Resource Management
Cultural Resources
Culture, Sport, Society
Culturefront
Curator
Current Events, a Weekly Reader Pub-
  lication
Current Literature
Current Opinion

Current Science
Cycle World

D Magazine
D.A.C. News
D & R Reports
Dallas Magazine
Database Programming & Design
Dawn Magazine
Dayton Daily News Magazine
Defense Law Journal
Delaware History
Delaware Journal of Corporate Law
Delaware Messenger
Dell Sports
The Denver Business Journal
Denver Corporate Connection
Denver Magazine
The Denver Quarterly
DePaul Law Review
Deporte Internacional
Design for Arts in Education
Design News
Details
Detroit
Dialectical Anthropology
Diamond Duds
Diamond Mind
Diamond Report
Diamondbacks Magazine
Dickinson Law Review
Diehard
Diesel Progress, North American Edi-
  tion
Dime Novel Roundup
Discover
Discovery
Dispute Resolution Journal
Diversity
Dodgers Dugout
Dodgers Magazine
Domestic Engineering
Doubletake
Down East
Dugout
Duke Law Journal
Dunn's Review

Early American Life
Early Canadian Life
Eastern Economic Journal
Ebony
Ecological Psychology
Economic Development Quarterly
Economic Inquiry
Economic Journal
Economics Letters
The Economist
Editor & Publisher
Editorial Research Reports
Education
Educational Record
El Andar
El Mensajero

Electric Journal
Electric Perspectives
Electrical Apparatus
Electrical West
Electrical World
Electronic Media
Elysian Fields Quarterly
Emedia
Emerge
Emmy
Emory Law Journal
Empirical Studies of the Arts
Employee Relations Law Journal
The Endless Vacation — Resort Condominiums International
English Journal
English Today
ENR
Enterpreneur
Enterprise
Entertainment and Sports Lawyer
Environment & Behavior
E.P.S. Education Physique et Sport (France)
Equipe Magazine
Escape to the Minnesota Good Times
ESPN: The Magazine
Esquire
Essays in Economic and Business HIstory
Ethos
Europe
European Planning Studies
European Sports History Review
Everybody's Magazine
Exceptional Parent
Experimental Techniques
The Explicator

50 Plus
Factory and Industrial Management
Facts on File
FAHPERD Journal of Health, Physical Education, Recreation, Dance and Driver Education
Fame
Family Circle
Family Life
Family Weekly
Fantasy Baseball
Far Eastern Economic Review
Farm Journal
Fate
Federal Communications Bar Journal
Federal Reserve Bank of Kansas City Economic Review
Feminisms
Film and History
Film Commentary
The Filson Club History Quarterly
Financial Post Magazine
Financial Post Moneywise Magazine
Financial World
First Aider

Flex
Florida Historical Quarterly
Florida Law Review
Florida State University Law Review
Florida Trend
Flower Grower
Folio
Folk Art
Food Management
Foodservice Equipment and Maintenance
Foot and Ankle International
Footsteps
For the Record
Forbes/Forbes FYI
Fordham Intellectual Property, Media, and Entertainment Law Journal
Fordham International Law Journal
Fordham Law Review
Fordham Urban Law Journal
Forecast
Forecast for Home Economics
Forest Products Journal
Fort Worth Business Press
Fortune
Found Object
Frank Leslie's Illustrated Weekly
Free China Review
Free Inquiry in Creative Sociology
The French Review: Journal of the American Association of Teachers of French
Friends of Financial History

Gallup Poll Monthly, The
Gateway Heritage
Genre
Gentry
Geo
The Geographical Bulletin
George
Georgetown Law Review
Georgia Law Review
Georgia Review
Georgia State University Law Review
Georgia Trend
Get Up and Go
The Gettysburg Review
Giant Gold
Giants Magazine
Giftware News
Glamour
Golden Notes: Sacramento County Historical Society
Golf Digest
Golf Magazine
Golfer and Sportsman
Good Housekeeping
Good Old Days
Gourmet
Governing
Government Finance Review
GQ — Gentlemen's Quarterly
Grand Rapids Business Journal

Great Lakes Review
Great Moments in Sports
Greeley Style Magazine
Grounds Maintenance
Groundsman
Group and Organization Management
Growth and Change

Hardball
Harper's
Harper's Bazaar
Harper's Weekly
Harper's Young People
Harvard Graduate Magazine
Harvard International Review
Harvard Journal of Legislation
Harvard Magazine
Hastings Communications and Entertainment Law Journal
Hastings Law Journal
Health
Health Education
Heating, Piping and Air Conditioning
The Hemingway Review
Hennepin County History
High Fidelity
High Plains Literary Review
High School Journal
Highlights for Children
Hippocrates
Hispanic
Hispanic Lifestyle
Histoire Sociale — Social History
Historian, The
Historic Preservation
Historical Messenger of the Milwaukee County Historical Society
Historical New Hampshire
History News
History of Education Quarterly
History Teacher
History Today
Hit and Run
Hitotsubashi Rouse
Hobbies
Hofstra Labor Law Journal
Holiday
Holy Cow — Newsletter of the Halsey Hall Chapter of SABR
Home Office Computing
Home PC
Honolulu
Hoosierisms Quarterly
Hopscotch
Horn Book
Hot Wire
Hotel and Motel Management
Houston
Houston Astros Magazine
Houston Business Journal
Houston Law Review
Houston Review: History and Culture on the Gulf Coast
Hudson Review

Hudson Valley Business Journal
Human Organization
Human Performance
Human Relations
Humanities

Idaho Statesman
IEEE Computer Graphics and Applications
Illinois History
Illinois Issues
Illinois Libraries
Illuminating Engineering
Illustrated Librarian
Illustrated Outdoor News
Illustrated World
In These Times
Inc
Incentive Marketing
Independent
Indian Historian
Indian History
Indiana Business Magazine
Indiana Journal of Global Legal Studies
Indiana Law Journal
Indiana Law Review
Indianapolis Business Journal
Indianapolis Monthly
Indians Ink
Industrial and Labor Relations Review
Industrial Finishing
Industrial Photography
Industrial Relations
Industry Week
Information Week
Ingram's
Inland Architect
Inside Sport (Canberra)
Inside Sports
Inside the Game: The Official Newsletter of SABR's Deadball Era Committee
Insight
Insight on the News
Institutional Investor
Instructor
Insurance Review
In Tech
Interfaces
International and Comparative Law Review
International Baseball Rundown
International Journal of Dermatology
International Journal of Instructional Media
International Journal of Sport Biomechanics
International Journal of Sport Psychology
International Journal of the History of Sport
International Library of Critical Writings in Economics

International Olympic Lifter
International Review of the Sociology of Sport
International Sports Journal
Internet World
Interview
InView
Iowa Law Review
Iowa Review
Iowan
Island Magazine, The

Jack & Jill
JAMA, The Journal of the American Medical Association
Japan and the World Economy
Japan Echo
Japan, Inc.
Japan Quarterly
Japan Weekly Chronicle
Japanese Journal of Psychology
JEN, Journal of Emergency Nursing
Jet
Jewish Life
Journal of Accounting
Journal of Adult Development
Journal of Advertising Research
Journal of African American Men
Journal of Aging and Physical Activity
Journal of American College Health
Journal of American Culture
Journal of American Ethnic History
Journal of American Folklore
Journal of American History
Journal of Applied Behavior Analysis
Journal of Applied Biomechanics
Journal of Applied Psychology
Journal of Applied Social Psychology
Journal of Applied Statistics
Journal of Athletic Training
Journal of Behavioral Economics
The Journal of Big Bend Studies
Journal of Black Studies
Journal of Blacks in Higher Education
Journal of Bone and Joint Surgery
Journal of Broadcasting and Electronic Media
Journal of Business
Journal of Business and Economic Statistics
Journal of Business Strategy
Journal of Career Development
Journal of Chemical Education
Journal of College and University Law
Journal of Commerce and Commercial
Journal of Communications
Journal of Computers in Mathematics and Science Teaching
Journal of Conflict Resolution
Journal of Consumer Marketing
Journal of Consumer Research
Journal of Contemporary Ethnography
Journal of Contemporary Law
Journal of Deferred Compensation

Journal of Drug Issues
Journal of East Tennessee History
Journal of Economic Education
Journal of Economic Literature
Journal of Economic Perspectives
Journal of Economic Studies
Journal of Economics and Business
Journal of Economics and Management Strategy
Journal of Educational Sociology
Journal of Ethnic Studies
Journal of Evolutionary Psychology
Journal of Experimental Psychology
Journal of Family and Consumer Sciences
Journal of Finance
Journal of Gambling Studies
Journal of Gender, Race and Justice
Journal of Geography
Journal of Gerontology
Journal of Health, Physical Education, and Recreation
Journal of Hispanic Higher Education
Journal of Hospitality & Leisure Marketing
Journal of Human Resources
Journal of Industrial Engineering
Journal of Interdisciplinary History
Journal of Irreproducible Results
Journal of Labor Economics
Journal of Labor Research
Journal of Legal Studies
Journal of Legal Studies Education
Journal of Leisure Research
Journal of Managerial Issues
Journal of Narrative Technique
Journal of Negro History
Journal of Orthopedic and Sports Physical Therapy
Journal of Orthopedics
Journal of Personnel and Social Psychology
Journal of Physical Education and Recreation
Journal of Physical Education, Recreation and Dance
Journal of Policy Analysis and Management
Journal of Political Economy
Journal of Popular Culture
Journal of Popular Literature
Journal of Professional Services Marketing
Journal of Promotion Management
Journal of Psychology
Journal of Recreational Mathematics
Journal of San Diego History
Journal of SMET Education: Innovations and Research
Journal of Social Behavior and Personality
Journal of Socioeconomics
Journal of Social Behavior and Personality

Opportunity
OR Insight
Orange County Business Journal
Orioles Gazette
The Other Side
Ottawa Journal Weekend Magazine
Our Sports
Our World
Outdoor Life
Outing
Outlook
Ovation
Overland Monthly and Out West
Magazine
Oxford American

Pacific Coast League Potpourri
Pacific Economic Review
Pacific Historian
Pacific Northwest Quarterly
Pacific Sociological Review
Palaestra
Palimpset
Panorama
Panstadia International Quarterly
Parade Magazine
Parents
Parent's Magazine
The Paris Review
Park Maintenance
Parking
Parks and Recreation
Parnassus: Poetry in Review
Pathfinder News Magazine
PC Magazine
Peace Review
Peacework
Pearson's Magazine (American Edition)
Pediatrics
Penn State Law Review
Pennsylvania Heritage
Pennsylvania History
Pennsylvania Journal of Health, Physical Education, Recreation, and
Dance
Pennsylvania Heritage
Pennsylvania Law Journal Report
Pennsylvania Magazine
Penny Power
Pensions and Investment Age
Pensions & Investments
Penthouse
People en Espanol
People Weekly
Pepperdine Law Review
Perceptual and Motor Skills
Personnel and Guidance Journal
Personnel and Social Psychology Bulletin
Perspectives
Perspectives in Mexican-American
Studies
Perspectives on Computing

Petersen's Photographic Magazine
Philadelphia
Philadelphia Business Journal
Philadelphia Enterpriser
Philadelphia Inquirer Magazine
Phillies Report
PhillySport
Phoenix
Photo District News
Phylon
Physian and Sports Medicine
Physical Education Digest
Physical Educator
Physics Teacher
Physics Today
Pitt Magazine
Pittsburgh
Pittsburgh Business Times
Pittsburgh History
Pittsburgh Magazine
Plain Dealer Magazine, The [Cleveland]
Planning
Platte Valley Review
Play and Culture
Playboy
Playground
PM Magazine
PM, Public Management
Poets and Writers
Policy Review
Policy Studies Review
Polyphony: The Bulletin of the Multicultural Society of Ontario
Popular Culture in Libraries
Popular Mechanics
Popular Music and Society
Popular Photogarphy
Popular Science
Population Today
Postgraduate Medicine
Prehospital Disaster Medicine
Premiere
Presbyterian Record
Preservation
Presidential Studies Quarterly
Presstime
Primus
Princeton Alumni Weekly
Print
Printer's Ink
Pro
Pro Sports
Proceedings of the American Antiquarian Society
Proceso
Professional Athlete
Professional Geographer
The Professional Photographer
Program Manager
Progress in Human Geography
The Progressive
Progressive Architecture
Prologue

Prospects
Prospects Report
PSA Journal
Psychology and Aging
Psychology Today
Public Administration Review
Public Culture
Public Finance Review
Public Interest, The
Public Library Quarterly
Public Management
Public Relations Review
Public Relations Tactics
Public Works
Publish Publisher's Weekly
Puget Sound Business Journal
Pulp and Paper
Purple Sages Review

Qualitative Sociology
Quality Progress
Quarry
Quarterly Journal of Business and
Economics
Quarterly Journal of Economics
Quarterly Review of Economics and
Finance
Queen City Heritage
Queen's Quarterly
Quest
Qui

Ragtime Sports
Ramsey County History
Reader's Digest
Reader's Digest (Canadian)
Reading Teacher
Real Estate Issues
Realities
Reason
Recreation
Recreation and Parks Law Reporter
Recreation Management
Recreation Research Review
Redbird Review
Redbook
Reds Report
Referee
Reference and User Services
Quarterly
Reformed Journal
Regardie's Magazine
The Regional Economist
Register of the Kentucky Historical
Society
Regulation
Reinforced Plastics
Report Newsmagazine
Reporter
Research in Politics and Society
Research in Urban Policy
Research on Men and Masculinities
Series
Research Quarterly

Research Quarterly for Exercise and
    Sports
Restaurant Business
Restaurants and Institutions
Rethinking History
Rethinking Marxism
The Review of Academic Life
Review of Black Political Economy
Review of Business and Economic
    Research
Review of Economics and Statistics
Review of Industrial Organization
Review of Litigation
Review of Reviews
Review of Sport Sociology
Review of Sports and Leisure
Revista de la Universidad de Yucatan
Revista Mexicana de Pedagogia
Revista/Review Interamericana
Roanoker
Rochester History
Rocky Mountain
Rolling Stone
Ron Schandler's Baseball Forecaster
Rosie
Rotarian
Rough Notes
Runner's World
Russian Life

S.A. Baseball Digest
Sabermetric Review
SABR Bulletin
SABR Review of Books
Sacramento Business Journal
St. Louis
St. Louis Business Journal
St. Louis Journalism Review
St. Louis University Law Journal
St. Nicholas Magazine
Sales and Marketing Management
San Antonio
San Antonio Business Journal
San Diego Business Journal
San Diego Magazine
San Diego Metropolitan
San Diego Padres Magazine
San Francisco
San Francisco Bay Guardian
San Francisco Business
San Francisco Business Times
San Francisco Examiner Image
San Francisco Tomorrow
Sandlapper
Santa Clara Law Review
Saskatchewan History
Saturday Evening Post
Saturday Night
Saturday Review of Literature
Savvy
Scandinavian Journal of Psychology
Scarboro Museum
Scholastic
Scholastic Coach

Scholastic Math
Scholastic Scope
Scholastic Update
School Activities
Science
Science '85
Science Digest
Science World
The Sciences
Scientific American
Scorebook
Scott Stamp Monthly
Scottish Journal of Political Economy
The Scrap Book
Scribner's Magazine
Seattle Business
Second Look
Security
Semiotic Inquiry
Sepia
Serial Review
Serials Librarian
Seton Hall Journal of Sports Law
Sex Roles: A Journal of Research
The Sewanee Review
Show
SIAM Journal on Discrete Mathemat-
    ics
SIECUS Report
Siempre
Signature
Skybox
Small Business Reports
Small Press
Smart Money
Smithsoanian
Social Behavior and Personality
Social Education
Social Forces
Social Science Quarterly
Social Science Research
The Social Studies
Society
Sociological Focus
Sociological Quarterly
Sociological Symposium
Sociologie et Societes
Sociology and Social Research
Sociology of Sport Journal
Sociology of Work and Occupations
Sociometry
Sojourners
Sound and Vibrations
Sound and Video Contractor
South Atlantic Quarterly
South Carolina Review
South Central Review
South Florida
South Florida Business Journal
Southern California Quarterly
The Southern Communications Journal
Southern Cultures
Southern Economic Journal
Southern Exposure

Southern Humanities Review
Southern Illinois Law Review
Southern Living
Southern Magazine
Southern Partisan
Southern Quarterly
Southern Review
Southern Social Science Quarterly
Southwest Historical Quarterly
Soviet Life
Sox Fan News
Spectator
Spinning Wheel
Spitball
Sport
Sport and Leisure Retailer
Sport Coach (Australia)
Sport Marketing Quarterly
Sport Place
Sport Psychologist
Sport Report (Canberra)
Sport Sociology Bulletin
Sport Style
Sport World
SportEurope (Italy)
Sportimes (Lahore)
Sporting Goods Business
Sporting Goods Review
Sporting Traditions
Sporting Traditions (Australia)
Sports Cards
Sports Coach
Sports Collector's Digest
Sports Engineeering
Sports Heritage
Sports History
Sports History Review
Sports Illustrated
Sports Illustrated Australia
Sports Illustrated Canada
Sports Illustrated for Kids
Sports Inc.
Sports Law Administration & Practice
Sports Link (Australia)
Sports Marketing Quarterly
Sports Medicine and Arthroscopy
    Review
Sports Medicine Digest
Sports Monthly (Melbourne)
Sports 'n Spokes
Sports, Parks and Recreation Law
    Reporter
Sports Retailer (Sydney)
Sports Science Reviews
Sports Scoup
Sports Today
Sports Trade
Sports Travel
SportsTURF
Sports TV Production
Sports World
Spotlight
Stadion: Journal of the History of
    Sport and Physical Education

Stamps
Stadion
Stanford Journal of Law, Business &
    Finance
Stanford Law Review
Stanford Magazine
State and Local Government
Stearns County Historical Society
    Crossings
Stetson Law Review
Stores
Strategies
Street & Smith's Sportsbusiness Journal
Strength and Conditioning
Studies in American Indian Literature
Studies in American Jewish Literature
Studies in Latin American Popular
    Culture
Studies in Short Fiction
Success
Successful Farming
Suffolk University Law Review
Sunday, the Pittsburgh Press Magazine
Sundial: West Virginia Wesleyan Col-
    lege
Sunset
Super Sports
Supermarket News
SuperVision
Symbolic Interaction
Syntax and Semantics
Syracuse Law Review

Tampa Bay Business Journal
Tampa Bay History
Tan
Tar Heel Junior Historian
Target Marketing
Tax Lawyer
Tax Notes
Taxes
TCI — Entertainment Design
Teachers College Record
Teaching Exceptional Children
Teaching PreK-8
Technical World
Teen
Telephony
Television
Television Quarterly
Television/Radio Age
TelevisionWeek
Temple Law Review
Temple Review
Tennessee Bar Journal
Tennessee Journal of Healthy, Physical
    Education, Recreation, and Dance
Texas Business Review
Texas Coach
Texas Historian
Texas Monthly
Texas Observer
Texas Tech Law Review
Theatrum

Thinking Pitcher
This Magazine
Thomas M. Cooley Journal of Practi-
    cal and Clinical Law, The
Threads Magazine
Tikkun
Time
Time & Society
Time Asia
Time International
Time-Life International
Timeline
Tobacco Control
Today
Today Magazine
Today's Health
Tokushima Journal of Experimental
    Medicine
Tokyo Weekender
Tomahawk
Top of the News
Topps Magazine
Toronto Life
Touchstone
Town and Country Monthly
Traces of Indiana and Midwestern
    History
Trademark Reporter
Tradition: A Journal of Orthodox Jew-
    ish Thought
Trailer Life
Trains
Transaction
Transportation and Distribution
Transportation Research Record
Travel and Leisure
Travel/Holiday
Travel in Taiwan
Travel Weekly
Traveler
Tree House
Trial
TriM
True
True Comics
True Detective Mysteries
Tube and Pipe Journal
Tuff Stuff
Tulsa Law Review
Turf & Recreation
Tusculum Magazine
TV Guide
TV Technology
Twin Cities
Twins Magazine
Two-Year College Mathematical Jour-
    nal

UCD Law Review
UCLA Law Review
UMAP Journal
UMKC Law Review
University of Alberta Sports Medicine
    Newsletter

University of Chicago Law School
    Roundtable
University of Colorado Law Review
University of Detroit Mercy Law
    Review
University of Florida Law
    Review
University of Illinois Law
    Review
University of Kansas Law
    Review
University of Miami Law
    Review
University of Minnesota Alumni News
University of Pennsylvania Journal of
    International Economic Law
University of Pennsylvania Journal of
    Labor and Employment Law
University of Pittsburgh Law Review
University of Toledo Law Review
University of Toledo Quarterly
Update-on-Law-Related Education
Urban Affairs Quarterly
Urban Affairs Review
Urban Lawyer
Urban Resources
U.S. Law Review
U.S. News & World Report
US
USA Today
USA Today Baseball Weekly
USA Weekend
USC Trojan Family Magazine
Utah Historical Quarterly
Utne Reader

Vanity Fair
Vanderbilt Law Review
Vaudeville TImes
Venture
Vermont History
Vermont Law Review
Vermont Life
Video Business
Video Review
Villanova Sports & Entertainment
    Law Journal
Vintage & Classic Baseball Collector
Virginia Cavalcade
Virginia Law Review
Virginia Quarterly Review
Vogue

War, Literature & the Arts: An Inter-
    national Journal of the Humanities
Waste Age
Washington Business Journal
Washington Journalism Review
Washington Magazine
Washington Monthly
Washington Post Magazine
Washington Post TV Week
Washington University Law Quarterly
Washingtonian

Wayne Law Review
Weatherwise
Web Techniques
Weekly Compilation of Presidential
   Documents
Week's Progress
Welding Design and Fabrication
Welding Journal
Westchester County Business Journal
West Virginia Libraries
Western Folklore
Western Humanities Review
Western Journal of Black Studies
Western Journal of Communications
Western Pennsylvania Historical
   Magazine
Western Report
Westways
What's Brewing
Where the Trails Cross
Whittier Law Review
Whole Earth Review

Wigwag
Wilson Library Bulletin
Wilson Quarterly, The
Win
Wisconsin Law Review
Wisconsin Magazine of History
Wisconsin Studies in Contemporary
   Literature
Wisconsin Trails
Witness
Woman's Day
Women and Language
Women Lawyer's Journal
Women's Sports and Fitness
Womensport
Wood and Wood Products
The Woodworker's Journal
Workforce
Working Woman
The World and I
World Baseball Magazine
World Monitor

World Progress
Worth
The Writer
Writer's Digest
Writing on the Edge

Yahoo Internet Life
Yale Alumni Magazine
Yale Journal of Criticism
Yale Journal of Law and the
   Humanities
Yale Law Review
Yale Review
Yankee
Yankees Magazine
Yellowback Library
You
Young Athlete
Youth Baseball
Youth's Companion

INDEX OF NAMES AND SUBJECTS

16948, 16951, 16998, 17005, 17024, 17075, 17173, 17224–17225, 17248, 17274, 17295, 17329; *see also* Maintenance; Playing surfaces; Groundskeepers (Specific) *see* Zwaska, Paul; HVAC 16931, 17139; • In specific locations: In Boston (MA) 17162; *see also* Fenway Park (MA); In California 17211, 17260; In Cincinnati (OH) 17117, 17253; *see also* Crosley Field (OH); Riverfront Stadium (OH); In Cleveland (OH) 16910; *see also* Jacobs Field; League Park; Municipal Stadium; In Denver (CO) 16993; *see also* Colorado (CO) Rockies; Denver Bears; In Florida 17096, 17298; In New York City 16932, 17303; *see also* Ebbets Field; Polo Grounds; Yankee Stadium; In North Carolina 17318; In Philadelphia (PA) 16893, 16930, 16986; *see also* Baker Bowl; Connie Mack Stadium; Shibe Park; Veterans Stadium; In St. Louis (MO) 17006, 17271; *see also* Busch Stadium (MO); Sportsman's Park; In San Diego (CA) 17231; In Texas 16915; In Washington, D.C. 17063; • Lighting 17086–17087, 17141, 17186, 17301, 17308; *see also* Night baseball; • Maintenance 16866, 16871, 16884, 16913–16914, 16921–16922, 16995, 17036, 17045, 17068, 17087, 17119, 17146, 17173, 17175–17177, 17262, 17278–17280, 17286, 17312, 17314, 17323; *see also* Playing surface; • Medical services 10038, 16920; • Naming 16897, 17016, 17219, 17298; • Organ music 16862, 16971; • Ownership/financing 8374–8375, 8423, 8473, 8555–8558, 8579–8580, 9577, 9593, 9610, 9678, 15570, 16863, 16872–16882, 16898, 16912, 16925, 16934, 16936–16937, 16939–16941, 16944–16946, 16966, 16976, 16985, 16990–16991, 16996–16997, 17007, 17015, 17028, 17034–17035, 17037, 17047–17048, 17052–17056, 17058–17062, 17070–17071, 17082, 17099–17100, 17111–17113, 17121, 17128–17129, 17137, 17143, 17145, 17188–17191, 17202–17206, 17220–17221, 17239–17243, 17258–17261, 17265–17266, 17268–17269, 17283, 17297, 17300, 17306–17307, 17319, 17324, 17327–17328; • PA systems 17023; • Pitchers' mounds 17019, 17067, 17078, 20442, 20727, 20841, 22953a, 22993c, 23111, 23163, 23202, 23241, 23262, 23427; • Playing surface (artificial) 10107, 16908, 16919, 16928, 16953, 16972, 16974, 16984, 16989, 16992, 16999, 17009, 17049, 17074, 17108, 17121a, 17130, 17138, 17169, 17251, 17291; *see also* Groundskeepers and groundskeeping; • Playing surface (grass) 16908, 16989, 17138, 17244, 17276, 17282; *see also* Groundskeeper and groundskeeping; • Renovation *see* Design and construction; • Roofs and domes 16885, 16905, 16968, 17009, 17080, 17311, 17325; *see also* names of specific domed stadiums, e.g., Astrodome; • Scoreboards 16918, 17069, 17209, 17215, 17236, 17353; • Security

/fire protection 16886, 16927, 16967, 17039, 17063, 17076, 17102; • Skyboxes and suites 16924, 17148; • Trivia 16909; • Vendors *see* Food and other concessions; • Specific *see* Names of individual parks and stadiums; • *See also* Fans — Legal rights/liabilities
Baseball shoes *see* Shoes
Baseball uniforms *see* Uniforms
Baseball writers/broadcasters 26260–26304; *see also* Broadcasters; Writers
Baseball Writers' Association of America 10448–10449, 10531
Baseballs: • General works 1878, 18217–18328, 19118; • Collectible 9406, 10700, 18323, 18326–18227, 18239, 18246, 18253, 18262, 18265, 18272, 18296, 18303, 18308–18310, 18318–18321, 18326; *see also* Bonds, Barry; McGwire, Mark; • Construction/doctoring 18241, 18244–18245, 18248–18251, 18258, 18260, 18261, 18263, 18267, 18273–18275, 18280, 18282, 18284, 18289, 18311–18312, 18317, 18328; • Dead ball 18240, 18285, 18288, 18295; • Liveliness 18218, 18231–18233, 18237, 18269, 18277–18279, 18281, 18288, 19297, 18315, 18324, 18382; • 62nd home run ball 18265, 18303; • 70th home run ball 18296, 18202, 18309, 18319
Bases, breakaway 10071, 17043
Basketball 672, 2226, 2999, 4199, 8386, 9612
Baserunners *see* Gaedel, Eddie; Gagliano, Ralph; Genovese, George; Stafford, Henry ("Heinie"); Washington, Herbert ("Herb")
Baserunning/basestealing: • General works 2432, 2967, 21524–21709; • Drills 21670, 21700; • *See also* Baserunning; Offense; Rules — Baserunning
Bases *see* Baseball parks and stadiums — Bases
Basestealing *see* Baserunning; Offense; Rules — Basestealing
Bass, Dick *see* Bass, Richard ("Dick")
Bass, Kevin 27765–27766
Bass, Randy 27767–27768
Bass, Richard ("Dick") 27769
Batavia (NY) Muckdogs 16071–16072
Batboys/Ballgirls 23866; *see also* Carrieri, Joe; Collins, Marla; Itaas, Mark; Reliford, Joe Louis
Bateman, John 27770–27771
Batikis, Annastasia 24446
Batista, Tony 27772–27773
Bats 18329–18490; *see also* Hitting; Pitches; Pitching; Rules — Bats
Battey, Earl Jesse 27774–27777
Batting *see* Hitting
Batting average *see* Statistics — Batting average
Batting helmets 18553, 18556–18557, 18562, 18564, 18571; *see also* Caps; Equipment — Protective equipment
Batting order *see* Managers/managing — Batting order
Battle Creek (MI) Golden Kazoos 16073; *see also* Michigan (MI) Battle Cats
Bauer, Hank 1730, 13540, 13590, 14840, 27778–27800

Bauman, Joe 25362, 27801–27806
Baumgardner, George 27807
Baumgartner, Stan 23857
Baumholtz, Frank 27808–27815
Bavasi, Emil ("Buzzie") 27816–27821; *see also* Brooklyn (N.L.) Dodgers; California (A.L.) Angels; Los Angeles (N.L.) Dodgers; San Diego (N.L.) Padres
Baxes, Jim 24446
Baylor, Don 27822–27841
Beadle and Adams, Publishers 5264; *see also* Novels
Beall, Vince 27842
Bean, Billy 27843–27844
Beane, Billy 27845–27850
Beanballs *see* Injuries and medical affairs — Specific — Beaning
Beanie babies (collectibles) 1805, 9414
Beard, Cramer ("Ted") 27851
Bearden, Henry ("Gene") 27852–27862
Bearnarth, Larry 27863–27864
"Beast" *see* Foxx, James ("Jimmie")
Beattie, Jim 7896; *see also* World Series — Specific years — 1979
Beaumont, Clarence ("Ginger") 27865–27867; *see also* World Series — Specific years — 1903
Beaumont (TX) Exporters 16074
Beazley, John 27868–27870
Becker, Rich 27871
Beckert, Glenn 27872–27875
Beckett, James 1575
Beckett, Josh 27876–27877
Beckley, Jake 23751, 27878–27882
Beckwith, John 27883
Becquer, Julio 27884
Bedient, Hugh 27885
Bedrosian, Steve 27886–27889
Beer *see* Baseball parks and stadiums — Food and other concessions; Drugs and doping — Alcohol; Fans — Alcohol consumption
Beer cans (collectibles) 1820
BEEP baseball 18902, 18987, 18997, 19025, 19045
Beeston, Paul 27890–27893; *see also* Toronto (A.L.) Blue Jays
Beggs, Joe 27894
Bejma, Aloysius ("Ollie") 27895
Belanger, Mark 27896–27901
Belcher, Tim 27902–27905
Belinda, Stan 27906
Belinsky, Bo 24702, 27907–27923
Bell, Buddy *see* Bell, David ("Buddy")
Bell, Cool Papa *see* Bell, James ("Cool Papa")
Bell, David ("Buddy") 27924–27935
Bell, David Michael 27936–27937
Bell, David Russell ("Gus") 27938–27944
Bell, Derek 27945
Bell, Gary 27946–27948
Bell, George 27949–27958
Bell, Gus *see* Bell, David Russell ("Gus")
Bell, James ("Cool Papa") 27959–27984
Bell, Jay Stuart 27985–27992
Bell, Les 27993
Belle, Albert 25799, 27994–28029
Belliard, Rafael 28030–28031